Corporate Finance

Corporate Finance
Third Edition

David Hillier

**Stephen Ross, Randolph Westerfield,
Jeffrey Jaffe, Bradford Jordan**

McGraw Hill Education

London Boston Burr Ridge, IL Dubuque, IA Madison, WI New York San Francisco
St. Louis Bangkok Bogotá Caracas Kuala Lumpur Lisbon Madrid Mexico City
Milan Montreal New Delhi Santiago Seoul Singapore Sydney Taipei Toronto

Corporate Finance, 3rd European Edition
David Hillier, Stephen Ross, Randolph Westerfield, Jeffrey Jaffe, Bradford Jordan
ISBN-13 9780077173630
ISBN-10 0077173635

Published by McGraw-Hill Education
Shoppenhangers Road
Maidenhead
Berkshire
SL6 2QL
Telephone: 44 (0) 1628 502 500
Fax: 44 (0) 1628 770 224
Website: www.mheducation.co.uk

British Library Cataloguing in Publication Data
A catalogue record for this book is available from the British Library

Library of Congress Cataloguing in Publication Data
The Library of Congress data for this book has been applied for from the Library of Congress

Content Acquisitions Manager: Emma Nugent
Product Developer: Rosie Churchill
Content Product Manager: Ben King

Text Design by Ian Youngs
Cover design by Adam Renvoize
Printed and bound by APP, Lebanon

ISBN-13 9780077173630
ISBN-10 0077173635
eISBN-10 0077173643

Dedication
To Mary-Jo

Brief Table of Contents

Detailed Table of Contents

Preface

I've been teaching Finance courses since 1994, first as a tutorial assistant in small group classes for masters and undergraduate students, all the way through to large lecture auditoriums of several hundred people. During that time, three books formed the basis of all my teaching (Ross, Westerfield and Jaffe, *Corporate Finance*; Brealey, Myers and Allen, *Principles of Corporate Finance*; and Grinblatt and Titman, *Financial Markets and Corporate Strategy*). In fact, coming from a mathematics background, I initially learned about finance through these textbooks.

When McGraw-Hill approached me to work on *Corporate Finance*, I was at first reluctant. The book is an institution. What could I do to improve on a text that has gone through so many editions and been taught in so many places? On reflection, however, I knew that there were many areas where the book needed to be changed for an international readership. Like many other lecturers, I had slipped into the habit of recommending RWJ and BMA, but then replacing more than half of the slides and examples so that the material was appropriate for my students. Differences in depreciation rules, taxes, accounting standards, and bankruptcy regulations, changed everything except the bare bones.

Now in its third edition, the book has had to change to reflect the enormous developments in the financial markets and the corporate world. Much has evolved over the past decade and business practice and economic fundamentals have experienced a major shift. Uncertainty is the keyword and financial managers are facing tighter financing conditions, very low interest rates and a considerably more difficult investment environment. Government bonds have negative yields, inflation is near zero and new economic power blocs are emerging. Now, more than ever, the principles and applications of corporate finance are needed to ensure companies can steer through these uncharted territories without taking too many casualties.

I have undertaken major updates of all chapters, introduced real world examples in each topic and updated the discussion to reflect new research findings. The text has also been sense checked for relevance and practice through my industry engagements. Finally, the references for each area have been comprehensively updated to the most recent research in the area.

I'm exceptionally honoured to be part of the RWJ history and very proud of this version in particular. I've thoroughly enjoyed writing the chapters and I sincerely hope you have the same enjoyment reading them.

David Hillier
5 January 2016

Real World Insight 23.1

Valuing Internet Firms

(Excerpts taken from 'Twitter's IPO and the dark side of valuing companies',
11 November 2013)
Social media darling Twitter ended last week with US$2.3 billion wiped off its market
a 7.24 per cent fall in its share price on the second day it traded. Despite the slip, the
US$41.64, significantly higher than the issue price of US$26.

The problems of valuing companies like Twitter are not new. Twitter is the latest exa
value business, but the same can be said of many listed companies including Google, Fac

As indicated by Mary Jo White, Chair of the US Securities Exchange Commission
selling recent IPOs like Google and Twitter to the public are not closely related to pro
of product. She identifies some of the recent measures that companies have touted as

... the number of users of the service, the number of players of an online game,
of people who quote 'liked' the company or something the company does.

To get a better sense of the problems faced in valuing these firms it is worth re
crisis of 2000. During this period it was often argued there was a pricing bubble in
with market prices arguably no longer reflecting value. Yet, when the crunch came it
new disclosures about the various measures of internet activity but earnings reports o
1999 year. These showed that predicted profits had not eventuated.

Mini Case

Exotic Cuisines Employee Share Options

As a new university graduate, you have taken a management position with Exotic Cuis
chain that just went public last year. The company's restaurants specialize in exoti
ingredients such as wild boar, crocodile and pheasant. A concern you had going in wa
the restaurant industry. It is widely thought that 90 per cent of new restaurants c
however, recent evidence suggests the failure rate is closer to 60 per cent over 3 y
business, although not as risky as you originally thought.

During your interview process, one of the benefits mentioned was employee share o
your employment contract, you received options with a strike price of £50 for 10,00
equity. As is fairly common, your share options have a 3-year vesting period and a
meaning that you cannot exercise the options for 3 years, and you lose them if you le
After the 3-year vesting period, you can exercise the options at any time. Thus, the em
are European (and subject to forfeit) for the first 3 years and American afterward. O
sell the options, nor can you enter into any sort of hedging agreement. If you leave th
options vest, you must exercise within 90 days or forfeit.

Exotic Cuisines equity is currently trading at £24.38 per share, a slight incre
offering price last year. There are no market-traded options on the company's
company has been traded for only about a year, you are reluctant to use t

Understanding and Application

The best way to understand corporate finance is to
explain it via situations and scenarios you can relate
to.

- **Example** boxes in every chapter to provide
  hypothetical examples to illustrate theoretical
  concepts.
- **Opening chapter vignettes** illustrate topical
  discussions that will be covered in the chapter.
- New to this edition are **Real World Insight**
  boxes which use real companies to show how
  they have applied corporate finance theories
  and concepts to their businesses and business
  decisions.
- **Practical case studies, mini cases** and
  additional reading further aid your
  understanding of concepts and to practise
  applying them.

Mastery of Mathematics

Many find the hardest part of learning finance
is mastering the jargon, maths, data and
standardized notation. *Corporate Finance* helps
you by:

- Making extensive use of **figures and
  tables** which use real data throughout the
  text.
- Listing the variables and acronyms you will
  encounter as you read the chapter in **key
  notation** boxes at the start of the chapter.
- Numbering **maths equations** the first time
  they appear in full for ease of reference and
  understanding.

The reason for this change in policy was that most executive share options were worthless as a result of the majo
market falls in the immediate aftermath of the global financial crisis. The main purpose for executive share options
is that they reward employees for good performance and loyalty
to their company. If the options are worth nothing, there is no
financial reason why the best executives should stay in a company
if their services are demanded elsewhere. Restricted stock units
are therefore better in a down market because executives always
receive something for their efforts.

KEY NOTATIONS

C	Value of a call option
P	Value of a put option
S	Current share price
E	Exercise price of option
R	Annual risk-free rate of return, continuously compounded
σ^2	Variance (per year) of the continuous share price return
t	Time (in years) to expiration date
$N(d)$	Probability that a standardized, normally distributed, random variable will be less than or equal to d

$$d_1 = [\ln(S/E) + (R + \sigma^2/2)t]/\sqrt{\sigma^2 t}$$

$$[0.45 \times (€2.10 - €2.74) \times 6 \text{ million} + 0.55. \times 0]/1.02 + €1,000,000,000 = -€694,118 \quad (23.1)$$

Value of the call option

revious chapter, we are valuing an option using risk-neutral pricing. The cash flows of
2.10 - €2.74) and €0 per litre are multiplied by their risk-neutral probabilities. The entire first
tion 23.1 is then discounted at €1.02 because the cash flows in that term occur on 1 December.
00 is not discounted because Mr Meyer receives it today, 1 September. Because the present value of
is negative, Mr Meyer would be wise to reject the contract.

before, the distributor has sold a call option to CECO. The first term in the preceding equation, which
94,118, can be viewed as the value of this call option. It is a negative number because the equation
ption from Mr Meyer's point of view. Therefore, the value of the call option would be +€1,694,118 to
er-litre basis, the value of the option to CECO is:

$$[0.45(€2.74 - €2.10) + 0.55 \times 0]/1.02 = €0.282 \quad (23.2)$$

shows that CECO will gain €0.64 (= €2.74 - €2.10) per litre in the up state because CECO can buy
orth €2.74 for only €2.10 under the contract. By contrast, the contract is worth nothing to CECO in the
ecause the utility will not pay €2.10 for oil selling for only €1.46 in the open market. Using risk-neutral
ormula tells us that the value of the call option on one litre of heating oil is €0.282.

e Example

receding example captures a number of aspects of the real world, it has one deficiency. It assume
heating oil can take on only two values on 1 December. This is clearly not plausible: oil can t

PART 6

Options, Futures and Corporate Finance

23.1 Executive Share Options

Why Options?

Executive compensation (see **Chapter 2**, section 2.2) usually made up of base salary plus some or all of the f

1 Base salary.

2 Annual bonuses.

3 Long-term incentives, such as retirement contributio

When stock markets are on an upward trajectory, the final compone biggest part of total compensation for many top executives. In many pa pay is not yet normal practice. However, this has not stopped politicia pay of executives, whose share options are a major component of their breakdown of chief executive pay in Europe in 2010. Bonuses represent the year and LTI is long-term incentives, which include executive share

Signposting and Navigation

To gain a full understanding of corporate finance it is important to understand how topics are linked together and how they relate to each other.

- New to this edition are **Chapter Links** which appear within the margin and are highlighted in the text; they provide a chapter and page reference for quick cross-referencing for information discussed in other chapters and they will aid in the enhancement of your understanding and background to topics.

- **Part Openers** are also new to this edition and provide a preface for the chapters that are to follow, linking the chapters together and explaining how and where topics are discussed within the chapters.

Practice and Proficiency

To obtain a solid understanding of finance it has been proven that practising questions is essential.

- At the end of every chapter there are **Questions and Problems;** they are presented by topic and level of difficulty and there are over 1,000 in the book altogether.

- These end of chapter questions and problems are all integrated into **Connect.**

- **Algorithmic** versions of the questions appear in Connect to ensure equations and calculations are not learnt by rote but by thorough understanding and practice.

- Also at the end of the chapters are **Exam Questions** designed to take 45 minutes and testing you on material learned in a more formal exam style.

- **LearnSmart** is also available to help you learn; it adaptively assesses your skill and knowledge levels to track which topics you have mastered and which require further instruction and practice.

connect®

McGraw-Hill Connect Finance is a learning and teaching environment that improves student performance and outcomes whilst promoting engagement and comprehension of content.

You can utilize publisher-provided materials, or add your own content to design a complete course to help your students achieve higher outcomes.

PROVEN EFFECTIVE

With Connect — Without Connect

MORE As and Bs
WITH CONNECT

A   B   C   D

INSTRUCTORS

With McGraw-Hill Connect Finance, instructors get:

- Simple **assignment management,** allowing you to spend more time teaching.
- **Auto-graded** assignments, quizzes and tests.
- **Detailed visual reporting** where students and section results can be viewed and analysed.
- Sophisticated **online testing** capability.
- A **filtering and reporting** function that allows you to easily assign and report on materials that are correlated to learning outcomes, topics, level of difficulty, and more. Reports can be accessed for individual students or the whole class, as well as offering the ability to drill into individual assignments, questions or categories.
- **Instructor materials** to help supplement your course.

Get Connected. Get Results.

Available online via Connect is a wealth of instructor support materials, including:

- Appendices that accompany the textbook
- Access to a wealth of videos discussing topics covered in the textbook on David Hillier's YouTube channel.
- Fully updated PowerPoint slides to use in lectures and an instructor's manual to support your course preparation.
- A solutions manual providing answers for the end of chapter questions in the textbook.
- Image library of artwork from the textbook.
- Case studies.

STUDENTS

With McGraw-Hill Connect Finance, students get:

Assigned content

- Easy **online access** to homework, tests and quizzes
- **Immediate feedback** and 24-hour tech support

With McGraw-Hill SmartBook, students can:

- Take control of your own learning with a personalized and adaptive reading experience.
- Understand what you know and don't know; SmartBook takes you through the stages of reading and practice, prompting you to recharge your knowledge throughout the course for maximum retention.
- Achieve the most efficient and productive study time by adapting to what you do and don't know.
- Hone in on concepts you are most likely to forget, to ensure knowledge of key concepts is learnt and retained.

connect®

Connect is an online assignment and assessment solution that offers a number of powerful tools and features that make managing assignments easier, so faculty can spend more time teaching. With Connect, students can engage with their coursework anytime and anywhere, making the learning process more accessible and efficient.

Excel Simulations

Provide students with an authentic Excel environment and experience which enables them to practise and learn to use Excel to solve finance problems just like they will in their future careers. These questions feature animated, narrated Help and Show Me tutorials for students, when enabled, as well as automatic feedback and grading for both students and professors.

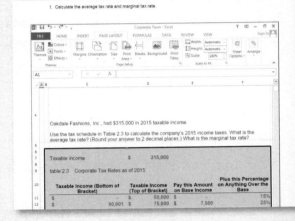

Algorithmic problem sets

Provide repeated opportunities for students to practise and master concepts with multiple versions of each problem. Or use the algorithmic problems in class testing to provide each student with a different version than that seen by their peers.

Calculation questions

Test students' mathematical understanding with auto-graded calculation questions.

Short-answer questions

Ensure students develop strong writing skills with short-answer and essay questions. Each question provides a guide answer and allows you to review and mark student responses. These questions are clearly marked as being manually graded, so you can include or skip these as you see fit.

Pre-built assignments

Assign all of the autogradable end of chapter or test bank material as a ready-made assignment with the simple click of a button.

Get Connected. Get Results.

SmartBook™

Fuelled by LearnSmart—the most widely used and intelligent adaptive learning resource—SmartBook is the first and only adaptive reading experience available today. Distinguishing what a student knows from what they don't, and honing in on concepts they are most likely to forget, SmartBook personalizes content for each student in a continuously adapting reading experience. Valuable reports provide instructors with insight as to how students are progressing through textbook content, and are useful for shaping in-class time or assessment.

LearnSmart™

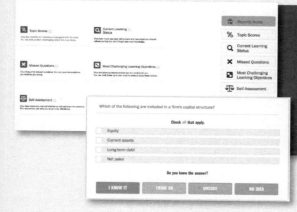

McGraw-Hill LearnSmart is an adaptive learning program that identifies what an individual student knows and doesn't know. LearnSmart's adaptive learning path helps students learn faster, study more efficiently, and retain more knowledge. Now with integrated learning resources which present topics and concepts in different and engaging formats, increases student engagement and promotes additional practice of key concepts. Reports available for both students and instructors indicate where students need to study more and assess their success rate in retaining knowledge.

About the Author

Adapting Author

David Hillier is a professor of Finance at the University of Strathclyde. Professor Hillier has published a wide range of peer-reviewed academic articles on corporate governance, corporate finance, insider trading, asset pricing, precious metals, auditing, and market microstructure. His research has attracted an ANBAR citation and a best paper prize from one of the top finance and management journals in Southeast Asia. He is on the editorial board and reviews for many of the world's top finance journals. Professor Hillier is an established teacher of executive programmes and has conducted courses for a variety of professional clients, including The World Bank and the UK National Health Service. Finally, he is a co-author of the European editions of *Financial Markets and Corporate Strategy* (McGraw-Hill, 2011) and *Fundamentals of Corporate Finance* (McGraw-Hill, 2011).

US Authors

Stephen A. Ross is the Franco Modigliani Professor of Finance and Economics at the Sloan School of Management, Massachusetts Institute of Technology.

Randolph W. Westerfield is Dean Emeritus of the University of Southern California's Marshall School of Business and is the Charles B. Thornton Professor of Finance.

Jeffrey F. Jaffe has been a frequent contributor to many finance and economics literatures for a number of years.

Bradford D. Jordan is Professor of Finance and holder of the Richard W. and Janis H. Furst Endowed Chair in Finance at the University of Kentucky.

Acknowledgements

I would like to acknowledge the following individuals who have all contributed in one way or another to the book.

First mention must go to Tom Hill and Rosie Churchill who worked with me tirelessly on this project from its inception. Tom and Rosie deserve as much credit as me in putting everything together and I am extremely grateful for all their support.

The review process has been extensive and many individuals have provided extensive advice and suggestions on how to make the text much more relevant and current to its intended readership. Every chapter has been scrutinized by several reviewers, leading to a substantial improvement in the quality of the text. In particular, I would like to recognize the efforts of

Tom Aabo, Aarhus University
Eser Arisoy, Lancaster University
Shantanu Banerjee, Lancaster University
Christina Bannier, Frankfurt School of Finance and
    Management
Edel Barnes, University College Cork
Mikael Bask, Uppsala University
Anthony Birts, University of Bath
Jaap Bos, Maastricht University
James Brown, Edinburgh Napier University
Evert Carlsson, University of Gothenburg
Jeremy Cheah, University of Sheffield
Peter Corvi, Warwick Business School
Twm Evans, Swansea University
Maria Gårdängen, Lund University

Peter de Goeij, Tilburg University
Manuel Goudie, Instituto de Estudios Bursatiles,
    Madrid
Ufuk Gucbilmez, University of Edinburgh
Stefan Hirth, Aarhus University
Jan Lemmen, Erasmus University
Maria-Teresa Marchica, University of Manchester
Kristian Miller, Aarhus University
Tomoe Moore, Brunel University
Arjen Mulder, Erasmus University
James Ryan, University of Limerick
Gert Sandhal, University of Gothenburg
Mohamed Sherif, Heriot-Watt University
Chris Veld, University of Glasgow
Steven Walters, Glasgow Caledonian Univeristy

A book of this type involves more than just writing the main text. The online learning materials have to be developed, checked and revised, and the drafts are typeset and proofread. The marketing endeavour is also something that often gets ignored but it is an exceptionally important component of the book's production process. Finally, I am truly indebted to the sales representatives who are on the coalface in raising sales. With this in mind, I would like to thank Jeffrey Egan, David Swift, Federico Parola, Nick Velander, Carina Boom, Claudia Leenen. I would also like to thank Emma Nugent, Beverley Shields, Sarah Fleming, Gill Colver, Elaine Bingham, Calum Crichton, Martin Kemmitt, George Hulene, Iain Clacher and Steve O'Callaghan for their contribution.

The whole project has taken more than a year of exceptionally hard work and my family, friends and colleagues have taken a lot of the burden in supporting me through this intensive period. I would like to thank the following colleagues for standing in for me at various meetings, helping with deadlines, and other sundry support: Emanuele Bajo, Marco Bigelli, Iain Clacher, Mehmet Demirbag, Helyn Gould, Susan Hart, Allan Hodgson, Suntharee Lhaopadchan, Morag McDonald, Alan McIntyre, Andy Marshall, Patrick McColgan and Krishna Paudyal.

The following friends deserve a special mention for their advice, support and good times during this time: Philip and Pauline Church, Anton Colella, Ronnie and Anne Convery, Paul and Clare Lombardi, Nicky and Ann McLuskey, Peter and Katherine McCudden, Monsignor Tom Monaghan, Kevin Page, Garry and Stella Stern, and Anne and Frank Walker.

I'm very grateful to my family, who mean everything to me: Benjy, Danny, Con, Maria, Patrick, Saoirse, Thomas, my mum, Marion, and my mother in law, Mary. Also, special mention must go to Chris and Bonnie, Margaret, Joe and Cathie, Liam, John and Christine, Patrick, and Quentin and Julie.

Finally, to Mary-Jo, my inspiration.

Mc Graw Hill Education

create

Let us help make our content your solution

At McGraw-Hill Education our aim is to help lecturers to find the most suitable content for their needs delivered to their students in the most appropriate way. Our **custom publishing solutions** offer the ideal combination of content delivered in the way which best suits lecturer and students.

Our custom publishing programme offers lecturers the opportunity to select just the chapters or sections of material they wish to deliver to their students from a database called CREATE™ at

create.mheducation.com/uk

CREATE™ contains over two million pages of content from:

- textbooks
- professional books
- case books – Harvard Articles, Insead, Ivey, Darden, Thunderbird and BusinessWeek
- Taking Sides – debate materials

Across the following imprints:

- McGraw-Hill Education
- Open University Press
- Harvard Business Publishing
- US and European material

There is also the option to include additional material authored by lecturers in the custom product – this does not necessarily have to be in English.

We will take care of everything from start to finish in the process of developing and delivering a custom product to ensure that lecturers and students receive exactly the material needed in the most suitable way.

With a **Custom Publishing Solution**, students enjoy the best selection of material deemed to be the most suitable for learning everything they need for their courses – something of real value to support their learning. Teachers are able to use exactly the material they want, in the way they want, to support their teaching on the course.

Please contact your local McGraw-Hill Education representative with any questions or alternatively contact Warren Eels e: warren.eels@mheducation.com

Make the grade!

Improve your grades!

20% off any Study Skills Book!

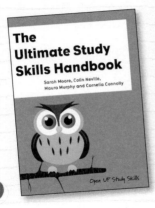

The Ultimate Study Skills Handbook

Sarah Moore, Colin Neville, Maura Murphy and Cornelia Connolly

Open UP Study Skills

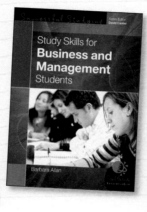

Study Skills for **Business and Management** Students

Barbara Allan

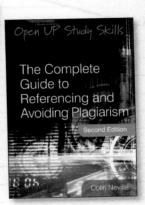

Open UP Study Skills

The Complete Guide to Referencing and Avoiding Plagiarism

Second Edition

Colin Neville

Our Study Skills books are packed with practical advice and tips that are easy to put into practice and will really improve the way you study.

Our books will help you:

- ✓ Improve your grades
- ✓ Avoid plagiarism
- ✓ Save time
- ✓ Develop new skills

- ✓ Write confidently
- ✓ Undertake research projects
- ✓ Sail through exams
- ✓ Find the perfect job

SPECIAL OFFER!

As a valued customer, buy online and receive 20% off any of our Study Skills books by entering the promo code **BRILLIANT**

www.openup.co.uk/studyskills

PART 1

Overview

You are at the beginning of a long but exceptionally rewarding journey. In this book, you will come to understand the decisions financial managers make in their day-to-day activities and take a large step forward towards being able to make these decisions yourself. Corporate finance is at the heart of all business activity. Whether you are in Marketing, Human Resources, Strategy or Communications; whether you are an entrepreneur setting up a new business, or an engineer or scientist trying to understand how companies invest in new projects; this book will give you that necessary insight to be a full member of the team that makes decisions to increase the value of your company.

In this first part of the book, we introduce you to the basic building blocks of corporate finance. Look on this section as the necessary overview of terms and concepts that form the foundations of the material covered later in the text. Key terminology and concepts will be explained and you will appreciate what is actually meant by the title of the book, 'Corporate Finance'. You will also come to appreciate why companies place financial management at the core of their business, and the differences between the fields of Accounting and Finance. Companies don't operate in a bubble, so we must also discuss the international environment in which businesses raise cash for their operations and do their business.

Ultimately, the decisions that financial managers make must be acceptable to the owners of the firm. However, the intuitive sense of this statement is not necessarily experienced in practice. In many companies across the world, managers prioritize their own welfare and personal earnings over that of the firm. In Chapter 2, we discuss in detail how to structure the leadership of a company so that managers are more likely to maximize firm value and make the best financial decisions. This is discussed in an international context so that the cultural variations which exist across countries can be fully understood.

Introduction to Corporate Finance

The last 10 years have led to a completely new understanding of Corporate Finance. Many established truths that existed prior to the global financial crisis of 2007 are now fiercely debated.

A common question is 'Are financial markets rational?'

Classic corporate finance is based on the premise that all decisions are rational and those who make financial decisions are also rational. Once we drop this fundamental axiom, many financial theories become much harder to prove. In fact, when we no longer expect decision-makers to be rational, many observed 'financial anomalies' can be easily explained.

Another massive change in finance is the widespread recognition that financial decisions should not ignore ethics and the wider non-financial impact of those decisions. Even today, with lessons apparently learned from the 2007 financial crisis, we still see misreporting, corporate fraud, excessive risk taking, and poor capital expenditure decisions. Fortunately, this has been accompanied by a concomitant increase in shareholder activism, especially from financial institutions that have become exceptionally vocal in their criticisms of corporate management when bad decisions are made.

Another change in finance is the integrated nature of global business, which has become a norm for every company. The international financial environment is now so central to business decision-making that any course on Finance must give consideration to the dynamics of currency movements, geopolitional risk and economics. Financial risk management is an area that has consequently come to the fore as a result of these changes, and it will remain essential for years to come.

Finally, the role of the corporate executive has also changed. Irrespective of his or her background (Marketing, Strategy, Human Resources, Consulting, etc.), today's managers must be fully loaded with financial tools to enable them to cope with the fast changing economic environment in which their companies

operate. The corporate executive must be an entrepreneur who not only understands risk but also knows how to use it to his or her advantage. More than that, the executive must be willing and have the confidence to implement investment and financing decisions that fully incorporate risky outcomes.

Bringing all of these issues together and integrating them into a coherent framework for optimal financial decision-making is the goal of this text. However, first of all, we require an understanding of what is meant by the term 'Corporate Finance', why it is so important to a successful business, the different financial environments in which businesses operate, and the emerging trends in global business – all of which we discuss in Chapter 1.

1.1 What Is Corporate Finance?

Suppose you decide to start a firm to make tennis balls. To do this you hire managers to buy raw materials, and you assemble a workforce that will produce and sell finished tennis balls. In the language of finance, you make an investment in assets such as inventory, machinery, land and labour. The amount of cash you invest in assets must be matched by an equal amount of cash raised by financing. When you begin to sell tennis balls, your firm will generate cash. This is the basis of value creation. The purpose of the firm is to create value for the owner, who may or may not be the manager of the firm. This concept of value is reflected in the framework of the simple balance sheet model of the firm.

The Balance Sheet Model of the Firm

**Chapter 3
Page 64**

Take a financial snapshot of the firm and its activities at a single point in time. Figure 1.1 shows a graphic conceptualization of the balance sheet, and it will help introduce you to the field of corporate finance. (See **Chapter 3** for more information on the balance sheet.)

The assets of the firm are on the left side of the balance sheet. These assets can be thought of as short-term (current) and long-term (non-current). *Non-current assets* are those that will last a long time, such as buildings. Some non-current assets are tangible, such as machinery and equipment. Other non-current assets are intangible, such as patents and trademarks. The other category of assets, *current assets*, comprises those that have short lives, such as inventory. For example, tennis balls that your firm has made but not yet sold are current assets. Unless you have overproduced, the tennis balls will leave the firm shortly and will not be in the company for a long time.

Before a company can invest in an asset, it must obtain financing, which means that it must raise the money to pay for the investment. The various forms of financing are represented on the right side of the balance sheet in Figure 1.1. A firm will issue (sell) pieces of paper called *bonds* (debt or loan agreements) or *shares* (certificates representing a fractional ownership of the firm). Just as assets are classified as long-lived or short-lived, so too are liabilities. Short-term debt is called a *current liability* and represents loans and other obligations that must be repaid within one year. *Non-current liabilities* include debt that does not have to be repaid within one year. Shareholders' equity represents the difference between the value of the assets and the liabilities of the firm. In this sense, it is a residual claim on the firm's assets.

Figure 1.1 The Balance Sheet Model of the Firm

From the balance sheet model of the firm, it is easy to see why corporate finance can be thought of as the study of the following three questions:

1   In what long-lived assets should the firm invest? This question concerns the left side of the balance sheet. Of course the types and proportions of assets the firm needs tend to be set by the nature of the business. We use the term **capital budgeting** to describe the process of making and managing expenditures on long-lived assets.

2   How can the firm raise cash for required capital expenditures? This question concerns the right side of the balance sheet. The answer to this question involves the firm's capital structure, which represents the proportions of the firm's financing from current and long-term debt and equity.

3   How should short-term operating cash flows be managed? This question concerns the upper portion of the balance sheet. There is often a mismatch between the timing of cash inflows and cash outflows during operating activities. Furthermore, the amount and timing of operating cash flows are not known with certainty. Financial managers must attempt to manage the gaps in cash flow. From a balance sheet perspective, short-term management of cash flow is associated with a firm's net working capital. Net working capital is defined as current assets minus current liabilities. From a financial perspective, short-term cash flow problems come from the mismatching of cash inflows and outflows. This is the subject of short-term finance.

Real World Insight 1.1

Vodafone is a global mobile telecommunications firm with operations in Europe, the Middle East, the US, the Asia Pacific region and Africa. The assets of Vodafone not only include infrastructure and telecommunications networks (tangible assets), but also licences to run mobile operations in many countries (intangible assets). In 2014, the company had £50.430 billion in tangible non-current assets and £46.688 billion in intangible non-current assets. Current assets amounted to £24.722 billion and current liabilities (liabilities due within one year) were £25.039 billion. Vodafone had £25.020 billion in non-current liabilities. A balance sheet for the company is presented below.

	£ billion		£ billion
Intangible Assets	46.688	Non-Current Liabilities	25.020
Tangible Assets	50.430	Current Liabilities	25.039
Non-Current Assets	97.118	Equity	71.781
Current Assets	24.722		
Total Assets	121.840	**Total Equity and Liabilities**	**121.840**

Net working capital is (Current Assets − Current Liabilities) = −£0.317 billion. Normally, one would expect a positive net working capital figure to ensure that the company has enough liquid assets to pay off its short-term liabilities. Vodafone's management would treat this as a priority over the next year.

Capital Structure

Financing arrangements determine how the value of the firm is sliced up. The people or institutions that buy debt from (i.e., lend money to) the firm are called *creditors*, *bondholders* or *debtholders*. The holders of equity are called *shareholders*.

Sometimes it is useful to think of the firm as a pie. Initially the size of the pie will depend on how well the firm has made its investment decisions. After a firm has made its investment decisions, it determines the value of its assets (e.g., its buildings, land and inventories).

The firm can then determine its capital structure. The firm might initially have raised the cash to invest in its assets by issuing more debt than equity; now it can consider changing that mix by issuing more equity and using the proceeds to buy back (pay off) some of its debt. Financing decisions like this can be made independently of the original investment decisions. The decisions to issue debt and equity affect how the pie is sliced.

The pie we are thinking of is depicted in Figure 1.2. The size of the pie is the value of the firm in the financial markets. We can write the value of the firm, V, as

$$V = D + E$$

Chapter 15
Page 396

where D is the market value of the debt (bonds) and E is the market value of the equity (shares). The pie diagrams consider two ways of slicing the pie: 50 per cent debt and 50 per cent equity, and 25 per cent debt and 75 per cent equity. The way the pie is sliced could affect its value. If so, the goal of the financial manager will be to choose the ratio of debt to equity that makes the value of the pie – that is, the value of the firm, V – as large as it can be. (See **Chapter 15** for more information on capital structure.)

Figure 1.2 Two Pie Models of the Firm

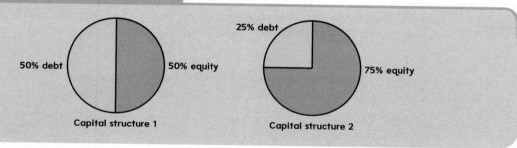

50% debt   50% equity

Capital structure 1

25% debt   75% equity

Capital structure 2

Real World Insight 1.2

Every company that requires cash will need to raise it from somewhere. Take London Stock Exchange, which is a company in its own right. In 2014, London Stock Exchange raised a total of $2.7 billion to fund a potential bid for the US firm, Russell Investments. The principal way of doing this was through issuing new equity. London Stock Exchange could also have borrowed $2.7 billion from a bank or issued bonds worth $2.7 billion as debt.

Why did the firm choose to issue new equity? Clearly the decision was based on what would maximize the value of the company and in London Stock Exchange's case, equity was the most sensible option. It is important to emphasize that although the London Stock Exchange management deals with security trading in its daily operations, it does not actually have the expertise to decide on the best choice of debt or equity for a particular issue. It also does not have any infrastructure to market its own security issue to investors.

This is where banks come in. Although they are most well known for lending funds to borrowers, banks are also very experienced in marketing and raising financing from other investors. We call this type of activity 'investment banking' and there are a number of banking institutions that specialize in this area. For the $2.7 billion London Stock Exchange issue, there were eight banks that were involved in finding buyers. These were: Barclays, RBC Capital Markets, Deutsche Bank, JPMorgan Cazenove, Banca IMI, Banco Santander, HSBC and Mitsubishi UFJ Securities. In total, the eight banks earned themselves $25 million from their involvement in the issue!

The Financial Manager

In large firms, the finance activity is usually associated with a top officer of the firm, such as the chief financial officer (CFO), and some lesser officers. Reporting to the chief financial officer are the treasurer and the financial controller. The treasurer is responsible for handling cash flows, managing capital expenditure decisions and making financial plans. The financial controller handles the accounting function, which includes taxes, financial and management accounting, and information systems.

In smaller firms, many of the roles within an organization are combined into one job. Although each firm will be different, there will always be someone who is responsible for the duties of a financial manager. The most important job of a financial manager is to create value from the firm's capital budgeting, financing and net working capital activities. How do financial managers create value? The answer is that the firm should:

1   Try to buy assets that generate more cash than they cost.
2   Sell bonds, shares and other financial instruments that raise more cash than they cost.

Thus, the firm must create more cash flow than it uses. The cash flows paid to bondholders and shareholders of the firm should be greater than the cash flows put into the firm by the bondholders and shareholders. To see how this is done, we can trace the cash flows from the firm to the financial markets and back again.

The interplay of the firm's activities with the financial markets is illustrated in Figure 1.3. The arrows in Figure 1.3 trace cash flow from the firm to the financial markets and back again. Suppose we begin with the firm's financing activities. To raise money, the firm sells debt (bonds) and equity (shares) to investors in the financial markets. This results in cash flows from the financial markets to the firm (A). This cash is invested in the investment activities (assets) of the firm (B) by the firm's management. The cash generated by the firm (C) is paid to shareholders and bondholders (F). The shareholders receive cash in the form of dividends; the bondholders who lent funds to the firm receive interest and, when the initial loan is repaid, principal. Not all of the firm's cash is paid out. Some is retained (E), and some is paid to the government as taxes (D).

Figure 1.3 Cash Flows between the Firm and the Financial Markets

Over time, if the cash paid to shareholders and bondholders (F) is greater than the cash raised in the financial markets (A), value will be created.

Identification of Cash Flows

Unfortunately, it is not easy to observe cash flows directly. Much of the information we obtain is in the form of accounting statements, and much of the work of financial analysis is to extract cash flow information from accounting statements. Example 1.1 illustrates how this is done.

Example 1.1

Accounting Profit versus Cash Flows

Midland plc is an Irish firm that refines and trades gold. At the end of the year, it sold 2,500 ounces of gold for €1.67 million. The company had acquired the gold for €1 million at the beginning of the year. The company paid cash for the gold when it was purchased. Unfortunately it has yet to collect from the customer to whom the gold was sold. The following is a standard accounting of Midland's financial circumstances at year-end:

The Midland plc Accounting view Income statement Year ended 31 December	
	€
Sales	1,670,000
– Costs	1,000,000
Profit	670,000

Under International Financial Reporting Standards (IFRS), the sale is recorded even though the customer has yet to pay. It is assumed that the customer will pay soon. From the accounting perspective,

Midland seems to be profitable. However, the perspective of corporate finance is different. It focuses on cash flows:

The Midland plc Financial view Income statement Year ended 31 December	
	€
Cash inflow	0
Cash outflow	− 1,000,000
Profit	− 1,000,000

Corporate finance is interested in whether cash flows are being created by the gold trading operations of Midland. Value creation depends on cash flows. For Midland, value creation depends on whether and when it actually receives €1.67 million.

Timing of Cash Flows

The value of an investment made by a firm depends on the timing of cash flows. One of the most important principles of finance is that individuals prefer to receive cash flows earlier rather than later. One euro received today is worth more than one euro received next year. See Example 1.2.

Example 1.2

Cash Flow Timing

The Italian firm Montana SpA is attempting to choose between two proposals for new products. Both proposals will provide additional cash flows over a 4-year period and will initially cost €10,000. The cash flows from the proposals are as follows:

Year	New product A (€)	New product B (€)
1	0	4,000
2	0	4,000
3	0	4,000
4	20,000	4,000
Total	20,000	16,000

At first it appears that new product A would be best because it earns more money. However, the cash flows from proposal B come earlier than those of A. Without more information, we cannot actually decide which set of cash flows would create the most value for the bondholders and shareholders. It depends on whether the value of getting cash from B up front outweighs the total extra cash from A. Bond and share prices reflect this preference for earlier cash, and we will see how to use them to decide between A and B.

Risk of Cash Flows

The firm must consider the risk of cash flows since their amount and timing are not usually known with certainty. Most investors have an aversion to risk.

Real World Insight 1.3

Risk

The Norwegian firm Fjell ASA is considering expanding operations overseas, and it is evaluating the Netherlands and South Africa as possible sites. The Netherlands is considered to be relatively safe, whereas operating in South Africa is seen as more risky. In both cases the company would close down operations after one year.

After undertaking a complete financial analysis, Fjell has come up with the following cash flows of the alternative expansion plans under three scenarios – pessimistic, most likely and optimistic:

	Pessimistic (NKr)	Most likely (NKr)	Optimistic (NKr)
Netherlands	750,000	1,000,000	1,250,000
South Africa	0	1,500,000	2,000,000

If we ignore the pessimistic scenario, perhaps South Africa is the best alternative. When we take the pessimistic scenario into account, the choice is unclear. South Africa appears to be riskier, but it also offers a higher expected level of cash flow.

What Is Risk and How Can it Be Defined?

Corporate finance cannot avoid coping with risky alternatives, and much of our book is devoted to developing methods for evaluating risky opportunities.

Real World Insight 1.4

Skills Needed for a Chief Financial Officer

One needs only to read the Employment Opportunities section in the financial press to appreciate the skills that are required for someone to be a successful chief financial officer. Below is presented an advert for a chief financial officer position based in Europe. The company is large and as a result, the successful candidate would have needed extensive experience in the role. As a budding financial manager yourself, it is useful to keep in mind the CV you must build to become an appropriate candidate for these types of jobs. It seems an awful lot at the moment, but experience and study will bring you to your required level if you keep focused on your target. The name of the company has been changed to FM GmbH to ensure anonymity.

Company: **FM GmbH**
Location: **Frankfurt, Germany**

The Chief Financial Officer will be responsible for the internal and external financial and accounting reporting requirements of the company. This position requires an individual whose business acumen, financial aptitude and professional initiative enable them to improve the organization's performance and enhance the effectiveness of the individuals within. The CFO will need to be committed to results and have a strong sense of personal responsibility for how the company performs. Financial aptitude and analytical skills need to translate into insightful corrective actions and proactive business improvement. FM is of a size where the CFO will need to blend both strategic and tactical skills. The candidate will need to maintain a 'big picture' perspective but also have a strong attention to detail.

Primary responsibilities:

- Oversee financial management of corporate operations, to include developing financial and budget policies and procedures.
- Responsible for cash management, banking relationships and debt management, as well as heavy involvement in any merger and acquisition activities.
- Create, coordinate and evaluate the financial programmes and supporting information systems of the company to include budgeting, tax planning, property and conservation of assets.
- Ensure compliance with local and international budgetary reporting requirements.
- Oversee the approval and processing of revenue, expenditure and position control documents, department budgets, mass salary updates, ledger and account maintenance.
- Co-ordinate the preparation of financial statements, financial reports, special analyses and information reports.

- Manage an accounting department including a controller and accounting staff.
- Implement finance, accounting, billing and auditing procedures.
- Establish and maintain appropriate internal control safeguards.
- Interact with other managers to provide consultative support to planning initiatives through financial and management information analyses, reports and recommendations.
- Ensure records systems are maintained in accordance with internationally accepted auditing standards.
- Strategic thinker who has the ability to manage with an operational perspective.
- Approve and co-ordinate changes and improvements in automated financial and management information systems for the company.
- Analyse cash flow, cost controls and expenses to guide business leaders. Analyse financial statements to pinpoint potential weak areas.
- Establish and implement short- and long-range departmental goals, objectives, policies and operating procedures.
- Serve on planning and policy-making committees.

1.2 The Goal of Financial Management

Assuming we restrict our discussion to for-profit businesses, the goal of financial management is to make money or add value for the owners. This goal is a little vague, of course, so we examine some different ways of formulating it to come up with a more precise definition. A clear definition is important because it leads to an objective basis for making and evaluating financial decisions.

Possible Goals

If we were to consider possible financial goals, we might come up with some ideas like the following:

- Survive
- Avoid financial distress and bankruptcy
- Beat the competition
- Maximize sales or market share
- Minimize costs
- Maximize profits
- Maintain steady earnings growth.

These are only a few of the goals we could list. Furthermore, each of these possibilities presents problems as a goal for the financial manager.

For example, it is easy to increase market share or unit sales: all we have to do is lower our prices or relax our credit terms. Similarly, we can always cut costs simply by doing away with things such as research and development. We can avoid bankruptcy by never borrowing any money or never taking any risks, and so on. It is not clear that any of these actions are in the shareholders' best interests.

Profit maximization would probably be the most commonly cited goal, but even this is not a precise objective. Do we mean profits this year? If so, then we should note that actions such as deferring maintenance, letting inventories run down, and taking other short-run cost-cutting measures will tend to increase profits now, but these activities are not necessarily desirable.

The goal of maximizing profits may refer to some sort of 'long-run' or 'average' profits, but it is still unclear exactly what this means. First, do we mean something like accounting net income or earnings per share? As we will see in more detail in Chapter 4, these accounting numbers may have little to do with what is good or bad for the firm. Second, what do we mean by the long run? As a famous economist once remarked, in the long run, we are all dead! More to the point, this goal does not tell us what the appropriate trade-off is between current and future profits.

The goals we have listed here are all different, but they tend to fall into two classes. The first of these relates to profitability. The goals involving sales, market share and cost control all relate, at least potentially, to different ways of earning or increasing profits. The goals in the second group, involving bankruptcy avoidance, stability and safety, relate in some way to controlling risk. Unfortunately, these two types of goals are somewhat contradictory. The pursuit of profit normally involves some element of risk, so it is not really possible to maximize both safety and profit. What we need, therefore, is a goal that encompasses both factors.

The Goal of Financial Management

The financial manager in a corporation makes decisions for the shareholders of the firm. So, instead of listing possible goals for the financial manager, we really need to answer a more fundamental question: from the shareholders' point of view, what is a good financial management decision?

If we assume that shareholders buy shares because they seek to gain financially, then the answer is obvious: good decisions increase the value of the company's shares, and poor decisions decrease the value of the shares.

From our observations, it follows that the financial manager acts in the shareholders' best interests by making decisions that increase the value of the company's shares. The appropriate goal for the financial manager can thus be stated quite easily:

The goal of financial management is to maximize the value of a company's equity shares.

Chapter 4
Page 93

The goal of maximizing share value avoids the problems associated with the different goals we listed earlier. There is no ambiguity in the criterion, and there is no short-run versus long-run issue. We explicitly mean that our goal is to maximize the *current* share price. (See **Chapter 4** for more information on value maximization.)

If this goal seems a little strong or one-dimensional to you, keep in mind that the shareholders in a firm are residual owners. By this we mean that they are entitled only to what is left after employees, suppliers and creditors (and everyone else with legitimate claims) are paid their due. If any of these groups go unpaid, the shareholders get nothing. So if the shareholders are winning in the sense that the leftover, residual portion is growing, it must be true that everyone else is winning also.

Because the goal of financial management is to maximize the value of the equity, we need to learn how to identify investments and financing arrangements that favourably impact share value. This is precisely what we will be studying. In fact, we could have defined *corporate finance* as the study of the relationship between business decisions and the value of the shares in the business.

A More General Goal

If our goal is as stated in the preceding section (to maximize the company's share price), an obvious question comes up: what is the appropriate goal when the firm has no traded shares? Corporations are certainly not the only type of business; and the shares in many corporations rarely change hands, so it is difficult to say what the value per share is at any particular time.

As long as we are considering for-profit businesses, only a slight modification is needed. The total value of the shares in a corporation is simply equal to the value of the owners' equity. Therefore, a more general way of stating our goal is as follows: maximize the market value of the existing owners' equity.

With this in mind, we do not care what the organizational form is, since good financial decisions increase the market value of the owners' equity, and poor financial decisions decrease it. In fact, although we choose to focus on corporations in the chapters ahead, the principles we develop apply to all forms of business. Many of them even apply to the not-for-profit sector.

Finally, our goal does not imply that the financial manager should take illegal or unethical actions in the hope of increasing the value of the equity in the firm. What we mean is that the financial manager best serves the owners of the business by identifying goods and services that add value to the firm because they are desired and valued in the free marketplace.

1.3 Financial Markets

When firms require cash to invest in new projects, they have to choose the most efficient and cost-effective financing option from a range of appropriate alternatives. First, they must choose whether to borrow money or give up a fraction of ownership in their firm. When borrowing, the company takes out a loan and agrees to later pay back the borrowed amount (principal), plus interest, to compensate the lender for giving the money to the borrower. If the firm decides to give up ownership, they sell a part of their company for a set cash amount. Irrespective, the firm will end up with the cash that they need.

If a firm borrows funds, they can go to a bank for a loan or they can issue *debt securities* in the financial markets. Debt securities are contractual obligations to repay corporate borrowing. If a firm gives up ownership, they can do this through private negotiation or a public sale. The public sale of ownership is undertaken through the marketing and sale of *equity securities*. Equity securities are shares (known as ordinary shares or common stock) that represent non-contractual claims to the residual cash flow of the firm. Issues of debt and equity that are publicly sold by the firm are then traded in the financial markets.

In many countries, the financial markets are not nearly as well developed as in Europe. For example in Africa, many stock exchanges are small and only a handful of companies have publicly traded equity or debt securities. For these firms, it is cheaper to get funding from banks and strategic investors.

The financial markets are composed of the money markets and the capital markets. Money markets are the markets for debt securities that will pay off in the short term (usually less than one year). Capital markets are the markets for long-term debt (with a maturity of over one year) and for equity shares.

The term *money market* applies to a group of loosely connected markets. They are dealer markets. Dealers are firms that make continuous quotations of prices for which they stand ready to buy and sell short-term financial instruments for their own inventory and at their own risk. Thus, the dealer is a principal in most transactions. This is different from a stockbroker acting as an agent for a customer in buying or selling shares on most stock exchanges; an agent does not actually acquire the securities.

Figure 1.4 illustrates the major difference between dealer and agency markets. In both cases, Trader A wishes to sell to Trader B. Moreover, in each scenario, Trader A sells shares for £100 and Trader B buys shares for £110. So what is the difference between the market types? In the dealer market, the dealer bears the risk of holding the shares before he can find a counterparty to buy them. In Figure 1.4, the dealer finds someone to buy the shares at £110. However, if they are unable to locate a counterparty, they may end up with shares that are less than the value at which they were purchased (£100). This is known as inventory risk, and constitutes a cost to the dealer. The difference between the dealer's buying and selling price is known as the *bid-ask spread*, which in this case is £10.

Figure 1.4 Comparison of Dealer and Agency Markets

In an agency market, Trader A hires an agent or broker to find a counterparty. The broker will hopefully find someone and then take a commission on the sale price, which in this case is £10. At no time does the broker own the shares that she is trying to sell and, as a result, does not bear inventory risk.

At the core of the money markets are the money market banks (these tend to be large banks located in Frankfurt, London and New York), government securities dealers (some of which are the same large banks), and many money brokers. Money brokers specialize in finding short-term money for borrowers and placing money for lenders. The financial markets can be classified further as the *primary market* and the *secondary markets*.

The Primary Market: New Issues

The primary market is used when governments and public corporations initially sell securities. Corporations engage in two types of primary market sales of debt and equity: public offerings and private placements.

Most publicly offered corporate debt and equity come to the market underwritten by a syndicate of investment banking firms. The *underwriting* syndicate buys the new securities from the firm for the syndicate's own account and resells them at a higher price. Publicly issued debt and equity must be registered with the local regulatory authority. *Registration* requires the corporation to disclose any and all material information in a registration statement.

Chapter 14 Page 376
Chapter 19 Page 514
Chapter 20 Page 541

The legal, accounting and other costs of preparing the registration statement are not negligible. In part to avoid these costs, privately placed debt and equity are sold on the basis of private negotiations to large financial institutions, such as insurance companies and mutual funds, and other investors. Private placements tend not to be registered with regulatory authorities in the same way as public issues. (See **Chapters 14, 19 and 20** for more information on financing decisions.)

Real World Insight 1.5

SSP

In 2014, the food company, SSP, issued 229.5 million shares at £2.10 per share to raise a total of £482 million. All of this money did not go to the company, however. First, the management and initial investors in the firm were paid £15 million. Then there were other parties that had to be compensated: Lazards advised SSP on the best format of the issue and several banks used their networks to build interest in the company among investors. The banks that were involved included Goldman Sachs, Bank of America Merrill Lynch, Morgan Stanley, Shore Capital and Nomura.

Every country has its own regulatory authority that deals with the registration of publicly traded securities. Corporations that wish to have traded securities in a country's securities exchange must register with the competent authority. Table 1.1 presents the names of regulators for a sample of countries.

Table 1.1 Corporate and Financial Regulators

Country	Regulator	Country	Regulator
Australia	Australian Securities and Investment Commission	Italy	Commissione Nazionale per le Società e la Borsa
		Malaysia	Securities Commission Malaysia
Austria	Financial Market Authority	The Netherlands	The Netherlands Authority for the Financial Markets
Bahrain	Central Bank of Bahrain	Norway	Financial Supervisory Authority (Finanstilsynet)
		Oman	Capital Market Authority
Belgium	Financial Services and Markets Authority	Poland	Financial Supervision Authority (KNF)
China	China Securities Regulatory Commission	Portugal	Comissão do Mercado de Valores Mobiliários
		Singapore	Money Authority of Singapore
		Slovenia	Securities Market Agency (ATVP)
Denmark	Financial Supervisory Authority (Finanstilsynet)	South Africa	Financial Services Board
Egypt	Egyptian Financial Supervisory Authority	Spain	Comisión Nacional del Mercado de Valores
Finland	Financial Supervision Authority	Sweden	Finansinspektionen

Country	Regulator	Country	Regulator
France	Autorité des Marchés Financiers (AMF)	Switzerland	Swiss Financial Market Supervisory Authority
Germany	Bundesanstalt für Finanzdienstleistungsaufsicht (BaFin)	Tanzania	Capital Markets and Securities Authority
Greece	Greek Capital Market Commission	Thailand	Securities and Exchange Commission
India	Securities and Exchange Board of India	Turkey	Capital Markets Board
Ireland	Central Bank of Ireland	United Kingdom	Financial Conduct Authority; Financial Policy Committee; Prudential Regulation Authority
Israel	Israel Securities Authority	United States	Securities and Exchange Commission

Secondary Markets

A secondary market transaction involves one owner or creditor selling to another. The secondary markets therefore provide the means for transferring ownership of corporate securities. Although a corporation is directly involved

Chapter 13 Page 343

only in a primary market transaction (when it sells securities to raise cash), the secondary markets are still critical to large corporations. The reason is that investors are much more willing to purchase securities in a primary market transaction when they know that those securities can later be resold if desired. (See **Chapter 13** for more information on secondary markets.)

Real World Insight 1.6

SSP

Following on from Real World Insight 1.5, on the day that SSP issued its new equity, the share price in the firm increased from the issue price of £2.10 to £2.20 on the back of heavy trading amongst investors. However, the money that was made on this day did not go to SSP but to investors who held the company's shares.

Dealer versus Auction Markets

There are two kinds of secondary markets: *dealer* markets and *auction* markets. Generally speaking, dealers buy and sell for themselves, at their own risk. A car dealer, for example, buys and sells automobiles. In contrast, brokers and agents match buyers and sellers, but they do not actually own the commodity that is bought or sold. An estate agent, for example, does not normally buy and sell houses.

Dealer markets in equities and long-term debt are called *over-the-counter* (OTC) markets. Most trading in debt securities takes place over the counter. The expression *over the counter* refers to days of old when securities were literally bought and sold at counters in offices around the country. Today a significant fraction of the market for equities and almost all of the market for long-term debt has no central location; the many dealers are connected electronically.

Auction markets differ from dealer markets in two ways. First, an auction market or exchange has a physical location (such as Wall Street in New York). Second, in a dealer market, most of the buying and selling is done by the dealer. The primary purpose of an auction market, on the other hand, is to match those who wish to sell with those who wish to buy. Dealers play only a limited role.

Trading in Corporate Securities

The equities of most large firms trade in organized auction markets. The largest such market is the New York Stock Exchange (NYSE). Other auction exchanges include Euronext (Amsterdam, Brussels, Paris and Lisbon Stock Exchanges) and the London Stock Exchange (largest securities only).

In addition to the stock exchanges, there is a large OTC market for equities. The National Association of Securities Dealers Automated Quotation System (NASDAQ) in the US and many equity securities traded on the London Stock Exchange are both examples of OTC markets. The fact that OTC markets have no physical location means that national borders do not present a great barrier, and there is now a huge international OTC debt market. Because of globalization, financial markets have reached the point where trading in many assets, commodities or securities never stops; it just travels around the world.

Stock market liquidity is very important to a financial manager because the easier and cheaper it is to trade the shares of a company, the more demand there will be in the firm. Recent research has actually shown that companies have higher values when their shares are liquid and heavily traded, even after taking out all other factors that may drive valuation differences. In addition, having numerous options on where to trade a company's shares does not harm the value, and in fact can make pricing of the shares more efficient.[1]

Exchange Trading of Listed Companies

The London Stock Exchange is ideal for describing how shares are traded in a dealer system and auction system since both operate simultaneously on the exchange. As of the beginning of 2015, there were more than 2,400 equities traded on the London Stock Exchange. Out of this number, most equities were traded on the exchange's auction system, SETS (Stock Exchange Trading System), and the rest were traded through dealers.

On SETS, traders are allowed to submit orders to buy or sell at a stated price within a reasonable time (limit order), or to buy or sell a stated number of shares immediately at the best price (market order). If a limit order cannot execute immediately (i.e. there are not enough shares at the stated price to fulfil the order), it will stay in the limit order book, which lists all outstanding limit orders.

Smaller companies (around 700 firms listed on the Alternative Investment Market, AIM) are traded through a dealer system, called SEAQ (Stock Exchange Automated Quotation System). Dealers compete with each other by posting buy and sell quotes for a maximum number of shares through an electronic system that lists every dealer's quotes. The dealer that quotes the highest buy price and the lowest sell price is most likely to trade.

Listing

Shares that trade on an organized exchange are said to be *listed* on that exchange or *publicly listed*. To be listed, firms must meet certain minimum criteria concerning, for example, asset size and number of shareholders. These criteria differ from one exchange to another. For example, Euronext has three main requirements for listing. One, a company must have at least 25 per cent of its shares listed on the exchange and the value of these shares must be at least €5 million. Unlike other exchanges, Euronext does not have a minimum threshold for asset size. The second requirement is that the listing firm has at least three years of financial accounts filed with the regulator. Finally, all of the company's financial statements follow recognized international financial reporting standards, also known as IFRS.

Table 1.2 gives a picture of the 30 largest stock exchanges around the world in 2015.

Table 1.2 World Stock Exchanges in 2015

Exchange	Region	Market Value ($m)	Exchange	Region	Market Value ($m)
NYSE	Americas	18,507,192	London SE Group	EAME	4,463,042
NASDAQ OMX	Americas	6,505,314	Euronext	EAME	3,623,096
TMX Group	Americas	2,423,747	Deutsche Börse	EAME	1,810,139
BM&FBOVESPA	Americas	1,102,538	SIX Swiss Exchange	EAME	1,545,221
Mexican Exchange	Americas	535,699	NASDAQ OMX Nordic Exchange	EAME	1,292,877
Santiago SE	Americas	248,783	BME Spanish Exchanges	EAME	1,212,965
Colombia SE	Americas	209,959	Johannesburg SE	EAME	1,036,222
Lima SE	Americas	83,762	Moscow Exchange	EAME	661,097
Buenos Aires SE	Americas	57,559	Saudi Stock Exchange – Tadawul	EAME	559,991
Bermuda SE	Americas	1,635	Oslo Børs	EAME	277,800
			Borsa Istanbul	EAME	228,694
Japan Exchange Group – Tokyo	Asia Pacific	4,658,418	Tel Aviv SE	EAME	218,067

Exchange	Region	Market Value ($m)	Exchange	Region	Market Value ($m)
Hong Kong Exchanges	Asia Pacific	3,290,333	Warsaw SE	EAME	190,335
Shanghai SE	Asia Pacific	2,615,035	Qatar Stock Exchange	EAME	189,576
Shenzhen SE	Asia Pacific	1,627,915	Irish SE	EAME	156,340
Australian SE	Asia Pacific	1,512,784	Tehran SE	EAME	130,513
BSE India	Asia Pacific	1,488,747	Abu Dhabi SE	EAME	126,121
National Stock Exchange India	Asia Pacific	1,459,150	Wiener Börse	EAME	112,750
Korea Exchange	Asia Pacific	1,333,695	Dubai Financial Market	EAME	94,381
Taiwan SE Corp.	Asia Pacific	889,047	Athens Exchange	EAME	89,027
Singapore Exchange	Asia Pacific	820,417	Luxembourg SE	EAME	73,468
Bursa Malaysia	Asia Pacific	529,983	Egyptian Exchange	EAME	70,224
Indonesia SE	Asia Pacific	436,438	Casablanca SE	EAME	54,827
The Stock Exchange of Thailand	Asia Pacific	427,492	Muscat Securities Market	EAME	39,423
Philippine SE	Asia Pacific	256,083	Kazakhstan SE	EAME	26,635
New Zealand Exchange	Asia Pacific	74,603	Amman SE	EAME	26,587
HoChiMinh SE	Asia Pacific	49,922	Budapest SE	EAME	16,651
Colombo SE	Asia Pacific	21,938	Mauritius SE	EAME	9,106
			Ljubljana SE	EAME	8,645
			Malta SE	EAME	4,053
			Cyprus SE	EAME	2,291

Source: © The World Federation of Exchanges Limited.

Real World Insight 1.7

The London Stock Exchange

At over 300 years of age, the London Stock Exchange is one of the world's oldest and largest exchanges. The stock exchange allows trading in equities, bonds and derivatives for UK companies as well as firms from all over the world. However, this isn't the end of the exchange's services. It is also involved in post-trade settlement and risk management for investors who use the exchange's products.

Data is an exceptionally valuable asset to any exchange, with information on all trading activity. A substantial part of its revenues come from the sale and subscription of real-time and reference data products that include stock quotes, orders and transaction prices. The exchange provides over 200,000 international equity, bond and alternative asset class indices, through its index provider, FTSE.

To fully exploit the power of data, the London Stock Exchange provides high performance trading platforms and capital markets software, as well as trading, surveillance and post-trade technology. Although the London Stock Exchange has its headquarters in London, it also has significant operations in Italy, France, North America and Sri Lanka, employing approximately 2,800 people.

Key dates in the history of the London Stock Exchange (from www.londonstockexchange.com)

Starting life in the coffee houses of 17th-century London, the London Stock Exchange quickly grew to become the City's most important financial institution.

1698   John Castaing begins to issue 'at this Office in Jonathan's Coffee-house' a list of stock and commodity prices called 'The Course of the Exchange and other things'.

1698	Stock dealers are expelled from the Royal Exchange for rowdiness and start to operate in the streets and coffee houses nearby, in particular in Jonathan's Coffee House in Change Alley.
1748	Fire sweeps through Change Alley, destroying most of the coffee houses. They are subsequently rebuilt.
1761	A group of 150 stock brokers and jobbers form a club at Jonathan's to buy and sell shares.
1773	The brokers erect their own building in Sweeting's Alley, with a dealing room on the ground floor and a coffee room above. Briefly known as 'New Jonathan's', members soon change the name to 'The Stock Exchange'.
1801	On 3 March, the business reopens under a formal membership subscription basis. On this date, the first regulated exchange comes into existence in London, and the modern Stock Exchange is born.
1812	The first codified rule book is created.
1836	The first regional exchanges open in Manchester and Liverpool.
1854	The Stock Exchange is rebuilt.
1914	The Great War means the Exchange market is closed from the end of July until the new year.
1923	The Exchange receives its own Coat of Arms, with the motto *Dictum Meum Pactum* (My word is my bond).
1972	The Exchange's new 26-storey office block with its 23,000 sq. ft trading floor is opened.
1973	First female members admitted to the market. The 11 British and Irish regional exchanges amalgamate with the London exchange.
1986	Deregulation of the market, known as 'Big Bang', and trading moves from being conducted face to face on a market floor to being performed via computer and telephone from separate dealing rooms. The Exchange becomes a private limited company.
1991	The governing Council of the London Stock Exchange is replaced with a Board of Directors drawn from the Exchange's executive, customer and user base. The trading name becomes 'The London Stock Exchange'.
1995	The Alternative Investment Market (AIM) for small companies is launched.
1997	SETS (Stock Exchange Electronic Trading Service) is launched to bring greater speed and efficiency to the market. The CREST settlement service is launched.
2000	The London Stock Exchange becomes a public limited company: London Stock Exchange plc.
2004	The Exchange moves to brand new headquarters in Paternoster Square, close to St Paul's Cathedral.
2007	The London Stock Exchange merges with Borsa Italiana, creating the London Stock Exchange Group.

Since this book is about corporate finance from a European perspective, it is useful to know what European companies look like. Table 1.3 is a summary of stock exchange listed European firms for the period 1994–2004 taken from a study by Bris et al. (2009). Several things stand out. First, the number of companies in Europe is quite large, with the UK being a major financial centre. Tobin's Q, which is approximately equal to the ratio of the market value of a firm to its accounting or book value, is roughly the same across the continent. Leverage (Total debt / Total assets) is quite variable across countries and ranges between 0.145 and 0.306. As will be seen in later chapters, leverage is strongly associated with industry characteristics and this is the main reason for inter-country differences. The means of other variables, such as CAPEX (capital expenditure), R&D (research and development) and NPPE (net property, plant and equipment) are also affected by the major industries that are in each country.

1.4 Corporate Finance in Action: The Case of Google

The verb 'To google' is defined in *Webster's New Millennium*™ *Dictionary of English* as 'to search for information on the internet'. This integration into everyday language is just one signal of the exceptional success of the Internet search engine that was started in 1996 by two Stanford PhD students, Sergey Brin and Larry Page. Google is now worth in excess of $130 billion. During its massive growth, the management of Google had to consider and deal with many issues, all of which are covered in this textbook over the next 30 chapters.

Table 1.3 European Firm Characteristics

Country	No. Firms	No. Firm-year Observations	Tobin's Q Mean	Sales (Million Euros) Mean	EBITDA/TA Mean	NPPE/TA Mean	Leverage Mean	CAPEX/TA Mean	R&D/TA Mean
Austria	79	671	1.205	549.4	0.108	0.369	0.249	0.062	0.006
Belgium	101	909	1.375	949.8	0.117	0.232	0.225	0.055	0.002
Finland	100	915	1.357	971.4	0.141	0.368	0.266	0.072	0.013
France	598	4,936	1.371	1,548.9	0.111	0.230	0.242	0.050	0.006
Germany	535	4,741	1.643	1,530.1	0.119	0.321	0.211	0.064	0.009
Ireland	41	380	1.396	935.6	0.102	0.416	0.268	0.063	0.004
Italy	175	1,589	1.261	2,115.6	0.089	0.245	0.283	0.042	0.004
Luxembourg	11	85	1.447	1,499.4	0.143	0.252	0.145	0.035	0.000
Netherlands	166	1,440	1.573	2,046.0	0.140	0.328	0.237	0.065	0.006
Portugal	73	578	1.127	567.3	0.107	0.383	0.288	0.047	0.000
Spain	138	1,256	1.328	1,528.1	0.108	0.380	0.224	0.047	0.001
All euro countries	2,017	17,500	1.434	1,489.0	0.115	0.297	0.238	0.061	0.006
Denmark	183	1,630	1.299	396.1	0.098	0.289	0.256	0.052	0.007
Norway	159	1,234	1.531	480.7	0.098	0.344	0.306	0.079	0.009
Sweden	201	1,659	1.631	1,107	0.112	0.320	0.253	0.060	0.012
Switzerland	169	1,551	1.451	1,234	0.114	0.367	0.260	0.047	0.016
UK	1,513	12,672	1.549	786.6	0.094	0.325	0.179	0.054	0.010
All non-euro countries	2,225	18,746	1.526	798.0	0.098	0.327	0.207	0.058	0.013
All countries	4,242	36,246	1.481	1,131.6	0.106	0.312	0.222	0.060	0.009

Notes: Tobin's Q is the (Market value of equity + Book value of debt) ÷ Total assets; EBITDA/TA is the Earnings before interest, taxes, and depreciation ÷ Total assets; NPPE/TA is the Net property, plant and equipment ÷ Total assets; Leverage is the Total debt ÷ Total assets; CAPEX/TA is the Annual capital expenditure of the firm ÷ Total assets; R&D/TA is the Annual research and development expenditure of the firm ÷ Total assets.

Source: Adapted from Bris et al. (2009).

Early Days

The foundation of any new business is the product or service idea. Through their research, Brin and Page believed they had a more efficient model of searching through Internet pages than the search engines that existed in 1996. Armed only with this idea and a few working algorithms, they approached several potential investors and successfully attracted $100,000 from one of the founders of Sun Microsystems to develop their business concept. Within a year, they had received a further $25 million from venture capitalists. To attract this financing, Brin and Page would have had to create a business plan and cash flow forecast that estimated their future costs and revenues. From business plans and cash flows, investors are able to arrive at a valuation of the potential company. Valuation of companies and projects is covered in Part Two of this text.

Google and Corporate Governance

By 2004, Google had been so successful with its business model and grown so much that they needed significant injections of cash to capture the emerging business opportunities that were becoming available. To the two founders, Brin and Page, it was paramount that they retained control of the company, but they also knew that they would have to issue many shares to investors so the firm could receive adequate funding. As a solution, Google restructured its ownership to have two types of equity shares, A and B class. B class shares, which were

Chapter 2
Page 25

predominantly owned by Brin and Page, awarded ten votes at company meetings for every share certificate, while A class shares received one vote for every share certificate. This meant that even though the number of shares held by outside investors was much higher than the two founders put together, the number of votes of outsiders was lower. Issues relating to ownership structure and corporate governance in general are covered in **Chapter 2**.

Google and Financing Decisions

When Google was thinking of raising capital, they had two choices. They could borrow the money (through a bank loan or public debt markets) or issue equity (through the equity markets). In the end, they chose to raise all the money in the form of equity financing. Google actually issued no long-term debt until 2011. There are a number of

Chapter 15
Page 396

reasons for this and there are many factors to take into consideration when a firm chooses its own debt to equity mix, which is also known as its capital structure. Companies may even choose to use more complex instruments such as options or warrants. Capital structure is covered in Part Four of the textbook and complex funding securities are discussed in detail in Part Six. For more information on financing decisions see **Chapter 15**.

Google and the Financing Process

Chapter 14 Page 376
Chapter 19 Page 514
Chapter 20 Page 541

The original Google share issue was highly unusual in that it was organized wholly over the Internet. However, several fundamental issues had to be decided upon. First, what should the value of the new shares be? Should A class shares have a different value to B class shares? How risky are the shares? These questions are of huge importance to investors who are planning to invest their cash in any new investment. Assessing the risk of investments is covered in Part Three and the process of issuing new securities is reviewed in Part Five. (See **Chapters 14, 19 and 20** for more information on the financing process.)

Google as a Business

Although Google is known as an Internet firm, its success and size makes it quite similar to other large firms in more capital intensive industries. As at the beginning of 2015, Google had over $12 billion invested in property and over 52,000 employees. In fact, the Google management were so concerned that the firm was losing a lot of its early values and culture that they appointed a chief cultural officer, whose remit was to develop and maintain the early Google working environment.

Google and Short-term Financing

Chapter 26 Page 698
Chapter 27 Page 721

Like all other firms, Google needs to ensure it has enough liquidity and cash available to pay off its creditors. Short-term financial planning is therefore crucial to its continued existence. Unlike many companies, Google is exceptionally cash rich. From its 2014 accounts, the company had over $48 billion in cash and highly marketable securities. Is this too much or too little? Short-term financing is covered in Part Seven of the text. (See **Chapters 26 and 27** for more information on short-term financing.)

Google and Acquisitions

Finally, Google has undertaken over 160 acquisitions since 2001. Most notably, it bought Motorola Mobility for $12.5 billion in 2011, YouTube ($1.65 billion) in 2006, DoubleClick ($3.1 billion) in 2007, and Nestlabs ($3.2 billion) in 2014. Its operations span many countries, making the firm's global reach enormous. It is one of the biggest companies in the world and will continue to evolve and develop in the future. The final part of this textbook deals with issues like corporate restructuring, financial distress and international finance. These are extremely important to all companies, and not just Google. (See **Chapter 28** for more information on mergers and acquisitions.)

Chapter 28
Page 755

So What is Corporate Finance?

Many people who think of corporate finance tend to consider valuation as being most important. Others think of risk assessment and risk management, while many think that capital structure should be emphasized. Hopefully, this section shows that for a business to be truly successful, the management of a firm and its shareholders must have a solid understanding of all corporate finance areas and not just one or two topics. Google was a success, not just because it had a fantastic business idea, but also because it understands the fundamental basis of good business and corporate finance.

Summary and Conclusions

This chapter introduced you to some of the basic ideas in corporate finance:

1   Corporate finance has three main areas of concern:

  (a) *Capital budgeting*: What long-term investments should the firm take?

  (b) *Capital structure*: Where will the firm get the long-term financing to pay for its investments? Also, what mixture of debt and equity should it use to fund operations?

  (c) *Working capital management*: How should the firm manage its everyday financial activities?

2   The goal of financial management in a for-profit business is to make decisions that increase the value of the shares, or, more generally, increase the market value of the equity.

Of the topics we have discussed thus far, the most important is the goal of financial management: maximizing share value. Throughout the text we will be analysing many different financial decisions, but we will always ask the same question: how does the decision under consideration affect the value of the equity?

Questions and Problems

CONCEPT

1 **What is Corporate Finance?**   What are the main elements of corporate finance? How might these elements relate to typical family life?

2 **Introduction to Corporate Finance**   Which of the following is **not** a core element of corporate finance?

  (a)   The investment decision

  (b)   The equity decision

  (c)   The financing decision

  (d)   Short-term capital management

3 **Goal of Financial Management**   Explain the assumption behind the statement: 'The goal of financial management is to maximize the current share price.' Why isn't the goal to maximize the future share price?

4 **Financial Markets**   Why do financial markets exist? Explain, in detail, how they facilitate the flow of capital around the economy.

REGULAR

5 **Financial Markets**   Describe 4 securities that are traded in financial markets.

6 **Corporate Finance in Action**   The section highlighting Google as a case study is special in many ways because of the firm's meteoric success. Extend the case study on Google by looking at the title of each chapter in this book and then identifying a similar event or news story about the firm that captures the material in the book. Write your own case study on Google.

7 **Balance Sheet Equation**   In 2011, Elan Corp plc, the Irish biotechnology firm had €619 million in current assets and €1,403 million in total assets. It had €338 million in current liabilities and €1,253 million in total liabilities. How much was the equity of Elan Corp plc worth? How much did it have in non-current assets and non-current liabilities?

8 **Capital Structure**   In the previous question, Elan Corp plc announced that it plans to increase its non-current assets by €100 million. If the company wishes to maintain its ratio of total liabilities to equity, how much long-term debt should it issue?

9 **Accounting and Cash Flows**   You work for a private airport that has just purchased a new radar system from the UK for £3.5 billion. You have paid £100 million up front with the rest to be paid in 3 months. Explain how these figures would appear on an accounting statement and cash flow statement.

10 **Timing of Cash Flows**   Your company has just purchased 20 fork-lift trucks and has two payment options. The first option is to pay £100,000 every month for 12 months. The second option is to pay £1,200,000 at the end of the year. Which option should you choose? Why?

11 **Risk of Cash Flows**   You are assessing the viability of two projects. Project A has a 25 per cent chance of losing €1,000,000, a 50 per cent chance of breaking even and a 25 per cent chance of making €1,000,000 profit. Project B has a 10 per cent chance of losing €2,000,000, an 80 per cent chance of breaking even, and a 10 per cent chance of making €2,000,000 profit. Which project should you choose? Why?

12 **Corporate Goals**   Explain what is meant by corporate social responsibility (CSR).

13 **Corporate Social Responsibility**   Do you consider corporate social responsibility (CSR) to be important to a firm's management? Explain.

14 **Financing Goals**   As a firm progresses throughout its life cycle it will typically move from seeking investment from private sources towards raising money on the capital markets. Explain why this is the case.

15 **Short-term Financing Goals**   In 2014 it was reported that Apple had twice as much cash as the US government. Why could this be a problem for the firm?

16 **Financial Management Goals**   You have read the first chapter of this textbook and have taken over a company that you now discover is losing £100,000 a week. At the rate things are going, the company will not have any cash left in 6 months to pay its creditors. What are your goals as a financial manager? Is this consistent with what you have read in this chapter? Explain.

17 **Financial Management Goals**   Explain what is meant by socially responsible investment (SRI). In your opinion, is this a necessary function of business?

18 **Ethical and Non-Ethical Funds**   You have just joined a graduate scheme in a fund management company, and your manager tells you that ethical funds do not significantly outperform non-ethical funds, according to the bulk of empirical evidence. Is this statement true or false?

19 **Financial Management Goals**   Many 'experts' suggest that maximizing profit should be the main financial goal of a corporation. Is this a correct view? Explain.

20 **Financial Management Goals**   If you are in charge of a private firm and it doesn't have a share price, what should be your goal as a financial manager? Explain.

21 **Financial Management Goals**   You have been manager of a small company for 20 years and have become great friends with your employees. In the last month, foreign owners have bought out the company's founding owner and have told you that they need to cut costs in order to maximize the value of the company. One of the things they suggest is to lay off 30 per cent of the workforce. However, you believe that the workforce is the company's greatest asset. On what basis do you argue against the new owners' opinions?

CHALLENGE

22 **Goals of the Firm**   Your company's new owners suggest the following changes to maximize the value of the firm. Write a brief report responding to each point in turn:

   (a) Add a cost of living adjustment to the pensions of your retired employees.

   (b) It is expected that high oil prices will increase your revenues by 25 per cent. The company wishes to increase its exploration costs by 15 per cent and pay the rest of the profit out to shareholders (i.e. themselves) in the form of increased cash dividends.

   (c) Begin new research and development into more advanced but untried exploration techniques.

   (d) Lay off 15 per cent of the workforce to keep costs down.

23 **Dealer versus Agency Markets**   Explain the difference between dealer and agency markets. Why do you think both types of markets exist? Is there one type of market that is the best? Explain.

24 **Statement of Financial Position**   If a firm is to cut costs as a result of falling revenues, how would this appear in the statement of financial position? Explain.

25 **Dual Class Shares**   The multinational media company News Corporation has a dual class share structure. Why might the company do this? Are there any drawbacks?

26 **Balance Sheet Equation**   You have the following information for the Swiss power and automation technology firm, ABB Ltd. All figures are in millions of Swiss francs (SFr).

	2015	2014	2013	2012	2011
Current assets	18,327	18,241	17,523	16,734	12,692
Non-current assets	7,915	6,868	6,344	5,680	5,485
Total assets	26,242	25,109	23,867	22,414	18,177
Current liabilities	12,102	10,541	11,499	10,468	9,027
Non-current liabilities	3,378	4,598	4,301	4,024	4,785
Total liabilities	15,480	15,139	15,800	14,492	13,812
Total equity	10,762	9,970	8,067	7,922	4,365
Total liabilities plus equity	26,242	25,109	23,867	22,414	18,177

   Give a brief interpretation of what you think ABB Ltd did over the period 2011–2015. Do you think they are in a better position now than in 2011?

27 **Balance Sheet**   Assume that ABB Ltd increased their non-current assets by SFr1 billion in 2016 and at the same time reduced their current assets by SFr500 million. Review the ways in which ABB would be able to finance this expansion.

28 **Statement of Financial Position**   Assume that, in 2016, ABB purchased a new automation technology for SFr500 million. They paid this on credit and won't be due to actually pay for the automation technology until 2018. The managers of ABB state that in the future, any increase in assets will be wholly funded by debt. What would the statement of financial position look like at the end of 2016? At the end of 2018?

29 **Statement of Financial Position**   Assume that instead of fully financing the expansion with debt, the managers of ABB Ltd say they wish to maintain the ratio of non-current liabilities to equity after the expansion. What would ABB's statement of financial position look like at the end of 2016?

30 **Financial Market Regulators**   The UK's financial markets regulator states that its objectives are to promote efficient, orderly and fair markets, help retail consumers achieve a fair deal, and improve the country's business capacity and effectiveness. The German financial markets regulator, BaFin, states that, 'The objective of securities supervision is to ensure the transparency and integrity of the financial market and the protection of investors.' Are the British and German objectives consistent with each other? Explain.

31 **Balance Sheet Model of the Firm**   The layout of financial accounts is rarely the same across companies and, sometimes, it can be difficult to establish a simple picture of a firm's balance sheet. The accounts below are for Logik plc. Construct a simple balance sheet model of the firm in the same way as Real World Insight 1.1 for years 2015 and 2014. Provide a brief report on how you think the company has changed.

Logik plc Annual Report 2015 Logik Consolidated Balance Sheet € million	31 Dec 2015	31 Dec 2014
Current assets		
Cash and cash equivalents	937.8	943.7
Marketable securities and financial assets	1,117.1	55.6
Trade accounts receivable	2,328.3	2,296.3
Inventories	1,691.1	1,673.5
Other current assets	250.2	564.7
Tax receivables	72.7	93.7
Assets held for sale	—	36.7
	6,397.2	**5,664.2**
Non-current assets		
Intangible assets	11,764.3	12,484.1
Property, plant and equipment	3,113.4	3,241.5
Investments at equity	—	5.0
Non-current financial assets	60.3	130.3
Financial assets covering pensions	—	216.9
Other non-current assets	54.9	52.9
Deferred tax assets	730.0	593.1
	15,722.9	**16,723.8**
Current liabilities		
Current financial liabilities	1,394.4	356.1
Trade accounts payable	1,100.8	1,200.1
Other current liabilities	1,102.1	1,054.6
Tax liabilities	399.4	368.4
Current provisions	365.5	374.5
Liabilities directly related to assets held for sale	—	5.9
	4,362.2	**3,359.6**
Non-current liabilities		
Non-current financial liabilities	4,144.9	5,127.4
Other non-current liabilities	43.6	42.9
Non-current provisions	619.5	524.2
Provisions for pensions and other post-employment benefits	1,136.9	1,581.6
Deferred tax liabilities	1,319.6	1,380.5
	7,264.5	**8,656.6**
Net equity		
Equity capital	565.2	565.2
Reserves	8,671.7	8,484.2
Gains/losses recognized immediately in equity	1,210.2	1,280.4
Equity attributable to Logik plc shareholders	**10,447.1**	**10,329.8**
Non-controlling interest	46.3	42.0
	10,493.4	**10,371.8**

32 Goals of a Financial Manager In 2012, the Argentinian government nationalized YPF, which is a subsidiary of Repsol, the Spanish oil giant. YPF was integral to the operations of Repsol. The firm was set up 10 years earlier, and had received more than €20 billion of capital investment from Repsol. The benefits to Repsol's shareholders from YPF were large and every year over €527 million of dividends were paid to the parent company. If you were the financial manager of YPF, how do you think your goals would change as a result of the change of owners (i.e. from Repsol to the Argentinian government)?

33 Stock Exchanges   The UK has a hybrid stock exchange where the largest companies are traded on an electronic order book and the smallest firms are traded through a competitive dealer market. Do you think this is a sensible system? If you were a new firm, on which system would you prefer to have your shares listed? Explain.

34 Life Cycle of Firms   Choose any company from your country and develop a chronology of the firm's life cycle, from the business start-up, through initial expansion, to stock exchange listing and then (if applicable) death through merger, acquisition or insolvency. In each stage, explain the company's evolution through the eyes of a financial manager.

Exam Question (45 minutes)

You have been hired to help a well-known artist to commercialize her oil and acrylic paintings. Your client has never worked in industry since leaving art college, having been funded by academic grants, and has very little understanding of how to develop a business that captures the true value of her artistic creations. In fact, she admits to you that she does not know one thing about running a business and asks you to define what you can do for her company. Specifically, she has a number of queries that she feels are important to understand before going forward:

1 As a financial manager, what will be your main activities in her new company? (12 marks)

2 What will be your first priority? Explain. (12 marks)

3 Will the company need to invest money? Explain. (12 marks)

4 Will the company need financing? Explain. (12 marks)

5 How will the company raise financing? Is it sensible to list the company on the stock market or issue debt? What about bank loans? (12 marks)

6 What are the benefits of holding cash? (12 marks)

7 What should be the goal of the company? (12 marks)

8 The artist has said to you that she does not wish to run a company that does not contribute to society. She asks whether it is sensible to run a company that donates 10 per cent of all profits to good causes. She asks you whether this is a sensible objective and, if not, are there other options to contribute to society? Explain your view in a way she can easily understand. (16 marks)

Practical Case Study

A skill any financial manager must have is to be able to find and understand financial information. Visit the websites of Volkswagen AG, Daimler AG and Renault SA. Download their financial accounts for the most recent year. At first you may find it difficult to find these, but persevere because the information is there.

1 For each firm, look at its statement of financial position and record the following:

   (a) Non-current assets

   (b) Current assets

   (c) Current liabilities

   (d) Non-current liabilities.

   Construct the balance sheet for each firm and calculate the value of shareholders' equity. What do the figures say about each company?

2 Visit the Yahoo! Finance website and find the share price of each firm. What does the share price history tell you about each company?

3 On Yahoo! Finance read the news for each company. What does the news tell you about the fortunes of each company?

4 Combining all the information, which company do you think is the best investment? Explain.

References

Bris, A., Y. Koskinen and M. Nilsson (2009) 'The Euro and Corporate Valuations', *Review of Financial Studies*, Vol. 22, No. 8, 3171–3209.

Fang, V.W., T. Hoe and S. Tice (2009) 'Stock Market Liquidity and Firm Value', *Journal of Financial Economics*, Vol. 94, 150–169.

O'Hara, M. and M. Ye (2011) 'Is Market Fragmentation Harming Market Quality?', *Journal of Financial Economics*, Vol. 100, 459–474.

Additional Reading

The field of corporate finance is enormous and evolves in conjunction with events in the global business environment. A couple of interesting papers for readers who wish to delve further are given below.

1   Rajan, R. G. (2012) 'Presidential Address: The Corporation in Finance', *The Journal of Finance*, Vol. 67, 1173–1217.

2   Zingales, L. (2000) 'In Search of New Foundations', *The Journal of Finance*, Vol. 55, No. 4, 1623–1653.

Since the financial crisis, many academics have reconsidered some of the fundamental paradigms of finance and ask whether these are still valid. Two interesting papers from the *Harvard Business Review* discuss this issue with respect to the way in which company performance is measured and the too focused nature of finance on figures (and too little on strategy).

3   Christensen, C. M. and D. Bever (2014) 'The Capitalist's Dilemma', *Harvard Business Review*, Vol. 92, No. 6, 60–68.

4   Mukunda, G. (2014) 'The Price of Wall Street's Power', *Harvard Business Review*, Vol. 92, No. 6, 70–78.

One question that has been approached in a very interesting way is 'What is more important? The business plan or the managers who carry it out?' This is examined in the following paper:

5   Kaplan, S., B. Sensoy and P. Stromberg (2009) 'Should Investors Bet on the Jockey or the Horse? Evidence from the Evolution of Firms from Early Business Plans to Public Companies', *The Journal of Finance*, Vol. 64, 75–115.

Studies of the financial markets are very common. Below are listed some papers on financial markets that are related to corporate finance and financial decision-making.

6   Bris, A., Y. Koskinen and M. Nilsson (2009) 'The Euro and Corporate Valuations', *Review of Financial Studies*, Vol. 22, No. 8, 3171–3209.

7   Doidge, C., G. A. Karolyi and R. M. Stulz (2009) 'Has New York Become Less Competitive than London in Global Markets? Evaluating Foreign Listing Choices over Time', *Journal of Financial Economics*, Vol. 91, No. 3, 253–277.

8   Fang, V. W., T. Hoe and S. Tice (2009) 'Stock Market Liquidity and Firm Value', *Journal of Financial Economics*, Vol. 94, 150–169.

9   O'Hara, M. and M. Ye (2011) 'Is Market Fragmentation Harming Market Quality?', *Journal of Financial Economics*, Vol. 100, 459–474.

10 Pukthuanthong, K. and R. Roll (2009) 'Global Market Integration: An Alternative Measure and its Application', *Journal of Financial Economics*, Vol. 94, 214–232.

11 Sarkissian, S. and M. J. Schill (2009) 'Are There Permanent Valuation Gains to Overseas Listing?' *Review of Financial Studies*, Vol. 22, No. 1, 372–412.

If you wish to understand what caused the financial crisis of 2008, the following paper is a very good academic study of the issue and, in particular, the risky mortgage market.

12 Demyanyk, Y. and O. van Hemert (2011) 'Understanding the Subprime Mortgage Crisis', *Review of Financial Studies*, Vol. 24, No. 6, 1848–1880.

Finally, Luigi Zingales has written a very interesting paper criticizing the approach finance academics sometimes take towards the subject. In the interests of humility, we present it here:

13 Zingales, L. (2015) 'DP10350, Does Finance Benefit Society?' CEPR Policy Paper.

Endnote

1   See Fang et al. (2009) and O'Hara and Ye (2011).

Corporate Governance

Does it matter how a company is structured for managers to make the best financial decisions? Does it matter who owns a company? Where do ethics come into the decision to invest a firm's resources and does this have any relevance for the financial manager? Do managers always follow the wishes of shareholders? Are lenders equally important to owners of a firm? How should a company manage its relationships with diverse stakeholder groups, such as employees, customers and suppliers? Are some shareholders more important than others?

All of the above are significant in understanding the various pressures managers face when running a business. Many finance textbooks assume that companies have an overriding objective to maximize firm value and that managers prioritize this over all others. However, there is nothing to stop managers from pursuing their personal agendas over that of the firm or its owners.

Recent years have seen major changes in the way shareholders engage with their own companies. The fall-out from the banking crisis of 2008 is still creating ripples in the corporate world and concepts such as managerial accountability and transparency have received much greater emphasis in recent times. Financial institutions have also become more involved in the strategic decisions of firms and shareholder activism is now common. Not only this, but more eclectic changes have affected the way companies are managed and run. The influx of money from international investors in China, India, South America and the Middle East has influenced corporate cultures in ways that would not have been imagined ten years ago.

Unfortunately, even with improvements in corporate governance, scandals are still occurring with worrying frequency. A recent case that reflects a number of distinct governance failures concerns Tesco, the multinational food retailer that has nearly 7,000 stores across Europe and South East Asia. Tesco, like many other retailers, has been struggling with increasing competition and weak consumer spending. The rise of budget retailers like Aldi and Lidl has also put stress on the firm's previously successful business model.

In late 2014, Tesco shocked investors when they announced their profits had been overstated by £250 million. Their share price immediately tumbled by more than 25 per cent and eight senior executives were suspended from the company. It will take years for all the reasons to be understood for the overstatement, but initially the £250 million error appeared to be a result of several contributory pressures.

A common understanding at the time was that Tesco used aggressive (but legal) accounting techniques to improve the annual accounting performance. For example, in the supermarket sector, it is difficult to predict future sales because a lot of business is directly linked to incentivization deals with suppliers, such as discounts when sales targets have been hit. In this setting, Tesco regularly brought forward predicted revenues in their accounting statements and delayed the recognition of expenses. Combining these, it is easy to see why profit forecasts overestimated what was happening in reality. A subsequent report by the accounting firm, Deloitte, stated that Tesco had been using aggressive (but legal) accounting practices for a number of years and so had systematically been recording higher trading profit.

Why did the firm pursue this policy and did regulators and investors do anything to curtail it? Clearly, when a firm is reporting healthy profits investors react in a positive way and increase their shareholdings. This would result in higher share prices and capital gains for investors. Questions must also be asked of the power and effectiveness of independent monitors such as Tesco's non-executive directors and their auditor, PWC. Why didn't they do anything?

In this chapter, we will cover the various issues involved with corporate governance, from the different corporate structures that can be created, through the various ways investors can put money into the firm, and the powers of regulators in incentivizing positive management behaviour. The topic is necessarily broad and so our purpose is to provide a broad introduction to corporate governance and how it affects financial decision-making. The interested reader is invited to review the articles presented in the reference list at the end of the chapter if they wish to investigate the area in more depth.

2.1   The Corporate Firm

A firm is a way of organizing the economic activity of many individuals. A basic problem faced by a firm is how to raise cash. The corporate form of business – that is, organizing the firm as a corporation – is the standard method for solving problems encountered in raising large amounts of cash. However, businesses can take other forms. In this section we consider the three basic legal forms of organizing firms, and we see how firms go about the task of raising large amounts of money under each form.

The Sole Proprietorship

A sole proprietorship is a business owned by one person. Suppose you decide to start a business to produce bagpipes. Going into business is simple: you announce to all who will listen, 'Today, I am going to build better bagpipes.'

A sole proprietorship is the most common form of business structure in the world. From London to Dar es Salaam, from Bangkok to Amsterdam, from Oman to Madrid, you will see people doing their business in the streets and at roadsides. These are all businesses owned by one person. Possibly, you, the reader, may come from a family that has a sole proprietorship business.

In many countries, you need a business licence to run a sole proprietorship but it is also common for sole proprietorships to be set up without any paperwork. Once started, a sole proprietorship can hire as many people as needed and borrow whatever money is required. At year-end, all the profits and losses will belong to the owner and this becomes his or her annual income.

Here are some factors that are important in considering a sole proprietorship:

1   The sole proprietorship is the cheapest business to form. No formal charter, articles or memoranda of association are required. Very few government regulations must be satisfied for most industries.

2   A sole proprietorship pays no corporate income taxes. All profits of the business are taxed as individual income.

3   The sole proprietorship has unlimited liability for business debts and obligations. No distinction is made between personal and business assets. This means that if a sole proprietorship owes money to creditors and cannot pay, the owner's own possessions must be used to pay off the firm's debts.

4   The life of the sole proprietorship is limited by the life of the owner of the firm.

5   Because the only money invested in the firm is the proprietor's, the cash that can be raised by the sole proprietor is limited to the proprietor's own personal wealth.

Example 2.1

JonMac Builders

JonMac Builders is a building contractor, owned as a sole proprietorship by John McAfee. Started in 1987 by a fresh-looking 24-year-old with his own savings, John leased a small van for £200, used his own tools, and began working on jobs garnered through word of mouth. The firm still exists as a sole proprietorship and now has four employees, all family members. All income from the company's activities is taxed at John's income tax rate and the firm's liabilities are secured by John's personal assets, such as his house.

The Partnership

Any two or more people can get together and form a **partnership**. Partnerships fall into two categories: (1) general partnerships, and (2) limited partnerships.

In a *general partnership* all partners agree to provide some fraction of the work and cash, and share the profits and losses of the firm. Each partner is liable for the debts of the partnership. A partnership agreement specifies the nature of the arrangement. The partnership agreement may be an oral agreement or a formal document setting forth the understanding.

Limited partnerships permit the liability of some of the partners to be limited to the amount of cash each has contributed to the partnership. Limited partnerships usually require that (1) at least one partner be a general partner, and (2) the limited partners do not participate in managing the business. Here are some things that are important when considering a partnership:

1   Partnerships are usually inexpensive and easy to form. Written documents are required in complicated arrangements, including general and limited partnerships. Business licences and filing fees may be necessary.

2   General partners have unlimited liability for all debts. The liability of limited partners is usually limited to the contribution each has made to the partnership. If one general partner is unable to meet his or her commitment, the shortfall must be made up by the other general partners.

3   The general partnership is terminated when a general partner dies or withdraws (but this is not so for a limited partner). It is difficult for a partnership to transfer ownership without dissolving. Usually all general partners must agree. However, limited partners may sell their interest in a business.

4   It is difficult for a partnership to raise large amounts of cash. Equity contributions are usually limited to a partner's ability and desire to contribute to the partnership. Many companies start life as a sole proprietorship or partnership, but at some point they choose to convert to corporate form.

5   Income from a partnership is taxed as personal income to the partners.

6   Management control resides with the general partners. Usually a majority vote is required on important matters, such as the amount of profit to be retained in the business.

It is difficult for large business organizations to exist as sole proprietorships or partnerships. The main advantage to a sole proprietorship or partnership is the cost of getting started. Afterward, the disadvantages, which may become severe, are (1) unlimited liability, (2) limited life of the enterprise, and (3) difficulty of transferring ownership. These three disadvantages lead to (4) difficulty in raising cash.

Example 2.2

NellaFola

NellaFola is a real estate broker consisting of 25 estate agents. Five of the estate agents are general partners who are responsible for the long-term strategy of the firm, in addition to managing their own clients. The other 20 estate agents have their own customers and earn commission for the partnership on real estate sales. Each estate agent will have a remuneration package that consists of a basic salary element plus a commission component. In addition to a basic salary and commission, the five general partners will also receive a component of the partnership's profits. Partnerships of this type are common in the law, medical and accounting professions.

The Corporation

Of the forms of business enterprises, the corporation is by far the most important. It is a distinct legal entity. This means that a corporation can have a name and enjoy many of the legal powers of natural persons. For example, corporations can acquire and exchange property. Corporations can enter contracts and may sue and be sued. For jurisdictional purposes the corporation is a citizen of its country of incorporation (it cannot vote, however).

The Articles of Incorporation and Memorandum of Association

Starting a corporation is more complicated than starting a proprietorship or partnership. The incorporators must prepare articles of incorporation and a memorandum of association (the terms differ from country to country but the general requirements are the same). The articles of incorporation must include the following:

1 Name of the corporation

2 Intended life of the corporation (it may be forever)

3 Business purpose

4 Number of shares that the corporation is authorized to issue, with a statement of limitations and rights of different classes of shares

5 Nature of the rights granted to shareholders

6 Number of members of the initial board of directors.

The memorandum of association contains the rules to be used by the corporation to regulate its own existence, and they concern its shareholders, directors and officers. The rules can range from the briefest possible statement of rules for the corporation's management to hundreds of pages of text.

Public versus Private Limited Corporations

A corporation will normally start off as a private limited corporation, in which the shares of the firm are not permitted to be traded or advertised in the public arena. The directors of the company will very likely also be the major shareholders. Private limited companies are usually very small with employees ranging between three and several thousand. Families are regularly the major shareholders in private limited companies.

In closely held corporations with few shareholders, there may be a large overlap among the shareholders, the directors and the top management. However, in larger corporations, the shareholders, directors and the top management are likely to be separate groups. At this point, the corporation will comprise three sets of distinct interests: the shareholders (the owners), the directors and senior management, and the firm's stakeholders (e.g. lenders, employees, local community).

The senior executives of a corporation make up the board of directors. On the board, someone will have the chairperson's role, and be responsible for ensuring that the interests of shareholders are actively considered in corporate decision-making. The chairperson is the most senior member of a corporation and leads all general meetings of the firm. The chief executive officer is the most senior manager of the corporation and is in ultimate charge of the day-to-day running of the firm. In many companies, the same person takes on the role of both chief executive and chairperson. The board also has other directors, and these are made up of two distinct categories. Executive directors are senior managers that work in the company on a day-to-day basis and non-executive directors are independent and are not involved in management. Non-executives usually attend monthly board meetings and will be individuals with significant business experience and possible political importance.

In countries (e.g. Belgium, Ireland, Italy, Portugal, Spain, Sweden, the UK and US) with single-tier, or unitary, board structures, the shareholders control the corporation's direction, policies and activities. The shareholders elect the board of directors, who in turn select top management. Members of top management serve as corporate officers and manage the operations of the corporation in the best interest of the shareholders.

In countries with two-tier board structures, a corporation's executive board (that is made up of directors and senior management) report to, and is elected by, a supervisory board which may consist of major shareholders, creditors, trade union representatives, major lenders and other important stakeholders. There are no non-executive directors on the executive board since the supervisory board has the responsibility of monitoring the actions of executive directors. Countries with two-tier boards include Austria, Denmark, Germany and the Netherlands. Countries where both unitary and two-tier boards can exist include Finland, France, Norway and Switzerland. However, things are never straightforward and there will always be country-specific differences. Belgium, for example, has a unitary board system but banks and insurance companies are allowed to have two-tier board structures.

Advantages of Corporations over Partnerships and Sole Partnerships

The potential separation of ownership from management gives the corporation several advantages over sole proprietorships and partnerships:

1   Because ownership in a corporation is represented by shares of equity, ownership can be readily transferred to new owners. Because the corporation exists independently of those who own its shares, there is no limit to the transferability of shares as there is in partnerships.

2   The corporation has unlimited life. Because the corporation is separate from its owners, the death or withdrawal of an owner does not affect the corporation's legal existence. The corporation can continue on after the original owners have withdrawn.

3   The shareholders' liability is limited to the amount invested in the ownership shares. For example, if a shareholder purchased €1,000 in shares of a corporation, the potential loss would be €1,000. In a partnership, a general partner with a €1,000 contribution could lose the €1,000 plus any other indebtedness of the partnership.

Limited liability, ease of ownership transfer and perpetual succession are the major advantages of the corporate form of business organization. These give the corporation an enhanced ability to raise cash.

There is, however, one great disadvantage to incorporation. Many countries tax corporate income in addition to the personal income tax that shareholders pay on dividend income they receive. Although there are normally tax rebates given to shareholders, this is, in effect, a double taxation when compared to taxation on sole proprietorships and partnerships. Table 2.1 summarizes our discussion of partnerships and corporations.

Table 2.1 A Comparison of Sole Proprietorships, Partnerships and Corporations

	Corporation	Partnership	Sole Proprietorship
Liquidity and marketability	Shares can be exchanged without termination of the corporation. Shares can be listed on a stock exchange.	Shares are subject to substantial restrictions on transferability. There is usually no established trading market for partnership shares.	Shares are exceptionally illiquid and there is no established trading market for shares.
Voting rights	In single-tier board structures, usually each share of equity entitles the holder to one vote per share on matters requiring a vote and on the election of the directors. Directors determine top management.	Some voting rights by limited partners. However, general partners have exclusive control and management of operations.	The sole-trader owns 100% of the firm and has exclusive control and management of operations.
Taxation	Corporations may have double taxation: corporate income is taxable, and dividends to shareholders are also taxable. Each country has its own approach to how it deals with double taxation and may give a full or partial rebate on the corporate tax payment.	Partnerships are not taxable. Partners pay personal taxes on partnership profits.	Sole traders pay personal taxes on company profits.
Reinvestment and dividend payout	Corporations have broad latitude on dividend payout decisions.	Partnerships are generally prohibited from reinvesting partnership profits. All profits are distributed to partners.	Sole proprietorships have a lot of freedom in reinvesting profits because they are treated as personal income.
Liability	Shareholders are not personally liable for obligations of the corporation.	Limited partners are not liable for obligations of partnerships. General partners may have unlimited liability.	Sole traders have unlimited liability for the obligations of the firm.
Continuity of existence	Corporations may have a perpetual life.	Partnerships have limited life.	Sole proprietorships have a limited life.

Real World Insight 2.1

Alcatel-Lucent SA Board Structure
(Drawn from www.alcatel-lucent.com)

The Franco-American firm, is the world's leading IP networking, ultra-broadband access, and cloud technology specialist. The company is managed by a Board of Directors. The duties of the Chairman of the Board and those of the Chief Executive Officer are separated.

The functions of Chairman of the Board of Directors and Chief Executive Officer have been respectively performed by Mr Philippe Camus since 1 October 2008 and by Mr Michel Combes since 1 April 2013. The Board of Directors appointed on 21 February 2013 Mr Jean C. Monty as Vice-Chairman of the Board of Directors in order to assist the Chairman for certain matters, including representing the Group at high-level meetings on the American continent, pursuant to specific requests of the Board of Directors.

As of 19 March 2014, the Alcatel-Lucent Board consisted of 11 Directors, three of whom were women, representing five different nationalities, and the average member age was 62. The term of office for each director is three years and the renewal of the Directors' terms of office is staggered in order to avoid replacing the entire Board of Directors. One-third of the Board of Directors members has been renewed each year since 2013.

Directors	Nationality	Position	Age	Independence	Term of Office
Mr Camus	French	Chairman	65	Yes	2013–2016
Mr Combes	French	CEO	52	No	2013–2016
Ms Cico	Italian	Director	52	Yes	2013–2016
Mr Monty	Canadian	Director	66	Yes	2013–2016
Mr Eizenstat	American	Director	71	Yes	2012–2015
Mr Hughes	American	Director	65	Yes	2012–2015
Mr Piou	French	Director	55	Yes	2012–2015
Ms Goodman	American	Director	48	Yes	2012–2014
Mr Bernard	French	Director	68	Yes	2011–2014
Lady Jay	British	Director	67	Yes	2011–2014
Mr Spinetta	French	Director	70	Yes	2011–2014

Source: Data from Alcatel.

The Board of Directors includes two Board Observers ('Censeurs'). The Board Observers are both employees of Alcatel-Lucent, or of an affiliate, and members of the Alcatel-Lucent mutual fund (in French 'fonds commun de placement'). The mutual fund owns Alcatel-Lucent shares and the employees of Alcatel-Lucent own a beneficial interest in this fund. The mutual fund designates, among its members, a number of candidates representing twice the number of Board Observers seats to be filled in at the Board of Directors of the Company. This list is addressed to the Chairman of the Board of Directors and then, upon recommendation of the Corporate Governance and Nominating Committee, the Board of Directors submits to the Shareholders' Meeting the appointment of one or several Board observers, as the case may be.

Independence of the Directors

The independence criteria selected are based on both the recommendations of the French Corporate Governance Code and the requirements of the NYSE. They comply with all of the necessary criteria, with the exception of the criterion that provides that a director's total term of office should not exceed 12 years. The Alcatel-Lucent Board of Directors favours each Director's competence and experience, as well as their good knowledge of the Group, since these assets do not represent a potential conflict of interest.

The independence criteria chosen by the Board of Directors is that 'A director is independent when he or she has no relationship of any kind whatsoever with the corporation, its group or the management of either that is such as to color his or her judgment.'

Using this statement, 10 of the 11 Directors were independent, with the exception of the CEO. In addition, in compliance with the legal requirements and Article 5 of the Board's Operating Rules, the Board of Directors has at least one independent Director – namely, Mr Jean C. Monty – with recognized financial and accounting expertise.

Selection Criteria of Directors

The appointment of new Directors must comply with the selection rules applied by Alcatel-Lucent's Corporate Governance and Nominating Committee. In the context of the multi-annual process of selecting new Directors, the Corporate Governance and Nominating Committee conducts its own studies on potential candidates, if necessary with the support of an outside consultant. On this basis, the Committee draws up a restricted list of candidates in order to fill each vacancy.

The Corporate Governance and Nominating Committee aims to combine a range of diverse skills and expertise capable of supporting the company's high-technology businesses as well as a telecom expertise and knowledge of the various geographic markets, the business environment in which Alcatel-Lucent operates in and sufficient financial expertise. These skills enable the Board of Directors to make informed and independent decisions about financial statements and compliance with accounting standards. Special attention is also paid to the quality and the complementary nature of the careers of the Directors, in terms of location, duties performed and business sector.

A Corporation by Another Name . . .

The corporate form of organization has many variations around the world. The exact laws and regulations differ from country to country, of course, but the essential features of public ownership and limited liability remain. These firms are often called *joint stock companies*, *public limited companies* or *limited liability companies*, depending on the specific nature of the firm and the country of origin.

Table 2.2 gives the names of a number of corporate abbreviations, their countries of origin, a translation of the abbreviation, and a description of its meaning.

Table 2.2 International Corporations

Type of Corporation	Country of Origin	In Original Language	Description
Pty Ltd.	Australia	Proprietary Limited	Private Limited
Limited	Australia	Limited	Publicly Listed
AG	Austria, Germany	Aktiengesellschaft	Publicly Listed
GmbH	Austria, Germany	Gesellschaft mit Beschränkter Haftung	Private Limited
NV	Belgium, Netherlands	Naamloze Vennootschap	Publicly Listed
BV	Belgium, Netherlands	Besloten Vennootschap	Private Limited
SA	Belgium, France, Luxembourg, Portugal, Spain	Société Anonyme/Sociedade	Publicly Listed
AD	Bulgaria	акционерно дружество	Publicly Listed
OOD	Bulgaria	дружество с ограничена отговорност	Private Limited
股 有 限 公 司	China Mainland	股 有 限 公 司	Publicly Listed
有 限 公 司	China Mainland	有 限 公 司	Private Limited
ApS	Denmark	Anpartsselskab	Private Limited
A/S	Denmark	Aktieselskab	Publicly Listed
SE	European Union	Societas Europaea	Publicly Listed
Oy	Finland	Osakeyhtiö	Private Limited
Oyj	Finland	Julkinen Osakeyhtiö	Publicly Listed

Type of Corporation	Country of Origin	In Original Language	Description
AB	Finland, Sweden	Aktiebolag	Private Limited
Abp	Finland	Publikt Aktiebolag	Publicly Listed
SARL	France, Luxembourg	Société à Responsibilité Limitée	Private Limited
Ltd	Hong Kong	Limited	Private/Public
Pvt. Ltd	India	Private Limited Company	Private Limited
Plc	India, Ireland, Thailand, UK	Public Limited Company	Publicly Listed
Srl	Italy	Società a Responsabilità Limitata	Private Limited
SpA	Italy	Società per Azioni	Publicly Listed
AS	Norway	Aksjeselskap	Private Limited
ASA	Norway	Allmennaksjeselskap	Publicly Listed
OOO	Russia	Общество сограниченной ответственностью	Private Limited
AO	Russia	Акционерн ое общество	Publicly Listed
(Pty) Ltd	South Africa	Privaat Maatskappy	Private Limited
LTD	South Africa	Publieke Maatskappy	Publicly Listed
S.L.	Spain	Sociedad Limitada	Private Limited
Ltd	Ireland, UK, US	Limited	Private Limited
Inc., Corp.	US	Incorporated, Corporation	Publicly Listed

2.2   The Agency Problem and Control of the Corporation

We have seen that the financial manager acts in the best interests of the shareholders when they take actions that increase the value of the company's equity. However, in many large corporations, particularly in the UK, Ireland and US, ownership can be spread over a huge number of shareholders. This dispersion of ownership arguably means that no one shareholder will have enough power to influence management, suggesting that managers effectively control the firm. In this case, will management necessarily act in the best interests of the shareholders, and might not management pursue their own goals at shareholders' expense?

A different type of problem exists in many European firms. Whereas large British and American firms have a dispersed ownership structure, many businesses in Europe have a dominant shareholder with a very large ownership stake. Primarily, these shareholders are family groups, banks or governments. In firms with a dominant shareholder it is possible that corporate objectives will be directed by only one individual or group at the expense of other smaller shareholders. In this case, managers will be acting in the interests of only a subset of the company's owners.

The issues we have discussed above are caused by what we call agency relationships. In the following pages, we briefly consider some of the arguments relating to this issue.

Type I Agency Relationships

The relationship between shareholders and management is called a Type I agency relationship. Such a relationship exists whenever someone (the principal) hires another (the agent) to represent his or her interests. For example, you might hire a company (the agent) to sell a car you own while you are away at university. In all such relationships, there is the possibility there may be a conflict of interest between the principal and the agent. Such a conflict is called a Type I agency problem.

Suppose you did hire a company to sell your car and agree to pay a flat fee when the firm sells the car. The agent's incentive in this case is to make the sale, not necessarily to get you the best price. If you offer a commission of, say, 10 per cent of the sales price instead of a flat fee, then this problem might not exist. This example illustrates that the way in which an agent is compensated is one factor that affects agency problems.

Management Goals

To see how management and shareholder interests might differ, imagine that a firm is considering a new investment. The new investment is expected to favourably impact the share value, but it is also a relatively risky venture. The owners of the firm will wish to take the investment (because the share value will rise), but management may not because there is the possibility that things will turn out badly and management jobs will be lost. If management do not invest, then the shareholders may lose a valuable opportunity. This is one example of a Type I agency cost.

In general, an *agency cost* is the cost of a conflict of interest between shareholders and management (we will consider later another agency relationship between controlling and minority shareholders). These costs can be indirect or direct. An indirect agency cost is a lost opportunity, such as the one we have just described.

Direct agency costs come in two forms. The first type is a corporate expenditure that benefits management but costs the shareholders. Perhaps the purchase of a luxurious and unneeded corporate jet would fall under this heading. The second type of direct agency cost is an expense that comes from the need to monitor management actions. Paying outside auditors to assess the accuracy of financial statement information could be one example.

It is sometimes argued that, left to themselves, managers would tend to maximize the amount of resources over which they have control or, more generally, corporate power or wealth. This goal could lead to an overemphasis on corporate size or growth. For example, sometimes management are accused of overpaying to acquire another company just to increase the business size or to demonstrate corporate power. Obviously, if overpayment does take place, such a purchase does not benefit the shareholders of the purchasing company.

Our discussion indicates that management may tend to prioritize organizational survival to protect job security. Also, executives may dislike outside interference, so independence and corporate self-sufficiency could be important managerial goals.

Do Managers Act in the Shareholders' Interests?

Whether managers will, in fact, act in the best interests of shareholders depends on two factors. First, how closely are management goals aligned with shareholder goals? This question relates, at least in part, to the way managers are compensated. Second, can managers be replaced if they do not pursue shareholder goals? This issue relates to control of the firm. As we will discuss, there are a number of reasons to think that even in the largest firms, management has a significant incentive to act in the interests of shareholders.

Managerial Compensation

Executives will frequently have a significant economic incentive to increase share value for two reasons. First, managerial compensation, particularly at the top, is usually tied to financial performance and often specifically to share value. For example, managers are frequently given the option to buy equity at a bargain price. The more the equity is worth, the more valuable is this option. In fact, options are often used to motivate employees of all types, not just top managers. For example, Google has issued share options to all of its employees, thereby giving its workforce a significant stake in the company's share price and better aligning employee and shareholder interests. Many other corporations, large and small, have similar policies.

The second incentive that managers have relates to job prospects. Better performers within the firm will tend to get promoted. More generally, managers who are successful in pursuing shareholder goals will be in greater demand in the labour market and thus command higher salaries.

In fact, managers who are successful in pursuing shareholder goals can reap enormous rewards. The five best paid executives in the UK (Sir Martin Sorrell of WPP, Peter Voser of Royal Dutch Shell, Stephen Stone of Crest Nicholson Holdings, Don Robert of Experian, and Vittorio Colao of Vodafone), all earned above £12 million. This compares to much higher pay in the US, where the top five executives earned more than $25 million. In fact, this was less than a third of the highest paid executive in the world, Larry Ellison of Oracle, who earned $78 million.

Annual remuneration is comprised of a number of different income streams. The executive will have a basic annual salary topped up with a variety of incentives. These are typically bonuses paid on the previous year's performance. A stock option grant is an award of executive share options. This is not actual cash but instead an offer (but not an obligation) to buy shares at some date in the future for a specified price. Executive share options

Chapter 23
Page 619

are discussed in Chapter 23. A restricted stock grant is equity that is issued to the executive but not allowed to be traded before a stated date. Finally, there are other performance awards consisting of perquisites and personal benefits, tax benefits, discounted equity purchases, company contributions to a corporate pension plan, or corporate payment of insurance premiums. (See **Chapter 23** for more information on managerial compensation.)

Executive Pay around the World

The structure of executive pay is markedly different across the world. Figure 2.1 presents a breakdown of executive remuneration into three different components for various parts of the world. Long-term incentives (LTI) represent stock– and option-based compensation and short-term incentives (STI) are annual bonuses and performance awards. In Asia, base salary is the largest component of an executive's pay with only 30 per cent of income coming from incentive plans. In Europe, the breakdown is roughly equal across all compensation categories. Even within Europe, there are significant differences in executive pay. The UK is similar to the US with a large proportion of executive remuneration in incentive plans compared to Sweden and Denmark, where salary is much more important.

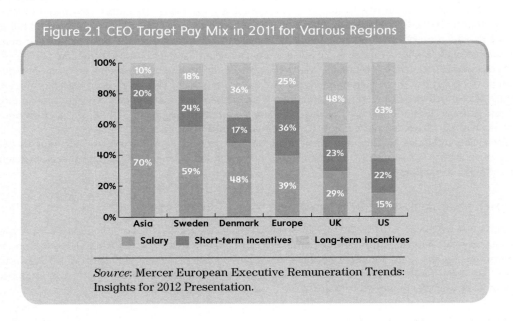

Figure 2.1 CEO Target Pay Mix in 2011 for Various Regions

Source: Mercer European Executive Remuneration Trends: Insights for 2012 Presentation.

Cable & Wireless Communications

Executive share options are very controversial and often attract the ire of major shareholders. A good case study is Cable & Wireless Communications (CWC) who faced a shareholder revolt in 2011 because of its executive share option award to the firm's executives. The terms of the incentive scheme were for senior management to receive restricted stock units equivalent to three times their annual basic salary as well as a bonus equivalent to 150 per cent of their basic salary.

This would have been fine if the share price of CWC had stayed at the same level or increased since the time the contract was drawn up in 2006. Unfortunately (or fortunately for the executives!), share prices in CWC had declined by 20 per cent and basic executive salaries had grown substantially, meaning that the CWC executives would have received significantly more shares than would have been expected in 2006. Since the executives would have to hold their restricted shares for a number of years, the expected bonus would have been massive.

Control of the Firm

Control of the firm ultimately rests with shareholders. They elect the board of directors, who in turn hire and fire managers. The fact that shareholders control the corporation was made abundantly clear by the late Steve Jobs's experience at Apple. Even though he was a founder of the corporation and largely responsible for its most successful products, there came a time when shareholders, through their elected directors, decided that Apple would be better off without him, so out he went. Of course, he was later rehired and helped turn Apple into the largest company in the world with great new products such as the iPod, iPhone and iPad.

Shareholder Rights

The conceptual structure of the corporation assumes that shareholders elect directors who, in turn, hire managers to carry out their directives. Shareholders, therefore, control the corporation through the right to elect the directors. In countries with single-tier boards, only shareholders have this right and in two-tier board countries, the supervisory board undertakes this task.

In two-tier board systems, the supervisory board (which consists of the main shareholder representatives, major creditors and employee representatives) chooses the executive board of directors. In companies with single-tier boards, directors are elected each year at an annual meeting. Although there are exceptions (discussed next), the general idea is 'one share, one vote' (not one shareholder, one vote). Directors are elected at an annual shareholders' meeting by a vote of the holders of a majority of shares who are present and entitled to vote. However, the exact mechanism for electing directors differs across companies. The most important difference is whether shares must be voted cumulatively or voted straight.

Example 2.3

Cumulative and Straight Voting

VanMore Ltd is considering two different voting procedures for four directors to be elected to the board. The firm has two shareholders: Smith with 20 shares and Jones with 80 shares. Both want to be a director. There are also three applicants from within the firm who are not shareholders. The key issue facing the company is that Jones does not want Smith to be a director!

Their first option is cumulative voting, which facilitates more minority shareholder participation. If cumulative voting is permitted, the total number of votes that each shareholder may cast is determined first. This is usually calculated as the number of shares (owned or controlled) multiplied by the number of directors to be elected. With cumulative voting, the directors are elected all at once. For VanMore Ltd, this means that the top four vote-getters will be the new directors. Each shareholder can distribute votes however he or she wishes.

Will Smith get a seat on the board? If we ignore the possibility of a five-way tie, then the answer is yes. Smith will cast $20 \times 4 = 80$ votes, and Jones will cast $80 \times 4 = 320$ votes. If Smith gives all his votes to himself, he is assured of a directorship. The reason is that Jones cannot divide 320 votes among four candidates in such a way as to give all of them more than 80 votes, so Smith will finish fourth at worst.

The second option is straight voting. With straight voting, the directors are elected one at a time. Each time, Smith can cast 20 votes and Jones can cast 80. As a consequence, Jones will elect all of the candidates.

In general, with cumulative voting, if there are N directors up for election, then $1/(N + 1)$ per cent of the shares plus one share will guarantee you a seat. In Example 2.3, this is $1/(4 + 1) = 20$ per cent. So the more seats that are up for election at one time, the easier (and cheaper) it is to win one. With straight voting, the only way to guarantee a seat is to own 50 per cent plus one share. This also guarantees that you will win every seat, so it is really all or nothing with this method.

Example 2.4

Buying the Election

Shares in Sole SpA sell for €20 each and feature cumulative voting. There are 10,000 shares outstanding. If three directors are up for election, how much does it cost to ensure yourself a seat on the board?

The question here is how many shares of equity it will take to get a seat. The answer is 2,501, so the cost is $2,501 \times €20 = €50,020$. Why 2,501? Because there is no way the remaining 7,499 votes can be divided among three people to give all of them more than 2,501 votes. For example, suppose two people receive 2,502 votes and the first two seats. A third person can receive at most $10,000 - 2,502 - 2,502 - 2,501 = 2,495$, so the third seat is yours.

As we have illustrated, straight voting can 'freeze out' minority shareholders; that is why many companies have mandatory cumulative voting. In companies where cumulative voting is mandatory, devices have been worked out to minimize its impact.

One such device is to stagger the voting for the board of directors. With staggered elections, only a fraction of the directorships are up for election at a particular time. Thus if only two directors are up for election at any one time, it will take $1/(2 + 1) = 33.33$ per cent of the equity plus one share to guarantee a seat.

Overall, staggering has two basic effects:

1   Staggering makes it more difficult for a minority to elect a director when there is cumulative voting because there are fewer directors to be elected at any one time.

2   Staggering makes takeover attempts less likely to be successful because it makes it more difficult to vote in a majority of new directors.

We should note that staggering may serve a beneficial purpose. It provides 'institutional memory' – that is, continuity on the board of directors. This may be important for corporations with significant long-range plans and projects.

Proxy Voting

A proxy is the grant of authority by a shareholder to someone else to vote his or her shares. For convenience, much of the voting in large public corporations is actually done by proxy. As we have seen, with straight voting, each share of equity has one vote. The owner of 10,000 shares has 10,000 votes. Large companies have hundreds of thousands or even millions of shareholders. In single-tier board environments, shareholders can come to the annual meeting and vote in person, or they can transfer their right to vote to another party.

Obviously, management always tries to get as many proxies as possible transferred to it. However, if shareholders are not satisfied with management, an 'outside' group of shareholders can try to obtain votes via proxy. They can vote by proxy in an attempt to replace management by electing enough directors. The resulting battle is called a proxy fight.

Classes of Shares

Chapter 19
Page 514

Some firms have more than one class of ordinary equity (see **Chapter 19** for more information on equities). Often the classes are created with unequal voting rights. Google, for example, has two classes of shares. The co-founders, Larry Page and Sergey Brin, own Class B shares, which have ten votes for each share. Other shareholders have Class A shares, which are entitled to one vote per share. So, although the founders only own 5.7 per cent of Google, they have 57 per cent of the voting power. Facebook, Alibaba and Groupon are further examples of firms with two classes of shares.

A primary reason for creating dual or multiple classes of equity has to do with control of the firm. If such shares exist, management can raise new equity capital by issuing non-voting or limited-voting shares while still maintaining control of the firm through voting power. The subject of unequal voting rights is controversial, and the idea of one share, one vote has a strong following and long history. Interestingly, however, shares with unequal voting rights are quite common in Europe.

Figure 2.2 presents the percentage of firms in each country (the sample is Europe's 30 largest firms) that have only one class of shares with one vote per share. As can be seen, there is a lot of heterogeneity in firms around Europe. In the UK, Germany and Belgium most firms have only one class of shares, which is substantially different to the situation in France, the Netherlands and Italy.

Investigating firms with multiple class shares further, there are a number of structures that firms can use to limit the power of any single shareholder. For example, *voting rate ceilings* restrict voting power for an investor to a specified percentage of shares irrespective of the actual shareholding. The actual ceiling percentage can vary but is usually between 5 and 20 per cent of total shares outstanding. *Ownership ceilings* forbid any shareholder from taking a holding of greater than a specified percentage of shares. *Priority shares* give the holders certain rights, such as being able to appoint a representative to the board of directors or veto a proposal at an annual general meeting. *Golden shares* are found in former state-owned enterprises and they give the government beneficial powers such as veto-capability against new shareholders. Finally, *depository receipts* are securities that have an equity ownership stake without the voting rights. Common in the Netherlands, a company's

Figure 2.2 Percentage of Companies with a 'One-Share-One-Vote' Structure by Country

Bar chart: % of companies

- UK: 88%
- FR: 31%
- DE: 97%
- CH: 59%
- SP: 59%
- IT: 68%
- NL: 14%
- SE: 25%
- BE: 100%
- Other: 69%
- All: 65%

Source: 'Application of the One Share One Vote System in Europe', Deminor-Rating commissioned by the Association of British Insurers (2005).

shares are held in a foundation which then issues depositary receipts to investors that mimic the cash flows of the underlying shares but have no voting rights. Frequently, the foundation's board of directors is linked to the underlying firm.

Table 2.3 presents detailed statistics on the different type of share characteristics of firms that have more than one type of share class. It is clear that, even within the Eurozone, there are broad differences in the way in which ownership is distributed across firms. In Germany, Italy and the UK, non-voting preference shares (see **Chapter 5**) are relatively common, whereas in France, the Netherlands and Sweden, there are a number of firms that have differential voting rights across share classes.

Chapter 5
Page 120

Table 2.3 Percentage of Dual Class Share Characteristics by Country (FTSE Eurofirst 300 Companies)

	Non-voting Preference Shares (%)	Multiple Voting Rights (%)	Voting Right Ceilings (%)	Ownership Ceilings (%)	Priority Shares (%)	Golden Shares (%)	Depositary Receipts (%)
UK	20	1	3	5	4	3	-
France	2	64	19	2	5	-	-
Germany	24	-	3	-	-	-	-
Switzerland	-	12	35	-	-	-	-
Spain	-	-	41	-	-	-	-
Italy	36	-	8	28	-	-	-
Netherlands	-	67	-	-	29	10	24
Sweden	-	75	6	-	-	-	-
Other	8	8	11	8	-	3	-

Source: 'Application of the One Share One Vote System in Europe', Deminor-Rating commissioned by the Association of British Insurers (2005).

Other Rights

The value of a share of equity in a corporation is directly related to the general rights of shareholders. In addition to the right to vote for directors, shareholders usually have the following rights:

1   The right to share proportionally in dividends paid.

2   The right to share proportionally in assets remaining after liabilities have been paid in a liquidation.

3   The right to vote on shareholder matters of great importance, such as a merger. Voting is usually done at the annual meeting or a special meeting.

Chapter 19
Page 514

In addition, shareholders sometimes have the right to share proportionally in any new equity sold. This is called the pre-emptive right (see **Chapter 19** for more information).

Essentially, a pre-emptive right means that a company that wishes to sell equity must first offer it to existing shareholders before marketing it to the general public. The purpose is to give shareholders the opportunity to protect their proportionate ownership in the firm.

Dividends

A distinctive feature of corporations is that they have shares of equity on which they are authorized by law to pay dividends to their shareholders. Dividends paid to shareholders represent a return on the capital directly or indirectly contributed to the corporation by the shareholders. The payment of dividends is at the discretion of the board of directors.

Some important characteristics of dividends include the following:

1   Unless a dividend is declared by the board of directors of a corporation, it is not a liability of the corporation. A corporation cannot default on an undeclared dividend. As a consequence, corporations cannot become bankrupt because of non-payment of dividends. The amount of the dividend and even whether it is paid are decisions based on the business judgement of the board of directors.

2   The payment of dividends by the corporation is not a business expense. Dividends are not deductible for corporate tax purposes. In short, dividends are paid out of the corporation's after-tax profits.

3   Dividends received by individual shareholders are taxable.

There is a common belief that shareholders prefer companies to issue dividends because it imposes a form of discipline on incumbent managers. If a company has high levels of cash, managers may invest in projects that will not normally be chosen simply because they can. By transferring the company's cash to shareholders through dividends, managers have less scope to squander resources.

The discussion so far has concerned the agency relationship between professional managers and outside shareholders. We will now discuss a different type of agency relationship, which is more subtle and complex, and is known as a Type II agency relationship. A Type II agency relationship exists between shareholders who own a significant amount of a company's shares (controlling shareholders) and other shareholders who own only a small proportional amount (minority shareholders).

Real World Insight 2.3

Alcatel-Lucent SA Group Ownership Structure
(*Drawn from www.alcatel-lucent.com*)

Consistent with its pre-eminent position as an international technology firm, Alcatel-Lucent SA is an exceptionally complex organization. The company is not a single entity but instead a network of different companies with product or geographical specialisms. The figure below illustrates the group structure of the company. All subsidiaries are 100 per cent owned by the parent unless explicitly stated in the chart.

As you can see, not only is the company split up into component parts, but the ownership of each component is a function of the ownership of the parent firms. Fortunately, International Accounting Standards and stock exchange listing requirements force companies to transparently show corporate and ownership structures in their financial reports.

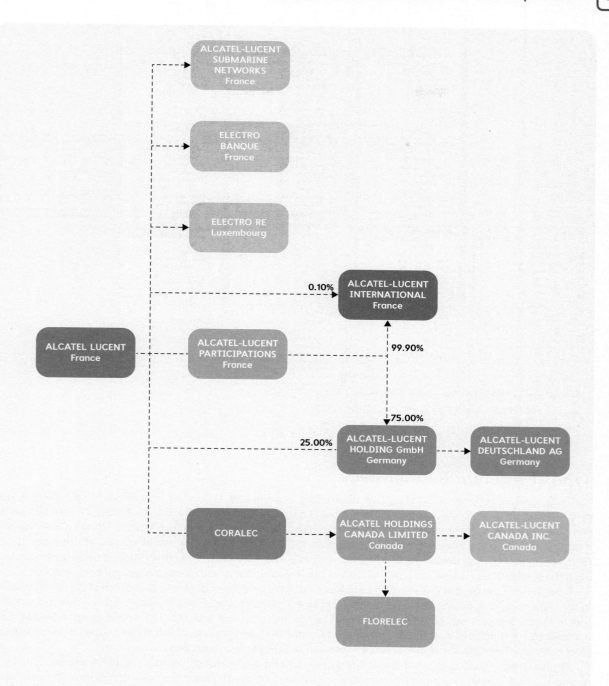

The figure above shows which companies Alcatel-Lucent owns, but who owns Alcatel-Lucent? This is presented below (the data comes from Osiris database). Public investors make up the largest group of Alcatel-Lucent's shareholders. However, there are two other large shareholders, Capital Group and Brandes Investment Partners. The interesting thing to note is that Capital Group are indirect shareholders of Alcatel-Lucent, since companies that they own have investments amounting to 11.39 per cent in Alcatel-Lucent. Capital Group do not own any Alcatel-Lucent shares directly. Also, Capital Group and Brandes are, in turn, owned by other shareholders. As you can see, ownership and corporate structure can be exceptionally complex in practice.

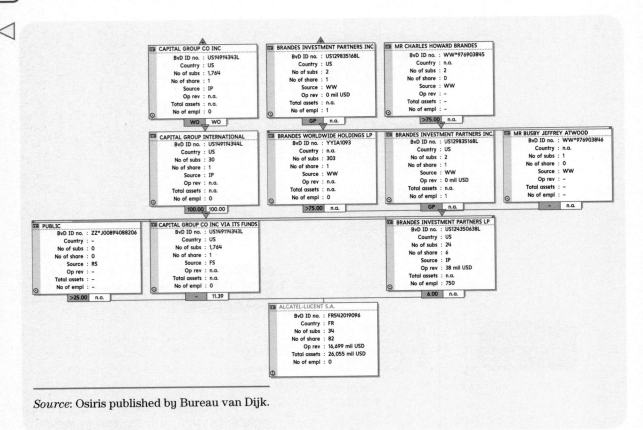

Source: Osiris published by Bureau van Dijk.

Type II Agency Relationships

The relationship between a dominant or controlling shareholder and other shareholders who have a small proportional ownership stake is known as a Type II agency relationship. Such a relationship exists whenever a company has a concentrated ownership structure, which is common in many countries. When an investor owns a large percentage of a company's shares, they have the ability to remove or install a board of directors through their voting power. This means that, indirectly, they can make the firm's objectives aligned to their own personal objectives, which may not be the same as that of other shareholders with a smaller proportionate stake.

It may seem strange that one set of shareholders can have a different objective to a different set of shareholders in the same company. Surely all shareholders want to maximize the value of their firm? Agency theory recognizes that everyone has personal objectives and these may not be congruent with other groups in an organization. Thus, for example, a dominant shareholder may benefit more from having one of her firms trading at advantageous prices with another firm she owns. This is known as a related party transaction.

Alternatively, a controlling shareholder may need cash for an investment in, for example, Company A and wish to take the cash from Company B through an extraordinary dividend. This will obviously not be in the interests of Company B's other shareholders, but in aggregate the action may be more profitable for the controlling shareholder of Company B if it stands to make more money from an investment in Company A.

Real World Insight 2.4

Ownership Structure of Iberdrola SA

The direct and indirect ownership structure of the multinational energy firm, Iberdrola, as of 2013 is presented in Table 2.4.

The share structure shows there are indirect voting rights and direct voting rights. Indirect voting rights mean that the owner indirectly has shares in Iberdrola through another company. So, for example, the Qatar

| Individual or company name of the shareholder | Indirect voting rights | | Number of direct voting rights | % of total voting rights |
	Direct holder of the interest	Number of voting rights		
Qatar Investment Authority	Qatar Holding Luxembourg II, S.À.R.L.	577,911,474	-	9.524
Qatar Investment Authority	DGIC Luxembourg, S.À.R.L.	16,395,153	-	
Actividades De Construcción Y Servicios, S.A.	Natixis, S.A.	164,352,702	-	5.645
Actividades De Construcción Y Servicios, S.A.	Funding Statement S.A.	125,000,000	-	
Actividades De Construcción Y Servicios, S.A.	Equity Share, S.L.	62,888,889	-	
Banco Financiero Y De Ahorros, S.A.	Bfa Participaciones Cotizadas, S.A.	314,887,559	-	5.069
Banco Financiero Y De Ahorros, S.A.	Bankia, S.A.	1,421,174	-	
Kutxabank, S.A.	Kartera 1, S.L.	249,976,993	-	4.006
Société Générale, S.A.	-		256,561,003	4.111
Blackrock, Inc.	Blackrock Group	189,860,019	-	3.043

Table 2.4 Ownership Structure of Iberdrola SA

Source: Iberdrola Corporate Governance Report, 2013.

Investment Authority (which is owned wholly by the Qatari Government) owns 9.524 per cent of Iberdrola through its investments in Qatar Holding Luxembourg II and DGIC Luxembourg. Unlike Société Générale, which owns 256 million shares of Iberdrola, the Qatar Investment Authority has no actual investment in the firm.

International Ownership Structure

Ownership structure varies considerably across the world. In the UK and US, most large companies are widely held, which means that no single investor has a large ownership stake in a firm. In such environments, Type I agency relationships tend to dominate. The rest of the world is characterized by closely held firms, where governments, families and banks are the main shareholders in firms. Type II agency relationships are more important in closely held firms and their corporate governance structure should reflect this.

Table 2.5 presents a breakdown of the ownership structure of the 20 largest corporations in a number of selected companies across the world. It is very clear from the table that no two countries are exactly the same. For example, the UK is characterized by a widely held ownership structure, whereas most of the large firms in Greece are run by families. Governments have a major role to play in many European countries with the Austrian government being the most involved in firms.

Table 2.5 Ownership Structure of 20 Largest Companies in Each Country

Country	Widely Held (%)	Family (%)	State (%)	Other (%)	Country	Widely held (%)	Family (%)	State (%)	Other (%)
Austria	5	15	70	10	Netherlands	30	20	5	45
Belgium	5	50	5	40	Norway	25	25	35	15
Denmark	40	35	15	10	Portugal	10	45	25	20
Finland	35	10	35	20	Spain	35	15	30	20

Country	Widely Held (%)	Family (%)	State (%)	Other (%)	Country	Widely held (%)	Family (%)	State (%)	Other (%)
France	60	20	15	5	Sweden	25	45	10	20
Germany	50	10	25	15	Switzerland	60	30	0	10
Italy	20	15	40	25	UK	100	0	0	0
Ireland	65	10	0	25	US	80	20	0	0

Source: Adapted from La Porta et al. (2000). The table presents the percentage of firms in a country that have a controlling shareholder with a greater than 20 per cent stake in the company. If no controlling shareholder exists, the firm is deemed to be widely held.

The identity of controlling owners will influence managerial objectives and whereas all shareholders wish to maximize the value of their investment, how value is assessed differs according to the individual. For example, if a firm is widely held in a market-based economy, such as the UK, corporate objectives are likely to be focused on maximizing share price performance. Family firms have slightly different objectives because not only do managers have to consider current shareholders but also the descendants of those shareholders. This would suggest that managers of family firms would have a longer-term perspective than other firms, which would influence the types of investments and funding they choose. Firms with the government as a major shareholder would have to consider political objectives in addition to maximizing share value.

The available theory and evidence are consistent with the view that shareholders control the firm and that shareholder wealth maximization is the relevant goal of the corporation. Even so, there will undoubtedly be times when management goals are pursued at the expense of some or all shareholders, at least temporarily.

Stakeholders

Our discussion thus far implies that management and shareholders are the only parties with an interest in the firm's decisions. This is an oversimplification, of course. Employees, customers, suppliers and even the government all have a financial interest in the firm.

Taken together, these various groups are called stakeholders. In general, a stakeholder is someone, other than a shareholder or creditor, who potentially has a claim on the cash flows of the firm. Such groups will also attempt to exert control over the firm, perhaps to the detriment of the owners. In countries with two-tier boards, such as the Netherlands and Germany, stakeholders are formally included in the decision-making activities of a firm, through its supervisory board to which the executive board must report.

2.3   The Governance Structure of Corporations

In this section, we review in more detail the different ways in which corporations can be governed. Because of cultural and regulatory differences, a variety of governance structures can be seen operating successfully across companies in many different countries. Moreover, company size is very important. The largest companies may have more than ten directors, a chairperson, a chief executive and other individuals on their executive board. Compare this with a private

Real World Insight 2.5

Ownership Structure of Samsung Electronics

While the Iberdrola share ownership structure in Real World Insight 2.4 may seem complex, it is nothing compared to many large Asian firms. Figure 2.3 is taken from a Credit Suisse trading note in June 2014, and it presents the web of ownership in Samsung Electronics.

Notice the different ways through which Chairman KH Lee's family owns Samsung. In addition, the ownership network is via many different firms with Samsung in the title. This type of ownership structure where there is a family of interconnected firms is known as a *Chaebol* in South Korea and *Kieretsu* in Japan, where they are common.

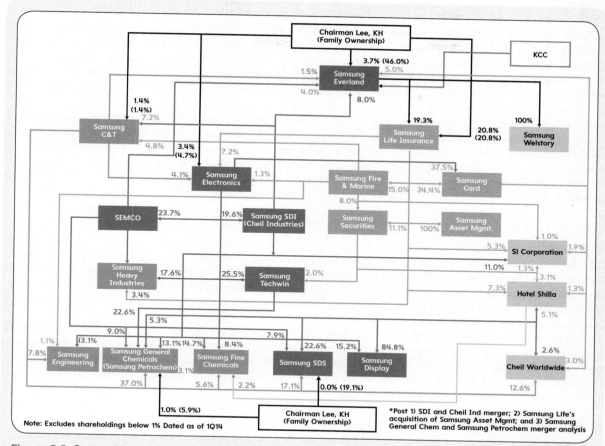

Figure 2.3 Ownership Structure of Samsung Electronics

Source: Credit Suisse Equity Research.

limited company, where the shareholders are also likely to be running the company, or, even more extreme, in a sole proprietorship where the manager is the owner. Some firms may be run by a family with many family members involved in the firm's management, or it may be state-owned and executive appointments made through political decisions.

In all businesses, there are a number of duties or responsibilities that must be carried out by corporate executives. For example, a firm must know and form its long-term business strategy. It must be in control of its financial affairs and actively seek out new and profitable investment opportunities. It should seek the most appropriate new financing when required and ensure it has complied with all relevant regulation.

As companies grow, these respective responsibilities become too large to be undertaken by only one individual and, consequently, must be delegated to a team or even a large department. Executives need to know what is happening in every sphere of their company's business activities and ensure that all aspects of business are operating at peak efficiency. Corporate governance is primarily concerned with ensuring that businesses are operating well, that business decisions are made rationally and that the appropriate individuals who make these decisions are held accountable when things go wrong.

Not all organizations are governed well. Just because a firm is listed on a stock exchange does not mean that correct business decisions are being made or that shareholder wealth is being maximized. In many companies, governance culture lags behind the growth of the firm. Small, successful companies are likely to have very different governance structures from large successful firms in the same industry. In many countries, individuals with political links are placed on corporate boards and their objectives are very different to that of shareholders.

While it is impossible to cover all the governance structures that exist in the business world, it is useful to see examples of the way in which different firms are governed.

The Sole Proprietorship

Let us return to JonMac Builders, the sole proprietorship that was introduced in Example 2.1. These types of firms are the easiest to understand since all the business activities are concentrated in one individual – the owner/manager. Business decisions, long-term strategy, short-term cash management and financing decisions are all made by John McAfee, the owner of JonMac Builders. John has no skill whatsoever in accounting, so he hires an accountant to draw up his financial accounts for the year. The main reason for hiring an accountant is to determine the amount of tax John has to pay based on the company's profits.

With the exception of the accounting function, everything in JonMac Builders is done informally and on a day-to-day basis. In these types of organizations, there is no real need for formal governance structures since there is nothing really to be governed. The only important formal aspect of the business, the financial accounting, has been outsourced to another company that specializes in the accounting function. It is hopefully clear that it is neither sensible nor cost-effective for JonMac builders to employ its own accountant or to introduce formal governance structures within the firm. This is the general position for most sole proprietorships.

Partnerships

A partnership is, in many ways, very similar to that of a sole proprietorship. Generally, partners will have unlimited liability, which means that they are personally liable for all of their firm's debts. Every partnership will have some form of formal agreement that governs the financial affairs of the firm, such as apportioning of profits among partners. Senior partners may receive a higher proportion of the company's profits than junior partners and this will be enshrined within the partnership agreement. Rules on partners resigning, new partners joining and major corporate decisions may also be included.

Partnership agreements need not be complicated or filled with legal jargon. They can also be quite short. Example 2.5 shows an actual partnership agreement for Twiga Export Partners, a partnership that sources materials, automobiles and electrical appliances from around the world and exports them to Sub-Saharan Africa. There are five partners in the firm, all concerned with different aspects of the business. Three of the partners are based in East Africa and two are based in Europe.

Example 2.5

Partnership Agreement of Twiga Export Company

This partnership agreement relates wholly, entirely and only to Twiga Export Partners, hereafter known as 'the business'. It does not convey rights or claim (partial, incidental or whole) towards any other activity or association to which any partner is involved.

This agreement applies as follows:

1 Each partner is due an equal share of all profits or losses accruing to the business. That is, each partner has claim to 20 per cent of profits or losses in any financial period.

2 Any injection of loan funds into the business will result in interest being paid, amounting to 8 per cent per annum compounded on an annual basis. Interest will be allocated against the partner's capital account.

3 Any withdrawal of funds from the business, not including any salary, will be charged interest at 8 per cent per annum compounded on an annual basis. Interest on drawings will be charged against the partner's capital account.

4 Any capital contributed by a partner must be agreed upon by all partners beforehand.

5 A partner will be paid a salary only on agreement by all partners. The level of salary must be agreed upon by all partners.

6 Before admission of any new partners, agreement and consent must be reached by all partners in business.

7 Upon leaving or retiring from business, a partner will be paid in cash their total capital invested in business as well as any goodwill owned by partner. Goodwill will be calculated as 20 per cent of average net profit over previous 5 years.

8 Changes in any of the points above must be agreed upon in writing by all partners.

Upon signing this document in the presence of two other partners, a partner will be deemed to accept the points in this document in full.

The partnership agreement only partially deals with the governance structure of a partnership. The firm must also have procedures in place for ensuring that all partners are carrying out their responsibilities fully. Normally, a partners' meeting will be held regularly to discuss business strategy and other long-term issues facing the business. They will also report on their own activity since the last partners' meeting. These may take place on a monthly basis or more frequently. In the case of Twiga Export Partners, the meeting takes place every 6 months because of the geographical distance between partners. More regular meetings would not be cost effective for Twiga, a trade-off that all companies must bear in mind when assessing the importance of better governance procedures.

Because the owners are also managers of the firm, partnerships do not normally require outside or independent individuals in the partners' meetings. In addition, they are also likely to appoint auditors and accountants to take care of the financial reporting of the firm.

Corporations

Because a corporation is a separate legal entity, the informality that is common in sole proprietorships and partnerships is substituted by formal corporate governance structures that are commonly seen in large organizations. Formal structures are necessary because the owners of the firm are less likely to be involved in management. As stated earlier, corporations must have articles of incorporation that govern the allocation and issuance of shares, the number of directors in the firm, as well as procedures for appointment and resignation from the board.

However, shareholders also require formal and explicit assurances that managers are running their company to maximize shareholder wealth. This is normally exhibited through the inclusion of external, non-executive and independent board members who attend all of the company's executive board meetings. In addition, there are usually a number of other governance structures ensuring that individuals do not have too much power within a firm, which could otherwise make them entrenched and less likely to pursue shareholder objectives over their own.

Whereas regulatory requirements can force board structures into a two-tier or unitary board structure, there are a number of principles to which all corporations are recommended to adhere in order to minimize governance failures. Individual countries have their own specific approach to corporate governance, but all follow the direction of the 2004 OECD Principles of Corporate Governance, published by the Organization for Economic Co-operation and Development. The principles themselves are not legally binding, but are recommendations on best governance practice within corporate organizations.

2.4 The OECD Principles of Corporate Governance

The principles are centred on six major areas and concern all aspects of corporate governance. It is important to emphasize that there is no 'one size fits all' for corporate governance. Companies must choose the level and type of structure that fits their environment, ownership structure and regulatory position. The principles are detailed below.

I. Ensuring the Basis for an Effective Corporate Governance Framework

The corporate governance framework should promote transparent and efficient markets, be consistent with the rule of law and clearly articulate the division of responsibilities among different supervisory, regulatory and enforcement authorities.

Real World Insight 2.6

Corruption

The index is graded between 0 and 100, with a lower score (darker shade) indicating a country in which the public sector is perceived to be exceptionally corrupt. Scandinavian countries are perceived to have very little public sector corruption, but this tends to get worse as one goes further south through

Europe. Consistent with their lack of economic development, emerging markets tend to have more public sector corruption than developed countries. Notably, the public sector in China and India is perceived to be exceptionally corrupt even with their incredible growth over the past 20 years.

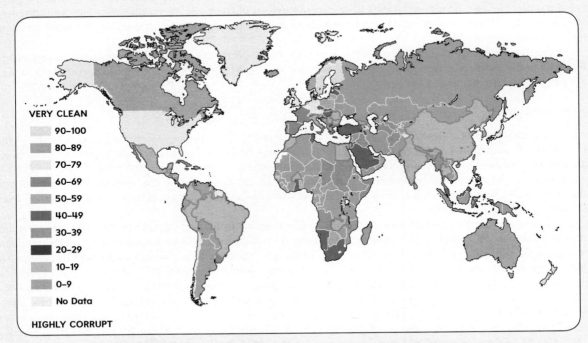

Figure 2.4 Corruption Around the World

Source: © Transparency International. All Rights Reserved. For more information, visit http://www.transparency. org. Transparency International's Corruption Perceptions Index measures the perceived level of public sector corruption in countries and territories around the world on a scale of 0 (highly corrupt) to 100 (very clean).

This principle emphasizes the need to recognize that corporations are fundamentally geared towards making money and corporate governance structures must be designed to ensure that this primary objective is not adversely affected. It also states that any governance regulation must be consistent with the legal and regulatory environment in which the firm operates. Finally, the principle argues that there should be a strict and transparent delineation of responsibilities in setting, monitoring and managing the governance of corporations.

II.   The Rights of Shareholders and Key Ownership Functions

The corporate governance framework should protect and facilitate the exercise of shareholders' rights.

The second principle focuses on the most important stakeholder of corporations – the shareholder. As owner, the shareholder is entitled to basic rights such as being able to register ownership of their shares, selling their shares to other parties, having access to important information about the company, being able to participate at general shareholder meetings, being able to elect and remove members from the board of directors, and to share in the profits of the corporation.

Shareholders should also be notified of, and participate in, their company's major decisions such as increasing the long-term financing of the company through debt or equity offerings, or when the company management decide to sell off a major proportion of the company's assets. Giving shareholders power to influence the direction of their company is the basic rationale underlying this principle and, as such, much of its discussion relates to putting in a framework that allows shareholders to vote and participate at general meetings. The principle recommends that structures should be put in place to allow shareholders to appoint the senior management and stop them from pursuing business objectives that are not consistent with maximizing shareholder wealth.

Real World Insight 2.7

Shareholder Activism at Aberdeen Ethical World Fund

In recent years, there has been a substantial growth in investment funds having a social, ethical, environmental or governance agenda. The funds have two main approaches: *voice* and *exit*. A *voice strategy* will mean that managers of funds that hold the equity of a firm will become directly and proactively involved in the management of the company. Managers with a voice strategy are called institutional shareholder activists. An *exit strategy* simply means that if a fund manager is unhappy with a company's behaviour, it will simply exit from the investment.

An example of an activist fund is Aberdeen Ethical World Fund. The fund has positive and negative screening investment criteria regarding the companies in which it will invest in addition to a proactive engagement policy. The following is an overview of the fund's voice strategy (*source*: EIRIS Green & Ethical Funds Directory):

Engagement   Aberdeen Asset Management (AAM) 'aims to visit all companies held within its ethical fund at least once every two years to discuss the socially responsible investment (SRI) issues covered by its SRI criteria. AAM maintains a dialogue on these topics with companies and follows up on issues to check to see if progress (if any) has been made'.

Methods of engagement   AAM communicates with company managers, investor relations representatives, and those responsible for policy making and/or policy implementation regarding SRI/ethical issues through visits, telephone conferences, letters and emails. AAM also collaborates with other shareholders on SRI issues and meets with other groups, such as non-government organizations, etc.

Examples of recent engagement   AAM states it has engaged with Asian, European and North American companies on SRI topics.

What further steps taken when engagement is considered unsuccessful?   AAM's stated policy is one of 'continued engagement with companies on important issues' with no cut-off period.

Voting   AAM's voting policy seeks to support good corporate governance through good quality management, transparency of corporate affairs and intentions, and fair and equal treatment of shareholders. This policy is set out on AAM's website (see section 'Aberdeen's policy on corporate governance, voting and SRI').

Are voting practices disclosed?   No.

The principle also encourages shareholder activism, especially for institutional shareholders who can exert significant pressure on the incumbent management of corporations because of the size of their shareholdings. The institutions themselves are recommended to publish their own governance structures and policies on voting in general meetings. They are also encouraged to consult with each other on issues concerning their basic shareholder rights.

III.   The Equitable Treatment of Shareholders

The corporate governance framework should ensure the equitable treatment of all shareholders, including minority and foreign shareholders. All shareholders should have the opportunity to obtain effective redress for violation of their rights.

In many firms, there is one shareholder or a group of shareholders that owns a very large fraction of the outstanding shares. It is important that dominant, or controlling, shareholders do not run the company in their interests at the expense of minority shareholders. There are several ways in which this could be done. For example, the controlling shareholder may vote for personal friends or family to be on the corporate board. Given that minority shareholders are not strong enough to force their view at general meetings, majority shareholders will always get their way.

The third OECD governance principle states that firms must ensure that minority shareholders are protected and that policies introduced by the company do not penalize them. Processes must ensure that the voice of minority and foreign shareholders is heard at company general meetings.

Corporate executive behaviour is also addressed in Principle III, where it is recommended that company insiders should be forbidden from trading when they have private specific and precise information that could be used to personally benefit themselves at the expense of other shareholders. This is known as insider dealing, which is illegal in most countries. Board members should also disclose any conflicts of interest or material interests in corporate decisions to shareholders.

Investing in Emerging Markets

Investing in emerging markets can be very risky. In 2015, the Middle East was aflame with conflict and in danger of exporting violence throughout the wider region. Ukraine and Russia were involved in a low level conflict themselves, and there was political instability and corruption in most emerging-market countries. Surprisingly, even with environments as volatile as these, golden opportunities can present themselves to the entrepreneurial manager. Most companies in emerging markets are privately owned by one or two dominant shareholder groups, so any wealth creation by companies is passed on directly to these controlling owners.

However, the story is different for foreign investors in emerging-market stock exchanges. The rule of law is often weak in emerging economies and there is little transparency in corporate decision-making and reporting. Corporate cultures can also vary from country to country, making an informed investment in publicly listed equities challenging.

Take, for example, Afren, the Nigerian oil exploration company that used to be listed on the London Stock Exchange but is now in bankruptcy. In 2015, it suspended its chief executive and chief operating officer because of allegations about 'unauthorised payments' to certain individuals.

Another example is Essar Energy, an Indian company that also used to be listed on the London Stock Exchange. In 2014, it was acquired by its controlling owner, the Ruia family. Minority investors had little choice but to accept the family's offer to buy their shares because if they refused they would have become a shareholder in a private company with virtually no chance of selling their equity stake after the acquisition.

IV.   The Role of Stakeholders in Corporate Governance

The corporate governance framework should recognize the rights of stakeholders established by law or through mutual agreements and encourage active co-operation between corporations and stakeholders in creating wealth, jobs, and the sustainability of financially sound enterprises.

Principle IV considers the other stakeholders of the corporation, such as employees and local communities. All rights of stakeholders that are enshrined in law should be respected by the corporation and if a firm violates any stakeholder rights, there should be a process or structure to allow them to seek redress from the firm. The principle also encourages the development of employee share ownership schemes and other performance-enhancing schemes.

If any stakeholder group feels that the company is not performing to its expectations or meeting its responsibilities to its stakeholders, they should be able to freely communicate their concerns to the company and expect the firm to proactively consider the concerns. Firms should also have a framework for dealing with insolvency procedures (to be used if needed) and effective enforcement of creditor rights.

V.   Disclosure and Transparency

The corporate governance framework should ensure that timely and accurate disclosure is made on all material matters regarding the corporation, including the financial situation, performance, ownership, and governance of the company.

Prompt disclosure of new information relating to the activities of a corporation is an absolute necessity for investors. If little is known about a company, it is almost impossible for outside shareholders to form an accurate estimate of the value of a firm or evaluate the performance of its management. Principle V states the main types of information that companies should disclose to the market.

These include the following:

(a) The main financial results, namely the profit and loss over the year, a statement of the firm's assets and liabilities (the balance sheet), and the cash flow position of the firm.

(b) Corporate objectives.

(c) The main shareholders and the various voting rights pertaining to different share classes.

(d) Information on the individuals that comprise the board of directors, their salaries and annual bonuses, and a statement on whether a director is an independent or executive director should be published regularly.

(e) Any trading of the company's shares undertaken by the firm's senior executives, their family, friends and other close associates.

(f) The major risks facing the firm's operations.

(g) Issues regarding employees and other stakeholders.

(h) The main governance structures and policies of the firm.

The principle maintains that all information disclosed by the firm should be made as rigorous and informative as possible. This means that financial statements should be prepared by qualified accountants and all the activities of a firm should be audited and assessed by an external professional firm, the auditor.

VI. The Responsibilities of the Board

The corporate governance framework should ensure the strategic guidance of the company, the effective monitoring of management by the board, and the board's accountability to the company and the shareholders.

The final OECD principle of corporate governance focuses on the corporate board itself. Board members are expected to make decisions on an informed and ethical basis and always take the company and shareholder objectives into account. The board must take all shareholders into account and act in their best interests whether they are minority shareholders, foreign shareholders or other groups that have little combined power to influence management. All of the firm's major stakeholders (e.g. lenders, employees, local community, creditors) must also be taken into account when making corporate decisions.

The principle states that a corporate board must fulfil a set number of functions, including:

(a) Reviewing and guiding corporate strategy, major plans of action, risk policy, annual budgets and business plans; setting performance objectives; monitoring implementation and corporate performance; and overseeing major capital expenditures, acquisitions and divestitures.

(b) Monitoring the effectiveness of the company's governance practices and making changes as needed.

(c) Selecting, compensating, monitoring and, when necessary, replacing key executives and overseeing succession planning.

(d) Aligning key executive and board remuneration with the longer-term interests of the company and its shareholders.

(e) Ensuring a formal and transparent board nomination and election process.

(f) Monitoring and managing potential conflicts of interest of management, board members and shareholders, including misuse of corporate assets and abuse in related party transactions.

(g) Ensuring the integrity of the corporation's accounting and financial reporting systems, including the independent audit, and that appropriate systems of control are in place, in particular, systems for risk management, financial and operational control, and compliance with the law and relevant standards.

(h) Overseeing the process of disclosure and communications.

It is expected that corporate boards approach the job of running a corporation in an objective and independent fashion. When there are conflicts of interest, non-executives should be used to manage potentially problematic situations. Sub-committees of the board, such as an audit committee, nomination committee and remuneration committee, should also be established to deal effectively with conflicts of interest.

Bringing it All Together

The basis of all good corporate finance decisions is a sound framework of corporate governance. This point cannot be emphasized too much because most of the problems that companies experience can usually be identified by failings in the way in which they are governed. When covering subjects in later chapters, the underlying assumption is that corporate executives are acting in the interests of shareholders and that the firm is well governed.

When a company does not have strong corporate governance, it may make decisions that do not maximize share value. For example, a firm may choose to invest in projects that maximize managerial wealth and not that of shareholders. They may also make financing decisions that minimize the risk of the firm for the management but not necessarily for the shareholders. This would lead them to make different investment and financing decisions to those that would be recommended in later chapters.

Transparency and timely information disclosure are major aspects of good governance. Without this, investors would find it extremely difficult to value a firm or assess the risk of its operations. Part Three of the textbook assumes that share prices efficiently incorporate information about a company. However, if the management of a firm do not see transparency and disclosure as an important part of their responsibilities, share prices will be uninformative and risk assessment would be meaningless.

The 2004 OECD Principles of Corporate Governance set the basis by which individual countries set their own corporate governance codes. This has led to a proliferation of codes issued by regulators specific to individual countries. Table 2.6 lists the main corporate governance codes and their date of publication for different countries. All codes can be downloaded from the European Corporate Governance Institute website (www.ecgi.org).

Table 2.6 Country Codes of Corporate Governance

Country	Code
Australia	Corporate Governance Principles and Recommendations (2014)
Austria	Austrian Code of Corporate Governance (2012)
Bahrain	Corporate Governance Code Kingdom of Bahrain (2010)
Belgium	The 2009 Belgian Code on Corporate Governance (2009)
China	The Code of Corporate Governance for Listed Companies in China (2001)
Denmark	Recommendations for Corporate Governance in Denmark (2014)
EU	EVCA Corporate Governance Guidelines (2005)
Finland	Finnish Corporate Governance Code (2010)
France	AFEP-MEDEF Corporate Governance Code of Listed Corporations (2013) Recommendations on Corporate Governance (2011)
Germany	German Corporate Governance Code (2013)
Greece	Hellenic Corporate Governance Code for Listed Companies (2013)
India	Corporate Governance Voluntary Guidelines (2009)
Ireland	Corporate Governance, Share Option and Other Incentive Schemes (1999)
Italy	Codice di Autodisciplina (2014)
Malaysia	Malaysian Code on Corporate Governance (2012)
Netherlands	Dutch Corporate Governance Code (2008)
Norway	The Norwegian Code of Practice for Corporate Governance (2012)
OECD	OECD Principles of Corporate Governance (2004)
Oman	Code of Corporate Governance for Public Listed Companies (2002)
Pakistan	Code of Corporate Governance (2012)
Poland	Code of Best Practice for WSE Companies (2012)
Portugal	CMVM Corporate Governance Code (2013)
Singapore	Code of Corporate Governance (2012)
Slovenia	Corporate Governance Code (2009)
South Africa	King Code of Corporate Governance for South Africa (2009)
Spain	Unified Good Governance Code (2006)
Sweden	Swedish Code of Corporate Governance (2010)
Switzerland	Swiss Code of Best Practice for Corporate Governance (2008)

Country	Code
Thailand	The Principles of Good Corporate Governance for Listed Companies (2006)
UAE	Corporate Governance Code for Small and Medium Enterprises Dubai (2009) Ministerial Resolution No. (518) of 2009 Concerning Governance Rules and Corporate Discipline Standards (2009)
UK	The UK Corporate Governance Code (2012) The UK Stewardship Code (2012)
US	Full CII Corporate Governance Policies (2013) Principles of Corporate Governance (2012)

2.5   International Corporate Governance

Why do countries have their own code of corporate governance and not just follow one generic code? The reason is that institutional differences exist across regions. Even in the European Union, there is a wide range of corporate governance practices and this, in turn, affects the way managers behave and make decisions. In this section, we will discuss some differences in corporate governance around the world and how they may impact upon the business decisions of corporations.

Investor Protection: The Legal Environment

The legal environment in which a corporation does business can have a big impact on its decisions. In a common law system, the law evolves as a result of the judgement decisions of courts whereas in a civil law system, judges interpret the law, they cannot change it. With respect to commercial decisions, the UK and Ireland follow a common law system whereas the rest of Europe follows civil law.

The third form of legal system is based on religious principles: Canon Law for Christianity, Halakha for Judaism, and Sharia for Islam. Under religious law, specific religious principles form the basis of legal decisions. This can have a considerable impact on business activity, especially when religion forbids specific activities. For example, Islam forbids the use of interest in any economic transaction and so financial loans are not allowed.

Figure 2.5 presents a snapshot of countries that follow different legal systems. Many countries do not follow one system alone, and the exact legal environment can be a hybrid of two systems. For example, India's legal

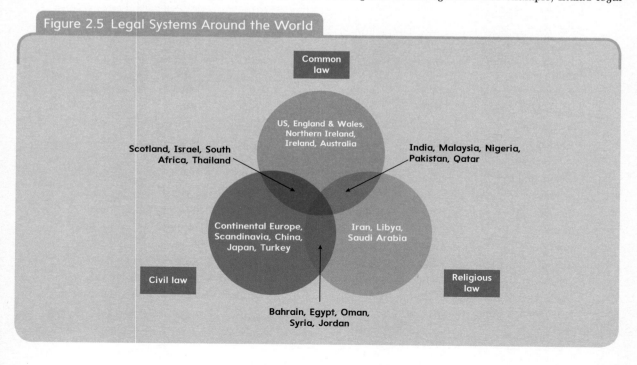

Figure 2.5 Legal Systems Around the World

Common law

US, England & Wales, Northern Ireland, Ireland, Australia

Scotland, Israel, South Africa, Thailand

India, Malaysia, Nigeria, Pakistan, Qatar

Continental Europe, Scandinavia, China, Japan, Turkey

Iran, Libya, Saudi Arabia

Civil law

Religious law

Bahrain, Egypt, Oman, Syria, Jordan

system is based on common law but personal laws are driven by religious law depending on an individual's religion. Scotland has a different legal system from the rest of the UK, with most laws based on continental or Roman civil law. Commercial law is an exception and it is similar to the rest of the UK in this regard.

Because the corporate environment must respond quickly to different economic events, common law systems are able to adapt faster to these changes. For example, if a company can identify a loophole in the law that allows them to legally expropriate wealth from shareholders, a common law system can quickly close this loophole through the courts. In a civil law system, any changes in regulation must be enacted through government statute, which can take a much longer time to process.

The inherent flexibility of common law legal environments ensures that shareholders and outside stakeholders are better protected than in civil law countries. This constrains the activities of corporate managers and, as a result, they are held more accountable. In addition, because investor protection is better in common law environments, it would be expected that raising capital through the equity markets would be more popular in countries that follow this system.

The type of legal system is not the only factor that affects corporate investors. Adherence to the rule of law and efficiency of law enforcement can have a major impact on corporate decision-making and regulatory compliance. Clearly, a country can have very comprehensive laws but if they are not enforced then their effect is meaningless.

The Financial System: Bank and Market-based Countries

In a bank-based financial system, banks play a major role in facilitating the flow of money between investors with surplus cash and organizations that require funding. In market-based systems, financial markets take on the role of the main financial intermediary. Corporations in countries with very well-developed financial markets find it easier to raise money by issuing debt and equity to the public than through bank borrowing. Countries with bank-based systems have very strong banks that actively monitor corporations and are often involved in long-term strategic decisions.

It has been argued that corporations in market-based countries have a shorter-term focus than in bank-based countries because of the emphasis on share price and market performance. When banks are the major source of funding to a company, managers may have longer investment horizons and be less willing to take risks. On the other hand, market-based systems have been argued to be more efficient at funding companies than bank systems. There are many ways in which a country's financial system can be classified as bank or market-based. Table 2.7 shows, for a number of countries, the level of domestic deposits in banks divided by stock market size. A country with a high ratio would be regarded as a bank-based financial system.

Table 2.7 Bank versus Market-based Financial Systems

Country	Domestic Bank Deposits/ Stock Market Capitalization	Country	Domestic Bank Deposits/ Stock Market Capitalization	Country	Domestic Bank Deposits/ Stock Market Capitalization
South Africa	0.40	Denmark	1.40	Finland	2.71
Malaysia	0.41	Thailand	1.44	Israel	2.76
Singapore	0.70	Netherlands	1.63	Greece	2.78
Hong Kong	0.76	Japan	1.66	France	3.11
Sweden	0.86	New Zealand	1.73	Belgium	3.31
United States	0.91	Kenya	1.80	Cyprus	3.73
United Kingdom	1.03	Switzerland	1.80	Italy	4.45
Australia	1.08	Nigeria	1.88	Iceland	4.50
Canada	1.12	Pakistan	2.17	Germany	5.01
India	1.24	Indonesia	2.67	Portugal	5.84
Turkey	1.35	Norway	2.69	Egypt	6.10
Ireland	1.36	Spain	3.20	Austria	10.24

Source: Demirgüç-Kunt and Levine (1999) 'Bank-based and Market-based Financial Systems: Cross-country Comparisons', World Bank Working Paper.

Culture and Corporate Governance

Most of the discussion so far has related to western governance environments where the principal–agent perspective is dominant. However, this is not fully accepted everywhere. For example, in the Middle East and parts of Asia and Africa, Islamic-based systems of governance are followed more closely. Furthermore, with governance scandals continuing to occur with regular frequency, western commentators are questioning whether other approaches to governance may be more appropriate. One of the most important alternatives to principal–agent theory is the Stewardship Theory of Corporate Governance, which regards the manager as a steward of the firm's assets rather than an agent of the firm's shareholders.

Agency Theory argues that managers are selfish agents who will pursue their own objectives at the expense of all other stakeholders, including shareholders. As a result, contractual obligations between the firm and management must exist that bring managerial objectives in line with shareholders. One way to do this is to construct a remuneration package that incentivizes (but not too much!) managers to do their job well and seek maximization of firm value. Another strategy is to reduce the power of the manager so that they will automatically be constrained in their behaviour. One typical governance innovation is to split the role of Chair and Chief Executive into two different jobs. Since the Chief Executive, who is responsible for the day-to-day running of the company, must report to the Chair there is less scope for non-value maximizing activities to continue without getting queried.

When you think about it, to say that a manager is selfish and only wanting to do their own thing at the expense of everyone else is quite insulting! It also does not capture the vast majority of managers in business who are completely loyal to their firm and employees. Most companies in the world are run via families, founder-entrepreneurs, or long-term investors. In such a situation, managerial tenures can be very long and people are employed at the same company for many years. Basically, Stewardship Theory argues that managers are motivated to do the very best for a company because they view themselves as stewards of the firm. The best way to do this is to have exceptionally strong relationships with the shareholders of a firm. In addition, Stewardship Theory would suggest that the role of Chair and Chief Executive should be combined so that the manager has enough power and authority to make decisions and take a long-term strategic perspective.

The Stewardship Theory concept is relevant in the Middle East and in those countries where long-term investors such as families are common, such as Southern Europe and most of Asia and Africa. Both theories argue that managers must be helped to make the best decisions for the firm, which will also be the best decisions for shareholders. How this happens and how a firm is structured contributes to the decision-making process and influences the financial choices made by managers.

Ethics and Corporate Governance

Many people confuse corporate governance with ethics and believe that if a company has strong corporate governance it will necessarily be more ethical. This is not necessarily the case and many of the most significant corporate crises in recent times have been in companies with the highest level of observed corporate governance. Take the banking sector as an example. Although the industry is one of the most well governed in the global economy, it still followed fairly unethical practices that led to the financial crisis and subsequent sovereign debt bailouts across the world. Another example is Tesco, which was discussed at the beginning of this chapter. Arguably, Tesco has an absolutely top quality governance structure with non-executive directors, split chairman/ chief executive position, a shareholder charter, and a corporate social responsibility policy, among other things. However, for years it continually presented optimistic profit forecasts that arguably led to wrong firm valuations. Is this ethical?

The key to understanding corporate governance is that its objective is to facilitate the optimal allocation of resources in a firm. Resources do not only include physical assets like plant, property and equipment, but also human capital like employees. For the best financial decisions to be made, they must reflect both financial and social/ethical concerns. In sum, managers should optimize firm value conditional on an ethical framework of decision-making. Corporate governance can facilitate ethical decision-making but it is not a necessary requisite nor does it lead to ethical decision-making. This is something that goes deeper than rules and regulations and cannot be mandated through simple corporate governance structures.

Given that this book concerns financial decisions and how to use these decisions to maximize firm value, it is implicitly understood that the decisions will be ethical. When necessary, appropriate reference will be made to ethics, but it will not be emphasized in the text unless it clarifies aspects of a corporate decision.

2.6 Corporate Governance in Action: Starbucks

Starbucks, the international coffee retailer chain, is frequently under scrutiny regarding its corporate governance policies. This is because much of its raw materials (coffee beans) is created in very poor, developing countries. The scope for manipulation and exploitation of the coffee farmers is massive, and the company has to proactively ensure that one of its stakeholder groups (the farmers) is not adversely and unfairly treated by the board's strategic decisions.

To see how Starbucks adheres to the main OECD corporate governance principles, it is useful to examine its Corporate Governance Principles and Practices. The company's corporate governance policy is available on its website and you can easily find it by searching for 'Starbucks Corporate Governance' on the Internet.

The Starbucks corporate governance document states that the board is responsible for looking after the Company's business and affairs to ensure they meet the objectives and goals outlined by the company. The role of the board of directors is to uphold the company's goals and responsibilities. Directors must be appropriately qualified and offer a wide variety of backgrounds and outlooks.

The board consists of 12 members, including the chairman and chief executive officer. In addition, the majority of board members must be independent non-executive directors.

Board Meetings

The board meets a minimum of five times per year and one of these meetings is solely concerned with long-term strategic planning. The chairman and chief executive officer are responsible for distributing the agenda of each meeting beforehand in a timely manner. All members of the board are expected to make every effort to attend the board meetings.

Authority and Responsibilities of the Board

Naturally, the company sees its shareholders as the main stakeholder group of the company. Starbucks states that the fundamental responsibility of the board is to promote the best interests of the Company and its shareholders by overseeing the management of the Company's business and affairs. This is the standard responsibility of a corporate board and translates itself into two basic legal obligations, namely (1) the duty of care, which imposes the obligation on the board to make appropriate decisions on behalf of the company and avoid unnecessary risk; and (2) the duty of loyalty, which requires that the board makes decisions that are in the interests of the company and its shareholders, without regard to any personal interest.

Policies and Practices

Starbucks is ahead of many other companies in that it has a corporate governance committee that reports directly to the board of directors. This places corporate governance at the same level of importance as the audit function, the remuneration of directors and their nomination to the board, which all have their separate committees.

The corporate governance document sets out detailed procedures for selecting new directorial candidates and their appointment to the board. It also describes the process by which agenda items are set for each board meeting.

Non-executive directors have time at each board meeting to meet on their own without any executive directors present. This is to ensure that a balanced discussion of the company's strategy can be carried out without the interference of the managers who are actually implementing the strategy.

Director Share Ownership

Starbucks insists that all its directors, whether they be executive or non-executive, hold shares in the company. This is important to the directors as it ensures some convergence of objectives of directors and shareholders. The minimum shareholding for directors, as of 2015, is $240,000. New directors have four years from the date of appointment to purchase these shares and must hold them for the period of appointment to the board.

Assessing Board Performance

Starbucks carries out an annual evaluation of the directors' performance, the effectiveness of the board of directors and all its subcommittees. An evaluation of the chairman and chief executive is also carried out. Both the chair and the chief executive of Starbucks are subjected to a formal evaluation each year based on a number of qualitative and quantitative benchmarks. The salaries of both chair and chief executive are consequently determined by this evaluation.

All the business and financing decisions of Starbucks are framed by the company's main corporate governance principles. By placing corporate governance at the very forefront of the Starbucks philosophy, shareholders and stakeholders know that their financial and human investment is governed in an appropriate manner.

Summary and Conclusions

All of the material in this textbook makes the assumption that firms are run properly, efficiently and ethically. Unfortunately, in practice, this may not be the case. Corporate governance is concerned with the way in which a firm is managed. There are a number of basic principles which should be followed to minimize the danger of firms getting into difficulty solely because of the way they are managed. The budding financial manager must be aware of and familiar with the basic principles underlying the way in which his or her company should be run. Without this knowledge, he or she will not be in a position to make the best financial decisions for the company's shareholders.

Questions and Problems

CONCEPT

1 **The Corporate Firm**   Differentiate between sole proprietorships, partnerships and corporations. What are the advantages and weaknesses of each?

2 **Agency Problems**   Suppose you own shares in a company. The current share price is £2.50. Another company has just announced that it wants to buy your company and will pay £3.50 per share to acquire all the outstanding equity. Your company's management immediately begins fighting off this hostile bid. Is management acting in the shareholders' best interests? Why or why not?

3 **The Governance Structure of Corporations**   Why do partnerships require formal agreements among the main shareholders when sole ownerships do not? Why are corporation articles and memoranda of understanding so complex compared to partnership agreements?

4 **The OECD Principles of Good Governance**   Review the OECD principles of corporate governance. Which principle relates to the ability of corporate executives to trade in the shares of their own company?

5 **Corporate Governance in Action**   Give an overview of the UK Stewardship Code (2012) and explain its importance. What is the most important principle? Does the Code have any weaknesses?

REGULAR

6 **Private vs Public Companies**   What are the main similarities and differences between private and public limited companies? Why are all firms not publicly listed?

7 **Macro Governance**   Why do you think corporate behaviour in bank-based financial systems would be different from market-based financial systems? How do you think other differences in the macro environment can affect corporate objectives?

8 **Corporate Governance**   An investor survey by McKinsey & Co in 2000 found that over 80 per cent of investors would pay a premium for the shares of a well-governed company compared to a poorly governed one. Why do shareholders value companies with an effective corporate governance system? Should the same corporate governance rules be applied to all companies? Why or why not?

9 **Corporate Governance**   Many regulators insist on public companies having board subcommittees such as the remuneration committee, audit committee and risk management committee. Why could this responsibility not simply be left to the board of directors? Explain.

10 **Corporate Governance across the World**   Give an overview of the basic underlying models of corporate governance that exist around the world today. How do these different systems influence share ownership? To what extent are these models converging? Explain.

11 **Corporate Governance around the World**   In the Middle East, many companies have a Sharia Supervisory Board to which the board of directors reports. Evaluate the merits of such a governance structure and argue whether this approach to governance could be extended to other areas where the supervisory board guides on ethical, social or environmental matters.

12 **Partnerships**   What are the differences between a general partnership and a limited partnership? Why do firms choose to be partnerships instead of limited liability corporations?

13 **Organizations**   Review the differences between various corporate forms. Why would an owner move from being a sole owner to a partner to a controlling shareholder in a limited corporation?

14 **Corporate Governance Principles**   Discuss the evolution of corporate governance in the United Kingdom. In what way are the Codes linked to each other? Explain.

15 **Corporate Governance Principles**   Is it possible to improve one governance principle in a firm but weaken another at the same time? Use an illustration to explain your answer.

16 **Corporate Governance Policy**   How do differences in the macro-environment affect corporate governance?

17 **Principles of Good Governance**   In 2004, the OECD published its document, 'Principles of Good Governance'. Discuss this report in detail and the major principles that are contained in it. In your opinion, what is the most important (if any) principle? Use practical examples to illustrate your answer.

18 **Regulatory Governance**   You have been appointed as a consultant for a very poor country in Africa, with no corporate governance regulations, and have been asked to formulate an appropriate corporate governance framework for the country's fledgling banking sector. Propose and justify five governance structures or systems that you would recommend to the country's regulators.

19 **Audit Committees**   The audit committee of a firm is an integral part of its corporate governance. Explain what an audit committee is, why it is important, its main responsibilities, and how you can evaluate the audit process within a company. Your answer should refer to real life examples where the audit process was ineffective or flawed.

20 **Agency Relationships**   Who owns a corporation? Describe the process whereby the owners control the firm's management. What is an agency relationship and what is the main reason that an agency relationship exists in the corporate form of organization? In this context, what kinds of problems can arise?

21 **Agency Problems and Corporate Ownership**   Corporate ownership varies around the world. Historically individuals have owned the majority of shares in public corporations in the United States. In Germany and Japan, however, banks and other large financial institutions own most of the equity in public corporations. Do you think agency problems are likely to be more or less severe in Germany and Japan than in the United States? Why? In recent years, large financial institutions such as mutual funds and pension funds have been becoming the dominant owners of shares in the UK, and these institutions are becoming more active in corporate affairs. What are the implications of this trend for agency problems and corporate control?

22 **Government Ownership**   In recent years, governments have taken control of banks through buying their shares. What impact does this have on the lending culture of these banks? Is this consistent with shareholder maximization? Banks have also been encouraged to shrink their balance sheets and focus more on expanding domestic lending operations. Is this consistent with achieving a good return for taxpayers? Use an example to illustrate your answer.

23 **Stakeholders**   Discuss what is meant by a stakeholder. In what ways are stakeholders represented in two-tier board structures? How does this differ from companies with a unitary board structure? Use real examples to illustrate your answer.

24 **Institutional Shareholders**   Regulators have developed a number of new policies with respect to institutional shareholder involvement in the running of firms. Review the reasons why regulators would prefer more or less involvement of institutions in the running of corporations. In addition, discuss the proposals that have been put forward by regulators in your own country and whether these are likely to be effective.

25 **Managerial Objectives**   Why would we expect managers of a corporation to pursue the objectives of shareholders? What about bondholders?

26 Codes of Corporate Governance   Choose a developed and an emerging market economy and identify any differences and similarities between your chosen countries.

27 Board of Directors   You have been hired as a consultant to evaluate the performance of a board of directors. What things would you look for? Why would shareholders want to hire a consultant to do such a job, when the share price is supposed to give an accurate reflection of corporate performance?

28 Managerial Ownership   How do agency costs in a firm change as managers build up their shareholdings? What does it mean when we say that managers are entrenched? Provide some examples of real life cases where managers have acted in a selfish fashion even when they are shareholders in the firm.

29 Executive Compensation   Critics have charged that compensation to top managers in the banking sector is simply too high and should be cut back. Look at the financial accounts of some banks in your region and determine the total pay of their chief executive officers. Are such amounts excessive? Do you think the European Union's plan to cap bankers' bonuses at the ratio of bonus pay to fixed pay at 1:1, or 2:1 if there is approval from shareholders is a good idea? Explain.

30 Managerial Objectives   In 2012, the Argentinian government nationalized YPF, which is a subsidiary of Repsol, the Spanish oil giant. YPF was integral to the operations of Repsol. The firm was set up 10 years earlier, and had received more than €20 billion of capital investment from Repsol. The benefits to Repsol's shareholders from YPF were large and every year, $600 million of dividends were paid to the parent company. How do you think the presence of a major state shareholder (the Argentinian government) will change the agency relationships within YPF? Explain.

Exam Question (45 minutes)

As the financial manager of an unlisted manufacturing company based in Amsterdam, you have been tasked with preparing your firm for potential listing on Euronext. The company is closely held with only five shareholders, each holding 20 per cent of the company's shares. The shareholders are all directors of the firm and they make up the board of directors. Because of the company's ownership structure, there has been no real consideration of corporate governance issues before.

The share listing will result in the total directors' cash ownership falling to 20 per cent of the total firm. This means that 80 per cent will be owned by external shareholders (mainly banks and financial institutions). However, the five directors have informed you that they do not wish to relinquish control of the firm. They have asked you to answer the following with respect to corporate governance issues:

1   How can the board maintain control of the firm while only having 20 per cent of the shares? (20 marks)

2   Should the company's board structure change? If so, what should be done and why? (20 marks)

3   What processes should be put in place to ensure that all shareholders have some say in the company's strategy? How should the company deal with foreign shareholders? (20 marks)

4   How should the company decide upon director remuneration? Are there any structures that should be put in place to ensure that the directors are fairly compensated for the work that they have done? (20 marks)

5   There is a proposal that the company should instead possibly list in London or Shanghai and move headquarters to the listing location. Are there any institutional differences that the directors should be aware of before making their decision? Explain. (20 marks)

Mini Case

Since the financial crisis, investors have become increasingly vocal about the size of executive pay and many companies have seen remuneration packages refused by shareholders at annual general meetings. Assume that you are on the remuneration committee of a 150-year-old family firm that has been proud of its family heritage for six generations of ownership. The company recently appointed its first ever non-family chief executive and the family shareholders are uncertain how they should structure her remuneration package. You have been tasked with putting together a sensible package that recognizes the specific objectives of the family but also the incentives required for an external non-family manager. Write a brief report to the board of directors on your proposed pay package, emphasizing its strengths and weaknesses.

Practical Case Study

Finance executives need to know and understand the corporate governance environment in which they operate.

1   Visit the European Corporate Governance Institute website (www.ecgi.org) and download the appropriate corporate governance code for your country. If your country does not have a governance code, download the OECD Principles of Good Governance.

2   Read over the document, identify five aspects of corporate governance that have been highlighted in the document, and explain their importance for your country.

Reference

La Porta, L., F. Lopez-de-Silanes, A. Shliefer and R. Vishny (2000) 'Investor Protection and Corporate Governance', *Journal of Financial Economics*, Vol. 58, Nos. 1 and 2, 3–27.

Additional Reading

Corporate governance is one of the fastest growing research areas in finance and the number of top quality papers that have been published over the last few years is enormous. In 2015 alone, more than 1,000 papers were submitted to the online research database SSRN with corporate governance as the topic. The ownership structure and governance environment, as well as their impact on all aspects of financial decision-making, have rightly been recognized as crucial to understanding how corporations make decisions. Consequently, the number of papers listed below is necessarily large. (The country of study is highlighted in bold.) A good starting point for readers is:

1   Bebchuk, L.A. and M.S. Weisbach (2010) 'The State of Corporate Governance Research', *Review of Financial Studies*, Vol. 23, No. 3, 939–961.

2   Fan, J.P.H., K.C.J. Wei and X. Xu (2011) 'Corporate Finance and Governance in Emerging Markets: A Selective Review and an Agenda for Future Research', *Journal of Corporate Finance*, Vol. 17, No. 2, 207–214. **International**.

3   Krüger, P. (2015) 'Corporate Goodness and Shareholder Wealth', *Journal of Financial Economics*, Vol. 115, No. 2, 304–329.

Macro Governance

Macro governance papers consider the impact of regulatory structures, culture and law on corporations. They normally examine more than one country and compare different regulatory and governance environments. Important papers are as follows:

4   Aggarwal, R., I. Erel, R. Stulz and R. Williamson (2009) 'Differences in Governance Practices between US and Foreign Firms: Measurement, Causes, and Consequences', *Review of Financial Studies*, Vol. 22, No. 8, 3131–3169. **International**.

5   Aggarwal, R., I. Erel, M. Ferreira and P. Matos (2011) 'Does Governance Travel around the World? Evidence from Institutional Investors', *Journal of Financial Economics*, Vol. 100, No. 1, 154–181. **International**.

6   Andres, C. and E. Theissen (2008) 'Setting a Fox to Keep the Geese: Does the Comply-or-Explain Principle Work?' *Journal of Corporate Finance*, Vol. 15, No. 3, 289–301.

7   Atanassov, J. and E.H. Kim (2009) 'Labor and Corporate Governance: International Evidence from Restructuring Decisions', *The Journal of Finance*, Vol. 64, No. 1, 341–374.

8   Ayyagari, M., A. Demirguc-Kunt and V. Maksimovic (2011) 'Firm Innovation in Emerging Markets: The Role of Finance, Governance, and Competition', *Journal of Financial and Quantitative Analysis*, Vol. 46, No. 6, 1545–1580. **International**.

9   Borisova, G. and W.L. Megginson (2011) 'Does Government Ownership Affect the Cost of Debt? Evidence from Privatization', *Review of Financial Studies*, Vol. 24, No. 8, 2693–2737. **International**.

10   Bortolotti, B. and M. Faccio (2009) 'Government Control of Privatized Firms', *Review of Financial Studies*, Vol. 22, 2907–2939.

11   Brockman, P. and E. Unlu (2009) 'Dividend Policy, Creditor Rights, and the Agency Costs of Debt', *Journal of Financial Economics*, Vol. 92, No. 2, 276–299. **International**.

12   Cornelli, F., Z. Kominek and A. Ljungqvist (2013) 'Monitoring Managers: Does it Matter?, *The Journal of Finance*, Vol. 68, No. 2, 431–481. **Central and Eastern Europe.**

13   Cuñat, V., M. Gine and M. Guadalupe (2012) 'The Vote Is Cast: The Effect of Corporate Governance on

Shareholder Value', *The Journal of Finance*, Vol. 67, No. 5, 1943–1977.

14   Doidge, C., G.A. Karolyi and R. Sultz (2007) 'Why Do Countries Matter so Much for Corporate Governance?', *Journal of Financial Economics*, Vol. 86, No. 1, 1–39.

15   Doidge, C., G.A. Karolyi, K.V. Lins, D.P. Miller and R. Sultz (2009) 'Private Benefits of Control Ownership and the Cross-Listing Decision', *The Journal of Finance*, Vol. 64, No. 1, 425–466.

16   Donghui, L., F. Moshirian, P.K. Pham and J. Zein (2006) 'When Financial Institutions Are Large Shareholders: The Role of Macro Corporate Governance Environments', *The Journal of Finance*, Vol. 61, No. 6, 2975–3007.

17   Dyck, A. and L. Zingales (2004) 'Private Benefits of Control: An International Comparison', *The Journal of Finance*, Vol. 59, No. 2, 537–600.

18   Erkens, D.H., M. Hung and P. Matos (2012) 'Corporate Governance in the 2007–2008 Financial Crisis: Evidence from Financial Institutions Worldwide', *Journal of Corporate Finance*, Vol. 18, No. 2, 389–411. **International**.

19   Ge, W., J-B. Kim and B.Y. Song (2012) 'Internal Governance, Legal Institutions and Bank Loan Contracting around the World', *Journal of Corporate Finance*, Vol. 18, No. 3, 413–432. **International**.

20   Giannetti, M. and Y. Koskinen (2010) 'Investor Protection, Equity Returns, and Financial Globalization', *Journal of Financial and Quantitative Analysis*, Vol. 45, No. 1, 135–168. **International**.

21   Goergen, M. and L. Renneboog (2008) 'Contractual Corporate Governance', *Journal of Corporate Finance*, Vol. 15, No. 3, 166–182.

22   Guiso, L., P. Sapienza and L. Zingales (2008) 'Trusting the Stock Market', *The Journal of Finance*, Vol. 63, No. 6, 2557–2600.

23   Hillier, D., V. Pereira de Queiroz, J. Pindado and C. De la Torre (2010) 'The Impact of Country-level Corporate Governance on Research and Development', *Journal of International Business Studies*, Vol. 42, No. 1, 76–98.

24   John, K., L. Litov and B. Yeung (2008) 'Corporate Governance and Risk-Taking', *The Journal of Finance*, Vol. 63, No. 4, 1679–1728.

25   Kim, K.A. P. Kitsabunnarat-Chatjuthamard and J.R. Nofsinger (2007) 'Large Shareholders, Board Independence, and Minority Shareholder Rights: Evidence from Europe', *Journal of Corporate Finance*, Vol. 13, No. 5, 859–880.

26   La Porta, L., F. Lopez-de-Silanes, A. Shliefer and R. Vishney (2000) 'Investor Protection and Corporate Governance', *Journal of Financial Economics*, Vol. 58, Nos. 1 and 2, 3–27.

27   Laeven, L. and R. Levine (2008) 'Complex Ownership Structures and Corporate Valuations', *Review of Financial Studies*, Vol. 21, No. 2, 579–604.

28   Laeven, L. and R. Levine (2009) 'Bank Governance, Regulation and Risk Taking', *Journal of Financial Economics*, Vol. 93, No. 2, 259–275. **International**.

29   Lel, U. (2012) 'Currency Hedging and Corporate Governance: A Cross-country Analysis', *Journal of Corporate Finance*, Vol. 18, No. 2, 221–237. **International**.

30   Leuz, C., K.V. Lins and F.E. Warnock (2009) 'Do Foreigners Invest Less in Poorly Governed Firms?', *Review of Financial Studies*, Vol. 22, No. 8, 3245–3285. **International**.

31   Lin, C., Y. Ma, P. Malatesta and Y. Xuan (2011) 'Ownership Structure and the Cost of Corporate Borrowing', *Journal of Financial Economics*, Vol. 100, No. 1, 1–23. **International**.

32   Martynova, M. and L. Renneboog (2011) 'Evidence on the International Evolution and Convergence of Corporate Governance Regulations', *Journal of Corporate Finance*, Vol. 17, No. 5, 1531–1557. **International**.

33   Morck, R., M.D. Yavuz and B. Yeung (2011) 'Banking System Control, Capital Allocation, and Economy Performance', *Journal of Financial Economics*, Vol. 100, No. 2, 264–283. **International**.

34   Spamann, H. (2010) 'The "Antidirector Rights Index" Revisited', *Review of Financial Studies*, Vol. 23, No. 2, 467–486. **International**.

There has also been a lot of research at the firm level in single countries. Researchers have examined a wide range of issues, but the general theme considers how governance structures or regulation affect the performance of firms and their strategic decisions. Another important area relates to ownership structure and how that affects a corporation. The listings below are categorized by general subject.

Board Characteristics

35   Acharya, V.V., S.C. Myers and R.G. Rajan (2011) 'The Internal Governance of Firms', *The Journal of Finance*, Vol. 66, No. 3, 689–720. **US**.

36   Adams, R.B. and D. Ferreira (2009) 'Women in the Boardroom and their Impact on Governance and Performance', *Journal of Financial Economics*, Vol. 94, No. 2, 291–309. **US**.

37   Aggarwal, R. (2009) 'Differences in Governance Practices between U.S. and Foreign Firms: Measurement, Causes, and Consequences', *Review of Financial Studies*, Vol. 22, No. 8, 3131–3169. **International**.

38   Armstrong, C.S., J.E. Core and W.R. Guay (2014) 'Do Independent Directors Cause Improvements in Firm Transparency?', *Journal of Financial Economics*, Vol. 113, No. 3, 383–403.

39   Bebchuk, L., A. Cohen and A. Ferrell (2009) 'What Matters in Corporate Governance?', *Review of Financial Studies*, Vol. 22, No. 2, 783–827. **US**.

40   Bebchuk, L.A., A. Cohen and C.C. Wang (2013) 'Learning and the Disappearing Association between Governance and Returns', *Journal of Financial Economics*, Vol. 108, No. 2, 323–348. **US**.

41   Belot, F., E. Ginglinger, M.B. Slovin and M.E. Sushka (2014) 'Freedom of Choice between Unitary and Two-tier Boards: An Empirical Analysis', *Journal of Financial Economics*, Vol. 112, No. 3, 364–385. **France**.

42   Bennedsen, M., H.C. Kongsted and K.M. Nielsen (2008) 'The Causal Effect of Board Size in the Performance of Small and Medium Sized Firms', *Journal of Banking and Finance*, Vol. 32, No. 6, 1098–1109. **Denmark**.

43   Bhagat, S. and B. Bolton (2008) 'Corporate Governance and Firm Performance', *Journal of Corporate Finance*, Vol. 15, No. 3, 257–273. **US**.

44   Bodnaruk, A., M. Massa and A. Simonov (2013) 'Alliances and Corporate Governance', *Journal of Financial Economics*, Vol. 107, No. 3, 671–693. **US**.

45   Chikh, S. and J.-Y. Filbien (2011) 'Acquisitions and CEO Power: Evidence from French Networks', *Journal of Corporate Finance*, Vol. 17, No. 5, 1221–1236. **France**.

46   Chung, K.H., J. Elder and J-C. Kim (2009) 'Corporate Governance and Liquidity', *Journal of Financial and Quantitative Analysis*, Vol. 45, 265–291. **US**.

47   Dahya, J. and J.J. McConnell (2007) 'Board Composition, Corporate Performance, and the Cadbury Committee Recommendation', *Journal of Financial and Quantitative Analysis*, Vol. 42, No. 3, 535–564. **UK**.

48   Doukas, J., M. Holmen and N. Travlos (2002) 'Diversification, Ownership and Control of Swedish Corporations', *European Financial Management*, Vol. 8, 281–314. **Sweden**.

49   Duchin, R., J.G. Matsusaka and O. Ozbas (2010) 'When Are Outside Directors Effective?', *Journal of Financial Economics*, Vol. 96, No. 2, 195–214. **US**.

50   Fahlenbrach, R., A. Low and R.M. Stulz (2010) 'Why Do Firms Appoint CEOs as Outside Directors?', *Journal of Financial Economics*, Vol. 97, No. 1, 12–32. **US**.

51   Falato, A., D. Kadyrzhanova and U. Lel (2014) 'Distracted Directors: Does Board Busyness Hurt Shareholder Value?', *Journal of Financial Economics*, Vol. 113, No. 3, 404–426.

52   Fich, E.M. and A. Shivdasani (2006) 'Are Busy Boards Effective Monitors?', *The Journal of Finance*, Vol. 61, No. 2, 689–724. **US**.

53   Field, L., M. Lowry and A. Mkrtchyan (2013) 'Are Busy Boards Detrimental?', *Journal of Financial Economics*, Vol. 109, No. 1, 63–82. **US**.

54   Ginglinger, E., W. Megginson and T. Waxin (2011) 'Employee Ownership, Board Representation, and Corporate Financial Policies', *Journal of Corporate Finance*, Vol. 17, No. 4, 868–887. **France**.

55   Goergen, M. and L. Renneboog (2011) 'Managerial Compensation', *Journal of Corporate Finance*, Vol. 17, No. 4, 1068–1077. **International**.

56   Guest, P.M. (2008) 'The Determinants of Board Size and Composition: Evidence from the UK', *Journal of Corporate Finance*, Vol. 15, No. 1, 51–72. **UK**.

57   Hafsi, T. and G. Turgut (2013) 'Boardroom Diversity and its Effect on Social Performance: Conceptualization and Empirical Evidence', *Journal of Business Ethics*, Vol. 112, No. 3, 463–479.

58   Hermalin, B.E. and M.S. Weisbach (2012) 'Information Disclosure and Corporate Governance', *The Journal of Finance*, Vol. 67, No. 1, 195–234. **US**.

59   Hillier, D. and P. McColgan (2006) 'An Analysis of Changes in Board Structure during Corporate Governance Reforms', *European Financial Management*, Vol. 12, No. 4, 575–607. **UK**.

60   Hilscher, J. and E. Şişli-Ciamarra (2013) 'Conflicts of Interest on Corporate Boards: The Effect of Creditor-Directors on Acquisitions', *Journal of Corporate Finance*, Vol. 19, 140–158. **US**.

61   Huang, J. and D.J. Kisgen (2013) 'Gender and Corporate Finance: Are Male Executives Overconfident Relative to Female Executives?', *Journal of Financial Economics*, Vol. 108, No. 3, 822–839.

62   Kaplan, S.N., M.M. Klebanov and M. Sorensen (2012) 'Which CEO Characteristics and Abilities Matter?', *The Journal of Finance*, Vol. 67, No. 3, 973–1007.

63   Lauterbach, B. and Y. Yafeh (2011) 'Long-term Changes in Voting Power and Control Structure Following the Unification of Dual Class Shares', *Journal of Corporate Finance*, Vol. 17, No. 2, 215–228. **Israel**.

64   Li, F. and S. Srinivasan (2011) 'Corporate Governance when Founders Are Directors', *Journal of Financial Economics*, Vol. 102, No. 2, 454–469. **US**.

65   Masulis, R.W. and S. Mobbs (2014) 'Independent Director Incentives: Where Do Talented Directors Spend their Limited Time and Energy?', *Journal of Financial Economics*, Vol. 111, No. 2, 406–429. **US**.

66   Masulis, R.W., C. Wang and F. Xie (2012) 'Globalizing the Boardroom: The Effects of Foreign Directors on Corporate Governance and Firm Performance', *Journal of Accounting and Economics*, Vol. 53, No. 3, 527–554. **US**.

67   Mura, R. (2007) 'Firm Performance: Do Non-Executive Directors Have Minds of their Own? Evidence from UK Panel Data', *Financial Management*, Vol. 36, No. 3, 81–112. **UK**.

68   Renneboog, L. and Y. Zhao (2011) 'Us Knows Us in the UK: On Director Networks and CEO Compensation', *Journal of Corporate Finance*, Vol. 17, No. 4, 1132–1157. **UK**.

69   Schwartz-Ziv, M. and M.S. Weisbach (2013) 'What Do Boards Really Do? Evidence from Minutes of Board Meetings', *Journal of Financial Economics*, Vol. 108, No. 2, 349–366. **Israel**.

Ownership Structure and Shareholder Activism

70 Anderson, R.C., D.M. Reeb and W. Zhao (2012) 'Family-Controlled Firms and Informed Trading: Evidence from Short Sales', *The Journal of Finance*, Vol. 67, No. 1, 351–386. **US**.

71 Barontini, R. and L. Caprio (2006) 'The Effect of Family Control on Firm Value and Performance: Evidence from Continental Europe', *European Financial Management*, Vol. 12, No. 5, 689–723. **Europe**.

72 Becht, M., J. Franks, C. Mayer and S. Rossi (2009) 'Returns to Shareholder Activism: Evidence from a Clinical Study of the Hermes UK Focus Fund', *Review of Financial Studies*, Vol. 22, No. 8, 3093–3129. **UK**.

73 Bena, J. and H. Ortiz-Molina (2013) 'Pyramidal Ownership and the Creation of New Firms', *Journal of Financial Economics*, Vol. 108, No. 3, 798–821. **Europe.**

74 Bigelli, M., V. Mehrotra and P.R. Rau (2011) 'Why Are Shareholders Not Paid to Give Up their Voting Privileges? Unique Evidence from Italy', *Journal of Corporate Finance*, Vol. 17, No. 5, 1619–1635. **Italy**.

75 Boubaker, S. and F. Labegorre (2008) 'Ownership Structure, Corporate Governance and Analyst Following: A Study of French Listed Firms', *Journal of Banking and Finance*, Vol. 32, No. 6, 961–976. **France**.

76 Boubakri, N., J.C. Cosset and W. Saffar (2013) 'The Role of State and Foreign Owners in Corporate Risk-taking: Evidence from Privatization', *Journal of Financial Economics*, Vol. 108, No. 3, 641–658. **International.**

77 Budsaratragoon, P., S. Lhaopadchan and D. Hillier (2010) 'Institutional Shareholder Activism and Limited Investor Attention', *Review of Behavioral Finance*, Vol. 2, No. 2, 106–125. **US**.

78 Chhaochharia, V., A. Kumar and A. Niessen-Ruenzi (2012) 'Local Investors and Corporate Governance', *Journal of Accounting and Economics*, Vol. 54, No. 1, 42–67. **US**.

79 Cronqvist, H., F. Heyman, M. Nilsson, H. Svaleryd and J. Vlachos (2009) 'Do Entrenched Managers Pay their Workers More?', *The Journal of Finance*, Vol. 64, No. 1, 309–339. **Sweden**.

80 Davies, J.R., D. Hillier and P. McColgan (2005) 'Ownership Structure, Managerial Behavior, and Corporate Value', *Journal of Corporate Finance*, Vol. 11, No. 4, 645–660. **UK**.

81 Doidge, C., G.A. Karolyi, K.V. Lins, D.P. Miller and R.M. Stulz (2009) 'Private Benefits of Control Ownership and the Cross-Listing Decision', *The Journal of Finance*, Vol. 64, No. 1, 425–466. **International**.

82 Faccio, M. and L.H.P. Lang (2002) 'The Ultimate Ownership of Western European Corporations', *Journal of Financial Economics*, Vol. 65, No. 3, 365–395. **Europe**.

83 Faccio, M., M-T. Marchica and R. Mura (2011) 'Large Shareholder Diversification and Corporate Risk-Taking', *Review of Financial Studies*, Vol. 24, No. 11, 3601–3641. **Europe**.

84 Fauver, L. and M.E. Fuerst (2006) 'Does Good Corporate Governance Include Employee Representation? Evidence from German Corporate Boards', *Journal of Financial Economics*, Vol. 82, No. 3, 673–710. **Germany**.

85 Ferreira, M.A., M. Massa and P. Matos (2010) 'Shareholders at the Gate? Institutional Investors and Cross-Border Mergers and Acquisitions', *Review of Financial Studies*, Vol. 23, No. 2, 601–644. **International**.

86 Franks, J., C. Mayer and S. Rossi (2009) 'Ownership: Evolution and Regulation', *Review of Financial Studies*, Vol. 22, 4009–4056. **UK**.

87 Gantchev, N. (2013) 'The Costs of Shareholder Activism: Evidence from a Sequential Decision Model', *Journal of Financial Economics*, Vol. 107, No. 3, 610–631.

88 Giannetti, M. and L. Laeven (2009) 'Pension Reform, Ownership Structure, and Corporate Governance: Evidence from a Natural Experiment', *Review of Financial Studies*, Vol. 22, No. 10, 4091–4127. **Sweden**.

89 Gugler, K., N. Ivanova and J. Zechner (2014) 'Ownership and Control in Central and Eastern Europe', *Journal of Corporate Finance*, Vol. 26, 145–163. **Central and Eastern Europe.**

90 Harbula, P. (2007) 'The Ownership Structure, Governance, and Performance of French Companies', *Journal of Applied Corporate Finance*, Vol. 19, No. 1, 88–101. **France**.

91 Kandel, E., M. Massa and A. Simonov (2011) 'Do Small Shareholders Count?', *Journal of Financial Economics*, Vol. 101, No. 3, 641–665. **Sweden**.

92 Klein, A. and E. Zur (2009) 'Entrepreneurial Shareholder Activism: Hedge Funds and Other Private Investors', *The Journal of Finance*, Vol. 64, No. 1, 187–229. **US**.

93 Li, D., Q.N. Nguyen, P.K. Pham and S. X. Wei (2011) 'Large Foreign Ownership and Firm-Level Stock Return Volatility in Emerging Markets', *Journal of Financial and Quantitative Analysis*, Vol. 46, No. 4, 1127–1155. **International**.

94 Lin, C., Y. Ma, P. Malatesta and Y. Xuan (2012) 'Corporate Ownership Structure and Bank Loan Syndicate Structure', *Journal of Financial Economics*, Vol. 104, No. 1, 1–22. **International**.

95 Maury, B. (2006) 'Family Ownership and Firm Performance: Empirical Evidence from Western European Corporations', *Journal of Corporate Finance*, Vol. 12, No. 2, 321–341. **Europe**.

96 Mehrotra, V., R. Morck, J. Shim and Y. Wiwattanakantang (2013) 'Adoptive Expectations: Rising Sons in Japanese Family Firms', *Journal of Financial Economics*, Vol. 108, No. 3, 840–854. **Japan**.

97   Norli, Ø., C. Ostergaard and I. Schindele (2015) 'Liquidity and Shareholder Activism', *Review of Financial Studies*, Vol. 28, No. 2, 486–520.

Executive Turnover and Managerial Succession

98   Amore, M.D., A. Minichilli and G. Corbetta (2011) 'How Do Managerial Successions Shape Corporate Financial Policies in Family Firms?', *Journal of Corporate Finance*, Vol. 17, No. 4, 1016–1027. **Italy**.

99   Ansari, I.F., M. Goergen and S. Mira (2014) 'The Determinants of the CEO Successor Choice in Family Firms', *Journal of Corporate Finance*, Vol. 28, 6–25. **France, Germany and UK.**

100   Cucculelli, M. and G. Micucci (2008) 'Family Succession and Firm Performance: Evidence from Italian Family Firms', *Journal of Corporate Finance*, Vol. 15, No. 1, 17–31. **Italy**.

101   Hazarika, S., J.M. Karpoff and R. Nahata (2012) 'Internal Corporate Governance, CEO Turnover, and Earnings Management', *Journal of Financial Economics*, Vol. 104, No. 1, 44–69. **US**.

102   Hillier, D. and P. McColgan (2009) 'Firm Performance and Managerial Succession in Family Managed Firms', *Journal of Business Finance and Accounting*, Vol. 36, 461–484. **UK**.

103   Hillier, D., S.C. Linn and P. McColgan (2005) 'Equity Issuance, CEO Turnover, and Corporate Governance', *European Financial Management*, Vol. 11, No. 4, 515–538. **UK**.

Regulation and Environment

104   Atanassov, J. (2013) 'Do Hostile Takeovers Stifle Innovation? Evidence from Antitakeover Legislation and Corporate Patenting', *The Journal of Finance*, Vol. 68, No. 3, 1097–1131.

105   Bajo, E., M. Bigelli, D. Hillier and B. Petracci (2009) 'The Determinants of Regulatory Compliance: An Analysis of Insider Trading Disclosures', *Journal of Business Ethics*, Vol. 90, No. 3, 331–343. **Italy**.

106   Benfratello, L., F. Schiantarelli and A. Sembenelli (2008) 'Banks and Innovation: Microeconometric Evidence on Italian Firms', *Journal of Financial Economics*, Vol. 90, No. 2, 197–217. **Italy**.

107   Cronqvist, H., F. Heyman, M. Nilsson, H. Svaleryd and J. Vlachos (2009) 'Do Entrenched Managers Pay their Workers More?', *The Journal of Finance*, Vol. 64, No. 1, 309–339. **Sweden**.

108   Hillier, D. and A. Marshall (2002) 'Are Trading Bans Effective? Exchange Regulation and Corporate Insider Trading', *Journal of Corporate Finance*, Vol. 8, No. 4, 393–410. **UK**.

109   Masulis, R.W., C. Wang and F. Xie (2009) 'Agency Problems at Dual-Class Companies', *The Journal of Finance*, Vol. 64, No. 4, 1697–1727. **US**.

Theoretical Papers (Advanced)

110   Baranchuk, N. and P.H. Dybvig (2009) 'Consensus in Diverse Corporate Boards', *Review of Financial Studies*, Vol. 22, No. 2, 715–747.

111   Boot, A.W.A. and A.V. Thakor (2011) 'Managerial Autonomy, Allocation of Control Rights, and Optimal Capital Structure', *Review of Financial Studies*, Vol. 24, No. 10, 3434–3485.

112   Carlin, B.I. and S. Gervais (2009) 'Work Ethic, Employment Contracts, and Firm Value', *The Journal of Finance*, Vol. 64, No. 2, 785–821.

113   Casamatta, C. and A. Guembel (2010) 'Managerial Legacies, Entrenchment, and Strategic Inertia', *The Journal of Finance*, Vol. 65, No. 6, 2403–2436.

114   Cohn, J.B. and U. Rajan (2013) 'Optimal Corporate Governance in the Presence of an Activist Investor', *Review of Financial Studies*, Vol. 26, No. 4, 985–1020.

115   Dhillon, A. and S. Rossetto (2015) 'Ownership Structure, Voting, and Risk', *Review of Financial Studies*, Vol. 28, No. 2. 521–560.

116   Harris, M. and A. Raviv (2010) 'Control of Corporate Decisions: Shareholders vs. Management', *Review of Financial Studies*, Vol. 23, No. 11, 4115–4147.

117   Inderst, R. and H.M. Mueller (2010) 'CEO Replacement under Private Information', *Review of Financial Studies*, Vol. 23, No. 8, 2935–2969.

118   Kind, A. and M. Poltera (2013) 'The Value of Corporate Voting Rights Embedded in Option Prices', *Journal of Corporate Finance*, Vol. 22, 16–34. **Europe**.

119   Manso, G. (2011) 'Motivating Innovation', *The Journal of Finance*, Vol. 66, No. 5, 1823–1860.

120   Morellec, E., B. Nikolov and N. Schürhoff (2012) 'Corporate Governance and Capital Structure Dynamics', *The Journal of Finance*, Vol. 67, No. 3, 803–848.

121   Noe, T.H. and M.J. Rebello (2012) 'Optimal Corporate Governance and Compensation in a Dynamic World', *Review of Financial Studies*, Vol. 25, No. 2, 480–521.

122   Robinson, D.T. (2009) 'Size, Ownership and the Market for Corporate Control', *Journal of Corporate Finance*, Vol. 15, No. 1, 80–84.

PART 2

Value and Capital Budgeting

One of the three central pillars of Corporate Finance is the investment decision. In Part 2, we will explore this topic in great detail and present a number of invaluable tools to assist you in making financial decisions. There are many types of information one can use to assess whether a potential project is worthwhile. In Finance, we almost always focus on cash flows, but there are other approaches (such as using accounting data) that provide valuable insights to the manager.

In Chapter 3 we start with the accounting figures of a company and, in particular, the income statement, balance sheet (or statement of financial position), and cash flow statement. A very common method of understanding the financial performance and health of a firm is to undertake a financial ratio analysis, and you are shown how to do this using an in-depth case study.

Chapter 4 is core to the remaining chapters of the book and introduces a concept called Time Value of Money. Time Value of Money takes both timing and risk into account to arrive at a present day value of any cash flow to be received in the future. Given the range of cash flow patterns that can be observed in business, Chapter 4 concerns itself with valuing these different cash flow streams.

The remaining chapters of Part 2 focus on practical applications. Chapter 5 shows how to value corporate bonds and equities, and Chapters 6 to 8 describe in some depth the various methods used by companies to value strategic investments. By the end of Part 2, you will be able to assess any investment or project and come to a conclusion on its value to your firm.

CHAPTER 3

Financial Statement Analysis

In November 2014, shares in the global engineering firm, Babcock International Group plc, were trading for about £10.89. At that price, Babcock had a price–earnings (PE) ratio of 24.66, meaning that investors were willing to pay £24.66 for every pound in income earned by Babcock. At the same time, investors were willing to pay £19.56 and £29.75 for each pound earned by BG Group and Smith & Nephew, respectively. Although their PE ratios are different from Babcock, the share prices were similar (£10.43 and £10.57 respectively). There are also many companies like Groupon and Facebook which, despite having very little or negative earnings (that is, they made a loss), have very high share prices. Meanwhile, the average equity in the FTSE 100 index, which contains 100 of the largest publicly traded companies in the United Kingdom, had a PE ratio of about 14.

Are the PE ratios of Babcock, BG Group and Smith & Nephew unnaturally high? What do PE ratios tell us and why are they important? To find out, this chapter explores a variety of ratios and their use in financial analysis and planning. However, before examining PE ratios, we need to spend some time on the source of this ratio – the company's financial statements.

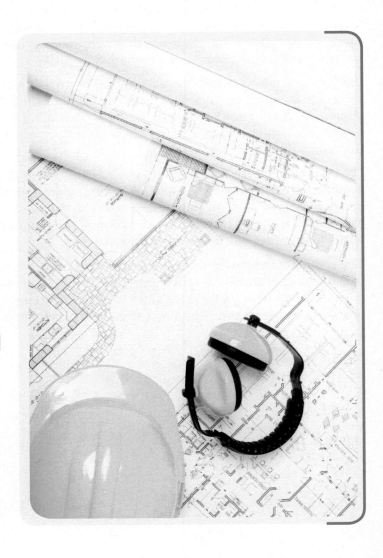

KEY NOTATIONS

ROE	Return on equity
ROA	Return on assets
EPS	Earnings per share
NCF	Net cash flow
$CF(O)$	Cash flow from operations
$CF(I)$	Cash flow from investing activities
$CF(F)$	Cash flow from financing activities
PE	Price–earnings ratio

3.1 The Statement of Financial Position

Chapter 1
Page 2

The statement of financial position or balance sheet is an accountant's snapshot of a firm's accounting value on a particular date, as though the firm stood momentarily still (see **Chapter 1**, Section 1.1 for more information). The statement of financial position has two sides: on the left are the *assets* and on the right are the *liabilities* and *shareholders' equity*. The statement of financial position states what the firm owns and how it is financed. The accounting definition that underlies the statement of financial position and describes the relationship is:

$$\text{Assets} \equiv \text{Liabilities} + \text{Shareholders' equity}$$

We have put a three-line equality in the balance equation to indicate that it must always hold, by definition. In fact, the shareholders' equity is *defined* to be the difference between the assets and the liabilities of the firm. In principle, equity is what the shareholders would have remaining after the firm discharged its obligations.

Table 3.1 gives the 2014 statement of financial position for the satellite media firm, Sky plc. The assets in the statement of financial position are listed in order by the length of time it normally would take an ongoing firm to convert them into cash. The asset side depends on the nature of the business and how management chooses to conduct it. Management must make decisions about cash versus marketable securities, credit versus cash sales, whether to make or buy inventory, whether to lease or purchase items, the types of business in which to engage, and so on. The liabilities and the shareholders' equity are also listed in the order in which they would typically be paid over time.

Table 3.1 2014 Statement of Financial Position (Balance Sheet) of Sky plc

Assets	£m	Equity and Liabilities	£m
Non-Current Assets		**Non-Current Liabilities**	
Intangible Assets	1,829	Bank and Other Borrowings	2,658
Property, Plant and Equipment	1,088	Non-Current Trade and Other Payables	56
Investments and Joint Ventures	706	Other Non-Current Liabilities	144
Other Non-Current Assets	253		
	3,876		2,858
Current Assets		**Current Liabilities**	
Inventories	546	Borrowings	11
Trade and Other Receivables	635	Trade and Other Payables	2,286
Short-Term Deposits	295	Other Current Liabilities	222
Cash and Cash Equivalents	1,082		2,519
Other Current Assets	15	**Total Liabilities**	5,377
	2,573	Total Equity	1,072
Total Assets	6,449	**Total Equity and Liabilities**	6,449

The liabilities and equity side reflects the types and proportions of financing, which depend on management's choice of capital structure, as between debt and equity and between current debt and long-term debt.

When analysing a statement of financial position, the financial manager should be aware of three concerns: liquidity, debt versus equity, and value versus cost.

Liquidity

Liquidity refers to the ease and quickness with which assets can be converted to cash (without significant loss in value). *Current assets* are the most liquid and include cash and assets that will be turned into cash within a year from the date of the statement of financial position. *Trade receivables* are amounts not yet collected from customers for goods or services sold to them (after adjustment for potential bad debts). *Inventories* are composed of raw materials to be used in production, work in progress and finished goods. *Non-current assets* are the least liquid kind of assets. Tangible non-current assets include property, plant and equipment. Non-current assets do not convert to cash from normal business activity, and they are not usually used to pay expenses such as payroll.

Some non-current assets are intangible. Intangible assets have no physical existence but can be very valuable. Examples of intangible assets are the value of a trademark or the value of a patent. Goodwill is an accounting term that reflects the premium paid by companies when they acquire other companies. Further analysis of Sky's intangible assets figure of £1,829 million is that it consists of £1,019 million in goodwill and £810 million in other intangibles such as brands, software and contractual business relationships.

The more liquid a firm's assets, the less likely the firm is to experience problems meeting short-term obligations. Thus, the probability that a firm will avoid financial distress can be linked to the firm's liquidity. Unfortunately, liquid assets frequently have lower rates of return than non-current assets; for example, cash generates no investment income. To the extent a firm invests in liquid assets, it sacrifices an opportunity to invest in more profitable investment vehicles.

Debt versus Equity

Liabilities are obligations of the firm that require a payout of cash within a stipulated period. Many liabilities involve contractual obligations to repay a stated amount and interest over a period. Thus, liabilities are debts and are frequently associated with nominally fixed cash burdens, called *debt service*, that put the firm in default of a contract if they are not paid. *Shareholders' equity* is a claim against the firm's assets that is residual and not fixed. In general terms, when the firm borrows, it gives the bondholders first claim on the firm's cash flow. Bondholders can sue the firm if the firm defaults on its bond contracts. This may lead the firm to declare itself bankrupt. Shareholders' equity is the residual difference between assets and liabilities:

$$\text{Assets} - \text{Liabilities} \equiv \text{Shareholders' equity}$$

This is the shareholders' ownership of the firm stated in accounting terms. The accounting value of shareholders' equity increases when retained earnings are added. This occurs when the firm retains part of its earnings instead of paying them out as dividends.

Value versus Cost

The accounting value of a firm's assets is frequently referred to as the *book value* of the assets. Firms in different countries use various accounting standards to report the value of their assets. All listed companies in the European Union are required to use International Financial Reporting Standards (IFRS). IFRS value assets at theoretically true market or fair values. *Market or fair value* is the price at which willing buyers and sellers would trade the assets. Unfortunately, even with fair value accounting (IFRS), the tradable value of assets is likely to be different from their accounting value. This is because in many cases there is no liquid market that allows the calculation of an asset's accounting fair value. In these situations, the financial manager must estimate a fair value from a similar asset or a theoretical model. In this book, we will treat IFRS as the main accounting system.

3.2   The Income Statement

The income statement measures performance over a specific period – say, a year. The accounting definition of income is:

$$\text{Revenue} - \text{Expenses} \equiv \text{Income}$$

If the statement of financial position is like a snapshot, the income statement is like a video recording of what the people did between two snapshots. Table 3.2 gives the income statement for Sky for year ending 2014.

The income statement usually includes several sections. The operations section reports the firm's revenues and expenses from principal operations. Among other things, the non-operating section of the income statement includes all financing costs, such as interest expense. Usually a second section reports as a separate item the amount of taxes levied on income. The last item on the income statement is the bottom line, or net income. Net income is frequently expressed per share of equity – that is, earnings per share.

When analysing an income statement, the financial manager should keep in mind non-cash items, time and costs.

Table 3.2 The 2014 Income Statement of Sky plc

	£m
Revenue	7,632
Operating Expenses	6,471
Operating Profit	**1,161**
Income from Joint Ventures and Investments	61
Profit Before Interest and Taxation	**1,222**
Finance Costs (Interest)	140
Profit before Tax	**1,082**
Tax	217
Profit After Tax	**865**
Number of Shares	**1,575.59**
Earnings per Share	0.549

$$\text{Earnings per share} = \frac{\text{Profit for the period attributable to equityholders}}{\text{Total shares outstanding}}$$

$$= \frac{\text{£865 million}}{\text{1,575.59 million}}$$

$$= \text{£0.549 per share}$$

Source: Sky plc annual accounts (2014).

Non-cash Items

The economic value of assets is naturally connected to their future incremental cash flows. However, cash flow does not appear on an income statement. There are several non-cash items that are expenses against revenues but do not affect cash flow. The most important of these is *depreciation*. Depreciation reflects the accountant's estimate of the cost of equipment used up in the production process. For example, suppose an asset with a 5-year life and no resale value is purchased for €1,000. According to accountants, the €1,000 cost must be expensed over the useful life of the asset. If straight-line depreciation is used, there will be five equal instalments, and €200 of depreciation expense will be incurred each year. From a finance perspective, the cost of the asset is the actual negative cash flow incurred when the asset is acquired (that is, €1,000, *not* the accountant's smoothed €200-per-year depreciation expense).

In practice, the difference between cash flows and accounting income can be quite dramatic, so it is important to understand the difference. For example, while Sky made a total profit of £865 million for the year ending 2014, their cash only increased by £267 million. We look at financial cash flow in more detail in Section 3.5.

Time and Costs

It is often useful to visualize all of future time as having two distinct parts, the *short run* and the *long run*. The short run is the period in which certain equipment, resources and commitments of the firm are fixed; but the time is long enough for the firm to vary its output by using more labour and raw materials. The short run is not a precise period that will be the same for all industries. However, all firms making decisions in the short run have some fixed costs – that is, costs that will not change because of fixed commitments. In real business activity, examples of fixed costs are bond interest, overhead and property taxes. Costs that are not fixed are variable. Variable costs change as the output of the firm changes; some examples are raw materials and wages for employees on the production line.

In the long run, all costs are variable. Accountants do not distinguish between variable costs and fixed costs. Instead, accounting costs usually fit into a classification that distinguishes product costs from period costs. Product costs are the total production costs incurred during a period – raw materials, direct labour and manufacturing overheads – and are reported on the income statement as cost of goods sold. Both variable and fixed costs are included in product costs. Period costs are costs that are allocated to a time period; they are called *selling*, *general* and *administrative expenses*. One period cost would be the company chief executive's salary.

3.3   Taxes

Taxes can be one of the largest cash outflows a firm experiences. For example, for the year ending 2013, Royal Dutch Shell's profit before taxes was €26.9 billion. Its tax bill for this period was €17.1 billion or about 63.6 per cent of its pretax earnings. The size of the tax bill is determined by the tax code of the region your firm operates in, an often amended set of rules, and any deferred taxes from an earlier year. In this section, we examine corporate tax rates and how taxes are calculated.

If the various rules of taxation seem a little bizarre or convoluted to you, keep in mind that the tax code is the result of political, not economic, forces. As a result, there is no reason why it has to make economic sense.

Corporate Tax Rates

An overview of corporate tax rates that were in effect for 2014 for a sample of countries is shown in Table 3.3. Corporate taxes are not normally a simple arithmetic deduction from profit before taxes. Almost all countries in the world allow firms to carry forward losses they have made in previous years to offset their tax bill in the future.

Chapter 15 Page 410
Chapter 16 Page 435

This is what happened to Royal Dutch Shell in 2013. Although the corporate tax rate in the UK is much lower than 63.6 per cent, Royal Dutch Shell would have had to pay tax in different jurisdictions, many of which would have been greater than in the UK, as well as past taxes deferred from earlier years. (See **Chapter 15**, Section 15.5 and **Chapter 16**, Section 16.4 for more information on corporate tax.)

Table 3.3 Corporate Tax Rates Around the World

Country	Corporation Tax (%)	Country	Corporation Tax (%)
Australia	30	New Zealand	30
Austria	25	Norway	28
Bahrain	0	Oman	12
Belgium	33.99	Poland	19
Canada	34	Portugal	23
China	25	Russia	20
Denmark	24.5	Singapore	17
Finland	20	South Africa	28
France	33.33	Spain	30
Germany	29.58	Sweden	22
Greece	26	Switzerland	11.48-24.43
India	33.99	Tanzania	30
Ireland	12.5	Thailand	20
Italy	31.4	Turkey	20
Japan	35.64	United Arab Emirates	0
Malaysia	25	United Kingdom	20
Netherlands	20/25	United States	40

Source: © KPMG 2014.

The tax rates presented in Table 3.3 are average tax rates for the largest companies. Many countries apply differential taxation depending on how much a company earns in any given year. In the Netherlands, for example, there are two corporation tax bands. Firms that earn between €0 and €200,000 per annum have a tax rate of 20 per cent. Firms that earn above €200,000 must pay 25 per cent (as presented in Table 3.3).

Average versus Marginal Tax Rates

In making financial decisions, it is frequently important to distinguish between average and marginal tax rates. Your average tax rate is your tax bill divided by your taxable income – in other words, the percentage of your income that goes to pay taxes. Your marginal tax rate is the tax you would pay (in per cent) if you earned one more unit of currency. The percentage tax rates shown in Table 3.3 for the Netherlands are marginal rates. The first €200,000 earned by Dutch firms must pay 20 per cent tax. Any extra earnings are charged 25 per cent tax. Put another way, marginal tax rates apply to the part of income in the indicated range only, not all income.

The difference between average and marginal tax rates can best be illustrated with a simple example. Suppose our Dutch corporation has a taxable income of €400,000. What is the tax bill? Using Table 3.3, we can figure our tax bill like this:

$$
\begin{aligned}
0.20 \times €200,000 &= €40,000 \\
0.25 \times (€400,000 - 200,000) &= \underline{50,000} \\
&\ €90,000
\end{aligned}
$$

Our total tax is thus €90,000.

In our example, what is the average tax rate? We had a taxable income of €400,000 and a tax bill of €90,000, so the average tax rate is €90,000/400,000 = 22.5 per cent. What is the marginal tax rate? If we made one more euro, the tax on that euro would be 25 cents, so our marginal rate is 25 per cent.

Example 3.1

Deep in the Heart of Taxes

Assume that TomTom, the Dutch satellite navigation firm, has a taxable income of €850,000. What is its tax bill? What is its average tax rate? Its marginal tax rate?

From Table 3.3, we see that the tax rate applied to the first €200,000 is 20 per cent; and the rate applied to the next €650,000 is 25 per cent. So TomTom must pay 0.20 × €200,000 + 0.25 × 650,000 = €202,500. The average tax rate is thus €202,500/850,000 = 23.82 per cent. The marginal rate is 25 per cent because TomTom's taxes would rise by 25 cents if it had another euro in taxable income.

With a *flat-rate* tax, there is only one tax rate, so the rate is the same for all income levels. With such a tax, the marginal tax rate is always the same as the average tax rate. As it stands now, corporate taxation in the United Kingdom is based on a modified flat-rate tax.

Normally, the marginal tax rate will be relevant for financial decision-making. The reason is that any new cash flows will be taxed at that marginal rate. Because financial decisions usually involve new cash flows or changes in existing ones, this rate will tell us the marginal effect of a decision on our tax bill.

3.4   Net Working Capital

Net working capital is current assets minus current liabilities. Net working capital is positive when current assets are greater than current liabilities. This means the cash that will become available over the next 12 months will be greater than the cash that must be paid out. The net working capital of Sky plc in 2014 was £54 million:

	Current assets (£ millions)	–	Current liabilities (£ millions)	=	Net working capital (£ millions)
2014	2,573	–	2,519	=	54
2013	2,569	–	2,317	=	252

In addition to investing in fixed assets (i.e., capital expenditure), a firm can invest in net working capital. This is called the change in net working capital. The change in net working capital in 2014 is the difference between the net working capital in 2014 and 2013. In Sky's case, this is £54 million − £252 million = −£198 million. What is causing the drop in net working capital? A further analysis of Sky's accounts shows that although current assets marginally increased by £4 million, its current liabilities jumped by £202 million, principally caused by a £200 million increase in Trade Payables.

3.5   Cash Flow

**Chapter 4
Page 93**

Perhaps the most important item that can be extracted from financial statements is the actual *cash flow* of the firm. An official accounting statement called the *statement of cash flows* helps to explain the change in accounting cash and equivalents, which for Sky was £267 million in 2014. (See **Chapter 4** for more information on cash flows.)

The first point we should mention is that cash flow is not the same as net working capital. For example, increasing inventory requires using cash. Because both inventories and cash are current assets, this does not affect net working capital. In this case, an increase in inventory is associated with decreasing cash flow.

A firm's cash flow comes from or goes to three main areas: operating activities, $CF(\text{O})$, investing activities, $CF(\text{I})$, and financing activities, $CF(\text{F})$. Just as we established that the value of a firm's assets is always equal to the combined value of the liabilities and the value of the equity, the net cash flow in a firm during a particular period is the sum of cash flows resulting from operating, investing and financing activities. A negative cash flow represents a movement of cash out of the firm.

$$NCF \equiv CF(\text{O}) + CF(\text{I}) + CF(\text{F})$$

The first step in determining cash flows of the firm is to figure out the *operating cash flow* or, more formally, *net cash provided by operating activities*. As can be seen in Table 3.4, operating cash flow is the cash flow generated by business activities, including sales of goods and services. Operating cash flow reflects tax payments, but not financing, capital spending or changes in net working capital.

Table 3.4 Cash Flow of Sky plc

	£m
Cash Flow from Operating Activities	
Cash Generated from Operations	1,769
Income from other activities	27
Tax Paid	−240
Net Cash from Operating Activities	1,556
Cash Flow from Investing Activities	
Purchase of Property, Plant & Equipment	−241
Purchase of Intangible Assets	−302
Decrease in Short-Term Deposits	300
Other Investments	−1
Net Cash used in Investing Activities	−244
Cash Flow from Financing Activities	
Interest Paid	−137
Dividends Paid	−485
Purchase of Own Shares	−430
Other Financing Activities	7
Net Cash used in Financing Activities	−1,045
Net Increase in Cash and Cash Equivalents	267

Another important component of cash flow involves *changes in cash flow from investing activities*. The net change in cash flow from investing activities equals the acquisition of non-current assets plus any security investments minus the sales of non-current assets. The result is the cash flow used for investment purposes. In Sky's cash flow statement, this amounts to a net outflow of £244 million in 2014.

Cash flows also come from financing purposes, such as the firm buying back its own shares, issuing new shares to the market and increasing or decreasing borrowing. For Sky in 2014, cash outflows from *financing activities* were £1,045 million. This was largely because the company paid interest of £137 million, dividends of £485 million, and bought back £430 million of its stock.

Total net cash flows generated by the firm's assets in 2014 were then equal to:

	(£ millions)
Net cash provided by operating activities	1,556
Net cash provided by investing activities	−244
Net cash provided by financing activities	−1,045
Net cash flow	267

Some important observations can be drawn from our discussion of cash flow:

1   Several types of cash flow are relevant to understanding the financial situation of the firm. Operating cash flow measures the cash generated from operations not counting cash flows arising from investment expenditure or financing. It is usually positive; a firm is in trouble if operating cash flow is negative for a long time because the firm is not generating enough cash to pay operating costs. The total cash flow of the firm includes adjustments for capital spending and new financing. It will frequently be negative. When a firm is growing at a rapid rate, spending on inventory and non-current assets can be higher than operating cash flow.

2   Profit is not cash flow. The profit made by Sky in 2014 was £865 million, whereas cash flow was only £267 million. The two numbers are not usually the same. In determining the economic and financial condition of a firm, cash flow is more revealing.

A firm's total cash flow sometimes goes by a different name, free cash flow. Of course, there is no such thing as 'free' cash. Instead, the name refers to cash that the firm is free to distribute to creditors and shareholders because it is not needed for working capital or investments. We will stick with 'total cash flow of the firm' as our label for this important concept because, in practice, there is some variation in exactly how free cash flow is computed. Nonetheless, whenever you hear the phrase 'free cash flow', you should understand that what is being discussed is cash flow from assets or something quite similar.

Real World Insight 3.1

BAE Systems Plc

BAE Systems is a global defence, aerospace and security company employing around 88,200 people worldwide. Its products and services cover air, land and naval forces, as well as advanced electronics, security, information technology, and support services. The company's income statement is presented below. All figures are in £millions.

Income Statement		
	2014 £m	2013 £m
Sales	16,637	18,180
Underlying EBITA	1,702	1,925
Return on sales	10.2%	10.6%
Non recurring items	-	6
EBITA	1,702	1,931
Amortisation of intangible assets	(184)	(189)

Income Statement		
	2014 £m	2013 £m
Impairment of intangible assets	(170)	(887)
Finance costs	(448)	(392)
Taxation expense	(148)	(287)
Profit for the year	752	176

Source: BAE Systems Annual Report 2014 from companieshouse.gov.uk.

There are many items of information a reader must take in when looking at an income statement. For example, have revenues increased or decreased over time? How have costs changed over the same period? Is any component of the cost base changing in an unusual way? What is the overall operating income of the company and is it improving? Is the company making a profit or loss? Is the profit acceptable to the firm?

3.6   Financial Statement Analysis

A good working knowledge of financial statements is desirable simply because such statements, and numbers derived from those statements, are the primary means of communicating financial information both within the firm and outside the firm. In short, much of the language of business finance is rooted in the ideas we discuss in this chapter.

Clearly, one important goal of the accountant is to report financial information to the user in a form useful for decision-making. Ironically, the information frequently does not come to the user in such a form. In other words, financial statements do not come with a user's guide. This chapter is a first step in filling this gap.

Standardizing Statements

One obvious thing we might want to do with a company's financial statements is to compare them to those of other, similar companies. We would immediately have a problem, however. It is almost impossible to directly compare the financial statements for two companies because of differences in size.

For example, Ryanair and Air France-KLM are obviously serious rivals in the European flights market, but Air France-KLM is much larger (in terms of assets), so it is difficult to compare them directly. For that matter, it is difficult even to compare financial statements from different points in time for the same company if the company's size has changed. The size problem is compounded if we try to compare Air France-KLM and, say, International Airlines Group (IAG, formerly British Airways and Iberia). Since IAG's financial statements are denominated in British pounds, we have size *and* currency differences.

To start making comparisons, one obvious thing we might try to do is to somehow standardize the financial statements. One common and useful way of doing this is to work with percentages instead of total monetary amounts. The resulting financial statements are called common-size statements.

Common-size statements of financial position can be constructed by expressing each item as a percentage of total assets. In this form, financial statements are relatively easy to read and compare. For example, just looking at the statement of financial position for Sky, we can see that current assets were 40 per cent of total assets in 2014. Current liabilities were 39 per cent of total assets over that same time. Similarly, shareholders' equity comprised 16.6 per cent of total asset value.

A useful way of standardizing the income statement shown in Table 3.2 (see page 67) is to express each item as a percentage of total revenues. A common-size income statement tells us what happens to each cash unit in revenues. For Sky, 2014 taxes ate up £0.0284 out of every pound made in revenues. When all is said and done, only £0.1133 of each pound in revenues flows through to the bottom line (net income). These percentages are useful in comparisons. For example, a relevant figure is the cost percentage. For Sky, £0.848 of each £1.00 in revenues goes in operating expenses. It would be interesting to compute the same percentage for Sky's main competitors to see how the firm stacks up in terms of cost control.

3.7 Ratio Analysis

Another way of avoiding the problems involved in comparing companies of different sizes is to calculate and compare financial ratios. Such ratios are ways of comparing and investigating the relationships between different pieces of financial information. We cover some of the more common ratios next (there are many others we do not discuss here).

One problem with ratios is that different people and different sources frequently do not compute them in exactly the same way, and this leads to much confusion. The specific definitions we use here may or may not be the same as ones you have seen or will see elsewhere. If you are using ratios as tools for analysis, you should be careful to document how you calculate each one; and, if you are comparing your numbers to those of another source, be sure you know how their numbers are computed.

We will defer much of our discussion of how ratios are used and some problems that come up with using them until later in the chapter. For now, for each ratio we discuss, several questions come to mind:

1   How is it computed?
2   What is it intended to measure, and why might we be interested?
3   What is the unit of measurement?
4   What might a high or low value be telling us? How might such values be misleading?
5   How could this measure be improved?

Financial ratios are traditionally grouped into the following categories:

1   Short-term solvency, or liquidity, ratios
2   Long-term solvency, or financial leverage, ratios
3   Asset management, or turnover, ratios
4   Profitability ratios
5   Market value ratios.

We will consider each of these in turn. In calculating these numbers for Sky, we will use the ending statement of financial position (2014) figures unless we explicitly say otherwise.

Short-term Solvency or Liquidity Measures

As the name suggests, short-term solvency ratios as a group are intended to provide information about a firm's liquidity, and these ratios are sometimes called *liquidity measures*. The primary concern is the firm's ability to pay its bills over the short run without undue stress. Consequently, these ratios focus on current assets and current liabilities.

For obvious reasons, liquidity ratios are particularly interesting to short-term creditors. Because financial managers are constantly working with banks and other short-term lenders, an understanding of these ratios is essential.

One advantage of looking at current assets and liabilities is that their book values and market values are likely to be similar. Often (though not always), these assets and liabilities just do not live long enough for the two to get seriously out of step. On the other hand, like any type of near-cash, current assets and liabilities can and do change fairly rapidly, so today's amounts may not be a reliable guide to the future.

Current Ratio

One of the best-known and most widely used ratios is the *current ratio*. As you might guess, the current ratio is defined as:

$$\text{Current ratio} = \frac{\text{Current assets}}{\text{Current liabilities}} \tag{3.1}$$

For Sky, the 2014 current ratio is:

$$\text{Current ratio} = \frac{£2,573}{£2,519} = 1.02 \text{ times}$$

Because current assets and liabilities are, in principle, converted to cash over the following 12 months, the current ratio is a measure of short-term liquidity. The unit of measurement is either in cash units (such as £s) or times. So, we could say Sky has £1.02 in current assets for every £1 in current liabilities, or we could say Sky has its current liabilities covered 1.02 times over.

To a creditor, particularly a short-term creditor such as a supplier, the higher the current ratio, the better. To the firm, a high current ratio indicates liquidity, but it also may indicate an inefficient use of cash and other short-term assets. Absent some extraordinary circumstances, we would expect to see a current ratio of at least 1; a current ratio of less than 1 would mean that net working capital (current assets less current liabilities) is negative. This would be unusual in a healthy firm, at least for most types of businesses.

The current ratio, like any ratio, is affected by various types of transactions. For example, suppose the firm borrows over the long term to raise money. The short-run effect would be an increase in cash from the issue proceeds and an increase in long-term debt. Current liabilities would not be affected, so the current ratio would rise.

Example 3.2

Current Events

Suppose a firm were to pay off some of its suppliers and short-term creditors. What would happen to the current ratio? Suppose a firm buys some inventory. What happens in this case? What happens if a firm sells some merchandise?

The first case is a trick question. What happens is that the current ratio moves away from 1. If it is greater than 1 (the usual case), it will get bigger, but if it is less than 1, it will get smaller. To see this, suppose the firm has £4 in current assets and £2 in current liabilities for a current ratio of 2. If we use £1 in cash to reduce current liabilities, the new current ratio is $(£4 - 1)/(£2 - 1) = 3$. If we reverse the original situation to £2 in current assets and £4 in current liabilities, the change will cause the current ratio to fall to 1/3 from 1/2.

The second case is not quite as tricky. Nothing happens to the current ratio because cash goes down while inventory goes up – total current assets are unaffected.

In the third case, the current ratio would usually rise because inventory is normally shown at cost and the sale would normally be at something greater than cost (the difference is the markup). The increase in either cash or receivables is therefore greater than the decrease in inventory. This increases current assets, and the current ratio rises.

Finally, note that an apparently low current ratio may not be a bad sign for a company with a large reserve of untapped borrowing power.

Quick (or Acid-test) Ratio

Inventory is often the least liquid current asset. It is also the one for which the book values are least reliable as measures of market value because the quality of the inventory is not considered. Some of the inventory may later turn out to be damaged, obsolete or lost.

More to the point, relatively large inventories are often a sign of short-term trouble. The firm may have overestimated sales and overbought or overproduced as a result. In this case, the firm may have a substantial portion of its liquidity tied up in slow-moving inventory.

To further evaluate liquidity, the *quick*, or *acid-test*, *ratio* is computed just like the current ratio, except inventory is omitted:

$$\text{Quick ratio} = \frac{\text{Current assets} - \text{Inventory}}{\text{Current liabilities}} \qquad (3.2)$$

Notice that using cash to buy inventory does not affect the current ratio, but it reduces the quick ratio. Again, the idea is that inventory is relatively illiquid compared to cash.

For Sky, this ratio in 2014 was:

$$\text{Quick ratio} = \frac{£2,573 - 546}{£2,519} = 0.80 \text{ times}$$

The quick ratio for Sky is lower because of the £546 million of inventory in the company. Managers would need to keep an eye on this ratio to ensure that inventory levels were not becoming too high, thereby reducing the quick ratio to unacceptably low levels.

To give an example of current versus quick ratios, based on recent financial statements, Sky and Inmarsat plc, the global satellite firm, had current ratios of 1.02 and 0.57, respectively. Inmarsat's current ratio is exceptionally low and concerning. Looking at the quick ratio, because Inmarsat has very little inventory, there is almost no difference between the quick ratio (0.53) and current ratio. Inmarsat would need to address the very low liquidity because it appears that it will have difficulty meeting its obligations over the coming year without some form of injection of cash.

Cash Ratio

A very short-term creditor might be interested in the *cash ratio*:

$$\text{Cash ratio} = \frac{\text{Cash and cash equivalents}}{\text{Current liabilities}} \qquad (3.3)$$

You can verify that this works out to be 0.43 times for Sky.

Long-term Solvency Measures

Long-term solvency ratios are intended to address the firm's long-run ability to meet its obligations or, more generally, its financial leverage. These ratios are sometimes called *financial leverage ratios* or just *leverage ratios*. We consider three commonly used measures and some variations.

Total Debt Ratio

The *total debt ratio* takes into account all debts of all maturities to all creditors. It can be defined in several ways, the easiest of which is this:

$$\text{Total debt ratio} = \frac{\text{Total assets} - \text{Total equity}}{\text{Total assets}}$$

$$= \frac{£6,449 - 1,072}{£6,449} = 0.8338 \text{ times} \qquad (3.4)$$

In this case, an analyst might say that Sky uses 83.38 per cent debt. Whether this is high or low or whether it even makes any difference depends on whether capital structure matters, a subject we discuss in a later chapter.

Sky has £0.8338 in debt for every £1 in assets. Therefore, there is £0.1662 in equity (£1 − 0.8338) for every £0.8338 in debt. With this in mind, we can define two useful variations on the total debt ratio, the *debt–equity ratio* and the *equity multiplier*:

$$\text{Debt–equity ratio} = \text{Total debt/Total equity}$$

$$= £0.8338/£0.1662 = 5.016 \text{ times} \qquad (3.5)$$

$$\text{Equity multiplier} = \text{Total assets/Total equity}$$

$$= £1/£0.1662 = 6.016 \text{ times} \qquad (3.6)$$

The fact that the equity multiplier is 1 plus the debt–equity ratio is not a coincidence:

$$\text{Equity multiplier} = \text{Total assets/Total equity} = £1/£0.1662 = 6.016 \text{ times}$$

$$= (\text{Total equity} + \text{Total debt})/\text{Total equity}$$

$$= 1 + (\text{Debt/equity ratio}) = 6.016 \text{ times}$$

The thing to notice here is that given any one of these three ratios, you can immediately calculate the other two, so they all say exactly the same thing.

Times Interest Earned

Another common measure of long-term solvency is the *times interest earned* (TIE) *ratio*. Once again, there are several possible (and common) definitions, but we will stick with the most traditional. The TIE formula is:

$$\text{Times interest earned ratio} = \frac{\text{Profit Before Interest and Taxes}}{\text{Interest}} = \frac{£1,222}{£140} = 8.73 \text{ times} \qquad (3.7)$$

Profit before Interest and Taxes is also known as Earnings before Interest and Taxes or EBIT. As the name suggests, this ratio measures how well a company has its interest obligations covered, and it is often called the *interest coverage ratio*. For Sky, the interest bill is covered 8.73 times over.

Cash Coverage

A problem with the TIE ratio is that it is based on EBIT, which is not really a measure of cash available to pay interest. The reason is that depreciation, a non-cash expense, has been deducted out. Because interest is most definitely a cash outflow (to creditors), one way to define the *cash coverage ratio* is:

$$\text{Cash coverage ratio} = \frac{\text{EBIT} + \text{Depreciation}}{\text{Interest}}$$

$$= \frac{£1,222 + 407}{£140} = 11.64 \text{ times} \qquad (3.8)$$

The numerator here, EBIT plus depreciation, is often abbreviated EBITD (earnings before interest, taxes and depreciation). It is a basic measure of the firm's ability to generate cash from operations, and it is frequently used as a measure of cash flow available to meet financial obligations. You may be wondering where the depreciation figure came from as it does not appear in any of the tables so far. This is because the information is taken from the notes to the financial reports, which is found in the full 2014 Sky plc annual report. Interested readers should check this from the company's website.

Asset Management or Turnover Measures

We next turn our attention to the efficiency with which Sky uses its assets. The measures in this section are sometimes called *asset management* or *utilization ratios*. The specific ratios we discuss can all be interpreted as measures of turnover. What they are intended to describe is how efficiently, or intensively, a firm uses its assets to generate sales. We first look at two important current assets: inventory and receivables.

Inventory Turnover and Days' Sales in Inventory

To calculate inventory turnover, one must first consider the cost of goods sold. This is the direct cost of earning the company's main revenues during the year. The costs should include materials used, labour costs, managerial salaries and other costs of earning the revenues. Depreciation is included in the figure if it is being charged on assets directly related to the main revenue stream. Otherwise, it is left out. In Sky's case, the depreciation would be charged for reduction in the value of their satellite equipment and so this figure should be included in the cost of goods sold figure.

For Sky, the concept of inventory turnover and days' sales in inventory is not appropriate because the firm does not have any real inventories to speak of. You would, therefore, not consider these ratios for this type of firm.

Normally, *inventory turnover* can be calculated as:

$$\text{Inventory turnover} = \frac{\text{Cost of goods sold}}{\text{Inventory}} \qquad (3.9)$$

As long as your company is not running out of stock and thereby forgoing sales, the higher this ratio is, the more efficiently your company is at managing inventory. For Sky, this is:

$$\text{Inventory turnover} = \frac{\text{Operating expenses}}{\text{Inventory}} = \frac{£6,471}{£546} = 11.85$$

The Inventory turnover figure of 11.85 tells us that Sky turned their inventory over 11.85 times during the year. We can immediately figure out how long it took them to turn it over on average. The result is the average *days' sales in inventory*:

$$\text{Days' sales in inventory} = \frac{365 \text{ days}}{\text{Inventory turnover}}$$

$$= \frac{365}{11.85} = 31 \text{ days} \qquad (3.10)$$

This tells us that, roughly speaking, inventory sits 31 days on average before it is sold. Alternatively, assuming we used the most recent inventory and cost figures, it will take about 31 days to work off our current inventory.

Receivables Turnover and Days' Sales in Receivables

Our inventory measures give some indication of how fast we can sell products. We now look at how fast we collect on those sales. The *receivables turnover* is defined in the same way as inventory turnover:

$$\text{Receivables turnover} = \frac{\text{Revenues}}{\text{Trade receivables}}$$

$$= \frac{\pounds 7,632}{635} = 12.02 \text{ times} \tag{3.11}$$

Loosely speaking, Sky collected its outstanding credit accounts and lent the money again 12.02 times during the year.

This ratio makes more sense if we convert it to days, so the *days' sales in receivables* is:

$$\text{Days' sales in receivables} = \frac{365 \text{ days}}{\text{Receivables turnover}}$$

$$= \frac{365}{12.02} = 30 \text{ days} \tag{3.12}$$

Therefore, on average, Sky collects on its credit sales in 30 days. For obvious reasons, this ratio is frequently called the *average collection period* (ACP). Also note that if we are using the most recent figures, we can also say that Sky has 30 days' worth of sales currently uncollected.

Unfortunately, this ratio illustrates the dangers of using financial ratios without really understanding their true meaning. The receivables turnover ratio and days' sales in receivables figure implicitly assumes that all sales in a firm are credit sales. When this is not true, only credit sales figures should be used – not total sales. For firms that take payment immediately, such as low budget airlines, credit sales will only make up a small proportion of total sales. If we had the data, we should have used only credit sales in the numerator of Equation (3.11).

Example 3.3

Payables Turnover

Here is a variation on the receivables collection period. How long, on average, does it take for Sky to *pay* its bills? To answer, we need to calculate the trade payables turnover rate using cost of goods sold. We will assume that Sky purchases everything on credit.

The operating expenses or cost of goods sold is £6,471 million, and trade payables are £2,286 million. The turnover is therefore £6,471/£2,286 = 2.83 times. So, payables turned over about every 365/2.83 = 129 days. On average, then, Sky takes 129 days to pay. As a potential creditor, we might take note of this fact.

Total Asset Turnover

Moving away from specific accounts like inventory or receivables, we can consider an important 'big picture' ratio, the *total asset turnover* ratio. As the name suggests, total asset turnover in 2014 for Sky is:

$$\text{Total asset turnover} = \frac{\text{Revenues}}{\text{Total assets}}$$

$$= \frac{\pounds 7,632}{\pounds 6,449} = 1.18 \text{ times} \tag{3.13}$$

In other words, for every pound in assets, Sky generated £1.18 in sales.

Example 3.4

More Turnover

Suppose you find that a particular company generates £0.40 in annual sales for every pound in total assets. How often does this company turn over its total assets?

The total asset turnover here is 0.40 times per year. It takes 1/0.40 = 2.5 years to turn assets over completely.

Profitability Measures

The three measures we discuss in this section are probably the best known and most widely used of all financial ratios. In one form or another, they are intended to measure how efficiently the firm uses its assets and how efficiently the firm manages its operations. The focus in this group is on the bottom line – net income, also labelled as Earnings after Tax or Profit after Tax.

Profit Margin

Companies pay a great deal of attention to their *profit margin*:

$$\text{Profit margin} = \frac{\text{Net income}}{\text{Revenues}}$$

$$= \frac{\pounds 865}{\pounds 7{,}632} = 11.33\% \tag{3.14}$$

This tells us that Sky, in an accounting sense, generated a little more than 11 pence in profit for every pound in sales during the year ending 2014.

All other things being equal, a relatively high profit margin is obviously desirable. This situation corresponds to low expense ratios relative to sales. However, we hasten to add that other things are often not equal.

For example, lowering our sales price will usually increase unit volume but will normally cause profit margins to shrink. Total profit (or, more importantly, operating cash flow) may go up or down, so the fact that margins are smaller is not necessarily bad.

Profit margins are very different for different industries. Grocery stores have a notoriously low profit margin, generally around 2 per cent. In contrast, the profit margin for the pharmaceutical industry is about 18 per cent.

Return on Assets

Return on assets (ROA) is a measure of profit per asset value. It can be defined several ways, but the most common is:

$$\text{Return on assets} = \frac{\text{Net income}}{\text{Total assets}}$$

$$= \frac{\pounds 865}{\pounds 6{,}449} = 13.41\% \tag{3.15}$$

Return on Equity

Return on equity (ROE) is a measure of how the shareholders fared during the year. Because benefiting shareholders is our goal, ROE is, in an accounting sense, the true bottom-line measure of performance. ROE is usually measured as:

$$\text{Return on equity} = \frac{\text{Net income}}{\text{Total equity}}$$

$$= \frac{\pounds 865}{\pounds 1{,}072} = 80.69\% \tag{3.16}$$

Therefore, for every pound in equity, Sky generated nearly 81 pence in profit during 2014; but, again, this is correct only in accounting terms.

Because ROA and ROE are such commonly cited numbers, we stress that it is important to remember they are accounting rates of return. For this reason, these measures should properly be called *return on book assets* and *return on book equity*. Whatever it is called, it would be inappropriate to compare the result to, for example, an interest rate observed in the financial markets.

The fact that ROE exceeds ROA reflects Sky's use of financial leverage. We will examine the relationship between these two measures in the next section.

Market Value Measures

Our final group of measures is based, in part, on information not necessarily contained in financial statements – the share price. Obviously, these measures can be calculated directly only for publicly traded companies.

At the end of November 2014, Sky had 1,575.59 million shares outstanding and its equity sold on the London Stock Exchange for £9.225. If we recall that Sky's net income was £865 million, then we can calculate that its earnings per share were:

$$\text{EPS} = \frac{\text{Net income}}{\text{Shares outstanding}} = \frac{\pounds 865}{1{,}575.59} = \pounds 0.549 \tag{3.17}$$

Price–Earnings Ratio

The first of our market value measures, the *price–earnings* (or PE) *ratio* (or multiple), is defined as:

$$\text{PE ratio} = \frac{\text{Price per share}}{\text{Earnings per share}}$$

$$= \frac{£9.225}{£0.549} = 16.80 \text{ times} \tag{3.18}$$

In the vernacular, we would say that Sky equity sells for just under 17 times earnings, or we might say that Sky shares have, or 'carry', a PE multiple of 16.80.

Because the PE ratio measures how much investors are willing to pay per unit of current earnings, higher PEs are often taken to mean that the firm has significant prospects for future growth. Of course, if a firm had no or almost no earnings, its PE would probably be quite large; so, as always, care is needed in interpreting this ratio.

Market-to-Book Ratio

A second commonly quoted measure is the *market-to-book ratio*:

$$\text{Market-to-book ratio} = \frac{\text{Market value per share}}{\text{Book value per share}}$$

$$= \frac{£9.225}{£1,072/1,575.69} = 13.56 \text{ times} \tag{3.19}$$

Notice also that book value per share is total equity (not just ordinary shares) divided by the total number of shares outstanding.

Book value per share is an accounting number that reflects historical costs. In a loose sense, the market-to-book ratio therefore compares the market value of the firm's investments to their cost. A value less than 1 could mean that the firm has not been successful overall in creating value for its shareholders. Sky plc's market-to-book ratio is exceptionally high at 13.56 and reflects the value and growth prospects of the firm.

This completes our definition of some common ratios. We could tell you about more of them, but these are enough for now. We will leave it here and go on to discuss some ways of using these ratios instead of just how to calculate them. Table 3.5 summarizes the ratios we have discussed.

Table 3.5 Common Financial Ratios

I. Short-term Solvency, or Liquidity, Ratios

$$\text{Current ratio} = \frac{\text{Current assets}}{\text{Current liabilities}}$$

$$\text{Quick ratio} = \frac{\text{Current assets} - \text{Inventory}}{\text{Current liabilities}}$$

$$\text{Cash ratio} = \frac{\text{Cash}}{\text{Current liabilities}}$$

$$\text{Days' sales in receivables} = \frac{365 \text{ days}}{\text{Receivables turnover}}$$

$$\text{Total asset turnover} = \frac{\text{Sales}}{\text{Total assets}}$$

$$\text{Capital intensity} = \frac{\text{Total assets}}{\text{Sales}}$$

II. Long-term Solvency, or Financial Leverage, Ratios

$$\text{Total debt ratio} = \frac{\text{Total assets} - \text{Total equity}}{\text{Total assets}}$$

Debt–equity ratio = Total debt/Total equity
Equity multiplier = Total assets/Total equity

$$\text{Times interest earned ratio} = \frac{\text{EBIT}}{\text{Interest}}$$

$$\text{Cash coverage ratio} = \frac{\text{EBIT} + \text{Depreciation}}{\text{Interest}}$$

IV. Profitability Ratios

$$\text{Profit margin} = \frac{\text{Net income}}{\text{Sales}}$$

$$\text{Return on assets (ROA)} = \frac{\text{Net income}}{\text{Total assets}}$$

$$\text{Return on equity (ROE)} = \frac{\text{Net income}}{\text{Total equity}}$$

$$\text{ROE} = \frac{\text{Net income}}{\text{Sales}} \times \frac{\text{Sales}}{\text{Assets}} \times \frac{\text{Assets}}{\text{Equity}}$$

III. Asset Utilization, or Turnover, Ratios	V. Market Value Ratios
$\text{Inventory turnover} = \dfrac{\text{Cost of goods sold}}{\text{Inventory}}$	$\text{Price-earnings ratio} = \dfrac{\text{Price per share}}{\text{Earnings per share}}$
$\text{Days' sales in inventory} = \dfrac{365 \text{ days}}{\text{Inventory turnover}}$	$\text{Market-to-book ratio} = \dfrac{\text{Market value per share}}{\text{Book value per share}}$
$\text{Receivables turnover} = \dfrac{\text{Sales}}{\text{Accounts receivable}}$	

3.8   The Du Pont Identity

As we mentioned in discussing ROA and ROE, the difference between these two profitability measures reflects the use of debt financing or financial leverage. We illustrate the relationship between these measures in this section by investigating a famous way of decomposing ROE into its component parts.

A Closer Look at ROE

To begin, let us recall the definition of ROE:

$$\text{Return on equity} = \frac{\text{Net income}}{\text{Total equity}}$$

If we were so inclined, we could multiply this ratio by Assets/Assets without changing anything:

$$\text{Return on equity} = \frac{\text{Net income}}{\text{Total equity}} = \frac{\text{Net income}}{\text{Total equity}} \times \frac{\text{Assets}}{\text{Assets}}$$

$$= \frac{\text{Net income}}{\text{Assets}} \times \frac{\text{Assets}}{\text{Total equity}}$$

Notice that we have expressed the ROE as the product of two other ratios – ROA and the equity multiplier:

$$\text{ROE} = \text{ROA} \times \text{Equity multiplier} = \text{ROA} \times (1 + \text{Debt–equity ratio})$$

Looking back at Sky, for example, we see that the debt–equity ratio was 5.016 and ROA was 13.41 per cent. Our work here implies that Sky's ROE, as we previously calculated, is:

$$\text{ROE} = 13.41\% \times (1 + 5.016) = 80.69\%$$

The difference between ROE and ROA can be substantial, as you can see for Sky plc. This is because of the amount of debt that the company has taken on.

We can further decompose ROE by multiplying the top and bottom by total sales:

$$\text{ROE} = \frac{\text{Sales}}{\text{Sales}} \times \frac{\text{Net income}}{\text{Assets}} \times \frac{\text{Assets}}{\text{Total equity}}$$

If we rearrange things a bit, ROE is:

$$\text{ROE} = \underbrace{\frac{\text{Net income}}{\text{Sales}} \times \frac{\text{Sales}}{\text{Assets}}}_{\text{Return on assets}} \times \frac{\text{Assets}}{\text{Total equity}}$$

$$= \text{Profit margin} \times \text{Total asset turnover} \times \text{Equity multiplier} \qquad (3.20)$$

What we have now done is to partition ROA into its two component parts, profit margin and total asset turnover. The last expression of the preceding equation is called the **Du Pont identity** after the Du Pont Corporation, which popularized its use.

We can check this relationship for Sky by noting that the profit margin was 11.33 per cent and the total asset turnover was 1.18. ROE should thus be:

$$ROE = \text{Profit margin} \times \text{Total asset turnover} \times \text{Equity multiplier}$$
$$= 11.33\% \quad \times \quad 1.18 \quad \times \quad 6.0159$$
$$= 80.69\%$$

This 80.69 per cent ROE is exactly what we had before.

The Du Pont identity tells us that ROE is affected by three things:

1 Operating efficiency (as measured by profit margin)

2 Asset use efficiency (as measured by total asset turnover)

3 Financial leverage (as measured by the equity multiplier).

Weakness in either operating or asset use efficiency (or both) will show up in a diminished return on assets, which will translate into a lower ROE.

Considering the Du Pont identity, it appears that the ROE could be leveraged up by increasing the amount of debt in the firm. However, notice that increasing debt also increases interest expense, which reduces profit margins, and this acts to reduce ROE. More important, the use of debt financing has a number of other effects, and, as we discuss at some length in later chapters, the amount of leverage a firm uses is governed by its capital structure policy.

The decomposition of ROE we have discussed in this section is a convenient way of systematically approaching financial statement analysis. If ROE is unsatisfactory by some measure, then the Du Pont identity tells you where to start looking for the reasons.

3.9   Using Financial Statement Information

Our next task is to discuss in more detail some practical aspects of financial statement analysis. In particular, we will look at reasons for doing financial statement analysis, how to go about getting benchmark information, and some of the problems that come up in the process.

Choosing a Benchmark

Given that we want to evaluate a division or a firm based on its financial statements, a basic problem immediately comes up. How do we choose a benchmark, or a standard of comparison? We describe some ways of getting started in this section.

Time Trend Analysis

One standard we could use is history. Suppose we found that the current ratio for a particular firm is 2.4 based on the most recent financial statement information. Looking back over the last 10 years, we might find that this ratio had declined fairly steadily over that period.

Based on this, we might wonder if the liquidity position of the firm has deteriorated. It could be, of course, that the firm has made changes that allow it to use its current assets more efficiently, that the nature of the firm's business has changed, or that business practices have changed. If we investigate, we might find any of these possible explanations behind the decline. This is an example of what we mean by management by exception – a deteriorating time trend may not be bad, but it does merit investigation.

Peer Group Analysis

The second means of establishing a benchmark is to identify firms similar in the sense that they compete in the same markets, have similar assets, and operate in similar ways. In other words, we need to identify a *peer group*. There are obvious problems with doing this: no two companies are identical. Ultimately, the choice of which companies to use as a basis for comparison is subjective.

One common way of identifying potential peers is based on Standard Industrial Classification (SIC) codes. In the UK, these are called UK Standard Industrial Classification (SIC) Codes and in the European Union, they are called the Industrial Classification System or 'Nomenclature des Activités Économiques dans la Communauté Européenne' (NACE). These are alphabetical categories subdivided by four-digit codes that are used for statistical reporting purposes. Both SIC and NACE codes are virtually identical and firms with the same SIC or NACE code are frequently assumed to be similar.

In total, there are 21 industry groups, categorized by alphabetical letter. The first SIC code digit establishes the general type of business. For example, firms engaged in finance, insurance and real estate have SIC codes beginning with 6. Each additional digit narrows the industry. Companies with SIC codes beginning with 64 are mostly banks and banklike businesses, those with codes beginning with 64.19 are mostly commercial banks, and SIC code 64.11 is assigned to central banks. Table 3.6 lists selected two-digit codes (the first two digits of the four-digit SIC codes) and the industries they represent.

Table 3.6 Selected Two-Digit SIC Codes

Code	Industry	Code	Industry
01–09	Agriculture, Forestry, Fishing	50–51	Wholesale Trade
10–14	Mining	52–59	Retail Trade
15–17	Construction	60–67	Finance, Insurance, Real Estate
20–39	Manufacturing	70–89	Services
40–49	Transportation & Public Utilities	91–99	Public Administration

Industry classification codes are far from perfect. For example, suppose you were examining financial statements for Tesco plc, one of the largest retailers in the world. However, Tesco are not just involved in supermarket retailing. They also have Tesco Telecom Services and Tesco Personal Finance, which includes credit cards and personal mortgages. Which industry code would Tesco plc have?

As this example illustrates, it is probably not appropriate to blindly use SIC code as the basis for carrying out a peer analysis. Instead, analysts often identify a set of primary competitors with similar activities and then compute a set of averages based on just this group. Also, we may be more concerned with a group of the top firms in an industry, not similar firms. Such a group is called an *aspirant group* because we aspire to be like its members. In this case, a financial statement analysis reveals how far we have to go.

There are many sources of financial information on the Internet that an analyst can access. For example, www.ft.com, Reuters and Yahoo! Finance show a variety of ratios for publicly traded companies. Table 3.7 shows a screenshot of some profitability ratios (called 'Management Effectiveness' on Reuters) for the German automobile firm, BMW, together with peer statistics ('TTM' stands for 'trailing twelve months').

Table 3.7 Management Effectiveness

	Industry	Sector	Company
Return on assets (TTM)	9.62	9.37	4.08
Return on assets – 5-year average	11.75	11.14	3.20
Return on investment (TTM)	17.19	16.12	6.38
Return on investment – 5-year average	19.93	18.56	5.07
Return on equity (TTM)	21.67	20.24	16.55
Return on equity – 5-year average	25.03	23.19	14.36

Source: Data from Reuters.

In looking at numbers such as these, recall our caution about analysing ratios that you do not calculate yourself: different sources frequently do their calculations somewhat differently, even if the ratio names are the same.

Problems with Financial Statement Analysis

We continue our chapter on financial statements by discussing some additional problems that can arise when using them. In one way or another, the basic problem with financial statement analysis is that there is no underlying theory to help us identify which quantities to look at and to guide us in establishing benchmarks.

As we discuss in other chapters, there are many cases in which financial theory and economic logic provide guidance in making judgements about value and risk. Little such help exists with financial statements. This is why we cannot say which ratios matter the most or what a high or low value might be.

One particularly severe problem is that many firms are conglomerates, owning more or less unrelated lines of business. Anglo American plc is a well-known example. Anglo American was originally founded in South Africa as a mining firm but is now involved in packaging, paper, coal and a variety of metal extraction activities. It is now listed on the London Stock Exchange and is commonly regarded as a metals conglomerate. Similar to Tesco plc, the consolidated financial statements of Anglo American do not really fit any neat industry category. More generally, the kind of peer group analysis we have been describing is going to work best when the firms are strictly in the same line of business, the industry is competitive, and there is only one way of operating.

Another problem that is becoming increasingly common is that major competitors and natural peer group members in an industry may be scattered around the globe. The automobile industry is an obvious example. The problem here is that financial statements in many countries do not necessarily conform to IFRS (i.e. the accounting standards used in most countries). For example, US firms follow US GAAP whereas European firms follow IFRS. The existence of different standards and procedures makes it difficult to compare financial statements across national borders.

Even companies that are clearly in the same line of business may not be comparable. For example, electric utilities engaged primarily in power generation are all classified in the same group. This group is often thought to be relatively homogeneous. However, most utilities operate as regulated monopolies, so they do not compete much with each other, at least not historically. Many have shareholders, and many are organized as cooperatives with no shareholders. There are several different ways of generating power, ranging from hydroelectric to nuclear, so the operating activities of these utilities can differ quite a bit. Finally, profitability is strongly affected by the regulatory environment, so utilities in different countries can be similar but show different profits.

Several other general problems frequently crop up. First, different firms use different accounting procedures, such as for inventories. This makes it difficult to compare statements. Second, different firms end their fiscal years at different times. For firms in seasonal businesses (such as a retailer with a large Christmas season), this can lead to difficulties in comparing statements of financial position because of fluctuations in accounts during the year. Finally, for any particular firm, unusual or transient events, such as a one-time profit from an asset sale, may affect financial performance. Such events can give misleading signals as we compare firms.

Real World Insight 3.2

BAE Systems Comparative Financial Ratio Analysis

As stated above, one can look at the financial ratios of a firm over time or compare them to other companies in the same industry. The table below shows a comparative analysis from Google Finance of key financial ratios for BAE Systems and its peers.

There is a lot of information to take in. The closest firm in size to BAE Systems is Rolls-Royce Holdings. A simple comparison shows that BAE Systems has less liquidity (current ratio) and more leverage (Long-Term Debt to Assets), but is performing better (Return on Assets, Return on Equity). Profitability (Margins) is roughly similar across both companies, with Rolls-Royce performing slightly better.

| | | Valuation | | Financial ratios | | | Operating metrics | | Margins | | |
	Company name	P/E ratio	Mkt Cap	Current ratio	Lt debt to assets	Lt debt to equity	Return on avg assets	Return on avg equity	Net profit margin	EBITD margin	Operating margin
BA	BAE Systems plc	22.99	16,934.67M	0.74	14.49	155.70	3.81	28.34	4.87	11.63	8.43
COB	Cobham plc	114.62	3,526.17M	1.58	40.38	130.18	0.97	2.67	1.57	18.46	3.11
MGGT	Meggitt plc	26.16	4,507.47M	1.51	15.77	29.05	4.58	8.39	11.39	25.80	15.20
BAB	Babcock Intl. Gro...	22.13	5,001.88M	0.77	21.13	65.88	6.13	18.50	5.66	10.99	7.02
CHG	Chemring Group plc		420.90M	1.94	24.41	51.95	−0.18	−0.41	−0.35	16.87	3.32
RR	Rolls-Royce Holdi...		17,422.09M	1.46	9.87	34.36	−0.37	−1.22	−0.61	15.58	10.07
QQ	QinetiQ Group plc		1,196.07M	1.37	14.85	40.74	−1.15	−3.11	−1.37	14.04	1.87
SPX	Spirax-Sarco Engi...	26.37	2,638.45M	2.80	6.64	11.13	14.01	23.78	14.83	25.94	21.83
ULE	Ultra Electronics...	56.84	1,189.09M	1.15	20.06	53.85	0.79	6.52	0.91	18.28	5.54
GKN	GKN plc	35.06	5,861.73M	1.33	13.13	59.30	2.69	10.39	2.49	12.30	4.14
WSG	Westminster Group...		14.75M	1.52	15.06	30.15	−40.11	−264.18	−21.95	−30.52	−20.64

Source: Google Finance. Google and the Google logo are registered trademarks of Google Inc., used with permission.

Summary and Conclusions

This chapter focuses on working with information contained in financial statements. Specifically, we studied standardized financial statements and ratio analysis.

1   We explained that differences in firm size make it difficult to compare financial statements.

2   Evaluating ratios of accounting numbers is another way of comparing financial statement information. We defined a number of the most commonly used ratios, and we discussed the famous Du Pont identity.

After you have studied this chapter, we hope that you have some perspective on the uses and abuses of financial statement information. You should also find that your vocabulary of business and financial terms has grown substantially.

In the online supplement to this chapter, we extend the discussion to include long-term financial planning and sustainable growth rates.

Questions and Problems

CONCEPT

1 **Accounting and Cash Flows** What does the term 'window dressing' mean in the context of financial statements? Identify three window-dressing techniques that companies use. What implications does this have for cash flows in terms of its relationship with reported revenue and cost figures?

2 **Book Values versus Market Values** Explain the difference between book value and market value. Under standard accounting rules, it is possible for a company's liabilities to exceed its assets. When this occurs, the owners' equity is negative. Can this happen with market values? Why or why not?

3 **Operating Cash Flow** Identify two circumstances where negative operating cash flow might not necessarily be a sign of deteriorating financial health. When can negative operating cash flow become problematic for a company?

4 **Financial Ratio Analysis** A financial ratio by itself tells us little about a company because financial ratios vary a great deal across industries. There are two basic methods for analysing financial ratios for a company: time trend analysis and peer group analysis. Why might each of these analysis methods be useful? What does each tell you about the company's financial health?

5 **Sales Forecast** Why do you think most long-term financial planning begins with sales forecasts? Put differently, why are future sales the key input?

6 **The DuPont Identity** Both ROA and ROE measure profitability. What does each of them measure, and which one is more useful for comparing two companies? Why?

7 **Building a Statement of Financial Position** According to AEB Systems plc financial statements as of June 2015, the firm had current assets of £6.642 billion, non-current assets of £16.521 billion, current liabilities of £11.283 billion, and non-current liabilities of £6.589 billion. What is the value of the shareholders' equity for AEB Systems? How much is net working capital?

8 **Building an Income Statement** In 2015, the UK insurance firm, Wheeler & Fox, had revenue of £38,440 million, total expenses of £37,133 million, tax of £487 million and zero depreciation. What is the net income for the firm? Wheeler & Fox paid out £238 million in cash dividends. What is the addition to retained earnings?

9 **Earnings per Share** In 2015, the Swedish bank, Nordicbank, had a price–earnings ratio of 6.35. If the firm's share price was SKr71.70, what was its earnings per share?

10 **Market Values and Book Values** Your company has just sealed a deal to sell a tract of land with accompanying warehouse for €3.2 million. This is significantly lower than the €7 million your firm paid when the plot was purchased at the height of the property boom. International Accounting Standards have been followed by your firm and so you will not make an accounting loss on the sale (why?). The company

has non-current assets of €4 million, non-current liabilities of €2.2 million and net working capital (current assets less current liabilities) of €0.9 million. What impact does the sale have on your firm's statement of financial position?

11 Calculating Taxes   The Dutch firm, Herrera NV, had €273,000 in taxable income. Using Table 3.3, what is the company's average tax rate? What is its marginal tax rate?

12 Calculating NCF   A firm has net revenues of £6,065 million (including net non-cash expenses). Net non-cash expenses (including depreciation) were £2,380 million. Cash outflows from investing activities (including capital expenditures) were £3,270 million. The firm paid a total cash dividend of £1,380 million and net interest expense was £3,410 million. What was the firm's net cash flow?

13 Calculating Net Capital Spending   Morena's Driving School's 2015 statement of financial position showed non-current assets of £4.2 million. One year later, the 2016 statement of financial position showed non-current assets of £4.7 million. The company's 2016 income statement showed a depreciation expense of £925,000. What was Morena's net capital spending for 2016?

14 Building a Statement of Financial Position   The following table presents the long-term debt and shareholders' equity of Tumbler SA one year ago:

	(€)
Long-term debt	60,000,000
Preference shares	18,000,000
Ordinary shares (€1 par value)	25,000,000
Capital surplus	49,000,000
Accumulated retained earnings	89,000,000

During the past year, Tumbler issued 20 million shares at a total price of €52 million, and issued €16 million in new long-term debt. The company generated €14 million in net income and paid €8 million in dividends. Construct the current statement of financial position reflecting the changes that occurred at Tumbler during the year.

REGULAR

15 Calculating the Du Pont Identity   Find the annual income statements and statement of financial positions for two firms in the same industry from your own country. Calculate the Du Pont identity for each company for the most recent 3 years. Comment on the changes in each component of the Du Pont identity for each company over this period and compare the components between the two companies. Are the results what you expected? Why or why not?

16 Return on Equity   Firm A and Firm B have debt–total asset ratios of 70 per cent and 30 per cent, and returns on total assets of 20 per cent and 30 per cent, respectively. Which firm has a greater return on equity?

17 Ratios and Foreign Companies   As of December 2014, the Royal Bank of Scotland plc made a net loss of £3.47 billion on revenues of £18.197 billion. What was the company's profit margin? Does the fact that these figures are quoted in pounds sterling make any difference to a Spanish investor. Why? In euros, revenues were €24.73 billion. What was the net loss in euros?

18 Cash Coverage Ratio   For the year ending 2015, TJC plc has revenues of £1,027 million and total costs (excluding interest) of £817 million. Net interest expense was £29 million and depreciation was £12 million. What is the firm's cash coverage ratio?

19 Days' Sales in Receivables   A company has net income of €173,000, a profit margin of 8.6 per cent, and a trade receivables balance of €143,200. Assuming 75 per cent of sales are on credit, what is the company's days' sales in receivables?

20 Ratios and Fixed Assets   Le Verd SA has a ratio of long-term debt to total assets of 0.70 and a current ratio of 1.20. Current liabilities are £850, revenues are £4,310, profit margin is 9.5 per cent, and ROE is 21.5 per cent. What is the amount of the firm's non-current assets?

21 Calculating the Cash Coverage Ratio   Titan SpA's net income for the most recent year was €4,850. The tax rate was 33 per cent. The firm paid €2,108 in total interest expense and deducted €1,687 in depreciation expense. What was Titan's cash coverage ratio for the year?

22 Cost of Goods Sold   Guthrie plc has current liabilities of £340,000, a quick ratio of 1.8, inventory turnover of 4.2 and a current ratio of 3.3. What is the cost of goods sold for the company?

CHALLENGE

For questions 23 and 24, consider the summarized financial statements for Sement AG (in € millions):

Summarized Statement of Income	
Revenue	77,327
Cost of goods sold	56,284
Operating income	21,043
Less:	
Depreciation	2,130
Other expenses	16,039
Income from continuing operations before income taxes	2,874

Summarized Statement of Income	
Income taxes	1,015
Income from continuing operations	**1,859**
Income from discontinued operations, net of taxes	4,027
Net income	**5,886**

Summarized Statement of Financial Position			
Assets		Liabilities	
Current assets		Current liabilities	
Cash and cash equivalents	6,893	Trade payables	8,860
Trade and other receivables	15,785	Other current liabilities	33,591
Inventories	14,509	Total current liabilities	42,451
Other current assets	6,055	Long-term debt	14,260
Total current assets	43,242	Other non-current liabilities	10,372
Non-current assets	51,221	Total liabilities	67,083
		Equity	4,391
		Retained earnings	22,989
Total assets	94,463	Total liabilities and equity	94,463

23 Financial Ratios   Calculate all relevant financial ratios for Sement AG.

24 Financial Statement Analysis   What are the weaknesses in the Sement examples for interpreting its financial well-being? Explain.

25 Financial Ratios   Lewellen (2004) makes a strong case for why financial ratios, such as dividend yield, book-to-market ratio and earnings per share, will predict prices. Discuss this argument and his main findings to support his view.

26 Cash Flow Volatility   Rountree et al. (2008) show that investors do not like cash flow volatility. Consider the financial ratios presented in this chapter. Can you adapt an existing financial ratio or construct a new one that may reflect the findings in Rountree et al. (2008)? Use your ratio to compare some firms in the same industry in your country. What are the strengths and weaknesses of your ratio?

Questions 27–37 relate to Montgomery Organizations plc, whose annual accounts are given below. The firm has 14,685,856 shares and the share price is £2.78.

Fixed Assets (£ millions)	2015	2014	2013	2012
Tangible assets	164	167	180	188
Land and buildings	71	70	68	66
Freehold land	71	70		
Fixtures and fittings	78	81	93	103
Plant and vehicles	15	15	19	19

Fixed Assets (£ millions)	2015	2014	2013	2012
Plant	15	15		
Intangible assets	832	832	832	832
Investments	520	521	509	518
Fixed assets	1,517	1,520	1,521	1,538

Current Assets				
Stock and WIP				1
Stock				1
WIP				0
Finished goods				
Trade debtors	2	4		1
Bank and deposits	47	58	43	34
Other current assets	662	35	28	26
Group loans (asset)	618	0	0	0
Directors loans (asset)	0	0	0	0
Other debtors	12	5	28	26
Prepayments	32	30		
Current assets	711	97	72	61

Current Liabilities				
Trade creditors	−7	−10	−14	−18
Short-term loans and overdrafts	−1,924	−1,325	−1,260	−1,255
Bank overdrafts	0	0	0	0
Group loans (short t.)	−1,923	−1,324	−1,259	−1,255
Director loans (short t.)	0	0	0	0
Hire purch. and leas. (short t.)	0	−1	−1	0
Hire purchase (short t.)				
Leasing (short t.)			−1	
Other short-term loans	0	0	0	0
Total other current liabilities	−105	−78	−102	−102
Corporation tax	−29	−28	−36	−29
Dividends	0	0	0	0
Accruals and def. inc. (sh. t.)	−33	−21	−41	−37
Social securities and VAT	−19	−18	−20	−21
Other current liabilities	−25	−11	−5	−15
Current liabilities	−2,035	−1,413	−1,376	−1,374
Net current assets (liab.)	−1,324	−1,316	−1,304	−1,313
Net tangible assets (liab.)	−639	−628	−615	−607
Working capital	−1,324	−1,316	−1,304	−1,313
Total assets	2,228	1,617	1,593	1,599
Total assets less cur. liab.	193	204	217	225

Long-Term Liabilities				
Provisions for other liab.	−12	−13	−31	−14
Deferred tax	−12	−13	−13	−12
Other provisions			−19	−2
Pension liabilities	−23	−31		
Long-term liabilities	−35	−44	−31	−14
Total assets less liabilities	158	160	186	210

▶

Shareholders' Funds				
Issued capital	1	1	1	1
Ordinary shares	1	1		
Preference shares				
Other shares				
Total reserves	157	158	184	209
Share premium account	3	3	3	3
Profit (loss) account	159	162	180	205
Other reserves	−5	−6	1	1
Shareholders' funds	158	160	186	210
Turnover	14,569	13,480	13,337	7,127
Cost of sales	−13,932	−12,870	−12,708	−6,800
Gross profit	637	610	629	327
Administration expenses		−388	−369	−502
Other operating income pre OP	−377			
Exceptional items pre OP		−13		
Operating profit	260	210	260	−175
Other income	10	33	30	486
Total other income and int. received	22	43	30	486
Exceptional items			−16	−18
Profit (loss) before interest paid	282	253	274	293
Interest received	12	10		
Interest paid	−28	−37	−84	−92
Other interest paid	−28	−37		
Net interest	−16	−27	−84	−92
Profit (loss) before tax	254	216	190	201
Taxation	−53	−46	−49	−18
Profit (loss) after tax	201	170	141	183
Dividends	−210	−175	−150	−20
Retained profit (loss)	−9	−6	−9	163
Depreciation	26	27	30	26

27 **Earnings per share**   What is the earnings per share for each year between 2012 and 2015 for Montgomery Organizations plc? What is your interpretation of these figures? Is EPS a reliable measure of performance?

28 **Tax Rate**   What is the effective tax rate for Montgomery Organizations plc for each year?

29 **Net Working Capital**   What is the net working capital of Montgomery Organizations plc in each year? What is the cause of the figures? Is this a healthy situation for the firm? Explain.

30 **Common-size Statements**   Construct common-size statements for Montgomery Organizations plc.

31 **Liquidity**   How would you rate the liquidity position of Montgomery Organizations plc between 2012 and 2015? Provide a brief report of the company's liquidity over time.

32 **Long-term solvency**   How would you rate the long-term solvency position of Montgomery Organizations plc between 2012 and 2015? Provide a brief report of the company's long-term solvency over time.

33 **Operations**   How efficient have Montgomery Organizations plc's operations been during 2015? Provide a brief report of the company's asset efficiency over time.

34 **Profitability**   What is the profitability of Montgomery Organizations plc like over the period 2012 and 2015? Provide a brief report of the company's profitability over time. Do profitability ratios give a good insight into company performance?

35 **Market Valuation**   Provide an overview on the company's relative market valuation over the period 2012–2015. What can be inferred from the company's relative market valuation?

36 **Du Point Identity**   Undertake a full Du Pont Identity analysis for the year 2015 to provide insights into the drivers of its return on equity.

37 **Du Point Identity**   Discuss the advantages and disadvantages of ratio analysis.

Exam Question (45 minutes)

You are tasked with analysing the last 2 years of accounts of a global mining firm. A simplified statement of financial position and income statement are provided below.

Period Ending	Yr-0	Yr-1	Yr-2	Yr-3
Total revenue	7,931	6,579	8,204	6,502
Cost of revenue	5,787	5,136	5,318	3,840
Gross profit	2,144	1,443	2,886	2,662
Depreciation	321	182	201	412
Other expenses	100	134	115	247
EBIT	1,723	1,127	2,570	2,003
Interest	1,135	957	1,272	1,009
EBT	588	170	1,298	994
Tax	153	44	337	258
Net income	435	126	961	736

Statement of Financial Position (£ millions)

Period Ending	Yr-0	Yr-1	Yr-2	Yr-3
Assets				
Current assets				
Cash and cash equivalents	390	381	458	1,585
Short-term investments	6,849	4,547	4,608	578
Net receivables	693	533	1,025	932
Inventory	1,261	909	1,299	880
Other current assets	200	250	86	74
Total current assets	9,393	6,620	7,476	4,049
Property, plant and equipment	10,201	10,920	10,300	10,350
Goodwill	21	23	28	40
Total non-current assets	10,222	10,943	10,328	10,390
Total assets	19,615	17,563	17,804	14,439
Liabilities				
Current liabilities				
Accounts payable	1,715	1,190	975	620
Short/current long-term debt	8,945	5,836	3,656	1,727
Other current liabilities	111	169	303	655
Total current liabilities	10,771	7,195	4,934	3,002
Long-term debt	7,161	3,816	1,557	1,478
Total liabilities	17,932	11,011	6,491	4,480
Shareholders' equity				
Total shareholders' equity	1,683	6,552	11,313	9,959
Equity plus liabilities	19,615	17,563	17,804	14,439

1 Using the information above, carry out a full financial statement analysis using a variety of financial ratios. (60 marks)

2 How do you think the company has been performing over the past 5 years? Has there been an improvement or deterioration in the firm's fortunes? What is driving the changing performance? Write a report, outlining your analysis and findings. (40 marks)

Mini Case

Ratios and Financial Planning at West Coast Yachts

Dan Ervin was recently hired by West Coast Yachts Ltd to assist the company with its short-term financial planning and also to evaluate the company's financial performance. Dan graduated from university 5 years ago with a finance degree, and he has been employed in the treasury department of a FTSE 100 company since then.

West Coast Yachts was founded 10 years ago by Larissa Warren. The company's operations are located in a well-known marina, Inverkip, on the west coast of Scotland. The firm is structured as a private limited company. The company has manufactured custom midsize, high-performance yachts for clients over this period, and its products have received high reviews for safety and reliability. The company's yachts have also recently received the highest award for customer satisfaction. The yachts are purchased primarily by wealthy individuals for pleasure use. Occasionally, a yacht is manufactured for purchase by a company for business purposes.

The custom yacht industry is fragmented, with a number of manufacturers. As with any industry, there are market leaders, but the diverse nature of the industry ensures that no manufacturer dominates the market. The competition in the market, as well as the product cost, ensures that attention to detail is a necessity. For instance, West Coast Yachts will spend 80 to 100 hours on hand-buffing the stainless steel stem-iron, which is the metal cap on the yacht's bow that conceivably could collide with a dock or another boat.

To get Dan started with his analyses, Larissa has provided the following financial statements. Larissa has gathered the industry ratios for the yacht manufacturing industry.

WEST COAST YACHTS Income Statement 2015		
	£	£
Operating revenues		128,700,000
Operating expenses		90,700,000
Operating profit		38,000,000
Depreciation		4,200,000
Other non-operating expenses		15,380,000
Interest		2,315,000
Profit before taxes		16,105,000
Taxes (28%)		4,509,400
Profit for period attributable to equity holders		11,595,600
Dividends	6,957,360	
Addition to retained earnings	4,638,240	

WEST COAST YACHTS Statement of Financial Position as of 31 December 2015			
Assets		**Liabilities and Equity**	
Current assets		**Current liabilities**	
	£		£
Cash	2,340,000	Trade payables	4,970,000

WEST COAST YACHTS			
Statement of Financial Position as of 31 December 2015			
Assets		**Liabilities and Equity**	
Trade receivables	4,210,000	Notes payable	10,060,000
Inventory	4,720,000		
Total	11,270,000	Total	15,030,000
Non-current assets		Non-current liabilities	25,950,000
Net plant and equipment	72,280,000		
		Shareholders' equity	
		Ordinary shares	4,000,000
		Retained earnings	38,570,000
		Total equity	42,570,000
Total assets	83,550,000	Total liabilities and equity	83,550,000

Yacht Industry Ratios			
	Lower Quartile	**Median**	**Upper Quartile**
Current ratio	0.50	1.43	1.89
Quick ratio	0.21	0.38	0.62
Total asset turnover	0.68	0.85	1.38
Inventory turnover	4.89	6.15	10.89
Receivables turnover	6.27	9.82	14.11
Debt ratio	0.44	0.52	0.61
Debt–equity ratio	0.79	1.08	1.56
Equity multiplier	1.79	2.08	2.56
Interest coverage	5.18	8.06	9.83
Profit margin (%)	4.05	6.98	9.87
Return on assets (%)	6.05	10.53	13.21
Return on equity (%)	9.93	16.54	26.15

1   Calculate all of the ratios listed in the industry table for West Coast Yachts.

2   Compare the performance of West Coast Yachts to the industry as a whole. For each ratio, comment on why it might be viewed as positive or negative relative to the industry. Suppose you create an inventory ratio calculated as inventory divided by current liabilities. How do you interpret this ratio? How does West Coast Yachts compare to the industry average?

3   Calculate the sustainable growth rate of West Coast Yachts. Calculate external funds needed (EFN) and prepare pro forma income statements and statements of financial position assuming growth at precisely this rate. Recalculate the ratios in the previous question. What do you observe?

4   As a practical matter, West Coast Yachts is unlikely to be willing to raise external equity capital, in part because the owners do not want to dilute their existing ownership and control positions. However, West Coast Yachts is planning for a growth rate of 20 per cent next year. What are your conclusions and recommendations about the feasibility of West Coast's expansion plans?

5   Most assets can be increased as a percentage of sales. For instance, cash can be increased by any amount. However, non-current assets often must be increased in specific amounts because it is impossible, as a practical matter, to buy part of a new plant or machine. In this case a company has a 'staircase' or 'lumpy' fixed cost structure. Assume that West Coast Yachts is currently producing at 100 per cent of capacity. As a result, to expand production, the company must set up an entirely new line at a cost of £25,000,000. Calculate the new EFN with this assumption. What does this imply about capacity utilization for West Coast Yachts next year?

Practical Case Study

Choose a listed company from your own country. Download the financial accounts from its website and carry out a full financial statement analysis. You should calculate financial ratios for not only the most recent year but past years as well. Write a brief report on your interpretation and the company's future well-being.

Relevant Accounting Standards

Given that this chapter is concerned with interpreting financial statements, all international accounting standards are relevant. However, the most important ones are IAS 1 *Presentation of Financial Statements*, IAS 7 *Statement of Cash Flows*, IAS 27 *Consolidated and Separate Financial Statements*, and IAS 33 *Earnings per Share*. For an excellent summary of these and other international accounting standards, visit the IASPlus website (www.iasplus.com).

Reference

Lewellen, J. (2004) 'Predicting Returns with Financial Ratios', *Journal of Financial Economics*, Vol. 74, No. 2, 209–235.

Rountree, B., J.P. Weston and G. Allayannis (2008) 'Do Investors Value Smooth Performance?' *Journal of Financial Economics*, Vol. 90, No. 3, 237–251.

Additional Reading

The interested reader can find a whole range of readings to peruse in accounting journals such as *Journal of Accounting Research*, *The Accounting Review*, *Journal of Accounting and Economics*, *Journal of Business Finance and Accounting* and *Accounting and Business Research*. Important recent papers that relate to corporate finance are:

1   Faulkender, M., M.J. Flannery, K. Watson Hankins and J.M. Smith (2012) 'Cash Flows and Leverage Adjustments', *Journal of Financial Economics*, Vol. 103, No. 3, 632–646. **US**.

2   Hutton, A.P., A.J. Marcus and H. Tehranian (2009) 'Opaque Financial Reports, R^2, and Crash Risk', *Journal of Financial Economics*, Vol. 94, No. 1, 67–86. **US**.

3   Lewellen, J. (2004) 'Predicting Returns with Financial Ratios', *Journal of Financial Economics*, Vol. 74, No. 2, 209–235.

4   Rountree, B., J.P. Weston and G. Allayannis (2008) 'Do Investors Value Smooth Performance?' *Journal of Financial Economics*, Vol. 90, No. 3, 237–251.

Endnote

1   Accounting conventions can be confusing and each country follows its own accounting standards. The most common one is published by the International Accounting Standards Board and is called International Financial Reporting Standards (IFRS). This is used by over 100 countries, including countries in the European Union, who made the standards mandatory for all listed companies from 2005. Unlisted and private companies have more flexibility in their approach to presenting financial statements. A major change in financial statement presentation took place in January 2009, when IFRS dropped the term 'balance sheet' and replaced it with 'statement of financial position'. Given that the focus of this textbook is on listed companies, we will adopt the conventions as laid out by the IASB.

CHAPTER 4

Discounted Cash Flow Valuation

Alibaba is the world's largest e-commerce firm with transactions in over 190 countries. In 2014, it also had the largest initial public offering in history with 368 million shares (14.9 per cent of the company) sold to investors amounting to $25 billion. Alibaba set the sale price to be $68 per share, but on the issue date it jumped by 35 per cent to over $90 per share. How did Alibaba value its shares? What was the correct price, $68 or $90? Was $68 too low or was $90 too high? What types of information should you use to value an investment? At the very minimum, Alibaba would have considered the risk of its operations and future potential cash flows before arriving at a decision.

This chapter gives you the 'basic tools of knowledge' to value companies such as Alibaba and assess whether market prices are sensible. You will also be able to value real investment projects using the same tools. Finally, the material in this chapter will form the foundation of the majority of techniques developed in the rest of the book, so make sure you fully understand the chapter before progressing.

The theoretical foundation of discounted cash flow valuation is very rich and can enhance understanding but some readers may feel that it is an unnecessary technical diversion at this stage. If you do wish to explore the theory underpinning this chapter, please refer to the online appendix. Although an appreciation of the theory is useful, it is not necessary to understand the intuition or practical application of the material in this chapter.

KEY NOTATIONS

PV	Present value
C_i	Cash flow at time i
r	Discount rate
NPV	Net present value
FV	Future value
m	Number of times that interest, r, is compounded in a year
APR	Annual Percentage Rate
g	Growth rate

ExxonMobile

As one of the world's largest energy firms, ExxonMobile is continually seeking out new opportunities and potential investments. Examples of ExxonMobile's major investment decisions include a $41 billion purchase of US gas explorer, XTO; major new exploration investments in Iraq and Kurdistan; and a strategic exploration partnership in the Russian Arctic with Rosneft, the Russian state oil company. All the decisions made by ExxonMobile senior management would have been based upon detailed Time Value of Money calculations using the concepts covered in this chapter.

4.1 Valuation: The One-period Case

Chapter 3
Page 64

Keith Vaughan is trying to sell a piece of undeveloped land in Wales. Yesterday he was offered £10,000 for the property. He was about ready to accept the offer when another individual offered him £11,424 to be paid a year from now. Keith has satisfied himself that both buyers are honest and financially solvent, so he has no fear that the offer he selects will fall through. These two offers are pictured as cash flows in Figure 4.1. Which offer should Keith choose? (See **Chapter 3**, Section 3.5 for more information on cash flows).

Figure 4.1 Cash Flow for Keith Vaughan's Sale

Alternative sale prices	£10,000	£11,424
Year	0	1

Mike Tuttle, Keith's financial adviser, points out that if Keith takes the first offer, he could invest the £10,000 in the bank at an insured rate of 12 per cent. At the end of one year, he would have:

$$£10,000 + (0.12 \times £10,000) = £10,000 \times 1.12 = £11,200$$

Return of   Interest
principal

Because this is less than the £11,424 Keith could receive from the second offer, Mike recommends that he take the latter. This analysis uses the concept of *future value (FV)* or *compound value*, which is the value of a sum after investing over one or more periods. The compound or future value of £10,000 at 12 per cent is £11,200.

An alternative method employs the concept of *present value (PV)*. One can determine present value by asking the following question: how much money must Keith put in the bank today so that he will have £11,424 next year? We can write this algebraically as:

$$PV \times 1.12 = £11,424$$

We want to solve for *PV*, the amount of money that yields £11,424 if invested at 12 per cent today. Solving for *PV*, we have:

$$PV = \frac{£11,424}{1.12} = £10,200$$

The formula for PV can be written as follows:

Present value of investment:

$$PV = \frac{C_1}{1 + r} \tag{4.1}$$

where $C1$ is cash flow at date 1 and r is the rate of return that Keith Vaughan requires on his land sale. It is sometimes referred to as the *discount rate*.

Present value analysis tells us that a payment of £11,424 to be received next year has a present value of £10,200 today. In other words, at a 12 per cent interest rate, Keith is indifferent between £10,200 today or £11,424 next year. If you gave him £10,200 today, he could put it in the bank and receive £11,424 next year.

Because the second offer has a present value of £10,200, whereas the first offer is for only £10,000, present value analysis also indicates that Keith should take the second offer. In other words, both future value analysis and present value analysis lead to the same decision. As it turns out, present value analysis and future value analysis must always lead to the same decision.

As simple as this example is, it contains the basic principles that we will be working with over the next few chapters. We now use another example to develop the concept of net present value.

Example 4.1

Present Value

Lida Jennings, a financial analyst at Kaufman & Broad, a leading real estate firm, is thinking about recommending that Kaufman & Broad invest in a piece of land that costs €85,000. She is certain that next year the land will be worth €91,000, a sure €6,000 gain. Given that the guaranteed interest rate in the bank is 10 per cent, should Kaufman & Broad undertake the investment in land? Ms Jennings' choice is described in Figure 4.2 with the cash flow time chart.

Figure 4.2 Cash Flows for Land Investment

A moment's thought should be all it takes to convince her that this is not an attractive business deal. By investing €85,000 in the land, she will have €91,000 available next year. Suppose, instead, that Kaufman & Broad puts the same €85,000 into the bank. At the interest rate of 10 per cent, this €85,000 would grow to:

$$(1 + 0.10) \times €85,000 = €93,500$$

next year.

It would be foolish to buy the land when investing the same €85,000 in the financial market would produce an extra €2,500 (that is, €93,500 from the bank minus €91,000 from the land investment). This is a future value calculation.

Alternatively, she could calculate the present value of the sale price next year as:

$$PV = \frac{€91,000}{1.10} = €82,727.27$$

Because the present value of next year's sales price is less than this year's purchase price of €85,000, present value analysis also indicates that she should not recommend purchasing the property.

Frequently, businesspeople want to determine the exact *cost* or *benefit* of a decision. In Example 4.1, the decision to buy this year and sell next year can be evaluated as:

$$-€2,273 = -€85,000 + \frac{€91,000}{1.10}$$

$$\times \qquad \times$$

Cost of land today   Present value of next year's sales price

The formula for *NPV* can be written as follows:

Net present value of investment:

$$NPV = -\text{Cost} + PV \tag{4.2}$$

Equation 4.2 says that the value of the investment is −€2,273, after stating all the benefits and all the costs as of date 0. We say that −€2,273 is the **net present value (NPV)** of the investment. That is, NPV is the present value of future cash flows minus the present value of the cost of the investment. Because the net present value is negative, Lida Jennings should not recommend purchasing the land.

Both the Vaughan and the Jennings examples deal with perfect certainty. That is, Keith Vaughan knows with perfect certainty that he could sell his land for £11,424 next year. Similarly, Lida Jennings knows with perfect certainty that Kaufman & Broad could receive €91,000 for selling its land. Unfortunately, businesspeople frequently do not know future cash flows. This uncertainty is treated in the next example.

Example 4.2

Uncertainty and Valuation

Professional Artworks plc is a firm that speculates in modern paintings. The manager is thinking of buying an original Picasso for £400,000 with the intention of selling it at the end of one year. The manager expects that the painting will be worth £480,000 in one year. The relevant cash flows are depicted in Figure 4.3.

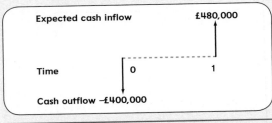

Figure 4.3 Cash Flows for Investment in Painting

Of course, this is only an expectation – the painting could be worth more or less than £480,000. Suppose the guaranteed interest rate granted by banks is 10 per cent. Should the firm purchase the piece of art?

Our first thought might be to discount at the interest rate, yielding:

$$\frac{£480,000}{1.10} = £436,364$$

Because £436,364 is greater than £400,000, it looks at first glance as if the painting should be purchased. However, 10 per cent is the return one can earn on a riskless investment. Because the painting is quite risky, a higher discount rate is called for. The manager chooses a rate of 25 per cent to reflect this risk. In other words, he argues that a 25 per cent expected return is fair compensation for an investment as risky as this painting.

The present value of the painting becomes:

$$\frac{£480,000}{1.25} = £384,000$$

Thus, the manager believes that the painting is currently overpriced at £400,000 and does not make the purchase.

The preceding analysis is typical of decision-making in today's corporations, though real-world examples are, of course, much more complex. Unfortunately, any example with risk poses a problem not presented by a riskless example. In an example with riskless cash flows, the appropriate interest rate can be determined by simply checking with a few banks. The selection of the discount rate for a risky investment is quite a difficult task. We simply do not know at this point whether the discount rate on the painting in Example 4.2 should be 11 per cent, 25 per cent, 52 per cent, or some other percentage.

Because the choice of a discount rate is so difficult, we merely wanted to broach the subject here. We must wait until the specific material on risk and return is covered in later chapters before a risk-adjusted analysis can be presented.

4.2   Valuation: The Multi-period Case

The previous section presented the calculation of future value and present value for one period only. We will now perform the calculations for the multi-period case.

Future Value and Compounding

Suppose an individual were to make a loan of £1. At the end of the first year, the borrower would owe the lender the principal amount of £1 plus the interest on the loan at the interest rate of r. For the specific case where the interest rate is, say, 9 per cent, the borrower owes the lender:

$$£1 \times (1 + r) = £1 \times 1.09 = £1.09$$

At the end of the year, though, the lender has two choices. She can either take the £1.09 – or, more generally, $(1 + r)$ – out of the financial market, or she can leave it in and lend it again for a second year. The process of leaving the money in the financial market and lending it for another year is called compounding.

Suppose the lender decides to compound her loan for another year. She does this by taking the proceeds from her first one-year loan, £1.09, and lending this amount for the next year. At the end of next year, then, the borrower will owe her:

$$£1 \times (1 + r) \times (1 + r) = £1 \times (1 + r)^2 = 1 + 2r + r^2$$

$$£1 \times (1.09) \times (1.09) = £1 \times (1.09)^2 = £1 + £0.18 + £0.0081 = £1.1881$$

This is the total she will receive 2 years from now by compounding the loan.

In other words, the capital market enables the investor, by providing a ready opportunity for lending, to transform £1 today into £1.1881 at the end of 2 years. At the end of 3 years, the cash will be £1 $\times$ $(1.09)^3$ = £1.2950.

The most important point to notice is that the total amount the lender receives is not just the £1 that she lent plus 2 years' worth of interest on £1:

$$2 \times r = 2 \times £0.09 = £0.18$$

The lender also gets back an amount r^2, which is the interest in the second year on the interest that was earned in the first year. The term $2 \times r$ represents simple interest over the 2 years, and the term r^2 is referred to as the *interest on interest*. In our example, this latter amount is exactly:

$$r^2 = (£0.09)^2 = £0.0081$$

When cash is invested at compound interest, each interest payment is reinvested. With simple interest, the interest is not reinvested. The difference between compound interest and simple interest is illustrated in Figure 4.4. In this example, the difference does not amount to much because the loan is for €1. If the loan were for €1 million, the lender would receive €1,188,100 in 2 years' time. Of this amount, €8,100 is interest on interest. The lesson is that those small numbers beyond the decimal point can add up to a lot when the transactions are for big amounts. In addition, the longer the loan lasts, the more important interest on interest becomes.

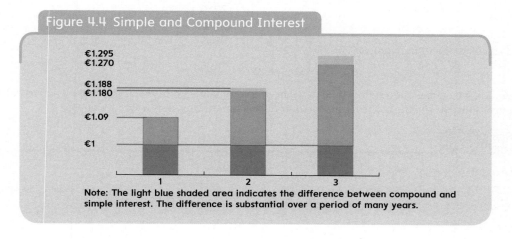

Figure 4.4 Simple and Compound Interest

Note: The light blue shaded area indicates the difference between compound and simple interest. The difference is substantial over a period of many years.

The general formula for an investment over many periods can be written as follows:

Future value of an investment:

$$FV = C_0 \times (1 + r)^T \qquad (4.3)$$

where C_0 is the cash to be invested at date 0 (i.e., today), r is the interest rate per period, and T is the number of periods over which the cash is invested.

Example 4.3

Interest on Interest

Suh-Pyng Ku has put £500 in a savings account at Barclays, a major bank. The account earns 7 per cent, compounded annually. How much will Ms Ku have at the end of 3 years? The answer is:

$$£500 \times 1.07 \times 1.07 \times 1.07 = £500 \times (1.07)^3 = £612.52$$

Figure 4.5 illustrates the growth of Ms Ku's account.

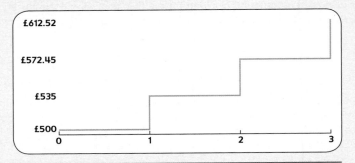

Figure 4.5 Suh-Pyng Ku's Savings Account

The previous example can be calculated in any one of several ways. The computations could be done by hand, by calculator, by spreadsheet, or with the help of a table. The appropriate table is Table A.3, which appears in the appendices on the Online Learning Centre. This table presents *future value of £1 at the end of T periods*. The table is used by locating the appropriate interest rate on the horizontal and the appropriate number of periods on the vertical. For example, Suh-Pyng Ku would look at the following portion of Table A.3:

Period	Interest Rate		
	6%	7%	8%
1	1.0600	1.0700	1.0800
2	1.1236	1.1449	1.1664
3	1.1910	1.2250	1.2597
4	1.2625	1.3108	1.3605

She could calculate the future value of her £500 as

$$£500 \times 1.2250 = £612.50$$

In Example 4.3, we gave you both the initial investment and the interest rate and then asked you to calculate the future value. Alternatively, the interest rate could have been unknown, as shown in Example 4.4.

Example 4.4

Finding the Rate

Carl Voigt, who recently won €10,000 in the lottery, wants to buy a car in 5 years' time. Carl estimates that the car will cost €16,105 at that time. His cash flows are displayed in Figure 4.6.

Figure 4.6 Cash Flows for Purchase of Carl Voigt's Car

What interest rate must he earn to be able to afford the car? The ratio of purchase price to initial cash is:

$$\frac{€16,105}{€10,000} = 1.6105$$

Thus, he must earn an interest rate that allows €1 to become €1.6105 in 5 years. Table A.3 tells us that an interest rate of 10 per cent will allow him to purchase the car.

We can express the problem algebraically as:

$$€10,000 \times (1 + r)^5 = €16,105$$

where r is the interest rate needed to purchase the car. Because €16,105/€10,000 = 1.6105, we have:

$$(1 + r)^5 = 1.6105$$
$$r = 10\%$$

Either the table or a calculator lets us solve for r.

The Power of Compounding: A Digression

Most people who have had any experience with compounding are impressed with its power over long periods. Take equities, for example. The average annual return on the 100 largest companies in the UK has been 8.47 per cent. Now assume that this is the average return on companies on the London Stock Exchange since it opened in 1801. If your great-great-grandmother invested £1 in the stock exchange on the very first day of trading, it would have been worth £39,045,648 in 2015! This is 8.47 per cent compounded annually for 215 years – that is, $(1.0847)^{215} =$ £39,045,648, ignoring a small rounding error.

The example illustrates the great difference between compound and simple interest. At 8.47 per cent, simple interest on £1 is 8.47 pence a year. Simple interest over 215 years is £18.21 (= 215 × £0.0847). That is, an individual withdrawing 8.47 pence every year would have withdrawn £18.21 (= 215 × £0.0847) over 215 years. This is quite a bit below the £39,045,648 that was obtained by reinvestment of all principal and interest.

Present Value and Discounting

We now know that an annual interest rate of 9 per cent enables the investor to transform £1 today into £1.1881 two years from now. In addition, we would like to know the following:

How much would an investor need to lend today so that she could receive £1 two years from today? Algebraically, we can write this as:

$$PV \times (1.09)^2 = £1$$

In the preceding equation, PV stands for present value, the amount of money we must lend today to receive £1 in 2 years' time.

Solving for PV in this equation, we have:

$$PV = \frac{£1}{1.1881} = £0.84$$

This process of calculating the present value of a future cash flow is called discounting. It is the opposite of compounding. To be certain that £0.84 is in fact the present value of £1 to be received in 2 years, we must check whether or not, if we lent £0.84 today and rolled over the loan for 2 years, we would get exactly £1 back. If this were the case, the capital markets would be saying that £1 received in 2 years' time is equivalent to having £0.84 today. Checking the exact numbers, we get:

$$£0.84168 \times 1.09 \times 1.09 = £1$$

In other words, when we have capital markets with a sure interest rate of 9 per cent, we are indifferent between receiving £0.84 today or £1 in 2 years. We have no reason to treat these two choices differently from each other because if we had £0.84 today and lent it out for 2 years, it would return £1 to us at the end of that time. The value 0.84 [= $1/(1.09)^2$] is called the **present value factor**. It is the factor used to calculate the present value of a future cash flow.

In the multi-period case, the formula for PV can be written as follows:

Present value of investment:

$$PV = \frac{C_T}{(1 + r)^T} \qquad (4.4)$$

Here, C_T is the cash flow at date T and r is the appropriate discount rate.

Example 4.5

Multi-period Discounting

Allan Wolf will receive €10,000 three years from now. He can earn 8 per cent on his investments, so the appropriate discount rate is 8 per cent. What is the present value of his future cash flow? The answer is:

$$PV = €10,000 \times \left(\frac{1}{1.08}\right)^3$$

$$= €10,000 \times 0.7938$$

$$= €7,938$$

Figure 4.7 illustrates the application of the present value factor to Allan's investment.

Figure 4.7 Discounting Allan's Opportunity

When his investments grow at an 8 per cent rate of interest, Allan is equally inclined toward receiving €7,938 now and receiving €10,000 in 3 years' time. After all, he could convert the €7,938 he receives today into €10,000 in 3 years by lending it at an interest rate of 8 per cent.

Allan could have reached his present value calculation in one of several ways. The computation could have been done by hand, by calculator, with a spreadsheet, or with the help of Table A.1 in the appendices on the Online Learning Centre. This table presents the *present value of £1 or €1 to be received after T periods*. We use the table by locating the appropriate interest rate on the horizontal and the appropriate number of periods on the vertical. The appropriate present value factor is 0.7938.

In the preceding example we gave both the interest rate and the future cash flow. Alternatively, the interest rate could have been unknown.

Example 4.6

Finding the Rate

A customer of Chaffkin GmbH wants to buy a tugboat today. Rather than paying immediately, he will pay €50,000 in 3 years. It will cost Chaffkin GmbH €38,610 to build the tugboat immediately. The relevant cash flows to Chaffkin GmbH are displayed in Figure 4.8. At what interest rate would Chaffkin GmbH neither gain nor lose on the sale?

Figure 4.8 Cash Flows for Tugboat

The ratio of construction cost (present value) to sale price (future value) is:

$$\frac{€38,610}{€50,000} = 0.7722$$

We must determine the interest rate that allows €1 to be received in 3 years to have a present value of €0.7722. Table A.1 tells us that 9 per cent is that interest rate.

Frequently, an investor or a business will receive more than one cash flow. The present value of the set of cash flows is simply the sum of the present values of the individual cash flows. This is illustrated in the following example.

Example 4.7

Cash Flow Valuation

Paul Wiggins has won a crossword competition and will receive the following set of cash flows over the next 2 years:

Year	Cash Flow
1	£2,000
2	£5,000

Paul can currently earn 6 per cent in his money market account, so the appropriate discount rate is 6 per cent. The present value of the cash flows is:

Year	Cash Flow × Present Value Factor = Present Value
1	$£2,000 \times \dfrac{1}{1.06} = £2,000 \times 0.943 = £1,887$
2	$£5,000 \times \left(\dfrac{1}{1.06}\right)^2 = £5,000 \times 0.890 = £4,450$
	Total £6,337

In other words, Paul is equally inclined toward receiving £6,337 today and receiving £2,000 and £5,000 over the next 2 years.

Example 4.8

NPV

Dratsel.com, an online broker based in Sweden, has an opportunity to invest in a new high-speed computer that costs SKr250,000. The computer will generate cash flows (from cost savings) of SKr125,000 one year from now, SKr100,000 two years from now, and SKr75,000 three years from now. The computer will be worthless after 3 years, and no additional cash flows will occur. Dratsel.com has determined that the appropriate discount rate is 7 per cent for this investment. Should Dratsel.com make this investment in a new high-speed computer? What is the net present value of the investment?

The cash flows and present value factors of the proposed computer are as follows:

Year	Cash Flows (SKr)	Present Value Factor
0	−250,000	$1 = 1$
1	125,000	$\dfrac{1}{1.07} = 0.9346$
2	100,000	$\left(\dfrac{1}{1.07}\right)^2 = 0.8734$
3	75,000	$\left(\dfrac{1}{1.07}\right)^3 = 0.8163$

The present value of the cash flows is:

Year	Cash Flows (SKr) × Present Value Factor	=	Present Value (SKr)
0	−250,000 × 1	=	−250,000
1	125,000 × 0.9346	=	116,825
2	100,000 × 0.8734	=	87,340
3	75,000 × 0.8163	=	61,225.5
		Total:	15,387.5

Dratsel.com should invest in the new high-speed computer because the present value of its future cash flows is greater than its cost. The NPV is SKr15,387.5.

The Algebraic Formula

To derive an algebraic formula for the net present value of a cash flow, recall that the PV of receiving a cash flow one year from now is:

$$PV = \frac{C_1}{(1 + r)}$$

and the PV of receiving a cash flow 2 years from now is:

$$PV = \frac{C_2}{(1 + r)^2}$$

We can write the NPV of a T-period project as:

$$NPV = -C_0 + \frac{C_1}{1 + r} + \frac{C_2}{(1 + r)^2} + \cdots + \frac{C_T}{(1 + r)^T}$$

$$= -C_0 + \sum_{t=1}^{T} \frac{C_t}{(1 + r)^t} \tag{4.5}$$

The initial flow, $-C_0$, is assumed to be negative because it represents an investment. The $\sum$ is shorthand for the sum of the series.

4.3   Compounding Periods

So far, we have assumed that compounding and discounting occur yearly. Sometimes, compounding may occur more frequently than just once a year. For example, imagine that a bank pays a 10 per cent interest rate 'compounded semi-annually'. This means that a £1,000 deposit in the bank would be worth £1,000 × 1.05 = £1,050 after 6 months, and £1,050 × 1.05 = £1,102.50 at the end of the year.

The end-of-year wealth can be written as:

$$£1,000 \left(1 + \frac{0.10}{2}\right)^2 = £1,000 \times (1.05)^2 = £1,102.50$$

Of course, a £1,000 deposit would be worth £1,100 (£1,000 × 1.10) with yearly compounding. Note that the future value at the end of one year is greater with semi-annual compounding than with yearly compounding. With yearly compounding, the original £1,000 remains the investment base for the full year. The original £1,000 is the investment base only for the first 6 months with semi-annual compounding. The base over the second 6 months is £1,050. Hence one gets *interest on interest* with semi-annual compounding.

Because £1,000 × 1.1025 = £1,102.50, 10 per cent compounded semi-annually is the same as 10.25 per cent compounded annually. In other words, a rational investor could not care less whether she is quoted a rate of 10 per cent compounded semi-annually or a rate of 10.25 per cent compounded annually.

Quarterly compounding at 10 per cent yields wealth at the end of 1 year of:

$$£1,000 \left(1 + \frac{0.10}{4}\right)^4 = £1,103.81$$

More generally, compounding an investment m times a year provides end-of-year wealth of:

$$C_0 \left(1 + \frac{r}{m}\right)^m \tag{4.6}$$

where C_0 is the initial investment and r is the stated annual interest rate. The stated annual interest rate is the annual interest rate without consideration of compounding.

Example 4.9

The Effective Annual Rate

What is the end-of-year wealth if Marie Van Bommel receives a stated annual interest rate of 24 per cent compounded monthly on a €1 investment?

Using Equation 4.6, her wealth is:

$$€1 \left(1 + \frac{0.24}{12}\right)^{12} = €1 \times (1.02)^{12}$$

$$= €1.2682$$

The annual rate of return is 26.82 per cent. This annual rate of return is called either the effective annual rate (EAR) or the effective annual yield (EAY). Due to compounding, the effective annual interest rate is greater than the stated annual interest rate of 24 per cent. Algebraically, we can rewrite the effective annual interest rate as follows:

Effective annual rate:

$$\left(1 + \frac{r}{m}\right)^m - 1 \tag{4.7}$$

Students are often bothered by the subtraction of 1 in Equation 4.7. Note that end-of-year wealth is composed of both the interest earned over the year and the original principal. We remove the original principal by subtracting 1 in Equation 4.7.

Example 4.10

Compounding Frequencies

If the stated annual rate of interest, 8 per cent, is compounded quarterly, what is the effective annual rate?

Using Equation 4.7, we have:

$$\left(1 + \frac{r}{m}\right)^m - 1 = \left(1 + \frac{0.08}{4}\right)^4 - 1 = 0.0824 = 8.24\%$$

Referring back to our original example where $C_0 = £1,000$ and $r = 10$ per cent, we can generate the following table:

$C_0(£)$	Compounding Frequency (m)	$C_1(£)$	Effective Annual Rate $= \left(1 + \frac{r}{m}\right)^m - 1$
1,000	Yearly ($m = 1$)	1,100.00	0.10
1,000	Semi-annually ($m = 2$)	1,102.50	0.1025
1,000	Quarterly ($m = 4$)	1,103.81	0.10381
1,000	Daily ($m = 365$)	1,105.16	0.10516

Compounding over Many Years

Equation 4.6 applies for an investment over one year. For an investment over one or more (T) years, the formula becomes:

Future value with compounding:

$$FV = C_0 \left(1 + \frac{r}{m}\right)^{mT} \tag{4.8}$$

Example 4.11

Multi-year Compounding

Harry DeAngelo is investing €5,000 at a stated annual interest rate of 12 per cent per year, compounded quarterly, for 5 years. What is his wealth at the end of 5 years?

Using Equation 4.8, his wealth is:

$$€5,000 \times \left(1 + \frac{0.12}{4}\right)^{4\times5} = €5,000 \times (1.03)^{20} = €5,000 \times 1.8061 = €9,030.50$$

The Annual Percentage Rate

Given the many different ways in which interest rates can be presented to the public, the European Union has a directive that harmonizes the way in which interest rates in any credit agreement for under €50,000 are presented. The UK extended the directive to all regulated loans and the Netherlands uses it for mortgage loans. This harmonized interest rate is called the Annual Percentage Rate (APR) and expresses the *total* cost of borrowing or investing as a percentage interest rate.

The reason for an APR is that a credit agreement may not just include interest payments, but also management fees, arrangement fees and other sundry costs that will affect the total charge for credit (TCC). In addition, knowing the interest rate is still not enough to guarantee full comparability of different loans or investments. As shown above, the compounding frequency and the date when interest is charged will influence the effective annual rate of interest.

Under the EU directive, all providers of credit must prominently show the APR in any document or advertising material that promotes a particular type of loan or investment. To calculate APR, we use the standard present value formula. The main difference is in the cash flows that are included in the calculation.

$$PV = C_0 + \frac{C_1}{1 + \text{APR}} + \frac{C_2}{(1 + \text{APR})^2} + \cdots + \frac{C_T}{(1 + \text{APR})^T}$$

$$= C_0 + \sum_{i=1}^{T} \frac{C_t}{(1 + \text{APR})^i} \tag{4.9}$$

The definition used by the European Union for APR is very different from the formula used in the United States and this can cause considerable confusion when Europeans read finance textbooks aimed at an American market. In the US, the APR is simply the stated annual interest. Remember this if you ever plan to take out a loan overseas!

Example 4.12

APR

After much deliberation, Mary Ennis decides to buy a new Mercedes Benz car for her family. The sale price of the car is £30,000. Mary arranges financing through the Mercedes dealer, who quotes a simple annual interest rate of 12 per cent on the original borrowed amount over 3 years, payable in 36 monthly instalments. This means that the lender will charge 12 per cent interest on the original loan of £30,000 every year for 3 years. Each year, the interest charge will be (12 per cent of £30,000) £3,600 making a total interest payment of £10,800 over 3 years.

The regular monthly instalments that Mary must pay are:

$$\text{Monthly instalment} = (\pounds30,000 + \pounds10,800)/36 = \pounds1,133.33$$

In addition to the interest payments, the Mercedes dealer charges a £250 administration fee, which must be paid when the financing agreement is made. We now solve for APR in Equation 4.9:

$$\pounds30,000 = \pounds250 + \frac{\pounds1,133.33}{(1 + \text{APR})^{\frac{1}{12}}} + \frac{\pounds1,133.33}{(1 + \text{APR})^{\frac{2}{12}}} + \cdots + \frac{\pounds1,133.33}{(1 + \text{APR})^{\frac{36}{12}}}$$

This gives an APR of 24.13 per cent! The lender must also state the total amount paid at the end of the loan, which, in this case, is £41,049.88 and the total charge for credit is £11,049.88 (£41,049.88 − £30,000).

Continuous Compounding

The previous discussion shows that we can compound much more frequently than once a year. We could compound semi-annually, quarterly, monthly, daily, hourly, each minute, or even more often. The limiting case would be to compound every infinitesimal instant, which is commonly called **continuous compounding**. Surprisingly, banks and other financial institutions sometimes quote continuously compounded rates, which is why we study them.

Though the idea of compounding this rapidly may boggle the mind, a simple formula is involved. With continuous compounding, the value at the end of T years is expressed as:

$$C_0 \times e^{rT} \tag{4.10}$$

where C_0 is the initial investment, r is the stated annual interest rate, and T is the number of years over which the investment runs. The number e is a constant and is approximately equal to 2.718. It is not an unknown like C_0, r and T.

Example 4.13

Continuous Compounding

Belinda LeTissier invested £1,000 at a continuously compounded rate of 10 per cent for 2 years. What is the value of her wealth at the end of 2 years?

From Equation 4.10 we have:

$$\pounds1,000 \times e^{0.10 \times 2} = \pounds1,000 \times 1.2214 = \pounds1,221.40$$

This number can easily be read from Table A.5 in the appendices on the Online Learning Centre. We merely set r, the value on the horizontal dimension, to 10 per cent and T, the value on the vertical dimension, to 2. For this problem the relevant portion of the table is shown here:

Period (T)	Continuously Compounded Rate (r)		
	9%	10%	11%
1	1.0942	1.1052	1.1163
2	1.1972	1.2214	1.2461
3	1.3100	1.3499	1.3910

Figure 4.9 illustrates the relationship among annual, semi-annual and continuous compounding. Semi-annual compounding gives rise to both a smoother curve and a higher ending value than does annual compounding. Continuous compounding has both the smoothest curve and the highest ending value of all.

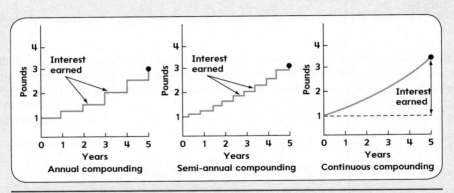

Figure 4.9 Annual, Semi-annual, and Continuous Compounding

Example 4.14

Present Value with Continuous Compounding

A crossword competition is going to pay you €1,000 at the end of 4 years. If the annual continuously compounded rate of interest is 8 per cent, what is the present value of this payment?

$$€1,000 \times \frac{1}{e^{0.08 \times 4}} = €1,000 \times \frac{1}{1.3771} = €726.16$$

4.4 Simplifications

The first part of this chapter has examined the concepts of future value and present value. Although these concepts allow us to answer a host of problems concerning the time value of money, the human effort involved can be excessive. For example, consider a bank calculating the present value of a 20-year monthly mortgage. This mortgage has 240 (= 20 × 12) payments, so a lot of time is needed to perform a conceptually simple task.

Because many basic finance problems are potentially time-consuming, we search for simplifications in this section. We provide simplifying formulas for four classes of cash flow streams:

- Perpetuity
- Growing perpetuity
- Annuity
- Growing annuity.

Perpetuity

A **perpetuity** is a constant stream of cash flows without end. If you are thinking that perpetuities have no relevance to reality, it will surprise you that there is a well-known case of an unending cash flow stream: the British bonds called *consols*. An investor purchasing a consol is entitled to receive yearly interest from the British government forever.

How can the price of a consol be determined? Consider a consol that pays a coupon of C each year and will do so forever. Simply applying the PV formula gives us:

$$PV = \frac{C}{1+r} + \frac{C}{(1+r)^2} + \frac{C}{(1+r)^3} + \dots$$

where the dots at the end of the formula stand for the infinite string of terms that continues the formula. Series like the preceding one are called *geometric series*. It is well known that even though they have an infinite number of terms, the whole series has a finite sum because each term is only a fraction of the preceding term. Before turning to our calculus books, though, it is worth going back to our original principles to see if a bit of financial intuition can help us find the PV.

The present value of the consol is the present value of all of its future coupons. In other words, it is an amount of money that, if an investor had it today, would enable him to achieve the same pattern of expenditures that the consol and its coupons would. Suppose an investor wanted to spend exactly C euros each year. If he had the consol, he could do this. How much money must he have today to spend the same amount? Clearly, he would need exactly enough so that the interest on the money would be C euros per year. If he had any more, he could spend more than C euros each year. If he had any less, he would eventually run out of money spending C euros per year.

The amount that will give the investor C euros each year, and therefore the present value of the consol, is simply:

$$PV = \frac{C}{r} \tag{4.11}$$

To confirm that this is the right answer, notice that if we lend the amount C/r, the interest it earns each year will be:

$$\text{Interest} = \frac{C}{r} \times r = C$$

which is exactly the consol payment. We have arrived at this formula for a consol:

Formula for present value of perpetuity:

$$PV = \frac{C}{1+r} + \frac{C}{(1+r)^2} + \frac{C}{(1+r)^3} + \cdots$$
$$= \frac{C}{r} \tag{4.12}$$

It is comforting to know how easily we can use a bit of financial intuition to solve this mathematical problem.

Example 4.15

Perpetuities

Consider a perpetuity paying £100 a year. If the relevant interest rate is 8 per cent, what is the value of the consol?
   Using Equation 4.11 we have:

$$PV = \frac{£100}{0.08} = £1,250$$

Now suppose that interest rates fall to 6 per cent. Using Equation 4.11 the value of the perpetuity is:

$$PV = \frac{£100}{0.06} = £1,666.67$$

Note that the value of the perpetuity rises with a drop in the interest rate. Conversely, the value of the perpetuity falls with a rise in the interest rate.

Growing Perpetuity

Imagine an apartment building where cash flows to the landlord after expenses will be €100,000 next year. These cash flows are expected to rise at 5 per cent per year. If one assumes that this rise will continue indefinitely, the cash flow stream is termed a **growing perpetuity**. The relevant interest rate is 11 per cent. Therefore, the appropriate discount rate is 11 per cent, and the present value of the cash flows can be represented as:

$$PV = \frac{€100,000}{1.11} + \frac{€100,000\,(1.05)}{(1.11)^2} + \frac{€100,000\,(1.05)^2}{(1.11)^3} + \cdots$$

$$+ \frac{€100,000\,(1.05)^{N-1}}{(1.11)^N} + \cdots$$

Algebraically, we can write the formula as:

$$PV = \frac{C}{1+r} + \frac{C \times (1+g)}{(1+r)^2} + \frac{C \times (1+g)^2}{(1+r)^3} + \cdots + \frac{C \times (1+g)^{N-1}}{(1+r)^N} + \cdots$$

where C is the cash flow to be received one period hence, g is the rate of growth per period, expressed as a percentage, and r is the appropriate discount rate.

Fortunately, this formula reduces to the following simplification:

Formula for present value of growing perpetuity:

$$PV = \frac{C}{r - g} \tag{4.13}$$

From Equation 4.13 the present value of the cash flows from the apartment building is:

$$\frac{€100,000}{0.11 - 0.05} = €1,666,667$$

There are three important points concerning the growing perpetuity formula:

1   *The numerator*: The numerator in Equation 4.13 is the cash flow one period hence, not at date 0.

2   *The discount rate and the growth rate*: The discount rate r must be greater than the growth rate g for the growing perpetuity formula to work. Consider the case in which the growth rate approaches the interest rate in magnitude. Then, the denominator in the growing perpetuity formula gets infinitesimally small and the present value grows infinitely large. The present value is in fact undefined when r is less than g.

3   *The timing assumption*: Cash generally flows into and out of real-world firms both randomly and nearly continuously. However, Equation 4.13 assumes that cash flows are received and disbursed at regular and discrete points in time. In the example of the apartment, we assumed that the net cash flows of €100,000 occurred only once a year. In reality, rent is usually paid every month. Payments for maintenance and other expenses may occur anytime within the year.

We can apply the growing perpetuity formula of Equation 4.13 only by assuming a regular and discrete pattern of cash flows. Although this assumption is sensible because the formula saves so much time, the user should never forget that it is an *assumption*. This point will be mentioned again in the chapters ahead.

A few words should be said about terminology. Authors of financial textbooks generally use one of two conventions to refer to time. A minority of financial writers treat cash flows as being received on exact *dates* – for example date 0, date 1, and so forth. Under this convention, date 0 represents the present time. However, because a year is an interval, not a specific moment in time, the great majority of authors refer to cash flows that occur at the end of a year (or alternatively, the end of a *period*). Under this *end-of-year* convention, the end of year 0 is the present, the end of year 1 occurs one period hence, and so on. (The beginning of year 0 has already passed and is not generally referred to.)[1]

The interchangeability of the two conventions can be seen from the following chart:

Date 0 = Now	Date 1	Date 2	Date 3	...
End of year 0 = Now	End of year 1	End of year 2	End of year 3	...

We strongly believe that the *dates convention* reduces ambiguity. However, we use both conventions because you are likely to see the *end-of-year convention* in later courses. In fact, both conventions may appear in the same example for the sake of practice.

Annuity

An annuity is a level stream of regular payments that lasts for a fixed number of periods. Not surprisingly, annuities are among the most common kinds of financial instruments. The pensions that people receive when they retire are often in the form of an annuity. Leases and mortgages are also often annuities.

To figure out the present value of an annuity we need to evaluate the following equation:

$$\frac{C}{1 + r} + \frac{C}{(1 + r)^2} + \frac{C}{(1 + r)^3} + \cdots + \frac{C}{(1 + r)^T}$$

The present value of receiving the coupons for only T periods must be less than the present value of a consol, but how much less? To answer this, we have to look at consols a bit more closely.

Consider the following time chart:

Date (or end of year)	Now 0	1	2	3	T		(T+1)	(T+2)
Consol 1		C	C	C...	C		C	C...
Consol 2							C	C...
Annuity		C	C	C...	C			

Consol 1 is a normal consol with its first payment at date 1. The first payment of consol 2 occurs at date $T + 1$.

The present value of having a cash flow of C at each of T dates is equal to the present value of consol 1 minus the present value of consol 2. The present value of consol 1 is given by:

$$PV = \frac{C}{r} \tag{4.14}$$

Consol 2 is just a consol with its first payment at date $T + 1$. From the perpetuity formula, this consol will be worth C/r at date T.[2] However, we do not want the value at date T. We want the value now, in other words, the present value at date 0. We must discount C/r back by T periods. Therefore, the present value of consol 2 is:

$$PV = \frac{C}{r} \left[\frac{1}{(1 + r)^T} \right] \tag{4.15}$$

The present value of having cash flows for T years is the present value of a consol with its first payment at date 1 minus the present value of a consol with its first payment at date $T + 1$. Thus the present value of an annuity is Equation 4.14 minus Equation 4.15. This can be written as:

$$\frac{C}{r} - \frac{C}{r} \left[\frac{1}{(1 + r)^T} \right]$$

This simplifies to the following:

Formula for present value of annuity:

$$PV = C \left[\frac{1}{r} - \frac{1}{r(1 + r)^T} \right]$$

This can also be written as:

$$PV = C \left[\frac{1 - \dfrac{1}{(1 + r)^T}}{r} \right] \tag{4.16}$$

Example 4.16

Lottery Valuation

Mark Lancaster has just won a competition paying £50,000 a year for 20 years. He is to receive his first payment a year from now. The competition organizers advertise this as the Million Pound Competition because £1,000,000 = £50,000 × 20. If the interest rate is 8 per cent, what is the true value of the prize?

Equation 4.16 yields:

$$\text{Present value of Million Pound Competition} = £50,000 \times \left[\frac{1 - \dfrac{1}{(1.08)^{20}}}{0.08} \right]$$

$$\text{Periodic payment} \times \text{Annuity factor}$$

$$= £50,000 \quad \times 9.8181$$

$$= £490,905$$

Rather than being overjoyed at winning, Mr Lancaster sues the company for misrepresentation and fraud. His legal brief states that he was promised £1 million but received only £490,905.

The term we use to compute the present value of the stream of level payments, C, for T years is called an *annuity factor*. The annuity factor in the current example is 9.8181. Because the annuity factor is used so often in PV calculations, we have included it in Table A.2 in the appendices on the Online Learning Centre. The table gives the values of these factors for a range of interest rates, r, and maturity dates, T.

The annuity factor as expressed in the brackets of Equation 4.16 is a complex formula. For simplification, we may from time to time refer to the annuity factor as:

$$A_r^T$$

This expression stands for the present value of £1 or €1 a year for T years at an interest rate of r.

We can also provide a formula for the future value of an annuity:

$$FV = C \left[\frac{(1 + r)^T}{r} - \frac{1}{r} \right] = C \left[\frac{(1 + r)^T - 1}{r} \right] \tag{4.17}$$

As with present value factors for annuities, we have compiled future value factors in Table A.4 in the appendices on the Online Learning Centre.

Example 4.17

Retirement Investing

Suppose you put £3,000 per year into a Cash Investment Savings Account. The account pays 6 per cent interest per year, tax free. How much will you have when you retire in 30 years?

This question asks for the future value of an annuity of £3,000 per year for 30 years at 6 per cent, which we can calculate as follows:

$$FV = C \left[\frac{(1 + r)^T - 1}{r} \right] = £3,000 \times \left[\frac{1.06^{30} - 1}{0.06} \right]$$
$$= £3,000 \times 79.0582$$
$$= £237,174.56$$

So, you will have close to a quarter million pounds in the account.

Our experience is that annuity formulas are not hard, but awkward, for the beginning student.
We present four tricks next.

Trick 1: A Delayed Annuity

One of the tricks in working with annuities or perpetuities is getting the timing exactly right. This is particularly true when an annuity or perpetuity begins at a date many periods in the future. We have found that even the brightest beginning student can make errors here. Consider the following example.

Example 4.18

Delayed Annuities

Roberta Barontelli will receive a 4-year annuity of €500 per year, beginning at date 6. If the interest rate is 10 per cent, what is the present value of her annuity? This situation can be graphed as follows:

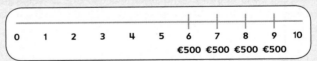

The analysis involves two steps:

1   Calculate the present value of the annuity using Equation 4.16:
    Present value of annuity at date 5:

$$€500 \left[\frac{1 - \dfrac{1}{(1.1)^4}}{0.1} \right] = €500 \times A^4_{0.10}$$
$$= €500 \times 3.1699$$
$$= €1,584.95$$

Note that €1,584.95 represents the present value at *date 5*.

Students frequently think that €1,584.95 is the present value at date 6 because the annuity begins at date 6. However, our formula values the annuity as of one period prior to the first payment. This can be seen in the most typical case where the first payment occurs at date 1. The formula values the annuity as of date 0 in that case.

2   Discount the present value of the annuity back to date 0:
    Present value at date 0:

$$\frac{€1,584.95}{(1.10)^5} = €984.13$$

Again, it is worthwhile mentioning that because the annuity formula brings Roberta's annuity back to date 5, the second calculation must discount over the remaining five periods.

Trick 2: Annuity Due

The annuity formula of Equation 4.16 assumes that the first annuity payment begins a full period hence. This type of annuity is sometimes called an *annuity in arrears* or an *ordinary annuity*. What happens if the annuity begins today – in other words, at date 0?

Example 4.19

Annuity Due

In a previous example, Mark Lancaster received £50,000 a year for 20 years from a competition. In that example, he was to receive the first payment a year from the winning date. Let us now assume that the first payment occurs immediately. The total number of payments remains 20.

Under this new assumption, we have a 19-date annuity with the first payment occurring at date 1 – plus an extra payment at date 0. The present value is:

$$\underset{\text{Payment at date 0}}{£50,000} \quad + \quad \underset{\text{19-year annuity}}{£50,000 \times A_{0.08}^{19}}$$

$$= £50,000 + (£50,000 \times 9.6036)$$

$$= £530,180$$

£530,180, the present value in this example, is greater than £490,905, the present value in the earlier competition example. This is to be expected because the annuity of the current example begins earlier. An annuity with an immediate initial payment is called an *annuity in advance* or, more commonly, an *annuity due*. Always remember that Equation 4.16 and Table A.2 in the appendices on the Online Learning Centre refer to an *ordinary annuity*.

Trick 3: The Infrequent Annuity

The following example treats an annuity with payments occurring less frequently than once a year.

Example 4.20

Infrequent Annuities

Ann Chen receives an annuity of £450, payable once every 2 years. The annuity stretches out over 20 years. The first payment occurs at date 2 – that is, 2 years from today. The annual interest rate is 6 per cent.

The trick is to determine the interest rate over a 2-year period. The interest rate over 2 years is:

$$(1.06 \times 1.06) - 1 = 12.36\%$$

That is, £100 invested over 2 years will yield £112.36.

What we want is the present value of a £450 annuity over 10 periods, with an interest rate of 12.36 per cent per period:

$$£450 \left[\frac{1 - \dfrac{1}{(1 + 0.1236)^{10}}}{0.1236} \right] = £450 \times A_{0.1236}^{10} = £2,505.57$$

Trick 4: Equating Present Value of Two Annuities

The following example equates the present value of inflows with the present value of outflows.

Example 4.21

Working with Annuities

You are saving for the university education of your newborn daughter, Susan, and estimate that university expenses will be €30,000 per year when she reaches university in 18 years. The annual interest rate over the next few decades will be 14 per cent. How much money must you deposit in the bank each year so that your daughter will be completely supported through 4 years of university?

To simplify the calculations, we assume that your daughter is born today. You will make the first of four annual tuition payments on her 18th birthday. You will also make equal bank deposits on each of her first 17 birthdays, but no deposit at date 0. This is illustrated as follows:

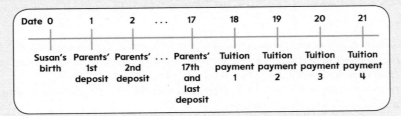

You will be making deposits to the bank over the next 17 years and will be withdrawing €30,000 per year over the following 4 years. We can be sure you will be able to withdraw fully €30,000 per year if the present value of the deposits is equal to the present value of the four €30,000 withdrawals.

This calculation requires three steps. The first two determine the present value of the withdrawals. The final step determines yearly deposits that will have a present value equal to that of the withdrawals.

1 We calculate the present value of the 4 years at university using the annuity formula:

$$€30,000 \left[\frac{1 - \dfrac{1}{(1.14)^4}}{0.14} \right] = €30,000 \times A_{0.14}^{10}$$

$$= €30,000 \times 2.9137 = €87,411$$

We assume that Susan enters university on her 18th birthday. Given our discussion in Trick 1, €87,411 represents the present value at date 17.

2 We calculate the present value of the university education at date 0 as:

$$\frac{€87,811}{(1.14)^{17}} = €9,422.91$$

3 Assuming that you make deposits to the bank at the end of each of the 17 years, we calculate the annual deposit that will yield a present value of all deposits of €9,422.91. This is calculated as:

$$C \times A_{0.14}^{17} = €9,422.91$$

Because $A_{0.14}^{17} = 6.3729$,

$$C = \frac{€9,422.91}{6.3729} = €1,478.59$$

Thus deposits of €1,478.59 made at the end of each of the first 17 years and invested at 14 per cent will provide enough money to make tuition payments of €30,000 over the following 4 years.

Growing Annuity

Cash flows in business are likely to grow over time, due either to real growth or to inflation. The growing perpetuity, which assumes an infinite number of cash flows, provides one formula to handle this growth. We now consider a growing annuity, which is a *finite* number of growing cash flows. Because perpetuities of any kind are rare, a formula for a growing annuity would be useful indeed. Here is the formula:

Formula for present value of growing annuity:

$$PV = C \left[\frac{1}{r-g} - \frac{1}{r-g} \times \left(\frac{1+g}{1+r} \right)^T \right] = C \left[\frac{1 - \left(\dfrac{1+g}{1+r} \right)^T}{r-g} \right] \tag{4.18}$$

As before, C is the payment to occur at the end of the first period, r is the interest rate, g is the rate of growth per period, expressed as a percentage, and T is the number of periods for the annuity.

Example 4.22

Growing Annuities

Stuart Gabriel, an MBA student, has just been offered a job at £80,000 a year. He anticipates his salary increasing by 9 per cent a year until his retirement in 40 years. Given an interest rate of 20 per cent, what is the present value of his lifetime salary?

   We simplify by assuming he will be paid his £80,000 salary exactly one year from now, and that his salary will continue to be paid in annual instalments. The appropriate discount rate is 20 per cent. From Equation 4.18, the calculation is:

$$\text{Present value of Stuart's lifetime salary} = £80,000 \times \left[\frac{1 - \left(\frac{1.09}{1.20} \right)^{40}}{0.20 - 0.09} \right] = £711,730.71$$

Example 4.23

More Growing Annuities

In Example 4.21, you planned to make 17 identical payments to fund the university education of your daughter, Susan. Alternatively, imagine that you planned to increase your payments at 4 per cent per year. What would their first payment be?

   The first two steps of Example 4.21 showed that the present value of the college costs was €9,422.91. These two steps would be the same here. However, the third step must be altered. Now we must ask how much your first payment should be so that, if payments increase by 4 per cent per year, the present value of all payments will be €9,422.91.

   We set the growing annuity formula equal to €9,422.91 and solve for C:

$$C \left[\frac{1 - \left(\frac{1+g}{1+r} \right)^{T}}{r - g} \right] = C \left[\frac{1 - \left(\frac{1.04}{1.14} \right)^{T}}{0.14 - 0.04} \right] = €9,422.91$$

Here, $C = €1,192.78$. Thus, the deposit on your daughter's first birthday is €1,192.78. The deposit on the second birthday is €1,240.49 (= 1.04 × €1,192.78), and so on.

Real World Insight 4.2

Research and Development in Drug Companies

How does a company value a new drug product? Research and development at large pharmaceutical firms is inherently risky because there is no guarantee that the drug will be accepted by regulatory authorities, be effective or have a receptive market wanting to buy the drug. Take Glybera, which reduces the likelihood of blood-clogging. The drug costs nearly €800,000 per patient!

   To justify such a high price, the costs are not only associated with very high research and development expense, but also the reduction in treatment costs associated with taking the drug. Since one course of Glybera provides a permanent cure, not having ongoing treatment costs are equivalent to an increase in cash flow, which clearly has value to the patient.

   Thus, buying Glybera entails a very high initial cash outflow but also a long-term annuity of cash inflows to represent the reduction in future costs. Taken together, the initial cost of the drug may not seem so high after all.

Summary and Conclusions

1   Two basic concepts, *future value* and *present value,* were introduced at the beginning of this chapter. With a 10 per cent interest rate, an investor with £1 today can generate a future value of £1.10 in a year, £1.21 [= £1 × $(1.10)^2$] in 2 years, and so on. Conversely, present value analysis places a current value on a future cash flow. With the same 10 per cent interest rate, one pound to be received in one year has a present value of £0.909 (= £1/1.10) in year 0. One pound to be received in 2 years has a present value of £0.826 [= £1/$(1.10)^2$].

2   We commonly express an interest rate as, say, 12 per cent per year. However, we can speak of the interest rate as 3 per cent per quarter. Although the stated annual interest rate remains 12 per cent (= 3 per cent × 4), the effective annual interest rate is 12.55 per cent [= $(1.03)^4$ × 1]. In other words, the compounding process increases the future value of an investment. The limiting case is continuous compounding, where funds are assumed to be reinvested every infinitesimal instant.

3   A basic quantitative technique for financial decision making is net present value analysis. The net present value formula for an investment that generates cash flows (C_i) in future periods is:

$$NPV = -C_0 + \frac{C_1}{(1+r)} + \frac{C_2}{(1+r)^2} + \cdots + \frac{C_r}{(1+r)^T} = -C_0 + \sum_{i=1}^{T} \frac{C_i}{(1+r)^i}$$

The formula assumes that the cash flow at date 0 is the initial investment (a cash outflow).

4   Frequently, the actual calculation of present value is long and tedious. The computation of the present value of a long-term mortgage with monthly payments is a good example of this. We presented four simplifying formulas:

$$\textit{Perpetuity: } PV = \frac{C}{r}$$

$$\textit{Growing Perpetuity: } PV = \frac{C}{r-g}$$

$$\textit{Annuity: } PV = C \left[\frac{1 - \dfrac{1}{(1+r)^T}}{r} \right]$$

$$\textit{Growing annuity: } PV = C \left[\frac{1 - \left(\dfrac{1+g}{1+r} \right)^T}{r-g} \right]$$

5   We stressed a few practical considerations in the application of these formulas:

   (a) The numerator in each of the formulas, C, is the cash flow to be received *one full period hence.*

   (b) Cash flows are generally irregular in practice. To avoid unwieldy problems, assumptions to create more regular cash flows are made both in this textbook and in the real world.

   (c) A number of present value problems involve annuities (or perpetuities) beginning a few periods hence. Students should practise combining the annuity (or perpetuity) formula with the discounting formula to solve these problems.

   (d) Annuities and perpetuities may have periods of every two or every n years, rather than once a year. The annuity and perpetuity formulas can easily handle such circumstances.

   (e) We frequently encounter problems where the present value of one annuity must be equated with the present value of another annuity.

Questions and Problems

CONCEPT

1   **Valuation: The One-period Case**   Your friend tells you that it does not matter when you receive money, since it is always worth the same. He tells you that £100 today is worth the same as £100 tomorrow. Is he correct? Would you be willing to pay £100 today in exchange for £150 in one year's time? What would be the key considerations in your decision?

2   **Valuation: The Multi-period Case**   You have taken out a loan that requires annual payments of £110 for each of the next 2 years. You wish to pay back the loan over 4 years. Should the payment be £55 per year? Should it be more or less? Explain your answer.

3   **Compounding Periods**   As you increase the length of time involved, what happens to future values? What happens to present values? What happens to the future value of an annuity if you increase the rate r? What happens to the present value?

4   **Simplifications**   Can the simplified formulae provided in this chapter work for every valuation problem? Explain your answer with an illustration.

5   **What is a Firm Worth?**   What is discounted cash flow (DCF) valuation? Can it be used to estimate the value of companies? What businesses could we value using DCF valuation? What are the advantages and disadvantages of such an approach?

REGULAR

6   **Interest**   You work for a jewellers and have sourced a good goldsmith who is able to sell you 100 ounces of gold for £100,000. You approach your two main customers. Mr Noel says he will buy the gold from you in 6 months for £104,000, whereas Ms Biggs tells you that she will be able to buy the gold from you in 2 years' time for £116,000. What is the annual percentage rate that Mr Noel and Ms Biggs are offering you? Which option should you go for?

7   **Calculating Future Values**   Calculate the future value of a £100 cash flow for the following combinations of rates and times:

   (a) $r = 8\%$; $t = 10$ years

   (b) $r = 8\%$; $t = 20$ years

   (c) $r = 4\%$; $t = 10$ years

   (d) $r = 4\%$; $t = 20$ years

8   **Calculating Future Values**   If you invest €1,000 in a savings account that pays 4 per cent every year, how long would it take you to triple your money?

9   **Calculating Present Values**   Calculate the present value of a £100 cash flow for the following rates and times:

   (a) $r = 8\%$; $t = 10$ years

   (b) $r = 8\%$; $t = 20$ years

   (c) $r = 4\%$; $t = 10$ years

   (d) $r = 4\%$; $t = 20$ years

10 **Calculating Rates of Return**   You own a property on the Isle of Arran, which you estimate will provide an annual income of £10,000 per year in perpetuity. If the property is valued at £250,000, what must be the discount rate?

11 **Calculating Rates of Return**   On 8 February 2009, John Madejski, chairman of Reading Football Club, sold the Edgar Degas bronze sculpture *Petite Danseuse de Quartorze Ans* at auction for a world record price of £13.3 million. He bought the statue in 2004 for £5 million. What was his annual rate of return on this sculpture?

12 **Perpetuities**   An investor purchasing a British consol is entitled to receive annual payments from the British government forever. What is the price of a consol that pays £4 annually if the next payment occurs one year from today? The market interest rate is 4 per cent.

13 Continuous Compounding   A zero coupon bond that will pay €1,000 in 10 years is selling today at €422.41. What is the continuously compounded annual interest rate on the bond?

14 Net Present Value   Your company has the opportunity to invest in a new computer system that requires an initial outlay of €20,000, and will increase the firm's cash flows by €4,000 per year for the next 8 years. The finance director has asked you to assess whether the system is worth installing if the required rate of return is (i) 9 per cent and (ii) 14 per cent. How high can the discount rate be before the project is rejected?

15 Calculating Annuity Present Value   An investment offers €4,000 per year for 10 years, with the first payment occurring one year from now. If the required return is 9 per cent, what is the value of the investment? What would the value be if the payments occurred for 20 years? For 50 years? Forever?

16 Calculating APR   Find the APR for the following 5-year loan: A principal of £15,000 with a stated annual interest rate of 7 per cent on the original principal amount to be paid in 60 monthly instalments. The loan has a £250 arrangement fee to be paid as soon as the contract is signed.

17 Present Value   A 25-year fixed-rate mortgage has monthly payments of €717 per month and a mortgage interest rate of 6.14 per cent per year compounded monthly. If a buyer purchases a home with the cash proceeds of the mortgage loan plus an additional 20 per cent deposit, what is the purchase price of the home?

18 Future Value   What is the future value in 4 years of €1,000 invested in an account with a stated annual interest rate of 10 per cent,

(a) Compounded annually

(b) Compounded semi-annually

(c) Compounded monthly

(d) Compounded continuously?

Why does the future value increase as the compounding period shortens?

19 Calculating Annuities   You are planning to save for retirement over the next 30 years. To do this, you will invest £500 a month in a share account and £500 a month in a bond account. The return of the share account is expected to be 7 per cent, and the bond account will pay 4 per cent. When you retire, you will combine your money into an account with a 6 per cent return. How much can you withdraw each month from your account assuming a 25-year withdrawal period?

20 Compounding   What is the annualized interest rate, compounded daily, that is equivalent to 12 per cent interest compounded semi-annually? What is the daily compounded rate that is equivalent to 12 per cent compounded continuously?

21 Growing Perpetuities   Oasis Telephony has been working on a new hands-free telephone that clips into your ear. The new gadget has now been cleared for manufacture and development. Oasis Telephony anticipates the first annual cash flow from the phone to be €200,000, received 2 years from today. Subsequent annual cash flows will grow at 5 per cent in perpetuity. What is the present value of the phone if the discount rate is 10 per cent?

22 Unusual Perpetuities   You have invested in a project that will pay you £1,000 every 2 years. If the interest rate is 8 per cent, how much is the project worth today?

23 Balloon Payments   Mario Guiglini has just sold his hotel and purchased a restaurant with the proceeds. The restaurant is on the Riccione seafront in northern Italy. The cost of the restaurant to Mario is €200,000 and the seller requires a 20 per cent up-front payment. Mario is able to pay the up-front payment from the proceeds of the hotel sale. He needs to take out a mortgage and has been able to arrange one with Unicredit Bank that charges a 12 per cent APR. Mario will make equal monthly payments over the next 20 years. His first payment will be due one month from now. However, the mortgage has a 10-year balloon payment option, meaning that the balance of the loan could be paid off at the end of year 10. There were no other transaction costs or finance charges. How much will Mario's balloon payment be in 8 years?

24 Calculating Interest Expense   You receive a credit card application from Shady Banks plc offering an introductory rate of 1.90 per cent per year, compounded monthly for the first 6 months, increasing thereafter to 16 per cent per year compounded monthly. Assuming you transfer the £4,000 balance from your existing credit card and make no subsequent payments, how much interest will you owe at the end of the first year?

25 Growing Annuity   Your job pays you only once a year for all the work you did over the previous 12 months. Today, 31 December, you just received your salary of £100,000, and plan to spend all of it.

However, you have also decided to join the company's employee pension scheme. Under the very generous scheme, your company contributes £2 for every £1 that you pay into the pension. You have decided that one year from today you will begin paying 2 per cent of your annual salary into the pension in which you are guaranteed to earn 8 per cent per year. Your salary will increase at 4 per cent per year throughout your career. How much money will you have on the date of your retirement 40 years from today?

26 **Calculating APR**   A local finance company quotes a 14 per cent interest rate on one-year loans. So, if you borrow €20,000, the interest for the year will be €2,800. Because you must repay a total of €22,800 in one year, the finance company requires you to pay €22,800/12, or €1,900, per month over the next 12 months. Is this a 14 per cent loan? What rate would legally have to be quoted?

27 **Calculating Present Values**   A 3-year annuity of six £5,000 semi-annual payments will begin 10 years from now, with the first payment coming 10.5 years from now. If the discount rate is 10 per cent compounded monthly, what is the value of this annuity 5 years from now? What is the value 3 years from now? What is the current value of the annuity?

28 **Calculating Annuities Due**   You want to lease a set of golf clubs from Pings Ltd. The lease contract is in the form of 36 equal monthly payments at a 14 per cent stated annual interest rate, compounded monthly. Because the clubs cost £4,000 retail, Pings wants the PV of the lease payments to equal £4,000. Suppose that your first payment is due immediately. What will your monthly lease payments be?

CHALLENGE

29 **Annuities**   A couple will retire in 50 years; they plan to spend about £30,000 a year in retirement, which should last about 25 years. They believe that they can earn 8 per cent interest on retirement savings. If they make annual payments into a savings plan, how much will they need to save each year? Assume the first payment comes in 1 year. How would this change if the couple also realize that in 20 years they will need to spend £30,000 on their child's college education?

30 **Balloon Payments**   On 1 September 2012, Susan Chao bought a motorcycle for £15,000. She paid £1,000 down and financed the balance with a 5-year loan at a stated annual interest rate of 9.6 per cent, compounded monthly. She started the monthly payments exactly one month after the purchase (i.e., 1 October 2012). Two years later, at the end of October 2014, Susan got a new job and decided to pay off the loan. If the bank charges her a 1 per cent prepayment penalty based on the loan balance, how much must she pay the bank on 1 November 2014?

31 **Calculating Annuity Values**   You are serving on a jury. A plaintiff is suing the city for injuries sustained after a freak doggie poo accident. In the trial, doctors testified that it will be 5 years before the plaintiff is able to return to work. The jury has already decided in favour of the plaintiff. You are the foreperson of the jury and propose that the jury give the plaintiff an award to cover the following: (1) The present value of 2 years' back pay. The plaintiff's annual salary for the last 2 years would have been €25,000 and €28,000, respectively. (2) The present value of 5 years' future salary. You assume the salary will be €28,000 per year. (3) €100,000 for pain, suffering and humiliation. (4) €20,000 for court costs. Assume that the salary payments are equal amounts paid at the end of each month. If the interest rate you choose is a 4 per cent APR, what is the size of the settlement? If you were the plaintiff, would you like to see a higher or lower interest rate?

32 **Annuities**   You have just read a life-enhancing book that tells you that if you believe things will happen, they will! You decide that you want to become a millionaire by the time you are 65. You have just turned 22 and you decide to play the stock market. Your fantastic corporate finance textbook leads you to believe that you can earn 11.8 per cent per annum from investing in equities. How much must you invest each year in order to realize your dream? You have decided that investing each year will be boring and so you just want to invest an amount today and leave it in an account for 43 years. How much should you invest today?

33 **Ordinary Annuities and Annuities Due**   As discussed in the text, an annuity due is identical to an ordinary annuity except that the periodic payments occur at the beginning of each period and not at the end of the period. Show that the relationship between the value of an ordinary annuity and the value of an otherwise equivalent annuity due is:

$$\text{Annuity due value} = \text{Ordinary annuity value} \times (1 + r)$$

Show this for both present and future values.

34 **Present Value of a Growing Perpetuity** What is the equation for the present value of a growing perpetuity with a payment of C one period from today if the payments grow by C each period?

35 **Rule of 72** A useful rule of thumb for the time it takes an investment to double with discrete compounding is the 'Rule of 72'. To use the Rule of 72, you simply divide 72 by the interest rate to determine the number of periods it takes for a value today to double. For example, if the interest rate is 6 per cent, the Rule of 72 says it will take $72/6 = 12$ years to double. This is approximately equal to the actual answer of 11.90 years. The Rule of 72 can also be applied to determine what interest rate is needed to double money in a specified period. This is a useful approximation for many interest rates and periods. At what rate is the Rule of 72 exact? A corollary to the Rule of 72 is the Rule of 69.3. The Rule of 69.3 is exactly correct except for rounding when interest rates are compounded continuously. Prove the Rule of 69.3 for continuously compounded interest.

Exam Question (45 minutes)

1 You have just started a new company to deliver mail and parcels to rural communities. At the moment, other companies either do not provide a service or are exceptionally expensive. The new company requires initial investment to purchase a fleet of 20 medium size vans. These cost £20,000 each and every one requires a down payment of 20 per cent. Your business plan anticipates the vans being fully paid off after 6 years and you wish to make monthly payments on the vans starting one month from now. The APR of the loan is 9.6 per cent. What are the monthly payments? (30 marks)

2 After 4 years, you are approached by another firm who wishes to buy the postal company. You wish to pay off the van loan completely and approach your bank for details. They have indicated that any early completion of your loan will incur a 1 per cent penalty. You have just paid an instalment and have 24 payments left (next payment in one month). How much will you need to pay the bank today to cancel the loan? (30 marks)

3 Explain how you would modify the present value of an annuity shortcut formula to accommodate an equal payment stream that begins immediately. How would you modify the present value of an annuity shortcut formula to accommodate an annuity that begins in year 5? How would you answer this question if the payment stream was a growing perpetuity? (40 marks)

Mini Case

The MBA Decision

Max Gruber graduated from university 6 years ago with a finance undergraduate degree. Although he is satisfied with his current job, his goal is to become an investment banker. He feels that an MBA would allow him to achieve this goal. After examining schools, he has narrowed his choice to either Universität des Geschäfts in Austria or Financez l'École d'affaires in France. Although internships are encouraged by both schools, to get class credit for the internship, no salary can be paid. Other than internships, neither school will allow its students to work while enrolled in its MBA programme.

Max currently works at the money management firm of Huber and Bauer. His annual salary at the firm is €75,000 per year, and his salary is expected to increase at 3 per cent per year until retirement. He is currently 28 years old and expects to work for 35 more years. His current job includes a fully paid health insurance plan, and his current average tax rate is 50 per cent. Max has a savings account with enough money to cover the entire cost of his MBA programme.

The Business School at Universität des Geschäfts is one of the top MBA programmes in Europe. The MBA degree requires 2 years of full-time enrolment at the university. The annual tuition is €60,000, payable at the beginning of each school year. Books and other supplies are estimated to cost €2,500 per year. Max expects that after graduation from Universität des Geschäfts, he will receive a job offer for about €125,000 per year, with a €25,000 signing bonus. The salary at this job will increase at 4 per cent per year. Because he will be working in Austria, his average income tax rate will remain at 50 per cent.

The Financez l'École d'affaires began its MBA programme 16 years ago. The Financez l'École d'affaires is smaller and less well known than the Universität des Geschäfts. However, the school offers an accelerated, one-year programme, with a tuition cost of €75,000 to be paid upon matriculation. Books and other supplies for the programme are expected to cost €3,500. Max thinks that he will receive an offer of €92,000 per year upon graduation, with a €10,000 signing bonus. The salary at this job will increase at 3.5 per cent per year. Because he will be working in France, Max's average tax rate at this level of income will be 41 per cent.

Both schools offer a discounted health insurance plan that will cost €3,000 per year, payable at the beginning of the year. Max also estimates that room and board expenses will cost €20,000 per year at either school. The appropriate discount rate is 6.5 per cent.

1 How does Max's age affect his decision to get an MBA?

2 What other, perhaps non-quantifiable factors affect Max's decision to get an MBA?

3 Assuming all salaries are paid at the end of each year, what is the best option for Max – from a strictly financial standpoint?

4 Max believes that the appropriate analysis is to calculate the future value of each option. How would you evaluate this statement?

5 What initial salary would Max need to receive to make him indifferent between attending Universität des Geschäfts and staying in his current position?

6 Suppose, instead of being able to pay cash for his MBA, Max must borrow the money. The current borrowing rate is 5.4 per cent. How would this affect his decision?

Practical Case Study

1 In Yahoo! Finance, find the closing price for a company in your country. Find the price exactly 4 years before. What was your annual return over the last 4 years assuming you purchased the equity at the closing price 4 years ago? (Assume no dividends were paid.) Using this same return, what price will the company sell for 5 years from now? And 10 years from now? What if the stock price increases at 11 per cent per year? Are these figures realistic? Explain.

2 Find the share price for a company in your country by visiting Yahoo! Finance. You find an analyst who projects the share price will increase 12 per cent per year for the foreseeable future. Based on the most recent share price, if the projection holds true, when will the share price be 10 times higher? When will it be 20 times higher?

Additional Reading

Because this is an introductory chapter on discounted cash flow valuation, there are not many entry level research papers that the reader would find of interest. However, if you are interested in a better understanding of the theoretical implications of discounted cash flow, the following paper is a worthwhile read:

Ruback, R.S. (2011) 'Downsides and DCF: Valuing Biased Cash Flow Forecasts', *Journal of Applied Corporate Finance*, Vol. 23, No. 2, 8–17.

Endnotes

1 Sometimes, financial writers merely speak of a cash flow in year x. Although this terminology is ambiguous, such writers generally mean the *end of year x*.

2 Students frequently think that C/r is the present value at date $T + 1$ because the consol's first payment is at date $T + 1$. However, the formula values the consol as of one period prior to the first payment.

CHAPTER 5

Bond, Equity and Firm Valuation

When the London Stock Exchange closed on 2 December 2014, the share price of the credit referencing firm, Experian plc, was £10.59. On that same day, Reed Elsevier plc closed at £10.99, while Capita plc, closed at £10.55. Because the share prices of these three companies were so similar, you might expect they would be offering similar dividends to their shareholders, but you would be wrong. In fact, Experian's dividend was 7.74 pence per share and Reed Elsevier's was 7.00 pence per share. In contrast, Capita paid a considerably higher dividend of 9.6 pence per share. How would one go about estimating the value of a company's equity? Are the methods used to calculate debt value the same? How would you value a firm? Although all the companies mentioned here have debt, finding information on their value can be very difficult. This is because companies can borrow privately (via bank loans) or publicly (via bonds). Even with public bond issues, getting current bond prices is problematic because most bonds are not traded frequently.

As a financial manager, you may be asked to value firms. With the difficulties experienced in equity and bond valuation, this is no easy task. As we will see in this chapter, the dividends currently being paid are one of the primary factors we look at when attempting to value the shares of a company. We also need to consider how likely earnings will grow in the future as well as the risk of a company's bonds. We begin our discussion with bond valuation and then consider equities. Finally, we look at ways in which you can value companies, even when equity and bond information is not available.

KEY NOTATIONS

C_i	Cash flow or coupon at time i
F	Face value of a bond
R	Discount rate
PV	Present value
T	Time period
Div_i	Dividend at time i
g	Growth rate
EPS	Earnings per share
NPVGO	Net present value of growth opportunities
$FCFF_i$	Free cash flow to the firm at time i

5.1   Definition and Example of a Bond

**Chapter 20
Page 541**

A *bond* is a certificate showing that a borrower owes a specified sum (see **Chapter 20** for more information on bonds). To repay the money, the borrower has agreed to make interest and principal payments on designated dates. For example, imagine that South African firm, Kreuger Enterprises just issued 100,000 bonds for 10,000 Rand each, where the bonds have a coupon rate of 5 per cent and a maturity of 2 years. Interest on the bonds is to be paid yearly. This means that:

1   R1 billion (=100,000 × R10,000) has been borrowed by the firm
2   The firm must pay interest of R50 million (=5% × R1 billion) at the end of one year
3   The firm must pay both R50 million of interest and R1 billion of principal at the end of 2 years.

There are many types of bonds that exist in the capital markets and issuers include corporations, private firms, banks and governments. In fact, the government bond market is one of the largest and most liquid markets in the world. Governments use bonds to manage their long- and short-term cash flow requirements and, as a result, almost every country will have government bonds. Corporate bonds are similar in structure to government bonds but, unlike governments, companies have the option to issue both debt and equity, and the corporate bond market is smaller.

Table 5.1 presents a sample of bonds that were issued in December 2014 across the world. Notice how the bond market is completely international. The Pakistani government issued $1 billion worth of bonds in the United States and GlaxoSmithKline issued bonds in euros. The bonds listed in Table 5.1 are all denominated in the currency of the country in which they were listed. 'Coupon %' is the coupon rate of the bond and 'Maturity' is the date the bond expires. For example, Table 5.1 shows that in December 2014, GlaxoSmithKline issued a 10-year bond that pays interest of 1.375 per cent per year at a price which was 98.856 per cent of the principal value of the bond.

There are a number of different bonds in Table 5.1. The Telefonica bond has a perpetual life, meaning that there is no end date for the bond. The BNZ bond has a floating rate note, which ties the coupon to a benchmark rate that varies on a daily basis. We also see that GlaxoSmithKline has issued two bonds with the same coupon rate but different maturities. These bonds have different prices from each other. Finally, several bonds are sold below the principal value (this is when the bond price is lower than 100). In the following section we will consider all of these cases and more.

Table 5.1 A Sample of International Bond Issues in December 2014

Borrower	Amount (millions)	Maturity Date	Coupon (%)	Issue Price
US dollars				
Pakistan	1,000	Dec 2019	6.750	100.000
Euros				
BNZ	300	Dec 2019	FRN	99.850
GlaxoSmithKline	1,000	Dec 2024	1.375	98.856
GlaxoSmithKline	1,500	Dec 2019	1.375	99.501
Telefonica	850	Perpetual	4.200	100.000
Sterling				
John Lewis	300	Dec 2034	4.250	98.380
Swiss francs				
Walliser KB/BCV	120	Dec 2023	0.625	100.282
Walliser KB/BCV	100	Dec 2021	0.375	100.138
Swedish Krona				
Rabobank	100	Nov 2019	FRN	100.000
Rikshem AB	300	Dec 2017	0.690	100.000

Notes: FRN denotes a bond with a floating coupon rate. Prices are quoted as a percentage of the face value.

Source: Data from Reuters.

5.2 How to Value Bonds

Pure Discount Bonds

The **pure discount bond** is perhaps the simplest kind of bond. It promises a single payment, say £1, at a fixed future date. If the payment is 1 year from now, it is called a *1-year discount bond;* if it is 2 years from now, it is called a *2-year discount bond,* and so on.

The date when the issuer of the bond makes the last payment is called the **maturity date** of the bond, or just its *maturity* for short. The bond is said to mature or *expire* on the date of its final payment. The payment at maturity (£1 in this example) is termed the bond's **face** or **par value.**

Pure discount bonds are often called *zero coupon bonds* to emphasize the fact that the holder receives no cash payments until maturity. We will use the terms *zero* and *discount* interchangeably to refer to bonds that pay no coupons.

The first row of Figure 5.1 shows the pattern of cash flows from a 4-year pure discount bond. Note that the face value, *F*, is paid when the bond expires in the 48th month. There are no payments of either interest or principal prior to this date.

Figure 5.1 Different Types of Bonds

Note: C, coupon paid every 6 months; *F,* face value at year 4 (maturity for pure discount and coupon bonds).

In the previous chapter, we indicated that one discounts a future cash flow to determine its present value. The present value of a pure discount bond can easily be determined by the techniques of the previous chapter. For short, we sometimes speak of the *value* of a bond instead of its present value.

Consider a pure discount bond that pays a face value of *F* in *T* years, where the interest rate is *R* in each of the *T* years. (We also refer to this rate as the *market interest rate.*) Because the face value is the only cash flow that the bond pays, the present value of this face amount is calculated as follows:

Value of a pure discount bond:

$$PV = \frac{F}{(1 + R)^T}$$

The present value formula can produce some surprising results. Suppose that the interest rate is 10 per cent. Consider a bond with a face value of €1 million that matures in 20 years. Applying the formula to this bond, its PV is given by:

$$PV = \frac{\text{€1 million}}{(1.1)^{20}}$$

$$= \text{€}148,644$$

or only about 15 per cent of the face value.

Level Coupon Bonds

Typical bonds issued by either governments or corporations offer cash payments not just at maturity, but also at regular times in between. For example, payments on government issues and corporate bonds tend to be made every 6 months until the bonds mature. These payments are called the coupons of the bond. The middle row of Figure 5.1 illustrates the case of a 4-year, *level coupon bond*: the coupon, C, is paid every 6 months in most countries (although annual and quarterly payments are also common) and is the same throughout the life of the bond.

Note that the face value of the bond, F, is paid at maturity (end of year 4). F is sometimes called the *principal* or the *denomination*. Bonds issued in the United Kingdom typically have face values of £100,000 and in the Eurozone, bonds tend to have face values of €1,000 or €10,000. However, this is not universally followed and can vary with the type of bond.

As we mentioned before, the value of a bond is simply the present value of its cash flows. Therefore, the value of a level coupon bond is merely the present value of its stream of coupon payments plus the present value of its repayment of principal. Because a level coupon bond is just an annuity of C each period, together with a payment at maturity of say, €1,000, the value of a level coupon bond is calculated as follows:

Value of a level coupon bond:

$$PV = \frac{C}{1+R} + \frac{C}{(1+R)^2} + \cdots + \frac{C}{(1+R)^T} + \frac{€1{,}000}{(1+R)^T}$$

where C is the coupon and the face value, F, is €1,000. The value of the bond can be rewritten like this:

Value of a level coupon bond:

$$PV = C \times A_R^T + \frac{€1{,}000}{(1+R)^T}$$

As mentioned in the previous chapter, A_R^T is the present value of an annuity of €1 per period for T periods at an interest rate per period of R.

Example 5.1

Bond Prices

Consider the GlaxoSmithKline bond from Table 5.1 that was issued in December 2014 in the UK. The coupon is 1.375 per cent and the face value is €10,000, implying that the yearly coupon is €137.5 (=1.375% × €10,000). Assume that the coupon is paid annually each December. The face value is paid out in December 2019, that is, 5 years from the issue date. By this we mean that the purchaser obtains claims to the following cash flows:

Dec 2015	Dec 2016	Dec 2017	Dec 2018	Dec 2019
€137.5	€137.5	€137.5	€137.5	€137.5 + €10,000

If the annual interest rate is 1.48 per cent per year, what is the present value of the bond?

Our work on compounding in the previous chapter showed that the present value of the bond is:

$$PV = \frac{€137.5}{(1.0148)} + \frac{€137.5}{(1.0148)^2} + \frac{€137.5}{(1.0148)^3} + \frac{€137.5}{(1.0148)^4} + \frac{€10{,}000 + €137.5}{(1.0148)^5}$$

$$= €9950.1$$

This figure is the same as the price quoted in Table 5.1. Traders will generally quote the bond as 99.501, indicating that it is selling at 99.501 per cent of the face value of €10,000.

One final note concerning level coupon bonds: although the preceding example concerns corporate bonds, government bonds are identical in form. There is no difference in the pricing of government bonds and corporate bonds – the principles are exactly the same.

Consols

Not all bonds have a final maturity date. As we mentioned in the previous chapter, consols are bonds that never stop paying a coupon, have no final maturity date, and therefore never mature. Thus, a consol is a perpetuity, which is the same as the Telefonica bond in Table 5.1.

Governments have also issued consols. In the 18th century, the Bank of England issued 'English consols'. These were bonds that the Bank of England guaranteed would pay the holder a cash flow forever. Through wars and depressions, the Bank of England has continued to honour this commitment, and you can still buy these bonds in London today.

Consols can be valued using the perpetuity formula of the previous chapter. For example, if the market-wide interest rate is 10 per cent, a consol with a yearly interest payment of €50 is valued at:

$$\frac{€50}{0.10} = €500$$

5.3   Bond Concepts

We complete our discussion of bonds by considering two concepts concerning them. First we examine the relationship between interest rates and bond prices. Then we define the concept of yield to maturity.

Interest Rates and Bond Prices

The discussion of level coupon bonds allows us to relate bond prices to interest rates. Consider the following example:

Example 5.2

Bond Valuation

The interest rate is 10 per cent. A 2-year bond with a 10 per cent coupon pays interest of £10 (=£100 × 10%). For simplicity we assume that the interest is paid annually. In this case, we see that the bond is priced at its face value of £100:

$$£100 = \frac{£10}{1.10} + \frac{£100 + £10}{(1.10)^2}$$

If the interest rate unexpectedly rises to 12 per cent, the bond sells at:

$$£96.62 = \frac{£10}{1.12} + \frac{£100 + £10}{(1.12)^2}$$

Because £96.62 is less than £100, the bond is said to sell at a discount. This is a sensible result. Now that the interest rate is 12 per cent, a newly issued bond with a 12 per cent coupon rate will sell at £100. This newly issued bond will have coupon payments of £12 (= 0.12 × £100). Because our bond has interest payments of only £10, investors will pay less than £100 for it.

If interest rates fell to 8 per cent, the bond would sell at:

$$£103.567 = \frac{£10}{1.08} + \frac{£100 + £10}{(1.08)^2}$$

Because £103.567 is more than £100, the bond is said to sell at a premium.

Thus, we find that bond prices fall with a rise in interest rates and rise with a fall in interest rates. Furthermore, the general principle is that a level coupon bond sells in the following ways:

1   At the face value if the coupon rate is equal to the market-wide interest rate
2   At a discount if the coupon rate is below the market-wide interest rate
3   At a premium if the coupon rate is above the market-wide interest rate.

Yield to Maturity

Let us now consider the previous example *in reverse*. If our bond is selling at £103.567, what return is a bondholder receiving? This can be answered by considering the following equation:

$$£103.567 = \frac{£10}{1 + \gamma} + \frac{£100 + £10}{(1 + \gamma)^2}$$

The unknown, γ, is the discount rate that equates the price of the bond with the discounted value of the coupons and face value. Our earlier work implies that $\gamma = 8$ per cent. Thus, traders state that the bond is yielding an 8 per cent return. Bond traders also state that the bond has a yield to maturity of 8 per cent. The yield to maturity is frequently called the bond's *yield* for short. So, we would say the bond with its 10 per cent coupon is priced to yield 8 per cent at £103.567.

The Present Value Formulas for Bonds

Pure discount bonds

$$PV = \frac{F}{(1 + R)^T}$$

Level coupon bonds

$$PV = C\left[\frac{1}{R} - \frac{1}{R \times (1 + R)^T}\right] + \frac{F}{(1 + R)^T} = C \times A_R^T + \frac{F}{(1 + R)^T}$$

where F is the face value.

Consols

$$PV = \frac{C}{R}$$

Real World Insight 5.1

Corporate Bond Yields in the Eurozone

Bond yields for many years have been exceptionally low both in the Eurozone and elsewhere in the world. As of 2015, less than a third of all corporate bonds issued in the Eurozone had a yield of more than 1 per cent. This had significant implications for borrowers and lenders, since it is very cheap to borrow but investors are not getting enough returns to compensate them for the perceived risk of investing in corporate bonds.

For example, half of all companies perceived to be risky by credit rating agencies had bonds with yields less than two per cent. Such low financing costs have pushed bond prices up and made debt financing very attractive to companies wishing to raise capital in the financial markets. As a result, Eurozone investment grade bond issues jumped by 41 per cent in 2014 to €97 billion. Even risky firms jumped on the bond bandwagon with high-yield Eurozone corporate bond issues jumping by 73 per cent in 2014 to €30 billion. All this extra investment is expected to kickstart growth in the Eurozone economy as firms invest in new projects using the money they raised from their bond issues.

5.4 The Present Value of Equity

Dividends versus Capital Gains

Chapter 20
Page 541

Our goal in this section is to value ordinary shares (see **Chapter 20** for more information). We learned in the previous chapter that an asset's value is determined by the present value of its future cash flows. Equities provide two kinds of cash flows. First, they often pay dividends on a regular basis. Second, the shareholder receives the sale price when they are sold. Thus, to value equity, we need to answer an interesting question. Which of the following is its value equal to?

1 The discounted present value of the sum of next period's dividend plus next period's share price
2 The discounted present value of all future dividends.

This is the kind of question that students would love to see in a multiple-choice exam: both (1) and (2) are right.

To see that (1) and (2) are the same, let us start with an individual who will buy the equity and hold it for one year. In other words, she has a one-year *holding period*. In addition, she is willing to pay P_0 for the share today. That is, she calculates:

$$P_0 = \frac{Div_1}{1 + R} + \frac{P_1}{1 + R}$$

(5.1)

Div_1 is the dividend paid at year's end, and P_1 is the price at year's end. P_0 is the PV of the equity investment. The term in the denominator, R, is the appropriate discount rate for the equity.

That seems easy enough; but where does P_1 come from? P_1 is not pulled out of thin air. Rather, there must be a buyer at the end of year 1 who is willing to purchase the equity for P_1. This buyer determines price as follows:

$$P_1 = \frac{Div_2}{1 + R} + \frac{P_2}{1 + R} \tag{5.2}$$

Substituting the value of P_1 from Equation 5.2 into Equation 5.1 yields:

$$P_0 = \frac{1}{1 + R}\left[Div_1 + \left(\frac{Div_2 + P_2}{1 + R}\right)\right]$$
$$= \frac{Div_1}{1 + R} + \frac{Div_2}{(1 + R)^2} + \frac{P_2}{(1 + R)^2} \tag{5.3}$$

We can ask a similar question for Equation 5.3: where does P_2 come from? An investor at the end of year 2 is willing to pay P_2 because of the dividend and share price at year 3. This process can be repeated *ad nauseam*. At the end, we are left with this:

$$P_0 = \frac{Div_1}{1 + R} + \frac{Div_2}{(1 + R)^2} + \frac{Div_3}{(1 + R)^3} + \cdots = \sum_{t=1}^{\infty} \frac{Div_t}{(1 + R)^t} \tag{5.4}$$

Thus, the value of a firm's equity to the investor is equal to the present value of all of the expected future dividends.

This is a very useful result. A common objection to applying present value analysis to equities is that investors are too shortsighted to care about the long-run stream of dividends. These critics argue that an investor will generally not look past his or her time horizon. Thus, prices in a market dominated by short-term investors will reflect only near-term dividends. However, our discussion shows that a long-run dividend discount model holds even when investors have short-term time horizons. Although an investor may want to cash out early, she must find another investor who is willing to buy. The price this second investor pays is dependent on dividends *after* his date of purchase.

Valuation of Different Types of Equities

The preceding discussion shows that the value of the firm is the present value of its future dividends. How do we apply this idea in practice? The above equation represents a very general model and is applicable regardless of whether the level of expected dividends is growing, fluctuating or constant. The general model can be simplified if the firm's dividends are expected to follow some basic patterns: (1) zero growth, (2) constant growth, and (3) differential growth. These cases are illustrated in Figure 5.2.

Figure 5.2 Zero Growth, Constant Growth and Differential Growth Patterns

Case 1 (Zero Growth)

The value of an equity with a constant dividend is given by

$$P_0 = \frac{Div_1}{1 + R} + \frac{Div_2}{(1 + R)^2} + \ldots = \frac{Div_1}{R}$$

Here it is assumed that $Div_1 = Div_2 = \ldots = Div$. This is just an application of the perpetuity formula from a previous chapter.

Case 2   (Constant Growth)

Dividends grow at rate g, as follows:
End of year dividend:

1	2	3	4	...
Div_1	$Div_1(1+g)$	$Div_1(1+g)^2$	$Div_1(1+g)^3$	

Note that Div_1 is the dividend at the end of the *first* period.

Example 5.3

Projected Dividends

Hampshire Products will pay a dividend of £4 per share a year from now. Financial analysts believe that dividends will rise at 6 per cent per year for the foreseeable future. What is the dividend per share at the end of each of the first 5 years? With 6 per cent growth we have this:

End of Year Dividend				
1	2	3	4	5
£4.00	£4 × (1.06) = £4.24	£4 × (1.06)² = £4.4944	£4 × (1.06)³ = £4.7641	£4 × (1.06)⁴ = £5.0499

The value of an equity security with dividends growing at a constant rate is:

$$P_0 = \frac{Div_1}{1+R} + \frac{Div_1(1+g)}{(1+R)^2} + \frac{Div_1(1+g)^2}{(1+R)^3} + \frac{Div_1(1+g)^3}{(1+R)^4} + \ldots = \frac{Div_1}{R-g}$$

where g is the growth rate. Div_1 is the dividend on the equity at the end of the first period. This is the formula for the present value of a growing perpetuity, which we derived in a previous chapter.

Example 5.4

Share Valuation

Suppose an investor is considering the purchase of a share of the Avila Mining Company. The equity will pay a €3 dividend a year from today. This dividend is expected to grow at 10 per cent per year ($g = 10\%$) for the foreseeable future. The investor thinks that the required return (R) on this equity is 15 per cent, given her assessment of Avila Mining's risk. (We also refer to R as the discount rate for the equity.) What is the share price of Avila Mining Company?

Using the constant growth formula of case 2, we assess the value to be €60:

$$€60 = \frac{€3}{0.15 - 0.10}$$

P_0 is quite dependent on the value of g. If g had been estimated to be 12.5 per cent, the share price would have been:

$$€120 = \frac{€3}{0.15 - 0.125}$$

The share price doubles (from €60 to €120) when g increases only 25 per cent (from 10 per cent to 12.5 per cent). Because of P_0's dependence on g, one must maintain a healthy sense of scepticism when using this constant growth of dividends model.

Furthermore, note that P_0 is equal to infinity when the growth rate, g, equals the discount rate, R. Because share prices do not grow infinitely, an estimate of g greater than R implies an error in estimation. More will be said about this point later.

Case 3 (Differential Growth)

In this case, an algebraic formula would be too unwieldy. Instead we present examples.

Example 5.5

Differential Growth

Consider the equity of Mint Drug Company, which has a new massage ointment and is enjoying rapid growth. The dividend per share a year from today will be €1.15. During the following 4 years the dividend will grow at 15 per cent per year ($g_1 = 15\%$). After that, growth (g_2) will equal 10 per cent per year. Can you calculate the present value of the equity if the required return (R) is 15 per cent?

Figure 5.3 displays the growth in the dividends. We need to apply a two-step process to discount these dividends. We first calculate the net present value of the dividends growing at 15 per cent per annum. That is, we first calculate the present value of the dividends at the end of each of the first 5 years. Second, we calculate the present value of the dividends that begin at the end of year 6.

Figure 5.3 Growth in Dividends for Mint Drug Company

Calculate present value of first five dividends   The present value of dividend payments in years 1 through 5 is as follows:

Future Year	Growth Rate (g_1)	Expected Dividend (€)	Present Value (€)
1	0.15	1.15	1
2	0.15	1.3225	1
3	0.15	1.5209	1
4	0.15	1.7490	1
5	0.15	2.0114	1
Years 1–5 The present value of dividends = €5			

The growing annuity formula of the previous chapter could normally be used in this step. However, note that dividends grow at 15 per cent, which is also the discount rate. Because $g = R$, the growing annuity formula cannot be used in this example.

Calculate present value of dividends beginning at end of year 6   This is the procedure for deferred perpetuities and deferred annuities that we mentioned in the previous chapter. The dividends beginning at the end of year 6 are as follows:

End of Year Dividend			
6	**7**	**8**	**9**
$Div_5 \times (1 + g_2)$	$Div_5 \times (1 + g_2)^2$	$Div_5 \times (1 + g_2)^3$	$Div_5 \times (1 + g_2)^4$
€2.0114 × (1.10)	€2.0114 × (1.10)²	€2.0114 × (1.10)³	€2.0114 × (1.10)⁴
= €2.2125	= €2.4338	= €2.6772	= €2.9449

As stated in the previous chapter, the growing perpetuity formula calculates present value as of one year prior to the first payment. Because the payment begins at the end of year 6, the present value formula calculates present value as of the end of year 5.

The price at the end of year 5 is given by

$$P_5 = \frac{Div_6}{R - g_2} = \frac{€2.2125}{0.15 - 0.10}$$

$$= €44.25$$

The present value of P_5 today is

$$\frac{P_5}{(1 + R)^5} = \frac{€44.25}{(1.15)^5} = €22$$

The present value of *all* dividends today is €27 (= €22 + 5).

5.5 Estimates of Parameters in the Dividend Growth Model

The value of the firm is a function of its growth rate, g, and its discount rate, R. How do we estimate these variables?

Where Does g Come From?

The previous discussion of equities assumed that dividends grow at the rate g. We now want to estimate this rate of growth. This section extends the discussion of growth contained in Chapter 3. Consider a business whose earnings next year are expected to be the same as earnings this year unless a *net investment* is made. This situation is likely to occur because net investment is equal to gross, or total, investment less depreciation. A net investment of zero occurs when *total investment* equals depreciation. If total investment is equal to depreciation, the firm's physical plant is maintained, consistent with no growth in earnings.

Net investment will be positive only if some earnings are not paid out as dividends – that is, only if some earnings are retained.[1] This leads to the following equation:

$$
\underset{\text{Increase in earnings}}{\underbrace{\begin{array}{ccccc} \text{Earnings} & & \text{Earnings} & & \text{Retained} & & \text{Return on} \\ \text{next} & = & \text{this} & + & \text{earnings} & \times & \text{retained} \\ \text{year} & & \text{year} & & \text{this year} & & \text{earnings} \end{array}}}
\qquad (5.5)
$$

The increase in earnings is a function of both the *retained earnings* and the *return on the retained earnings*.

We now divide both sides of Equation 5.5 by earnings this year, yielding

$$\frac{\text{Earnings next year}}{\text{Earnings this year}} = \frac{\text{Earnings this year}}{\text{Earnings this year}} + \left(\frac{\text{Retained earnings this year}}{\text{Earnings this year}} \right)$$

$$\times \text{ Return on retained earnings} \qquad (5.6)$$

The left side of Equation 5.6 is simply 1 plus the growth rate in earnings, which we write as $1 + g$. The ratio of retained earnings to earnings is called the **retention ratio**. Thus we can write

$$1 + g = 1 + (\text{Retention ratio} \times \text{Return on retained earnings}) \qquad (5.7)$$

It is difficult for a financial analyst to determine the return to be expected on currently retained earnings: the details on forthcoming projects are not generally public information. However, it is frequently assumed that the projects selected in the current year have an anticipated return equal to returns from projects in other years. Here we can estimate the anticipated return on current retained earnings by the historical return on equity or ROE. After all, ROE is simply the return on the firm's entire equity, which is the return on the accumulation of all the firm's past projects.

From Equation 5.7, we have a simple way to estimate growth:

Formula for firm's growth rate:

$$g = \text{Retention ratio} \times \text{Return on retained earnings} \tag{5.8}$$

Previously, g referred to growth in dividends. However, the growth in earnings is equal to the growth rate in dividends in this context, because as we will presently see, the ratio of dividends to earnings is held constant.[2]

Example 5.6

Earnings Growth

Pagemaster plc just reported earnings of £2 million. It plans to retain 40 per cent of its earnings. The historical return on equity (ROE) has been 16 per cent, a figure that is expected to continue into the future. How much will earnings grow over the coming year?

We first perform the calculation without reference to Equation 5.8. Then, we use Equation 5.8 as a check.

Calculation without reference to Equation 5.8   The firm will retain £800,000 (= 40% × £2 million). Assuming that historical ROE is an appropriate estimate for future returns, the anticipated increase in earnings is:

$$£800,000 \times 0.16 = £128,000$$

The percentage growth in earnings is:

$$\frac{\text{Change in earnings}}{\text{Total earnings}} = \frac{£128,000}{£2\text{ million}} = 0.064$$

This implies that earnings in one year will be £2,128,000 (= £2,000,000 × 1.064).

Check using Equation 5.8   We use g = Retention ratio × ROE. We have:

$$g = 0.4 \times 0.16 = 0.064$$

Where Does R Come From?

Thus far, we have taken the required return, or discount rate R, as given. We will have quite a bit to say about this subject in later chapters. For now, we want to examine the implications of the dividend growth model for this required return. Earlier we calculated P_0 as follows:

$$P_0 = Div_1/(R - g)$$

If we rearrange this to solve for R, we get:

$$R - g = Div_1/P_0$$
$$R = Div_1/P_0 + g \tag{5.9}$$

This tells us that the total return, R, has two components. The first of these, Div_1/P_0, is called the dividend yield. Because this is calculated as the expected cash dividend divided by the current price, it is conceptually similar to the current yield on a bond, which is the annual coupon divided by the bond's price.

The second part of the total return is the growth rate, g. As we will verify shortly, the dividend growth rate is also the rate at which the share price grows. Thus, this growth rate can be interpreted as the capital gains yield – that is, the rate at which the value of the investment grows.

To illustrate the components of the required return, suppose we observe an equity selling for €20 per share. The next dividend will be €1 per share. You think that the dividend will grow by 10 per cent per year more or less indefinitely. What return does this equity offer you if this is correct?

The dividend growth model calculates total return as:

$$R = \text{Dividend yield} + \text{Capital gains yield}$$
$$R = Div_1/P_0 \quad + \quad g$$

In this case, total return works out to be:

$$R = €1/€20 + 10\%$$
$$= 5\% + 10\%$$
$$= 15\%$$

This equity, therefore, has an expected return of 15 per cent.

We can verify this answer by calculating the price in one year, P_1, using 15 per cent as the required return. Based on the dividend growth model, this price is:

$$P_1 = Div_1 \times (1 + g)/(R - g)$$
$$= €1 \times 1.10/(0.15 - 0.10)$$
$$= €1.10/0.05$$
$$= €22$$

Notice that this €22 is €20 × 1.1, so the share price has grown by 10 per cent as it should. If you pay €20 for the shares today, you will get a €1 dividend at the end of the year, and you will have a €22 − 20 = €2 gain. Your dividend yield is thus €1/20 = 5 per cent. Your capital gains yield is €2/20 = 10 per cent, so your total return would be 5 per cent + 10 per cent = 15 per cent.

To get a feel for actual numbers in this context, according to FT.com (who surveyed 25 analysts), the dividends of BP plc, the British energy firm, were expected to grow from $0.365 per share in 2013 to $0.393 in 2014. The share price at that time was $4.294 per share. What is the return investors require on BP? Here, the dividend yield is 9.15 per cent (= $0.393/$4.294) and the capital gains yield is 7.67 per cent (= [$0.393/$0.365] − 1), giving a total estimated required return of 16.82 per cent on BP shares.

Example 5.7

Calculating the Required Return

Pagemaster plc, the company examined in the previous example, has 1,000,000 shares outstanding. The equity is selling at £10. What is the required return on the shares?

Because the retention ratio is 40 per cent, the **payout ratio** is 60 per cent (= 1 − retention ratio). The payout ratio is the ratio of dividends/earnings. Because earnings one year from now will be £2,128,000 (= £2,000,000 × 1.064), dividends will be £1,276,800 (= 0.60 × £2,128,000). Dividends per share will be £1.28 (= £1,276,800/1,000,000). Given our previous result that $g = 0.064$, we calculate R from (5.9) as follows:

$$0.192 = \frac{£1.28}{10.00} + 0.064$$

A Healthy Sense of Scepticism

Our approach merely *estimates* g; it does not *determine* g precisely. The one-year growth rate may not be the appropriate estimate of a long-term sustainable growth rate. For example, if one was to use the growth rate in BP dividends between 2012 and 2013 as the estimate of g, we would have recorded a growth rate for the company of 10.5 per cent, not 7.67 per cent. A possible solution is to consider growth rates over a longer period. So, in the case of BP, the dividend in 2010 was $0.140; in 2011 it was $0.2722; and in 2012 it was $0.330. Taking the 2010 dividend of $0.140, a number of dividend growth rates may be calculated. Closer analysis reveals that the 2010 dividend was abnormally low because of the US Gulf oil spill that the company experienced at that time, so it may be sensible to ignore the 2010 dividend and focus on those from 2011 and 2012. In this situation, it would be wise to use the differential dividend growth rate methodology presented earlier.

Our estimate of g can be based on a number of assumptions. For example, we assume that the return on reinvestment of future retained earnings is equal to the firm's past ROE. We assume that the future retention ratio is equal to the past retention ratio. Our estimate for g will be off if these assumptions prove to be wrong.

Unfortunately, the determination of R is highly dependent on g. For example, if g is estimated to be 0 in Example 5.6, R equals 12.8 per cent (= £1.28/£10.00). If g is estimated to be 12 per cent, R equals 24.8 per cent (= £1.28/£10.00 + 12%). Thus, one should view estimates of R with a healthy sense of scepticism.

Because of the preceding, some financial economists generally argue that the estimation error for R or a single security is too large to be practical. Therefore, they suggest calculating the average R for an entire industry. This R would then be used to discount the dividends of a particular equity in the same industry.

One should be particularly sceptical of two polar cases when estimating R for individual securities. First, consider a firm currently paying no dividend. The share price will be above zero because investors believe that the firm may initiate a dividend at some point or the firm may be acquired at some point. However, when a firm goes from no dividends to a positive number of dividends, the implied growth rate is *infinite*. Thus, Equation 5.9 must be used with extreme caution here, if at all – a point we emphasize later in this chapter.

Second, we mentioned earlier that the value of the firm is infinite when g is equal to R. Because share prices do not grow infinitely, an analyst whose estimate of g for a particular firm is equal to or above R will clearly be wrong. Firms simply cannot maintain an abnormally high growth rate *forever*.

Real World Insight 5.2

Valuing Smartphone App Companies

How do you value a company that sells smartphone and tablet apps? Take the Swedish firm, King Digital Entertainment, which makes the Candy Crush Saga game for Android and IOS platforms. In 2015, the firm announced plans to issue its shares on the New York Stock Exchange for a total value of $5 billion.

King Digital Entertainment has seen huge growth in recent years and by the end of 2014 had 324 million monthly users. According to its prospectus, adjusted earnings before interest, tax, depreciation and amortization rose from $4m in 2011 to $825m in 2013. Full-year sales rose to $1.8bn with a pre-tax profit of $714m. The average revenue per employee in 2013 was $2.7m.

To value King Digital Entertainment, you would need to estimate its growth in future revenues. However, with a single game company, a key factor will be the likelihood of the company making more smash-hit games in the future. This is clearly a difficult task!

To illustrate, Zynga is a similar company to King Digital Entertainment, and is famous for its Farmville series of games. Zynga listed its equity in 2011 at just under $10 and very quickly the share price reached $14.69. However, as opportunities failed to emerge, the price fell to $2.24, to reflect the changing expectations of future revenue growth.

5.6   Growth Opportunities

We previously spoke of the growth rate of dividends. We now want to address the related concept of growth opportunities. Imagine a company with a level stream of earnings per share in perpetuity. The company pays all of these earnings out to shareholders as dividends.

Hence we have:

$$EPS = Div$$

where *EPS* is *earnings per share* and *Div* is dividends per share. A company of this type is frequently called a *cash cow*.

The perpetuity formula of the previous chapter gives the value of a share of equity:

Value of a share of equity when a firm acts as a cash cow:

$$\frac{EPS}{R} = \frac{Div}{R}$$

where R is the discount rate on the firm's equity.

This policy of paying out all earnings as dividends may not be the optimal one. Many firms have *growth opportunities*: opportunities to invest in profitable projects. Because these projects can represent a significant fraction of the firm's value, it would be foolish to forgo them in order to pay out all earnings as dividends.

Although firms frequently think in terms of a *set* of growth opportunities, let us focus on only one opportunity – that is, the opportunity to invest in a single project. Suppose the firm retains the entire dividend at date 1 to invest in a particular capital budgeting project. The net present value *per share* of the project as of date 0 is *NPVGO*, which stands for the *net present value (per share) of the growth opportunity*.

What is the share price at date 0 if the firm decides to take on the project at date 1? Because the per share value of the project is added to the original share price, the share price must now be this:

Share price after firm commits to new project:

$$\frac{EPS}{R} + NPVGO \qquad (5.10)$$

Thus Equation 5.10 indicates that the share price can be viewed as the sum of two different items. The first term (*EPS/R*) is the value of the firm if it rested on its laurels – that is, if it simply distributed all earnings to the shareholders. The second term is the *additional* value if the firm retains earnings to fund new projects.

Example 5.8

Growth Opportunities

Sarro Shipping plc expects to earn £1 million per year in perpetuity if it undertakes no new investment opportunities. There are 100,000 shares of equity outstanding, so earnings per share equal £10 (=£1,000,000/100,000). The firm will have an opportunity at date 1 to spend £1,000,000 on a new marketing campaign. The new campaign will increase earnings in every subsequent period by £210,000 (or £2.10 per share). This is a 21 per cent return per year on the project. The firm's discount rate is 10 per cent. What is the share price before and after deciding to accept the marketing campaign?

The share price of Sarro Shipping before the campaign is

Share price of Sarro when firm acts as a cash cow:

$$\frac{EPS}{R} = \frac{£10}{0.1} = £100$$

The value of the marketing campaign as of date 1 is

Value of marketing campaign at date 1:

$$-£1,000,000 + \frac{£210,000}{0.1} = £1,100,000 \qquad (5.11)$$

Because the investment is made at date 1 and the first cash inflow occurs at date 2, Equation 5.11 represents the value of the marketing campaign as of date 1. We determine the value at date 0 by discounting back one period as follows:

Value of marketing campaign at date 0:

$$\frac{£1,100,000}{1.1} = £1,000,000$$

Thus NPVGO per share is £10 (= £1,000,000/100,000).

The share price is

$$EPS/R + NPVGO = £100 + 10 = £110$$

The calculation in our example can also be made on a straight net present value basis. Because all the earnings at date 1 are spent on the marketing effort, no dividends are paid to shareholders at that date. Dividends in all subsequent periods are £1,210,000 (= £1,000,000 + £210,000). In this case £1,000,000 is the annual dividend when Sarro is a cash cow. The additional contribution to the dividend from the marketing effort is £210,000. Dividends per share are £12.10 (= £1,210,000/100,000). Because these dividends start at date 2, the share price at date 1 is £121 (= £12.10/0.1). The share price at date 0 is £110 (= £121/1.1).

Note that value is created in this example because the project earned a 21 per cent rate of return when the discount rate was only 10 per cent. No value would have been created had the project earned a 10 per cent rate of return. The NPVGO would have been zero, and value would have been negative had the project earned a percentage return below 10 per cent. The NPVGO would be negative in that case.

Two conditions must be met in order to increase value:

1   Earnings must be retained so that projects can be funded[3]
2   The projects must have positive net present value.

Surprisingly, a number of companies seem to invest in projects known to have *negative* net present values. For example, in the late 1970s, oil companies and tobacco companies were flush with cash. Due to declining markets in both industries, high dividends and low investment would have been the rational action. Unfortunately, a number of companies in both industries reinvested heavily in what were widely perceived to be negative NPVGO projects.

Given that NPV analysis (such as that presented in the previous chapter) is common knowledge in business, why would managers choose projects with negative NPVs? One conjecture is that some managers enjoy controlling a large company. Because paying dividends in lieu of reinvesting earnings reduces the size of the firm, some managers find it emotionally difficult to pay high dividends.

Growth in Earnings and Dividends versus Growth Opportunities

As mentioned earlier, a firm's value increases when it invests in growth opportunities with positive NPVGOs. A firm's value falls when it selects opportunities with negative NPVGOs. However, dividends grow whether projects with positive NPVs or negative NPVs are selected. This surprising result can be explained by the following example.

Example 5.9

NPV versus Dividends

Lane Supermarkets, a new firm, will earn €100,000 a year in perpetuity if it pays out all its earnings as dividends. However, the firm plans to invest 20 per cent of its earnings in projects that earn 10 per cent per year. The discount rate is 18 per cent. An earlier formula tells us that the growth rate of dividends is:

$$g = \text{Retention ratio} \times \text{Return on retained earnings} = 0.2 \times 0.10 = 2\%$$

For example, in this first year of the new policy, dividends are €80,000 [= (1 − 0.2) × €100,000]. Dividends next year are €81,600 (= €80,000 × 1.02). Dividends the following year are €83,232 [= €80,000 × $(1.02)^2$] and so on. Because dividends represent a fixed percentage of earnings, earnings must grow at 2 per cent a year as well.

However, note that the policy reduces value because the rate of return on the projects of 10 per cent is less than the discount rate of 18 per cent. That is, the firm would have had a higher value at date 0 if it had a policy of paying all its earnings out as dividends. Thus, a policy of investing in projects with negative NPVs rather than paying out earnings as dividends will lead to growth in dividends and earnings, but will reduce value.

Dividends or Earnings: Which to Discount?

As mentioned earlier, this chapter applied the growing perpetuity formula to the valuation of equity. In our application, we discounted dividends, not earnings. This is sensible because investors select shares for what they can get out of them. They get only two things out of shares: dividends and the ultimate sale price, which is determined by what future investors expect to receive in dividends.

The calculated share price would be too high were earnings to be discounted instead of dividends. As we saw in our estimation of a firm's growth rate, only a portion of earnings goes to the shareholders as dividends. The remainder is retained to generate future dividends. In our model, retained earnings are equal to the firm's investment. To discount earnings instead of dividends would be to ignore the investment a firm must make today to generate future returns.

The No-dividend Firm

Students frequently ask the following question: if the dividend discount model is correct, why aren't no-dividend shares selling at zero? This is a good question and gets at the goals of the firm. A firm with many growth opportunities faces a dilemma. The firm can pay out dividends now, or it can forgo dividends now so that it can make investments that will generate even greater dividends in the future.[4] This is often a painful choice because a strategy of dividend deferment may be optimal yet unpopular among certain shareholders.

Many firms choose to pay no dividends – and these firms sell at positive prices. For example, most Internet firms, such as Facebook, Groupon, Amazon.com, Google and eBay, pay no dividends. Rational shareholders believe that either they will receive dividends at some point or they will receive something just as good. That is, the firm will be acquired in a merger, with the shareholders receiving either cash or shares of equity at that time.

Of course, the actual application of the dividend discount model is difficult for firms of this type. Clearly the model for constant growth of dividends does not apply. Though the differential growth model can work in theory, the difficulties of estimating the date of first dividend, the growth rate of dividends after that date, and the ultimate merger price make application of the model quite difficult in reality.

Empirical evidence suggests that firms with high growth rates are likely to pay lower dividends, a result consistent with the analysis here. For example, consider Microsoft Corporation. The company started in the 1970s and grew rapidly for many years. It paid its first dividend in 2003, though it was a billion-dollar company (in both sales and market value of shareholders' equity) prior to that date. Why did it wait so long to pay a dividend? It waited because it had so many positive growth opportunities (additional locations for new outlets) of which to take advantage.

5.7   The Dividend Growth Model and the NPVGO Model

This chapter has revealed that the share price is the sum of its price as a cash cow plus the per-share value of its growth opportunities. The Sarro Shipping example illustrated this formula using only one growth opportunity. We also used the growing perpetuity formula to price an equity security with a steady growth in dividends. When the formula is applied to shares, it is typically called the *dividend growth model*. A steady growth in dividends results from a continual investment in growth opportunities, not just investment in a single opportunity. Therefore, it is worthwhile to compare the dividend growth model with the *NPVGO model* when growth occurs through continual investing.

We can use an example to illustrate the main points. Suppose Manama Books has EPS of €10 at the end of the first year, a dividend payout ratio of 40 per cent, a discount rate of 16 per cent, and a return on its retained earnings of 20 per cent. Because the firm retains some of its earnings each year, it is selecting growth opportunities each year. This is different from Sarro Shipping, which had a growth opportunity in only one year. We wish to calculate the price per share using both the dividend growth model and the NPVGO model.

The Dividend Growth Model

The dividends at date 1 are $0.40 \times €10 = €4$ per share. The retention ratio is $0.60 \ (1 - 40)$, implying a growth rate in dividends of $0.12 \ (= 0.60 \times 0.20)$.

From the dividend growth model, the price of a share today is

$$\frac{Div_1}{R - g} = \frac{€4}{0.16 - 0.12} = €100$$

The NPVGO Model

Using the NPVGO model, it is more difficult to value a firm with growth opportunities each year (like Manama) than a firm with growth opportunities in only one year (like Sarro). To value according to the NPVGO model, we need to calculate on a per-share basis (1) the net present value of a single growth opportunity, (2) the net present value of all growth opportunities, and (3) the share price if the firm acts as a cash cow – that is, the value of the firm without these growth opportunities. The value of the firm is the sum of (2) + (3).

1   *Value per share of a single growth opportunity*: Out of the earnings per share of €10 at date 1, the firm retains €6 $(= 0.6 \times €10)$ at that date. The firm earns €1.20 $(= €6 \times 0.20)$ per year in perpetuity on that €6 investment. The NPV from the investment is calculated as follows:

Per-share NPV generated from investment at date 1:

$$-€6 + \frac{€1.20}{0.16} = €1.50 \tag{5.12}$$

That is, the firm invests €6 to reap €1.20 per year on the investment. The earnings are discounted at 16 per cent, implying a value per share from the project of €1.50. Because the investment occurs at date 1 and the first cash flow occurs at date 2, €1.50 is the value of the investment at *date 1*. In other words, the NPV from the date 1 investment has *not* yet been brought back to date 0.

2   *Value per share of all opportunities*: As pointed out earlier, the growth rate of earnings and dividends is 12 per cent. Because retained earnings are a fixed percentage of total earnings, retained earnings must also grow at 12 per cent a year. That is, retained earnings at date 2 are €6.72 $(= €6 \times 1.12)$, retained earnings at date 3 are €7.5264 $[= €6 \times (1.12)^2]$, and so on.

Let us analyse the retained earnings at date 2 in more detail. Because projects will always earn 20 per cent per year, the firm earns €1.344 (= €6.72 × 0.20) in each future year on the €6.72 investment at date 2.

Here is the NPV from the investment:

NPV per share generated from investment at date 2:

$$-€6.72 + \frac{€1.344}{0.16} = €1.68 \tag{5.13}$$

€1.68 is the NPV as of date 2 of the investment made at date 2. The NPV from the date 2 investment has *not* yet been brought back to date 0.

Now consider the retained earnings at date 3 in more detail. The firm earns €1.5053 (= €7.5264 × 0.20) per year on the investment of €7.5264 at date 3.

The NPV from the investment is thus:

NPV per share generated from investment at date 3:

$$-€7.5264 + \frac{€1.5053}{0.16} = €1.882 \tag{5.14}$$

From Equations 5.12, 5.13 and 5.14, the NPV per share of all of the growth opportunities, discounted back to date 0, is:

$$\frac{€1.50}{1.16} + \frac{€1.68}{(1.16)^2} + \frac{€1.882}{(1.16)^3} + \dots \tag{5.15}$$

Because it has an infinite number of terms, this expression looks quite difficult to compute. However, there is an easy simplification. Note that retained earnings are growing at 12 per cent per year. Because all projects earn the same rate of return per year, the NPVs in Equations 5.12, 5.13 and 5.14 are also growing at 12 per cent per year. Hence, we can write Equation 5.15 as:

$$\frac{€1.50}{1.16} + \frac{€1.50 \times 1.12}{(1.16)^2} + \frac{€1.50 \times (1.12)^2}{(1.16)^3} + \dots$$

This is a growth perpetuity whose value is:

$$\text{NPVGO} = \frac{€1.50}{0.16 - 0.12} = €37.50$$

Because the first NPV of €1.50 occurs at date 1, the NPVGO is €37.50 as of date 0. In other words, the firm's policy of investing in new projects from retained earnings has an NPV of €37.50.

3   *Value per share if the firm is a cash cow:* We now assume that the firm pays out all of its earnings as dividends. The dividends would be €10 per year in this case. Because there would be no growth, the value per share would be evaluated by the perpetuity formula:

$$\frac{Div}{R} = \frac{€10}{0.16} = €62.50$$

Summation

Equation 5.10 states that share price is the value of a cash cow plus the value of the growth opportunities. This is

$$€100 = €62.50 + €37.50$$

Hence, value is the same whether calculated by a discounted dividend approach or a growth opportunities approach. The share prices from the two approaches must be equal because the approaches are different yet equivalent methods of applying concepts of present value.

5.8   Stock Market Reporting

If you visit Yahoo! Finance, Reuters or FT.com, you will find information about a large number of equities in several different markets. Figure 5.4 reproduces a small section of the FT.com page from 5 December 2014 for BP plc, listed on the London Stock Exchange. Information on most listed equities is reported in the same way.

Figure 5.4 FT.com Listing for BP plc on 5 December 2014

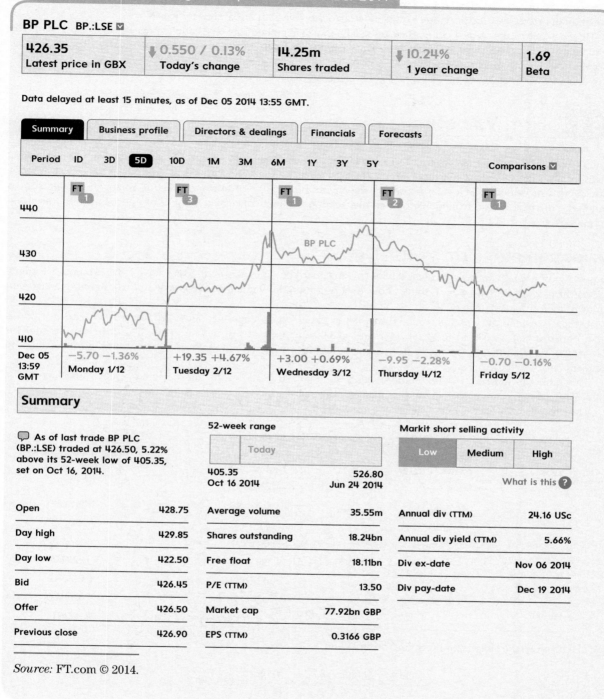

BP PLC BP.:LSE ▾

| **426.35** Latest price in GBX | ↓ **0.550 / 0.13%** Today's change | **14.25m** Shares traded | ↓ **10.24%** 1 year change | **1.69** Beta |

Data delayed at least 15 minutes, as of Dec 05 2014 13:55 GMT.

| Summary | Business profile | Directors & dealings | Financials | Forecasts |

| Period | ID | 3D | **5D** | 10D | 1M | 3M | 6M | 1Y | 3Y | 5Y | Comparisons ▾ |

| Dec 05 13:59 GMT | −5.70 −1.36% Monday 1/12 | +19.35 +4.67% Tuesday 2/12 | +3.00 +0.69% Wednesday 3/12 | −9.95 −2.28% Thursday 4/12 | −0.70 −0.16% Friday 5/12 |

Summary

💬 As of last trade BP PLC (BP.:LSE) traded at 426.50, 5.22% above its 52-week low of 405.35, set on Oct 16, 2014.

52-week range

Today

| 405.35 Oct 16 2014 | 526.80 Jun 24 2014 |

Markit short selling activity

| Low | Medium | High |

What is this ❓

Open	428.75	Average volume	35.55m	Annual div (TTM)	24.16 USc
Day high	429.85	Shares outstanding	18.24bn	Annual div yield (TTM)	5.66%
Day low	422.50	Free float	18.11bn	Div ex-date	Nov 06 2014
Bid	426.45	P/E (TTM)	13.50	Div pay-date	Dec 19 2014
Offer	426.50	Market cap	77.92bn GBP		
Previous close	426.90	EPS (TTM)	0.3166 GBP		

Source: FT.com © 2014.

Chapter 10
Page 253

The first line has the name of the firm plus its identifying code (LSE: BP.L). These identify the company's equity on the London Stock Exchange. Latest Price refers to the last trade in the equity prior to the time of the printout. In this case, the last transaction price was at 1.55 p.m. The table also shows that the price has fallen by £0.0055 from the previous day's closing price of £4.2690 (£4.2635 + £0.0055), and by 10.24 per cent from the one year before. As of 1.55 p.m., 14.25 million shares of BP had been traded on 5 December 2014. The Beta of BP plc is a measure of risk, which will be discussed in much greater detail in **Chapter 10**.

The opening price of £4.2875 is the price that the equity started trading on 5 December 2014. The Bid and Offer prices are the prices that an investor can sell and buy BP plc shares on the London Stock Exchange. Looking at the variation in prices over the previous 5 days illustrates the volatility of BP share prices.

BP plc is one of the largest companies in the UK, and 35.55 million shares change hands on an average day. The total value of BP's shares was £77.92 billion. The earnings per share of BP over the past 12 months (TTM stands for 'Trailing Twelve Months') was £0.3166.

5.9   Firm Valuation

A look back at Chapter 1 shows that the assets of a firm are equal in value to the sum of a firm's liabilities and equity. Using the techniques in this chapter to value bonds and equity can assist you in the valuation process. However, firm valuation is a very imprecise science and the range of uncertainties the financial manager faces can make the task a very formidable one. In this section, we will consider a number of approaches that are used in practice.

Valuation of a Firm's Cash Flows

Suppose you are a business appraiser trying to determine the value of small companies. How can you determine what a firm is worth? One way to think about the question of how much a firm is worth is to calculate the present value of its future cash flows.

Let us consider the example of a firm that is expected to generate net cash flows (cash inflows minus cash outflows) of £5,000 in the first year and £2,000 for each of the next 5 years. The firm can be sold for £10,000 in 7 years' time. The owners of the firm would like to be able to make 10 per cent on their investment in the firm.

The value of the firm is found by multiplying the net cash flows by the appropriate present value factor. The value of the firm is simply the sum of the present values of the individual net cash flows.

The present value of the net cash flows is given next.

The Present Value of the Firm			
End of Year	Net Cash Flow of the Firm (£)	Present Value Factor (10%)	Present Value of Net Cash Flows (£)
1	5,000	0.90909	4,545.45
2	2,000	0.82645	1,652.90
3	2,000	0.75131	1,502.62
4	2,000	0.68301	1,366.02
5	2,000	0.62092	1,241.84
6	2,000	0.56447	1,128.94
7	10,000	0.51316	5,131.58
		Present value of firm	16,569.35

We can also use the simplifying formula for an annuity:

$$\frac{£5,000}{1.1} + \frac{(2,000 \times A^5_{0.10})}{1.1} + \frac{10,000}{(1.1)^7} = £16,569.35$$

Suppose you have the opportunity to acquire the firm for £12,000. Should you acquire the firm? The answer is yes because the NPV is positive:

$$NPV = PV - Cost$$

$$£4,569.35 = £16,569.35 - £12,000$$

The incremental value (NPV) of acquiring the firm is £4,569.35.

Example 5.10

Firm Valuation

Del Piero's Pizza Company is contemplating investing €1 million in four new outlets in Italy. Mr Prandelli, the firm's chief financial officer (CFO), has estimated that the investments will pay out cash flows of €200,000 per year for 9 years and nothing thereafter. (The cash flows will occur at the end of each year and there will be no cash flow after year 9.) Mr Prandelli has determined that the relevant discount rate for this investment is 15 per cent. This is the rate of return that the firm can earn on comparable projects. Should Del Piero make the investments in the new outlets?

The decision can be evaluated as follows:

$$NPV = -€1,000,000 + \frac{€200,000}{1.15} + \frac{€200,000}{(1.15)^2} + \ldots + \frac{€200,000}{(1.15)^9}$$

$$= -€1,000,000 + €200,000 \times A^9_{0.15}$$

$$= -€1,000,000 + €954,316.78$$

$$= -€45,683.22$$

The present value of the four new outlets is only €954,316.78. The outlets are worth less than they cost. Del Piero should not make the investment because the NPV is −€45,683.22. If Del Piero requires a 15 per cent rate of return, the new outlets are not a good investment.

Chapter 3
Page 64

When valuing another firm, the financial manager will not normally have estimates of future cash flows to hand. As a result, other sources of information must be used. **Chapter 3** illustrated the use of financial statements in assessing a firm's performance and growth rate. If the firm is listed on a stock exchange, past share price performance and volatility can also be used. Finally, comparative information on a firm's peers is necessary to calibrate your initial valuations.

The Price–Earnings Ratio

Chapter 3
Page 73

We argued earlier that one should not discount earnings to determine the share price. Nevertheless, financial analysts frequently relate earnings and share price, as made evident by their heavy reliance on the price–earnings (or PE) ratio (see **Chapter 3**, section 3.7 for more information).

Our previous discussion stated that:

$$\text{Price per share} = \frac{EPS}{R} + NPVGO$$

Dividing by *EPS* yields:

$$\frac{\text{Price per share}}{EPS} = \frac{1}{R} + \frac{NPVGO}{EPS}$$

The left side is the formula for the price–earnings ratio. The equation shows that the PE ratio is related to the net present value of growth opportunities. As an example, consider two firms, each having just reported earnings per share of £1. However, one firm has many valuable growth opportunities, whereas the other firm has no growth opportunities at all. The firm with growth opportunities should sell at a higher price because an investor is buying both current income of £1 and growth opportunities. Suppose that the firm with growth opportunities sells for £16 and the other firm sells for £8. The £1 earnings per share number appears in the denominator of the PE ratio for both firms. Thus, the PE ratio is 16 for the firm with growth opportunities but only 8 for the firm without the opportunities.

This explanation seems to hold fairly well in the real world. Electronic and other high-tech shares generally sell at very high PE ratios (or *multiples*, as they are often called) because they are perceived to have high growth rates. In fact, some technology shares sell at high prices even though the companies have never earned a profit. Conversely, railroads, utilities and steel companies sell at lower multiples because of the prospects of lower growth. Table 5.2 contains PE ratios in 2015 for different UK industries. Notice the variation across industries and how the PE ratios are related to growth opportunities. They are also much higher than the historical average for the stock market of around 14. Is this a sign of real growth opportunities for firms or are stock market valuations too high? Only time will tell!

Table 5.2 Selected PE Ratios

Industry	PE Ratio	Industry	PE Ratio
Oil and Gas	12.91	Utilities	17.02
Basic Materials	9.53	Financials	18.38
Industrials	18.92	Non-financials	33.64
Consumer Goods	18.41	Technology	35.74
Health Care	22.73	Travel and Leisure	22.90
Consumer Services	18.41	Oil Equipment and Services	12.66
Telecommunications	9.93	General Retailers	17.92

Source: Datastream, 2015.

Of course, the market is merely pricing *perceptions* of the future, not the future itself. We will argue later in the text that the stock market generally has realistic perceptions of a firm's prospects. However, this is not always true. In the late 1960s, many electronics firms were selling at multiples of 200 times earnings. The high perceived growth rates did not materialize, causing great declines in share prices during the early 1970s. In earlier decades, fortunes were made in equities like IBM and Xerox because the high growth rates were not anticipated by investors. More recently, we have experienced the dot-com collapse when many Internet stocks were trading at multiples of thousands of times annual earnings. In fact, most Internet stocks had no earnings.

There is an additional factor that explains the PE ratio, and this is the discount rate, R. The previous formula shows that the PE ratio is *negatively* related to the firm's discount rate. We have already suggested that the discount rate is positively related to the equity's risk or variability. Thus the PE ratio is negatively related to the equity's risk. To see that this is a sensible result, consider two firms, A and B, behaving as cash cows. The stock market *expects* both firms to have annual earnings of €1 per share forever. However, the earnings of firm A are known with certainty, whereas the earnings of firm B are quite variable. A rational investor is likely to pay more for a share of firm A because of the absence of risk. If a share of firm A sells at a higher price and both firms have the same EPS, the PE ratio of firm A must be higher.

Free Cash Flow to the Firm

Chapter 3
Page 64

In many countries, firms also repurchase equity from shareholders as a substitute for paying dividends.[5] This makes the dividend valuation models presented in this chapter more difficult to implement because we must not only value dividends but also value the present value of future share repurchases. An alternative solution is to value the cash flows that could accrue to the firm taking out the effect of financing. This is done through the cash flow statement that is provided every year in the financial accounts (see **Chapter 3**). Free cash flow to the firm (FCFF) can be calculated from either the income statement or the cash flow statement. Under International Accounting Standards, it is fairly straightforward to arrive at FCFF from the statement of cash flows and this is what we will do in this section. The formula for FCFF (taking outflows as negative) is as follows:

$$\text{FCFF} = \text{Cash flow from operations} + \text{Cash flow from investing activities} \tag{5.16}$$

Under International Accounting Standards, firms will normally include interest expense under the heading *Cash Flow from Financing Activities*. However, they have the option to include interest under *Cash Flow from Operations* if the interest is viewed to be part of a firm's operations. When this is the case, Equation 5.16 should be modified as follows:

$$\text{FCFF} = \text{Cash flow from operations} + \text{Cash flow from investing activities}$$
$$+ \text{Net interest payment} \times (1 - \text{Tax rate}) \tag{5.17}$$

Example 5.11

Free Cash Flow to the Firm

BP plc had the following statement of cash flows ($ millions) for 2013. What is the free cash flow to the firm?

Cash flow from operations	21,100
Cash flow from investing activities	−7,855
Cash flow from financing activities	−10,400

The statement of cash flows included interest payments of $1,084 million under *Cash Flow from Operations*. The tax rate is 26 per cent.

FCFF is calculated as follows:

$$FCFF = \$21,100 - \$7,855 + (1 - 0.26) \times \$1,084 = \$14,047.16$$

Once FCFF has been calculated, it is a simple matter to discount the cash flows using the appropriate discount for the firm's operations. It is important to note that the discount rate used in the free cash flow valuation method will be different from the rate used for the dividend growth model. This is because the FCFF discount rate reflects the risk of the firm whereas the discount rate used in the dividend growth model reflects the risk of the firm's equity. When a firm has no debt, the two discount rates will be the same.[6]

Example 5.12

FCFF Valuation

In Example 5.11, we estimated that BP plc had a FCFF of $14,047.16 million in 2013. If the appropriate discount rate for BP is 12 per cent and the company's cash flows are expected to grow at 3 per cent every year, what was the value of BP in 2013?

To estimate the value of BP we use the following valuation formula:

$$V_0 = \frac{FCFF_1}{r-g} = \frac{FCFF_0\,(1+g)}{r-g} = \frac{\$14,047.16(1.03)}{0.12 - 0.03}$$

$$= \$160,761.94 \text{ million}$$

Summary and Conclusions

In this chapter, we used general present value formulas from the previous chapter to price bonds and equities.

1   Pure discount bonds and perpetuities can be viewed as the polar cases of bonds. The value of a pure discount bond (also called a zero coupon bond) is:

$$PV = \frac{F}{(1+R)^T}$$

The value of a perpetuity (also called a *consol*) is:

$$PV = \frac{C}{R}$$

2   Level payment bonds can be viewed as an intermediate case. The coupon payments form an annuity, and the principal repayment is a lump sum. The value of this type of bond is simply the sum of the values of its two parts.

3   The yield to maturity on a bond is the single rate that discounts the payments on the bond to its purchase price.

4   An equity can be valued by discounting its dividends. We mentioned three types of situations:

(a) The case of zero growth of dividends

(b) The case of constant growth of dividends

(c) The case of differential growth.

5   An estimate of the growth rate of an equity is needed for the formulas for situations 4(b) or 4(c). A useful estimate of the growth rate is

$$g = \text{Retention ratio} \times \text{Return on retained earnings}$$

6   It is worthwhile to view a share as the sum of its worth if the company behaves like a cash cow (the company does no investing) and the value per share of its growth opportunities. We write the value of a share as:

$$\frac{EPS}{R} + NPVGO$$

We showed that, in theory, the share price must be the same whether the dividend growth model or the formula here is used.

7   From accounting, we know that earnings are divided into two parts: dividends and retained earnings. Most firms continually retain earnings to create future dividends. One should not discount earnings to obtain the share price because part of earnings must be reinvested. Only dividends reach the shareholders, and only they should be discounted to obtain share price.

8   We suggested that a firm's price–earnings ratio is a function of three factors:

(a) The per-share amount of the firm's valuable growth opportunities

(b) The risk of the share price

(c) The type of accounting method used by the firm.

9   A firm can be valued via its free cash flow by estimating the amount of cash available to the company to either invest or pay out as dividends. The free cash flow to the firm (FCFF) formula is:

$$V_0 = \frac{FCFF_1}{r - g}$$

where $FCFF_1$ is the free cash flow to the firm at time 1, r is the discount rate of the firm and g is the growth rate in the cash flows of the firm.

Questions and Problems

CONCEPT

1   **Definition of a Bond**   What are the main characteristics of a bond? Provide examples of different types of bonds in terms of coupons, maturity and face value.

2   **Bond Valuation**   Show how you would value a level coupon bond and a zero coupon bond. How would you value a bond with a changing coupon rate?

3   **Bond Concepts**   Explain the difference between a coupon rate and a yield to maturity. Show, using examples, how changing the coupon rate and yield to maturity affects the bond price.

4   **The Present Value of Equity**   Explain why the share price depends on dividends and capital gains.

5   **The Dividend Growth Model**   Under what two assumptions can we use the dividend growth model to determine the share price? Comment on the reasonableness of these assumptions.

6   **Growth Opportunities**   In the context of the dividend growth model, is it true that the growth rate in dividends and the growth rate in the share price are identical?

7   **Net Present Value of Growth Opportunities**   Explain what is meant by NPVGO. In what circumstances is calculating the NPVGO better than other methods of share valuation?

8 **Price–Earnings Ratio**   What are the three factors that determine a company's price–earnings ratio? Explain the possible reasons why the PE ratios vary between firms within the same sector, and between firms in different sectors.

9 **Stock Market Reporting**   What information might a financial analyst need when valuing a company's prospects? Comment on the usefulness of this information.

> REGULAR

10 **Valuing Bonds**   A 30-year gilt is issued with face value of £100, paying interest of £20 per year. If market yields increase shortly after the bond is issued, what happens to the:

   (a) Coupon rate

   (b) Price

   (c) Yield to maturity

   (d) Current yield?

11 **Bond Yields**   In March 2012, the French bank, RCI Banque, issued an 18-month bond with a face value of €10,000, and an annual coupon rate of 2 per cent, paid every quarter. The issue price was €9,984.50. What was its YTM?

12 **Share Values**   Your manager has obtained the following information on comparable stocks A and B, both of which are estimated to have a discount rate of 15 per cent.

	Stock A	Stock B
Return on equity	15%	10%
Earnings per share	£2.00	£1.50
Dividends per share	£ 1.00	£1.00

Calculate the dividend payout ratios for each firm, the expected dividend growth rates for each firm and the 'true' stock price for each firm.

13 **Share Values**   A2A SpA is an Italian utility firm. Its most recent dividend was €0.013 per share. In the past year, the company has experienced financial difficulties and the share price has dropped by more than 20 per cent. However, long-term growth in dividends is anticipated to be 7 per cent forever. If A2A shares currently sell for €0.52, what is the required return? Does this make sense? Explain.

14 **Share Values**   ABC plc pays dividends that are expected to grow at 5 per cent each year. These will stop in year 5, at which point the company will pay out all its earnings as dividends. Next year's dividend is £0.87 and its EPS at the time will be £2.02. If the appropriate discount rate on ABC plc shares is 14 per cent, what is its share price today?

15 **Growth Opportunities**   If Severn Trent plc were to distribute all its earnings, it could maintain a level dividend stream of £0.67 per share. How much is the market actually paying per share for growth opportunities?

16 **Equity Valuation**   XYZ plc will pay a dividend next year of 40p per share, and it is estimated that XYZ's dividend will increase by 4 per cent per year forever. Investors in XYZ require a rate of return of 10 per cent. What is the share price of XYZ plc?

17 **Bond Price Movements**   Define each of the following terms:

   (i) Treasury bill

   (ii) Pure discount bond

   (iii) Index-linked bond.

   Which G7 country has the highest average maturity of debt stock? Why do you think this is?

18 **Bond Returns**   The UK government issues a 5-year bond which makes annual coupon payments of 5 per cent and offers a yield of 3 per cent annually compounded. Suppose that one year later the bond still yields 3 per cent. What return has the bondholder earned over the 12-month period? Now suppose that the bond yields 2 per cent at the end of the year. What return would the bondholder earn in this case?

19 **Non-constant Growth**   Dylan Bearings is a young start-up company. No dividends will be paid on the shares over the next 9 years because the firm needs to plough back its earnings to fuel growth. The company will pay an £8 per share dividend in 10 years and will increase the dividend by 6 per cent per year thereafter. If the required return is 13 per cent, what is the current share price?

20 **Valuing Preference Shares** Mark Bank has just issued some new preference shares. The issue will pay a £5 annual dividend in perpetuity, beginning 4 years from now. If the market requires an 8 per cent return on this investment, how much do preference shares cost today?

21 **Non-constant Growth** The return on equity (ROE) of Child SA is 14 per cent and it has a payout ratio of 0.5. Current book value per share is €50 and the book value will grow as the firm reinvests earnings. Assume that the ROE and payout ratio stay constant for the next 4 years. After that, competition forces ROE down to 11.5 per cent, and the payout ratio increases to 0.8. The appropriate discount rate is 11.5 per cent. What are Child's EPS and dividends next year? How will EPS and dividends grow in years 2, 3, 4, 5 and subsequent years? What is Child's share price? How does that value depend on the payout ratio and growth rate after year 4?

22 **Semi-annual Dividends** The Belgian food group, Delhaize, has just paid a dividend of €1.08. This is paid in semi-annual instalments. The firm has a policy to pay out 75 per cent of its annual dividend after 6 months and the remaining amount at the end of the year. If the annual discount rate on Delhaize shares is 8 per cent and the dividend is expected to grow at 3 per cent per year, what is the current share price of Delhaize?

23 **Finding the Required Return** Regenboog NV earned €68 million for the fiscal year ending yesterday. The firm also paid out 25 per cent of its earnings as dividends yesterday. The firm will continue to pay out 25 per cent of its earnings as annual, end-of-year dividends. The remaining 75 per cent of earnings is retained by the company for use in projects. The company has 1.25 million shares of equity outstanding. The current share price is €272. The historical return on equity (ROE) of 12 per cent is expected to continue in the future. What is the required rate of return on the equity?

24 **Price–Earnings Ratio** The market consensus is that Pinto plc has an ROE of 9 per cent, a beta of 1.25, and plans to maintain its plowback ratio of 0.67. This year's earnings per share was €3. The consensus view of the expected market return is 14 per cent, and the return on Treasury Bills is currently 6 per cent. What is the current PE ratio for the company? What is the prospective PE ratio for the company?

25 **Growth Opportunities** For Pinto plc in question 24 above, what is the present value of growth opportunities?

26 **Growth Opportunities** Yorkshire Property Ltd expects to earn £60 million per year in perpetuity if it does not undertake any new projects. The firm has an opportunity to invest £10 million today and £12 million in one year in real estate. The new investment will generate annual earnings of £15 million in perpetuity, beginning 2 years from today. The firm has 10 million shares outstanding, and the required rate of return on the equity is 12 per cent. Land investments are not depreciable. Ignore taxes.

(a) What is the share price if the firm does not undertake the new investment?

(b) What is the value of the investment?

(c) What is the share price if the firm undertakes the investment?

27 **Firm Valuation** The ABC plc cash flow statement for the latest financial year is given below. The appropriate discount and growth rates are 14 per cent and 4 per cent, respectively. Assume the marginal corporate tax rate is 23 per cent. What is the value of the firm?

Year Ended 31 March		
£m	Notes	2011
Net cash flows, from operating activities		
Cash generated from (used in) operations		611.6
Interest paid		(234.0)
Purchase of interest rate caps		–
Interest received		1.9
Corporate income tax (paid) refunded		(24.6)
Net cash generated from operating activities		354.9
Cash flows from investing activities		
Acquisition of subsidiary undertakings, net of cash acquired	23	(12.8)
Increased investment in subsidiary undertakings		–
Purchase of property, plant and equipment and software		(77.4)
Loans made to Group companies		–
Net cash used in investing activities		(90.2)

£m	Year Ended 31 March		
		Notes	2011
Free cash flow			**264.7**
Cash flows from financing activities			
Net proceeds from share issues			0.8
Purchase of own shares			(0.2)
Treasury shares sold by trust			–
Repayment of borrowings			(216.5)
Net payments on revolving and short-term credit facilities			(6.6)
Financing fees paid			(0.4)
Net cash (used in) generated from financing activities			**(222.9)**
Net increase (decrease) in cash and cash equivalents			**41.8**
Cash and cash equivalents at beginning of the year			160.4
Exchange losses on cash and cash equivalents			(1.7)
Cash and cash equivalents at year end			**200.5**

28 Growth Opportunities   The annual earnings of Avalanche Skis will be 6 Swedish kroner per share in perpetuity if the firm makes no new investments. Under such a situation the firm would pay out all of its earnings as dividends. Assume the first dividend will be received exactly one year from now.

Alternatively, assume that 3 years from now, and in every subsequent year in perpetuity, the company can invest 25 per cent of its earnings in new projects. Each project will earn 40 per cent at year-end in perpetuity. The firm's discount rate is 14 per cent.

(a) What is the share price of Avalanche Skis today without the company making the new investment?

(b) If Avalanche announces that the new investment will be made, what will the share price be today?

CHALLENGE

29 Firm Valuation   Larsen & Toubro Ltd (www.larsentoubro.com) is an Indian multinational conglomerate listed on the Bombay Stock Exchange. In the financial year 2011, the company's net income was 4,456 crore, EPS was 73.56 crore, and the dividend payout ratio was 23.7 per cent. The return on equity of the firm was 17.83 per cent and its debt to equity ratio is 1.31. The appropriate discount rate for L&T is 18 per cent. What is the value of the firm's equity? What is L&T's share price? What is the value of the firm's bonds? What is the value of the firm?

30 Components of Bond Returns   Bond P is a premium bond with a 10 per cent coupon. Bond D is a 7 per cent coupon bond currently selling at a discount. Both bonds make annual payments, have a YTM of 9 per cent, and have 5 years to maturity. What is the current yield for Bond P? For Bond D? If interest rates remain unchanged, what is the expected capital gains yield over the next year for Bond P? For Bond D? Explain your answers and the interrelationship among the various types of yields.

31 Holding Period Yield   The YTM on a bond is the interest rate you earn on your investment if interest rates do not change. If you actually sell the bond before it matures, your realized return is known as the holding period yield (HPY).

(a) Suppose that today you buy an 8 per cent annual coupon bond for €1,150. The bond has 10 years to maturity. What rate of return do you expect to earn on your investment?

(b) Two years from now, the YTM on your bond has declined by 1 per cent, and you decide to sell. What price will your bond sell for? What is the HPY on your investment? Compare this yield to the YTM when you first bought the bond. Why are they different?

32 Discount Rate   Man SE is a German commercial vehicle manufacturer. Its DPS and EPS for 2011 were €2 and €4.62, respectively. The RoE of the firm was 11.85 per cent and the share price is €99.63. How would you calculate the appropriate discount rate for the firm's equity?

33 Valuing Bonds   Mallory plc has two different bonds currently outstanding. Bond M has a face value of £20,000 and matures in 20 years. The bond makes no payments for the first 6 years, then pays £1,200 every

6 months over the subsequent 8 years, and finally pays £1,500 every 6 months over the last 6 years. Bond N also has a face value of £20,000 and a maturity of 20 years; it makes no coupon payments over the life of the bond. If the required return on both these bonds is 10 per cent compounded semi-annually, what is the current price of Bond M? Of Bond N?

34 **Capital Gains versus Income**   Consider four different equities, all of which have a required return of 15 per cent and a most recent dividend of £4.00 per share. Equities W, X and Y are expected to maintain constant growth rates in dividends for the foreseeable future of 10 per cent, 0 per cent, and −5 per cent per year, respectively. Z is a growth stock that will increase its dividend by 20 per cent for the next two years and then maintain a constant 12 per cent growth rate thereafter. What is the dividend yield for each of these four equities? What is the expected capital gains yield? Discuss the relationship among the various returns that you find for each of these equities.

35 **Equity Valuation**   Most corporations pay semi-annual rather than annual dividends on their equity. Barring any unusual circumstances during the year, the board raises, lowers or maintains the current dividend once a year and then pays this dividend out in equal biannual instalments to its shareholders.

   (a) Suppose a company currently pays a €3.00 annual dividend on its equity in a single annual instalment, and management plans on raising this dividend by 6 per cent per year indefinitely. If the required return on this equity is 14 per cent, what is the current share price?

   (b) Now suppose that the company in (a) actually pays its annual dividend in equal 6-monthly instalments; thus this company has just paid a £1.50 dividend per share, as it has in the previous 6 months. What is the current share price now? (*Hint*: Find the equivalent annual end-of-year dividend for each year. Assume the dividends grew by 6 per cent every 6 months.) Comment on whether you think that this model of share valuation is appropriate.

36 **Growth Opportunities**   Nakamura has earnings of £10 million and is projected to grow at a constant rate of 5 per cent forever because of the benefits gained from the learning curve. Currently all earnings are paid out as dividends. The company plans to launch a new project 2 years from now that would be completely internally funded and require 20 per cent of the earnings that year. The project would start generating revenues one year after the launch of the project, and the earnings from the new project in any year are estimated to be constant at £5 million. The company has 10 million shares outstanding. Estimate the value of Nakamura. The discount rate is 10 per cent.

37 **Equity Valuation**   Michelin's share price is €56.99. You wish to value the company's equity and compare your valuation to the share price. The dividend that has just been paid is €1.78 and the earnings per share is €7.96. From FT.com, the return on equity for Michelin is 18.66 per cent. There are a number of estimated growth rates for the firm and these are given below:

Source	Growth Rate (%)
DPS growth (5 yr)	9.52
EPS growth (5 yr)	16.85
EPS growth (1 yr)	16.01
DPS growth (1 yr)	17.98

What is Michelin's estimated discount rate for each growth rate? Which estimate makes most sense and why? Using your chosen discount rate, value the company based on your own growth rate calculation.

Exam Question (45 minutes)

1 Kalvin SA pays dividends that are expected to grow at 7 per cent each year. These will stop in year 5, at which point the company will pay out all its earnings as dividends. Next year's dividend is €10 and its EPS at the time will be €15. If the appropriate discount rate on Kalvin shares is 9 per cent, what is its share price today? (20 marks)

2 If Kalvin SA were to distribute all its earnings, it could maintain a level dividend stream of €15 per share. How much is the market actually paying per share for growth opportunities? (20 marks)

3   A 6-year government bond makes annual coupon payments of 4 per cent and offers a yield of 8 per cent annually compounded. Suppose that one year later the bond still yields 8 per cent. What return has the bondholder earned over the 12-month period? Now suppose that the bond yields 6 per cent at the end of the year. What return would the bondholder earn in this case? The face value of the bond is £1,000. (20 marks)

4   How would you value a firm that pays no dividends? Explain, using a quantitative example to illustrate your answer. (40 marks)

Mini Case

Equity Valuation at Ragan Thermal Systems

Ragan Thermal Systems plc was founded 9 years ago by brother and sister Carrington and Genevieve Ragan. The company manufactures and installs commercial heating, ventilation and cooling (HVAC) units. Ragan has experienced rapid growth because of a proprietary technology that increases the energy efficiency of its systems. The company is equally owned by Carrington and Genevieve. The original agreement between the siblings gave each 50,000 shares. In the event either wished to sell the shares, they first had to be offered to the other at a discounted price.

Although neither sibling wants to sell any shares at this time, they have decided they should value their holdings in the company for financial planning purposes. To accomplish this, they have gathered the following information about their main competitors.

Ragan Thermal Systems plc Competitors					
	EPS (€)	DPS (€)	Share Price (€)	ROE (%)	R (%)
Arctic Cooling Ltd	0.82	0.16	15.19	11	10
National Heating & Cooling	1.32	0.52	12.49	14	13
Expert HVAC plc	−0.47	0.54	48.60	14	12
Industry average	0.56	0.41	25.43	13	11.67

Expert HVAC plc's negative earnings per share (EPS) were the result of an accounting write-off last year. Without the write-off, EPS for the company would have been €2.34.

Last year, Ragan had an EPS of €4.32 and paid a dividend to Carrington and Genevieve of €54,000 each. The company also had a return on equity of 25 per cent. The siblings believe a required return for the company of 20 per cent is appropriate.

1   Assuming the company continues its current growth rate, what is the share price of the company's equity?

2   To verify their calculations, Carrington and Genevieve have hired Josh Jobby as a consultant. Josh was previously an equity analyst, and he has covered the HVAC industry. Josh has examined the company's financial statements as well as those of its competitors. Although Ragan currently has a technological advantage, Josh's research indicates that Ragan's competitors are investigating other methods to improve efficiency. Given this, Josh believes that Ragan's technological advantage will last for only the next 5 years. After that period, the company's growth will likely slow to the industry average. Additionally, Josh believes that the required return the company uses is too high. He believes the industry average required return is more appropriate. Under Josh's assumptions, what is the estimated share price?

3   What is the industry average price–earnings ratio? What is Ragan's price–earnings ratio? Comment on any differences and explain why they may exist.

4   Assume the company's growth rate declines to the industry average after 5 years. What percentage of the equity's value is attributable to growth opportunities?

5   Assume the company's growth rate slows to the industry average in 5 years. What future return on equity does this imply?

6   After discussions with Josh, Carrington and Genevieve agree that they would like to try to increase the value of the company equity. Like many small business owners, they want to retain control of the company and do not want to sell shares to outside investors. They also feel that the company's debt is at a manageable level and do not want to borrow more money. What steps can they take to increase the share price? Are there any conditions under which this strategy would not increase the share price?

Practical Case Study

For these problems, use any web service that provides financial information. Good examples are Yahoo! Finance, Hemscott, Reuters and FT.com. You can also go to the company's website and download financial accounts from there. Get used to accessing financial websites as it is a basic skill required by all financial managers.

1   **Dividend Discount Model**   Choose any large company from your country and download its most recent statement of financial position and income statement. Using the financial figures in the accounts, calculate the sustainable growth rate for your company. Now go to Yahoo! Finance or any other financial website and find the closing share price for the same month as the financial accounts you used. What is the implied required return on your company according to the dividend growth model? Does this number make sense? Why or why not?

2   **Growth Opportunities**   Assume that investors require an 8 per cent return on the company you have studied in Question 1. Using this share price and the EPS for the most recent year, calculate the NPVGO for your company. What is the appropriate PE ratio for your company using these calculations? What is the PE ratio on Yahoo! Finance? Can you explain the difference, if any?

Relevant Accounting Standards

Accounting standards are very relevant for security valuation because you need to be able to interpret the correct growth rates from the accounting figures. Important standards relating to this chapter are IAS 33 *Earnings per Share* and IAS 39 *Financial Instruments: Recognition and Measurement*. IAS 39 provides definitions for different types of financial securities. This can sometimes be problematic for an accountant because many securities have equity and bond-like features. Visit the IASPlus website (www.iasplus.com) for more information.

Additional Reading

A major challenge in share and bond valuation is measuring growth rates. The following papers investigate this issue (country or region of study is given in bold):

1   Beck, T., A. Demirguc-Kunt and V. Maksimovic (2005) 'Financial and Legal Constraints to Growth: Does Firm Size Matter?' *The Journal of Finance*, Vol. 60, No. 1, 137–177. **International**.

2   Chen, L. (2009) 'On the Reversal of Return and Dividend Growth Predictability: A Tale of Two Periods', *Journal of Financial Economics*, Vol. 92, No. 1, 128–151. **US**.

3   Claessens, S. and L. Laeven (2003) 'Financial Development, Property Rights, and Growth', *The Journal of Finance*, Vol. 58, No. 6, 2401–2436. **International**.

4   Penman, S. (2011) 'Accounting for Risk and Return in Valuation', *Journal of Applied Corporate Finance*, Vol. 23, No. 2, 50–58.

The following papers are also of interest:

5   Bris, A., Y. Koskinen and M. Nilsson (2009) 'The Euro and Corporate Valuations', *Review of Financial Studies*, Vol. 22, No. 8, 3171–3209. **Europe**.

6   Penman, S. (2006) 'Handling Valuation Models', *Journal of Applied Corporate Finance*, Vol. 18, No. 2, 48–55. **Theoretical**.

Endnotes

1   We ignore the possibility of the issuance of equities or bonds to raise capital. These possibilities are considered in later chapters.

2   If you have read the online supplement to Chapter 3, you will have probably figured out that g is the sustainable growth rate.

3   Later in the text, we speak of issuing shares or debt to fund projects.

4   A third option is to issue equity so the firm has enough cash both to pay dividends and to invest. This possibility is explored in a later chapter.

5   A full discussion of dividend policy, including share repurchases, is provided in Chapter 18.

6   The appropriate discount rate to use is discussed in detail in Chapter 12.

Net Present Value and Other Investment Rules

Irrespective of the state of the economy, companies need to invest to maintain existing operations or exploit new opportunities. Companies must decide whether the return from investing in a particular project, acquiring a new firm or expanding operations is enough to offset the costs of undertaking the investment. This is one of the financial manager's most important decisions and considerable time is taken up in companies assessing the viability of investment decisions.

Take, for example, oil exploration and extraction. One of the key inputs into deciding whether to build a new oil rig and initiate a new exploration project is the price of oil. In years when the oil price is high (above \$100 a barrel), the returns from finding oil can be lucrative. However, when the oil price falls, the returns are often not enough to justify the expense of starting a new oil field. This is what faced the oil industry at the beginning of 2015, when oil fell to \$70 a barrel. New exploration projects were postponed because it simply wasn't profitable enough to invest. Decisions such as these, with a price tag of many millions of pounds each, are obviously major undertakings, and the risks and rewards must be carefully weighed. In this chapter, we discuss the basic tools used in making such decisions.

In Chapter 1, we saw that increasing the value of a company's equity is the goal of financial management. Thus, we need to know how a particular investment will achieve that. This chapter considers a variety of techniques that are used in practice for this purpose. More important, it shows how many of these techniques can be misleading when used on their own, and it explains why the net present value approach is the right approach in theory but may not be the best approach in practice.

KEY NOTATIONS

NPV	Net present value
AAR	Average accounting return
IRR	Internal rate of return
PI	Profitability index
R	Discount rate

6.1 Why Use Net Present Value?

Chapter 4
Page 93

This chapter, as well as the next two, focuses on *capital budgeting*, the decision-making process for accepting or rejecting projects. We develop the basic capital budgeting methods, leaving much of the practical application to subsequent chapters. Fortunately, we do not have to develop these methods from scratch. In **Chapter 4**, we pointed out that one pound or euro received in the future is worth less than a pound or euro received today. The reason, of course, is that today's money can be reinvested, yielding a greater amount in the future. And we showed in Chapter 4 that the exact worth of a pound or euro to be received in the future is its present value. Furthermore, Section 4.1 suggested calculating the *net present value* of any project. That is, the section suggested calculating the difference between the sum of the present values of the project's future cash flows and the initial cost of the project.

The net present value (NPV) method is the first one to be considered in this chapter. We begin by reviewing the approach with a simple example. Then, we ask why the method leads to good decisions.

Example 6.1

Net Present Value

Alpha Corporation is considering investing in a riskless project costing £100. The project receives £107 in one year and has no other cash flows. The discount rate is 6 per cent.

The NPV of the project can easily be calculated as:

$$£0.94 = -£100 + \frac{£100}{1.06} \tag{6.1}$$

From Chapter 4, we know that the project should be accepted because its NPV is positive. Had the NPV of the project been negative, as would have been the case with an interest rate greater than 7 per cent, the project should be rejected.

The basic investment rule can be generalized thus:

Accept a project if the NPV is greater than zero. Reject a project if NPV is less than zero.

We refer to this as the NPV rule.

Why does the NPV rule lead to good decisions? Consider the following two strategies available to the managers of Alpha Corporation:

1 Use £100 of corporate cash to invest in the project. The £107 will be paid as a dividend in one year.
2 Forgo the project and pay the £100 of corporate cash as a dividend today.

If strategy 2 is employed, the shareholder might deposit the dividend in a bank for one year. With an interest rate of 6 per cent, strategy 2 would produce cash of £106 (=£100 × 1.06) at the end of the year. The shareholder would prefer strategy 1 because strategy 2 produces less than £107 at the end of the year.

Our basic point is this: accepting positive NPV projects benefits shareholders.

How do we interpret the exact NPV of £0.94? This is the increase in the value of the firm from the project. For example, imagine that the firm today has productive assets worth £V and has £100 of cash. If the firm forgoes the project, the value of the firm today would simply be:

$$£V + £100$$

If the firm accepts the project, the firm will receive £107 in one year but will have no cash today. Thus, the firm's value today would be:

$$£V + \frac{£107}{1.06}$$

The difference between these equations is just £0.94, the present value of Equation 6.1. Thus, the value of the firm rises by the NPV of the project.

Note that the value of the firm is merely the sum of the values of the different projects, divisions or other entities within the firm. This property, called value additivity, is quite important. It implies that the contribution of any project to a firm's value is simply the NPV of the project. As we will see later, alternative methods discussed in this chapter do not generally have this nice property.

One detail remains. We assumed that the project was riskless, a rather implausible assumption. Future cash flows of real-world projects are invariably risky. In other words, cash flows can only be estimated, rather than known. Imagine that the managers of Alpha *expect* the cash flow of the project to be £107 next year. That is, the cash flow could be higher, say £117, or lower, say £97. With this slight change, the project is risky. Suppose the project is about as risky as the stock market as a whole, where the expected return this year is perhaps 10 per cent. Then 10 per cent becomes the discount rate, implying that the NPV of the project would be:

$$-£2.73 = -£100 + \frac{£107}{1.10}$$

Because the NPV is negative, the project should be rejected. This makes sense. A shareholder of Alpha receiving a £100 dividend today could invest it in the stock market, expecting a 10 per cent return. Why accept a project with the same risk as the market but with an expected return of only 7 per cent?

Conceptually, the discount rate on a risky project is the return that one can expect to earn on a financial asset of comparable risk. This discount rate is often referred to as an *opportunity cost* because corporate investment in the project takes away the shareholder's opportunity to invest the dividend in a financial asset. If the actual calculation of the discount rate strikes you as extremely difficult in the real world, you are right. Although you can call a bank to find out the current interest rate, whom do you call to find the expected return on the market this year? And, if the risk of the project differs from that of the market, how do you make the adjustment? However, the calculation is by no means impossible. We forgo the calculation in this chapter, but we present it in later chapters of the text.

Having shown that NPV is a sensible approach, how can we tell whether alternative methods are as good as NPV? The key to NPV is its three attributes:

1 *NPV uses cash flows.* Cash flows from a project can be used for other corporate purposes (such as dividend payments, other capital budgeting projects or payments of corporate interest). By contrast, earnings are an artificial construct. Although earnings are useful to accountants, they should not be used in capital budgeting because they do not represent cash.

2 *NPV uses all the cash flows of the project.* Other approaches ignore cash flows beyond a particular date; beware of these approaches.

3 *NPV discounts the cash flows properly.* Other approaches may ignore the time value of money when handling cash flows. Beware of these approaches as well.

6.2 The Payback Period Method

Defining the Rule

One of the most popular alternatives to NPV is payback. Here is how payback works: consider a project with an initial investment of −€50,000. Cash flows are €30,000, €20,000 and €10,000 in the first 3 years, respectively. These flows are illustrated in Figure 6.1.

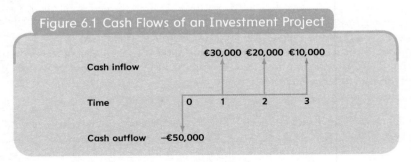

Figure 6.1 Cash Flows of an Investment Project

A useful way of writing down investments like the preceding is with the notation:

(−€50,000, €30,000, €20,000, €10,000)

The minus sign in front of the €50,000 reminds us that this is a cash outflow for the investor, and the commas between the different numbers indicate that they are received – or if they are cash outflows, that they are paid out – at different times. In this example we are assuming that the cash flows occur one year apart, with the first one occurring the moment we decide to take on the investment.

The firm receives cash flows of €30,000 and €20,000 in the first 2 years, which add up to the €50,000 original investment. This means that the firm has recovered its investment within 2 years. In this case 2 years is the *payback period* of the investment.

The payback period rule for making investment decisions is simple. A particular cut-off date, say 2 years, is selected. All investment projects that have payback periods of 2 years or less are accepted, and all of those that pay off in more than 2 years – if at all – are rejected.

Problems with the Payback Method

There are at least three problems with payback. To illustrate the first two problems, we consider the three projects in Table 6.1. All three projects have the same 3-year payback period, so they should all be equally attractive – right?

Table 6.1 Expected Cash Flows for Projects A through C

Year	A (£)	B (£)	C (£)
0	−100	−100	−100
1	20	50	50
2	30	30	30
3	50	20	20
4	60	60	60,000
Payback period (years)	3	3	3

Actually, they are not equally attractive, as can be seen by a comparison of different *pairs* of projects.

Problem 1: Timing of Cash Flows within the Payback Period

Let us compare project A with project B. In years 1 through 3, the cash flows of project A rise from £20 to £50, while the cash flows of project B fall from £50 to £20. Because the large cash flow of £50 comes earlier with project B, its net present value must be higher. Nevertheless, we just saw that the payback periods of the two projects are identical. Thus, a problem with the payback method is that it does not consider the timing of the cash flows within the payback period. This example shows that the payback method is inferior to NPV because, as we pointed out earlier, the NPV method *discounts the cash flows properly.*

Problem 2: Payments after the Payback Period

Now consider projects B and C, which have identical cash flows within the payback period. However, project C is clearly preferred because it has a cash flow of £60,000 in the fourth year. Thus, another problem with the payback method is that it ignores all cash flows occurring after the payback period. Because of the short-term orientation of the payback method, some valuable long-term projects are likely to be rejected. The NPV method does not have this flaw because, as we pointed out earlier, this method *uses all the cash flows of the project.*

Problem 3: Arbitrary Standard for Payback Period

We do not need to refer to Table 6.1 when considering a third problem with the payback method. Capital markets help us estimate the discount rate used in the NPV method. The riskless rate, perhaps proxied by the yield on a Treasury instrument, would be the appropriate rate for a riskless investment. Later chapters of this textbook show how to use historical returns in the capital markets to estimate the discount rate for a risky project. However, there is no comparable guide for choosing the payback cut-off date, so the choice is somewhat arbitrary.

Managerial Perspective

The payback method is often used by large, sophisticated companies when making relatively small decisions. The decision to build a small warehouse, for example, or to pay for a tune-up for a truck is the sort of decision that is often made by lower-level management. Typically, a manager might reason that a tune-up would cost, say, £200, and if it saved £120 each year in reduced fuel costs, it would pay for itself in less than two years. On such a basis the decision would be made.

Although the treasurer of the company might not have made the decision in the same way, the company endorses such decision-making. Why would upper management condone or even encourage such retrograde activity in its employees? One answer would be that it is easy to make decisions using payback. Multiply the tune-up decision into 50 such decisions a month, and the appeal of this simple method becomes clearer.

The payback method also has some desirable features for managerial control. Just as important as the investment decision itself is the company's ability to evaluate the manager's decision-making ability. Under the NPV method, a long time may pass before one decides whether a decision was correct. With the payback method we know in 2 years whether the manager's assessment of the cash flows was correct.

It has also been suggested that firms with good investment opportunities but no available cash may justifiably use payback. For example, the payback method could be used by small, privately held firms with good growth prospects but limited access to the capital markets. Quick cash recovery enhances the reinvestment possibilities for such firms. Payback period is also useful when firms invest in emerging markets. The uncertainty involved with such investments means that firms like to know they are getting their money back within a certain period. A short payback period equates roughly to a very high discount rate, where cash flows in the future have little present value.

Finally, practitioners often argue that standard academic criticisms of payback overstate any real-world problems with the method. For example, textbooks typically make fun of payback by positing a project with low cash inflows in the early years but a huge cash inflow right after the payback cut-off date. This project is likely to be rejected under the payback method, though its acceptance would, in truth, benefit the firm. Project C in Table 6.1 is an example of such a project. Practitioners point out that the pattern of cash flows in these textbook examples is much too stylized to mirror the real world. In fact, a number of executives have told us that for the overwhelming majority of real-world projects, both payback and NPV lead to the same decision. In addition, these executives indicate that if an investment like project C were encountered in the real world, decision-makers would almost certainly make ad hoc adjustments to the payback rule so that the project would be accepted.

Notwithstanding all of the preceding rationale, it is not surprising to discover that as the decisions grow in importance, which is to say when firms look at bigger projects, NPV becomes the order of the day. When questions of controlling and evaluating the manager become less important than making the right investment decision, payback is used less frequently. For big-ticket decisions, such as whether or not to buy a machine, build a factory, or acquire a company, the payback method is seldom used.

Summary of Payback

The payback method differs from NPV and is therefore conceptually wrong. With its arbitrary cut-off date and its blindness to cash flows after that date, it can lead to some flagrantly foolish decisions if it is used too literally. Nevertheless, because of its simplicity, as well as its other mentioned advantages, companies often use it as a screen for making the myriad minor investment decisions they continually face.

Although this means that you should be wary of trying to change approaches such as the payback method when you encounter them in companies, you should probably be careful not to accept the sloppy financial thinking they represent. After this course, you would do your company a disservice if you used payback instead of NPV when you had a choice.

Real World Insight 6.1

Patisserie Valerie

Investment appraisal methods can be used in a variety of situations and not just for specific projects. As an investor in new companies, you can use the methods in this chapter to work out if it is worthwhile to put your cash into a business.

Patisserie Valerie, a speciality cafe chain and cake maker from London's Soho, planned to raise £33 million in 2015. The company has five brands: Patisserie Valerie (cafes and cakes), Druckers Vienna Patisserie (cakes), Philpotts (sandwiches and salads), Baker & Spice (delicatessens and bakeries), and Flour Power City Baker (bakers). The company has seven bakeries and all produce is made in-house and delivered to its outlets every day. Patisserie Valerie has also built up an online presence which is growing very fast.

The most recent financial figures prior to the listing showed that Patisserie Valerie had earnings before interest, tax, depreciation and amortization of £12 million, with revenues of £60.1 million. Breaking these figures down, the company had 89 stores across all its brands with average weekly sales of £14,000 for each store. On average, each store had 1,583 customers who each spent £8.84 per visit.

To value Patisserie Valerie using investment appraisal methods, you would need to estimate overall cash flows for each year using data like that given above and forecast changes in efficiency and cash flow growth. Not an easy task, but don't worry – we show you how to do this and more in the next chapter.

6.3   The Discounted Payback Period Method

Aware of the pitfalls of payback, some decision-makers use a variant called the discounted payback period method. Under this approach, we first discount the cash flows. Then we ask how long it takes for the discounted cash flows to equal the initial investment.

For example, suppose that the discount rate is 10 per cent and the cash flows on a project are given by:

$$(-£100, £50, £50, £20)$$

This investment has a payback period of 2 years because the investment is paid back in that time.

To compute the project's discounted payback period, we first discount each of the cash flows at the 10 per cent rate. These discounted cash flows are:

$$[-£100, £50/1.1, £50/(1.1)^2, £20/(1.1)^3] = (-£100, £45.45, £41.32, £15.03)$$

The discounted payback period of the original investment is simply the payback period for these discounted cash flows. The payback period for the discounted cash flows is slightly less than 3 years because the discounted cash flows over the 3 years are £101.80 (=£45.45 + 41.32 + 15.03). As long as the cash flows and discount rate are positive, the discounted payback period will never be smaller than the payback period because discounting reduces the value of the cash flows.

At first glance discounted payback may seem like an attractive alternative, but on closer inspection we see that it has some of the same major flaws as payback. Like payback, discounted payback first requires us to make a somewhat magical choice of an arbitrary cut-off period, and then it ignores all cash flows after that date.

If we have already gone to the trouble of discounting the cash flows, any small appeal to simplicity or to managerial control that payback may have has been lost. We might just as well add up all the discounted cash flows and use NPV to make the decision. Although discounted payback looks a bit like NPV, it is just a poor compromise between the payback method and NPV.

6.4   The Average Accounting Return Method

Defining the Rule

Another attractive, but fatally flawed, approach to financial decision-making is the average accounting return. The average accounting return is the average project earnings after taxes and depreciation, divided by the average book value of the investment during its life. In spite of its flaws, the average accounting return method is worth examining because it is used frequently in the real world.

It is worth examining Table 6.2 carefully. In fact, the first step in any project assessment is a careful look at projected cash flows. First-year sales for the store are estimated to be £433,333. Before-tax cash flow will be £233,333. Sales are expected to rise and expenses are expected to fall in the second year, resulting in a before-tax cash flow of £300,000. Competition from other stores and the loss in novelty will reduce before-tax cash flow to £166,667, £100,000 and £33,333, respectively, in the next 3 years.

Example 6.2

Average Accounting Return

Consider a company that is evaluating whether to buy a store in a new shopping centre. The purchase price is £500,000. We will assume that the store has an estimated life of 5 years and will need to be completely scrapped or rebuilt at the end of that time. For simplicity's sake, the asset will be depreciated using straight line depreciation (this does not occur in countries that use International Accounting Standards but suits to illustrate the method). The projected yearly sales and expense figures are shown in Table 6.2.

	Year 1 (£)	Year 2 (£)	Year 3 (£)	Year 4 (£)	Year 5 (£)
Revenue	433,333	450,000	266,667	200,000	133,333
Expenses	200,000	150,000	100,000	100,000	100,000
Before-tax cash flow	233,333	300,000	166,667	100,000	33,333
Depreciation	100,000	100,000	100,000	100,000	100,000
Profit before taxes	133,333	200,000	66,667	0	−66,667
Taxes (t_c = 25%)*	33,333	50,000	16,667	0	−16,667
Net income	100,000	150,000	50,000	0	−50,000

$$\text{Average net income} = \frac{£100,000 + 150,000 + 50,000 + 0 - 50,000}{5} = £50,000$$

$$\text{Average investment} = \frac{£500,000 + 0}{2} = £250,000$$

$$\text{AAR} = \frac{£50,000}{£250,000} = 20\%$$

*Corporate tax rate = t_c. The tax rebate in year 5 of −£16,667 occurs if the rest of the firm is profitable. Here the loss in the project reduces the taxes of the entire firm.

Table 6.2 Projected Yearly Revenue and Costs for Average Accounting Return

To compute the average accounting return (AAR) on the project, we divide the average net income by the average amount invested. This can be done in three steps.

Step 1: Determining Average Net Income

Net income in any year is net cash flow minus depreciation and taxes. Depreciation is *not* a cash outflow.[1] Rather, it is a charge reflecting the fact that the investment in the store becomes less valuable every year.

We assume the project has a useful life of 5 years, at which time it will be worthless. Because the initial investment is £500,000 and because it will be worthless in 5 years, we assume that it loses value at the rate of £100,000 each year. This steady loss in value of £100,000 is called *straight-line depreciation*. The method used in countries that employ International Accounting Standards is known as the *reducing balance method*, which will be discussed in detail later. We subtract both depreciation and taxes from before-tax cash flow to derive net income, as shown in Table 6.2. Net income is £100,000 in the first year, £150,000 in year 2, £50,000 in year 3, zero in year 4, and −£50,000 in the last year. The average net income over the life of the project is therefore:

Average net income:

$$[£100,000 + 150,000 + 50,000 + 0 + (-50,000)]/5 = £50,000$$

Step 2: Determining Average Investment

We stated earlier that, due to depreciation, the investment in the store becomes less valuable every year. Because depreciation is £100,000 per year, the value at the end of year zero is £500,000, the value at the end of year 1 is £400,000, and so on. What is the average value of the investment over the life of the investment?

The mechanical calculation is:

$$(\text{£}500{,}000 + 400{,}000 + 300{,}000 + 200{,}000 + 100{,}000 + 0)/6 = \text{£}250{,}000 \qquad (6.2)$$

We divide by 6, not 5, because £500,000 is what the investment is worth at the beginning of the 5 years and £0 is what it is worth at the beginning of the sixth year. In other words, there are six terms in the parentheses of Equation 6.2.

Step 3: Determining AAR

The average return is simply:

$$\text{AAR} = \frac{\text{£}50{,}000}{\text{£}250{,}000} = 20\%$$

If the firm had a targeted accounting rate of return greater than 20 per cent, the project would be rejected; if its targeted return were less than 20 per cent, it would be accepted.

Analysing the Average Accounting Return Method

By now you should be able to see what is wrong with the AAR method.

The most important flaw with AAR is that it does not work with the right raw materials. It uses net income and book value of the investment, both of which come from the accounting figures. Accounting numbers are somewhat arbitrary. For example, certain cash outflows, such as the cost of a building, are depreciated under specific accounting rules. Other flows, such as maintenance, are expensed. In real-world situations, the decision to depreciate or expense an item involves judgement. Thus, the basic inputs of the AAR method, income and average investment, are affected by the accountant's judgement. Conversely, the NPV method *uses cash flows*. Accounting judgements do not affect cash flow.

Second, AAR takes no account of timing. In the previous example, the AAR would have been the same if the £100,000 net income in the first year had occurred in the last year. However, delaying an inflow for 5 years would have lowered the NPV of the investment. As mentioned earlier in this chapter, the NPV approach *discounts properly*.

Third, just as payback requires an arbitrary choice of the cut-off date, the AAR method offers no guidance on what the right targeted rate of return should be. It could be the discount rate in the market. But then again, because the AAR method is not the same as the present value method, it is not obvious that this would be the right choice.

Given these problems, is the AAR method employed in practice? Like the payback method, the AAR (and variations of it) is frequently used as a 'backup' to discounted cash flow methods. Perhaps this is so because it is easy to calculate and uses accounting numbers readily available from the firm's accounting system. In addition, both shareholders and the media pay a lot of attention to the overall profitability of a firm. Thus, some managers may feel pressured to select projects that are profitable in the near term, even if the projects come up short in terms of NPV. These managers may focus on the AAR of individual projects more than they should.

6.5 The Internal Rate of Return

Now we come to the most important alternative to the NPV method: the internal rate of return, universally known as the IRR. The IRR is about as close as you can get to the NPV without actually being the NPV. The basic rationale behind the IRR method is that it provides a single number summarizing the merits of a project. That number does not depend on the interest rate prevailing in the capital market. That is why it is called the internal rate of return; the number is internal or intrinsic to the project and does not depend on anything except the cash flows of the project.

For example, consider the simple project (−£100, £110) in Figure 6.2. For a given rate, the net present value of this project can be described as:

$$NPV = -\text{£}100 + \frac{\text{£}110}{1 + R}$$

where R is the discount rate. What must the discount rate be to make the NPV of the project equal to zero?

We begin by using an arbitrary discount rate of 0.08, which yields:

$$\text{£}1.85 = -\text{£}100 + \frac{\text{£}110}{1.08}$$

Because the NPV in this equation is positive, we now try a higher discount rate, such as 0.12. This yields:

$$-£1.79 = -£100 + \frac{£110}{1.12}$$

Because the NPV in this equation is negative, we try lowering the discount rate to 0.10. This yields:

$$0 = -£100 + \frac{£110}{1.10}$$

Figure 6.2 Cash Flows for a Simple Project

This trial-and-error procedure tells us that the NPV of the project is zero when R equals 10 per cent.[2] Thus, we say that 10 per cent is the project's **internal rate of return (IRR)**. In general, the IRR is the rate that causes the NPV of the project to be zero. The implication of this exercise is very simple. The firm should be equally willing to accept or reject the project if the discount rate is 10 per cent. The firm should accept the project if the discount rate is below 10 per cent. The firm should reject the project if the discount rate is above 10 per cent.

The general investment rule is clear:

Accept the project if the IRR is greater than the discount rate. Reject the project if the IRR is less than the discount rate.

We refer to this as the **basic IRR rule**. Now we can try the more complicated example ($-€200$, €100, €100, €100) in Figure 6.3.

Figure 6.3 Cash Flows for a More Complex Project

As we did previously, let us use trial and error to calculate the internal rate of return. We try 20 per cent and 30 per cent, yielding the following:

Discount rate (%)	NPV (€)
20	10.65
30	−18.39

After much more trial and error, we find that the NPV of the project is zero when the discount rate is 23.37 per cent. Thus, the IRR is 23.37 per cent. With a 20 per cent discount rate, the NPV is positive and we would accept it. However, if the discount rate were 30 per cent, we would reject it.

Algebraically, IRR is the unknown in the following equation:[3]

$$0 = -€200 + \frac{€100}{1 + IRR} + \frac{€100}{(1 + IRR)^2} + \frac{€100}{(1 + IRR)^3}$$

Figure 6.4 illustrates what the IRR of a project means. The figure plots the NPV as a function of the discount rate. The curve crosses the horizontal axis at the IRR of 23.37 per cent because this is where the NPV equals zero.

Figure 6.4 Net Present Value (NPV) and Discount Rates for a More Complex Project

> The NPV is positive for discount rates below the IRR and negative for discount rates above the IRR.

It should also be clear that the NPV is positive for discount rates below the IRR and negative for discount rates above the IRR. This means that if we accept projects like this one when the discount rate is less than the IRR, we will be accepting positive NPV projects. Thus, the IRR rule coincides exactly with the NPV rule.

If this were all there were to it, the IRR rule would always coincide with the NPV rule. This would be a wonderful discovery because it would mean that just by computing the IRR for a project we would be able to tell where it ranks among all of the projects we are considering. For example, if the IRR rule really works, a project with an IRR of 20 per cent will always be at least as good as one with an IRR of 15 per cent.

Unfortunately, the world of finance is not so kind. The IRR rule and the NPV rule are the same only for examples like the one just discussed. Several problems with the IRR approach occur in more complicated situations.

6.6 Problems with the IRR Approach

Definition of Independent and Mutually Exclusive Projects

An **independent project** is one whose acceptance or rejection is independent of the acceptance or rejection of other projects. For example, imagine that Starbucks is considering putting a coffee outlet on a remote island in the north of Scotland. Acceptance or rejection of this outlet is likely to be unrelated to the acceptance or rejection of any other coffee outlet that Starbucks is thinking of opening. This is because the remoteness of the Scottish outlet ensures that it will not pull sales away from other outlets.

Now consider the other extreme, **mutually exclusive investments.** What does it mean for two projects, A and B, to be mutually exclusive? You can accept A or you can accept B or you can reject both of them, but you cannot accept both of them. For example, A might be a decision to build a house on a corner lot that you own, and B might be a decision to build a cinema on the same lot.

We now present two general problems with the IRR approach that affect both independent and mutually exclusive projects. Then we deal with two problems affecting mutually exclusive projects only.

Two General Problems Affecting Both Independent and Mutually Exclusive Projects

We begin our discussion with project A, which has the following cash flows:

$$(-£100, £130)$$

The IRR for project A is 30 per cent. Table 6.3 provides other relevant information about the project. The relationship between NPV and the discount rate is shown for this project in Figure 6.5. As you can see, the NPV declines as the discount rate rises.

Table 6.3 The Internal Rate of Return and Net Present Value

	Project A			Project B			Project C		
Dates:	0	1	2	0	1	2	0	1	2
Cash flows (£)	−100	130		100	−130		−100	230	−132
IRR (%)		30			30		10	and	20
NPV @10% (£)		18.2			−18.2			0	
Accept if market rate		<30%			>30%		>10%	but	<20%
Financing or investing		Investing			Financing			Mixture	

Figure 6.5 Net Present Value and Discount Rates for Projects A, B and C

Project A has a cash outflow at date 0 followed by a cash inflow at date 1. Its NPV is negatively related to the discount rate.

Project B has a cash inflow at date 0 followed by a cash outflow at date 1. Its NPV is positively related to the discount rate.

Project C has two changes of sign in its cash flows. It has an outflow at date 0, an inflow at date 1, and an outflow at date 2.

Projects with more than one change of sign can have multiple rates of return.

Problem 1: Investing or Financing?

Now consider project B, with cash flows of:

$$(£100, -£130)$$

These cash flows are exactly the reverse of the flows for project A. In project B, the firm receives funds first and then pays out funds later. While unusual, projects of this type do exist. For example, consider a company conducting a seminar where the participants pay in advance. Because large expenses are frequently incurred at the seminar date, cash inflows precede cash outflows.

Consider our trial-and-error method to calculate IRR:

$$-£4 = +£100 - \frac{£130}{1.25}$$

$$£0 = +£100 - \frac{£130}{1.30}$$

$$£3.70 = +£100 - \frac{£130}{1.35}$$

As with project A, the internal rate of return is 30 per cent. However, notice that the net present value is *negative* when the discount rate is *below* 30 per cent. Conversely, the net present value is positive when the discount rate is above 30 per cent. The decision rule is exactly the opposite of our previous result. For this type of a project, the following rule applies:

Accept the project when the IRR is less than the discount rate. Reject the project when the IRR is greater than the discount rate.

This unusual decision rule follows from the graph of project B in Figure 6.5. The curve is upward sloping, implying that NPV is *positively* related to the discount rate.

The graph makes intuitive sense. Suppose the firm wants to obtain £100 immediately. It can either (1) accept project B, or (2) borrow £100 from a bank. Thus, the project is actually a substitute for borrowing. In fact, because the IRR is 30 per cent, taking on project B is tantamount to borrowing at 30 per cent. If the firm can borrow from a bank at, say, only 25 per cent, it should reject the project. However, if a firm can borrow from a bank only at, say, 35 per cent, it should accept the project. Thus project B will be accepted if and only if the discount rate is *above* the IRR.[4]

This should be contrasted with project A. If the firm has £100 of cash to invest, it can either (1) accept project A, or (2) lend £100 to the bank. The project is actually a substitute for lending. In fact, because the IRR is 30 per cent, taking on project A is tantamount to lending at 30 per cent. The firm should accept project A if the lending rate is below 30 per cent. Conversely, the firm should reject project A if the lending rate is above 30 per cent.

Because the firm initially pays out money with project A but initially receives money with project B, we refer to project A as an *investing type project* and project B as a *financing type project*. Investing type projects are the norm. Because the IRR rule is reversed for financing type projects, be careful when using it with this type of project.

Problem 2: Multiple Rates of Return

Suppose the cash flows from a project are:

$$(-£100, £230, -£132)$$

Because this project has a negative cash flow, a positive cash flow, and another negative cash flow, we say that the project's cash flows exhibit two changes of sign, or 'flip-flops'. Although this pattern of cash flows might look a bit strange at first, many projects require outflows of cash after receiving some inflows. An example would be a strip-mining project. The first stage in such a project is the initial investment in excavating the mine. Profits from operating the mine are received in the second stage. The third stage involves a further investment to reclaim the land and satisfy the requirements of environmental protection legislation. Cash flows are negative at this stage.

It is easy to verify that this project has not one but two IRRs, 10 per cent and 20 per cent.[5] In a case like this, the IRR does not make any sense. What IRR are we to use – 10 per cent or 20 per cent? Because there is no good reason to use one over the other, IRR simply cannot be used here.

Why does this project have multiple rates of return? Project C generates multiple internal rates of return because both an inflow and an outflow occur after the initial investment. In general, these flip-flops or changes in sign produce multiple IRRs. In theory, a cash flow stream with K changes in sign can have up to K sensible internal rates of return (IRRs above –100 per cent). Therefore, because project C has two changes in sign, it can have as many as two IRRs. As we pointed out, projects whose cash flows change sign repeatedly can occur in the real world.

NPV Rule

Of course, we should not be too worried about multiple rates of return. After all, we can always fall back on the NPV rule. Figure 6.5 plots the NPV of project C (−£100, £230, −£132) as a function of the discount rate. As the figure shows, the NPV is zero at both 10 per cent and 20 per cent and negative outside the range. Thus, the NPV rule tells us to accept the project if the appropriate discount rate is between 10 per cent and 20 per cent. The project should be rejected if the discount rate lies outside this range.

The Guarantee against Multiple IRRs

If the first cash flow of a project is negative (because it is the initial investment) and if all of the remaining flows are positive, there can only be a single, unique IRR, no matter how many periods the project lasts. This is easy to understand by using the concept of the time value of money. For example, it is simple to verify that project A in Table 6.3 has an IRR of 30 per cent because using a 30 per cent discount rate gives

$$NPV = -£100 + £130/(1.3)$$
$$= 0$$

How do we know that this is the only IRR? Suppose we were to try a discount rate greater than 30 per cent. In computing the NPV, changing the discount rate does not change the value of the initial cash flow of −£100 because that cash flow is not discounted. But raising the discount rate can only lower the present value of the future cash flows. In other words, because the NPV is zero at 30 per cent, any increase in the rate will push the NPV into the negative range. Similarly, if we try a discount rate of less than 30 per cent, the overall NPV of the project will be positive. Though this example has only one positive flow, the above reasoning still implies a single, unique IRR if there are many inflows (but no outflows) after the initial investment.

If the initial cash flow is positive – and if all of the remaining flows are negative – there can only be a single, unique IRR. This result follows from similar reasoning. Both these cases have only one change of sign or flip-flop in the cash flows. Thus, we are safe from multiple IRRs whenever there is only one sign change in the cash flows.

General Rules

The following chart summarizes our rules:

Flows	Number of IRRs	IRR criterion	NPV criterion
First cash flow is negative and all remaining cash flows are positive	1	Accept if IRR $>R$ Reject if IRR $< R$	Accept if NPV > 0 Reject if NPV < 0
First cash flow is positive and all remaining cash flows are negative	1	Accept if IRR $< R$ Reject if IRR $> R$	Accept if NPV > 0 Reject if NPV < 0
Some cash flows after first are positive and some cash flows after first are negative	May be more than 1	No valid IRR	Accept if NPV > 0 Reject if NPV < 0

Note that the NPV criterion is the same for each of the three cases. In other words, NPV analysis is always appropriate. Conversely, the IRR can be used only in certain cases.

Problems Specific to Mutually Exclusive Projects

As mentioned earlier, two or more projects are mutually exclusive if the firm can accept only one of them. We now present two problems dealing with the application of the IRR approach to mutually exclusive projects. These two problems are quite similar, though logically distinct.

The Scale Problem

A professor we know motivates class discussions of this topic with the statement: Students, I am prepared to let one of you choose between two mutually exclusive 'business' propositions: Opportunity 1 – You give me €1 now and I'll give you €1.50 back at the end of the class period. Opportunity 2 – You give me €10 and I'll give you €11 back at the end of the class period. You can choose only one of the two opportunities. And you cannot choose either opportunity more than once. I'll pick the first volunteer.

Which would you choose? The correct answer is opportunity 2. To see this, look at the following chart:

	Cash Flow at Beginning of Class	Cash Flow at End of Class (90 Minutes Later)	NPV[6]	IRR
Opportunity 1	−€1	+€1.50	€0.50	50%
Opportunity 2	−€10	+€11.00	€1.00	10%

As we have stressed earlier in the text, one should choose the opportunity with the highest NPV. This is opportunity 2 in the example.

This business proposition illustrates a defect with the internal rate of return criterion. The basic IRR rule indicates the selection of opportunity 1 because the IRR is 50 per cent. The IRR is only 10 per cent for opportunity 2.

Where does IRR go wrong? The problem with IRR is that it ignores issues of *scale*. Although opportunity 1 has a greater IRR, the investment is much smaller. In other words, the high percentage return on opportunity 1 is more than offset by the ability to earn at least a decent return on a much bigger investment under opportunity 2.

Because IRR seems to be misguided here, can we adjust or correct it? We illustrate how in the next example.

Example 6.3

NPV versus IRR

Stanley Jaffe and Sherry Lansing have just purchased the rights to *Corporate Finance: The Motion Picture*. They will produce this major motion picture on either a small budget or a big budget. Here are the estimated cash flows:

	Cash Flow at Date 0 (€)	Cash Flow at Date 1 (€)	NPV @25% (€)	IRR (%)
Small budget	−10 million	40 million	22 million	300
Large budget	−25 million	65 million	27 million	160

Because of high risk, a 25 per cent discount rate is considered appropriate. Sherry wants to adopt the large budget because the NPV is higher. Stanley wants to adopt the small budget because the IRR is higher. Who is right?

For the reasons espoused in the classroom example, NPV is correct. Hence Sherry is right. However, Stanley is very stubborn where IRR is concerned. How can Sherry justify the large budget to Stanley using the IRR approach?

This is where *incremental IRR* comes in. Sherry calculates the incremental cash flows from choosing the large budget instead of the small budget as follows:

	Cash Flow at Date 0 (€ millions)	Cash Flow at Date 1 (€ millions)
Incremental cash flows from choosing large budget instead of small budget	−25 − (−10) = −15	65 − 40 = 25

This chart shows that the incremental cash flows are −€15 million at date 0 and €25 million at date 1.
Sherry calculates incremental IRR as follows:

Formula for calculating the incremental IRR:

$$0 = -€15 \text{ million} + \frac{€25 \text{ million}}{1 + \text{IRR}}$$

IRR equals 66.67 per cent in this equation, implying that the incremental IRR is 66.67 per cent. Incremental IRR is the IRR on the incremental investment from choosing the large project instead of the small project.
In addition, we can calculate the NPV of the incremental cash flows:

NPV of incremental cash flows:

$$-€15 \text{ million} + \frac{€25 \text{ million}}{1.25} = €5 \text{ million}$$

We know the small-budget picture would be acceptable as an independent project because its NPV is positive. We want to know whether it is beneficial to invest an additional €15 million to make the large-budget picture instead of the small-budget picture. In other words, is it beneficial to invest an additional €15 million to receive an additional €25 million next year? First, our calculations show the NPV on the incremental investment to be positive. Second, the incremental IRR of 66.67 per cent is higher than the discount rate of 25 per cent. For both reasons, the incremental investment can be justified, so the large-budget movie should be made. The second reason is what Stanley needed to hear to be convinced.

In review, we can handle this example (or any mutually exclusive example) in one of three ways:

1 *Compare the NPVs of the two choices.* The NPV of the large-budget picture is greater than the NPV of the small-budget picture. That is, €27 million is greater than €22 million.

2 *Calculate the incremental NPV from making the large-budget picture instead of the small-budget picture.* Because the incremental NPV equals €5 million, we choose the large-budget picture.

3 *Compare the incremental IRR to the discount rate.* Because the incremental IRR is 66.67 per cent and the discount rate is 25 per cent, we take the large-budget picture.

All three approaches always give the same decision. However, we must *not* compare the IRRs of the two pictures. If we did, we would make the wrong choice. That is, we would accept the small-budget picture.

Although students frequently think that problems of scale are relatively unimportant, the truth is just the opposite. No real-world project comes in one clear-cut size. Rather, the firm has to *determine* the best size for the project. The movie budget of €25 million is not fixed in stone. Perhaps an extra €1 million to hire a bigger star or to film at a better location will increase the movie's gross revenues. Similarly, an industrial firm must decide whether it wants a warehouse of, say, 500,000 square feet or 600,000 square feet. And, earlier in the chapter, we imagined Starbucks opening an outlet on a remote island. If it does this, it must decide how big the outlet should be. For almost any project, someone in the firm has to decide on its size, implying that problems of scale abound in the real world.

One final note here. Students often ask which project should be subtracted from the other in calculating incremental flows. Notice that we are subtracting the smaller project's cash flows from the bigger project's cash flows. This leaves an *outflow* at date 0. We then use the basic IRR rule on the incremental flows.[7]

The Timing Problem

Next we illustrate another, quite similar problem with the IRR approach to evaluating mutually exclusive projects.

Example 6.4

Mutually Exclusive Investments

Suppose that Kaufold plc has two alternative uses for a warehouse. It can store toxic waste containers (investment A) or electronic equipment (investment B). The cash flows are as follows:

	Cash Flow at Year				NPV			IRR (%)
Year:	0 (£)	1 (£)	2 (£)	3 (£)	@0% (£)	@10% (£)	@15% (£)	
Investment A	−10,000	10,000	1,000	1,000	2,000	669	109	16.04
Investment B	−10,000	1,000	1,000	12,000	4,000	751	−484	12.94

We find that the NPV of investment B is higher with low discount rates, and the NPV of investment A is higher with high discount rates. This is not surprising if you look closely at the cash flow patterns. The cash flows of A occur early, whereas the cash flows of B occur later. If we assume a high discount rate, we favour investment A because we are implicitly assuming that the early cash flow (for example, £10,000 in year 1) can be reinvested at that rate. Because most of investment B's cash flows occur in year 3, B's value is relatively high with low discount rates.

Project A has an NPV of £2,000 at a discount rate of zero. This is calculated by simply adding up the cash flows without discounting them. Project B has an NPV of £4,000 at the zero rate. However, the NPV of project B declines more rapidly as the discount rate increases than does the NPV of project A. As we mentioned, this occurs because the cash flows of B occur later. Both projects have the same NPV at a discount rate of 10.55 per cent. The IRR for a project is the rate at which the NPV equals zero. Because the NPV of B declines more rapidly, B actually has a lower IRR.

As with the movie example, we can select the better project with one of three different methods:

1 *Compare NPVs of the two projects.* If the discount rate is below 10.55 per cent, we should choose project B because B has a higher NPV. If the rate is above 10.55 per cent, we should choose project A because A has a higher NPV.

2 *Compare incremental IRR to discount rate.* Method 1 employed NPV. Another way of determining that B is a better project is to subtract the cash flows of A from the cash flows of B and then to calculate the IRR. This is the incremental IRR approach we spoke of earlier.

Here are the incremental cash flows:

					NPV of Incremental Cash Flows			
	0	1	2	3	Incremental	@0%	@10%	@15%
Year:	(£)	(£)	(£)	(£)	IRR (%)	(£)	(£)	(£)
B − A	0	−9,000	0	11,000	10.55	2,000	83	−593

This chart shows that the incremental IRR is 10.55 per cent. In other words, the NPV on the incremental investment is zero when the discount rate is 10.55 per cent. Thus, if the relevant discount rate is below 10.55 per cent, project B is preferred to project A. If the relevant discount rate is above 10.55 per cent, project A is preferred to project B.[8]

3 *Calculate NPV on incremental cash flows.* Finally, we could calculate the NPV on the incremental cash flows. The incremental NPV is positive when the discount rate is either 0 per cent or 10 per cent. The incremental NPV is negative if the discount rate is 15 per cent. If the NPV is positive on the incremental flows, we should choose B. If the NPV is negative, we should choose A.

In summary, the same decision is reached whether we (1) compare the NPVs of the two projects, (2) compare the incremental IRR to the relevant discount rate, or (3) examine the NPV of the incremental cash flows. However, as mentioned earlier, we should *not* compare the IRR of project A with the IRR of project B.

We suggested earlier that we should subtract the cash flows of the smaller project from the cash flows of the bigger project. What do we do here when the two projects have the same initial investment? Our suggestion in this case is to perform the subtraction so that the *first* non-zero cash flow is negative. In the Kaufold plc example we achieved this by subtracting A from B. In this way, we can still use the basic IRR rule for evaluating cash flows.

The preceding examples illustrate problems with the IRR approach in evaluating mutually exclusive projects. Both the professor–student example and the motion picture example illustrate the problem that arises when mutually exclusive projects have different initial investments. The Kaufold plc example illustrates the problem that arises when mutually exclusive projects have different cash flow timing. When working with mutually exclusive projects, it is not necessary to determine whether it is the scale problem or the timing problem that exists. Very likely both occur in any real-world situation. Instead, the practitioner should simply use either an incremental IRR or an NPV approach.

Redeeming Qualities of IRR

IRR probably survives because it fills a need that NPV does not. People seem to want a rule that summarizes the information about a project in a single rate of return. This single rate gives people a simple way of discussing projects. For example, one manager in a firm might say to another, 'Remodelling the north wing has a 20 per cent IRR.'

To their credit, however, companies that employ the IRR approach seem to understand its deficiencies. For example, companies frequently restrict managerial projections of cash flows to be negative at the beginning and strictly positive later. Perhaps, then, the ability of the IRR approach to capture a complex investment project in a single number and the ease of communicating that number explain the survival of the IRR.

A Test

To test your knowledge, consider the following two statements:

1 You must know the discount rate to compute the NPV of a project, but you compute the IRR without referring to the discount rate.

2 Hence, the IRR rule is easier to apply than the NPV rule because you do not use the discount rate when applying IRR.

The first statement is true. The discount rate is needed to *compute* NPV. The IRR is *computed* by solving for the rate where the NPV is zero. No mention is made of the discount rate in the mere computation. However, the second statement is false. To *apply* IRR, you must compare the internal rate of return with the discount rate. Thus the discount rate is needed for making a decision under either the NPV or IRR approach.

6.7   The Profitability Index

Another method used to evaluate projects is called the profitability index. It is the ratio of the present value of the future expected cash flows *after* initial investment divided by the amount of the initial investment. The profitability index can be represented like this:

$$\text{Profitability index (PI)} = \frac{\text{PV of cash flows } subsequent \text{ to initial investment}}{\text{Initial investment}}$$

Example 6.5

Profitability Index

Hiram Finnegan Int. (HFI) applies a 12 per cent discount rate to two investment opportunities.

Project	Cash Flows (€000,000)			PV @ 12% of Cash Flows Subsequent to Initial Investment (€000,000)	Profitability Index	NPV @ 12% (€000,000)
	C_0	C_1	C_2			
1	−20	70	10	70.5	3.53	50.5
2	−10	15	40	45.3	4.53	35.3

Calculation of Profitability Index

The profitability index is calculated for project 1 as follows. The present value of the cash flows *after* the initial investment is:

$$€70.5 = \frac{€70}{1.12} + \frac{€10}{(1.12)^2}$$

The profitability index is obtained by dividing this result by the initial investment of €20. This yields:

$$3.53 = \frac{€70.5}{€20}$$

Application of the Profitability Index

How do we use the profitability index? We consider three situations:

1 *Independent projects*: Assume that HFI's two projects are independent. According to the NPV rule, both projects should be accepted because NPV is positive in each case. The profitability index (PI) is greater than 1 whenever the NPV is positive. Thus, the PI *decision rule* is

- Accept an independent project if PI > 1.
- Reject it if PI < 1.

2 *Mutually exclusive projects*: Let us now assume that HFI can only accept one of its two projects. NPV analysis says accept project 1 because this project has the bigger NPV. Because project 2 has the higher PI, the profitability index leads to the wrong selection.

   The problem with the profitability index for mutually exclusive projects is the same as the scale problem with the IRR that we mentioned earlier. Project 2 is smaller than project 1. Because the PI is a ratio, this index misses the fact that project 1 has a larger investment than project 2 has. Thus, like IRR, PI ignores differences of scale for mutually exclusive projects.

   However, like IRR, the flaw with the PI approach can be corrected using incremental analysis. We write the incremental cash flows after subtracting project 2 from project 1 as follows:

Project	Cash Flows (€000,000)			PV @ 12% of Cash Flows Subsequent to Initial Investment (€000,000)	Profitability Index	NPV @ 12% (€000,000)
	C_0	C_1	C_2			
1 − 2	−10	55	−30	25.2	2.52	15.2

   Because the profitability index on the incremental cash flows is greater than 1.0, we should choose the bigger project – that is, project 1. This is the same decision we get with the NPV approach.

3 *Capital rationing*: The first two cases implicitly assumed that HFI could always attract enough capital to make any profitable investments. Now consider the case when the firm does not have enough capital to fund all positive NPV projects. This is the case of capital rationing.

Imagine that the firm has a third project, as well as the first two. Project 3 has the following cash flows:

Project	Cash Flows (€000,000)			PV @ 12% of Cash Flows Subsequent to Initial Investment (€000,000)	Profitability Index	NPV @ 12% (€000,000)
	C_0	C_1	C_2			
3	−10	−5	60	43.4	4.34	33.4

Further, imagine that (1) the projects of Hiram Finnegan Int. are independent, but (2) the firm has only €20 million to invest. Because project 1 has an initial investment of €20 million, the firm cannot select both this project and another one. Conversely, because projects 2 and 3 have initial investments of €10 million each, both these projects can be chosen. In other words, the cash constraint forces the firm to choose either project 1 or projects 2 and 3.

What should the firm do? Individually, projects 2 and 3 have lower NPVs than project 1 has. However, when the NPVs of projects 2 and 3 are added together, the sum is higher than the NPV of project 1. Thus, common sense dictates that projects 2 and 3 should be accepted.

What does our conclusion have to say about the NPV rule or the PI rule? In the case of limited funds, we cannot rank projects according to their NPVs. Instead we should rank them according to the ratio of present value to initial investment. This is the PI rule. Both project 2 and project 3 have higher PI ratios than does project 1. Thus they should be ranked ahead of project 1 when capital is rationed.

It should be noted that the profitability index does not work if funds are also limited beyond the initial time period. For example, if heavy cash outflows elsewhere in the firm were to occur at date 1, project 3, which also has a cash outflow at date 1, might need to be rejected. In other words, the profitability index cannot handle capital rationing over multiple time periods.

In addition, what economists term *indivisibilities* may reduce the effectiveness of the PI rule. Imagine that HFI has €30 million available for capital investment, not just €20 million. The firm now has enough cash for projects 1 and 2. Because the sum of the NPVs of these two projects is greater than the sum of the NPVs of projects 2 and 3, the firm would be better served by accepting projects 1 and 2. But because projects 2 and 3 still have the highest profitability indexes, the PI rule now leads to the wrong decision. Why does the PI rule lead us astray here? The key is that projects 1 and 2 use up all of the €30 million, whereas projects 2 and 3 have a combined initial investment of only €20 million (=€10 + 10). If projects 2 and 3 are accepted, the remaining €10 million must be left in the bank.

This situation points out that care should be exercised when using the profitability index in the real world. Nevertheless, while not perfect, the profitability index goes a long way toward handling capital rationing.

Real World Insight 6.2

Statoil

Even when market conditions are very poor, there are still opportunities for investment for sharp-eyed companies. Take Statoil, the international oil company, who invested $31 billion in a new North Sea oil field (the Johann Sverdrup field on the Norwegian side of the North Sea) in 2015. With oil prices only $60 per barrel, and down from $110 just months before, it doesn't appear to make sense that an oil field investment would be worthwhile. In fact, many oil firms had made significant redundancies and sold assets just to stay afloat in this new regime of low oil prices and dwindling revenues.

So why did Statoil invest in the Johann Sverdrup field? It all comes down to investment appraisal. According to Statoil, total production revenues over 50 years may amount to as much as NOK1,350 billion, from investments of NOK120 billion. Production would be in the range of 315,000–380,000 barrels per day, so it would be easy to predict revenues based on different oil price forecasts. According to Wood MacKenzie, the energy consultancy firm, the IRR of this investment is about 23 per cent at an oil price of only $41 per barrel. At a price of $60 per barrel, the IRR would be significantly greater.

6.8   The Practice of Capital Budgeting

So far this chapter has asked 'Which capital budgeting methods should companies be using?' An equally important question is this: which methods *are* companies using? Table 6.4 helps answer this question. As can be seen from the table, there is quite strong variation in the frequency with which different techniques are utilized.

Chapter 8
Page 204

Other more advanced techniques, such as real options, and sensitivity analysis, are covered in **Chapter 8**. The hurdle rate is known as the break-even approach and is also covered in Chapter 8. Most companies use the IRR and NPV methods. This is not surprising, given the theoretical advantages of these approaches. The most interesting point is that for the UK, Germany and France, payback period is the most popular technique to appraise new projects, which is surprising given the conceptual problems with this approach. However, the flaws of payback period, as mentioned in the current chapter, may be relatively easy to correct. For example, while the payback method ignores all cash flows after the payback period, an alert manager can make ad hoc adjustments for a project with back-loaded cash flows.

Table 6.4 Percentage of Firms in Selected Countries who use Capital Budgeting Techniques

	UK	Germany	France	Netherlands	US
Net present value	46.97	47.58	35.09	70.00	74.93
Internal rate of return	53.13	42.15	44.07	56.00	75.61
Accounting rate of return	38.10	32.17	16.07	25.00	20.29
Profitability index	15.87	16.07	37.74	8.16	11.87
Payback period	69.23	50.00	50.88	64.71	56.74
Discounted payback	25.40	30.51	11.32	25.00	29.45
Sensitivity analysis	42.86	28.07	10.42	36.73	51.54
Real options	29.03	44.04	53.06	34.69	26.56

Source: Adapted from Brounen et al. (2004).

Capital expenditures by individual corporations can add up to enormous sums for the economy as a whole. For example, for the financial year 2013, the energy firm, Centrica, showed an outflow of £2.351 billion in investing activities. You may think this is a large amount but it is dwarfed by Shell, who invested more than £25.6 billion in capital expenditure over the same period.

The use of quantitative techniques in capital budgeting varies with the industry. As one would imagine, firms that are better able to estimate cash flows are more likely to use NPV. For example, estimation of cash flow in certain aspects of the oil business is quite feasible. Because of this, energy-related firms were among the first to use NPV analysis. Conversely, the cash flows in the motion picture business are very hard to project. The grosses of the great hits like *Titanic*, *Harry Potter* and *Avatar* were far, far greater than anyone imagined. The big failures like *Knight and Day* and *John Carter* were unexpected as well. Because of this, NPV analysis is frowned upon in the movie business.

Another important insight from Table 6.4 is that companies use a combination of investment appraisal methods to make capital expenditure decisions. This is without doubt the most sensible strategy, and combinations of the methods introduced in this chapter can be the basis for excellent hybrid decision rules for investment appraisal. For example, consider an energy firm that is capital rationed and experiences large winding down costs for projects (such as dismantling oil rigs and clean-up costs at the end of an oilfield life). An appropriate combination would be NPV and payback period. NPV tells the financial manager whether the project will add value and includes all cash flows including the very large final cash flow, while payback period will say how long it takes to get the initial investment back. A decision rule that requires both a payback period less than 4 years and a positive NPV would be a potential decision rule. As can be seen, combining investment appraisal methods can open up a whole set of innovative decision rules to make financial decisions.

Summary and Conclusions

1   In this chapter, we covered different investment decision rules. We evaluated the most popular alternatives to the NPV: the payback period, the discounted payback period, the accounting rate of return, the internal rate of return and the profitability index. In doing so we learned more about the NPV.

2   While we found that the alternatives have some redeeming qualities, when all is said and done, they are not the NPV rule; for those of us in finance, that makes them decidedly second-rate.

3   Of the competitors to NPV, IRR must be ranked above both payback and accounting rate of return. In fact, IRR always reaches the same decision as NPV in the normal case where the initial outflows of an independent investment project are followed only by a series of inflows.

4   We classified the flaws of IRR into two types. First, we considered the general case applying to both independent and mutually exclusive projects. There appeared to be two problems here:

   (a) Some projects have cash inflows followed by one or more outflows. The IRR rule is inverted here: one should accept when the IRR is *below* the discount rate.

   (b) Some projects have a number of changes of sign in their cash flows. Here, there are likely to be multiple internal rates of return. The practitioner must use either NPV or modified internal rate of return here.

5   Next, we considered the specific problems with the NPV for mutually exclusive projects. We showed that, due to differences in either size or timing, the project with the highest IRR need not have the highest NPV. Hence, the IRR rule should not be applied. (Of course, NPV can still be applied.)

   However, we then calculated incremental cash flows. For ease of calculation, we suggested subtracting the cash flows of the smaller project from the cash flows of the larger project. In that way the incremental initial cash flow is negative. One can always reach a correct decision by accepting the larger project if the incremental IRR is greater than the discount rate.

6   We described capital rationing as the case where funds are limited to a fixed dollar amount. With capital rationing the profitability index is a useful method of adjusting the NPV.

Questions and Problems

CONCEPT

1   **Net Present Value**   What is meant by a project's NPV, and what is the decision rule? List the main strengths of the net present value method. What do you think are the weaknesses of NPV in practical capital budgeting analysis?

2   **Payback Period**   What is a project's payback period? Discuss the advantages and disadvantages of the payback period method. If a project has a payback period less than the lifetime of the project, can we know for sure whether the NPV will be positive or negative?

3   **Discounted Payback Period**   Why would a manager use discounted payback period? Can the discounted payback ever be longer than the conventional payback?

4   **Average Accounting Return**   Average accounting return is a popular method with accountants. Review the main strengths and weaknesses of the methodology for practical capital budgeting.

5   **Internal Rate of Return**   In many countries, internal rate of return is the most popular capital budgeting technique, yet in almost all academic textbooks, NPV is put forward as the best method. Why do you think this is the case?

6   **Problems with IRR**   Review the main problems that arise when one uses only IRR to evaluate potential projects. In spite of these pitfalls, why do many managers use IRR instead of NPV to evaluate projects?

7   **Profitability Index**   What is the profitability index, and how is it calculated? Discuss the main applications of the profitability index in capital budgeting. When is it most useful and what are its weaknesses? What is its relationship with NPV?

8   **The Practice of Capital Budgeting**   Why do you think certain capital budgeting techniques are used more often in some countries than in others? If NPV is theoretically the best methodology and most managers of large European corporations have studied corporate finance, why do not all companies use the method?

REGULAR

9 **Calculating Payback Period and NPV** Shire plc has the following mutually exclusive projects.

Year	Project A (£)	Project B (£)
0	−14,000	−6,000
1	4,000	4,500
2	5,500	2,200
3	8,000	200

(a) Suppose Shire's payback period cut-off is 2 years. Which of these two projects should be chosen?

(b) Suppose Shire uses the NPV rule to rank these two projects. Which project should be chosen if the appropriate discount rate is 12 per cent?

10 **Investment Criteria** Which of the following statements is correct:

(a) The NPV and the IRR always result in the same accept/reject decisions.

(b) The NPV cannot rank mutually exclusive projects.

(c) The IRR cannot rank mutually exclusive projects.

(d) The NPV cannot be used in cases of multiple IRRs.

11 **Discounted Payback and Discount Rates** A project has annual cash flows of −€45,000, €35,000, €15,000 and €5,000. What is the payback period for this project? What is the maximum discount rate that would result in a positive NPV?

12 **Calculating Discounted Payback** An investment project has annual cash inflows of £20,000, £35,400, £48,000 and £54,500, and a discount rate of 14 per cent. What is the discounted payback period for these cash flows if the initial cost is £100,000? What if the initial cost is £120,000? What if it is £170,000?

13 **Average Accounting Return** Your firm is considering purchasing a machine which requires an annual investment of €16,000. Depreciation is calculated using 20 per cent reducing balance (i.e. instead of depreciating the machine by the same amount each year, we depreciate the residual value of the investment by 20 per cent). The machine generates, on average, €4,500 per year in additional net income. Assume that the estimated economic life is 5 years.

(a) What is the average accounting return for this machine?

(b) What three flaws are inherent in this decision rule?

14 **Average Accounting Return** Vedanta Resources has invested £8 million in a new mining project lasting 3 years. Depreciation is charged on a straight line basis to zero over the course of the project. The project generates pre-tax income of £2 million each year. The pre-tax income already includes the depreciation expense. If the tax rate is 23 per cent, what is the project's average accounting return (AAR)?

15 **Calculating NPV** Calculate the NPV of the following project for discount rates of 5, 12 and 19 per cent.

Year	0	1	2
Cash flow	−£77,000	+£55,000	+£320,000

16 **Calculating IRR** Marielle Machinery Works is considering a project which has an initial investment of £10,000 and has expected cash flows of £0 in year 1, £7,500 in year 2, and £8,500 in year 3. The company uses the IRR rule to accept or reject projects, and has asked for your assessment on what to do if the required rate of return is 12 per cent.

17 **Calculating Profitability Index** What is the profitability index for a project with an initial investment of €14,000, and has cash flows of €7,300 in year 1, €6,900 in year 2, and €5,700 in year 3? Should the project be accepted or rejected if the discount rate is 14 per cent?

18 **Calculating Profitability Index** Suppose the following two independent investment opportunities are available to Greenplain Ltd. The appropriate discount rate is 10 per cent.

Year	Project Alpha (€)	Project Beta (€)
0	−500	−2,000
1	300	300
2	700	1,800
3	600	1,700

(a) Compute the profitability index for each of the two projects.

(b) Which project(s) should Greenplain accept based on the profitability index rule?

19 **Problems with IRR** Suppose you are offered £5,000 today but must make the following payments:

Year	Cash Flows (£)
0	5,000
1	−2,500
2	−2,000
3	−1,000
4	−1,000

(a) What is the IRR of this offer?

(b) If the appropriate discount rate is 10 per cent, should you accept this offer?

(c) If the appropriate discount rate is 20 per cent, should you accept this offer?

(d) What is the NPV of the offer if the appropriate discount rate is 10 per cent? 20 per cent?

(e) Are the decisions under the NPV rule in part (d) consistent with those of the IRR rule?

20 **NPV versus IRR** Consider the following cash flows on two mutually exclusive projects for Tomatina Recreation SA. Both projects require an annual return of 15 per cent.

Year	Deepwater Fishing (€)	New Submarine Ride (€)
0	−600,000	−1,800,000
1	270,000	1,000,000
2	350,000	700,000
3	300,000	900,000

As a financial analyst for Tomatina, you are asked the following questions:

(a) If your decision rule is to accept the project with the greater IRR, which project should you choose?

(b) Because you are fully aware of the IRR rule's scale problem, you calculate the incremental IRR for the cash flows. Based on your computation, which project should you choose?

(c) To be prudent, you compute the NPV for both projects. Which project should you choose? Is it consistent with the incremental IRR rule?

21 **Capital Budgeting Tools** Consider the following cash flows:

Year	0	1	2	3	4	5
Cash flow	−£15,000	£4,000	£5,000	−£2,000	£7,000	£7,000

(a) What is the payback period for the above project? Assume the cash flows are received continuously throughout each year.

(b) If the discount rate is 10 per cent, what is the NPV of the project?

(c) If the discount rate is 10 per cent, what is the IRR of the project? How many IRRs does the project have? Explain how you would deal with this problem.

(d) If the discount rate is 10 per cent, what is the PI of the project?

22 **Comparing Investment Criteria** Software games company, Avalanche Entertainment, is considering expanding its highly successful online game franchise to the board game or trading card environment. The company has decided that it will invest in one project but not both. Consider the following cash flows of the two mutually exclusive projects. Assume the discount rate for Avalanche Entertainment is 10 per cent.

Year	Trading Cards (€)	Board Game (€)
0	−200	−2,000
1	300	2,200
2	100	900
3	100	500

(a) Based on the payback period rule, which project should be chosen?

(b) Based on the NPV, which project should be chosen?

(c) Based on the IRR, which project should be chosen?

(d) Based on the incremental IRR, which project should be chosen?

23 **Capital Budgeting** Sandy Grey Ltd is in the process of deciding whether or not to revise its line of mobile phones which it manufactures and sells. Their sole market is large corporations and they have not as yet focused on the retail sector. They have estimated that the revision will cost £220,000. Cash flows from increased sales will be £80,000 in the first year. These cash flows will increase by 5 per cent per year. The firm estimates that the new line will be obsolete 5 years from now. Assume the initial cost is paid now and all revenues are received at the end of each year. If the company requires a 10 per cent return for such an investment, should it undertake the revision? Use three investment evaluation techniques to arrive at your answer.

24 **Comparing Investment Criteria** Pinto plc is considering spending €10,000 on insulating its office, which will save it €1,000 per year in heating expenses in perpetuity.

(a) What is the NPV of the investment when the cost of capital is 8 per cent?

(b) What is the IRR of the investment?

(c) What is the payback period of the investment?

25 **Comparing Investment Criteria** The treasurer of Amaro Canned Fruits has projected the cash flows of projects A, B and C as follows.

Year	Project A (€)	Project B (€)	Project C (€)
0	−100,000	−200,000	−100,000
1	70,000	130,000	75,000
2	70,000	130,000	60,000

Suppose the relevant discount rate is 12 per cent a year.

(a) Compute the profitability index for each of the three projects.

(b) Compute the NPV for each of the three projects.

(c) Suppose these three projects are independent. Which project(s) should Amaro accept based on the profitability index rule?

(d) Suppose these three projects are mutually exclusive. Which project(s) should Amaro accept based on the profitability index rule?

(e) Suppose Amaro's budget for these projects is €300,000. The projects are not divisible. Which project(s) should Amaro accept?

26 **Comparing Investment Criteria** Consider the following cash flows of two mutually exclusive projects for Tadcaster Rubber Company. Assume the discount rate for Tadcaster Rubber Company is 10 per cent.

Year	Dry Prepreg (€)	Solvent Prepreg (€)
0	−800,000	−600,000
1	500,000	400,000
2	300,000	600,000
3	900,000	200,000

(a) Based on the payback period, which project should be taken?

(b) Based on the NPV, which project should be taken?

(c) Based on the IRR, which project should be taken?

(d) Based on this analysis, is incremental IRR analysis necessary? If yes, please conduct the analysis.

CHALLENGE

27 **Cash Flow Intuition** A project has an initial cost of I, has a required return of R, and pays C annually for N years.

(a) Find C in terms of I and N such that the project has a payback period just equal to its life.

(b) Find C in terms of I, N, and R such that this is a profitable project according to the NPV decision rule.

(c) Find C in terms of I, N, and R such that the project has a benefit–cost ratio of 2.

28 **Comparing Investment Criteria** You are a senior manager at Airbus and have been authorized to spend up to €200,000 for projects. The three projects you are considering have the following characteristics:

Project A: Initial investment of €150,000. Cash flow of €50,000 at year 1 and €100,000 at year 2. This is a plant expansion project, where the required rate of return is 10 per cent.

Project B: Initial investment of €200,000. Cash flow of €200,000 at year 1 and €111,000 at year 2. This is a new product development project, where the required rate of return is 20 per cent.

Project C: Initial investment of €100,000. Cash flow of €100,000 at year 1 and €100,000 at year 2. This is a market expansion project, where the required rate of return is 20 per cent.

Assume the corporate discount rate is 10 per cent.

Please offer your recommendations, backed by your analysis:

	A	B	C	Implications
Payback period				
IRR				
Incremental IRR				
PI				
NPV				

29 **Project Valuation** The financial manager of Solsken is evaluating a proposal to purchase a new solar machine unit that has a lifetime of 10 years. The new machine would allow the company to make cost savings of SKr4 million per annum. The new fully solar machine would cost SKr9 million and have a resale value of SKr1 million at the end of the project. The required rate of return on such investments is 14 per cent. Use four methods to appraise the value of this investment.

30 **Payback and NPV** An investment under consideration has a payback of 7 years and a cost of £483,000. If the required return is 12 per cent, what is the worst-case NPV? What is the best-case NPV? Explain. Assume the cash flows are conventional.

31 **Multiple IRRs** This problem is useful for testing the ability of financial calculators and computer software. Consider the following cash flows. How many different IRRs are there? (*Hint*: Search between 20 per cent and 70 per cent.) When should we take this project?

Year	Cash Flow (£)
0	−504
1	2,862
2	−6,070
3	5,700
4	−2,000

32 **NPV Valuation** Yuvhadit Ltd wants to set up a private cemetery business. According to the CFO, Barry M. Deep, business is 'looking up'. As a result, the cemetery project will provide a net cash inflow of €80,000 for the firm during the first year, and the cash flows are projected to grow at a rate of 6 per cent per year forever. The project requires an initial investment of €800,000.

(a) If Yuvhadit requires a 12 per cent return on such undertakings, should the cemetery business be started?

(b) The company is somewhat unsure about the assumption of a 6 per cent growth rate in its cash flows. At what constant growth rate would the company just break even if it still required a 12 per cent return on investment?

33 **Calculating IRR** Moshi Mining is set to open a gold mine in northern Tanzania. The mine will cost 6 million rand to open and will have an economic life of 12 years. It will generate a cash inflow of 1 million rand at the end of the first year, and the cash inflows are projected to grow at 10 per cent per year for the next 11 years. After 12 years, the mine will be abandoned. Abandonment costs will be 500,000 rand at the end of year 12.

(a) What is the IRR for the gold mine?

(b) Moshi Mining requires a 10 per cent return on such undertakings. Should the mine be opened?

34 **IRR and NPV** You are out having dinner with your two colleagues who are also studying finance. John, who loves the IRR method, tells you that ranking projects by IRR is fine as long as each project's cash flows can be reinvested at the project's IRR. Your other friend, Beverley, is confused and asks whether NPV

assumes that cash flows are always reinvested at the opportunity cost of capital. Take a deep breath and explain whether John and Beverley are correct.

35 **Investment Appraisal** Many companies have a set of appraisal methods that they recommend their managers use when considering new project investments. Assume that your company uses three methods: NPV (hurdle rate of 20 per cent on all new projects), payback period (2–3 years maximum), and accounting rate of return (20 per cent on all new projects). Explain to your manager why the firm's investment policy may lead to conflicting recommendations. Why do you think your firm has this policy? Is your manager correct to argue that you should focus mainly on the NPV method, using the other criteria as supplementary methodologies? What should the firm do if the project has an NPV of zero?

36 **Calculating Incremental Cash Flows** Darin Clay, the CFO of MakeMoney.com, has to decide between the following two projects:

Year	Project Million	Project Billion
0	−£1,500	−£I_0
1	I_0 + 200	I_0 + 500
2	1,200	1,500
3	1,500	2,000

The expected rate of return for either of the two projects is 12 per cent. What is the range of initial investment (I_0) for which Project Billion is more financially attractive than Project Million?

37 **Problems with IRR** Kikmaheedin Ltd has a project with the following cash flows:

Year	Cash Flow (£)
0	20,000
1	−26,000
2	13,000

What is the IRR of the project? What is happening here?

Exam Question (45 minutes)

1 Assume you are the new financial manager of the bed mattress firm, Fairy Tale Lullaby Ltd. The firm has always used payback period and accounting rate of return to appraise new investments. With your trusty copy of 'Corporate Finance' to hand, you believe that other methods may be more appropriate for the firm. Write a report to the owners of Fairy Tale Lullaby Ltd reviewing the different methods that can be used in investment appraisal together with their strengths and weaknesses. Comment on any practical issues that Fairy Tale Lullaby may face in implementing these methods. (50 marks)

2 A solar panel production firm Soleil SA, is considering an investment in new solar production technology. The new investment would require initial funding of €4 million today and further expenditure on manufacture of €1 million in each of the years 6 and 7. The net cash inflow for the years 1 to 4 is €2.34 million per year. Some equipment could be sold at the end of year 5 when the production ends and together with the cash flows from operation would produce a net cash flow of €4.85 million. Evaluate the investment using four investment appraisal criteria. The required rate of return of Soleil SA is 12 per cent and Soleil has been known to use a payback period of 2 years in the past. However, the firm's managers believe that this payback period may be too short. (50 marks)

Mini Case

Davies Gold Mining

Dick Davies, the owner of Davies Gold Mining, is evaluating a new gold mine in Tanzania. Barry Koch, the company's geologist, has just finished his analysis of the mine site. He has estimated that the mine would be productive for 8 years, after which the gold would be completely mined. Barry has taken an estimate of the gold deposits to Andy Marshall, the company's financial officer. Andy has been asked by Dick to perform an analysis of the new mine and present his recommendation on whether the company should open the new mine.

Andy has used the estimates provided by Barry to determine the revenues that could be expected from the mine. He has also projected the expense of opening the mine and the annual operating expenses. If the company opens the mine, it will cost £500 million today, and it will have a cash outflow of £80 million 9 years from today in costs associated with closing the mine and reclaiming the area surrounding it. The expected cash flows each year from the mine are shown in the following table. Davies Gold Mining has a 12 per cent required return on all of its gold mines.

Year	Cash Flow (£)
0	−500,000,000
1	60,000,000
2	90,000,000
3	170,000,000
4	230,000,000
5	205,000,000
6	140,000,000
7	110,000,000
8	70,000,000
9	−80,000,000

1   Construct a spreadsheet to calculate the payback period, internal rate of return, modified internal rate of return, and net present value of the proposed mine.

2   Based on your analysis, should the company open the mine?

3   Bonus question: Most spreadsheets do not have a built-in formula to calculate the payback period. Write a VBA script that calculates the payback period for a project.

Practical Case Study

In recent years, many firms have experienced significant difficulties in running their operations. This has primarily been down to the stagnant global economic environment, but is also a result of exceptionally high volatility in the financial markets. Undertake your own research and identify a firm that has undergone a significant restructuring of its business.

1   Use NPV and other capital budgeting theories to explain the reasoning behind their restructuring.

2   Is it possible for the value of distressed firms' shares to go up even though their sales revenues are extremely likely to fall as a result of their decisions? Explain your answer.

3   What do you think would be the effect of your firm's business decisions on its risk? How would this factor into the value of your company's operations?

4   Can you think of any other business decisions your company could have made to protect itself against future economic conditions? Give some reasons why you think it did not choose these.

5   Look up the share price of your firm and search the Internet (FT.com, Yahoo! Finance, Reuters, Google News are examples) for information on your company over the last 3 years. What was the main reason for the financial distress your company is currently in? Do you think its restructuring strategy will be successful? Explain.

Additional Reading

The techniques presented in this chapter are used in all industries to assess the value of potential investments. The papers below give the reader some insight into their strengths and weaknesses:

1   Chiang, Y.H., E.W.L. Cheng and P.T.I. Lam (2010) 'Employing the Net Present Value – Consistent IRR Methods for PFI Contracts', *Journal of Construction Engineering and Management*, Vol. 136, No. 7, 811–814.

2   Johnson, N.H. and B.D. Solomon (2010) 'A Net-Present Value Analysis for a Wind Turbine Purchase at a Small US College', *Energies*, Vol. 3, No. 5, 943–959.

3   Kahn, M.J. and E.F. Nelling (2010) 'Estimating the Value of Medical Education: A Net Present Value Approach', *Teaching and Learning in Medicine: An International Journal*, Vol. 22, No. 3, 205–208.

Endnotes

1   Depreciation will be treated in more detail in the next chapter.

2   Of course, we could have directly solved for R in this example after setting NPV equal to zero. However, with long series of cash flows, one cannot generally directly solve for R. Instead, one is forced to use trial and error (or let a machine use trial and error).

3   One can derive the IRR directly for a problem with an initial outflow and up to four subsequent inflows. In the case of two subsequent inflows, for example, the quadratic formula is needed. In general, however, only trial and error will work for an outflow and five or more subsequent inflows.

4   This paragraph implicitly assumes that the cash flows of the project are risk-free. In this way we can treat the borrowing rate as the discount rate for a firm needing £100. With risky cash flows, another discount rate would be chosen. However, the intuition behind the decision to accept when the IRR is less than the discount rate would still apply.

5   The calculations are

$$-£100 + \frac{£230}{1.1} - \frac{£132}{(1.1)^2}$$
$$-£10 + 209.09 - 109.09 = 0$$

and

$$-£100 + \frac{£230}{1.2} - \frac{£132}{(1.2)^2}$$
$$-£100 + 191.67 - 91.67 = 0$$

Thus, we have multiple rates of return.

6   We assume a zero rate of interest because his class lasted only 90 minutes. It just seemed like a lot longer.

7   Alternatively, we could have subtracted the larger project's cash flows from the smaller project's cash flows. This would have left an *inflow* at date 0, making it necessary to use the IRR rule for financing situations. This would work, but we find it more confusing.

8   In this example, we first showed that the NPVs of the two projects are equal when the discount rate is 10.55 per cent. We next showed that the incremental IRR is also 10.55 per cent. This is not a coincidence; this equality must *always* hold. The incremental IRR is the rate that causes the incremental cash flows to have zero NPV. The incremental cash flows have zero NPV when the two projects have the same NPV.

Making Capital Investment Decisions

Corporate financial managers have a responsibility to identify and exploit investment opportunities wherever they can. One such area that came to prominence in 2015 was the rise of superbugs and exceptionally hazardous diseases, like Ebola. It may seem tasteless to think of financial gain when so many people are dying, but investments in technology and medicine may result in the eradication of these microscopic killers and prevent the emergence of new and as yet unknown biological dangers.

At the end of 2014, Merck (the multinational pharmaceuticals firm) invested $9.5 billion in the US biotech company, Cubist Inc., which is focused on developing new antibiotics to combat the ever-growing range of drug-resistant harmful bacteria. When more than 23,000 people are dying of bacterial related infections every year, there is a great opportunity for pharmaceutical firms to create value and resolve a fundamental danger to mankind at the same time. It's not often one can say that!

This chapter follows up on our previous one by delving more deeply into capital budgeting and the evaluation of projects similar to Merck's decision to buy a biotech firm. We identify the relevant cash flows of a project, including initial investment outlays, requirements for net working capital and operating cash flows. Further, we look at the effects of depreciation and taxes. We also examine the impact of inflation, and show how to consistently evaluate the NPV analysis of a project.

KEY NOTATIONS

NPV	Net present value
EBIT	Earnings before interest and taxes
OCF	Operating cash flows
t_c	Corporate tax rate
C_i	Cash flow at time i
PV	Present value

7.1   Incremental Cash Flows

Cash Flows – Not Accounting Income

You may not have thought about it, but there is a big difference between corporate finance courses and financial accounting courses. Techniques in corporate finance generally use cash flows, whereas financial accounting generally stresses income or earnings numbers. Certainly our text follows this tradition: our net present value techniques discount cash flows, not earnings. When considering a single project, we discount the cash flows that the firm receives from the project. When valuing the firm as a whole, we discount dividends – not earnings – because dividends are the cash flows that an investor receives. With the *free cash flow to the firm* method (see **Chapter 5**), we use cash flows themselves to value a firm.

Chapter 5
Page 120

Example 7.1

Relevant Cash Flows

Weber-Decker GmbH just paid €1 million in cash for a building as part of a new capital budgeting project. This entire €1 million is an immediate cash outflow. However, assuming 20 per cent reducing balance depreciation over 20 years, only €200,000 (=€1 million × 20 per cent) is considered an accounting expense in the current year. Current earnings are thereby reduced by only €200,000. The remaining €800,000 is expensed over the following 19 years. For capital budgeting purposes, the relevant cash outflow at date 0 is the full €1 million, not the reduction in earnings of only €200,000.

Always discount cash flows, not earnings, when performing a capital budgeting calculation. Earnings do not represent real money. You cannot spend out of earnings, you cannot eat out of earnings, and you cannot pay dividends out of earnings. You can do these things only out of cash flow.

In addition, it is not enough to use cash flows. In calculating the NPV of a project, only cash flows that are *incremental* to the project should be used. These cash flows are the changes in the firm's cash flows that occur as a direct consequence of accepting the project. That is, we are interested in the difference between the cash flows of the firm with the project and the cash flows of the firm without the project.

The use of incremental cash flows sounds easy enough, but pitfalls abound in the real world. We describe how to avoid some of the pitfalls of determining incremental cash flows.

Sunk Costs

A sunk cost is a cost that has already occurred. Because sunk costs are in the past, they cannot be changed by the decision to accept or reject the project. Just as we 'let bygones be bygones', we should ignore such costs. Sunk costs are not incremental cash outflows.

Example 7.2

Sunk Costs

Hill Electronics Ltd is currently evaluating the NPV of establishing a line of 3D televisions. As part of the evaluation, the company had paid a consulting firm £100,000 to perform a test marketing analysis. The expenditure was made last year. Is this cost relevant for the capital budgeting decision now confronting the management of Hill Electronics Ltd?

The answer is no. The £100,000 is not recoverable, so the £100,000 expenditure is a sunk cost. Of course, the decision to spend £100,000 for a marketing analysis was a capital budgeting decision itself and was perfectly relevant *before* it was sunk. Our point is that once the company incurred the expense, the cost became irrelevant for any future decision.

Opportunity Costs

Your firm may have an asset that it is considering selling, leasing or employing elsewhere in the business. If the asset is used in a new project, potential revenues from alternative uses are lost. These lost revenues can meaningfully be viewed as costs. They are called opportunity costs because, by taking the project, the firm forgoes other opportunities for using the assets. Clearly, opportunity costs assume that another valuable opportunity will be forgone if the project is adopted. This, in itself, is a prediction of the future and estimated with a degree of uncertainty.

Example 7.3

Opportunity Costs

Suppose Martinez Trading has an empty warehouse in Salamanca that can be used to store a new line of e-readers. The company hopes to sell these e-readers to affluent European consumers. Should the warehouse be considered a cost in the decision to sell the machines?

The answer is yes. The company could sell the warehouse if the firm decides not to market the e-readers. Thus, the sales price of the warehouse is an opportunity cost in the e-reader decision.

Side Effects

Another difficulty in determining incremental cash flows comes from the side effects of the proposed project on other parts of the firm. A side effect is classified as either erosion (also cannibalization) or synergy. Erosion occurs when a new product reduces the sales and, hence, the cash flows of existing products. Synergy occurs when a new project increases the cash flows of existing projects. Because side effects predict the spending habits of customers, they are necessarily hypothetical and difficult to estimate.

Example 7.4

Synergies

Suppose Innovative Motors (IM) is determining the NPV of a new convertible sports car. Some of the customers who would purchase the car are owners of IM's SUVs. Are all sales and profits from the new convertible sports car incremental?

The answer is no because some of the cash flow represents transfers from other elements of IM's product line. This is erosion, which must be included in the NPV calculation. Without taking erosion into account, IM might erroneously calculate the NPV of the sports car to be, say, £100 million. If half the customers are transfers from the SUV and lost SUV sales have an NPV of −£150 million, the true NPV is −£50 million (=£100 million − £150 million).

IM is also contemplating the formation of a racing team. The team is forecast to lose money for the foreseeable future, with perhaps the best projection showing an NPV of −£35 million for the operation. However, IM's managers are aware that the team will likely generate great publicity for all of IM's products. A consultant estimates that the increase in cash flows elsewhere in the firm has a present value of £65 million. Assuming that the consultant's estimates of synergy are trustworthy, the net present value of the team is £30 million (=£65 million − £35 million). The managers should form the team.

Allocated Costs

Frequently a particular expenditure benefits a number of projects. Accountants allocate this cost across the different projects when determining income. However, for capital budgeting purposes, this allocated cost should be viewed as a cash outflow of a project only if it is an incremental cost of the project.

Example 7.5

Allocated Costs

Voetmann Consulting NV devotes one wing of its suite of offices to a library requiring a cash outflow of €100,000 a year in upkeep. A proposed capital budgeting project is expected to generate revenue equal to 5 per cent of the overall firm's sales. An executive at the firm, H. Sears, argues that €5,000 (=5 per cent × €100,000) should be viewed as the proposed project's share of the library's costs. Is this appropriate for capital budgeting?

The answer is no. One must ask what the difference is between the cash flows of the entire firm with the project and the cash flows of the entire firm without the project. The firm will spend €100,000 on library upkeep whether or not the proposed project is accepted. Because acceptance of the proposed project does not affect this cash flow, the cash flow should be ignored when calculating the NPV of the project.

7.2 Energy Renewables Ltd: An Example

We next consider the example of a proposed investment in an innovative renewable energy project. Our example involves the hypothetical firm, Energy Renewables Ltd and the development of a new wind turbine technology. In any capital budgeting analysis, the broad steps to follow are the same. These are:

1 Calculation of depreciation for each year
2 Generation of the Income Statement to identify the tax that is due to be paid
3 Construction of the cash flow forecast to generate cash flows
4 Investment appraisal analysis using the techniques introduced in Chapter 6.

In this case study, we will take you through a detailed capital budgeting case completing each step at a time. However, there is more than one way to arrive at the final decision so just try and understand the calculations and what is happening at each step.

History

Energy Renewables Ltd was originally established in 2001 to manufacture and research new solar power technology. However, in recent years, the company has moved away from its roots as a solar power expert to wind energy as the market in this area has grown. Energy Renewables management has sought opportunities in whatever businesses seem to have potential for cash flow. Recently the firm identified a niche segment for small-scale wind turbines to provide low cost energy to manufacturers that have an explicit environment policy relating to industrial waste. Although there are a number of options that environmental-friendly firms can pursue, Energy Renewables believes its wind technology will be very attractive to firms that have an explicit policy towards environment waste. They also believe that it would be difficult for competitors to take advantage of the opportunity because of the cost advantages from Energy Renewable's wind turbines and the firm's highly developed marketing skills in the sector.

Market Research

Market research has been carried out throughout Europe and the feedback was much better than expected. The company that Energy Renewables hired to undertake the analysis supported the conclusion that the new wind turbines could achieve a 10 to 15 per cent share of the market. Of course, some people at Energy Renewables complained about the £250,000 cost of the market research. (As we shall see later, this is a sunk cost and should not be included in project evaluation.)

The Proposal

As a result of the positive market research, Energy Renewables is considering an investment to build high value manufacturing facilities to produce its wind turbines. The turbines would be manufactured in a large vacant lot owned by the firm. The vacant lot has been valued by an independent surveyor, who estimates that it could be sold now for £1,500,000 after taxes.

Your team has come up with the following estimates:

1 The technology underlying the wind turbines is expected to be obsolete after five years, at which point the project will be terminated.
2 The cost of the manufacturing facilities is £3,000,000. The facilities are expected to have an estimated market value at the end of 5 years of £1,000,000.
3 Production of wind turbines by year during the 5-year life of the project is expected to be as follows: 8 units, 12 units, 24 units, 20 units and 12 units.

4   The price of turbines in the first year will be £200,000. The turbine market is uncertain, so you expect that the price of turbines will increase at only 2 per cent per year, as compared to the anticipated general inflation rate of 5 per cent.

5   The rare metals used to produce wind turbines are rapidly becoming more expensive. Because of this, production cash outflows are expected to grow at 10 per cent per year. First-year production costs will be £100,000 per unit.

6   Net working capital (that is, investment in raw materials and inventory) will immediately (year 0) grow to £100,000. This will remain level till year 2, when it will grow to £160,000, then increase again to £250,000 in year 3. By year 4 the project will be winding down and net working capital will be £210,000. At the end of the project, net working capital will return to zero as all inventory and raw materials are sold off.

7   Based on Energy Renewables' taxable income, the appropriate incremental corporate tax rate in the wind turbine project is 20 per cent. The appropriate discount rate for this type of investment is 12 per cent.

Step 1: Depreciation

In Europe, assets are depreciated for tax purposes using a system called capital allowances or tax depreciation. This effectively entails that assets are depreciated by a certain percentage each year. Assume the capital allowances rate on plant and machinery is 20 per cent per annum. That is, plant and machinery depreciate by 20 per cent per year. Depreciation of this kind is known as the reducing balance method, in contrast to straight line depreciation, where asset values fall by the same amount each year.

The cost of the facilities is £3,000,000 and so depreciation in year 1 is £600,000 (20 per cent of £3,000,000). This leaves a residual value of £2,400,000 and in year 2, the depreciation will be (20 per cent of £2,400,000 =) £480,000. The residual value at the end of year 2 will be (£2,400,000 − £480,000 =) £1,920,000. Depreciation is calculated for the remaining life of the project in the same way. Table 7.1 provides a detailed breakdown of the depreciation calculation for the new project.

Table 7.1 Depreciation Calculation using Capital Allowances (20 per cent Reducing Balance, £s)

	1	2	3	4	5
Initial Value	3,000,000	2,400,000	1,920,000	1,536,000	1,228,800
Depreciation	600,000	480,000	384,000	307,200	228,800
Residual Value	2,400,000	1,920,000	1,536,000	1,228,800	1,000,000

Important Note: In Table 7.1, we took the year 5 resale value of £1,000,000 and used this as the terminal value of the facilities. This resulted in a depreciation of £228,800 in the final year.

An alternative way of calculating the depreciation in the final year is to calculate depreciation as normal (that is, 20 per cent of £1,228,800 = £245,760), which gives a new terminal value of £1,228,800 − £245,760 = £983,040. There will then be a taxable gain of £16,960 on the sale of the facilities, which is the difference between the terminal value (£983,040) and the resale value (£1,000,000). The year 5 depreciation (£245,760) less the gain on the sale of the facilities (£16,960) is equal to £228,800, which is the same as the depreciation for year 5 in the approach taken in Table 7.1. Therefore, both approaches end up with the same overall impact on Net Income and tax paid (check this for yourself).

In our alternative approach to depreciation, the market value of the facilities (£1,000,000) is greater than the book value (£983,040), giving a profit on sale. Taxes must be paid on the profit because the difference between the market value and the book value is 'excess' depreciation, and it must be 'recaptured' when the asset is sold. In this case, Energy Renewables would have over-depreciated the asset by £16,960. Because the depreciation was too high, the company paid too little in taxes.

Notice this is not a tax on a long-term capital gain. Further, what is and what is not a capital gain is ultimately up to taxing authorities, and the specific rules can be very complex. We will ignore capital gains taxes for the most part. Finally, if the book value exceeds the market value, then the difference is treated as a loss for tax purposes. For example, if Energy Renewables sold the facilities for £900,000, then the book value exceeds the market value by £83,040. In this case, Energy Renewables would make a tax savings.

Step 2: The Income Statement

In any capital budgeting analysis, an income statement must be prepared so that the firm's incremental tax costs can be calculated. Unlike depreciation, tax is a cash flow that must be estimated. Table 7.2 presents the operating revenues and costs of Energy Renewables and these follow from assumptions made by the corporate planning staff at the firm. In other words, the estimates critically depend on the fact that product prices are projected to increase at 2 per cent per year and costs per unit are projected to increase at 10 per cent per year.

Table 7.2 Operating Revenues and Costs of Energy Renewables (£s)

Year	1	2	3	4	5
Quantity Produced	8	12	24	20	12
Price	200,000	204,000	208,080	212,242	216,486
Sales Revenues	**1,600,000**	**2,448,000**	**4,993,920**	**4,244,832**	**2,597,837**
Cost per unit	100,000	110,000	121,000	133,100	146,410
Operating Costs	**800,000**	**1,320,000**	**2,904,000**	**2,662,000**	**1,756,920**

Note: Prices rise at 2 per cent per year; unit costs rise at 10 per cent per year.

The information in Table 7.2 is now used to prepare the project's income statement (see **Chapter 3**, Section 3.2 for more information on the income statement). The two main items are the sales revenues and operating costs. Table 7.3 gives the information that is used to calculate Energy Renewables' net income and tax payments. Remember that cash outflows are negative values and inflows are positive.

Chapter 3 Page 66

The key figure from Table 7.3 is the tax paid since this is a cash flow that needs to be included in step 3 of the capital budgeting analysis.

Table 7.3 Income Statement of Energy Renewables (£s)

Year	1	2	3	4	5
Sales	1,600,000	2,448,000	4,993,920	4,244,832	2,597,837
Operating Costs	800,000	1,320,000	2,904,000	2,662,000	1,756,920
Depreciation	600,000	480,000	384,000	307,200	228,800
Income before Taxes	200,000	648,000	1,705,920	1,275,632	612,117
Tax (at 20%)	40,000	129,600	341,184	255,126	122,423
Net Income	160,000	518,400	1,364,736	1,020,506	489,694

Step 3: Cash Flow Forecast

In Step 3, we estimate the actual cash flows that will arise as a result of investing in the project. First we need to calculate Investment Cash Flows and then Operating Cash Flows.

Investment Cash Flows

Investment cash flows arise from any expenditure in assets that are required to undertake the project. This include inventory, property, machinery and other assets. We begin with Net Working Capital.

Chapter 26 Page 699

Net working capital is defined as the difference between current assets and current liabilities (see **Chapter 26**, Section 26.1 for more information on managing net working capital). Like any other manufacturing firm, Energy Renewables finds that it must maintain an investment in working capital. It will purchase raw materials before production and sale, giving rise to an investment in inventory. It will maintain cash as a buffer against unforeseen expenditures. Its credit sales will generate trade receivables.

Management determines that an immediate (year 0) investment in the different items of working capital of £100,000 is required. Working capital is forecast to rise in the early years of the project as expansion occurs and then to fall to £0 by the project's end. In other words, the investment in working capital is to be completely recovered by the end of the project's life. This is a common assumption in capital budgeting and reflects the situation that all inventory is sold by the end, the cash balance maintained as a buffer is liquidated, and all outstanding credit sales (trade receivables) are collected.

Increases in working capital in the early years must be funded by cash generated elsewhere in the firm. Hence, these increases are viewed as cash *outflows*. To reiterate, it is the *increase* in working capital over a year that leads to a cash outflow in that year. Even if working capital is at a high level, there will be no cash outflow over a year if working capital stays constant over that year. Conversely, decreases in working capital in the later years are viewed as cash inflows. All of these cash flows are presented in Table 7.4. A more complete discussion of working capital is provided later in this section.

Net working capital represents an investment of cash flows in the current assets and liabilities of the firm. These are short term in nature since they are used in the operationalization of the project. Long-term investment cash flows represent the investment in the manufacturing facilities themselves. We must also include any opportunity costs that are incurred as a result of undertaking the project.

Table 7.4 Change in Net Working Capital (£s)

Year	0	1	2	3	4	5
Net Working Capital	100,000	100,000	160,000	250,000	210,000	—
Change in Net Working Capital	100,000	—	60,000	90,000	−40,000	−210,000
Cash Flow	−100,000	—	−60,000	−90,000	40,000	210,000

The investment outlays for the project are summarized in Table 7.5. They consist of three parts:

1 *The production facilities*: The purchase requires an immediate (year 0) cash outflow of £3,000,000. The firm realizes a cash inflow when the facilities are sold in year 5. These cash flows are shown in line 1 of Table 7.5.

2 *The opportunity cost of not selling the vacant lot*: If Energy Renewables accepts the wind turbine project, it will use a vacant lot and land that could otherwise be sold. The estimated sale price of the vacant lot and land is therefore included as an *opportunity cost* in year 0, as presented in line 2. Opportunity costs are treated as cash outflows for purposes of capital budgeting. However, note that if the project is accepted, management assumes that the vacant lot and land will be sold for £1,500,000 (after taxes) in year 5.

3 The market research cost of £250,000 is not included. The tests occurred in the past and should be viewed as a *sunk cost*.

4 *The investment in working capital*: To recap, there are three investments in this example: the manufacturing facilities, the opportunity cost of the vacant lot and land, and the changes in working capital. The total cash flow from these three investments is shown in line 4 of Table 7.5.

Table 7.5 Investment Cash Flows (£s; all cash flows occur at the end of the year)

Year	0	1	2	3	4	5
Manufacturing Facilities	−3,000,000					1,000,000
Opportunity Cost (Vacant Lot)	−1,500,000					1,500,000
Net Working Capital	−100,000	0	−60,000	−90,000	40,000	210,000
Investment Cash Flows	**−4,600,000**	**0**	**−60,000**	**−90,000**	**40,000**	**2,710,000**

Operating Cash Flow

Chapter 3
Page 70

Operating cash flows arise from the investment itself (see **Chapter 3**, Section 3.5 for more information on cash flows). Clearly, these need to be positive for the project to be worthwhile. There are a number of ways to calculate operating cash flows and these are discussed in Section 7.4. For now, we will follow one approach by working from the Net Income figure in Stage 2 of the Capital Budgeting analysis and adding back all non-cash accounting items. In our example, the only non-cash item in the Income Statement is depreciation and so we simply add this to our net income figure to generate the operating cash flow for each year. Table 7.6 shows how the operating cash flow is calculated.

Table 7.6 Operating Cash Flows (£s; all cash flows occur at the *end* of the year)

Year	1	2	3	4	5
Net Income	160,000	518,400	1,364,736	1,020,506	489,694
Add Depreciation	600,000	480,000	384,000	307,200	228,800
Operating Cash Flow	760,000	998,400	1,748,736	1,327,706	718,494

Net Cash Flow

Net Cash flow is finally determined in Table 7.7 by adding the Investment Cash Flow and Operating Cash Flow together.

Table 7.7 Incremental Cash Flows for Energy Renewables (£s)

Year	0	1	2	3	4	5
Investment Cash Flow	−4,600,000	0	−60,000	−90,000	40,000	2,710,000
Operating Cash Flow		760,000	998,400	1,748,736	1,327,706	718,494
Net Cash Flow	−4,600,000	760,000	938,400	1,658,736	1,367,706	3,428,494

Step 4: Investment Appraisal

Net Present Value

The NPV of the Energy Renewables wind turbine project can be calculated from the net cash flows of Table 7.7. If the discount rate is 12 per cent, the NPV is as follows:

$$\text{NPV} = -£4,600,000 + \frac{£760,000}{1.12} + \frac{£938,400}{1.12^2} + \frac{£1,658,736}{1.12^3} + \frac{£1,367,706}{1.12^4} + \frac{£3,428,494}{1.12^5}$$

This gives an NPV of £821,934.75. If the discount rate is 17.48 per cent, the project will have a zero NPV. In other words, the project's internal rate of return is 17.48 per cent. If the discount rate of the Energy Renewables wind turbine project is above 17.48 per cent, it should not be accepted because its NPV would be negative.

A Note about Net Working Capital

The investment in net working capital is an important part of any capital budgeting analysis. While we explicitly considered net working capital in Table 7.4, readers may wonder where the numbers in these lines came from. An investment in net working capital arises whenever (1) inventory is purchased, (2) cash is kept in the project as a buffer against unexpected expenditures, and (3) credit sales are made, generating trade receivables rather than cash. (The investment in net working capital is reduced by credit purchases, which generate trade payables.) This investment in net working capital represents a cash outflow because cash generated elsewhere in the firm is tied up in the project.

To see how the investment in net working capital is built from its component parts, we focus on year 1. We see in Table 7.2 that Energy Renewables' managers predict sales in year 1 to be £1,600,000 and operating costs to be £800,000. If both the sales and costs were cash transactions, the firm would receive £800,000 (=£1,600,000 − £800,000). As stated earlier, this cash flow would occur at the *end* of year 1.

Now let us give you more information. The managers:

1   Forecast that there will be £1,490,000 of trade sales on credit but that £90,000 will still be owed at the end of year 1, implying accounts receivable of £90,000 will be collected at the end of year 2.

2   Believe that they can defer payment on £30,000 of the £800,000 of costs until year 2.

3   Decide that inventory of £25,000 should be left on hand at the end of year 1 to avoid *stockouts* (that is, running out of inventory).

4   Decide that cash of £15,000 should be earmarked for the project at the end of year 1 to avoid running out of cash.

Thus, net working capital at the end of year 1 is:

$$\underset{\substack{\text{Trade}\\\text{receivables}}}{£90,000} - \underset{\substack{\text{Trade}\\\text{payables}}}{£30,000} + \underset{\substack{\text{Inventory}}}{£25,000} + \underset{\substack{\text{Cash}}}{£15,000} = \underset{\substack{\text{Net working}\\\text{capital}}}{£100,000}$$

Because £100,000 of cash generated elsewhere in the firm must be used to offset this requirement for net working capital, Energy Renewables' managers correctly view the investment in net working capital as a cash outflow of the project. As the project grows over time, needs for net working capital increase. *Changes* in net working capital from year to year represent further cash flows, as indicated by the negative numbers for the first few years on line 3 of Table 7.4. However, in the declining years of the project, net working capital is reduced – ultimately to zero. That is, trade receivables are finally collected, the project's cash buffer is returned to the rest of the corporation, and all remaining inventory is sold off. This frees up cash in the later years, as indicated by positive numbers in years 4 and 5 on line 3.

Typically corporate worksheets treat net working capital as a whole. The individual components of working capital (receivables, inventory and the like) do not generally appear in the worksheets. However, the reader should remember that the working capital numbers in the worksheets are not pulled out of thin air. Rather, they result from a meticulous forecast of the components, just as we illustrated for year 1.

A Note about Depreciation

The Energy Renewables case made some assumptions about depreciation. Where did these assumptions come from? Assets are depreciated according to the tax rules that apply in each country. In general there are two main asset categories for depreciation: plant and machinery, and land/buildings. However, other countries may have more complex systems for estimating depreciation expenses and these should be considered before carrying out a capital budgeting analysis.

Depreciation rates change regularly and a financial manager must be up to date with the current applicable rates. For example, as of 2015, the rate is 18 per cent reducing balance on plant and machinery for the UK. Buildings and land tend not to be depreciated but should be revalued periodically to reflect value increases or decreases.

Currently, each country in the European Union has its own tax system and this is seen as one of the major obstacles for full integration of the different European economies. However, a working group has been set up to develop a Common Consolidated Corporate Tax Base (CCCTB) for all countries. Although it will take several years for it to be enacted, the CCCTB is definitely a step in the right direction. The main recommendations of the working group are that all countries will work from a common tax basis so that European companies can easily operate in all countries within the EU.

Interest Expense

It may have bothered you that interest expense was ignored in the Energy Renewables example. After all, many projects are at least partially financed with debt, particularly wind turbine facilities that are likely to increase the debt capacity of the firm. As it turns out, our approach of assuming no debt financing is rather standard in the real world. Firms typically calculate a project's cash flows under the assumption that the project is financed only with equity. Any adjustments for debt financing are reflected in the discount rate, not the cash flows. The treatment of debt in capital budgeting will be covered in depth later in the text. Suffice it to say at this time that the full ramifications of debt financing are well beyond our current discussion.

7.3   Inflation and Capital Budgeting

Chapter 30
Page 824

Inflation is an important fact of economic life, and it must be considered in capital budgeting. We begin our examination of inflation by considering the relationship between interest rates and inflation (Inflation is discussed in more detail in **Chapter 30**, Section 30.4 in the context of international finance.)

Interest Rates and Inflation

Suppose a bank offers a one-year interest rate of 10 per cent. This means that an individual who deposits £1,000 will receive £1,100 (=£1,000 × 1.10) in one year. Although 10 per cent may seem like a handsome return, one can put it in perspective only after examining the rate of inflation.

Imagine that the rate of inflation is 6 per cent over the year and it affects all goods equally. For example, a restaurant that charges £1.00 for a hamburger today will charge £1.06 for the same hamburger at the end of the year. You can use your £1,000 to buy 1,000 hamburgers today (date 0). Alternatively, if you put your money in the bank, you can buy 1,038 (=£1,100/£1.06) hamburgers at date 1. Thus, lending increases your hamburger consumption by only 3.8 per cent.

Because the prices of all goods rise at this 6 per cent rate, lending lets you increase your consumption of any single good or any combination of goods by only 3.8 per cent. Thus, 3.8 per cent is what you are *really* earning through your savings account, after adjusting for inflation. Economists refer to the 3.8 per cent number as the *real interest rate*. Economists refer to the 10 per cent rate as the *nominal interest rate* or simply the *interest rate*. This discussion is illustrated in Figure 7.1.

We have used an example with a specific nominal interest rate and a specific inflation rate. In general, the formula between real and nominal interest rates can be written as follows:

$$1 + \text{Nominal interest rate} = (1 + \text{Real interest rate}) \times (1 + \text{Inflation rate})$$

Rearranging terms, we have:

$$\text{Real interest rate} = \frac{1 + \text{Nominal interest rate}}{1 + \text{Inflation rate}} - 1 \qquad (7.1)$$

The formula indicates that the real interest rate in our example is 3.8 per cent (=1.10/1.06 − 1).

Figure 7.1 Calculation of Real Rate of Interest

Today (Date 0)
Individual invests £1,000 in bank.

---------- 10% ---------->

Interest rate

3.8%

(Because hamburgers sell for £1 at date 0, £1,000 would have purchased 1,000 hamburgers.)

Date 1
Individual receives £1,100 from bank.

Inflation rate has been 6% over year.

Because each hamburger sells for £1.06 at date 1, 1,038 (=£1,100/£1.06) hamburgers can be purchased

Hamburger is used as an illustrative good. 1,038 hamburgers can be purchased on date 1 instead of 1,000 hamburgers at date 0. Real interest rate = 1,038/1,000 − 1 = 3.8%.

Equation 7.1 determines the real interest rate precisely. The following formula is an approximation:

$$\text{Real interest rate} \cong \text{Nominal interest rate} - \text{Inflation rate} \qquad (7.2)$$

The symbol ≅ indicates that the equation is approximately true. This latter formula calculates the real rate in our example like this:

$$4\% = 10\% - 6\%$$

The student should be aware that, although Equation 7.2 may seem more intuitive than Equation 7.1, 7.2 is only an approximation and should not be used in a formal analysis.

Cash Flow and Inflation

The previous analysis defines two types of interest rates, nominal rates and real rates, and relates them through Equation 7.1. Capital budgeting requires data on cash flows as well as on interest rates. Like interest rates, cash flows can be expressed in either nominal or real terms.

A nominal cash flow refers to the actual money in cash to be received (or paid out). A real cash flow refers to the cash flow's purchasing power. These definitions are best explained by an example.

Example 7.6

Nominal versus Real Cash Flow

Lioness Publishing has just purchased the rights to the next book of famed romantic novelist, Barbara Musk. Still unwritten, the book should be available to the public in 4 years. Currently, romantic novels sell for €10.00 in paperback. The publishers believe that inflation will be 6 per cent a year over the next 4 years. Because romantic novels are so popular, the publishers anticipate that their prices will rise about 2 per cent per year more than the inflation rate over the next 4 years. Lioness Publishing plans to sell the novel at €13.60 [$=(1.08)^4 \times €10.00$] 4 years from now, anticipating sales of 100,000 copies.

The expected cash flow in the fourth year of €1.36 million (= €13.60 × 100,000) is a *nominal cash flow*. That is, the firm expects to receive €1.36 million at that time. In other words, a nominal cash flow refers to the actual cash flow in euros to be received in the future.

The purchasing power of €1.36 million in 4 years is:

$$€1.08 \text{ million} = \frac{€1.36 \text{ million}}{(1.06)^4}$$

The figure of €1.08 million is a *real cash flow* because it is expressed in terms of purchasing power.

Discounting: Nominal or Real?

Our previous discussion showed that interest rates can be expressed in either nominal or real terms. Similarly, cash flows can be expressed in either nominal or real terms. Given these choices, how should one express interest rates and cash flows when performing capital budgeting?

Financial practitioners correctly stress the need to maintain *consistency* between cash flows and discount rates. That is:

- *Nominal* cash flows must be discounted at the *nominal* rate.
- *Real* cash flows must be discounted at the *real* rate.

As long as one is consistent, either approach is correct. To minimize computational error, it is generally advisable in practice to choose the approach that is easiest. This idea is illustrated in the following two examples.

Example 7.7

Real and Nominal Discounting

Shields Electric forecasts the following nominal cash flows on a particular project:

	0	1	2
Cash flow	−£1,000	£600	£650

The nominal discount rate is 14 per cent, and the inflation rate is forecast to be 5 per cent. What is the value of the project?

Using Nominal Quantities   The NPV can be calculated as:

$$£26.47 = −£1,000 + \frac{£600}{1.14} + \frac{£650}{(1.14)^2}$$

The project should be accepted.

Using Real Quantities   The real cash flows are these:

	0	1	2
Cash flow	−£1,000	£571.43 $\left(\dfrac{£600}{1.05}\right)$	£589.57 $\left(\dfrac{£650}{(1.05)^2}\right)$

As we have discussed, the real discount rate is 8.57143 per cent (=1.14/1.05 − 1).
The NPV can be calculated as:

$$£26.47 = -£1,000 + \frac{£571.43}{1.0857143} + \frac{£589.57}{(1.0857143)^2}$$

The NPV is the same whether cash flows are expressed in nominal or in real quantities. It must always be the case that the NPV is the same under the two different approaches.

Because both approaches always yield the same result, which one should be used? Use the approach that is simpler because the simpler approach generally leads to fewer computational errors. The Shields Electric example begins with nominal cash flows, so nominal quantities produce a simpler calculation here.

Example 7.8

Real and Nominal NPV

Bella SpA generated the following forecast for a capital budgeting project:

	Year		
	0 (€)	1 (€)	2 (€)
Capital expenditure	1,210		
Revenues (in real terms)		1,900	2,000
Cash expenses (in real terms)		950	1,000
Depreciation (straight-line)		605	605

The president, Mrs Bella, estimates inflation to be 10 per cent per year over the next 2 years. In addition, she believes that the cash flows of the project should be discounted at the nominal rate of 15.5 per cent. Her firm's tax rate is 40 per cent.

Mrs Bella forecasts all cash flows in *nominal* terms, leading to the following spreadsheet:

	Year		
	0 (€)	1 (€)	2 (€)
Capital expenditure	−1,210		
Revenues		2,090 (=1,900 × 1.10)	2,420 [=2,000 × (1.10)²]
−Expenses		−1,045 (=950 × 1.10)	−1,210 [=1,000 × (1.10)²]
−Depreciation		−605 (=1,210/2)	−605
Taxable income		440	605
−Taxes (40%)		−176	−242
Income after taxes		264	363
+Depreciation		+605	+605
Cash flow		869	968

$$\text{NPV} = -€1,210 + \frac{€869}{1.155} + \frac{€968}{(1.155)^2} = €268$$

Mrs Bella's sidekick, Mr Barbi, prefers working in real terms. He first calculates the real rate to be 5 per cent ($=1.155/1.10 - 1$). Next, he generates the following spreadsheet in *real* quantities:

	Year		
	0 (€)	1 (€)	2 (€)
Capital expenditure	−1,210		
Revenues		1,900	2,000
−Expenses		−950	−1,000
−Depreciation		−550 (= 605/1.1)	−500 [= 605/(1.1)²]
Taxable income		400	500
−Taxes (40%)		−160	−200
Income after taxes		240	300
+Depreciation		+550	+500
Cash flow		790	800

$$\text{NPV} = -€1{,}210 + \frac{€790}{1.05} + \frac{€800}{(1.05)^2} = €268$$

In explaining his calculations to Mrs Bella, Mr Barbi points out these facts:

1 The capital expenditure occurs at date 0 (today), so its nominal value and its real value are equal.

2 Because yearly depreciation of €605 is a nominal quantity, one converts it to a real quantity by discounting at the inflation rate of 10 per cent.

It is no coincidence that both Mrs Bella and Mr Barbi arrive at the same NPV number. Both methods must always generate the same NPV.

7.4 Alternative Definitions of Operating Cash Flow

Chapter 3
Page 70

The analysis we went through in the previous section is quite general and can be adapted to just about any capital investment problem. In the next section, we illustrate a particularly useful variation. Before we do so, we need to discuss the fact that different definitions of project operating cash flow are commonly used, both in practice and in finance texts (see **Chapter 3**, Section 3.5 for more detail on cash flow statements).

As we will see, the different approaches to operating cash flow all measure the same thing. If they are used correctly, they all produce the same answer, and one is not necessarily any better or more useful than another. Unfortunately, the fact that alternative definitions are used sometimes leads to confusion. For this reason, we examine several of these variations next to see how they are related.

In the discussion that follows, keep in mind that when we speak of cash flow, we literally mean *cash in less cash out*. This is all we are concerned with. Different definitions of operating cash flow simply amount to different ways of manipulating basic accounting information about sales, costs, depreciation and taxes to get at cash flow.

For a particular project and year under consideration, suppose we have the following estimates:

$$\text{Sales} = £1{,}500$$
$$\text{Costs} = £700$$
$$\text{Depreciation} = £600$$

With these estimates, notice that earnings before interest and taxes (EBIT) is:

$$\begin{aligned}\text{EBIT} &= \text{Sales} - \text{Costs} - \text{Depreciation} \\ &= £1{,}500 - 700 - 600 \\ &= £200\end{aligned}$$

Once again, we assume that no interest is paid, so the tax bill is:

$$\text{Taxes} = \text{EBIT} \times t_c$$
$$= £200 \times 0.28 = £56$$

where t_c, the corporate tax rate, is 28 per cent.

When we put all of this together, we see that project operating cash flow, OCF, is:

$$\text{OCF} = \text{EBIT} + \text{Depreciation} - \text{Taxes}$$
$$= £200 + 600 - 56 = £744$$

It turns out there are some other ways to determine OCF that could be (and are) used. We consider these next.

The Bottom-up Approach

Because we are ignoring any financing expenses, such as interest, in our calculations of project OCF, we can write project net income as:

$$\text{Project net income} = \text{EBIT} - \text{Taxes}$$
$$= £200 - 56$$
$$= £144$$

If we simply add the depreciation to both sides, we arrive at a slightly different and very common expression for OCF:

$$\text{OCF} = \text{Net income} + \text{Depreciation}$$
$$= £144 + 600 = £744 \qquad (7.3)$$

This is the *bottom-up* approach. Here, we start with the accountant's bottom line (net income) and add back any non-cash deductions such as depreciation. It is crucial to remember that this definition of operating cash flow as net income plus depreciation is correct only if there is no interest expense subtracted in the calculation of net income.

The Top-down Approach

Perhaps the most obvious way to calculate OCF is this:

$$\text{OCF} = \text{Sales} - \text{Costs} - \text{Taxes}$$
$$= £1,500 - 700 - 56 = £744 \qquad (7.4)$$

This is the *top-down* approach, the second variation on the basic OCF definition. Here we start at the top of the income statement with sales and work our way down to net cash flow by subtracting costs, taxes and other expenses. Along the way, we simply leave out any strictly non-cash items such as depreciation.

The Tax Shield Approach

The third variation on our basic definition of OCF is the *tax shield* approach. This approach will be very useful for some problems we consider in the next chapter. The tax shield definition of OCF is:

$$\text{OCF} = (\text{Sales} - \text{Costs}) \times (1 - t_c) + \text{Depreciation} \times t_c \qquad (7.5)$$

where t_c is again the corporate tax rate. Assuming that $t_c = 28$ per cent, the OCF works out to be:

$$\text{OCF} = (£1,500 - 700) \times 0.72 + 600 \times 0.28$$
$$= £576 + 168$$
$$= £744$$

This is just as we had before.

This approach views OCF as having two components. The first part is what the project's cash flow would be if there were no depreciation expense. In this case, this would-have-been cash flow is £576.

The second part of OCF in this approach is the depreciation deduction multiplied by the tax rate. This is called the depreciation tax shield. We know that depreciation is a non-cash expense. The only cash flow effect of deducting depreciation is to reduce our taxes, a benefit to us. At the current 28 per cent corporate tax rate, every pound in depreciation expense saves us 28 pence in taxes. So, in our example, the £600 depreciation deduction saves us £600 × 0.28 = £168 in taxes.

Conclusion

Now that we have seen that all of these approaches are the same, you are probably wondering why everybody does not just agree on one of them. One reason is that different approaches are useful in different circumstances. The best one to use is whichever happens to be the most convenient for the problem at hand.

7.5 Investments of Unequal Lives: The Equivalent Annual Cost Method

Suppose a firm must choose between two machines of unequal lives. Both machines can do the same job, but they have different operating costs and will last for different time periods. A simple application of the NPV rule suggests taking the machine whose costs have the lower present value. This choice might be a mistake, however, because the lower cost machine may need to be replaced before the other one.

Let us consider an example. The Downtown Athletic Club must choose between two mechanical tennis ball throwers. Machine A costs less than machine B but will not last as long. The cash *outflows* from the two machines are shown here:

Machine	Date				
	0 (€)	1 (€)	2 (€)	3 (€)	4 (€)
A	500	120	120	120	
B	600	100	100	100	100

Machine A costs €500 and lasts 3 years. There will be maintenance expenses of €120 to be paid at the end of each of the 3 years. Machine B costs €600 and lasts 4 years. There will be maintenance expenses of €100 to be paid at the end of each of the 4 years. We place all costs in real terms, an assumption greatly simplifying the analysis. Revenues per year are assumed to be the same, regardless of machine, so they are ignored in the analysis. Note that all numbers in the previous chart are *outflows*.

To get a handle on the decision, let us take the present value of the costs of each of the two machines. Assuming a discount rate of 10 per cent, we have:

$$\text{Machine A: } €798.42 = €500 + \frac{€120}{1.1} + \frac{€120}{(1.1)^2} + \frac{€120}{(1.1)^3}$$

$$\text{Machine B: } €916.99 = €600 + \frac{€100}{1.1} + \frac{€100}{(1.1)^2} + \frac{€100}{(1.1)^3} + \frac{€100}{(1.1)^4}$$

Machine B has a higher present value of outflows. A naive approach would be to select machine A because of its lower present value. However, machine B has a longer life, so perhaps its cost per year is actually lower.

Chapter 4
Page 93
How might one properly adjust for the difference in useful life when comparing the two machines? Perhaps the easiest approach involves calculating something called the *equivalent annual cost* of each machine (looking again at **Chapter 4**, Section 4.4 on annuities will help with this section). This approach puts costs on a per-year basis.

The previous equation showed that payments of (€500, €120, €120, €120) are equivalent to a single payment of €798.42 at date 0. We now wish to equate the single payment of €798.42 at date 0 with a 3-year annuity. Using techniques of previous chapters, we have:

$$€798.42 = C \times A_{0.10}^3$$

$A_{0.10}^3$ is an annuity of €1 a year for 3 years, discounted at 10 per cent. C is the unknown – the annuity payment per year such that the present value of all payments equals €798.42. Because $A_{0.10}^3$ equals 2.4869, C equals €321.05 (=€798.42/2.4869). Thus, a payment stream of (€500, €120, €120, €120) is equivalent to annuity payments of €321.05 made at the *end* of each year for 3 years. We refer to €321.05 as the *equivalent annual cost* of machine A.

This idea is summarized in the following chart:

	Date			
	0 (€)	1 (€)	2 (€)	3 (€)
Cash outflows of machine A	500.00	120.00	120.00	120.00
Equivalent annual cost of machine A		321.05	321.05	321.05

The Downtown Athletic Club should be indifferent between cash outflows of (€500, €120, €120, €120) and cash outflows of (€0, €321.05, €321.05, €321.05). Alternatively, one can say that the purchase of the machine is financially equivalent to a rental agreement calling for annual lease payments of €321.05.

Now let us turn to machine B. We calculate its equivalent annual cost from:

$$€916.99 = C \times A_{0.10}^4$$

Because $A_{0.10}^4$ equals 3.1699, C equals €916.99/3.1699, or €289.28.

As we did for machine A, we can create the following chart for machine B:

	Date				
	0 (€)	1 (€)	2 (€)	3 (€)	4 (€)
Cash outflows of machine B	600.00	100.00	100.00	100.00	100.00
Equivalent annual cost of machine B		289.28	289.28	289.28	289.28

The decision is easy once the charts of the two machines are compared. Would you rather make annual lease payments of €321.05 or €289.28? Put this way, the problem becomes a no-brainer: a rational person would rather pay the lower amount. Thus, machine B is the preferred choice.

Two final remarks are in order. First, it is no accident that we specified the costs of the tennis ball machines in real terms. Although B would still have been the preferred machine had the costs been stated in nominal terms, the actual solution would have been much more difficult. As a general rule, always convert cash flows to real terms when working through problems of this type.

Second, such analysis applies only if one anticipates that both machines can be replaced. The analysis would differ if no replacement were possible. For example, imagine that the only company that manufactured tennis ball throwers just went out of business and no new producers are expected to enter the field. In this case, machine B would generate revenues in the fourth year whereas machine A would not. Here, simple net present value analysis for mutually exclusive projects including both revenues and costs would be appropriate.

The General Decision to Replace

The previous analysis concerned the choice between machine A and machine B, both of which were new acquisitions. More typically firms must decide when to replace an existing machine with a new one. This decision is actually quite straightforward. One should replace if the annual cost of the new machine is less than the annual cost of the old machine. As with much else in finance, an example clarifies this approach better than further explanation.

Example 7.9

Replacement Decisions

Consider the situation of BIKE, which must decide whether to replace an existing machine. BIKE currently pays no taxes. The replacement machine costs £9,000 now and requires maintenance of £1,000 at the end of every year for 8 years. At the end of 8 years, the machine would be sold for £2,000 after taxes.

The existing machine requires increasing amounts of maintenance each year, and its salvage value falls each year, as shown:

Year	Maintenance (£)	After-tax Salvage (£)
Present	0	4,000
1	1,000	2,500
2	2,000	1,500
3	3,000	1,000
4	4,000	0

This chart tells us that the existing machine can be sold for £4,000 now after taxes. If it is sold one year from now, the resale price will be £2,500 after taxes, and £1,000 must be spent on maintenance during the year to keep it running. For ease of calculation, we assume that this maintenance fee is paid at the end of the year.

The machine will last for 4 more years before it falls apart. In other words, salvage value will be zero at the end of year 4. If BIKE faces an opportunity cost of capital of 15 per cent, when should it replace the machine?

Our approach is to compare the annual cost of the replacement machine with the annual cost of the old machine. The annual cost of the replacement machine is simply its *equivalent annual cost* (EAC). Let us calculate that first.

Equivalent Annual Cost of New Machine The present value of the cost of the new replacement machine is as follows:

$$PV_{costs} = £9,000 + £1,000 \times A_{0.15}^8 - \frac{£2000}{(1.15)^8}$$
$$= £9,000 + £1,000 \times (4.4873) - £2,000 \times (0.3269)$$
$$= £12,833$$

Notice that the £2,000 salvage value is an inflow. It is treated as a *negative* number in this equation because it *offsets* the cost of the machine.

The EAC of a new replacement machine equals:

$$\text{PV/8-year annuity factor at } 15\% = \frac{PV}{A_{0.15}^8} = \frac{£12,833}{4.4873} = £2,860$$

This calculation implies that buying a replacement machine is financially equivalent to renting this machine for £2,860 per year.

Cost of Old Machine This calculation is a little trickier. If BIKE keeps the old machine for one year, the firm must pay maintenance costs of £1,000 a year from now. But this is not BIKE's only cost from keeping the machine for one year. BIKE will receive £2,500 at date 1 if the old machine is kept for one year but would receive £4,000 today if the old machine were sold immediately. This reduction in sales proceeds is clearly a cost as well.

Thus the PV of the costs of keeping the machine one more year before selling it equals:

$$£4,000 + \frac{£1,000}{1.15} - \frac{£2,500}{1.15} = £2,696$$

That is, if BIKE holds the old machine for one year, BIKE does *not* receive the £4,000 today. This £4,000 can be thought of as an opportunity cost. In addition, the firm must pay £1,000 a year from now. Finally, BIKE does receive £2,500 a year from now. This last item is treated as a negative number because it offsets the other two costs.

Although we normally express cash flows in terms of present value, the analysis to come is easier if we express the cash flow in terms of its future value one year from now. This future value is:

$$£2,696 \times 1.15 = £3,100$$

In other words, the cost of keeping the machine for one year is equivalent to paying £3,100 at the end of the year.

Making the Comparison Now let us review the cash flows. If we replace the machine immediately, we can view our annual expense as £2,860, beginning at the end of the year. This annual expense occurs forever if we replace the new machine every 8 years. This cash flow stream can be written as follows:

	Year 1	Year 2	Year 3	Year 4	...
Expenses from replacing machine immediately	£2,860	£2,860	£2,860	£2,860	...

If we replace the old machine in one year, our expense from using the old machine for that final year can be viewed as £3,100, payable at the end of the year. After replacement, our annual expense is £2,860, beginning at the end of 2 years. This annual expense occurs forever if we replace the new machine every 8 years. This cash flow stream can be written like this:

	Year 1	Year 2	Year 3	Year 4	...
Expenses from using old machine for one year and then replacing it	£3,100	£2,860	£2,860	£2,860	...

Put this way, the choice is a no-brainer. Anyone would rather pay £2,860 at the end of the year than £3,100 at the end of the year. Thus, BIKE should replace the old machine immediately to minimize the expense at year 1.[1]

Two final points should be made about the decision to replace. First, we have examined a situation where both the old machine and the replacement machine generate the same revenues. Because revenues are unaffected by the choice of machine, revenues do not enter our analysis. This situation is common in business. For example, the decision to replace either the heating system or the air conditioning system in one's home office will likely not affect firm revenues. However, sometimes revenues will be greater with a new machine. The approach here can easily be amended to handle differential revenues.

Second, we want to stress the importance of the current approach. Applications of this approach are pervasive in business because *every* machine must be replaced at some point.

Summary and Conclusions

This chapter discussed a number of practical applications of capital budgeting.

1 Capital budgeting must be placed on an incremental basis. This means that sunk costs must be ignored, whereas both opportunity costs and side effects must be considered.

2 In the Energy Renewables case we computed NPV using the following two steps:

(a) Calculate the net cash flow from all sources for each period.

(b) Calculate the NPV using these cash flows.

3 Inflation must be handled consistently. One approach is to express both cash flows and the discount rate in nominal terms. The other approach is to express both cash flows and the discount rate in real terms. Because either approach yields the same NPV calculation, the simpler method should be used. The simpler method will generally depend on the type of capital budgeting problem.

4 A firm should use the equivalent annual cost approach when choosing between two machines of unequal lives.

Questions and Problems

CONCEPT

1 **Incremental Cash Flows**   Why is it important for the financial analyst to focus on incremental cash flows? Which of the following should be treated as an incremental cash flow when computing the NPV of an investment?

(a) A reduction in the sales of a company's other products caused by the investment.

(b) An expenditure on plant and equipment that has not yet been made and will be made only if the project is accepted.

(c) Costs of developing a prototype of the product.

(d) Annual depreciation expense from the investment.

(e) Share buybacks by the firm.

(f) The resale value of plant and equipment at the end of the project's life.

(g) Salary and medical costs for production personnel who will be employed only if the project is accepted.

2 **Incremental Cash Flows**

(a) In the context of capital budgeting, what is an opportunity cost? Why do we include this in a capital budgeting analysis? Give an example to support your answer.

(b) What is meant by operating cash flow? Review the different ways in which operating cash flow can be calculated.

3   Inflation and Capital Budgeting   In a hyperinflationary environment, how would you incorporate inflation into a capital budgeting analysis? Explain your methodology in words to a manager who is worried about the power of capital budgeting when inflation is very high. How do increases in expected inflation affect the firm's accept/reject decision at the margin?

4   Equivalent Annual Cost   Explain what is meant by the equivalent annual cost method. When is EAC analysis appropriate for comparing two or more projects? Why is this method used? Are there any implicit assumptions required by this method that you find troubling? Explain.

REGULAR

5   Depreciation   What is meant by the terms 'straight line depreciation' and 'reducing balance depreciation'? What are the advantages and disadvantages of each? Explain.

6   Calculating Project NPV   You have been appointed by a retail store as its new financial manager. The firm has opened a new store in the south of France that is specifically targeted at holiday makers. The firm has decided that it will install a rotisserie which allows customers to directly pick cooked chickens to eat. The cost of the rotisserie is €37,000. Because the food is made on the premises, the store must pay a one-off insurance fee of €8,000 to avoid any liability from food poisoning. The chief executive has asked you to deal with the transaction. Should you include the insurance fee as capital investment or is it an expense? The tax rate is 33.3 per cent and the relevant discount rate is 12 per cent. If the insurance is treated as a capital investment cost, what is the present value of tax savings using a depreciation method of 20 per cent reducing balance? Assume that the rotisserie will be scrapped for nothing in 5 years. Which is better for the store: treating the insurance cost as a capital investment or as an expense?

7   Calculating Project NPV   Carlsberg is considering a new retail lager investment in Copenhagen. Financial projections for the investment are tabulated here. The Danish corporate tax rate is 25 per cent and the investment is depreciated using 20 per cent reducing balances. Assume all sales revenue is received in cash, all operating costs and income taxes are paid in cash, and all cash flows occur at the end of the year. All net working capital is recovered at the end of the project and the investment is sold at its residual value after depreciation.

	Year 0 (€)	Year 1 (€)	Year 2 (€)	Year 3 (€)	Year 4 (€)
Investment	325,000	–	–	–	–
Sales revenue	–	105,000	105,000	105,000	105,000
Operating costs	–	20,000	20,000	20,000	20,000
Net working capital spending	10,000	2,000	3,000	4,000	?

(a)   Compute the incremental net income of the investment for each year.

(b)   Compute the incremental cash flows of the investment for each year.

(c)   Suppose the appropriate discount rate is 12 per cent. What is the NPV of the project?

8   Calculating Project Cash Flow from Assets   In the previous problem, suppose the project requires an initial investment in net working capital of €2,000 and the investment will have a market value of €1,000 at the end of the project. Assume the discounting rate to be 12 per cent. What is the project's year 0 net cash flow? Year 1? Year 2? Year 3? Year 4? What is the new NPV?

9   NPV and Accelerated Depreciation   In the previous problem, suppose the investment is depreciated using the reducing balance method at 25 per cent per annum. All the other facts are the same. What is the project's year 1 net income now? Year 2? Year 3? Year 4? What is the new NPV?

10   Project Evaluation   Your firm is contemplating the purchase of a new £925,000 computer-based order entry system. The system will be depreciated using reducing balance at 20 per cent per annum over its 5-year life. It will be worth £90,000 at the end of that time. You will save £360,000 before taxes per year in order processing costs, and you will be able to reduce working capital by £125,000 (this is a one-time reduction). If the tax rate is 28 per cent, what is the IRR for this project?

11   Project Evaluation   Dog Up! Franks is looking at a new sausage system with an installed cost of €390,000. This cost will be depreciated straight-line to zero over the project's 5-year life, at the end of which the sausage system can be scrapped for €60,000. The sausage system will save the firm €120,000 per year in pre-tax operating costs, and the system requires an initial investment in net working capital of €28,000. If the tax rate is 34 per cent and the discount rate is 10 per cent, what is the NPV of this project?

12 **Calculating Salvage Value**   An asset used in a 4-year project is depreciated at 20 per cent reducing balance for tax purposes. The asset has an acquisition cost of £9,300,000 and will be sold for £3,100,000 at the end of the project. If the tax rate is 28 per cent, what is the after-tax salvage value of the asset?

13 **Calculating NPV**   Howell Petroleum is considering a new project that complements its existing business. The machine required for the project costs €2 million. The marketing department predicts that sales related to the project will be €1.2 million per year for the next 4 years, after which the market will cease to exist. The machine will be depreciated using a 20 per cent reducing balance method. At the end of 4 years it will be sold at its residual value. Cost of goods sold and operating expenses related to the project are predicted to be 25 per cent of sales. Howell also needs to add net working capital of €100,000 immediately. The additional net working capital will be recovered in full at the end of the project's life. The corporate tax rate is 35 per cent. The required rate of return for Howell is 14 per cent. Should Howell proceed with the project?

14 **Calculating EAC**   Machine A costs £10,000 and costs £3,000 per year to maintain. It is expected to last 3 years. Machine B costs £8,000 and costs £5,000 per year to maintain. It is expected to last 2 years. Assume the discount rate is 7 per cent. Which machine should be purchased?

15 **Comparing Mutually Exclusive Projects**   Hagar Industrial Systems Company (HISC) is trying to decide between two different conveyor belt systems. System A costs 430,000 Norwegian kroner (NKr), has a 4-year life, and requires NKr120,000 in pre-tax annual operating costs. System B costs NKr540,000, has a 6-year life, and requires NKr80,000 in pre-tax annual operating costs. Both systems are to be depreciated using the reducing balance method of 50 per cent per annum and will have zero salvage value at the end of their life. Whichever system is chosen, it will *not* be replaced when it wears out. If the tax rate is 28 per cent and the discount rate is 20 per cent, which system should the firm choose?

16 **Comparing Mutually Exclusive Projects**   Suppose in the previous problem that HISC always needs a conveyor belt system; when one wears out, it must be replaced. Which system should the firm choose now?

17 **Inflation and Company Value**   Small Hours LLC, a music events firm based in Dubai, expects to sell 10,000 festival tickets for different musical events around the world in perpetuity. This year, the average ticket will sell for AED300 in real terms. The total cost of running a festival is AED2 million and each festival will attract an average of 10,000 people. Sales income and costs occur at year-end. Revenues will rise at a real rate of 7 per cent annually, while real costs will rise at a real rate of 5 per cent annually. The real discount rate is 18 per cent. There is no corporate tax in Dubai. What is Small Hours LLC worth today?

18 **Calculating Nominal Cash Flow**   Etonic SA is considering an investment of €250,000 in an asset with an economic life of 5 years. The firm estimates that the nominal annual cash revenues and expenses at the end of the first year will be €200,000 and €50,000, respectively. Both revenues and expenses will grow thereafter at the annual inflation rate of 3 per cent. Etonic will use the 20 per cent reducing balance method to depreciate its asset over 5 years. The salvage value of the asset is estimated to be €30,000 in nominal terms at that time. The one-time net working capital investment of €10,000 is required immediately and will be recovered at the end of the project. All corporate cash flows are subject to a 34 per cent tax rate. What is the project's total nominal cash flow from assets for each year?

19 **Equivalent Annual Cost**   Yell Group plc, the global advertising company, is evaluating the viability of a new machine to print telephone directories in emerging markets. The baseline machine costs £65,000, has a 3-year life, and costs £12,000 per year to operate. The relevant discount rate is 10 per cent. Assume that the reducing balance (20 per cent) depreciation method is used. Furthermore, assume the equipment has a salvage value of £20,000 at the end of the project's life. The relevant tax rate is 24 per cent. All cash flows occur at the end of the year. What is the equivalent annual cost (EAC) of this equipment?

20 **Calculating NPV and IRR for a Replacement**   A firm is considering an investment in a new machine with a price of £32 million to replace its existing machine. The current machine has a book value of £8 million and a market value of £9 million. The new machine is expected to have a 4-year life, and the old machine has 4 years left in which it can be used. If the firm replaces the old machine with the new machine, it expects to save £5 million in operating costs each year over the next 4 years. Both machines will have no salvage value in 4 years. If the firm purchases the new machine, it will also need an investment of £500,000 in net working capital. The required return on the investment is 10 per cent, and the tax rate is 39 per cent.

(a) What are the NPV and IRR of the decision to replace the old machine?

(b) The new machine saves £32 million over the next 4 years and has a cost of £32 million. When you consider the time value of money, how is it possible that the NPV of the decision to replace the old machine has a positive NPV?

21 Calculating Project NPV With the growing popularity of casual surf print clothing, two recent MBA graduates decided to broaden this casual surf concept to encompass a 'surf lifestyle for the home'. With limited capital, they decided to focus on surf print table and floor lamps to accent people's homes. They projected unit sales of these lamps to be 5,000 in the first year, with growth of 15 per cent each year for the next 5 years. Production of these lamps will require £28,000 in net working capital to start. Total fixed costs are £75,000 per year, variable production costs are £20 per unit, and the units are priced at £45 each. The equipment needed to begin production will cost £60,000. The equipment will be depreciated using the reducing balance (20 per cent) method and is not expected to have a salvage value. The effective tax rate is 28 per cent, and the required rate of return is 25 per cent. What is the NPV of this project?

22 Calculating Project NPV Industrial Hooks plc is deciding when to replace its old machine. The machine's current salvage value is £3 million. Its current book value is £4 million. If not sold, the old machine will require maintenance costs of £300,000 at the end of the year for the next 5 years. Depreciation on the old machine is calculated using 20 per cent reducing balances. At the end of 5 years, it will have a salvage value of £100,000. A replacement machine costs £5 million now and requires maintenance costs of £100,000 at the end of each year during its economic life of 5 years. At the end of the 5 years, the new machine will have a salvage value of £1,000,000. It will be depreciated by the reducing balance method (20 per cent). In 5 years a replacement machine will cost £6,000,000. Industrial Hooks will need to purchase this machine regardless of what choice it makes today. The corporate tax rate is 24 per cent and the appropriate discount rate is 12 per cent. The company is assumed to earn sufficient revenues to generate tax shields from depreciation. Should Industrial Hooks replace the old machine now or at the end of 5 years?

23 Inflation Your company manufactures non-stick frying pans. However, it outsources the production of the glass covers for the pans. Until now, this has been a good option. However, your supplier has become unreliable and doubled his prices. As a result, you feel that now might be the time to start producing your own glass covers. At the moment, your company produces 200,000 non-stick pans per year. The producer charges you €2 per cover and you estimate the costs of producing your own cover to be €1.50. A new machine will be required to produce the covers and this costs €150,000 in the market. The machine will last for 10 years, at which point it will have no value. The expansion will require an increase in working capital of €30,000. Your company pays 28 per cent tax and the appropriate discount rate is 15 per cent. Inflation is expected to be 4 per cent per year for the next 10 years. Assume you use the 20 per cent reducing balance method for depreciation. Should you undertake this investment? State clearly any additional assumptions you have made in your analysis.

24 Project Analysis and Inflation Dickinson Brothers is considering investing in a machine to produce computer keyboards. The price of the machine will be £400,000, and its economic life is 5 years. The machine will be depreciated by the reducing balance (20 per cent) method but will be worthless in 5 years. The machine will produce 10,000 keyboards each year. The price of each keyboard will be £40 in the first year and will increase by 5 per cent per year. The production cost per keyboard will be £20 in the first year and will increase by 10 per cent per year. The project will have an annual fixed cost of £50,000 and require an immediate investment of £25,000 in net working capital. The corporate tax rate for the company is 28 per cent. If the appropriate discount rate is 15 per cent, what is the NPV of the investment?

CHALLENGE

25 Project Evaluation Aguilera Acoustics (AA) projects unit sales for a new seven-octave voice emulation implant as follows:

Year	Unit Sales
1	85,000
2	98,000
3	106,000
4	114,000
5	93,000

Production of the implants will require €1,500,000 in net working capital to start and additional net working capital investments each year equal to 15 per cent of the projected sales increase for the following year. Total fixed costs are €900,000 per year, variable production costs are €240 per unit, and the units are priced at €325 each. The equipment needed to begin production has an installed cost of €21,000,000. Because the implants are intended for professional singers, this equipment is considered industrial machinery and is thus depreciated by reducing balance method at 20 per cent per annum. In 5 years, this equipment can be sold for about 20 per cent of its acquisition cost. AA is in the 35 per cent marginal tax bracket and has a required return on all its projects of 18 per cent. Based on these preliminary project estimates, what is the NPV of the project? What is the IRR?

26 **Calculating Required Savings**   A proposed cost-saving device has an installed cost of £360,000. The device will be used in a 5-year project and be depreciated using the reducing balance method at 20 per cent per annum. The required initial net working capital investment is £20,000, the marginal tax rate is 24 per cent, and the project discount rate is 12 per cent. The device has an estimated year 5 salvage value of £60,000. What level of pre-tax cost savings do we require for this project to be profitable?

27 **Calculating a Bid Price**   Another utilization of cash flow analysis is setting the bid price on a project. To calculate the bid price, we set the project NPV equal to zero and find the required price. Thus the bid price represents a financial break-even level for the project. Guthrie Enterprises needs someone to supply it with 150,000 cartons of machine screws per year to support its manufacturing needs over the next 5 years, and you have decided to bid on the contract. It will cost you €780,000 to install the equipment necessary to start production; you will depreciate this cost using 20 per cent reducing balances over the project's life. You estimate that in 5 years this equipment can be salvaged for €50,000. Your fixed production costs will be €240,000 per year, and your variable production costs should be €8.50 per carton. You also need an initial investment in net working capital of €75,000. If your tax rate is 35 per cent and you require a 16 per cent return on your investment, what bid price should you submit?

28 **Financial Break-Even Analysis**   The technique for calculating a bid price can be extended to many other types of problems. Answer the following questions using the same technique as setting a bid price; that is, set the project NPV to zero and solve for the variable in question.

(a) In the previous problem, assume that the price per carton is €13 and calculate the project NPV. What does your answer tell you about your bid price? What do you know about the number of cartons you can sell and still break even? How about your level of costs?

(b) Solve the previous problem again with the price still at €13 and calculate the quantity of cartons per year that you can supply and still break even.

(c) Repeat (b) with a price of €13 and the quantity at 150,000 cartons per year, then calculate the highest level of fixed costs you could afford and still break even.

29 **Calculating a Bid Price**   Your company has been approached to bid on a contract to sell 10,000 voice recognition (VR) computer keyboards a year for 4 years. Due to technological improvements, beyond that time they will be outdated and no sales will be possible. The equipment necessary for production will cost £2.4 million and will be depreciated on a reducing balance (25 per cent) method. Production will require an investment in net working capital of £75,000 to be returned at the end of the project, and the equipment can be sold for £200,000 at the end of production. Fixed costs are £500,000 per year, and variable costs are £165 per unit. In addition to the contract, you feel your company can sell 3,000, 6,000, 8,000 and 5,000 additional units to companies in other countries over the next 4 years, respectively, at a price of £275. This price is fixed. The tax rate is 24 per cent, and the required return is 13 per cent. Additionally, the managing director of the company will undertake the project only if it has an NPV of £100,000. What bid price should you set for the contract?

30 **Project Analysis**   Benson Enterprises is evaluating alternative uses for a three-story manufacturing and warehousing building that it has purchased for £225,000. The company can continue to rent the building to the present occupants for £12,000 per year. The present occupants have indicated an interest in staying in the building for at least another 15 years. Alternatively, the company could modify the existing structure to use for its own manufacturing and warehousing needs. Benson's production engineer feels the building could be adapted to handle one of two new product lines. The cost and revenue data for the two product alternatives are as follows:

	Product A	Product B
Initial cash outlay for building modifications	£ 36,000	£ 54,000
Initial cash outlay for equipment	144,000	162,000
Annual pre-tax cash revenues (generated for 15 years)	105,000	127,500
Annual pre-tax expenditures (generated for 15 years)	60,000	75,000

The building will be used for only 15 years for either product A or product B. After 15 years the building will be too small for efficient production of either product line. At that time, Benson plans to rent the building to firms similar to the current occupants. To rent the building again, Benson will need to restore the building to its present layout. The estimated cash cost of restoring the building if product A has been undertaken is £3,750. If product B has been manufactured, the cash cost will be £28,125. These cash costs can be deducted for tax purposes in the year the expenditures occur.

Benson will depreciate the original building shell (purchased for £225,000) over a 30-year life to zero, regardless of which alternative it chooses. The building modifications and equipment purchases for either product are estimated to have a 15-year life. They will be depreciated by the 20 per cent reducing balance method. At the end of the project's life, the salvage value of the equipment will be equal to the residual value. The firm's tax rate is 28 per cent, and its required rate of return on such investments is 12 per cent.

For simplicity, assume all cash flows occur at the end of the year. The initial outlays for modifications and equipment will occur today (year 0), and the restoration outlays will occur at the end of year 15. Benson has other profitable ongoing operations that are sufficient to cover any losses. Which use of the building would you recommend to management? Assume the production of Product A and B as Project A and Project B respectively.

31 Project Analysis and Inflation Genetic Engineering Research Studies Ltd (GERS) has hired you as a consultant to evaluate the NPV of its proposed toad house. GERS plans to breed toads and sell them as ecologically desirable insect control mechanisms. They anticipate that the business will continue into perpetuity. Following the negligible start-up costs, GERS expects the following nominal cash flows at the end of the year:

Revenues	£150,000
Labour costs	80,000
Other costs	40,000

The company will lease machinery for £20,000 per year. The lease payments start at the end of year 1 and are expressed in nominal terms. Revenues will increase by 5 per cent per year in real terms. Labour costs will increase by 3 per cent per year in real terms. Other costs will decrease by 1 per cent per year in real terms. The rate of inflation is expected to be 6 per cent per year. GERS' required rate of return is 10 per cent in real terms. The company has a 28 per cent tax rate. All cash flows occur at year-end. What is the NPV of GERS' proposed toad house today?

32 Project Analysis and Inflation Sony International has an investment opportunity to produce a new 100-inch widescreen TV. The required investment on 1 January of this year is $32 million. The firm will depreciate the investment to zero using the straight-line method over 4 years. The investment has no resale value after completion of the project. The firm is in the 34 per cent tax bracket. The price of the product will be $400 per unit, in real terms, and will not change over the life of the project. Labour costs for year 1 will be $15.30 per hour, in real terms, and will increase at 2 per cent per year in real terms. Energy costs for year 1 will be $5.15 per physical unit, in real terms, and will increase at 3 per cent per year in real terms. The inflation rate is 5 per cent per year. Revenues are received and costs are paid at year-end. Refer to the following table for the production schedule:

	Year 1	Year 2	Year 3	Year 4
Physical production, in units	100,000	200,000	200,000	150,000
Labour input, in hours	2,000,000	2,000,000	2,000,000	2,000,000
Energy input, physical units	200,000	200,000	200,000	200,000

The real discount rate for Sony is 8 per cent. Calculate the NPV of this project.

33 Project Analysis and Inflation After extensive medical and marketing research, Pill plc believes it can penetrate the pain reliever market. It is considering two alternative products. The first is a medication for headache pain. The second is a pill for headache and arthritis pain. Both products would be introduced at a price of £4 per package in real terms. The headache-only medication is projected to sell 5 million packages a year, whereas the headache and arthritis remedy would sell 10 million packages a year. Cash costs of production in the first year are expected to be £1.50 per package in real terms for the headache-only brand. Production costs are expected to be £1.70 in real terms for the headache and arthritis pill. All prices and costs are expected to rise at the general inflation rate of 5 per cent.

Either product requires further investment. The headache-only pill could be produced using equipment costing £10.2 million. That equipment would last 3 years and have no resale value. The machinery required to produce the broader remedy would cost £12 million and last 3 years. The firm expects that equipment to have a £1 million resale value (in real terms) at the end of year 3.

Pill plc uses reducing balance (20 per cent) depreciation. The firm faces a corporate tax rate of 24 per cent and believes that the appropriate real discount rate is 13 per cent. Which pain reliever should the firm produce?

34 **Calculating Project NPV**   Petracci SpA manufactures fine furniture. The company is deciding whether to introduce a new mahogany dining room table set. The set will sell for €5,600, including a set of eight chairs. The company feels that sales will be 1,300, 1,325, 1,375, 1,450 and 1,320 sets per year for the next 5 years, respectively. Variable costs will amount to 45 per cent of sales, and fixed costs are €1.7 million per year. The new tables will require inventory amounting to 10 per cent of sales, produced and stockpiled in the year prior to sales. It is believed that the addition of the new table will cause a loss of 200 tables per year of the oak tables the company produces. These tables sell for €4,500 and have variable costs of 40 per cent of sales. The inventory for this oak table is also 10 per cent. Petracci currently has excess production capacity. If the company buys the necessary equipment today, it will cost €10.5 million. However, the excess production capacity means the company can produce the new table without buying the new equipment. The company controller has said that the current excess capacity will end in 2 years with current production. This means that if the company uses the current excess capacity for the new table, it will be forced to spend the €10.5 million in 2 years to accommodate the increased sales of its current products. In 5 years, the new equipment will have a market value of €2.8 million if purchased today, and €6.1 million if purchased in 2 years. The equipment is depreciated using reducing balances at 20 per cent per annum. The company has a tax rate of 38 per cent, and the required return for the project is 14 per cent.

(a)   Should Petracci undertake the new project?

(b)   Can you perform an IRR analysis on this project? How many IRRs would you expect to find?

(c)   How would you interpret the profitability index?

Exam Question (45 minutes)

Kicvarom Plc is considering the manufacture of a new product. The company has existing buildings that could be sold to buyers for €120,000. The balance sheet records the buildings as having a value of €60,000. The new product, which has a life of 5 years, will require installation of sophisticated machinery. This will cost €200,000. At the end of its life, the machine can be sold for €10,000. Depreciation should be charged on the machine at 25 per cent using the reducing balance method. Demand for the new product is expected to be 4,000 units in year 1 and 7,000 units in each of years 2 to 5. The sale price will be €110 per unit; direct labour, direct material and variable overheads will cost €60 per unit and additional fixed expenses of €50,000 per annum will be incurred. An investment in working capital is required in year 0 of €75,000. This will be increased to €100,000 in year 1. No further increases are required over the life of the project. Assume that the company pays corporation tax at 24 per cent on its taxable profit one year after the end of the year and requires a rate of return of 10 per cent per annum after tax on this type of project. Should the company undertake the investment? Use four investment appraisal methods and state all your assumptions. (100 marks)

Mini Case

Bethesda Mining Company

Bethesda Mining is a mid-sized coal mining company with 20 mines located in England and Scotland. The company operates deep mines as well as strip mines. Most of the coal mined is sold under contract, with excess production sold on the spot market.

The coal mining industry, especially high-sulphur coal operations such as Bethesda, has been hit hard by environmental regulations. Recently, however, a combination of increased demand for coal and new pollution reduction technologies has led to an improved market demand for high-sulphur coal. Bethesda has just been approached by Scottish Power with a request to supply coal for its electric generators for the next 4 years. Bethesda Mining does not have enough excess capacity at its existing mines to guarantee the contract. The company is considering opening a strip mine in Auchtermuchty on 5,000 acres of land purchased 10 years ago for £6 million. Based on a recent appraisal, the company feels it could receive £5 million on an after-tax basis if it sold the land today.

Strip mining is a process where the layers of topsoil above a coal vein are removed and the exposed coal is removed. Some time ago, the company would simply remove the coal and leave the land in an unusable condition. Changes in mining regulations now force a company to reclaim the land; that is, when the mining is completed, the land must be restored to near its original condition. The land can then be used for other purposes. Because it is currently operating at full capacity, Bethesda will need to purchase additional necessary equipment, which will cost £30 million. The equipment will be depreciated using capital allowances (reducing balance) at 20 per cent per annum. The contract runs for only 4 years. At that time the coal from the site will be entirely mined. The company feels that the equipment can be sold for 60 per cent of its initial purchase price. However, Bethesda plans to open another strip mine at that time and will use the equipment at the new mine.

The contract calls for the delivery of 600,000 tons of coal per year at a price of £34 per ton. Bethesda Mining feels that coal production will be 650,000 tons, 725,000 tons, 810,000 tons and 740,000 tons, respectively, over the next 4 years. The excess production will be sold in the spot market at an average of £40 per ton. Variable costs amount to £13 per ton, and fixed costs are £2,500,000 per year. The mine will require a net working capital investment of 5 per cent of sales. The NWC will be built up in the year prior to the sales.

Bethesda will be responsible for reclaiming the land at termination of the mining. This will occur in year 5. The company uses an outside company for reclamation of all the company's strip mines. It is estimated the cost of reclamation will be £4 million. After the land is reclaimed, the company plans to donate the land to the National Trust for use as a public park and recreation area. This will occur in year 6 and result in a charitable expense deduction of £6 million. Bethesda faces a 28 per cent tax rate and has a 12 per cent required return on new strip mine projects. Assume that a loss in any year will result in a tax credit.

You have been approached by the chairman of the company with a request to analyse the project. Calculate the payback period, profitability index, average accounting return, net present value, internal rate of return, and modified internal rate of return for the new strip mine. Should Bethesda Mining take the contract and open the mine?

Practical Case Study

In many emerging market countries, concepts such as discount rates are significantly more cumbersome to estimate with any degree of accuracy. Furthermore, capital budgeting techniques can become significantly more difficult to use in practice. The following case is based on real experience, with identities and numbers changed for confidentiality. As part of a consultancy assignment in Dar es Salaam, Tanzania, you have been asked by a private cement manufacturing company to consider the viability of expanding its business operations into the north of the country.

The company has two main rivals in Tanzania: Tanga Cement Company Limited (SIMBA) (http://www.simbacement.co.tz/) and Tanzania Portland Cement Company Limited (TWIGA) (http://www.heidelbergcement.com/africa/en/twigacement/home.htm). Both SIMBA and TWIGA are listed on the Dar es Salaam Stock Exchange (www.dse.co.tz). The company that has hired you as a consultant earns about one-quarter the revenues of SIMBA.

The new expansion requires an investment of 5 billion Tanzanian shillings (TSh) and as a result of the investment, you expect a permanent increase in total operating revenues for the firm of TSh800 million. While SIMBA is your closest rival in Dar es Salaam, TWIGA has more extensive operations in the north of Tanzania and so they are more likely to be your rivals in the new investment.

Growth in earnings is possible, but this depends on several factors. First, growth in the economy is uncertain. While Tanzania's economy has been fairly stable, analysts are uncertain as to how the country will fare in the future. This is largely because of uncertainty in international donor funding as a result of the recession affecting donor countries. Second, inflation appears to be higher on the streets than the government statistics suggest. Your estimates are that a more appropriate inflation figure is 3 per cent higher than existing government statistics present. Third, the demand for industrial expansion (and consequently cement) has in the past been vibrant in Tanzania but the future is less certain. Tanzanian economists are predicting that the country will continue to grow as in the past, less about 1.5 per cent. This is because they expect the global recession will largely bypass Tanzania given that the country's economy is not tightly integrated into other developed country economies. However, you are not too sure. Table 30.1 in this textbook shows the main import and export partners for Tanzania and the fortunes of these partners will naturally affect the Tanzanian economy.

Later chapters explore the estimate of discount rates in more detail, but for now, we will approach the issue in a more basic way. Given that the financial markets in Tanzania are not well developed, you have decided to survey experts in each sector on the appropriate discount rates to use for your closest rivals, TWIGA and SIMBA. The survey responses have been surprising:

Dar es Salaam Stock Exchange	Pension Funds	Insurance Companies	Brokers and Dealers	Bank of Tanzania
12%	16%	14%	22%	10%

A rule of thumb that you have been given is that you can approximate the growth rate in the economy as a whole by adding GDP growth to the rate of inflation. To then estimate the cost of capital for a private firm, you must add on a risk premium to reflect the increased risk.

The challenge facing you as a consultant is daunting but it reflects reality in many parts of the world. The company has asked you to prepare a report on how you plan to carry out your analysis. Specifically, you must consider the following:

1 *Cash Flows*: What factors will affect the estimated cash flows? Carry out your own analysis on Tanzania, its economy, the cement industry and its rivals.

2 *Growth Rates*: What factors will affect the growth rates of the firm? From your own analysis of the company and the project, report on the possible growth rates you may use.

3 *Discount Rates*: Many of the models presented in later chapters do not work well in emerging markets because good quality price data is not available. Carry out your own investigations into possible discount rates for the project.

4 *Funding*: We cover financing in detail in later chapters. However, carry out your own analysis into the different sources of funding that are available in Tanzania for a project of this type and size.

5 *Capital Budgeting Methods*: There are many methods available that you can use. Which ones will you focus on? Explain.

Relevant Accounting Standards

The main reason that accounting standards are important for capital budgeting is in the estimation of tax payments. Given that tax is derived from accounting statements and reduces cash flow, all the accounting standards are relevant. However, depreciation is possibly the most important issue and so IAS 16 *Property, Plant and Equipment*, IFRS 3 *Business Combinations*, and IAS 38 *Intangible Assets* are particularly relevant. The analyst should also be aware of current practice in depreciating assets. This can be quite complex and more information will be found on each country's government tax site (for the UK, this is www.hmrc.gov.uk). Readers in the European Union should also be familiar with developments and harmonization towards a common tax base (http://ec.europa.eu).

Other important accounting standards include IAS 2 *Inventories*, IAS 17 *Leases*, IAS 21 *The Effects of Changes in Foreign Exchange Rates*, and IAS 36 *Impairment of Assets*. Visit the IASPlus website (www.iasplus.com) for good summaries of each standard.

While it is easy to be overwhelmed by the number of accounting standards, everything that is needed to carry out a capital budgeting analysis is provided in this textbook, so do not worry. The accounting standards are for reference and should only be consulted when a real capital budgeting analysis is undertaken.

Additional Reading

A very interesting paper that links stock market efficiency and capital budgeting is Durnev et al. (2004). This has implications for capital budgeting when carried out in emerging and developed markets. Although the research uses US data, the authors do present a nice figure of stock market synchronicity (Figure 1) for many countries and link this to market efficiency and capital budgeting.

1 Durnev, A., R. Morck and B. Yeung (2004) 'Value-Enhancing Capital Budgeting and Firm-Specific Stock Return Variation', *The Journal of Finance*, Vol. 59, No. 1, 65–105.

Some other interesting papers on capital budgeting methods include:

2 Brunzell, T., E. Liljeblom and M. Vaikekoski (2012) 'Determinants of Capital Budgeting Methods and Hurdle Rates in Nordic Firms', *Accounting and Finance* (Forthcoming). **Nordic Countries**.

3 Duchin, R. and D. Sosyura (2013) 'Divisional Managers and Internal Capital Markets', *The Journal of Finance*, Vol. 68, No. 2, 387–429.

4 Holmén, M. and B. Pramborg (2009) 'Capital Budgeting and Political Risk: Empirical Evidence', *Journal of International Financial Management and Accounting*, Vol. 20, No. 2, 105–134. **Sweden**.

Endnote

1 One caveat is in order. Perhaps the old machine's maintenance is high in the first year but drops after that. A decision to replace immediately might be premature in that case. Therefore, we need to check the cost of the old machine in future years.

The cost of keeping the existing machine a second year is:

$$\text{PV of costs at time } 1 = £2,500 + \frac{£2,000}{1.15} - \frac{£1,500}{1.15}$$
$$= £2,935$$

which has a future value of £3,375 (=£2,935 × 1.15).

The costs of keeping the existing machine for years 3 and 4 are also greater than the EAC of buying a new machine. Thus, BIKE's decision to replace the old machine immediately is still valid.

Risk Analysis, Real Options and Capital Budgeting

For several years, companies have made strategic investment decisions in an exceptionally uncertain and tough economic environment. Europe, in particular, has experienced unprecedented upheaval with the Eurozone crisis affecting every country in the union. Firms that have operations in the oil and gas sector have similarly faced exceptionally difficult challenges to forecast cash flows. In recent years, oil exporting countries such as Russia, Venezuela and Saudi Arabia have had to forecast oil prices for several years in order to determine their future revenue streams.

Strategic decisions that reflect future uncertainty, such as a potential euro break-up or extreme economic conditions, need to be analysed in such a way that incorporates all potential future events. Standard net present value valuation does not adequately capture alternative scenarios and so a modification of the methods must be developed. This chapter explores how firms can assess strategic investments in uncertain environments and what they can do to possibly mitigate the risk of their decisions.

KEY NOTATIONS

NPV	Net present value
EAC	Equivalent annual cost
t_c	Corporate tax rate

8.1 Sensitivity Analysis, Scenario Analysis and Break-even Analysis

One main point of this book is that NPV analysis is a superior capital budgeting technique. In fact, because the NPV approach uses cash flows rather than profits, uses all the cash flows, and discounts the cash flows properly, it is hard to find any theoretical fault with it. However, in our conversations with businesspeople, we hear the phrase 'a false sense of security' frequently. These people point out that the documentation for capital budgeting proposals is often quite impressive. Cash flows are projected down to the last few pounds or euros for each year (or even each month). Opportunity costs and side effects are handled quite properly. Sunk costs are ignored – also quite properly. When a high net present value appears at the bottom, one's temptation is to say 'yes' immediately. Nevertheless, the projected cash flow often goes unmet in practice, and the firm ends up with a money loser.

Sensitivity Analysis and Scenario Analysis

How can the firm get the net present value technique to live up to its potential? One approach is *sensitivity analysis*, which examines how sensitive a particular NPV calculation is to changes in underlying assumptions. Sensitivity analysis is also known as *what-if* analysis and *bop* (best, optimistic and pessimistic) analysis.

Consider the following example. Solar Electronics (SE) has recently developed a solar-powered jet engine and wants to go ahead with full-scale production. The initial (year 0) investment is £1,500 million, followed by production and sales over the next 5 years. The preliminary cash flow projection appears in Table 8.1.

Table 8.1 Cash Flow Forecasts for Solar Electronics' Jet Engine: Base Case (millions)*

	Year 0 (£)	Years 1–5 (£)
Revenues		6,000
Variable costs		3,000
Fixed costs		1,791
Depreciation		300
Pre-tax profit		909
Tax ($t_c = 0.28$)		255
Net profit		654
Cash flow		954
Initial investment costs	1,500	

*Assumptions: (1) Investment is depreciated in years 1 through 5 using the straight-line method for simplicity; (2) tax rate is 28 per cent; (3) the company receives no tax benefits for initial development costs.

If SE were to go ahead with investment in and production of the jet engine, the NPV at a discount rate of 15 per cent would be (in millions):

$$NPV = -£1,500 + \sum_{t=1}^{5} \frac{£954}{(1.15)^t}$$

$$= -£1,500 + £954 \times A_{0.15}^5$$

$$= £1,700$$

Because the NPV is positive, basic financial theory implies that SE should accept the project. However, is this all there is to say about the venture? Before actual funding, we ought to check out the project's underlying assumptions about revenues and costs.

Revenues

Let us assume that the marketing department has projected annual sales to be:

$$\begin{array}{ccccc} \text{Number of jet engines} \\ \text{sold per year} & = & \text{Market share} & \times & \begin{array}{c}\text{Size of jet engine} \\ \text{market per year}\end{array} \end{array}$$

$$3{,}000 \quad = \quad 0.30 \quad \times \quad 10{,}000$$

$$\begin{array}{ccccc} \text{Annual sales} \\ \text{revenues} & = & \begin{array}{c}\text{Number of jet} \\ \text{engines sold}\end{array} & \times & \text{Price per engine} \end{array}$$

$$\text{£6,000 million} \quad = \quad 3{,}000 \quad \times \quad \text{£2 million}$$

Thus, it turns out that the revenue estimates depend on three assumptions:

1 Market share
2 Size of jet engine market
3 Price per engine.

Costs

Financial analysts frequently divide costs into two types: variable costs and fixed costs. Variable costs change as the output changes, and they are zero when production is zero. Costs of direct labour and raw materials are usually variable. It is common to assume that a variable cost is constant per unit of output, implying that total variable costs are proportional to the level of production. For example, if direct labour is variable and one unit of final output requires £10 of direct labour, then 100 units of final output should require £1,000 of direct labour.

Fixed costs are not dependent on the amount of goods or services produced during the period. Fixed costs are usually measured as costs per unit of time, such as rent per month or salaries per year. Naturally, fixed costs are not fixed forever. They are fixed only over a predetermined time period.

The engineering department has estimated variable costs to be £1 million per engine. Fixed costs are £1,791 million per year. The cost breakdowns are:

$$\begin{array}{ccccc} \text{Variable cost} \\ \text{per year} & = & \begin{array}{c}\text{Variable cost} \\ \text{per unit}\end{array} & \times & \begin{array}{c}\text{Number of jet engines} \\ \text{sold per year}\end{array} \end{array}$$

$$\text{£3,000 million} \quad = \quad \text{£1 million} \quad \times \quad 3{,}000$$

$$\begin{array}{ccccc} \text{Total cost before} \\ \text{taxes per year} & = & \begin{array}{c}\text{Variable cost} \\ \text{per year}\end{array} & + & \begin{array}{c}\text{Fixed cost} \\ \text{per year}\end{array} \end{array}$$

$$\text{£4,791 million} \quad = \quad \text{£3,000 million} \quad + \quad \text{£1,791 million}$$

These estimates for market size, market share, price, variable cost and fixed cost, as well as the estimate of initial investment, are presented in the middle column of Table 8.2. These figures represent the firm's expectations or best estimates of the different parameters. For comparison, the firm's analysts also prepared both optimistic and pessimistic forecasts for each of the different variables. These forecasts are provided in the table as well.

Table 8.2 Different Estimates for Solar Electronics' Solar Plane Engine

Variable	Pessimistic	Expected or Best	Optimistic
Market size (per year)	5,000	10,000	20,000
Market share (%)	20	30	50
Price (£ million)	1.9	2	2.2
Variable cost (per engine) (£ million)	1.2	1	0.8
Fixed cost (per year) (£ million)	1,891	1,791	1,741
Investment (£ million)	1,900	1,500	1,000

Standard sensitivity analysis calls for an NPV calculation for all three possibilities of a single variable, along with the expected forecast for all other variables. This procedure is illustrated in Table 8.3. For example, consider the NPV calculation of £8,940 million provided in the upper right corner of this table. This NPV occurs when the optimistic forecast of 20,000 units per year is used for market size while all other variables are set at their expected forecasts from Table 8.2. Note that each row of the middle column of Table 8.3 shows a value of £1,700 million. This occurs because the expected forecast is used for the variable that was singled out, as well as for all other variables.

Table 8.3 NPV Calculations for the Solar Plane Engine Using Sensitivity Analysis

	Pessimistic (£m)	Expected or Best (£m)	Optimistic (£m)
Market size	−1,921*	1,700	8,940
Market share	−714*	1,700	6,527
Price	976	1,700	3,148
Variable cost	251	1,700	3,148
Fixed cost	1,458	1,700	1,820
Investment	1,300	1,700	2,200

Under sensitivity analysis, one input is varied while all other inputs are assumed to meet their expectation. For example, an NPV of −£1,921 million occurs when the pessimistic forecast of 5,000 is used for market size, while all other variables are set at their expected forecasts from Table 8.2.

*We assume that the other divisions of the firm are profitable, implying that a loss on this project can offset income elsewhere in the firm, thereby reducing the overall taxes of the firm.

Table 8.3 can be used for a number of purposes. First, taken as a whole, the table can indicate whether NPV analysis should be trusted. In other words, it reduces the false sense of security we spoke of earlier. Suppose that NPV is positive when the expected forecast for each variable is used. However, further suppose that every number in the pessimistic column is highly negative and every number in the optimistic column is highly positive. A change in a single forecast greatly alters the NPV estimate, making one wary of the net present value approach. A conservative manager might well scrap the entire NPV analysis in this situation. Fortunately, the solar plane engine does not exhibit this wide dispersion because all but two of the numbers in Table 8.3 are positive. Managers viewing the table will likely consider NPV analysis to be useful for the solar-powered jet engine.

Second, sensitivity analysis shows where more information is needed. For example, an error in the estimate of investment appears to be relatively unimportant because, even under the pessimistic scenario, the NPV of £1,300 million is still highly positive. By contrast, the pessimistic forecast for market share leads to a negative NPV of −£714 million, and a pessimistic forecast for market size leads to a substantially negative NPV of −£1,921 million. Because the effect of incorrect estimates on revenues is so much greater than the effect of incorrect estimates on costs, more information about the factors determining revenues might be needed.

Unfortunately, sensitivity analysis also suffers from some drawbacks. For example, sensitivity analysis may unwittingly *increase* the false sense of security among managers. Suppose all pessimistic forecasts yield positive NPVs. A manager might feel that there is no way the project can lose money. Of course the forecasters may simply have an optimistic view of a pessimistic forecast. To combat this, some companies do not treat optimistic and pessimistic forecasts subjectively. Rather, their pessimistic forecasts are always, say, 20 per cent less than expected. Unfortunately, the cure in this case may be worse than the disease: a deviation of a fixed percentage ignores the fact that some variables are easier to forecast than others.

In addition, sensitivity analysis treats each variable in isolation when, in reality, the different variables are likely to be related. For example, if ineffective management allows costs to get out of control, it is likely that variable costs, fixed costs and investment will all rise above expectation at the same time. If the market is not receptive to a solar plane engine, both market share and price should decline together.

Managers frequently perform scenario analysis, a variant of sensitivity analysis, to minimize this problem. Simply put, this approach examines a number of different likely scenarios, where each scenario involves a confluence of factors. As a simple example, consider the effect of a few airline crashes. These crashes are likely to reduce flying in total, thereby limiting the demand for any new engines. Furthermore, even if the crashes do not involve solar-powered aircraft, the public could become more averse to any innovative and controversial technologies. Hence, SE's market share might fall as well. Perhaps the cash flow calculations would look like those in Table 8.4 under the scenario of a plane crash. Given the calculations in the table, the NPV (in millions) would be:

$$-£2,162 = -£1,500 - £198 \times A_{0.15}^{5}$$

Table 8.4 Cash Flow Forecast under the Scenario of a Plane Crash*

	Year 1 (£m)	Years 1–5 (£m)
Revenues		2,800
Variable costs		1,400
Fixed costs		1,791
Depreciation		300
Pre-tax profit		−691
Tax ($t_c = 0.28$)[†]		193
Net profit		−498
Cash flow		−198
Initial investment cost	−1,500	

*Assumptions are
  Market size 7,000 (70% of expectation)
  Market share 20% (2/3 of expectation)
Forecasts for all other variables are the expected forecasts as given in Table 8.2.
[†]Tax loss offsets income elsewhere in firm.

A series of scenarios like this might illuminate issues concerning the project better than the standard application of sensitivity analysis would.

Real World Insight 8.1

Modelling the Impact of Changing Oil Prices

What price will oil eventually stabilize at? The figure below presents the price of oil between 1998 and 2015. As you can see, prices have varied between $40 and $140 over the time period.

Investment proposals that require the oil price as a revenue component or raw material cost must forecast oil prices for a number of years into the future. If you were undertaking a capital budgeting analysis in 2010, it would be unlikely that you could ever have predicted oil to drop so precipitously. As a result, your net present values will have probably misjudged the true net present value arising from a project. Sensitivity and scenario analysis allows you to consider such events and help you to make better investment decisions in the presence of price volatility.

Break-even Analysis

Our discussion of sensitivity analysis and scenario analysis suggests that there are many ways to examine variability in forecasts. We now present another approach, break-even analysis. As its name implies, this approach determines the sales needed to break even. The approach is a useful complement to sensitivity analysis because it also sheds light on the severity of incorrect forecasts. We calculate the break-even point in terms of both accounting profit and present value.

Accounting Profit

Annual net profit under four different sales forecasts is as follows:

Annual Unit Sales	Net Profit (£m)
0	−1,506
1,000	−786
3,000	654
10,000	5,694

A more complete presentation of costs and revenues appears in Table 8.5.

Table 8.5 Revenues and Costs of Project under Different Sales Assumptions

Year 0	Years 1-5								
Initial Investment (£m)	Annual Unit Sales	Revenues (£m)	Variable Costs (£m)	Fixed Costs (£m)	Depreciation (£m)	Taxes* ($t_c = 0.28$) (£m)	Net Profit (£m)	Operating Cash Flows (£m)	NPV (evaluated date 0) (£m)
1,500	0	0	0	−1,791	−300	585	−1,506	−1,206	−5,541
1,500	1,000	2,000	−1,000	−1,791	−300	305	−786	−486	−3,128
1,500	3,000	6,000	−3,000	−1,791	−300	−255	654	954	1,700
1,500	10,000	20,000	−10,000	−1,791	−300	−2,215	5,694	5,994	18,594

*Loss is incurred in the first two rows. For tax purposes, this loss offsets income elsewhere in the firm.

We plot the revenues, costs and profits under the different assumptions about sales in Figure 8.1. The revenue and cost curves cross at 2,091 jet engines. This is the break-even point – that is, the point where the project generates no profits or losses. As long as annual sales are above 2,091 jet engines, the project will make a profit.

Figure 8.1 Break-even Point Using Accounting Numbers

This break-even point can be calculated very easily. Because the sales price is £2 million per engine and the variable cost is £1 million per engine,[1] the difference between sales price and variable cost per engine is:

$$\text{Sales price} - \text{Variable cost} = £2 \text{ million} - £1 \text{ million}$$
$$= £1 \text{ million}$$

This difference is called the pre-tax contribution margin because each additional engine contributes this amount to pre-tax profit. (Contribution margin can also be expressed on an after-tax basis.)

Fixed costs are £1,791 million and depreciation is £300 million, implying that the sum of these costs is:

$$\text{Fixed costs} + \text{Depreciation} = \text{£1,791 million} + \text{£300 million}$$
$$= \text{£2,091 million}$$

That is, the firm incurs costs of £2,091 million per year, regardless of the number of sales. Because each engine contributes £1 million, annual sales must reach the following level to offset the costs:

Accounting profit break-even point:

$$\frac{\text{Fixed costs} + \text{Depreciation}}{\text{Sales price} - \text{Variable costs}} = \frac{\text{£2,091 million}}{\text{£1 million}} = 2,091$$

Thus, 2,091 engines is the break-even point required for an accounting profit.

The astute reader might be wondering why taxes have been ignored in the calculation of break-even accounting profit. The reason is that a firm with a pre-tax profit of £0 will also have an after-tax profit of £0 because no taxes are paid if no pre-tax profit is reported. Thus, the number of units needed to break even on a pre-tax basis must be equal to the number of units needed to break even on an after-tax basis.

Present Value

As we have stated many times, we are more interested in present value than we are in profit. Therefore, we should calculate break-even in terms of present value. Given a discount rate of 15 per cent, the solar plane engine has the following net present values for different levels of annual sales:

Annual Unit Sales	NPV (£m)
0	−5,541
1,000	−3,128
3,000	1,700
10,000	18,594

These NPV calculations are reproduced from the last column of Table 8.5.

Figure 8.2 relates the net present value of both the revenues and the costs to output. There are at least two differences between Figure 8.2 and Figure 8.1, one of which is quite important and the other is much less so. First the less important point: the monetary amounts on the vertical dimension of Figure 8.2 are greater than those on the vertical dimension of Figure 8.1 because the net present values are calculated over 5 years. More important, accounting break-even occurs when 2,091 units are sold annually, whereas NPV break-even occurs when 2,296 units are sold annually.

Of course the NPV break-even point can be calculated directly. The firm originally invested £1,500 million. This initial investment can be expressed as a 5-year equivalent annual cost[2] (EAC), determined by dividing the initial investment by the appropriate 5-year annuity factor:

$$\text{EAC} = \frac{\text{Initial investment}}{\text{5-year annuity factor at 15\%}} = \frac{\text{Initial investment}}{A_{0.15}^{5}}$$

$$= \frac{\text{£1,500 million}}{3.3522} = \text{£447.5 million}$$

Note that the EAC of £447.5 million is greater than the yearly depreciation of £300 million. This must occur because the calculation of EAC implicitly assumes that the £1,500 million investment could have been invested at 15 per cent.

After-tax costs, regardless of output, can be viewed like this:

$$\underset{\text{million}}{\text{£1,653}} = \underset{\text{million}}{\text{£447.5}} + \underset{\text{million}}{\text{£1,791}} \times 0.72 - \underset{\text{million}}{\text{£300}} \times 0.28$$

$$= \text{EAC} + \text{Fixed costs} \times (1 - t_c) - \text{Depreciation} \times t_c$$

Figure 8.2 Break-even Point Using Net Present Value

Net present value of revenues

Net present value of total costs

Net present value of variable costs

£ millions

£11,082

£5,541

Net present value of fixed costs (including depreciation)

2,296

Output (in terms of annual sales units)

Net present values of both revenues and costs are calculated on an after-tax basis. Break-even in terms of NPV occurs at a higher level of sales than does break-even for accounting income. Companies that just break even on an accounting basis are not recovering the opportunity cost of the initial investment.

That is, in addition to the initial investment's equivalent annual cost of £447.5 million, the firm pays fixed costs each year and receives a depreciation tax shield each year. The depreciation tax shield is written as a negative number because it offsets the costs in the equation. Each plane contributes £0.72 million to after-tax profit, so it will take the following sales to offset the costs:

Present value break-even point:

$$\frac{\text{EAC} + \text{Fixed costs} \times (1 - t_c) - \text{Depreciation} \times t_c}{(\text{Sales price} - \text{Variable costs}) \times (1 - t_c)} = \frac{\text{£1.653 million}}{\text{£0.72 million}} = 2,296$$

Thus, 2,296 planes is the break-even point from the perspective of present value.

Why is the accounting break-even point different from the financial break-even point? When we use accounting profit as the basis for the break-even calculation, we subtract depreciation. Depreciation for the solar jet engines project is £300 million per year. If 2,091 solar jet engines are sold per year, SE will generate sufficient revenues to cover the £300 million depreciation expense plus other costs. Unfortunately, at this level of sales SE will not cover the economic opportunity costs of the £1,500 million laid out for the investment. If we take into account that the £1,500 million could have been invested at 15 per cent, the true annual cost of the investment is £447.5 million, not £300 million. Depreciation understates the true costs of recovering the initial investment. Thus companies that break even on an accounting basis are really losing money. They are losing the opportunity cost of the initial investment.

Is break-even analysis important? Very much so: all corporate executives fear losses. Breakeven analysis determines how far down sales can fall before the project is losing money, either in an accounting sense or an NPV sense.

8.2   Monte Carlo Simulation

Both sensitivity analysis and scenario analysis attempt to answer the question 'What if?'. However, while both analyses are frequently used in the real world, each has its own limitations. Sensitivity analysis allows only one variable to change at a time. By contrast, many variables are likely to move at the same time in the real world. Scenario analysis follows specific scenarios, such as changes in inflation, government regulation, or the number of competitors. Although this methodology is often quite helpful, it cannot cover all sources of variability. In fact, projects are likely to exhibit a lot of variability under just one economic scenario.

Monte Carlo simulation is a further attempt to model real-world uncertainty. This approach takes its name from the famous European casino because it analyses projects the way one might analyse gambling strategies. Imagine a serious blackjack player who wonders if he should take a third card whenever his first two cards total 16. Most likely, a formal mathematical model would be too complex to be practical here. However, he could play thousands of hands in a casino, sometimes drawing a third card when his first two cards add to 16 and sometimes not drawing that third card. He could compare his winnings (or losings) under the two strategies to determine which were better. Of course he would probably lose a lot of money performing this test in a real casino, so simulating the results from the two strategies on a computer might be cheaper. Monte Carlo simulation of capital budgeting projects is in this spirit.

Imagine that Backyard Barbeques (BB), a manufacturer of both charcoal and gas grills, has a blueprint for a new grill that cooks with compressed hydrogen. The CFO, Edward H. Comiskey, being dissatisfied with simpler capital budgeting techniques, wants a Monte Carlo simulation for this new grill. A consultant specializing in the Monte Carlo approach, Lester Mauney, takes him through the five basic steps of the method.

Step 1: Specify the Basic Model

Les Mauney breaks up cash flow into three components: annual revenue, annual costs and initial investment. The revenue in any year is viewed as:

$$\text{Number of grills sold} \atop \text{by entire industry} \quad \times \quad \text{Market share of BB's} \atop \text{hydrogen grill (in per cent)} \quad \times \quad \text{Price per} \atop \text{hydrogen grill} \qquad (8.1)$$

The cost in any year is viewed as:

$$\text{Fixed manufacturing costs} + \text{Variable manufacturing costs} + \text{Marketing costs} \atop + \text{Selling costs}$$

Initial investment is viewed as:

$$\text{Cost of patent} + \text{Test marketing costs} + \text{Cost of production facility}$$

In step 1, you define the key inputs into your model. From above, revenues are a function of three components (the number of grills sold, market share and price per grill), annual costs are a function of four components (fixed costs, variable costs, marketing costs, selling costs), and the initial investment is a function of three components (patent, test marketing, and cost of the facility).

As an analyst, you can make your Monte Carlo simulation as simple or as complex as you desire. You may, for example, decide to focus only on revenues and assume that costs are fixed. Alternatively, you may believe that every component is important and wish to simulate each separately.

Step 2: Specify a Distribution for Each Variable in the Model

Here comes the hard part. Let us start with revenue, which has three components in Equation 8.1. The consultant first models overall market size – that is, the number of grills sold by the entire industry. The trade publication *Outdoor Food (OF)* reported that 10 million grills of all types were sold in Europe last year, and it forecasts sales of 10.5 million next year. Mr Mauney, using *OF*'s forecast and his own intuition, creates the following distribution for next year's sales of grills by the entire industry:

Probability (%)	20	60	20
Next year's industry-wide unit sales	10 million	10.5 million	11 million

The tight distribution here reflects the slow but steady historical growth in the grill market. This probability distribution is graphed in Panel A of Figure 8.3.

Lester Mauney realizes that estimating the market share of BB's hydrogen grill is more difficult. Nevertheless, after a great deal of analysis, he determines the distribution of next year's market share:

Probability (%)	10	20	30	25	10	5
Market share of BB's hydrogen grill next year (%)	1	2	3	4	5	8

Whereas the consultant assumed a symmetrical distribution for industry-wide unit sales, he believes a skewed distribution makes more sense for the project's market share. In his mind there is always the small possibility that sales of the hydrogen grill will really take off. This probability distribution is graphed in Panel B of Figure 8.3.

These forecasts assume that unit sales for the overall industry are unrelated to the project's market share. In other words, the two variables are *independent* of each other. Mr Mauney reasons that although an economic boom might increase industry-wide grill sales and a recession might decrease them, the project's market share is unlikely to be related to economic conditions.

Now Mr Mauney must determine the distribution of price per grill. Mr Comiskey, the CFO, informs him that the price will be in the area of €200 per grill, given what other competitors are charging. However, the consultant believes that the price per hydrogen grill will almost certainly depend on the size of the overall market for grills. As in any business, you can usually charge more if demand is high.

After rejecting a number of complex models for price, Mr Mauney settles on the following specification:

$$\text{Next year's price per hydrogen grill} = €190 + €11 \times \text{Industrywide unit sales (in millions)} + /-€3 \tag{8.2}$$

The grill price in Equation 8.2 depends on the unit sales of the industry. In addition, random variation is modelled via the term '+/−€3', where a drawing of +€3 and a drawing of −€3 each occur 50 per cent of the time. For example, if industry-wide unit sales are 11 million, the price per unit would be either of the following:

$$€190 + €11 + €3 = €204 \quad (50\% \text{ probability})$$

$$€190 + €11 − €3 = €198 \quad (50\% \text{ probability})$$

The relationship between the price of a hydrogen grill and industry-wide unit sales is graphed in Panel C of Figure 8.3.

Figure 8.3 Probability Distributions for Industry-wide Unit Sales, Market Share of BB's Hydrogen Grill, and Price of Hydrogen Grill

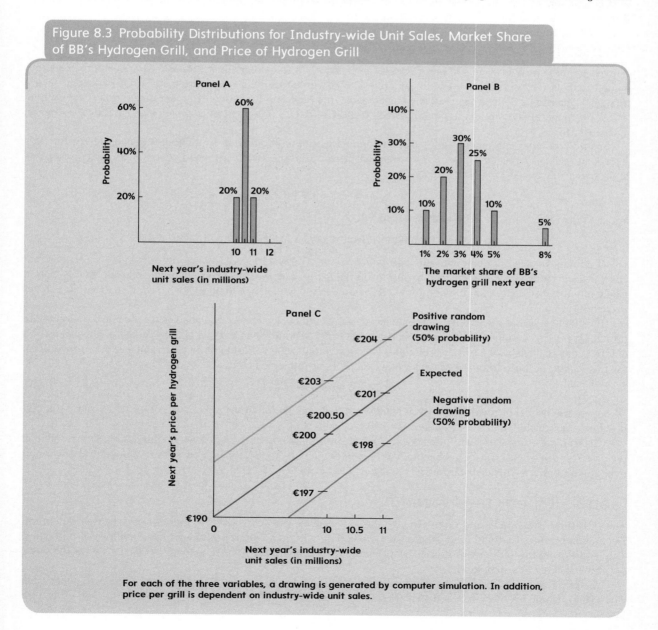

For each of the three variables, a drawing is generated by computer simulation. In addition, price per grill is dependent on industry-wide unit sales.

The consultant now has distributions for each of the three components of next year's revenue. However, he needs distributions for future years as well. Using forecasts from *Outdoor Food* and other publications, Mr Mauney forecasts the distribution of growth rates for the entire industry over the second year:

Probability (%)	20	60	20
Growth rate of industry-wide unit sales in second year (%)	1	3	5

Given both the distribution of next year's industry-wide unit sales and the distribution of growth rates for this variable over the second year, we can generate the distribution of industry-wide unit sales for the second year. A similar extension should give Mr Mauney a distribution for later years as well, though we will not go into the details here. And just as the consultant extended the first component of revenue (industry-wide unit sales) to later years, he would want to do the same thing for market share and unit price.

The preceding discussion shows how the three components of revenue can be modelled. Step 2 would be complete once the components of cost and investment are modelled in a similar way. Special attention must be paid to the interactions between variables here because ineffective management will likely allow the different cost components to rise together. However, you are probably getting the idea now, so we will skip the rest of this step.

Step 3: The Computer Draws One Outcome

As we said, next year's revenue in our model is the product of three components. Step 3 requires you to randomly sample values for each component to generate a constructed random observation for each key input in the analysis. This can be done in a spreadsheet using dedicated functions for random number generation (for example, '=RAND$_{()}$' generates a random number between 0 and 1 in Excel) or with more sophisticated statistical software, such as Stata.

Imagine that the computer randomly picks industry-wide unit sales of 10 million, a market share for BB's hydrogen grill of 2 per cent, and a +€3 random price variation. Given these drawings, next year's price per hydrogen grill will be:

$$€190 + €10 + €3 = €203$$

and next year's revenue for BB's hydrogen grill will be:

$$10 \text{ million} \times 0.02 \times €203 = €40.6 \text{ million}$$

Of course, we are not done with the entire *outcome* yet. We would have to perform drawings for revenue and costs in each future year. Finally, a drawing for initial investment would have to be made as well. In this way, a single outcome, made up of a drawing for each variable in the model, would generate a cash flow from the project in each future year.

How likely is it that the specific outcome discussed would be drawn? We can answer this because we know the probability of each component. Because industry sales of €10 million has a 20 per cent probability, a market share of 2 per cent also has a 20 per cent probability, and a random price variation of +€3 has a 50 per cent probability, the probability of these three drawings together in the same outcome is:

$$0.02 = 0.20 \times 0.20 \times 0.50 \tag{8.3}$$

Of course the probability would get even smaller once drawings for future revenues, future costs and the initial investment are included in the outcome.

This step generates the cash flow for each year from a single outcome. What we are ultimately interested in is the *distribution* of cash flow each year across many outcomes. We ask the computer to randomly draw over and over again to give us this distribution, which is just what is done in the next step.

Step 4: Repeat the Procedure

The first three steps generate one outcome, but the essence of Monte Carlo simulation is repeated outcomes. Depending on the situation, the computer may be called on to generate thousands or even millions of outcomes. The result of all these drawings is a distribution of cash flow for each future year. This distribution is the basic output of Monte Carlo simulation.

Consider Figure 8.4. Here, repeated drawings have produced the simulated distribution of the third year's cash flow. There would be, of course, a distribution like the one in this figure for each future year. This leaves us with just one more step.

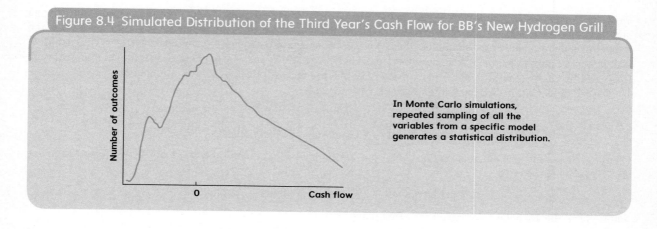

Figure 8.4 Simulated Distribution of the Third Year's Cash Flow for BB's New Hydrogen Grill

In Monte Carlo simulations, repeated sampling of all the variables from a specific model generates a statistical distribution.

Step 5: Calculate NPV

Given the distribution of cash flow for the third year in Figure 8.4, one can determine the expected cash flow for this year. In a similar manner, one can also determine the expected cash flow for each future year and then calculate the net present value of the project by discounting these expected cash flows at an appropriate rate.

Monte Carlo simulation is often viewed as a step beyond either sensitivity analysis or scenario analysis. Interactions between the variables are explicitly specified in Monte Carlo, so (at least in theory) this methodology provides a more complete analysis. And, as a by-product, having to build a precise model deepens the forecaster's understanding of the project.

One of the great benefits of Monte Carlo simulation is that the financial manager has a distribution of NPVs, instead of a single point estimate. This provides not only an insight into the scale of the NPV estimate (and any other investment appraisal method for that matter) but also the range of potential outcomes through the spread of simulated observations. These two pieces of information provide substantially more insight into the possible success of a proposed investment than a single value, which will considerably improve investment decisions.

8.3 Real Options

In Chapter 6, we stressed the superiority of net present value (NPV) analysis over other approaches when valuing capital budgeting projects. However, both scholars and practitioners have pointed out problems with NPV. The basic idea here is that NPV analysis, as well as all the other approaches in Chapter 6, ignores the adjustments that a firm can make after a project is accepted. These adjustments are called **real options**. In this respect NPV underestimates the true value of a project. NPV's conservatism is best explained through a series of examples (**Chapters 22 and 23** cover options and their valuation in a lot of detail).

Chapter 22 Page 586
Chapter 23 Page 619

The value of real option analysis comes from its ability to value managerial flexibility and corporate strategy. In almost all investments, managers continually assess and reassess ways in which costs can be reduced and revenues maximized. This activity requires identification of any possibility to expand, reduce, delay or even abandon production of an asset. Strategic flexibility provides an option to managers and, as with any option (see **Chapters 22 and 23**), it has value. Real option analysis is a methodology that allows you to value the strategic flexibility inherent in every project.

The Option to Expand

Conrad Willig, an entrepreneur, recently learned of a chemical treatment causing water to freeze at 20 degrees Celsius rather than 0 degrees. Of all the many practical applications for this treatment, Mr Willig liked the idea of hotels made of ice more than anything else. Conrad estimated the annual cash flows from a single ice hotel to be £2 million, based on an initial investment of £12 million. He felt that 20 per cent was an appropriate discount rate, given the risk of this new venture. Believing that the cash flows would be perpetual, Mr Willig determined the NPV of the project to be:

$$-£12,000,000 + £2,000,000/0.20 = -£2 \text{ million}$$

Most entrepreneurs would have rejected this venture, given its negative NPV. But Conrad was not your typical entrepreneur. He reasoned that NPV analysis missed a hidden source of value. While he was pretty sure that the initial investment would cost £12 million, there was some uncertainty concerning annual cash flows. His cash flow estimate of £2 million per year actually reflected his belief that there was a 50 per cent probability that annual cash flows will be £3 million and a 50 per cent probability that annual cash flows will be £1 million.

The NPV calculations for the two forecasts are given here:

Optimistic forecast: −£12 million + £3 million/0.20 = £3 million

Pessimistic forecast: −£12 million + £1 million/0.20 = −£7 million

On the surface, this new calculation does not seem to help Mr Willig much. An average of the two forecasts yields an NPV for the project of:

50% × £3 million + 50% × (−£7 million) = −£2 million

which is just the value he calculated in the first place.

However, if the optimistic forecast turns out to be correct, Mr Willig would want to *expand*. If he believes that there are, say, 10 locations in the country that can support an ice hotel, the true NPV of the venture would be:

50% × 10 × £3 million + 50% × (−£7 million) = £11.5 million

Figure 8.5, which represents Mr Willig's decision, is often called a decision tree. The idea expressed in the figure is both basic and universal. The entrepreneur has the option to expand if the pilot location is successful. For example, think of all the people that start restaurants, most of them ultimately failing. These individuals are not necessarily overly optimistic. They may realize the likelihood of failure but go ahead anyway because of the small chance of starting the next McDonald's or Starbucks.

The Option to Abandon

Managers also have the option to abandon existing projects. Abandonment may seem cowardly, but it can often save companies a great deal of money. Because of this, the option to abandon increases the value of any potential project.

The example of ice hotels, which illustrated the option to expand, can also illustrate the option to abandon. To see this, imagine that Mr Willig now believes that there is a 50 per cent probability that annual cash flows will be £6 million and a 50 per cent probability that annual cash flows will be −£2 million. The NPV calculations under the two forecasts become:

Optimistic forecast: −£12 million + £6 million/0.2 = £18 million

Pessimistic forecast: −£12 million − £2 million/0.2 = −£22 million

yielding an NPV for the project of:

50% × £18 million + 50% × (−£22 million) = −£2 million   (8.4)

Furthermore, now imagine that Mr Willig wants to own, at most, just one ice hotel, implying that there is no option to expand. Because the NPV in Equation 8.4 is negative, it looks as if he will not build the hotel.

But things change when we consider the abandonment option. As of date 1, the entrepreneur will know which forecast has come true. If cash flows equal those under the optimistic forecast, Conrad will keep the project alive. If, however, cash flows equal those under the pessimistic forecast, he will abandon the hotel. If Mr Willig knows these possibilities ahead of time, the NPV of the project becomes:

50% × £18 million + 50% × (−£12 million − £2 million/1.20) = £2.17 million

Because Mr Willig abandons after experiencing the cash flow of −£2 million at date 1, he does not have to endure this outflow in any of the later years. The NPV is now positive, so Conrad will accept the project.

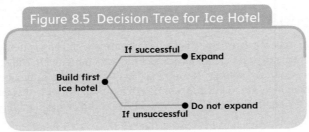

Figure 8.5 Decision Tree for Ice Hotel

Build first ice hotel

If successful • Expand

If unsuccessful • Do not expand

The example here is clearly a stylized one. Whereas many years may pass before a project is abandoned in the real world, our ice hotel was abandoned after just one year. And, while salvage values generally accompany abandonment, we assumed no salvage value for the ice hotel. Nevertheless, abandonment options are pervasive in the real world.

For example, consider the film-making industry. As shown in Figure 8.6, films begin with either the purchase or the development of a script. A completed script might cost a film studio a few million pounds and potentially lead to actual production. However, the great majority of scripts (perhaps well in excess of 90 per cent) are abandoned. Why would studios abandon scripts that they commissioned in the first place? The studios know ahead of time that only a few scripts will be promising, and they do not know which ones. Thus, they cast a wide net, commissioning many scripts to get a few good ones. The studios must be ruthless with the bad scripts because the expenditure here pales in comparison to the huge losses from producing a bad film.

Figure 8.6 The Abandonment Option in the Film Industry

Film studios have abandonment options throughout the production of a film.

The few lucky scripts then move into production, where costs might be budgeted in the tens of millions of pounds, if not much more. At this stage, the dreaded phrase is that on-location production gets 'bogged down', creating cost overruns. But the studios are equally ruthless here. Should these overruns become excessive, production is likely to be abandoned midstream. Interestingly, abandonment almost always occurs due to high costs, not due to the fear that the film will not be able to find an audience. Little information on that score will be obtained until the film is actually released.

Release of the film is accompanied by significant advertising expenditures, perhaps in the range of £5 to £10 million and sometimes even more. Advertising will continue following strong ticket sales, but it will likely be abandoned after a few weeks of poor box office performance.

Film-making is one of the riskiest businesses around, with studios receiving hundreds of millions of pounds or euros in a matter of weeks from a blockbuster while receiving practically nothing during this period from a flop. The abandonment options contain costs that might otherwise bankrupt the industry.

A recent example of companies actually exercising the option concerns the housing market in many European countries in the immediate aftermath of the global financial crisis in 2008. In the UK, for example, major house builders were reporting sales of only one house per month throughout the whole country. Rather than continue to build new plots and estates, companies such as Barratt, Taylor Wimpey and Persimmon Homes abandoned many sites.

Timing Options

One often finds urban land that has been vacant for many years. Yet this land is bought and sold from time to time. Why would anyone pay a positive price for land that has no source of revenue? Certainly, one could not arrive at a positive price through NPV analysis. However, the paradox can easily be explained in terms of real options.

Suppose that the land's highest and best use is as an office building. Total construction costs for the building are estimated to be €1 million. Currently, net rents (after all costs) are estimated to be €90,000 per year in perpetuity, and the discount rate is 10 per cent. The NPV of this proposed building would be:

$$-€1 \text{ million} + €90{,}000/0.10 = -€100{,}000$$

Because this NPV is negative, one would not currently want to build. However, suppose that the government is planning various urban revitalization programmes for the city. Office rents will likely increase if the programmes succeed. In this case the property's owner might want to erect the office building after all. Conversely, office rents will remain the same, or even fall, if the programmes fail. The owner will not build in this case.

We say that the property owner has a *timing option*. Although she does not currently want to build, she will want to build in the future should rents in the area rise substantially. This timing option explains why vacant land often has value. There are costs, such as taxes, from holding raw land, but the value of an office building after a substantial rise in rents may more than offset these holding costs. Of course the exact value of the vacant land depends on both the probability of success in the revitalization programme and the extent of the rent increase. Figure 8.7 illustrates this timing option.

Figure 8.7 Decision Tree for Vacant Land

Rents rise substantially — Erect office building

Do not build yet because rents are too low

Rents either stay the same or fall — Do not build yet

Vacant land may have value today because the owner can erect a profitable office building if rents rise.

Mining operations almost always provide timing options as well. Suppose you own a copper mine where the cost of mining each ton of copper exceeds the sales revenue. It is a no-brainer to say that you would not want to mine the copper currently. And because there are costs of ownership such as property taxes, insurance and security, you might actually want to pay someone to take the mine off your hands. However, we would caution you not to do so hastily. Copper prices in the future might increase enough so that production is profitable. Given that possibility, you could likely find someone to pay a positive price for the property today.

8.4 Decision Trees

As shown in the previous section, managers adjust their decisions on the basis of new information. For example, a project may be expanded if early experience is promising, whereas the same project might be abandoned in the wake of bad results. As we said earlier, the choices available to managers are called *real options* and an individual project can often be viewed as a series of real options, leading to valuation approaches beyond the basic present value methodology of earlier chapters.

Earlier in this chapter, we considered Solar Electronics' (SE's) solar-powered jet engine project, with cash flows as shown in Table 8.1. In that example, SE planned to invest £1,500 million at year 0 and expected to receive £954 million per year in each of the next 5 years. Our calculations showed an NPV of £1,700 million, so the firm would presumably want to go ahead with the project.

To illustrate decision trees in more detail, let us move back one year prior to year 0, when SE's decision was more complicated. At that time, the engineering group had developed the technology for a solar-powered plane engine, but test marketing had not begun. The marketing department proposed that SE develop some prototypes and conduct test marketing of the engine. A corporate planning group, including representatives from production, marketing and engineering, estimated that this preliminary phase would take a year and cost £100 million. Furthermore, the group believed there was a 75 per cent chance that the marketing test would prove successful. After completion of the marketing tests, SE would decide whether to engage in full-scale production, necessitating the investment of £1,500 million.

The marketing tests add a layer of complexity to the analysis. Our previous work on the example assumed that the marketing tests had already proved successful. How do we analyse whether we want to go ahead with the marketing tests in the first place? This is where decision trees come in.

To recap, SE faces two decisions, both of which are represented in Figure 8.8. First the firm must decide whether to go ahead with the marketing tests. And if the tests are performed, the firm must decide whether the results of the tests warrant full-scale production. The important point here, as we will see, is that decision trees answer the two questions in *reverse* order. So let us work backward, first considering what to do with the results of the tests, which can be either successful or unsuccessful.

- *Assume tests have been successful (75 per cent probability).* Table 8.1 tells us that full-scale production will cost £1,500 million and will generate an annual cash flow of £954 million for 5 years, yielding an NPV of:

$$= -£1,500 + \sum_{t=1}^{5} \frac{£954}{(1.15)^t}$$

$$= -£1,500 + £954 \times A^5_{0.15}$$

$$= £1,700$$

Because the NPV is positive, successful marketing tests should lead to full-scale production. (Note that the NPV is calculated as of year 1, the time at which the investment of £1,500 million is made. Later we will discount this number back to year 0, when the decision on test marketing is to be made.)

- *Assume tests have not been successful (25 per cent probability).* Here, SE's £1,500 million investment would produce an NPV of −£3,611 million, calculated as of year 1. (To save space, we will not provide the raw numbers leading to this calculation.) Because the NPV here is negative, SE will not want full-scale production if the marketing tests are unsuccessful.

- *Decision on marketing tests.* Now we know what to do with the results of the marketing tests. Let us use these results to move back one year. That is, we now want to figure out whether SE should invest £100 million for the test marketing costs in the first place.

The expected pay-off evaluated at date 1 (in millions) is:

$$\text{Expected} \atop \text{pay-off} = \begin{pmatrix} \text{Probability} \\ \text{of} \\ \text{success} \end{pmatrix} \times \begin{pmatrix} \text{Pay-off} \\ \text{if} \\ \text{successful} \end{pmatrix} + \begin{pmatrix} \text{Probability} \\ \text{of} \\ \text{failure} \end{pmatrix} \times \begin{pmatrix} \text{Pay-off} \\ \text{if} \\ \text{failure} \end{pmatrix}$$

$$= (0.75 \times £1,700) + (0.25 \times £0) = £1,275$$

The NPV (in millions) of testing computed one year prior to year 0 is:

$$\text{NPV} = -£100 + \frac{£1,275}{1.15}$$

$$= £1,008$$

Because the NPV is positive, the firm should test the market for solar-powered jet engines.

Warning

We have used a discount rate of 15 per cent for both the testing and the investment decisions. Perhaps a higher discount rate should have been used for the initial test marketing decision, which is likely to be riskier than the investment decision.

Recap

As mentioned above, the analysis is graphed in Figure 8.8. As can be seen from the figure, SE must make the following two decisions:

1 Whether to develop and test the solar-powered jet engine.
2 Whether to invest for full-scale production following the results of the test.

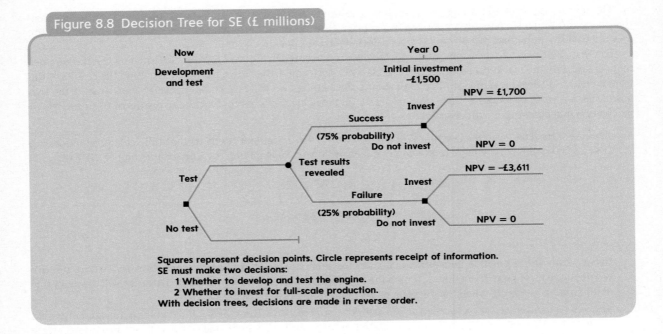

Figure 8.8 Decision Tree for SE (£ millions)

Squares represent decision points. Circle represents receipt of information.
SE must make two decisions:
   1 Whether to develop and test the engine.
   2 Whether to invest for full-scale production.
With decision trees, decisions are made in reverse order.

Using a decision tree, we answered the second question before we answered the first one.

Decision trees represent the best approach to solving SE's problem, given the information presented so far in the text. However, we will examine a more sophisticated approach to valuing options in a later chapter. Though this approach was first used to value financial options traded on organized option exchanges, it can be used to value real options as well.

Summary and Conclusions

This chapter discussed a number of practical applications of capital budgeting.

1   Though NPV is the best capital budgeting approach conceptually, it has been criticized in practice for giving managers a false sense of security. Sensitivity analysis shows NPV under varying assumptions, giving managers a better feel for the project's risks. Unfortunately sensitivity analysis modifies only one variable at a time, but many variables are likely to vary together in the real world. Scenario analysis examines a project's performance under different scenarios (such as war breaking out or oil prices skyrocketing). Finally, managers want to know how bad forecasts must be before a project loses money. Break-even analysis calculates the sales figure at which the project breaks even. Though break-even analysis is frequently performed on an accounting profit basis, we suggest that a net present value basis is more appropriate.

2   Monte Carlo simulation begins with a model of the firm's cash flows, based on both the interactions between different variables and the movement of each individual variable over time. Random sampling generates a distribution of these cash flows for each period, leading to a net present value calculation.

3   We analysed the hidden options in capital budgeting, such as the option to expand, the option to abandon, and timing options.

4   Decision trees represent an approach for valuing projects with these hidden, or real, options.

Questions and Problems

CONCEPT

1 **NPV, Sensitivity Analysis, Monte Carlo Simulation, and Decision Trees** *'NPV is just a tool and as with any tool, it can be dangerous in the wrong hands.'*

   (a) Discuss this statement. In what way do sensitivity analysis, break-even analysis and scenario analysis improve things? Surely they are just tools as well?

   (b) Explain the rationale underlying Monte Carlo simulation. How does it improve upon other forms of sensitivity analysis? Does it have any weaknesses? If so, what are they? How could you improve on the methodology?

   (c) When should you stop decision tree analysis on a capital budgeting project?

2 **Risk-neutral Valuation** Explain why a company might use a risk-neutral valuation approach for valuing real options. Is this method appropriate for traditional NPV?

3 **Ross (1995)** Ross (1995) puts forward that there are three sources of value in a typical capital budgeting project. Explain these three sources using examples.

4 **Real Options** When Microsoft launched its Xbox console in 2001 the NPV from the project was negative. However, the company proceeded with the project. Why do you think this was?

REGULAR

5 **Sensitivity Analysis and Break-even Point** A retail clothing firm is evaluating the development of a new range of all-weather coats. These coats contain an internal solar battery to provide heating whenever the garment is worn. The solar battery cost £3.2 million to make and the expectation is that the project will last for 5 years. At the end of the project, the machinery to make the battery will be worthless because of new technological developments. Assume that depreciation is 20 per cent reducing balance method. Sales are projected at 250,000 units per year. Price per battery is £10, variable cost per unit is £2.50, and fixed costs are £900,000 per year. The tax rate is 23 per cent, and we require a 13 per cent return on this project.

   (a) Calculate the accounting break-even point.

   (b) Calculate the base-case cash flow and NPV. What is the sensitivity of NPV to changes in the sales figure? Explain what your answer tells you about a 50,000-unit decrease in projected sales.

   (c) What is the sensitivity of OCF to changes in the variable cost figure? Explain what your answer tells you about a £1 decrease in estimated variable costs.

6 **Scenario Analysis** A retail clothing firm is evaluating the development of a new range of all-weather coats. These coats contain an internal solar battery to provide heating whenever the garment is worn. The solar battery cost £3.2 million to make and the expectation is that the project will last for 5 years. At the end of the project, the machinery to make the battery will be worthless because of new technological developments. Assume that depreciation is 20 per cent reducing balance method. Sales are projected at 250,000 units per year. Price per battery is £10, variable cost per unit is £1.50, and fixed costs are £900,000 per year. The tax rate is 23 per cent, and we require a 13 per cent return on this project. Suppose the projections given for price, quantity, variable costs and fixed costs are all accurate to within ± 10 per cent. Calculate the best-case and worst-case NPV figures.

7 **Financial Break-even** L.J.'s Toys has just purchased a £200,000 machine to produce toy cars. The machine will be fully depreciated using 20 per cent reducing balances over its 5-year economic life. Each toy sells for £25. The variable cost per toy is £5, and the firm incurs fixed costs of £350,000 each year. The corporate tax rate for the company is 25 per cent. The appropriate discount rate is 12 per cent. What is the financial break-even point for the project?

8 **Option to Wait** Your company is deciding whether to invest in a new machine. The new machine will increase cash flow by €280,000 per year. You believe the technology used in the machine has a 10-year life; in other words, no matter when you purchase the machine, it will be obsolete 10 years from today. The machine is currently priced at €1,500,000 and should be depreciated using 25 per cent reducing balance method. If your required return is 12 per cent, should you purchase the machine? If so, when should you purchase it?

9 **Decision Trees** Ang Electronics has developed a new DVDR. If the DVDR is successful, the present value of the pay-off (when the product is brought to market) is £20 million. If the DVDR fails, the present value of the pay-off is £5 million. If the product goes directly to market, there is a 50 per cent chance of success. Alternatively, Ang can delay the launch by one year and spend £2 million to test market the DVDR. Test marketing would allow the firm to improve the product and increase the probability of success to 75 per cent. The appropriate discount rate is 15 per cent. Should the firm conduct test marketing?

10 **Option to Wait Versus Immediate Investment** Global Investments has hired you as a financial consultant to advise them on whether to enter the shoe market, an investment opportunity which has an initial outlay of £35 million. During a Board meeting, the CEO tells you that due to the upcoming summer season there is high demand in the shoe market, and he believes the time is right to open a shoe business today. However, with the country hosting a major sporting event next summer, the finance director of the company argues that waiting exactly one year from now would also be a good opportunity. He argues that in one year from now there should be even higher demand, and hence shoes can be sold at higher prices. After a further meeting with the company's management, you are given the following information:

- The value of a shoe company is estimated to be £40 million.

- Due to a high degree of market competition the flow of customers is uncertain, so that value of the company is volatile, and based on the standard deviation of the company's stock price you estimate this to be 25 per cent per year.

- 15 per cent of the value of the company is attributable to the value of the free cash flows expected in the first year.

- The one-year risk-free rate is 4 per cent.

The Board cannot reach agreement, and so they ask for your opinion on when and if the company should go ahead with the project. What is your recommendation? Should they wait or invest?

11 **Decision Trees** B&B has a new baby powder ready to market. If the firm goes directly to the market with the product, there is only a 55 per cent chance of success. However, the firm can conduct customer segment research, which will take a year and cost €1 million. By going through research, B&B will be able to better target potential customers and will increase the probability of success to 70 per cent. If successful, the baby powder will bring a present value profit (at time of initial selling) of €30 million. If unsuccessful, the present value pay-off is only €3 million. Should the firm conduct customer segment research or go directly to market? The appropriate discount rate is 15 per cent.

12 **Financial Break-even Analysis** You are considering investing in a company that cultivates abalone for sale to local restaurants. Use the following information:

Sales price per abalone	£2.00
Variable costs per abalone	£0.72
Fixed costs per year	£340,000
Depreciation per year	£20,000
Tax rate	35%

The discount rate for the company is 15 per cent, the initial investment in equipment is £140,000, and the project's economic life is 7 years. Assume, for simplicity, that the equipment is depreciated on a straight-line basis over the project's life.

(a) What is the accounting break-even level for the project?

(b) What is the financial break-even level for the project?

13 **Scenario Analysis** You have been given the following figures to assess the viability of a new portable hospital scanner. It is expected that you will be able to capture 10 per cent of the total market of 1.1 million units. The market price will be €400,000 and the unit variable cost is 90 per cent of the market price. Fixed costs of running and manufacture amount to €2 billion per annum.

(a) What is the net income of the project?

(b) You have been approached by the management, who disagree on the figures that were originally used in the analysis. They want you to consider the following scenarios proposed by different directors in the company.

	Director A	Director B	Director C
Market size	0.8 million	1 million	1.2 million
Market share (%)	4	10	16
Unit price (€)	300,000	375,000	400,000
Variable cost (%)	116	80	70
Fixed cost (€)	5 billion	3 billion	1 billion

Carry out a sensitivity analysis of the project. What are the main uncertainties in the project?

14 **Break-even Intuition** Consider a project with a required return of R per cent that costs £I and will last for N years. The project uses straight-line depreciation to zero over the N-year life; there are neither salvage value nor net working capital requirements.

(a) At the accounting break-even level of output, what is the IRR of this project? The payback period? The NPV?

(b) At the cash break-even level of output, what is the IRR of this project? The payback period? The NPV?

(c) At the financial break-even level of output, what is the IRR of this project? The payback period? The NPV?

15 **Project Analysis** You are considering a new product launch. The project will cost £460,000, have a 4-year life, and have no salvage value; depreciation is 20 per cent reducing balance. Sales are projected at 150 units per year; price per unit will be £24,000; variable costs are 75 per cent of sales; and fixed costs will be £200,000 per year. The required return on the project is 15 per cent, and the relevant tax rate is 24 per cent.

(a) Based on your experience, you think the unit sales, variable cost and fixed cost projections given here are probably accurate to within ±10 per cent. What are the upper and lower bounds for these projections? What is the base-case NPV? What are the best-case and worst-case scenarios?

(b) Evaluate the sensitivity of your base-case NPV to changes in fixed costs.

(c) What is the accounting break-even level of output for this project?

16 **Project Analysis** McGilla Golf has decided to sell a new line of golf clubs. The clubs will sell for £700 per set and have a variable cost of £320 per set. The company has spent £150,000 for a marketing study that determined the company will sell 55,000 sets per year for 7 years. The marketing study also determined that the company will lose sales of 13,000 sets of its high-priced clubs. The high-priced clubs sell at £1,100 and have variable costs of £600. The company will also increase sales of its cheap clubs by 10,000 sets. The cheap clubs sell for £400 and have variable costs of £180 per set. The fixed costs each year will be £7,500,000. The company has also spent £1,000,000 on research and development for the new clubs. The plant and equipment required will cost £18,200,000 and will be depreciated on a 20 per cent reducing balance basis. At the end of the 7 years, the salvage value of the plant and equipment will be equal to the written down or residual value. The new clubs will also require an increase in net working capital of £950,000 that will be returned at the end of the project. The tax rate is 28 per cent, and the cost of capital is 14 per cent.

(a) Calculate the payback period, the NPV and the IRR for base case.

(b) You feel that the values are accurate to within only ± 10 per cent. What are the best-case and worst-case NPVs? (*Hint:* The price and variable costs for the two existing sets of clubs are known with certainty; only the sales gained or lost are uncertain.)

(c) McGilla would like to know the sensitivity of NPV to changes in the price of the new clubs and the quantity of new clubs sold. What is the sensitivity of the NPV to each of these variables?

17 **Abandonment Value** We are examining a new project. We expect to sell 7,000 units per year at €60 net cash flow apiece for the next 10 years. In other words, the annual operating cash flow is projected to be €60 × 7,000 = €420,000. The relevant discount rate is 16 per cent, and the initial investment required is €1,800,000.

(a) What is the base-case NPV?

(b) After the first year, the project can be dismantled and sold for €1,400,000. If expected sales are revised based on the first year's performance, when would it make sense to abandon the investment? In other words, at what level of expected sales would it make sense to abandon the project?

(c) Explain how the €1,400,000 abandonment value can be viewed as the opportunity cost of keeping the project in one year.

(d) Suppose you think it is likely that expected sales will be revised upward to 9,000 units if the first year is a success and revised downward to 4,000 units if the first year is not a success. If success and failure are equally likely, what is the NPV of the project? Consider the possibility of abandonment in answering. What is the value of the option to abandon?

18 **Abandonment and Expansion** In the previous problem, suppose the scale of the project can be doubled in one year in the sense that twice as many units can be produced and sold. Naturally, expansion would be desirable only if the project were a success. This implies that if the project is a success, projected sales after expansion will be 18,000. Again assuming that success and failure are equally likely, what is the NPV of the project? Note that abandonment is still an option if the project is a failure. What is the value of the option to expand?

19 **Decision Trees** Young screenwriter Carl Draper has just finished his first script. It has action, drama and humour, and he thinks it will be a blockbuster. He takes the script to every film studio in town and tries to sell it but to no avail. Finally, ACME studios offers to buy the script for either (a) $5,000 or (b) 1 per cent of the film's profits. There are two decisions the studio will have to make. First is to decide if the script is good or bad, and second if the film is good or bad. First, there is a 90 per cent chance that the script is bad. If it is bad, the studio does nothing more and throws the script out. If the script is good, they will shoot the film. After the film is shot, the studio will review it, and there is a 70 per cent chance that the film is bad. If the film is bad, it will not be promoted and will not turn a profit. If the film is good, the studio will promote heavily; the average profit for this type of film is $10 million. Carl rejects the $5,000 and says he wants the 1 per cent of profits. Was this a good decision by Carl?

20 **Accounting Break-even** Samuelson GmbH has just purchased a €600,000 machine to produce calculators. The machine will be fully depreciated using the 20 per cent reducing balance method over its economic life of 5 years and will produce 20,000 calculators each year. The salvage value of the machine will be equal to its residual or written down value. The variable production cost per calculator is €15, and total fixed costs are €900,000 per year. The corporate tax rate for the company is 30 per cent. For the firm to break even in terms of accounting profit, how much should the firm charge per calculator?

21 **Real Options** Petrofac Ltd, the international provider of oil and gas building facilities, has entered into an agreement with a number of Kenyan oil exploration firms to support development of oil wells in the Turkana region after a very large oil well was found there in 2012. The cost of setting up new facilities is £12 million and the well is expected to have a life of 5 years. Oil is currently fetching £84 per barrel in the international markets and production and extraction costs stand at 85 per cent of the oil price. The appropriate discount rate for this project is 18 per cent. What is the break-even number of barrels that can be sold?

22 **Abandonment Decisions** Allied Products is considering a new product launch. The firm expects to have an annual operating cash flow of AED60 million for the next 6 years. Allied Products uses a discount rate of 14 per cent for new product launches. The initial investment is AED200 million. Assume that the project has no salvage value at the end of its economic life.

(a) What is the NPV of the new product?

(b) After the first year, the project can be dismantled and sold for AED50 million. If the estimates of remaining cash flows are revised based on the first year's experience, at what level of expected cash flows does it make sense to abandon the project?

23 **Expansion Decisions** Applied Nanotech is thinking about introducing a new surface cleaning machine. The marketing department has come up with the estimate that Applied Nanotech can sell 10 units per year at £0.3 million net cash flow per unit for the next 5 years. The engineering department has come up with the estimate that developing the machine will take a £10 million initial investment. The finance department has estimated that a 25 per cent discount rate should be used.

(a) What is the base-case NPV?

(b) If unsuccessful, after the first year the project can be dismantled and will have an after-tax salvage value of £5 million. Also, after the first year, expected cash flows will be revised up to 20 units per year or to 0 units, with equal probability. What is the revised NPV?

24 Scenario Analysis You are the financial analyst for a tennis racket manufacturer. The company is considering using a graphite-like material in its tennis rackets. The company has estimated the information in the following table about the market for a racket with the new material. The company expects to sell the racket for 5 years. The equipment required for the project has no salvage value. The required return for projects of this type is 13 per cent, and the company has a 40 per cent tax rate. Should you recommend the project? Assume 20 per cent reducing balance depreciation.

	Pessimistic	Expected	Optimistic
Market size	110,000	120,000	130,000
Market share (%)	22	25	27
Selling price (€)	115	120	125
Variable costs per unit (€)	72	70	68
Fixed costs per year (€)	850,000	800,000	750,000
Initial investment (€)	1,500,000	1,500,000	1,500,000

CHALLENGE

25 The Capital Budgeting Process This question takes a step back from the quantitative analysis and makes you think about how you would manage a capital budgeting project in a firm. You have just graduated from university and taken up your first job in a local distribution firm. The firm stores alcoholic beverages for breweries and distributes these to pubs and restaurants depending on the specific orders placed with your customers. Your firm does not own any stock. It just holds it for others and distributes it when needed. The directors are considering expanding their business by building two new warehouses to increase capacity and hopefully revenues. As a corporate finance expert, you have been tasked with the job of managing the capital budgeting analysis from the initial idea to the start of operations.

Prepare a flow chart or mind map for presentation to the directors that will deal with the following issues:

(a) Who will prepare the initial proposal?

(b) What information will the proposal contain?

(c) How will you evaluate it?

(d) What approvals will be needed and who will give them?

(e) What happens if the expenditure is 25 per cent more than the original forecast?

(f) What will happen when the warehouses have been built?

26 Scenario Analysis Consider a project to supply Italy with 40,000 tons of machine screws annually for automobile production. You will need an initial €1,500,000 investment in threading equipment to get the project started; the project will last for 5 years. The accounting department estimates that annual fixed costs will be €600,000 and that variable costs should be €210 per ton; accounting will depreciate the initial fixed asset investment using 20 per cent reducing balance method over the 5-year project life. It also estimates a salvage value of €800,000 after dismantling costs. The marketing department estimates that the automakers will let the contract at a selling price of €230 per ton. The engineering department estimates you will need an initial net working capital investment of €450,000. You require a 13 per cent return and face a marginal tax rate of 32 per cent on this project.

(a) What is the estimated OCF for this project? The NPV? Should you pursue this project?

(b) Suppose you believe that the accounting department's initial cost and salvage value projections are accurate only to within ±15 per cent; the marketing department's price estimate is accurate only to within ±10 per cent; and the engineering department's net working capital estimate is accurate only to within ±5 per cent. What is your worst-case scenario for this project? Your best-case scenario? Do you still want to pursue the project?

27 Sensitivity Analysis In Problem 26, suppose you are confident about your own projections, but you are a little unsure about Italy's actual machine screw requirement. What is the sensitivity of the project OCF to changes in the quantity supplied? What about the sensitivity of NPV to changes in quantity supplied? Given the sensitivity number you calculated, is there some minimum level of output below which you would not want to operate? Why?

28 **Abandonment Decisions** Consider the following project for Hand Clapper. The company is considering a 4-year project to manufacture clap-command garage door openers. This project requires an initial investment of €10 million that will be depreciated using the 20 per cent reducing balance method over the project's life. The salvage value at the end of the project's life is assumed to be equal to its residual or written-down value. An initial investment in net working capital of €3 million is required to support spare parts inventory; this cost is fully recoverable whenever the project ends. The company believes it can generate €8 million in pre-tax revenues with €2 million in total pre-tax operating costs. The tax rate is 34 per cent, and the discount rate is 17 per cent. The market value of the equipment over the life of the project is as follows:

Year	Market value (€ millions)
1	6.50
2	6.00
3	3.00
4	0.00

(a) Assuming Hand Clapper operates this project for 4 years, what is the NPV?

(b) Now compute the project NPVs assuming the project is abandoned after only 1 year, after 2 years and after 3 years. What economic life for this project maximizes its value to the firm? What does this problem tell you about not considering abandonment possibilities when evaluating projects?

29 **Abandonment Decisions** M.V.P. Games has hired you to perform a feasibility study of a new video game that requires a $9 million initial investment. M.V.P. expects a total annual operating cash flow of $1,750,000 for the next 10 years. The relevant discount rate is 12 per cent. Cash flows occur at year-end.

(a) What is the NPV of the new video game?

(b) After one year, the estimate of remaining annual cash flows will be revised either upward to $2.5 million or downward to $520,000. Each revision has an equal probability of occurring. At that time, the video game project can be sold for $2,000,000. What is the revised NPV given that the firm can abandon the project after one year?

30 **Financial Break-even** The Wheatchopper Company is considering the purchase of a new harvester. Wheatchopper has hired you to determine the break-even purchase price in terms of present value of the harvester. This break-even purchase price is the price at which the project's NPV is zero. Base your analysis on the following facts:

- The new harvester is not expected to affect revenues, but pre-tax operating expenses will be reduced by €10,000 per year for 10 years.

- The old harvester is now 5 years old, with 10 years of its scheduled life remaining. It was originally purchased for €45,000 and has been depreciated using the 20 per cent reducing balance method.

- The old harvester can be sold for €20,000 today.

- The new harvester will be depreciated by the 20 per cent reducing balance method over its 10-year life.

- The corporate tax rate is 34 per cent.

- The firm's required rate of return is 15 per cent.

- The initial investment, the proceeds from selling the old harvester, and any resulting tax effects occur immediately.

- All other cash flows occur at year-end.

- The market value of each harvester at the end of its economic life is equal to its residual or written down value.

31 **Sensitivity Analysis** Unmondo SpA is proposing to replace its old DVD stamping machinery with more modern equipment geared towards the blu-ray technology. The new machinery costs €9 million (the existing machinery has no value). The attraction of the blu-ray stamper is that it is expected to cut manufacturing costs from their current level of €8 per DVD to €4 per blu-ray disc. However, as the following table shows, there is some uncertainty about future sales and the performance of the blu-ray technology.

	Pessimistic	Expected	Optimistic
Sales, millions of units	0.4	0.5	0.6
Manufacturing cost, €/unit	6	4	3
Life of new machine	7 years	10 years	13 years

(a) Carry out a sensitivity analysis of the replacement decision, assuming a discount rate of 12 per cent. Unmondo does not pay taxes.

(b) Unmondo SpA could commission engineering tests to determine the actual improvement in manufacturing costs generated by the proposed new blu-ray disc stamper. The study would cost €450,000. Would you advise Unmondo to go ahead with the study?

32 **Option to Abandon** You own an unused gold mine that will cost $800,000 to reopen. If you open the mine, you expect to be able to extract 1,000 ounces of gold a year for each of 3 years. After that, the deposit will be exhausted. The gold price is currently $2,000 an ounce, and each year the price is equally likely to rise or fall by $100 from its level at the start of the year. The extraction cost is $920 an ounce and the discount rate is 14 per cent.

(a) Should you open the mine now or delay one year in the hope of a rise in the gold price?

(b) What difference would it make to your decision if you could costlessly (but irreversibly) shut down the mine at any stage?

33 **Options to Abandon and Expand** Grace and Danger plc is introducing a new product this year. If its luminous golf balls (with integrated beeper) are a success, the firm expects to be able to sell 50,000 units a year at a price of £60 each (they will not go missing so you will pay a lot for them!). If the new golf balls are not well received, only 30,000 units can be sold at a price of £55. The variable cost of each golf ball is £30 and the fixed costs are zero. The cost of the manufacturing equipment is £6 million, and the project life is estimated to be 10 years. The firm will use 20 per cent reducing balances as their method of depreciation and at the end of the project's life, the machine will be worth nothing. Grace and Danger's tax rate is 28 per cent and the appropriate discount rate is 12 per cent.

(a) If each outcome is equally likely, what is the expected NPV? Will the firm accept the project?

(b) Suppose now that the firm can abandon the project and sell off the manufacturing equipment for £5.4 million if demand for the golf balls turns out to be weak. The firm will make the decision to continue or abandon after the first year of sales. Does the option to abandon change the firm's decision to accept the project?

(c) Now suppose Grace and Danger can expand production if the project is successful. By paying its workers overtime, it can increase production by 25,000 golf balls; the variable cost of each ball will be higher, however, equal to £35 per golf ball. By how much does this option to expand production increase the NPV of the project?

Exam Question (45 minutes)

1 You are the financial analyst for Weir Group plc, the global engineering firm. The company is considering the development of a new slurry pump in its existing products. The pump is expected to improve market share for the company if it is fully integrated into its existing product line-up. With the pace of new technological developments, you expect the slurry pump to be obsolete by the end of 5 years. The equipment required for the project has no salvage value. The required return for projects of this type is 20 per cent, and the company has a 24 per cent tax rate. Should you recommend the project? Assume 20 per cent reducing balance depreciation. (75 marks)

	Pessimistic	Expected	Optimistic
Market size	1,000	1,500	1,700
Market share (%)	15	20	25
Selling price (£)	10,000	15,000	20,000
Variable costs per unit (%)	72	70	68
Fixed costs per year (£)	400,000	450,000	550,000
Initial investment (£)	2,500,000	2,500,000	2,500,000

2 Explain the difference between sensitivity analysis, scenario analysis and break-even analysis. In the context of the problem in part (a), what do you think is the most appropriate investment appraisal method? Explain your answer. (25 marks)

Mini Case

Bunyan Lumber, LLC

Bunyan Lumber Ltd harvests timber and delivers logs to timber mills for sale. The company was founded 70 years ago by Pete Bunyan. The current CEO is Paula Bunyan, the granddaughter of the founder. The company is currently evaluating a 5,000-acre forest it owns in the Scottish Highlands. Paula has asked Steve Boles, the company's finance officer, to evaluate the project. Paula's concern is when the company should harvest the timber.

Lumber is sold by the company for its 'pond value'. Pond value is the amount a mill will pay for a log delivered to the mill location. The price paid for logs delivered to a mill is quoted in pounds per thousands of board feet (MBF), and the price depends on the grade of the logs. The forest Bunyan Lumber is evaluating was planted by the company 20 years ago and is made up entirely of Douglas fir trees. The table here shows the current price per MBF for the three grades of timber the company feels will come from the stand:

Timber Grade	Price Per MBF (£)
1P	1,050
2P	925
3P	770

Steve believes that the pond value of lumber will increase at the inflation rate. The company is planning to thin the forest today, and it expects to realize a positive cash flow of £1,000 per acre from thinning. The thinning is done to increase the growth rate of the remaining trees, and it is always done 20 years following a planting.

The major decision the company faces is when to log the forest. When the company logs the forest, it will immediately replant saplings, which will allow for a future harvest. The longer the forest is allowed to grow, the larger the harvest becomes per acre. Additionally, an older forest has a higher grade of timber. Steve has compiled the following table with the expected harvest per acre in thousands of board feet, along with the breakdown of the timber grades:

Years From Today to Begin Harvest	Harvest (MBF) Per Acre	Timber Grade		
		1P (%)	2P (%)	3P (%)
20	6	10	40	50
25	7.6	12	42	46
30	9	15	42	43
35	10	16	43	41

The company expects to lose 5 per cent of the timber it cuts due to defects and breakage.

The forest will be clear-cut when the company harvests the timber. This method of harvesting allows for faster growth of replanted trees. All of the harvesting, processing, replanting and transportation is to be handled by subcontractors hired by Bunyan Lumber. The cost of the logging is expected to be £140 per MBF. A road system has to be constructed and is expected to cost £50 per MBF on average. Sales preparation and administrative costs, excluding office overhead costs, are expected to be £18 per MBF.

As soon as the harvesting is complete, the company will reforest the land. Reforesting costs include the following:

	Per Acre Cost (£)
Excavator piling	150
Broadcast burning	300
Site preparation	145
Planting costs	225

All costs are expected to increase at the inflation rate.

Assume all cash flows occur at the year of harvest. For example, if the company begins harvesting the timber 20 years from today, the cash flow from the harvest will be received 20 years from today. When the company logs the land, it will immediately replant the land with new saplings. The harvest period chosen will be repeated for the foreseeable future. The company's nominal required return is 10 per cent, and the inflation rate is expected to be 3.7 per cent per year. Bunyan Lumber has a 35 per cent tax rate.

Clear-cutting is a controversial method of forest management. To obtain the necessary permits, Bunyan Lumber has agreed to contribute to a conservation fund every time it harvests the lumber. If the company harvested the forest today, the required contribution would be £100,000. The company has agreed that the required contribution will grow by 3.2 per cent per year. When should the company harvest the forest?

Practical Case Study

Let us return to the practical cement case study from Chapter 7. The executives of the cement company have decided to go ahead with the investment appraisal and have retained you for the more detailed analysis. In any capital budgeting investigation, you need an estimate of future net cash flows, future growth rates and appropriate discount rates. We will leave a detailed discussion of discount rates until later in the text.

Cash Flows   In the first stage of the consultancy, you were informed that the investment will be TSh5 billion and operating revenues are expected to increase by TSh800 million per year. That was just an estimate and after several interviews, you have come up with a more detailed cash flow forecast. First, the TSh5 billion investment is made up of three components. The cement company will need to purchase the land for TSh2 billion and spend TSh2 billion on property, plant and machinery. The other TSh1 billion will be paid out in salaries, wages and other cash expenses every year.

You need to find out about taxation and depreciation in Tanzania. You know that the country follows International Accounting Standards and so all the material in this textbook is appropriate. However, you need the actual depreciation rules, which differ in every country. The first place you should look is the Tanzanian Ministry of Finance website (http://www.mof.go.tz/mofdocs/revenue/incometax/start.htm). At this site you will find the appropriate corporate tax rate and all depreciation rates for your company.

Operating revenues are based on the expected total demand for cement and the current cement price of TSh90,000 per tonne. If the expansion goes ahead, the company expects to sell an additional 20,000 tonnes of cement at a constant gross profit margin of 44 per cent. However, these figures may change depending on economic conditions and changing costs. The company expects to run the new operations indefinitely.

Growth Rates   In the previous chapter, you spent a lot of time thinking about the factors that drive growth rates. Now, with this information, you should consider several growth rate scenarios for your company. You should also be able to defend your assumptions.

Discount Rates   Similarly, you should consider the information you have been given by the experts as well as all other information available in the markets to come up with several discount rate scenarios. You should be able to defend your choices here as well.

Activities

1   Carry out a full capital budgeting analysis on the above problem using one or more techniques you feel are appropriate here.

2   As with any real life capital budgeting analysis, the leeway in assumptions can really make your analysis difficult. Carry out a full sensitivity analysis on the project based on your own private analysis.

3   Clearly state and explain all assumptions in your analysis.

4 Discuss some factors, costs, inputs or assumptions that have not appeared in the analysis and suggest ways in which you can gather this information for an extension of the analysis.

5 Write a consultancy report on the analysis.

Many students will be put off by the complexity of this analysis but the practice of actually working with real and often poor data is one of the best skills you can develop. Corporate finance consultants get paid very handsomely for their work and this is primarily because the investment decision is one of the most important facing a firm. If managers get it right, a good investment can add millions to firm value. Get it wrong and the firm can go bankrupt!

Relevant Accounting Standards

This chapter is concerned with deepening the capital budgeting analysis and does not require specific accounting standards. See Chapter 7 for those standards that are relevant for capital budgeting.

Reference

Ross, S. (1995) 'Uses, Abuses, and Alternatives to the Net-Present-Value Rule', *Financial Management*, Vol. 24, No. 3, 96–102.

Additional Reading

Real options is an emerging field of valuation and few accessible applied papers are written on the topic. The ones listed below come from a variety of different fields that serve to present the variety of areas in which real options can be used.

1 Aguerrevere, F.L. (2009) 'Real Options, Product Market Competition, and Asset Returns', *The Journal of Finance*, Vol. 64, No. 2, 957–983.

2 Brouthers, K.B. and D. Dikova (2010) 'Acquisitions and Real Options: The Greenfield Alternative', *Journal of Management Studies*, Vol. 47, No. 6, 1048–1071. **Europe**.

3 Driouchi, T., M. Leseure and D. Bennett (2009) 'A Robustness Framework for Monitoring Real Options Under Uncertainty', *Omega*, Vol. 37, No. 3, 698–710.

Endnotes

1 Though the previous section considered both optimistic and pessimistic forecasts for sales price and variable cost, break-even analysis uses just the expected or best estimates of these variables.

2 Please refer to Chapter 7 for full details on how to calculate equivalent annual cost.

PART 3

Risk

The two key factors one must know before estimating the present value of a cash flow is (a) when it is likely to occur in the future; and (b) the risk of the cash flow. Forecasting the timing of a cash flow is straightforward and linked to the characteristics of the project or investment. However, estimating and quantifying risk is much more problematic. In this section, we will consider the different approaches to undertaking this task. It is important to recognize that there is no single approach to calculating the risk of an investment. In addition, most techniques use historical information and there is no guarantee that the past will predict the future.

The first three chapters of Part 3 develop different approaches to measuring risk. In Chapter 9, we consider the link between risk and the expected return on an investment by looking at the financial markets. Investors should be compensated for taking on risk, and we examine whether this is true by looking at different financial investments over time. The discussion then becomes quite theoretical in Chapter 10 when we explore portfolio theory and develop one of the most important theories in finance, the Capital Asset Pricing Model or CAPM. Factor models and the Arbitrage Pricing Theory (APT) are then introduced in Chapter 11.

In Chapter 12, the material in Chapters 9, 10 and 11 is brought together and we look at their relevance for capital budgeting and corporate finance. In particular, we introduce the concept of Cost of Capital for a project and a company, which is the discount rate applied in a capital budgeting analysis.

One of the implicit assumptions of Corporate Finance is that market prices and valuations are correct, unbiased and reflect all available information. Otherwise, it would be impossible to accurately measure risk and use this for business decisions. In Chapter 13, we investigate whether financial markets are efficient in practice. Part 3 then finishes with a general discussion of the different types of financial securities companies can issue to finance their operations.

Risk and Return: Lessons from Market History

On any single day, the stock market will see winners and losers. Take, for example, Wednesday 24 December 2014. The news that week was not positive with the oil price hitting lows of $60 a barrel (from over $100 a few months before); political instability in Ukraine, Syria and Iraq causing uncertainty in markets; and deflation in China and South East Asia as a result of falling global demand. However, there was some good news at the same time. The Spanish economy was showing strong signs of recovery; there was an improvement in British productivity and stock market indices closed up as 2014 drew to a close.

Could an investor have made money from buying shares in the morning and selling at night on 24 December 2014? The answer is yes. In the UK, Smith & Nephew, the global medical technology firm, increased by 7.71 per cent. Another technology firm, Alent plc, saw its share price rise by 4.59 per cent. Could an investor have lost money following the same strategy? The answer is also a definite yes. In the UK, shares in the mining firm, Centamin, were down by 6.52 per cent. In Sweden, AstraZeneca dropped by 2.33 per cent and in Norway, Nattopharma, fell by 13.21 per cent. These examples show that there are tremendous potential profits to be made, irrespective of whether markets are falling or growing. However, there is also the risk of losing money – lots of it. So what should you, as a stock market investor, expect when you invest your own money? In this chapter, we study decades of market history to find out.

KEY NOTATIONS

C_i	Cash flow at time i
Div_i	Dividend at time i
P_i	Price at time i
R_i	Total return; discount rate
VaR	Value at risk

9.1   Returns

Monetary Returns

Suppose the Video Concept Company has several thousand shares of equity outstanding and you are a shareholder. Further suppose that you purchased some of the shares in the company at the beginning of the year; it is now year-end and you want to figure out how well you have done on your investment. The return you get on an investment in shares, like that in bonds or any other investment, comes in two forms.

First, over the year most companies pay dividends to shareholders. As the owner of shares in the Video Concept Company, you are a part owner of the company. If the company is profitable, it will generally distribute some of its profits to the shareholders. Therefore, as the owner of shares, you will receive some cash, called a *dividend*, during the year. This cash is the *income component* of your return. In addition to the dividends, the other part of your return is the *capital gain* – or, if it is negative, the *capital loss* (negative capital gain) – on the investment.

For example, suppose we are considering the cash flows of the investment in Figure 9.1, showing that you purchased 100 shares at the beginning of the year at a price of £37 per share. Your total investment, then, was:

$$C_0 = £37 \times 100 = £3{,}700$$

Figure 9.1 Monetary Returns

Suppose that over the year the shares paid a dividend of £1.85 per share. During the year, then, you received income of:

$$\text{Div} = £1.85 \times 100 = £185$$

Suppose, finally, that at the end of the year the market price of the equity is £40.33 per share. Because the shares increased in price, you had a capital gain of:

$$\text{Gain} = (£40.33 - £37) \times 100 = £333$$

The capital gain, like the dividend, is part of the return that shareholders require to maintain their investment in the Video Concept Company. Of course, if the price of Video Concept shares had dropped in value to, say, £34.78, you would have recorded this capital loss:

$$\text{Loss} = (£34.78 - £37) \times 100 = -£222$$

The *total monetary return* on your investment is the sum of the dividend income and the capital gain or loss on the investment:

$$\text{Total monetary return} = \text{Dividend income} + \text{Capital gain (or loss)}$$

(From now on we will refer to *capital losses* as *negative capital gains* and not distinguish between them.) In our first example the total monetary return is given by:

$$\text{Total monetary return} = £185 + £333 = £518$$

Notice that if you sold the shares at the end of the year, your total amount of cash would be the initial investment plus the total monetary return. In the preceding example you would have:

$$\text{Total cash if equity is sold} = \text{Initial investment} + \text{Total monetary return}$$
$$= £3,700 + £518$$
$$= £4,218$$

As a check, notice that this is the same as the proceeds from the sale of shares plus the dividends:

$$\text{Proceeds from equity sale} + \text{Dividends} = £40.33 \times 100 + £185$$
$$= £4,033 + £185$$
$$= £4,218$$

Suppose, however, that you hold your Video Concept shares and do not sell them at year-end. Should you still consider the capital gain as part of your return? Does this violate our previous present value rule that only cash matters?

The answer to the first question is a strong yes, and the answer to the second question is an equally strong no. The capital gain is every bit as much a part of your return as is the dividend, and you should certainly count it as part of your total return. That you have decided to hold onto the shares and not sell or *realize* the gain or the loss in no way changes the fact that, if you want to, you could get the cash value of the shares. After all, you could always sell the shares at year-end and immediately buy them back. The total amount of cash you would have at year-end would be the £518 gain plus your initial investment of £3,700. You would not lose this return when you bought back 100 shares. In fact, you would be in exactly the same position as if you had not sold the shares (assuming, of course, that there are no tax consequences and no brokerage commissions from selling the equity).

Percentage Returns

It is more convenient to summarize the information about returns in percentage terms than in monetary terms because the percentages apply to any amount invested. The question we want to answer is this: How much return do we get for each unit of currency invested? To find this out, let t stand for the year we are looking at, let P_t be the price of the equity at the beginning of the year, and let Div_{t+1} be the dividend paid on the equity during the year. Consider the cash flows in Figure 9.2.

Figure 9.2 Percentage Returns

In our example, the price at the beginning of the year was £37 per share and the dividend paid during the year on each share was £1.85. Hence the percentage income return, sometimes called the *dividend yield*, is:

$$\text{Dividend yield} = Div_{t+1}/P_t$$
$$= £1.85/£37$$
$$= 0.05$$
$$= 5\%$$

The capital gain (or loss) is the change in the price of shares divided by the initial price. Letting P_{t+1} be the price of the equity at year-end, we can compute the capital gain as follows:

$$\text{Capital gain} = (P_{t+1} - P_t)/P_t$$
$$= (£40.33 - £37)/£37$$
$$= £3.37/£37$$
$$= 0.09$$
$$= 9\%$$

Combining these two results, we find that the *total return* on the investment in Video Concept shares over the year, which we will label R_{t+1}, was:

$$R_{t+1} = \frac{Div_{t+1}}{P_t} + \frac{(P_{t+1} - P_t)}{P_t}$$
$$= 5\% + 9\%$$
$$= 14\%$$

From now on, we will refer to returns in percentage terms.

To give a more concrete example, shares in the sportswear firm Adidas began 2014 at €92.64 a share. Adidas paid a dividend of €1.125 during 2014, and the share price at the end of the year was €56.74. What was the annual return on Adidas? For practice, see if you agree that the answer is −37.54 per cent. Of course, positive returns occur as well. For example, in 2013, the Adidas share price grew from €67.33 in January to €92.64 at the end of December, with a €0.9937 dividend paid during the year. Verify that the annual return was 39.07 per cent.

Example 9.1

Calculating Returns

Suppose an equity begins the year with a price of €25 per share and ends with a price of €35 per share. During the year it paid a €2 dividend per share. What are its dividend yield, its capital gain, and its total return for the year? We can imagine the cash flows in Figure 9.3.

$$R_1 = \frac{Div_1}{P_0} + \frac{P_1 - P_0}{P_0}$$
$$= \frac{€2}{€25} + \frac{€35 - 25}{€25} = \frac{€12}{€25}$$
$$= 8\% + 40\% \qquad = 48\%$$

Figure 9.3 Cash Flow – An Investment Example

Thus, the equity's dividend yield, its capital gain yield and its total return are 8 per cent, 40 per cent and 48 per cent, respectively.

Suppose you had €5,000 invested. The total return you would have received on an investment in the shares is €5,000 × 0.48 = €2,400. If you know the total return on the equity, you do not need to know how many shares you would have had to purchase to figure out how much money you would have made on the €5,000 investment. You just use the total return.

9.2   Holding Period Returns

In this section, we will discuss the rates of return on a number of different securities in different countries across Europe and the world. The countries we look at are China, Denmark, France, Germany, India, Italy, the Netherlands, Norway, Spain, Sweden, Switzerland, the UK and the US. The large company share portfolios are based on indices representing the largest companies in each country. In turn, these are the China Shanghai Composite Index (China), OMX Copenhagen 20 (Denmark), CAC40 (France), DAX30 (Germany), BSE SENSEX (India), FTSE MIB (Italy), Amsterdam SE All Shares (the Netherlands), Oslo Exchange All Shares (Norway), IBEX35 (Spain), OMXS30 (Sweden), Swiss Market Index (SMI), FTSE 100 (UK) and S&P500 (US).

Figure 9.4 shows the relative performance of different stock markets over the period 2005–2015. None of the returns are adjusted for taxes, transaction costs or inflation.[1] During this time, the financial crisis erupted in 2007 and its effect through 2008 is clear. The emergence of China and India as financial powerhouses is also evidenced, although their collapse in 2008 and much greater volatility provides strong support for their emerging market status. Europe, on the other hand, did not recover from the crisis particularly well and financial markets were only slightly higher at the beginning of 2015 than they were at the beginning of 2005. Finally, note that after the collapse of the Chinese and Indian stock markets at the end of 2007, whereas India recovered very well, the Chinese stock market only presented the same performance as European markets and arguably underperformed relative to Europe since mid-2008.

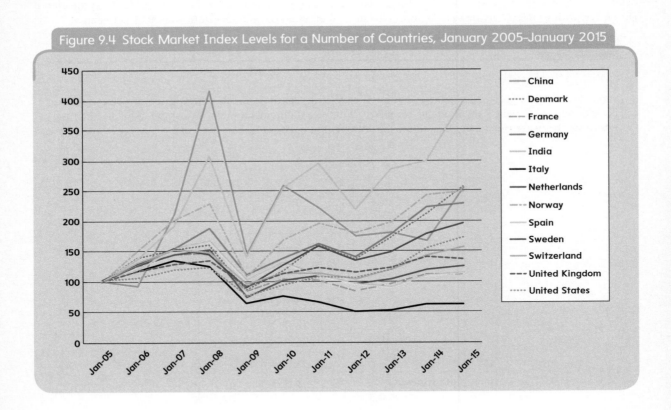

Figure 9.4 Stock Market Index Levels for a Number of Countries, January 2005–January 2015

Table 9.1 presents the index values for each stock market for every year between 2005 and 2015. Notice how most markets fell in late 2007 and early 2008. This was a result of the global credit crunch and subsequent financial crisis. The turning point in countries' fortunes was the autumn of 2008 and most markets saw sustained performance over the next 2 years. The main insight from Figure 9.4 is that emerging markets (such as China and India) are inherently more risky than developed economies. This is evidenced by the exceptionally high growth rate in 2007 followed by the equally dramatic crash early 2008. A brief assessment of European countries suggests that the markets started to show sustained recovery in 2012 and this continued into 2015. Of all the countries examined in Table 9.1, the clear loser is the Italian Stock Market, which was only 61.52 per cent of its 2005 value at the beginning of 2015.

Table 9.1 Year-by-Year Stock Market Index Levels for Different Countries, 2005–2015

Date	China	Denmark	France	Germany	India	Italy	Netherlands	Norway	Spain	Sweden	Switzerland	UK	US
Jan 2005	100	100	100	100	100	100	100	100	100	100	100	100	100
Jan 2006	91.67	137.96	123.32	126.99	136.44	115.99	125.25	151.81	118.22	128.84	131.47	116.71	103.84
Jan 2007	211.25	152.45	143.73	153.72	192.40	133.64	144.55	201.94	155.05	153.43	152.30	129.22	117.99
Jan 2008	415.44	160.27	145.61	187.98	308.79	124.35	151.50	229.11	166.40	144.62	147.08	134.12	122.15
Jan 2009	143.77	85.54	83.46	112.09	141.05	62.76	73.48	108.61	100.79	88.58	95.94	92.10	75.14
Jan 2010	258.76	116.26	102.09	138.82	254.32	74.98	100.59	168.86	130.86	127.28	113.47	112.43	92.76
Jan 2011	221.72	159.50	101.17	162.87	295.25	65.91	109.40	197.03	108.38	157.38	112.57	122.55	105.81
Jan 2012	173.66	137.47	83.57	141.57	218.86	49.85	95.69	179.58	95.61	133.66	102.90	115.74	104.62
Jan 2013	179.17	171.33	94.43	177.38	286.44	52.49	102.13	197.17	89.52	147.74	118.27	122.51	118.64
Jan 2014	167.07	212.54	111.42	222.58	300.64	61.18	117.37	242.30	108.69	178.26	142.20	140.19	153.76
Jan 2015	255.40	257.07	110.82	228.49	398.06	61.32	125.12	249.11	112.66	195.86	155.73	136.39	171.28

The data in Table 9.1 clearly show that an investor must be careful when reading information on company or stock market performance. For example, if one was to look at the holding period return for Switzerland between January 2005 and January 2008, and compare this to the holding period return for the same country between January 2008 and January 2012, conflicting messages would be given. The holding period return for the years 2005–2007 is 47.08 per cent, compared to the holding period return for the years 2008–2010 of −23.46 per cent! Which is the correct performance measure? Unfortunately, both are correct from different perspectives.

Figure 9.4 gives the growth of an investment in various stock markets between January 2005 and January 2015. In other words, it shows what the worth of the investment would have been if the money that was initially invested had been left in the stock market and if each year the dividends from the previous year had been reinvested in more shares. If R_t is the return in year t (expressed in decimals), the value you would have at the end of year T is the product of 1 plus the return in each of the years:

$$(1 + R_1)\times(1 + R_2)\times \ldots \times(1 + R_t)\times \ldots \times(1 + R_T)$$

For example, in Table 9.2, the index values in Table 9.1 are presented as annual percentage returns.

Table 9.2 Year-by-Year Stock Market Returns for Different Countries, 2005–2014

Date	China	Denmark	France	Germany	India	Italy	Netherlands	Norway	Spain	Sweden	Switzerland	UK	US
2005	−8.33	37.96	23.32	26.99	36.44	15.99	25.25	51.81	18.22	28.84	31.47	16.71	3.84
2006	130.43	10.50	16.55	21.04	41.01	15.22	15.41	33.02	31.15	19.09	15.85	10.71	13.62
2007	96.66	5.13	1.31	22.29	60.49	−6.95	4.81	13.45	7.32	−5.74	−3.43	3.80	3.53
2008	−65.39	−46.63	−42.68	−40.37	−54.32	−49.53	−51.50	−52.59	−39.43	−38.75	−34.77	−31.33	−38.49
2009	79.98	35.92	22.32	23.85	80.30	19.47	36.90	55.47	29.84	43.69	18.27	22.07	23.45
2010	−14.31	37.19	−0.90	17.33	16.09	−12.10	8.76	16.68	−17.18	23.66	−0.79	9.00	14.06
2011	−21.68	−13.81	−17.40	−13.08	−25.87	−24.38	−12.53	−8.85	−11.78	−15.08	−8.59	−5.55	−1.12
2012	3.17	24.63	13.00	25.30	30.88	5.30	6.73	9.79	−6.38	10.54	14.93	5.84	13.41
2013	−6.75	24.05	17.99	25.48	4.96	16.56	14.93	22.89	21.42	20.66	20.24	14.43	29.60
2014	52.87	20.95	−0.54	2.65	32.40	0.23	6.60	2.81	3.66	9.87	9.51	−2.71	11.39

Consider the returns for Italy in 2012 (5.30 per cent), 2013 (16.56 per cent) and 2014 (0.23 per cent). An investment of €1 at the beginning of 2012 would have been worth at the end of 2014:

$$(1 + R_1) \times (1 + R_2) \times (1 + R_3) = (€1 + .0530) \times (€1 + .1656) \times (€1 + .0023) = €1.2302$$

at the end of 2014. Notice that 0.2302 or 23.02 per cent is the total return and that it includes the return from reinvesting the first-year dividends in the stock market for 2 more years and reinvesting the second-year dividends for the final year. The 23.02 per cent is called a 3-year holding period return.

9.3 Return Statistics

The history of capital market returns is too complicated to be handled in its undigested form. To use the history, we must first find some manageable ways of describing it, dramatically condensing the detailed data into a few simple statements.

This is where two important numbers summarizing the history come in. The first and most natural number is some single measure that best describes the past annual returns on the stock market. In other words, what is our best estimate of the return that an investor could have realized in a particular year over a period? This is the *average return*.

Figure 9.5 plots the histogram of the yearly stock market returns for the UK FTSE All Share Index of the UK's largest companies between 1801 and 2011. This plot is the frequency distribution of the returns. The height of the graph gives the number of sample observations in the range on the horizontal axis.

Figure 9.5 Histogram of Returns on UK Equities, 1801–2011

Source: www.finfacts.com © Finfacts Multimedia Limited.

Example 9.2

Calculating Average Returns

From Table 9.2, the returns on large Danish company shares between 2012 and 2014 are 0.2463, 0.2405 and 0.2095, respectively. The average, or arithmetic mean, return over these 3 years is:

$$\bar{R} = \frac{0.2463 + 0.2405 + 0.2095}{3} = 0.2321$$

Given a frequency distribution like that in Figure 9.5, we can calculate the *average* or *mean* of the distribution. To compute the average of the distribution, we add up all of the values and divide by the total (*T*) number (211 in our case because we have 211 years of data). The bar over the *R* is used to represent the mean, and the formula is the ordinary formula for the average:

$$\text{Mean} = \overline{R} = \frac{(R_1 + \cdots + R_T)}{T}$$

The mean of the 211 annual large-company share price returns from 1801 to 2011 is only 3.73 per cent.

Real World Insight 9.1

Christian Dior SE

Christian Dior is a luxury goods firm with retail outlets all over the world. It is listed on NYSE Euronext and its share price performance between January 2000 and April 2015 is presented below.

Since 2009, Christian Dior's share price performance has been on a strict upward trajectory. However, during this period there have been some poor years, such as 2011. Using different periods to estimate average returns would clearly give different estimates and this would impact upon any future analysis. The financial manager should be aware of this when working with historical data. The table below gives different average return estimates for various estimation periods.

Period	Average Return
1 year (1 April 2014 – 1 April 2015)	25.21%
2 years (1 April 2013 – 1 April 2015)	19.76%
3 years (1 April 2012 – 1 April 2015)	19.29%
4 years (1 April 2011 – 1 April 2015)	16.72%
5 years (1 April 2010 – 1 April 2015)	21.04%
6 years (1 April 2009 – 1 April 2015)	27.74%
7 years (1 April 2008 – 1 April 2015)	19.77%
8 years (1 April 2007 – 1 April 2015)	14.65%
9 years (1 April 2006 – 1 April 2015)	14.93%
10 years (1 April 2005 – 1 April 2015)	19.67%

9.4 Average Stock Returns and Risk-free Returns

Now that we have computed the average return on the stock market, it seems sensible to compare it with the returns on other securities. The most obvious comparison is with the low-variability returns in the government bond market. These are free of most of the volatility we see in the stock market.

Governments borrow money by issuing bonds, which the investing public holds. As we discussed in an earlier chapter, these bonds come in many forms, and the ones we will look at here are called *Treasury bills*, or *T-bills*. Once a week the government sells some bills at an auction. A typical bill is a pure discount bond that will mature in a year or less. Because governments can raise taxes to pay for the debt they incur – a trick that many of us would like to be able to perform – this debt is virtually free of the risk of default. Thus we will call this the *risk-free return* over a short time (one year or less).

An interesting comparison, then, is between the virtually risk-free return on T-bills and the very risky return on equity. This difference between risky returns and risk-free returns is often called the *excess return on the risky asset*. It is called *excess* because it is the additional return resulting from the riskiness of equities and is interpreted as an equity risk premium.

Figure 9.6 shows the average risk premium of equities in a number of countries over the period 1900 to 2010. The equity risk premium relates to two securities: long-term government bonds and short-term treasury bills.

Figure 9.6 Worldwide Annualized Equity Risk Premium (%) Relative to Bills and Bonds, 1900–2010

Source: Adapted from Dimson et al. (2002, 2011) Premiums for Germany are based on 109 years, excluding hyperinflationary 1922–23.

One of the most significant observations of stock market data is this long-term excess of the share price return over the risk-free return in every country that appears in Figure 9.6. An investor for this period was rewarded for investment in the stock market with an extra or excess return over what would have been achieved by simply investing in T-bills.

Why was there such a reward? Does it mean that it never pays to invest in T-bills and that someone who invested in them instead of in the stock market needs a course in finance? A complete answer to these questions lies at the heart of modern finance, and Chapter 10 is devoted entirely to this. However, part of the answer can be found in the variability of the various types of investments. We see in Table 9.2 years when an investment in equities resulted in a loss of money (negative returns). The returns from an investment in equities are frequently negative across all countries, whereas an investment in T-bills never produces a negative return. So, we now turn our attention to measuring the variability of returns and an introductory discussion of risk.

We first look more closely at the underlying data in Figure 9.6. We see that the standard deviation of T-bills is substantially less than that of equities, and suggests that the risk of T-bills is less than that of equities. Because the answer turns on the riskiness of investments in equities, we next turn our attention to measuring this risk.

9.5 Risk Statistics

The second number that we use to characterize the distribution of returns is a measure of the risk in returns. There is no universally agreed-upon definition of risk. One way to think about the risk of returns on company shares is in terms of the spread of returns over a period. The spread, or dispersion, of a distribution is a measure of how much a particular return can deviate from the mean return. If the distribution is very spread out, the returns that will occur are very uncertain. By contrast, a distribution whose returns are all within a few percentage points of each other is tight, and the returns are less uncertain. The measures of risk we will discuss are variance and standard deviation.

Variance

The variance and its square root, the standard deviation, are the most common measures of variability or dispersion. We will use Var and σ^2 to denote the variance and SD and σ to represent the standard deviation. σ is, of course, the Greek letter sigma.

Example 9.3

Volatility

Consider the returns on India's stock market between 2010 and 2014. These are, respectively, 0.1609, −0.2587, 0.3088, 0.0496, and 0.3240. The variance of this sample is computed as follows:

$$Var = \frac{1}{T-1}[(R_1 - \overline{R})^2 + (R_2 - \overline{R})^2 + (R_3 - \overline{R})^2 + (R_4 - \overline{R})^2 + (R_5 - \overline{R})^2]$$

$$1.8088 = \frac{1}{4}[(0.1609 - 0.1169)^2 + (-0.2587 - 0.1169)^2 + (0.3088 - 0.1169)^2$$

$$+ (0.0496 - 0.1169)^2 + (0.3240 - 0.1169)^2]$$

$$SD = \sqrt{0.0568} = 0.2384 \text{ or } 23.84\%$$

This formula tells us just what to do: take the T individual returns (R_1, R_2, ...) and subtract the average return $\overline{R}$, square the result, and add them up. Finally, this total must be divided by the number of returns less one ($T - 1$). The standard deviation is always just the square root of the variance.

Using the UK share price returns for the 211-year period from 1801 through 2011 (see Figure 9.5) in this formula, the resulting standard deviation is 17.82 per cent. The standard deviation is the standard statistical measure of the spread of a sample, and it will be the measure we use most of the time. Its interpretation is facilitated by a discussion of the normal distribution.

Normal Distribution and its Implications for Standard Deviation

A large enough sample drawn from a normal distribution looks like the bell-shaped curve drawn in Figure 9.7. As you can see, this distribution is *symmetric* about its mean, not *skewed*, and has a much cleaner shape than the actual distribution of yearly returns drawn in Figure 9.5. Of course, if we had been able to observe stock market returns for 1,000 years, we might have filled in a lot of the jumps and jerks in Figure 9.5 and had a smoother curve.

In classical statistics, the normal distribution plays a central role, and the standard deviation is the usual way to represent the spread of a normal distribution. For the normal distribution, the probability of having a return that is above or below the mean by a certain amount depends only on the standard deviation. For example, the probability of having a return that is within one standard deviation of the mean of the distribution is approximately 0.68 or 2/3, and the probability of having a return that is within two standard deviations of the mean is approximately 0.95.

We can also discuss the normal distribution in an alternative way. For example, we can say that there is only a 1 per cent probability that a return will be 2.33 standard deviations from the mean and only a 5 per cent probability that a return will be 1.645 standard deviations from the mean. Note that this way of discussing probabilities is only looking at one side of the normal distribution instead of both sides.

Figure 9.7 The Normal Distribution

In the case of a normal distribution there is a 68.26 per cent probability that a return will be within one standard deviation of the mean. In this example there is a 68.26 per cent probability that a yearly return will be between –7.9 per cent and 32.5 per cent.
There is a 95.44 per cent probability that a return will be within two standard deviations of the mean. In this example, there is a 95.44 per cent probability that a yearly return will be between –28.1 per cent and 52.7 per cent.
Finally, there is a 99.74 per cent probability that a return will be within three standard deviations of the mean. In this example, there is a 99.74 per cent probability that a yearly return will be between –48.3 per cent and 72.9 per cent.

The 17.82 per cent standard deviation we found for UK stock returns from 1801 through 2011 can now be interpreted in the following way: if equity returns are roughly normally distributed, the probability that a yearly return will fall within 17.82 per cent of the mean of 3.73 per cent will be approximately 2/3. That is, about 2/3 of the yearly returns will be between −14.09 per cent and 21.55 per cent. (Note that −14.09 = 3.73 − 17.82 and 21.55 = 3.73 + 17.82.) The probability that the return in any year will fall within two standard deviations is about 0.95. That is, about 95 per cent of yearly returns will be between −31.91 per cent and 39.37 per cent.[2]

Other Measures of Risk

Although variance and standard deviation are the most common risk measures, there are other approaches to assessing risk that are sometimes utilized by investors. One of the major drawbacks of variance and standard deviation is that they implicitly assume that increases in share prices are just as risky as price falls. However, many investors perceive a decrease in the value of their investment to be significantly more risky than when their investment grows in value. This asymmetry in personal perspectives is seen to be the major weakness of the variance and standard deviation measures.

Asymmetric measures of risk use only the downside variation in returns from some target return, which could be the mean historical return or some benchmark return set by the investor. The semi-variance is calculated as follows:

$$\text{Semi-variance} = \frac{1}{n-1}\left[\sum_{r_i < \text{target}}^{n} (\text{target} - r_i)^2\right]$$

where n is the number of observations below the target; r_t is the observed return; and 'target' is the target return, which could be the historical mean return. The semi-variance has the advantage that only those deviations that are below the target or benchmark return are considered in the risk measure.

Another measure of risk that incorporates asymmetry in investment returns is that of skewness. Skewness refers to the extent to which a distribution is skewed to the left or right. In Figure 9.7, the normal distribution is symmetric, which means that downside and upside observations are equally likely. However, many return series have an asymmetric distribution, and skewness measures the degree to which observations are likely to be on the downside or upside. Consider Figure 9.8, which presents two skewed distributions. In the first diagram, negative returns are more likely, whereas in the second diagram positive returns are more likely. To measure the degree to which a return series is skewed, also known as skewness risk, simply divide the proportion of variation that is caused by upside deviations from the mean by the proportion of variation caused by downside deviations from the mean. Values of skewness risk above one correspond to positive skewness, where values of skewness risk below one correspond to negative skewness.

Figure 9.8 Skewed Distributions

Negative skew

Positive skew

A second measure of risk that is related to the distribution of returns is kurtosis. Kurtosis is a measure of the frequency of very negative and very positive returns. The normal distribution predicts that approximately 4.56 per cent of all observed returns will be greater than two standard deviations away from the mean return. However, in many cases, share price returns have a much greater prevalence of extreme values and this is reflected in the size of the kurtosis measure. The formula for kurtosis is quite complex but, fortunately, all statistical packages and spreadsheets calculate this for you. For example, in Microsoft Excel, the formula for kurtosis is KURT. Similarly, the formula for skewness is SKEW.

Value at Risk

A measure of risk that is commonly used for risk management purposes is called value at risk (or VaR). There are many ways to measure VaR but for our purposes, we will focus on the approach that uses the normal distribution. VaR tells you how much you can potentially lose from an investment. More formally, it measures the potential loss in an asset's value within a specified time period with a specified probability. For example, if the VaR on an equity portfolio is €100 million with a one-week holding period and a 5 per cent probability, you would say that there is a 5 per cent probability that you may lose more than €100 million in the value of your portfolio within the next week.

Measuring VaR is a relatively simple process and we will show how to calculate it with an example. We start off by stating the measurement period and probability for which we wish to measure VaR. Let us say that we have a weekly holding period and a 1 per cent probability. This means that we wish to find the largest expected drop in value over the next week with a 99 per cent probability.

Example 9.4

Calculating VaR

Assume that we have invested £1 million in a fund that perfectly tracks the FTSE 100 Index for large UK company stocks. What is the biggest drop in value that we could expect over the next month with a 99 per cent probability?

Step 1: Find the monthly mean and standard deviation of the fund's returns

If data are available, you could calculate the mean and standard deviation using historical returns. A second approach is to use your own forward-looking estimate. In this example, we will use the information in Table 9.2, which is annualized. To calculate monthly returns from annual data, we simply divide the annualized figure by 12. The average annual return for the FTSE 100 is the average return between 2005 and 2014, which is 4.2974 per cent (check this for yourself):

$$\overline{R}^{\text{Monthly}} = \frac{\overline{R}^{\text{Annual}}}{12} = \frac{4.2974\%}{12} = 0.3581\%$$

The conversion from annual standard deviation is slightly more complex in that you divide the annualized standard deviation by the square root of 12. The average annual standard deviation for the FTSE 100 is 15.1067 per cent (again, check this for yourself).

$$\overline{\sigma}^{\text{Monthly}} = \frac{\overline{\sigma}^{\text{Annual}}}{\sqrt{12}} = \frac{15.1067\%}{\sqrt{12}} = 4.3609\%$$

Step 2: **Calculate the negative return that will occur 1 per cent of the time**

Since we assume that the FTSE 100 fund returns are normally distributed, we can say that a return that is 2.33 standard deviations below the mean will only occur 1 per cent of the time. In the FTSE 100 case, this return is:

$$R_{VaR}^{1\%,\ \text{Monthly}} = 0.3581\% - 2.33(4.3609\%) = -9.8029\%$$

Step 3: **Calculate VaR**

With a €1 million investment, the VaR would be 9.8029 per cent of £1 million = £98,029.

9.6 More on Average Returns

Thus far in this chapter we have looked closely at simple average returns. But there is another way of computing an average return. The fact that average returns are calculated two different ways leads to some confusion, so our goal in this section is to explain the two approaches and also the circumstances under which each is appropriate.

Arithmetic versus Geometric Averages

Let us start with a simple example. Suppose you buy a particular equity for £100. Unfortunately, the first year you own it, it falls to £50. The second year you own it, it rises back to £100, leaving you where you started (no dividends were paid).

What was your average return on this investment? Common sense seems to say that your average return must be exactly zero because you started with £100 and ended with £100. But if we calculate the returns year-by-year, we see that you lost 50 per cent the first year (you lost half of your money). The second year, you made 100 per cent (you doubled your money). Your average return over the 2 years was thus (−50 per cent + 100 per cent)/2 = 25 per cent.

So which is correct, 0 per cent or 25 per cent? The answer is that both are correct; they just answer different questions. The 0 per cent is called the **geometric average return**. The 25 per cent is called the **arithmetic average return**. The geometric average return answers the question, '*What was your average compound return per year over a particular period?*' The arithmetic average return answers the question, '*What was your return in an average year over a particular period?*'

Notice that in previous sections, the average returns we calculated were all arithmetic averages, so we already know how to calculate them. What we need to do now is (1) learn how to calculate geometric averages, and (2) learn the circumstances under which one average is more meaningful than the other.

Calculating Geometric Average Returns

First, to illustrate how we calculate a geometric average return, suppose a particular investment had annual returns of 10 per cent, 12 per cent, 3 per cent and −9 per cent over the last 4 years. The geometric average return over this 4-year period is calculated as $(1.10 \times 1.12 \times 1.03 \times 0.91)^{1/4} - 1 = 3.66$ per cent. In contrast, the average arithmetic return we have been calculating is $(0.10 + 0.12 + 0.03 - 0.09)/4 = 4.0$ per cent.

In general, if we have T years of returns, the geometric average return over these T years is calculated using this formula:

$$\text{Geometric average return} = [(1 + R_1) \times (1 + R_2) \times \ldots \times (1 + R_T)]^{1/T} - 1 \tag{9.1}$$

This formula tells us that four steps are required:

1   Take each of the T annual returns $R_1, R_2, \ldots, R_T$ and add 1 to each (after converting them to decimals).
2   Multiply all the numbers from step 1 together.
3   Take the result from step 2 and raise it to the power of $1/T$.
4   Finally, subtract 1 from the result of step 3. The result is the geometric average return.

Example 9.5

Calculating the Geometric Average Return

Calculate the geometric average return for Norwegian stocks for 2010–2014 using the numbers given here. First convert percentages to decimal returns, add 1, and then calculate their product:

Norwegian Returns	Product
16.68	1.1668
−8.85	×0.9115
9.79	×1.0979
22.89	×1.2289
2.81	×1.0281
	1.4753

Notice that the number 1.4753 is what our investment is worth after 5 years if we started with a 1 krone investment. The geometric average return is then calculated as:

$$\text{Geometric average return} = 1.4753^{1/5} - 1 = 0.0809, \text{ or } 8.09\%$$

Thus the geometric average return is about −8.09 per cent in this example. Here is a tip: if you are using a financial calculator, you can put 1 in as the present value, 1.4753 as the future value, and 5 as the number of periods. Then solve for the unknown rate. You should get the same answer we did.

Table 9.3 shows the arithmetic averages and standard deviations along with the geometric average returns and other data.

Table 9.3 Worldwide Risk Premiums Relative to Bonds, 1900–2010

Country	Geometric Mean (%)	Arithmetic Mean (%)	Standard Dev. (%)	Min. Return (%)	Max. Return (%)
Belgium	2.6	4.9	21.4	−60.3	84.4
Canada	3.7	5.3	18.2	−40.7	48.6
Denmark	2	3.4	17.2	−54.3	74.9
Finland	5.6	9.2	30.3	−56.3	173.1
France	3.2	5.6	22.9	−50.3	84.3
Germany	5.4	8.8	28.4	−50.8	116.6
Ireland	2.9	4.9	19.8	−66.6	83.2
Italy	3.7	7.2	29.6	−49.4	152.2
The Netherlands	3.5	2.1	22.2	−55.6	107.6
Norway	2.5	5.5	28	−57.8	192.1
South Africa	5.5	1.9	19.6	−34.3	70.9
Spain	2.3	4.3	20.8	−42.7	69.1
Sweden	3.8	6.1	22.3	−48.1	87.5
Switzerland	2.1	3.6	17.6	−40.6	52.2
UK	3.9	1.6	17	−38.4	80.8

Country	Geometric Mean (%)	Arithmetic Mean (%)	Standard Dev. (%)	Min. Return (%)	Max. Return (%)
US	4.4	1.9	20.5	−50.1	57.2
Europe	3.9	5.2	16.6	−47.6	67.9

Note: All statistics for Germany are based on 109 years, excluding hyperinflationary 1922–23.

Source: Adapted from Dimson et al. (2002, 2011).

Finally, we have to look at what is meant by arithmetic and geometric average returns and this we do in the next section.

Arithmetic Average Return or Geometric Average Return?

When we look at historical returns, the difference between the geometric and arithmetic average returns is not too hard to understand. To put it slightly differently, the geometric average tells you what you actually earned per year on average, compounded annually. The arithmetic average tells you what you earned in a typical year. You should use whichever one answers the question you want answered.

A somewhat trickier question concerns forecasting the future, and there is a lot of confusion about this point among analysts and financial planners. The problem is this: if we have *estimates* of both the arithmetic and geometric average returns, then the arithmetic average is probably too high for longer periods and the geometric average is probably too low for shorter periods.

The good news is that there is a simple way of combining the two averages, which we will call *Blume's formula*. Suppose we calculated geometric and arithmetic return averages from N years of data and we wish to use these averages to form a T-year average return forecast, $R(T)$, where T is less than N. Here is how we do it:

$$R(T) = \frac{T - 1}{N - 1} \times \text{Geometric average} + \frac{N - T}{N - 1} \times \text{Arithmetic average} \qquad (9.2)$$

For example, suppose that from 25 years of annual returns data, we calculate an arithmetic average return of 12 per cent and a geometric average return of 9 per cent. From these averages, we wish to make 1-year, 5-year and 10-year average return forecasts. These three average return forecasts are calculated as follows:

$$R(1) = \frac{1 - 1}{24} \times 9\% + \frac{25 - 1}{24} \times 12\% = 12\%$$

$$R(5) = \frac{5 - 1}{24} \times 9\% + \frac{25 - 5}{24} \times 12\% = 11.5\%$$

$$R(10) = \frac{10 - 1}{24} \times 9\% + \frac{25 - 10}{24} \times 12\% = 10.875\%$$

Thus, we see that 1-year, 5-year and 10-year forecasts are 12 per cent, 11.5 per cent and 10.875 per cent, respectively. This concludes our discussion of geometric versus arithmetic averages. One last note: in subsequent chapters, when we say 'average return', we mean arithmetic average unless we explicitly say otherwise.

Summary and Conclusions

1   This chapter presented returns for a number of different asset classes. The general conclusion is that equities have outperformed bonds over most of the past 200 years, though equities have also exhibited more risk.

2   The statistical measures in this chapter are necessary building blocks for the material of the next three chapters. In particular, standard deviation and variance measure the variability of the return on an individual security and on portfolios of securities. In the next chapter, we will argue that standard deviation and variance are appropriate measures of the risk of an individual security if an investor's portfolio is composed of that security only.

Questions and Problems

CONCEPT

1 Returns What is meant by the term 'return'? What is the difference between monetary returns and percentage returns? Do monetary or percentage returns matter more to investors? Provide an example to explain your answer.

2 Holding Period Returns In what situations would you use a holding period return or a percentage return? Are the two measures the same?

3 Return Statistics Why would you wish to present return distributions? How do you think the distributions would change when you incorporated inflation into the return statistics?

4 Risk Statistics What do we mean by risk? In long-term investments, equities tend to give higher returns than bonds. Why then, do all investors not invest in equities? Are such investors irrational?

5 Other Return Measures What is the difference between arithmetic and geometric returns? Suppose you have invested in a company's shares for the last 10 years. Which number is more important to you, the arithmetic or geometric return?

REGULAR

6 Investment Selection Given that the Venezuela Caracas Stock Exchange was up by over 80 per cent for 2011, why didn't all investors put their money in Venezuela?

7 Investment Selection Given that the Cyprus stock exchange was down 75.8 per cent in 2011, why did investors continue to hold shares in Cyprus? Why didn't they sell out before the market declined so sharply?

8 Equities versus Gambling Critically evaluate the following statement: 'Investing in the stock market is just like gambling. It has no social value and investors do it purely to give them a thrill.'

9 Risk Premiums Is it possible for the risk premium to be negative before an investment is undertaken? Can the risk premium be negative after the fact? Explain.

10 Returns Two years ago, General Materials' and Standard Fixtures' share prices were the same. During the first year, General Materials' share price increased by 10 per cent while Standard Fixtures' share price decreased by 10 per cent. During the second year, General Materials' share price decreased by 10 per cent and Standard Fixtures' share price increased by 10 per cent. Do these two equities have the same price today? Explain.

11 Historical Returns The historical returns presented in the chapter are not adjusted for inflation. What would happen to the estimated risk premium if we did account for inflation? The returns are also not adjusted for taxes. What would happen to the returns if we accounted for taxes? What would happen to the volatility?

12 Calculating Returns Suppose you bought an 8 per cent coupon bond one year ago for €1,200. The bond sells for €1,074 today.

(a) Assuming a €1,000 face value, what was your total euro return on this investment over the past year?

(b) What was your total nominal rate of return on this investment over the past year?

(c) If the inflation rate last year was 3 per cent, what was your total real rate of return on this investment?

13 Calculating Returns and Variability The returns of Lockhart Group plc and TJC plc are given below. Using the following returns, calculate the average returns, the variances, and the standard deviations for Lockhart Group and TJC:

Year	Lockhart Group (%)	TJC (%)
2015	−60.7	−3.6
2014	24.1	37.5
2013	33.6	105.5
2012	−62.3	−61.8
2011	−21.8	−33.2

14 **Risk Premiums**   Refer to Table 9.1 in the text and look at the period from 2005 through 2012.

  (a) Calculate the arithmetic average returns for each country's stock market over this period.

  (b) Calculate the standard deviation of the returns for each country over this period.

15 **Calculating Returns and Variability**   You have observed the following prices for British Auto, the luxury car maker, for a number of years. Jan 2006: €26.87; Jan 2007: €35.19; Jan 2008: €32.17; Jan 2009: €37.23; Jan 2010: €46.84; Jan 2011: €36.80; Jan 2012: €18.61; Jan 2013: €30.96; Jan 2014: €56.08; Jan 2015: €65.39. The company paid the following dividends: 2006: €0.52; 2007: €0.58; 2008: €0.62; 2009: €0.64; 2010: €0.70; 2011: Nil; 2012: €0.30; 2013: €0.30; 2014: Nil.

  (a) What was the arithmetic average return on British Auto's shares over this period?

  (b) What was the variance of British Auto's returns over this period? The standard deviation?

16 **Calculating Real Returns and Risk Premiums**   In Problem 15, suppose the average inflation rate over this period was 4.2 per cent and the average T-bill rate over the period was 5.1 per cent.

  (a) What was the average real return on British Auto's shares?

  (b) What was the average nominal risk premium on British Auto's shares?

  (c) What was the average real risk-free rate over this time period? What was the average real risk premium?

17 **Holding Period Return**   A firm had the following share prices: Jan 2010: £1.12; Jan 2011: £1.34; Jan 2012: £1.68; Jan 2013: £1.8825; Jan 2014: £2.18; Jan 2015: £2.07. The equity paid no dividends. What was the holding period return?

18 **Return Distributions**   Refer back to Table 9.3. What range of risk premiums would you expect to see 68 per cent of the time for Europe? What about 95 per cent of the time?

19 **Blume's Formula**   Over a 30-year period an asset had an arithmetic return of 12 per cent and a geometric return of 10 per cent. Using Blume's formula, what is your best estimate of the future annual returns over 5 years? 10 years? 20 years?

20 **Arithmetic and Geometric Returns**   An equity has had returns of 10 per cent, 15 per cent, 20 per cent, −12 per cent, 2 per cent, and −5 per cent over the last 6 years. What are its arithmetic and geometric returns?

21 **Arithmetic and Geometric Returns**   An equity has had the following year-end prices and dividends:

Year	Price (£)	Dividend (£)
1	43.12	—
2	49.07	0.55
3	51.19	0.60
4	47.24	0.63
5	56.09	0.72
6	67.21	0.81

What are the arithmetic and geometric returns?

22 **Calculating Investment Returns**   You bought one of Bergen Manufacturing's 8 per cent coupon bonds one year ago for NKr1,028.50. These bonds make annual payments and mature 6 years from now. Suppose you decide to sell your bonds today, when the required return on the bonds is 7 per cent. If the inflation rate was 4.8 per cent over the past year, what would be your total real return on the investment?

23 **Using Return Distributions**   Suppose the returns on your company are normally distributed. The historical average share price return for your firm is 5.8 per cent with a standard deviation of 9.3 per cent. What is the approximate probability that your return will be less than −3.5 per cent in a given year? What range of returns would you expect to see 95 per cent of the time? What range would you expect to see 99 per cent of the time?

24 **Using Return Distributions**   Assume that the returns from holding French shares are normally distributed. From Table 9.2, what is the approximate normal distribution probability that your money will double in value in a single year? Triple in value?

25 **Distributions**   In the previous problem, what is the probability that the return is less than −100 per cent? (Think.) What are the implications for the distribution of returns?

26 Using Return Distributions Suppose the mean returns on long-term government bonds are 5.8 per cent, and are normally distributed with a standard deviation of 9.3 per cent. Based on the historical record, what is the approximate probability that your return on these bonds will be less than –3.5 per cent in a given year? What range of returns would you expect to see 95 per cent of the time? What range would you expect to see 99 per cent of the time?

27 Distributions Your investment portfolio has earned returns of 400 per cent once in the last 10 years, zero per cent in 8 years out of the last 10 years and lost 90 per cent one year. Use Table 9.2. What was the average arithmetic return and standard deviation of returns for this portfolio?

28 Inflation The inflation rates for the UK have been as follows, 2015: 4.8 per cent; 2014: 4.8 per cent; 2013: 2.4 per cent; 2012: 0.9 per cent; and in 2011: 4.0 per cent. Calculate the average real return of Lockhart Group and TJC from Question 13.

CHALLENGE

29 Calculating Returns Go to the Yahoo! Finance website and look up any FTSE 100 company of your choice. Click on the Historical Prices link. Find its closing price yesterday and its closing price exactly one year earlier. From the historical prices in Yahoo! Finance you will see the total dividend paid out in the last year. What has been the annual return on the company? What was the dividend yield? The capital gains yield?

30 Value at Risk The monthly prices for Banco Ruida are as follows:

Date	Adj Close
01/03/2015	514.2
01/02/2015	518
03/01/2015	493.35
01/12/2014	492.75
01/11/2014	473
03/10/2014	533
01/09/2014	539
01/08/2014	564
01/07/2014	640
01/06/2014	715
03/05/2014	720
01/04/2014	763
01/03/2014	714
01/02/2014	758
04/01/2014	764.5
01/12/2013	685.5
01/11/2013	610.5
18/10/2013	796.24

Assume you have €1 million invested in the bank. Calculate the analytical VaR for Banco Ruida using a monthly holding period and 1 per cent loss probability. What is the main limitation of the value-at-risk method?

Exam Question (45 minutes)

You have invested in the UK stock market. Details on the performance of the market are given below:

Date	UK
Jan-05	100
Jan-06	117.36
Jan-07	131.46

▶

Date	UK
Jan-08	122.47
Jan-09	86.136
Jan-10	110.06
Jan-11	126.16
Jan-12	116.00

1   Calculate the average arithmetic returns, the variances, and the standard deviations for the UK. (30 marks)

2   Calculate the geometric return on the UK and compare it to the arithmetic return. Comment on and explain the differences between the UK arithmetic and geometric return. (20 marks)

3   What was the holding period return on UK equities over the period? (10 marks)

4   Suppose the returns on UK equities are normally distributed. Based on the data above, what is the approximate probability that your return on these will be less than –2 per cent in a given year? What range of returns would you expect to see 95 per cent of the time? What range would you expect to see 99 per cent of the time? (20 marks)

5   Review the difficulties in using historical data to measure expected returns on an investment. (20 marks)

Mini Case

A Job at West Coast Yachts

You recently graduated from university, and your job search led you to West Coast Yachts at Kip Marina. Because you felt the company's business was seaworthy, you accepted a job offer. The first day on the job, while you are finishing your employment paperwork, Dan Ervin, who works in Finance, stops by to inform you about the company's retirement plan.

Retirement plans are offered by many companies and are tax-deferred savings vehicles, meaning that any deposits you make into the plan are deducted from your current pretax income, so no current taxes are paid on the money. For example, assume your salary will be £50,000 per year. If you contribute £3,000 to the plan, you will pay taxes on only £47,000 in income. There are also no taxes paid on any capital gains or income while you are invested in the plan, but you do pay taxes when you withdraw money at retirement. As is fairly common, the company also has a 5 per cent matched-funding. This means that the company will match your contribution up to 5 per cent of your salary, but you must contribute to get the match.

The retirement plan has several options for investments, most of which are mutual funds. A mutual fund is a portfolio of assets. When you purchase shares in a mutual fund, you are actually purchasing partial ownership of the fund's assets. The return of the fund is the weighted average of the return of the assets owned by the fund, minus any expenses. The largest expense is typically the management fee, paid to the fund manager. The management fee is compensation for the manager, who makes all of the investment decisions for the fund.

West Coast Yachts uses Skandla Life Assurance Company Ltd as its retirement plan administrator. Here are the investment options offered for employees:

• **Company Shares**   One option in the retirement plan is equity ownership of West Coast Yachts. The company is currently privately held. However, when you interviewed with the owner, Larissa Warren, she informed you the company shares were expected to go public in the next 3 to 4 years. Until then, a company share price is simply set each year by the board of directors.

• **Skandla Market Index Fund**   This mutual fund tracks the FTSE 100 index. Equities in the fund are weighted exactly the same as the FTSE 100. This means the fund return is approximately the return on the FTSE 100, minus expenses. Because an index fund purchases assets based on the composition of the index it is following, the fund manager is not required to research stocks and make investment decisions. The result is that the fund expenses are usually low. The Skandla Index Fund charges expenses of 0.15 per cent of assets per year.

• **Skandla Small-Cap Fund**   This fund invests primarily in small-capitalization companies. As such, the returns of the fund are more volatile. The fund can also invest 10 per cent of its assets in companies based outside the United Kingdom. This fund charges 1.70 per cent in expenses.

- **Skandla Large-Company Equity Fund** This fund invests primarily in large-capitalization companies based in the United Kingdom. The fund is managed by Evan Skandla and has outperformed the market in six of the last eight years. The fund charges 1.50 per cent in expenses.

- **Skandla Bond Fund** This fund invests in long-term corporate bonds issued by UK-domiciled companies. The fund is restricted to investments in bonds with an investment-grade credit rating. This fund charges 1.40 per cent in expenses.

- **Skandla Money Market Fund** This fund invests in short-term, high-credit quality debt instruments, which include Treasury bills. As such, the return on the money market fund is only slightly higher than the return on Treasury bills. Because of the credit quality and short-term nature of the investments, there is only a very slight risk of negative return. The fund charges 0.60 per cent in expenses.

1 What advantages do the mutual funds offer compared to the company equity?

2 Assume that you invest 5 per cent of your salary and receive the full 5 per cent match from West Coast Yachts. What APR do you earn from the match? What conclusions do you draw about matching plans?

3 Assume you decide you should invest at least part of your money in large-capitalization companies based in the United Kingdom. What are the advantages and disadvantages of choosing the Skandla Large-Company Equity Fund compared to the Skandla Market Index Fund?

4 The returns on the Skandla Small-Cap Fund are the most volatile of all the mutual funds offered in the retirement plan. Why would you ever want to invest in this fund? When you examine the expenses of the mutual funds, you will notice that this fund also has the highest expenses. Does this affect your decision to invest in this fund?

5 A measure of risk-adjusted performance that is often used is the Sharpe ratio. The Sharpe ratio is calculated as the risk premium of an asset divided by its standard deviation. The standard deviation and return of the funds over the past 10 years are listed here. Calculate the Sharpe ratio for each of these funds. Assume that the expected return and standard deviation of the company equity will be 18 per cent and 70 per cent, respectively. Calculate the Sharpe ratio for the company shares. How appropriate is the Sharpe ratio for these assets? When would you use the Sharpe ratio?

	10-year Annual Return (%)	Standard Deviation (%)
Skandla Market Index Fund	11.48	15.82
Skandla Small-Cap Fund	16.68	19.64
Skandla Large-Company Equity Fund	11.85	15.41
Skandla Bond Fund	9.67	10.83

6 What portfolio allocation would you choose? Why? Explain your thinking carefully.

Practical Case Study

1 **Calculating Yields** Download the historical monthly share prices for Alcatel-Lucent from Yahoo! Finance. Find the closing share price for yesterday and for exactly 2 years ago. The dividends should also be listed in the monthly price series. What was the capital gains yield and dividend yield for Alcatel-Lucent equity for each of these years? Now calculate the capital gains yield and dividend yield for Alstom, the French design and infrastructure construction firm. How do the returns for these two companies compare?

2 **Calculating Average Returns** Download the Monthly Adjusted Prices for Deutsche Telekom AG. What is the return on the equity over the past 12 months? Now use the 1 Month Total Return and calculate the average monthly return. Is this one-twelfth of the annual return you calculated? Why or why not? What is the monthly standard deviation of Deutsche Telekom's shares over the past year?

Relevant Accounting Standards

Now that we are moving into the realms of financial markets, accountancy standards take on less importance. However, one standard that has received a lot of attention in recent years is IAS 39 *Financial Instruments: Recognition and Measurement*. This standard guides the accountant on how all financial instruments should be presented in a company's financial statements. In addition, you should also be aware of IFRS 7 *Financial Instruments: Disclosure*. Visit the IASPlus website (www.iasplus.com) for more information.

References

Dimson, E., P. Marsh and M. Staunton (2002) *Triumph of the Optimists* (Princeton, NJ: Princeton University Press).

Dimson, E., P. Marsh and M. Staunton (2011) 'Equity Premia around the World', in P.B. Hammond, M.L. Leibowitz and L.B. Siegel (eds), *Rethinking the Equity Risk Premium* (CFA Institute).

Additional Reading

The number of research papers about the financial markets would fill a whole book and more. As a result, we have had to be exceptionally selective in picking those papers that are most appropriate to the understanding and study of corporate finance. The first two papers study the US market and look at broad relationships between returns and corporate characteristics. Fama and French (2006) show that share price returns are related to profitability and the book to market equity ratio. Lundblad (2007) reports a positive link between risk and return over a very long period.

1   Fama, E.F. and K.R. French (2006) 'Profitability, Investment and Average Returns', *Journal of Financial Economics*, Vol. 82, No. 3, 491–518.

2   Lundblad, C. (2007) 'The Risk Return Tradeoff in the Long Run: 1836–2003', *Journal of Financial Economics*, Vol. 85, No. 1, 123–150.

Another paper that the advanced reader may find interesting relates to stock market bubbles:

3   O'Hara, M. (2008) 'Bubbles: Some Perspectives (and Loose Talk) from History', *Review of Financial Studies*, Vol. 21, No. 1, 11–17.

The following paper considers return comovements across countries:

4   Bekaert, G., R.J. Hodrick and X. Zhang (2009) 'International Stock Return Comovements', *The Journal of Finance*, Vol. 64, No. 6, 2591–2626.

Finally, the use of value at risk to measure risk exposure to a certain asset class is given below for the oil market.

5   Marimoutoi, V., B. Raggad and A. Tabelsi (2009) 'Extreme Value Theory and Value at Risk: Application to Oil Market', *Energy Economics*, Vol. 31, No. 4, 519–530.

Endnotes

1   The data used in this chapter are available on the book's website: www.mcgraw-hill.co.uk/textbook/hillier

2   In this example we have used the data from the period 1801–2011. However, if we were to use the data that appear in Table 9.3 for the period 1900–2010, we would get different answers.

Risk and Return: The Capital Asset Pricing Model

Expected returns on equities can vary quite a bit. One important determinant is the industry in which a company operates. For example, in Europe, the Food and Drug Retail sector (representing the big supermarkets among other retail firms) fell over 30 per cent in 2014, whereas the Healthcare Equipment and Services sector grew more than 30 per cent in the same period.

These estimates raise some obvious questions. First, why do industry returns differ so much, and how are these specific numbers calculated? Also, does the higher return offered by Healthcare Equipment and Services mean that investors should prefer these to, say, the Food and Drug Retail sector? As we will see in this chapter, the answers to these questions form the basis of our modern understanding of risk and return.

KEY NOTATIONS

R_{it}	Return on security i at time t
Var or σ^2	Variance
SD or σ	Standard deviation
ρ_{AB}	Correlation between A and B
Cov(A,B)	Covariance between A and B
X_A	Weight of an asset or security, A, in a portfolio
N	Number of assets or securities in a portfolio
R_F	Risk-free rate of return
R_M	Market rate of return
β	Beta or systematic risk of a security
SML	Security Market Line
CAPM	Capital Asset Pricing Model
PE	Price–earnings ratio
BM	Book value of equity to market value of equity ratio

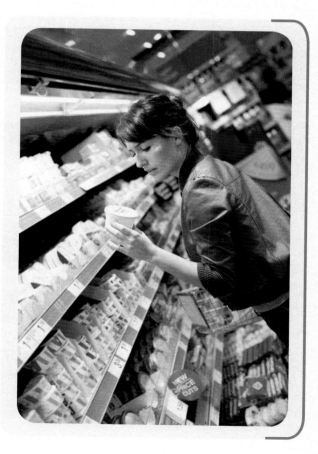

10.1   Individual Securities

In the first part of Chapter 10 we will examine the characteristics of individual securities. In particular, we will discuss:

1   *Expected return*: This is the return that an individual expects a security to earn over the next period. Of course, because this is only an expectation, the actual return may be either higher or lower. An individual's expectation may simply be the average return per period a security has earned in the past. Alternatively, it may be based on a detailed analysis of a firm's prospects, on some computer-based model, or on special (or inside) information.

2   *Variance and standard deviation*: There are many ways to assess the volatility of a security's return. One of the most common is variance, which is a measure of the squared deviations of a security's return from its expected return. Standard deviation is the square root of the variance.

3   *Covariance and correlation*: Returns on individual securities are related to one another. Covariance is a statistic measuring the interrelationship between two securities. Alternatively, this relationship can be restated in terms of the correlation between the two securities. Covariance and correlation are building blocks to an understanding of the beta coefficient.

10.2   Expected Return, Variance and Covariance

Expected Return and Variance

Suppose financial analysts believe that there are four equally likely states of the economy: depression, recession, normal and boom. The returns on 'Supertech' are expected to follow the economy closely, while the returns on 'Slowburn' are not. The return predictions are as follows:

	Supertech Returns R_{At} (%)	Slowburn Returns R_{Bt} (%)
Depression	−20	5
Recession	10	20
Normal	30	−12
Boom	50	9

Variance can be calculated in four steps. An additional step is needed to calculate standard deviation. (The calculations are presented in Table 10.1.) The steps are these:

1   Calculate the expected return:

Supertech

$$\frac{-0.20 + 0.10 + 0.30 + 0.50}{4} = 0.175 = 17.5\% = \overline{R}_A$$

Table 10.1 Calculating Variance and Standard Deviation

(1) State of Economy	(2) Rate of Return Supertech*	(3) Deviation from Expected Return (Expected Return = 0.175)	(4) Squared Value of Deviation
	R_{At}	$(R_{At} - \overline{R}_A)$	$(R_{At} - \overline{R}_A)^2$
Depression	−0.20	−0.375	0.140625
		$(=-0.20 - 0.175)$	$[= (-0.375)^2]$
Recession	0.10	−0.075	0.005625
Normal	0.30	0.125	0.015625

(1) State of Economy	(2) Rate of Return Supertech*	(3) Deviation from Expected Return (Expected Return = 0.175)	(4) Squared Value of Deviation
Boom	0.50	0.325	0.105625
			0.267500
	Slowburn†	(Expected Return = 0.055)	
	R_{Bt}	$(R_{Bt} - \overline{R}_B)$	$(R_{Bt} - \overline{R}_B)^2$
Depression	0.05	−0.005	0.000025
		(= 0.05 − 0.055)	[= (−0.005)²]
Recession	0.20	0.145	0.021025
Normal	−0.12	−0.175	0.030625
Boom	0.09	0.035	0.001225
			0.052900

$$*\overline{R}_A = \frac{-0.20 + 0.10 + 0.30 + 0.50}{4} = 0.175 = 17.5\%$$

$$Var(R_A) = \sigma_A^2 = \frac{0.2675}{4} = 0.066875$$

$$SD(R_A) = \sigma_A = \sqrt{0.066875} = 0.2586 = 25.86\%$$

$$†\overline{R}_B = \frac{0.05 + 0.20 - 0.12 + 0.09}{4} = 0.055 = 5.5\%$$

$$Var(R_B) = \sigma_B^2 = \frac{0.0529}{4} = 0.013225$$

$$SD(R_B) = \sigma_B = \sqrt{0.013225} = 0.1150 = 11.50\%$$

Slowburn

$$\frac{0.05 + 0.20 - 0.12 + 0.09}{4} = 0.055 = 5.5\% = \overline{R}_B$$

2 For each company, calculate the deviation of each possible return from the company's expected return given previously. This is presented in the third column of Table 10.1.

3 The deviations we have calculated are indications of the dispersion of returns. However, because some are positive and some are negative, it is difficult to work with them in this form. For example, if we were to simply add up all the deviations for a single company, we would get zero as the sum.

To make the deviations more meaningful, we multiply each one by itself. Now all the numbers are positive, implying that their sum must be positive as well. The squared deviations are presented in the last column of Table 10.1.

4 For each company, calculate the average squared deviation, which is the variance:[1]

Supertech

$$\frac{0.140625 + 0.005625 + 0.015625 + 0.105625}{4} = 0.066875$$

Slowburn

$$\frac{0.000025 + 0.021025 + 0.030625 + 0.001225}{4} = 0.013225$$

Thus, the variance of Supertech is 0.066875, and the variance of Slowburn is 0.013225.

5 Calculate standard deviation by taking the square root of the variance:

Supertech

$$\sqrt{0.066875} = 0.2586 = 25.86\%$$

Slowburn

$$\sqrt{0.013225} = 0.1150 = 11.50\%$$

Algebraically, the formula for variance can be expressed as:

$$\text{Var}(R) = \text{Expected value of } (R - \overline{R})^2$$

where $\overline{R}$ is the security's expected return and R is the actual return.

A look at the four-step calculation for variance makes it clear why it is a measure of the spread of the sample of returns. For each observation we square the difference between the actual return and the expected return. We then take an average of these squared differences. Squaring the differences makes them all positive. If we used the differences between each return and the expected return and then averaged these differences, we would get zero because the returns that were above the mean would cancel the ones below.

Chapter 9
Page 241

However, because the variance is still expressed in squared terms, it is difficult to interpret. Standard deviation has a much simpler interpretation, which was provided in **Chapter 9**, Section 9.5. Standard deviation is simply the square root of the variance. The general formula for the standard deviation is:

$$\text{SD}(R) = \sqrt{\text{Var}(R)}$$

Covariance and Correlation

Variance and standard deviation measure the variability of individual securities. We now wish to measure the relationship between the return on one security and the return on another. This brings us to covariance and correlation.

Covariance and correlation measure how two random variables are related. We explain these terms by extending the Supertech and Slowburn example.

Example 10.1

Calculating Covariance and Correlation

We have already determined the expected returns and standard deviations for both Supertech and Slowburn. (The expected returns are 0.175 and 0.055 for Supertech and Slowburn, respectively. The standard deviations are 0.2586 and 0.1150, respectively.) In addition, we calculated the deviation of each possible return from the expected return for each firm. Using these data, we can calculate covariance in two steps. An extra step is needed to calculate correlation.

1   For each state of the economy, multiply Supertech's deviation from its expected return and Slowburn's deviation from its expected return together. For example, Supertech's rate of return in a depression is -0.20, which is 0.375 ($= -0.20 - 0.175$) from its expected return. Slowburn's rate of return in a depression is 0.05, which is 0.005 ($= 0.05 - 0.055$) from its expected return. Multiplying the two deviations together yields 0.001875 [$= (-0.375) \times (0.005)$]. The actual calculations are given in the last column of Table 10.2. This procedure can be written algebraically as:

$$(R_{At} - \overline{R}_A) \times (R_{Bt} - \overline{R}_B) \tag{10.1}$$

where R_{At} and R_{Bt} are the returns on Supertech and Slowburn in state t. $\overline{R}_A$ and $\overline{R}_B$ are the expected returns on the two securities.

$$\sigma_{A,B} = \text{Cov}(R_A, R_B) = \frac{-0.0195}{4} = -0.004875$$

$$\rho_{A,B} = \text{Corr}(R_A, R_B) = \frac{\text{Cov}(R_A, R_B)}{\text{SD}(R_A) \times \text{SD}(R_B)} = \frac{-0.004875}{0.2586 \times 0.1150} = -0.1639$$

2   Calculate the average value of the four states in the last column. This average is the covariance. That is:[2]

$$\sigma_{A,B} = \text{Cov}(R_A, R_B) = \frac{-0.0195}{4} = -0.004875$$

Note that we represent the covariance between Supertech and Slowburn as either $\text{Cov}(R_A, R_B)$ or $\sigma_{A,B}$. Equation 10.1 illustrates the intuition of covariance. Suppose Supertech's return is generally above

State of Economy	Rate of Return of Supertech R_{At}	Deviation from Expected Return $(R_{At} - \overline{R}_A)$ (Expected return = 0.175)	Rate of Return of Slowburn R_{Bt}	Deviation from Expected Return $(R_{Bt} - \overline{R}_B)$ (Expected return = 0.055)	Product of Deviations $(R_{At} - \overline{R}_A) \times (R_{Bt} - \overline{R}_B)$
Depression	−0.20	−0.375 ($=-0.20 - 0.175$)	0.05	−0.005 ($=0.05 - 0.055$)	0.001875 ($= -0.375 \times -0.005$)
Recession	0.10	−0.075	0.20	0.145	−0.010875 ($= -0.075 \times 0.145$)
Normal	0.30	0.125	−0.12	−0.175	−0.021875 ($=0.125 \times (= -0.175)$)
Boom	0.50	0.325	0.09	0.035	0.011375 ($=0.325 \times 0.035$)
	0.70		0.22		−0.0195

Table 10.2 Calculating Covariance and Correlation

its average when Slowburn's return is above its average, and Supertech's return is generally below its average when Slowburn's return is below its average. This shows a positive dependency or a positive relationship between the two returns. Note that the term in Equation 10.1 will be *positive* in any state where both returns are *above* their averages. In addition, 10.1 will still be *positive* in any state where both terms are *below* their averages. Thus a positive relationship between the two returns will give rise to a positive value for covariance.

Conversely, suppose Supertech's return is generally above its average when Slowburn's return is below its average, and Supertech's return is generally below its average when Slowburn's return is above its average. This demonstrates a negative dependency or a negative relationship between the two returns. Note that the term in Equation 10.1 will be *negative* in any state where one return is above its average and the other return is below its average. Thus a negative relationship between the two returns will give rise to a negative value for covariance.

Finally, suppose there is no relationship between the two returns. In this case, knowing whether the return on Supertech is above or below its expected return tells us nothing about the return on Slowburn. In the covariance formula, then, there will be no tendency for the deviations to be positive or negative together. On average, they will tend to offset each other and cancel out, making the covariance zero.

Of course, even if the two returns are unrelated to each other, the covariance formula will not equal zero exactly in any actual history. This is due to sampling error; randomness alone will make the calculation positive or negative. But for a historical sample that is long enough, if the two returns are not related to each other, we should expect the covariance to come close to zero.

The covariance formula seems to capture what we are looking for. If the two returns are positively related to each other, they will have a positive covariance, and if they are negatively related to each other, the covariance will be negative. Last, and very important, if they are unrelated, the covariance should be zero.

The formula for covariance can be written algebraically as:

$$\sigma_{A,B} = \text{Cov}(R_A, R_B) = \text{Expected value of } [(R_A - \overline{R}_A) \times (R_B - \overline{R}_B)]$$

where $\overline{R}_A$ and $\overline{R}_B$ are the expected returns for the two securities, and R_A and R_B are the actual returns. The ordering of the two variables is unimportant. That is, the covariance of A with B is equal to the covariance of B with A. This can be stated more formally as $\text{Cov}(R_A, R_B) = \text{Cov}(R_B, R_A)$ or $\sigma_{A,B} = \sigma_{B,A}$.

The covariance we calculated is −0.004875. A negative number like this implies that the return on one security is likely to be above its average when the return on the other security is below its average, and vice versa. However, the size of the number is difficult to interpret. Like the variance figure, the covariance is in squared deviation units. Until we can put it in perspective, we do not know what to make of it.

We solve the problem by computing the correlation.

3 To calculate the correlation, divide the covariance by the standard deviations of both of the two securities. For our example, we have:

$$\rho_{A,B} = \text{Corr}(R_A, R_B) = \frac{\text{Cov}(R_A, R_B)}{\sigma_A \times \sigma_B} = \frac{-0.004875}{0.2586 \times 0.1150} = -0.1639 \tag{10.2}$$

where σ_A and σ_B are the standard deviations of Supertech and Slowburn, respectively. Note that we represent the correlation between Supertech and Slowburn either as $\text{Corr}(R_A, R_B)$ or $\rho_{A,B}$. As with covariance, the ordering of the two variables is unimportant. That is, the correlation of A with B is equal to the correlation of B with A. More formally, $\text{Corr}(R_A, R_B) = \text{Corr}(R_B, R_A)$ or $\rho_{A,B} = \rho_{B,A}$.

Because the standard deviation is always positive, the sign of the correlation between two variables must be the same as that of the covariance between the two variables. If the correlation is positive, we say that the variables are *positively correlated*; if it is negative, we say that they are *negatively correlated*; and if it is zero, we say that they are *uncorrelated*. Furthermore, it can be proved that the correlation is always between −1 and +1. This is due to the standardizing procedure of dividing by the two standard deviations.

We can compare the correlation between different *pairs* of securities. For example, it turns out that the correlation between Persimmon and Bovis (both construction companies) is much higher than the correlation between Persimmon and Antofagasta (a pharmaceutical firm). Hence, we can state that the first pair of securities is more interrelated than the second pair.

Figure 10.1 shows the three benchmark cases for two assets, A and B. The figure shows two assets with return correlations of +1, −1, and 0. This implies perfect positive correlation, perfect negative correlation, and no correlation, respectively. The graphs in the figure plot the separate returns on the two securities through time.

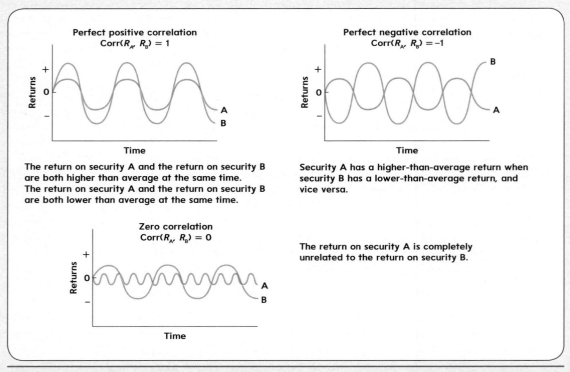

Figure 10.1 Examples of Different Correlation Coefficients – Graphs Plotting the Separate Returns on Two Securities through Time

Real World Insight 10.1

Deutsche Bank and Deutsche Telekom

As their names suggest, both Deutsche Bank and Deutsche Telekom are German firms operating in the banking and telecommunications sectors. Given that they are large companies and come from the same country, it is likely that the returns on each company will be correlated with each other. This is the case with the correlation between both company's monthly returns equal to 0.33 using data between 2010 and 2015. A scatterplot of monthly returns is given below. Although the correlation is quite high, there is still a lot of variation between the two companies.

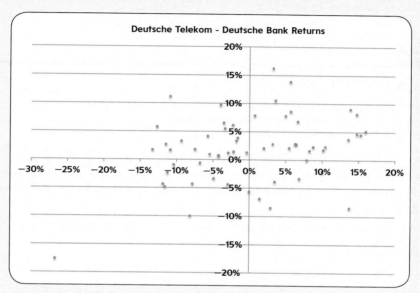

Deutsche Telekom - Deutsche Bank Returns

10.3   The Return and Risk for Portfolios

Suppose an investor has estimates of the expected returns and standard deviations on individual securities and the correlations between securities. How does the investor choose the best combination or portfolio of securities to hold? Obviously, the investor would like a portfolio with a high expected return and a low standard deviation of return. It is therefore worthwhile to consider:

1 The relationship between the expected return on individual securities and the expected return on a portfolio made up of these securities.

2 The relationship between the standard deviations of individual securities, the correlations between these securities, and the standard deviation of a portfolio made up of these securities.

To analyse these two relationships, we will use the same example of Supertech and Slowburn. The relevant calculations follow.

The Expected Return on a Portfolio

The formula for expected return on a portfolio is very simple:

The expected return on a portfolio is simply a weighted average of the expected returns on the individual securities.

Relevant Data from Example of Supertech and Slowburn		
Item	Symbol	Value
Expected return on Supertech	$\overline{R}_{\text{Super}}$	0.175 = 17.5%
Expected return on Slowburn	$\overline{R}_{\text{Slow}}$	0.055 = 5.5%

Relevant Data from Example of Supertech and Slowburn		
Item	Symbol	Value
Variance of Supertech	σ^2_{Super}	0.066875
Variance of Slowburn	σ^2_{Slow}	0.013225
Standard deviation of Supertech	σ_{Super}	0.2586 = 25.86%
Standard deviation of Slowburn	σ_{Slow}	0.1150 = 11.50%
Covariance between Supertech and Slowburn	$\sigma_{\text{Super, Slow}}$	−0.004875
Correlation between Supertech and Slowburn	$\rho_{\text{Super, Slow}}$	−0.1639

Example 10.2

Portfolio Expected Returns

Consider Supertech and Slowburn. From our earlier calculations, we find that the expected returns on these two securities are 17.5 per cent and 5.5 per cent, respectively.

The expected return on a portfolio of these two securities alone can be written as:

$$\text{Expected return on portfolio} = X_{\text{Super}} (17.5\%) + X_{\text{Slow}} (5.5\%) = \overline{R}_p$$

where X_{Super} is the percentage of the portfolio in Supertech and X_{Slow} is the percentage of the portfolio in Slowburn. If the investor with £100 invests £60 in Supertech and £40 in Slowburn, the expected return on the portfolio can be written as:

$$\text{Expected return on portfolio} = 0.6 \times 17.5\% + 0.4 \times 5.5\% = 12.7\%$$

Algebraically, we can write:

$$\text{Expected return on portfolio} = X_A \overline{R}_A + X_A \overline{R}_B = \overline{R}_p \qquad (10.3)$$

where X_A and X_B are the proportions of the total portfolio in the assets A and B, respectively. (Because our investor can invest in only two securities, $X_A + X_B$ must equal 1 or 100 per cent.) $\overline{R}_A$ and $\overline{R}_B$ are the expected returns on the two securities.

Now consider two securities, each with an expected return of 10 per cent. The expected return on a portfolio composed of these two securities must be 10 per cent, regardless of the proportions of the two securities held. This result may seem obvious at this point, but it will become important later. The result implies that you do not reduce or *dissipate* your expected return by investing in a number of securities. Rather, the expected return on your portfolio is simply a weighted average of the expected returns on the individual assets in the portfolio.

Variance and Standard Deviation of a Portfolio

The formula for the variance of a portfolio composed of two securities, A and B, is:

The variance of the portfolio

$$\text{Var(portfolio)} = X_A^2 \sigma_A^2 + 2X_A X_B \sigma_{A,B} + X_B^2 \sigma_B^2$$

Note that there are three terms on the right side of the equation. The first term involves the variance of A, (σ_A^2), the second term involves the covariance between the two securities, $(\sigma_{A,B})$, and the third term involves the variance of B, (σ_B^2). (As stated earlier in this chapter, $\sigma_{A,B} = \sigma_{B,A}$. That is, the ordering of the variables is not relevant when we are expressing the covariance between two securities.)

The formula indicates an important point. The variance of a portfolio depends on both the variances of the individual securities and the covariance between the two securities. The variance of a security measures the variability of an individual security's return. Covariance measures the relationship between the two securities. For given variances of the individual securities, a positive relationship or covariance between the two securities increases the variance of the entire portfolio. A negative relationship or covariance between the two securities decreases the variance of the entire portfolio. This important result seems to square with common sense.

If one of your securities tends to go up when the other goes down, or vice versa, your two securities are offsetting each other. You are achieving what we call a *hedge* in finance, and the risk of your entire portfolio will be low. However, if both your securities rise and fall together, you are not hedging at all. Hence, the risk of your entire portfolio will be higher.

The variance formula for our two securities, Super and Slow, is:

$$\text{Var(portfolio)} = X^2_{\text{Super}}\sigma^2_{\text{Super}} + 2X_{\text{Super}}X_{\text{Slow}}\sigma_{\text{Super,Slow}} + X^2_{\text{Slow}}\sigma^2_{\text{Slow}} \tag{10.4}$$

Given our earlier assumption that an individual with £100 invests £60 in Supertech and £40 in Slowburn, X Super $= 0.6$ and X Slow $= 0.4$. Using this assumption and the relevant data from our previous calculations, the variance of the portfolio is:

$$0.023851 = 0.36 \times 0.066875 + 2 \times [0.6 \times 0.4 \times (-0.004875)] + 0.16 \times 0.013225 \tag{10.4'}$$

The Matrix Approach

Alternatively, Equation 10.4 can be expressed in the following matrix format:

	Supertech	Slowburn
Supertech	$X^2_{\text{Super}}\sigma^2_{\text{Super}}$ $0.024075 = 0.36 \times 0.066875$	$X_{\text{Super}}X_{\text{Slow}}\sigma_{\text{Super,Slow}}$ $-0.00117 = 0.6 \times 0.4 \times (-0.004875)$
Slowburn	$X_{\text{Super}}X_{\text{Slow}}\sigma_{\text{Super,Slow}}$ $-0.00117 = 0.6 \times 0.4 \times (-0.004875)$	$X^2_{\text{Super}}\sigma^2_{\text{Slow}}$ $0.002116 = 0.16 \times 0.013225$

There are four boxes in the matrix. We can add the terms in the boxes to obtain Equation 10.4, the variance of a portfolio composed of the two securities. The term in the upper left corner involves the variance of Supertech. The term in the lower right corner involves the variance of Slowburn. The other two boxes contain the term involving the covariance. These two boxes are identical, indicating why the covariance term is multiplied by 2 in Equation 10.4.

At this point, students often find the box approach to be more confusing than Equation 10.4. However, the box approach is easily generalized to more than two securities, a task we perform later in this chapter.

Standard Deviation of a Portfolio

Given Equation 10.4′, we can now determine the standard deviation of the portfolio's return. This is:

$$\sigma_p = \text{SD(portfolio)} = \sqrt{\text{Var(portfolio)}} = \sqrt{0.023851} \tag{10.5}$$

$$= 0.1544 = 15.44\%$$

The interpretation of the standard deviation of the portfolio is the same as the interpretation of the standard deviation of an individual security. The expected return on our portfolio is 12.7 per cent. A return of −2.74 per cent ($= 12.7\% - 15.44\%$) is one standard deviation below the mean, and a return of 28.14 per cent ($= 12.7\% + 15.44\%$) is one standard deviation above the mean. If the return on the portfolio is normally distributed, a return between −2.74 per cent and +28.14 per cent occurs about 68 per cent of the time.[3]

The Diversification Effect

It is instructive to compare the standard deviation of the portfolio with the standard deviation of the individual securities. The weighted average of the standard deviations of the individual securities is:

$$\text{Weighted average of standard deviations} = X_{\text{Super}}\,\sigma_{\text{Super}} + X_{\text{Slow}}\,\sigma_{\text{Slow}} \tag{10.6}$$

$$0.2012 = 0.6 \times 0.2586 + 0.4 \times 0.115$$

One of the most important results in this chapter concerns the difference between Equations 10.5 and 10.6. In our example, the standard deviation of the portfolio is *less* than a weighted average of the standard deviations of the individual securities.

We pointed out earlier that the expected return on the portfolio is a weighted average of the expected returns on the individual securities. Thus, we get a different type of result for the standard deviation of a portfolio than we do for the expected return on a portfolio.

It is generally argued that our result for the standard deviation of a portfolio is due to diversification. For example, Supertech and Slowburn are slightly negatively correlated ($\rho = -0.1639$). Supertech's return is likely to be a little below average if Slowburn's return is above average. Similarly, Supertech's return is likely to be a little above average if Slowburn's return is below average. Thus, the standard deviation of a portfolio composed of the two securities is less than a weighted average of the standard deviations of the two securities.

Our example has negative correlation. Clearly, there will be less benefit from diversification if the two securities exhibit positive correlation. How high must the positive correlation be before all diversification benefits vanish?

To answer this question, let us rewrite Equation 10.4 in terms of correlation rather than covariance. The covariance can be rewritten as:[4]

$$S_{\text{Super, Slow}} = \rho_{\text{Super, Slow}} \sigma_{\text{Super}} \sigma_{\text{Slow}} \qquad (10.7)$$

This formula states that the covariance between any two securities is simply the correlation between the two securities multiplied by the standard deviations of each. In other words, covariance incorporates both (1) the correlation between the two assets, and (2) the variability of each of the two securities as measured by standard deviation.

From our calculations earlier in this chapter we know that the correlation between the two securities is -0.1639. Given the variances used in Equation 10.4′, the standard deviations are 0.2586 and 0.115 for Supertech and Slowburn, respectively. Thus, the variance of a portfolio can be expressed as follows:

Variance of the portfolio's return

$$= X_{\text{Super}}^2 \sigma_{\text{Super}}^2 + 2X_{\text{Super}} X_{\text{Slow}} \rho_{\text{Super,Slow}} \sigma_{\text{Super}} \sigma_{\text{Slow}} + X_{\text{Slow}}^2 \sigma_{\text{Slow}}^2$$

$$0.023851 = 0.36 \times 0.066875 + 2 \times 0.6 \times 0.4 \times (-0.1639)$$
$$\times 0.2586 \times 0.115 + 0.16 \times 0.013225 \qquad (10.8)$$

The middle term on the right side is now written in terms of correlation, ρ, not covariance.

Suppose $\rho_{\text{Super, Slow}} = 1$, the highest possible value for correlation. Assume all the other parameters in the example are the same. The variance of the portfolio is:

Variance of the portfolio's return

$$= 0.040466 = 0.36 \times 0.066875 + 2 \times (0.6 \times 0.4 \times 1 \times 0.2586 \times 0.115) + 0.16 \times 0.013225$$

The standard deviation is:

$$\text{Standard deviation of portfolio's return} = \sqrt{0.040466} = 0.2012 = 20.12\% \qquad (10.9)$$

Note that Equations 10.9 and 10.6 are equal. That is, the standard deviation of a portfolio's return is equal to the weighted average of the standard deviations of the individual returns when $\rho = 1$. Inspection of Equation 10.8 indicates that the variance and hence the standard deviation of the portfolio must fall as the correlation drops below 1. This leads to the following result:

> **As long as $\rho < 1$, the standard deviation of a portfolio of two securities is *less* than the weighted average of the standard deviations of the individual securities.**

In other words, the diversification effect applies as long as there is less than perfect correlation (as long as $\rho < 1$). Thus, our Supertech–Slowburn example is a case of overkill. We illustrated diversification by an example with negative correlation. We could have illustrated diversification by an example with positive correlation – as long as it was not *perfect* positive correlation.

An Extension to Many Assets

The preceding insight can be extended to the case of many assets. That is, as long as correlations between pairs of securities are less than 1, the standard deviation of a portfolio of many assets is less than the weighted average of the standard deviations of the individual securities.

Now consider Table 10.3, which shows the standard deviation of the Dow Jones Euro Stoxx 50 (a portfolio of the 50 largest companies in the Eurozone) and the standard deviations of some of the individual securities listed in the index over a recent 5-year period. Note that all of the individual securities in the table have higher standard deviations than that of the index. In general, the standard deviations of most of the individual securities in an index will be above the standard deviation of the index itself, though a few of the securities could have lower standard deviations than that of the index.

Table 10.3 Standard Deviations for Dow Jones Euro Stoxx 50 Index and for Selected Equities in the Index

Asset	Standard Deviation (%)
DJ Euro Stoxx 50 Index	13.10
Carrefour SA	41.08
Ageas	65.55
Vinci SA	35.17
Intesa SanPaolo	31.53
Saint Gobain	48.80
Telecom Italia	32.22
Arcelormittal	41.07
Credit Agricole	57.92
Adidas	29.47

Source: Yahoo! Finance © 2015 Yahoo! Inc.

As long as the correlations between pairs of securities are less than 1, the standard deviation of an index will always be less than the weighted average of the standard deviations of the individual securities within the index.

10.4 The Efficient Set for Two Assets

Our results for expected returns and standard deviations are graphed in Figure 10.2. The figure shows a dot labelled Slowburn and a dot labelled Supertech. Each dot represents both the expected return and the standard deviation for an individual security. As can be seen, Supertech has both a higher expected return and a higher standard deviation.

Figure 10.2 Expected Returns and Standard Deviations for Supertech, Slowburn and a Portfolio Composed of 60 Per cent in Supertech and 40 Per cent in Slowburn

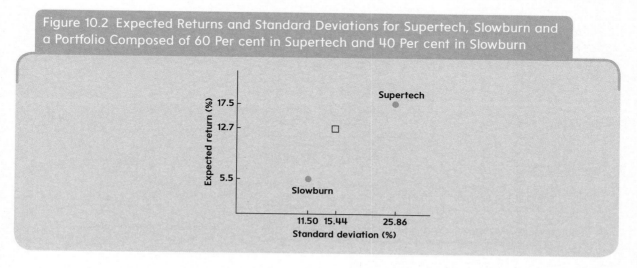

The box or '□' in the graph represents a portfolio with 60 per cent invested in Supertech and 40 per cent invested in Slowburn. You will recall that we previously calculated both the expected return and the standard deviation for this portfolio. The choice of 60 per cent in Supertech and 40 per cent in Slowburn is just one of an infinite number of portfolios that can be created. The set of portfolios is sketched by the curved line in Figure 10.3.

Consider portfolio 1. This is a portfolio composed of 90 per cent Slowburn and 10 per cent Supertech. Because it is weighted so heavily toward Slowburn, it appears close to the Slowburn point on the graph. Portfolio 2 is higher on the curve because it is composed of 50 per cent Slowburn and 50 per cent Supertech. Portfolio 3 is close to the Supertech point on the graph because it is composed of 90 per cent Supertech and 10 per cent Slowburn.

There are a few important points concerning this graph:

1   We argued that the diversification effect occurs whenever the correlation between the two securities is below 1. The correlation between Supertech and Slowburn is −0.1639. The diversification effect can be illustrated by comparison with the straight line between the Supertech point and the Slowburn point. The straight line represents points that would have been generated had the correlation coefficient between the two securities been 1. The diversification effect is illustrated in the figure because the curved line is always to the left of the straight line. Consider point 1'. This represents a portfolio composed of 90 per cent in Slowburn and 10 per cent in Supertech *if* the correlation between the two were exactly 1. We argue that there is no diversification effect if $\rho = 1$. However, the diversification effect applies to the curved line because point 1 has the same expected return as point 1' but has a lower standard deviation. (Points 2' and 3' are omitted to reduce the clutter of Figure 10.3.)

Though the straight line and the curved line are both represented in Figure 10.3, they do not simultaneously exist in the same world. *Either* $\rho = -0.1639$ and the curve exists *or* $\rho = 1$ and the straight line exists. In other words, though an investor can choose between different points on the curve if $\rho = -0.1639$, she cannot choose between points on the curve and points on the straight line.

2   The point MV represents the minimum variance portfolio. This is the portfolio with the lowest possible variance. By definition, this portfolio must also have the lowest possible standard deviation. (The term *minimum variance portfolio* is standard in the literature, and we will use that term. Perhaps minimum standard deviation would actually be better because standard deviation, not variance, is measured on the horizontal axis of Figure 10.3.)

Figure 10.3 Set of Portfolios Composed of Holdings in Supertech and Slowburn (correlation between the two securities is −0.1639)

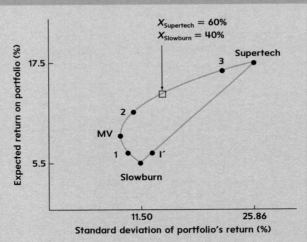

Portfolio 1 is composed of 90 per cent Slowburn and 10 per cent Supertech ($\rho = -0.1639$).
Portfolio 2 is composed of 50 per cent Slowburn and 50 per cent Supertech ($\rho = -0.1639$).
Portfolio 3 is composed of 10 per cent Slowburn and 90 per cent Supertech ($\rho = -0.1639$).
Portfolio 1' is composed of 90 per cent Slowburn and 10 per cent Supertech ($\rho = 1$).
Point MV denotes the minimum variance portfolio. This is the portfolio with the lowest possible variance. By definition, the same portfolio must also have the lowest possible standard deviation.

3   An individual contemplating an investment in a portfolio of Slowburn and Supertech faces an opportunity set or feasible set represented by the curved line in Figure 10.3. That is, he can achieve any point on the curve by selecting the appropriate mix between the two securities. He cannot achieve any point above the curve because he cannot increase the return on the individual securities, decrease the standard deviations of

the securities, or decrease the correlation between the two securities. Neither can he achieve points below the curve because he cannot lower the returns on the individual securities, increase the standard deviations of the securities, or increase the correlation. (Of course, he would not want to achieve points below the curve, even if he were able to do so.)

Were he relatively tolerant of risk, he might choose portfolio 3. (In fact, he could even choose the end point by investing all his money in Supertech.) An investor with less tolerance for risk might choose portfolio 2. An investor wanting as little risk as possible would choose MV, the portfolio with minimum variance or minimum standard deviation.

4　Note that the curve is backward bending between the Slowburn point and MV. This indicates that, for a portion of the feasible set, standard deviation actually decreases as we increase expected return. Students frequently ask, 'How can an increase in the proportion of the risky security, Supertech, lead to a reduction in the risk of the portfolio?'

This surprising finding is due to the diversification effect. The returns on the two securities are negatively correlated with each other. One security tends to go up when the other goes down and vice versa. Thus, an addition of a small amount of Supertech acts as a hedge to a portfolio composed only of Slowburn. The risk of the portfolio is reduced, implying backward bending. Actually, backward bending always occurs if $\rho < 0$. It may or may not occur when $\rho \geq 0$. Of course, the curve bends backward only for a portion of its length. As we continue to increase the percentage of Supertech in the portfolio, the high standard deviation of this security eventually causes the standard deviation of the entire portfolio to rise.

5　No investor would want to hold a portfolio with an expected return below that of the minimum variance portfolio. For example, no investor would choose portfolio 1. This portfolio has less expected return but more standard deviation than the minimum variance portfolio. We say that portfolios such as portfolio 1 are *dominated* by the minimum variance portfolio. Though the entire curve from Slowburn to Supertech is called the *feasible set*, investors consider only the curve from MV to Supertech. Hence the curve from MV to Supertech is called the efficient set or the efficient frontier.

Figure 10.3 represents the opportunity set where $\rho = -0.1639$. It is worthwhile to examine Figure 10.4, which shows different curves for different correlations. As can be seen, the lower the correlation, the more bend there is in the curve. This indicates that the diversification effect rises as ρ declines. The greatest bend occurs in the limiting case where $\rho = -1$. This is perfect negative correlation. While this extreme case where $\rho = -1$ seems to fascinate students, it has little practical importance. Most pairs of securities exhibit positive correlation. Strong negative correlations, let alone perfect negative correlation, are unlikely occurrences indeed.[5]

Figure 10.4　Opportunity Sets Composed of Holdings in Supertech and Slowburn

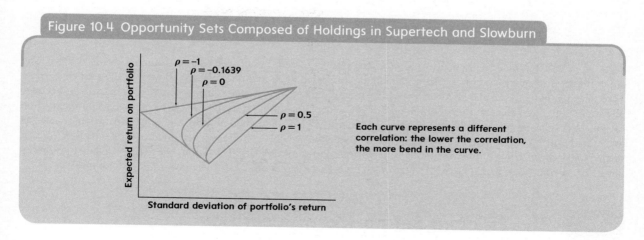

Each curve represents a different correlation: the lower the correlation, the more bend in the curve.

Note that there is only one correlation between a pair of securities. We stated earlier that the correlation between Slowburn and Supertech is -0.1639. Thus, the curve in Figure 10.4 representing this correlation is the correct one, and the other curves should be viewed as merely hypothetical.

The graphs we examined are not mere intellectual curiosities. Rather, efficient sets can easily be calculated in the real world. As mentioned earlier, data on returns, standard deviations and correlations are generally taken from past observations, though subjective notions can be used to determine the values of these parameters as well. Once the parameters have been determined, any one of a whole host of software packages can be purchased to generate an efficient set. However, the choice of the preferred portfolio within the efficient set is up to you. As with other important decisions like what job to choose, what house or car to buy, and how much time to allocate to this course, there is no computer program to choose the preferred portfolio.

An efficient set can be generated where the two individual assets are portfolios themselves. For example, the two assets in Figure 10.5 are a diversified portfolio of US equities and a diversified portfolio of non-US equities. Expected returns, standard deviations and the correlation coefficient were calculated over the recent past. No subjectivity entered the analysis. The US equity portfolio with a standard deviation of about 0.173 is less risky than the non-US equity portfolio, which has a standard deviation of about 0.222. However, combining a small percentage of the non-US equity portfolio with the US portfolio actually reduces risk, as can be seen by the backward-bending nature of the curve. In other words, the diversification benefits from combining two different portfolios more than offset the introduction of a riskier set of equities into our holdings. The minimum variance portfolio occurs with about 80 per cent of our funds in US equities and about 20 per cent in non-US equities. The addition of non-US securities beyond this point increases the risk of the entire portfolio.

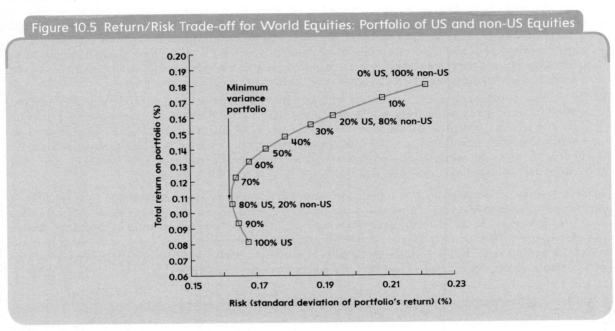

Figure 10.5 Return/Risk Trade-off for World Equities: Portfolio of US and non-US Equities

A point worth pondering concerns the potential pitfalls of using only past data to estimate future returns. The stock markets of many countries, especially China and India, have had phenomenal growth in the past few years. Thus, a graph like Figure 10.5 makes a large investment in these foreign markets seem attractive. However, because abnormally high returns cannot be sustained forever, some subjectivity must be used in forecasting future expected returns. A good example concerns the Indian stock market. At the beginning of 2013, if you used historical returns as an estimate of future returns, India would have had a heavy weighting in your investment portfolio. However, as it turned out, India was one of the world's worst performing stock markets in 2013. If you then used 2013 data to estimate 2014 performance, you would have lost again with India since it was one of the best performing stock markets!

10.5   The Efficient Set for Many Securities

The previous discussion concerned two securities. We found that a simple curve sketched out all the possible portfolios. Because investors generally hold more than two securities, we should look at the same graph when more than two securities are held. The shaded area in Figure 10.6 represents the opportunity set or feasible set when many securities are considered. The shaded area represents all the possible combinations of expected return and standard deviation for a portfolio. For example, in a universe of 100 securities, point 1 might represent a portfolio of, say, 40 securities. Point 2 might represent a portfolio of 80 securities. Point 3 might represent a different set of 80 securities, or the same 80 securities held in different proportions, or something else. Obviously, the combinations are virtually endless. However, note that all possible combinations fit into a confined region. No security or combination of securities can fall outside the shaded region. That is, no one can choose a portfolio with an expected return above that given by the shaded region. Furthermore, no one can choose a portfolio with a standard deviation below that given in the shaded area. Perhaps more surprisingly, no one can choose an expected return below that given in the curve. In other words, the capital markets actually prevent a self-destructive person from taking on a guaranteed loss.[6]

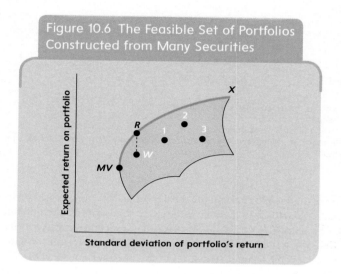

Figure 10.6 The Feasible Set of Portfolios Constructed from Many Securities

So far, Figure 10.6 is different from the earlier graphs. When only two securities are involved, all the combinations lie on a single curve. Conversely, with many securities the combinations cover an entire area. However, notice that an individual will want to be somewhere on the upper edge between *MV* and *X*. The upper edge, which we indicate in Figure 10.6 by a thick curve, is called the *efficient set*. Any point below the efficient set would receive less expected return and the same standard deviation as a point on the efficient set. For example, consider *R* on the efficient set and *W* directly below it. If *W* contains the risk level you desire, you should choose *R* instead to receive a higher expected return.

In the final analysis, Figure 10.6 is quite similar to Figure 10.3. The efficient set in Figure 10.3 runs from *MV* to Supertech. It contains various combinations of the securities Supertech and Slowburn. The efficient set in Figure 10.6 runs from *MV* to *X*. It contains various combinations of many securities. The fact that a whole shaded area appears in Figure 10.6 but not in Figure 10.3 is just not an important difference; no investor would choose any point below the efficient set in Figure 10.6 anyway.

We mentioned before that an efficient set for two securities can be traced out easily in the real world. The task becomes more difficult when additional securities are included because the number of observations grows. For example, using subjective analysis to estimate expected returns and standard deviations for, say, 100 or 500 securities may very well become overwhelming, and the difficulties with correlations may be greater still. There are almost 5,000 correlations between pairs of securities from a universe of 100 securities.

Though much of the mathematics of efficient set computation had been derived in the 1950s,[7] the high cost of computer time restricted application of the principles. In recent years this cost has been almost eliminated and an efficient frontier can now be easily computed with standard spreadsheet software.

Variance and Standard Deviation in a Portfolio of Many Assets

We earlier calculated the formulas for variance and standard deviation in the two-asset case. Because we considered a portfolio of many assets in Figure 10.6, it is worthwhile to calculate the formulas for variance and standard deviation in the many-asset case. The formula for the variance of a portfolio of many assets can be viewed as an extension of the formula for the variance of two assets.

To develop the formula, we employ the same type of matrix that we used in the two-asset case. This matrix is displayed in Table 10.4. Assuming that there are N assets, we write the numbers 1 through N on the horizontal axis and 1 through N on the vertical axis. This creates a matrix of $N \times N = N^2$ boxes. The variance of the portfolio is the sum of the terms in all the boxes.

Table 10.4 Matrix Used to Calculate the Variance of a Portfolio

Security	1	2	3	...	N
1	$X_1^2\sigma_1^2$	$X_1X_2\text{Cov}(R_1,R_2)$	$X_1X_3\text{Cov}(R_1,R_3)$		$X_1X_N\text{Cov}(R_1,R_N)$
2	$X_2\,X_1\text{Cov}(R_2,R_1)$	$X_2^2\sigma_2^2$	$X_2X_3\text{Cov}(R_2,R_3)$		$X_2X_N\text{Cov}(R_2,R_N)$
3	$X_3\,X_1\text{Cov}(R_3,R_1)$	$X_3X_2\text{Cov}(R_3,R_2)$	$X_3^2\sigma_3^2$		$X_3X_N\text{Cov}(R_3,R_N)$
.					
.					
.					
N	$X_NX_1\text{Cov}(R_N,R_1)$	$X_NX_2\text{Cov}(R_N,R_2)$	$X_NX_3\text{Cov}(R_N,R_3)$		$X_N^2\sigma_N^2$

Notes: The variance of the portfolio is the sum of the terms in all the boxes.
σ_i is the standard deviation of security i.
$\text{Cov}(R_i,\ R_j)$ is the covariance between security i and security j.
Terms involving the standard deviation of a single security appear on the diagonal. Terms involving covariance between two securities appear off the diagonal.

Consider, for example, the box in the second row and the third column. The term in the box is $X_2\,X_3\,\text{Cov}(R_2,R_3)$. X_2 and X_3 are the percentages of the entire portfolio that are invested in the second asset and the third asset, respectively. For example, if an individual with a portfolio of €1,000 invests €100 in the second asset, $X_2 = 10$ per cent (= €100/€1,000). $\text{Cov}(R_3, R_2)$ is the covariance between the returns on the third asset and the returns on the second asset. Next, note the box in the third row and the second column. The term in this box is $X_3\,X_2\,\text{Cov}(R_3, R_2)$. Because $\text{Cov}(R_3, R_2) = \text{Cov}(R_2, R_3)$, both boxes have the same value. The second security and the third security make up one pair. In fact, every pair of securities appears twice in the table: once in the lower left side and once in the upper right side.

Now consider boxes on the diagonal. For example, the term in the first box on the diagonal is $X_1^2\sigma_1^2$. Here, σ_1^2 is the variance of the return on the first security.

Thus, the diagonal terms in the matrix contain the variances of the different securities. The off-diagonal terms contain the covariances. Table 10.5 relates the numbers of diagonal and off-diagonal elements to the size of the matrix. The number of diagonal terms (number of variance terms) is always the same as the number of securities in the portfolio. The number of off-diagonal terms (number of covariance terms) rises much faster than the number of diagonal terms. For example, a portfolio of 100 securities has 9,900 covariance terms. Because the variance of a portfolio's return is the sum of all the boxes, we have the following:

The variance of the return on a portfolio with many securities is more dependent on the covariances between the individual securities than on the variances of the individual securities.

Table 10.5 Number of Variance and Covariance Terms as a Function of the Number of Securities in the Portfolio

Number of Securities in Portfolio	Total Number of Terms	Number of Variance Terms (number of terms on diagonal)	Number of Covariance Terms (number of terms off diagonal)
1	1	1	0
2	4	2	2
3	9	3	6
10	100	10	90
100	10,000	100	9,900
.	.	.	.
.	.	.	.
.	.	.	.
N	N^2	N	$N^2 - N$

In a large portfolio, the number of terms involving covariance between two securities is much greater than the number of terms involving variance of a single security.

To give a recent example of the impact of diversification, consider an investment in large Chinese and German stocks. From Chapter 9, 2013 saw a fall in the Chinese market of 6.75 per cent while Germany grew by 25.48 per cent. In 2014, the markets experience the opposite performance with Germany only growing by 2.65 per cent and China jumped 52.87 per cent in value. A portfolio containing Germany and China would have offset the poor returns in China for 2013 and Germany for 2014 with very high returns in the other country.

10.6 Diversification: An Example

The preceding point can be illustrated by altering the matrix in Table 10.4 slightly. Suppose we make the following three assumptions:

1. All securities possess the same variance, which we write as $\overline{var}$. In other words, $\sigma_i^2 = \overline{var}$ for every security.
2. All covariances in Table 10.4 are the same. We represent this uniform covariance as $\overline{cov}$. In other words. $Cov(R_i, R_j) = \overline{cov}$ for every pair of securities. It can easily be shown that $\overline{var} > \overline{cov}$.
3. All securities are equally weighted in the portfolio. Because there are N assets, the weight of each asset in the portfolio is $1/N$. In other words, $X_i = 1/N$ for each security i.

Table 10.6 is the matrix of variances and covariances under these three simplifying assumptions. Note that all of the diagonal terms are identical. Similarly, all of the off-diagonal terms are identical. As with Table 10.4, the variance of the portfolio is the sum of the terms in the boxes in Table 10.6. We know that there are N diagonal terms involving variance. Similarly, there are $N \times (N - 1)$ off-diagonal terms involving covariance. Summing across all the boxes in Table 10.6, we can express the variance of the portfolio as:

$$\text{Variance of portfolio} = \underset{\substack{\text{Number of} \\ \text{diagonal} \\ \text{terms}}}{N} \times \underset{\substack{\text{Each} \\ \text{diagonal} \\ \text{term}}}{\left[\frac{1}{N^2}\right]\overline{var}} + \underset{\substack{\text{Number of} \\ \text{off-diagonal} \\ \text{terms}}}{N(N-1)} \times \underset{\substack{\text{Each} \\ \text{off-diagonal} \\ \text{term}}}{\left[\frac{1}{N^2}\right]\overline{cov}}$$

$$= \left[\frac{1}{N}\right]\overline{var} + \left[\frac{N^2 - N}{N^2}\right]\overline{cov}$$

$$= \left[\frac{1}{N}\right]\overline{var} + \left[\frac{N^2 - N}{N^2}\right]\overline{cov} \tag{10.10}$$

Equation 10.10 expresses the variance of our special portfolio as a weighted sum of the average security variance and the average covariance.[8]

Table 10.6 Matrix Used to Calculate the Variance of a Portfolio When (a) All Securities Possess the Same Variance, Which We Represent as $\overline{var}$; (b) All Pairs of Securities Possess the Same Covariance, Which We Represent as $\overline{cov}$; (c) All Securities Are Held in the Same Proportion, Which is $1/N$

Security	1	2	3	...	N
1	$(1/N^2)\,\overline{var}$	$(1/N^2)\,\overline{cov}$	$(1/N^2)\,\overline{cov}$	...	$(1/N^2)\,\overline{cov}$
2	$(1/N^2)\,\overline{cov}$	$(1/N^2)\,\overline{var}$	$(1/N^2)\,\overline{cov}$	...	$(1/N^2)\,\overline{cov}$
3	$(1/N^2)\,\overline{cov}$	$(1/N^2)\,\overline{cov}$	$(1/N^2)\,\overline{var}$	...	$(1/N^2)\,\overline{cov}$
.					
.					
.					
N	$(1/N^2)\,\overline{cov}$	$(1/N^2)\,\overline{cov}$	$(1/N^2)\,\overline{cov}$		$(1/N^2)\,\overline{var}$

Now, let us increase the number of securities in the portfolio without limit. The variance of the portfolio becomes:

$$\text{Variance of portfolio (when } N \to \infty) = \overline{cov} \tag{10.11}$$

This occurs because (1) the weight on the variance term, $1/N$, goes to 0 as N goes to infinity, and (2) the weight on the covariance term, $1 - 1/N$, goes to 1 as N goes to infinity.

Equation 10.11 provides an interesting and important result. In our special portfolio, the variances of the individual securities completely vanish as the number of securities becomes large. However, the covariance terms remain. In fact, the variance of the portfolio becomes the average covariance, $\overline{cov}$. We often hear that we should diversify. In other words, we should not put all our eggs in one basket. The effect of diversification on the risk of a portfolio can be illustrated in this example. The variances of the individual securities are diversified away, but the covariance terms cannot be diversified away.

The fact that part, but not all, of our risk can be diversified away should be explored. Consider Mr Smith, who brings £1,000 to the roulette table at a casino. It would be very risky if he put all his money on one spin of the wheel. For example, imagine that he put the full £1,000 on red at the table. If the wheel showed red, he would get £2,000; but if the wheel showed black, he would lose everything. Suppose instead he divided his money over 1,000 different spins by betting £1 at a time on red. Probability theory tells us that he could count on winning about 50 per cent of the time. This means he could count on pretty nearly getting all his original £1,000 back.[9] In other words, risk is essentially eliminated with 1,000 different spins.

Now, let us contrast this with our stock market example, which we illustrate in Figure 10.7. The variance of the portfolio with only one security is, of course $\overline{var}$ because the variance of a portfolio with one security is the variance of the security. The variance of the portfolio drops as more securities are added, which is evidence of the diversification effect. However, unlike Mr Smith's roulette example, the portfolio's variance can never drop to zero. Rather it reaches a floor of $\overline{cov}$, which is the covariance of each pair of securities.[10]

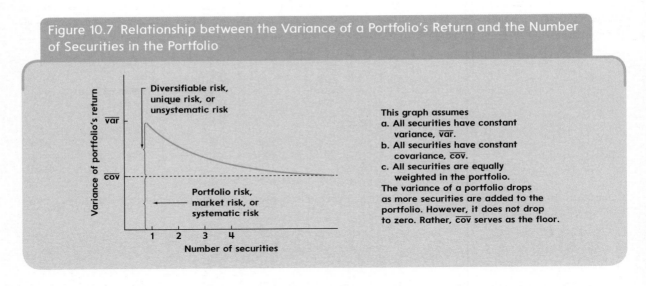

Figure 10.7 Relationship between the Variance of a Portfolio's Return and the Number of Securities in the Portfolio

Because the variance of the portfolio asymptotically approaches $\overline{cov}$, each additional security continues to reduce risk. Thus, if there were neither commissions nor other transactions costs, it could be argued that we can never achieve too much diversification. However, there is a cost to diversification in the real world. Commissions per unit of money invested fall as we make larger purchases in a single security. Unfortunately, we must buy fewer shares of each security when buying more and more different securities. Comparing the costs and benefits of diversification, Meir Statman (1987) argues that a portfolio of about 30 equities is needed to achieve optimal diversification.

We mentioned earlier that $\overline{var}$ must be greater than $\overline{cov}$. Thus, the variance of a security's return can be broken down in the following way:

$$\begin{array}{ccc} \text{Total risk of} & \text{Portfolio} & \text{Unsystematic or} \\ \text{individual security} = & \text{risk} & + \text{ diversifiable risk} \\ (\overline{var}) & (\overline{cov}) & (\overline{var} - \overline{cov}) \end{array}$$

Total risk, which is $\overline{var}$ in our example, is the risk we bear by holding onto one security only. *Portfolio risk* is the risk we still bear after achieving full diversification, which is $\overline{cov}$ in our example. Portfolio risk is often called systematic or market risk as well. Diversifiable, unique, or unsystematic risk is the risk that can be diversified away in a large portfolio, which must be $(\overline{var} - \overline{cov})$ by definition.

To an individual who selects a diversified portfolio, the total risk of an individual security is not important. When considering adding a security to a diversified portfolio, the individual cares about only that portion of the risk of a security that cannot be diversified away. This risk can alternatively be viewed as the *contribution* of a security to the risk of an entire portfolio. We will talk later about the case where securities make different contributions to the risk of the entire portfolio.

Risk and the Sensible Investor

Having gone to all this trouble to show that unsystematic risk disappears in a well-diversified portfolio, how do we know that investors even want such portfolios? What if they like risk and do not want it to disappear?

We must admit that, theoretically at least, this is possible, but we will argue that it does not describe what we think of as the typical investor. Our typical investor is risk-averse. Risk-averse behaviour can be defined in many ways, but we prefer the following example: a fair gamble is one with zero expected return; a risk-averse investor would prefer to avoid fair gambles.

Why do investors choose well-diversified portfolios? Our answer is that they are risk-averse, and risk-averse people avoid unnecessary risk, such as the unsystematic risk on an equity. If you do not think this is much of an answer, consider whether you would take on such a risk. For example, suppose you had worked all summer and had saved €5,000, which you intended to use for your university expenses. Now, suppose someone came up to you and offered to flip a coin for the money: heads, you would double your money, and tails, you would lose it all.

Would you take such a bet? Perhaps you would, but most people would not. Leaving aside any moral question that might surround gambling and recognizing that some people would take such a bet, it is our view that the average investor would not.

To induce the typical risk-averse investor to take a fair gamble, you must sweeten the pot. For example, you might need to raise the odds of winning from 50–50 to 70–30 or higher. The risk-averse investor can be induced to take fair gambles only if they are sweetened so that they become unfair to the investor's advantage.

10.7 Riskless Borrowing and Lending

Figure 10.6 assumes that all the securities in the efficient set are risky. Alternatively, an investor could combine a risky investment with an investment in a riskless or *risk-free* security, such as an investment in government treasury bills. This is illustrated in the following example.

Example 10.3

Riskless Lending and Portfolio Risk

Ms Bagwell is considering investing in the equity of Merville Enterprises. In addition, Ms Bagwell will either borrow or lend at the risk-free rate. The relevant parameters are these:

	Equity of Merville (%)	**Risk-Free Asset (%)**
Expected return	14	10
Standard deviation	20	0

Suppose Ms Bagwell chooses to invest a total of £1,000, £350 of which is to be invested in Merville Enterprises and £650 placed in the risk-free asset. The expected return on her total investment is simply a weighted average of the two returns:

$$\text{Expected return on portfolio composed of one riskless and one risky asset} = 0.114 = (0.35 \times 0.14) + (0.65 \times 0.10) \qquad (10.12)$$

Because the expected return on the portfolio is a weighted average of the expected return on the risky asset (Merville Enterprises) and the risk-free return, the calculation is analogous to the way we treated two risky assets. In other words, Equation 10.3 applies here.

Using Equation 10.4, the formula for the variance of the portfolio can be written as:

$$X_{\text{Merville}}^2 \, \sigma_{\text{Merville}}^2 + 2X_{\text{Merville}} X_{\text{Risk-free}} \sigma_{\text{Merville,Risk-free}} + X_{\text{Merville}}^2 \sigma_{\text{Risk-free}}^2$$

However, by definition, the risk-free asset has no variability. Thus both $\sigma_{\text{Merville, Risk-free}}$ and $\sigma^2_{\text{Risk-free}}$ are equal to zero, reducing the above expression to:

$$\text{Variance of portfolio composed of one riskless and one risky asset} = X^2_{\text{Merville}} \, \sigma^2_{\text{Merville}}$$

$$= (0.35)^2 \times (0.20)^2 \qquad (10.13)$$

$$= 0.0049$$

The standard deviation of the portfolio is:

$$\text{Standard deviation of portfolio composed of one riskless and one risky asset} = X_{\text{Merville}} \, \sigma_{\text{Merville}}$$

$$= 0.35 \times 0.20 \qquad (10.14)$$

$$= 0.07$$

The relationship between risk and expected return for one risky and one riskless asset can be seen in Figure 10.8. Ms Bagwell's split of 35–65 per cent between the two assets is represented on a *straight* line between the risk-free rate and a pure investment in Merville Enterprises. Note that, unlike the case of two risky assets, the opportunity set is straight, not curved.

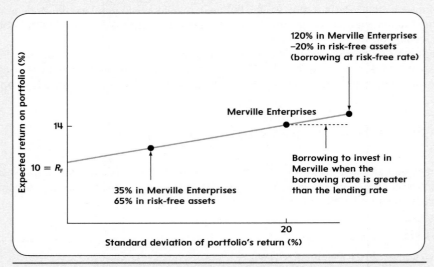

Figure 10.8 Relationship between Expected Return and Risk for a Portfolio of One Risky Asset and One Riskless Asset

Suppose that, alternatively, Ms Bagwell borrows £200 at the risk-free rate. Combining this with her original sum of £1,000, she invests a total of £1,200 in Merville. Her expected return would be:

$$\begin{array}{l} \text{Expected return on portfolio} \\ \text{formed by borrowing} \\ \text{to invest in risky asset} \end{array} = 14.8\% = 1.20 \times 0.14 + (-0.2 \times 0.10)$$

Here, she invests 120 per cent of her original investment of £1,000 by borrowing 20 per cent of her original investment. Note that the return of 14.8 per cent is greater than the 14 per cent expected return on Merville Enterprises. This occurs because she is borrowing at 10 per cent to invest in a security with an expected return greater than 10 per cent.

The standard deviation is:

$$\begin{array}{l} \text{Standard deviation of portfolio} \\ \text{formed by borrowing to invest} \\ \text{in risky asset} \end{array} = 0.24 = 1.20 \times 0.2$$

The standard deviation of 0.24 is greater than 0.20, the standard deviation of the Merville investment, because borrowing increases the variability of the investment. This investment also appears in Figure 10.8.

So far, we have assumed that Ms Bagwell is able to borrow at the same rate at which she can lend.[11] Now let us consider the case where the borrowing rate is above the lending rate. The dotted line in Figure 10.8 illustrates the opportunity set for borrowing opportunities in this case. The dotted line is below the solid line because a higher borrowing rate lowers the expected return on the investment.

The Optimal Portfolio

The previous section concerned a portfolio formed between one riskless asset and one risky asset. In reality, an investor is likely to combine an investment in the riskless asset with a *portfolio* of risky assets. This is illustrated in Figure 10.9.

Figure 10.9 Relationship between Expected Return and Standard Deviation for an Investment in a Combination of Risky Securities and the Riskless Asset

Portfolio Q is composed of 30 per cent Carrefour, 45 per cent LVMH, and 25 per cent Vinci.

Consider point Q, representing a portfolio of securities. Point Q is in the interior of the feasible set of risky securities. Let us assume the point represents a portfolio of 30 per cent in Carrefour, the French supermarket chain, 45 per cent in LVMH, the luxury designer goods group, and 25 per cent in Vinci SA, the European road-builder. Individuals combining investments in Q with investments in the riskless asset would achieve points along the straight line from R_F to Q. We refer to this as line I. For example, point 1 on the line represents a portfolio of 70 per cent in the riskless asset and 30 per cent in equities represented by Q. An investor with €100 choosing point 1 as his portfolio would put €70 in the risk-free asset and €30 in Q. This can be restated as €70 in the riskless asset, €9 (= 0.3 × €30) in Carrefour, €13.50 (= 0.45 × €30) in LVMH, and €7.50 (= 0.25 × €30) in Vinci. Point 2 also represents a portfolio of the risk-free asset and Q, with more (65 per cent) being invested in Q.

Point 3 is obtained by borrowing to invest in Q. For example, an investor with €100 of her own would borrow €40 from the bank or broker to invest €140 in Q. This can be stated as borrowing €40 and contributing €100 of her money to invest €42 (= 0.3 × €140) in Carrefour, €63 (= 0.45 × €140) in LVMH, and €35 (= 0.25 × €140) in Vinci. These investments can be summarized as follows:

	Point Q (€)	Point 1 (Lending €70) (€)	Point 3 (Borrowing €40) (€)
Carrefour	30.00	9.00	42.00
LVMH	45.00	13.50	63.00
Vinci	25.00	7.50	35.00
Risk-free	0	70.00	−40.00
Total investment	100.00	100.00	100.00

Though any investor can obtain any point on line I, no point on the line is optimal. To see this, consider line II, a line running from R_F through A. Point A represents a portfolio of risky securities. Line II represents portfolios formed by combinations of the risk-free asset and the securities in A. Points between R_F and A are portfolios in which some money is invested in the riskless asset and the rest is placed in A. Points past A are achieved by borrowing at the riskless rate to buy more of A than we could with our original funds alone.

As drawn, line II is tangent to the efficient set of risky securities. Whatever point an individual can obtain on line I, he can obtain a point with the same standard deviation and a higher expected return on line II. In fact, because line II is tangent to the efficient set of risky assets, it provides the investor with the best possible opportunities. In other words, line II can be viewed as the efficient set of *all* assets, both risky and riskless. An investor with a fair degree of risk aversion might choose a point between R_F and A, perhaps point 4. An individual with less risk aversion might choose a point closer to A or even beyond A. For example, point 5 corresponds to an individual borrowing money to increase investment in A.

The graph illustrates an important point. With riskless borrowing and lending, the portfolio of *risky* assets held by any investor would always be point A. Regardless of the investor's tolerance for risk, she would never choose any other point on the efficient set of risky assets (represented by curve *XAY*) nor any point in the interior of the feasible region. Rather, she would combine the securities of A with the riskless assets if she had high aversion to risk. She would borrow the riskless asset to invest more funds in A had she low aversion to risk.

This result establishes what financial economists call the separation principle. That is, the investor's investment decision consists of two separate steps:

1 After estimating (a) the expected returns and variances of individual securities, and (b) the covariances between pairs of securities, the investor calculates the efficient set of risky assets, represented by curve *XAY* in Figure 10.9. He then determines point A, the tangency between the risk-free rate and the efficient set of risky assets (curve *XAY*). Point A represents the portfolio of risky assets that the investor will hold. This point is determined solely from his estimates of returns, variances and covariances. No personal characteristics, such as degree of risk aversion, are needed in this step.

2 The investor must now determine how he will combine point A, his portfolio of risky assets, with the riskless asset. He might invest some of his funds in the riskless asset and some in portfolio A. He would end up at a point on the line between R_F and A in this case. Alternatively, he might borrow at the risk-free rate and contribute some of his own funds as well, investing the sum in portfolio A. He would end up at a point on line II beyond A. His position in the riskless asset – that is, his choice of where on the line he wants to be – is determined by his internal characteristics, such as his ability to tolerate risk.

10.8　Market Equilibrium

Definition of the Market Equilibrium Portfolio

The preceding analysis concerns one investor. His estimates of the expected returns and variances for individual securities and the covariances between pairs of securities are his and his alone. Other investors would obviously have different estimates of these variables. However, the estimates might not vary much because all investors would be forming expectations from the same data about past price movements and other publicly available information.

Financial economists often imagine a world where all investors possess the *same* estimates of expected returns, variances and covariances. Though this can never be literally true, it can be thought of as a useful simplifying assumption in a world where investors have access to similar sources of information. This assumption is called homogeneous expectations.[12]

If all investors had homogeneous expectations, Figure 10.9 would be the same for all individuals. That is, all investors would sketch out the same efficient set of risky assets because they would be working with the same inputs. This efficient set of risky assets is represented by the curve *XAY*. Because the same risk-free rate would apply to everyone, all investors would view point A as the portfolio of risky assets to be held.

This point A takes on great importance because all investors would purchase the risky securities that it represents. Investors with a high degree of risk aversion might combine A with an investment in the riskless asset, achieving point 4, for example. Others with low aversion to risk might borrow to achieve, say, point 5. Because this is a very important conclusion, we restate it:

In a world with homogeneous expectations, all investors would hold the portfolio of risky assets represented by point A.

If all investors choose the same portfolio of risky assets, it is possible to determine what that portfolio is. Common sense tells us that it is a market value weighted portfolio of all existing securities. It is the market portfolio.

In practice, economists use a broad-based index such as the FTSE 100, Dow Jones Euro Stoxx 50, or Standard & Poor's (S&P) 500 as a proxy for the market portfolio, depending on the country they analyse. Of course all investors do not hold the same portfolio in practice. However, we know that many investors hold diversified portfolios, particularly when mutual funds or pension funds are included. A broad-based index is a good proxy for the highly diversified portfolios of many investors.

Definition of Risk When Investors Hold the Market Portfolio

The previous section states that many investors hold diversified portfolios similar to broad-based indexes. This result allows us to be more precise about the risk of a security in the context of a diversified portfolio.

Researchers have shown that the best measure of the risk of a security in a large portfolio is the *beta* of the security. We illustrate beta by an example.

Example 10.4

Beta

Consider the following possible returns both on the equity of Hicks plc and on the market:

State	Type of Economy	Return on Market (%)	Return on Hicks plc (%)
I	Bull	15	25
II	Bull	15	15
III	Bear	−5	−5
IV	Bear	−5	−15

Though the return on the market has only two possible outcomes (15 per cent and −5 per cent), the return on Hicks has four possible outcomes. It is helpful to consider the expected return on a security for a given return on the market. Assuming each state is equally likely, we have:

Type of Economy	Return on Market (%)	Expected Return on Hicks plc (%)
Bull	15	$20\% = 25\% \times \frac{1}{2} + 15\% \times \frac{1}{2}$
Bear	−5	$-10\% - 25\% \times \frac{1}{2} + (-15\%) \times \frac{1}{2}$

Hicks plc responds to market movements because its expected return is greater in bullish states than in bearish states. We now calculate exactly how responsive the security is to market movements. The market's return in a bullish economy is 20 per cent [= 15% − (−5%)] greater than the market's return in a bearish economy. However, the expected return on Hicks in a bullish economy is 30 per cent [= 20% − (−10%)] greater than its expected return in a bearish state. Thus Hicks plc has a responsiveness coefficient of 1.5 (= 30%/20%).

This relationship appears in Figure 10.10. The returns for both Hicks and the market in each state are plotted as four points. In addition, we plot the expected return on the security for each of the two possible returns on the market. These two points, each of which we designate by an X, are joined by a line called the characteristic line of the security. The slope of the line is 1.5, the number calculated in the previous paragraph. This responsiveness coefficient of 1.5 is the beta of Hicks.

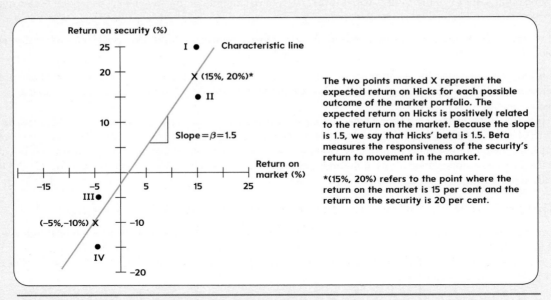

Figure 10.10 Performance of Hicks plc and the Market Portfolio

The interpretation of beta from Figure 10.10 is intuitive. The graph tells us that the returns of Hicks are magnified 1.5 times over those of the market. When the market does well, Hicks' equity is expected to do even better. When the market does poorly, Hicks' equity is expected to do even worse. Now imagine an individual with a portfolio near that of the market who is considering the addition of Hicks to her portfolio. Because of Hicks' *magnification factor* of 1.5, she will view this security as contributing much to the risk of the portfolio. (We will show shortly that the beta of the average security in the market is 1.) Hicks contributes more to the risk of a large, diversified portfolio than does an average security because Hicks is more responsive to movements in the market.

Further insight can be gleaned by examining securities with negative betas. One should view these securities as either hedges or insurance policies. The security is expected to do well when the market does poorly and vice versa. Because of this, adding a negative-beta security to a large, diversified portfolio actually reduces the risk of the portfolio.[13]

Table 10.7 presents empirical estimates of betas for individual securities. As can be seen, some securities are more responsive to the market than others. For example, Siemens has a beta of 1.51. This means that for every 1 per cent movement in the market, Siemens is expected to move 1.51 per cent in the same direction. Conversely, SAP has a beta of only 0.56. This means that for every 1 per cent movement in the market, SAP is expected to move 0.56 per cent in the same direction.

Table 10.7 Estimates of Beta for Selected Individual Equities

Stock	Beta
Alcatel-Lucent	1.44
L'Oreal	0.45
SAP	0.56
Siemens	1.51
Daimler	1.25
Philips	0.92
Renault	1.64
Volkswagen	0.40

Source: Yahoo! Finance © 2015 Yahoo! Inc.

The beta is defined as $\text{Cov}(R_i, R_M)/\text{Var}(R_M)$, where $\text{Cov}(R_i, R_M)$ is the covariance of the return on an individual equity, R_i, and the return on the market, R_M. $\text{Var}(R_M)$ is the variance of the return on the market, R_M.

We can summarize our discussion of beta by saying this:

Beta measures the responsiveness of a security to movements in the market portfolio.

The Formula for Beta

Our discussion so far has stressed the intuition behind beta. The actual definition of beta is:

$$\beta_i = \frac{\text{Cov}(R_i, R_M)}{\sigma^2(R_M)} \tag{10.15}$$

where $\text{Cov}(R_i, R_M)$ is the covariance between the return on asset i and the return on the market portfolio and $\sigma^2(R_M)$ is the variance of the market.

One useful property is that the average beta across all securities, when weighted by the proportion of each security's market value to that of the market portfolio, is 1. That is:

$$\sum_{i=1}^{N} X_i \beta_i = 1 \tag{10.16}$$

where X_i is the proportion of security i's market value to that of the entire market and N is the number of securities in the market.

Equation 10.16 is intuitive, once you think about it. If you weight all securities by their market values, the resulting portfolio is the market. By definition, the beta of the market portfolio is 1. That is, for every 1 per cent movement in the market, the market must move 1 per cent – *by definition*.

A Test

We have put these questions on past corporate finance examinations:

1   What sort of investor rationally views the variance (or standard deviation) of an individual security's return as the security's proper measure of risk?

2   What sort of investor rationally views the beta of a security as the security's proper measure of risk?

A good answer might be something like the following:

> A rational, risk-averse investor views the variance (or standard deviation) of her portfolio's return as the proper measure of the risk of her portfolio. If for some reason the investor can hold only one security, the variance of that security's return becomes the variance of the portfolio's return. Hence, the variance of the security's return is the security's proper measure of risk.
>
> If an individual holds a diversified portfolio, she still views the variance (or standard deviation) of her portfolio's return as the proper measure of the risk of her portfolio. However, she is no longer interested in the variance of each individual security's return. Rather, she is interested in the contribution of an individual security to the variance of the portfolio.

Under the assumption of homogeneous expectations, all individuals hold the market portfolio. Thus, we measure risk as the contribution of an individual security to the variance of the market portfolio. This contribution, when standardized properly, is the beta of the security. Although few investors hold the market portfolio exactly, many hold reasonably diversified portfolios. These portfolios are close enough to the market portfolio so that the beta of a security is likely to be a reasonable measure of its risk.

10.9   The Capital Asset Pricing Model

It is commonplace to argue that the expected return on an asset should be positively related to its risk. That is, individuals will hold a risky asset only if its expected return compensates for its risk. In this section, we first estimate the expected return on the stock market as a whole. Next, we estimate expected returns on individual securities.

Expected Return on Market

Economists frequently argue that the expected return on the market can be represented as:

$$\overline{R}_M = R_F + \text{Risk premium}$$

In words, the expected return on the market is the sum of the risk-free rate plus some compensation for the risk inherent in the market portfolio. Note that the equation refers to the *expected* return on the market, not the actual return in a particular month or year. Because equities have risk, the actual return on the market over a particular period can, of course, be below R_F or can even be negative.

Because investors want compensation for risk, the risk premium is presumably positive. But exactly how positive is it? It is generally argued that the place to start looking for the risk premium in the future is the average risk premium in the past. As reported in Chapter 9, the average return on large UK companies was 6.35 per cent over 1900–2010. The average risk-free rate over the same interval was 4.96 per cent. Thus, the average difference between the two was 1.39 per cent (= 6.35% − 4.96%). Financial economists find this to be a useful estimate of the difference to occur in the future.

For example, if the risk-free rate, estimated by the current yield on a one-year Treasury bill, is 1 per cent, the expected return on the market is:

$$2.39\% = 1\% + 1.39\%$$

Of course, the future equity risk premium could be higher or lower than the historical equity risk premium. This could be true if future risk is higher or lower than past risk or if individual risk aversions are higher or lower than those of the past.

Expected Return on an Individual Security

Now that we have estimated the expected return on the market as a whole, what is the expected return on an individual security? We have argued that the beta of a security is the appropriate measure of risk in a large, diversified portfolio. Because most investors are diversified, the expected return on a security should be positively related to its beta. This is illustrated in Figure 10.11.

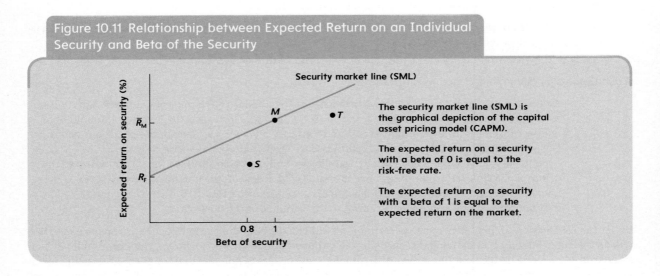

Figure 10.11 Relationship between Expected Return on an Individual Security and Beta of the Security

The security market line (SML) is the graphical depiction of the capital asset pricing model (CAPM).

The expected return on a security with a beta of 0 is equal to the risk-free rate.

The expected return on a security with a beta of 1 is equal to the expected return on the market.

Actually, economists can be more precise about the relationship between expected return and beta. They posit that under plausible conditions the relationship between expected return and beta can be represented by the following equation.[14]

Capital asset pricing model

$$\overline{R} = R_F + \beta \times (\overline{R}_M - R_F)$$

$\overline{R}$	R_F	β	$(\overline{R}_M - R_F)$	
Expected return on a security	Risk-free rate	Beta of the security	Difference between expected return on market and risk-free rate	(10.17)

This formula, which is called the **capital asset pricing model** (or **CAPM** for short), implies that the expected return on a security is linearly related to its beta. Because the average return on the market has been higher than the average risk-free rate over long periods of time, $\overline{R}_M - R_F$ is presumably positive. Thus, the formula implies that the expected return on a security is *positively* related to its beta. The formula can be illustrated by assuming a few special cases:

- *Assume that* $\beta = 0$. Here $\overline{R} = R_F$ — that is, the expected return on the security is equal to the risk-free rate. Because a security with zero beta has no relevant risk, its expected return should equal the risk-free rate.

- *Assume that* $\beta = 1$. Equation 10.17 reduces to $\overline{R} = \overline{R}_M$. That is, the expected return on the security is equal to the expected return on the market. This makes sense because the beta of the market portfolio is also 1.

Equation 10.17 can be represented graphically by the upward-sloping line in Figure 10.11. Note that the line begins at R_F and rises to $\overline{R}_M$ when beta is 1. This line is frequently called the security market line (SML).

As with any line, the SML has both a slope and an intercept. R_F, the risk-free rate, is the intercept. Because the beta of a security is the horizontal axis, $R_M - R_F$ is the slope. The line will be upward-sloping as long as the expected return on the market is greater than the risk-free rate. Because the market portfolio is a risky asset, theory suggests that its expected return is above the risk-free rate. As mentioned, the empirical evidence of the previous chapter showed that the average return per year on the market portfolio (for large UK companies as an example) over the past 111 years was 1.39 per cent above the risk-free rate.

Example 10.5

The shares of Aardvark Enterprises have a beta of 1.5 and that of Zebra Enterprises have a beta of 0.7. The risk-free rate is assumed to be 3 per cent, and the difference between the expected return on the market and the risk-free rate is assumed to be 8.0 per cent. The expected returns on the two securities are

Expected return for Aardvark

$$15.0\% = 3\% + 1.5 \times 8.0\% \tag{10.18}$$

Expected return for Zebra

$$8.6\% = 3\% + 0.7 \times 8.0\%$$

Three additional points concerning the CAPM should be mentioned:

1 *Linearity*: The intuition behind an upwardly sloping curve is clear. Because beta is the appropriate measure of risk, high-beta securities should have an expected return above that of low-beta securities. However, both Figure 10.11 and Equation 10.17 show something more than an upwardly sloping curve: the relationship between expected return and beta corresponds to a *straight* line.

   It is easy to show that the line of Figure 10.11 is straight. To see this, consider security S with, say, a beta of 0.8. This security is represented by a point below the security market line in the figure. Any investor could duplicate the beta of security S by buying a portfolio with 20 per cent in the risk-free asset and 80 per cent in a security with a beta of 1. However, the homemade portfolio would itself lie on the SML. In other words, the portfolio dominates security S because the portfolio has a higher expected return and the same beta.

   Now consider security T with, say, a beta greater than 1. This security is also below the SML in Figure 10.11. Any investor could duplicate the beta of security T by borrowing to invest in a security with a beta of 1. This portfolio must also lie on the SML, thereby dominating security T.

   Because no one would hold either S or T, their prices would drop. This price adjustment would raise the expected returns on the two securities. The price adjustment would continue until the two securities lay on the security market line. The preceding example considered two overpriced equities and a straight SML. Securities lying above the SML are *underpriced*. Their prices must rise until their expected returns lie on the line. If the SML is itself curved, many equities would be mispriced. In equilibrium, all securities would be held only when prices changed so that the SML became straight. In other words, linearity would be achieved.

2 *Portfolios as well as securities*: Our discussion of the CAPM considered individual securities. Does the relationship in Figure 10.11 and Equation 10.17 hold for portfolios as well?

   Yes. To see this, consider a portfolio formed by investing equally in our two securities from Example 10.5, Aardvark and Zebra. The expected return on the portfolio is:

Expected return on portfolio

$$11.8\% = 0.5 \times 15.0\% + 0.5 \times 8.6\% \qquad (10.19)$$

The beta of the portfolio is simply a weighted average of the betas of the two securities. Thus, we have:

Beta of portfolio

$$1.1 = 0.5 \times 1.5 + 0.5 \times 0.7$$

Under the CAPM, the expected return on the portfolio is

$$11.8\% = 3\% + 1.1 \times 8.0\% \qquad (10.20)$$

Because the expected return in Equation 10.19 is the same as the expected return in Equation 10.20, the example shows that the CAPM holds for portfolios as well as for individual securities.

3   *A potential confusion*: Students often confuse the SML in Figure 10.11 with line II in Figure 10.9. Actually, the lines are quite different. Line II traces the efficient set of portfolios formed from both risky assets and the riskless asset. Each point on the line represents an entire portfolio. Point A is a portfolio composed entirely of risky assets. Every other point on the line represents a portfolio of the securities in A combined with the riskless asset. The axes of Figure 10.9 are the expected return on a *portfolio* and the standard deviation of a *portfolio*. Individual securities do not lie along line II.

The SML in Figure 10.11 relates expected return to beta. Figure 10.11 differs from Figure 10.9 in at least two ways. First, beta appears in the horizontal axis of Figure 10.11, but standard deviation appears in the horizontal axis of Figure 10.9. Second, the SML in Figure 10.11 holds both for all individual securities and for all possible portfolios, whereas line II in Figure 10.9 holds only for efficient portfolios.

We stated earlier that, under homogeneous expectations, point A in Figure 10.9 becomes the market portfolio. In this situation, line II is referred to as the capital market line (CML).

Real World Insight 10.2

Enel SpA

Enel is Italy's largest power company and Europe's second largest utility firm with operations in over 40 countries. To find the expected return on Enel equity using the CAPM, you must collect three data items: the company's beta, the risk-free rate, and the expected market risk premium.

Beta:

Go to any financial website (examples include Yahoo! Finance, Google Finance, Reuters) and search for Enel. According to FT.Com, Enel's beta is 1.04.

Enel SpA ENEL:MIL ☑				
4.40	↑ 0.01 / 0.23%	8.27m	↑ 9.13%	1.04
Latest price in EUR	Today's change	Shares traded	1 year change	Beta

Source: FT.com.

Risk-Free Rate:

When using CAPM for corporate finance purposes, such as investment decisions, the rule of thumb is to use the 10-year government bond yield. This is because we are matching the term of the risk-free security with a typical life of an investment. A search of the markets data page on FT.com shows that Italian 10-year government bond yields are 1.3 per cent.

Expected Market Risk Premium:

There are many ways to forecast future market returns, but all methods suffer from the fact that you are trying to predict the future. For our purposes, we will use the information in Table 9.3 from Chapter 9 and go with the historical Italian market risk premium of 7.2 per cent.

Ten Year Government Bond Spreads			
Country	Latest Yield	Spread vs Bund	Spread vs T-bonds
Austria	2.4%	+2.21	+0.42
Australia	0.3%	+0.14	−1.65
Belgium	0.4%	+0.27	−1.52
Canada	1.4%	+1.21	−0.58
Denmark	0.3%	+0.13	−1.65
Finland	0.3%	+0.13	−1.66
France	0.5%	+0.29	−1.50
Germany	0.2%	—	−1.79
Greece	11.1%	+10.92	+9.14
Ireland	0.7%	+0.55	−1.24
Italy	1.3%	+1.10	−0.69

Using this information, we can now estimate the expected return on Enel SpA shares.

$$E(R_{Enel}) = r_f + \beta(E(R_m) - r_f) = 1.3 + 1.04(7.2) = 8.788\%$$

10.10   Criticisms of the CAPM

The capital asset pricing model represents one of the most important advances in financial economics. It is clearly useful for investment purposes because it shows how the expected return on an asset is related to its beta. In addition, we will show in Chapter 12 that it is useful in corporate finance because the discount rate on a project is a function of the project's beta. However, never forget that, as with any other model, the CAPM is not revealed truth but, rather, a construct to be empirically tested and give some insights into what is reality. Nobody who works in finance will ever say that they believe the CAPM fully explains the returns on securities, investments or financial portfolios. All the CAPM does, as with any other theoretical model, is give insights into the truth.

Roll's (1977) Critique of CAPM

Before we discuss empirical tests, it is important to understand whether CAPM can be tested at all. Richard Roll, in the *Journal of Financial Economics*, argued that, because it is practically impossible to construct a portfolio that contains every single security (i.e. the true market portfolio), any test of the CAPM that uses a market proxy (e.g. FTSE 100, DAX, CAC 40, etc.) will be testing that specific portfolio, and not the true market portfolio. This means that, for all intents and purposes, the CAPM is empirically untestable because the underlying market portfolio is unobservable. Any tests of the CAPM that use market proxies will be affected by this criticism.

Academics have spent a lot of time debating the merits of Roll's (1977) critique. However, use of the model in corporate finance and investment is widespread. Financial websites, such as Yahoo! Finance, Bloomberg, and FT.com, frequently provide estimates of the beta of listed firms. Given its massive popularity, and taking into account the weaknesses associated with any empirical tests, it is important to know whether the CAPM is successful in explaining at least some of the variation in security returns.

Empirical Tests of the CAPM

The first empirical tests of the CAPM occurred over 30 years ago and were quite supportive of the model. Using data from the 1930s to the 1960s on US stock markets, researchers showed that the average return on a portfolio of stocks was positively related to the beta of the portfolio[15] – a finding consistent with the CAPM. Though some evidence in these studies was less consistent with the CAPM,[16] financial economists were quick to embrace the model following these empirical papers.

Although a large body of empirical work developed in the following decades, often with varying results, the CAPM was not seriously called into question until the 1990s. Two papers by Fama and French (1992, 1993) present evidence inconsistent with the model. Their work has received a great deal of attention, both in academic circles and in the popular press, with newspaper articles displaying headlines such as 'Beta Is Dead!' These papers make two related points. First, they conclude that, for US firms, the relationship between average return and beta is weak over the period from 1941 to 1990 and virtually non-existent from 1963 to 1990. Second, they argue that the average return on a security is negatively related to both the firm's price–earnings (PE) ratio and the firm's market-to-book (MB) ratio. Other research has provided strong evidence against the CAPM by showing that securities which have performed well in the recent past tend to have higher returns in the near future (Carhart's (1997) momentum factor). In addition, Ang et al. (2006) found that equities with a greater sensitivity to stock market volatility have lower returns than control firms with the same systematic risk. Finally, it is possible that these results are only applicable in the United States. However, the poor performance of beta has also been found in other countries by Fama and French (1998).

These contentions, if confirmed by other research, would be quite damaging to the CAPM. After all, the CAPM states that the expected returns on equities should be related only to beta, and not to other factors such as PE, MB, momentum or market volatility.

A number of researchers have criticized this type of research carried out by Fama and French. We avoid an in-depth discussion of the fine points of the debate, but we mention a few issues. First, although Fama and French, Carhart and Ang et al. cannot reject the hypothesis that average returns are unrelated to beta, they also cannot reject the hypothesis that average returns are related to beta exactly as specified by the CAPM. In other words, although 50 years of data seem like a lot, they may simply not be enough to test the CAPM properly. Second, the results may be due to a statistical fallacy called a hindsight bias.[17] Third, PE, MB, momentum and market volatility are merely four of an infinite number of possible factors. Thus, the relationship between average return and these variables may be spurious, being nothing more than the result of data mining. Fourth, average returns on US stocks are positively related to beta over the period from 1927 to the present. There appears to be no compelling reason for emphasizing a shorter period than this one. Fifth, average returns are actually positively related to beta over shorter periods when annual data, rather than monthly data, are used to estimate beta.[18] There appears to be no compelling reason for preferring either monthly data over annual data or vice versa. Thus, we believe that although the results of Fama and French, Carhart, Ang et al. and others are quite intriguing, they cannot be viewed as the final word.

10.11 Variations of the CAPM

The CAPM relates an individual security's expected return to the expected return on the market portfolio through its systematic risk, beta. Beta measures the sensitivity of an investor's wealth to movements in the underlying market portfolio. Many academics have argued that wealth, in itself, is not important in pricing securities. Instead, it is the effect of an investment on the consumption, or spending power of an investor that is relevant. So, the more that an investment makes consumption riskier, the higher should be its expected returns.

This view has led to a variation of the CAPM, known as the Consumption Capital Asset Pricing Model, or CCAPM. Systematic risk, or beta, in the CAPM measures the covariance of security returns with market returns. However, in the CCAPM, beta is slightly more complex. The CCAPM is expressed as follows:

$$\underset{\substack{\text{Expected} \\ \text{return} \\ \text{on a security}}}{\overline{R}} \quad = \quad \underset{\substack{\text{Risk-free} \\ \text{rate}}}{R_F} \quad + \quad \underset{\substack{\text{Consumption} \\ \text{beta of the} \\ \text{security}}}{\beta_c} \quad \times \quad \underset{\substack{\text{Difference between} \\ \text{expected return on market} \\ \text{and risk-free rate}}}{(\overline{R}_M - R_F)}$$
(10.21)

where the consumption beta, β_c, is equal to:

$$\beta_C = \frac{\text{Cov}(\overline{R}, \text{consumption growth})}{\text{Cov}(\overline{R}_M, \text{consumption growth})}$$

In the CCAPM, if a security has a higher expected return when consumption growth is higher, its consumption beta will be high. Similarly, a low covariance between security returns and consumption growth will lead to a lower CCAPM beta.

Another variation in the CAPM recognizes that not all of an individual's wealth comes from financial assets. In recent years, many people increased their wealth through investment in non-financial (human capital) assets such as housing and property. This was particularly true in Europe (especially the UK and Spain) where property values (until 2008) had been growing at more than 10 per cent per annum and more recently in high growth emerging markets like China and India. The Human Capital CAPM, or HCAPM, incorporates both sources of wealth creation. According to the HCAPM, the return on the expected market portfolio is a linear combination (weighted by the relative investment of assets) of the expected return on the underlying financial portfolio and the underlying non-financial portfolio. If δ represents the fraction of total wealth that is invested in non-financial assets (or human capital), and $\overline{R}_{NF}$ and $\overline{R}_F$ represent the expected returns on non-financial and financial assets respectively, the expected return on the market is equal to:

$$\overline{R}_M = \delta\,\overline{R}_{NF} + (1 - \delta)\overline{R}_F$$

The expected return on financial assets is simply the market portfolio of the CAPM, whereas the expected return on non-financial assets is normally taken to be the growth in average earnings, or labour income. The HCAPM has the same form as the normal CAPM. However, if the expected return on the market portfolio is disaggregated into its two components, the expected return on a security can be expressed as a linear function of its financial and non-financial betas. In this form, the expected return on a security is expressed as follows:

$$\overline{R} = \beta_0 + \beta_F\overline{R}_F + \beta_{NF}\,\overline{R}_{NF}$$

Although both the CCAPM and HCAPM are theoretically sound, because of the difficulties in using the model with real data, the models do not tend to be used in practice. The CCAPM requires reliable data on total consumption growth, and the HCAPM utilizes data on non-financial wealth, both of which are rarely available on a continuing basis. For this reason, the standard CAPM is the most commonly used theoretical model in corporate finance.

Summary and Conclusions

This chapter set forth the fundamentals of modern portfolio theory. Our basic points are these:

1. This chapter showed us how to calculate the expected return and variance for individual securities, and the covariance and correlation for pairs of securities. Given these statistics, the expected return and variance for a portfolio of two securities A and B can be written as:

    $$\text{Expected return on portfolio} = X_A\overline{R}_A + X_B\overline{R}_B$$
    $$\text{Var (portfolio)} = X_A^2\,\sigma_A^2 + 2X_A X_B\,\sigma_{AB} + X_B^2\,\sigma_B^2$$

2. In our notation, X stands for the proportion of a security in a portfolio. By varying X we can trace out the efficient set of portfolios. We graphed the efficient set for the two-asset case as a curve, pointing out that the degree of curvature or bend in the graph reflects the diversification effect: the lower the correlation between the two securities, the greater the bend. The same general shape of the efficient set holds in a world of many assets.

3   Just as the formula for variance in the two-asset case is computed from a 2×2 matrix, the variance formula is computed from an $N \times N$ matrix in the N-asset case. We showed that with a large number of assets, there are many more covariance terms than variance terms in the matrix. In fact the variance terms are effectively diversified away in a large portfolio, but the covariance terms are not. Thus, a diversified portfolio can eliminate some, but not all, of the risk of the individual securities.

4   The efficient set of risky assets can be combined with riskless borrowing and lending. In this case a rational investor will always choose to hold the portfolio of risky securities represented by point A in Figure 10.9. Then he can either borrow or lend at the riskless rate to achieve any desired point on line II in the figure.

5   The contribution of a security to the risk of a large, well-diversified portfolio is proportional to the covariance of the security's return with the market's return. This contribution, when standardized, is called the beta. The beta of a security can also be interpreted as the responsiveness of a security's return to that of the market.

6   The CAPM states that:

$$\overline{R} = R_F + \beta(\overline{R}_M - R_F)$$

In other words, the expected return on a security is positively (and linearly) related to the security's beta.

7   The CAPM is a theoretical construct and only gives an insight into reality. Other theoretical models exist that do just as good a job at explaining variation in expected security returns.

Questions and Problems

CONCEPT

1   **Individual Securities**   What are the main characteristics of individual security returns? Provide a definition of each characteristic and why it is important.

2   **Expected Return, Variance and Covariance**   Explain what is meant by correlation and how it is used to measure the relationship between the returns on two securities. How is correlation related to variance and covariance? Use mathematical formulae to illustrate your answer. If a portfolio has a positive investment in every asset, can the expected return on the portfolio be greater or less than on every asset in the portfolio?

3   **Portfolio Risk and Return**   Why does naïve diversification reduce the risk of a portfolio? What benefits does naïve diversification bring to international investment strategies?

4   **The Efficient Set for Two Assets**   What is a minimum variance portfolio? In a world with only two assets, is it possible to have two portfolios with the same risk but different expected return? Explain your answer using a practical example. What is the two-fund spanning property of the efficient frontier?

5   **The Efficient Set for Many Securities**   In a portfolio of many securities, all having positive correlation with each other, is it possible for the minimum variance portfolio to have zero risk? What happens to the efficient frontier when a risk-free asset exists?

6   **Diversification**   Assume that every asset has the same expected return and variance. Furthermore, all assets have the same covariance with each other. As the number of assets in the portfolio grows, which becomes more important: variance or covariance? Clarify your answer using words, diagrams, formulae or a practical example.

7   **Riskless Borrowing and Lending**   Explain what is meant by an optimal portfolio. What are the conditions that must exist for there to be only one optimal portfolio? Do you think these conditions are likely to persist in the real world? Explain.

8   **Market Equilibrium**   Your company is following two stocks, ABC plc and XYZ plc, and your manager tells you the following:

'The shares of ABC plc have traded close to £15 for most of the past 4 years, and because of this lack of price movement the stock has a very low beta. XYZ plc, on the other hand, has traded as high as £90 and as low as its current £20. Since this stock has demonstrated a large amount of price movement, the stock has a very high beta.'

Do you agree with your manager's analysis?

9 **Relationship between Risk and Expected Return** Is it possible that a risky asset could have a beta of zero? Explain. Based on the CAPM, what is the expected return on such an asset? Is it possible that a risky asset could have a negative beta? What does the CAPM predict about the expected return on such an asset? Can you give an explanation for your answer? Discuss the central predictions of the CAPM and give an overview of the empirical evidence.

10 **Criticisms of the CAPM** Define the market portfolio and provide a brief overview of Roll's Critique. Do you agree or disagree with it? Why?

11 **Variations of the CAPM** Explain what is meant by the CCAPM and the HCAPM. Why do you think these models are not popular with practitioners? Give an overview of the empirical evidence concerning these models and their performance relative to the CAPM.

REGULAR

12 **Systematic Versus Unsystematic Risk** Classify the following events as mostly systematic or mostly unsystematic:

(a) The Bank of England's base rate increases unexpectedly.

(b) A company renegotiates its bank debt after breaching a covenant agreement.

(c) Oil prices unexpectedly decline.

(d) No clear winner in the British general election.

(e) A bank loses a multimillion-pound lawsuit for the mis-selling of derivative products.

13 **Short Selling** Explain what is meant by short selling. When is short selling profitable?

14 **Risk** A broker has advised you not to invest in technology stocks because they have high standard deviations. Is the broker's advice sound for a risk-averse investor like yourself? Why or why not?

15 **Using CAPM** An equity has a beta of 0.9 and an expected return of 9 per cent. A risk-free asset currently earns 2 per cent.

(a) What is the expected return on a portfolio that is equally invested in the two assets?

(b) If a portfolio of the two assets has a beta of 0.6, what are the portfolio weights?

(c) If a portfolio of the two assets has an expected return of 6 per cent, what is its beta?

(d) If a portfolio of the two assets has a beta of 1.50, what are the portfolio weights? How do you interpret the weights for the two assets in this case? Explain.

16 **Portfolio Risk** Assume that the risk-free rate is 3 per cent and the expected return on the FTSE 100 index is 9 per cent. The standard deviation of the market index is 23 per cent. You are managing the pension fund of your company and would like to achieve an expected return of 5 per cent. How should your company's pension portfolio be structured so as to achieve this expected return? What is the risk of this portfolio?

17 **Using the SML** W has an expected return of 12 per cent and a beta of 1.2. If the risk-free rate is 3 per cent, complete the following table for portfolios of W and a risk-free asset. Illustrate the relationship between portfolio expected return and portfolio beta by plotting the expected returns against the betas. What is the slope of the line that results?

Percentage of Portfolio in W	Portfolio Expected Return	Portfolio Beta
0		
25		
50		
75		
100		
125		
150		

18 **Reward-to-Risk Ratios** Y has a beta of 1.50 and an expected return of 17 per cent. Z has a beta of 0.80 and an expected return of 10.5 per cent. If the risk-free rate is 5.5 per cent and the market risk premium is 7.5 per cent, are these equities correctly priced? What would the risk-free rate have to be for the two equities to be correctly priced?

19 **Portfolio Returns and Deviations** Shares in Hellenic Telecom have an expected return of 15 per cent and the standard deviation of these returns is 30 per cent. National Bank of Greece's shares are expected to produce a return of 16 per cent with a standard deviation of 40 per cent. What would be the rate of return and risk of a portfolio made up of 40 per cent of Hellenic Telecom's shares and 60 per cent of National Bank of Greece's shares, if the returns on these shares have a correlation of 0.6?

20 **Analysing a Portfolio** You want to create a portfolio equally as risky as the market, and you have €1,000,000 to invest. Given this information, fill in the rest of the following table:

Asset	Investment (€)	Beta
Equity A	200,000	0.80
Equity B	250,000	1.30
Equity C		1.50
Risk-free asset		

21 **Analysing a Portfolio** You have £24,000 to invest in a portfolio containing X, Y and a risk-free asset. You must invest all of your money. Your goal is to create a portfolio that has an expected return of 8.5 per cent and that has only 70 per cent of the risk of the overall market. If X has an expected return of 12 per cent and a beta of 1.5, Y has an expected return of 9 per cent and a beta of 1.2, and the risk-free rate is 3 per cent, how much money will you invest in X? How do you interpret your answer?

22 **Covariance and Correlation** Based on the following information, calculate the expected return and standard deviation of each of the following equities. Assume each state of the economy is equally likely to happen. What are the covariance and correlation between the returns of the two equities?

State of Economy	Return on A	Return on B
Bear	0.063	−0.037
Normal	0.105	0.064
Bull	0.156	0.253

23 **Covariance and Correlation** Based on the following information, calculate the expected return and standard deviation for each of the following equities. What are the covariance and correlation between the returns of the two equities?

State of Economy	Probability of State of Economy	Return on J	Return on K
Bear	0.25	−0.020	0.050
Normal	0.60	0.092	0.062
Bull	0.15	0.154	0.074

24 **Portfolio Standard Deviation** Suppose the expected returns and standard deviations of A and B are $E(R_A) = 0.15$, $E(R_B) = 0.25$, $\sigma_A = 0.40$, and $\sigma_B = 0.65$, respectively.

(a) Calculate the expected return and standard deviation of a portfolio that is composed of 40 per cent A and 60 per cent B when the correlation between the returns on A and B is 0.5.

(b) Calculate the standard deviation of a portfolio that is composed of 40 per cent A and 60 per cent B when the correlation coefficient between the returns on A and B is −0.5.

(c) How does the correlation between the returns on A and B affect the standard deviation of the portfolio?

25 **Correlation and Beta** You have been provided the following data about the equities of three firms, the market portfolio, and the risk-free asset:

	Expected Return	Standard Deviation	Correlation*	Beta
Firm A	0.13	0.38	(i)	0.9
Firm B	0.16	(ii)	0.40	1.1
Firm C	0.25	0.65	0.35	(iii)

	Expected Return	Standard Deviation	Correlation*	Beta
The market portfolio	0.15	0.20	(iv)	(v)
The risk-free asset	0.05	(vi)	(vii)	(viii)

*With the market portfolio.

(a) Fill in the missing values in the table.

(b) Is the equity of Firm A correctly priced according to the capital asset pricing model (CAPM)? What about the equity of Firm B? Firm C? If these securities are not correctly priced, what is your investment recommendation for someone with a well-diversified portfolio?

26 CML The market portfolio has an expected return of 12 per cent and a standard deviation of 10 per cent. The risk-free rate is 5 per cent.

(a) What is the expected return on a well-diversified portfolio with a standard deviation of 7 per cent?

(b) What is the standard deviation of a well-diversified portfolio with an expected return of 20 per cent?

27 CAPM The expected rates of return on the French firms, Publicis and Renault, the market portfolio (CAC 40) and the risk-free asset are given below, along with the standard deviations of these returns.

Asset	Expected Return (%)	Standard Deviation (%)
Publicis	17	40
Renault	10	20
CAC 40	14	17
Risk-free asset	3	0

(a) Assuming that the returns are explained by the capital asset pricing model, specify the betas for Publicis and Renault and the risk of a portfolio of Publicis and Renault with an expected return the same as the CAC 40.

(b) Specify the composition of a portfolio consisting of the CAC 40 and the risk-free asset that will produce an expected return of 10 per cent. Contrast the risk on this portfolio with the risk of Renault.

28 Portfolios Below is given the standard deviation and correlation information on three South African companies, Afgri, Harmony Gold and SABMiller.

	Afgri	Harmony Gold	SABMiller	Standard Deviation (%)
Afgri	1	−0.2	0.5	29
Harmony Gold		1	0.4	21
SABMiller			1	23

(a) If a portfolio is made up of 30 per cent of Afgri, 40 per cent of Harmony Gold and 30 per cent of SABMiller, estimate the portfolio's standard deviation.

(b) If you were asked to design a portfolio using just Harmony Gold and Afgri, what percentage investment in each share would produce a zero standard deviation?

CHALLENGE

29 Systematic versus Unsystematic Risk Consider the following information about I and II:

State of Economy	Probability of State of Economy	Rate of Return if State Occurs	
		I	II
Recession	0.15	0.09	−0.30
Normal	0.70	0.42	0.12
Irrational exuberance	0.15	0.26	0.44

The market risk premium is 10 per cent, and the risk-free rate is 4 per cent. Which security has the most systematic risk? Which one has the most unsystematic risk? Which stock is 'riskier'? Explain.

30 CML and SML Explain in detail, using diagrams to illustrate your answer, what is meant by the terms 'capital market line' and 'security market line'.

31 SML   Suppose you observe the following situation:

Security	Beta	Expected Return
Renewable Energy Corp	1.3	0.23
STATOIL	0.6	0.13

Assume these securities are correctly priced. Based on the CAPM, what is the expected return on the market? What is the risk-free rate?

32 Portfolio Theory   This question is designed to test your understanding of the mean standard deviation diagram.

(a) Draw a mean-standard deviation diagram to illustrate combinations of a risky asset and the risk-free asset.

(b) Extend this concept to a diagram of the risk-free asset and all possible risky portfolios.

(c) Why does one line, the capital market line, dominate all other possible portfolio combinations?

(d) Label the capital market line and that optimal portfolio.

(e) What condition must hold at the optimal portfolio?

33 Covariance and Portfolio Standard Deviation   There are three securities in the market. The following chart shows their possible pay-offs:

State	Probability of Outcome	Return on Security 1	Return on Security 2	Return on Security 3
1	0.10	0.25	0.25	0.10
2	0.40	0.20	0.15	0.15
3	0.40	0.15	0.20	0.20
4	0.10	0.10	0.10	0.25

(a) What are the expected return and standard deviation of each security?

(b) What are the covariances and correlations between the pairs of securities?

(c) What are the expected return and standard deviation of a portfolio with half of its funds invested in security 1 and half in security 2?

(d) What are the expected return and standard deviation of a portfolio with half of its funds invested in security 1 and half in security 3?

(e) What are the expected return and standard deviation of a portfolio with half of its funds invested in security 2 and half in security 3?

(f) What do your answers in parts (a), (c), (d) and (e) imply about diversification?

34 SML   Suppose you observe the following situation:

		Return if State Occurs	
State of Economy	Probability of State	A	B
Bust	0.25	−0.10	−0.30
Normal	0.50	0.10	0.05
Boom	0.25	0.20	0.40

(a) Calculate the expected return on each equity.

(b) Assuming the capital asset pricing model holds and A's beta is greater than B's beta by 0.25, what is the expected market risk premium?

35 Standard Deviation and Beta   There are two securities in the market, A and B. The price of A today is €50. The price of A next year will be €40 if the economy is in a recession, €55 if the economy is normal, and €60 if the economy is expanding. The probabilities of recession, normal times and expansion are 0.1, 0.8 and 0.1, respectively. A pays no dividends and has a correlation of 0.8 with the market portfolio. B has an expected return of 9 per cent, a standard deviation of 12 per cent, a correlation with the market portfolio of 0.2, and a correlation with A of 0.6. The market portfolio has a standard deviation of 10 per cent. Assume the CAPM holds.

(a) If you are a typical, risk-averse investor with a well-diversified portfolio, which security would you prefer? Why?

(b) What are the expected return and standard deviation of a portfolio consisting of 70 per cent of A and 30 per cent of B?

(c) What is the beta of the portfolio in part (b)?

36 Company Beta   Weir Group plc has three main divisions: Oil & Gas, Minerals, Power & Industrial. Oil & Gas accounts for 40 per cent of the company's assets and Minerals accounts for 35 per cent of the assets. It has been estimated that the asset betas for these divisions are 1.2, 0.8 and 0.6 respectively. The company employs 30 per cent debt in its capital structure. Estimate the beta of Weir Group's equity if the debt is risk-free.

37 Minimum Variance Portfolio   Assume A and B have the following characteristics:

Equity	Expected Return (%)	Standard Deviation (%)
A	5	10
B	10	20

The covariance between the returns on the two equities is 0.001.

(a)   Suppose an investor holds a portfolio consisting of only A and B. Find the portfolio weights, X_A and X_B, such that the variance of her portfolio is minimized. (*Hint:* Remember that the sum of the two weights must equal 1.)

(b)   What is the expected return on the minimum variance portfolio?

(c)   If the covariance between the returns on the two equities is -0.02, what are the minimum variance weights?

(d)   What is the variance of the portfolio in part (c)?

38 CAPM   An investor holds a portfolio of 3 securities. She invests 30 per cent in A, 30 per cent in B, and 40 per cent in C. The betas on A, B, and C are 1.5, 0.6 and 1.1 respectively. If $E(R_M) = 12\%$ and $R_F = 4\%$, calculate the expected return and beta of the portfolio.

39 Minimum Variance Portfolio   Consider the table below. Using either the historical return or expected return and Solver, compute the minimum variance portfolio for the universe of three Norwegian shares, Crew Gold, GGS and Marine Harvest, described below. Assume the risk-free return is 6 per cent. Which return measure did you use and why?

Stock	Correlation with			Expected Return (%)	Historical Return (%)	Variance
	Crew Gold	GGS	Marine Harvest			
Crew Gold	1	0.40	0.45	16	20.65	168
GGS	0.40	1	-0.09	10	-34.15	231
Marine Harvest	0.45	-0.09	1	30	68.6	433

40 Beta   The following prices are for the British insurer ADX plc and the FTSE 100 Index.

Date	ADX plc	FTSE 100
Mar-15	1,187.00	5,768.50
Feb-15	1,077.00	5,871.50
Jan-15	941.00	5,681.60
Dec-14	852.00	5,572.30
Nov-14	922.50	5,505.40
Oct-14	1,179.00	5,544.20
Sep-14	1,263.00	5,128.50
Aug-14	1,365.00	5,394.50
Jul-14	1,549.00	5,815.20
Jun-14	1,661.00	5,945.70
May-14	1,723.00	5,990.00
Apr-14	1,692.00	6,069.90
Mar-14	1,554.00	5,908.80

Use a spreadsheet to calculate ADX plc's beta for the full period. Now calculate the beta using data for March 2014 to September 2014. Calculate the beta for October 2014 to March 2015. What can you say about the different beta estimates? Is this evidence for or against CAPM? Explain your answer.

Exam Question (45 minutes)

Below, you are given the expected returns and standard deviations of L'Oreal and Daimler AG, the Euro Stoxx 50 Index of largest Eurozone firms, and the risk-free asset.

Asset	Expected Return (%)	Standard Deviation (%)
L'Oreal	16	30
Daimler	12	25
Euro Stoxx 50	13	12
Risk-free asset	3	0

1   Assuming that the returns are explained by the capital asset pricing model, calculate the betas of L'Oreal and Daimler and the risk of a portfolio holding L'Oreal and Daimler with an expected return the same as the Euro Stoxx 50 Index return. (20 marks)

2   Construct a portfolio consisting of the Euro Stoxx 50 Index and the risk-free asset that will produce an expected return of 12 per cent. Contrast the risk on this portfolio with the risk of Daimler. (20 marks)

3   Assuming that the expected return on an average security is 13 per cent with a standard deviation of 26 per cent and the average covariance of returns between securities is +100, determine the expected risk of a portfolio with 28 securities and a portfolio with 1,000 securities. Comment briefly on your results. (20 marks)

4   Now assume that the returns on securities are independent. Continuing to assume that the expected return on an average security is 13 per cent with a standard deviation of 26 per cent, determine the risk of a portfolio with 28 securities and 1,000 securities. Comment on your results. (20 marks)

5   Explain what is meant by the separation principle. (20 marks)

Mini Case

A Job at West Coast Yachts, Part 2

You are discussing your retirement plan with Dan Ervin when he mentions that Sarah Brown, a representative from Skandla Financial Services, is visiting West Coast Yachts today. You decide that you should meet with Sarah, so Dan sets up an appointment for you later in the day.

When you sit down with Sarah, she discusses the various investment options available in the company's retirement account. You mention to Sarah that you researched West Coast Yachts before you accepted your new job. You are confident in management's ability to lead the company. Analysis of the company has led to your belief that the company is growing and will achieve a greater market share in the future. Given these considerations, you are leaning toward investing 100 per cent of your retirement account in West Coast Yachts.

Assume the risk-free rate is the return on a 30-day T-bill. The correlation between the Skandla bond fund and large-cap equity fund is 0.27.

1   Considering the effects of diversification, how should Sarah respond to the suggestion that you invest 100 per cent of your retirement account in West Coast Yachts?

2   Sarah's response to investing your retirement account entirely in West Coast Yachts has convinced you that this may not be the best alternative. You now consider that a 100 per cent investment in the bond fund may be the best alternative. Is it?

3   Using the returns for the Skandla Large-Cap Equity Fund and the Skandla Bond Fund, graph the opportunity set of feasible portfolios.

4   After examining the opportunity set, you notice that you can invest in a portfolio consisting of the bond fund and the large-cap equity fund that will have exactly the same standard deviation as the bond fund. This portfolio will also have a greater expected return. What are the portfolio weights and expected return of this portfolio?

5   Examining the opportunity set, notice there is a portfolio that has the lowest standard deviation. This is the minimum variance portfolio. What are the portfolio weights, expected return, and standard deviation of this portfolio? Why is the minimum variance portfolio important?

6   A measure of risk-adjusted performance that is often used is the Sharpe ratio. The Sharpe ratio is calculated as the risk premium of an asset divided by its standard deviation. The portfolio with the highest possible Sharpe ratio on the opportunity set is called the Sharpe optimal portfolio. What are the portfolio weights, expected return, and standard deviation of the Sharpe optimal portfolio? How does the Sharpe ratio of this portfolio compare to the Sharpe ratios of the bond fund and the large-cap equity fund? Do you see a connection between the Sharpe optimal portfolio and the CAPM?

Practical Case Study

Using CAPM In Yahoo! Finance, you can find estimates of beta for companies under the 'Detailed Data' link. Locate the beta for Associated British Foods (ABF.L) and Diageo (DGE.L). Using an estimate of the historical risk-free rate and market risk premium, calculate the expected return for each company based on the most recent beta. Is the expected return for each company what you would expect? Why or why not?

References

Ang, A., R.J. Hodrick, Y. Xing and X. Zhang (2006) 'The Cross-section of Volatility and Expected Returns', *The Journal of Finance*, Vol. 51, 259–299.

Black, F., M.C. Jensen and M.S. Scholes (1972) 'The Capital Asset Pricing Model: Some Empirical Tests', in M. Jensen (ed.), *Studies in the Theory of Capital Markets* (New York: Praeger).

Breen, W.J. and R.A. Koraczyk (1993) 'On Selection Biases in Book-to-Market Based Tests of Asset Pricing Models', unpublished paper, Northwestern University, November.

Carhart, M. (1997) 'On Persistence in Mutual Fund Performance', *The Journal of Finance*, Vol. 52, 57–82.

Fama, E.F. and K.R. French (1992) 'The Cross-Section of Expected Stock Returns', *The Journal of Finance*, Vol. 47, 427–466.

Fama, E.F. and K.R. French (1993) 'Common Risk Factors in the Returns on Stocks and Bonds', *Journal of Financial Economics*, Vol. 17, 3–56.

Fama, E.F. and K.R. French (1998) 'Value versus Growth: The International Evidence', *The Journal of Finance*, Vol. 53, 1975–1999.

Fama, E.F. and J. MacBeth (1973) 'Risk, Return and Equilibrium: Some Empirical Tests', *Journal of Political Economy*, Vol. 8, 607–636.

Kothari, S.P., J. Shanken and R.G. Sloan (1995) 'Another Look at the Cross-Section of Expected Stock Returns', *The Journal of Finance*, Vol. 50, No. 1, 185–224.

Markowitz, H. (1959) *Portfolio Selection* (New York: John Wiley and Sons).

Roll, R. (1977) 'A Critique of the Asset Pricing Theory's Tests', *Journal of Financial Economics*, Vol. 4, 129–176.

Statman, M. (1987) 'How Many Stocks Make a Diversified Portfolio?', *Journal of Financial Quantitative Analysis*, Vol. 22, No. 3, 353–363.

Additional Reading

Capital asset pricing theory is probably the most tested theory in modern investment finance. Given this, it is important that the interested reader is directed to the most relevant recent research in the area. A number of papers listed below directly test the power of the CAPM or market model beta under a variety of environments and with a number of other control variables. While it is easy to say that the range of CAPM anomalies suggests that the model is inferior to other, more complex, models, it is still the most commonly used way to estimate the cost of equity (discount rate) of a listed firm. Most of the papers listed below study the US markets. Those papers that consider other countries are highlighted in bold. The list does not follow any real theme, as is the case in other chapters. Moreover, the listing is a very small representation of recent research in the area. Those who wish to specialize should view the references as the tip of the iceberg and use them to build up their own reading list.

1   Ang, A., R. Hodrick, Y. Xing and X. Zhang (2009) 'High Idiosyncratic Volatility and Low Returns: International and Further Evidence', *Journal of Financial Economics*, Vol. 91, No. 1, 1–23. **International**.

2   Bodnaruk, A., and P. Ostberg (2009) 'Does Investor Recognition Predict Returns?', *Journal of Financial Economics*, Vol. 91, No. 2, 208–226. **Sweden**.

3   Burlacu, R., P. Fontaine, S. Jimenez-Garcès and M.S. Seasholes (2012) 'Risk and the Cross Section of Stock Returns', *Journal of Financial Economics*, Vol. 105, No. 3, 511–522.

4   Fama, E.F. and K.R. French (2006) 'The Value Premium and the CAPM', *The Journal of Finance*, Vol. 61, No. 5, 2163–2185. **US**.

5   Fama, E.F. and K.R. French (2012) 'Size, Value, and Momentum in International Stock Returns' *Journal of Financial Economics*, Vol. 105, No. 3, 457–472.

6   Fu, F. (2009) 'Idiosyncratic Risk and the Cross-Section of Expected Stock Returns', *Journal of Financial Economics*, Vol. 91, No. 1, 24–37. **US**.

7   Gârleanu, N., L. Kogan and S. Panageas (2012) 'Displacement Risk and Asset Returns', *Journal of Financial Economics*, Vol. 105, No. 3, 491–510.

8   Kearney, C. and V. Poti (2008) 'Have European Stocks Become More Volatile? An Empirical Investigation of Idiosyncratic and Market Risk in the Euro Area', *European Financial Management*, Vol. 14, No. 3, 419–444. **Europe**.

9   Kumar, P., S.M. Sorescu, R.D. Boehme and B.R. Danielsen (2008) 'Estimation Risk, Information, and the Conditional CAPM: Theory and Evidence', *Review of Financial Studies*, Vol. 21, No. 3, 1037–1075. **US**.

10   Lewellen, J. and S. Nagel (2006) 'The Conditional CAPM Does Not Explain Asset-Pricing Anomalies', *Journal of Financial Economics*, Vol. 82, No. 2, 289–314. **US**.

11   Novy-Marx, R. (2013) 'The Other Side of Value: The Gross Profitability Premium', *Journal of Financial Economics*, Vol. 108, No. 1, 1–28.

12   Pastor, L. (2000) 'Portfolio Selection and Asset Pricing Models', *The Journal of Finance*, Vol. 55, No. 1, 179–223. **US**.

13   Piazzesi, M., M. Schneider and S. Tuzel (2007) 'Housing, Consumption and Asset Pricing', *Journal of Financial Economics*, Vol. 83, No. 3, 531–569. **US**.

14   Trigeorgis, L. and N. Lambertides (2014) 'The Role of Growth Options in Explaining Stock Returns', *Journal of Financial and Quantitative Analysis*, Vol. 49, No. 3, 749–771.

Endnotes

1   In this example, the four states give rise to four *possible* outcomes for each security. Had we used past data, the outcomes would have actually occurred. In that case, statisticians argue that the correct divisor is $N - 1$, where N is the number of observations. Thus the denominator would be 3 $[= (4 - 1)]$ in the case of past data, not 4. Note that the example in Section 9.5 involved past data and we used a divisor of $N - 1$. While this difference causes grief to both students and textbook writers, it is a minor point in practice. In the real world, samples are generally so large that using N or $N - 1$ in the denominator has virtually no effect on the calculation of variance.

2   As with variance, we divided by N (4 in this example) because the four states give rise to four possible outcomes. However, had we used past data, the correct divisor would be $N - 1$ (3 in this example).

3   There are only four equally probable returns for Supertech and Slowburn, so neither security possesses a normal distribution. Thus, probabilities would be slightly different in our example.

4   As with covariance, the ordering of the two securities is not relevant when we express the correlation between the two securities. That is, $\rho_{\text{Super, Slow}} = \rho_{\text{Slow, Super}}$.

5   A major exception occurs with derivative securities. For example, the correlation between an equity share and a put on the equity is generally strongly negative. Puts will be treated later in the text.

6   Of course, someone dead set on parting with their money can do so. For example, one can trade frequently without purpose, so that commissions more than offset the positive expected returns on the portfolio.

7   The classic treatise is Harry Markowitz, *Portfolio Selection* (1959). Markowitz won the Nobel Prize in economics in 1990 for his work on modern portfolio theory.

8   Equation 10.10 is actually a weighted *average* of the variance and covariance terms because the weights, $1/N$ and $1 - 1/N$, sum to 1.

9   This example ignores the casino's cut.

10   Though it is harder to show, this risk reduction effect also applies to the general case where variances and covariances are *not* equal.

11   Surprisingly, this appears to be a decent approximation because many investors can borrow from a stockbroker (called *going on margin*) when purchasing securities. The borrowing rate here is very near the riskless rate of interest, particularly for large investors. More will be said about this in a later chapter.

12   The assumption of homogeneous expectations states that all investors have the same beliefs concerning

returns, variances and covariances. It does not say that all investors have the same aversion to risk.

13 Unfortunately, empirical evidence shows that virtually no equities have negative betas.

14 This relationship was first proposed independently by John Lintner and William F. Sharpe. The plausible conditions are as follows: (1) Investors are only interested in the mean and variance of their investment returns; (2) Markets are frictionless; (3) Investors have homogeneous expectations.

15 Perhaps the two most well-known papers were Black et al. (1972) and Fama and MacBeth (1973).

16 For example, the studies suggest that the average return on a zero-beta portfolio is above the risk-free rate, a finding inconsistent with the CAPM.

17 For example, see Breen and Koraczyk (1993) and Kothari et al. (1995).

18 Points 4 and 5 are addressed in Kothari et al. (1995).

Factor Models and the Arbitrage Pricing Theory

To paint a picture of the exceptionally complex financial situation facing companies in recent years, one can look at the impact of oil on operations and ultimately share prices. Without any doubt, the oil price has been more volatile than it has been for many years. Given its centrality to almost every sector of the economy, the oil price can have a major impact on corporate profitability and the viability of existing or potential investments. If oil forms the basis of revenues (for example, in BP and Shell), increases in the oil price will normally improve the share price performance of these firms. If oil is a major cost (for example, in manufacturing and airline travel), increases in the oil price will increase the cost of doing business and have an adverse effect on share prices. Even countries are dependent on the oil price. Many oil exporting countries can only balance their budget when the oil price exceeds $100 a barrel. When the oil price falls below this level, country budgets are in deficit and cuts needs to be made in public spending. This clearly raises the question, should we consider changes in oil prices when we forecast the share price returns of companies or is the market return enough? Oil is just one factor – what about the gold price or interest rates? This chapter explores the fundamental concepts of risk and return in detail and considers advanced asset pricing models for the estimation of risk and return.

KEY NOTATIONS

R	Total return in a period
$E(R)$	Expected return, and
U	Unexpected return
β_F	Systematic risk with respect to factor, F
HML	High minus low Fama French factor
SMB	Small minus big Fama French factor
MOM	Carhart momentum factor
X_i	Weight of asset i in portfolio
N	Number of assets in portfolio
R_M	Market return
R_F	Risk-free rate of return

Factor Models: Announcements, Surprises and Expected Returns

11.1

We learned in the previous chapter how to construct portfolios and how to evaluate their returns. We now step back and examine the returns on individual securities more closely. By doing this we will find that the portfolios inherit and alter the properties of the securities they comprise.

To be concrete, let us consider the return on the shares of the global technology firm, Apple. What will determine their share price return over, say, a monthly period?

Chapter 10
Page 254

The return on any equity traded in a financial market consists of two parts. First, the *normal* or *expected return* from the equity is the part of the return that shareholders in the market predict or expect (for more information on expected returns see **Chapter 10**, Section 10.2). It depends on all of the information shareholders have that bears on the company, and it uses all of our understanding of what will influence the share price in the next month.

The second part is the *uncertain* or *risky return* on the equity. This is the portion that comes from information that will be revealed within the month. The list of such information is endless, but here are some examples:

- News about Apple's research.
- Government figures released for the gross national product (GNP).
- Results of the patent policy enforcement in Asia.
- Discovery that a rival's product has been tampered with.
- News that Apple's sales figures are higher than expected.
- A sudden drop in interest rates.
- The unexpected retirement of Apple's founder and chairman.

A way to write the return on Apple's shares in the coming month, then, is:

$$R = E(R) + U$$

where R is the actual total return in the month, $E(R)$ is the expected part of the return, and U stands for the unexpected part of the return.

We must exercise some care in studying the effect of these or other news items on the return. For example, the government might give us GNP or unemployment figures for this month, but how much of that is new information for shareholders? Surely, at the beginning of the month, shareholders will have some idea or forecast of what the monthly GNP will be. The expectations of shareholders should be factored into the expected part of the return as of the beginning of the month, $E(R)$. On the other hand, insofar as the announcement by the government is a surprise and to the extent to which it influences the return on the shares, it will be part of U, the unanticipated part of the return.

As an example, suppose shareholders in the market had forecast that the GNP increase this month would be 0.5 per cent. If GNP influences our company's share price, this forecast will be part of the information shareholders use to form the expectation, $E(R)$, of the monthly return. If the actual announcement this month is exactly 0.5 per cent, the same as the forecast, then the shareholders learned nothing new, and the announcement is not news. It is like hearing a rumour about a friend when you knew it all along.

On the other hand, suppose the government announced that the actual GNP increase during the year was 1.5 per cent. Now shareholders have learned something – that the increase is one percentage point higher than they had forecast. This difference between the actual result and the forecast, one percentage point in this example, is sometimes called the *innovation* or *surprise*.

Any announcement can be broken into two parts, the anticipated or expected part and the surprise or innovation:

$$\text{Announcement} = \text{Expected part} + \text{Surprise}$$

The expected part of any announcement is part of the information the market uses to form the expectation, $E(R)$, of the return on the equity. The surprise is the news that influences the unanticipated return on the equity, U.

Returning to the Apple example, consider the historical iPad sales between Q1 of 2010 and Q4 of 2013. At the end of Q4, 2013, analysts expected the same growth rate in iPad sales between 2013 (Q1) and 2014 (Q1), as they were between the same periods in 2012 and 2013. As you can see from Figure 11.1, although sales of iPads in 2014 (Q1) broke all previous records, they did not meet the level expected by the market. As a result, the surprise component to the annual results was negative and the announcement day return was significantly negative!

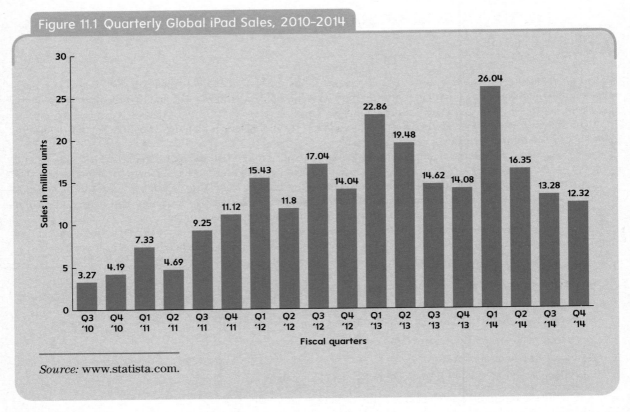

Figure 11.1 Quarterly Global iPad Sales, 2010–2014

Source: www.statista.com.

When we speak of news, then, we only refer to the surprise part of any announcement and not any portion that the market has expected and therefore has already discounted.

11.2   Risk: Systematic and Unsystematic

The unanticipated part of the return – that portion resulting from surprises – is the true risk of any investment. After all, if we got what we had expected, there would be no risk and no uncertainty.

There are important differences, though, among various sources of risk. Look at our previous list of news stories. Some of these stories are directed specifically at Apple, and some are more general. Which of the news items are of specific importance to Apple?

Chapter 10
Page 269

Announcements about interest rates or GNP are clearly important for nearly all companies, whereas news about the Apple chairman, its research, its sales, or the affairs of a rival company are of specific interest to Apple's shareholders. We will divide these two types of announcements and the resulting risk, then, into two components: a systematic portion, called *systematic risk,* and the remainder, which we call *specific* or *unsystematic risk* (for more information on systematic and unsystematic risk, see **Chapter 10**, Section 10.6). The following definitions describe the difference:

- A *systematic risk* is any risk that affects a large number of assets, each to a greater or lesser degree.
- An *unsystematic risk* is a risk that specifically affects a single asset or a small group of assets.[1]

Uncertainty about general economic conditions, such as GNP, interest rates or inflation, is an example of systematic risk. These conditions affect nearly all securities to some degree. An unanticipated or surprise increase in inflation affects wages and the costs of the supplies that companies buy, the value of the assets that companies own, and the prices at which companies sell their products. These forces to which all companies are susceptible are the essence of systematic risk.

In contrast, the announcement of a small technological innovation by Apple may affect that company alone or a few other companies. Certainly, it is unlikely to have an effect on the global technology prices. To stress that such information is unsystematic and affects only some specific companies, we sometimes call it an *idiosyncratic risk.*

This permits us to break down the risk of Apple's equity into its two components: the systematic and the unsystematic. As is traditional, we will use the Greek epsilon, ε, to represent the unsystematic risk and write:

$$R = E(R) + U$$
$$= E(R) + m + \varepsilon$$

where we have used the letter m to stand for the systematic risk. Sometimes systematic risk is referred to as *market risk*. This emphasizes the fact that m influences all assets in the market to some extent.

The important point about the way we have broken the total risk, U, into its two components, m and ε, is that ε, because it is specific to the company, is unrelated to the specific risk of most other companies. For example, the unsystematic risk on Apple's equity, ε_R, is unrelated to the unsystematic risk of a company, such as Chevron, in another industry, ε_V. The risk that Apple's equity will go up or down because of a discovery by its research team – or its failure to discover something – probably is unrelated to any of the specific uncertainties that affect Chevron's equity.

Using the terms of the previous chapter, this means that the unsystematic risks of Apple's equity and Chevron's equity are unrelated to each other, or uncorrelated. In the symbols of statistics:

$$\text{Corr}(\varepsilon_{\text{Apple}}, \varepsilon_{\text{Chevron}}) = 0$$

11.3   Systematic Risk and Betas

The fact that the unsystematic parts of the returns on two companies are unrelated to each other does not mean that the systematic portions are unrelated. On the contrary, because both companies are influenced by the same systematic risks, their total returns will also be related.

For example, a surprise about inflation will influence almost all companies to some extent. How sensitive is Apple's share price return to unanticipated changes in inflation? If the Apple share price tends to go up on news that inflation is exceeding expectations, we would say that it is positively related to inflation. If the share price goes down when inflation exceeds expectations and up when inflation falls short of expectations, it is negatively related. In the unusual case where an equity's return is uncorrelated with inflation surprises, inflation has no effect on it.

We capture the influence of a systematic risk by using the beta coefficient. The beta coefficient, β, tells us the response of the equity's return to a systematic risk. In the previous chapter, beta measured the responsiveness of a security's return to a specific risk factor, the return on the market portfolio. We used this type of responsiveness to develop the capital asset pricing model. Because we now consider many types of systematic risks, our current work can be viewed as a generalization of our work in the previous chapter.

If a company's share price return is positively related to the risk of inflation, it has a positive inflation beta. If it is negatively related to inflation, its inflation beta is negative; and if it is uncorrelated with inflation, its inflation beta is zero.

It is not hard to imagine some equities with positive inflation betas and others with negative inflation betas. The equity of a company owning gold mines will probably have a positive inflation beta because an unanticipated rise in inflation is usually associated with an increase in gold prices. On the other hand, an automobile company facing stiff foreign competition might find that an increase in inflation means that the wages it pays are higher, but that it cannot raise its prices to cover the increase. This profit squeeze, as the company's expenses rise faster than its revenues, would give its equity a negative inflation beta.

Some structure is useful at this point. Suppose we have identified three systematic risks on which we want to focus. We may believe that these three are sufficient to describe the systematic risks that influence share price returns. Three likely candidates are inflation, GNP and interest rates. Thus, every equity will have a beta associated with each of these systematic risks: an inflation beta, a GNP beta and an interest rate beta. We can write the return on the equity, then, in the following form:

$$R = E(R) + U$$
$$= E(R) + m + \varepsilon$$
$$= E(R) + \beta_I F_I + \beta_{\text{GNP}} F_{\text{GNP}} + \beta_r F_r + \varepsilon$$

where we have used the symbol β_I to denote the equity's inflation beta, β_{GNP} for its GNP beta, and β_r to stand for its interest rate beta. In the equation, F stands for a surprise, whether it be in inflation, GNP or interest rates.

Let us go through an example to see how the surprises and the expected return add up to produce the total return, R, on a given security. To make it more familiar, suppose that the return is over a horizon of a year and not just a month. Suppose that at the beginning of the year, annual inflation is forecast to be 5 per cent, GNP is forecast to increase by 2 per cent and interest rates are not expected to change. Suppose the security we are looking at has the following betas:

$$\beta_I = 2$$
$$\beta_{GNP} = 1$$
$$\beta_r = -1.8$$

The magnitude of the beta describes how great an impact a systematic risk has on a security's returns. A beta of $+1$ indicates that the security's return rises and falls one for one with the systematic factor. This means, in our example, that because the security has a GNP beta of 1, it experiences a 1 per cent increase in return for every 1 per cent surprise increase in GNP. If its GNP beta were -2, it would fall by 2 per cent when there was an unanticipated increase of 1 per cent in GNP, and it would rise by 2 per cent if GNP experienced a surprise 1 per cent decline.

Let us suppose that during the year the following events occur: inflation rises by 7 per cent, GNP rises by only 1 per cent, and interest rates fall by 2 per cent. Suppose we learn some good news about the company, perhaps that it is succeeding quickly with some new business strategy, and that this unanticipated development contributes 5 per cent to its return. In other words:

$$\varepsilon = 5\%$$

Let us assemble all of this information to find what return the security had during the year.

First we must determine what news or surprises took place in the systematic factors. From our information we know that:

$$\text{Expected inflation} = 5\%$$
$$\text{Expected GNP change} = 2\%$$

and:

$$\text{Expected change in interest rates} = 0\%$$

This means that the market had discounted these changes, and the surprises will be the difference between what actually takes place and these expectations:

$$
\begin{aligned}
F_I &= \text{Surprise in inflation} \\
&= \text{Actual inflation} - \text{Expected inflation} \\
&= 7\% - 5\% \\
&= 2\%
\end{aligned}
$$

Similarly:

$$
\begin{aligned}
F_{GNP} &= \text{Surprise in GNP} \\
&= \text{Actual GNP} - \text{Expected GNP} \\
&= 1\% - 2\% \\
&= -1\%
\end{aligned}
$$

and:

$$
\begin{aligned}
F_I &= \text{Surprise in change in interest rates} \\
&= \text{Actual change} - \text{Expected change} \\
&= -2\% - 0\% \\
&= -2\%
\end{aligned}
$$

The total effect of the systematic risks on the security return, then, is:

$$
\begin{aligned}
m &= \text{Systematic risk portion of return} \\
&= \beta_I F_I + \beta_{GNP} F_{GNP} + \beta_r F_r \\
&= [2 \times 2\%] + [1 \times (-1\%)] + [(-1.8) \times (-2\%)] \\
&= 6.6\%
\end{aligned}
$$

Combining this with the unsystematic risk portion, the total risky portion of the return on the security is:

$$m + \varepsilon = 6.6\% + 5\% = 11.6\%$$

Last, if the expected return on the security for the year was, say, 4 per cent, the total return from all three components will be:

$$R = E(R) + m + \varepsilon$$

$$= 4\% + 6.6\% + 5\%$$

$$= 15.6\%$$

The model we have been looking at is called a factor model, and the systematic sources of risk, designated F, are called the *factors*. To be perfectly formal, a *k-factor model* is a model where each security's return is generated by:

$$R = E(R) + \beta_1 F_1 + \beta_2 F_2 + \cdots + \beta_k F_k + \varepsilon$$

where ε is specific to a particular security and uncorrelated with the ε term for other securities. In our preceding example we had a three-factor model. We used inflation, GNP and the change in interest rates as examples of systematic sources of risk, or factors. Researchers have not settled on what is the correct set of factors. Like so many other questions, this might be one of those matters that is never laid to rest.

In practice, researchers frequently use different models for returns. They do not use all of the economic factors we used previously as examples; instead they use an index of stock market returns – like the FTSE 100 or DAX, in addition to returns on arbitrage portfolios representing factors that have been identified as being important from earlier research. Using the single-factor model we can write returns like this:

$$R = E(R) + \beta[R_{\text{FTSE100}} - E(R_{\text{FTSE100}})] + \varepsilon$$

Where there is only one factor (such as the returns on the FTSE 100 or DAX index), we do not need to put a subscript on the beta. In this form (with minor modifications) the factor model is called a market model. This term is employed because the index that is used for the factor is an index of returns on the whole market. The market model is written as:

$$R = E(R) + \beta[R_M - E(R_M)] + \varepsilon$$

where R_M is the return on the market portfolio.[2] The single β is called the *beta coefficient*.

In the past 20 years, practice has changed quite significantly in the area of factor models because of two seminal research articles published by Eugene Fama and Kenneth French in 1993, and Mark Carhart in 1997. Both papers recognized that the market index alone cannot fully explain the variation in asset returns. Fama and French introduced the three-factor model using two new factors HML and SMB. HML stands for 'High Minus Low Book-to-Market Equity' and represents the return on an arbitrage portfolio that is long (a positive investment) in high book-to-market equity companies and short (a negative investment or borrowing) in low book-to-market equity companies. An arbitrage portfolio has a zero net investment because the positive weights completely cancel out the negative weights on assets. Similarly, SMB means 'Small Minus Big Companies' and corresponds to an arbitrage portfolio that is long in small companies and short in big companies. Carhart (1997) added another factor that represented a momentum effect that is measured by the return on an arbitrage portfolio that is long in the best performing equities of the previous year and short in the worst performing equities of the previous year. Algebraically, the four-factor model is expressed as:

$$R - r_f = E(R) + \beta_1(R_M - r_f) + \beta_2 HML + \beta_3 SMB + \beta_4 MOM + \varepsilon$$

where there are four factors representing the market risk premium, High minus Low B/M, Small minus Big, and momentum arbitrage portfolios respectively. The Fama–French three-factor model is simply the four-factor model without the momentum factor. In 2015, Fama and French published new work on the three-factor model and found that a five-factor model based on size, value, profitability and investment patterns performed better. The Fama–French five factor model is presented below:

$$R - r_f = E(R) + \beta_1(R_M - r_f) + \beta_2 HML + \beta_3 SMB + \beta_4 RMW + \beta_5 CMA + \varepsilon$$

where RMW is the difference between the returns on diversified equity portfolios of high and low profitability, CMA is the difference between the returns on diversified equity portfolios of low and high investment firms, and other variables are as defined earlier.

Real World Insight 11.1

Glencore plc

Glencore is one of the world's largest diversified natural resource firms and a major producer and marketer of over 90 commodities worldwide. With Glencore's international reach and reliance on commodities, it could be argued that an additional risk factor related to commodities will be important in explaining the company's equity returns. For this analysis, we will hypothesize that the market return, oil price returns, and gold price returns explain the returns on Glencore. We will use monthly data between 2011 and 2015 and assume that expected returns on each of the three factors is zero. This is a common assumption in estimations of this type.

The model is specified as:

$$R - r_f = E(R) + \beta_1(R_M - r_f) + \beta_2 R_{Oil} + \beta_3 R_{Gold} + \varepsilon$$

We will use the FTSE 100 as the market index, the 10-year government bond yield as the risk free rate, and the historical oil and gold price returns for the commodity factors. A multiple regression model provides the following estimates (with t-statistics below).

$$R - r_f = -0.003 + 0.765(R_M - r_f) + 0.596R_{Oil} + 0.017R_{Gold} + \varepsilon$$

$$(-0.32) \qquad (2.18) \qquad\qquad (3.67) \qquad\quad (0.27)$$

The t-statistics tell us which variables are important in the model, and in this case both the market and oil factors are significant. Surprisingly, the gold factor is not statistically significant.

11.4   Portfolios and Factor Models

Chapter 10
Page 269

Now let us see what happens to portfolios of equities when each follows a one-factor model (the properties of portfolios and effect of diversification are also discussed in **Chapter 10**, Section 10.6). For purposes of discussion, we will take the coming one-month period and examine returns. We could have used a day or a year or any other period. If the period represents the time between decisions, however, we would rather it be short than long, and a month is a reasonable time frame to use.

We will create portfolios from a list of N securities, and use a one-factor model to capture the systematic risk. The ith security in the list will therefore have returns:

$$R_i = E(R_i) + \beta_i F + \varepsilon_i \tag{11.1}$$

where we have subscripted the variables to indicate that they relate to the ith security. Notice that the factor F is not subscripted. The factor that represents systematic risk could be a surprise in GNP, or we could use the market model and let the difference between the market return and what we expect that return to be, $R_{\text{market}} - E(R_{\text{market}})$, be the factor. In either case, the factor applies to all of the securities in the portfolio.

The β_i is subscripted because it represents the unique way the factor influences the ith security. To recapitulate our discussion of factor models, if β_i is zero, the returns on the ith security are:

$$R_i = E(R_i) + \varepsilon_i$$

In words, the ith security's returns are unaffected by the factor, F, if β_i is zero. If β_i is positive, positive changes in the factor raise the ith security's returns, and negative changes lower them. Conversely, if β_i is negative, its returns and the factor move in opposite directions.

Figure 11.2 illustrates the relationship between a security's excess returns, $R_i - E(R_i)$, and the factor F for different betas, where $\beta_i > 0$. The lines in Figure 11.2 plot Equation 11.1 on the assumption that there has been no unsystematic risk. That is, $\varepsilon_i = 0$. Because we are assuming positive betas, the lines slope upward, indicating that the return rises with F. Notice that if the factor is zero ($F = 0$), the line passes through zero on the y-axis.

Figure 11.2 The One-Factor Model

Each line represents a different security, where each security has a different beta.

Now let us see what happens when we create equity portfolios where each equity follows a one-factor model. Let X_i be the proportion of equity i in the portfolio. That is, if an individual with a portfolio of €100 wants €20 in Axa, we say $X_{AXA} = 20$ per cent. Because the Xs represent the proportions of wealth we are investing in each of the equities, we know that they must add up to 100 per cent or 1:

$$X_1 + X_2 + X_3 + \cdots + X_N = 1$$

We know that the portfolio return is the weighted average of the returns on the individual assets in the portfolio. Algebraically, this can be written as follows:

$$R_P = X_1 R_1 + X_2 R_2 + X_3 R_3 + \cdots + X_N R_N \tag{11.2}$$

We saw from Equation 11.1 that each asset, in turn, is determined by both the factor F and the unsystematic risk of ε_i. Thus by substituting Equation 11.1 for each R_i in Equation 11.2, we have:

$$R_P = \underbrace{X_1[E(R_1) + \beta_1 F + \varepsilon_1]}_{\text{(Return on equity 1)}} + \underbrace{X_2[E(R_2) + \beta_2 F + \varepsilon_2]}_{\text{(Return on equity 2)}}$$

$$+ \underbrace{X_3(E(R_3) + \beta_3 F + \varepsilon_3)}_{\text{(Return on equity 3)}} + \cdots + \underbrace{X_N(E(R_N) + \beta_N F + \varepsilon_N)}_{\text{(Return on equity N)}} \tag{11.3}$$

Equation 11.3 shows us that the return on a portfolio is determined by three sets of parameters:

1 The expected return on each individual security, $E(R_i)$.

2 The beta of each security multiplied by the factor F.

3 The unsystematic risk of each individual security, ε_i.

We express Equation 11.3 in terms of these three sets of parameters like this:

Weighted average of expected returns

$$R_P = X_1 E(R_1) + X_2 E(R_2) + X_3 E(R_3) + \cdots + X_N E(R_N) \tag{11.4}$$

Weighted average of betas × F

$$+ (X_1 \beta_1 + X_2 \beta_2 + X_3 \beta_3 + \cdots + X_N \beta_N) F$$

Weighted average of unsystematic risks

$$+ X_1 \varepsilon_1 + X_2 \varepsilon_2 + X_3 \varepsilon_3 + \cdots + X_N \varepsilon_N$$

This rather imposing equation is actually straightforward. The first row is the weighted average of each security's expected return. The items in the parentheses of the second row represent the weighted average of each security's beta. This weighted average is, in turn, multiplied by the factor F. The third row represents a weighted average of the unsystematic risks of the individual securities.

Where does uncertainty appear in Equation 11.4? There is no uncertainty in the first row because only the expected value of each security's return appears there. Uncertainty in the second row is reflected by only one item, F. That is, while we know that the expected value of F is zero, we do not know what its value will be over a particular period. Uncertainty in the third row is reflected by each unsystematic risk, ε_i.

Portfolios and Diversification

In the previous sections of this chapter, we expressed the return on a single security in terms of our factor model. Portfolios were treated next. Because investors generally hold diversified portfolios, we now want to know what Equation 11.4 looks like in a *large* or diversified portfolio.[3]

As it turns out, something unusual occurs to Equation 11.4: the third row actually *disappears* in a large portfolio. To see this, consider a gambler who divides £1,000 by betting on red over many spins of the roulette wheel. For example, he may participate in 1,000 spins, betting £1 at a time. Though we do not know ahead of time whether a particular spin will yield red or black, we can be confident that red will win about 50 per cent of the time. Ignoring the house take, the investor can be expected to end up with just about his original £1,000.

Though we are concerned with securities, not roulette wheels, the same principle applies. Each security has its own unsystematic risk, where the surprise for one security is unrelated to the surprise of another security. By investing a small amount in each security, we bring the weighted average of the unsystematic risks close to zero in a large portfolio.[4]

Although the third row completely vanishes in a large portfolio, nothing unusual occurs in either row 1 or row 2. Row 1 remains a weighted average of the expected returns on the individual securities as securities are added to the portfolio. Because there is no uncertainty at all in the first row, there is no way for diversification to cause this row to vanish. The terms inside the parentheses of the second row remain a weighted average of the betas. They do not vanish, either, when securities are added. Because the factor F is unaffected when securities are added to the portfolios, the second row does not vanish.

Why does the third row vanish while the second row does not, though both rows reflect uncertainty? The key is that there are many unsystematic risks in row 3. Because these risks are independent of each other, the effect of diversification becomes stronger as we add more assets to the portfolio. The resulting portfolio becomes less and less risky, and the return becomes more certain. However, the systematic risk, F, affects all securities because it is outside the parentheses in row 2. Because we cannot avoid this factor by investing in many securities, diversification does not occur in this row.

Example 11.1

Diversification and Unsystematic Risk

The preceding material can be further explained by the following example. We keep our one-factor model here but make three specific assumptions:

1 All securities have the same expected return of 10 per cent. This assumption implies that the first row of Equation 11.4 must also equal 10 per cent because this row is a weighted average of the expected returns of the individual securities.

2 All securities have a beta of 1. The sum of the terms inside the parentheses in the second row of Equation 11.4 must equal 1 because these terms are a weighted average of the individual betas. Because the terms inside the parentheses are multiplied by F, the value of the second row is $1 \times F = F$.

3 In this example, we focus on the behaviour of one individual, Walter V. Bagehot. Mr Bagehot decides to hold an equally weighted portfolio. That is, the proportion of each security in his portfolio is $1/N$.

We can express the return on Mr Bagehot's portfolio as follows:

Return on Walter V. Bagehot's portfolio

$$R_P = \underbrace{10\%}_{\substack{\text{From} \\ \text{row 1 of} \\ \text{Equation 11.4}}} + \underbrace{F}_{\substack{\text{From} \\ \text{row 2 of} \\ \text{Equation 11.4}}} + \underbrace{\left(\frac{1}{N}\varepsilon_1 + \frac{1}{N}\varepsilon_2 + \frac{1}{N}\varepsilon_3 + \cdots + \frac{1}{N}\varepsilon_N\right)}_{\text{From row 3 of Equation 11.4}} \qquad (11.4')$$

We mentioned before that as N increases without limit, row 3 of Equation 11.4 becomes equal to zero.[5] Thus, the return to Walter Bagehot's portfolio when the number of securities is very large is

$$R_P = 10\% + F \qquad (11.4'')$$

The key to diversification is exhibited in Equation 11.4″. The unsystematic risk of row 3 vanishes while the systematic risk of row 2 remains.

This is illustrated in Figure 11.3. Systematic risk, captured by variation in the factor F, is not reduced through diversification. Conversely, unsystematic risk diminishes as securities are added, vanishing as the number of securities becomes infinite. Our result is analogous to the diversification example of the previous chapter. In that chapter, we said that undiversifiable or systematic risk arises from positive covariances between securities. In this chapter, we say that systematic risk arises from a common factor F. Because a common factor causes positive covariances, the arguments of the two chapters are parallel.

Total risk decreases as the number of securities in the portfolio rises. This drop occurs only in the unsystematic risk component. Systematic risk is unaffected by diversification.

Figure 11.3 Diversification and the Portfolio Risk for an Equally Weighted Portfolio

11.5 Betas and Expected Returns

The Linear Relationship

We have argued many times that the expected return on a security compensates for its risk. In the previous chapter we showed that market beta (the standardized covariance of the security's returns with those of the market) was the appropriate measure of risk under the assumptions of homogeneous expectations and riskless borrowing and lending. The capital asset pricing model, which posited these assumptions, implied that the expected return on a security was positively (and linearly) related to its beta. We will find a similar relationship between risk and return in the one-factor model of this chapter.

We begin by noting that the relevant risk in large and well-diversified portfolios is all systematic because unsystematic risk is diversified away. An implication is that when a well-diversified shareholder considers changing her holdings of a particular security, she can ignore its unsystematic risk.

Notice that we are not claiming that equities, like portfolios, have no unsystematic risk. Nor are we saying that the unsystematic risk of an equity will not affect its returns. Shares do have unsystematic risk, and their actual returns do depend on the unsystematic risk. Because this risk washes out in a well-diversified portfolio, however, shareholders can ignore this unsystematic risk when they consider whether to add an equity to their portfolio. Therefore, if shareholders are ignoring the unsystematic risk, only the systematic risk of a security can be related to its *expected* return.

This relationship is illustrated in the security market line of Figure 11.4. Points P, C, A and L all lie on the line emanating from the risk-free rate of 10 per cent. The points representing each of these four assets can be created by combinations of the risk-free rate and any of the other three assets. For example, because A has a beta of 2.0 and P has a beta of 1.0, a portfolio of 50 per cent in asset A and 50 per cent in the riskless rate has the same beta as asset P. The risk-free rate is 10 per cent and the expected return on security A is 35 per cent, implying that the combination's return of 22.5 per cent [(10% + 35%)/2] is identical to security P's expected return. Because security P has both the same beta and the same expected return as a combination of the riskless asset and security A, an individual is equally inclined to add a small amount of security P and to add a small amount of this combination to her portfolio. However, the unsystematic risk of security P need not be equal to the unsystematic risk of the combination of security A and the risk-free rate because unsystematic risk is diversified away in a large portfolio.

Figure 11.4 A Graph of Beta and Expected Return for Individual Securities under the One-Factor Model

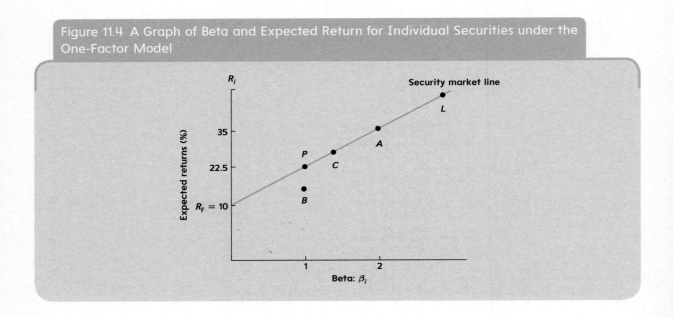

Of course, the potential combinations of points on the security market line are endless. We can duplicate P by combinations of the risk-free rate and either C or L (or both of them). We can duplicate C (or A or L) by borrowing at the risk-free rate to invest in P. The infinite number of points on the security market line that are not labelled can be used as well.

Now consider security B. Because its expected return is below the line, no investor would hold it. Instead, the investor would prefer security P, a combination of security A and the riskless asset, or some other combination. Thus, security B's price is too high. Its price will fall in a competitive market, forcing its expected return back up to the line in equilibrium.

The preceding discussion allows us to provide an equation for the security market line of Figure 11.4. We know that a line can be described algebraically from two points. It is perhaps easiest to focus on the risk-free rate and asset P because the risk-free rate has a beta of 0 and P has a beta of 1.

Because we know that the return on any zero-beta asset is R_F and the expected return on asset P is $E(R_P)$, it can easily be shown that:

$$E(R) = R_F + \beta[E(R_P) - R_F].$$ (11.5)

In Equation 11.5, $E(R)$ can be thought of as the expected return on any security or portfolio lying on the security market line. β is the beta of that security or portfolio.

The Market Portfolio and the Single Factor

Chapter 10
Page 277

In the CAPM (see **Chapter 10**, Section 10.9), the beta of a security measures its responsiveness to movements in the market portfolio. In the one-factor model of the arbitrage pricing theory (APT) the beta of a security measures its responsiveness to the factor. We now relate the market portfolio to the single factor.

A large, diversified portfolio has no unsystematic risk because the unsystematic risks of the individual securities are diversified away. Assuming enough securities so that the market portfolio is fully diversified and assuming that no security has a disproportionate market share, this portfolio is fully diversified and contains no unsystematic risk.[6] In other words, the market portfolio is perfectly correlated with the single factor, implying that the market portfolio is really a scaled-up or scaled-down version of the factor. After scaling properly, we can treat the market portfolio as the factor itself.

The market portfolio, like every security or portfolio, lies on the security market line. When the market portfolio is the factor, the beta of the market portfolio is 1 by definition. This is shown in Figure 11.5. (We deleted the securities and the specific expected returns from Figure 11.4 for clarity: the two graphs are otherwise identical.) With the market portfolio as the factor, Equation 11.5 becomes:

$$E(R) = R_\text{F} + \beta[\text{E}(R_\text{M}) - R_\text{F}]$$

where $E(R_\text{M})$ is the expected return on the market. This equation shows that the expected return on any asset, $E(R)$, is linearly related to the security's beta. The equation is identical to that of the CAPM, which we developed in the previous chapter.

Figure 11.5 A Graph of Beta and Expected Return for Individual Equities under the One-Factor Model

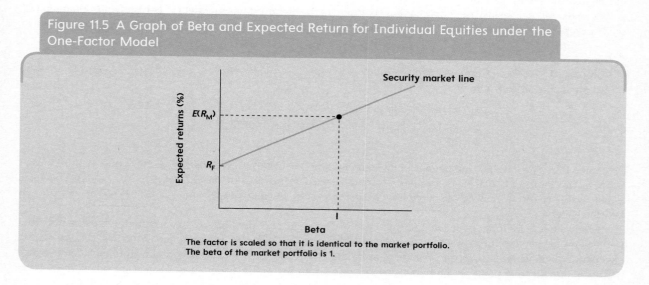

The factor is scaled so that it is identical to the market portfolio.
The beta of the market portfolio is 1.

11.6 The Capital Asset Pricing Model and the Arbitrage Pricing Theory

The CAPM and the APT are alternative models of risk and return. It is worthwhile to consider the differences between the two models, both in terms of pedagogy and in terms of application.

Differences in Pedagogy

We feel that the CAPM has at least one strong advantage from the student's point of view. The derivation of the CAPM necessarily brings the reader through a discussion of efficient sets. This treatment – beginning with the case of two risky assets, moving to the case of many risky assets, and finishing when a riskless asset is added to the many risky ones – is of great intuitive value. This sort of presentation is not as easily accomplished with the APT.

However, the APT has an offsetting advantage. The model adds factors until the unsystematic risk of any security is uncorrelated with the unsystematic risk of every other security. Under this formulation, it is easily shown that (1) unsystematic risk steadily falls (and ultimately vanishes) as the number of securities in the portfolio increases, but (2) the systematic risks do not decrease. This result was also shown in the CAPM, though the intuition was cloudier because the unsystematic risks could be correlated across securities.

Differences in Application

One advantage of the APT is that it can handle multiple factors while the CAPM ignores them. Although the bulk of our presentation in this chapter focused on the one-factor model, a multifactor model, like the Carhart (1997) four-factor model, is probably more reflective of reality. That is, we must abstract from many marketwide and industrywide factors before the unsystematic risk of one security becomes uncorrelated with the unsystematic risks of other securities. Under the four-factor model, the relationship between risk and return can be expressed as:

$$R - r_f = E(R) + \beta[E(R_M) - r_f] + \gamma HML + \delta SMB + \eta MOM + \varepsilon \tag{11.6}$$

In this equation, β stands for the security's beta with respect to the first factor, γ stands for the security's beta with respect to the second factor, and so on. The equation states that the security's expected return is related to the security's factor betas. The intuition in Equation 11.6 is straightforward. Each factor represents risk that cannot be diversified away. The higher a security's beta with regard to a particular factor, the higher is the risk that the security bears. In a rational world, the expected return on the security should compensate for this risk. Equation 11.6 states that the expected return is a summation of the base expected return plus the compensation for each type of risk that the security bears.

As an example, consider the hypothetical coefficients for the four-factor model for British Land Company plc, the UK property developer. Assume that the expected monthly return on any equity, $E(R_S)$, can be described as:

$$E(R_S) = 0.0041 + 0.0136\beta - 0.0001\gamma - 0.0006\delta + 0.0072\mu$$

Suppose British Land Company had the following betas: $\beta = 1.1$, $\gamma = 2$, $\delta = 3$, $\mu = 0.1$. The expected monthly return on that security would be:

$$\overline{R}_{BLC} = 0.0041 + 0.0136 \times 1.1 - 0.0001 \times 2 - 0.0006 \times 3 + 0.0072 \times 0.1$$
$$= 0.0041 + 0.01496 - 0.0002 - 0.0018 + 0.00072$$
$$= 0.01778$$

Assuming that British Land Company is unlevered and that one of the firm's projects has risk equivalent to that of the firm, this value of 0.01778 (i.e., 1.78 per cent) can be used as the monthly discount rate for the project. (Because annual data are often supplied for capital budgeting purposes, the annual rate of 0.2355 [= $(1.01778)^{12} - 1$] might be used instead.)

Because many factors appear on the right side of Equation 11.6, the four-factor formulation has the potential to measure expected returns more accurately than does the CAPM. However, as we mentioned earlier, we cannot easily determine whether these factors are appropriate. The factors in the preceding study were included because they were found to explain a significant proportion of returns for US companies. They were not derived from theory and they may not be particularly appropriate for European, Middle Eastern or African companies.

By contrast, the use of the market index in the CAPM formulation is implied by the theory of the previous chapter. We suggested in earlier chapters that market indices (such as the FTSE 100 and DJ Euro Stoxx 50) mirror stock market movements quite well.

Summary and Conclusions

The previous chapter developed the capital asset pricing model (CAPM). As an alternative, this chapter developed the arbitrage pricing theory (APT) and introduced the Fama–French three-factor model and Carhart four-factor model.

1   The APT assumes that security returns are generated according to factor models. For example, we might describe a stock's return as:

$$R = E(R) + \beta_I F_I + \beta_{GNP} F_{GNP} + \beta_r F_r + \varepsilon$$

where I, GNP and r stand for inflation, gross national product and the interest rate, respectively. The three factors F_I, F_{GNP}, and F_r represent systematic risk because these factors affect many securities. The term ε is considered unsystematic risk because it is unique to each individual security.

2   For convenience, we frequently describe a security's return according to a one-factor model:

$$R = E(R) + \beta F + \varepsilon$$

3   The Fama–French and Carhart factor models are now frequently used by financial analysts. The Carhart four-factor model is expressed as follows:

$$R - r_f = E(R) + \beta[E(R_M) - r_f] + \gamma HML + \delta SMB + \eta MOM + \varepsilon$$

where $[E(R_M) - r_f]$ is the market risk premium, HML is the return on an arbitrage portfolio that is long in high B/M equities and short in low B/M stocks, SMB is the return on an arbitrage portfolio that is long in small market capitalization equities and short in large market capitalization equities, and MOM is the return on an arbitrage portfolio that is long in the best performing equities and short in the worst performing equities. The term ε is considered unsystematic risk because it is unique to each individual security. The Fama–French three-factor model is simply the Carhart model without the momentum factor.

4   The Fama–French five factor model is presented below:

$$R - r_f = E(R) + \beta_1(R_M - r_f) + \beta_2 HML + \beta_3 SMB + \beta_4 RMW + \beta_5 CMA + \varepsilon$$

where RMW is the difference between the returns on diversified equity portfolios of high and low profitability, CMA is the difference between the returns on diversified equity portfolios of low and high investment firms, and other variables are as defined earlier.

5   As securities are added to a portfolio, the unsystematic risks of the individual securities offset each other. A fully diversified portfolio has no unsystematic risk but still has systematic risk. This result indicates that diversification can eliminate some, but not all, of the risk of individual securities.

6   Because of this, the expected return on a security is related to its systematic risk. In a one-factor model, the systematic risk is simply the beta of the CAPM. Thus, the implications of the CAPM and the one-factor APT are identical. However, each security has many risks in a multifactor model such as the Carhart model. The expected return on a security is related to the beta of the security with each factor.

Questions and Problems

CONCEPT

1   **Announcements, Surprises and Expected Returns**   What is the difference between an expected return and observed return? Is it possible to predict the surprise component of an observed return?

2   **Systematic versus Unsystematic Risk**   You own equity in Lewis-Striden Drugs plc. Suppose you had expected the following events to occur last month:

(a) The government would announce that real GNP had grown 1.2 per cent during the previous quarter. The returns of Lewis-Striden are positively related to real GNP.

(b) The government would announce that inflation over the previous quarter was 3.7 per cent. The returns of Lewis-Striden are negatively related to inflation.

(c) Interest rates would rise 2.5 percentage points. The returns of Lewis-Striden are negatively related to interest rates.

(d) The chairman of the firm would announce his retirement. The retirement would be effective 6 months from the announcement day. The chairman is well liked: in general, he is considered an asset to the firm.

(e) Research data would conclusively prove the efficacy of an experimental drug. Completion of the efficacy testing means the drug will be on the market soon.

Suppose the following events actually occurred:

(a) The government announced that real GNP grew 2.3 per cent during the previous quarter.

(b) The government announced that inflation over the previous quarter was 3.7 per cent.

(c) Interest rates rose 2.1 percentage points.

(d) The chairman of the firm died suddenly of a heart attack.

(e) Research results in the efficacy testing were not as strong as expected. The drug must be tested for another 6 months, and the efficacy results must be resubmitted to the FDA.

(f) Lab researchers had a breakthrough with another drug.

(g) A competitor announced that it will begin distribution and sale of a medicine that will compete directly with one of Lewis-Striden's top-selling products.

Discuss how each of the actual occurrences affects the returns on your Lewis-Striden shares. Which events represent systematic risk? Which events represent unsystematic risk?

3 **Systematic Risk and Betas** What is data mining? Is there anything wrong with measuring the performance of an Irish growth fund portfolio manager against a benchmark composed of Greek equities?

4 **Portfolios and Factor Models** You have recently been employed as a finance consultant to Bread plc. The CEO wants to use an APT model to estimate the required return on the company's stock, and the risk factors he plans to use in his model are the stock market risk premium, the inflation rate, and the price of wheat (since wheat is one of the major costs his company face). He has asked for your opinion on his choice of risk factors. Is there anything he has overlooked? Is there anything he has not included that should be? Explain.

5 **Betas and Expected Returns** Why does the market portfolio lie on the security market line? What does it mean if a security lies below the security market line? What would happen to the returns of the security if traders exploit any possible arbitrage opportunities?

6 **APT** Your manager tells you that for the APT to be useful, the number of systematic risk factors must be small. Is your manager right? Explain.

REGULAR

7 **Market Model versus APT** What are the differences between a k-factor model and the market model?

8 **APT** As financial director of Renault SA, you have been tasked with estimating the required return on the company's equity. What risk factors should you use? Explain your choice.

9 **Market Model versus the Carhart (1997) Model** What are the differences between the Carhart (1997) model and the market model?

10 **APT** What is the relationship between the one-factor model and the CAPM? In contrast to the CAPM, the APT does not indicate which factors are expected to determine the risk premium of an asset. How can we determine which factors should be included?

11 **Factor Models** How can the return on a portfolio be expressed in terms of a factor model?

12 **Factor Models** You plan to purchase a company and wish to estimate the expected return on the company's equity using a three-factor model. You believe the appropriate factors are the market return, the percentage change in GNP and the oil price return. The market is expected to grow by 6 per cent, GNP is expected to grow by 2 per cent, and the oil price is expected to fall by 5 per cent. The company has betas of 0.8, 0.3 and −0.1 for the market, GNP and oil respectively. The expected rate of return on the equity is 15 per cent. What is the revised expected return if the market falls by 8 per cent, GNP contracts by 0.3 per cent and the oil price grows by 9 per cent?

13 **Factor Models** Suppose a factor model is appropriate to describe stock returns for a company, with information about these factors set out in the table below. The expected return on the stock is 10.5 per cent.

Factor	β	Expected Value	Actual Value
GNP growth	2.05	3%	3.5%
Inflation	−2	5.5%	5%

(a) What is the systematic risk of the stock return?

(b) The firm announced that its market share had unexpectedly increased from 23 per cent to 27 per cent. Investors know from past experience that the stock return will increase by 0.36 per cent for every 1 per cent increase in its market share. What is the unsystematic risk of the stock?

(c) What is the total return on this stock?

14 Factor Models Suppose the Fama–French three-factor model is appropriate to describe the returns of an equity. Information about those three factors is presented in the following table:

Factor	β	Expected Value (%)	Actual Value (%)
$(R_m - r_f)$	1.50	8.4	8.1
HML	−1.40	3.1	3.8
SMB	−0.67	9.5	10.3

(a) What is the systematic risk of the equity return?

(b) Suppose unexpected bad news about the firm was announced that causes the share price to drop by 2.6 per cent. If the expected return is 9.5 per cent, what is the total return on this equity?

15 Factor Models Suppose the Carhart (1997) factor model is appropriate to describe the returns on an equity. The current expected return on the equity is 10.5 per cent. Information about the factors is presented in the following table:

Factor	β	Expected Value (%)	Actual Value (%)
$(R_m - r_f)$	1.04	3.5	4.8
HML	−1.90	7.1	7.8
SMB	0.60	2.4	6.4
Momentum	0.44	0.23	−3.2

(a) What is the systematic risk of the equity return?

(b) The firm announced that its market share had unexpectedly increased from 23 per cent to 27 per cent. Investors know from past experience that the share price return will increase by 0.36 per cent for every 1 per cent increase in its market share. What is the equity's unsystematic risk?

(c) What is the equity's total return?

16 Factor Models Suppose equity returns can be explained by the Fama–French three-factor model:

$$R = \overline{R} + \beta(R_M - r_f) + \gamma HML + \delta SMB + \varepsilon$$

Assume there is no firm-specific risk. The information for each equity is presented here:

	β	γ	δ
Equity A	1.20	0.90	0.20
Equity B	0.80	1.40	−0.30
Equity C	0.95	−0.05	1.50

The risk premiums for the three factors are 5.5 per cent, 4.2 per cent, and 4.9 per cent, respectively. If you create a portfolio with 20 per cent invested in A, 20 per cent invested in B, and the remainder in C, what is the expression for the return of your portfolio? Assuming that the base return for each equity is 5 per cent and the risk free rate is 5 per cent, what is the expected return of your portfolio?

17 Multifactor Models Suppose equity returns can be explained by the Fama–French three-factor model. The firm-specific risks for all equities are independent. The following table shows the information for three diversified portfolios:

	β	γ	δ	$E(R)$ (%)
Portfolio A	0.75	1.20	0.04	18
Portfolio B	1.60	−0.20	0.07	14
Portfolio C	0.85	1.20	0.65	22

Assuming that the base return on each portfolio is 6 per cent and the risk free rate is 5 per cent, what are the risk premiums for each factor in this model?

18 Market Model Assume that the market model is given by:

$$R_{i,t} = \alpha + \beta R_{M,t} + \varepsilon_{i,t}$$

In this equation, $R_{i,t}$ represents the return on asset i at time t; $R_{M,t}$ represents the return on a portfolio containing all risky assets in the same proportion at time t; and both $R_{M,t}$ and $\varepsilon_{i,t}$ are statistically independent variables. Short selling is allowed in the market. You are provided with the information set out in the table below:

Asset	β	Expected return (%)	$Var(\varepsilon_{i,t})$
A	0.7	8.41	0.0100
B	1.2	12.06	0.0144
C	1.5	13.95	0.0225

The variance of the market is 0.0121. Assume that there are no transaction costs.

(a) Calculate the standard deviation of returns for each asset.

(b) Calculate the variance of return of three portfolios containing an infinite number of asset types A, B or C, respectively.

(c) Assume the risk-free rate is 3.3 per cent and the expected return on the market is 10.6 per cent. Which asset will not be held by rational investors?

(d) What equilibrium state will emerge such that no arbitrage opportunities exist? Why?

19 Portfolio Risk You are forming an equally weighted portfolio of equities. Many equities have the same beta of 0.84 for factor 1 and the same beta of 1.69 for factor 2. They also have the same expected return of 11 per cent. Assume a two-factor model describes the return on each of these equities.

(a) Write the equation of the returns on your portfolio if you place only five equities in it.

(b) Write the equation of the returns on your portfolio if you place in it a very large number of equities that all have the same expected returns and the same betas.

20 Arbitrage Pricing Theory The returns on three equities, A, B and C, are given by the following:

$$R_A = 2.4\% + 0.5F_1$$
$$R_B = 4.6\% + 1.2F_1 - 0.5F_2$$
$$R_C = 4.1\% - 0.4F_1 + 0.6F_2$$

(a) Are the returns correlated? Explain.

(b) Assume that you have another equity, D. This equity's returns are generated as:

$$R_D = \alpha + F_1 + F_2$$

If there are no arbitrage possibilities, what is the value of α?

21 Factor Models The UK is found to have two factors, GDP growth and the inflation rate, that generate the returns of all equities. The expected GDP growth rate in the next year is 2 per cent and the expected inflation rate is 1.5 per cent. Pinto plc has an expected return of 10 per cent, a GDP growth rate factor loading of 1.6 and an inflation rate factor loading of –0.5. If the actual GDP growth rate turns out to be 3 per cent and inflation is 2.3 per cent, what is your estimate of the expected return on Pinto plc?

CHALLENGE

22 APT There are two equity markets, each driven by the same common force F with an expected value of zero and standard deviation of 10 per cent. There are many securities in each market; thus you can invest in as many stocks as you wish. Due to restrictions, however, you can invest in only one of the two markets. The expected return on every security in both markets is 10 per cent.

The returns for each security i in the first market are generated by the relationship:

$$R_{1i} = 0.10 + 1.5F + \varepsilon_{1i}$$

where ε_{1i} is the term that measures the surprises in the returns of security i in the first market. These surprises are normally distributed; their mean is zero. The returns for security j in the second market are generated by the relationship

$$R_{2j} = 0.10 + 0.5F + \varepsilon_{2j}$$

where ε_{2j} is the term that measures the surprises in the returns of security j in market 2. These surprises are normally distributed; their mean is zero. The standard deviation of ε_{1i} and ε_{2j} for any two securities, i and j, is 20 per cent.

(a) If the correlation between the surprises in the returns of any two securities in the first market is zero, and if the correlation between the surprises in the returns of any two securities in the second market is zero, in which market would a risk-averse person prefer to invest? (*Note:* The correlation between ε_{1i} and ε_{1j} for any i and j is zero, and the correlation between ε_{2i} and ε_{2j} for any i and j is zero.)

(b) If the correlation between ε_{1i} and ε_{1j} in the first market is 0.9 and the correlation between ε_{2i} and ε_{2j} in the second market is zero, in which market would a risk-averse person prefer to invest?

(c) If the correlation between ε_{1i} and ε_{1j} in the first market is zero and the correlation between ε_{2i} and ε_{2j} in the second market is 0.5, in which market would a risk-averse person prefer to invest?

(d) In general, what is the relationship between the correlations of the disturbances in the two markets that would make a risk-averse person equally willing to invest in either of the two markets?

23 **APT**   Assume that the following market model adequately describes the return-generating behaviour of risky assets:

$$R_{it} = \alpha_i + \beta_i R_{Mt} + \varepsilon_{it}$$

Here:

R_{it} = the return for the ith asset at time t

R_{Mt} = the return on a portfolio containing all risky assets in some proportion at time t

R_{Mt} and ε_{it} are statistically independent.

Short selling (i.e., negative positions) is allowed in the market. You are given the following information:

Asset	β_i	$E(R_i)$ (%)	$Var(\varepsilon_i)$
A	0.7	8.41	0.0100
B	1.2	12.06	0.0144
C	1.5	13.95	0.0225

The variance of the market is 0.0121, and there are no transaction costs.

(a) Calculate the standard deviation of returns for each asset.

(b) Calculate the variance of return of three portfolios containing an infinite number of asset types A, B or C, respectively.

(c) Assume the risk-free rate is 3.3 per cent and the expected return on the market is 10.6 per cent. Which asset will not be held by rational investors?

(d) What equilibrium state will emerge such that no arbitrage opportunities exist? Why?

24 **APT**   Assume that the returns of individual securities are generated by the following two-factor model:

$$R_{it} = E(R_{it}) + \beta_{ij}F_{1t} + \beta_{i2}F_{2t}$$

Here:

R_{it} is the return for security i at time t

F_{1t} and F_{2t} are market factors with zero expectation and zero covariance.

In addition, assume that there is a capital market for four securities, and the capital market for these four assets is perfect in the sense that there are no transaction costs and short sales (i.e., negative positions) are permitted. The characteristics of the four securities follow:

Security	β_1	β_2	$E(R)$ (%)
1	1.0	1.50	20
2	0.5	2.00	20
3	1.0	0.50	10
4	1.5	0.75	10

(a) Construct a portfolio containing (long or short) securities 1 and 2, with a return that does not depend on the market factor, F_1, in any way. (*Hint:* Such a portfolio will have $\beta_1 = 0$.) Compute the expected return and β_2 coefficient for this portfolio.

(b) Following the procedure in (a), construct a portfolio containing securities 3 and 4 with a return that does not depend on the market factor F_1. Compute the expected return and β_2 coefficient for this portfolio.

(c) There is a risk-free asset with expected return equal to 5 per cent, $\beta_1 = 0$, and $\beta_2 = 0$. Describe a possible arbitrage opportunity in such detail that an investor could implement it.

(d) What effect would the existence of these kinds of arbitrage opportunities have on the capital markets for these securities in the short and long run? Graph your analysis.

25 **Factor Models**   The returns on Ericsson, Electrolux and Swedbank are generated as follows:

$$R_{it} = \alpha_i + \beta_{i,SMB}\, R_{SMB} + \beta_{i,HML\ RHML} + \varepsilon_{it}$$

Name	α(%)	β_{HML}	β_{SMB}
Ericsson	3	1.2	−0.3
Electrolux	5	0.9	−0.25
Swedbank	7	−0.5	1.3

How would you determine the return on an equally weighted portfolio of all three equities?

26 **Factor Models**   Prove that the portfolio-weighted average of a security's sensitivity to a particular factor is the same as the covariance between the return of the portfolio and the factor divided by the variance of the factor if the factors are uncorrelated with each other.

27 **Factor Models**   How can the return on a portfolio be expressed in terms of a factor model? What is the minimum number of factors needed to explain the expected returns of a group of five securities if the securities' returns have no firm-specific risk? Why?

28 **Factor Models**   Consider the following two-factor model for the returns of three securities. Assume that the factors and epsilons have means of zero. Also, assume the factors have variances of 0.1 and are uncorrelated with each other.

$$\tilde{r}_A = 0.13 + 0.6\tilde{F}_1 + 0.4\tilde{F}_2 + \tilde{\epsilon}_A$$
$$\tilde{r}_B = 0.15 + 0.2\tilde{F}_1 + 0.2\tilde{F}_2 + \tilde{\epsilon}_B$$
$$\tilde{r}_C = 0.07 + 0.5\tilde{F}_1 + 0.1\tilde{F}_2 + \tilde{\epsilon}_C$$

If $var(\tilde{\epsilon}_A) = 0.01\, var(\tilde{\epsilon}_B) = 0.04\, var(\tilde{\epsilon}_C) = 0.02$ what are the variances of the returns of the three securities, as well as the covariances and correlations between them?

29 **Factor Models**   A portfolio manager wants to create a simple portfolio from only two stocks, A and B. The returns for stocks A and B are given by the following equations:

$$R_A = 0.09 - 1F_{INF} + 1F_{GDP} + \varepsilon_A \text{ and } R_B = 0.12 + 2F_{INF} + 4F_{GDP} + \varepsilon_B$$

The manager forms a portfolio with market value weights of 40 per cent in stock A and 60 per cent in stock B. What is the sensitivity to the portfolio of a 1 per cent rise in inflation, in basis points?

Exam Question (45 minutes)

Assume a two-factor APT model is appropriate for asset returns, and there are an infinite number of assets in the economy. Two factors drive expected return: the percentage change in GDP and interest rates. The cross-sectional relationship between expected return and factor betas indicates that GDP is expected to grow by 5 per cent and interest rates will grow by 2 per cent. You have estimated factor betas for equities X and Y as follows:

Equity	β_1	β_2
X	2.3	1.9
Y	0.6	−0.5

1 The expected return on an asset having zero betas (with respect to both factors) is 0.03. According to the APT, what are the approximate equilibrium returns on each of the two equities? (25 marks)

2 Discuss what the theoretical results in the APT say about the number of factors used in this question. (25 marks)

3 The APT expected return relationship looks very similar to the security market line which was derived in the capital asset pricing model. Review the differences between the APT and CAPM. (25 marks)

4 You determine that there are two factors under the APT which affect the portfolios you have constructed for your limited clientele, who invest only in gold equities: the rate of inflation and the growth rate of all gold stocks in relation to the growth rate of all commodity equities. You determine that the two factors will grow by 0.08 and 0.20, respectively, with zero covariance between the two factors, and the zero beta portfolio's expected rate of return is 3 per cent. The beta for your gold portfolio is 1.2 with respect to both factors. Calculate the expected rate of return for your portfolio. (25 marks)

Mini Case

The Fama–French Multifactor Model and Mutual Fund Returns

Dawn Browne, an investment broker, has been approached by client Jack Thomas about the risk of his investments. Dawn has recently read several articles concerning the risk factors that can potentially affect asset returns, and she has decided to examine Jack's mutual fund holdings. Jack is currently invested in the Fidelity Magellan Fund (FMAGX), the Fidelity Low-Priced Stock Fund (FLPSX), and the Baron Small Cap Fund (BSCFX).

Dawn would like to estimate the well-known multifactor model proposed by Mark Carhart in 1997 to determine the risk of each mutual fund.

$$R_{it} - R_{Ft} = \alpha_i + \beta_1(R_{Mt} - R_{Ft}) + \beta_2(SMB_t) + \beta_3(HML_t) + \beta_4(MOM) + \varepsilon_t$$

In models such as the one Dawn is considering, the alpha (α) term is of particular interest. It is the regression intercept; but more important, it is also the excess return the asset earned. In other words, if the alpha is positive, the asset earned a return greater than it should have given its level of risk; if the alpha is negative, the asset earned a return lower than it should have given its level of risk. This measure is called 'Jensen's alpha', and it is a very widely used tool for mutual fund evaluation.

1 For a large-company equity mutual fund, would you expect the betas to be positive or negative for each of the factors in a Carhart multifactor model?

2 The SMB, HML, MOM factors, and risk-free rates for the US are available at Ken French's website: mba.tuck.dartmouth.edu/pages/faculty/ken.french/. Download the monthly factors and save the most recent 60 months for each factor. The historical prices for each of the mutual funds can be found on various websites, including finance.yahoo.com. Find the prices of each mutual fund for the same time as the Carhart factors and calculate the returns for each month. Be sure to include dividends. For each mutual fund, estimate the multifactor regression equation using the Carhart factors. How well do the regression estimates explain the variation in the return of each mutual fund?

3   What do you observe about the beta coefficients for the different mutual funds? Comment on any similarities or differences.

4   If the market is efficient, what value would you expect for alpha? Do your estimates support market efficiency?

5   Which fund has performed best considering its risk? Why?

References

Carhart, M. (1997) 'On Persistence in Mutual Fund Performance', *The Journal of Finance*, Vol. 52, 57–82.

Fama, E.F., and K.R. French (1993) 'Common Risk Factors in the Returns on Stocks and Bonds', *Journal of Financial Economics,* Vol. 17, 3–56.

Fama, E.F., and K.R. French (2015) 'A Five-Factor Asset Pricing Model', *Journal of Financial Economics*, Vol. 116, No. 1, 1–22.

Additional Reading

Much of the research into asset pricing overlaps that of Chapter 10. A good review of the literature is the paper by Avanidhar Subrahmanyam:

1   Subrahmanyam, A. (2010) 'The Cross-Section of Expected Stock Returns: What Have We Learnt from the Past Twenty-Five Years of Research?' *European Financial Management*, Vol. 16, No. 1, 27–42.

The three papers that are listed below consider several factors that can influence share price returns. As with the previous chapter, the range of anomalies and factors that have been investigated is vast and the listing is simply an example of research in this area.

2   Baker, M. and J. Wurgler (2006) 'Investor Sentiment and the Cross-Section of Stock Returns', *The Journal of Finance*, Vol. 61, No. 4, 1645–1680. **US**.

3   Davis, J.L., E.F. Fama and K.R. French (2000) 'Characteristics, Covariances, and Average Returns: 1927 to 1997', *The Journal of Finance*, Vol. 55, No. 1, 389–406. **US**.

4   Scowcroft, A. and J. Sefton (2005) 'Understanding Momentum', *Financial Analysts Journal*, Vol. 61, No. 2, 64–82. **International**.

Endnotes

1   In the previous chapter, we briefly mentioned that unsystematic risk is risk that can be diversified away in a large portfolio. This result will also follow from the present analysis.

2   Alternatively, the market model could be written as:

$$R = \alpha + \beta R_M + \varepsilon$$

Here alpha (α) is an intercept term equal to $\bar{R} - \beta \bar{R}_M$.

3   Technically, we can think of a large portfolio as one where an investor keeps increasing the number of securities without limit. In practice, *effective* diversification would occur if at least a few dozen securities were held.

4   More precisely, we say that the weighted average of the unsystematic risk approaches zero as the number of equally weighted securities in a portfolio approaches infinity.

5   Our presentation on this point has been non-rigorous. The student interested in more rigour should note that the variance of row 3 is:

$$\frac{1}{N^2}\sigma_\varepsilon^2 + \frac{1}{N^2}\sigma_\varepsilon^2 + \frac{1}{N^2}\sigma_\varepsilon^2 + \cdots + \frac{1}{N^2}\sigma_\varepsilon^2 = \frac{1}{N^2}\sigma_\varepsilon^2$$

where σ_ε^2 is the variance of each ε. This can be rewritten as σ_ε^2/N, which tends to 0 as N goes to infinity.

6   This assumption is plausible in the real world. For example, the market value of Royal Dutch Shell, which is the biggest company in the FTSE 100, is only 3 per cent to 4 per cent of the market value of the index.

Risk, Cost of Capital and Capital Budgeting

Risk is integral to any type of financial decision for a business. Without understanding how risky an investment or project is, it is impossible to undertake any valuation appraisal. Risk is captured by the discount rate of a project, but what is actually meant by a discount rate? The discount rate to an investor is the rate of return expected for undertaking the project, given its risk. The discount rate to a corporate manager is the cost of raising capital to fund the company's investments. To arrive at a sensible value for discount rates, one must always keep in mind this duality in investor and management perspectives, and this is why the investor's rate of return is also called the cost of capital.

In this chapter, we learn how to compute a firm's cost of capital and find out what it means to the firm and its investors. We will also learn when to use the firm's cost of capital – and perhaps more important, when not to use it.

KEY NOTATIONS

R_E	Return on shares; cost of equity capital
R_D	Return on debt; cost of debt capital
β	Systematic risk; beta
R_M	Market return
R_F	Risk-free rate of return
$\text{Cov}(R_i, R_M); \sigma_{i,M}$	Covariance between security i and the market, M
$\text{Var}(R_M); \sigma_M^2$	Variance of the market return
S	Market value of equity
B	Market value of debt
R_{WACC}	Weighted average cost of capital
EVA	Economic value added

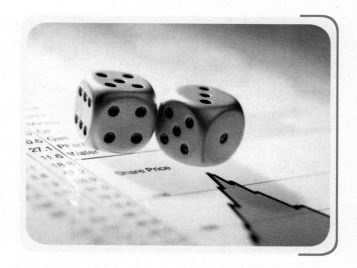

12.1 The Cost of Equity Capital

Whenever a firm has extra cash, it can take one of two actions. It can pay out the cash immediately as a dividend, or alternatively, the firm can invest extra cash in a project, paying out the future cash flows of the project as dividends. Which procedure would shareholders prefer? If a shareholder can reinvest the dividend in a financial asset (an equity or bond) with the same risk as that of the project, the shareholders would desire the alternative with the highest expected return. In other words, the project should be undertaken only if its expected return is greater than that of a financial asset of comparable risk. This is illustrated in Figure 12.1. This discussion implies a very simple capital budgeting rule:

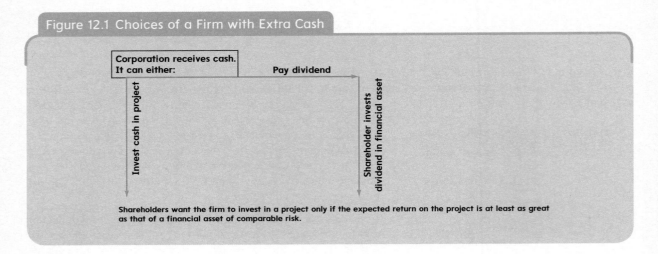

Figure 12.1 Choices of a Firm with Extra Cash

Corporation receives cash. It can either:

Invest cash in project

Pay dividend

Shareholder invests dividend in financial asset

Shareholders want the firm to invest in a project only if the expected return on the project is at least as great as that of a financial asset of comparable risk.

The discount rate of a project should be the expected return on a financial asset of comparable risk.

From the firm's perspective, the expected return is the cost of equity capital. Under the CAPM, the expected return on a security can be written as:

$$R_E = R_F + \beta \times (R_M - R_F) \tag{12.1}$$

where R_F is the risk-free rate and $R_M - R_F$ is the difference between the expected return on the market portfolio and the riskless rate. This difference is often called the expected *excess* market return or market risk premium. Note we have dropped the bar denoting expectations from our expression to simplify the notation, but remember that we are always thinking about expected returns with the CAPM.

We now have the tools to estimate a firm's cost of equity capital. To do this, we need to know three things:

- The risk-free rate, R_F
- The market risk premium, $R_M - R_F$
- The company beta, β.

Example 12.1

Cost of Equity

According to Reuters, the beta of the French bank Société Générale SA is 2.29. Assume, for now, that the firm is 100 per cent equity financed; that is, it has no debt. Société Générale is considering a number of expansion projects that will double its size. Because these new projects are similar to the firm's existing ones, the average beta on the new projects is assumed to be equal to Société Générale's existing beta. Assume that the risk-free rate is 1.5 per cent. What is the appropriate discount rate for these new projects, assuming a market risk premium of 7.2 per cent?

We estimate the cost of equity, R_E, for Société Générale as:

$$R_E = 1.5\% + (7.2\% \times 2.29)$$
$$= 1.5\% + 16.488\%$$
$$= 17.988\%$$

Two key assumptions were made in this example: (1) The beta risk of the new projects is the same as the risk of the firm, and (2) the firm is all equity financed. Given these assumptions, it follows that the cash flows of the new projects should be discounted at the 12.16 per cent rate.

Example 12.2

Project Evaluation and Beta

Glencore plc is a diversified natural resource company listed on the London Stock Exchange. Suppose Glencore is an all-equity firm. According to Reuters, the firm has a beta of 1.24. Further, suppose the market risk premium is 7.5 per cent, and the risk-free rate is 2 per cent. We can determine the expected return on the equity of Glencore by using the SML of Equation 12.1. We find that the expected return is:

$$2\% + (1.24 \times 7.5\%) = 11.3\%$$

Because this is the return that shareholders can expect in the financial markets on an equity with a β of 1.24, it is also the return they expect on Glencore plc.

Further suppose Glencore is evaluating the following non-mutually exclusive projects in Greece:

Project	Project's Beta (β)	Project's Expected Cash Flows Next Year (£)	Project's Internal Rate of Return (%)	Project's NPV When Cash Flows are Discounted at 11.3% (£)	Accept or Reject
A	1.24	140	40	25.79	Accept
B	1.24	120	20	7.82	Accept
C	1.24	110	10	−1.17	Reject

Each project initially costs £100. All projects are assumed to have the same risk as the firm as a whole. Because the cost of equity capital is 11.3 per cent, projects in an all-equity firm are discounted at this rate. Projects A and B have positive NPVs, and C has a negative NPV. Thus, only A and B will be accepted. This is illustrated in Figure 12.2.

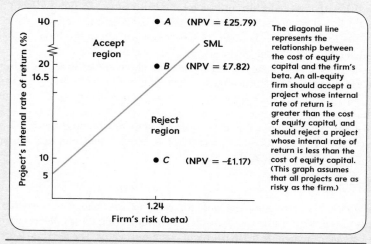

Figure 12.2 Using the Security Market Line to Estimate the Risk-Adjusted Discount Rate for Risky Projects

12.2   Estimation of Beta

Chapter 10 Page 277
Chapter 11 Page 297

In the previous section, we assumed that the beta of the company was known (see **Chapter 11**, Section 11.3 and **Chapter 10**, Section 10.9 for more information on betas). Of course, beta must be estimated in the real world. We pointed out earlier that the beta of a security is the standardized covariance of a security's return with the return on the market portfolio. As we have seen, the formula for security i is

$$\text{Beta of security } i = \frac{\text{Cov}(R_i, R_M)}{\text{Var}(R_M)} = \frac{\sigma_{i,M}}{\sigma_M^2}$$

In words, the beta is the covariance of a security with the market, divided by the variance of the market. Because we calculated both covariance and variance in earlier chapters, calculating beta involves no new material.

Measuring Company Betas

The basic method of measuring company betas is to estimate:

$$\frac{\text{Cov}(R_i, R_M)}{\text{Var}(R_M)}$$

using $t = 1, 2, \ldots, T$ observations

Problems

1 Betas may vary over time.
2 The sample size may be inadequate.
3 Betas are influenced by changing financial leverage and business risk.

Solutions

1 Problems 1 and 2 can be moderated by more sophisticated statistical techniques.
2 Problem 3 can be lessened by adjusting for changes in business and financial risk.
3 Look at average beta estimates of several comparable firms in the industry.

Real-world Betas

It is instructive to see how betas are determined for actual real-world companies. Figure 12.3 plots monthly returns for two large European firms against monthly returns on the Euro Stoxx 50 index. Using a standard regression technique, we fit a straight line through data points. The result is called the 'characteristic' line for the security. The slope of the characteristic line is beta. Though we have not shown it in the table, we can also determine the intercept (commonly called alpha) of the characteristic line by regression.

We use 5 years of monthly data for each plot. Although this choice is arbitrary, it is in line with calculations performed in the real world. Practitioners know that the accuracy of the beta coefficient is suspect when too few observations are used. Conversely, because firms may change their industry over time, observations from the distant past are out of date.

Because beta is a measure of the risk of a single security for someone holding a large, diversified portfolio, our results indicate that Koninklijke (Royal) KPN has relatively lower risk than Unicredit. A more detailed discussion of the determinants of beta is presented in Section 12.3.

Using an Industry Beta

Our approach to estimating the beta of a company from its own past data may seem sensible to you. However, it is frequently argued that people can better estimate a firm's beta by involving the whole industry. Consider Table 12.1, which shows the betas of some prominent firms in the global banking sector. The average beta across all of the firms in the sector is 0.985. Imagine a financial executive at Credit Agricole trying to estimate the firm's beta. Because beta estimation is subject to large random variation in this volatile industry, the executive may be uncomfortable with the estimate of 2.046. However, the error in beta estimation on a single equity is much higher than the error for a portfolio of securities. Thus the executive of Santander may use the industry beta of 0.985 as the estimate of its own firm's beta.

Figure 12.3 Plots of 5 Years of Monthly Returns (2007–2012) on Two Individual Securities against 5 Years of Monthly Returns on the Euro Stoxx 50 Index

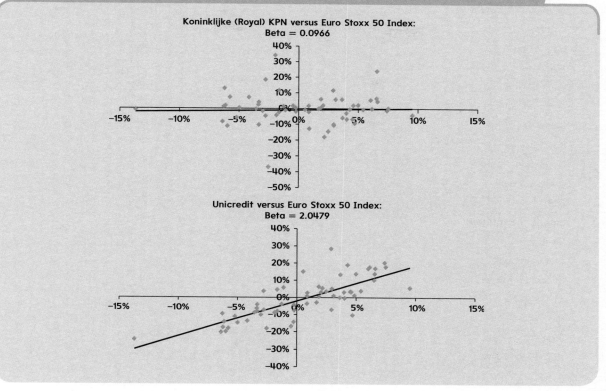

Table 12.1 Betas for Firms in the Global Banking Industry, 2015

Name	Beta
Bank of Ireland	2.327
Société Générale	2.170
Popular	2.092
Credit Agricole	2.046
Citigroup	1.756
BNP Paribas	1.733
Unicredit	1.724
Credit Suisse Group N	1.689
Pacwest Bancorp	1.668
Philippine National Bank	1.663
Intesa Sanpaolo RSP	1.661
Raiffeisen Bank Intl.	1.638
Intesa Sanpaolo	1.608
Emirates NBD	1.604
Bank Muscat	1.589
Lloyds Banking Group	1.561
Ing Groep	1.555

Name	Beta
JP Morgan Chase & Co.	1.538
Barclays	1.532
UBS Group	1.496
Mediobanca BC.Fin	1.487
Bank of America	1.485
National Bank of Greece	1.476
Banco Popolare	1.460
Royal Bank of Scotland Group	1.459
Dubai Islamic Bank	1.402
Deutsche Bank	1.277
BCI	1.250
Standard Chartered	1.214
Swedbank 'A'	1.203
Commerzbank	1.172
Banco Santander	1.114
Nordea Bank	1.055
HSBC Holdings	0.970
Bankia	0.860
Hang Seng Bank	0.853

In contrast, consider Royal Bank of Scotland. Assuming a risk-free rate of 2 per cent and a risk premium of 6 per cent, Royal Bank of Scotland might estimate its cost of equity capital as:

$$2\% + 1.459 \times 6\% = 10.75\%$$

However, if Royal Bank of Scotland believed the industry beta contained less estimation error, it could estimate its cost of equity capital as:

$$2\% + 0.985 \times 6\% = 7.910\%$$

The difference is substantial here, presenting a difficult choice for a financial executive at Royal Bank of Scotland.

While there is no formula for selecting the right beta, there is a very simple guideline. If you believe that the operations of a firm are similar to the operations of the rest of the industry, you should use the industry beta simply to reduce estimation error.[1] However, if an executive believes that the operations of the firm are fundamentally different from those in the rest of the industry, the firm's beta should be used.

Chapter 3
Page 64

When we discussed financial statement analysis in **Chapter 3**, we noted that a problem frequently comes up in practice – namely, what is the industry? For example, Tesco is normally regarded as a supermarket. However, the company is also involved in financial services. The risk of these different business operations can be quite different.

12.3   Determinants of Beta

The regression analysis approach in the previous section does not tell us where beta comes from. Of course, the beta of a security does not come out of thin air. Rather, it is determined by the characteristics of the firm. We consider three factors: the cyclical nature of revenues, operating leverage and financial leverage.

Cyclicality of Revenues

The revenues of some firms are quite cyclical. That is, these firms do well in the expansion phase of the business cycle and do poorly in the contraction phase. Empirical evidence suggests hi-tech firms, retailers and automotive firms fluctuate with the business cycle. Firms in industries such as utilities, railroads, food and airlines are less dependent on the cycle. Because beta is the standardized covariance of a security's return with the market's return, it is not surprising that highly cyclical securities have high betas.

It is worthwhile to point out that cyclicality is not the same as variability. For example, a film-making firm has highly variable revenues because hits and flops are not easily predicted. However, because the revenues of a studio are more dependent on the quality of its releases than the phase of the business cycle, motion picture companies are not particularly cyclical. In other words, securities with high standard deviations need not have high betas, a point we have stressed before.

Operating Leverage

We distinguished fixed costs from variable costs earlier in the text. At that time, we mentioned that fixed costs do not change as quantity changes. Conversely, variable costs increase as the quantity of output rises. This difference between variable and fixed costs allows us to define operating leverage.

Example 12.3

Operating Leverage Illustrated

Consider a typical problem faced by Carlsberg, the Danish alcoholic drinks firm. As part of the brewing process, Carlsberg often needs to choose between two production technologies. Assume that Carlsberg can choose either technology A or technology B when making a particular drink. The relevant differences between the two technologies are displayed here:

Technology A	Technology B
Fixed cost: DKr1,000/year	Fixed cost: DKr2,000/year
Variable cost: DKr8/unit	Variable cost: DKr6/unit
Price: DKr10/unit	Price: DKr10/unit
Contribution margin: DKr2 (=£10 − £8)	Contribution margin: DKr4 (=DKr10 −DKr6)

Technology A has lower fixed costs and higher variable costs than does technology B. Perhaps technology A involves less mechanization than does B. Or the equipment in A may be leased, whereas the equipment in B must be purchased. Alternatively, perhaps technology A involves few employees but many subcontractors, whereas B involves only highly skilled employees who must be retained in bad times. Because technology B has both lower variable costs and higher fixed costs, we say that it has higher operating leverage.

Figure 12.4 graphs the costs under both technologies. The slope of each total cost line represents variable costs under a single technology. The slope of A's line is steeper, indicating greater variable costs.

Technology A has higher variable costs and lower fixed costs than does technology B. Technology B has higher operating leverage.

Figure 12.4 Illustration of Two Different Technologies

Because the two technologies are used to produce the same drinks, a unit price of DKr10 applies for both cases. An unexpected sale increases profit by DKr2 under A but increases profit by DKr4 under B. Similarly, an unexpected sale cancellation reduces profit by DKr2 under A but reduces profit by DKr4 under B. This is illustrated in Figure 12.5. This figure shows the change in earnings before interest and taxes for a given change in volume. The slope of the right graph is greater, indicating that technology B is riskier.

Technology B has lower variable costs than A, implying a higher contribution margin. The profits of the firm are more responsive to changes in volume under technology B than under A.

Figure 12.5 Illustration of the Effect of a Change in Volume on the Change in Earnings before Interest and Taxes (EBIT)

The cyclicality of a firm's revenues is a determinant of the firm's beta. Operating leverage magnifies the effect of cyclicality on beta. As mentioned earlier, business risk is generally defined as the risk of the firm without financial leverage. Business risk depends both on the responsiveness of the firm's revenues to the business cycle and on the firm's operating leverage.

Although the preceding discussion concerns firms, it applies to projects as well. If we cannot estimate a project's beta in another way, we can examine the project's revenues and operating leverage. Projects whose revenues appear strongly cyclical and whose operating leverage appears high are likely to have high betas. Conversely, weak cyclicality and low operating leverage imply low betas. As mentioned earlier, this approach is unfortunately qualitative in nature. Because start-up projects have little data, quantitative estimates of beta generally are not feasible.

Financial Leverage and Beta

As suggested by their names, operating leverage and financial leverage are analogous concepts. Operating leverage refers to the firm's fixed costs of *production*. Financial leverage is the extent to which a firm relies on debt, and a levered firm is a firm with some debt in its capital structure. Because a *levered* firm must make interest payments regardless of the firm's sales, financial leverage refers to the firm's fixed costs of *finance*.

Chapter 10
Page 275

Consider our discussion in **Chapter 10** (Example 10.4) concerning the beta of Hicks plc. In that example, we estimated beta from the returns on Hicks' *equity*. Furthermore, the betas in Figure 12.3 from real-world firms were estimated from returns on equity. Thus, in each case, we estimated the firm's equity beta. The beta of the assets of a levered firm is different from the beta of its equity. As the name suggests, the asset beta is the beta of the assets of the firm. The asset beta could also be thought of as the beta of the firm's shares had the firm been financed only with equity.

Imagine an individual who owns all the firm's debt and all its equity. In other words, this individual owns the entire firm. What is the beta of her portfolio of the firm's debt and equity?

As with any portfolio, the beta of this portfolio is a weighted average of the betas of the individual items in the portfolio. Let D stand for the market value of the firm's debt and E stand for the market value of the firm's equity. We have:

$$\beta_{\text{Asset}} = \frac{E}{D+E} \times \beta_{\text{Equity}} + \frac{D}{D+E} \times \beta_{\text{Debt}} \qquad (12.2)$$

where β_{Equity} is the beta of the equity of the *levered* firm. Notice that the beta of debt, β_{Debt}, is multiplied by $D/(D+E)$, the percentage of debt in the capital structure. Similarly, the beta of equity is multiplied by the percentage of equity in the capital structure. Because the portfolio contains both the debt of the firm and the equity of the firm, the beta of the portfolio is the *asset beta*. As we have just said, the asset beta can also be viewed as the beta of the company's shares had the firm been all equity.

The beta of debt is very low in practice. If we make the common assumption that the beta of debt is zero, we have:

$$\beta_{Asset} = \frac{E}{D+E} \times \beta_{Equity} \tag{12.3}$$

Because $E/(D + E)$ must be below 1 for a levered firm, it follows that $\beta_{Asset} < \beta_{Equity}$. Rearranging this equation, we have:

$$\beta_{Equity} = \beta_{Asset}\left(1 + \frac{D}{E}\right)$$

The equity beta will always be greater than the asset beta with financial leverage (assuming the asset beta is positive).[2]

Example 12.4

Asset versus Equity Betas

Consider a Swedish tree-growing company, Rapid Firs, which is currently all equity and has a beta of 0.8. The firm has decided to move to a capital structure of one part debt to two parts equity. Because the firm is staying in the same industry, its asset beta should remain at 0.8. However, assuming a zero beta for its debt, its equity beta would become:

$$\beta_{Equity} = \beta_{Asset}\left(1 + \frac{D}{E}\right)$$
$$1.2 = 0.8\left(1 + \frac{1}{2}\right)$$

If the firm had one part debt to one part equity in its capital structure, its equity beta would be:

$$1.6 = 0.8(1 + 1)$$

However, as long as it stayed in the same industry, its asset beta would remain at 0.8. The effect of leverage, then, is to increase the equity beta.

12.4 Extensions of the Basic Model

The Firm versus the Project

We now assume that the risk of a project differs from that of the firm, while going back to the all-equity assumption. We began the chapter by pointing out that each project should be paired with a financial asset of comparable risk. If a project's beta differs from that of the firm, the project should be discounted at the rate commensurate with its own beta. This is a very important point because firms frequently speak of a *corporate discount rate*. (*Hurdle rate, cutoff rate, benchmark* and *cost of capital* are frequently used synonymously.) Unless all projects in the corporation are of the same risk, choosing the same discount rate for all projects is incorrect.

Example 12.5

Project Risk

D.D. Ronnelley, a publishing firm, may accept a project to adapt its existing textbooks into interactive textbook apps for the Apple and Android operating systems. Noting that computer software companies have high betas, the publishing firm views the software venture as more risky than the rest of its business. It should discount the project at a rate commensurate with the risk of software companies. For example, it might use the average beta of a portfolio of publicly traded software firms. Instead, if all projects in D.D. Ronnelley were discounted at the same rate, a bias would result. The firm would accept too many high-risk projects (software ventures) and reject too many low-risk projects (books and magazines). This point is illustrated in Figure 12.6.

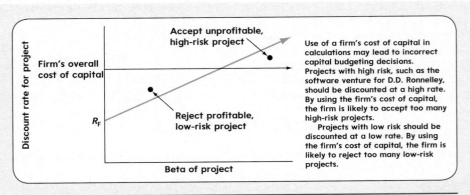

Figure 12.6 Relationship between the Firm's Cost of Capital and the Security Market Line

The D.D. Ronnelley example assumes that the proposed project has identical risk to that of the software industry, allowing the industry beta to be used. However, the beta of a new project may be greater than the beta of existing firms in the same industry because the very newness of the project likely increases its responsiveness to economy-wide movements. For example, a start-up computer venture may fail in a recession, whereas Dell or Apple will still be around. Conversely, in an economy-wide expansion, the venture may grow much faster than the oldline computer firms.

Fortunately, a slight adjustment is all that is needed here. The new venture should be assigned a somewhat higher beta than that of the industry to reflect added risk. The adjustment is necessarily ad hoc, so no formula can be given. Our experience indicates that this approach is widespread in practice today.

The Cost of Capital with Debt

Section 12.1 showed how to choose the discount rate when a project is all equity financed. In this section we discuss an adjustment when the project is financed with both debt and equity.

Suppose a firm uses both debt and equity to finance its investments. If the firm pays R_D for its debt financing and R_E for its equity, what is the overall or average cost of its capital? The cost of equity is R_E, as discussed in earlier sections. The cost of debt is the firm's borrowing rate, R_D, which we can often observe by looking at the yield to maturity on the firm's debt. If a firm uses both debt and equity, the cost of capital is a weighted average of each. This works out to be:

$$\frac{E}{D+E} \times R_E + \frac{D}{D+E} \times R_D$$

The weights in the formula are, respectively, the proportion of total value represented by the equity:

$$\left(\frac{E}{D+E}\right)$$

and the proportion of total value represented by debt:

$$\left(\frac{D}{D+E}\right)$$

This is only natural. If the firm had issued no debt and was therefore an all-equity firm, its average cost of capital would equal its cost of equity, R_E. At the other extreme, if the firm had issued so much debt that its equity was valueless, it would be an all-debt firm, and its average cost of capital would be its cost of debt, R_D.

Of course, interest is tax deductible at the corporate level, a point to be treated in more detail in a later chapter. The after-tax cost of debt is:

$$\text{Cost of debt (after corporate tax)} = R_D \times (1 - t_C)$$

where t_C is the corporation's tax rate.

Assembling these results, we get the average cost of capital (after tax) for the firm:

$$\text{Average cost of capital} = \left(\frac{E}{D+E} \right) \times R_E + \left(\frac{D}{D+E} \right) \times R_D \times (1 - t_C) \qquad (12.4)$$

Because the average cost of capital is a weighting of its cost of equity and its cost of debt, it is usually referred to as the **weighted average cost of capital**, R_{WACC}, and from now on we will use this term.

Example 12.6

WACC

According to the ArcelorMittal website, the European steelmaker has debt with a market value of €4.4 billion and equity with a market value of €71.4 billion. ArcelorMittal has eight different types of bonds in issue, four of which were issued in Luxembourg (denominated in euros) and the other four denominated in dollars. For the purposes of this question, assume that the bonds are all the same, denominated in dollars and pay interest of 6 per cent per annum. The company's shares have a beta of 1.81. Because of the range of countries and tax codes in regimes in which Arcelormittal operates, the effective tax rate for the company is 13.1 per cent. Assume that the SML holds, that the risk premium on the market is 9.5 per cent (slightly higher than the historical equity risk premium), and that the current Treasury bill rate is 4.5 per cent. What is this firm's R_{WACC}?

To compute the R_{WACC} using Equation 12.4, we must know (1) the after-tax cost of debt, $R_D \times (1 - t_C)$, (2) the cost of equity, R_E, and (3) the proportions of debt and equity used by the firm. These three values are computed next:

1. The pre-tax cost of debt is 6 per cent, implying an after-tax cost of 5.214 per cent [6% × (1 − 0.131)].

2. We compute the cost of equity capital by using the SML:

$$R_E = R_F + \beta(R_M - R_F)$$
$$= 4.5\% + 1.81 \times 9.5\%$$
$$= 21.695\%$$

3. We compute the proportions of debt and equity from the market values of debt and equity. Because the market value of the firm is €75.8 billion (= €4.4 billion + €71.4 billion), the proportions of debt and equity are 5.8 and 94.2 per cent, respectively.

The cost of equity, R_E, is 21.695 per cent, and the after-tax cost of debt, $R_D \times (1 - t_C)$, is 5.214 per cent. D is €4.4 billion and E is €71.4 billion. Therefore:

$$R_{WACC} = \frac{D}{D+E} \times R_D \times (1 - t_C) + \frac{E}{D+E} \times R_E$$
$$= \left(\frac{4.4}{75.8} \times 5.214\% \right) + \left(\frac{71.4}{75.8} \times 21.695\% \right)$$
$$= 20.738\%$$

This procedure is presented in table form next:

(1) Financing Components	(2) Market Values (€)	(3) Weight	(4) Cost of Capital (After Corporate Tax)	(5) Weighted Cost of Capital (%)
Debt	4.4 billion	0.058	6% × (1 − 0.131) = 5.214%	0.302
Equity	71.4 billion	0.942	4.5% + 1.81 × 9.5% = 21.695%	20.436
	75.8 billion	1.000		20.738

The weights we used in the previous example were market value weights. Market value weights are more appropriate than book value weights because the market values of the securities are closer to the actual money that would be received from their sale. Actually, it is usually useful to think in terms of 'target' market weights. These are the market weights expected to prevail over the life of the firm or project.

Example 12.7

Project Evaluation and the WACC

Suppose a firm has both a current and a target debt–equity ratio of 0.6, a cost of debt of 15.15 per cent, and a cost of equity of 20 per cent. The corporate tax rate is 34 per cent.

Our first step calls for transforming the debt–equity (*D/E*) ratio to a debt–value ratio. A *D/E* ratio of 0.6 implies 6 parts debt for 10 parts equity. Because value is equal to the sum of the debt plus the equity, the debt–value ratio is 6/(6 + 10) = 0.375. Similarly, the equity–value ratio is 10/(6 + 10) = 0.625. The R_{WACC} will then be:

$$R_{\text{WACC}} = \left(\frac{E}{D + E}\right) \times R_E + \left(\frac{D}{D + E}\right) \times R_D \times (1 - t_C)$$
$$= 0.625 \times 20\% + 0.375 \times 15.15\% \times 0.66$$
$$= 16.25\%$$

Suppose the firm is considering taking on a warehouse renovation costing £50 million that is expected to yield cost savings of £12 million a year for 6 years. Using the NPV equation and discounting the 6 years of expected cash flows from the renovation at the R_{WACC}, we have:

$$\text{NPV} = -£50 + \frac{£12}{(1 + R_{\text{WACC}})} + \ldots + \frac{£12}{(1 + R_{\text{WACC}})^6}$$
$$= -£50 + £12 \times A_{0.1625}^6$$
$$= -£50 + (12 \times 3.66)$$
$$= -£6.07$$

Should the firm take on the warehouse renovation? The project has a negative NPV using the firm's R_{WACC}. This means that the financial markets offer superior projects in the same risk class (namely, the firm's risk class). The answer is clear: the firm should reject the project.

Real World Insight 12.1

Regulators and the WACC of Utilities

For all companies, WACC is a function of the risk of the company's operations. That is, the risk of the assets drives the risk of equity and debt. With utilities, the government decides what the WACC should be, meaning that the risk of operations is constrained by the regulators, which has a knock-on effect on the returns provided by utility companies' debt and equity securities.

In 2015, the UK regulator stated that water utility WACCs should be no more than 3.85 per cent. This meant that the cost of debt would be in the range of 2.2 to 2.8 per cent and the cost of equity should be around 5.6 per cent.

12.5   Estimating Carrefour Group's Cost of Capital

In the previous section, we calculated the cost of capital of Arcelormittal and simplified a number of important inputs such as the annual interest payment. We will now calculate the cost of capital for Carrefour Group, the French supermarket chain, in the same way that a financial analyst would. Carrefour has stores in Europe, North and South America, as well as Asia operating under the names Carrefour, Pryca, Stoc, Marche Plus, Optique and Comod.

Carrefour Group's Cost of Equity

Our first stop for Carrefour is www.reuters.com. Search for the company using its code (CARR.PA). As of January 2015, Carrefour has 734.91 million shares outstanding. The share price is €28.42 and the market value of the equity is 734.91 × €28.42 = €20,886 million.

To estimate Carrefour's cost of equity, we will assume a market risk premium of 7 per cent. This is a subjective estimate based upon the sentiment of a number of analysts. Given that the rate on European T-bills is around 0.6 per cent (*source*: FT.com), a market risk premium of 7 per cent implies that the market is expected to go up by 7.6 per cent in the next year. Carrefour's beta on Reuters is 1.22. Table 12.2 shows the betas for other food distribution and convenience stores. As you can see, the industry average beta is 0.75, which is a little bit lower than Carrefour's beta. Using Carrefour's own beta in the CAPM to estimate the cost of equity, we find:

$$R_E = 0.006 + 1.22(0.076) = 0.0987 \text{ or } 9.87\%$$

If we use the industry beta, we would find that the estimate for the cost of equity capital is:

$$R_E = 0.006 + 0.75(0.076) = 0.0630 \text{ or } 6.30\%$$

Notice that the estimates for the cost of equity are quite different because Carrefour's beta is much higher than the industry beta. The decision of which cost of equity estimate to use is up to the financial executive, based on knowledge and experience of both the company and the industry. In this case, we will choose to use the cost of equity using Carrefour's own estimated beta.

Table 12.2 Snapshot of Betas for Companies in the Food Distribution and Convenience Stores Industry

Name	Beta
MktCap Weighted Average	**0.75**
O'Key Group SA	1.73
Ontsu Co Ltd	1.50
Premier Foods PLC	1.39
Uoki Co Ltd	1.32
Tori Holdings Co Ltd	1.21
Safeway Inc	1.13
Tesco PLC	0.90
J. Sainsbury PLC	0.81
Asian Tea & Exports Ltd	0.48
WM Morrison Supermarkets PLC	0.43
Booker Group PLC	0.42
Majestic Wine PLC	0.41

Source: Data from Reuters. © 2015 Thomson Reuters.

Carrefour's Cost of Debt

We must now find out about the different bonds that Carrefour has issued. To do this, download the Carrefour financial accounts from the company's website and read the information on bonds. A snapshot of the information is reproduced below and the figure in the last column is the value of each bond tranche in millions of euros:

Breakdown of Bonds (Nominal Value)	Maturity	Amount (€m)
7-year 5.375% Fixed Rate Euro Bonds in euros	2015	1,000
10-year 3.825% Fixed Rate Euro Bonds in euros	2015	50
10-year 3.85% Fixed Rate Euro Bonds in euros	2015	50

Breakdown of Bonds (Nominal Value)	Maturity	Amount (€m)
10-year 4.375% Fixed Rate Euro Bonds in euros	2016	600
4-year 4.375% EMTNs in euros	2016	500
8-year 4.678% EMTNs in euros	2017	250
5-year 1.875% EMTNs in euros	2017	1,000
7-year 5.25% Fixed Rate Euro Bonds in euros	2018	500
10-year 4.00% EMTNs in euros	2020	1,000
11-year 3.875% EMTNs in euros	2021	1,000

Unlike in the US, corporate bonds are not traded frequently in Europe and the rest of the world. This brings difficulties when calculating the weighted average cost of debt. If one does not have a current price, it is impossible to accurately calculate the yield to maturity. A search of Euronext (where Carrefour bonds are listed) gives no information on the bonds. Therefore, we must work with the breakdown of bonds given above.

To make things simple, we will assume that Carrefour issues its bonds so that the coupon rate is equal to the yield to maturity. This means that the cost of debt for Carrefour ranges between 1.875 per cent and 5.25 per cent. The actual estimate we use will be based on an assessment of the general risk of Carrefour debt and, for the purposes of the present case, we will use an estimate of 4 per cent since it is in the region of the most recent Carrefour bond issues. Clearly, this is subjective and a full analysis would consider a variety of cost of debt estimates.

Carrefour's WACC

We now have the various pieces necessary to calculate Carrefour's WACC. First, we need to calculate the capital structure weights. Carrefour's equity and debt are worth €20,886 million and (from the annual report) €37,483 million, respectively. The capital structure weight for equity is €20,886 million/€58,369 million = 0.358 and for debt it is €37,483 million/€58,369 million = 0.642, so the equity percentage is lower. According to Carrefour's page on www.reuters.com (check the *Financials* link), the effective tax rate for Carrefour is 38.72 per cent.

With these weights, Carrefour's R_{WACC} is:

$$R_{WACC} = 0.358 \times 9.87\% + 0.642 \times 4.00\% \times (1 - 0.3872)$$
$$= 5.11\%$$

Thus, using market value weights, we get 5.11 per cent for Carrefour's R_{WACC}.

So how does our estimate of the R_{WACC} for Carrefour compare to others? Carrefour's own annual report suggests that it has a WACC of 5.3 per cent in France, which is very similar to our own estimate. Carrefour also considers WACCs in other countries and these range from 5.1 per cent for Belgian operations to 21.0 per cent for its business in Argentina. Clearly, country and political risk will have an impact on the discount rate used for doing business in each country.

12.6   Reducing the Cost of Capital

Chapters 9–12 develop the idea that both the expected return on an equity and the cost of capital of the firm are positively related to risk. Recently, a number of academics have argued that expected return and cost of capital are negatively related to liquidity as well.[3] In addition, these scholars make the interesting point that although it is quite difficult to lower the risk of a firm, it is much easier to increase the liquidity of the firm's equity. Therefore they suggest that a firm can actually lower its cost of capital through liquidity enhancement. We develop this idea next.

What Is Liquidity?

Anyone who owns a home probably thinks of liquidity in terms of the time it takes to buy or sell the home. For example, apartments in city centre areas are generally quite liquid. Particularly in good times, an apartment may sell within days of being placed on the market. By contrast, single-family homes in suburban areas may take weeks or months to sell. Special properties such as multimillion-pound mansions may take even longer.

The concept of liquidity is similar, but not identical, for equities. Here, we speak of the *cost* of buying and selling instead. That is, equities that are expensive to trade are considered less liquid than those that trade cheaply. What do we mean by the cost to trade? We generally think of three costs here: brokerage fees, the bid–ask spread, and market impact costs.

Brokerage fees are the easiest to understand because you must pay a broker to execute a trade. More difficult is the bid–ask spread. Consider the London Stock Exchange. If you want to trade 100 shares of XYZ plc, your broker will use a specialized trading terminal to get the best price that you can buy and sell. Suppose the broker provides a quote of 100.00–100.07. This means that you can buy at £100.07 per share and sell at £100 per share. The spread of £0.07 is a cost to you because you are losing £0.07 per share over a round-trip transaction (over a purchase and a subsequent sale).

Finally, we have *market impact costs*. Suppose a trader wants to sell 10,000 shares instead of just 100 shares. Here, someone has to take on extra risk when buying. First, she has to pay out £1,000,000 (= 10,000 × £100), cash that may not be readily available. Second, the trader may be selling this large amount because she has special information that the share price will fall imminently. The counterparty bears the risk of losing a lot of money on that trade. Consequently, to compensate for these risks, the transaction price may not be £100 per share but a lower price. Similarly, a counterparty may be willing to sell a large block of equity only at a price above £100.07. The price drop associated with a large sale and the price rise associated with a large purchase are the market impact costs.

Liquidity, Expected Returns and the Cost of Capital

The cost of trading non-liquid shares reduces the total return that an investor receives. That is, if you buy a share for £100 and sell it later for £105, the gain before trading costs is £5. If you must pay £1 in commission when buying and another £1 when selling, the gain after trading costs is only £3. Both the bid–ask spread and market impact costs would reduce this gain still further.

As we will see later, trading costs vary across securities. In the last four chapters we have stressed that investors demand a high expected return as compensation when investing in high-risk (e.g., high-beta) equities. Because the expected return to the investor is the cost of capital to the firm, the cost of capital is positively related to beta. Now we are saying the same thing for trading costs. Investors demand a high expected return when investing in equities with high trading costs – that is, with low liquidity. This high expected return implies a high cost of capital to the firm. This idea is illustrated in Figure 12.7.

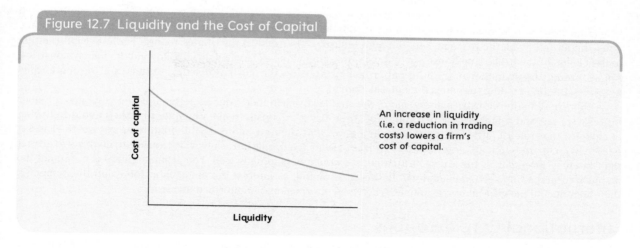

Figure 12.7 Liquidity and the Cost of Capital

An increase in liquidity (i.e. a reduction in trading costs) lowers a firm's cost of capital.

Liquidity and Adverse Selection

Although there are a number of factors that influence liquidity, we focus on just one: *adverse selection*. As mentioned before, a counterparty will lose money on a trade if the trader has information that the counterparty does not have. If you have special information that the share is worth £110 in the preceding example, you will want to buy shares at £100.07. Conversely, if you know that the equity is worth only £90 and you currently own 100 shares, you will be happy to sell these shares at £100. In either of these cases, we say that the counterparty has been *picked off*, or has been subject to adverse selection.

Traders in the market must protect themselves in some way here. Of course, they cannot forbid informed individuals from trading with them because they do not know ahead of time who these investors are. The next best alternative is to reduce the price at which you are willing to buy or increase the price at which you are willing to sell. The effect of this is that the bid–ask spread will widen, thereby increasing the costs of trading to *all* traders – both informed and uninformed. That is, if the spread is widened to, say, £99.98 − £100.11, each trader pays a round-trip cost of £0.13 per share.

The key here is that the spread should be positively related to the ratio of informed to uninformed traders. That is, informed traders will pick off the market and uninformed traders will not. Thus, informed traders in an equity raise the required return on equity, thereby increasing the cost of capital.

What the Corporation Can Do

The corporation has an incentive to lower trading costs because (given the preceding discussion) a lower cost of capital should result. Amihud and Mendelson (2000) identify two general strategies for corporations. First, they argue that firms should try to bring in more uninformed investors. Stock splits may be a useful tool here. Imagine that a company has 1 million shares outstanding with a share price of £100. Because investors generally buy in round lots of 100 shares, these investors would need £10,000 (= £100 × 100 shares) for a purchase. A number of small investors might be 'priced out' of the equity, although large investors would not be. Thus, the ratio of large investors to small investors would be high. Because large investors are generally more likely than small investors to be informed, the ratio of informed to uninformed investors will likely be high.

A 2:1 stock split would give two shares of equity for every one share that the investor previously held. Because every investor would still hold the same proportional interest in the firm, each investor would be no better off than before. Thus, it is likely that the share price will fall to £50 from £100. Here, an individual with 100 shares worth £10,000 (= £100 × 100 shares) finds them still worth £10,000 (= £50 × 200 shares) after the split.

However, a round lot becomes more affordable, thereby bringing more small and uninformed investors into the firm. Consequently, the adverse selection costs are reduced, leading to lower bid–ask spreads. In turn, it is hoped that the expected return on the equity, and the cost of equity capital, will fall as well. If this happens, the shares might actually trade at a price slightly above £50.

Another strategy to lower the cost of capital is to disclose more information. This narrows the gap between uninformed and informed investors, thereby lowering the cost of capital. Suggestions include providing more financial data about corporate segments and more management forecasts. An interesting study by Coller and Yohn (1997) concludes that the bid–ask spread is reduced after the release of these forecasts.

This section would not be complete without a discussion of security analysts. Analysts are employed by brokerage houses to follow companies in individual industries. For example, an analyst for a particular brokerage house might follow all the firms in, say, the auto industry. This analyst distributes reports and other information to the clients of the brokerage house. Virtually all brokerage houses have analysts following the major industries. Again, through dissemination of the information, analysts narrow the gap between the informed and the uninformed investors, thereby tending to reduce the bid–ask spread.

Although all major industries are covered, the smaller firms in industries are often ignored, implying a higher bid–ask spread and a higher cost of capital for these firms. Analysts frequently state that they avoid following companies that release little information, pointing out that they are more trouble than they are worth. Thus, it behooves companies that are not followed to release as much information as possible to security analysts to attract their interest. Friendliness toward security analysts would be helpful as well. The argument here is not to get the analysts to make buy recommendations. Rather, it is simply to interest the analysts in following the company, thereby reducing the information asymmetry between informed and uninformed investors.

International Considerations

Thirty years ago, most companies raised funds in their own country. However, now there is significantly greater choice on where firms raise capital. Naturally, the costs of capital across countries have become an important issue to financial managers who wish to minimize the cost of raising funds.

A few years ago, the London Stock Exchange hired a financial consulting firm, Oxera, to compare the costs of capital in London with its regional competitors.[4] They decomposed the cost of raising capital into two main groups: the costs of going through an IPO and the ongoing costs of maintaining a public listing. Note that these costs are in addition to the return required by investors. Thus, if investors required a 10 per cent return on an investment in a firm and the costs of raising the funds was 3 per cent, the cost of capital for the company would be 13 per cent.

Taking IPOs first, the costs can be decomposed into several components including underwriting fees, professional fees, listing fees and price discounts. The costs of maintaining a listing include regulatory, corporate governance and professional fees, annual listing fees and trading costs. Table 12.3 presents an overview of the comparative costs of capital across Europe and the US.

Table 12.3 Costs of Raising Capital across Europe and US

Costs	Evidence	Quantitative Impact on Cost of Capital
IPO costs		
Initial underwriting fees	Higher in US than in UK, Germany and France	3–4% in Europe, 6.5–7% in US
IPO price discounts	Differs across countries	10–15%
Initial listing fees	Deutsche Börse and LSE are lowest	<0.1%
Professional fees	US highest, then UK; France and Germany are lowest	3–6%
Ongoing costs		
Trading costs and liquidity: fees	Lowest on LSE, then NYSE; highest on Euronext, Deutsche Börse and Nasdaq	
Trading costs and liquidity: spreads	Lowest on NYSE; higher in Europe	
Annual exchange fees	For smaller firms, European exchanges are cheaper than the US; for larger firms, Deutsche Börse and Euronext are cheaper	<0.1%

Source: Partially reproduced from Oxera Consulting (2006).

Lee et al. (2006) estimate the cost of equity capital and WACC for different industries in Europe and the estimates are summarized in Table 12.4. In general, the cost of equity is lower in the UK than in the rest of Europe, which reflects the relative importance of the London Stock Exchange in the region. However, for a financial manager, the weighted average cost of capital is most important for capital budgeting. A look at Table 12.4 shows very little difference across the UK and Europe for WACC. In contrast to the UK, debt markets are more efficient in Europe and so, overall, the weighted average cost of capital is quite stable for European industries. The figures in Table 12.4 do not include an adjustment for corporation tax. This will depend on the actual country in which the industry is based.

Table 12.4 Costs of Equity and WACC across Europe by Industry

Industry	Cost of Equity Premium		WACC Premium	
	Europe	UK	Europe	UK
Aerospace and Defence	5.51	4.14	3.25	3.20
Automobile and Parts	6.90	5.76	3.45	3.80
Beverages	3.70	2.36	2.30	1.96
Chemicals	6.18	3.74	3.99	2.81
Construction	5.22	5.26	3.27	3.77
Diversified Industry	6.44	6.41	3.52	4.46
Electricity	2.45	0.70	1.67	0.61
Electronic	6.98	5.25	4.83	3.95
Engineering	6.98	5.30	4.55	3.66
Food and Drug Retail	4.27	2.63	2.71	2.19
Food Producer	4.52	3.76	2.94	2.70
Forest and Paper	9.11	4.24	4.91	2.71
Healthcare	5.46	4.40	4.18	3.48
Household Goods	5.85	8.07	3.97	5.64
IT Hardware	8.09	6.20	5.63	5.04

Industry	Cost of Equity Premium		WACC Premium	
	Europe	UK	Europe	UK
IT Software	7.06	5.64	5.42	4.62
Leisure and Hotel	5.31	4.56	3.27	3.22
Media and Entertainment	4.94	3.69	3.53	2.85
Mining	8.15	7.65	4.90	5.37
Oil and Gas	6.40	5.18	3.83	3.81
Personal Care	3.14	4.74	2.43	3.61
Pharmaceutical and Biotech	3.95	4.06	3.28	3.39
Retail General	5.43	4.53	3.16	3.67
Steel and Materials	8.88	9.41	4.98	6.54
Support Services	5.75	4.74	4.00	3.44
Telecom	4.95	4.23	3.71	3.18
Tobacco	4.04	3.28	2.81	2.35
Transport	6.54	3.79	3.15	2.67
Utilities and Other	2.26	1.64	1.37	1.26

Note: The figures in the table are the cost of equity and WACC premium, which is measured by subtracting the yield on 10-year government bonds from the estimated cost of equity and WACC.

Source: Lee et al. (2006).

12.7 How Do Corporations Estimate Cost of Capital in Practice?

Chapter 5 Page 125
Chapter 9 Page 238
Chapter 10 Page 277
Chapter 11 Page 294

The material in this chapter is quite complex and the reader may be left wondering what firms actually do when they calculate the cost of capital in practice. Brounen et al. (2004) surveyed executives in France, Germany, the Netherlands and the UK on the methods they used to estimate the cost of capital for their firm and the responses are presented in Table 12.5. Historical returns are covered in **Chapter 9**, Section 9.3, CAPM is introduced in **Chapter 10**, Section 10.9, **Chapter 11** discusses a wide range of multifactor models and **Chapter 5**, Section 5.4 derives and explains the Dividend Growth Model.

Table 12.5 Of Firms that Estimate Cost of Capital, the Percentage that Use Specific Methods

	US	UK	The Netherlands	Germany	France
Capital asset pricing model	73.49	47.06	55.56	33.96	45.16
Historical returns	39.41	31.25	30.77	18.00	27.27
Multifactor models	34.29	27.27	15.38	16.07	30.30
Backed out from dividend growth model (i.e. $P = Div/r$)	15.74	10.00	10.71	10.42	10.34
Determined by investors	13.93	18.75	44.83	39.22	34.38
Determined by regulators	7.04	16.13	3.70	0.00	16.13

Source: Brounen et al. (2004: Table 2).

There are notable differences across countries, but the most commonly used method is CAPM and beta. Historical returns on share prices are also frequently used and in the Netherlands, a surprisingly large number of companies use a cost of capital estimate that is set by investors. Regulators play an important role in the UK and France, whereas in Germany they are not considered at all. It is interesting to note the popularity of historical returns across countries. This is essentially saying that the return investors received in the past is the best predictor of the return investors will receive in the future. Some argue that with such volatility in financial markets, this is the most rational predictor!

12.8 Economic Value Added and the Measurement of Financial Performance

This chapter shows how to calculate the appropriate discount rate for capital budgeting and other valuation problems. We now consider the concept of economic value added, which uses the same discount rate developed for capital budgeting. Consider the following simple example.

Many years ago, Henry Bodenheimer started Bodie's Blimps, one of the largest high-speed blimp manufacturers. Because growth was so rapid, Henry put most of his effort into capital budgeting. He forecast cash flows for various projects and discounted them at the cost of capital appropriate to the beta of the blimp business. However, these projects have grown rapidly, in some cases becoming whole divisions. He now needs to evaluate the performance of these divisions to reward his division managers. How does he perform the appropriate analysis?

Henry is aware that capital budgeting and performance measurement are essentially mirror images of each other. Capital budgeting is forward-looking because we must estimate future cash flows to value a project. By contrast, performance measurement is backward-looking. As Henry stated to a group of his executives, 'Capital budgeting is like looking through the windshield while driving a car. You need to know what lies farther down the road to calculate a net present value. Performance measurement is like looking into the rearview mirror. You find out where you have been.'

> **Chapter 3**
> **Page 64**

Henry first measured the performance of his various divisions by return on assets (ROA), an approach that we treated in **Chapter 3**. For example, if a division had earnings after tax of €1,000 and had assets of €10,000, the ROA would be:

$$\frac{€1,000}{€10,000} = 10\%$$

He calculated the ROA ratio for each of his divisions, paying a bonus to each of his division managers based on the size of that division's ROA. However, while ROA was generally effective in motivating his managers, there were a number of situations where it appeared that ROA was counterproductive.

For example, Henry always believed that Sharon Smith, head of the supersonic division, was his best manager. The ROA of Smith's division was generally in the high double digits, but the best estimate of the weighted average cost of capital for the division was only 20 per cent. Furthermore, the division had been growing rapidly. However, as soon as Henry paid bonuses based on ROA, the division stopped growing. At that time, Smith's division had after-tax earnings of €2,000,000 on an asset base of €2,000,000, for an ROA of 100 per cent (= €2 million/€2 million).

Henry found out why the growth stopped when he suggested a project to Smith that would earn €1,000,000 per year on an investment of €2,000,000. This was clearly an attractive project with an ROA of 50 per cent (= €1 million/€2 million). He thought that Smith would jump at the chance to place his project into her division because the ROA of the project was much higher than the cost of capital of 20 per cent. However, Smith did everything she could to kill the project. And, as Henry later figured out, Smith was rational to do so. Smith must have realized that if the project were accepted, the division's ROA would become:

$$\frac{€2,000,000 + €1,000,000}{€2,000,000 + €2,000,000} = 75\%$$

Thus the ROA of Smith's division would fall from 100 per cent to 75 per cent if the project were accepted, with Smith's bonus falling in tandem.

Henry was later exposed to the economic value added (EVA®) approach,[5] which seems to obviate this particular problem. The formula for EVA is:

$$(\text{ROA} - \text{Weighted average cost of capital}) \times \text{Total capital}$$

Without the new project, the EVA of Smith's division would be:

$$(100\% - 20\%) \times \text{€}2{,}000{,}000 = \text{€}1{,}600{,}000$$

This is an annual number. That is, the division would bring in €1.6 million above and beyond the cost of capital to the firm each year.

With the new project included, the EVA would jump to:

$$(75\% - 20\%) \times \text{€}4{,}000{,}000 = \text{€}2{,}200{,}000$$

If Sharon Smith knew that her bonus was based on EVA, she would now have an incentive to accept, not reject, the project. Although ROA appears in the EVA formula, EVA differs substantially from ROA. The big difference is that ROA is a percentage number and EVA is a monetary value. In the preceding example, EVA increased when the new project was added even though the ROA actually decreased. In this situation, EVA correctly incorporates the fact that a high return on a large division may be better than a very high return on a smaller division. The situation here is quite similar to the scale problem in capital budgeting that we discussed in Section 6.6.

Further understanding of EVA can be achieved by rewriting the EVA formula. Because ROA × total capital is equal to earnings after tax, we can write the EVA formula as

Earnings after tax − Weighted average cost of capital × Total capital

Thus, EVA can simply be viewed as earnings after capital costs. Although accountants subtract many costs (including depreciation) to get the earnings number shown in financial reports, they do not subtract out capital costs. We can see the logic of accountants because the cost of capital is very subjective. By contrast, costs such as COGS (cost of goods sold), SGA (sales, general and administration) and even depreciation can be measured more objectively. However, even if the cost of capital is difficult to estimate, it is hard to justify ignoring it completely. After all, this textbook argues that the cost of capital is a necessary input to capital budgeting. Shouldn't it also be a necessary input to performance measurement?

The preceding example shows that EVA can increase investment for firms that are currently underinvesting. However, there are many firms in the reverse situation: the managers are so focused on increasing earnings that they take on projects for which the profits do not justify the capital outlays. These managers either are unaware of capital costs or, knowing these costs, choose to ignore them. Because the cost of capital is right in the middle of the EVA formula, managers will not easily ignore these costs when evaluated on an EVA system.

One other advantage of EVA® is that it is so stark: the number is either positive or it is negative. Plenty of divisions have negative EVAs for a number of years. Because these divisions are destroying more value than they are creating, a strong point can be made for liquidating these divisions. Although managers are generally emotionally opposed to this type of action, EVA analysis makes liquidation harder to ignore.

Criticisms of EVA

We now focus on two well-known problems with EVA. First, the preceding example uses EVA for performance measurement, where we believe it properly belongs. To us, EVA seems a clear improvement over ROA and other financial ratios. However, EVA has little to offer for capital budgeting because EVA focuses only on current earnings. By contrast, net present value analysis uses projections of all future cash flows, where the cash flows will generally differ from year to year. Thus, as far as capital budgeting is concerned, NPV analysis has a richness that EVA does not have. Although supporters may argue that EVA correctly incorporates the weighted average cost of capital, remember that the discount rate in NPV analysis is the same weighted average cost of capital. That is, both approaches take the cost of equity capital based on beta and combine it with the cost of debt to get an estimate of this weighted average.

A second problem with EVA is that it may increase the shortsightedness of managers. Under EVA, a manager will be well rewarded today if earnings are high today. Future losses may not harm the manager because there is a good chance that she will be promoted or have left the firm by then. Thus, the manager has an incentive to run a division with more regard for short-term than long-term value. By raising prices or cutting quality, the manager may increase current profits (and therefore current EVA). However, to the extent that customer satisfaction is reduced, future profits (and, therefore, future EVA) are likely to fall. But we should not be too harsh with EVA here because the same problem occurs with ROA. A manager who raises prices or cuts quality will increase current ROA at the expense of future ROA. The problem, then, is not EVA per se but with the use of accounting numbers in general. Because shareholders want the discounted present value of all cash flows to be maximized, managers with bonuses based on some function of current profits or current cash flows are likely to behave in a shortsighted way.

Summary and Conclusions

Earlier chapters about capital budgeting assumed that projects generate riskless cash flows. The appropriate discount rate in that case is the riskless interest rate. Of course, most cash flows from real world capital budgeting projects are risky. This chapter discussed the discount rate when cash flows are risky.

1   A firm with excess cash can either pay a dividend or make a capital expenditure. Because shareholders can reinvest the dividend in risky financial assets, the expected return on a capital budgeting project should be at least as great as the expected return on a financial asset of comparable risk.

2   The expected return on any asset is dependent on its beta. Thus, we showed how to estimate the beta of an equity. The appropriate procedure employs regression analysis on historical returns.

3   We considered the case of a project whose beta risk was equal to that of the firm. If the firm is unlevered, the discount rate on the project is equal to:

$$R_F + \beta \times (R_M - R_F)$$

where R_M is the expected return on the market portfolio and R_F is the risk-free rate. In words, the discount rate on the project is equal to the CAPM's estimate of the expected return on the security.

4   If the project's beta differs from that of the firm, the discount rate should be based on the project's beta. We can generally estimate the project's beta by determining the average beta of the project's industry.

5   The beta of a company is a function of a number of factors. Perhaps the three most important are:
   • cyclicality of revenues
   • operating leverage
   • financial leverage.

6   Sometimes we cannot use the average beta of the project's industry as an estimate of the beta of the project. For example, a new project may not fall neatly into any existing industry. In this case, we can estimate the project's beta by considering the project's cyclicality of revenues and its operating leverage. This approach is qualitative.

7   If a firm uses debt, the discount rate to use is the R_{WACC}. To calculate R_{WACC}, we must estimate the cost of equity and the cost of debt applicable to a project. If the project is similar to the firm, the cost of equity can be estimated using the SML for the firm's equity. Conceptually, a dividend growth model could be used as well, though it is likely to be far less accurate in practice.

8   Liquidity probably plays a role in determining a firm's cost of capital. A firm may be able to reduce its cost of capital by taking steps to improve liquidity.

Questions and Problems

CONCEPT

1   **The Cost of Equity Capital**   Explain what is meant by the cost of equity capital. How is the cost of equity capital linked to the risk of the assets of a firm? How would you use cost of equity in a capital budget analysis?

2   **Determinants and Estimation of Beta**   What factors determine the beta of a security? Define and describe each. Explain why an equity's beta is important in capital budgeting. How do you calculate beta and what are the pitfalls you may face in its calculation? Can you foresee any problems with using a historical beta for future capital budgeting projects? Explain.

3   **The Capital Budgeting Process**   What are the six major steps involved in the capital budget process?

4   **Extensions of the Basic Model**   How would you estimate the cost of capital for a project if its risk is different from the rest of the company? Similarly, how would you estimate the cost of capital for a project when the company has debt in its capital structure? When estimating the cost of debt, does it make a difference if the company's debt is privately or publicly held?

5   **Practical Concerns**   What are the main issues you need to consider when estimating the cost of capital of a project in practice? State any potential problems or challenges you may face.

6   **Reducing the Cost of Capital**   Why would a firm wish to reduce its cost of capital? Review different ways in which this can be done. Which way do you think is the most effective? Explain.

7   **Estimating the Cost of Capital in Practice**   Corporations use many methods to estimate the cost of capital. Why do you think there is no consensus on the best method? If you were estimating the cost of capital in an emerging market, what method would you use? Explain.

8   **EVA**   Explain what is meant by Economic Value Added and show how it can be used to evaluate the performance of a firm.

REGULAR

9   **Project Risk**   'My company can borrow at 5 per cent so it means that its cost of capital for all new projects is 5 per cent.' Do you agree with this statement? Explain.

10   **Company Beta**   The beta of Ericsson, the Swedish communications technology firm, is 0.70. What do you think is the main determinant of Ericsson's beta and why?

11   **WACC and Taxes**   'If I use the after-tax cost of debt for my project analysis then I should use the after-tax cost of equity as well.' Do you agree with this statement? Explain.

12   **SML Cost of Equity Estimation**   If you use the equity beta and the security market line to compute the discount rate for a project, what assumptions are you implicitly making? What are the advantages of using the SML approach to finding the cost of equity capital? What are the disadvantages? What are the specific pieces of information needed to use this method? Are all of these variables observable, or do they need to be estimated? What are some of the ways in which you could get these estimates?

13   **Industry Beta**   What are the benefits of using an industry beta instead of a company beta when undertaking a capital budgeting analysis? Explain, using an example.

14   **Cost of Debt Estimation**   How do you determine the appropriate cost of debt for a company? Does it make a difference if the company's debt is privately placed as opposed to being publicly traded? How would you estimate the cost of debt for a firm whose only debt issues are privately held by institutional investors?

15   **Cost of Capital**   How would a manager of a new stock exchange-listed company reduce its cost of equity capital?

16   **Cost of Capital**   As financial manager of Cosco Pacific Limited, you have been tasked with determining your firm's cost of debt and cost of equity capital.

    (a)   The shares currently sell for HK$10.40, and the dividend per share will probably be about HK$0.05736. Your assistant argues, 'It will cost us HK$0.05736 per share to use the shareholders' money this year, so the cost of equity is only equal to 0.55 per cent (HK$0.05736/HK$10.40).' What's wrong with this conclusion?

    (b)   Based on the most recent financial statements, Cosco Pacific Limited's total liabilities are HK$2.5 billion. Total interest expense for the coming year will be about HK$58 million. Your assistant therefore reasons, 'We owe HK$2.5 billion, and we will pay HK$58 million interest. Therefore, our cost of debt is obviously HK$58 million/HK$2.5 billion = 2.32 per cent.' What's wrong with this conclusion?

    (c)   Based on his own analysis, your assistant is recommending that the company increase its use of equity financing because 'debt costs 2.32 per cent, but equity only costs 0.55 per cent; thus equity is cheaper'. Ignoring all the other issues, what do you think about the conclusion that the cost of equity is less than the cost of debt?

17   **Company Risk versus Project Risk**   Both AstraZeneca plc, a large pharmaceutical firm, and Shire plc, a major prescription medicine manufacturer, are thinking of investing in an Indian generic drugs company. Assume that both AstraZeneca and Shire have no debt and both firms are considering identical projects. They have analysed their respective investments, which would involve a negative cash flow now and positive expected cash flows in the future. These cash flows would be the same for both firms. No debt would be used to finance the projects. Both companies estimate that their projects would have a net present value of £10 million at a 12 per cent discount rate and a −£12 million NPV at a 15 per cent discount

rate. AstraZeneca has a beta of 1.25, whereas Shire has a beta of 0.75. The expected risk premium on the market is 8 per cent, and risk-free bonds are yielding 3 per cent. Should either company proceed? Should both? Explain.

18 **Divisional Cost of Capital** Under what circumstances would it be appropriate for a firm to use different costs of capital for its different operating divisions? If the overall firm WACC were used as the hurdle rate for all divisions, would the riskier divisions or the more conservative divisions tend to get most of the investment projects? Why? If you were to try to estimate the appropriate cost of capital for different divisions, what problems might you encounter? What are two techniques you could use to develop a rough estimate for each division's cost of capital?

19 **SML and Cost of Capital** An all-equity firm is considering the following projects:

Project	Beta	Expected Return
A	0.6	11%
B	0.9	13%
C	1.2	14%
D	1.7	16%

The expected return on the market is 12 per cent, and the current rate on UK gilts is 5 per cent.

(a) Which projects have a higher expected return than the firm's 12 per cent cost of capital?

(b) Which projects should be accepted?

(c) Which projects would incorrectly be accepted or rejected if the firm's overall cost of capital were used as a hurdle rate?

20 **Calculating Cost of Equity** The Dybvig Corporation's equity has a beta of 1.3. If the risk-free rate is 4.5 per cent and the expected return on the market is 12 per cent, what is Dybvig's cost of equity capital?

21 **Calculating Cost of Debt** Advance plc is trying to determine its cost of debt. The firm has a debt issue outstanding with 7 years to maturity that is quoted at 92 per cent of face value. The issue makes semi-annual payments and has a coupon rate of 4 per cent annually. What is Advance's pre-tax cost of debt? If the tax rate is 24 per cent, what is the after-tax cost of debt?

22 **Calculating Cost of Debt** Shanken NV issued a 30-year, 10 per cent semi-annual bond 7 years ago. The bond currently sells for 108 per cent of its face value. The company's tax rate is 35 per cent.

(a) What is the pre-tax cost of debt?

(b) What is the after-tax cost of debt?

(c) Which is more relevant, the pre-tax or the after-tax cost of debt? Why?

23 **Calculating Cost of Debt** For the firm in the previous problem, suppose the book value of the debt issue is €20 million. In addition, the company has a second debt issue on the market, a zero coupon bond with 7 years left to maturity; the book value of this issue is €80 million and the bonds sell for 58 per cent of par. What is the company's total book value of debt? The total market value? What is your best estimate of the after-tax cost of debt now?

24 **Calculating WACC** Mullineaux Corporation has a target capital structure of 55 per cent equity and 45 per cent debt. Its cost of equity is 16 per cent, and the cost of debt is 9 per cent. The relevant tax rate is 35 per cent. What is Mullineaux's WACC?

25 **Calculating Beta** The returns of Siracha plc have a standard deviation of 40 per cent per annum and have a correlation with the FTSE 100 of 0.65. The standard deviation of the FTSE 100 is 20 per cent. What is Siracha's beta?

26 **Taxes and WACC** Miller Manufacturing has a target debt–equity ratio of 0.60. Its cost of equity is 18 per cent, and its cost of debt is 10 per cent. If the tax rate is 35 per cent, what is Miller's WACC?

27 **Leverage** Consider a levered firm's projects that have similar risks to the firm as a whole. Is the discount rate for the projects higher or lower than the rate computed using the security market line? Why/why not?

28 **Finding the Capital Structure** Fama's Llamas has a weighted average cost of capital of 11.5 per cent. The company's cost of equity is 16 per cent, and its cost of debt is 8.5 per cent. The tax rate is 35 per cent. What is Fama's debt–equity ratio?

29   **Book Value versus Market Value**   Filer Manufacturing has 9.5 million shares of equity outstanding. The current share price is £53, and the book value per share is £5. Filer Manufacturing also has two bond issues outstanding. The first bond issue has a face value of £75 million and an 8 per cent coupon and sells for 93 per cent of par. The second issue has a face value of £60 million and a 7.5 per cent coupon and sells for 96.5 per cent of par. The first issue matures in 10 years, the second in 6 years.

    (a)   What are Filer's capital structure weights on a book value basis?

    (b)   What are Filer's capital structure weights on a market value basis?

    (c)   Which are more relevant, the book or market value weights? Why?

30   **Calculating the WACC**   In the previous problem, suppose the company's equity has a beta of 1.2. The risk-free rate is 5.2 per cent, and the market risk premium is 9 per cent. Assume that the overall cost of debt is the weighted average implied by the two outstanding debt issues. Both bonds make semi-annual payments. The tax rate is 35 per cent. What is the company's WACC?

31   **WACC**   Kose SA has a target debt–equity ratio of 0.80. Its WACC is 10.5 per cent, and the tax rate is 35 per cent.

    (a)   If Kose's cost of equity is 15 per cent, what is its pre-tax cost of debt?

    (b)   If instead you know that the after-tax cost of debt is 6.4 per cent, what is the cost of equity?

32   **Finding the WACC**   Given the following information for Huntington Power, find the WACC. Assume the company's tax rate is 28 per cent.

    Debt: 40,000 7 per cent coupon bonds outstanding, £100 par value, 20 years to maturity, selling for 103 per cent of par; the bonds make semi-annual payments.

    Equity: 90,000 shares outstanding, selling for £57 per share; the beta is 1.10.

    Market: 8 per cent market risk premium and 6 per cent risk-free rate.

33   **Finding the WACC**   The power systems firm, Raging Volts, has a market value of equity of £15.77 billion and total debt of £1.21 billion. The cost of equity capital is 19.96 per cent and the cost of debt is 5 per cent. If the company has a marginal tax rate of 24 per cent, what is its WACC?

34   **Finding the WACC**   Titan Mining Corporation has 9 million shares of equity outstanding and 1,200,000 8.5 per cent semi-annual bonds outstanding, par value £100 each. The equity currently sells for £34 per share and has a beta of 1.20, and the bonds have 15 years to maturity and sell for 93 per cent of par. The market risk premium is 10 per cent, T-bills are yielding 5 per cent, and Titan Mining's tax rate is 28 per cent.

    (a)   What is the firm's market value capital structure?

    (b)   If Titan Mining is evaluating a new investment project that has the same risk as the firm's typical project, what rate should the firm use to discount the project's cash flows?

35   **SML and WACC**   An all-equity firm is considering the following projects:

Project	Beta	Expected return (%)
W	0.80	6
X	0.70	5
Y	1.15	9
Z	1.70	13

    The T-bill rate is 3 per cent, and the expected return on the market is 7.5 per cent.

    (a)   Which projects have a higher expected return than the firm's 12 per cent cost of capital?

    (b)   Which projects should be accepted?

    (c)   Which projects would be incorrectly accepted or rejected if the firm's overall cost of capital were used as a hurdle rate?

36   **WACC and NPV**   Och SpA is considering a project that will result in initial after-tax cash savings of €3.5 million at the end of the first year, and these savings will grow at a rate of 5 per cent per year indefinitely. The firm has a target debt–equity ratio of 0.65, a cost of equity of 15 per cent, and an after-tax cost of debt of 5.5 per cent. The cost-saving proposal is somewhat riskier than the usual project the firm undertakes; management uses the subjective approach and applies an adjustment factor of +2 per cent to the cost of capital for such risky projects. Under what circumstances should Och take on the project?

37 Preference Shares and WACC   Bottled Water is a listed European company which has a corporate finance structure as shown below. What is the company's WACC?

Debt:	50,000 bonds with a quoted price of 119.80, providing an 8 per cent coupon rate. The bonds have 25 years to maturity. There are also 150,000 zero-coupon bonds outstanding, with a quoted price of 13.85 and 30 years until maturity.
Preferred stock:	120,000 shares of 6.5 per cent preferred with a current price of €112 and a par value of €100.
Common stock:	2 million shares of common stock. The current share price is €65, and the beta of the stock is 1.1.
Market:	The corporate tax rate is 40 per cent, the market risk premium is 5 per cent, and the risk-free rate is 4 per cent.

CHALLENGE

38 WACC and NPV   Photochronograph Corporation (PC) manufactures time series photographic equipment. It is currently at its target debt–equity ratio of 1.3. It is considering building a new £45 million manufacturing facility. This new plant is expected to generate after-tax cash flows of £5.7 million in perpetuity. There are three financing options:

- A new issue of equity. The required return on the company's equity is 17 per cent.

- A new issue of 20-year bonds. If the company issues these new bonds at an annual coupon rate of 9 per cent, they will sell at par.

- Increased use of trade payables financing. Because this financing is part of the company's ongoing daily business, the company assigns it a cost that is the same as the overall firm WACC. Management has a target ratio of accounts payable to long-term debt of 0.20. (Assume there is no difference between the pre-tax and after-tax accounts payable cost.)

What is the NPV of the new plant? Assume that PC has a 28 per cent tax rate.

39 Project Evaluation   This is a comprehensive project evaluation problem bringing together much of what you have learned in this and previous chapters. Suppose you have been hired as a financial consultant to Defence Electronics International (DEI), a large, publicly traded firm that is the market share leader in radar detection systems (RDSs). The company is looking at setting up a manufacturing plant overseas to produce a new line of RDSs. This will be a 5-year project. The company bought some land three years ago for £7 million in anticipation of using it as a toxic dump site for waste chemicals, but it built a piping system to safely discard the chemicals instead. If the company sold the land today, it would receive £6.5 million after taxes. In 5 years the land can be sold for £4.5 million after taxes and reclamation costs. The company wants to build its new manufacturing plant on this land; the plant will cost £15 million to build. The following market data on DEI's securities are current:

Debt:	150,000 7 per cent coupon bonds outstanding, 15 years to maturity, selling for 92 per cent of par; the bonds have a £100 par value each and make semi-annual payments.
Equity:	300,000 shares outstanding, selling for £75 per share; the beta is 1.3.
Preference shares:	20,000 shares with 5 per cent dividends outstanding, selling for £72 per share.
Market:	8 per cent expected market risk premium; 5 per cent risk-free rate.

DEI's tax rate is 28 per cent. The project requires £900,000 in initial net working capital investment to become operational.

(a) Calculate the project's initial time 0 cash flow, taking into account all side effects.

(b) The new RDS project is somewhat riskier than a typical project for DEI, primarily because the plant is being located overseas. Management has told you to use an adjustment factor of +2 per cent to account for this increased riskiness. Calculate the appropriate discount rate to use when evaluating DEI's project.

(c) The manufacturing plant has an 8-year tax life, and DEI uses 20 per cent reducing balance depreciation for the plant. At the end of the project (i.e., the end of year 5), the plant can be scrapped for £5 million. What is the after-tax salvage value of this manufacturing plant?

(d) The company will incur £400,000 in annual fixed costs. The plan is to manufacture 12,000 RDSs per year and sell them at £10,000 per machine; the variable production costs are £9,000 per RDS. What is the annual operating cash flow (OCF) from this project?

(e) DEI's comptroller is primarily interested in the impact of DEI's investments on the bottom line of reported accounting statements. What will you tell her is the accounting break-even quantity of RDSs sold for this project?

(f) Finally, DEI's president wants you to throw all your calculations, assumptions and everything else into the report for the chief financial officer; all he wants to know is the RDS project's internal rate of return, IRR, and net present value, NPV. What will you report?

Exam Question (45 minutes)

1   Fresnillo plc explores and mines gold and silver in Mexico. The gold production accounts for 55 per cent of the activities of the firm, with the rest of the effort involved in silver mining. Other gold mining firms have an average beta of 0.8 and a debt to equity ratio of 1/3. Silver mining is less risky and the average beta of silver mining firms is 0.6. However, these companies tend to have more debt, with an average of 1/2. Fresnillo has a market capitalization of equity of £11.93 billion and it has no debt. Determine the expected return on Fresnillo's shares if the expected return on the FTSE 100 is 12 per cent and the risk-free rate is 3 per cent. (40 marks)

2   Discuss the primary determinants of beta and how they can be measured. In Fresnillo's case, what do you think will be the most important determinant? Explain. (30 marks)

3   How could Fresnillo reduce its equity cost of capital? Explain, using examples to illustrate your answer. (30 marks)

Mini Case

The Cost of Capital for Martyn Airlines

You have recently been hired by Martyn Airlines (MA), a budget airline based in and around the Eurozone region. MA was founded 8 years ago by John Martyn and currently operates 74 flights in the Eurozone. MA is privately owned by John and his family and had sales of £97 million last year.

MA sells primarily to online customers. Customers visit the MA website and choose the flight and fare combination appropriate to their requirements. All transactions are immediately paid via credit card.

MA's growth to date has been financed from its profits. Whenever the company had sufficient capital, it would open a new flight destination. Relatively little formal analysis has been used in the capital budgeting process. John has just read about capital budgeting techniques and has come to you for help. The company has never attempted to determine its cost of capital, and Chris would like you to perform the analysis. Because the company is privately owned, it is difficult to determine the cost of equity for the company. You have determined that to estimate the cost of capital for MA, you will use Ryanair Holdings Ltd as a representative company. The following steps will allow you to calculate this estimate:

1   Go to Ryanair's website and download their most recent financial accounts. Seek out the details on their borrowings and look for the coupon on their debt. If you cannot find it, you will need to go onto the Internet to seek out similar budget airline debt issues. The objective is to find an indicative yield for MA bonds.

2   To estimate the cost of equity for MA, go to www.reuters.com and enter the ticker symbol 'RYA.L'. Follow the various links to find answers to the following questions: What is the most recent share price listed for Ryanair? What is the market value of equity, or market capitalization? How many shares of equity does Ryanair have outstanding? What is the beta for Ryanair? Now go to www.ft.com, follow the 'Markets Data' link and then the 'Bonds and Rates' link. What is the yield on 3-month UK Treasury bills?

3   We now need to estimate the historical market risk premium. Go to Yahoo! Finance, download the monthly historical prices for the FTSE 100 index for the last 5 years. Calculate the monthly returns, take the average, multiply this by 12 to get the annualized historical return on the FTSE 100. What is the historical market risk premium for UK? Using the historical market risk premium, what is the cost of equity for Ryanair using the CAPM?

4 Go to www.reuters.com and find the list of competitors in the industry. Find the beta for each of these competitors, and then calculate the industry average beta. Using the industry average beta, what is the cost of equity? Does it matter if you use the beta for Ryanair or the beta for the industry in this case?

5 You now need to calculate the cost of debt for Ryanair. Use the information on Ryanair bonds to find the weighted average cost of debt for Ryanair using the book value weights. Try and find bond prices for Ryanair debt. What should you do if no information is available? Does it make a difference in this case if you use book value weights or market value weights? Explain.

6 You now have all the necessary information to calculate the weighted average cost of capital for Ryanair. Calculate the weighted average cost of capital for Ryanair using book value weights and market value weights assuming Ryanair has a 24 per cent tax rate. Which cost of capital number is more relevant?

7 You used Ryanair as a representative company to estimate the cost of capital for MA. What are some of the potential problems with this approach in this situation? What improvements might you suggest?

References

Amihud, Y. and H. Mendelson (2000) 'The Liquidity Route to a Lower Cost of Capital', *Journal of Applied Corporate Finance*, Vol. 12, No. 4, 8–25.

Brennan, M.J. and C. Tamarowski (2000) 'Investor Relations, Liquidity, and Stock Prices', *Journal of Applied Corporate Finance*, Vol. 12, No. 4, 26–37.

Brounen, D., A. de Jong, and K. Koedijk (2004) 'Corporate Finance in Europe: Confronting Theory with Practice', *Financial Management*, Vol. 33, No. 4, 71–101.

Coller, M. and T. Yohn (1997) 'Management Forecasts and Information Asymmetry: An Examination of Bid–Ask Spreads', *Journal of Accounting Research* (Fall 1997).

Lee, E., M. Walker and H. Christensen (2006) *The Cost of Capital in Europe: an Empirical Analysis and the Preliminary Impact of International Accounting Harmonisation*, ACCA Research Report No. 4, London: ACCA.

Oxera Consulting (2006) *The Cost of Capital: An International Comparison*, available at: www.oxera.com

Additional Reading

The following papers consider the cost of capital for both debt and equity, and how it is affected by different factors, such as default risk, growth opportunities, and information quality. Brav (2009) considers the much wider issue of financing choices for private and public firms and should also be read as additional reading for Chapters 14, 19 and 20.

1 Brav, O. (2009) 'Access to Capital, Capital Structure, and the Funding of the Firm', *The Journal of Finance*, Vol. 64, No. 1, 263–308. **UK.**

2 Chen, K.C.W., Z. Chen and K.C.J. Wei (2009) 'Legal protection of investors, corporate governance, and the cost of equity capital', *Journal of Corporate Finance*, Vol. 15, No. 3, 273–289. **International.**

3 Driessen, J. (2005) 'Is Default Event Risk Priced in Corporate Bonds?', *Review of Financial Studies*, Vol. 18, No. 1, 165–195. **US.**

4 Easley, D. and M. O'Hara (2004) 'Information and the Cost of Capital', *The Journal of Finance*, Vol. 59, No. 4, 1553–1583. **US.**

5 Hail, L. and C. Leuz (2009) 'Cost of Capital Effects and Changes in Growth Expectations around U.S. Cross-Listings', *Journal of Financial Economics*, Vol. 93, No. 3, 428–454. **International.**

6 Hirst, I., J. Danbolt and E. Jones (2008) 'Required Rates of Return for Corporate Investment Appraisal in the Presence of Growth Opportunities', *European Financial Management*, Vol. 14, No. 5, 989–1006. **UK.**

7 Kisgen, D.J. and P.E. Strahan (2010) 'Do Regulations Based on Credit Ratings Affect a Firm's Cost of Capital?' *Review of Financial Studies*, Vol. 23, No. 12, 4324–4347.

8 Sabal, J. (2004) 'The Discount Rate in Emerging Markets: A Guide', *Journal of Applied Corporate Finance*, Vol. 16, Nos. 2 and 3, 155–166.

9 Zou, H. and M.B. Adams (2008) 'Debt Capacity, Cost of Debt, and Corporate Insurance', *Journal of Financial and Quantitative Analysis*, Vol. 43, No. 2, 433–466. **China.**

Endnotes

1   As we will see later, an adjustment must be made when the debt level in the industry is different from that of the firm. However, we ignore this adjustment here for simplicity to ensure the basic concept is clear.

2   It can be shown that the relationship between a firm's asset beta and its equity beta with corporate taxes is

$$\beta_{\text{Equity}} = \beta_{\text{Asset}} \left[1 + (1 - t_c)\frac{B}{S} \right]$$

In this expression, t_c is the corporate tax rate. Tax effects are considered in more detail in a later chapter.

3   For example, see Amihud and Mendelson (2000), and Brennan and Tamarowski (2000).

4   The full document, 'The Cost of Capital: An International Comparison', can be downloaded from Oxera's website, www.oxera.com.

5   EVA is a registered trademark of Stern Stewart & Company.

Efficient Capital Markets and Behavioural Finance

The Chinese stock markets experienced explosive growth in 2006 and 2007, gaining 130 per cent and 97 per cent, respectively. Of course, that spectacular run came to a jarring halt after the global credit crisis when the Shanghai Composite lost over 60 per cent in 2008. In 2009, fantastic performance returned with a 72 per cent annual return. Since then, however, the Chinese stock market has performed very poorly, unlike its real economy which has consistently been one of the strongest performers across the world (see **Chapter 9** for more information).

Chapter 9
Page 232

What caused the incredible growth in 2006, 2007 and 2009 or the disastrous performance in 2008 for China? Even when the stock market was falling, the Chinese economy still grew at more than 10 per cent. Could prices have been inflated because investors were irrationally buying equities because of positive media attention about the Chinese economy? What made investors reverse their views so quickly? Did the Chinese stock markets experience a 'bubble' in prices, in which equity valuations are ridiculously high? Could other macroeconomic factors have been the root cause?

In this chapter, we discuss the competing ideas, present some evidence on both sides, and then examine the implications for financial managers.

KEY NOTATIONS

NPV	Net present value
P_t	Price at time t
AR	Abnormal return
R	Actual return
E(R)	Expected return
CAR	Cumulative abnormal return

13.1   Can Financing Decisions Create Value?

Earlier parts of the book showed how to evaluate projects according to the net present value criterion. The real world is a competitive one where projects with positive net present value are not always easy to come by. However, through hard work or through good fortune, a firm can identify winning projects. For example, to create value from capital budgeting decisions, the firm is likely to:

1   Locate an unsatisfied demand for a particular product or service.

2   Create a barrier to make it more difficult for other firms to compete.

3   Produce products or services at lower cost than the competition.

4   Be the first to develop a new product.

The next five chapters concern *financing* decisions. Typical financing decisions include how much debt and equity to sell, what types of debt and equity to sell, and when to sell them. Just as the net present value criterion was used to evaluate capital budgeting projects, we now want to use the same criterion to evaluate financing decisions.

Though the procedure for evaluating financing decisions is identical to the procedure for evaluating projects, the results are different. It turns out that the typical firm has many more capital expenditure opportunities with positive net present values than financing opportunities with positive net present values. In fact, we later show that some plausible financial models imply that no valuable financial opportunities exist at all.

Though this dearth of profitable financing opportunities will be examined in detail later, a few remarks are in order now. We maintain that there are basically three ways to create valuable financing opportunities:

1   *Investors lack an understanding of the risk and valuation of complex securities.* Assume that a firm can raise capital either by issuing equity or by issuing a more complex security – say, a combination of shares and warrants. Suppose that, in truth, 100 shares are worth the same as 50 units of our complex security. If investors have a misguided, overly optimistic view of the complex security, perhaps the 50 units can be sold for more than the 100 shares of equity can be. Clearly this complex security provides a valuable financing opportunity because the firm is getting more than fair value for it.

Financial managers try to package securities to receive the greatest value. Many have argued that the global credit crisis in 2007 and 2008 was caused by investors (including financial institutions) not understanding how to quantify the risk and value of the complex securities that banks issued on the back of sub-prime mortgage loans.

The theory of efficient capital markets implies that investors cannot, in general, be easily fooled. It says that all securities are appropriately priced at all times, implying that the market as a whole is shrewd indeed. In our example, 50 units of the complex security would sell for the same price as 100 shares of equity. Thus, corporate managers cannot attempt to create value by fooling investors. Instead, managers must create value in other ways.

2   *Reduce costs or increase subsidies.* We show later that certain forms of financing have greater tax advantages than other forms. Clearly, a firm packaging securities to minimize taxes can increase firm value. In addition, any financing technique involves other costs. For example, investment bankers, lawyers and accountants must be paid. A firm packaging securities to minimize these costs can also increase its value.

Example 13.1

Valuing Financial Subsidies

Suppose Salamanca Electronics Company is thinking about relocating its plant to Mexico where labour costs are lower. In the hope that it can stay in Salamanca, the company has submitted an application to the Castille y Leon autonomous region to issue €2 million in 5-year, tax-exempt industrial bonds. The coupon rate on industrial revenue bonds in Castille y Leon is currently 5 per cent. This is an attractive rate because the normal cost of debt capital for Salamanca Electronics Company is 10 per cent. What is the NPV of this potential financing transaction?

If the application is accepted and the industrial revenue bonds are issued by the Salamanca Electronics Company, the NPV (ignoring corporate taxes) is:

$$NPV = €2,000,000 - \left[\frac{€100,000}{1.1} + \frac{€100,000}{(1.1)^2} + \frac{€100,000}{(1.1)^3} + \frac{€100,000}{(1.1)^4} + \frac{€2,100,000}{(1.1)^5}\right]$$

$$= €2,000,000 - €1,620,921$$

$$= €379,079$$

This transaction has a positive NPV. The Salamanca Electronics Company obtains subsidized financing where the value of the subsidy is €379,079. Note that we used the normal cost of debt capital, 10 per cent, to discount the cash flows because this is the rate that accurately reflects the cost of debt for securities of similar risk in the markets.

3   *Create a new security.* In recent decades there has been a massive surge in financial innovation. Though the advantage of each instrument is different, one general theme is that new complex securities cannot easily be duplicated by combinations of existing securities. Thus, a previously unsatisfied clientele may pay extra for a specialized security catering to its needs. For example, putable bonds let the purchaser sell the bond at a fixed price back to the firm. This innovation creates a price floor, allowing the investor to reduce his or her downside risk. Perhaps risk-averse investors or those with little knowledge of the bond market would find this feature particularly attractive.

Corporations gain by issuing these unique securities at high prices. However, the value captured by the innovator may well be small in the long run because the innovator usually cannot patent or copyright an idea. Soon many firms are issuing securities of the same kind, forcing prices down as a result.

Since 2008, the amount of complex securities issued in the financial markets has fallen drastically. The collapse of banks like Washington Mutual (WaMu), Lehman Brothers, Bear Stearns, Northern Rock, HBOS, Bradford & Bingley, and others, was initially caused by the whole banking sector embracing complex securities to offset the risk of speculative lending policies. Looking forward, it remains to be seen whether investor appetite for complex securities will return.

This brief introduction sets the stage for the next several chapters of the book. The rest of this chapter examines the efficient capital markets hypothesis. We show that if capital markets are efficient, corporate managers cannot create value by fooling investors. This is quite important because managers must create value in other, perhaps more difficult, ways. The following chapters concern the costs and subsidies of various forms of financing.

13.2 A Description of Efficient Capital Markets

An efficient capital market is one in which share prices fully reflect available information. To illustrate how an efficient market works, suppose F-stop Smartphone Cameras plc (FSC) is attempting to develop a camera that will double the speed of the auto-focusing system now available in smart phones. FSC believes this research has positive NPV.

Now consider a share of equity in FSC. What determines the willingness of investors to hold shares of FSC at a particular price? One important factor is the probability that FSC will be the first company to develop the new auto-focusing system. In an efficient market, we would expect the price of the shares of FSC to increase if this probability increases.

Suppose FSC hires a well-known engineer to develop the new auto-focusing system. In an efficient market, what will happen to FSC's share price when this is announced? If the well-known scientist is paid a salary that fully reflects his or her contribution to the firm, the share price will not necessarily change. Suppose instead that hiring the scientist is a positive NPV transaction. In this case, the share price of FSC will increase because the firm can pay the scientist a salary below his or her true value to the company.

When will the increase in the share price of FSC occur? Assume that the hiring announcement is made in a press release on Wednesday morning. In an efficient market, the FSC share price will *immediately* adjust to this new information. Investors should not be able to buy the shares on Wednesday afternoon and make a profit on Thursday. This would imply that it took the equity market a day to realize the implication of the FSC press release. The efficient market hypothesis predicts that the FSC share price on Wednesday afternoon will already reflect the information contained in the Wednesday morning press release.

The efficient market hypothesis (EMH) has implications for investors and for firms:

- Because information is reflected in prices immediately, investors should only expect to obtain a normal rate of return. Awareness of information when it is released does an investor no good. The price adjusts before the investor has time to trade on it.

- Firms should expect to receive fair value for securities that they sell. *Fair* means that the price they receive from issuing securities is the present value. Thus, valuable financing opportunities that arise from fooling investors are unavailable in efficient capital markets.

Figure 13.1 presents several possible adjustments in equity prices. The solid line represents the path taken by the security in an efficient market. In this case the price adjusts immediately to the new information with no further price changes. The dotted line depicts a slow reaction. Here it takes the market 30 days to fully absorb the information. Finally, the broken line illustrates an overreaction and subsequent correction back to the true price. The broken line and the dotted line show the paths that the share price might take in an inefficient market. If the share price takes several days to adjust, trading profits would be available to investors who suitably timed their purchases and sales.

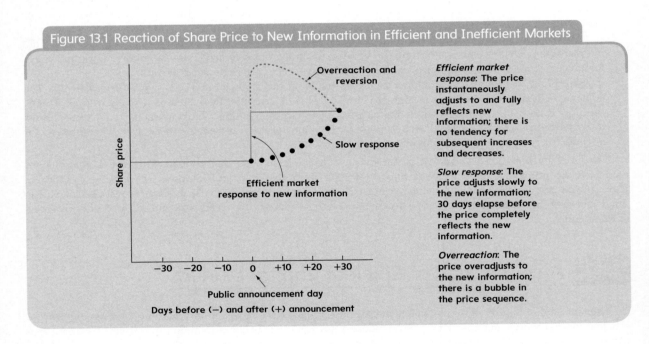

Figure 13.1 Reaction of Share Price to New Information in Efficient and Inefficient Markets

Efficient market response: The price instantaneously adjusts to and fully reflects new information; there is no tendency for subsequent increases and decreases.

Slow response: The price adjusts slowly to the new information; 30 days elapse before the price completely reflects the new information.

Overreaction: The price overadjusts to the new information; there is a bubble in the price sequence.

Foundations of Market Efficiency

Figure 13.1 shows the consequences of market efficiency. But what are the conditions that *cause* market efficiency? Andrei Shleifer (2000) argues that there are three conditions, any one of which will lead to efficiency: (1) rationality, (2) independent deviations from rationality, and (3) arbitrage. A discussion of these conditions follows.

Rationality

Imagine that all investors are rational. When new information is released in the marketplace, all investors will adjust their estimates of share prices in a rational way. In our example, investors will use the information in FSC's press release, in conjunction with existing information about the firm, to determine the NPV of FSC's new venture. If the information in the press release implies that the NPV of the venture is £10 million and there are 2 million shares, investors will calculate that the NPV is £5 per share. While FSC's old share price might be, say,

£40, no one would now transact at that price. Anyone interested in selling would sell only at a price of at least £45 (= £40 + £5). Anyone interested in buying would now be willing to pay up to £45. In other words, the price would rise by £5. And the price would rise immediately because rational investors would see no reason to wait before trading at the new price.

Of course, we all know times when family members, friends, and yes, even we seem to behave less than perfectly rationally. Thus, perhaps it is too much to ask that *all* investors behave rationally. But the market will still be efficient if the following scenario holds.

Independent Deviations from Rationality

Suppose that FSC's press release is not all that clear. How many new cameras are likely to be sold? At what price? What is the likely cost per camera? Will other camera companies be able to develop competing products? How long will this likely take? If these and other questions cannot be answered easily, it will be difficult to estimate NPV.

Now imagine that with so many questions going unanswered, many investors do not think clearly. Some investors might get caught up in the romance of a new product, hoping for and ultimately believing in sales projections well above what is rational. They would overpay for new shares. And if they needed to sell shares (perhaps to finance current consumption), they would do so only at a high price. If these individuals dominate the market, the share price would likely rise beyond what market efficiency would predict.

However, due to emotional resistance, investors could just as easily react to new information in a pessimistic manner. After all, business historians tell us that investors were initially quite sceptical about the benefits of the telephone, the copier, the automobile, and the motion picture. Certainly, they could be overly sceptical about this new camera. If investors were primarily of this type, the share price would likely rise less than market efficiency would predict.

But suppose that about as many individuals were irrationally optimistic as were irrationally pessimistic. Prices would likely rise in a manner consistent with market efficiency, even though most investors would be classified as less than fully rational. Thus market efficiency does not require rational individuals – only countervailing irrationalities.

However, this assumption of offsetting irrationalities at *all* times may be unrealistic. Perhaps at certain times most investors are swept away by excessive optimism and at other times are caught in the throes of extreme pessimism. But even here there is an assumption that will produce efficiency.

Arbitrage

Imagine a world with two types of individuals: the irrational amateurs and the rational professionals. The amateurs get caught up in their emotions, at times believing irrationally that an equity is undervalued and at other times believing the opposite. If the passions of the different amateurs do not cancel each other out, these amateurs, by themselves, would tend to carry shares either above or below their efficient prices.

Now let us bring in the professionals. Suppose professionals go about their business methodically and rationally. They study companies thoroughly, they evaluate the evidence objectively, they estimate share prices coldly and clearly, and they act accordingly. If an equity is underpriced, they would buy it. If it is overpriced, they would sell it. And their confidence would likely be greater than that of the amateurs. Whereas an amateur might risk only a small sum, these professionals might risk large ones, *knowing* as they do that the security is mispriced. Furthermore, they would be willing to rearrange their entire portfolio in search of a profit. *Arbitrage* is the word that comes to mind here because arbitrage generates profit from the simultaneous purchase and sale of different, but substitute, securities. If the arbitrage of professionals dominates the speculation of amateurs, markets would still be efficient.

13.3   The Different Types of Efficiency

In our previous discussion, we assumed that the market responds immediately to all available information. In actuality, certain information may affect share prices more quickly than other information. To handle differential response rates, researchers separate information into different types. The most common classification system identifies three types: information about past prices, publicly available information and all information. The effect of these three information sets on prices is examined next.

The Weak Form

Imagine a trading strategy that recommends buying a share after it has gone up 3 days in a row and recommends selling a share after it has gone down 3 days in a row. This strategy uses information based only on past prices. It does not use any other information, such as earnings, forecasts, merger announcements or money supply figures. A capital market is said to be *weakly efficient* or to satisfy weak form efficiency if it fully incorporates the information in past share prices. Thus, the preceding strategy would not be able to generate profits if weak form efficiency holds.

Often weak form efficiency is represented mathematically as:

$$P_t = P_{t-1} + \text{Expected return} + \text{Random error}_t \qquad (13.1)$$

Equation 13.1 states that the price today is equal to the sum of the last observed price plus the expected return on the equity (in currency) plus a random component occurring over the interval. The last observed price could have occurred yesterday, last week or last month, depending on the sampling interval. The expected return is a function of a security's risk and would be based on the models of risk and return in previous chapters. The random component is due to new information about the company. It could be either positive or negative and has an expectation of zero. The random component in a period is unrelated to the random component in any past period. Hence this component is not predictable from past prices. If share prices follow Equation 13.1 they are said to follow a random walk.[1]

Weak form efficiency is about the weakest type of efficiency that we would expect a financial market to display because historical price information is the easiest kind of information about a company's equity to acquire. If it were possible to make extraordinary profits simply by finding patterns in share price movements, everyone would do it, and any profits would disappear in the scramble.

This effect of competition can be seen in Figure 13.2. Suppose a company's share price displays a cyclical pattern, as indicated by the wavy curve. Shrewd investors would buy at the low points, forcing those prices up. Conversely, they would sell at the high points, forcing prices down. Via competition, cyclical regularities would be eliminated, leaving only random fluctuations.

Figure 13.2 Investor Behaviour Tends to Eliminate Cyclical Patterns

Share price / Time

Sell / Sell / Sell / Buy / Buy / Buy

If an equity's price follows a cyclical pattern, the pattern will be quickly eliminated in an efficient market. A random pattern will emerge as investors buy at the trough and sell at the peak of a cycle.

The Semi-strong and Strong Forms

If weak form efficiency is controversial, even more contentious are the two stronger types of efficiency, semi-strong form efficiency and strong form efficiency. A market is semi-strong form efficient if prices reflect (incorporate) all publicly available information, including information such as published accounting statements for the firm as well as historical price information. A market is strong form efficient if prices reflect all information, public or private.

The information set of past prices is a subset of the information set of publicly available information, which in turn is a subset of all information. This is shown in Figure 13.3. Thus, strong form efficiency implies semi-strong form efficiency, and semi-strong form efficiency implies weak form efficiency. The distinction between semi-strong form efficiency and weak form efficiency is that semi-strong form efficiency requires not only that the

Figure 13.3 Relationship among Three Different Information Sets

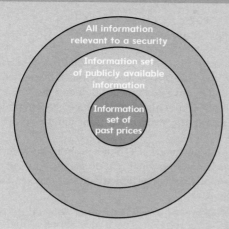

All information relevant to a security

Information set of publicly available information

Information set of past prices

The information set of past prices is a subset of the set of all publicly available information, which in turn is a subset of all information. If today's price reflects only information about past prices, the market is weak form efficient. If today's price reflects all publicly available information, the market is semi-strong form efficient. If today's price reflects all information, both public and private, the market is strong form efficient.

Semi-strong form efficiency implies weak form efficiency, and strong form efficiency implies semi-strong form efficiency.

market be efficient with respect to historical price information, but that *all* of the information available to the public be reflected in prices.

To illustrate the different forms of efficiency, imagine an investor who always sold a particular equity after its price had risen. A market that was only weak form efficient and not semi-strong form efficient would still prevent such a strategy from generating positive profits. According to weak form efficiency, a recent price rise does not imply that the equity is overvalued.

Now consider a firm reporting increased earnings. An individual might consider investing in the company's shares after reading the news release providing this information. However, if the market is semi-strong form efficient, the price should rise immediately upon the news release. Thus, the investor would end up paying the higher price, eliminating all chance for profit.

At the furthest end of the spectrum is strong form efficiency. This form says that anything that is pertinent to the value of the security and that is known to at least one investor is, in fact, fully incorporated into the share price. A strict believer in strong form efficiency would deny that an insider who knew whether a company mining operation had struck gold could profit from that information. Such a devotee of the strong form efficient market hypothesis might argue that as soon as the insider tried to trade on his or her information, the market would recognize what was happening, and the price would shoot up before he or she could buy any of the shares. Alternatively, believers in strong form efficiency argue that there are no secrets, and as soon as the gold is discovered, the secret gets out.

One reason to expect that markets are weak form efficient is that it is so cheap and easy to find patterns in share prices. Anyone who can program a computer and knows a little bit of statistics can search for such patterns. It stands to reason that if there were such patterns, people would find and exploit them, in the process causing them to disappear.

Semi-strong form efficiency, though, implies more sophisticated investors than does weak form efficiency. An investor must be skilled in accounting, finance and statistics and steeped in the idiosyncrasies of individual industries and companies. Furthermore, to acquire and use such skills requires talent, ability and time. In the jargon of the economist, such an effort is costly, and the ability to be successful at it is probably in scarce supply.

As for strong form efficiency, this is just further down the road than semi-strong form efficiency. It is difficult to believe that the market is so efficient that someone with valuable inside information cannot prosper from it. And empirical evidence tends to be unfavourable to this form of market efficiency.

Some Common Misconceptions about the Efficient Market Hypothesis

No idea in finance has attracted as much attention as that of efficient markets, and not all of the attention has been flattering. To a certain extent this is because much of the criticism has been based on a misunderstanding of what the hypothesis does and does not say. We illustrate three misconceptions next.

The Efficacy of Dart Throwing

When the notion of market efficiency was first publicized and debated in the popular financial press, it was often characterized by the following quote: '. . . throwing darts at the financial page will produce a portfolio that can be expected to do as well as any managed by professional security analysts' (Malkiel, 2003). This is almost, but not quite, true.

All the efficient market hypothesis really says is that, on average, the manager will not be able to achieve an abnormal or excess return. The excess return is defined with respect to some benchmark expected return, such as that from the security market line (SML) of Chapter 11. The investor must still decide how risky a portfolio he or she wants. In addition, a random dart thrower might wind up with all of the darts sticking into one or two high-risk stocks that deal in genetic engineering. Would you really want all of your equity investments in two such stocks?

The failure to understand this has often led to confusion about market efficiency. For example, sometimes it is wrongly argued that market efficiency means that it does not matter what you do because the efficiency of the market will protect the unwary. However, someone once remarked, 'The efficient market protects the sheep from the wolves, but nothing can protect the sheep from themselves.'

What efficiency does say is that the price that a firm obtains when it sells a share of its equity is a fair price in the sense that it reflects the value of that equity given the information that is available about it. Shareholders need not worry that they are paying too much for an equity with a low dividend or some other characteristic because the market has already incorporated it into the price. However, investors still have to worry about such things as their level of risk exposure and their degree of diversification.

Price Fluctuations

Much of the public is sceptical of efficiency because share prices fluctuate from day to day. However, daily price movement is in no way inconsistent with efficiency; an equity in an efficient market adjusts to new information by changing price. A great deal of new information comes into the stock market each day. In fact, the *absence* of daily price movements in a changing world might suggest an inefficiency.

Shareholder Disinterest

Many laypeople are sceptical that the market price can be efficient if only a fraction of the outstanding shares changes hands on any given day. However, the number of traders in a company's shares on a given day is generally far fewer than the number of people following the shares. This is true because an individual will trade only when his appraisal of the value of the equity differs enough from the market price to justify incurring brokerage commissions and other transaction costs. Furthermore, even if the number of traders following an equity is small relative to the number of outstanding shareholders, the company's shares can be expected to be efficiently priced as long as a number of interested traders use the publicly available information. That is, the share price can reflect the available information even if many shareholders never follow the company and are not considering trading in the near future.

13.4 The Evidence

The evidence on the efficient market hypothesis is extensive, with studies covering the broad categories of weak form, semi-strong form, and strong form efficiency. In the first category we investigate whether share price changes are random. We review both *event studies* and studies of the performance of mutual funds in the second category. In the third category, we look at the performance of corporate insiders.

The Weak Form

Weak form efficiency implies that a security's price movement in the past is unrelated to its price movement in the future. The work of Chapter 10 allows us to test this implication. In that chapter we discussed the concept of correlation between the returns on two different securities. For example, the correlation between the return on HSBC and the return on Lloyds Banking Group is likely to be relatively high because both companies are in the same industry. Conversely, the correlation between the return on HSBC and the return on the shares of, say, an Australian fast-food chain is likely to be low.

Financial economists frequently speak of serial correlation, which involves only one security. This is the correlation between the current return on a security and the return on the same security over a later period. A positive coefficient of serial correlation for a particular share indicates a tendency toward *continuation*. That is, a higher-than-average return today is likely to be followed by higher-than-average returns in the future. Similarly, a lower-than-average return today is likely to be followed by lower-than-average returns in the future.

A negative coefficient of serial correlation for a particular equity indicates a tendency toward *reversal*. A higher-than-average return today is likely to be followed by lower-than-average returns in the future. Similarly, a lower-than-average return today is likely to be followed by higher-than-average returns in the future. Both significantly positive and significantly negative serial correlation coefficients are indications of market inefficiencies; in either case, returns today can be used to predict future returns.

Serial correlation coefficients for share price returns near zero would be consistent with weak form efficiency. Thus, a current share price return that is higher than average is as likely to be followed by lower-than-average returns as by higher-than-average returns. Similarly, a current return that is lower than average is as likely to be followed by higher-than-average returns as by lower-than-average returns.

Table 13.1 shows the serial correlation for daily share price changes for eight large UK companies. These coefficients indicate whether there are relationships between yesterday's return and today's return. As can be seen, the correlation coefficients are predominantly negative, implying that a higher-than-average return today makes a lower-than-average return tomorrow slightly more likely. Conversely, Admiral Group's coefficient is slightly positive, implying that a higher-than-average return today makes a higher-than-average return tomorrow slightly more likely.

Table 13.1 Serial Correlation Coefficients for Selected Companies, January 2011–January 2015

Company Name	Serial correlation coefficient
Admiral Group	0.0154
Laura Ashley	−0.2502
British Land	−0.0526
HSBC	−0.0356
JD Sports Fashion	−0.1248
Premier Foods	0.1325
Rathbone Brothers	−0.0971
Rolls-Royce Holdings	−0.0006
Shaftesbury	−0.0463
Sky	0.0151
SSE	−0.0808
Standard Life	0.0109
Ted Baker	−0.0971
Wetherspoon (JD)	−0.0874
Wolseley	0.1000

However, because correlation coefficients can, in principle, vary between −1 and 1, the reported coefficients are quite small. In fact, for all the companies in Table 13.1, apart from Laura Ashley, the coefficients are so small relative to both estimation errors and transaction costs that the results are generally considered to be consistent with weak form efficiency. Laura Ashley has a serial correlation coefficient that is probably large enough to suggest that for some firms there is some predictability of returns. The weak form of the efficient market hypothesis has been tested in many other ways and, taken as a whole, the research on predictability of past returns is supportive of weak form efficiency.

This research raises an interesting thought: if price changes are truly random, why do so many believe that prices follow patterns? The work of both psychologists and statisticians suggests that most people simply do not know what randomness looks like. For example, consider Figure 13.4. One line was generated by a computer using random numbers and Equation 13.1 and the other is the share price series for Deutsche Telekom AG, the German telecommunications firm. Do you see a pattern in either series? Different people see different patterns and forecast different future price movements. However, in our experience, viewers are all quite confident of the patterns they see. Both lines may look quite non-random to some, suggesting weak form inefficiency. However, the Deutsche Telekom price series bears a close visual resemblance to the simulated price series, and statistical tests indicate that it indeed behaves like a purely random series. Further, the correlation between the returns (not the prices) of Deutsche Telekom and the simulated series is only 0.03. Thus, in our opinion, people claiming to see patterns in historical share price data may simply be seeing optical illusions.

Figure 13.4 Simulated and Actual Share Price Movements

The Semi-strong Form

The semi-strong form of the efficient market hypothesis implies that prices should reflect all publicly available information. We present two types of tests of this form.

Event Studies

The *abnormal return* (AR) on a given security for a particular day can be calculated by subtracting the market's return on the same day (R_m) – as measured by a broad-based index such as the FTSE All Share or Euro Stoxx 50 index – from the actual return (R) on the equity for that day.[2] We write this algebraically as:

$$AR = R - R_m$$

The following system will help us understand tests of the semi-strong form:

$$\text{Information released at time } t - 1 \rightarrow AR_{t-1}$$
$$\text{Information released at time } t \quad\;\; \rightarrow AR_t$$
$$\text{Information released at time } t + 1 \rightarrow AR_{t+1}$$

The arrows indicate that the abnormal return in any time period is related only to the information released during that period.

According to the efficient market hypothesis, a company's abnormal return at time t, AR_t, should reflect the release of information at the same time, t. Any information released before then should have no effect on abnormal returns in this period because all of its influence should have been felt before. In other words, an efficient market would already have incorporated previous information into prices. Because a company's share price return today cannot depend on what the market does not yet know, information that will be known only in the future cannot influence the company's return either. Hence the arrows point in the direction that is shown, with information in any period affecting only that period's abnormal return. *Event studies* are statistical studies that examine whether the arrows are as shown or whether the release of information influences returns on other days.

These studies also speak of *cumulative abnormal returns* (CARs), as well as abnormal returns (ARs). As an example, consider a firm with ARs of 1 per cent, −3 per cent and 6 per cent for dates −1, 0 and 1, respectively, relative to a corporate announcement. The CARs for dates −1, 0 and 1 would be 1 per cent, −2 per cent [= 1 per cent + (−3 per cent)] and 4 per cent [= 1 per cent + (−3 per cent) + 6 per cent], respectively.

As an example, consider the cumulative abnormal returns around a major profit warning issued by Tesco plc on 8 December 2014. Figure 13.5 shows the plot of CARs and because a profit warning is generally considered to be bad news, we would expect abnormal returns to be negative around the time of the announcement. They are, as evidenced by a drop in the CAR on the day of the announcement (day 0). The CARs then fall over the next 3 days before stabilizing at around −4 per cent. This implies that the bad news is fully incorporated into the stock price by the announcement day, a result consistent with market efficiency. More research on profit warnings is required to ascertain whether this is just confined to the Tesco event or more generally.

Figure 13.5 Cumulative Abnormal Returns for Companies Announcing Profit Warnings

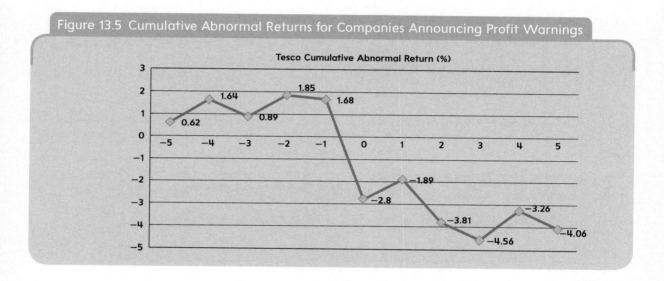

Over the years this type of methodology has been applied to many events. Announcements of dividends, earnings, mergers, capital expenditures and new issues of equity are a few examples of the vast literature in the area. The early event study tests generally supported the view that the market is semi-strong form (and therefore also weak form) efficient. However, a number of more recent studies present evidence that the market does not impound all relevant information immediately. Some conclude from this that the market is not efficient. Others argue that this conclusion is unwarranted, given statistical and methodological problems in the studies. This issue will be addressed in more detail later in the chapter.

The Record of Investment Funds

If the market is efficient in the semi-strong form, then no matter what publicly available information fund managers rely on to pick equities, their average returns should be the same as those of the average investor in the market as a whole. We can test efficiency, then, by comparing the performance of these professionals with that of a market index.

Consider Figure 13.6, which presents the performance of various types of US mutual funds relative to the stock market as a whole. The far left of the figure shows that the universe of all funds covered in the study underperforms the market by 2.13 per cent per year after an appropriate adjustment for risk. Thus, rather than outperforming the market, the evidence shows underperformance. This underperformance holds for a number of types of funds as well. Returns in this study are net of fees, expenses and commissions, so fund returns would be higher if these costs were added back. However, the study shows no evidence that funds, as a whole, are *beating* the market.

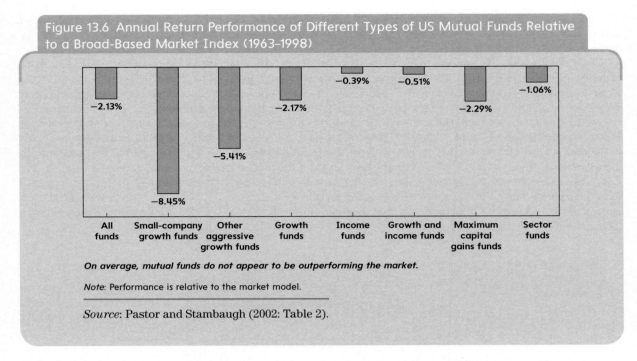

Figure 13.6 Annual Return Performance of Different Types of US Mutual Funds Relative to a Broad-Based Market Index (1963-1998)

On average, mutual funds do not appear to be outperforming the market.

Note: Performance is relative to the market model.

Source: Pastor and Stambaugh (2002: Table 2).

European evidence is conflicting. Whereas Otten and Bams (2002) report consistently positive performance for funds in four out of five European countries (see Table 13.2), Fletcher and Marshall (2005) find that for most UK unit trusts with international objectives, performance is significantly negative.

Table 13.2 European Fund Performance After and Before Management Fees 1991-1998

Country	After Fees (%)	Before Fees (%)
France	0.80	**2.04**
Germany	−2.17	−1.32
Italy	0.43	**2.32**
Netherlands	**3.08**	3.59
UK	**1.40**	**2.59**

Note: Figures are annualized alphas and bold indicates the figure is statistically significant from zero.

Source: Adapted from Otten and Bams (2002: Table 8).

By and large, fund managers rely on publicly available information. Thus the finding that they do not outperform market indexes is consistent with semi-strong form and weak form efficiency. Obviously, Otten and Bams (2002) cast some doubt on this hypothesis but, in general, research has shown that mutual funds do not consistently outperform the market.

Does the overall evidence imply that, in general, mutual funds are bad investments for individuals? Not necessarily. Though many funds fail to achieve better returns than some indices of the market, they do permit the investor to buy a portfolio of many securities (the phrase 'a well-diversified portfolio' is often used). They might also provide a variety of services such as keeping custody and records of all the company's shares.

The Strong Form

Even the strongest adherents to the efficient market hypothesis would not be surprised to find that markets are inefficient in the strong form. After all, if an individual has information that no one else has, it is likely that she can profit from it.

One group of studies of strong form efficiency investigates trading by senior executives in a company. Insiders, such as directors and chief executives, have access to information that is not generally available. But if the strong form of the efficient market hypothesis holds, they should not be able to profit by trading on their information. Most government agencies require corporate insiders to reveal any trading they might do in their own company's stock. By examining the record of such trades, we can see whether they made abnormal returns.

Figure 13.7 shows the cumulative abnormal returns that UK directors earned from their trading between 1994 and 2005. It is clear that there is a strong market reaction in the days after insider trading and that their trades were abnormally profitable. This view is supported using data in other countries. Given that it seems one can make abnormal profits from private information, strong form efficiency does not seem to be substantiated by the evidence.

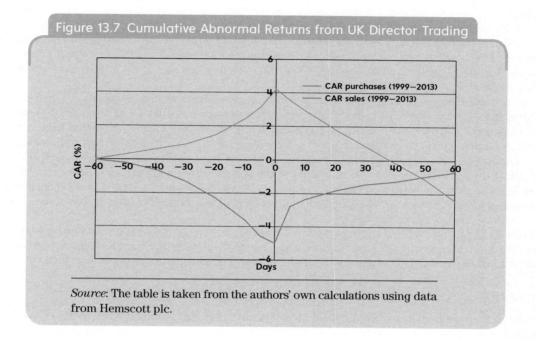

Figure 13.7 Cumulative Abnormal Returns from UK Director Trading

Source: The table is taken from the authors' own calculations using data from Hemscott plc.

13.5 The Behavioural Challenge to Market Efficiency

In Section 13.2 we presented Professor Shleifer's three conditions, any one of which will lead to market efficiency. In that section we made a case that at least one of the conditions is likely to hold in the real world. However, there is definitely disagreement here. Many members of the academic community (including Professor Shleifer) argue that none of the three conditions is likely to hold in reality. This point of view is based on what is called *behavioural finance*. Let us examine the behavioural view of each of these three conditions.

Rationality

Are people really rational? Not always. Just travel to any casino to see people gambling, sometimes with large sums of money. The casino's take implies a negative expected return for the gambler. Because gambling is risky and has a negative expected return, it can never be on the efficient frontier of our Chapter 10. In addition, gamblers will often bet on black at a roulette table after black has occurred a number of consecutive times, thinking that the run will continue. This strategy is faulty because roulette tables have no memory.

But, of course, gambling is only a sideshow as far as finance is concerned. Do we see irrationality in financial markets as well? The answer may well be yes. Many investors do not achieve the degree of diversification that they should. Others trade frequently, generating both commissions and taxes. In fact, taxes can be handled optimally by selling losers and holding onto winners. Although some individuals invest with tax minimization in mind, plenty of them do just the opposite. Many are more likely to sell their winners than their losers, a strategy leading to high tax payments.[3] The behavioural view is not that *all* investors are irrational, but that some, perhaps many, investors are.

Independent Deviations from Rationality

Are deviations from rationality generally random, and thereby likely to cancel out in a whole population of investors? To the contrary, psychologists have long argued that people deviate from rationality in accordance with a number of basic principles. Not all of these principles have an application to finance and market efficiency, but at least two seem to do so.

The first principle, called *representativeness*, can be explained with the gambling example just used. The gambler believing a run of black will continue is in error because the probability of a black spin is still only about 50 per cent. Gamblers behaving in this way exhibit the psychological trait of representativeness. That is, they draw conclusions from insufficient data. In other words, the gambler believes the small sample he observed is more representative of the population than it really is.

How is this related to finance? Perhaps a market dominated by representativeness leads to bubbles. People see a sector of the market – for example, sub-prime mortgages – having a short history of high revenue growth and extrapolate that it will continue forever. When the growth inevitably stalls, prices have nowhere to go but down.

The second principle is *conservatism*, which means that people are too slow in adjusting their beliefs to new information. Suppose that your goal since childhood was to become a dentist. Perhaps you came from a family of dentists, perhaps you liked the security and relatively high income that comes with that profession, or perhaps teeth always fascinated you. As things stand now, you could probably look forward to a long and productive career in that occupation. However, suppose a new drug was developed that would prevent tooth decay. That drug would clearly reduce the demand for dentists. How quickly would you realize the implications as stated here? If you were emotionally attached to dentistry, you might adjust your beliefs slowly. Family and friends could tell you to switch out of dental courses at university, but you just might not be psychologically ready to do that. Instead, you might cling to your rosy view of dentistry's future.

Perhaps there is a relationship to finance here. For example, many studies report that prices seem to adjust slowly to the information contained in earnings announcements. Could it be that because of conservatism, investors are slow in adjusting their beliefs to new information? More will be said about this in the next section.

Arbitrage

In Section 13.2 we suggested that professional investors, knowing that securities are mispriced, could buy the underpriced ones while selling correctly priced (or even overpriced) substitutes. This might undo any mispricing caused by emotional amateurs.

Trading of this sort is likely to be more risky than it appears at first glance. Suppose professionals generally believed that the shares of the copper mining firm, Vedanta Resources plc, were underpriced. They would buy them while selling their holdings in other mining firms, say, Anglo American and Rio Tinto plc. However, if amateurs were taking opposite positions, prices would adjust to correct levels only if the positions of amateurs were small relative to those of the professionals. In a world of many amateurs, a few professionals would have to take big positions to bring prices into line, perhaps even engaging heavily in short selling. Buying large amounts of one company's shares and short selling large amounts of another company's shares is quite risky, even if the two shares are in the same industry. Here, unanticipated bad news about Vedanta Resources and unanticipated good news about the other two companies would cause the professionals to register large losses.

In addition, if amateurs mispriced Vedanta Resources today, what is to prevent Vedanta from being even *more* mispriced tomorrow? This risk of further mispricing, even in the presence of no new information, may also cause professionals to cut back their arbitrage positions. As an example, imagine a shrewd professional who believed technology equities were underpriced in early 2014. Had he bet on technology equities rising at that time, he would have lost in the near term: prices fell through the first 4 months of 2014. Yet, he would have eventually made money because prices later increased. The key insight is that near-term risk may reduce the size of arbitrage strategies.

In conclusion, the arguments presented here suggest that the theoretical underpinnings of the efficient capital markets hypothesis, presented in Section 13.2, might not hold in reality. That is, investors may be irrational, irrationality may be related across investors rather than cancelling out across investors, and arbitrage strategies may involve too much risk to eliminate market efficiencies.

13.6 Empirical Challenges to Market Efficiency

Section 13.4 presented empirical evidence supportive of market efficiency. We now present evidence challenging this hypothesis. (Adherents of market efficiency generally refer to results of this type as *anomalies*.)

Limits to Arbitrage

Royal Dutch Petroleum and Shell Transport merged their interests in 1907, with all subsequent cash flows being split on a 60–40 per cent basis between the two companies. However, both companies continued to be publicly traded separately until 2005. You might imagine that before 2005, the market value of Royal Dutch would always have been 1.5 (= 60/40) times that of Shell. That is, if Royal Dutch ever became overpriced, rational investors would buy Shell instead of Royal Dutch. If Royal Dutch were underpriced, investors would buy Royal Dutch. In addition, arbitrageurs would go further by buying the underpriced security and selling the overpriced security short.

However, Figure 13.8 shows that Royal Dutch and Shell rarely traded at parity (i.e., 60/40) before their shares were combined in 2005. Why would these deviations have occurred? As stated in the previous section, behavioural finance suggests that there are limits to arbitrage. That is, an investor buying the overpriced asset and selling the underpriced asset does not have a sure thing. Deviations from parity could actually *increase* in the short run, implying losses for the arbitrageur. The well-known statement, 'Markets can stay irrational longer than you can stay solvent', attributed to John Maynard Keynes, applies here. Thus, risk considerations may force arbitrageurs to take positions that are too small to move prices back to parity.

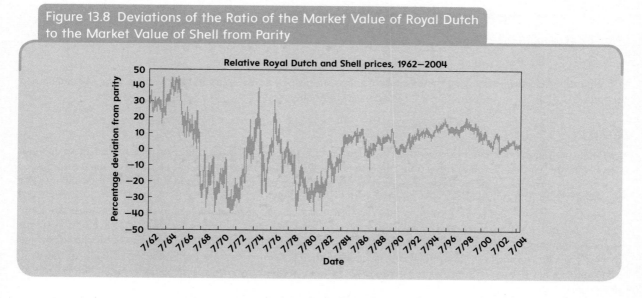

Figure 13.8 Deviations of the Ratio of the Market Value of Royal Dutch to the Market Value of Shell from Parity

Academics have documented a number of these deviations from parity. Froot and Dabora (1999) show similar results for both the twin companies of Unilever N.V. and Unilever plc and for two classes of SmithKline Beecham shares. Lamont and Thaler (2003) present similar findings for 3Com and its subsidiary Palm Inc. Other researchers find price behaviour in closed-end mutual funds suggestive of parity deviations.

Earnings Surprises

Common sense suggests that prices should rise when earnings are reported to be higher than expected and prices should fall when the reverse occurs. However, market efficiency implies that prices will adjust immediately to the announcement, while behavioural finance would predict another pattern. Kolasinski and Li (2010) rank US companies by the extent of their *earnings surprise* – that is, the difference between current quarterly earnings and quarterly earnings four quarters ago, divided by the current share price. They form a portfolio of companies with the most extreme positive surprises and another portfolio of companies with the most extreme negative surprises. Figure 13.9 shows returns from buying the two portfolios, net of the return on the overall market. As can be seen, prices adjust slowly to the earnings announcements, with the portfolio with the positive surprises outperforming the portfolio with the negative surprises over both the next month and the next 6 months. Gerard (2012) extends this research to a large sample of European firms and finds the same post-earnings announcement drift.

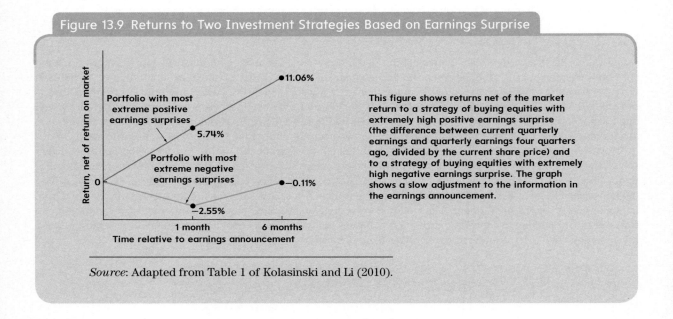

Figure 13.9 Returns to Two Investment Strategies Based on Earnings Surprise

This figure shows returns net of the market return to a strategy of buying equities with extremely high positive earnings surprise (the difference between current quarterly earnings and quarterly earnings four quarters ago, divided by the current share price) and to a strategy of buying equities with extremely high negative earnings surprise. The graph shows a slow adjustment to the information in the earnings announcement.

Source: Adapted from Table 1 of Kolasinski and Li (2010).

Why do prices adjust slowly? Behavioural finance suggests that investors exhibit conservatism because they are slow to adjust to the information contained in the announcements.

Size

In 1981, two important papers presented evidence that in the United States, the returns on equities with small market capitalizations were greater than the returns on equities with large market capitalizations over most of the 20th century.[4] The studies have since been replicated over different periods and in different countries. For example, Table 13.3 shows average returns over the period from 1986 to 2002 for 25 portfolios of European and US equities ranked by size and book to market equity. As can be seen, the average return on small stocks in Europe is quite a bit higher than the average return on large equities, whereas for the US, the anomaly seems to have disappeared. Although much of the differential performance is merely compensation for the extra risk of small firms, researchers have generally argued that not all of it can be explained by risk differences. In addition, Donald Keim (1983) presented evidence that most of the difference in performance occurs in the month of January.[5]

Value versus Growth

A number of papers have argued that equities with high book-value-to-share-price ratios and/or high earnings-to-price ratios (generally called *value stocks*) outperform equities with low ratios (*growth stocks*). For example, Fama and French find that for 12 of 13 major international stock markets, the average return on equities with high book-value-to-share-price ratios is above the average return on equities with low book-value-to-share-price ratios.[6] Figure 13.10 shows the returns for a number of European countries for the period 1991 to 2013. In every country, with the exception of Finland, value stocks outperformed growth stocks.

Because the return difference is so large and because these ratios can be obtained so easily for individual companies, the results may constitute strong evidence against market efficiency. However, a number of papers suggest that the unusual returns are due to biases in commercial databases or to differences in risk, not to a true inefficiency.[7] Because the debate revolves around arcane statistical issues, we will not pursue the issue further. However, it is safe to say that no conclusion is warranted at this time. As with so many other topics in finance and economics, further research is needed.

Table 13.3 Average Monthly Returns for European, US and Country or Sector-neutral European size-B/M Portfolios

	USA						Europe					
	Low	2	3	4	High	H-L	Low	2	3	4	High	H-L
Small	-0.24	0.72	0.86	1.11	0.98	1.22*	2.35	1.19	0.60	0.92	1.20	-1.15*
2	0.22	0.60	0.87	0.92	0.84	0.62	1.00	0.70	0.54	0.87	1.19	0.19
3	0.39	0.69	0.70	0.80	1.03	0.64	0.48	0.44	0.36	0.79	1.16	0.68*
4	0.74	0.75	0.75	0.90	0.85	0.11	0.41	0.34	0.56	0.87	1.08	0.67*
Big	0.76	0.79	0.71	0.73	0.65	-0.10	0.52	0.45	0.56	0.72	1.08	0.30
S-B	-0.99*	-0.06	0.15	0.39	0.33		1.83*	0.73*	0.05	0.20	0.38	

Average monthly value-weighted returns for size-B/M stock portfolios between February 1986 through June 2002. H-L is the value premium for a given size quintile defined as the average of the time-series of monthly differences between the return for the highest B/M quintile and the return for the lowest B/M quintile. Similarly S-B is the size premium for a given B/M quintile defined as the average of the time-series of monthly differences between the return for the smallest size quintile and the return for the largest size quintile within a B/M group.

Source: Based on Bauer, Cosemans and Schotman (2010: Table 2).

Figure 13.10 Annual Percentage Returns on Low Book-to-Price Firms and High Book-to-Price Firms in Selected Countries for the period 1991–2013

Source: The figures are the authors' own calculations based on data taken from Kenneth French's website (http://mba.tuck.dartmouth.edu/pages/faculty/ken.french/index.html).

Crashes and Bubbles

The US stock market crash of 6 May 2010 is extremely puzzling. At 2:45 p.m., the market dropped 1,000 points only to recover in minutes. A drop of this magnitude for no apparent reason is not consistent with market efficiency. Because the US crash of 1987 is still an enigma, it is doubtful that the more recent 2010 debacle will be explained anytime soon. The recent comments of an eminent historian are apt here. When asked what, in his opinion, the effect of the French Revolution of 1789 was, he replied that it was too early to tell.

Perhaps market crashes are evidence consistent with the bubble theory of speculative markets. That is, security prices sometimes move wildly above their true values. Eventually, prices fall back to their original level, causing great losses for investors. Consider, for example, the behaviour of Internet stocks of the late 1990s. Figure 13.11 shows values of an index of Internet stocks from 1996 through 2002. The index rose over ten-fold from January 1996 to its high in March 2000 before retreating to approximately its original level in 2002. For comparison, the figure also shows price movement for the Standard & Poor's 500 index. While this index rose and fell over the same period, the price movement was quite muted relative to that of Internet stocks.

Figure 13.11 Value of Index of Internet Stocks

The index of Internet stocks rose over ten-fold from the beginning of 1996 to its high in March 2000 before falling to approximately its original level in 2002.

Many commentators describe the rise and fall of Internet stocks as a *bubble*. Is it correct to do so? Unfortunately, there is no precise definition of the term. Some academics argue that the price movement in the figure is consistent with rationality. Prices rose initially, they say, because it appeared that the Internet would soon capture a large chunk of international commerce. Prices fell when later evidence suggested this would not occur quite so quickly. However, others argue that the initial rosy scenario was never supported by the facts. Rather, prices rose due to nothing more than 'irrational exuberance'.

Real World Insight 13.1

Understanding Negative Bond Yields

It is fair to say that the financial markets have behaved very strangely in recent years. Government bond yields are negative, stock markets are at 10-year highs, and China appears to be in a financial bubble. What does this all mean for concepts like Market Efficiency? Take negative government bond yields, which means that the return you receive on these instruments is expected to be negative. On one level, you would argue that this is definitely proof that the market is inefficient since the risk-expected return relation is violated. However, it could also mean that investors are expecting deflation, where overall price levels are falling. In such a situation, if the positive return on bonds to compensate for risk (which is to be expected) is not larger than the drop in overall price levels, negative yields will result.

13.7   Reviewing the Differences

It is fair to say that the controversy over efficient capital markets has not yet been resolved. Rather, academic financial economists have sorted themselves into three camps, with some adhering to market efficiency, some believing in behavioural finance and others (perhaps the majority) not yet convinced that either side has won the argument. This state of affairs is certainly different from, say, 20 years ago, when market efficiency went unchallenged. In addition, the controversy here is perhaps the most contentious of any area of financial economics.

Because of the controversy, it does not appear that our textbook, or any textbook, can easily resolve the differing points of view. However, we can illustrate the differences between the camps by relating the two psychological principles mentioned earlier, representativeness and conservatism, to share price returns.

Representativeness

This principle implies overweighting the results of small samples, as with the gambler who thinks a few consecutive spins of black on the roulette wheel make black a more likely outcome than red on the next spin. Financial economists have argued that representativeness leads to *overreaction* in share price returns. We mentioned earlier that financial bubbles are likely overreactions to news. Internet companies showed great revenue growth for a short time in the late 1990s, causing many to believe that this growth would continue indefinitely. Share prices rose (too much) at this point. Similarly, most people in the banking sector thought that subprime mortgages would provide strong returns at little risk. It was only when these loans started to go bad in 2008 and banks such as Washington Mutual, Lehmann Brothers, Bear Stearns, Northern Rock, Royal Bank of Scotland and HBOS, got into serious financial distress that they realized how wrong they were. In both cases, when investors realized that they were wrong, prices plummeted.

Conservatism

This principle states that individuals adjust their beliefs too slowly to new information. A market composed of this type of investor would likely lead to share prices that *underreact* in the presence of new information. The example concerning earnings surprises may illustrate this underreaction. Prices rose slowly following announcements of positive earnings surprises. Announcements of negative surprises had a similar, but opposite, reaction.

The global credit crisis of 2008 gives us another good example of conservatism in financial markets. When the British bank, Northern Rock, was nationalized in the early part of the year, investors thought or hoped that it would only be that bank which was affected. Then Bear Stearns, the US investment bank, had to be purchased by JP Morgan Chase in May 2008, and although investors were shaken they still clung to hopes that the credit crisis was nearly over. Fast forward to September 2008 and the banking sector had ground to a halt. In the space of one week, Lehmann Brothers went bankrupt in the world's largest ever bankruptcy. HBOS, Britain's largest mortgage lender, had to be purchased by Lloyds TSB after its share price collapsed. The US and UK governments temporarily halted the practice of short selling and the Russian stock markets had to close for a day because prices became too volatile. With hindsight, it is easy to see that the credit crisis had only really started when Northern Rock was nationalized. It could be argued that if investors had acted rationally 3 years earlier, the disaster that hit the world's economies may have been averted.

The Academic Viewpoints

The academic camps have different views of these results. The efficient market believers stress that representativeness and conservatism have opposite implications for share prices. Which principle, they ask, should dominate in any particular situation? In other words, why should investors overreact to news about Internet stocks but underreact to banking stocks? Proponents of market efficiency say that unless behaviourists can answer these two questions satisfactorily, we should not reject market efficiency in favour of behavioural finance. In addition, Eugene Fama (1998) reviewed the academic studies on anomalies, finding that about half of them show overreaction and half show underreaction. He concluded that this evidence is consistent with the market efficiency hypothesis that anomalies are chance events.

Adherents of behavioural finance see things a little differently. First, they point out that, as discussed in Section 13.5, the three theoretical foundations of market efficiency appear to be violated in the real world. Second, there are simply too many anomalies, with a number of them being replicated in out-of-sample tests. This argues against anomalies being mere chance events. Finally, though the field has not yet determined why either overreaction or underreaction should dominate in a particular situation, much progress has already been made in a short time.[8]

13.8   Implications for Corporate Finance

So far this chapter has examined both theoretical arguments and empirical evidence concerning efficient markets. We now ask whether market efficiency has any relevance for corporate financial managers. The answer is that it does. Next we consider four implications of efficiency for managers.

Accounting Choices, Financial Choices and Market Efficiency

The accounting profession provides firms with a significant amount of leeway in their reporting practices. Managers clearly prefer high share prices to low share prices. Should managers use the leeway in accounting choices to report the highest possible income? Not necessarily. That is, accounting choice should not affect share price if two conditions hold. First, enough information must be provided in the annual report so that financial analysts can construct earnings under the alternative accounting methods. This appears to be the case for many, though not necessarily all, accounting choices. Second, the market must be efficient in the semi-strong form. In other words, the market must appropriately use all of this accounting information in determining the market price.

Of course, the issue of whether accounting choice affects share price is ultimately an empirical matter. A number of academic papers have addressed this issue. Kaplan and Roll (1972) found that the switch from accelerated to straight-line depreciation did not affect share prices.

Several other accounting procedures have been studied. Hong et al. (1978) found no evidence that the stock market was affected by the artificially higher earnings reported using the pooling method, compared to the purchase method, for reporting mergers and acquisitions.[9] In summary, empirical evidence suggests that accounting changes do not fool the market. Therefore, the evidence does not suggest that managers can boost share price through accounting practices. In other words, the market appears efficient enough to see through different accounting choices.

One caveat is called for here. Our discussion specifically assumed that 'financial analysts can construct earnings under the alternative accounting methods'. However, many companies (like Enron, WorldCom, Global Crossing, Parmalat, Xerox, Olympus Corporation and Satyam Computer Services) have simply reported fraudulent numbers in recent years. There was no way for financial analysts to construct alternative earnings numbers because these analysts were unaware how the reported numbers were determined. So it was not surprising that the share prices of these companies initially rose well above fair value. Yes, managers can boost prices in this way – as long as they are willing to serve time once they are caught!

The Timing Decision

Imagine a firm whose managers are contemplating the date to issue equity. This decision is frequently called the *timing* decision. If managers believe that their equity is overpriced, they are likely to issue shares immediately. Here, they are creating value for their current shareholders because they are selling shares for more than they are worth. Conversely, if the managers believe that their equity is underpriced, they are more likely to wait, hoping that the equity price will eventually rise to its true value.

However, if markets are efficient, securities are always correctly priced. Efficiency implies that equity is sold for its true worth, so the timing decision becomes unimportant. Figure 13.12 shows three possible share price adjustments to the issuance of new equity.

Figure 13.12 Three Share Price Adjustments after Issuing Equity

Share price movement if managers have inferior timing ability

Efficient market movement

Share price movement if managers have superior timing ability

Studies show that shares are more likely to be issued after equity prices have increased. No inferences about market efficiency can be drawn from this result. Rather, market efficiency implies that the share price of the issuing firm, on average, neither rises nor falls (relative to equity market indices) after issuance of equity.

Consistent with the behavioural belief, Ritter (2003) presents evidence that annual equity returns over the 5 years following an initial public offering (IPO) are about 2 per cent less for the issuing company than the returns on a non-issuing company of similar book-to-market ratio. Annual share price returns over this period following a seasoned equity offering (SEO) are between 3 per cent and 4 per cent less for the issuing company than for a comparable non-issuing company. The upper half of Figure 13.13 shows average annual returns of both IPOs and their control group, and the lower half of the figure shows average annual returns of both SEOs and their control group.

The evidence in Ritter's (2003) paper suggests that corporate managers issue SEOs when the company's equity is overpriced. In other words, managers appear to time the market successfully. The evidence that managers time their IPOs is less compelling: returns following IPOs are closer to those of their control group. Dong et al. (2012) extend this research and examine the level of financing and equity issuance for overvalued firms. Similar to Ritter (2003), they find that managers definitely take advantage of high stock prices and issue new shares when their equity is overvalued.

Does the ability of a corporate official to issue an SEO when the security is overpriced indicate that the market is inefficient in the semi-strong form or the strong form? The answer is actually somewhat more complex than it may first appear. On the one hand, officials are likely to have special information that the rest of us do not have, suggesting that the market need only be inefficient in the strong form. On the other hand, if the market were truly semi-strong efficient, the price would drop immediately and completely upon the announcement of an upcoming SEO. That is, rational investors would realize that equity is being issued because corporate officials have special information that the shares are overpriced. Indeed, many empirical studies report a price drop on the announcement date. However, Figure 13.13 shows a further price drop in the subsequent years, suggesting that the market is inefficient in the semi-strong form.

If firms can time the issuance of shares, perhaps they can also time the repurchase of shares. Here a firm would like to repurchase when its equity is undervalued. Ikenberry et al. (1995) find that equity returns of repurchasing firms are abnormally high in the 2 years following repurchase, suggesting that timing is also effective here.

Speculation and Efficient Markets

We normally think of individuals and financial institutions as the primary speculators in financial markets. However, industrial corporations speculate as well. For example, many companies make interest rate bets. If the managers of a firm believe that interest rates are likely to rise, they have an incentive to borrow because the present value of the liability will fall with the rate increase. In addition, these managers will have an incentive to

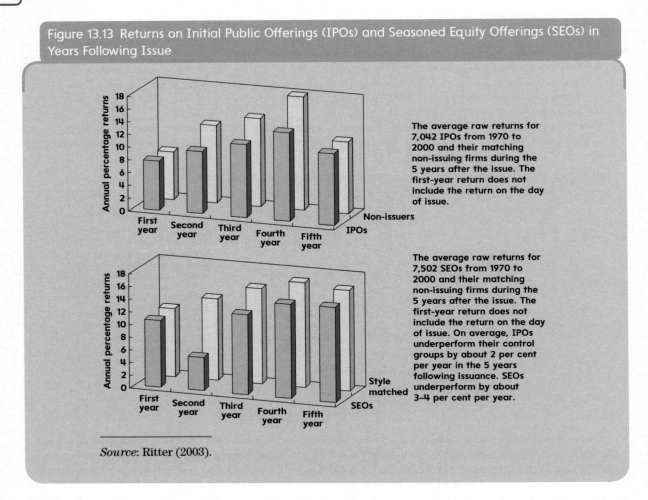

Figure 13.13 Returns on Initial Public Offerings (IPOs) and Seasoned Equity Offerings (SEOs) in Years Following Issue

The average raw returns for 7,042 IPOs from 1970 to 2000 and their matching non-issuing firms during the 5 years after the issue. The first-year return does not include the return on the day of issue.

The average raw returns for 7,502 SEOs from 1970 to 2000 and their matching non-issuing firms during the 5 years after the issue. The first-year return does not include the return on the day of issue. On average, IPOs underperform their control groups by about 2 per cent per year in the 5 years following issuance. SEOs underperform by about 3–4 per cent per year.

Source: Ritter (2003).

borrow long term rather than short term in order to lock in the low rates for a longer period. The thinking can get more sophisticated. Suppose that the long-term rate is already higher than the short-term rate. The manager might argue that this differential reflects the market's view that rates will rise. However, perhaps he anticipates a rate increase even greater than what the market anticipates, as implied by the upward-sloping term structure. Again, the manager will want to borrow long term rather than short term.

Firms also speculate in foreign currencies. Suppose that the CFO of a multinational corporation based in the United Kingdom believes that the euro will decline relative to sterling. She would probably issue euro-denominated debt rather than sterling-denominated debt because she expects the value of the foreign liability to fall. Conversely, she would issue debt domestically if she believes foreign currencies will appreciate relative to the British pound.

We are perhaps getting a little ahead of our story: the subtleties of the term structure and exchange rates are treated in other chapters, not this one. However, the big question is this: what does market efficiency have to say about such activity? The answer is clear. If financial markets are efficient, managers should not waste their time trying to forecast the movements of interest rates and foreign currencies. Their forecasts will likely be no better than chance. And they will be using up valuable executive time. This is not to say, however, that firms should flippantly pick the maturity or the denomination of their debt in a random fashion. A firm must *choose* these parameters carefully. However, the choice should be based on other rationales, not on an attempt to beat the market. For example, a firm with a project lasting 5 years might decide to issue 5-year debt. A firm might issue renminbi-denominated debt because it anticipates expanding into China in a big way.

The same thinking applies to acquisitions. Many corporations buy up other firms because they think these targets are underpriced. Unfortunately, the empirical evidence suggests that the market is too efficient for this type of speculation to be profitable. And the acquirer never pays just the current market price. The bidding firm must pay a premium above market to induce a majority of shareholders of the target firm to sell their shares. However, this is not to say that firms should never be acquired. Rather, managers should consider an acquisition if there are benefits (synergies) from the union. Improved marketing, economies in production, replacement of bad management, and even tax reduction are typical synergies. These synergies are distinct from the perception that the acquired firm is underpriced.

One final point should be mentioned. We talked earlier about empirical evidence suggesting that equity issues are timed to take advantage of overpriced equity. This makes sense – managers are likely to know more about their own firms than the market does. However, while managers may have special information about their own firms, it is unlikely that they have special information about interest rates, foreign currencies and other firms. There are simply too many participants in these markets, many of whom are devoting all of their time to forecasting. Managers typically spend most of their effort running their own firms, with only a small amount of time devoted to studying financial markets.

Information in Market Prices

The previous section argued that it is quite difficult to forecast future market prices. However, the current and past prices of any asset are known – and of great use. Consider, for example, Becher's (2000) study of bank mergers. The author finds that share prices of acquired banks rise about 23 per cent on average upon the first announcement of a merger. This is not surprising because companies are generally bought out at a premium above current share price. However, the same study shows that prices of acquiring banks fall almost 5 per cent on average upon the same announcement. This is pretty strong evidence that bank mergers do not benefit, and may even hurt, acquiring companies. The reason for this result is unclear, though perhaps acquirers simply overpay for acquisitions. Regardless of the reason, the *implication* is clear. A bank should think deeply before acquiring another bank.

Furthermore, suppose you are the CFO of a company whose share price drops much more than 5 per cent upon announcement of an acquisition. The market is telling you that the merger is bad for your firm. Serious consideration should be given to cancelling the merger, even if, prior to the announcement, you thought the merger was a good idea.

Of course, mergers are only one type of corporate event. Managers should pay attention to the share price reaction to any of their announcements, whether it concerns a new venture, a divestiture, a restructuring, or something else. Hill and Hillier (2009) find that managers do exactly that. They look at how managers respond to negative share price performance in the days following a new equity offering and report that they significantly scale back their investment activities as a result.

This is not the only way in which corporations can use the information in market prices. Suppose you are on the board of directors of a company whose share price has declined precipitously since the current chief executive officer (CEO) was hired. In addition, the prices of competitors have risen over the same time. Though there may be extenuating circumstances, this can be viewed as evidence that the CEO is doing a poor job. Perhaps he should be fired. If this seems harsh, consider that Warner et al. (1988) find a strong negative correlation between managerial turnover and prior stock performance. Figure 13.14 shows that share prices fall on average about 40 per cent in price (relative to market movements) in the 3 years prior to the forced departure of a top manager.

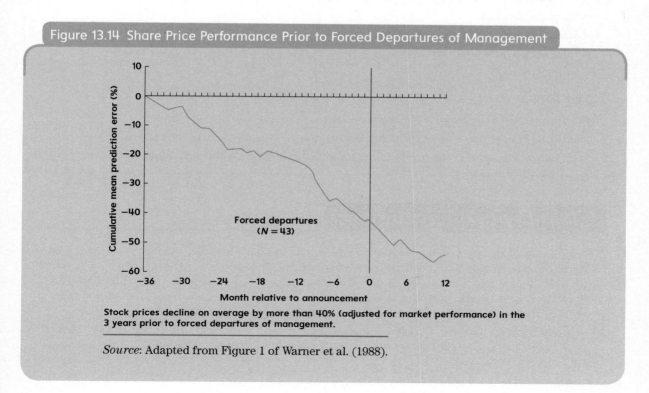

Figure 13.14 Share Price Performance Prior to Forced Departures of Management

Stock prices decline on average by more than 40% (adjusted for market performance) in the 3 years prior to forced departures of management.

Source: Adapted from Figure 1 of Warner et al. (1988).

Market efficiency implies that share prices reflect all available information. We recommend using this information as much as possible in corporate decisions as long as the manager feels that share prices accurately reflect the true value of company equity. In most emerging market countries, stock markets may not be very efficient and you should be careful about using available share prices. In developed economies, at least with respect to executive firings and executive compensation, it looks as if real-world corporations do pay attention to market prices. The following box summarizes some key issues in the efficient markets debate:

Efficient Market Hypothesis: A Summary

Does not say

- Prices are uncaused.
- Investors are foolish and too stupid to be in the market.
- All shares of stock have the same expected returns.
- Investors should throw darts to select shares.
- There is no upward trend in share prices.

Does say

- Prices reflect underlying value.
- Financial managers cannot time equity and bond sales.
- Managers cannot profitably speculate in foreign currencies.
- Managers cannot boost share prices through creative accounting.

Why doesn't everybody believe it?

- There are optical illusions, mirages and apparent patterns in charts of stock market returns.
- The truth is less interesting.
- There is evidence against efficiency:
  - Two different, but financially identical, classes of shares of the same firm selling at different prices.
  - Earnings surprises.
  - Small versus large company share price returns.
  - Value versus growth stocks.
  - Crashes and bubbles.

Three forms

1 *Weak form*: Current prices reflect past prices; chartism (technical analysis) is useless.
2 *Semi-strong form*: Prices reflect all public information; most financial analysis is useless.
3 *Strong form*: Prices reflect all that is knowable; nobody consistently makes superior profits.

Summary and Conclusions

1 An efficient financial market processes the information available to investors and incorporates it into the prices of securities. Market efficiency has two general implications. First, in any given time period, an equity's abnormal return depends on information or news received by the market in that period. Second, an investor who uses the same information as the market cannot expect to earn abnormal returns. In other words, systems for playing the market are doomed to fail.

2 What information does the market use to determine prices? The weak form of the efficient market hypothesis says that the market uses the history of prices and is therefore efficient with respect to these

past prices. This implies that security selection based on patterns of past share price movements is no better than random selection.

3   The semi-strong form states that the market uses all publicly available information in setting prices.

4   Strong form efficiency states that the market uses all of the information that anybody knows about equities, even inside information.

5   Much evidence from different financial markets supports weak form and semi-strong form efficiency but not strong form efficiency.

6   Behavioural finance states that the market is not efficient. Adherents argue that:

   (a)   Investors are not rational.

   (b)   Deviations from rationality are similar across investors.

   (c)   Arbitrage, being costly, will not eliminate inefficiencies.

7   Behaviourists point to many studies, including those showing that small company shares outperform large company shares, value stocks outperform growth stocks, and share prices adjust slowly to earnings surprises, as empirical confirmation of their beliefs.

8   Four implications of market efficiency for corporate finance are:

   (a)   Managers cannot fool the market through creative accounting.

   (b)   Firms cannot successfully time issues of debt and equity.

   (c)   Managers cannot profitably speculate in foreign currencies and other instruments.

   (d)   Managers can reap many benefits by paying attention to market prices.

Questions and Problems

CONCEPT

1   **Financing Decisions and Firm Value**   What rule should a firm follow when making financing decisions? How can firms create valuable financing opportunities?

2   **Efficient Capital Markets**   What are the three conditions under which Fama (1970) argues markets may be efficient? Describe these in detail and provide a practical example illustrating each condition in practice. What are the three categories of market efficiency identified by Fama (1991)?

3   **Efficient Market Hypothesis**   Explain what is meant by the efficient market hypothesis. Define the three forms of market efficiency and explain why a characteristic of an efficient market is that investments in that market have zero NPVs. Does market efficiency mean you can randomly pick stocks from an exchange to form your portfolio? Explain.

4   **Efficient Market Hypothesis: The Evidence**   Suppose XYZ plc announced this morning that its profit from last quarter has dropped 15 per cent compared to the previous quarter, and that its closing price at the end of the day is up 2 per cent from yesterday. Is this evidence against the efficiency market hypothesis?

5   **Behavioural Finance**   In recent years, a new interpretation of market behaviour has emerged. Explain this theory and review what it says about Shleifer's three conditions of market efficiency. Compare and contrast both theories. In your opinion, which is the most reflective of market behaviour? Explain.

6   **Empirical Challenges to Market Efficiency**   Discuss some of the anomalies to market efficiency that have been detected in academic research. Taken together, do these anomalies provide concrete evidence that the market is inefficient? Why or why not? Explain.

7   **Efficient Market Theory versus Behavioural Finance**   The efficient market hypothesis implies that abnormal returns are expected to be zero. Yet in order for markets to be efficient, arbitrageurs must be able to force prices back into equilibrium. If they earn profits in doing so, is this fact inconsistent with market efficiency?

8   **Implications for Corporate Finance**   What does efficient market theory and behavioural finance imply for corporate decision making? Provide three examples of how each theory may affect managerial behaviour.

REGULAR

9 **Efficient Market Hypothesis**   Which of the following statements are true about the efficient market hypothesis?

(a) It implies perfect forecasting ability.

(b) It implies that prices reflect all available information.

(c) It implies an irrational market.

(d) It implies that prices do not fluctuate.

(e) It results from keen competition among investors.

10 **Technical Trading** 'Every day I check the price patterns from the day before to identify the shares I wish to trade that day.' What do the efficient markets hypothesis and behavioural finance hypothesis say about this statement? Which explanation do you believe as being most valid?

11 **Investment Gurus** Warren Buffett and several other investors earned significantly positive returns during the financial crisis, 2008–2009. How can you explain this using the efficient markets hypothesis and behavioural finance theory?

12 **Competitive Product Markets** Assume that markets are efficient, and that investment firms have decided to retire all portfolio managers and financial analysts, letting random choice via a computer determine their security selection process. What mistake is implicit in this action?

13 **Corporate Insider Trading** The cumulative abnormal returns pattern for British insider trading (Figure 13.7) suggests that executives have private information that they exploit to their advantage. Is there a behavioural interpretation for the pattern? Does this violate any of the three forms of market efficiency? Explain.

14 **Investor Sentiment** Some people believe that following the European Consumer Confidence Index (see chart below) allows you to predict future market movements. What is the Consumer Confidence Index intended to capture? How might it be useful in technical analysis? Look at the stock market indices of any European country. Do you think it is a good indicator? Explain.

15 **Efficient Markets** Since 2005, all publicly listed European companies follow International Accounting Standards. This means that financial statements are based largely on market values instead of historical cost measures. Assuming the market is semi-strong form efficient, what does this say about market efficiency pre- and post-2005?

16 **Efficient Markets Hypothesis** Kasetsart Agriculture, a Thai agricultural technology research firm, announced this morning that it has hired the world's most knowledgeable and prolific agriculture researchers. Before today Kasetsart's equity had been selling for 100 baht. Assume that no other information is received over the next week and the Thai stock market as a whole does not move.

(a) What do you expect will happen to Kasetsart's share price?

(b) Consider the following scenarios:

(i) The share price jumps to 118 baht on the day of the announcement. In subsequent days it floats up to 123 baht, then falls back to 116 baht.

(ii) The share price jumps to 116 baht and remains at that level.

(iii) The share price gradually climbs to 116 baht over the next week.

Which scenario(s) indicate market efficiency? Which do not? Why? Provide a behavioural interpretation for each scenario.

17 **Behavioural Finance** Do you think emerging markets will be more or less efficient? Do you think they will be more or less sensitive to market sentiment? Explain.

18 **Efficient Markets Hypothesis** When the 56-year-old founder of the Turkish firm, Gulf Oil and Minerals, died of a heart attack, the share price immediately jumped from 18.00 Lira a share to 20.25 Lira, a 12.5 per cent increase. This is evidence of market inefficiency because an efficient stock market would have anticipated his death and adjusted the price beforehand. Assume that no other information is received and the stock market as a whole does not move. Is this statement about market efficiency true or false? Explain.

19 **Efficient Markets Hypothesis** Newtech GmbH is going to adopt a new chip-testing device that can greatly improve its production efficiency. Do you think the lead engineer can profit from purchasing the firm's shares before the news release on the device? After reading the announcement in *Spiegel*, should you be able to earn an abnormal return from purchasing the equity if the market is efficient?

20 **Efficient Markets Hypothesis** In 2005, all companies in the European Union adopted IFRS, International Financial Reporting Standards. TransTrust NV changed how it accounts for inventory. Taxes are unaffected, although the resulting earnings report released once IFRS had been adopted is 20 per cent higher than what it would have been under the old accounting system. There is no other surprise in the earnings report, and the change in the accounting treatment was publicly announced. If the market is efficient, will the share price be higher when the market learns that the reported earnings are higher?

21 **Efficient Markets Hypothesis** The Durkin Investing Agency has been the best stock picker in the country for the past two years. Before this rise to fame occurred, the Durkin newsletter had 200 subscribers. Those subscribers beat the market consistently, earning substantially higher returns after adjustment for risk and transaction costs. Subscriptions have skyrocketed to 10,000. Now, when the Durkin Investing Agency recommends an equity, the price instantly rises several points. The subscribers currently earn only a normal return when they buy recommended shares because the price rises before anybody can act on the information. Briefly explain this phenomenon. Is Durkin's ability to pick winners consistent with market efficiency?

22 **Efficient Markets Hypothesis** Your broker commented that well-managed firms are better investments than poorly managed firms. As evidence your broker cited a recent study examining 100 small manufacturing firms that 8 years earlier had been listed in an industry magazine as the best-managed small manufacturers in the country. In the ensuing 8 years, the 100 firms listed have not earned more than the normal market return. Your broker continued to say that if the firms were well managed, they should have produced better-than-average returns. If the market is efficient, do you agree with your broker?

23 **Efficient Markets Hypothesis** A famous economist just announced in the *Financial Times* his findings that the recession is over and the economy is again entering an expansion. Assume market efficiency. Can you profit from investing in the stock market after you read this announcement? Assume behavioural finance is true. What do you think will happen in the stock market and why?

24 **Efficient Markets Hypothesis** Suppose the market is strong form efficient. Can you expect to earn excess returns if you make trades based on:

(a) An analyst's forecasts about future company earnings?

(b) Rumours about the takeover of a firm?

(c) A company's announcement of a successful prototype launch?

25 **Efficient Markets Hypothesis** Imagine that a particular macroeconomic variable that influences your firm's net earnings is positively serially correlated. Assume market efficiency. Would you expect price changes in your shares to be serially correlated? Why or why not?

26 **Efficient Markets Hypothesis** The efficient market hypothesis implies that all mutual funds should obtain the same expected risk-adjusted returns. Therefore, we can simply pick mutual funds at random. Is this statement true or false? Explain.

27 **Efficient Markets Hypothesis** Assume that markets are efficient. During a trading day, British Golf plc announces that it has lost a contract for a large golfing project that, prior to the news, it was widely believed to have secured. If the market is efficient, how should the stock price react to this information if no additional information is released?

28 **Efficient Markets Hypothesis** Prospectors plc is a publicly traded gold prospecting company with operations in Northern Tanzania. Although the firm's searches for gold usually fail, the prospectors occasionally find a rich vein of ore. What pattern would you expect to observe for Prospectors' cumulative abnormal returns if the market is efficient?

29   **Evidence on Market Efficiency**   Some people argue that the efficient market hypothesis cannot explain the 2010 US flash market crash or the high price-to-earnings ratio of European shares in 2005 and 2006. What alternative hypothesis is currently used for these two phenomena?

30   **Shareholder Activism**   Many financial institutions use the media to drive shareholder activism strategies so that pressure is maximized on the target firm managers. Is this evidence that institutional shareholders believe in efficient markets, behavioural finance or both? What would happen to market efficiency if all investors follow a passive buy-and-hold investment strategy? Explain.

31   **Initial Public Offerings**   Research has shown that managers of newly listed firms rein in their capital expenditure plans if the market share price performance is not particularly strong around the IPO date. This is regularly put down to 'poor market sentiment'. Is this evidence that corporate managers believe in efficient markets, behavioural finance or both? Explain.

32   **Insider Trading**   When corporate executives trade the shares of their own company, the share price normally responds in a correlated way (i.e. share price increases after buy transactions and share price falls after sale transactions). Is this evidence of efficient markets, behavioural finance, or both? Explain.

CHALLENGE

33   **Cumulative Abnormal Returns**   National Airlines Group, Air France-KLM and Lufthansa announced purchases of planes on 18 July (18/7), 12 February (12/2), and 7 October (7/10), respectively. Given the following information, calculate the cumulative abnormal return (CAR) for these equities as a group. Graph the result and provide an explanation. All of the stocks have a beta of 1, and no other announcements are made.

National Airlines Group			Air France-KLM			Lufthansa		
Date	Market return	Company return	Date	Market return	Company return	Date	Market return	Company return
12/7	−0.3	−0.5	8/2	−0.9	−1.1	1/10	0.5	0.3
13/7	0.0	0.2	9/2	−1.0	−1.1	2/10	0.4	0.6
16/7	0.5	0.7	10/2	0.4	0.2	3/10	1.1	1.1
17/7	−0.5	−0.3	11/2	0.6	0.8	6/10	0.1	−0.3
18/7	−2.2	1.1	12/2	−0.3	−0.1	7/10	−2.2	−0.3
19/7	−0.9	−0.7	15/2	1.1	1.2	8/10	0.5	0.5
20/7	−1.0	−1.1	16/2	0.5	0.5	9/10	−0.3	−0.2
23/7	0.7	0.5	17/2	−0.3	−0.2	10/10	0.3	0.1
24/7	0.2	0.1	18/2	0.3	0.2	13/10	0.0	−0.1

34   **Cumulative Abnormal Returns**   The following diagram shows the cumulative abnormal returns (CAR) for 386 oil exploration companies announcing oil discoveries between 1950 and 1980. Month 0 in the diagram is the announcement month. Assume that no other information is received and the equity market as a whole does not move. Is the diagram consistent with market efficiency? Why or why not?

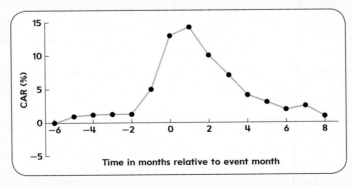

35   **Cumulative Abnormal Returns**   The following figures present the results of four cumulative abnormal returns (CAR) studies. Indicate whether the results of each study support, reject or are inconclusive about the semi-strong form of the efficient market hypothesis. In each figure time 0 is the date of an event.

36 **Cumulative Abnormal Returns** A study analysed the behaviour of the equity prices of firms that had lost monopoly cases. Included in the diagram are all firms that lost the initial court decision, even if the decision was later overturned on appeal. The event at time 0 is the initial, pre-appeal court decision. Assume no other information was released, aside from that disclosed in the initial trial. The stock prices all have a beta of 1. Is the diagram consistent with market efficiency? Why or why not?

Exam Question (45 minutes)

1 Explain what is meant by efficient market theory and discuss some of its implications for corporate financial management. (25 marks)

2 *'Even in an efficient market it is still valid to seek out a "favourable" rate of return from an equity investment.'*

   Consider the argument that, in an efficient market 'one security is as good as any other'. (25 marks)

3 Explain how behavioural finance can provide insights to corporate financial managers. (25 marks)

4 What strategies can financial managers follow if they believe behavioural finance is a valid hypothesis? (25 marks)

Mini Case

Your Retirement Account at West Coast Yachts

You have been at your job for West Coast Yachts for a week now and have decided you need to sign up for the company's retirement plan. Even after your discussion with Sarah Brown, the Skandla Financial Services representative, you are still unsure which investment option you should choose. Recall that the options available to you are owning shares of West Coast Yachts, the Skandla Market Index Fund, the Skandla Large Company Equity Fund, the Skandla Small-Cap Fund, the Skandla Bond Fund, and the Skandla Money

Market Fund. You have decided that you should invest in a diversified portfolio, with 70 per cent of your investment in equity, 25 per cent in bonds, and 5 per cent in the money market fund. You have also decided to focus your equity investment on large-cap company shares, but you are debating whether to select the Market Index Fund or the Large-Company Equity Fund.

In thinking it over, you understand the basic difference in the two funds. One is a purely passive fund that replicates a widely followed large-cap index, the FTSE 100, and has low fees. The other is actively managed with the intention that the skill of the portfolio manager will result in improved performance relative to an index. Fees are higher in the latter fund. You are just not certain which way to go, so you ask Dan Ervin, who works in the company's finance area, for advice.

After discussing your concerns, Dan gives you some information comparing the performance of equity mutual funds and the FTSE 100 Index Fund. The FTSE 100 Index Fund replicates the FTSE 100, and its return is only negligibly different from the Index itself. Fees are very low. As a result, the FTSE 100 Index Fund is essentially identical to the Skandla Market Index Fund offered in the retirement plan, but it has been in existence for much longer, so you can study its track record for over two decades. The graph shown summarizes Dan's comments by showing the percentage of equity mutual funds that outperformed the FTSE 100 Index Fund over the previous 10 years. So for example, from January 2001 to December 2001, about 20 per cent of equity mutual funds outperformed the FTSE 100 Index Fund. Dan suggests that you study the graph and answer the following questions:

1   What implications do you draw from the graph for mutual fund investors?

2   Is the graph consistent or inconsistent with market efficiency? Explain carefully.

3   What investment decision would you make for the equity portion of your retirement account? Why?

Practical Case Study

In many countries, regulators have moved to ban an activity called equity short-selling. In order to sell equity short, a trader would open an account with a broker, borrow shares from existing shareholders for a fee and promise to give them back at some point in the future. Short-selling is normally used as an effective hedging tool. However, it can also be used to speculate against future falls in prices.

The practice of short selling came under intense scrutiny when it was blamed for the collapsing share prices of banks in 2008. Regulators argued that hedge funds were contributing to the collapse in share prices by irrationally forcing them down below their true level. As bank share prices imploded, there was clear evidence that many banks had very high levels of short selling. As a result, the British government imposed a short-selling ban on 18 September 2008 until 16 January 2009. Other countries imposed similar bans.

If share prices were forced down by a small number of hedge funds (and their short-selling followers) purely because of speculative activity, it would be clear evidence against the efficient market hypothesis.

1 Visit Yahoo! Finance and download the share prices of five British banks for the dates 1 August 2008 to 31 January 2009. Also download the FTSE 100 index for the same period.

2 Track each bank's share price before the ban, during the ban, and after the ban. Do the share price movements support the view that the market was irrationally depressed because of speculative activity?

3 Carry out your own investigation of short-selling in Europe. How did other European governments deal with the short-selling controversy?

4 Write a report about the short-selling controversy in the context of the efficient markets hypothesis and behavioural finance. What does it say about the validity (if at all) of either theory?

Relevant Accounting Standards

If there is one area where International Financial Reporting Standards have faced a lot of criticism, it is with respect to their effect on market prices. Because financial assets and liabilities have to be reported at fair or market value, volatility in the stock markets inevitably leads to volatility in the accounting statements. The main standard is IAS 39 *Financial Instruments: Recognition and Measurement*. IAS 39 provides definitions for different types of financial securities and how to measure their value. Another is FRS 7 *Financial Instruments: Disclosure*. Given their hypothesized impact on accounting statements and the corresponding reinforced share price revisions, it is very likely that both standards will change over the next few years. Keep updated by visiting the IASPlus website (www.iasplus.com).

References

Baker, M. and J. Wurgler (2011) 'Behavioral Corporate Finance: An Updated Survey', NBER Working Paper.

Banz, R.W. (1981) 'The Relationship between Return and Market Value of Common Stocks', *Journal of Financial Economics*, Vol. 9, No. 1, 3–18.

Barber, B. and T. Odean (1999) 'The Courage of Misguided Convictions', *Financial Analysts Journal*, Vol. 56, No. 6, 41–55.

Barberis, N. and R. Thaler (2003) 'A Survey of Behavioural Finance', in G. Constantinides, M. Harris and R. Stultz (eds), *The Handbook of the Economics of Finance* (Amsterdam: North Holland).

Bauer, R., M. Cosemans and P.C. Schotman (2010) 'Conditional Asset Pricing and Stock Market Anomalies in Europe', *European Financial Management*, Vol. 16, 165–190.

Becher, D.A. (2000) 'The Valuation Effects of Bank Mergers', *Journal of Corporate Finance*, Vol. 6, No. 2, 189–214.

Dong, M., D. Hirshleifer and S.H. Teoh (2012) 'Overvalued Equity and Financing Decisions', *Review of Financial Studies*, Vol. 25, No. 12, 3645–3683.

Easterday, K. (2005) 'The Declining January Effect? An Examination of Monthly Returns for Firms Trading on NYSE, AMEX, and NASDAQ', unpublished paper, University of Cincinnati.

Fama, E.F. (1970) 'Efficient Capital Markets: A Review of Theory and Empirical Work', *The Journal of Finance*, Vol. 25, No. 2, 383–417.

Fama, E.F. (1991) 'Efficient Capital Markets: II', *The Journal of Finance*, Vol. 46, 1575–1617.

Fama, E.F. (1998) 'Market Efficiency, Long-term Returns, and Behavioral Finance', *Journal of Financial Economics*, Vol. 49, No. 3, 283–307.

Fama, E.F. and K.R. French (1996) 'Multifactor Explanations of Asset Pricing Anomalies', *The Journal of Finance*, Vol. 51, No. 1, 55–84.

Fama, E.F. and K.R. French (1998) 'Value versus Growth: The International Evidence', *The Journal of Finance*, Vol. 53, 1975–1999.

Fletcher, J. and A. Marshall (2005) 'The Performance of UK International Unit Trusts', *European Financial Management*, Vol. 11, 365–386.

Forbes, W. (2009) *Behavioural Finance* (Chichester: John Wiley & Sons).

Froot, K.A. and E.M. Dabora (1999) 'How Are Stock Prices Affected by the Location of Trade?', *Journal of Financial Economics,* Vol. 53, No. 2, 189–216.

Gerard, X. (2012) 'Information Uncertainty and the Post-earnings Announcement Drift in Europe', *Financial Analysts Journal,* Vol. 68, No. 2, 51–69.

Hill, P. and D. Hillier (2009) 'Market Feedback, Investment Constraints and Managerial Behavior', *European Financial Management,* Vol. 15, No. 3, 584–605.

Hong, H., R.S. Kaplan and G. Mandelker (1978) 'Pooling vs. Purchase: The Effects of Accounting for Mergers on Stock Prices', *Accounting Review,* Vol. 53, 31–47.

Ikenberry, D., J. Lakonishok and T. Vermaelen (1995) 'Market Underreaction to Open Market Share Repurchases', *Journal of Financial Economics,* Vol. 29, Nos. 2–3, 181–208.

Kaplan, R.S. and Roll, R. (1972) 'Investor Evaluation of Accounting Information: Some Empirical Evidence', *The Journal of Business,* Vol. 45, No. 2, 225–257.

Keim, D.B. (1983) 'Size-related Anomalies and Stock Return Seasonality: Further Empirical Evidence', *Journal of Financial Economics,* Vol. 12, 13–32.

Kolasinski, A. and X. Li (2010) 'Are Corporate Managers Savvy about their Stock Price? Evidence from Insider Trading after Earnings Announcements', *Journal of Accounting and Public Policy,* Vol. 29, 27–44.

Kothari, P., J. Shanken and R.G. Sloan (1995) 'Another Look at the Cross-Section of Stock Returns', *The Journal of Finance,* Vol. 50, No. 1, 185–224.

Lamont, O. and R. Thaler (2003) 'Can the Market Add and Subtract? Mispricing in Tech Stock Carve-Outs', *Journal of Political Economy,* Vol. 111, No. 2, 227–268.

Malkiel, B.G. (2003) *A Random Walk Down Wall Street,* 8th edn (New York: Norton).

Otten, R. and D. Bams (2002) 'European Mutual Fund Performance', *European Financial Management Journal,* Vol. 8, 75–101.

Pastor, L. and R.F. Stambaugh (2002) 'Mutual Fund Performance and Seemingly Unrelated Assets', *Journal of Financial Economics,* Vol. 63, No. 3, 315–349.

Reinganum, M.R. (1981) 'Misspecification of Capital Asset Pricing: Empirical Anomalies Based on Earnings Yields and Market Values', *Journal of Financial Economics,* Vol. 9, 19–46.

Ritter, J. (2003) 'Investment Banking and Security Issuance', in G. Constantinides, M. Harris and R. Stultz (eds), *The Handbook of the Economics of Finance* (Amsterdam: North Holland).

Shleifer, A. (2000) *Inefficient Markets: An Introduction to Behavioural Finance* (Oxford: Oxford University Press).

Warner, J.B., R.L. Watts and K.H. Wruck (1988) 'Stock Prices and Top Management Changes', *Journal of Financial Economics,* Vol. 20, 461–492.

Additional Reading

In recent years, the debate about market efficiency has exploded with the arrival of a new and very intuitive portfolio of research findings in the behavioural finance paradigm. Subrahmanyam (2008) provides a very readable review of this research. The other papers in the list consider different aspects of market efficiency, such as predictability in returns and whether managers are more informed than the aggregate market about their own company. Conrad et al. (2003) is notable because it criticizes extant research because of biases in research design. This is always a danger in finance research because, unlike deterministic science experiments, the laboratory for financial markets and the economy is inherently random in nature. Keep this in mind when reading any empirical financial research.

1   Bailey, W., A. Kumar and D. Ng (2011) 'Behavioral Biases of Mutual Fund Investors', *Journal of Financial Economics,* Vol. 102, 1–27. **US.**

2   Bajgrowicz, P. and O. Scaillet (2012) 'Technical Trading Revisited: False Discoveries, Persistence Tests, and Transaction Costs', *Journal of Financial Economics,* Vol. 106, No. 3, 473–491.

3   Barton, J., G.S. Berns and A.M. Brooks (2014) 'The Neuroscience Behind the Stock Market's Reaction to Corporate Earnings News', *The Accounting Review,* Vol. 89, No. 6, 1945–1977.

4   Bessembinder, H. and F. Zhang (2013) 'Firm Characteristics and Long-run Stock Returns after Corporate Events', *Journal of Financial Economics,* Vol. 109, No. 1, 83–102.

5   Chui, A.C.W., S. Titman and K.C.J. Wei (2010) 'Individualism and Momentum around the World', *The Journal of Finance,* Vol. 65, No. 1, 361–392. **International.**

6   Conrad, J., M. Cooper and G. Kaul (2003) 'Value versus Glamour', *The Journal of Finance,* Vol. 58, No. 5, 1969–1996. **US.**

7   Cronqvist, H., A.K. Makhija and S.E. Yonker (2012) 'Behavioral Consistency in Corporate Finance: CEO Personal and Corporate Leverage', *Journal of Financial Economics,* Vol. 103, No. 1, 20–40.

8   Da, Z., J. Engelberg and P. Gao (2011) 'In Search of Attention', *The Journal of Finance,* Vol. 66, No. 5, 1461–1499.

9   Dong, M., D. Hirshleifer and S.H. Teoh (2012) 'Overvalued Equity and Financing Decisions', *Review of Financial Studies,* Vol. 25, No. 12, 3645–3683.

10 Gennaioli, N., A. Shleifer and R. Vishny (2015) 'Money Doctors', *The Journal of Finance*, Vol. 70, No. 1, 91–114.

11 Green, T.C. and R. Jame (2013) 'Company Name Fluency, Investor Recognition, and Firm Value', *Journal of Financial Economics*, Vol. 109, No. 3, 813–834.

12 Greenwood, R. and A. Shleifer (2014) 'Expectations of Returns and Expected Returns', *Review of Financial Studies*, Vol. 27, No. 3, 714–746.

13 Hartzmark, S.M. and D.H. Solomon (2013) 'The Dividend Month Premium', *Journal of Financial Economics*, Vol. 109, No. 3, 640–660.

14 Hill, P. and D. Hillier (2009) 'Market Feedback, Investment Constraints and Managerial Behavior', *European Financial Management*, Vol. 15, No. 3, 584–605. **UK**.

15 Hwang, S., A. Keswani and M.B. Shackleton (2008) 'Surprise vs Anticipated Information Announcements: Are Prices Affected Differently? An Investigation in the Context of Stock Splits', *Journal of Banking and Finance*, Vol. 32, No. 5, 643–653. **US**.

16 Lilienfeld-Toal, U.V. and S. Ruenzi (2014) 'CEO Ownership, Stock Market Performance, and Managerial Discretion', *The Journal of Finance*, Vol. 69, No. 3, 1013–1050.

17 Savor, P.G. (2012) 'Stock Returns after Major Price Shocks: The Impact of Information', *Journal of Financial Economics*, Vol. 106, No. 3, 635–659.

18 Subrahmanyam, A. (2008) 'Behavioural Finance: A Review and Synthesis', *European Financial Management*, Vol. 14, No. 1, 12–29.

Endnotes

1 For purposes of this text, the random walk can be considered synonymous with weak form efficiency. Technically, the random walk is a slightly more restrictive hypothesis because it assumes that share price returns are identically distributed through time. The random walk model is normally used to predict price movements, not explain them (as the CAPM does). Two main assumptions of investor behaviour are required for it to hold. First, investors are rational and their predictions of what will happen in the future are neither optimistic nor pessimistic. That is, they are unbiased. The other assumption is that price changes are caused by the arrival of new information only. Given that new information arrives randomly, prices must evolve randomly, hence the term random walk.

2 We can also measure the abnormal return by using the market model. In this case the abnormal return is:

$$AR = R - (\alpha + \beta R_{M})$$

3 For example, see Barber and Odean (1999).

4 See Banz (1981) and Reinganum (1981).

5 Also see Easterday (2005) for similar conclusions with more recent data.

6 Taken from Table III of Fama and French (1998).

7 For example, see Kothari et al. (1995) and Fama and French (1996).

8 Excellent reviews of this progress can be found in Shleifer (2000), Barberis and Thaler (2003), Baker and Wurgler (2011) and Forbes (2009).

9 The pooling method for mergers is no longer allowed under generally accepted accounting principles.

Long-term Financing: An Introduction

Companies that require cash to fund new investments have a variety of options to consider. They can take on more debt via bank loans or through the issue of bonds in the public markets. Alternatively, they can give up part ownership and issue new equity. Companies will not go through just one funding round but many, and the choice of debt or equity type instruments will change over time. Over the last few years, bank credit has become a lot more scarce, and this has led to a growth in public issues as well as alternative financing models such as crowdfunding (an informal source of financing for small start-up companies). In 2014 alone, the equity offering market was particularly active with 1,245 global issues raising $263 billion in funds, the biggest of which was by Alibaba Group for $25 billion. Global debt markets were similarly buoyant with $5.7 trillion raised (both corporate and government debt) in 2014 alone.

What forms of long-term financing are available to companies? This chapter introduces the basic sources of long-term financing: ordinary shares, preference shares and long-term debt. Subsequent chapters address the optimal mix of these sources. We will also discuss how companies have financed themselves in recent years.

14.1   Ordinary Shares

Chapter 5
Page 125

Under International Financial Reporting Standards (IFRS), the term ordinary shares has no precise meaning. It is usually applied to equity (see **Chapter 5**, Sections 5.4–5.8 on how to value equities) that has no special preference in either dividends or in bankruptcy. Let us take a typical firm as an example. Below is a description of the equity share capital of the energy firm ABB for the year ending 31 December 2014. ABB has equity listed on the SIX Swiss Exchange in Zurich, the NASDAQ OMX in Stockholm and the NYSE in New York.

Shareholders' Equity ($millions)	31 Dec 2014	31 Dec 2013
Capital Stock and Additional Paid-In Capital (2,314,743,264 issued shares at December 31, 2014 and 2013)	1,777	1,750
Retained Earnings	19,939	19,186
Accumulated Other Comprehensive Loss	−4,241	−2,012
Treasury Stock, at cost (55,843,639 and 14,093,960 shares at 31 December 2014 and 2013, respectively)	−1,206	−246
Total ABB shareholders' equity	16,269	18,678

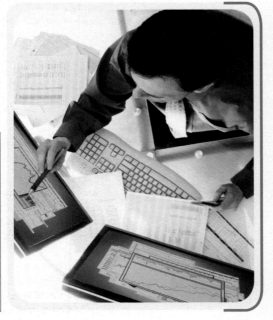

Par and No-par Shares

Owners of ordinary shares in a corporation are referred to as *shareholders* or *stockholders*. They receive share certificates for the *shares* they own. There is usually a stated value on each share certificate called the *par value, face value, stated value* or *nominal value,* which is similar in concept to the face value of a bond. Par value comes from a time when stock markets were not well regulated, but is now no longer needed. Many shares have no par value. Vodafone's shares have a par value of £0.072.

The total par value is the number of shares issued multiplied by the par value of each share and is sometimes referred to as the *dedicated* or *called-up capital* of a corporation.

Authorized versus Outstanding Shares

Ordinary shares are the fundamental ownership units of the corporation. The articles of incorporation of a new company must state the number of ordinary shares the corporation is authorized to issue.

The board of directors of the corporation, after an agreement from the shareholders (in unitary board systems) or the supervisory board (in two-tier board systems) can amend the articles of incorporation to increase the number of shares authorized; there is no limit to the number of shares that can be authorized.[1] In 2014, ABB had issued 2,314,743,264 shares. Although there are no legal limits to authorizing shares of equity, some practical considerations may exist:

1   Some governments impose taxes based on the number of authorized shares.

2   Authorizing a large number of shares may create concern on the part of investors because authorized shares can be issued later *with* the approval of the board of directors but *without* a vote of the shareholders or supervisory board.

Additional paid-in capital usually refers to amounts of directly contributed equity capital in excess of the par value.

Example 14.1

Par Value and Additional Paid-in Capital

Suppose 100 shares of equity have a par value of £2 each and are sold to shareholders for £10 per share. The additional paid in capital would be $(£10 − £2) × 100 = £8 × 100 = £800$, and the total par value would be $£2 × 100 = £200$. What difference does it make if the total capital contribution is reported as par value or additional paid-in capital?

About the only difference is that the par value is locked in and cannot be distributed to shareholders except upon the liquidation of the corporation.

The additional paid-in capital of Vodafone is £153,760 million. This figure indicates that the price of new shares issued by Vodafone has exceeded the par value and the difference has been entered as *additional paid-in capital.*

Retained Earnings

In 2014, ABB paid out 72 per cent of its net income as dividends. The rest of the net income was retained in the business and is called retained earnings. Year on year, a company's retained earnings will accumulate and if earnings in the past have been positive, this can be a substantial amount. For ABB, the cumulative retained earnings (since original incorporation) by the end of 2014 were $19,939 million.

The sum of the equity components, or the total equity, can be referred to as the firm's book value. The book value represents the amount contributed directly and indirectly to the corporation by equity investors.

Example 14.2

Equity Accounting

Suppose Louest Rouge plc was formed in 1910 with 10,000 shares of equity issued with each share valued at £1 par value. Because the shares were sold for £1, the first balance sheet showed a zero amount for capital surplus. By 2015, the company had become very profitable and had retained profits of £100,000. The shareholders' equity of Louest Rouge in 2015 is as follows:

Louest Rouge plc Equity Accounts 1 January 2015	
Ordinary shares; par £1; 10,000 shares outstanding	£ 10,000
Additional paid-in capital	0
Retained earnings	100,000
Total shareholders' equity	£110,000

$$\text{Book value per share} = \frac{£110,000}{10,000} = £11$$

Suppose the company has profitable investment opportunities and decides to sell 10,000 shares of new equity. The current market price is £20 per share. The effect of the sale of shares on the balance sheet at the end of the year will be:

Louest Rouge plc Equity Accounts 31 December 2015	
Ordinary shares, £1 par, 20,000 shares outstanding	£ 20,000
Additional paid-in capital (£20 − £1) × 10,000 shares	190,000
Retained earnings	100,000
Total shareholders' equity	£310,000

$$\text{Book value per share} = \frac{£310,000}{20,000} = £15.5$$

What happened?

1   Because 10,000 shares of new equity were issued with par value of £1, the par value rose £10,000.

2   The total amount raised by the new issue was £20 × 10,000 = £200,000, and £190,000 was entered into additional paid-in capital.

3   The book value per share increased because the market price of the new equity was higher than the book value of the old equity.

Market Value and Book Value

The book value of ABB for year ending 31 December 2014 was $16,269 million. The company had bought back approximately $1,206 million worth of shares. The shares bought back are called *treasury stock* or *treasury shares*.

The book value per share was equal to:

$$\frac{\text{Total equity}}{\text{Shares outstanding}} = \frac{\$16,269 \text{ million}}{(2,314,743,264 - 55,843,639) \text{ million}} = \$7.20$$

Since ABB is a very large publicly owned company and listed in Zurich, Stockholm and New York, thousands of shares change hands every day throughout the world. In February 2015, the share price of ABB equity was $20.76 on the NYSE, 174.10 krona in Stockholm and 19.27 Swiss francs in Zurich. Using the dollar valuation, the market price ($20.76) was substantially higher than the book value ($7.20). However, market valuations are volatile and over the previous 52 weeks, ABB's share price fluctuated between $19.14 and $26.35.

Shareholders' Rights

The value of a share of equity in a corporation is directly related to the general rights of shareholders. In addition to the right to vote for directors, shareholders usually have the following rights:

1   The right to share proportionally in dividends paid.

2   The right to share proportionally in assets remaining after liabilities have been paid in a liquidation.

3   The right to vote on matters of great importance to shareholders, such as a merger, usually decided at the annual meeting or a special meeting.

4   The right to share proportionally in any new equity sold. This is called the *pre-emptive right* and will be discussed in detail in later chapters.

Dividends

A distinctive feature of corporations is that they issue shares of equity and are authorized by law to pay dividends to the holders of those shares. Dividends paid to shareholders represent a return on the capital directly or indirectly contributed to the corporation by the shareholders. The payment of dividends occurs at the discretion of the board of directors.

Here are some important characteristics of dividends:

1 Unless a dividend is declared by the board of directors of a corporation, it is not a liability of the corporation. A corporation cannot *default* on an undeclared dividend. As a consequence, corporations cannot become *bankrupt* because of non-payment of dividends. The amount of the dividend – and even whether or not it is paid – is a decision based on the business judgement of the board of directors.

2 The payment of dividends by the corporation is not a business expense. Dividends are not deductible for corporate tax purposes. In short, dividends are paid out of after-tax profits of the corporation.

3 Dividends received by individual shareholders are for the most part considered ordinary income by the tax authorities and are fully or partially taxable depending on the specific tax rules of the country in which the dividends are paid. Corporations that own shares in other corporations are normally permitted to exclude some component of the amounts they receive as dividends. In other words, they are taxed only on a certain percentage of the dividends.

Classes of Shares

Some firms issue more than one class of ordinary shares. The classes are usually created with unequal voting rights. All Chinese firms have two classes of equity, A and B class shares. The A class shares can only be owned by Chinese nationals whereas B class shares can be owned by anyone. The number of A class shares is almost always more than the number of B class shares, ensuring that Chinese firms are ultimately controlled by Chinese nationals. A good example of an individual firm with dual class shares is Google, the Web search company. Google has two classes of equity, A and B. Class A shares are held by the public, and each share has one vote. Class B shares are held by company insiders, and each class B share has 10 votes. As a result, Google's founders and management control the company.

Many companies issue dual classes of equity. The reason has to do with control of the firm. Management of a firm can raise equity capital by issuing non-voting shares while maintaining voting control. Harry and Linda DeAngelo (1985) found that managements' equity holdings are usually tilted toward the shares with the superior voting rights. Moreover, Luigi Zingales (1994) found the premium associated with superior voting rights in Italian companies to be around 60 per cent. Thus, vote ownership is an important element of corporate control structure.

14.2 Corporate Long-term Debt: The Basics

Chapter 5 Page 121
Chapter 20 Page 541

Securities issued by corporations may be classified roughly as *equity* securities and *debt* securities. The distinction between equity and debt is fundamental to much of the modern theory and practice of corporate finance (see **Chapter 20** for further discussion).

At its crudest level, debt represents something that must be repaid; it is the result of borrowing money (in **Chapter 5**, Sections 5.1–5.3 you are shown how to value bonds). When corporations borrow, they promise to make regularly scheduled interest payments and to repay the original amount borrowed (that is, the *principal*). The person or firm making the loan is called a *creditor* or *lender*.

Interest versus Dividends

The corporation borrowing the money is called a *debtor* or *borrower*. The amount owed to the creditor is a liability of the corporation; however, it is a liability of limited value. The corporation can legally default at any time on its liability. This can be a valuable option. The creditors benefit if the assets have a value greater than the value of the liability, but this would happen only if management were foolish. On the other hand, the corporation and the equity investors benefit if the value of the assets is less than the value of the liabilities because equity investors can walk away from the liabilities and default on their payment.

From a financial point of view, the main differences between debt and equity are the following:

1 Debt is not an ownership interest in the firm. Creditors do not usually have voting power. The device used by creditors to protect themselves is the loan contract (that is, the *indenture*).

2 The corporation's payment of interest on debt is considered a cost of doing business and is fully tax deductible. Thus interest expense is paid out to creditors before the corporate tax liability is computed. Dividends on ordinary and preference shares are paid to shareholders after the tax liability has been determined. Dividends are considered a return to shareholders on their contributed capital. Because interest expense can be used to reduce taxes, governments provide a direct tax subsidy on the use of debt when compared to equity. This point is discussed in detail in the next two chapters.

3 Unpaid debt is a liability of the firm. If it is not paid, the creditors can legally claim the assets of the firm. This action may result in *liquidation* and *bankruptcy*. Thus, one of the costs of issuing debt is the possibility of *financial failure*, which does not arise when equity is issued.

Is it Debt or Equity?

Sometimes it is not clear whether a particular security is debt or equity. For example, suppose a 50-year bond is issued with interest payable solely from corporate income if and only if earned, and repayment is subordinate to all other debts of the business. Corporations are very adept at creating hybrid or compound securities that look like equity but are called *debt*. Obviously the distinction between debt and equity is important for tax purposes. When corporations try to create a debt security that is really equity, they are trying to obtain the tax benefits of debt while eliminating its bankruptcy costs.

According to International Accounting Standard 32 (IAS 32), a debt instrument has a contractual obligation to deliver cash or another financial asset, whereas equity is a security that has a residual cash flow after all other liabilities have been paid. When accounting for hybrid or compound securities, the instrument should be disaggregated into its equity and debt components and recorded accordingly. So, for example, a debt instrument that can be converted into equity, would have its value arising from the debt and equity components valued and recorded separately in the company's accounts.

Basic Features of Long-term Debt

Long-term corporate debt usually is denominated in multiples of 100 (e.g. £100,000 or €1,000), called the *principal* or *face value*. Long-term debt is a promise by the borrowing firm to repay the principal amount by a certain date, called the *maturity date*. Debt price is often expressed as a percentage of the par or face value. For example, it might be said that Swedbank AB's debt is selling at 90, which means that a bond with a par value of SKr1,000 can be purchased for SKr900. In this case, the debt is selling at a discount because the market price is less than the par value. Debt can also sell at a premium with respect to par value. The borrower using long-term debt generally pays interest at a rate expressed as a fraction of par value. Thus, at SKr1,000 par value, Swedbank's 7 per cent debt means that SKr70 of interest is paid to holders of the debt, usually in semi-annual instalments (for example, SKr35 on 30 June and 31 December). These payments are referred to as 'coupons', and the 7 per cent is called the *coupon rate*.

Different Types of Debt

Typical debt securities are called *bills*, *notes*, *debentures* or *bonds*. A debenture is an unsecured corporate debt, whereas a bond is secured by a mortgage on the corporate property. However, in common parlance the word *bond* is used indiscriminately and often refers to both secured and unsecured debt. A note usually refers to an unsecured debt with a maturity shorter than that of a debenture, perhaps under 10 years. A bill usually refers to a short-term debt instrument with a maturity less than a year. In the UK, government bonds are known as *gilts*.

Debentures and bonds are long-term debt or non-current liabilities. *Long-term debt* is any obligation that is payable more than one year from the date it was originally issued. Sometimes long-term debt is called *funded debt*. Debt that is due in less than one year is unfunded and is accounted for as a current liability. Some debt is perpetual and has no specific maturity. This type of debt is referred to as a *consol*.

Repayment

Long-term debt is typically repaid in regular amounts over the life of the debt. The payment of long-term debt by instalments is called *amortization*. At the end of the amortization the entire indebtedness is said to be *extinguished*. Amortization is typically arranged by a *sinking fund*. Each year the corporation places money into a sinking fund, and the money is used to buy back the bonds.

Debt may be extinguished before maturity by a call. Historically, almost all publicly issued corporate long-term debt has been *callable*. These are debentures or bonds for which the firm has the right to pay a specific amount, the *call price*, to retire (extinguish) the debt before the stated maturity date. The call price is always higher than the par value of the debt. Debt that is callable at 105 is debt that the firm can buy back from the holder at a price of £105 or €1,050 per debenture or bond, regardless of what the market value of the debt might be. Call prices are always specified when the debt is originally issued. As discussed in an earlier chapter, 'make-whole' call provisions have become the norm.

Seniority

In general terms seniority indicates preference in position over other lenders. Some debt is subordinated. In the event of default, holders of subordinated debt must give preference to other specified creditors. Usually, this means that the subordinated lenders will be paid off only after the specified creditors have been compensated. However, debt cannot be subordinated to equity. This is discussed in more detail in Section 14.5.

Security

Security is a form of attachment to property; it provides that the property can be sold in the event of default to satisfy the debt for which security is given. A mortgage is used for security in tangible property; for example, debt can be secured by mortgages on plant and equipment. Holders of such debt have prior claim on the mortgaged assets in case of default. Debentures are not secured by a mortgage. Thus, if mortgaged property is sold in the event of default, debenture holders will obtain something only if the mortgage bondholders have been fully satisfied.

Indenture

The written agreement between the corporate debt issuer and the lender, setting forth maturity date, interest rate and all other terms, is called an *indenture*. We treat this in detail in later chapters. For now, we note that:

1 The indenture completely describes the nature of the indebtedness.

2 It lists all restrictions placed on the firm by the lenders. These restrictions are placed in *restrictive covenants*.

Some typical restrictive covenants are the following:

1 Restrictions on further indebtedness.

2 A maximum on the amount of dividends that can be paid.

3 A minimum level of working capital.

Real World Insight 14.1

Long-term Debt

The following table shows some of the many debt securities of Siemens AG at the end of 2014 (in millions), listed in order of priority (highest first). Libor, Euribor and US$ Libor are the rates that British, European and US banks lend to each other, respectively.

(interest/issued/maturity)	September 30, 2013 Carrying amount in millions of €[1]	September 30, 2014 Carrying amount in millions of €[1]
5.625%/2006/March 2016/US$ fixed-rate instruments	412	425
5.375%/2008/June 2014/EUR fixed-rate instruments[2]	1,031	–
5.625%/2008/June 2018/EUR fixed-rate instruments	1,844	1,839
5.125%/2009/February 2017/EUR fixed-rate instruments	2,136	2,122
US$ 3m LIBOR+1.4%/2012/February 2019/US$ floating-rate instruments	296	318

(interest/issued/maturity)	September 30, 2013 Carrying amount in millions of €[1]	September 30, 2014 Carrying amount in millions of €[1]
0.375%/2012/September 2014/EUR fixed-rate instruments[2]	400	–
1.5%/2012/March 2020/EUR fixed-rate instruments	994	995
2.75%/2012/September 2025/GBP fixed-rate instruments	416	448
3.75%/2012/September 2042/GBP fixed-rate instruments	760	819
1.75%/2013/March 2021/EUR fixed-rate instruments	1,242	1,276
2.875%/2013/March 2028/EUR fixed-rate instruments	995	996
1.5%/2013/March 2018/US$ fixed-rate instruments	368	396
3.5%/2013/March 2028/US$ fixed-rate instruments	72	77
2013/June 2020/US$ floating-rate instruments	295	317
2014/March 2019/US$ floating-rate instruments	–	238
2014/September 2021/US$ floating-rate instruments	–	317
Total Debt Issuance Program	11,262	10,582
5.75%/2006/October 2016/US$ fixed-rate instruments	1,389	1,457
6.125%/2006/August 2026/US$ fixed-rate instruments	1,759	1,843
Total US$ Bonds	3,147	3,301
5.25%/2006/September 2066/EUR fixed-rate instruments	976	959
6.125%/2006/September 2066/GBP fixed-rate instruments	986	1,025
Total Hybrid Capital Bond	1,962	1,984
1.05%/2012/August 2017/US$ fixed-rate instruments	1,068	1,158
1.65%/2012/August 2019/US$ fixed-rate instruments	1,052	1,140
Total Bond with Warrant Units	**2,120**	**2,298**
	18,491	**18,165**

1 Includes adjustments for fair value hedge accounting.
2 Redeemed at face value at maturity in fiscal 2014.

Siemens AG has different bonds that are denominated in several currencies (dollars, euros and sterling). As can be seen, there are different maturities and coupon rates (fixed and floating).

14.3   Preference Shares

Preference shares represent equity of a corporation, but they are different from ordinary shares because they are preferred in the payment of dividends and in the assets of the corporation in the event of bankruptcy. *Preference* means only that the holder of the preference share must receive a dividend (in the case of an ongoing firm) before holders of ordinary shares are entitled to anything. Preference shares are the most common form of compound security and can be viewed as equity or debt depending on the exact characteristics of the security.

In some companies, a subsidiary will issue preference shares to raise funds and lend these funds to the parent company in order to minimize tax payments for the firm as a whole. The loan will be tax-deductible from the perspective of the parent company. From the subsidiary's perspective, the dividend paid to the preference shareholders will be completely offset by the interest paid by the parent company. This type of complex transaction is more likely to occur when the parent and the subsidiary operate in different tax locales.

Stated Value

Preference shares have a stated liquidating value, usually £100 or €100 per share. The dividend preference is described in terms of pounds or euros per share. For example, '£5 preferred' translates into a dividend yield of 5 per cent of stated value.

Cumulative and Non-cumulative Dividends

A preference share dividend is not like interest on a bond. The board of directors may decide not to pay the dividends on preference shares, and their decision may not have anything to do with current net income of the corporation. Dividends payable on preference shares are either *cumulative* or *non-cumulative*. If preference share dividends are cumulative and are not paid in a particular year, they will be carried forward. Usually both the cumulated (past) preference share dividends plus the current preference share dividends must be paid before the ordinary shareholders can receive anything. Unpaid preference share dividends are *not* debts of the firm. Directors elected by the ordinary shareholders can defer preference share dividends indefinitely. However, if so,

1 Ordinary shareholders must forgo dividends.

2 Though holders of preference shares do not always have voting rights, they will typically be granted these rights if preference share dividends have not been paid for some time.

Because preference shareholders receive no interest on the cumulated dividends, some have argued that firms have an incentive to delay paying preferred dividends.

Are Preference Shares Really Debt?

A good case can be made that preference shares are really debt in disguise. Preference shareholders receive a stated dividend only, and if the corporation is liquidated, they get a stated value. In recent years, many new issues of preference shares have had obligatory sinking funds.

The yields on preference shares are typically very low. For example, BP plc has an 8 per cent preference share with a stated £0.08 dividend. This dividend is perpetual – that is, it will be paid each year by BP plc forever unless called. However, at a board meeting, holders of the 8 per cent preference shares have two votes for every five shares held, compared to one vote for every ordinary share held.

The IFRS, in the document IAS 32 *Financial Instruments – Presentation*, discuss in detail how preference shares should be regarded. The fundamental issue is whether the preference share has predominantly debt characteristics or equity characteristics. For example, the preference share would be viewed as debt if it contractually pays a fixed dividend and expires or is redeemed at a mandatory fixed future date. On the other hand, it will be regarded as equity if is not obligated to pay a dividend or has a maturity date. When the preference share has clear debt and equity components, IFRS recommends that the equity and debt components are valued and reported separately in the financial accounts.

Equity versus Debt

Feature	Equity	Debt
Income	Dividends	Interest
Tax status	Dividends are taxed as personal income. Dividends are not a business expense.	Interest is taxed as personal income. Interest is a business expense, and corporations can deduct interest when computing corporate tax liability.
Control	Ordinary shares usually have voting rights.	Control is exercised with loan agreement.
Default	Firms cannot be forced into bankruptcy for non-payment of dividends.	Unpaid debt is a liability of the firm. Non-payment results in bankruptcy.

Bottom line: Tax status favours debt, but default favours equity. Control features of debt and equity are different, but one is not better than the other.

14.4 Patterns of Financing

Chapter 15
Page 396

Firms receive funding from three main sources. First, they can reinvest their profits from existing operations. Second, they can borrow from the banking sector and third, they can issue securities (debt and equity) to the public. (In **Chapter 15**, we look in detail at the capital structure decision, which is the amount of debt that is used to finance a firm's operations.)

Table 14.1 summarizes the patterns of funding for a number of countries.

Table 14.1 Financing Patterns Around the World

Country	External Finance	Bank	Equity	Leasing	Supplier Credit	Development Bank	Informal
China	29.93	10.17	2.41	1.63	2.41	4.63	5.93
Croatia	41.31	19.79	3.02	0.31	8.19	6.23	2.47
Czech Republic	32.50	13.90	0.66	3.90	3.75	6.84	3.46
France	30.91	6.76	5.76	4.30	7.36	1.42	1.67
Germany	54.29	16.84	23.13	0.74	0.94	8.52	4.13
Italy	77.71	49.67	6.88	1.67	5.83	1.17	4.17
Pakistan	43.13	29.96	5.63	1.50	2.92	1.04	2.08
Poland	58.60	15.44	27.58	4.50	4.60	4.33	1.72
Singapore	45.17	28.06	7.67	1.16	6.14	0.58	0.00
Spain	39.78	23.00	0.67	8.04	4.22	2.62	1.22
Sweden	43.42	19.70	8.33	1.22	6.16	3.43	1.12
Turkey	43.98	20.41	9.68	4.85	1.42	6.21	1.17
United Kingdom	36.12	13.14	11.56	2.91	7.47	0.58	0.47
United States	47.12	21.47	3.24	6.09	6.62	6.76	2.94

Figures given are firm averages for each country, and they are the proportion of investment financed by each source. External finance is the sum of bank, equity, leasing, supplier credit, development bank and informal finance. Bank finance includes financing from domestic as well as foreign banks. Development bank includes funding from both development and public sector banks. Informal includes funding from money lenders and traditional or informal sources.

Source: Beck and Demirgüç-Kunt (2008).

Corporations mostly rely on internal financing for their investment expenditure. In all countries, apart from Italy, firms draw on internal cash flow more than external funding sources. However, looking at the overall picture, it can be seen that there is a financial gap between the level of funds available from ongoing operations and the total investment expenditure. One of the challenges of the financial manager is to finance the gap.

Internal financing comes from internally generated cash flow and is defined as net income plus depreciation minus dividends. External financing is net new debt and new shares of equity net of buybacks.

Several features of long-term financing seem clear from Table 14.1:

1 Internally generated cash flow has dominated as a source of financing. Typically, over 50 per cent of long-term financing comes from cash flows that corporations generate internally.

2 Typically, total firm spending is greater than internally generated cash flow. A financial deficit is created by the difference between total firm spending and internally generated cash flow. For example, in Germany, 45.71 (= 100 − 54.29) per cent of financing came from internal cash flow, implying a financial deficit over the period of 54.29 per cent.

3 In most countries, bank loans constitute the largest source of external financing. However, there are notable exceptions. In Germany and Poland, the equity markets have been very popular routes to raise cash. Leasing (**Chapter 21**) is normally regarded as short-term financing but in Spain and the US, it is a common method of financing long-term projects. Companies in the UK, France and Croatia use trade finance and supplier credit (**Chapter 28**) to raise new capital. Finally, informal financing is the second largest source of external capital in China. Informal financing comes from non-contractual sources such as families, individuals and money lenders.

Chapter 21 Page 565
Chapter 28 Page 755

International Patterns in Capital Structure

Chapter 2
Page 25

Chapter 2 of this book established that there are many different corporate and ownership structures around the world. Firms that operate in China can look very different from similar firms doing business in the United Kingdom. State ownership is prevalent in many countries. There are even very large differences in the ownership levels and board structures of firms that are incorporated in Europe. These differences suggest the question: are there differences in the capital structure of firms in different parts of the world?

Figure 14.1 presents the average leverage ratios (debt to market value of the firm) for many countries between 1991 and 2006. While countries like Pakistan and Thailand have very high debt levels, most other countries use very little debt. The Pakistani example is surprising given that it is largely a Muslim country and Islamic financing forbids the use of debt. The figures are also in market value terms and not book value terms. Given that the value of debt does not change very much, countries with vibrant and strongly performing equity markets would tend to have lower leverage ratios. Likewise, in markets that are bearish and not performing well, leverage ratios will be higher.

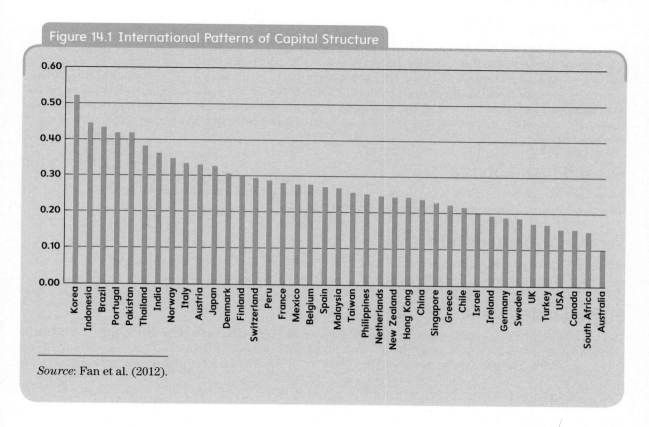

Figure 14.1 International Patterns of Capital Structure

Source: Fan et al. (2012).

Which Are Best: Book or Market Values?

In general, financial economists prefer the use of market values when measuring debt ratios. This is true because market values reflect current rather than historical values. Most financial economists believe that current market values better reflect true intrinsic values than do historically based values. However, the use of market values contrasts with the perspective of many corporate practitioners.

Our conversations with corporate treasurers suggest to us that the use of book values is popular because of the volatility of the stock market, which has been a significant problem in recent times. It is frequently claimed that the inherent volatility of the stock market makes market-based debt ratios move around too much. It is also true that restrictions of debt in bond covenants are usually expressed in book values rather than market values. Moreover, firms such as Standard & Poor's and Moody's use debt ratios expressed in book values to measure creditworthiness.

A key fact is that whether we use book or market values, debt ratios for most non-financial firms generally have been well below 100 per cent of total equity in recent years; that is, firms generally use less debt than equity.

14.5 Hierarchies in Long-term Financing

In Real World Insight 14.1, it was shown that Siemens AG had many different types of debt. These were identified as senior and junior unsecured debt. If Siemens were to go bankrupt, the security holders would want as much of their initial investment back as possible. The hierarchy or priority of a company's securities determines who gets a claim on the assets of a bankrupt company first. In this section, we will review in more detail the different types of long-term financing and their priority in the list of corporate claims.

Senior Secured Debt

Senior secured debt is a debt instrument that is backed by a claim on the assets of the issuing company. This claim is known as collateral and may comprise buildings, manufacturing facilities, airplanes, or any other fixed asset. Mortgaged debt is debt secured by property and buildings and non-recourse debt is debt that is only partially secured by some assets in the company. Typically, the value of the collateral in non-recourse debt will be around 80 to 90 per cent of the total value of the debt. If the borrower defaults on the debt, the lender can only claim against the value of the collateral and no more. Senior secured debt has the first and highest claim on the assets of a defaulting company.

Second Lien Loans

Second lien loans are debt instruments that are normally secured to some form of collateral but are second in line for a claim of a company's assets behind senior secured debt.

Senior Unsecured Debt

The next financial security in the hierarchy is senior unsecured debt. Senior debt has a claim above other forms of debt but in contrast to secured debt, the issue is not supported by any collateral.

Subordinated or Junior Debt

The ranking of debt below senior debt is commonly known as either subordinated or junior debt. Subordinated debt has a claim below all other senior debt instruments. Subordinated debt is fairly risky because in the event of a corporate default, it is unlikely that the subordinated bondholders will receive any of their money back.

Shareholder Loans

Shareholder loans are very long-term low-interest loans given to a company by dominant shareholders. Because the loans are owned by the shareholders, they are commonly regarded as equity. For example, it would not make sense for the shareholder who gave a loan to make their firm bankrupt because this would directly hurt their shareholdings in the company. Given their unique nature, shareholder loans are the lowest ranking of all debt instruments.

Preference Shares

Preference shares have been discussed in Section 14.3. They fall below debt in the seniority of financial claims but sit above ordinary equity.

Ordinary Equity

Equity holders are at the very bottom of the financing hierarchy and are also known as residual claimants. This is because, in the event of a corporate bankruptcy, shareholders are the very last of all financial claimants to receive their money back. Normally, they would receive nothing at all.

14.6   Long-term Islamic Financing

In recent years, many countries have developed financial instruments and business practices reflecting the religious values of Islam. This is known as Islamic financing, with the main characteristic being that interest of any kind is not allowed to be charged on financial securities. The United Kingdom is at the forefront of Islamic financing in Western Europe followed by Switzerland, France and Luxembourg. In the Middle East, Bahrain is the Islamic financing centre and Malaysia is the main country in South East Asia. Islamic financing need not be confined only to Muslims and in Malaysia, for example, nearly a quarter of all users of Islamic products are non-Muslims.

Not having interest-bearing securities presents a number of challenges to firms wishing to raise financing for investment projects. In response, banks have created a number of innovative instruments and financing methods that are consistent with Islamic or Shariah principles and have debt-like characteristics. The most common of these involve elements of profit-sharing, known as *mudharabah*, joint ventures (*musharakah*), leasing (*ijarah*), and compensation for facilitating the financing activity (*murabahah*). Islamic securities that can be traded on exchanges are known as *sukuk*.

Types of Islamic Financing Methods

An Advanced Payment Sale

A *bai salam* is a contract where two parties trade today in return for a good to be delivered at some specified date in the future. The transfer of cash must be made today and the quality and quantity of the good must be specified at the time of the trade. One of the requirements of *bai salam* is that there can be no uncertainty in the quality or quantity of a good or commodity. Therefore, raw agricultural produce is not allowed to be traded in this way because flooding or an earthquake may result in loss of quality or quantity.

Example 14.3

Bai Salam

Shukran plc is undertaking a new warehouse expansion and has commissioned a company, Temsaah Ltd, to build it on the site of an existing warehouse. The warehouse with full facilities will take one year to build and the price of the new warehouse will be £3,000,000 in one year. In a *bai salam* sale, Shukran may pay £2.7 million today for the warehouse (fully specified at the time of the contract) to be ready for use exactly one year from the date of the trade.

Stated Cost plus Profit

Murabahah is one of the most common forms of Islamic financing contracts. In this transaction, the seller of a commodity expressly states the cost that has been incurred in producing, manufacturing or buying a commodity or asset. A pre-agreed mark-up or profit margin is then applied to the cost in order to find the price of the trade. Clearly, a *murabahah* contract requires the seller to be honest about the base cost of the commodity. *Murabahah* is used for the financing of asset purchases and property investments. So that there is no doubt that it was the underlying asset that has been traded (to avoid accusations of interest payments in another form), the seller of the commodity or asset must be the owner before selling it. As in other Islamic financing contracts, a seller may consult the debt markets to ascertain competitive mark-up rates.

In a *murabahah* sale, the purchaser may pay the stated amount in fixed instalments. When only one payment in the future is made, this is known as a *bai' bithaman ajil* contract.

Example 14.4

Murabahah

Shukran plc is undertaking a new warehouse expansion and has commissioned a company, Temsaah Ltd, to build it on the site of an existing warehouse. Temsaah need cash equalling the construction costs of

£2.7 million today to finance the building of the warehouse. Unfortunately, Shukran does not have the funds in place. The CEO of Shukran goes to Bahrain Bank and enters into a *murabahah* transaction.

Bahrain Bank agrees to pay £2.7 million today to Temsaah and notifies Shukran's CEO of the cost. Given market conditions, with comparable loans currently at 10 per cent, the manager of Bahrain Bank enters into an agreement with the CEO of Shukran to charge a mark-up of £270,000 on the building to be paid in one year. This markup of 10 per cent makes the *murabahah* contract competitive with Western financing deals.

In this transaction, Bahrain Bank owns the warehouse until the date of the trade. In one year, Bahrain Bank sells the warehouse for £2,970,000 (£2,700,000 cost plus £270,000 mark-up) and the transfer of title deeds to Shukran takes place at that date. As you will have noticed, this transaction is actually a *bai' bithaman ajil* contract, which is a subtype of *murabahah* financing.

Goodwill Loan

Perhaps unique to the global financial markets, a *qard hassan* is a loan without any interest. The lender will provide the borrower with funds and, at some point in the future, these will be paid back to the bank. The borrower may, at his own discretion, repay an extra amount to compensate the lender for supplying the funds. A *qard hassan* is normally very small, say £2,000, and is given to pay for school education, medical fees or some other social improving purpose.

Hire Purchase

Hire purchase agreements originally came from the United Kingdom and are most commonly used in the automobile industry. In a Western hire purchase agreement, the buyer of an asset puts down an initial deposit on the price of an asset and agrees to hire or rent it for a set period. When the sum of the rental payments reaches a certain amount, the buyer may purchase the asset outright for a pre-agreed price and take ownership.

With a little modification, hire purchase agreements are ideal instruments for Islamic financing. In an *ijarah thumma al bai'* contract, the buyer agrees to first lease or rent the asset for a certain period. When this period has expired, the buyer may purchase the asset for a specific price that is agreed at the very beginning of the contract.

Example 14.5

Using Western Loans to Determine Payments in an *Ijarah Thumma Al Bai'*

Shufaa Al Beity wishes to purchase a car whose sale price is €25,000. Unfortunately, she is a student and cannot afford to part with that amount of money today. She decides to enter into an *ijarah thumma al bai'* contract to buy the car over 5 years in monthly instalments. How much would she pay?

To determine a set of monthly payments that is competitive with other Western lenders, an Islamic bank would study the range of Western loans that are on offer today. Assume that most banks are giving personal loans with an APR of 10 per cent. This is the effective interest rate on car loans for €25,000 over 5 years and equates to a rate of 0.7974 per cent per month (work it out yourself!). Using the standard annuity formula, the monthly payment on a loan of €25,000 paid over 60 monthly instalments at a rate of 0.7974 per cent per month is:

$$C = \frac{€25,000}{A^{60}_{0.007974}} = \frac{€25,000}{47.5385} = €525.89$$

The total payments that Shufaa will need to make if she takes out a Western loan is 60 × €525.89 = €31,553.37. For an Islamic bank to be competitive with its Western counterpart, the total amount paid in an *ijarah thumma al bai'* must be equal to or less than €31,553.37.

Shufaa can only afford a monthly payment of €500, so she enters into an *ijarah thumma al bai'* contract where the Islamic bank buys the car from the car dealer for €25,000. It then leases the car to Shufaa for a monthly payment of €500 a month for 60 months. At the end of the term of the *ijarah thumma al bai'*, she will have paid a total of €30,000. To be competitive with Western loans, the final payment must be less than or equal to €31,553.37 − €30,000 = €1,553.37.

Joint Venture

A *musharakah* is a contract between two parties to invest in a joint venture and share in any profit or losses that may arise from the investment. Companies that require partial funding for an investment can go to an Islamic bank and enter into a *musharakah* agreement and raise the required funds.

This type of financing alternative is an important alternative to standard bank loans and illustrates the cooperative nature of the Islamic approach to doing business. In each transaction, the supplier and demander of funds directly bears the cash flow risk of the underlying investment.

Leasing

Leasing or *ijarah* is a form of financing that is available to companies. With a lease, the lessee pays rent for an asset for a period of time from the lessor. In this type of contract, the payments are for the use of the asset. Lease financing is covered in more detail later in the text.

Profit Sharing

In a *mudharabah* contract, a businessman uses the funds of a bank or lender to invest in a project. The two parties share the profits of the business according to predetermined ratios. In this transaction, the lender bears the financial risk of the investment but gains from the specialized skills of the entrepreneur. Both parties benefit financially from the joint investment through the contribution of different skills or assets.

Safekeeping

Like Western banks, Islamic banks require deposits to fund their activities. A company or individual may lodge funds at an Islamic bank and is able to draw those funds at any time from the bank. In some situations, the bank may give the depositor a *hibah*, which is a small sum of money to compensate the depositor for leaving the funds with the Islamic bank. This is known as *wadiah*. Although this could be seen as an interest payment in any other name, because the *hibah* payment is not contractual, it is not viewed as such under Shariah law.

Sale and Buyback

With a *bai' al-inah* agreement, a company buys an asset from a seller and agrees to pay for it at some point in the future. The seller immediately buys the asset back at a discount.

Example 14.6

Bai' Al-inah

Shukran plc needs £2,700,000 to undertake a new warehouse expansion. They approach an Islamic bank, which agrees to participate in a *bai' al-inah* agreement. In this transaction, the bank sells a building today to Shukran for £3,000,000 to be paid in one year. Immediately, the bank buys the building back for £2,700,000 today. In this transaction, Shukran now has £2,700,000 but must pay £3,000,000 to the bank in one year. This is very similar to a one-year loan but the crucial thing is that a real asset and not money is driving the payments. This is acceptable under Islamic law.

Real World Insight 14.2

Petronas Islamic Bond Issue

In April 2015, the Malaysian energy firm, Petronas, issued $5 billion of bonds to enthusiastic investors. The bond issue contained four tranches: a $1.25 billion sukuk, and three fixed coupon bonds. The sukuk was priced at 1.1 per cent higher than the US five-year government bond yield, to give an overall yield of 2.7 per cent. The pricing of the bond shows that although there is no interest paid on the bond, its price is linked to an underlying interest rate. The bond issue was in response to the collapse in oil prices which saw Petronas cutting back on strategic investments and existing projects. By taking advantage of low interest rates, the company was able to restructure its debt to lower its overall interest payments.

Summary and Conclusions

The basic sources of long-term financing are long-term debt, preference shares and ordinary shares. This chapter described the essential features of each.

1 We emphasized that ordinary shareholders have:
   (a) residual risk and return in a corporation
   (b) voting rights
   (c) limited liability if the corporation elects to default on its debt and must transfer some or all of its assets to the creditors.

2 Long-term debt involves contractual obligations set out in indentures. There are many kinds of debt, but the essential feature is that debt involves a stated amount that must be repaid. Interest payments on debt are considered a business expense and are tax deductible.

3 Preference shares have some of the features of debt and some of the features of ordinary equity. Holders of preference shares have preference in liquidation and in dividend payments compared to holders of ordinary equity.

4 Firms need financing for capital expenditures, working capital and other long-term uses. Most of the financing is provided from internally generated cash flow.

5 In many parts of the world where the Muslim faith is common, standard investment instruments that involve interest payments are not acceptable. In response, Islamic financing has developed to counter the problems associated with raising capital for firms wishing to adhere to Islamic principles.

Questions and Problems

CONCEPT

1 **Ordinary Shares**   What is a proxy? What is the difference between voting rights and cash flow rights? Do you think this will have an impact on share values?

2 **Corporate Long-term Debt**   Why do you think companies have issued bonds in different currencies, maturities and coupon rates? Shouldn't the coupon be the same on every bond? Explain.

3 **Preference Shares**   Preference shares do not offer a corporate tax shield on the dividends paid. Why do we still observe some firms issuing preference shares?

4 **Patterns of Financing**   Why do you think companies in certain countries prefer different forms of financing? Carry out your own research and comment on capital structure choice among firms in the G7 countries.

5 **Hierarchies**   What is meant by hierarchies in long-term financing and why are bonds higher in priority than shares?

6 **Islamic Financing**   Explain what is meant by Islamic financing. What are the different types of securities that are used in this sector? In this context, explain what is meant by a 'sukuk'. Construct a practical example of a sukuk and explain the issues that arise in its use. [Challenge: discuss some of the specific transactions, rather than simply the type of transactions, that are commonly used in Islamic banking.]

REGULAR

7 **Preference Shares and Bond Yields**   The yields on non-convertible preference shares are lower than the yields on corporate bonds. Why is there a difference? Which investors are the primary holders of preference shares? Why?

8 **Corporate Financing**   What are the main differences between corporate debt and equity? Why do some firms try to issue equity in the guise of debt? How would you categorize preference shares?

9 **Par Values** International Energy plc was formed in 1912 with 100,000 shares of equity with a £1 par value. Today, the company's share price is £9 and retained earnings are £213,000. International Energy has just decided that it wishes to issue 25,000 new shares. What will be the total par value, additional paid-in capital and book value per share after the issue?

10 **Corporate Financing** The Cable Company has £1 million of positive NPV projects it would like to accept. If Cable's managers follow the historical pattern of long-term financing for UK industrial firms, what will their financing strategy be?

11 **Preference Shares** Do you think preference shares are more like debt or equity? Why?

12 **Islamic Financing** Explain why leasing is consistent with Islamic financing principles. [Challenge: Explain what is meant by a 'musharaka' transaction in Islamic finance. Give an example to illustrate your answer.]

13 **Long-term Financing** New equity issues are generally only a small portion of all new issues. At the same time, companies continue to issue new debt. Why do companies tend to issue little new equity but continue to issue new debt?

14 **Internal versus External Financing** What is the difference between internal financing and external financing? What factors influence a firm's choices of external versus internal equity financing?

15 **Security Priority** A company has €25 million in equity, €18 million in preference shares, €15 million in secured bonds, and €34 million in unsecured bonds. Assume, because of financial distress, that the managers have decided to liquidate the firm's assets and pay off the funders. The asset sale (after legal expenses) resulted in €50 million being raised. Explain how much each funder gets from the asset sale.

16 **Islamic Financing** You plan to raise funds through following Islamic principles. You require funding today of 3 billion Bahrain dinars and would like to pay it back in equal amounts over 10 years in monthly instalments. How would you do this?

CHALLENGE

17 **Equity Accounts** Following are the equity accounts for Dawn Technologies:

Ordinary shares, £0.12 par value	120,000
Additional paid-in capital	4,526,123
Retained earnings	?
Total	6,421,830

(a) What are the retained earnings of Dawn Technologies?
(b) How many shares are outstanding?
(c) At what average price were the shares sold?
(d) What is the book value per share?

18 **Equity Accounts** The equity accounts for ABC plc are as follows:

Ordinary shares, £2 par value 500 shares outstanding	?
Capital surplus	250,000
Retained earnings	750,000
Total	?

(a) What are the ordinary share and total equity values for the equity account?
(b) The company has decided to issue 5,000 shares of equity at a price of £30 per share. Show the effects of the new issue on the equity accounts.

19 **Equity Accounts** Ulrich plc's articles of incorporation authorize the firm to issue 500,000 shares of £5 par value ordinary equity, of which 410,000 shares have been issued. Those shares were sold at an average of 30 per cent over par. In the quarter that ended last week, net income was £650,000; 30 per cent of that income was paid as a dividend. The previous balance sheet showed a retained earnings balance of £3,545,000.

(a) Create the equity statement for the company.
(b) Suppose the company sells 25,000 of the authorized but unissued shares at the price of £4 per share. What will the new equity statement look like?

20 **Corporate Voting** The shareholders of Unicorn plc need to elect seven new directors. There are 500,000 shares outstanding currently trading at £34 per share. You would like to serve on the board of directors;

unfortunately no one else will be voting for you. How much will it cost you to be certain that you can be elected if the company uses straight voting? How much will it cost you if the company uses cumulative voting?

21 **Murabahah**   You manage an Islamic financing division and have been approached by a company for funding of 6 billion Bahrain dinars. The company wish to pay the funding back in equal instalments over 10 years through Islamic principles. Western banks quote comparable interest paying loans of 8 per cent. Construct a *murabahah* contract that makes you competitive with your Western counterparts.

22 **Ijarah Thumma Al Bai'**   You run an Islamic financing division and have been approached by a customer for a 40,000 Bahrain dinar *ijarah thumma al bai'* financing deal. The customer wishes to pay a maximum of 1,000 Bahrain dinars per month over 5 years. Comparable loans in Western banks are quoted at 12 per cent interest. Construct a financing deal for your customer.

23 **Bai' Al-Inah**   You run an Islamic financing bank and have been approached by a company to construct a sale and buyback financing deal. The firm requires financing of £8 billion and wishes to pay back the financing over 7 years. Comparable Western loans quote 7 per cent interest for financing of this type. Construct a *bai' al-inah* contract for your customer.

24 **Share Capital**   The Akva Group ASA equity accounts for 2008–2010 are given below. Explain what each item is and how it changed over time.

	Note	2010	2009	2008
EQUITY				
Paid-in capital				
Share capital	15	17,223	17,223	17,223
Share premium reserve		256,178	256,178	256,178
Other paid-in capital		2,337	2,175	1,951
Total paid-in capital		275,738	275,576	275,352

25 **Shareholdings**   In 2012, Rangers Football Club had a majority shareholder, Craig Whyte, who owned 83.5 per cent of the firm. The same individual also owned secured debt worth £18 million and was Rangers' largest secured creditor. Why would an individual choose to be a major lender at the same time as the main shareholder? Does this make sense? Explain.

26 **Cumulative Voting**   An election is being held to fill three seats on the Board of Directors of a firm in which you are a shareholder. The company has 2,500 shares outstanding. If the election is conducted under cumulative voting and you own 300 shares, how many more shares must you buy to be assured of earning a seat on the Board?

27 **Family Firms and Long-term Financing**   Assume that you are the manager of a family firm and the company wishes to expand its operations into a new unrelated business sector. The expansion requires funding. What type of financing (debt or equity) would you choose and why?

28 **Financial Flexibility**   Your company plans to expand into a new business sector that requires higher levels of capital investment and fixed costs. Holding all else equal, what type of financing (debt or equity) would you choose to fund the expansion and why?

29 **R&D Intensive Firms**   If you are the manager of a young research-intensive firm, which type of financing would you prefer and why? Carry out research on research-intensive firms in your country. What is the preferred financing choice of firms in practice?

Exam Question (45 minutes)

1 Your company, Living Planet plc, was formed in 1985 to develop technologies that combat climate change. You started the firm with £80,000 financing which consisted of 3,000 shares of equity amounting to £60,000 and a £20,000 bank loan. The company is listed on the small companies exchange and has accumulated earnings of £120,000. The share price is £7.50. You plan to expand the firm into solar technologies and have agreed to issue 1,000 new shares to a local investor. Construct the equity statement for your company before and after the share issue. The statement must include the total par value, additional paid-in capital, and book value per share. (40 marks)

2 You are concerned that possibly other forms of financing may be more appropriate and in particular you have heard about hybrid securities. Explain what these are and why companies use them. (30 marks)

3 If a company was to go into liquidation, which claims would have higher priority: bonds or equity? Why? How would you deal with hybrid securities in liquidation? (30 marks)

Mini Case

The Islamic Bank of Britain (IBB) released a new product in 2012 called a Home Purchase Plan (HPP). This product allows individuals to invest over the long term in a mortgage-equivalent financing deal. According to their publicity materials the Home Purchase Plan consists of two components:

1 **Co-ownership agreement.** IBB will agree to sell its share of the property to you at an agreed monthly amount over a fixed period (known as the term). Your share in the property increases with every monthly payment made towards acquiring IBB's share in the property.

2 **Lease agreement.** IBB will then agree to lease its share in the property to you for which you will pay a monthly rent.

Your monthly HPP payment is therefore made up of two elements: an acquisition payment and a rental payment. As you make your monthly payments, your share in the property increases as IBB's share gets smaller, and although your monthly payments remain constant (subject to quarterly reviews) the rental payment element will decrease while your acquisition payment element increases. Rent is reviewed every three months in March, June, September and December. The rent rate may increase, decrease or stay the same at each rent review.

Explain this product in terms of a normal mortgage. Assume the interest rate for similar risk mortgages is 4.19 per cent. Construct a home purchase plan so that it has the exact same cash flows as a normal mortgage. Is this possible? Explain.

Practical Case Study

Choose a company from your country. Download its financial accounts and find out how its long-term funding is structured. Does it have more debt than equity? Are there any securities that have debt and equity characteristics? Try and ascertain the funding hierarchy for the company.

Relevant Accounting Standard

As with all the chapters dealing with financial instruments, the main accounting standard is IAS 39 *Financial Instruments: Recognition and Measurement*. IAS 39 provides definitions for different types of financial securities and how these should be treated in the financial accounts. This can sometimes be problematic because many securities have equity and bond-like features. Visit the IASPlus website (www.iasplus.com) for more information.

References

Beck, T. and A. Demirgüç-Kunt (2008) 'Access to Finance', *The World Bank Economic Review*, Vol. 22, No. 3, 383–396.

DeAngelo, H. and L. DeAngelo (1985) 'Managerial Ownership of Voting Rights: A Study of Public Corporations with Dual Classes of Common Stock', *Journal of Financial Economics*, Vol. 14, No. 1, 33–69.

Fan, J.P.H., S. Titman and G. Twite (2012) 'An International Comparison of Capital Structure and Debt Maturity Choices', *Journal of Financial and Quantitative Analysis*, Vol. 47, No. 1, 23.

Zingales, L. (1994) 'The Value of a Voting Right: A Study of the Milan Stock Exchange Experience', *The Journal of Finance*, Vol. 7, No. 1, 125–148.

Additional Reading

The literature in this section investigates the factors that determine long-term financing decisions. References 5, 6 and 7 are particularly relevant given their international focus. Dittmann and Ulbricht (2008) consider equity restructuring and should also be read for Chapter 19.

1   Brophy, D., P. Ouimet and C. Sialm (2009) 'Hedge Funds as Investors of Last Resort?', *Review of Financial Studies*, Vol. 22, No. 2, 541–574. **US**.

2   Chang, X., S. Dasgupta and G. Hilary (2006) 'Analyst Coverage and Financing Decisions', *The Journal of Finance*, Vol. 61, No. 6, 3009–3048. **US**.

3   Dittmann, I. and N. Ulbricht (2008) 'Timing and Wealth Effects of German Dual Class Stock Unifications', *European Financial Management*, Vol. 14, No. 1, 163–196. **Germany**.

4   Dittmar, A.K. and R.F. Dittmar (2008) 'The Timing of Financing Decisions: An Examination of the Correlation in Financing Waves', *Journal of Financial Economics*, Vol. 90, No. 1, 59–83. **US**.

5   Iannotta, G. and M. Navone (2008) 'Which Factors Affect Bond Underwriting Fees? The Role of Banking Relationships', *European Financial Management*, Vol. 14, No. 5, 944–961. **International**.

6   Martinsson, G. (2010) 'Equity Financing and Innovation: Is Europe Different from the United States?' *Journal of Banking and Finance*, Vol. 34, No. 6, 1215–1224. **International**.

7   Megginson, W.L., R.C. Nash, J.M. Netter and A.B. Poulsen (2004) 'The Choice of Private versus Public Capital Markets: Evidence from Privatizations', *The Journal of Finance*, Vol. 59, No. 6, 2835–2870. **International**.

8   Mitton, T. (2008) 'Why Have Debt Ratios Increased For Firms in Emerging Markets?', *European Financial Management*, Vol. 14, No. 1, 127–151. **International**.

Endnote

1   In the UK, regulation (Companies Act 2006) abolished the term 'authorised share capital' and now all British firms can issue capital without limit and when required.

PART 4

Capital Structure and Dividend Policy

The second pillar of corporate finance is capital structure. Capital structure refers to the proportion of debt and equity used to finance a company's operations. Part 2 of the text showed you how to increase the value of your firm through making investment decisions. In Part 4, you investigate ways to increase corporate value through capital structure decisions and a firm's dividend policy.

We begin our discussion of capital structure with the theoretical basics and fundamental concepts underlying the topic. Chapter 15 introduces the Modigliani–Miller propositions for capital structure and asks if firm value and equity risk are affected by capital structure. Tax is introduced into the discussion and its transformational effect on business decisions is shown. Chapter 15 is necessarily theoretical and so Chapter 16 presents limitations to the theory and explores more practical issues related to capital structure.

In Chapter 17, we return once again to capital budgeting and look at three new investment appraisal methods that incorporate the capital structure decision into the valuation analysis. Part 4 ends with an in-depth discussion of dividend policy, the reasons underlying different dividend decisions, and whether dividends can increase firm value.

CHAPTER 15

Capital Structure: Basic Concepts

In recent years, analysts of European soccer clubs have become seriously concerned about the level of indebtedness in their largest football institutions. In some countries, such as England, Germany and Spain, football has seen unparalleled injections of cash from global television deals. This additional spending power has inflated transfer fees, which in turn has required more funding. Several clubs, including Valencia, Arsenal and Manchester United, have incredible levels of debt, which will expire at some point in the future. Several questions arise: Is the level of debt in European football too high? Will we see a fallout in the football sector in the same way as the banking sector experienced in 2007? How should a company choose a capital structure for itself and what are the important factors driving this? We will explore this and other issues in the following chapters.

KEY NOTATIONS

V	Market value of firm
E	Market value of equity
D	Market value of bonds
ROA	Return on assets
ROE	Return on equity
EBI	Earnings before interest
EPS	Earnings per share
R_E	Return on equity; cost of equity capital
R_D	Return on debt; cost of debt capital
R_{WACC}	Weighted average cost of capital
MM	Modigliani Miller Proposition I or II
t_C	Corporate tax rate
NPV	Net present value
EBIT	Earnings before interest and taxes
V_U	Value of an unlevered firm
R_A	Cost of capital to an all-equity firm
V_L	Value of a levered firm
t_E	Personal tax rate on dividends
t_D	Personal tax rate on debt interest income

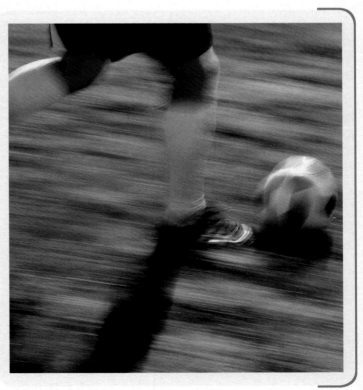

15.1 The Capital Structure Question and the Pie Theory

How should a firm choose its debt–equity ratio? We call our approach to the capital structure question the pie model. If you are wondering why we chose this name, just take a look at Figure 15.1. The pie in question is the sum of the financial claims of the firm, debt and equity in this case. We *define* the value of the firm to be this sum. Hence the value of the firm, V, is:

$$V = D + E \qquad (15.1)$$

where D is the market value of the debt and E is the market value of the equity. Figure 15.1 presents two possible ways of slicing this pie between equity and debt: 40 per cent–60 per cent and 60 per cent–40 per cent. If the goal of the management of the firm is to make the firm as valuable as possible, then the firm should pick the debt–equity ratio that makes the pie – the total value – as big as possible.

Figure 15.1 Two Pie Models of Capital Structure

This discussion begs two important questions:

1 Why should the shareholders in the firm care about maximizing the value of the entire firm? After all, the value of the firm is, by definition, the sum of both the debt and the equity. Instead, why should the shareholders not prefer the strategy that maximizes their interests only?

2 What ratio of debt to equity maximizes the shareholders' interests?

Let us examine each of the two questions in turn.

Real World Insight 15.1

Intercontinental Hotels Group Plc

How much is too much leverage? Intercontinental Hotels Group plc (IHG) is a global hotel firm that owns nearly 5,000 hotels in over 100 countries. Its brand names include Intercontinental Hotels, Crowne Plaza and Holiday Inn. IHG has reported increasing revenues and operating income every year since 2010 and the company's share price has more than doubled during this time.

A look at the capital structure of IHG can provide insights into how this growth has been funded. Total debt grew from $2.5 billion to $3.5 billion between 2010 and 2015, while the market value of its equity grew from around $3 billion to $6.5 billion. This gave a 2015 debt-equity ratio of 0.54, which means that only about one third of IHG's assets were funded by debt.

15.2 Maximizing Firm Value versus Maximizing Shareholder Interests

The following example illustrates that the capital structure that maximizes the value of the firm is the one that financial managers should choose for the shareholders.

Example 15.1

Debt and Firm Value

Suppose the market value of J.J. Sprint plc is £1,000. The company currently has no debt, and each of J.J. Sprint's 100 shares sells for £10. A company such as J.J. Sprint with no debt is called an *unlevered* company. Further suppose that J.J. Sprint plans to borrow £500 and pay the £500 proceeds to shareholders as an extra cash dividend of £5 per share. After the issuance of debt, the firm becomes *levered*. The investments of the firm will not change as a result of this transaction. What will the value of the firm be after the proposed restructuring?

Management recognizes that, by definition, only one of three outcomes can occur from restructuring. Firm value after restructuring can be (1) greater than the original firm value of £1,000, (2) equal to £1,000, or (3) less than £1,000. After consulting with investment bankers, management believes that restructuring will not change firm value more than £250 in either direction. Thus it views firm values of £1,250, £1,000 and £750 as the relevant range. The original capital structure and these three possibilities under the new capital structure are presented next:

| | No Debt (Original Capital Structure) (£) | Value of Debt Plus Equity after Payment of Dividend (Three Possibilities) | | |
		I (£)	II (£)	III (£)
Debt	0	500	500	500
Equity	1,000	750	500	250
Firm value	1,000	1,250	1,000	750

Note that the value of equity is below £1,000 under any of the three possibilities. This can be explained in one of two ways. First, the table shows the value of the equity *after* the extra cash dividend is paid. Because cash is paid out, a dividend represents a partial liquidation of the firm. Consequently there is less value in the firm for the equityholders after the dividend payment. Second, in the event of a future liquidation, shareholders will be paid only after bondholders have been paid in full. Thus the debt is an encumbrance of the firm, reducing the value of the equity.

Of course management recognizes that there are infinite possible outcomes. These three are to be viewed as *representative* outcomes only. We can now determine the pay-off to shareholders under the three possibilities:

| | Pay-off to Shareholders after Restructuring | | |
	I (£)	II (£)	III (£)
Capital gains	−250	−500	−750
Dividends	500	500	500
Net gain or loss to shareholders	250	0	−250

No one can be sure ahead of time which of the three outcomes will occur. However, imagine that managers believe that outcome I is most likely. They should definitely restructure the firm because the shareholders would gain £250. That is, although the price of the shares declines by £250 to £750, they receive £500 in dividends. Their net gain is £250 = −£250 + £500. Also, notice that the value of the firm would rise by £250 = £1,250 − £1,000.

Alternatively, imagine that managers believe that outcome III is most likely. In this case they should not restructure the firm because the shareholders would expect a £250 loss. That is, the equity falls by £750 to £250 and they receive £500 in dividends. Their net loss is −£250 = −£750 + £500. Also, notice that the value of the firm would change by −£250 = £750 − £1,000.

Finally, imagine that the managers believe that outcome II is most likely. Restructuring would not affect the shareholders' interest because the net gain to shareholders in this case is zero. Also notice that the value of the firm is unchanged if outcome II occurs.

This example explains why managers should attempt to maximize the value of the firm. In other words, it answers question (1) in Section 15.1. We find in this example the following wisdom:

Changes in capital structure benefit the shareholders *if and only if* the value of the firm increases.

Conversely, these changes hurt the shareholders if and only if the value of the firm decreases. This result holds true for capital structure changes of many different types.[1] As a corollary, we can say the following:

Managers should choose the capital structure that they believe will have the highest firm value because this capital structure will be most beneficial to the firm's shareholders.

Note, however, that this example does not tell us which of the three outcomes is most likely to occur. Thus it does not tell us whether debt should be added to J.J. Sprint's capital structure. In other words, it does not answer question (2) in Section 15.1. This second question is treated in the next section.

15.3 Financial Leverage and Firm Value: An Example

Leverage and Returns to Shareholders

The previous section shows that the capital structure producing the highest firm value is the one that maximizes shareholder wealth. In this section, we wish to determine that optimal capital structure. We begin by illustrating the effect of capital structure on returns to shareholders. We will use a detailed example that we encourage students to study carefully. Once we fully understand this example, we will be ready to determine the optimal capital structure.

Autoveloce SpA currently has no debt in its capital structure. The firm is considering issuing debt to buy back some of its equity. Both its current and proposed capital structures are presented in Table 15.1. The firm's assets are €8,000. There are 400 shares of the all-equity firm, implying a market value per share of €20. The proposed debt issue is for €4,000, leaving €4,000 in equity. The interest rate is 10 per cent. Assume in all our examples that debt is issued at par.

Table 15.1 Financial Structure of Autoveloce SpA

	Current	Proposed
Assets (€)	8,000	8,000
Debt (€)	0	4,000
Equity (market and book) (€)	8,000	4,000
Interest rate (%)	10	10
Market value/share (€)	20	20
Shares outstanding	400	200

The proposed capital structure has leverage, whereas the current structure is all equity.

The effect of economic conditions on earnings per share is shown in Table 15.2 for the current capital structure (all-equity). Consider first the middle column where earnings are expected to be €1,200. Because assets are €8,000, the return on assets (ROA) is 15 per cent (= €1,200/€8,000). Assets equal equity for this all-equity firm, so return on equity (ROE) is also 15 per cent. Earnings per share (EPS) is €3.00 (= €1,200/400). Similar calculations yield EPS of €1.00 and €5.00 in the cases of recession and expansion, respectively.

Table 15.2 Autoveloce's Current Capital Structure: No Debt

	Recession	Expected	Expansion
Return on assets (%)	5	15	25
Earnings (€)	400	1,200	2,000
Return on equity = Earnings/Equity (%)	5	15	25
Earnings per share (€)	1.00	3.00	5.00

The case of leverage is presented in Table 15.3. ROA in the three economic states is identical in Tables 15.2 and 15.3 because this ratio is calculated before interest is considered. Debt is €4,000 here, so interest is €400 (= 0.10 × €4,000). Thus earnings after interest are €800 (= €1,200 − €400) in the middle (expected) case. Because equity is €4,000, ROE is 20 per cent (= €800/€4,000). Earnings per share are €4.00 (= €800/200). Similar calculations yield earnings of €0 and €8.00 for recession and expansion, respectively.

Table 15.3 Autoveloce's Proposed Capital Structure

	Recession	Expected	Expansion
Return on assets (%)	5	15	25
Earnings before interest (€)	400	1,200	2,000
Interest (€)	−400	−400	−400
Earnings after interest (€)	0	800	1,600
Return on equity = Earnings after interest/Equity (%)	0	20	40
Earnings per share (€)	0	4.00	8.00

Tables 15.2 and 15.3 show that the effect of financial leverage depends on the company's earnings before interest. If earnings before interest are equal to €1,200, the return on equity (ROE) is higher under the proposed structure. If earnings before interest are equal to €400, the ROE is higher under the current structure.

This idea is represented in Figure 15.2. The solid line represents the case of no leverage. The line begins at the origin, indicating that earnings per share (EPS) would be zero if earnings before interest (EBI) were zero. The EPS rise in tandem with a rise in EBI.

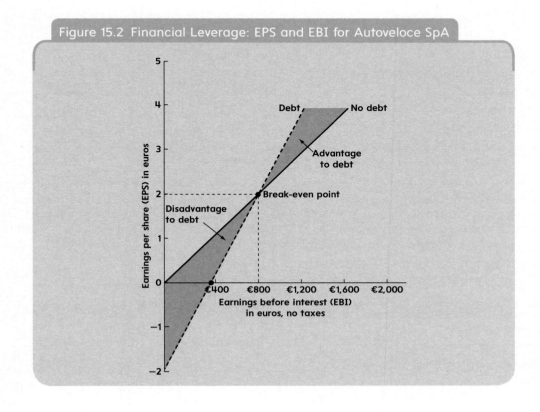

Figure 15.2 Financial Leverage: EPS and EBI for Autoveloce SpA

The dotted line represents the case of €4,000 of debt. Here EPS are negative if EBI are zero. This follows because €400 of interest must be paid regardless of the firm's profits.

Now consider the slopes of the two lines. The slope of the dotted line (the line with debt) is higher than the slope of the solid line. This occurs because the levered firm has *fewer* shares of equity outstanding than the unlevered firm. Therefore, any increase in EBI leads to a greater rise in EPS for the levered firm because the earnings increase is distributed over fewer shares of equity.

Because the dotted line has a lower intercept but a higher slope, the two lines must intersect. The *break-even* point occurs at €800 of EBI. Were earnings before interest to be €800, both firms would produce €2 of earnings per share (EPS). Because €800 is break-even, earnings above €800 lead to greater EPS for the levered firm. Earnings below €800 lead to greater EPS for the unlevered firm.

The Choice between Debt and Equity

Tables 15.2 and 15.3 and Figure 15.2 are important because they show the effect of leverage on earnings per share. Students should study the tables and figure until they feel comfortable with the calculation of each number in them. However, we have not yet presented the punch line. That is, we have not yet stated which capital structure is better for Autoveloce.

At this point many students believe that leverage is beneficial because EPS are expected to be €4.00 with leverage and only €3.00 without leverage. However, leverage also creates *risk*. Note that in a recession, EPS are higher (€1.00 versus €0) for the unlevered firm. Thus a risk-averse investor might prefer the all-equity firm, whereas a risk-neutral (or less risk-averse) investor might prefer leverage. Given this ambiguity, which capital structure *is* better?

Modigliani and Miller (MM) have a convincing argument that a firm cannot change the total value of its outstanding securities by changing the proportions of its capital structure. In other words, the value of the firm is always the same under different capital structures. In still other words, no capital structure is any better or worse than any other capital structure for the firm's shareholders. This rather pessimistic result is the famous MM Proposition I.[2]

Their argument compares a simple strategy, which we call strategy A, with a two-part strategy, which we call strategy B. Both of these strategies for shareholders of Autoveloce are illustrated in Table 15.4. Let us now examine the first strategy.

Table 15.4 Pay-Off and Cost to Shareholders of Autoveloce SpA Under the Proposed Structure and Under the Current Structure with Homemade Leverage

	Recession (€)	Expected (€)	Expansion (€)
Strategy A: Buy 100 Shares of Levered Equity			
EPS of *levered* equity (taken from last line of Table 15.3)	0	4	8
Earnings per 100 shares	0	400	800
Initial cost = 100 shares @ €20/share = €2,000			
Strategy B: Homemade Leverage			
Earnings per 200 shares in current	1 × 200 =	3 × 200 =	5 × 200 =
unlevered Autoveloce	200	600	1,000
Interest at 10% on €2,000	−200	−200	−200
Net earnings	0	400	800
Initial cost = 200 shares @ €20/share− €2,000 = €2,000			
Cost of equity Amount borrowed			

Investor receives the same pay-off whether she (1) buys shares in a levered corporation or (2) buys shares in an unlevered firm and borrows on personal account. Her initial investment is the same in either case. Thus the firm neither helps nor hurts her by adding debt to capital structure.

Strategy A: Buy 100 shares of the levered equity

The first line in the top panel of Table 15.4 shows EPS for the proposed levered equity in the three economic states. The second line shows the earnings in the three states for an individual buying 100 shares. The next line shows that the cost of these 100 shares is €2,000.

Let us now consider the second strategy, which has two parts to it.

Strategy B: Homemade Leverage

1 Borrow €2,000 from either a bank or, more likely, a brokerage house. (If the brokerage house is the lender, we say that this activity is *going on margin.*)

2 Use the borrowed proceeds plus your own investment of €2,000 (a total of €4,000) to buy 200 shares of the current unlevered equity at €20 per share.

The bottom panel of Table 15.4 shows pay-offs under strategy B, which we call the *homemade leverage* strategy. First observe the middle column, which indicates that 200 shares of the unlevered equity are expected to generate €600 of earnings. Assuming that the €2,000 is borrowed at a 10 per cent interest rate, the interest expense is €200 (= 0.10 × €2,000). Thus the net earnings are expected to be €400. A similar calculation generates net earnings of either €0 or €800 in recession or expansion, respectively.

Now let us compare these two strategies, both in terms of earnings per year and in terms of initial cost. The top panel of the table shows that strategy A generates earnings of €0, €400 and €800 in the three states. The bottom panel of the table shows that strategy B generates the *same* net earnings in the three states.

The top panel of the table shows that strategy A involves an initial cost of €2,000. Similarly, the bottom panel shows an *identical* net cost of €2,000 for strategy B.

This shows a very important result. Both the cost and the pay-off from the two strategies are the same. Thus we must conclude that Autoveloce is neither helping nor hurting its shareholders by restructuring. In other words, an investor is not receiving anything from corporate leverage that she could not receive on her own.

Note that, as shown in Table 15.1, the equity of the unlevered firm is valued at €8,000. Because the equity of the levered firm is €4,000 and its debt is €4,000, the value of the levered firm is also €8,000. Now suppose that, for whatever reason, the value of the levered firm were actually greater than the value of the unlevered firm. Here strategy A would cost more than strategy B. In this case an investor would prefer to borrow on his own account and invest in the equity of the unlevered firm. He would get the same net earnings each year as if he had invested in the equity of the levered firm. However, his cost would be less. The strategy would not be unique to our investor. Given the higher value of the levered firm, no rational investor would invest in the shares of the levered firm. Anyone desiring shares in the levered firm would get the same euro return more cheaply by borrowing to finance a purchase of the unlevered firm's shares. The equilibrium result would be, of course, that the value of the levered firm would fall and the value of the unlevered firm would rise until they became equal. At this point individuals would be indifferent between strategy A and strategy B.

This example illustrates the basic result of Modigliani–Miller (MM) and is, as we have noted, commonly called their Proposition I. We restate this proposition as follows:

MM Proposition I (no taxes): The value of the levered firm is the same as the value of the unlevered firm.

This is perhaps the most important result in all of corporate finance. In fact, it is generally considered the beginning point of modern corporate finance. Before MM, the effect of leverage on the value of the firm was considered complex and convoluted. Modigliani and Miller showed a blindingly simple result: if levered firms are priced too high, rational investors will simply borrow on their personal accounts to buy shares in unlevered firms. This substitution is often called *homemade leverage.* As long as individuals borrow (and lend) on the same terms as the firms, they can duplicate the effects of corporate leverage on their own.

The example of Autoveloce SpA shows that leverage does not affect the value of the firm. Because we showed earlier that shareholders' welfare is directly related to the firm's value, the example also indicates that changes in capital structure cannot affect the shareholders' welfare.

A Key Assumption

The MM result hinges on the assumption that individuals can borrow as cheaply as corporations. If, alternatively, individuals can borrow only at a higher rate, we can easily show that corporations can increase firm value by borrowing.

Is this assumption of equal borrowing costs a good one? Individuals who want to buy shares and borrow can do so by establishing a margin account with a broker. Under this arrangement the broker lends the individual a portion of the purchase price. For example, the individual might buy €10,000 of equity by investing €6,000 of her own funds and borrowing €4,000 from the broker. Should the shares be worth €9,000 on the next day, the individual's net worth or equity in the account would be €5,000 = €9,000 − €4,000.[3]

The broker fears that a sudden price drop will cause the equity in the individual's account to be negative, implying that the broker may not get the loan repaid in full. To guard against this possibility, stock exchange rules require that the individual makes additional cash contributions (replenishes her margin account) as the share price falls. Because (1) the procedures for replenishing the account have developed over many years, and (2) the broker holds the equity as collateral, there is little default risk to the broker. In particular, if margin contributions are not made on time, the broker can sell the shares to satisfy the loan. Therefore, brokers generally charge low interest, with many rates being only slightly above the risk-free rate.

By contrast, corporations frequently borrow using illiquid assets (e.g., plant and equipment) as collateral. The costs to the lender of initial negotiation and ongoing supervision, as well as of working out arrangements in the event of financial distress, can be quite substantial. Thus it is difficult to argue that individuals must borrow at higher rates than corporations.

15.4 Modigliani and Miller: Proposition II (No Taxes)

Risk to Equityholders Rises with Leverage

At an Autoveloce board meeting, a director said, 'Well, maybe it does not matter whether the corporation or the individual levers – as long as some leverage takes place. Leverage benefits investors. After all, an investor's expected return rises with the amount of the leverage present.' He then pointed out that, as shown in Tables 15.2 and 15.3, the expected return on unlevered equity is 15 per cent whereas the expected return on levered equity is 20 per cent.

However, another director replied, 'Not necessarily. Though the expected return rises with leverage, the *risk* rises as well.' This point can be seen from an examination of Tables 15.2 and 15.3. With earnings before interest (EBI) varying between €400 and €2,000, earnings per share (EPS) for the shareholders of the unlevered firm vary between €1.00 and €5.00. EPS for the shareholders of the levered firm vary between €0 and €8.00. This greater range for the EPS of the levered firm implies greater risk for the levered firm's shareholders. In other words, levered shareholders have better returns in good times than do unlevered shareholders but have worse returns in bad times. The two tables also show greater range for the ROE of the levered firm's shareholders. The earlier interpretation concerning risk applies here as well.

The same insight can be taken from Figure 15.2. The slope of the line for the levered firm is greater than the slope of the line for the unlevered firm. This means that the levered shareholders have better returns in good times than do unlevered shareholders but have worse returns in bad times, implying greater risk with leverage. In other words, the slope of the line measures the risk to shareholders because the slope indicates the responsiveness of ROE to changes in firm performance (earnings before interest).

Proposition II: Required Return to Equityholders Rises with Leverage

Because levered equity has greater risk, it should have a greater expected return as compensation. In our example, the market *requires* only a 15 per cent expected return for the unlevered equity, but it requires a 20 per cent expected return for the levered equity.

This type of reasoning allows us to develop MM Proposition II. Here MM argue that the expected return on equity is positively related to leverage because the risk to equityholders increases with leverage.

To develop this position recall that the firm's weighted average cost of capital, R_{WACC}, can be written as:[4]

$$R_{\text{WACC}} = \frac{E}{D+E} \times R_E + \frac{D}{D+E} \times R_D \qquad (15.2)$$

where R_D is the cost of debt; R_E is the expected return on equity, also called the *cost of equity* or the *required return on equity*; R_{WACC} is the firm's weighted average cost of capital; D is the market value of the firm's debt or bonds; and E is the market value of the firm's shares or equity.

Equation 15.2 is quite intuitive. It simply says that a firm's weighted average cost of capital is a weighted average of its cost of debt and its cost of equity. The weight applied to debt is the proportion of debt in the capital structure, and the weight applied to equity is the proportion of equity in the capital structure. Calculations of R_{WACC} from Equation 15.2 for both the unlevered and the levered firm are presented in Table 15.5.

Table 15.5 Cost of Capital Calculations for Autoveloce

$$R_{WACC} = \frac{E}{D+E} \times R_E + \frac{D}{D+E} \times R_D$$

Unlevered firm:

$$15\% = \frac{0}{\text{€8,000}} \times 10\%^* + \frac{\text{€8,000}}{\text{€8,000}} \times 15\%^\dagger$$

Levered firm:

$$15\% = \frac{\text{€4,000}}{\text{€8,000}} \times 10\%^* + \frac{\text{€4,000}}{\text{€8,000}} \times 20\%^\ddagger$$

*10% is the cost of debt.

†From the 'Expected' column in Table 15.2, we learn that expected earnings after interest for the unlevered firm are €1,200. From Table 15.1 we learn that equity for the unlevered firm is

$$\frac{\text{Expected earnings after interest}}{\text{Equity}} = \frac{\text{€1,200}}{\text{€8,000}} = 15\%$$

‡ From the 'Expected' column in Table 15.3, we learn that expected earnings after interest for the levered firm are €800. From Table 15.1 we learn that equity for the levered firm is €4,000. Thus R_E for the levered firm is

$$\frac{\text{Expected earnings after interest}}{\text{Equity}} = \frac{\text{€800}}{\text{€4,000}} = 20\%$$

An implication of MM Proposition I is that R_{WACC} is a constant for a given firm, regardless of the capital structure.[5] For example, Table 15.5 shows that R_{WACC} for Autoveloce is 15 per cent, with or without leverage.

Let us now define R_A to be the *cost of capital for an all-equity firm*. For Autoveloce SpA, R_A is calculated as

$$R_A = \frac{\text{Expected earnings to unlevered firm}}{\text{Unlevered equity}} = \frac{\text{€1,200}}{\text{€8,000}} = 15\%$$

As can be seen from Table 15.5, R_{WACC} is equal to R_A for Autoveloce. In fact, R_{WACC} must *always* equal R_A in a world without corporate taxes.[6]

Proposition II states the expected return on equity, R_E, in terms of leverage. The exact relationship, derived by setting $R_{WACC} = R_A$ and then rearranging Equation 15.2, is[7]

MM Proposition II (no taxes)

$$R_E = R_A + \frac{D}{E}(R_A - R_D) \tag{15.3}$$

Equation 15.3 implies that the required return on equity is a linear function of the firm's debt–equity ratio. Examining Equation 15.3, we see that if R_A exceeds the cost of debt, R_D, then the cost of equity rises with increases in the debt–equity ratio, D/E. Normally R_A should exceed R_D. That is, because even unlevered equity is risky, it should have an expected return greater than that of riskless debt. Note that Equation 15.3 holds for Autoveloce in its levered state:

$$0.20 = 0.15 + \frac{\text{€4,000}}{\text{€4,000}}(0.15 - 0.10)$$

Figure 15.3 graphs Equation 15.3. As you can see, we have plotted the relation between the cost of equity, R_E, and the debt–equity ratio, D/E, as a straight line. What we witness in Equation 15.3 and illustrate in Figure 15.3 is the effect of leverage on the cost of equity. As the firm raises the debt–equity ratio, each euro of equity is levered with additional debt. This raises the risk of equity and therefore the required return, R_E, on the equity.

Figure 15.3 The Cost of Equity, the Cost of Debt, and the Weighted Average Cost of Capital: MM Proposition II with no Corporate Taxes

$$R_E = R_A + (R_A - R_D)D/E$$

R_E is the cost of equity.
R_D is the cost of debt.
R_A is the cost of capital for an all-equity firm.
R_{WACC} is a firm's weighted average cost of capital. In a world with no taxes, R_{WACC} for a levered firm is equal to R_A.
R_A is a single point whereas R_E, R_D and R_{WACC} are all entire lines.

The cost of equity capital, R_E, is positively related to the firm's debt–equity ratio. The firm's weighted average cost of capital, R_{WACC}, is invariant to the firm's debt-equity ratio.

Figure 15.3 also shows that R_{WACC} is unaffected by leverage, a point we have already made. (It is important for students to realize that R_A, the cost of capital for an all-equity firm, is represented by a single dot on the graph. By contrast, R_{WACC} is an entire line.)

MM Propositions I and II

Canary Motors, an all-equity firm, has expected earnings of £10 million per year in perpetuity. The firm pays all of its earnings out as dividends, so the £10 million may also be viewed as the shareholders' expected cash flow. There are 10 million shares outstanding, implying expected annual cash flow of £1 per share. The cost of capital for this unlevered firm is 10 per cent. In addition, the firm will soon build a new plant for £4 million. The plant is expected to generate additional cash flow of £1 million per year. These figures can be described as follows:

Current Company	New Plant	
Cash flow: £10 million	Initial outlay: £4 million	
Number of outstanding shares: 10 million	Additional annual cash flow: £1 million	

The project's net present value is

$$-\text{£4 million} + \frac{\text{£1 million}}{0.1} = \text{£6 million}$$

assuming that the project is discounted at the same rate as the firm as a whole. Before the market knows of the project, the *market value* balance sheet of the firm is this:

CANARY MOTORS		
Market Value Balance Sheet (All Equity)		
Old assets: $\frac{\text{£10 million}}{0.1} = \text{£100 million}$	Equity	£100 million (10 million shares)

The value of the firm is £100 million because the cash flow of £10 million per year is capitalized (discounted) at 10 per cent. A share of equity sells for £10 (= £100 million/10 million) because there are 10 million shares outstanding.

The firm will issue £4 million of either equity or debt. Let us consider the effect of equity and debt financing in turn.

Equity Financing

Imagine that the firm announces that in the near future it will raise £4 million in equity to build a new plant. The share price, and therefore the value of the firm, will rise to reflect the positive net present value of the plant. According to efficient markets, the increase occurs immediately. That is, the rise occurs on the day of the announcement, not on the date of either the onset of construction of the plant or the forthcoming equity offering. The market value balance sheet becomes this:

CANARY MOTORS Market Value Balance Sheet (upon announcement of equity issue to construct plant)			
	(£)		(£)
Old assets	100 million	Equity	106 million (10 million shares)
NPV of plant: $-£4$ million $+ \dfrac{£1 \text{ million}}{0.1}$	6 million		
Total assets	106 million		

Note that the NPV of the plant is included in the market value balance sheet. Because the new shares have not yet been issued, the number of outstanding shares remains 10 million. The price per share has now risen to £10.60 (= £106 million/10 million) to reflect news concerning the plant.

Shortly thereafter, £4 million of equity is issued or *floated*. Because the shares are selling at £10.60 per share, 377,358 (= £4 million/£10.60) shares are issued. Imagine that funds are put in the bank *temporarily* before being used to build the plant. The market value balance sheet becomes this:

CANARY MOTORS Market Value Balance Sheet (upon issuance of equity but before construction begins on plant)			
	(£)		(£)
Old assets	100 million	Equity	110 million (10,377,358 shares)
NPV of plant	6 million		
Proceeds from new issue of equity (currently placed in bank)	4 million		
Total assets	110 million		

The number of shares outstanding is now 10,377,358 because 377,358 new shares were issued. The share price is £10.60 (= £110,000,000/10,377,358). Note that the price has not changed. This is consistent with efficient capital markets because the share price should move due only to new information.

Of course the funds are placed in the bank only temporarily. Shortly after the new issue, the £4 million is given to a contractor who builds the plant. To avoid problems in discounting, we assume that the plant is built immediately. The market value balance sheet then looks like this:

CANARY MOTORS Market Value Balance Sheet (upon completion of the plant)			
	(£)		(£)
Old assets	100 million	Equity	110 million (10,377,358 shares)
PV of plant $\dfrac{£1 \text{ million}}{0.1} =$	10 million		
Total assets	110 million		

Though total assets do not change, the composition of the assets does change. The bank account has been emptied to pay the contractor. The present value of cash flows of £1 million a year from the plant is reflected as an asset worth £10 million. Because the building expenditures of £4 million have already been paid, they no longer represent a future cost. Hence they no longer reduce the value of the plant. According to efficient capital markets, the share price remains £10.60.

Expected yearly cash flow from the firm is £11 million, £10 million of which comes from the old assets and £1 million from the new. The expected return to shareholders is

$$R_E = \frac{\text{£11 million}}{\text{£110 million}} = 0.10$$

Because the firm is all equity, $R_E = R_A = 0.10$.

Debt Financing

Alternatively, imagine the firm announces that in the near future it will borrow £4 million at 6 per cent to build a new plant. This implies yearly interest payments of £240,000 (= £4,000,000 × 6 per cent). Again the share price rises immediately to reflect the positive net present value of the plant. Thus we have the following:

CANARY MOTORS Market Value Balance Sheet (upon announcement of debt issue to construct plant)			
	(£)		(£)
Old assets	100 million	Equity	106 million (10 million shares)
NPV of plant: $-\text{£4 million} + \dfrac{\text{£1 million}}{0.1} =$	6 million		
Total assets	106 million		

The value of the firm is the same as in the equity financing case because (1) the same plant is to be built, and (2) MM proved that debt financing is neither better nor worse than equity financing.

At some point £4 million of debt is issued. As before, the funds are placed in the bank temporarily. The market value balance sheet becomes this:

CANARY MOTORS Market Value Balance Sheet (upon debt issuance but before construction begins on plant)			
	(£)		(£)
Old assets	100 million	Debt	4 million
NPV of plant	6 million	Equity	106 million (10 million shares)
Proceeds from debt issue (currently invested in bank)	4 million		
Total assets	110 million	Debt plus equity	110 million

Note that debt appears on the right side of the market value balance sheet. The share price is still £10.60 in accordance with our discussion of efficient capital markets.

Finally, the contractor receives £4 million and builds the plant. The market value balance sheet turns into this:

CANARY MOTORS Market Value Balance Sheet (upon completion of the plant)			
	(£)		(£)
Old assets	100 million	Debt	4 million
PV of plant	10 million	Equity	106 million (10 million shares)
Total assets	110 million	Debt plus equity	110 million

The only change here is that the bank account has been depleted to pay the contractor. The shareholders expect yearly cash flow after interest of

$$
\underset{\substack{\text{Cash flow on}\\\text{old assets}}}{£10,000,000} + \underset{\substack{\text{Cash flow on}\\\text{new assets}}}{£1,000,000} - \underset{\substack{\text{Interest:}\\£4 \text{ million} \times 6\%}}{£240,000} = £10,760,000
$$

The shareholders expect to earn a return of

$$
\frac{£10,760,000}{£106,000,000} = 10.15\%
$$

This return of 10.15 per cent for levered shareholders is higher than the 10 per cent return for the unlevered shareholders. This result is sensible because, as we argued earlier, levered equity is riskier. In fact, the return of 10.15 per cent should be exactly what MM Proposition II predicts. This prediction can be verified by plugging values into

$$
R_E = R_A + \frac{D}{E}(R_A - R_D)
$$

We obtain

$$
10.15\% = 10\% + \frac{£4,000,000}{£106,000,000} \times (10\% - 6\%)
$$

This example was useful for two reasons. First, we wanted to introduce the concept of market value balance sheets, a tool that will prove useful elsewhere in the text. Among other things, this technique allows us to calculate the share price of a new issue of shares. Second, the example illustrates three aspects of Modigliani and Miller:

1 The example is consistent with MM Proposition I because the value of the firm is £110 million after either equity or debt financing.

2 Students are often more interested in share price than in firm value. We show that the share price is always £10.60, regardless of whether debt or equity financing is used.

3 The example is consistent with MM Proposition II. The expected return to shareholders rises from 10 to 10.15 per cent, just as Equation 15.3 states. This rise occurs because the shareholders of a levered firm face more risk than do the shareholders of an unlevered firm.

MM: An Interpretation

The Modigliani–Miller results indicate that managers cannot change the value of a firm by repackaging the firm's securities. Though this idea was considered revolutionary when it was originally proposed in the late 1950s, the MM approach and proof have since met with wide acclaim.[8]

MM argue that the firm's overall cost of capital cannot be reduced as debt is substituted for equity, even though debt appears to be cheaper than equity. The reason for this is that as the firm adds debt, the remaining equity becomes more risky. As this risk rises, the cost of equity capital rises as a result. The increase in the cost of the remaining equity capital offsets the higher proportion of the firm financed by low-cost debt. In fact, MM prove that the two effects exactly offset each other, so that both the value of the firm and the firm's overall cost of capital are invariant to leverage.

Food found its way into this chapter earlier when we viewed the firm as a pie. MM argue that the size of the pie does not change no matter how shareholders and bondholders divide it. MM say that a firm's capital structure is irrelevant; it is what it is by some historical accident. The theory implies that firms' debt–equity ratios could be anything. They are what they are because of whimsical and random managerial decisions about how much to borrow and how much equity to issue.

In Their Own Words

In Professor Miller's Words . . .

[The Modigliani–Miller results are not easy to understand fully. This point is related in a story told by Merton Miller.*]

How difficult it is to summarize briefly the contribution of the [Modigliani–Miller] papers was brought home to me very clearly last October after Franco Modigliani was awarded the Nobel Prize in Economics in part – but, of course, only in part – for the work in finance. The television camera crews from our local stations in Chicago immediately descended upon me. 'We understand,' they said, 'that you worked with Modigliani some years back in developing these M and M theorems and we wonder if you could explain them briefly to our television viewers.'

'How briefly?' I asked.

'Oh, take ten seconds,' was the reply.

Ten seconds to explain the work of a lifetime! Ten seconds to describe two carefully reasoned articles, each running to more than thirty printed pages and each with sixty or so long footnotes! When they saw the look of dismay on my face, they said, 'You don't have to go into details. Just give us the main points in simple, commonsense terms.'

The main point of the first or cost-of-capital article was, in principle at least, simple enough to make. It said that in an economist's ideal world of complete and perfect capital markets and with full and symmetric information among all market participants, the total market value of all the securities issued by a firm was governed by the earning power and risk of its underlying real assets and was independent of how the mix of securities issued to finance it was divided between debt instruments and equity capital. . . .

Such a summary, however, uses too many shorthanded terms and concepts, like perfect capital markets, that are rich in connotations to economists but hardly so to the general public. So I thought, instead, of an analogy that we ourselves had invoked in the original paper. . . .

'Think of the firm,' I said, 'as a gigantic tub of whole milk. The farmer can sell the whole milk as is. Or he can separate out the cream and sell it at a considerably higher price than the whole milk would bring. (That's the analogy of a firm selling low-yield and hence high-priced debt securities.) But, of course, what the farmer would have left would be skim milk with low butterfat content and that would sell for much less than whole milk. That corresponds to the levered equity. The M and M proposition says that if there were no costs of separation (and, of course, no government dairy support programme), the cream plus the skim milk would bring the same price as the whole milk.'

The television people conferred among themselves and came back to inform me that it was too long, too complicated, and too academic.

'Don't you have anything simpler?' they asked. I thought of another way that the M and M proposition is presented these days, which emphasizes the notion of market completeness and stresses the role of securities as devices for 'partitioning' a firm's pay-offs in each possible state of the world among the group of its capital suppliers.

'Think of the firm,' I said, 'as a gigantic pizza, divided into quarters. If now you cut each quarter in half into eighths, the M and M proposition says that you will have more pieces but not more pizza.'

Again there was a whispered conference among the camera crew, and the director came back and said:

'Professor, we understand from the press releases that there were two M and M propositions. Can we try the other one?'

[Professor Miller tried valiantly to explain the second proposition, though this was apparently even more difficult to get across. After his attempt:]

Once again there was a whispered conversation. They shut the lights off. They folded up their equipment. They thanked me for giving them the time. They said that they'd get back to me. But I knew that I had somehow lost my chance to start a new career as a packager of economic wisdom for TV viewers in convenient ten-second bites. Some have the talent for it . . . and some just don't.

*Taken from *GSB Chicago*, University of Chicago (Autumn 1986).

Although scholars are always fascinated with far-reaching theories, students are perhaps more concerned with real-world applications. Do real-world managers follow MM by treating capital structure decisions with indifference? Unfortunately for the theory, virtually all companies in certain industries, such as banking, choose high debt–equity ratios. Conversely, companies in other industries, such as pharmaceuticals, choose low debt–equity ratios. In fact, almost any industry has a debt–equity ratio to which companies in that industry tend to adhere. Thus companies do not appear to be selecting their degree of leverage in a frivolous or random manner. Because of this, financial economists (including MM themselves) have argued that real-world factors may have been left out of the theory.

Though many of our students have argued that individuals can borrow only at rates above the corporate borrowing rate, we disagreed with this argument earlier in the chapter. But when we look elsewhere for unrealistic assumptions in the theory, we find two:[9]

1   Taxes were ignored.

2   Bankruptcy costs and other agency costs were not considered.

We turn to taxes in the next section. Bankruptcy costs and other agency costs will be treated in the next chapter. A summary of the main Modigliani–Miller results without taxes is presented in the boxed section below.

Summary of Modigliani–Miller Propositions without Taxes

Assumptions

- No taxes.
- No transaction costs.
- Individuals and corporations borrow at same rate.

Results

Proposition I: $V_L = V_U$ (Value of levered firm equals value of unlevered firm)

Proposition II: $R_E = R_A + \dfrac{D}{E}(R_A - R_D)$

Intuition

Proposition I: Through homemade leverage individuals can either duplicate or undo the effects of corporate leverage.

Proposition II: The cost of equity rises with leverage because the risk to equity rises with leverage.

15.5   Corporate Taxes

The Basic Insight

Chapter 3
Page 64

The previous part of this chapter showed that firm value is unrelated to debt in a world without taxes. We now show that in the presence of corporate taxes, the firm's value is positively related to its debt (taxes are introduced in **Chapter 3**, Section 3.3). The basic intuition can be seen from a pie chart, such as the one in Figure 15.4. Consider the all-equity firm on the left. Here both shareholders and tax authorities have claims on the firm. The value of the all-equity firm is, of course, that part of the pie owned by the shareholders. The proportion going to taxes is simply a cost.

The pie on the right for the levered firm shows three claims: shareholders, debtholders and taxes. The value of the levered firm is the sum of the value of the debt and the value of the equity. In selecting between the two capital structures in the picture, a financial manager should select the one with the higher value. Assuming that the total area is the same for both pies,[10] value is maximized for the capital structure paying the least in taxes. In other words, the manager should choose the capital structure that the government hates the most.

We will show that due to a quirk in corporate tax law, the proportion of the pie allocated to taxes is less for the levered firm than it is for the unlevered firm. Thus, managers should select high leverage.

Figure 15.4 Two Pie Models of Capital Structure Under Corporate Taxes

All-equity firm

Equity | Taxes

Levered firm

Debt | Taxes | Equity

The levered firm pays less in taxes than does the all-equity firm. Thus the sum of the debt plus the equity of the levered firm is greater than the equity of the unlevered firm.

Example 15.3

Taxes and Cash Flow

Wasserprodukte GmbH has a corporate tax rate, t_C, of 35 per cent and expected earnings before interest and taxes (EBIT) of €1 million each year. Its entire earnings after taxes are paid out as dividends.

The firm is considering two alternative capital structures. Under Plan I, Wasserprodukte would have no debt in its capital structure. Under Plan II, the company would have €4,000,000 of debt, D. The cost of debt, R_D, is 10 per cent.

The chief financial officer for Wasserprodukte makes the following calculations:

	Plan I (€)	Plan II (€)
Earnings before interest and corporate taxes (EBIT)	1,000,000	1,000,000
Interest ($R_D D$)	0	400,000
Earnings before taxes (EBT) = (EBIT − $R_D D$)	1,000,000	600,000
Taxes ($t_C = 0.35$)	350,000	210,000
Earnings after corporate taxes (EAT) = [(EBIT − $R_D D$) × (1 − t_C)]	650,000	390,000
Total cash flow to both shareholders and bondholders [EBIT × (1 − t_C) + $t_C R_D D$]	650,000	790,000

The most relevant numbers for our purposes are the two on the bottom line. Dividends, which are equal to earnings after taxes in this example, are the cash flow to shareholders, and interest is the cash flow to bondholders. Here we see that more cash flow reaches the owners of the firm (both shareholders and bondholders) under Plan II. The difference is €140,000 = €790,000 − €650,000. It does not take us long to realize the source of this difference. The government receives less tax under Plan II (€210,000) than it does under Plan I (€350,000). The difference here is €140,000 = €350,000 − €210,000.

This difference occurs because the way governments treat interest is different from the way they treat earnings going to shareholders.[11] Interest totally escapes corporate taxation, whereas earnings after interest but before corporate taxes (EBT) are taxed at the corporate tax rate.

Present Value of the Tax Shield

The previous discussion shows a tax advantage to debt or, equivalently, a tax disadvantage to equity. We now want to value this advantage. The interest in monetary terms is

$$\text{Interest} = \underbrace{R_D}_{\text{Interest rate}} \times \underbrace{D}_{\text{Amount borrowed}}$$

This interest is €400,000 (= 10 per cent × €4,000,000) for Wasserprodukte. All this interest is tax deductible. That is, whatever the taxable income of Wasserprodukte would have been without the debt, the taxable income is now €400,000 *less* with the debt.

Because the corporate tax rate is 0.35 in our example, the reduction in corporate taxes is €140,000 (= 0.35 × €400,000). This number is identical to the reduction in corporate taxes calculated previously.

Algebraically, the reduction in corporate taxes is

$$\underbrace{t_C}_{\text{Corporate tax rate}} \times \underbrace{R_D \times D}_{\text{Interest paid}} \qquad (15.4)$$

That is, whatever the taxes that a firm would pay each year without debt, the firm will pay $t_C R_D D$ less with the debt of D. Expression 15.4 is often called the *tax shield from debt*. Note that it is an *annual* amount.

As long as the firm expects to be paying tax, we can assume that the cash flow in Expression 15.4 has the same risk as the interest on the debt. Thus its value can be determined by discounting at the cost of debt, R_D. Assuming that the cash flows are perpetual, the present value of the tax shield is

$$\frac{t_C R_D D}{R_D} = t_C D$$

Value of the Levered Firm

We have just calculated the present value of the tax shield from debt. Our next step is to calculate the value of the levered firm. The annual after-tax cash flow of an unlevered firm is

$$\text{EBIT} \times (1 - t_C)$$

where EBIT is earnings before interest and taxes. The value of an unlevered firm (that is, a firm with no debt) is the present value of EBIT × (1 − t_C):

$$V_U = \frac{\text{EBIT} \times (1 - t_C)}{R_A}$$

Here V_U is the present value of an unlevered firm; EBIT × (1 − t_C) represents firm cash flows after corporate taxes; t_C is the corporate tax rate; R_A is the cost of capital to an all-equity firm. As can be seen from the formula, R_A now discounts *after-tax* cash flows.

As shown previously, leverage increases the value of the firm by the tax shield, which is $t_C D$ for perpetual debt. Thus we merely add this tax shield to the value of the unlevered firm to get the value of the levered firm.

We can write this algebraically as follows:[12]

MM Proposition I (Corporate Taxes)

$$V_L = \frac{\text{EBIT} \times (1 - t_C)}{R_A} + \frac{t_C R_D D}{R_D} = V_U + t_C D \qquad (15.5)$$

Equation 15.5 is MM Proposition I under corporate taxes. The first term in Equation 15.5 is the value of the cash flows of the firm with no debt tax shield. In other words, this term is equal to V_U, the value of the all-equity firm. The value of the levered firm is the value of an all-equity firm plus $t_C D$, the tax rate times the value of the debt. $t_C D$ is the present value of the tax shield in the case of perpetual cash flows.[13] Because the tax shield increases with the amount of debt, the firm can raise its total cash flow and its value by substituting debt for equity.

Example 15.4

MM with Corporate Taxes

Divided Airlines is currently an unlevered firm. The company expects to generate €153.85 in earnings before interest and taxes (EBIT) in perpetuity. The corporate tax rate is 35 per cent, implying after-tax earnings of €100. All earnings after tax are paid out as dividends.

The firm is considering a capital restructuring to allow €200 of debt. Its cost of debt capital is 10 per cent. Unlevered firms in the same industry have a cost of equity capital of 20 per cent. What will the new value of Divided Airlines be?

The value of Divided Airlines will be equal to

$$V_L = \frac{\text{EBIT} \times (1 - t_C)}{R_A} + \frac{t_C R_D D}{R_D} = V_U + t_C D$$

$$V_L = \frac{\text{EBIT} \times (1 - t_C)}{R_A} + t_C D$$

$$= \frac{€100}{0.20} + (0.35 \times €200)$$

$$= €500 + €70 = €570$$

The value of the levered firm is €570, which is greater than the unlevered value of €500. Because $V_L = D + E$, the value of levered equity, E, is equal to €570 − €200 = €370. The value of Divided Airlines as a function of leverage is illustrated in Figure 15.5.

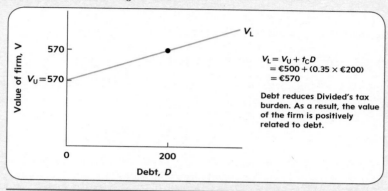

Figure 15.5 The Effect of Financial Leverage on Firm Value: MM with Corporate Taxes in the Case of Divided Airlines

Expected Return and Leverage under Corporate Taxes

MM Proposition II under no taxes posits a positive relationship between the expected return on equity and leverage. This result occurs because the risk of equity increases with leverage. The same intuition also holds in a world of corporate taxes. The exact formula in a world of corporate taxes is this:[14]

MM Proposition II (Corporate Taxes)

$$R_E = R_A + \frac{D}{E} \times (1 - t_C) \times (R_A - R_D) \tag{15.6}$$

Applying the formula to Divided Airlines, we get

$$R_E = 0.2351 = 0.20 + \frac{200}{370} \times (1 - 0.35) \times (0.20 - 0.10)$$

This calculation is illustrated in Figure 15.6.

Figure 15.6 The Effect of Financial Leverage on the Cost of Debt and Equity Capital

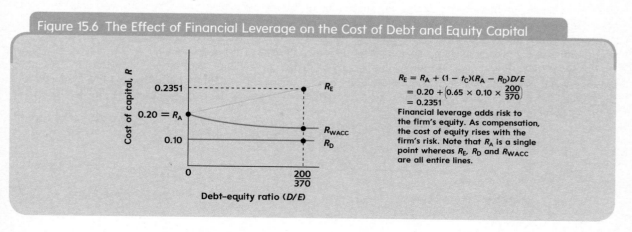

Whenever $R_A > R_D$, R_E increases with leverage, a result that we also found in the no-tax case. As stated earlier in this chapter, R_A should exceed R_D. That is, because equity (even unlevered equity) is risky, it should have an expected return greater than that on the less risky debt.

Let us check our calculations by determining the value of the levered equity in another way. The algebraic formula for the value of levered equity is

$$E = \frac{(\text{EBIT} - R_D D) \times (1 - t_C)}{R_E}$$

The numerator is the expected cash flow to levered equity after interest and taxes. The denominator is the rate at which the cash flow to equity is discounted.

For Divided Airlines we get

$$\frac{(€153.85 - 0.10 \times €200)(1 - 0.35)}{0.2351} = €370$$

which is the same result we obtained earlier (ignoring a small rounding error).

The Weighted Average Cost of Capital, R_{WACC}, and Corporate Taxes

Chapter 12
Page 315

In **Chapter 12** we defined the weighted average cost of capital (with corporate taxes) as follows (note that $V_L = D + E$):

$$R_{\text{WACC}} = \frac{E}{V_L} R_E + \frac{D}{V_L} R_D (1 - t_C)$$

Note that the cost of debt capital, R_D, is multiplied by $(1 - t_C)$ because interest is tax deductible at the corporate level. However, the cost of equity, R_E, is not multiplied by this factor because dividends are not deductible. In the no-tax case, R_{WACC} is not affected by leverage. This result is reflected in Figure 15.3, which we discussed earlier. However, because debt is tax advantaged relative to equity, it can be shown that R_{WACC} declines with leverage in a world with corporate taxes. This result can be seen in Figure 15.6.

For Divided Airlines, R_{WACC} is equal to

$$R_{\text{WACC}} = \left(\frac{370}{570} \times 0.2351\right) + \left(\frac{200}{570} \times 0.10 \times 0.65\right) = 0.1754$$

Divided Airlines has reduced its R_{WACC} from 0.20 (with no debt) to 0.1754 with reliance on debt. This result is intuitively pleasing because it suggests that when a firm lowers its R_{WACC}, the firm's value will increase. Using the R_{WACC} approach, we can confirm that the value of Divided Airlines is €570:

$$V_L = \frac{\text{EBIT} \times (1 - t_C)}{R_{\text{WACC}}} = \frac{€100}{0.1754} = €570$$

Share Prices and Leverage under Corporate Taxes

At this point students often believe the numbers – or at least are too intimidated to dispute them. However, they sometimes think we have asked the wrong question. 'Why are we choosing to maximize the value of the firm?' they will say. 'If managers are looking out for the shareholders' interest, why aren't they trying to maximize the share price?' If this question occurred to you, you have come to the right section.

Our response is twofold. First, we showed in the first section of this chapter that the capital structure that maximizes firm value is also the one that most benefits the interests of the shareholders.

However, that general explanation is not always convincing to students. As a second procedure, we calculate the share price of Divided Airlines both before and after the exchange of debt for equity. We do this by presenting a set of market value balance sheets. The market value balance sheet for the company in its all-equity form can be represented as follows:

DIVIDED AIRLINES Market Value Balance Sheet (all-equity firm)			
Physical assets		Equity	€500
$\frac{€153.85}{0.20} \times (1 - 0.35) =$	€500		(100 shares)

Assuming that there are 100 shares outstanding, each share is worth €5 = €500/100.

Next, imagine the company announces that in the near future it will issue €200 of debt to buy back €200 of equity. We know from our previous discussion that the value of the firm will rise to reflect the tax shield of debt. If we assume that capital markets efficiently price securities, the increase occurs immediately. That is, the rise occurs on the day of the announcement, not on the date of the debt-for-equity exchange. The market value balance sheet now becomes this:

DIVIDED AIRLINES Market Value Balance Sheet (upon announcement of debt issue)			
	(€)		(€)
Physical assets	500	Equity	570
			(100 shares)
Present value of tax shield:			
$t_C D = 35\% \times €200 =$	70		
Total assets	570		

Note that the debt has not yet been issued. Therefore, only equity appears on the right side of the balance sheet. Each share is now worth €570/100 = €5.70, implying that the shareholders have benefited by €70. The shareholders gain because they are the owners of a firm that has improved its financial policy.

The introduction of the tax shield to the balance sheet is perplexing to many students. Although physical assets are tangible, the ethereal nature of the tax shield bothers these students. However, remember that an asset is any item with value. The tax shield has value because it reduces the stream of future taxes. The fact that one cannot touch the shield in the way that one can touch a physical asset is a philosophical, not financial, consideration.

At some point the exchange of debt for equity occurs. Debt of €200 is issued, and the proceeds are used to buy back shares. How many shares are repurchased? Because shares are now selling at €5.70 each, the number of shares that the firm acquires is €200/€5.70 = 35.09. This leaves 64.91 (= 100 − 35.09) shares outstanding. The market value balance sheet is now this:

DIVIDED AIRLINES Market Value Balance Sheet (after exchange has taken place)			
	(€)		(€)
Physical assets	500	Equity	370
		(100 − 35.09 = 64.91 shares)	
Present value of tax shield	70	Debt	200
Total assets	570	Debt plus equity	570

Each share is worth €370/64.91 = €5.70 after the exchange. Notice that the share price does not change on the exchange date. As we mentioned, the share price moves on the date of the announcement only. Because the shareholders participating in the exchange receive a price equal to the market price per share after the exchange, they do not care whether they exchange their equity.

This example was provided for two reasons. First, it shows that an increase in the value of the firm from debt financing leads to an increase in the price of the shares. In fact, the shareholders capture the entire €70 tax shield. Second, we wanted to provide more work with market value balance sheets.

A summary of the main results of Modigliani–Miller with corporate taxes is presented in the following box.

Summary of Modigliani–Miller Propositions with Corporate Taxes

Assumptions

- Corporations are taxed at the rate t_C, on earnings after interest.
- No transaction costs.
- Individuals and corporations borrow at same rate.

Results

Proposition I: $V_L = V_U + t_C D$ (for a firm with perpetual debt)

Proposition II: $R_E = R_A + \dfrac{D}{E} \times (1 - t_C)(R_A - R_D)$

Intuition

Proposition I: Because corporations can deduct interest payments but not dividend payments, corporate leverage lowers tax payments.

Proposition II: The cost of equity rises with leverage because the risk to equity rises with leverage.

15.6 Personal Taxes

So far in this chapter, we have considered corporate taxes only. Because interest on debt is tax deductible whereas dividends on equity are not deductible, we argued that the tax system gives firms an incentive to issue debt. But corporations are not the only ones paying taxes; individuals must pay taxes on both the dividends and the interest that they receive. We cannot fully understand the effect of taxes on capital structure until all taxes, both corporate and personal, are considered.

The Basics of Personal Taxes

Let us begin by examining an all-equity firm that receives €1 of pre-tax earnings. If the corporate tax rate is t_C, the firm pays taxes t_C, leaving itself with earnings after taxes of $1 - t_C$. Let us assume that this entire amount is distributed to the shareholders as dividends. If the personal tax rate on share dividends is t_E, the shareholders pay taxes of $(1 - t_C) \times t_E$, leaving them with $(1 - t_C) \times (1 - t_E)$ after taxes.

Alternatively, imagine that the firm is financed with debt. Here, the entire €1 of earnings will be paid out as interest because interest is deductible at the corporate level. If the personal tax rate on interest is t_D, the bondholders pay taxes of t_D, leaving them with $1 - t_D$ after taxes.

The Effect of Personal Taxes on Capital Structure

To explore the effect of personal taxes on capital structure, let us consider three questions:

1. Ignoring costs of financial distress, what is the firm's optimal capital structure if dividends and interest are taxed at the same personal rate – that is, $t_E = t_D$?

   The firm should select the capital structure that gets the most cash into the hands of its investors. This is tantamount to selecting a capital structure that minimizes the total amount of taxes at both the corporate and personal levels.

   As we have said, beginning with €1 of pre-tax corporate earnings, shareholders receive $(1 - t_C) = (1 - t_E)$, and bondholders receive $1 - t_D$. We can see that if $t_E = t_D$, bondholders receive more than shareholders. Thus, the firm should issue debt, not equity, in this situation. Intuitively, income is taxed twice – once at the corporate level and once at the personal level – if it is paid to shareholders. Conversely, income is taxed only at the personal level if it is paid to bondholders.

   Note that the assumption of no personal taxes, which we used in the previous chapter, is a special case of the assumption that both interest and dividends are taxed at the same rate. Without personal taxes, the shareholders receive $1 - t_C$ while the bondholders receive £1. Thus, as we stated in a previous section, firms should issue debt in a world without personal taxes.

2. Under what conditions will the firm be indifferent between issuing equity or debt?

   The firm will be indifferent if the cash flow to shareholders equals the cash flow to bondholders. That is, the firm is indifferent when:

   $$(1 - t_C) \times (1 - t_E) = 1 - t_D \tag{15.7}$$

3. What should companies do in the real world?

   Although this is clearly an important question, it is, unfortunately, a hard one – perhaps too hard to answer definitively. Nevertheless, let us begin by working with the highest tax rates for a specific country, the UK. As of

2015, the corporate tax rate was 21 per cent. For investors in the highest tax bracket, interest income was taxed at 45 per cent. Investors in this highest bracket faced an effective 30.56 per cent tax rate on dividends.[15]

At these rates, the left side of Equation 15.7 becomes $(1 - 0.21) \times (1 - 0.3056)$, which equals 0.535. The right side of the equation becomes $1 - 0.45$, which equals 0.55. Because any rational firm would rather put £0.55 instead of £0.549 into its investors' hands, it appears at first glance that firms should prefer debt over equity, just as we argued earlier. The relative differences between debt and equity in the UK have become considerably less in recent years with changes in tax rates. However, this does not necessarily apply to other countries, where either debt or equity may have a distinct tax advantage.

Does anything else in the real world alter this conclusion? Perhaps: our discussion on equity income is not yet complete. Firms can repurchase shares with excess cash instead of paying a dividend. Although capital gains in the UK are taxed at 28 per cent (for individuals who earn more than £31,865), the shareholder pays a capital gains tax only on the gain from sale, not on the entire proceeds from the repurchase. Thus, the *effective* tax rate on capital gains is actually lower than 28 per cent. Because firms both pay dividends and repurchase shares, the effective personal tax rate on *share distributions* must be below 28 per cent.

This lower effective tax rate makes equity issuance less burdensome. For example, suppose that the effective tax rate on share distributions is 20 per cent. From every pound of pre-tax corporate income, shareholders in the UK receive $(1 - 0.21) \times (1 - 0.20)$, which equals £0.632. This amount is now more than the £0.55 that bondholders receive.

Given that bonds appear to have the tax advantage in the UK against cash dividends but not against share repurchases, does this mean that companies should issue equities and have share repurchases instead of paying dividends? It looks as if many firms have actually followed this logic with share repurchases now significantly more common than cash dividends.

There is also another reason for issuing equity instead of debt, and this is financial distress. We previously said that financial distress costs are an offset to debt's tax advantage, causing firms to employ less than 100 per cent leverage. The same point applies in the presence of personal taxes. And as long as the personal tax rate on equity income is below the personal tax rate on interest, the tax advantage to debt is smaller in a world with personal taxes than in a world without personal taxes. Thus, the optimal amount of debt will be lower in a world with personal taxes than in a world without them.

In a large scale research study of US firms, Lin and Flannery (2013) examined the impact of new tax regulation which led to a tax cut only for individual investors. They found that the tax cut reduced firm leverage by about 5 per cent, and this effect was stronger for firms with lower marginal corporate tax rates and for firms without financial constraints. This was perhaps the strongest evidence to date that personal tax does have an important impact on capital structure.

International Comparison of Tax Rates

Tax systems across the world are extremely varied and the various combinations of corporation tax, income tax and capital gains tax make a lot of the discussion on tax and capital structure very country specific. The previous section considered the UK's tax system in detail. However, this has little relevance to an Italian financial manager whose shareholders are all from Italy. A sample of country tax rates is presented in Table 15.6. However, the reader should be mindful of these figures for several reasons. First, every country's tax system is a complex set of rules that includes credits, discounts and exemptions for various taxpayer groups. The figures are effective tax rates for listed firms that will not correspond exactly to every individual's situation. Second, tax systems and tax rates change regularly. This means that some of the figures may become out of date over time (the figures are correct at February 2015). In fact, the authors fully expect these rates to change as the governments respond to changes in the global economic landscape.

Table 15.6 Tax Rates Around the World, 2015

Country	Corporation Tax (%)	Income Tax (%)	Dividend Tax (%)	Capital Gains Tax (%)
Australia	30	45	15	45% (halved if asset is held for 1 year)
Austria	25	50	25	25

Country	Corporation Tax (%)	Income Tax (%)	Dividend Tax (%)	Capital Gains Tax (%)
Bahrain	0	0	0	0
Belgium	33.99	50	25	0% (25.75% if shares sold within 1 year)
China	25	45	10	10
Denmark	24.5	55.56	0	42
Finland	20	51.25	41.76	32
France	33.33	45	30	20.5
Germany	29.58	45	25	30.5
Greece	26	42	25	15
India	33.99	33.99	0	33.99% if asset is held for less than 3 years; 20% if held for more.
Ireland	12.5	48	20	33
Italy	31.4	43	26	26
Netherlands	25	52	25	0
Norway	27	47.2	27	27
Oman	12	0	0	0
Poland	19	32	19	19
Portugal	23	48	0	20
Qatar	10	0	0	0
Romania	16	16	16	16
Russia	20	13	0	0% if asset owned for 3 years, otherwise 13%
Saudi Arabia	20	0	0	20
Singapore	17	20	0	0
Slovenia	17	50	15	25
South Africa	28	40	15	13.3
Spain	30	52	27	24; 23% from January 2016
Sweden	22	57	0	30
Switzerland	17.92	40	35	0
Tanzania	30	30	5	30
Thailand	20	35	10	35
Turkey	20	35	15	0
United Arab Emirates	55	0	0	0
United Kingdom	21	45	30.56	28
United States	40	39.6	15	20

Source: Federation of International Trade Associations, KPMG. © GlobalTrade.net

Summary and Conclusions

1. We began our discussion of the capital structure decision by arguing that the particular capital structure that maximizes the value of the firm is also the one that provides the most benefit to the shareholders.

2. In a world of no taxes, the famous Proposition I of Modigliani and Miller proves that the value of the firm is unaffected by the debt–equity ratio. In other words, a firm's capital structure is a matter of indifference in that world. The authors obtain their results by showing that either a high or a low corporate ratio of debt to equity can be offset by homemade leverage. The result hinges on the assumption that individuals can borrow at the same rate as corporations, an assumption we believe to be quite plausible.

3. MM's Proposition II in a world without taxes states that

$$R_E = R_A + \frac{D}{E}(R_A - R_D)$$

This implies that the expected rate of return on equity (also called the *cost of equity* or the *required return on equity*) is positively related to the firm's leverage. This makes intuitive sense because the risk of equity rises with leverage, a point illustrated by Figure 15.2.

4. Although the above work of MM is quite elegant, it does not explain the empirical findings on capital structure very well. MM imply that the capital structure decision is a matter of indifference, whereas the decision appears to be a weighty one in the real world. To achieve real-world applicability, we next considered corporate taxes.

5. In a world with corporate taxes but no bankruptcy costs, firm value is an increasing function of leverage. The formula for the value of the firm is

$$V_L = V_U + t_C D$$

Expected return on levered equity can be expressed as

$$R_E = R_A + (1 - t_C) \times (R_A - R_D) \times \frac{D}{E}$$

Here, value is positively related to leverage. This result implies that firms should have a capital structure almost entirely composed of debt. Because real-world firms select more moderate levels of debt, the next chapter considers modifications to the results of this chapter.

6. If distributions to shareholders are taxed at a lower effective personal tax rate than are interest payments, the tax advantage to debt at the corporate level is partially offset.

Questions and Problems

CONCEPT

1. **Capital Structure, the Pie Theory and MM** Use a pizza analogy to explain why capital structure should not influence firm value in a world with no taxes, transaction costs or financial distress costs. List three assumptions that lie behind the Modigliani–Miller theory in a world without taxes. Are these assumptions reasonable in the real world? Explain.

2. **Maximizing Firm Value versus Maximizing Shareholder Interests** Explain why, in a world with no taxes, transaction costs or financial distress costs, maximizing firm value is the same as maximizing share value. Are business risk and financial risk the same thing? If Firm A has greater business risk than Firm B, will it also have a higher cost of equity capital? Explain.

3. **Financial Leverage and Firm Value** In a world with no taxes, no transaction costs and no costs of financial distress, is the following statement true, false or uncertain? If a firm issues equity to repurchase some of its debt, the share price of the firm's equity will rise because the shares are less risky. Explain.

4   **Financial Leverage and Firm Value: An Example**   In a world with no taxes, no transaction costs, and no costs of financial distress, does moderate borrowing increase the required return on a firm's equity? Does it necessarily follow that increases in debt increase the riskiness of the firm? Explain.

5   **Corporate Taxes**   How do corporate taxes affect the Modigliani–Miller theory of capital structure? Illustrate your answer with a practical example.

6   **Personal Taxes**   Show the impact of personal taxes on the firm value in an MM universe. When would a firm be indifferent between issuing debt or equity? Illustrate your answer with a practical example.

REGULAR

7   **Return on Equity**   Explain, using an example, how a change in the capital structure of a firm can affect the company's return on equity.

8   **Capital Structure**   What is the basic goal of financial management with respect to capital structure? Is there an easily identifiable capital structure that will maximize the value of the firm? Why or why not?

9   **Return on Equity**   Mayou plc currently has no debt in its capital structure but has decided to issue new debt to replace the equity so that the debt to equity ratio is 1:1. On the firm's accounting statements, the total asset value is £120,000. Equity book and market values are the same and there are currently 300 shares outstanding. The coupon on the bonds is 10 per cent and the bond issue will be at par. Assume that there are three possible economic states: recession, expected and boom time. The earnings in each state are £8,000, £10,000 and £12,000 respectively. Estimate the return on equity of Mayou plc in each state under the original capital structure and the capital structure including debt.

10 **EBIT and Gearing**   Penybont plc is planning to raise funds to finance a major new development, and its management is considering borrowing on a long-term basis for the first time. It has been established that it is possible to borrow £600 million at an interest rate of 8 per cent to meet its funding requirements. Alternatively, it could issue 400 million shares at the prevailing market price of £1.50 through a private placement. The market has been kept informed of the company's investment plans and it is anticipated that such an issue will leave the share price unchanged. The company currently has 900 million shares outstanding, and its expected earnings before interest and tax have been estimated at £180 million.

   (a) Assuming a corporate tax rate of 30 per cent, determine the expected earnings per share of the company under both forms of financing.

   (b) Determine the level of earnings before interest and tax at which both plans will produce the same level of earnings per share.

11 **EBIT, Taxes and Leverage**   Fresenius SE & Co has no debt outstanding and a total market value of €12.68 billion. Earnings before interest and taxes (EBIT) are projected to be €2.56 billion if economic conditions are normal. If there is strong expansion in the economy, then EBIT will be 30 per cent higher. If there is a recession, then EBIT will be 60 per cent lower. Fresenius is considering a €2 billion debt issue with a 5 per cent interest rate. The proceeds will be used to repurchase shares of equity. There are currently 1 billion shares outstanding. Fresenius has a tax rate of 15 per cent.

   (a) Calculate earnings per share (EPS) under each of the three economic scenarios before any debt is issued.

   (b) Calculate the percentage changes in EPS when the economy expands or enters a recession.

12 **ROE and Leverage**   Using the information in the question above on Fresenius SE & Co, suppose Fresenius has a book value of €12.68 billion.

   (a) Calculate return on equity, ROE, under each of the three economic scenarios before any debt is issued. Also calculate the percentage changes in ROE for economic expansion and recession, assuming no taxes.

   (b) Repeat part (a) assuming the firm goes through with the proposed recapitalization.

   (c) Repeat parts (a) and (b) of this problem assuming the firm has a tax rate of 20 per cent.

13 **Break-even EBIT**   Hammerson plc is comparing two different capital structures: an all-equity plan (Plan I) and a levered plan (Plan II). Under Plan I, Hammerson would have 712 million shares of equity outstanding. Under Plan II, there would be 475 million shares of equity outstanding and £1 billion in debt outstanding. The interest rate on the debt is 5 per cent and there are no taxes.

(a) If EBIT is £459 million, which plan will result in the higher EPS?

(b) If EBIT is £80 million, which plan will result in the higher EPS?

(c) What is the break-even EBIT?

14 **MM and Share Value**   In Problem 13, use MM Proposition I to find the share price under each of the two proposed plans. What is the value of the firm?

15 **Break-even EBIT and Leverage**   Taiyuan Coal Gasification Ltd is comparing two different capital structures. Plan I would result in 1.62 billion shares of equity and 798 million yuan in debt. Plan II would result in 1 billion shares of equity and 2.1 billion yuan in debt. The interest rate on the debt is 11 per cent.

(a) Ignoring taxes, compare both of these plans to an all-equity plan assuming that EBIT will be 370 million yuan. The all-equity plan would result in 2 billion shares of equity outstanding. Which of the three plans has the highest EPS? The lowest?

(b) In part (a) what are the break-even levels of EBIT for each plan as compared to that for an all-equity plan? Is one higher than the other? Why?

(c) Ignoring taxes, when will EPS be identical for Plans I and II?

(d) Repeat parts (a), (b), and (c) assuming that the corporate tax rate is 25 per cent. Are the break-even levels of EBIT different from before? Why or why not?

16 **Leverage and Share Value**   ABC plc is comparing two different capital structures. Plan I would result in 1,100 shares of stock and €16,500 in debt. Plan II would result in 900 shares of stock and €27,500 in debt, on which it would pay interest of 8 per cent. What is the price per share of equity under Plan I? Plan II? What principle is illustrated by your answers?

17 **Homemade Leverage**   Star plc, a prominent consumer products firm, is debating whether or not to convert its all-equity capital structure to one that is 40 per cent debt. Currently there are 2,000 shares outstanding and the share price is £70. EBIT is expected to remain at £16,000 per year forever. The interest rate on new debt is 8 per cent, and there are no taxes.

(a) Ms Brown, a shareholder of the firm, owns 100 shares of equity. What is her cash flow under the current capital structure, assuming the firm has a dividend payout rate of 100 per cent?

(b) What will Ms Brown's cash flow be under the proposed capital structure of the firm? Assume that she keeps all 100 of her shares.

(c) Suppose Star does convert, but Ms Brown prefers the current all-equity capital structure. Show how she could unlever her shares to recreate the original capital structure.

(d) Using your answer to part (c), explain why Star's choice of capital structure is irrelevant.

18 **Homemade Leverage and WACC**   ABC AG and XYZ AG are identical firms in all respects except for their capital structure. ABC is all equity financed with NKr600,000 in equity shares. XYZ uses both shares and perpetual debt; its equity is worth NKr300,000 and the interest rate on its debt is 10 per cent. Both firms expect EBIT to be NKr73,000. Ignore taxes.

(a) Knut owns NKr30,000 worth of XYZ's shares. What rate of return is he expecting?

(b) Show how Knut could generate exactly the same cash flows and rate of return by investing in ABC and using homemade leverage.

(c) What is the cost of equity for ABC? What is it for XYZ?

(d) What is the WACC for ABC? For XYZ? What principle have you illustrated?

19 **MM**   Nina plc uses no debt. The weighted average cost of capital is 13 per cent. If the current market value of the equity is £35 million and there are no taxes, what is EBIT?

20 **MM and Taxes**   In the previous question, suppose the corporate tax rate is 28 per cent. What is EBIT in this case? What is the WACC? Explain.

21 **Calculating WACC**   Strade plc is an all equity financed company. The Finance Director suggested in a recent meeting with the Board of Directors a capital restructuring to introduce some debt in the company's financing to take advantage of the tax benefits of debt. With a corporate tax rate of 40 per cent, he argued that the advantages make the adjustment worthwhile. His proposal is to repurchase 30 million of the company's 100 million ordinary shares outstanding, which will be financed by an issue of debt at 8 per cent. The company's shares are currently trading at £0.75. Whilst the company has no growth prospects, it is anticipated that the company can sustain its expected earnings for the next year of £200 million before

tax indefinitely into the future. The proposal has been discussed with the company's investment bank and no problems are anticipated in its implementation.

(a)   Determine the firm's weighted average cost of capital following the restructuring.

(b)   Find the value of the geared firm.

22   **Calculating WACC**   Shadow plc has no debt but can borrow at 8 per cent. The firm's WACC is currently 12 per cent, and the tax rate is 28 per cent.

(a)   What is Shadow's cost of equity?

(b)   If the firm converts to 25 per cent debt, what will its cost of equity be?

(c)   If the firm converts to 50 per cent debt, what will its cost of equity be?

(d)   What is Shadow's WACC in part (b)? In part (c)?

23   **MM and Taxes**   Bruce & Co. expects its EBIT to be £100,000 every year forever. The firm can borrow at 10 per cent. Bruce currently has no debt, and its cost of equity is 20 per cent. If the tax rate is 21 per cent, what is the value of the firm? What will the value be if Bruce borrows £80,000 and uses the proceeds to repurchase shares?

24   **MM and Taxes**   In Problem 23, what is the cost of equity after recapitalization? What is the WACC? What are the implications for the firm's capital structure decision?

25   **MM Proposition I**   Levered plc and Unlevered plc are identical in every way except their capital structures. Each company expects to earn £96 million before interest per year in perpetuity, with each company distributing all its earnings as dividends. Levered's perpetual debt has a market value of £275 million and costs 8 per cent per year. Levered has 4.5 million shares outstanding, currently worth £100 per share. Unlevered has no debt and 10 million shares outstanding, currently worth £80 per share. Neither firm pays taxes. Is Levered's equity a better buy than Unlevered's equity?

26   **MM**   Tool Manufacturing has an expected EBIT of £35,000 in perpetuity and a tax rate of 28 per cent. The firm has £70,000 in outstanding debt at an interest rate of 9 per cent, and its unlevered cost of capital is 14 per cent. What is the value of the firm according to MM Proposition I with taxes? Should Tool change its debt–equity ratio if the goal is to maximize the value of the firm? Explain.

27   **Firm Value**   Old School Corporation expects an EBIT of £9,000 every year forever. Old School currently has no debt, and its cost of equity is 17 per cent. The firm can borrow at 10 per cent. If the corporate tax rate is 28 per cent, what is the value of the firm? What will the value be if Old School converts to 50 per cent debt? To 100 per cent debt?

28   **MM Proposition I with Taxes**   Bigelli SpA is financed entirely with equity. The company is considering a loan of €1 million. The loan will be repaid in equal instalments over the next 2 years, and it has an 8 per cent interest rate. The company's tax rate is 35 per cent. According to MM Proposition I with taxes, what would be the increase in the value of the company after the loan?

29   **MM Proposition I without Taxes**   Alpha NV and Beta NV are identical in every way except their capital structures. Alpha NV, an all-equity firm, has 5,000 shares of equity outstanding, currently worth €20 per share. Beta NV uses leverage in its capital structure. The market value of Beta's debt is €25,000, and its cost of debt is 12 per cent. Each firm is expected to have earnings before interest of €35,000 in perpetuity. Neither firm pays taxes. Assume that every investor can borrow at 12 per cent per year.

(a)   What is the value of Alpha NV?

(b)   What is the value of Beta NV?

(c)   What is the market value of Beta NV's equity?

(d)   How much will it cost to purchase 20 per cent of each firm's equity?

(e)   Assuming each firm meets its earnings estimates, what will be the euro return to each position in part (d) over the next year?

(f)   Construct an investment strategy in which an investor purchases 20 per cent of Alpha's equity and replicates both the cost and dollar return of purchasing 20 per cent of Beta's equity.

(g)   Is Alpha's equity more or less risky than Beta's equity? Explain.

30   **Cost of Capital**   Acetate SA has equity with a market value of €20 million and debt with a market value of €10 million. Treasury bills that mature in one year yield 8 per cent per year, and the expected return on the market portfolio over the next year is 18 per cent. The beta of Acetate's equity is 0.90. The firm pays no taxes.

(a) What is Acetate's debt–equity ratio?

(b) What is the firm's weighted average cost of capital?

(c) What is the cost of capital for an otherwise identical all-equity firm?

31 **Homemade Leverage** The Veblen Company and the Knight Company are identical in every respect except that Veblen is not levered. The market value of Knight Company's 6 per cent bonds is SKr1 million. Financial information for the two firms appears here. All earnings streams are perpetuities. Neither firm pays taxes. Both firms distribute all earnings available to ordinary shareholders immediately.

	Veblen (SKr)	Knight (SKr)
Projected operating income	300,000	300,000
Year-end interest on debt	—	60,000
Market value of stock	2,400,000	1,714,000
Market value of debt	—	1,000,000

(a) An investor who can borrow at 6 per cent per year wishes to purchase 5 per cent of Knight's equity. Can he increase his Krona return by purchasing 5 per cent of Veblen's equity if he borrows so that the initial net costs of the two strategies are the same?

(b) Given the two investment strategies in (a), which will investors choose? When will this process cease?

32 **MM Propositions** Locomotive plc is planning to repurchase part of its ordinary share equity by issuing corporate debt. As a result, the firm's debt–equity ratio is expected to rise from 40 per cent to 50 per cent. The firm currently has £7.5 million worth of debt outstanding. The cost of this debt is 10 per cent per year. Locomotive expects to have an EBIT of £3.75 million per year in perpetuity. Locomotive pays no taxes.

(a) What is the market value of Locomotive plc before and after the repurchase announcement?

(b) What is the expected return on the firm's equity before the announcement of the share repurchase plan?

(c) What is the expected return on the equity of an otherwise identical all-equity firm?

(d) What is the expected return on the firm's equity after the announcement of the share repurchase plan?

33 **Share Value and Leverage** Green Manufacturing plc plans to announce that it will issue £2 million of perpetual debt and use the proceeds to repurchase equity. The bonds will sell at par with a 6 per cent annual coupon rate. Green is currently an all-equity firm worth £10 million with 500,000 shares of equity outstanding. After the sale of the bonds, Green will maintain the new capital structure indefinitely. Green currently generates annual pre-tax earnings of €1.5 million. This level of earnings is expected to remain constant in perpetuity. Green is subject to a corporate tax rate of 28 per cent.

(a) What is the expected return on Green's equity before the announcement of the debt issue?

(b) Construct Green's market value balance sheet before the announcement of the debt issue. What is the price per share of the firm's equity?

(c) Construct Green's market value balance sheet immediately after the announcement of the debt issue.

(d) What is Green's share price immediately after the repurchase announcement?

(e) How many shares will Green repurchase as a result of the debt issue? How many shares of equity will remain after the repurchase?

(f) Construct the market value balance sheet after the restructuring.

(g) What is the required return on Green's equity after the restructuring?

34 **MM with Taxes** Williamsen GmbH has a debt–equity ratio of 2.5. The firm's weighted average cost of capital is 15 per cent, and its pre-tax cost of debt is 10 per cent. Williamsen is subject to a corporate tax rate of 35 per cent.

(a) What is Williamsen's cost of equity capital?

(b) What is Williamsen's unlevered cost of equity capital?

(c) What would Williamsen's weighted average cost of capital be if the firm's debt–equity ratio were 0.75? What if it were 1.5?

CHALLENGE

35 **Weighted Average Cost of Capital** In a world of corporate taxes only, show that the R_{WACC} can be written as $R_{WACC} = R_A \times [1 - t_C (B/V)]$.

36 **Cost of Equity and Leverage**   Assuming a world of corporate taxes only, show that the cost of equity, R_S, is as given in the chapter by MM Proposition II with corporate taxes.

37 **Business and Financial Risk**   Assume a firm's debt is risk-free, so that the cost of debt equals the risk-free rate, R_f. Define β_A as the firm's *asset* beta – that is, the systematic risk of the firm's assets. Define β_S to be the beta of the firm's equity. Use the capital asset pricing model, CAPM, along with MM Proposition II to show that $\beta_E = \beta_A \times (1 + D/E)$, where D/E is the debt–equity ratio. Assume the tax rate is zero.

38 **Shareholder Risk**   Suppose a firm's business operations mirror movements in the economy as a whole very closely – that is, the firm's asset beta is 1.0. Use the result of the previous problem to find the equity beta for this firm for debt–equity ratios of 0, 1, 5 and 20. What does this tell you about the relationship between capital structure and shareholder risk? How is the shareholders' required return on equity affected? Explain.

39 **Unlevered Cost of Equity**   Beginning with the cost of capital equation – that is:

$$R_{\text{WACC}} = \frac{E}{D + E} R_E + \frac{D}{D + E} R_D$$

show that the cost of equity capital for a levered firm can be written as follows:

$$R_E = R_A + \frac{D}{E}(R_A - R_D)$$

Exam Question (45 minutes)

Sapphire is an all-equity financed company, which is valued at €250 million. The firm's shares are expected to produce a return of 15 per cent. The company has decided to modify its capital structure to capture the tax benefits of debt. The plan is to have a target debt/equity ratio of 25 per cent. The company has been told that any borrowings made by them will attract a rate of 7 per cent.

1 Calculate the return on equity of Sapphire before and after the restructuring. (20 marks)

2 Write a brief report to the management of Sapphire explaining why the return on equity has changed as a result of restructuring. (20 marks)

3 What is meant by gearing? How does gearing affect the financial risk of a firm? (20 marks)

4 Assume that the corporate tax rate is 35 per cent, capital gains tax is zero and the personal income tax rate is 45 per cent. What is the value of Sapphire before the restructuring? What is its value after? (20 marks)

5 What would the personal rate of tax on interest income have to be to push the tax advantage of debt to zero? (20 marks)

Mini Case

Stephenson Real Estate Recapitalization

Stephenson Real Estate was founded 25 years ago by the current CEO, Robert Stephenson. The company purchases real estate, including land and buildings, and rents the property to tenants. The company has shown a profit every year for the past 18 years, and the shareholders are satisfied with the company's management. Prior to founding Stephenson Real Estate, Robert was the founder and CEO of a failed sheep farming operation. The resulting bankruptcy made him extremely averse to debt financing. As a result, the company is entirely equity financed, with 15 million shares outstanding. The shares currently trade at £32.50 per share.

Stephenson is evaluating a plan to purchase a huge tract of land in south-eastern England for £100 million. The land will subsequently be leased to tenant farmers. This purchase is expected to increase Stephenson's annual pre-tax earnings by £25 million in perpetuity. Kim Weyand, the company's new CFO, has been put in charge of the project. Kim has determined that the company's current cost of capital is 12.5 per cent. She feels that the company would be more valuable if it included debt in its capital structure, so she is evaluating whether the company should issue debt to entirely finance the project. Based on some conversations with investment banks, she thinks that the company can issue bonds at par value with an 8 per cent coupon rate. Based on her analysis, she also believes that a capital structure in the range of 70 per cent equity/30 per cent debt would be optimal. If the company goes beyond 30 per cent debt, its bonds would carry a lower rating and a much higher coupon because the possibility of financial distress and the associated costs would rise sharply. Stephenson has a 28 per cent corporate tax rate.

1   If Stephenson wishes to maximize its total market value, would you recommend that it issue debt or equity to finance the land purchase? Explain.

2   Construct Stephenson's market value balance sheet before it announces the purchase.

3   Suppose Stephenson decides to issue equity to finance the purchase.

   (a)   What is the net present value of the project?

   (b)   Construct Stephenson's market value balance sheet after it announces that the firm will finance the purchase using equity. What would be the new price per share of the firm's equity? How many shares will Stephenson need to issue to finance the purchase?

   (c)   Construct Stephenson's market value balance sheet after the equity issue but before the purchase has been made. How many shares of equity does Stephenson have outstanding? What is the price per share of the firm's equity?

   (d)   Construct Stephenson's market value balance sheet after the purchase has been made.

4   Suppose Stephenson decides to issue debt to finance the purchase.

   (a)   What will be the market value of the Stephenson company if the purchase is financed with debt?

   (b)   Construct Stephenson's market value balance sheet after both the debt issue and the land purchase. What is the price per share of the firm's equity?

5   Which method of financing maximizes the per-share price of Stephenson's equity?

Practical Case Study

1   Locate the annual balance sheets for the British firms, Thomson Reuters plc, Capita Group plc, and Next plc. For each company calculate the long-term debt–equity ratio for the prior 2 years. Why would these companies use such different capital structures?

2   Download the annual income statements for Marks and Spencer plc. For the most recent year, calculate the average tax rate and EBIT, and find the total interest expense. From the annual balance sheets calculate the total long-term debt (including the portion due within one year). Using the interest expense and total long-term debt, calculate the average cost of debt. Next, find the estimated beta for Marks and Spencer on the Yahoo! Finance website. Use this reported beta, a current T-bill rate for the UK, and the historical average market risk premium found in a previous chapter to calculate the levered cost of equity. Now calculate the unlevered cost of equity, then the unlevered EBIT. What is the unlevered value of Marks and Spencer? What is the value of the interest tax shield and the value of the levered Marks and Spencer?

References

Lin, L. and M.J. Flannery (2013) 'Do Personal Taxes Affect Capital Structure? Evidence from the 2003 Tax Cut', *Journal of Financial Economics*, Vol. 109, No. 2, 549–565.

Miles, J.A. and J.R. Ezzel (1980) 'The Weighted Average Cost of Capital, Perfect Capital Markets and Project

Life', *Journal of Financial and Quantitative Analysis*, Vol. 15, No. 3, 719–730.

Modigliani, F. and M. Miller (1958) 'The Cost of Capital, Corporation Finance and the Theory of Investment', *American Economic Review*, Vol. 48, 261–297.

Additional Reading

If you wish to delve deeper into the theory of capital structure and how it affects corporate strategy, you should read:

1   Hillier, D., M. Grinblatt and S. Titman (2012) *Financial Markets and Corporate Strategy: European Edition*, 2nd edn (McGraw-Hill).

An excellent paper that looks at the determinants of capital structure in a number of different countries is given below. The paper should also be read as part of your reading for Chapter 2 on macro-governance and Chapter 16.

2   Antoniou, A., Y. Guney and K. Paudyal (2008) 'The Determinants of Capital Structure: Capital Market-Oriented versus Bank-Oriented Institutions', *Journal*

of Financial and Quantitative Analysis, Vol. 43, No. 1, 59–92. **International**.

The following paper considers a multinational firm's capital structure when there are different country taxes. It is a theoretical paper but tests this on European firms.

3   Huizinga, H., L. Laeven and G. Nicodeme (2008) 'Capital Structure and International Debt Shifting', *Journal of Financial Economics*, Vol. 88, No. 1, 80–118.

Another paper of interest is given below:

4   De Jong, A., R. Kabir and T.T. Nguyen (2008) 'Capital Structure around the World: The Roles of Firm- and Country-specific Determinants', *Journal of Banking and Finance*, Vol. 32, No. 9, 1954–1969.

Endnotes

1   This result may not hold exactly in a more complex case where debt has a significant possibility of default. Issues of default are treated in the next chapter.

2   The original paper is Modigliani and Miller (1958).

3   We are ignoring the one-day interest charge on the loan.

4   Because we do not have taxes here, the cost of debt is R_D, not $R_D(1 - t_C)$ as it was in Chapter 12.

5   This statement holds in a world of no taxes. It does not hold in a world with taxes, a point to be brought out later in this chapter (see Figure 15.6).

6   This statement holds in a world of no taxes. It does not hold in a world with taxes, a point to be brought out later in this chapter (see Figure 15.6).

7   This can be derived from Equation 15.2 by setting $R_{WACC} = R_A$, yielding

$$\frac{D}{D + E} R_D + \frac{E}{D + E} R_E = R_A$$

Multiplying both sides by $(D + E)/E$ yields

$$\frac{D}{E} R_D + R_E = \frac{D + E}{E} R_A$$

We can rewrite the right side as

$$\frac{D}{E} R_D + R_E = \frac{D}{E} R_A + R_A$$

Moving $(D/E) R_D$ to the right side and rearranging yields

$$R_E = R_A + \frac{D}{E} (R_A - R_D)$$

8   Both Merton Miller and Franco Modigliani were awarded separate Nobel Prizes, in part for their work on capital structure.

9   MM were aware of both of these issues, as can be seen in their original paper (Modigliani and Miller, 1958).

10 Under the MM propositions developed earlier, the two pies should be of the same size.

11 Note that shareholders actually receive more under Plan I (€650,000) than under Plan II (€390,000). Students are often bothered by this because it seems to imply that they are better off without leverage. However, remember that there are more shares outstanding in Plan I than in Plan II. A full-blown model would show that earnings *per share* are higher with leverage.

12 This relationship holds when the debt level is assumed to be constant through time. A different formula would apply if the debt–equity ratio was assumed to be a non-constant over time. For a deeper treatment of this point, see Miles and Ezzel (1980).

13 The following example calculates the present value if we assume the debt has a finite life. Suppose Maxwell plc has £1 million in debt with an 8 per cent coupon rate. If the debt matures in 2 years and the cost of debt capital, R_D, is 10 per cent, what is the present value of the tax shields if the corporate tax rate is 28 per cent? The debt is amortized in equal instalments over 2 years.

Year	Loan Balance (£)	Interest (£)	Tax Shield (£)	Present Value of Tax Shield (£)
0	1,000,000			
1	500,000	80,000	0.28 × 80,000	22,400
2	0	40,000	0.28 × 40,000	11,200
				33,600

The present value of the tax saving is

$$PV = \frac{0.28 \times £80{,}000}{1.10} + \frac{0.28 \times £80{,}000}{(1.10)^2} = £33{,}600$$

Maxwell plc's value is higher than that of a comparable unlevered firm by £33,600.

14 This relationship can be shown as follows: Given MM Proposition I under taxes, a levered firm's market value balance sheet can be written as:

V_U = Value of unlevered firm	D = Debt
$t_C D$ = Tax shield	E = Equity

The value of the unlevered firm is simply the value of the assets without benefit of leverage. The balance sheet indicates that the firm's value increases by $t_C D$ when debt of D is added. The expected cash flow *from* the left side of the balance sheet can be written as

$$V_U R_A + t_C D R_D \qquad (a)$$

Because assets are risky, their expected rate of return is R_A. The tax shield has the same risk as the debt, so its expected rate of return is R_D.

The expected cash *to* bondholders and shareholders together is

$$E R_E + D R_D \qquad (b)$$

Expression (b) reflects the fact that equity earns an expected return of R_E and debt earns the interest rate R_D.

Because all cash flows are paid out as dividends in our no-growth perpetuity model, the cash flows going into the firm equal those going to shareholders. Hence (a) and (b) are equal:

$$E R_E + D R_E = V_U R_A + t_C D R_D \qquad (c)$$

Dividing both sides of (c) by E, subtracting $D R_D$ from both sides, and rearranging yields

$$R_E = \frac{V_U}{E} \times R_A - (1 - t_C) \times \frac{D}{E} R_D \qquad (d)$$

Because the value of the levered firm, V_L, equals $V_U + t_C D = D + E$, it follows that $V_U = E + (1 - t_C) \times D$. Thus (d) can be rewritten as

$$R_E = \frac{E + (1 - t_C) \times D}{E} \times R_A - (1 - t_C) \times \frac{D}{E} R_D \qquad (e)$$

Bringing the terms involving $(1 - t_C) \times (D/E)$ together produces Equation 15.6.

15 The UK dividend tax rate is fairly complex and uses tax credits to augment payments. To summarize, for the year 2015, there are three basic dividend tax rates. If total taxable income is below £41,865, the tax rate on dividend income is 10 per cent. If taxable income is between £41,865 and £150,000, the tax rate on dividend income is 32.5 per cent. Higher earners have a tax rate on dividend income of 37.5 per cent. All taxpayers receive a dividend tax credit of 10 per cent on dividend income. Dividend income is the sum of the original dividend plus the tax credit. This means that the effective rate of dividend tax is significantly lower at 0 per cent, 25 per cent and 30.56 per cent for the three taxable income bands, respectively. An example will help to illustrate the calculation.

Three individuals, A, B and C, are paid a dividend of £100. A is in the lower tax bracket, B is in the middle tax bracket and C is in the upper tax bracket. Dividend calculations are given in the table below:

	A	B	C
Dividend	£100	£100	£100
Dividend income (£100/(1−10%))	£111.11	£111.11	£111.11
Tax credit	£11.11	£11.11	£11.11
Dividend tax rate	10%	32.5%	37.5%
Tax charged	£11.11	£36.11	£41.67
Tax paid (Tax charged − Tax credit)	£0	£25	£30.56
Effective tax rate (Tax paid/Dividend)	0%	25%	30.56%

Capital Structure: Limits to the Use of Debt

Although the use of debt brings benefits in the form of tax shields, there are dangers from having too much debt. Take Italy's flagship airline, Alitalia, which despite having government support never made a profit in any year between 2009 and 2015, when it was purchased by Etihad Airways. Basically, Alitalia's debt of €900 million meant that every year they were paying out a large portion of their revenues in the form of interest, and as a result, the debt and interest payments had effectively crippled the airline making it unsustainable.

As the Alitalia situation suggests, financial leverage has a number of drawbacks and there is a limit to the financial leverage a company can bear. The risk of too much leverage is bankruptcy. Chapter 29 covers bankruptcy law and the turnaround strategies that firms follow once they are in financial distress. In this chapter, we discuss the costs associated with bankruptcies and how companies attempt to avoid this process.

KEY NOTATIONS

E	Market value of equity
D	Market value of debt
V	Market value of firm
EBIT	Earnings before interest and taxes

16.1 Costs of Financial Distress

Bankruptcy Risk or Bankruptcy Cost?

Chapter 29
Page 794

Debt puts pressure on the firm because interest and principal payments are obligations. If these obligations are not met, the firm may risk some sort of financial distress. The ultimate distress is *bankruptcy*, where ownership of the firm's assets is legally transferred from the shareholders to the bondholders (financial distress is covered in a lot more detail in **Chapter 29**). These debt obligations are fundamentally different from equity obligations. Although shareholders like and expect dividends, they are not legally entitled to them in the way bondholders are legally entitled to interest and principal payments.

We show next that bankruptcy costs, or more generally financial distress costs, tend to offset the advantages to debt. We begin by positing a simple example of bankruptcy. All taxes are ignored to focus only on the costs of debt.

16.2 Description of Financial Distress Costs

Example 16.1 shows that bankruptcy costs can lower the value of the firm. In fact, the same general result holds even if a legal bankruptcy is prevented. Thus *financial distress costs* may be a better phrase than *bankruptcy costs*. It is worthwhile to describe these costs in more detail.

Example 16.1

Bankruptcy Costs

Knight NV plans to be in business for one more year. It forecasts a cash flow of either €100 or €50 in the coming year, each occurring with 50 per cent probability. The firm has no other assets. Previously issued debt requires payments of €49 of interest and principal. Day NV has identical cash flow prospects but has €60 of interest and principal obligations. The cash flows of these two firms can be represented as follows:

	Knight NV		Day NV	
	Boom Times (prob. 50%) (€)	Recession (prob. 50%) (€)	Boom Times (prob. 50%) (€)	Recession (prob. 50%) (€)
Cash flow	100	50	100	50
Payment of interest and principal on debt	49	49	60	50
Distribution to shareholders	51	1	40	0

For Knight NV in both boom times and recession and for Day NV in boom times, cash flow exceeds interest and principal payments. In these situations the bondholders are paid in full, and the shareholders receive any residual. However, the most interesting of the four columns involves Day NV in a recession. Here the bondholders are owed €60, but the firm has only €50 in cash. Because we assumed that the firm has no other assets, the bondholders cannot be satisfied in full. If bankruptcy occurs, the bondholders will receive all of the firm's cash, and the shareholders will receive nothing. Importantly, the shareholders do not have to come up with the additional €10 (= €60 − €50). Corporations have limited liability in Europe and most other countries, implying that bondholders cannot sue the shareholders for the extra €10.[1]

We assume that (1) both bondholders and shareholders are risk-neutral, and (2) the interest rate is 10 per cent. Due to this risk neutrality, cash flows to both shareholders and bondholders are to be discounted at the 10 per cent rate.[2] We can evaluate the debt, the equity and the entire firm for both Knight and Day as follows:

$$E_{\text{KNIGHT}} = \text{€}23.64 = \frac{\text{€}51 \times \frac{1}{2} \times \text{€}1 \times \frac{1}{2}}{1.10} \qquad E_{\text{DAY}} = \text{€}18.18 = \frac{\text{€}40 \times \frac{1}{2} \times 0 \times \frac{1}{2}}{1.10}$$

$$D_{\text{KNIGHT}} = \text{€}44.54 = \frac{\text{€}49 \times \frac{1}{2} \times \text{€}49 \times \frac{1}{2}}{1.10} \qquad D_{\text{DAY}} = \text{€}50 = \frac{\text{€}60 \times \frac{1}{2} \times \text{€}50 \times \frac{1}{2}}{1.10}$$

$$V_{\text{KNIGHT}} = \overline{\text{€}68.18} \qquad\qquad V_{\text{DAY}} = \overline{\text{€}68.18}$$

Note that the two firms have the same value, even though Day runs the risk of bankruptcy. Furthermore, notice that Day's bondholders are valuing the bonds with 'their eyes open'. Though the promised payment of principal and interest is €60, the bondholders are willing to pay only €50. Hence their *promised* return or yield is:

$$\frac{\text{€}60}{\text{€}50} - 1 = 20\%$$

Day's debt can be viewed as a *junk bond* because the probability of default is so high. As with all junk bonds, Day's bondholders demand a high promised yield.

Day's example is not realistic because it ignores an important cash flow to be discussed next. A more realistic set of numbers might be these:

	Day NV			
	Boom Times (prob. 50%) (€)	Recession (prob. 50%) (€)		
Earnings	100	50	$E_{DAY} = \text{€}18.18 =$	$\dfrac{\text{€}40 \times \frac{1}{2} + 0 \times \frac{1}{2}}{1.10}$
Debt repayment	60	35	$D_{DAY} = \text{€}43.18 =$	$\dfrac{\text{€}60 \times \frac{1}{2} + \text{€}35 \times \frac{1}{2}}{1.10}$
Distribution to stockholders	$\overline{40}$	$\overline{0}$	$V_{DAY} = \overline{\text{€}61.36}$	

Why do the bondholders receive only €35 in a recession? If cash flow is only €50, bondholders will be informed that they will not be paid in full. These bondholders are likely to hire lawyers to negotiate or even to sue the company. Similarly, the firm is likely to hire lawyers to defend itself. Further costs will be incurred if the case gets to a bankruptcy court. These fees are always paid before the bondholders get paid. In this example, we are assuming that bankruptcy costs total €15 (= €50 − 35).

The value of the firm is now €61.36, an amount below the €68.18 figure calculated earlier. By comparing Day's value in a world with no bankruptcy costs to Day's value in a world with these costs, we conclude the following:

The possibility of bankruptcy has a negative effect on the value of the firm. However, it is not the *risk* of bankruptcy itself that lowers value. Rather it is the costs associated with bankruptcy that lower value.

The explanation follows from our pie example. In a world without bankruptcy costs, the bondholders and the shareholders share the entire pie. However, bankruptcy costs eat up some of the pie in the real world, leaving less for the shareholders and bondholders.

Because the bondholders are aware that they would receive little in a recession, they pay the low price of €43.18. In this case, their promised return is:

$$\frac{\text{€}60}{\text{€}43.18} - 1 = 39.0\%$$

The bondholders are paying a fair price if they are realistic about both the probability and the cost of bankruptcy. It is the *shareholders* who bear these future bankruptcy costs. To see this, imagine that Day NV was originally all equity. The shareholders want the firm to issue debt with a promised payment of €60 and use the proceeds to pay a dividend. If there had been no bankruptcy costs, our results show that bondholders would pay €50 to purchase debt with a promised payment of €60. Hence, a dividend of €50 could be paid to the shareholders. However, if bankruptcy costs exist, bondholders would only pay €43.18 for the debt. In that case, only a dividend of €43.18 could be paid to the shareholders. Because the dividend is smaller with bankruptcy costs, the shareholders are hurt by these costs.

Direct Costs of Financial Distress: Legal and Administrative Costs of Liquidation or Reorganization

As mentioned earlier, lawyers are involved throughout all the stages before and during bankruptcy. With fees often in the hundreds of pounds or euros an hour, these costs can add up quickly. Someone once remarked that bankruptcies are to lawyers what blood is to sharks. In addition, administrative and accounting fees can substantially add to the total bill. If a trial takes place, we must not forget expert witnesses. Each side may hire a number of these witnesses to testify about the fairness of a proposed settlement and their fees can easily rival those of lawyers or accountants.

Real World Insight 16.1

Lehman Brothers Bankruptcy

The largest ever bankruptcy concerned Lehman Brothers, at the time one of the biggest banks in the world. This bankruptcy followed large write-downs on subprime mortgage assets and a general collapse in interbank credit in September 2008. Estimates vary on the total cost of the bank's collapse but a conservative estimate is around $2 billion, and it is very likely to be much higher. According to Lehman Brothers' official documentation, the total fees that were paid to administrators, lawyers and other parties amounted to $1.05 billion within just two years of the bankruptcy. Given its enormous size, the bankruptcy affected nearly every country in Europe and the cost of winding up Lehman's European subsidiaries was almost as high at $900 million. These are just the direct costs. The total (direct and indirect) costs of the bankruptcy will have been astronomical once the company's demise is considered more broadly in terms of impacting the local community and the wider financial sector.

A number of academic studies have measured the direct costs of financial distress. Although large in absolute amount, these costs are actually small as a percentage of firm value. Warner and White (1983), Altman (1984) and Weiss (1990) estimate the direct costs of financial distress to be about 3 per cent of the market value of the firm. Bris et al. (2006) find that direct costs are about 8 per cent of pre-bankruptcy assets. However, since the costs are fixed, irrespective of the size of the firm, the proportional costs can be between 20 and 25 per cent for smaller firms.[3]

Of course, few firms end up in bankruptcy. Thus, the preceding cost estimates must be multiplied by the probability of bankruptcy to yield the *expected* cost of bankruptcy. For example, consider a firm that has a 5 per cent probability of going into bankruptcy each year. If the firm declares bankruptcy, the direct costs it incurs amount to 8 per cent of the total value of the firm. The *expected* bankruptcy cost must be then 0.4 per cent ($= 0.05 \times 0.08$).

Indirect Costs of Financial Distress

Impaired Ability to Conduct Business

Bankruptcy hampers conduct with customers and suppliers. Sales are frequently lost because of both fear of impaired service and loss of trust. For example, in 2015, Japan's third largest airline, Skymark, announced that it filed for bankruptcy because of excessive debt and a potential €680 million compensation bill to Airbus for a cancelled airplane order. Although the company was still operating during bankruptcy, many potential customers refused to use the airline because of doubts that the firm would be able to service flights in the future.

Though indirect costs clearly exist, it is quite difficult to measure them. Altman (1984) estimates that both direct and indirect costs of financial distress are frequently greater than 20 per cent of firm value. Andrade and Kaplan (1998) estimate total distress costs to be between 10 per cent and 20 per cent of firm value. Bar-Or (2000) estimates expected future distress costs for firms that are currently healthy to be 8–10 per cent of operating value, a number below the estimates of either Altman or Andrade and Kaplan. However, unlike Bar-Or, these authors consider distress costs for firms already in distress, not expected distress costs for currently healthy firms.

Agency Costs

When a firm has debt, conflicts of interest arise between shareholders and bondholders. Because of this, shareholders are tempted to pursue selfish strategies. These conflicts of interest, which are magnified when financial distress is incurred, impose agency costs on the firm. We describe three kinds of selfish strategies that shareholders use to hurt the bondholders and help themselves. These strategies are costly because they will lower the market value of the whole firm.

Selfish Investment Strategy 1: Incentive to Take Large Risks

Firms near bankruptcy often take great chances because they believe that they are playing with someone else's money. To see this, imagine a levered firm considering two *mutually exclusive* projects, a low-risk one and a high-risk one. There are two equally likely outcomes, recession and boom. The firm is in such dire straits that should a recession hit, it will come near to bankruptcy with one project and actually fall into bankruptcy with the other. The cash flows for the entire firm if the low-risk project is taken can be described as follows:

	Value of Entire Firm if Low-Risk Project is Chosen					
	Probability	Value of Firm (£)	=	Shares (£)	+	Bonds (£)
Recession	0.5	100	=	0	+	100
Boom	0.5	200	=	100	+	100

If recession occurs, the value of the firm will be £100; if a boom occurs, the value of the firm will be £200. The expected value of the firm is £150 (= 0.5 × £100 + 0.5 × £200).

The firm has promised to pay bondholders £100. Shareholders will obtain the difference between the total pay-off and the amount paid to the bondholders. In other words, the bondholders have the prior claim on the pay-offs, and the shareholders have the residual claim.

Now suppose that the riskier project can be substituted for the low-risk project. The pay-offs and probabilities are as follows:

	Value of Entire Firm if High-Risk Project is Chosen					
	Probability	Value of Firm (£)	=	Shares (£)	+	Bonds (£)
Recession	0.5	50	=	0	+	50
Boom	0.5	240	=	140	+	100

The expected value of the *firm* is £145 (= 0.5 × £50 + 0.5 × £240), which is lower than the expected value of the firm with the low-risk project. Thus the low-risk project would be accepted if the firm were all equity. However, note that the expected value of the *equity* is £70 (= 0.5 × 0 + 0.5 × £140) with the high-risk project, but only £50 (= 0.5 × 0 + 0.5 × £100) with the low-risk project. Given the firm's present levered state, shareholders will select the high-risk project, even though the high-risk project has a *lower* NPV.

The key is that relative to the low-risk project, the high-risk project increases firm value in a boom and decreases firm value in a recession. The increase in value in a boom is captured by the shareholders because the bondholders are paid in full (they receive £100) regardless of which project is accepted. Conversely, the drop in value in a recession is lost by the bondholders because they are paid in full with the low-risk project but receive only £50 with the high-risk one. The shareholders will receive nothing in a recession anyway, whether the high-risk or low-risk project is selected. Thus, financial economists argue that shareholders expropriate value from the bondholders by selecting high-risk projects.

Selfish Investment Strategy 2: Incentive toward Underinvestment

Shareholders of a firm with a significant probability of bankruptcy often find that new investment helps the bondholders at the shareholders' expense. The simplest case might be a property owner facing imminent bankruptcy. If he took €100,000 out of his own pocket to refurbish the building, he could increase the building's value by, say, €150,000. Though this investment has a positive net present value, he will turn it down if the increase in value cannot prevent bankruptcy. 'Why,' he asks, 'should I use my own funds to improve the value of a building that the bank will soon repossess?'

This idea is formalized by the following simple example. Consider the firm in Table 16.1, which must decide whether to accept or reject a new project. The first two columns in the table show cash flows without the project. The firm receives cash inflows of £5,000 and £2,400 under a boom and a recession, respectively. Because the firm must pay principal and interest of £4,000, the firm will default in a recession.

Table 16.1 Example Illustrating Incentive to Underinvest

	Firm without Project		Firm with Project Costing £1,000	
	Boom (£)	Recession (£)	Boom (£)	Recession (£)
Firm cash flows	5,000	2,400	6,700	4,100
Bondholders' claim	4,000	2,400	4,000	4,000
Shareholders' claim	1,000	0	2,700	100

The project has positive NPV. However, much of its value is captured by bondholders. Rational managers, acting in the shareholders' interest, will reject the project.

Alternatively, as indicated in the next two columns of the table, the firm could raise equity to invest in a new project. The project brings in £1,700 in either state, which is enough to prevent bankruptcy even in a recession. Because £1,700 is much greater than the project's cost of £1,000, the project has a positive NPV at any plausible interest rate. Clearly, an all-equity firm would accept the project.

However, the project hurts the shareholders of the levered firm. To see this, imagine the old shareholders contribute the £1,000 *themselves*.[4] Assuming that a boom and a recession are equally likely, the expected value of the shareholders' interest without the project is £500 (= 0.5 × £1,000 + 0.5 × 0). The expected value with the project is £1,400 (= 0.5 × £2,700 + 0.5 × £100). The shareholders' interest rises by only £900 (= £1,400 − £500) while costing £1,000.

Why does a project with a positive NPV hurt the shareholders? The key is that the shareholders contribute the full £1,000 investment, but the shareholders and bondholders *share* the benefits. The shareholders take the entire gain if boom times occur. Conversely, the bondholders reap most of the cash flow from the project in a recession.

The discussion of selfish strategy 1 is quite similar to the discussion of selfish strategy 2. In both cases, an investment strategy for the levered firm is different from the one for the unlevered firm. Thus, leverage results in distorted investment policy. Whereas the unlevered corporation always chooses projects with positive net present value, the levered firm may deviate from this policy.

Selfish Investment Strategy 3: Milking the Property

Another strategy is to pay out extra dividends or other distributions in times of financial distress, leaving less in the firm for the bondholders. This is known as *milking the property*, a phrase taken from real estate. Strategies 2 and 3 are very similar. In Strategy 2, the firm chooses not to raise new equity. Strategy 3 goes one step further because equity is actually withdrawn through the dividend.

Summary of Selfish Strategies

The distortions just discussed occur only when there is a probability of bankruptcy or financial distress. Thus, these distortions *should not* affect, say, Vodafone because bankruptcy is not a realistic possibility for a diversified blue-chip firm such as this. In other words, Vodafone's debt will be virtually risk-free, regardless of the projects it accepts. The same argument could be made for nationalized banks, such as the Royal Bank of Scotland, that are protected by the government. By contrast, small firms in risky industries, such as computers, are more likely to experience financial distress and, in turn, to be affected by such distortions.

Who pays for the cost of selfish investment strategies? We argue that it is ultimately the shareholders. Rational bondholders know that when financial distress is imminent, they cannot expect help from shareholders. Rather, shareholders are likely to choose investment strategies that reduce the value of the bonds. Bondholders protect themselves accordingly by raising the interest rate that they require on the bonds. Because the shareholders must pay these high rates, they ultimately bear the costs of selfish strategies. For firms that face these distortions, debt will be difficult and costly to obtain. These firms will have low leverage ratios.

The relationship between shareholders and bondholders is very similar to the relationship between Erroll Flynn and David Niven, good friends and film stars in the 1930s. Niven reportedly said that the good thing about Flynn was that you knew exactly where you stood with him. When you needed his help, you could always count on him to let you down.

16.3   Can Costs of Debt Be Reduced?

Chapter 20
Page 541

Each of the costs of financial distress we have mentioned is substantial in its own right. The sum of them may well affect debt financing severely. Thus, managers have an incentive to reduce these costs. We now turn to some of their methods. However, it should be mentioned at the outset that the methods here can, at most, reduce the costs of debt. They cannot *eliminate* them entirely (check out **Chapter 20** to find out more about the process of raising debt financing).

Protective Covenants

Because shareholders must pay higher interest rates as insurance against their own selfish strategies, they frequently make agreements with bondholders in the hope of lower rates. These agreements, called protective covenants, are incorporated as part of the loan document (or *indenture*) between shareholders and bondholders. The covenants must be taken seriously because a broken covenant can lead to default. Protective covenants can be classified into two types: negative covenants and positive covenants.

A negative covenant limits or prohibits actions that the company may take. Here are some typical negative covenants:

1   Limitations are placed on the amount of dividends a company may pay.
2   The firm may not pledge any of its assets to other lenders.
3   The firm may not merge with another firm.
4   The firm may not sell or lease its major assets without approval by the lender.
5   The firm may not issue additional long-term debt.

A positive covenant specifies an action that the company agrees to take or a condition the company must abide by. Here are some examples:

1   The company agrees to maintain its working capital at a minimum level.
2   The company must furnish periodic financial statements to the lender.

These lists of covenants are not exhaustive. The authors have seen loan agreements with more than 30 covenants.

Smith and Warner (1979) examined public issues of debt and found that 91 per cent of the bond indentures included covenants that restricted the issuance of additional debt, 23 per cent restricted dividends, 39 per cent restricted mergers, and 36 per cent limited the sale of assets. Qi et al. (2011) consider foreign bond issuance in the US and provide evidence which highlights the importance of a country's creditor rights. Firms that come from countries with stronger creditor rights have fewer bond indentures.

With this in mind, protective covenants should reduce the costs of bankruptcy, ultimately increasing the value of the firm. Thus, shareholders are likely to favour all reasonable covenants. To see this, consider three choices by shareholders to reduce bankruptcy costs:

1   *Issue no debt.* Because of the tax advantages to debt, this is a very costly way of avoiding conflicts.
2   *Issue debt with no restrictive and protective covenants.* In this case, bondholders will demand high interest rates to compensate for the unprotected status of their debt.
3   *Write protective and restrictive covenants into the loan contracts.* If the covenants are clearly written, the creditors may receive protection without large costs being imposed on the shareholders. The creditors will gladly accept a lower interest rate.

Thus, bond covenants, even if they reduce flexibility, can increase the value of the firm. They can be the lowest-cost solution to the shareholder–bondholder conflict. A list of typical bond covenants and their uses appears in Table 16.2.

Table 16.2 Loan Covenants

Shareholder Action or Firm Circumstances	Covenant Type	Reason for Covenant
As firm approaches financial distress, shareholders may want firm to make high-risk investments.	Financial statement restrictions 1 Minimum working capital 2 Minimum interest coverage 3 Minimum net worth	High-risk investments transfer value from bondholders to shareholders when financial distress is a realistic possibility. Covenants reduce probability of financial distress.
Shareholders may attempt to transfer corporate assets to themselves.	Restrictions on asset disposition 1 Limit on dividends 2 Limit on sale of assets 3 Collateral and mortgages	Covenants limit the ability of shareholders to transfer assets to themselves and to *underinvest*.
Shareholders may attempt to increase risk of firm.	Restrictions on switching assets	Increased firm risk helps shareholders and hurts bondholders.
Shareholders may attempt to issue new debt of equal or greater priority.	Dilution restrictions 1 Limit on leasing 2 Limit on further borrowing	Covenants restrict dilution of the claim of existing bondholders.

Consolidation of Debt

One reason bankruptcy costs are so high is that different creditors (and their lawyers) contend with each other. This problem can be alleviated by proper arrangement of bondholders and shareholders. For example, perhaps one, or at most a few, lenders can shoulder the entire debt. Should financial distress occur, negotiating costs are minimized under this arrangement. In addition, bondholders can purchase equity as well. In this way, shareholders and debtholders are not pitted against each other because they are not separate entities. This appears to be the approach in Japan, where large banks generally take significant equity positions in the firms to which they lend money.[5]

16.4 Integration of Tax Effects and Financial Distress Costs

Chapter 15
Page 396

Modigliani and Miller argue that the firm's value rises with leverage in the presence of corporate taxes (the impact of taxation on capital structure was introduced in **Chapter 15**, Sections 15.6 and 15.7). Because this relationship implies that all firms should choose maximum debt, the theory does not predict the behaviour of firms in the real world. Other authors have suggested that bankruptcy and related costs reduce the value of the levered firm.

The integration of tax effects and distress costs appears in Figure 16.1. In the top graph of the figure, the diagonal straight line represents the value of the firm in a world without bankruptcy costs. The hump-shaped curve represents the value of the firm with these costs. This curve rises as the firm moves from all equity to a small amount of debt. Here, the present value of the distress costs is minimal because the probability of distress is so small. However, as more and more debt is added, the present value of these costs rises at an *increasing* rate. At some point, the increase in the present value of these costs from an additional unit of debt equals the increase in the present value of the tax shield. This is the debt level maximizing the value of the firm and is represented by D^* in Figure 16.1. In other words, D^* is the optimal amount of debt. Bankruptcy costs increase faster than the tax shield beyond this point, implying a reduction in firm value from further leverage.

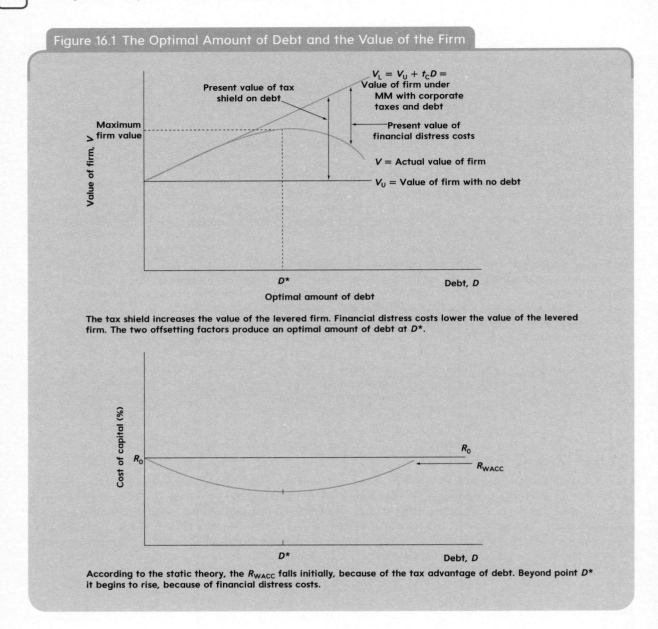

Figure 16.1 The Optimal Amount of Debt and the Value of the Firm

The tax shield increases the value of the levered firm. Financial distress costs lower the value of the levered firm. The two offsetting factors produce an optimal amount of debt at D*.

According to the static theory, the R_{WACC} falls initially, because of the tax advantage of debt. Beyond point D* it begins to rise, because of financial distress costs.

In the bottom graph of Figure 16.1, the weighted average cost of capital (R_{WACC}) falls as debt is added to the capital structure. After reaching D* the weighted average cost of capital rises. The optimal amount of debt produces the lowest weighted average cost of capital.

Our discussion implies that a firm's capital structure decision involves a trade-off between the tax benefits of debt and the costs of financial distress. In fact, this approach is frequently called the *trade-off* or the *static trade-off* theory of capital structure. The implication is that there is an optimal amount of debt for any individual firm. This amount of debt becomes the firm's target debt level. Because financial distress costs cannot be expressed in a precise way, no formula has yet been developed to determine a firm's optimal debt level exactly. However, the last section of this chapter offers some rules of thumb for selecting a debt–equity ratio in the real world.

Pie Again

Now that we have considered bankruptcy costs, let us return to the pie approach of the previous chapter. The cash flows of the firm go to four different claimants: shareholders, bondholders, the government (in the form of taxes) and, during the bankruptcy process, lawyers (and others). Algebraically, we must have:

$$\text{CF} = \text{Payments to shareholders}$$
$$+$$
$$\text{Payments to bondholders}$$
$$+$$
$$\text{Payments to the government}$$
$$+$$
$$\text{Payments to lawyers (and others)}$$

It follows that the total value of the firm, V_T, equals the sum of the following four components:

$$V_T = E + D + G + L$$

where E is the value of the equity, D is the value of the bonds, G is the value of the government claims from taxes, and L stands for the value that lawyers and others receive when the firm is under financial distress. This relationship is illustrated in Figure 16.2.

Nor have we even begun to exhaust the list of financial claims to the firm's cash flows. To give an unusual example, everyone reading this book has an economic claim to the cash flows of Mercedes-Benz. After all, if you are injured in an accident, you might sue Mercedes-Benz. Win or lose, Mercedes-Benz will expend resources dealing with the matter. If you think this is farfetched and unimportant, ask yourself what Mercedes-Benz might be willing to pay every man, woman and child in the world to have them promise that they would never sue Mercedes-Benz, no matter what happened. The law does not permit such payments, but that does not mean that a value to all of those potential claims does not exist. We guess that it would run into the billions of euros, and, for Mercedes-Benz or any other company, there should be a slice of the pie labelled LS for 'potential lawsuits'.

Figure 16.2 illustrates the essence of MM's intuition. While V_T is determined by the firm's cash flows, the firm's capital structure merely cuts V_T into slices. Capital structure does *not* affect the total value, V_T.

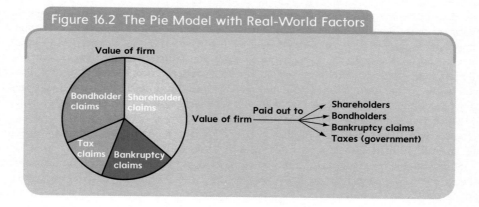

Figure 16.2 The Pie Model with Real-World Factors

There is, however, a difference between claims such as those of shareholders and bondholders on the one hand and those of government and potential litigants in lawsuits on the other. The first set of claims are marketable claims, and the second set are non-marketable claims. Marketable claims can be bought and sold in financial markets, and the non-marketable claims cannot. This distinction between marketable and non-marketable claims is important. When equity is issued, shareholders pay cash to the firm for the privilege of later receiving dividends. Similarly, bondholders pay cash to the firm for the privilege of receiving interest in the future. However, the government pays nothing to the firm for the privilege of receiving taxes in the future. Similarly, lawyers pay nothing to the firm for the privilege of receiving fees from the firm in the future.

When we speak of the *value of the firm*, we are referring just to the value of the marketable claims, V_M, and not the value of non-marketable claims, V_N. What we have shown is that capital structure does not affect the total value:

$$V_T = E + D + G + L$$
$$= V_M - V_N$$

But as we saw, the value of the marketable claims, V_M, can change with changes in the capital structure.

By the pie theory, any increase in V_M must imply an identical decrease in V_N. Rational financial managers will choose a capital structure to maximize the value of the marketable claims, V_M. Equivalently, rational managers will work to minimize the value of the non-marketable claims, V_N. These are taxes and bankruptcy costs in the previous example, but they also include all the other non-marketable claims such as the potential lawsuits, LS, claim.

16.5   Signalling

The previous section pointed out that the corporate leverage decision involves a trade-off between a tax subsidy and financial distress costs. This idea was graphed in Figure 16.1, where the marginal tax subsidy of debt exceeds the distress costs of debt for low levels of debt. The reverse holds for high levels of debt. The firm's capital structure is optimized where the marginal subsidy to debt equals the marginal cost.

Let us explore this idea a little more. What is the relationship between a company's profitability and its debt level? A firm with low anticipated profits will likely take on a low level of debt. A small interest deduction is all that is needed to offset all of this firm's pre-tax profits. And too much debt would raise the firm's expected distress costs. A more successful firm would probably take on more debt. This firm could use the extra interest to reduce the taxes from its greater earnings. Being more financially secure, this firm would find its extra debt increasing the risk of bankruptcy only slightly. In other words, rational firms raise debt levels (and the concomitant interest payments) when profits are expected to increase.

How do investors react to an increase in debt? Rational investors are likely to infer a higher firm value from a higher debt level. Thus, these investors are likely to bid up a firm's share price after the firm has, say, issued debt in order to buy back equity. We say that investors view debt as a *signal* of firm value.

Now we get to the incentives of managers to fool the public. Consider a firm whose level of debt is optimal. That is, the marginal tax benefit of debt exactly equals the marginal distress costs of debt. However, imagine that the firm's manager desires to increase the firm's current share price, perhaps because he knows that many of his shareholders want to sell their equity soon. This manager might want to increase the level of debt just to make investors *think* that the firm is more valuable than it really is. If the strategy works, investors will push up the price of the shares.

This implies that firms can fool investors by taking on *some* additional leverage. Now let us ask the big question. Are there benefits to extra debt but no costs, implying that all firms will take on as much debt as possible? The answer, fortunately, is that there are costs as well. Imagine that a firm has issued extra debt just to fool the public. At some point, the market will learn that the company is not that valuable after all. At this time the share price should actually fall *below* what it would have been had the debt never been increased. Why? Because the firm's debt level is now above the optimal level. That is, the marginal tax benefit of debt is below the marginal cost of debt. Thus if the current shareholders plan to sell, say, half of their shares now and retain the other half, an increase in debt will help them on immediate sales but likely hurt them on later ones.

Now here is the important point. We said that in a world where managers do not attempt to fool investors, valuable firms issue more debt than less valuable ones. It turns out that even when managers attempt to fool investors, the more valuable firms will still want to issue more debt than the less valuable firms. That is, while all firms will increase debt levels somewhat to fool investors, the costs of extra debt prevent the less valuable firms from issuing more debt than the more valuable firms issue. Thus, investors can still treat debt level as a signal of firm value. In other words, investors can still view an announcement of debt as a positive sign for the firm.

The foregoing is a simplified example of debt signalling, and you might argue that it is too simplified. For example, perhaps the shareholders of some firms want to sell most of their equity immediately, whereas the shareholders of other firms want to sell only a little of theirs now. It is impossible to tell here whether the firms with the most debt are the most valuable or merely the ones with the most impatient shareholders. Because other objections can be brought up as well, signalling theory is best validated by empirical evidence. And fortunately, the empirical evidence tends to support the theory.

For example, consider the evidence concerning exchange offers. Firms often change their debt levels through exchange offers, of which there are two types. The first type of offer allows shareholders to exchange some of their equity for debt, thereby increasing leverage. The second type allows bondholders to exchange some of their debt for equity, decreasing leverage. Figure 16.3 shows the share price behaviour of firms that change their proportions of debt and equity via exchange offers. The solid line in the figure indicates that share prices rise substantially on the date when an exchange offering increasing leverage is announced. (This date is referred to as date 0 in the figure.) Conversely, the dotted line in the figure indicates that the share price falls substantially when an offer decreasing leverage is announced.

Figure 16.3 Equity Returns at the Time of Announcements of Exchange Offers

Exchange offers change the debt–equity ratios of firms. The graph shows that share prices increase for firms whose exchange offers increase leverage. Conversely, share prices decrease for firms whose offers decrease leverage.

Source: Shah (1994).

The market infers from an increase in debt that the firm is better off, leading to a share price rise. Conversely, the market infers the reverse from a decrease in debt, implying a share price fall. Thus, we say that managers signal information when they change leverage.

16.6 Shirking, Perquisites and Bad Investments: A Note on Agency Cost of Equity

Chapter 2
Page 25

A previous section introduced the static trade-off model, where a rise in debt increases both the tax shield and the costs of distress. We now extend the trade-off model by considering an important agency cost of equity (agency costs are first introduced in **Chapter 2**, Section 2.2). A discussion of this cost of equity is contained in a well-known quote from Adam Smith:

The directors of such [joint-stock] companies, however, being the managers of other people's money than of their own, it cannot well be expected that they should watch over it with the same anxious vigilance with which the partners in a private copartnery frequently watch over their own. Like the stewards of a rich man, they are apt to consider attention to small matters as not for their master's honor, and very easily give themselves a dispensation from having it. Negligence and profusion, therefore, must always prevail, more or less, in the management of the affairs of such a company.[6]

This elegant prose can be restated in modern vocabulary. An individual will work harder for a firm if she is one of its owners than if she is just an employee. In addition, the individual will work harder if she owns a large percentage of the company than if she owns a small percentage. This idea has an important implication for capital structure, which we illustrate with the following example.

Example 16.2

Agency Costs

Ms Wolfe is an owner–entrepreneur running a computer services firm worth £1 million. She currently owns 100 per cent of the firm. Because of the need to expand, she must raise another £2 million. She can either issue £2 million of debt at 12 per cent interest or issue £2 million in equity. The cash flows under the two alternatives are presented here:

	Debt Issue				Equity Issue			
Work Intensity	Cash Flow (£)	Interest (£)	Cash Flow to Equity (£)	Cash Flow to Ms Wolfe (100% of Equity) (£)	Cash Flow (£)	Interest (£)	Cash Flow to Equity (£)	Cash Flow to Ms Wolfe (33⅓% of equity) (£)
6-hour days	300,000	240,000	60,000	60,000	300,000	0	300,000	100,000
10-hour days	400,000	240,000	160,000	160,000	400,000	0	400,000	133,333

Like any entrepreneur, Ms Wolfe can choose the degree of intensity with which she works. In our example, she can work either a 6- or a 10-hour day. With the debt issue, the extra work brings her £100,000 (= £160,000 − £60,000) more income. However, let us assume that with an equity issue she retains only a one-third interest in the equity. Here, the extra work brings her merely £33,333 (= £133,333 − £100,000). Being human, she is likely to work harder if she issues debt. In other words, she has more incentive to *shirk* if she issues equity.

In addition, she is likely to obtain more *perquisites* (a big office, a company car, more expense account meals) if she issues equity. If she is a one-third shareholder, two-thirds of these costs are paid for by the other shareholders. If she is the sole owner, any additional perquisites reduce her equity stake alone.

Finally, she is more likely to take on capital budgeting projects with negative net present values. It might seem surprising that a manager with any equity interest at all would take on negative NPV projects: the share price would clearly fall here. However, managerial salaries generally rise with firm size, providing managers with an incentive to accept some unprofitable projects after all the profitable ones have been taken on. That is, when an unprofitable project is accepted, the loss in share value to a manager with only a small equity interest may be less than the increase in salary. In fact, it is our opinion that losses from accepting bad projects are far greater than losses from either shirking or excessive perquisites. Hugely unprofitable projects have bankrupted whole firms, something that even the largest expense account is unlikely to do.

Thus, as the firm issues more equity, our entrepreneur will likely increase leisure time, work-related perquisites and unprofitable investments. These three items are called *agency costs* because managers of the firm are agents of the shareholders.[7]

This example is quite applicable to a small company considering a large equity offering. Because a manager–owner will greatly dilute his or her share of the total equity in this case, a significant drop in work intensity or a significant increase in fringe benefits is possible. However, the example may be less applicable for a large corporation with many shareholders. For example, consider a large company such as ICI issuing shares for the umpteenth time. The typical manager there already has such a small percentage stake in the firm that any temptation for negligence has probably been experienced before. An additional offering cannot be expected to increase this temptation.

Who bears the burden of these agency costs? Shareholders do not bear these costs as long as they invest with their eyes open. Knowing that Ms Wolfe may work shorter hours, they will pay only a low price for the equity. Thus, it is the owner who is hurt by agency costs. However, Ms Wolfe can protect herself to some extent. Just as shareholders reduce bankruptcy costs through protective covenants, an owner may allow monitoring by new shareholders. However, though proper reporting and surveillance may reduce the agency costs of equity, these techniques are unlikely to eliminate them.

It is commonly suggested that leveraged buyouts (LBOs) significantly reduce these costs of equity. In an LBO, a purchaser (usually a team of existing management) buys out the shareholders at a price above the current market. In other words, the company goes private: the equity is placed in the hands of only a few people. Because the managers now own a substantial chunk of the business, they are likely to work harder than when they were simply hired hands.

Effect of Agency Costs of Equity on Debt–Equity Financing

The preceding discussion of the agency costs of equity should be viewed as an extension of the static trade-off model. That is, we stated in Section 16.4 that the change in the value of the firm when debt is substituted for equity is the difference between (1) the tax shield on debt and (2) the increase in the costs of financial distress (including the agency costs of debt). Now the change in the value of the firm is (1) the tax shield on debt, plus (2) the reduction in the agency costs of equity, minus (3) the increase in the costs of financial distress (including the agency costs of debt). The optimal debt–equity ratio would be higher in a world with agency costs of equity than in a world without these costs. However, because costs of financial distress are so significant, the costs of equity do not imply 100 per cent debt financing.

Free Cash Flow

Any reader of murder mysteries knows that a criminal must have both motive and opportunity. The discussion thus far has been about motive. Managers with only a small ownership interest have an incentive for wasteful behaviour. For example, they bear only a small portion of the costs of, say, excessive expense accounts, and they reap all of the benefits.

Now let us talk about opportunity. A manager can pad his expense account only if the firm has the cash flow to cover it. Thus, we might expect to see more wasteful activity in a firm with a capacity to generate large cash flows than in one with a capacity to generate only small cash flows. This simple idea, which is formally called the *free cash flow hypothesis*,[8] is backed by a fair amount of empirical research. For example, a frequently cited paper found that firms with high free cash flow are more likely to make bad acquisitions than firms with low free cash flow (Lang et al., 1989).

The hypothesis has important implications for capital structure. Since dividends leave the firm, they reduce free cash flow. Thus, according to the free cash flow hypothesis, an increase in dividends should benefit the shareholders by reducing the ability of managers to pursue wasteful activities. Furthermore, since interest and principal also leave the firm, debt reduces free cash flow as well. In fact, interest and principal should have a greater effect than dividends have on the free-spending ways of managers, because bankruptcy will occur if the firm is unable to make future debt payments. By contrast, a future dividend reduction will cause fewer problems to the managers, since the firm has no legal obligation to pay dividends. Because of this, the free cash flow hypothesis argues that a shift from equity to debt will boost firm value.

In summary, the free cash flow hypothesis provides still another reason for firms to issue debt. We previously discussed the cost of equity; new equity dilutes the holdings of managers with equity interests, increasing their *motive* to waste corporate resources. We now state that debt reduces free cash flow, because the firm must make interest and principal payments. The free cash flow hypothesis implies that debt reduces the *opportunity* for managers to waste resources.

16.7 The Pecking Order Theory

Although the trade-off theory has dominated corporate finance circles for a long time, attention has also been paid to the *pecking order theory*.[9] To understand this view of the world, let us put ourselves in the position of a corporate finance manager whose firm needs new capital. The manager faces a choice between issuing debt and issuing equity. Previously, we evaluated the choice in terms of tax benefits, distress costs and agency costs. However, there is one consideration that we have so far neglected: timing.

Imagine the manager saying:

> *I want to issue equity in one situation only – when it is overvalued. If the equity of my firm is selling at £50 per share, but I think that it is actually worth £60, I will not issue equity. I would actually be giving new shareholders a gift because they would receive equity worth £60 but would only have to pay £50 for it. More important, my current shareholders would be upset because the firm would be receiving £50 in cash but giving away something worth £60. So if I believe that my equity is undervalued, I would issue bonds. Bonds, particularly those with little or no risk of default, are likely to be priced correctly. Their value is determined primarily by the marketwide interest rate, a variable that is publicly known.*
>
> *But suppose our equity is selling at £70. Now I'd like to issue equity. If I can get some fool to buy our shares for £70 while the equity is really worth only £60, I will be making £10 for our current shareholders.*

Although this may strike you as a cynical view, it seems to square well with reality. For example, managers seem more willing to issue equity after the price of their shares has risen than after their shares have fallen in price. So timing might be an important motive in equity issuance, perhaps even more important than the motives in the trade-off model. After all, the firm in the preceding example *immediately* makes £10 by properly timing the issuance of equity. £10 worth of agency costs and bankruptcy cost reduction might take many years to realize.

The key that makes the example work is *asymmetric information:* the manager must know more about his firm's prospects than does the typical investor. If the manager's estimate of the true worth of the company is no better than the estimate of a typical investor, any attempts by the manager to time the market will fail. This assumption of asymmetry is quite plausible. Managers should know more about their company than do outsiders because managers work at the company every day. (One caveat is that some managers are perpetually optimistic about their firm, blurring good judgement.)

But we are not done with this example yet; we must consider the investor. Imagine an investor saying:

> I make investments carefully because they involve my hard-earned money. However, even with all the time I put into studying shares, I can't possibly know what the managers themselves know. After all, I've got a day job to be concerned with. So I watch what the managers do. If a firm issues equity, the firm was likely overvalued beforehand. If a firm issues debt, it was likely undervalued.

When we look at both issuers and investors, we see a kind of poker game, with each side trying to outwit the other. What should the issuing firm do in this poker game? Clearly, the firm should issue debt if the equity is undervalued. But what if the equity is overvalued? Here it gets tricky because a first thought is that the firm should issue equity. However, if a firm issues equity, investors will infer the shares are overvalued. They will not buy them until the share price has fallen enough to eliminate any advantage from equity issuance. In fact, it can be shown that only the most overvalued firms have any incentive to issue equity. Should even a moderately overpriced firm issue equity, investors will infer that this firm is among the *most* overpriced, causing the shares to fall more than is deserved. Thus, the end result is that virtually no one will issue equity.[10]

This result that essentially all firms should issue debt is clearly an extreme one. It is as extreme as (1) the Modigliani–Miller (MM) result that in a world without taxes, firms are indifferent to capital structure, and (2) the MM result that in a world of corporate taxes but no financial distress costs, all firms should be 100 per cent debt-financed. Perhaps we in finance have a penchant for extreme models!

But just as we can temper MM's conclusions by combining financial distress costs with corporate taxes, we can temper those of the pure pecking order theory. This pure version assumes that timing is the financial manager's only consideration. In reality, a manager must consider taxes, financial distress costs and agency costs as well. Thus, a firm may issue debt only up to a point. If financial distress becomes a real possibility beyond that point, the firm may issue equity instead.

Rules of the Pecking Order

The previous discussion presented the basic ideas behind the pecking order theory. What are the practical implications of the theory for financial managers? The theory provides the following two rules for the real world.

Rule 1: Use Internal Financing

For expository purposes, we have oversimplified by comparing equity to *riskless* debt. Managers cannot use special knowledge of their firm to determine if this type of debt is mispriced because the price of riskless debt is determined solely by the marketwide interest rate. However, in reality, corporate debt has the possibility of default. Thus, just as managers tend to issue equity when they think it is overvalued, managers also tend to issue debt when they think it is overvalued.

When would managers view their debt as overvalued? Probably in the same situations when they think their equity is overvalued. For example, if the public thinks that the firm's prospects are rosy but the managers see trouble ahead, these managers would view their debt – as well as their equity – as being overvalued. That is, the public might see the debt as nearly risk-free, whereas the managers see a strong possibility of default.

Thus, investors are likely to price a debt issue with the same scepticism that they have when pricing an equity issue. The way managers get out of this box is to finance projects out of retained earnings. You do not have to worry about investor scepticism if you can avoid going to investors in the first place. So the first rule of the pecking order is this:

Use internal financing.

Rule 2: Issue Safe Securities First

Although investors fear mispricing of both debt and equity, the fear is much greater for equity. Corporate debt still has relatively little risk compared to equity because if financial distress is avoided, investors receive a fixed return. Thus, the pecking order theory implies that if outside financing is required, debt should be issued before equity. Only when the firm's debt capacity is reached should the firm consider equity.

Of course, there are many types of debt. For example, because convertible debt is more risky than straight debt, the pecking order theory implies that managers should issue straight debt before issuing convertibles. So, the second rule of pecking order theory is this:

Issue the safest securities first.

Implications

A number of implications associated with the pecking order theory are at odds with those of the trade-off theory.

1 *There is no target amount of leverage.* According to the trade-off model, each firm balances the benefits of debt, such as the tax shield, with the costs of debt, such as distress costs. The optimal amount of leverage occurs where the marginal benefit of debt equals the marginal cost of debt.

   By contrast, the pecking order theory does not imply a target amount of leverage. Rather, each firm chooses its leverage ratio based on financing needs. Firms first fund projects out of retained earnings. This should lower the percentage of debt in the capital structure because profitable, internally funded projects raise both the book value and the market value of equity. Additional projects are funded with debt, clearly raising the debt level. However, at some point the debt capacity of the firm may be exhausted, giving way to equity issuance. Thus, the amount of leverage is determined by the happenstance of available projects. Firms do not pursue a target ratio of debt to equity.

2 *Profitable firms use less debt.* Profitable firms generate cash internally, implying less need for outside financing. Because firms desiring outside capital turn to debt first, profitable firms end up relying on less debt. The trade-off model does not have this implication. Here the greater cash flow of more profitable firms creates greater debt capacity. These firms will use that debt capacity to capture the tax shield and the other benefits of leverage.

3 *Companies like financial slack.* The pecking order theory is based on the difficulties of obtaining financing at a reasonable cost. A sceptical investing public thinks an equity is overvalued if the managers try to issue more of it, thereby leading to a share price decline. Because this happens with bonds only to a lesser extent, managers rely first on bond financing. However, firms can only issue so much debt before encountering the potential costs of financial distress.

Wouldn't it be easier to have the cash ahead of time? This is the idea behind *financial slack*. Because firms know that they will have to fund profitable projects at various times in the future, they accumulate cash today. They are then not forced to go to the capital markets when a project comes up. However, there is a limit to the amount of cash a firm will want to accumulate. As mentioned earlier in this chapter, too much free cash may tempt managers to pursue wasteful activities.

16.8   Growth and the Debt–Equity Ratio

Although the trade-off between the tax shield and bankruptcy costs (as illustrated in Figure 16.1) is often viewed as the 'standard model' of capital structure, it has its critics. For example, some point out that bankruptcy costs in the real world appear to be much smaller than the tax subsidy. Thus, the model implies that the optimal debt/value ratio should be near 100 per cent, an implication at odds with reality.[11]

Perhaps the pecking order theory is more consistent with the real world here. That is, firms are likely to have more equity in their capital structure than implied by the static trade-off theory because internal financing is preferred to external financing.

**Chapter 5
Page 129**

There is another approach that implies significant equity financing, even in a world with low bankruptcy costs. This idea, developed by Berens and Cuny (1995), argues that equity financing follows from growth (the effect of growth on equity valuation is discussed in **Chapter 5**, Section 5.5). To explain the idea, we first consider an example of a no-growth firm. Next, we examine the effect of growth on firm leverage.

No Growth

Imagine a world of perfect certainty[12] where a firm has annual earnings before interest and taxes (EBIT) of €100. In addition, the firm has issued €1,000 of debt at an interest rate of 10 per cent, implying interest payments of €100 per year. Here are the cash flows to the firm:

	Date			
	1 **(€)**	**2** **(€)**	**3** **(€)**	**4 . . .** **(€)**
Earnings before interest and taxes (EBIT)	100	100	100	100 . . .
Interest	−100	−100	−100	−100 . . .
Taxable income	0	0	0	0

The firm has issued just enough debt so that all EBIT are paid out as interest. Because interest is tax deductible, the firm pays no taxes. In this example, the equity is worthless because shareholders receive no cash flows. Since debt is worth €1,000, the firm is also valued at €1,000. Therefore the debt-to-value ratio is 100 per cent (= €1,000/€1,000).

Had the firm issued less than €1,000 of debt, the corporation would have positive taxable income and, consequently, would have ended up paying some taxes. Had the firm issued more than €1,000 of debt, interest would have exceeded EBIT, causing default. Consequently, the optimal debt-to-value ratio is 100 per cent.

Growth

Now imagine another firm where EBIT are also €100 at date 1 but are growing at 5 per cent per year.[13] To eliminate taxes, this firm also wants to issue enough debt so that interest equals EBIT. Because EBIT are growing at 5 per cent per year, interest must also grow at this rate. This is achieved by increasing debt by 5 per cent per year.[14] The debt, EBIT, interest and taxable income levels are these:

	Date				
	0 **(€)**	**1** **(€)**	**2** **(€)**	**3** **(€)**	**4 . . .** **(€)**
Debt	1,000	1,050	1,102.50	1,157.63 . . .	
New debt issued		50	52.50	55.13 . . .	
EBIT		100	105	110.25	115.76 . . .
Interest		−100	−105	−110.25	−115.76 . . .
Taxable income		0	0	0	0

Note that interest on a particular date is always 10 per cent of the debt on the previous date. Debt is set so that interest is exactly equal to EBIT. As in the no-growth case, the levered firm has the maximum amount of debt at each date. Default would occur if interest payments were increased.

Because growth is 5 per cent per year, the value of the firm is:[15]

$$V_{\text{Firm}} = \frac{€100}{0.10 - 0.05} = €2,000$$

The equity at date 0 is the difference between the value of the firm at that time, €2,000, and the debt of €1,000. Hence, equity must be equal to €1,000,[16] implying a debt-to-value ratio of 50 per cent (= €1,000/€2,000). Note the important difference between the no-growth and the growth example. The no-growth example has no equity; the value of the firm is simply the value of the debt. With growth, there is equity as well as debt.

We can also value the equity in another way. It may appear at first glance that the shareholders receive nothing because the EBIT are paid out as interest each year. However, the new debt issued each year can be paid as a dividend to the shareholders. Because the new debt is €50 at date 1 and grows at 5 per cent per year, the value of the shareholders' interest is:

$$\frac{€50}{0.10 - 0.05} = €1,000$$

which is the same number that we obtained in the previous paragraph.

As we mentioned earlier, any further increase in debt above €1,000 at date 0 would lower the value of the firm in a world with bankruptcy costs. Thus, with growth, the optimal amount of debt is less than 100 per cent. Note, however, that bankruptcy costs need not be as large as the tax subsidy. In fact, even with infinitesimally small bankruptcy costs, firm value would decline if promised interest rose above €100 in the first year. The key to this example is that *today's* interest is set equal to *today's* income. Although the introduction of future growth opportunities increases firm value, it does not increase the current level of debt needed to shield today's income from today's taxes. Because equity is the difference between firm value and debt, growth increases the value of equity.

The preceding example captures an essential feature of the real world: growth. The same conclusion is reached in a world of inflation but with no growth opportunities. Thus, the result of this section, that 100 per cent debt financing is suboptimal, holds whether inflation or growth opportunities are present. Furthermore, high-growth firms should have lower debt ratios than low-growth firms. Most firms have growth opportunities and inflation has been with us for most of this and the previous centuries, so this section's example is based on realistic assumptions.[17]

16.9 Market Timing Theory

In recent years, a new view of capital structure has come to the fore that believes leverage ratios have nothing to do with a pecking order or optimal capital structure. The view, which was originally put forward by Baker and Wurgler (2002), suggests that differentials between market and book valuations drive capital structure levels in firms. For example, if a firm requires funding during a period when its market value to book value ratio is high, it is more likely to raise equity. Similarly, in low market to book value periods, debt is likely to be the funding vehicle of choice. This has a permanent effect on capital structures that have nothing to do with bankruptcy costs or pecking orders.

The pecking order theory also puts forward a timing motivation for funding choices. However, this theory argues that asymmetric information between managers and outside shareholders drives managers to always issue debt before equity, whenever it is possible to do so. Market timing theory disagrees and states that asymmetric information is irrelevant. Managers simply take advantage of market conditions when they decide to raise capital.

Capital structure is one area (of many!) in which finance academics are divided and there are supporters in each of the three camps (trade-off, pecking order and market timing). So how does the empirical evidence stack up? Fama and French (2002) showed that leverage ratios took too long to move back to mean levels after markets received a shock. This would indicate that, over the short term at least, there is no target capital structure. Similarly, Welch (2003) finds that companies tend to issue shares when market valuations are high. In contrast, Kayhan and Titman (2007) show that over the longer term, capital structures do move towards a target level. Finally, Lemmon and Zender (2010) show that profitable and low leverage firms accumulate debt capacity for potential future investment needs.

Finally, almost all research has only examined US securities and very little work comparing the validity of the three theories has focused on Europe or the rest of the world. Given the institutional and ownership differences between the US and the rest of the world, it is possible that the relationship between financing decisions and managerial behaviour will be different.

16.10 How Firms Establish Capital Structure

The theories of capital structure are among the most elegant and sophisticated in the field of finance. Financial economists should (and do!) pat themselves on the back for contributions in this area. However, the practical applications of the theories are less than fully satisfying. Consider that our work on net present value produced an *exact* formula for evaluating projects. Prescriptions for capital structure under either the trade-off model, the pecking order theory, or market timing are vague by comparison. No exact formula is available for evaluating the optimal debt–equity ratio. Because of this, we turn to evidence from the real world.

The following empirical regularities are worthwhile to consider when formulating capital structure policy.

1   *Most corporations have low debt–asset ratios.* How much debt is used in the real world? The average debt ratio is never greater than 100 per cent. Figure 16.4 shows the debt-to-market value of the firm ratios of firms in different countries in recent years. The main thing to notice is that there is quite a lot of variation in the debt ratios.

Should we view these ratios as being high or low? Because academics generally see corporate tax reduction as the chief motivation for debt, we might wonder if real-world companies issue enough debt to greatly reduce, if not downright eliminate, corporate taxes. The empirical evidence suggests that this is not the case. For example, corporate taxes in the United Kingdom for 2011 were just over £42 billion. Thus, it is clear that corporations do not issue debt up to the point where tax shelters are completely used up. There are clearly limits to the amount of debt corporations can issue, perhaps because of the financial distress costs discussed earlier in this chapter.

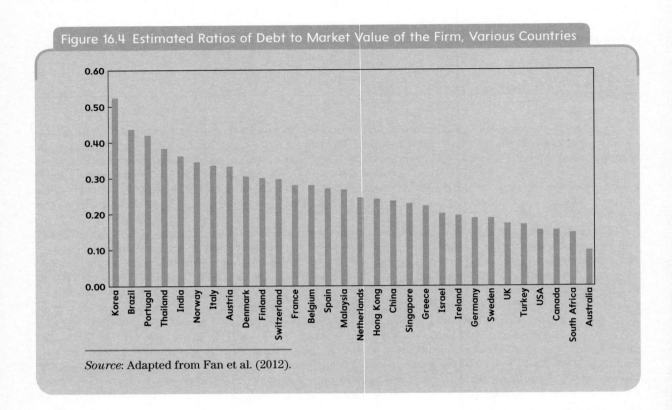

Figure 16.4 Estimated Ratios of Debt to Market Value of the Firm, Various Countries

Source: Adapted from Fan et al. (2012).

2   *A number of firms use no debt.* In a fascinating study, Strebulaev and Yang (2013) found that approximately 10.2 per cent of non-financial US firms have zero debt and 22 per cent have less than 5 per cent debt. These firms pay higher dividends, are more profitable, pay higher taxes, issue less equity and have more cash balances. In addition, firms with higher CEO ownership and longer CEO tenure are more likely to have zero debt. In another study, Agrawal and Nagarajan (1990) examined approximately 100 firms on the New York Stock Exchange without long-term debt. They found that these firms are averse to leverage of any kind, with little short-term debt as well. In addition, they have levels of cash and marketable securities well above their levered counterparts. Typically, the managers of these firms have high equity ownership. Furthermore, there is significantly greater family involvement in all-equity firms than in levered firms.

Thus, a story emerges. Managers of all-equity firms are less diversified than the managers of similar, but levered, firms. Because of this, significant leverage represents an added risk that the managers of all-equity firms are loath to accept.

3   *There are differences in the capital structures of different industries.* There are considerable inter-industry differences in debt ratios that persist over time. As can be seen in Table 16.3, debt/asset ratios tend to be quite low in high-growth industries with ample future investment opportunities, such as the healthcare and technology industries. This is true even when the need for external financing is great. Industries with large investments in tangible assets, such as utilities, tend to have high leverage.

4   *Most corporations employ target debt–equity ratios.* Brounen et al. (2006) asked 313 chief financial officers (CFOs) of European firms whether they use target debt–equity ratios, with the results being presented in

Table 16.3 Distribution of Capital Structure Ratios for Various Industries in the European Union, 2015

Debt to equity	From 0 to 10% (%)	From 10 to 50% (%)	From 50 to 70% (%)	From 70 to 100% (%)	More than 100% (%)	Number of Companies
Basic Materials	39.27	24.77	12.99	10.57	12.39	331
Consumer Goods	24.42	31.16	12	14.53	17.89	475
Consumer Services	31.34	25.35	8.27	8.98	26.06	568
Financials	41.99	19.52	5.43	5.62	27.44	1086
Health Care	47.92	28.82	5.21	6.6	11.46	288
Industrials	24.28	32.13	11.56	10.39	21.63	943
Oil & Gas	45.59	25.49	9.31	5.88	13.73	204
Technology	47.22	32.74	8.91	2.9	8.24	449
Telecommunications	35.94	21.88	3.13	15.63	23.44	64
Utilities	15.84	14.85	7.92	11.88	49.5	101
N.A.	25	25	0	0	50	4
Total	1592	1201	399	380	941	4513

Source: Datastream. Countries included in the sample are Austria, Belgium, Croatia, Denmark, Finland, France, Germany, Greece, Hungary, Ireland, Italy, Lithuania, Luxembourg, Malta, Netherlands, Poland, Portugal, Spain, Sweden, UK.

Figure 16.5. As can be seen, the great majority of the firms across countries use targets, though the strictness of the targets varies across companies. A notable exception to this is France, where most firms do not pursue a target debt ratio. Even in the UK, nearly half of all firms do not consider a target debt ratio to be important.

Figure 16.5 Survey Results on the Use of Target Debt-Equity Ratios

US   UK   France

Netherlands   Germany

☐ No target debt ratio
☐ Flexible target debt ratio
■ Somewhat tight target debt rati
☐ Strict target debt ratio

Source: Figure 1 of Brounen et al. (2006).

How should companies establish target debt–equity ratios? While there is no mathematical formula for establishing a target ratio, we present three important factors affecting the ratio:

- *Taxes*: As we pointed out earlier, firms can deduct interest for tax purposes only to the extent of their profits before interest. Thus, highly profitable firms are more likely to have larger target ratios than less profitable firms.[18]

- *Types of assets*: Financial distress is costly with or without formal bankruptcy proceedings. The costs of financial distress depend on the types of assets that the firm has. For example, if a firm has a large investment in land, buildings and other tangible assets, it will have smaller costs of financial distress than a firm with a large investment in research and development. Research and development typically has less resale value than land;

thus, most of its value disappears in financial distress. Therefore, firms with large investments in tangible assets are likely to have higher target debt–equity ratios than firms with large investments in research and development.

- *Uncertainty of operating income*: Firms with uncertain operating income have a high probability of experiencing financial distress, even without debt. Thus, these firms must finance mostly with equity. For example, pharmaceutical firms have uncertain operating income because no one can predict whether today's research will generate new, profitable drugs. Consequently, these firms issue little debt. By contrast, the operating income of firms in regulated industries, such as utilities, generally has low volatility. Relative to other industries, utilities use a great deal of debt.

5 *Peer firms influence capital structures.* Leary and Roberts (2014) found that peer firms play an important role in determining a company's capital structures. Peer effects dominated other factors and smaller, less successful firms were very sensitive to larger, more successful peer capital structure choice. However, the opposite was not the case.

6 *Capital structures are unstable over time.* Average capital structures change markedly over time. Many firms have high and low leverage at different times, and only a very few consistently keep debt/asset ratios above 0.5. The only situation where capital structure appears stable is for low leverage firms. The graphs in Figure 16.6 show the time series of capital structures for a number of large multinational companies. As you can see, they vary massively over time.

Figure 16.6 Capital Structures

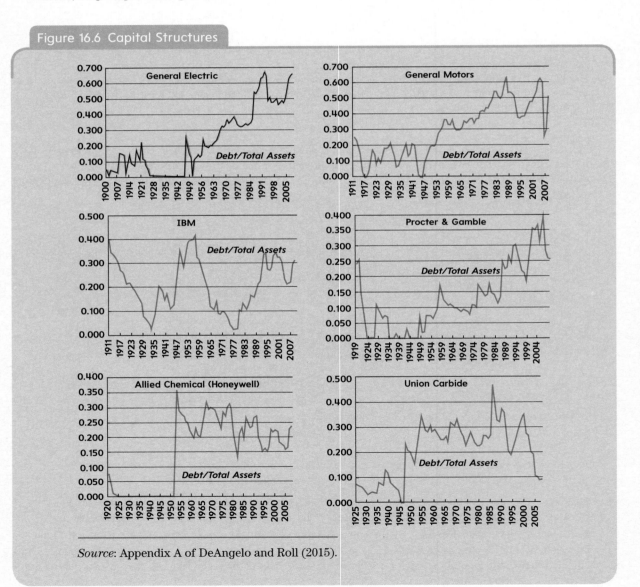

Source: Appendix A of DeAngelo and Roll (2015).

One final note is in order. Because no formula supports them, the preceding points may seem too nebulous to assist financial decision-making. Instead, many real-world firms simply base their capital structure decisions on industry averages. This may strike some as a cowardly approach, but it at least keeps firms from deviating far from accepted practice. After all, the existing firms in any industry are the survivors. Therefore we should pay at least some attention to their decisions.

Summary and Conclusions

1 We mentioned in the last chapter that according to theory, firms should create all-debt capital structures under corporate taxation. Because firms generally employ moderate amounts of debt in the real world, the theory must have been missing something at that point. We stated in this chapter that costs of financial distress cause firms to restrain their issuance of debt. These costs are of two types: direct and indirect. Lawyers' and accountants' fees during the bankruptcy process are examples of direct costs. We mentioned four examples of indirect costs:

   (a) Impaired ability to conduct business

   (b) Incentive to take on risky projects

   (c) Incentive toward underinvestment

   (d) Distribution of funds to shareholders prior to bankruptcy.

2 Because financial distress costs are substantial and the shareholders ultimately bear them, firms have an incentive to reduce costs. Protective covenants and debt consolidation are two common cost reduction techniques.

3 Because costs of financial distress can be reduced but not eliminated, firms will not finance entirely with debt. Figure 16.1 illustrates the relationship between firm value and debt. In the figure, firms select the debt–equity ratio at which firm value is maximized.

4 Signalling theory argues that profitable firms are likely to increase their leverage because the extra interest payments will offset some of the pre-tax profits. Rational shareholders will infer higher firm value from a higher debt level. Thus investors view debt as a signal of firm value.

5 Managers owning a small proportion of a firm's equity can be expected to work less, maintain more lavish expense accounts, and accept more pet projects with negative NPVs than managers owning a large proportion of equity. Because new issues of equity dilute a manager's percentage interest in the firm, such agency costs are likely to increase when a firm's growth is financed through new equity rather than through new debt.

6 The pecking order theory implies that managers prefer internal to external financing. If external financing is required, managers tend to choose the safest securities, such as debt. Firms may accumulate slack to avoid external equity.

7 The market timing theory suggests that there is no pecking order or trade-off of capital structure choices. Observed debt ratios are simply a function of past market to book valuations and the timing of funding requirements. Firms will have more equity if they needed funding when market to book valuations were high. Conversely, if financing was required during low market to book periods, debt will tend to dominate.

8 Berens and Cuny (1995) argue that significant equity financing can be explained by real growth and inflation, even in a world of low bankruptcy costs.

9 Debt–equity ratios vary across industries. We present three factors determining the target debt–equity ratio:

   (a) *Taxes*: Firms with high taxable income should rely more on debt than firms with low taxable income.

   (b) *Types of assets*: Firms with a high percentage of intangible assets such as research and development should have low debt. Firms with primarily tangible assets should have higher debt.

   (c) *Uncertainty of operating income*: Firms with high uncertainty of operating income should rely mostly on equity.

Questions and Problems

CONCEPT

1   **Costs of Financial Distress**   What are the direct and indirect costs of bankruptcy? Briefly explain each and provide a practical example of these costs.

2   **Description of Financial Distress Costs**   Are managers liable to act differently when their firm is in financial distress? Explain your answer using practical examples.

3   **Rationale for the Tax Benefits of Debt**   Despite the significant costs of high leverage, tax systems around the world have a built-in debt bias. Why do you think this is?

4   **Trade-off Theory**   Explain what is meant by the trade-off theory of capital structure choice. Your answer should discuss the main costs and benefits of debt within this model and its empirical limitations.

5   **Signalling**   Explain how managers can signal to the market the value of their firm through their capital structure decisions. Do you think this is an effective strategy? Explain.

6   **Agency Costs of Equity**   What are the sources of agency costs of equity?

7   **Pecking Order Theory**   Explain what is meant by the pecking order theory and how it relates to observed capital structures of companies. Where does a deeply discounted equity rights issue fit into the pecking order of financing choices? Explain your answer.

8   **Growth and the Debt–Equity Ratio**   How does growth affect the desired debt to equity ratio of a company? Explain the impact of growth opportunities in the context of the static trade-off theory and pecking order theory of capital structure.

9   **Market Timing Theory**   Is the market timing theory of financing choices consistent with the pecking order theory or trade-off theory? Explain your answer.

10   **Observed Capital Structures**   In all countries, it appears that some firms have a target debt ratio while others do not have one. What does this say about the validity of the trade-off theory, pecking order theory, and market timing theory? Explain.

REGULAR

11   **Shareholder Incentives**   Do you agree or disagree with the following statement? 'A firm's shareholders will never want the firm to invest in projects with negative net present values.' Why? What steps can shareholders take to reduce the costs of debt?

12   **Debt and Risk**   You have been asked the following questions: 'If debt can reduce the weighted average cost of capital for project appraisal, why does it then increase the risk of a company? Is it possible for a financial manager to diversify bankruptcy risk away like other risks?' What are your answers?

13   **Capital Structure Decisions**   During the last few years, many companies have suffered major trading losses because of the poor economic climate. Assume your firm has found itself in this situation and is considering a major redevelopment investment to exploit nascent growth opportunities. Due to the large losses incurred in recent years, your firm has significant tax loss carry-forwards, which means that it does not need to pay any tax for 3 years. Should you use debt or equity to finance the firm's redevelopment investment? Explain your choice.

14   **Observed Capital Structures**   Refer to the observed capital structures given in Table 16.3 of the text. What do you notice about the types of industries with respect to their average debt–asset ratios? Are certain types of industries more likely to be highly leveraged than others? What are some possible reasons for this observed segmentation? Do the operating results and tax history of the firms play a role? How about their future earnings prospects? What about the different institutional characteristics of each country? Explain.

15   **Costs of Bankruptcy**   What is the average cost of bankruptcy for a firm in the United States? How does this compare to other countries? Why do bankruptcy costs differ both within a country and between countries?

16   **Bankruptcy and Corporate Ethics**   Explain the ethical considerations of the following:

(a)   Firms sometimes use the threat of a bankruptcy filing to force creditors to renegotiate terms. Critics argue that in such cases the firm is using bankruptcy laws 'as a sword rather than a shield'.

(b)   A company files for bankruptcy as a means of reducing labour costs.

17 **Firm Value** Hoy plc has a profit before interest and taxes of £900,000 per year that is expected to continue in perpetuity. The unlevered cost of equity for the company is 17 per cent, and the corporate tax rate is 20 per cent. The company also has a perpetual bond issue outstanding with a market value of £2 million. What is the value of the company?

18 **Agency Costs** Tom Scott is the owner, chairman and primary salesperson for Scott Manufacturing. Because of this, the company's profits are driven by the amount of work Tom does. If he works 40 hours each week, the company's profit before interest and taxes will be £500,000 per year; if he works a 50-hour week, the company's profit before interest and taxes will be £600,000 per year. The company is currently worth £3 million. The company needs a cash infusion of £2 million, and it can issue equity or issue debt with an interest rate of 9 per cent. Assume there are no corporate taxes.

(a) What are the cash flows to Tom under each scenario?

(b) Under which form of financing is Tom likely to work harder?

(c) What specific new costs will occur with each form of financing?

19 **Capital Structure and Growth** Transvaal Ltd currently has debt outstanding with a market value of R980,000 and a cost of 10 per cent. The company has an EBIT of R98,000 that is expected to continue in perpetuity. Assume there are no taxes.

(a) What is the value of the company's equity? What is the debt-to-value ratio?

(b) What are the equity value and debt-to-value ratio if the company's growth rate is 4 per cent?

(c) What are the equity value and debt-to-value ratio if the company's growth rate is 8 per cent?

20 **Capital Structure and Non-marketed Claims** Suppose the chief executive of the company in the previous problem stated that the company should increase the amount of debt in its capital structure because of the tax-advantaged status of its interest payments. His argument is that this action would increase the value of the company. How would you respond?

21 **Costs of Financial Distress** Steinberg plc and Dietrich plc are identical firms except that Dietrich is more levered. Both companies will remain in business for one more year. The companies' economists agree that the probability of the continuation of the current expansion is 80 per cent for the next year, and the probability of a recession is 20 per cent. If the expansion continues, each firm will generate profit before interest and taxes of £2 million. If a recession occurs, each firm will generate profit before interest and taxes of £800,000. Steinberg's debt obligation requires the firm to pay £750,000 at the end of the year. Dietrich's debt obligation requires the firm to pay £1 million at the end of the year. Neither firm pays taxes. Assume a discount rate of 15 per cent.

(a) What are the potential pay-offs in one year to Steinberg's shareholders and bondholders? What about those for Dietrich's?

(b) Steinberg's CEO recently stated that Steinberg's value should be higher than Dietrich's because the firm has less debt and therefore less bankruptcy risk. Do you agree or disagree with this statement?'

22 **Agency Costs** Kašna Corporation's economists estimate that a good business environment and a bad business environment are equally likely for the coming year. The managers of Kašna must choose between two mutually exclusive projects. Assume that the project Kašna chooses will be the firm's only activity and that the firm will close one year from today. Kašna is obligated to make a CHK50,000 payment to bondholders at the end of the year. The projects have the same systematic risk but different volatilities. Consider the following information pertaining to the two projects:

Economy	Probability	Low-Volatility Project Pay-off (CHK)	High-Volatility Project Pay-off (CHK)
Bad	0.50	50,000	10,000
Good	0.50	70,000	80,000

(a) What is the expected value of the firm if the low-volatility project is undertaken? What if the high-volatility project is undertaken? Which of the two strategies maximizes the expected value of the firm?

(b) What is the expected value of the firm's equity if the low-volatility project is undertaken? What is it if the high-volatility project is undertaken?

(c)   Which project would Kašna's shareholders prefer? Explain.

(d)   Suppose bondholders are fully aware that shareholders might choose to maximize equity value rather than total firm value and opt for the high-volatility project. To minimize this agency cost, the firm's bondholders decide to use a bond covenant to stipulate that the bondholders can demand a higher payment if Kašna chooses to take on the high-volatility project. What payment to bondholders would make shareholders indifferent between the two projects?

23   **Financial Distress**   Good Time plc is a regional chain department store. It will remain in business for one more year. The probability of a boom year is 60 per cent and the probability of a recession is 40 per cent. It is projected that the company will generate a total cash flow of £250 million in a boom year and £100 million in a recession. The company's required debt payment at the end of the year is £150 million. The market value of the company's outstanding debt is £108.93 million. The company pays no taxes. Assume a discount rate of 12 per cent.

(a)   What pay-off do bondholders expect to receive in the event of a recession?

(b)   What is the promised return on the company's debt?

(c)   What is the expected return on the company's debt?

CHALLENGE

24   **Personal Taxes, Bankruptcy Costs and Firm Value**   When personal taxes on interest income and bankruptcy costs are considered, the general expression for the value of a levered firm in a world in which the tax rate on equity distributions equals zero is:

$$V_L = V_U + \{1 - [(1 - t_C)/(1 - t_B)]\} \times D - C(D)$$

where V_L is the value of a levered firm; V_U is the value of an unlevered firm; D is the value of the firm's debt; t_C is the tax rate on corporate income; t_B is the personal tax rate on interest income; $C(D)$ is the present value of the costs of financial distress.

(a)   In their no-tax model, what do Modigliani and Miller assume about t_C, t_B, and C (B)? What do these assumptions imply about a firm's optimal debt–equity ratio?

(b)   In their model with corporate taxes, what do Modigliani and Miller assume about t_C, t_B, and $C(B)$? What do these assumptions imply about a firm's optimal debt–equity ratio?

(c)   Consider an all-equity Belgian firm that is certain to be able to use interest deductions to reduce its corporate tax bill. If the corporate tax rate is 33.99 per cent, the personal tax rate on interest income is 50 per cent, and there are no costs of financial distress, by how much will the value of the firm change if it issues €1 million in debt and uses the proceeds to repurchase equity?

(d)   Consider another all-equity Belgian firm that does not pay taxes due to large tax loss carry-forwards from previous years. The personal tax rate on interest income is 50 per cent, and there are no costs of financial distress. What would be the change in the value of this firm from adding €1 of perpetual debt rather than €1 of equity?

25   **Personal Taxes, Bankruptcy Costs and Firm Value**   Overnight Publishing SA (OP) has €2 million in excess cash. The firm plans to use this cash either to retire all of its outstanding debt or to repurchase equity. The firm's debt is held by one institution that is willing to sell it back to OP for €2 million. The institution will not charge OP any transaction costs. Once OP becomes an all-equity firm, it will remain unlevered forever. If OP does not retire the debt, the company will use the €2 million in cash to buy back some of its equity on the open market. Repurchasing equity also has no transaction costs. The company will generate €1,100,000 of annual earnings before interest and taxes in perpetuity regardless of its capital structure. The firm immediately pays out all earnings as dividends at the end of each year. OP is subject to a corporate tax rate of 33.33 per cent, and the required rate of return on the firm's unlevered equity is 20 per cent. The personal tax rate on interest income is 40 per cent, and there are no taxes on equity distribution. Assume there are no bankruptcy costs.

(a)   What is the value of OP if it chooses to retire all of its debt and become an unlevered firm?

(b)   What is the value of OP if it decides to repurchase equity instead of retiring its debt? (*Hint:* Use the equation for the value of a levered firm with personal tax on interest income from the previous problem.)

(c)   Assume that expected bankruptcy costs have a present value of €300,000. How does this influence OP's decision?

26 **Islamic Financing** Islamic financing forbids the use of interest in any financial security, and this will clearly have an impact on the capital structure decisions of firms that follow Shariah principles. At the same time, many Islamic securities have the same cash flows requirements as Western financial securities. Explain how the costs of financial distress are affected in the event a firm with Islamic securities finds itself near insolvency. Are Islamic securities better in this regard? Explain why or why not.

27 **Corporate Pension Plans** Many firms have pension plans for their employees that are heavily in deficit (i.e. the asset value of the fund is less than the present value of its future pension payments). How does this affect the risk of firms? How would you incorporate the pension fund deficit or surplus into the Modigliani–Miller framework?

28 **Guaranteed Debt** Many companies in emerging markets use AAA rated firms in the West to guarantee any debt issue that is made by the firm. A good example is the Bakrie family in Indonesia, who used Bumi plc in the UK to guarantee a loan of $473 million. In 2012, the Bakrie family's operations were not performing well and their firm was in financial distress. As a result, the share price of the guarantor, Bumi plc, fell 60 per cent on the possibility that the Bakrie family may default on its loan, thus engaging the guarantor, Bumi plc, to repay the full amount. How would you incorporate a guarantor contract in the Modigliani–Miller framework?

29 **Debt Buybacks** In the aftermath of the global financial crisis in the late 2000s, many companies sought to bring their leverage ratios down to much lower levels. In 2012, Lloyds Banking Group began to repurchase their own debt. If debt brings tax benefits and gearing is not abnormally high, why would this be a sensible strategy?

30 **Market Timing Theory** Look again at Table 16.3. Can you provide a market timing interpretation to the distribution of gearing ratios in the table? Can you provide a more plausible or intuitive interpretation of the figures? Write a brief report, justifying your views.

Exam Question (45 minutes)

Biller Industries plc is a global haulage equipment and scaffolding manufacturer. The company has never borrowed before but feels that in order to maximize growth and increase value, a debt issue is required. Currently the firm has 50 million shares outstanding with a share price of £1.50. The profit before taxes is forecast to be £25 million. Biller Industries requires £30 million to fund its expansion plans. The firm feels that it could borrow £45 million and use the additional £15 million to also buy back shares in the company. The corporate tax rate is 23 per cent.

1 Determine the expected earnings per share for the company before and after the debt issue. (20 marks)

2 Using your answer to part (1), discuss the use of earnings per share as a basis for financial decision taking. (20 marks)

3 Determine the value of Biller Industries plc after restructuring and the value of its equity using the Modigliani–Miller model with corporate taxes. (15 marks)

4 Determine the cost of equity for Biller Industries plc before and after the debt issue. (15 marks)

5 If the Miller (Debt and Taxes) model holds and capital gains tax is 28 per cent, corporation tax is 23 per cent and personal tax rate on interest income is 45 per cent, estimate the value of Biller Industries plc. (15 marks)

6 Determine the personal tax rate on interest income at which the tax advantage of debt is zero. (15 marks)

Mini Case

McKenzie Restaurants plc's Capital Budgeting

Sam McKenzie is the founder and CEO of McKenzie Restaurants plc, a British company. Sam is considering opening several new restaurants. Sally Thornton, the company's CFO, has been put in charge of the capital budgeting analysis. She has examined the potential for the company's expansion and determined that the success of the new restaurants will depend critically on the state of the economy over the next few years.

McKenzie currently has a bond issue outstanding with a face value of £25 million that is due in one year. Covenants associated with this bond issue prohibit the issuance of any additional debt. This restriction means that the expansion will be entirely financed with equity at a cost of £9 million. Sally has summarized her analysis in the following table, which shows the value of the company in each state of the economy next year, both with and without expansion:

Economic growth	Probability	Without Expansion (£)	With Expansion (£)
Low	0.30	20,000,000	24,000,000
Normal	0.50	34,000,000	45,000,000
High	0.20	41,000,000	53,000,000

1   What is the expected value of the company in one year, with and without expansion? Would the company's shareholders be better off with or without expansion? Why?

2   What is the expected value of the company's debt in one year, with and without the expansion?

3   One year from now, how much value creation is expected from the expansion? How much value is expected for shareholders? For bondholders?

4   If the company announces that it is not expanding, what do you think will happen to the price of its bonds? What will happen to the price of the bonds if the company does expand?

5   If the company opts not to expand, what are the implications for the company's future borrowing needs? What are the implications if the company does expand?

6   Because of the bond covenant, the expansion would have to be financed with equity. How would it affect your answer if the expansion were financed with cash on hand instead of new equity?

Practical Case Study

For this case study, you will need to access Yahoo! Finance. For your own country, choose an industry and find the debt to equity ratio of each company in the industry. Now choose another country and find the debt to equity ratios of all the companies in the same industry. Is the median leverage different between countries? If so, explain why you think this might be the case. If not, what does this tell you about the three theories (trade-off, pecking order, market timing) of capital structure? Write a brief report on your findings.

References

Agrawal, A. and N. Nagarajan (1990) 'Corporate Capital Structure, Agency Costs, and Ownership Control: The Case of All-Equity Firms', *The Journal of Finance*, Vol. 45, No. 4, 1325–1331.

Altman, E.I. (1984) 'A Further Empirical Investigation of the Bankruptcy Cost Question', *The Journal of Finance*, Vol. 39, No. 4, 1067–1089.

Andrade, G. and S.N. Kaplan (1998) 'How Costly Is Financial (Not Economic) Distress? Evidence from Highly Leveraged Transactions that Became Distressed', *The Journal of Finance*, Vol. 53, No. 5, 1443–1493.

Ang, J., J. Chua and J. McConnell (1982) 'The Administrative Costs of Bankruptcy: A Note', *The Journal of Finance*, Vol. 37, No. 1, 219–226.

Baker, M. and J. Wurgler (2002) 'Market Timing and Capital Structure', *The Journal of Finance*, Vol. 57, No. 1, 1–32.

Bar-Or, Y. (2000) 'An Investigation of Expected Financial Distress Costs', unpublished paper, Wharton School, University of Pennsylvania.

Berens, J.L. and C.L. Cuny (1995) 'Inflation, Growth and Capital Structure', *Review of Financial Studies*, Vol. 8, 1185–1208.

Bris, A., I. Welch and N. Zhu (2006) 'The Costs of Bankruptcy: Chapter 7 Liquidation versus Chapter 11 Reorganization', *The Journal of Finance*, Vol. 61, No. 3, 1253–1303.

Brounen, D., A. de Jong and K. Koedijk (2006) 'Capital Structure Policies in Europe: Survey Evidence', *Journal of Banking and Finance*, Vol. 30, No. 5, 1409–1442.

DeAngelo, H. and R. Roll (2015) 'How Stable Are Corporate Capital Structures?', *The Journal of Finance*, Vol. 70, No. 1, 373–418.

Fama, E. and K. French (2002) 'Testing Trade-Off and Pecking Order Predictions about Dividends and Debt', *Review of Financial Studies*, Vol. 15, No. 1, 1–33.

Fan, J.P.H., S. Titman and G. Twite (2012) 'An International Comparison of Capital Structure and Debt Maturity Choices', *Journal of Financial and Quantitative Analysis*, Vol. 47, No. 1, 23–56.

Jensen, M.C. (1986) 'The Agency Costs of Free Cash Flow: Corporate Finance and Takeovers', *American Economic Review*, Vol. 76, No. 2, 323–339.

Jensen, M.C. and W. Meckling (1978) 'Theory of the Firm: Managerial Behavior, Agency Costs, and Ownership Structure', *Journal of Financial Economics*, Vol. 3, No. 4, 305–360.

Kayhan, A. and S. Titman (2007) 'Firms' Histories and their Capital Structures', *Journal of Financial Economics*, Vol. 83, No. 1, 1–32.

Lang, L., R. Stulz and R. Walkling (1989) 'Managerial Performance, Tobin's *Q* and the Gains in Tender Offers', *Journal of Financial Economics*, Vol. 24, 137–154.

Leary, M.T. and M.R. Roberts (2014) 'Do Peer Firms Affect Corporate Financial Policy?', *The Journal of Finance*, Vol. 69, No. 1, 139–178.

Lemmon, M. and J. Zender (2010) 'Debt Capacity and Tests of Capital Structure Theories', *Journal of Financial and Quantitative Analysis*, Vol. 45, 1161–1187.

Miller, M. (1977) 'Debt and Taxes', *The Journal of Finance*, Vol. 32, 261–275.

Myers, S.C. (1984) 'The Capital Structure Puzzle', *The Journal of Finance*, Vol. 39, No. 3, 574–592.

Qi, Y., L. Roth and J.K. Wald (2011) 'How Legal Environments Affect the Use of Bond Covenants', *Journal of International Business Studies*, Vol. 42, 235–262.

Shah, K. (1994) 'The Nature of Information Conveyed by Pure Capital Structure Changes', *Journal of Financial Economics*, Vol. 36, No. 1, 81–126.

Smith, A. (1937) *The Wealth of Nations* [1776], Cannon edition (New York: Modern Library).

Smith, C.W. and J.B. Warner (1979) 'On Financial Contracting: An Analysis of Bond Covenants', *Journal of Financial Economics*, Vol. 7, 117–161.

Strebulaev, I.A. and B. Yang (2013) 'The Mystery of Zero-leverage Firms', *Journal of Financial Economics*, Vol. 109, No. 1, 1–23.

Warner, J.B. and M.J. White (1983) 'Bankruptcy Costs and the New Bankruptcy Code', *The Journal of Finance*, Vol. 38, 477–488.

Weiss, L.A. (1990) 'Bankruptcy Resolution: Direct Costs and Violation of Priority of Claims', *Journal of Financial Economics*, Vol. 27, No. 2, 285–314.

Welch, I. (2003) 'Capital Structure and Stock Returns', *Journal of Political Economy*, Vol. 112, No. 1, 106–131.

Additional Reading

Since Baker and Wurgler's (2002) paper on market timing, the capital structure literature has taken on a completely new lease of life. For many years, researchers believed that pecking orders and static trade-offs were the only intuitive reasons why managers chose capital structures in practice. Now we have market timing and dynamic trade-offs to consider and things are uncertain again. The references to papers discussed in the main text are provided above. The following papers will add to your reading pleasure.

Trade-offs, Pecking Orders and Market Timing

1   Alti, A. (2006) 'How Persistent Is the Impact of Market Timing on Capital Structure?', *The Journal of Finance*, Vol. 61, No. 4, 1681–1710. **US**.

2   Byoun, S. (2008) 'How and When Do Firms Adjust their Capital Structures toward Targets?', *The Journal of Finance*, Vol. 63, No. 6, 3069–3096. **US**.

3   Chang, X. and S. Dasgupta (2009) 'Target Behavior and Financing: How Conclusive is the Evidence?', *The Journal of Finance*, Vol. 64, No. 4, 1767–1796. **US**.

4   Elliott, W.B., J. Koeter-Kant and R.S. Warr (2007) 'A Valuation-Based Test of Market Timing', *Journal of Corporate Finance*, Vol. 13, No. 1, 112–128. **US**.

5   Elliott, W.B., J. Koeter-Kant and R.S. Warr (2008) 'Market Timing and the Debt–Equity Choice', *Journal of Financial Intermediation*, Vol. 17, No. 2, 175–197. **US**.

6   Graham, J.R. (2003) 'Taxes and Corporate Finance: A Review', *Review of Financial Studies*, Vol. 16, No. 4, 1075–1129. **Review Paper**.

7   Graham, J.R. and A.L. Tucker (2006) 'Tax Shelters and Corporate Debt Policy', *Journal of Financial Economics*, Vol. 81, No. 3, 563–594. **US**.

8   Hennessy, C. and T.M. Whited (2005) 'Debt Dynamics', *The Journal of Finance*, Vol. 60, No. 3, 1129–1165. **US**.

9   Hovakimian, A. (2006) 'Are Observed Capital Structures Determined by Equity Market Timing?', *Journal of Financial and Quantitative Analysis*, Vol. 41, No. 1, 221–243. **US**.

10 Huang, R. and J.R. Ritter (2009) 'Testing Theories of Capital Structure and Estimating the Speed of Adjustment', *Journal of Financial and Quantitative Analysis*, Vol. 44, 237–271.

11 Kayhan, A. and S. Titman (2007) 'Firm's Histories and their Capital Structures', *Journal of Financial Economics*, Vol. 83, No. 1, 1–32. **US**.

12 Leary, M.T. and M.R. Roberts (2005) 'Do Firms Rebalance their Capital Structures?', *The Journal of Finance*, Vol. 60, No. 6, 2575–2619. **US**.

13   Lemmon, M.L. and J.F. Zender (2010) 'Debt Capacity and Tests of Capital Structure Theories', *Journal of Financial and Quantitative Analysis*, Vol. 45, No. 5, 1161–1187.

14   Lemmon, M.L., M.R. Roberts and J.F. Zender (2008) 'Back to the Beginning: Persistence and the Cross-Section of Corporate Capital Structure', *The Journal of Finance*, Vol. 63, No. 4, 1575–1608. **US**.

15   Mahajan, A. and S. Tartaroglu (2008) 'Equity Market Timing and Capital Structure: International Evidence', *Journal of Banking and Finance*, Vol. 32, No. 5, 754–766. **International**.

Other Papers on Capital Structure Choice

16   Almeida, H. and T. Philippon (2007) 'The Risk-Adjusted Cost of Financial Distress', *The Journal of Finance*, Vol. 62, No. 6, 2557–2586. **US**.

17   Booth, L., V. Aivazian, A. Demirguc-Kunt and V. Maksimovic (2001) 'Capital Structures in Developing Countries', *The Journal of Finance*, Vol. 56, No. 1, 87–130. **International**.

18   Danis, A., D.A. Rettl and T.M. Whited (2014) 'Refinancing, Profitability, and Capital Structure', *Journal of Financial Economics*, Vol. 114, No. 3, 424–443.

19   Desai, M.A., C.F. Foley and J.R. Hines (2004) 'A Multinational Perspective on Capital Structure Choice and Internal Capital Markets', *The Journal of Finance*, Vol. 59, No. 6, 2451–2487. **International**.

20   Dittmar, A. and A. Thakor (2007) 'Why Do Firms Issue Equity?', *The Journal of Finance*, Vol. 62, No. 1, 1–54. **US**.

21   Fama, E.F. and K.R. French (2005) 'Financing Decisions: Who Issues Stock?', *Journal of Financial Economics*, Vol. 76, No. 3, 549–582. **US**.

22   Fan, J.P.H., S. Titman and G. Twite (2012) 'An International Comparison of Capital Structure and Debt Maturity Choices', *Journal of Financial and Quantitative Analysis*, Vol. 47, No. 1, 23–56. **International**.

23   Faulkender, M. and M.A. Petersen (2006) 'Does the Source of Capital Affect Capital Structure?', *Review of Financial Studies*, Vol. 19, No. 1, 45–79. **US**.

24   Frank, M.Z. and V.K. Goyal (2009) 'Capital Structure Decisions: Which Factors Are Reliably Important?', *Financial Management*, Vol. 38, No. 1, 1–37.

25   Gonzalez, V.M. and F. Gonzalez (2008) 'Influence of Bank Concentration and Institutions on Capital Structure: New International Evidence', *Journal of Corporate Finance*, Vol. 14, No. 4, 363–375. **International**.

26   Kisgen, D.J. (2006) 'Credit Ratings and Capital Structure', *The Journal of Finance*, Vol. 61, No. 3, 1035–1072. **US**.

27   Molina, C.A. (2005) 'Are Firms Underleveraged? An Examination of the Effect of Leverage on Default Probabilities', *The Journal of Finance*, Vol. 60, No. 3, 1427–1459. **US**.

To access the appendixes for this chapter, please visit **www.mheducation.co.uk/textbooks/hillier3**.

Endnotes

1   There are situations where the limited liability of corporations can be 'pierced'. Typically, fraud or misrepresentation must be present.

2   Normally, we assume that investors are *averse* to risk. In that case, the cost of debt capital, R_D, is less than the cost of equity capital, R_E, which rises with leverage, as shown in the previous chapter. In addition, R_D may rise when the increase in leverage allows the possibility of default.

   For simplicity, we assume *risk neutrality* in this example. This means that investors are indifferent to the level of risk. Here, $R_E = R_D$ because risk-neutral investors do not demand compensation for bearing risk. In addition, neither R_E nor R_D rises with leverage. Because the interest rate is 10 per cent, our assumption of risk neutrality implies that $R_E = 10$ per cent as well.

   Though financial economists believe that investors are risk-averse, they frequently develop examples based on risk neutrality to isolate a point unrelated to risk. This is our approach because we want to focus on bankruptcy costs – not bankruptcy risk. The same qualitative conclusions from this example can be drawn in a world of risk aversion, albeit with *much* more difficulty for the reader.

3   Bris et al. (2006); Ang et al. (1982).

4   The same qualitative results will obtain if the £1,000 is raised from new shareholders. However, the arithmetic becomes much more difficult because we must determine how many new shares are issued.

5   Legal limitations may prevent this practice in other countries.

6   Adam Smith, *The Wealth of Nations* [1776], Cannon edition (New York: Modern Library, 1937), p. 700, as quoted in Jensen and Meckling (1978).

7   As previously discussed, *agency costs* are generally defined as the costs from the conflicts of interest among shareholders, bondholders and managers. See Chapter 2 for more information.

8 The seminal theoretical article is Jensen (1986).

9 The pecking order theory is generally attributed to Myers (1984).

10 In the interest of simplicity, we have not presented our results in the form of a rigorous model. To the extent that a reader wants a deeper explanation, we refer him or her to Myers (1984).

11 See Merton Miller's Presidential Address to the American Finance Association, reprinted as 'Debt and Taxes' (1977).

12 The same qualitative results occur under uncertainty, though the mathematics is more troublesome.

13 For simplicity, assume that growth is achieved without earnings retention. The same conclusions would be reached with retained earnings, though the arithmetic would become more involved. Of course, growth without earnings retention is less realistic than growth with retention.

14 Because the firm makes no real investment, the new debt is used to buy back shares of equity.

15 The firm can also be valued by a variant of Equation 15.5:

$$V_L = V_U + PVTS$$
$$= \frac{€100(1 - t_C)}{0.10 - 0.05} + \frac{t_C \times €100}{0.10 - 0.05} = €2,000$$

Because of firm growth, both V_U and $PVTS$ are growing perpetuities.

16 Students are often surprised that equity has value when taxable income is zero. Actually, the equityholders are receiving cash flow each period. The proceeds from the new debt can be used either to pay dividends or to buy back shares.

17 Our example assumes a single perpetual bond with level coupon payments. Berens and Cuny (1995: p. 1201) point out that, with a number of different bonds, a firm might be able to construct an equally optimal capital structure with a greater debt-to-value (D/V) ratio. Because both capital structures are equally optimal, a firm might choose either one.

Although the analysis with many financing instruments is more complex, a firm can still choose a low D/V with no ill effect. Thus, Berens and Cuny's conclusion that firms *can* employ a significant amount of equity in a world with a low level of bankruptcy costs still holds.

18 By contrast, the pecking order theory argues that profitable firms will employ less debt because they can invest out of retained earnings. However, the pecking order theory argues against the use of target ratios in the first place.

CHAPTER
17

Valuation and Capital Budgeting for the Levered Firm

The Private Finance Initiative (PFI) is a UK scheme that brings together the private and public sector in big social infrastructure projects. Under PFI, a private consortium of firms will design, build, finance and operate an asset or service according to specifications imposed by the public sector. In return, the government will pay the private consortium periodic payments for this collaboration. The rationale underlying PFI is that private organizations are more efficient at running big investment projects and this brings cost savings in addition to improved service and quality.

An example of the PFI is the building of the British Embassy in Berlin in 2000. Under this scheme, Arteos (a subsidiary of Bilfinger Berger, the German construction firm) financed and built the building. In addition, they were contracted to operate it until 2030, after which ownership reverts to the British government. Why did Bilfinger Berger enter into the contract? One of the reasons was the attractive financial package offered to the company by the British government to undertake the collaboration.

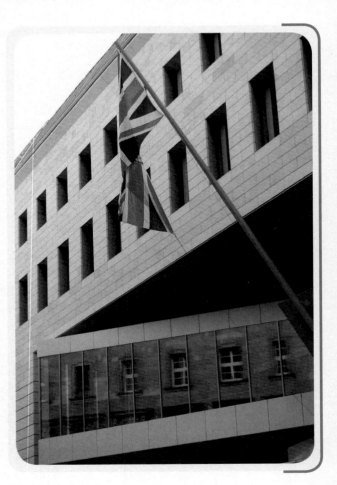

KEY NOTATIONS

APV	Adjusted present value
FTE	Flow to equity
NPV	Net present value
NPVF	Net present value of financing
t_C	Corporate tax rate
R_0	Cost of capital for an all-equity firm
R_E	Cost of equity capital
R_D	Cost of debt capital
UCF	Unlevered cash flow
LCF	Levered cash flow
D	Value of debt
E	Value of shares
R_{WACC}	Weighted average cost of capital
β	Beta of systematic risk
R_F	Risk-free rate

Similarly, when a corporation opens a major plant or considers relocation, municipalities or regions often create a package loaded with subsidies, including tax credits, subsidized debt, educational training, road and infrastructure creation, and other incentives.

With subsidized debt, the government or region guarantees the debt, which allows the company to borrow at a much lower interest rate. If the interest rate on the debt is lower than the company's normal cost of debt, how does a company evaluate the financial benefits of this and other such subsidies? In this chapter, we illustrate how to evaluate projects using the adjusted present value and some flow to equity approaches in capital budgeting that allow us to answer this question.

17.1 Adjusted Present Value Approach

Chapter 7
Page 177

When financing issues are an important part of an investment proposal, a good methodology to use is the adjusted present value method (it is worthwhile reading over **Chapter 7** again to refresh your mind on the more commonly used investment appraisal methods). The approach separates the project cash flows from the financing cash flows and values these separately. If the combined present values are positive, the project should be taken. The adjusted present value (APV) method is described by the following formula:

$$APV = NPV + NPVF$$

In words, the value of a project to a levered firm (APV) is equal to the value of the project to an unlevered firm (NPV) plus the net present value of the financing side effects (NPVF). We can generally think of four side effects:

Chapter 15
Page 396

1 *The tax subsidy to debt*: This was discussed in **Chapter 15**, where we pointed out that for perpetual debt the value of the tax subsidy is $t_C D$. (t_C is the corporate tax rate, and D is the value of the debt.) The material about valuation under corporate taxes in Chapter 15 is actually an application of the APV approach.

2 *The costs of issuing new securities*: As we will discuss in detail in **Chapter 20**, bankers participate in the public issuance of corporate debt. These bankers must be compensated for their time and effort, a cost that lowers the value of the project.

Chapter 20
Page 541

3 *The costs of financial distress*: The possibility of financial distress, and bankruptcy in particular, arises with debt financing. As stated in the previous chapter, financial distress imposes costs, thereby lowering value.

4 *Subsidies to debt financing*: The interest on debt issued by state and local governments may not be taxable to the investor or the tax may be discounted. Because of this, the yield on government debt can be substantially below the yield on taxable debt. Frequently corporations can obtain financing from a municipality at the tax-exempt rate because the municipality can borrow at that rate as well. As with any subsidy, this subsidy adds value.

Although each of the preceding four side effects is important, the tax deduction to debt almost certainly has the highest value in most actual situations. For this reason, the following example considers the tax subsidy but not the other three side effects. (A later example will deal with these three.)

Consider a project of P.B. Singer plc with the following characteristics:

* Cash inflows: £500,000 per year for the indefinite future.
* Cash costs: 72 per cent of sales.
* Initial investment: £520,000.
* $t_C = 28$ per cent
* $R_A = 20$ per cent, where R_0 is the cost of capital for a project of an all-equity firm.

If both the project and the firm are financed with only equity, the project's cash flows are as follows:

	£
Cash inflows	500,000
Cash costs	−360,000

	£
Profit before tax	140,000
Corporate tax (28% tax rate)	−39,200
Unlevered cash flow (UCF)	100,800

The distinction between present value and net present value is important for this example. The *present value* of a project is determined before the initial investment at date 0 is subtracted. The initial investment is subtracted for the calculation of *net* present value.

Given a discount rate of 20 per cent, the present value of the project is:

$$\frac{£100,800}{0.20} = £504,000$$

The net present value (NPV) of the project – that is, the value of the project to an all-equity firm – is:

$$£504,000 - £520,000 = -£16,000$$

Because the NPV is negative, the project would be rejected by an all-equity firm.

Now imagine that the firm finances the project with exactly £135,483.90 in debt, so that the remaining investment of £384,516.10 (= £520,000 − £135,483.90) is financed with equity. The net present value of the project under leverage, which we call the adjusted present value, or the APV, is:

$$APV = NPV + t_C \times D$$

$$£21,935 = -£16,000 + 0.28 \times £135,483.90$$

That is, the value of the project when financed with some leverage is equal to the value of the project when financed with all equity plus the tax shield from the debt. Because this number is positive, the project should be accepted.

You may be wondering why we chose such a precise amount of debt. Actually, we chose it so that the ratio of debt to the present value of the project under leverage is 0.25.[1]

In this example, debt is a fixed proportion of the present value of the project, not a fixed proportion of the initial investment of £520,000. This is consistent with the goal of a target debt-to-*market*-value ratio, which we find is followed by companies in many countries. For example, banks typically lend to property developers a fixed percentage of the appraised market value of a project, not a fixed percentage of the initial investment.

17.2 Flow to Equity Approach

Chapter 5
Page 120

The **flow to equity (FTE)** approach is an alternative capital budgeting approach and is similar to the free cash flow to the firm (FCFF) method that was used to value firms in **Chapter 5**. The formula simply calls for discounting the cash flow from the project to the shareholders of the levered firm at the cost of equity capital, R_E. For a perpetuity this becomes:

$$\frac{\text{Cash flow from project to equityholders of the levered firm}}{R_E}$$

There are three steps to the FTE approach.

Step 1: Calculating Levered Cash Flow (LCF)[2]

Assuming an interest rate of 10 per cent, the perpetual cash flow to shareholders in our P.B. Singer plc example is:

	£
Cash inflows	500,000
Cash costs	−360,000
Interest (10% × £135,483.90)	−13,548
Income after interest	126,452
Corporate tax (28% tax rate)	−35,407
Levered cash flow (LCF)	91,045

Alternatively, we can calculate levered cash flow (LCF) directly from unlevered cash flow (UCF). The key here is that the difference between the cash flow that shareholders receive in an unlevered firm and the cash flow that shareholders receive in a levered firm is the after-tax interest payment. (Repayment of principal does not appear in this example because the debt is perpetual.) We write this algebraically as:

$$UCF - LCF = (1 - t_C)R_D BD$$

The term on the right side of this expression is the after-tax interest payment. Thus, because cash flow to the unlevered shareholders (UCF) is £100,800 and the after-tax interest payment is £9,754.84 [= 0.72 × 0.10 × £135,483.90], cash flow to the levered shareholders (LCF) is:

$$£100,800 - £9,755 = £91,045$$

which is exactly the number we calculated earlier.

Step 2: Calculating R_E

The next step is to calculate the discount rate, R_E. Note that we assumed that the discount rate on unlevered equity, R_A, is 0.20. As we saw in an earlier chapter, the formula for R_E is:

$$R_E = R_A + \frac{D}{E}(1 - t_C)(R_A - R_D)$$

Note that our target debt-to-value ratio of 1/4 implies a target debt-to-equity ratio of 1/3. Applying the preceding formula to this example, we have:

$$R_E = 0.20 + \frac{1}{3}(0.72)(0.20 - 0.10)$$

$$= 0.224$$

Step 3: Valuation

The present value of the project's LCF is:

$$\frac{LCF}{R_E} = \frac{£91,045}{0.224} = £406,451$$

Because the initial investment is £520,000 and £135,483.90 is borrowed, the firm must advance the project £384,516.10 (=£520,000 − £135,483.90) out of its own cash reserves. The *net* present value of the project is simply the difference between the present value of the project's LCF and the investment not borrowed. Thus, the NPV is:

$$£406,451 - £384,516.10 = £21,935$$

which is identical to the result found with the APV approach.

17.3   Weighted Average Cost of Capital Method

Chapter 12
Page 326

Finally, we can value a project using the **weighted average cost of capital (WACC)** method. Although this method was discussed in earlier chapters (WACC is first discussed in **Chapter 12**, Section 12.5), it is worthwhile to review it here. The WACC approach begins with the insight that projects of levered firms are simultaneously financed with both debt and equity. The cost of capital is a weighted average of the cost of debt and cost of equity. The cost of equity is R_S. Ignoring taxes, the cost of debt is simply the borrowing rate, R_D. However, with corporate taxes, the appropriate cost of debt is $(1 - t_C) R_D$, the after-tax cost of debt.

The formula for determining the weighted average cost of capital, R_{WACC}, is:

$$R_{WACC} = \frac{E}{D + E}R_E + \frac{D}{D + E}R_D (1 - t_C)$$

The weight for equity, $E/(D + E)$, and the weight for debt, $D/(D + E)$, are target ratios. Target ratios are generally expressed in terms of market values, not accounting values. (Recall that another phrase for accounting value is *book value*.)

The formula calls for discounting the *unlevered* cash flow of the project (UCF) at the weighted average cost of capital, R_{WACC}. The net present value of the project can be written algebraically as:

$$\sum_{t=1}^{\infty} \frac{UCF_t}{(1 + R_{\text{WACC}})^t} - \text{Initial investment}$$

If the project is a perpetuity, the net present value is:

$$\frac{UCF}{R_{\text{WACC}}} - \text{Initial investment}$$

We previously stated that the target debt-to-value ratio of our project is 1/4 and the corporate tax rate is 0.28, implying that the weighted average cost of capital is:

$$R_{\text{WACC}} = \frac{3}{4} \times 0.224 + \frac{1}{4} \times 0.10 \times 0.72 = 0.186$$

Note that R_{WACC}, 0.186, is lower than the cost of equity capital for an all-equity firm, 0.20. This must always be the case because debt financing provides a tax subsidy that lowers the average cost of capital.

We previously determined the UCF of the project to be £100,800, implying that the present value of the project is:

$$\frac{£100{,}800}{0.186} = £541{,}935$$

This initial investment is £520,000, so the NPV of the project is:

$$£541{,}935 - £520{,}000 = £21{,}935$$

Note that all three approaches yield the same value.

17.4   A Comparison of the APV, FTE and WACC Approaches

Capital budgeting techniques in the early chapters of this text applied to all-equity firms. Capital budgeting for the levered firm could not be handled earlier in the book because the effects of debt on firm value were deferred until the previous two chapters. We learned there that debt increases firm value through tax benefits but decreases value through bankruptcy and related costs.

In this chapter, we provide three approaches to capital budgeting for the levered firm. The adjusted present value (APV) approach first values the project on an all-equity basis. That is, the project's after-tax cash flows under all-equity financing (called unlevered cash flows, or UCF) are placed in the numerator of the capital budgeting equation. The discount rate, assuming all-equity financing, appears in the denominator. At this point, the calculation is identical to that performed in the early chapters of this book. We then add the net present value of the debt. We point out that the net present value of the debt is likely to be the sum of four parameters: tax effects, flotation costs, bankruptcy costs and interest subsidies.

Chapter 15
Page 396

The flow to equity (FTE) approach discounts the after-tax cash flow from a project going to the shareholders of a levered firm (LCF). LCF, which stands for levered cash flow, is the residual to shareholders after interest has been deducted. The discount rate is R_E, the cost of capital to the shareholders of a levered firm. For a firm with leverage, R_E must be greater than R_A, the cost of capital for an unlevered firm. This follows from our material in **Chapter 15** showing that leverage raises the risk to the shareholders.

The last approach is the weighted average cost of capital (WACC) method. This technique calculates the project's after-tax cash flows assuming all-equity financing (UCF). The UCF is placed in the numerator of the capital budgeting equation. The denominator, R_{WACC}, is a weighted average of the cost of equity capital and the cost of debt capital. The tax advantage of debt is reflected in the denominator because the cost of debt capital is determined net of corporate tax. The numerator does not reflect debt at all.

Which Method Is Best?

The net present value of our project is exactly the same under each of the three methods. In theory, this should always be the case.[3] However, one method usually provides an easier computation than another, and, in many cases, one or more of the methods are virtually impossible computationally. We first consider when it is best to use the WACC and FTE approaches.

If the risk of a project stays constant throughout its life, it is plausible to assume that R_A remains constant throughout the project's life. This assumption of constant risk appears to be reasonable for most real-world projects. In addition, if the debt-to-value ratio remains constant over the life of the project, both R_E and R_{WACC} will remain constant as well. Under this latter assumption, either the FTE or the WACC approach is easy to apply. However, if the debt-to-value ratio varies from year to year, both R_S and R_{WACC} vary from year to year as well. Using the FTE or the WACC approach when the denominator changes every year is computationally quite complex, and when computations become complex, the error rate rises. Thus, both the FTE and WACC approaches present difficulties when the debt-to-value *ratio* changes over time.

The APV approach is based on the *level* of debt in each future period. Consequently, when the debt level can be specified precisely for future periods, the APV approach is quite easy to use. However, when the debt level is uncertain, the APV approach becomes more problematic. For example, when the debt-to-value ratio is constant, the debt level varies with the value of the project. Because the value of the project in a future year cannot be easily forecast, the level of debt cannot be easily forecast either.

Thus, we suggest the following guideline:

Use WACC or FTE if the firm's target debt-to-value *ratio* applies to the project over its life. Use APV if the project's *level* of debt is known over the life of the project.

There are a number of situations where the APV approach is preferred. For example, in a leveraged buyout (LBO) the firm begins with a large amount of debt but rapidly pays down the debt over a number of years. Because the schedule of debt reduction in the future is known when the LBO is arranged, tax shields in every future year can be easily forecast. Thus, the APV approach is easy to use here. By contrast, the WACC and FTE approaches are virtually impossible to apply here because the debt-to-equity value cannot be expected to be constant over time. In addition, situations involving interest subsidies and flotation costs are much easier to handle with the APV approach. Finally, the APV approach handles the lease-versus-buy decision much more easily than does either the FTE or the WACC approach.

The preceding examples are special cases. Typical capital budgeting situations are more amenable to either the WACC or the FTE approach than to the APV approach. In many countries, financial managers think in terms of target debt-to-value *ratios*. If a project does better than expected, both its value and its debt capacity will likely rise. The manager will increase debt correspondingly here. Conversely, the manager would be likely to reduce debt if the value of the project were to decline unexpectedly. Of course, because financing is a time-consuming task, the ratio cannot be adjusted daily or monthly. Rather, the adjustment can be expected to occur over the long run. As mentioned before, the WACC and FTE approaches are more appropriate than is the APV approach when a firm focuses on a target debt-to-value ratio.

Because of this, we recommend that the WACC and the FTE approaches, rather than the APV approach, be used in most real-world situations. In addition, frequent discussions with business executives have convinced us that the WACC is by far the most widely used method in the real world. Thus, practitioners seem to agree with us that, outside of the special situations mentioned, the APV approach is a less important method of capital budgeting.

The Three Methods of Capital Budgeting with Leverage

1 Adjusted present value (APV) method:

$$\sum_{t=1}^{\infty} \frac{UCF_t}{(1+R_A)^t} + \text{Additional effects of debt} - \text{Initial investment}$$

where UCF_t is the project's cash flow at date t to the equityholders of an unlevered firm and R_A is the cost of capital for a project in an unlevered firm.

2 Flow to equity (FTE) method:

$$\sum_{t=1}^{\infty} \frac{LCF_t}{(1+R_E)^t} - (\text{Initial investment} - \text{Amount borrowed})$$

where LCF_t is the project's cash flow at date t to the equityholders of a levered firm and R_E is the cost of equity capital with leverage.

3 Weighted average cost of capital (WACC) method:

$$\sum_{t=1}^{\infty} \frac{UCF_t}{(1+R_{WACC})^t} - \text{Initial investment}$$

where R_{WACC} is the weighted average cost of capital.

Notes

1 The middle term in the APV formula implies that the value of a project with leverage is greater than the value of the project without leverage. Because $R_{WACC} < R_A$, the WACC formula implies that the value of a project with leverage is greater than the value of the project without leverage.

2 In the FTE method, cash flow *after interest* (LCF) is used. Initial investment is reduced by *amount borrowed* as well.

Guidelines

1 Use WACC or FTE if the firm's target debt-to-value *ratio* applies to the project over its life.

2 Use APV if the project's *level* of debt is known over the life of the project.

17.5 Capital Budgeting When the Discount Rate Must Be Estimated

The previous sections of this chapter introduced APV, FTE and WACC – the three basic approaches to valuing a levered firm. However, one important detail remains. The example in Sections 17.1 through 17.3 *assumed* a discount rate. We now want to show how this rate is determined for real-world firms with leverage, with an application to the three preceding approaches. The example in this section brings together the work in Chapters 9–12 on the discount rate for unlevered firms with that in Chapter 15 on the effect of leverage on the cost of capital.

Example 17.1

Cost of Capital

World-Wide Enterprises (WWE) is a large conglomerate thinking of entering the widget business, where it plans to finance projects with a debt-to-value ratio of 25 per cent (or, alternatively, a debt-to-equity ratio of 1/3). There is currently one firm in the widget industry, Asian Widgets (AW). This firm is financed with 40 per cent debt and 60 per cent equity. The beta of AW's equity is 1.5. AW has a borrowing rate of 12 per cent, and WWE expects to borrow for its widget venture at 10 per cent. The corporate tax rate for both firms is 0.40, the market risk premium is 8.5 per cent, and the riskless interest rate is 8 per cent. What is the appropriate discount rate for WWE to use for its widget venture?

As shown in Sections 17.1–17.3, a corporation may use one of three capital budgeting approaches: APV, FTE or WACC. The appropriate discount rates for these three approaches are R_A, R_E and R_{WACC}, respectively. Because AW is WWE's only competitor in widgets, we look at AW's cost of capital to calculate R_A, R_E and R_{WACC} for WWE's widget venture. The following four-step procedure will allow us to calculate all three discount rates:

1 *Determining AW's cost of equity capital*: First, we determine AW's cost of equity capital using the security market line (SML):

AW's cost of equity capital

$$R_E = R_F + \beta \times (\overline{R}_M - R_F)$$
$$= 8\% + 1.5 \times 8.5\%$$
$$= 20.75\%$$

where $\overline{R}_M$ is the expected return on the market portfolio and R_F is the risk-free rate.

2 *Determining AW's hypothetical all-equity cost of capital*: We must standardize the preceding number in some way because AW and WWE's widget ventures have different target debt-to-value ratios. The

easiest approach is to calculate the hypothetical cost of equity capital for AW, assuming all-equity financing. This can be determined from MM's Proposition II under taxes:

AW's cost of capital if all equity

$$R_E = R_A + \frac{D}{E}(1 - t_C)(R_A - R_D)$$

$$= R_A + \frac{0.4}{0.6}(0.60)(R_A - 12\%)$$

$$= 20.75\%$$

By solving the equation, we find that $R_A = 0.1825$. Of course, R_A is less than R_A because the cost of equity capital would be less when the firm employs no leverage.

At this point, firms in the real world generally make the assumption that the business risk of their venture is about equal to the business risk of the firms already in the business. Applying this assumption to our problem, we assert that the hypothetical discount rate of WWE's widget venture if all equity financed is also 0.1825.[4] This discount rate would be employed if WWE uses the APV approach because the APV approach calls for R_A, the project's cost of capital in a firm with no leverage.

3 *Determining R_E for WWE's widget venture*: Alternatively, WWE might use the FTE approach, where the discount rate for levered equity is determined like this:

Cost of equity capital for WWE's widget venture

$$R_E = R_A + \frac{D}{E}(1 - t_C)(R_A - R_D)$$

$$= 18.25\% + \frac{1}{3}(0.60)(18.25\% - 10\%)$$

$$= 19.9\%$$

Note that the cost of equity capital for WWE's widget venture, 0.199, is less than the cost of equity capital for AW, 0.2075. This occurs because AW has a higher debt-to-equity ratio. (As mentioned, both firms are assumed to have the same business risk.)

4 *Determining R_{WACC} for WWE's widget venture*: Finally, WWE might use the WACC approach. Here is the appropriate calculation:

R_{WACC} for WWE's widget venture

$$R_{WACC} = \frac{D}{D + E}R_D(1 - t_C) + \frac{E}{D + E}R_E$$

$$= \frac{1}{4}10\%(0.60) + \frac{3}{4}19.9\%$$

$$= 16.425\%$$

The preceding example shows how the three discount rates, R_A, R_E and R_{WACC}, are determined in the real world. These are the appropriate rates for the APV, FTE and WACC approaches, respectively. Note that R_E for Asian Widgets is determined first because the cost of equity capital can be determined from the beta of the firm's equity. As discussed in an earlier chapter, beta can easily be estimated for any publicly traded firm such as AW.

17.6 APV Example

As mentioned earlier in this chapter, firms generally set a target debt-to-equity ratio, allowing the use of WACC and FTE for capital budgeting. APV does not work as well here. However, as we also mentioned earlier, APV is the preferred approach when there are side benefits and side costs to debt. Because the analysis can be tricky, we now devote an entire section to an example where, in addition to the tax subsidy to debt, both flotation costs and interest subsidies come into play.

Example 17.2

APV

Bicksler Enterprises is considering a £10 million project that will last 5 years. The investment will be depreciated at 25 per cent reducing balance for tax purposes. At the end of the 5 years, the investment will be sold for its residual book value. The cash revenues less cash expenses per year are £3,500,000. The corporate tax bracket is 28 per cent. The risk-free rate is 10 per cent, and the cost of unlevered equity is 20 per cent.

First we will calculate the depreciation in each year.

	C_0	C_1	C_2	C_3	C_4	C_5
Initial outlay	−£10,000,000					
Depreciation		0.25 × (£10,000,000) =£2,500,000	0.25 × (£7,500,000) =£1,875,000	0.25 × (£5,625,000) =£1,406,250	0.25 × (£4,218,750) =£1,054,688	0.25 × (£3,164,063) =£791,016
Residual value		£7,500,000	£5,625,000	£4,218,750	£3,164,063	£2,373,047

The cash flow projections each year are below. Because the investment is sold at its residual value, there are no tax implications for the final cash flow of £2,373,047. If, for example, Bicksler sold the investment for £3,000,000 it would be liable to pay tax on the profit of £626,953 (£3,000,000 − £2,373,047):

	C_0	C_1	C_2	C_3	C_4	C_5	C_6
Initial outlay	−£10,000,000						£2,373,047
Depreciation tax shield		0.28 × £2,500,000 =£700,000	0.28 × £1,875,000 =£525,000	0.28 × £1,406,250 =£393,750	0.28 × £1,054,688 =£295,313	0.28 × £791,016 =£197,754	
Revenue less expenses		(1 − 0.28) × £3,500,000 =£2,520,000	£2,520,000	£2,520,000	£2,520,000	£2,520,000	

We stated before that the APV of a project is the sum of its all-equity value plus the additional effects of debt. We examine each in turn.

All-equity Value

Assuming the project is financed with all equity, we will discount the revenues and initial outlay cash flows by the cost of unlevered equity. The depreciation tax shield should be discounted at the risk-free rate. The present value of each cash flow is given below:

	C_0	C_1	C_2	C_3	C_4	C_5	C_6
Initial outlay	−£10,000,000						£794,729
Depreciation tax shield		£636,364	£433,884	£295,830	£201,703	£122,790	
Revenue less expenses		£2,100,000	£1,750,000	£1,458,333	£1,215,278	£1,012,731	
Present value	−£10,000,000	£2,736,364	£2,183,884	£1,754,164	£1,416,981	£1,135,521	£794,729

The net present value is thus:

$$-£10,000,000 + £2,736,364 + £1,754,164 + £1,416,981 + £1,135,521 + £794,729 = £21,642$$

This calculation uses the techniques presented in the early chapters of this book. Notice again that the depreciation tax shield is discounted at the riskless rate of 10 per cent. The revenues and expenses are discounted at the higher rate of 20 per cent.

An all-equity firm would accept the project because the NPV is £21,642. However, equity flotation costs and economic volatility (not mentioned yet) would more than likely make the NPV negative. However, debt financing may add enough value to the project to justify acceptance. We consider the effects of debt next.

Additional Effects of Debt

Bicksler Enterprises can obtain a 5-year, non-amortizing loan for £7,500,000 after flotation costs at the risk-free rate of 10 per cent. Flotation costs are fees paid when equity or debt is issued. These fees may go to printers, lawyers and bankers, among others. Bicksler Enterprises is informed that flotation costs will be 1 per cent of the gross proceeds of its loan. The previous chapter indicates that debt financing alters the NPV of a typical project.

Flotation Costs

Given that flotation costs are 1 per cent of the gross proceeds, we have:

$$£7,500,000 = (1 - 0.01) \times \text{Gross proceeds} = 0.99 \times \text{Gross proceeds}$$

Thus, the gross proceeds are:

$$\frac{£7,500,000}{1 - 0.01} = \frac{£7,500,000}{0.99} = £7,575,758$$

This implies flotation costs of £75,758 ($= 1\% \times £7,575,758$). To check the calculation, note that net proceeds are £7,500,000 ($= £7,575,758 - £75,758$). In other words, Bicksler Enterprises receives only £7,500,000. The flotation costs of £75,758 are received by intermediaries such as bankers.

Under International Financial Reporting Standards, flotation costs directly attributable to an investment in a particular asset should be depreciated using the same method as the asset itself. In our case, depreciation would be charged on the flotation costs using 25 per cent reducing balance. The tax shield can then be calculated accordingly. Flotation costs are paid immediately but are deducted from taxes by amortizing on a 25 per cent reducing balance basis over the life of the loan. The depreciation schedule on the flotation costs is presented below:

	C_0	C_1	C_2	C_3	C_4	C_5
Flotation costs	−£75,758					
Depreciation		$0.25 \times$ (£75,758) =£18,940	$0.25 \times$ (£56,818) =£14,205	$0.25 \times$ (£42,613) =£10,653	$0.25 \times$ (£31,960) =£7,990	$0.25 \times$ (£23,970) =£5,993
Residual value		£56,818	£42,613	£31,960	£23,970	£17,977

The cash flows from flotation costs are as follows:

	Date 0	Date 1	Date 2	Date 3	Date 4	Date 5	Date 6
Flotation costs	−£75,758						
Deduction		£18,940	£14,205	£10,653	£7,990	£5,993	£17,977
Tax shield from flotation costs		0.28(£18,940) =£5,303	0.28(£14,205) =£3,977	0.28(£10,653) =£2,983	0.28(£7,990) =£2,237	0.28(£5,993) =£1,678	0.28(£17,977) =£5,034
PV(Costs)	−£75,758	£4,821	£3,287	£2,241	£1,528	£1,042	£2,841

When we discount at 10 per cent, the net cost of flotation is:

$$-£75,758 + £4,821 + £3,287 + £2,241 + £1,528 + £1,042 + £2,841 = -£59,998$$

The net present value of the project after the flotation costs of debt but before the benefits of debt is:

$$£21,642 - £59,998 = -£38,356$$

Tax Subsidy

Interest must be paid on the gross proceeds of the loan, even though intermediaries receive the flotation costs. Because the gross proceeds of the loan are £7,575,578, annual interest is £757,576 ($= £7,575,758 \times 0.10$).

The interest cost after taxes is £545,455 [=£757,576 × (1 − 0.28)]. Because the loan is non-amortizing, the entire debt of £7,575,758 is repaid at date 5. These terms are indicated here:

	Date 0	Date 1	Date 2	Date 3	Date 4	Date 5
Loan (gross proceeds)	£7,575,758					
Interest paid		10% × £7,575,758 = £757,576	£757,576	£757,576	£757,576	£757,576
Interest cost after taxes		(1 − 0.28) × £757,576 = £545,455	£545,455	£545,455	£545,455	£545,455
Repayment of debt						£7,575,758

The relevant cash flows are listed in boldface in the preceding table. They are (1) loan received, (2) annual interest cost after taxes, and (3) repayment of debt. Note that we include the *gross* proceeds of the loan as an inflow because the flotation costs have previously been subtracted.

In Chapter 15 we mentioned that the financing decision can be evaluated in terms of net present value. The net present value of the loan is simply the sum of the net present values of each of the three cash flows. This can be represented as follows:

$$\text{NPV (loan)} = +\text{ Amount borrowed} - \frac{\text{Present value of after-tax interest payments}}{} - \frac{\text{Present value of loan repayments}}{} \qquad (17.1)$$

The calculations for this example are:

$$£804,105 = +£7,575,758 - \frac{£545,455}{0.10} \times \left[1 - \left(\frac{1}{1.10}\right)^5\right] - \frac{£7,575,758}{(1.10)^5} \qquad (17.1')$$

The NPV (loan) is positive, reflecting the interest tax shield.[5]

The adjusted present value of the project with this financing is:

$$\text{APV} = \text{All-equity value} - \text{Flotation cost of debt} + \text{NPV (loan)} \qquad (17.2)$$

$$£768,749 = £21,642 - £59,998 + £804,105 \qquad (17.2')$$

Though we previously saw that an all-equity firm would probably not accept the project (once equity flotation costs were taken into account), a firm would *accept* the project if a £7,500,000 (net) loan could be obtained.

Because the loan just discussed was at the market rate of 10 per cent, we have considered only two of the three additional effects of debt (flotation costs and tax subsidy) so far. We now examine another loan where the third effect arises.

Non-Market-Rate Financing

A number of companies are fortunate enough to obtain subsidized financing from a governmental authority. Suppose that the project of Bicksler Enterprises is deemed socially beneficial and the British government grants the firm a £7,500,000 loan at 8 per cent interest. In addition, all flotation costs are absorbed by the state. Clearly, the company will choose this loan over the one we previously calculated. Here are the cash flows from the loan:

	Date 0	Date 1	Date 2	Date 3	Date 4	Date 5
Loan received	£7,500,000					
Interest paid		8% × £7,500,000 = £600,000	£600,000	£600,000	£600,000	£600,000
After-tax interest		(1 − 0.28) £600,000 = £432,000	£432,000	£432,000	£432,000	£432,000
Repayment of debt						£7,500,000

The relevant cash flows are listed in boldface in the preceding table. Using Equation 17.1, the NPV (loan) is:

$$£1,205,470 = +£7,500,000 - \frac{£432,000}{0.10} \times \left[1 - \left(\frac{1}{1.10}\right)^5\right] - \frac{£7,500,000}{(1.10)^5} \qquad (17.1'')$$

Why do we discount the cash flows in Equation 17.1" at 10 per cent when the firm is borrowing at 8 per cent? We discount at 10 per cent because that is the fair or market-wide rate. That is, 10 per cent is the rate at which the firm could borrow *without* benefit of subsidization. The net present value of the subsidized loan is larger than the net present value of the earlier loan because the firm is now borrowing at the below-market rate of 8 per cent. Note that the NPV (loan) calculation in Equation 17.1" captures both the tax effect *and* the non-market-rate effect.

The net present value of the project with subsidized debt financing is:

$$APV = \text{All-equity value} - \text{Flotation costs of debt} + \text{NPV (loan)} \qquad (17.2)$$

$$£1,227,112 = £21,642 - £0 + £1,205,470 \qquad (17.2'')$$

The preceding example illustrates the adjusted present value (APV) approach. The approach begins with the present value of a project for the all-equity firm. Next, the effects of debt are added in. The approach has much to recommend it. It is intuitively appealing because individual components are calculated separately and added together in a simple way. And, if the debt from the project can be specified precisely, the present value of the debt can be calculated precisely.

17.7 Beta and Leverage

A previous chapter provides the formula for the relationship between the beta of the equity and leverage of the firm in a world without taxes. We reproduce this formula here:

The no-tax case

$$\beta_{\text{Equity}} = \beta_{\text{Asset}} \left(1 + \frac{\text{Debt}}{\text{Equity}} \right) \qquad (17.3)$$

As pointed out earlier, this relationship holds under the assumption that the beta of debt is zero.

Because firms must pay corporate taxes in practice, it is worthwhile to provide the relationship in a world with corporate taxes. It can be shown that the relationship between the beta of the unlevered firm and the beta of the levered equity is this:[6]

The corporate tax case

$$\beta_{\text{Equity}} = \left[1 + \frac{(1 - t_C)\text{Debt}}{\text{Equity}} \right] \beta_{\text{Unlevered firm}} \qquad (17.4)$$

when (1) the corporation is taxed at the rate of t_C, and (2) the debt has a zero beta.

Because $[1 + (1 - t_C)\text{ Debt/Equity}]$ must be more than 1 for a levered firm, it follows that $\beta_{\text{Unlevered firm}} < \beta_{\text{Equity}}$. The corporate tax case of Equation 17.4 is quite similar to the no-tax case of Equation 17.3 because the beta of levered equity must be greater than the beta of the unlevered firm in either case. The intuition that leverage increases the risk of equity applies in both cases.

However, notice that the two equations are not equal. It can be shown that leverage increases the equity beta less rapidly under corporate taxes. This occurs because, under taxes, leverage creates a *riskless* tax shield, thereby lowering the risk of the entire firm.

Example 17.3

Unlevered Betas

Barajas SA is considering a scale-enhancing project. The market value of the firm's debt is €100 million, and the market value of the firm's equity is €200 million. The debt is considered riskless. The corporate tax rate is 28 per cent. Regression analysis indicates that the beta of the firm's equity is 2. The risk-free rate is 10 per cent, and the expected market premium is 8.5 per cent. What would the project's discount rate be in the hypothetical case that Barajas SA is all-equity?

◁

We can answer this question in two steps.

1 *Determining beta of hypothetical all-equity firm*: Rearranging Equation 17.4, we have this:

Unlevered beta

$$\frac{\text{Equity}}{\text{Equity} + (1 - t_C) \times \text{Debt}} \times \beta_{\text{Equity}} = \beta_{\text{Unlevered firm}}$$

$$\frac{\text{€200 million}}{\text{€200 million} + (1 - 0.28) \times \text{€100 million}} \times 2 = 1.47 \qquad (17.5)$$

2 *Determining discount rate*: We calculate the discount rate from the security market line (SML) as follows:

Discount rate

$$R_E = R_F + \beta \times (R_M - R_F)$$
$$= 10\% + 1.47 \times 8.5\%$$
$$= 22.5\%$$

The Project Is Not Scale Enhancing

Because the previous example assumed that the project is scale enhancing, we began with the beta of the firm's equity. If the project is not scale enhancing, we could begin with the equity betas of firms in the industry of the project. For each firm, we could calculate the hypothetical beta of the unlevered equity by Equation 17.5. The SML could then be used to determine the project's discount rate from the average of these betas.

Example 17.4

More Unlevered Betas

The Irish firm, J. Lowes plc, which currently manufactures staples, is considering a €1 million investment in a project in the aircraft adhesives industry. The corporation estimates unlevered after-tax cash flows (UCF) of €300,000 per year into perpetuity from the project. The firm will finance the project with a debt-to-value ratio of 0.5 (or, equivalently, a debt-to-equity ratio of 1:1).

The three competitors in this new industry are currently unlevered, with betas of 1.2, 1.3 and 1.4. Assuming a risk-free rate of 5 per cent, a market risk premium of 9 per cent and a corporate tax rate of 12.5 per cent, what is the net present value of the project?

We can answer this question in five steps.

1 *Calculating the average unlevered beta in the industry*: The average unlevered beta across all three existing competitors in the aircraft adhesives industry is:

$$\frac{1.2 + 1.3 + 1.4}{3} = 1.3$$

2 *Calculating the levered beta for J. Lowes's new project*: Assuming the same unlevered beta for this new project as for the existing competitors, we have, from Equation 17.4:

Levered beta

$$\beta_{\text{Equity}} = \left[1 + \frac{(1 - t_C)\text{Debt}}{\text{Equity}}\right] \beta_{\text{Unlevered firm}}$$

$$= \left(1 + \frac{0.875 \times 1}{1}\right) \times 1.3$$

$$= 2.4375$$

3 *Calculating the cost of levered equity for the new project*: We calculate the discount rate from the security market line (SML) as follows:

Discount rate

$$R_E = R_F + \beta \times (R_M - R_F)$$
$$= 0.05 + 2.4375 \times 0.09$$
$$= 0.269$$

4   *Calculating the WACC for the new project*: The formula for determining the weighted average cost of capital, R_{WACC}, is:

$$R_{\text{WACC}} = \frac{D}{D + E} R_D (1 - t_C) + \frac{E}{D + E} R_E$$

$$= \frac{1}{2} \times 0.05 \times 0.875 + \frac{1}{2} \times 0.269$$

$$= 0.156$$

5   *Determining the project's value*: Because the cash flows are perpetual, the NPV of the project is:

$$\frac{\text{Unlevered cash flows } (UCF)}{R_{\text{WACC}}} - \text{Initial investment}$$

$$\frac{\text{€}300,000}{0.156} - \text{£1 million} = \text{£923,077}$$

Real World Insight 17.1

Investing in Student Apartments

A major growth area for investment in the UK is student accommodation. With more universities charging premium fees for their programmes, incoming students are becoming increasingly more choosy about the indirect impact of moving to a new city to study. Affordable but pleasant accommodation is a key input in deciding which university to attend and this has attracted a wave of entrepreneurs who seek to leverage the excess demand for student apartments.

One such entrepreneur, Russian billionaire Mikhail Fridman, has invested millions in UK student accommodation. His first investment was a £61 million purchase of apartments from McLaren Property, which doubled as a ballet school. At the same time, Fridman spent £83 million to buy more apartments in other parts of the UK. Finally, in 2015, he acquired Pure Student Living (five London-based luxury student tower blocks) for £535 million.

Summary and Conclusions

Earlier chapters of this text showed how to calculate net present value for projects of all-equity firms. We pointed out in the last two chapters that the introduction of taxes and bankruptcy costs changes a firm's financing decisions. Rational corporations should employ some debt in a world of this type. Because of the benefits and costs associated with debt, the capital budgeting decision is different for levered firms than for unlevered firms. The present chapter has discussed three methods for capital budgeting by levered firms: the adjusted present value (APV), flows to equity (FTE), and weighted average cost of capital (WACC) approaches.

1   The APV formula can be written as:

$$\sum_{t=1}^{\infty} \frac{UCF_t}{(1 + R_A)^t} + \text{Additional effects of debt} - \text{Initial investment}$$

There are four additional effects of debt:

(a) Tax shield from debt financing

(b) Flotation costs

(c) Bankruptcy costs

(d) Benefit of non-market-rate financing.

2   The FTE formula can be written as:

$$\sum_{t=1}^{\infty} \frac{LCF_t}{(1 + R_E)^t} - (\text{Initial investment} - \text{Amount borrowed})$$

3   The WACC formula can be written as:

$$\sum_{t=1}^{\infty} \frac{UCF_t}{(1 + R_{\text{WACC}})^t} - \text{Initial investment}$$

4   Corporations frequently follow this guideline:

    (a)   Use WACC or FTE if the firm's target debt-to-value *ratio* applies to the project over its life.

    (b)   Use APV if the project's *level* of debt is known over the life of the project.

5   The APV method is used frequently for special situations like interest subsidies, LBOs and leases. The WACC and FTE methods are commonly used for more typical capital budgeting situations. The APV approach is a rather unimportant method for typical capital budgeting situations.

6   The beta of the equity of the firm is positively related to the leverage of the firm.

Questions and Problems

CONCEPT

1   **Adjusted Present Value**   How is the APV of a project calculated? What about the FTE? What is the main difference between the APV, FTE and WACC?

2   **Capital Budgeting Assumptions**   What assumptions are commonly made in a capital budgeting analysis?

3   **Weighted Average Cost of Capital**   Is WACC consistent with a target debt–equity ratio? Explain.

4   **APV, FTE and WACC**   Compare and contrast the three methods of capital budgeting. What are their strengths and weaknesses? When and why should you use each method instead of the other two? Are the three methods consistent when a firm does not have a target debt-to-equity ratio? Explain.

5   **Discount Rate in Capital Budgeting**   Review the steps required in calculating the correct discount rate for capital budgeting when a firm has a high level of debt in its capital structure.

6   **Beta and Leverage**   What are the two types of risk that are measured by a levered beta?

REGULAR

7   **Capital Budgeting**   You are determining whether your company should undertake a new project and have calculated the NPV of the project using the WACC method when the CFO, a former accountant, notices that you did not use the interest payments in calculating the cash flows of the project. What should you tell him? If he insists that you include the interest payments in calculating the cash flows, what method can you use? The former accountant also tells you to assume the opportunity cost of the company's idle asset is zero. Is he correct? Why / why not?

8   **NPV and APV**   Zoso is a rental car company that is considering whether to add 25 cars to its fleet. The company depreciates all its rental cars using 20 per cent reducing balance, and at the end of 5 years assumes that the cars will be sold at residual value. The new cars are expected to generate £120,000 per year in earnings before taxes and depreciation for 5 years. The company is financed entirely by equity and has a 28 per cent tax rate. The required return on the company's unlevered equity is 10 per cent, and the new fleet will not change the risk of the company.

    (a)   What is the maximum price that the company should be willing to pay for the new fleet of cars if it remains an all-equity company?

    (b)   Suppose the company can purchase the fleet of cars for £375,000. Additionally, assume the company can issue £250,000 of 5-year, 8 per cent debt to finance the project. All principal will be repaid in one balloon payment at the end of the fifth year. What is the adjusted present value (APV) of the project?

9 **NPV Capital Budgeting**   Bose plc has developed a design for a new iPod docking station, and is considering whether it is viable to produce the product as a replacement for its existing product, whose popularity has decreased in the last year. The company publishes its financial accounts at 31 December 2014, and today is 1 January 2015. As the financial manager of the business you have been provided with the following information:

- The machinery required to produce the station will cost £100 million today. The project is likely to become obsolete after 5 years, at which time the machinery will have an expected resale value of £30 million.
- The company has already spent £20 million on market research and development of the prototype for the product.
- Production will take place on premises currently owned but rented out by the company for 35 million per annum.
- The annual sales volume over the life of the project is expected to be 100,000; 100,000; 200,000; 300,000; and 200,000 in years 1–5, respectively. The selling price per unit will be £300 throughout the life of the project.
- The variable costs per unit produced are expected to be as follows:

Materials	£90 per machine
Wages	£30 per machine
Others	£30 per machine

- The firm's fixed costs are currently £50 million, and are expected to increase to £55 million as a direct result of this project.
- The project's working capital requirements for the project are as follows:

Raw materials	one-tenth of annual material requirements
Finished goods	one-tenth of annual total costs of production
Debtors	one-fifth of annual sales
Creditors	one-fifth of annual material requirements.

- Tax depreciation on the purchase of the machine is allowed at 25 per cent on a reducing balance basis.
- The company pays corporation tax at 35 per cent, which is payable one year in arrears.
- The opportunity cost of capital for the project is 10 per cent.

Produce a working capital schedule and tax depreciation schedule for the project. Also prepare a change in income statement and show the change in cash flows. Calculate the project's NPV. Should the project be accepted?

10 **APV**   Gemini plc, an all-equity firm, is considering a €2.4 million investment that will be depreciated according to 25 per cent reducing balances. At the end of its 4-year life, the investment will be sold for its residual value. The project is expected to generate earnings before taxes and depreciation of €850,000 per year for 4 years. The investment will not change the risk level of the firm. The company can obtain a 4-year, 9.5 per cent loan to finance the project from a local bank. All principal will be repaid in one balloon payment at the end of the fourth year. The bank will charge the firm €24,000 in flotation fees, which will be amortized over the 4-year life of the loan. If the company financed the project entirely with equity, the firm's cost of capital would be 13 per cent. The corporate tax rate is 12.5 per cent. Using the adjusted present value method, determine whether the company should undertake the project.

11 **Flow to Equity**   Milano Pizza owns three identical restaurants popular for their specialty pizzas. Each restaurant has a debt–equity ratio of 40 per cent and makes interest payments of €29,500 at the end of each year. The cost of the firm's levered equity is 19 per cent. Each store estimates that annual sales will be €1 million; annual cost of goods sold will be €450,000; and annual general and administrative costs will be €325,000. These cash flows are expected to remain the same forever. The corporate tax rate is 37.2 per cent.

(a) Use the flow to equity approach to determine the value of the company's equity.

(b) What is the total value of the company?

12 **WACC**   Cryo NV is an all-equity firm involved in property and casualty insurance. However, Cryo is about to issue a 10-year bond issued at par with a coupon of 8 per cent. Prior to the bond issue, the firm has a beta of 0.8 but recognizes that this will change once the firm moves to its new target debt–equity ratio of 0.25. The expected return on the Euro Stoxx 50 index is 13 per cent and Treasury bills currently yield 3.4 per cent. What

will be Cryo NV's cost of debt, cost of equity and WACC once the bond is issued? The corporate tax rate is 23 per cent.

13 **WACC** If Wild Widgets were an all-equity company, it would have a beta of 1.1. The company has a target debt–equity ratio of 0.40. The expected return on the market portfolio is 13 per cent, and Treasury bills currently yield 7 per cent. The company has one bond issue outstanding that matures in 20 years and has a 9 per cent coupon rate. The bond currently sells for £97.50. The corporate tax rate is 28 per cent.

   (a) What is the company's cost of debt?
   (b) What is the company's cost of equity?
   (c) What is the company's weighted average cost of capital?

14 **Beta and Leverage** Maersk A/S and Lundberg A/S would have identical equity betas of 0.9 if both were all equity financed. The market value information for each company is shown here:

	Maersk A/S (DKr)	Lundberg A/S (DKr)
Debt	11,400,000	25,600,000
Equity	25,600,000	11,400,000

The expected return on the market portfolio is 9 per cent, and the risk-free rate is 2.3 per cent. Both companies are subject to a corporate tax rate of 25 per cent. Assume the beta of debt is zero.

   (a) What is the equity beta of each of the two companies?
   (b) What is the required rate of return on each of the two companies' equity?

15 **NPV of Loans** Daniel Kaffe, CFO of Kendrick Enterprises, is evaluating a 6-year, 13 per cent loan with gross proceeds of €9,000,000. The interest payments on the loan will be made annually. Flotation costs are estimated to be 1 per cent of gross proceeds and will be amortized using a 25 per cent reducing balance method over the 6-year life of the loan. The company has a tax rate of 35 per cent, and the loan will not increase the risk of financial distress for the company.

   (a) Calculate the net present value of the loan excluding flotation costs.
   (b) Calculate the net present value of the loan including flotation costs.

16 **NPV** Station GmbH is a German all-equity firm which is about to issue a new 10-year, 17 per cent bond with interest paid annually. The debt issue of €10 million is to fund an expansion of the firm's activities into Switzerland. Flotation costs are 0.8 per cent of gross proceeds, amortized over the life of the bond using 20 per cent reducing balances. Station's tax rate is 33 per cent and the bond will not increase the risk of financial distress. You believe that the company may be better off issuing the bond in Switzerland (rather than Germany) to raise visibility of the company among its new customer base. You estimate that a Swiss bond issue will increase cash flows by €200,000 per annum over 10 years from additional Swiss revenues. However, flotation costs are 1.2 per cent in Switzerland. What is the net present value of the loan if it is made in Germany? Is a Swiss bond issue a better decision? Explain.

17 **NPV for an All-equity Company** Shattered Glass plc is an all-equity firm. The cost of the company's equity is currently 22 per cent, and the risk-free rate is 3 per cent. The company is currently considering a project that will cost £8 million and last 5 years. The project will generate revenues minus expenses each year (excluding depreciation) in the amount of £2.3 million. If the company has a tax rate of 23 per cent, should it accept the project? The initial investment is depreciated using 20 per cent reducing balance and will have zero salvage value at the end of its life.

18 **WACC** XYZ plc is considering purchasing new equipment that would cost £40 million. The expected unlevered cash flows from this investment are £13 million per annum for the next 5 years. The company's stock returns have a covariance with the market portfolio of 0.048. The standard deviation of the returns on the market portfolio is 20 per cent, and the expected market risk premium is 7.5 per cent. XYZ currently have bonds outstanding with a market value of £30 million and a yield to maturity of 8 per cent. The company also has 5 million shares of ordinary shares outstanding, currently selling at £20 per share. The company's CEO considers the current debt–equity ratio as optimal. Government debt is currently selling at a yield of 6 per cent, and the company pays a corporation tax rate of 21 per cent.

   (a) Use the WACC approach to determine whether XYZ plc should purchase the equipment.
   (b) If the company decides to buy the equipment financed solely with debt, what is the cost of capital for the project?

19 WACC Bolero plc has compiled the following information on its financing costs:

Type of financing	Book value (£)	Market value (£)	Cost (%)
Long-term debt	2,000,000	2,000,000	3.5
Short-term debt	9,000,000	8,000,000	6.8
Ordinary shares	6,000,000	22,000,000	14.5
Total	17,000,000	32,000,000	

The company is in the 28 per cent tax bracket and has a target debt–equity ratio of 60 per cent. The target short-term debt/long-term debt ratio is 20 per cent.

(a) What is the company's weighted average cost of capital using book value weights?

(b) What is the company's weighted average cost of capital using market value weights?

(c) What is the company's weighted average cost of capital using target capital structure weights?

(d) What is the difference between WACCs? Which is the correct WACC to use for project evaluation?

20 APV Letlago plc has established a joint venture with Wannako Ltd to build a new gold mine in Kenya. The initial investment in paving equipment is £12 million. The equipment will be depreciated using the 20 per cent reducing balance method over its economic life of 5 years, at the end of which it will be sold for its residual value. Earnings before interest, taxes and depreciation collected from the gold mine are projected to be £0.8 million per annum for 20 years starting from the end of the first year. The corporate tax rate is 23 per cent. The required rate of return for the project under all-equity financing is 19 per cent. The pre-tax cost of debt for the joint partnership is 8.5 per cent. To encourage investment in the country's infrastructure, the Kenyan government will subsidize the project with a £10 million, 15-year loan at an interest rate of 7 per cent per year. All principal will be repaid in one balloon payment at the end of year 15. What is the adjusted present value of this project?

21 APV For the company in the previous problem, what is the value of being able to issue subsidized debt instead of having to issue debt at the terms it would normally receive? Assume the face amount and maturity of the debt issue are the same.

22 APV MVP GmbH has produced football supplies for over 20 years. The company currently has a debt–equity ratio of 50 per cent and is in the 29.8 per cent tax bracket. The required return on the firm's levered equity is 16 per cent. MVP is planning to expand its production capacity. The equipment to be purchased is expected to generate the following unlevered cash flows:

Year	Cash flow (€)
0	−24,000,000
1	8,000,000
2	13,000,000
3	10,000,000

The company has arranged a €12 million debt issue to partially finance the expansion. Under the loan, the company would pay interest of 9 per cent at the end of each year on the outstanding balance at the beginning of the year. The company would also make year-end principal payments of €4 million per year, completely retiring the issue by the end of the third year. Using the adjusted present value method, should the company proceed with the expansion?

23 WACC Neon Corporation's share price returns have a covariance with the market portfolio of 0.048. The standard deviation of the returns on the market portfolio is 20 per cent, and the expected market risk premium is 7.5 per cent. The company has bonds outstanding with a total market value of £30 million and a yield to maturity of 8 per cent. The company also has 5 million ordinary shares outstanding, each selling for £20. The company's CEO considers the firm's current debt–equity ratio optimal. The corporate tax rate is 28 per cent, and Treasury bills currently yield 6 per cent. The company is considering the purchase of additional equipment that would cost £40 million. The expected unlevered cash flows from the equipment are £13 million per year for 5 years. Purchasing the equipment will not change the risk level of the firm.

(a) Use the weighted average cost of capital approach to determine whether Neon should purchase the equipment.

(b) Suppose the company decides to fund the purchase of the equipment entirely with debt. What is the cost of capital for the project now? Explain.

CHALLENGE

24 **APV, FTE and WACC** Seger plc is an unlevered firm with expected annual earnings before taxes of £35 million in perpetuity. The current required return on the firm's equity is 20 per cent, and the firm distributes all of its earnings as dividends at the end of each year. The company has 1.5 million ordinary shares outstanding and is subject to a corporate tax rate of 28 per cent. The firm is planning a recapitalization under which it will issue £40 million of perpetual 9 per cent debt and use the proceeds to buy back shares.

(a) Calculate the value of the company before the recapitalization plan is announced. What is the value of equity before the announcement? What is the price per share?

(b) Use the APV method to calculate the company value after the recapitalization plan is announced. What is the value of equity after the announcement? What is the price per share?

(c) How many shares will be repurchased? What is the value of equity after the repurchase has been completed? What is the price per share?

(d) Use the flow to equity method to calculate the value of the company's equity after the recapitalization.

25 **APV, FTE and WACC** Mojito Mint Company has a debt–equity ratio of 0.45. The required return on the company's unlevered equity is 17 per cent, and the pre-tax cost of the firm's debt is 9 per cent. Sales revenue for the company is expected to remain stable indefinitely at last year's level of £23,500,000. Variable costs amount to 60 per cent of sales. The tax rate is 28 per cent, and the company distributes all its earnings as dividends at the end of each year.

(a) If the company were financed entirely by equity, how much would it be worth?

(b) What is the required return on the firm's levered equity?

(c) Use the weighted average cost of capital method to calculate the value of the company. What is the value of the company's equity? What is the value of the company's debt?

(d) Use the flow to equity method to calculate the value of the company's equity.

26 **APV, FTE and WACC** Lone Star Industries has just issued £160,000 of perpetual 10 per cent debt and used the proceeds to repurchase equity. The company expects to generate £75,000 of earnings before interest and taxes in perpetuity. The company distributes all its earnings as dividends at the end of each year. The firm's unlevered cost of capital is 18 per cent, and the corporate tax rate is 28 per cent.

(a) What is the value of the company as an unlevered firm?

(b) Use the adjusted present value method to calculate the value of the company with leverage.

(c) What is the required return on the firm's levered equity?

(d) Use the flow to equity method to calculate the value of the company's equity.

27 **Projects that Are Not Scale Enhancing** Blue Angel Ltd, a private firm in the holiday gift industry, is considering a new project. The company currently has a target debt–equity ratio of 0.40, but the industry target debt–equity ratio is 0.35. The industry average beta is 1.2. The market risk premium is 8 per cent, and the risk-free rate is 7 per cent. Assume all companies in this industry can issue debt at the risk-free rate. The corporate tax rate is 28 per cent. The project requires an initial outlay of £450,000 and is expected to result in a £75,000 cash inflow at the end of the first year. The project will be financed at Blue Angel's target debt–equity ratio. Annual cash flows from the project will grow at a constant rate of 5 per cent until the end of the fifth year and remain constant forever thereafter. Should Blue Angel invest in the project?

28 **Equivalence of WACC and APV** Read the paper by M. Massari, F. Roncaglio and L. Zanetti, 'On the Equivalence between the APV and the WACC Approach in a Growing Leveraged Firm', *European Financial Management*, Vol. 14, No. 1, 2008, pp. 152–162. Provide an overview of the main findings and discuss the implications of the research for investment evaluation.

29 **Equivalence of WACC and APV** Select a range of empirical studies on capital budgeting and discuss their findings. What, in your opinion, are the most interesting findings?

30 **NPV** After graduating from university you get a job for a non-dividend paying company which has recently listed on the stock exchange. Your manager tells you that the company does not favour the NPV approach to capital budgeting. Do you think this is a good decision by the company's management?

Exam Question (45 minutes)

Electrolar AB is planning to set up new operations in northern Sweden. Having established that the investment has a positive net present value, they now have to consider their financing decision. The underwriters to the company state that the total funding required amounts to SKr0.5 billion and that this can be raised through a debt issue or an equity issue.

1 Their first option concerns the use of debt financing. The underwriters suggest that a 10-year bond issue with a 7 per cent coupon may be a sensible route to raising these funds. If interest payments are tax deductible and the tax rate is 26.33 per cent, estimate the required rate of return for debt financing to the nearest half per cent. (25 marks)

2 The second option relates to equity financing. The underwriters believe that if the company were to issue shares to fund the proposed project, they would have to be sold at a discount of 20 per cent. Issue expenses will be 1 per cent of the funding requirement. Estimate the return required by investors when investing in Electrolar plc's new share issue. (25 marks)

3 Review the ways in which positive net present value opportunities may arise when a company wishes to raise funds in the financial markets. Use an example to illustrate your answer. (25 marks)

4 Compare and contrast the strengths and weaknesses of the adjusted present value, weighted average cost of capital, and flow to equity approaches to investment appraisal. Which method, in your opinion, is the best? Explain. (25 marks)

Mini Case

The Leveraged Buyout of Cheek Products Ltd

Cheek Products Ltd was founded 53 years ago by Joe Cheek and originally sold snack foods such as crisps and biscuits. Through acquisitions, the company has grown into a conglomerate with major divisions in the snack food industry, home security systems, cosmetics and plastics. Additionally, the company has several smaller divisions. In recent years the company has been underperforming, but the company's management does not seem to be aggressively pursuing opportunities to improve operations (and the share price).

Meg Whalen is a financial analyst specializing in identifying potential buyout targets. She believes that two major changes are needed at Cheek Products. First, she thinks that the company would be better off if it sold several divisions and concentrated on its core competencies in snack foods and home security systems. Second, the company is financed entirely with equity. Because the cash flows of the company are relatively steady, Meg thinks the company's debt–equity ratio should be at least 0.25. She believes these changes would significantly enhance shareholder wealth, but she also believes that the existing board and company management are unlikely to take the necessary actions. As a result, Meg thinks the company is a good candidate for a leveraged buyout.

A leveraged buyout (LBO) is the acquisition by a small group of equity investors of a public or private company. Generally, an LBO is financed primarily with debt. The new shareholders service the heavy interest and principal payments with cash from operations and/or asset sales. Shareholders generally hope to reverse the LBO within 3 to 7 years by way of a public offering or sale of the company to another firm. A buyout is therefore likely to be successful only if the firm generates enough cash to serve the debt in the early years and if the company is attractive to other buyers a few years down the road.

Meg has suggested the potential LBO to her partners, Ben Feller and Brenton Flynn. Ben and Brenton have asked Meg to provide projections of the cash flows for the company. Meg has provided the following estimates (in millions):

	2011 (£)	2012 (£)	2013 (£)	2014 (£)	2015 (£)
Sales	1,627	1,824	1,965	2,012	2,106
Costs	432	568	597	645	680
Depreciation	287	305	318	334	340

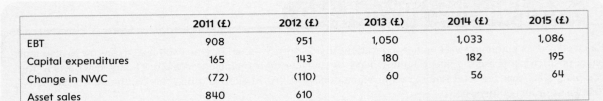

	2011 (£)	2012 (£)	2013 (£)	2014 (£)	2015 (£)
EBT	908	951	1,050	1,033	1,086
Capital expenditures	165	143	180	182	195
Change in NWC	(72)	(110)	60	56	64
Asset sales	840	610			

At the end of 5 years, Meg estimates that the growth rate in cash flows will be 3.5 per cent per year. The capital expenditures are for new projects and the replacement of equipment that wears out. Additionally, the company would realize cash flow from the sale of several divisions. Even though the company will sell these divisions, overall sales should increase because of a more concentrated effort on the remaining divisions.

After ploughing through the company's financials and various pro forma scenarios, Ben and Brenton feel that in 5 years they will be able to sell the company to another party or take it public again. They are also aware that they will have to borrow a considerable amount of the purchase price. The interest payments on the debt for each of the next 5 years if the LBO is undertaken will be these (in millions):

	2011	2012	2013	2014	2015
Interest payments (£)	1,140	1,100	1,180	1,150	1,190

The company currently has a required return on assets of 14 per cent. Because of the high debt level, the debt will carry a yield to maturity of 12.5 per cent for the next 5 years. When the debt is refinanced in 5 years, they believe the new yield to maturity will be 8 per cent.

Check Products Ltd currently has 104 million shares of equity outstanding that sell for £53 per share. The corporate tax rate is 28 per cent. If Meg, Ben and Brenton decide to undertake the LBO, what is the most they should offer per share?

Practical Case Study

We now return to our Cement example in Chapters 7 and 8. So far, we have gone with a consensus discount rate and assumed away any complications from leverage. The cement company for which you are carrying out consultancy has no debt funding. However, it wishes to borrow from a multinational bank in Tanzania the total amount required for the loan. If it does this, its debt–equity ratio will increase to 50 per cent. Assuming that the surveyed discount rates (see Chapter 7 case study) are for the firm prior to any debt increase, how would you now alter the analysis to take into account the increased debt? Use all information available to you, including the financial statements of other relevant companies.

Reference

Inselbag, I. and Kaufold, H. (1997) 'Two Approaches for Valuing Companies under Alternative Financial Strategies (and How to Choose between Them)', *Journal of Applied Corporate Finance,* Vol. 10, No. 1, 114–122.

Additional Reading

For recent developments, see:

1   Booth, L. (2002) 'Finding Value Where None Exists: Pitfalls in Using Adjusted Present Value', *Journal of Applied Corporate Finance,* Vol. 15, No. 1, 8–17.

2   Booth, L. (2007) 'Capital Cash Flows, APV and Valuation', *European Financial Management,* Vol. 13, No. 1, 29–48.

3 Dempsey, M. (2013) 'Consistent Cash Flow Valuation with Tax-Deductible Debt: A Clarification', *European Financial Management*, Vol. 19, No. 4, 830–836.

4 Massari, M., F. Roncaglio and L. Zanetti (2008) 'On the Equivalence between the APV and WACC Approach in a Growing Leveraged Firm', *European Financial Management*, Vol. 14, No. 1, 152–162.

Endnotes

1 That is, the present value of the project after the initial investment has been made is £541,935.49 (= £21,935.49 + £520,000). Thus, the debt-to-value ratio of the project is 0.25 (£135,483.90/£541,935.49).

This level of debt can be calculated directly. Note that:

Present value of levered project = Present value of unlevered project + $t_C \times D$

$$V_{\text{With debt}} = £504,000 + 0.28 \times 0.25 \times V_{\text{With debt}}$$

Rearranging the last line, we have:

$$V_{\text{With debt}} \times (1 - 0.28 \times 0.25) = £504,000$$

$$V_{\text{With debt}} = £541,935.50$$

Debt is 0.25 of value: £135,483.90 (= 0.25 × £541,935.50).

2 We use the term *levered cash flow* (LCF) for simplicity. A more complete term would be *cash flow from the project to the shareholders of a levered firm*. Similarly, a more complete term for *unlevered cash flow* (UCF) would be *cash flow from the project to the shareholders of an unlevered firm*.

3 See Inselbag and Kaufold (1997).

4 Alternatively, a firm might assume that its venture would be somewhat riskier because it is a new entrant. Thus, the firm might select a discount rate slightly higher than 0.1825. Of course, no exact formula exists for adjusting the discount rate upward.

5 The NPV (loan) must be zero in a no-tax world because interest provides no tax shield there. To check this intuition, we calculate:

No-tax case: $0 = +£7,575,758 - \dfrac{£757,576}{0.10} \times$

$$\left[1 - \left(\frac{1}{1.10}\right)^5\right] - \frac{£7,575,758}{(1.10)^5}$$

6 This result holds only if the beta of debt equals zero. To see this, note that:

$$V_U + t_C D = V_L = D + E \qquad \text{(a)}$$

where: V_U is the value of unlevered firm; V_L is the value of levered firm; D is the market value of debt in a levered firm; and E is the market value of equity in a levered firm.

As we stated in the text, the beta of the levered firm is a weighted average of the debt beta and the equity beta:

$$\frac{D}{D + E} \times \beta_D + \frac{E}{D + E} \times \beta_E$$

where β_D and β_E are the betas of the debt and the equity of the levered firm, respectively. Because $V_L = D + E$, we have:

$$\frac{D}{V_L} \times \beta_D + \frac{E}{V_L} \times \beta_E \qquad \text{(b)}$$

The beta of the levered firm can *also* be expressed as a weighted average of the beta of the unlevered firm and the beta of the tax shield:

$$\frac{V_U}{V_U + t_C D} \times \beta_U + \frac{t_C D}{V_U + t_C D} \times \beta_D$$

where β_U is the beta of the unlevered firm. This follows from Equation (a). Because $V_L = V_U + t_C D$, we have:

$$\frac{V_U}{V_L} \times \beta_U + \frac{t_C D}{V_L} \times \beta_D \qquad \text{(c)}$$

We can equate (b) and (c) because both represent the beta of a levered firm. Equation (a) tells us that $V_U = S + (1 - t_C) \times D$. Under the assumption that $\beta_D = 0$, equating (b) and (c) and using Equation (a) yields Equation 17.4.

The generalized formula for the levered beta (where β_D is not zero) is:

$$\beta_E = \beta_U + (1 - t_C)(\beta_U - \beta_D)\frac{D}{E}$$

and

$$\beta_U = \frac{E}{D(1 - t_C) + E}\beta_E + \frac{D(1 - t_C)}{D(1 - t_C) + E}\beta_D$$

Dividends and Other Payouts

During uncertain economic periods, many companies maintain or raise their dividends even though simultaneously providing cautious statements about future operations and the economy. The combination of positive news (dividend increases) with negative information (caution about future) often leaves investors uncertain of the sustainability of the dividend increases. In an interview with Reuters, Stuart Reeve (Blackrock Global Equity) summed up the feeling with the following words:

> *There are two things that threaten dividends – the first is that you pay out too much cash in a cyclical business and the second is that you're just too leveraged. We want to know what investment stream we can expect delivered and the capital growth we can reasonably hope for. We don't plan for what might come our way in buybacks. We want to know what the sustainable underlying dividend is.*

Why are dividends so important? What is meant by buybacks? This chapter explores the importance of dividends to corporate managers and the reasons why firms like to pay them. We also consider other forms of payouts to investors and why they are becoming more relevant.

KEY NOTATIONS

V_i	Value at time i
Div_i	Dividend at time i
R_E	Cost of equity capital; discount rate

18.1 Different Types of Dividends

The term *dividend* usually refers to a cash distribution of earnings. If a distribution is made from sources other than current or accumulated retained earnings, the term *distribution* rather than dividend is used. However, it is acceptable to refer to a distribution from earnings as a *dividend* and a distribution from capital as a *liquidating dividend*. More generally, any direct payment by the corporation to shareholders may be considered part of dividend policy.

The most common type of dividend is in the form of cash. Public companies usually pay regular cash dividends two times a year. Sometimes firms will pay a regular cash dividend and an *extra cash dividend*. Paying a cash dividend reduces corporate cash and retained earnings – except in the case of a liquidating dividend (where paid-in capital may be reduced).

Another type of dividend is paid out in shares of equity. This dividend is referred to as a stock dividend. It is not a true dividend because no cash leaves the firm. Rather, a stock dividend increases the number of shares outstanding, thereby reducing the value of each share. A stock dividend is commonly expressed as a ratio; for example, with a 2 per cent stock dividend a shareholder receives 1 new share for every 50 currently owned.

When a firm declares a stock split, it increases the number of shares outstanding. Because each share is now entitled to a smaller percentage of the firm's cash flow, the share price should fall. For example, if the managers of a firm whose equity is selling at €90 declare a 3:1 stock split, the price of a share of equity should fall to about €30. A stock split strongly resembles a stock dividend except that it is usually much larger.

18.2 Standard Method of Cash Dividend Payment

The decision to pay a dividend rests in the hands of the board of directors of the corporation. A dividend is distributable to shareholders of record on a specific date. When a dividend has been declared, it becomes a liability of the firm and cannot be easily rescinded by the corporation. The amount of dividend is expressed as pounds/euros/currency per share (*dividend per share*), as a percentage of the market price (*dividend yield*), or as a percentage of earnings per share (*dividend payout*).

The mechanics of a dividend payment can be illustrated by the example in Figure 18.1 and the following chronology:

1. *Declaration date*: On 15 January (the declaration date), the board of directors passes a resolution to pay a dividend of £1 per share on 16 February to all holders of record on 30 January.

2. *Date of record*: The corporation prepares a list on 30 January of all individuals believed to be shareholders as of this date. The word *believed* is important here: the dividend will not be paid to individuals whose notification of purchase is received by the company after 30 January.

3. *Ex-dividend date*: The procedure for the date of record would be unfair if efficient brokerage houses could notify the corporation by 30 January of a trade occurring on 29 January, whereas the same trade might not reach the corporation until 2 February if executed by a less efficient house. To eliminate this problem, all brokerage firms entitle shareholders to receive the dividend if they purchased the equity three business days before the date of record. The second day before the date of record, which is Wednesday, 28 January, in our example, is called the *ex-dividend date*. Before this date the shares are said to trade *cum dividend*.

4. *Date of payment*: The dividend cheques are mailed to the shareholders on 16 February.

Obviously, the ex-dividend date is important because an individual purchasing the security before the ex-dividend date will receive the current dividend, whereas another individual purchasing the security on or after this date will not receive the dividend. The share price will therefore fall on the ex-dividend date (assuming no other events occur). It is worthwhile to note that this drop is an indication of efficiency, not inefficiency, because the market rationally attaches value to a cash dividend. In a world with neither taxes nor transaction costs, the share price would be expected to fall by the amount of the dividend (illustrated in Figure 18.2):

Before ex-dividend date   Price $= £(P + 1)$
On or after ex-dividend date   Price $= £P$

Figure 18.1 Example of Procedure for Dividend Payment

Thursday, 15 January	Wednesday, 28 January	Friday, 30 January	Monday, 16 February
Declaration date	Ex-dividend date	Record date	Payment date

1 *Declaration date*: The board of directors declares a payment of dividends.
2 *Record date*: The declared dividends are distributable to shareholders of record on a specific date.
3 *Ex-dividend date*: A share of equity becomes ex dividend on the date the seller is entitled to keep the dividend; under stock exchange rules, shares are traded ex dividend on and after the second business day before the record date.
4 *Payment date*: The dividend cheques are mailed to shareholders of record.

Figure 18.2 Price Behaviour around the Ex-Dividend Date for a £1 Cash Dividend

Perfect world case
Ex-date

Price = £(P+1)

−t ... −2 −1 0 +1 +2 ... t

£1 is the ex-dividend price drop

Price = £P

In a world without taxes, the share price will fall by the amount of the dividend on the ex-date (time 0). If the dividend is £1 per share, the price will be equal to P on the ex-date.

Before ex-date (−1)   Price = £(P+1)
Ex-date (0)   Price = £P

The amount of the price drop may depend on tax rates. For example, consider the case with no capital gains taxes. On the day before an equity goes ex dividend, a purchaser must decide either (1) to buy the shares immediately and pay tax on the forthcoming dividend or (2) to buy the shares tomorrow, thereby missing the dividend. If all investors are in the 25 per cent bracket and the dividend is £1, the share price should fall by £0.75 on the ex-dividend date. That is, if the share price falls by this amount on the ex-dividend date, purchasers will receive the same return from either strategy.

As an example of the price drop on the ex-dividend date, consider an extraordinary dividend paid by Microsoft in 2004. The shares went ex dividend on 15 November 2004, with a total dividend of $3.08 per share, consisting of a $3 special dividend and a $0.08 regular dividend. The following share price chart shows the price of Microsoft shares on each of the 4 days prior to the ex-dividend date and on the ex-dividend date:

Figure 18.3 Microsoft Share Price

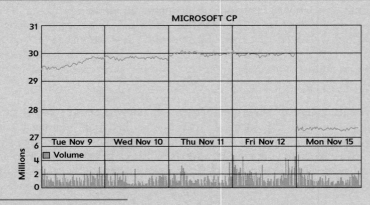

Source: Data drawn from Yahoo! Finance.

The shares closed at $29.97 on 12 November (a Friday) and opened at $27.34 on 15 November, a drop of $2.63. With a 15 per cent tax rate on dividends, we would have expected a drop of $2.62, and the actual price drop was almost exactly that amount.

18.3 The Benchmark Case: An Illustration of the Irrelevance of Dividend Policy

A powerful argument can be made that dividend policy does not matter. This will be illustrated with the Bristol Corporation. Bristol is an all-equity firm started 10 years ago. The current financial managers know at the present time (date 0) that the firm will dissolve in one year (date 1). At date 0 the managers are able to forecast cash flows with perfect certainty. The managers know that the firm will receive a cash flow of £10,000 immediately and another £10,000 next year. Bristol has no additional positive NPV projects.

Current Policy: Dividends Set Equal to Cash Flow

At the present time, dividends (Div) at each date are set equal to the cash flow of £10,000. The value of the firm can be calculated by discounting these dividends. This value is expressed as:

$$V_0 = Div_0 + \frac{Div_1}{1 + R_E}$$

where Div_0 and Div_1 are the cash flows paid out in dividends, and R_E is the discount rate. The first dividend is not discounted because it will be paid immediately.

Assuming $R_E = 10$ per cent, the value of the firm is:

$$£10,000 + \frac{£10,000}{1.1} = £19,090.91$$

If 1,000 shares are outstanding, the value of each share is:

$$£10 + \frac{£10}{1.1} = £19.09 \qquad (18.1)$$

To simplify the example, we assume that the ex-dividend date is the same as the date of payment. After the imminent dividend is paid, the share price will immediately fall to £9.09 (= £19.09 − £10). Several members of Bristol's board have expressed dissatisfaction with the current dividend policy and have asked you to analyse an alternative policy.

Alternative Policy: Initial Dividend Is Greater than Cash Flow

Another policy is for the firm to pay a dividend of £11 per share immediately, which is, of course, a total dividend payout of £11,000. Because the cash run-off is only £10,000, the extra £1,000 must be raised in one of a few ways. Perhaps the simplest would be to issue £1,000 of bonds or equity now (at date 0). Assume that equity is issued and the new shareholders will desire enough cash flow at date 1 to let them earn the required 10 per cent return on their date 0 investment. The new shareholders will demand £1,100 of the date 1 cash flow, leaving only £8,900 to the old shareholders. The dividends to the old shareholders will be these:

	Date 0 (£)	Date 1 (£)
Aggregate dividends to old shareholders	11,000	8,900
Dividends per share	11.00	8.90

The present value of the dividends per share is therefore:

$$£11 + \frac{£8.90}{1.1} = £19.09 \qquad (18.2)$$

Students often find it instructive to determine the price at which the new equity is issued. Because the new shareholders are not entitled to the immediate dividend, they would pay £8.09 (= £8.90/1.1) per share. Thus, 123.61 (= £1,000/£8.09) new shares are issued.

The Indifference Proposition

Note that the values in Equations 18.1 and 18.2 are equal. This leads to the initially surprising conclusion that the change in dividend policy did not affect the value of a share of equity. However, on reflection, the result seems sensible. The new shareholders are parting with their money at date 0 and receiving it back with the appropriate return at date 1. In other words, they are taking on a zero NPV investment. As illustrated in Figure 18.4, old shareholders are receiving additional funds at date 0 but must pay the new shareholders their money with the appropriate return at date 1. Because the old shareholders must pay back principal plus the appropriate return, the act of issuing new equity at date 0 will not increase or decrease the value of the old shareholders' holdings. That is, they are giving up a zero NPV investment to the new shareholders. An increase in dividends at date 0 leads to the necessary reduction of dividends at date 1, so the value of the old shareholders' holdings remains unchanged.

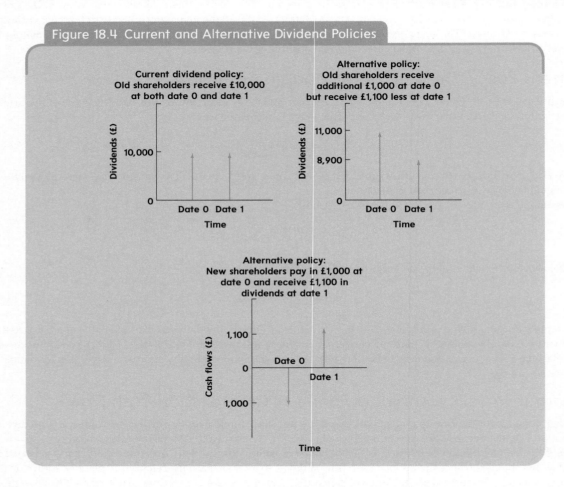

Figure 18.4 Current and Alternative Dividend Policies

This illustration is based on the pioneering work of Miller and Modigliani (MM). Although our presentation is in the form of a numerical example, the MM paper proves that investors are indifferent to dividend policy in a more general setting.

Homemade Dividends

To illustrate the indifference investors have toward dividend policy in our example, we used present value equations. An alternative and perhaps more intuitively appealing explanation avoids the mathematics of discounted cash flows.

Suppose individual investor X prefers dividends per share of £10 at both dates 0 and 1. Would she be disappointed when informed that the firm's management is adopting the alternative dividend policy (dividends of £11 and £8.90 on the two dates, respectively)? Not necessarily: she could easily reinvest the £1 of unneeded funds received on date 0, yielding an incremental return of £1.10 at date 1. Thus, she would receive her desired net cash flow of £11 − £1 = £10 at date 0 and £8.90 + £1.10 = £10 at date 1.

Conversely, imagine investor Z preferring £11 of cash flow at date 0 and £8.90 of cash flow at date 1, who finds that management will pay dividends of £10 at both dates 0 and 1. He can sell off shares of equity at date 0 to receive the desired amount of cash flow. That is, if he sells off shares (or fractions of shares) at date 0 totalling £1, his cash flow at date 0 becomes £10 + £1 = £11. Because a £1 sale of shares at date 0 will reduce his dividends by £1.10 at date 1, his net cash flow at date 1 would be £10 − £1.10 = £8.90.

The example illustrates how investors can make homemade dividends. In this instance, corporate dividend policy is being undone by a potentially dissatisfied shareholder. This homemade dividend is illustrated by Figure 18.5. Here the firm's cash flows of £10 per share at both dates 0 and 1 are represented by point A. This point also represents the initial dividend payout. However, as we just saw, the firm could alternatively pay out £11 per share at date 0 and £8.90 per share at date 1, a strategy represented by point B. Similarly, by either issuing new equity or buying back old equity, the firm could achieve a dividend payout represented by any point on the diagonal line.

Figure 18.5 Homemade Dividends: A Trade-Off between Dividends per Share at Date 0 and Dividends per Share at Date 1

The graph illustrates both (a) how managers can vary dividend policy, and (b) how individuals can undo the firm's dividend policy.

Managers varying dividend policy. A firm paying out all cash flows immediately is at point A on the graph. The firm could achieve point B by issuing equity to pay extra dividends or achieve point C by buying back old equity with some of its cash.

Individuals undoing the firm's dividend policy. Suppose the firm adopts the dividend policy represented by point B: dividends per share of £11 at date 0 and £8.90 at date 1. An investor can reinvest £1 of the dividends at 10 per cent, which will place her at point A. Suppose, alternatively, the firm adopts the dividend policy represented by point A. An investor can sell off £1 of equity at date 0, placing him at point B. No matter what dividend policy the firm establishes, a shareholder can undo it.

The previous paragraph describes the choices available to the managers of the firm. The same diagonal line also represents the choices available to the shareholder. For example, if the shareholder receives a per-share dividend distribution of (£11, £8.90), he or she can either reinvest some of the dividends to move down and to the right on the graph or sell off shares of equity and move up and to the left.

The implications of the graph can be summarized in two sentences:

1   By varying dividend policy, managers can achieve any payout along the diagonal line in Figure 18.5.

2   Either by reinvesting excess dividends at date 0 or by selling off shares of equity at this date, an individual investor can achieve any net cash payout along the diagonal line.

Thus, because both the corporation and the individual investor can move only along the diagonal line, dividend policy in this model is irrelevant. The changes the managers make in dividend policy can be undone by an individual who, by either reinvesting dividends or selling off equity, can move to a desired point on the diagonal line.

A Test

You can test your knowledge of this material by examining these true statements:

1   Dividends are relevant.

2   Dividend policy is irrelevant.

The first statement follows from common sense. Clearly, investors prefer higher dividends to lower dividends at any single date if the dividend level is held constant at every other date. In other words, if the dividend per share at a given date is raised while the dividend per share for each other date is held constant, the share price will rise. This act can be accomplished by management decisions that improve productivity, increase tax savings, or strengthen product marketing. In fact, you may recall that in Chapter 5 we argued that the value of a firm's equity is equal to the discounted present value of all its future dividends.

The second statement is understandable once we realize that dividend policy cannot raise the dividend per share at one date while holding the dividend level per share constant at all other dates. Rather, dividend policy merely establishes the trade-off between dividends at one date and dividends at another date. As we saw in Figure 18.5, an increase in date 0 dividends can be accomplished only by a decrease in date 1 dividends. The extent of the decrease is such that the present value of all dividends is not affected.

Thus, in this simple world, dividend policy does not matter. That is, managers choosing either to raise or to lower the current dividend do not affect the current value of their firm. This theory is powerful, and the work of MM is generally considered a classic in modern finance. With relatively few assumptions, a rather surprising result is shown to be perfectly true. Nevertheless, because we want to examine many real-world factors ignored by MM, their work is only a starting point in this chapter's discussion of dividends. Later parts of this chapter investigate these real-world considerations.

Dividends and Investment Policy

The preceding argument shows that an increase in dividends through issuance of new shares neither helps nor hurts the shareholders. Similarly, a reduction in dividends through share repurchases neither helps nor hurts shareholders.

What about reducing capital expenditures to increase dividends? Earlier chapters show that a firm should accept all positive net present value projects. To do otherwise would reduce the value of the firm. Thus, we have an important point:

Firms should never give up a positive NPV project to increase a dividend (or to pay a dividend for the first time).

This idea was implicitly considered by Miller and Modigliani. One of the assumptions underlying their dividend irrelevance proposition was this: 'The investment policy of the firm is set ahead of time and is not altered by changes in dividend policy.'

As later sections will show, there is always more to real life than theory predicts.

18.4   Share Repurchases

Instead of paying dividends, a firm may use cash to repurchase shares of its own equity. Share repurchases have taken on increased importance in recent years. Consider the situation in Europe, where in recent years, share repurchase activity exploded to now comprise over half the value of all cash dividends in the European Union.[1] Table 18.1 shows the trend in share repurchases over the period 1989 to 2005. It is clear that in all countries, share repurchases have become a much more important part of payout policy since 1999.

Share repurchases are typically accomplished in one of three ways. First, companies may simply purchase their own equity, just as anyone would buy shares of a particular company. In these *open market purchases*, the firm does not reveal itself as the buyer. Thus, the seller does not know whether the shares were sold back to the firm or to just another investor.

Second, the firm could institute a *tender offer*. Here, the firm announces to all of its shareholders that it is willing to buy a fixed number of shares at a specific price. For example, suppose Arts and Crafts (A&C) has 1 million shares outstanding, with a share price of €50. The firm makes a tender offer to buy back 300,000 shares at €60 per share. A&C chooses a price above €50 to induce shareholders to sell – that is, tender – their shares. In fact, if the tender price is set high enough, shareholders may want to sell more than the 300,000 shares. In the extreme case where all outstanding shares are tendered, A&C will buy back 3 out of every 10 shares that a shareholder has.

Finally, firms may repurchase shares from specific individual shareholders, a procedure called a *targeted repurchase*. For example, suppose International Biotechnology AB purchased approximately 10 per cent of the outstanding shares of Prime Robotics Ltd (P-R Ltd) in April at around SKr38 per share. At that time, International Biotechnology announced to the Stockholm Stock Exchange that it might eventually try to take control of P-R Ltd. In May, P-R Ltd repurchased International Biotechnology holdings at SKr48 per share, well above the market price at that time. This offer was not extended to other shareholders.

Companies engage in targeted repurchases for a variety of reasons. In some rare cases, a single large shareholder can be bought out at a price lower than that in a tender offer. The legal fees in a targeted repurchase may also be lower than those in a more typical buyback. In addition, the shares of large shareholders are often repurchased to avoid a takeover unfavourable to management.

We now consider an example of a repurchase presented in the theoretical world of a perfect capital market. We next discuss real-world factors involved in the repurchase decision.

Table 18.1 Share Repurchases in Europe (€ millions) between 1989 and 2005

Year	Austria	Belgium	Denmark	Finland	France	Germany	Greece	Ireland	Italy	Luxembourg	Netherlands	Portugal	Spain	Sweden	United Kingdom	All countries
1989	0	0	8	129	577	0	0	0	260	0	114	6	46	40	4965	6146
1990	0	0	27	134	278	54	0	0	366	0	19	0	37	3	1543	2461
1991	0	0	0	22	99	0	0	0	99	0	19	0	2	17	316	575
1992	0	0	0	83	−11	210	0	5	202	0	18	3	6	35	462	1013
1993	0	5	1	9	91	45	0	58	1	0	1	−14	33	14	1049	1293
1994	0	0	16	5	151	70	0	6	0	0	432	11	23	0	1100	1813
1995	0	0	2	40	252	2	0	71	0	5	5	7	59	2	898	1344
1996	0	0	0	104	86	1	0	1	0	3	140	16	82	363	1152	1946
1997	1	0	16	20	472	71	0	13	27	2	540	17	67	1743	6726	9717
1998	0	0	331	388	888	4	0	66	182	3	1405	60	218	610	13569	17723
1999	24	0	463	247	5019	1601	0	29	153	1	1464	36	177	408	6706	16329
2000	105	107	665	542	4291	4583	4	16	697	0	1443	38	173	2874	10518	26056
2001	160	190	176	689	11875	2289	162	43	1797	6	1639	39	168	1685	9695	30611
2002	19	341	449	351	5883	1164	0	65	824	2	1176	28	257	415	13409	24382
2003	4	57	492	1595	5917	1424	4	13	658	35	837	54	189	477	10123	21880
2004	0	363	704	2727	8419	2234	43	34	182	265	1091	32	382	1001	13335	30814
2005	35	1076	984	4428	6184	3508	256	349	1355	48	7383	31	1126	2733	29344	58841
Total	349	2138	4336	11515	50473	17259	468	767	6804	370	17726	363	3047	12420	124909	252943

Source: von Eije and Megginson (2008).

Dividend versus Repurchase: Conceptual Example

Imagine that Telephonic Industries has excess cash of £300,000 (or £3 per share) and is considering an immediate payment of this amount as an extra dividend. The firm forecasts that, after the dividend, earnings will be £450,000 per year, or £4.50 for each of the 100,000 shares outstanding. Because the price–earnings ratio is 6 for comparable companies, the shares of the firm should sell for £27 (= £4.50 × 6) after the dividend is paid. These figures are presented in the top half of Table 18.2. Because the dividend is £3 per share, the equity would have sold for £30 a share *before* payment of the dividend.

Table 18.2 Dividend versus Repurchase Example for Telephonic Industries

	For Entire Firm (£)	Per Share (£)
Extra Dividend		(100,000 shares outstanding)
Proposed dividend	300,000	3.00
Forecast annual earnings after dividend	450,000	4.50
Market value of equity after dividend	2,700,000	27.00
Repurchase		(90,000 shares outstanding)
Forecast annual earnings after repurchase	450,000	5.00
Market value of equity after repurchase	2,700,000	30.00

Alternatively, the firm could use the excess cash to repurchase some of its own equity. Imagine that a tender offer of £30 a share is made. Here, 10,000 shares are repurchased so that the total number of shares remaining is 90,000. With fewer shares outstanding, the earnings per share will rise to £5 (= £450,000/90,000). The price–earnings ratio remains at 6 because both the business and financial risks of the firm are the same in the repurchase case as they were in the dividend case. Thus, the price of a share after the repurchase is £30 (= £5 × 6). These results are presented in the bottom half of Table 18.2.

If commissions, taxes and other imperfections are ignored in our example, the shareholders are indifferent between a dividend and a repurchase. With dividends each shareholder owns a share worth £27 and receives £3 in dividends, so that the total value is £30. This figure is the same as both the amount received by the selling shareholders and the value of the equity for the remaining shareholders in the repurchase case.

This example illustrates the important point that, in a perfect market, the firm is indifferent between a dividend payment and a share repurchase. This result is quite similar to the indifference propositions established by MM for debt versus equity financing and for dividends versus capital gains.

You may often read in the popular financial press that a repurchase agreement is beneficial because earnings per share increase. Earnings per share do rise for Telephonic Industries if a repurchase is substituted for a cash dividend: the EPS is £4.50 after a dividend and £5 after the repurchase. This result holds because the drop in shares after a repurchase implies a reduction in the denominator of the EPS ratio.

However, the financial press frequently places undue emphasis on EPS figures in a repurchase agreement. Given the irrelevance propositions we have discussed, the increase in EPS here is not beneficial. Table 18.2 shows that, in a perfect capital market, the total value to the shareholder is the same under the dividend payment strategy as under the repurchase strategy.

Dividends versus Repurchases: Real-world Considerations

Why do some firms choose repurchases over dividends? Here are perhaps five of the most common reasons.

1 Flexibility

Firms often view dividends as a commitment to their shareholders and are quite hesitant to reduce an existing dividend. Repurchases do not represent a similar commitment. Thus, a firm with a permanent increase in cash flow is likely to increase its dividend. Conversely, a firm whose cash flow increase is only temporary is likely to repurchase shares of equity.

2 Executive Compensation

Executives are frequently given share options as part of their overall compensation. Let us revisit the Telephonic Industries example of Table 18.2, where the firm's equity was selling at £30 when the firm was considering either a dividend or a repurchase. Further imagine that Telephonic had granted 1,000 share options to its CEO, Ralph Taylor, 2 years earlier. At that time, the share price was, say, only £20. This means that Mr Taylor can buy 1,000 shares for £20 a share at any time between the grant of the options and their expiration, a procedure called *exercising* the options. His gain from exercising is directly proportional to the rise in the share price above £20. As we saw in the example, the price of the equity would fall to £27 following a dividend but would remain at £30 following a repurchase. The CEO would clearly prefer a repurchase to a dividend because the difference between the share price and the exercise price of £20 would be £10 (= £30 − £20) following the repurchase but only £7 (= £27 − £20) following the dividend. Existing share options will always have greater value when the firm repurchases shares instead of paying a dividend because the share price will be greater after a repurchase than after a dividend.

3 Offset to Dilution

In addition, the exercise of share options increases the number of shares outstanding. In other words, exercise causes dilution of the shares. Firms frequently buy back shares of equity to offset this dilution. However, it is hard to argue that this is a valid reason for repurchase. As we showed in Table 18.2, repurchase is neither better nor worse for the shareholders than a dividend. Our argument holds whether or not share options have been exercised previously.

4 Undervaluation

Many companies buy back shares because they believe that a repurchase is their best investment. This occurs more frequently when managers believe that the share price is temporarily depressed.

The fact that some companies repurchase their equity when they believe it is undervalued does not imply that the management of the company must be correct; only empirical studies can make this determination. The immediate market reaction to the announcement of a share repurchase is usually quite favourable. In addition, some empirical work has shown that the long-term share price performance of securities after a buyback is better than the share price performance of comparable companies that do not repurchase.

5 Taxes

Because taxes for both dividends and share repurchases are treated in depth in the next section, suffice it to say at this point that repurchases provide a tax advantage over dividends.

18.5   Personal Taxes and Dividends

Chapter 15 Page 416

Section 18.3 asserted that in a world without taxes and other frictions, dividend policy is irrelevant. Similarly, Section 18.4 concluded that the choice between a share repurchase and a dividend is irrelevant in a world of this type. This section examines the effect of taxes on both dividends and repurchases (see also **Chapter 15**, Section 15.6 for the effect of personal taxes on capital structure). Our discussion is facilitated by classifying firms into two types: those without sufficient cash to pay a dividend and those with sufficient cash to do so.

Firms without Sufficient Cash to Pay a Dividend

It is simplest to begin with a firm without cash and owned by a single entrepreneur. If this firm should decide to pay a dividend of £100, it must raise capital. The firm might choose among a number of different equity and bond issues to pay the dividend. However, for simplicity, we assume that the entrepreneur contributes cash to the firm by issuing shares to himself. This transaction, diagrammed in the left side of Figure 18.6, would clearly be a *wash* in a world of no taxes. The £100 cash goes into the firm when equity is issued and is immediately paid out as a dividend. Thus, the entrepreneur neither benefits nor loses when the dividend is paid, a result consistent with Miller–Modigliani.

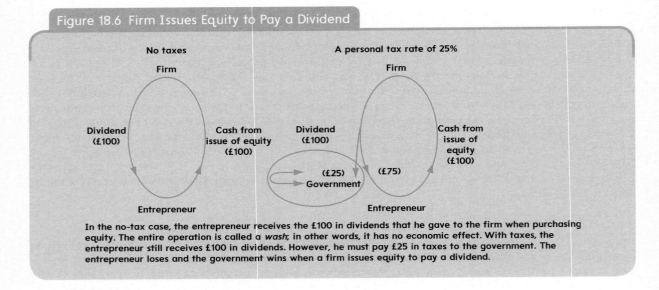

Figure 18.6 Firm Issues Equity to Pay a Dividend

In the no-tax case, the entrepreneur receives the £100 in dividends that he gave to the firm when purchasing equity. The entire operation is called a *wash;* in other words, it has no economic effect. With taxes, the entrepreneur still receives £100 in dividends. However, he must pay £25 in taxes to the government. The entrepreneur loses and the government wins when a firm issues equity to pay a dividend.

Now assume that dividends are taxed at the owner's personal tax rate of 25 per cent (in the UK, this is the effective tax rate on dividend income for individuals earning over £35,000 but below £150,000).[2] The firm still receives £100 upon issuance of equity. However, the entrepreneur does not get to keep the full £100 dividend. Instead the dividend payment is taxed, implying that the owner receives only £75 net after tax. Thus, the entrepreneur loses £25.

Though the example is clearly contrived and unrealistic, similar results can be reached for more plausible situations. Thus, financial economists generally agree that in a world of personal taxes, firms should not issue equity to pay dividends.

The direct costs of issuance will add to this effect. Bankers must be paid when new capital is raised. Thus, the net receipts due to the firm from a new issue are less than 100 per cent of total capital raised. Because the size of new issues can be lowered by a reduction in dividends, we have another argument in favour of a low-dividend policy.

Of course, our advice not to finance dividends through new equity issues might need to be modified somewhat in the real world. A company with a large and steady cash flow for many years in the past might be paying a regular dividend. If the cash flow unexpectedly dried up for a single year, should new equity be issued so that dividends could be continued? Although our previous discussion would imply that new equity should not be issued, many managers might issue the equity anyway for practical reasons. In particular, shareholders appear to prefer dividend stability. Thus, managers might be forced to issue equity to achieve this stability, knowing full well the adverse tax consequences.

Firms with Sufficient Cash to Pay a Dividend

The previous discussion argued that in a world with personal taxes, a firm should not issue equity to pay a dividend. Does the tax disadvantage of dividends imply the stronger policy, 'Never, under any circumstances, pay dividends in a world with personal taxes'?

We argue next that this prescription does not necessarily apply to firms with excess cash. To see this, imagine a firm with £1 million in extra cash after selecting all positive NPV projects and determining the level of prudent cash balances. The firm might consider the following alternatives to a dividend:

1 *Select additional capital budgeting projects.* Because the firm has taken all the available positive NPV projects already, it must invest its excess cash in negative NPV projects. This is clearly a policy at variance with the principles of corporate finance.

**Chapter 16
Page 428**

In spite of our distaste for this policy, researchers have suggested that many managers purposely take on negative NPV projects in lieu of paying dividends.[3] The idea here is that managers would rather keep the funds in the firm because their prestige, pay and perquisites are often tied to the firm's size. Although managers may help themselves here, they are hurting shareholders. We broached this subject in the section titled 'Free Cash Flow' in **Chapter 16**, and we will have more to say about it later in this chapter.

2   *Acquire other companies.* To avoid the payment of dividends, a firm might use excess cash to acquire another company. This strategy has the advantage of acquiring profitable assets. However, a firm often incurs heavy costs when it embarks upon an acquisition programme. In addition, acquisitions are invariably made above the market price. Premiums of 20 to 80 per cent are not uncommon. Because of this, a number of researchers have argued that mergers are not generally profitable to the acquiring company, even when firms are merged for a valid business purpose. Therefore, a company making an acquisition merely to avoid a dividend is unlikely to succeed.

3   *Purchase financial assets.* The strategy of purchasing financial assets in lieu of a dividend payment can be illustrated with the following example.

Example 18.1

Dividends and Taxes

The Dutch firm, Regional Electric NV, has €1,000 of extra cash. It can retain the cash and invest it in Treasury bills yielding 10 per cent, or it can pay the cash to shareholders as a dividend. Shareholders can also invest in Treasury bills with the same yield. In the Netherlands, the effective corporate tax rate is 30 per cent and the dividend tax rate is 15 per cent. The personal tax rate is an incremental system whereby different tax rates are levied on different salary bands. This means that each individual will have a unique personal tax rate dependent on their individual salary. Assume, for simplicity, that the effective personal tax rate for shareholders is 28 per cent. How much cash will investors have after 5 years under each policy?

If dividends are paid now, shareholders will receive:

$$€1,000 \times (1 - 0.15) = €850$$

today after taxes. Because their return after personal tax on Treasury bills is 7.2 [$= 10 \times (1 - 0.28)$] per cent, shareholders will have:

$$€850 \times (1.072)^5 = €1,203.35 \tag{18.3}$$

in 5 years. Note that interest income is taxed at the personal tax rate (28 per cent in this example), but dividends are taxed at the lower rate of 15 per cent.

If Regional Electric NV retains the cash to invest in Treasury bills, its after-tax interest rate will be 0.07 [$= 0.10 \times (1 - 0.3)$]. At the end of 5 years, the firm will have:

$$€1,000 \times (1.07)^5 = €1,402.55$$

If these proceeds are then paid as a dividend, the shareholders will receive:

$$€1,402.55 \times (1 - 0.15) = €1,192.17 \tag{18.4}$$

after personal taxes at date 5. The value in Equation 18.3 is greater than that in Equation 18.4, implying that cash to shareholders will be greater if the firm pays the dividend now.

This example shows that for a firm with extra cash, the dividend payout decision will depend on personal and corporate tax rates. If personal tax rates are higher than corporate tax rates, a firm will have an incentive to reduce dividend payouts. However, if personal tax rates are lower than corporate tax rates, a firm will have an incentive to pay out any excess cash as dividends.

Table 15.6 shows quite clearly that tax systems differ considerably across countries. In some countries, many investors face marginal tax rates that are above the corporate tax rate. However, at the same time, many investors face marginal tax rates well below the maximum. The interaction between personal and corporate tax rates within a country will mean that the environment faced by investors will be unique and a function of where they stay. As a result, firms may or may not have an incentive not to hoard cash. This is an important point because many US textbooks (which only consider the US environment) would argue that firms will pay dividends because of tax reasons. However, from a European or Asian perspective, this may not necessarily be a valid assertion.

4   *Repurchase shares*. The example we described in the previous section showed that investors are indifferent between share repurchase and dividends in a world without taxes and transaction costs. However, under current international tax laws, shareholders will generally prefer a repurchase to a dividend.

As an example, consider an individual receiving a dividend of €1 on each of 100 shares of an equity. With a 15 per cent tax rate, that individual would pay taxes of €15 on the dividend. Selling shareholders would pay lower taxes if the firm repurchased €100 of existing shares. This occurs because taxes are paid only on the *profit* from a sale. The individual's gain on a sale would be only €40 if the shares sold for €100 were originally purchased for, say, €60. The capital gains tax would be €6 ($= 0.15 \times €40$), a number below the tax on dividends of €15. Note that the tax from a repurchase is less than the tax on a dividend even though the same 15 per cent tax rate applies to both the repurchase and the dividend.

Of all the alternatives to dividends mentioned in this section, the strongest case can be made for repurchases. In fact, academics have long wondered why firms *ever* pay a dividend instead of repurchasing shares. There have been at least two possible reasons for avoiding repurchases. First, in many countries, including the UK, there is the fear that share repurchase programmes can lead to illegal price manipulation. Second, tax authorities can penalize firms repurchasing their own shares if the only reason is to avoid the taxes that would be levied on dividends. However, this threat has not materialized with the growth in corporate repurchases.

Summary of Personal Taxes

This section suggests that because of personal taxes, firms have an incentive to reduce dividends. For example, they might increase capital expenditures, acquire other companies or purchase financial assets. However, due to financial considerations and legal constraints, rational firms with large cash flows will likely exhaust these activities with plenty of cash left over for dividends.

It is harder to explain why firms pay dividends instead of repurchasing shares. The tax savings from buybacks are significant, and fear of either the stock exchange or tax authorities seems overblown. Academics are of two minds here. Some argue that corporations were simply slow to grasp the benefits from repurchases. However, since the idea has now firmly caught on, the trend toward replacement of dividends with buybacks will continue. We might even conjecture that dividends will be as unimportant in the future as repurchases were in the past. Conversely, others argue that companies have paid dividends all along for good reason. Perhaps the legal hassles, particularly from tax authorities, are significant after all. Or there may be other, more subtle benefits from dividends. We consider potential benefits of dividends in the next section.

18.6   Real-world Factors Favouring a High-dividend Policy

The previous section pointed out that because individuals pay taxes on dividends, financial managers might seek ways to reduce dividends. While we discussed the problems with taking on more capital budgeting projects, acquiring other firms, and hoarding cash, we stated that share repurchase has many of the benefits of a dividend with less of a tax disadvantage. This section considers reasons why a firm might pay its shareholders high dividends even in the presence of personal taxes on these dividends.

Desire for Current Income

It has been argued that many individuals desire current income. The classic example is the group of retired people and others living on a fixed income. The argument further states that these individuals would bid up the share price should dividends rise and bid down the share price should dividends fall.

This argument does not hold in Miller and Modigliani's theoretical model. An individual preferring high current cash flow but holding low-dividend securities could easily sell off shares to provide the necessary funds. Thus in a world of no transaction costs, a high current dividend policy would be of no value to the shareholder.

However, the current income argument is relevant in the real world. Equity sales involve brokerage fees and other transaction costs – direct cash expenses that could be avoided by an investment in high-dividend securities. In addition, equity sales are time-consuming, further leading investors to buy high-dividend securities.

To put this argument in perspective, remember that financial intermediaries such as mutual funds can perform repackaging transactions at low cost. Such intermediaries could buy low-dividend equities and, by a controlled policy of realizing gains, pay their investors at a higher rate.

Behavioural Finance

Suppose it turned out that the transaction costs in selling no-dividend securities could not account for the preference of investors for dividends. Would there still be a reason for high dividends? We introduced the topic of behavioural finance in Chapter 13, pointing out that the ideas of behaviourists represent a strong challenge to the theory of efficient capital markets. It turns out that behavioural finance also has an argument for high dividends.

The basic idea here concerns *self-control*, a concept that, though quite important in psychology, has received virtually no emphasis in finance. Although we cannot review all that psychology has to say about self-control, let us focus on one example – losing weight. Suppose Alfred Martin, a university student, just got back from the Christmas break more than a few pounds heavier than he would like. Alfred wishes to lose weight through doing yoga. Each day Alfred would balance the costs and the benefits of doing yoga. Perhaps he would choose to exercise on most days because losing the weight is important to him. However, when he is too busy with exams, he might rationally choose not to exercise because he cannot afford the time. So he may rationally choose to avoid doing yoga on days when other social commitments become too time-consuming.

Unfortunately, Alfred must make a proactive choice to do yoga every day, and there may be too many days when his lack of self-control gets the better of him. He may tell himself that he does not have the time to exercise on a particular day, simply because he is starting to find yoga boring, not because he really does not have the time. Before long, he is avoiding yoga on most days – and overeating in reaction to the guilt from not exercising!

Is there an alternative? One way would be to set rigid rules. Perhaps Alfred may decide to do yoga every day *no matter what*. This is not necessarily the best approach for everyone, but there is no question that many of us (perhaps most of us) live by a set of rules.

What does this have to do with dividends? Investors must also deal with self-control. Suppose a retiree wants to consume £20,000 a year from savings, in addition to her pension. On one hand, she could buy shares with a dividend yield high enough to generate £20,000 in dividends. On the other hand, she could place her savings in no-dividend shares, selling off £20,000 each year for consumption. Though these two approaches seem equivalent financially, the second one may allow for too much leeway. If lack of self-control gets the better of her, she might sell off too much, leaving little for her later years. Better, perhaps, to short-circuit this possibility by investing in dividend-paying equities with a firm personal rule of *never* 'dipping into principal'. Although behaviourists do not claim that this approach is for everyone, they argue that enough people think this way to explain why firms pay dividends – even though, as we said earlier, dividends are tax disadvantaged.

Does behavioural finance argue for increased share repurchases as well as increased dividends? The answer is no because investors will sell the shares that firms repurchase. As we have said, selling shares involves too much leeway. Investors might sell too many shares, leaving little for later years. Thus, the behaviourist argument may explain why companies pay dividends in a world with personal taxes.

Agency Costs

Although shareholders, bondholders and management form firms for mutually beneficial reasons, one party may later gain at the other's expense. For example, take the potential conflict between bondholders and shareholders. Bondholders would like shareholders to leave as much cash as possible in the firm so that this cash would be available to pay the bondholders during times of financial distress. Conversely, shareholders would like to keep this extra cash for themselves. That is where dividends come in. Managers, acting on behalf of the shareholders, may pay dividends simply to keep the cash away from the bondholders. In other words, a dividend can be viewed as a wealth transfer from bondholders to shareholders. There is empirical evidence for this view of things. For example, DeAngelo and DeAngelo (1990) find that firms in financial distress are reluctant to cut dividends.[4] Of course, bondholders know about the propensity of shareholders to transfer money out of the firm. To protect themselves, bondholders frequently create loan agreements stating that dividends can be paid only if the firm has earnings, cash flow and working capital above specified levels.

Although managers may be looking out for shareholders in any conflict with bondholders, managers may pursue selfish goals at the expense of shareholders in other situations. For example, as discussed in a previous chapter, managers might pad expense accounts, take on pet projects with negative NPVs, or simply not work hard. Managers find it easier to pursue these selfish goals when the firm has plenty of free cash flow. After all, one cannot squander funds if the funds are not available in the first place. And that is where dividends come in. Several scholars have suggested that the board of directors can use dividends to reduce agency costs.[5] By paying dividends equal to the amount of 'surplus' cash flow, a firm can reduce management's ability to squander the firm's resources.

This discussion suggests a reason for increased dividends, but the same argument applies to share repurchases as well. Managers, acting on behalf of shareholders, can just as easily keep cash from bondholders through repurchases as through dividends. And the board of directors, also acting on behalf of shareholders, can reduce the cash available to spendthrift managers just as easily through repurchases as through dividends. Thus, the presence of agency costs is not an argument for dividends over repurchases. Rather, agency costs imply firms may increase either dividends or share repurchases rather than hoard large amounts of cash.

Information Content of Dividends and Dividend Signalling

Information Content

While there are many things researchers do not know about dividends, we know one thing for sure: the share price of a firm generally rises when the firm announces a dividend increase and generally falls when a dividend reduction is announced. For example, Asquith and Mullins (1983) estimate that share prices rise about 3 per cent following announcements of dividend initiations. Michaely et al. (1995) find that share prices fall about 7 per cent following announcements of dividend omissions.

The question is how we should *interpret* this empirical evidence. Consider the following three positions on dividends:

1   From the homemade dividend argument of MM, dividend policy is irrelevant, given that future earnings (and cash flows) are held constant.

2   Because of tax effects, a firm's share price is negatively related to the current dividend when future earnings (or cash flows) are held constant.

3   Because of shareholders' desire for current income, a firm's share price is positively related to its current dividend, even when future earnings (or cash flows) are held constant.

At first glance, the empirical evidence that share prices rise when dividend increases are announced may seem consistent with position 3 and inconsistent with positions 1 and 2. In fact, many writers have said this. However, other authors have countered that the observation itself is consistent with all three positions. They point out that companies do not like to cut a dividend. Thus, firms will raise the dividend only when future earnings, cash flow and so on are expected to rise enough so that the dividend is not likely to be reduced later to its original level. A dividend increase is management's *signal* to the market that the firm is expected to do well.

It is the expectation of good times, and not only the shareholders' affinity for current income, that raises a share price. The rise in the share price following the dividend signal is called the information content effect of the dividend. To recapitulate, imagine that the share price is unaffected or even negatively affected by the level of dividends, given that future earnings (or cash flows) are held constant. Nevertheless, the information content effect implies that share prices may rise when dividends are raised – if dividends simultaneously cause shareholders to *increase* their expectations of future earnings and cash flows.

Dividend Signalling

We just argued that the market infers a rise in earnings and cash flows from a dividend increase, leading to a higher share price. Conversely, the market infers a decrease in cash flows from a dividend reduction, leading to a drop in share price. This raises an interesting corporate strategy: could management increase dividends just to make the market *think* that cash flows will be higher, even when management knows that cash flows will not rise?

While this strategy may seem dishonest, academics take the position that managers frequently attempt the strategy. Academics begin with the following accounting identity for an all-equity firm:

$$\text{Cash flow}^6 = \text{Capital expenditures} + \text{Dividends} \qquad (18.5)$$

Equation 18.5 must hold if a firm is neither issuing nor repurchasing equity. That is, the cash flow from the firm must go somewhere. If it is not paid out in dividends, it must be used in some expenditure. Whether the expenditure involves a capital budgeting project or a purchase of Treasury bills, it is still an expenditure.

Imagine that we are in the middle of the year and investors are trying to make some forecast of cash flow over the entire year. These investors may use Equation 18.5 to estimate cash flow. For example, suppose the firm announces that current dividends will be £50 million and the market believes that capital expenditures are £80 million. The market would then determine cash flow to be £130 million (= £50 + 80).

Now, suppose that the firm had, alternatively, announced a dividend of £70 million. The market might assume that cash flow remains at £130 million, implying capital expenditures of £60 million (= £130 − 70). Here, the increase in dividends would hurt the share price because the market anticipates valuable capital expenditures will be crowded out. Alternatively, the market might assume that capital expenditures remain at £80 million, implying the estimate of cash flow to be £150 million (= £70 + 80). The share price would likely rise here because share prices usually increase with cash flow. In general, academics believe that models where investors assume capital expenditures remain the same are more realistic. Thus, an increase in dividends raises the share price.

Now we come to the incentives of managers to fool the public. Suppose you are a manager who wants to boost the share price, perhaps because you are planning to sell some of your personal holdings of the company's equity immediately. You might increase dividends so that the market would raise its estimate of the firm's cash flow, thereby also boosting the current share price.

If this strategy is appealing, would anything prevent you from raising dividends without limit? The answer is yes because there is also a *cost* to raising dividends. That is, the firm will have to forgo some of its profitable projects. Remember that cash flow in Equation 18.5 is a constant, so an increase in dividends is obtained only by a reduction in capital expenditures. At some point the market will learn that cash flow has not increased, but instead profitable capital expenditures have been cut. Once the market absorbs this information, the share price should fall below what it would have been had dividends never been raised. Thus, if you plan to sell, say, half of your shares and retain the other half, an increase in dividends should help you on the immediate sale but hurt you when you sell your remaining shares years later. So your decision on the level of dividends will be based, among other things, on the timing of your personal equity sales.

This is a simplified example of dividend signalling, where the manager sets dividend policy based on maximum benefit for himself.[7] Alternatively, a given manager may have no desire to sell his shares immediately but knows that, at any one time, plenty of ordinary shareholders will want to do so. Thus, for the benefit of shareholders in general, a manager will always be aware of the trade-off between current and future share price. And this, then, is the essence of signalling with dividends. It is not enough for a manager to set dividend policy to maximize the true (or intrinsic) value of the firm. He must also consider the effect of dividend policy on the current share price, even if the current share price does not reflect true value.

Does a motive to signal imply that managers will increase dividends rather than share repurchases? The answer is likely no: most academic models imply that dividends and share repurchases are perfect substitutes.[8] Rather, these models indicate that managers will consider reducing capital spending (even on projects with positive NPVs) to increase either dividends or share repurchases.

18.7   The Clientele Effect

In the previous two sections, we pointed out that the existence of personal taxes favours a low-dividend policy, whereas other factors favour high dividends. The finance profession had hoped that it would be easy to determine which of these sets of factors dominates. Unfortunately, after years of research, no one has been able to conclude which of the two is more important. This is surprising: we might be sceptical that the two sets of factors would cancel each other out so perfectly.

However, one particular idea, known as the *clientele effect*, implies that the two sets of factors are likely to cancel each other out after all. To understand this idea, let us separate investors in high tax brackets from those in low tax brackets. Individuals in high tax brackets likely prefer either no or low dividends. Low tax bracket investors generally fall into two categories. First, there are individual investors in low brackets. They are likely to prefer some dividends if they desire current income. Second, in many countries, pension funds pay no taxes on either dividends or capital gains. Because they face no tax consequences, pension funds will also prefer dividends if they have a preference for current income. Suppose that 40 per cent of all investors prefer high dividends and 60 per cent prefer low dividends, yet only 20 per cent of firms pay high dividends while 80 per cent pay low dividends. Here, the high-dividend firms will be in short supply, implying that their equity should be bid up while the shares of low-dividend firms should be bid down.

However, the dividend policies of all firms need not be fixed in the long run. In this example, we would expect enough low-dividend firms to increase their payout so that 40 per cent of the firms pay high dividends and 60 per cent pay low dividends. After this adjustment, no firm will gain from changing its dividend policy. Once payouts of corporations conform to the desires of shareholders, no single firm can affect its market value by switching from one dividend strategy to another.

Clienteles are likely to form in the following way:

Group	Equities
Individuals in high tax brackets	Zero- to low-payout shares
Individuals in low tax brackets	Low- to medium-payout shares
Tax-free institutions	Medium- to high-payout shares

To see if you understand the clientele effect, consider the following statement: 'In a world where many investors like high dividends, a firm can boost its share price by increasing its dividend payout ratio.' True or false?

The statement is likely to be false. As long as there are already enough high-dividend firms to satisfy dividend-loving investors, a firm will not be able to boost its share price by paying high dividends. A firm can boost its share price only if an *unsatisfied* clientele exists.

Our discussion of clienteles followed from the fact that tax brackets vary across investors. If shareholders care about taxes, equities should attract clienteles based on dividend yield. Is there any evidence that this is the case?

Consider Figure 18.7. Here, John Graham and Alok Kumar (2006) rank equities by their dividend yields (the ratio of dividend to share price) and place them into five portfolios, called quintiles. The bottom quintile contains the 20 per cent of shares with the lowest dividend yields; the next quintile contains the 20 per cent of shares with the next lowest dividend yields; and so on. The figure shows the weight of each quintile in the portfolios of low-, medium-, and high-income investors. As can be seen, relative to low-income investors, high-income investors put a greater percentage of their assets into low-dividend securities. Conversely, again relative to low-income investors, high-income investors put a smaller percentage of their assets into high-dividend securities.

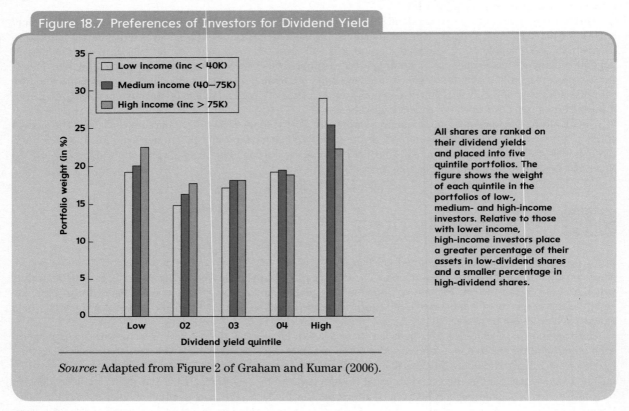

Figure 18.7 Preferences of Investors for Dividend Yield

All shares are ranked on their dividend yields and placed into five quintile portfolios. The figure shows the weight of each quintile in the portfolios of low-, medium- and high-income investors. Relative to those with lower income, high-income investors place a greater percentage of their assets in low-dividend shares and a smaller percentage in high-dividend shares.

Source: Adapted from Figure 2 of Graham and Kumar (2006).

18.8   A Catering Theory of Dividends

A recent perspective on why companies pay dividends has been proposed by Malcolm Baker and Jeffrey Wurgler (2004). The basic premise is that there are times when companies are mispriced in the stock market or when there are changes in the demand for dividend-paying equities. This may be because of the clientele effect, which predicts that if the proportion of dividend-paying companies in a market increases or decreases, the demand for dividend-paying shares will shift to a new equilibrium temporarily imparting a premium or discount on shares of companies that pay dividends.

Instead of focusing on investor decisions, the catering theory of dividends predicts that managers will rationally respond to time variation in investor demand for dividends by modifying their company's dividend policy. In effect, the theory makes less of a statement about market efficiency or behavioural finance than it does about the logical business decisions by corporate management. Baker and Wurgler (2004) show that management behaviour in the US is consistent with this theory. They consider dividend initiation and omission decisions and relate them to share price premiums for dividend-paying shares. For initiations in particular, the relationship with a price premium for dividends is exceptionally strong. This is clearly shown by Figure 18.8 where the link between dividend premium (market to book value) and dividend initiation is presented.

Figure 18.8 The Dividend Premium and the Rate of Dividend Initiation, 1962 to 2000

The log difference in the market-to-book ratio of dividend payers and non-payers (the dividend premium, dashed line–left axis) and one-year-ahead rate of dividend initiations (solid line–right axis). A firm is defined as a dividend payer at time *t* if it has positive dividends per share by the ex date. The initiation rate Initiate in *t* + 1 is defined as the percentage rate of new dividend payers at time *t* + 1 among surviving non-payers from *t*.

Source: Based on Figure 2 of Baker and Wurgler (2004).

So according to the catering theory, will dividend increases lead to a positive price reaction? Not necessarily. If the time-varying demand for dividend-paying shares is low, an announcement by a company that it is increasing its dividend will not likely be met with a positive reaction. In this situation, a dividend omission may elicit a more positive market response.

18.9   What We Know and Do Not Know about Dividend Policy

Corporate Dividends Are Substantial

We pointed out earlier in the chapter that dividends are tax disadvantaged relative to capital gains because dividends are taxed upon payment whereas taxes on capital gains are deferred until sale. Nevertheless, the total monetary value of dividends paid by companies is substantial. In Europe, the total real dividends (share repurchases and cash dividends) have increased significantly since 2000. For example, consider Figure 18.9, which shows the total real cash dividends and share repurchases by the EU15 companies between 1989 and 2005. Share repurchases increase from virtually zero in 1996 to €60 billion (2000 prices) in 2005. Similarly, cash dividends grow from approximately €40 billion in 1993 to nearer €120 billion in 2005.

We could argue that the taxation on dividends is actually minimal, perhaps because dividends are paid primarily to individuals in low tax brackets or because institutions such as pension funds, which normally pay no taxes, are the primary recipients. However, Peterson et al. (1985) conducted an in-depth study of dividends for one representative year, 1979. They found that about two-thirds of dividends went to individuals and that the average marginal tax bracket for these individuals was about 40 per cent. Thus, we must conclude that large amounts of dividends are paid, even in the presence of substantial taxation.

Fewer Companies Pay Dividends

Although dividends are substantial, von Eije and Megginson (2008) point out that the percentage of European companies paying cash dividends has fallen over the last few decades. They show that these have largely been replaced by share repurchases. Fama and French (2001) argue that the decline was caused primarily by an explosion of small, currently unprofitable companies that have recently listed on various stock exchanges. For the most part, firms of this type do not pay dividends. Figure 18.10 shows that the proportion of cash dividend payers among European industrial firms dropped substantially between 1989 and 2005.

Figure 18.9 Dividends and Share Repurchases in the European Union

Source: Adapted from Figure 4 of von Eije and Megginson (2008).

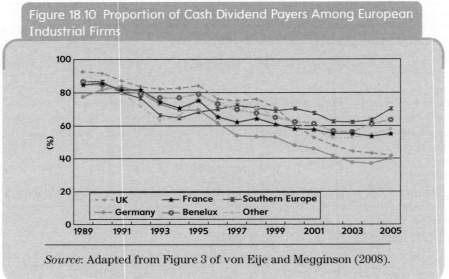

Figure 18.10 Proportion of Cash Dividend Payers Among European Industrial Firms

Source: Adapted from Figure 3 of von Eije and Megginson (2008).

This figure also shows an *increase* in the proportion of dividend payers across the whole of Europe from 2002 to 2005. Interestingly, this is the same pattern as seen in the US (Julio and Ikenberry, 2004). One reason given for the US was the cut in the maximum tax rate on dividends to 15 per cent, signed into law in May 2003. However, clearly this cannot be the reason for Europe. Furthermore, the resurgence in dividend payers has been observed only over the 2- and 3-year period from 2002 to 2005. Perhaps this trend is just a statistical aberration.

Figure 18.10 does not imply that dividends across *all* firms declined from 1989 to 2005. DeAngelo et al. (2004) point out that while small firms have shied away from dividends, the largest firms have substantially increased their dividends over recent decades. This increase has created such concentration in dividends that the 25 top dividend-paying firms accounted for more than 50 per cent of aggregate dividends in the United States in 2000. DeAngelo and colleagues conclude (p. 425): 'Industrial firms exhibit a two-tier structure in which a small number of firms with very high earnings collectively generates the majority of earnings and dominates the dividend supply, while the vast majority of firms has at best a modest collective impact on aggregate earnings and dividends.'

Corporations Smooth Dividends

In 1956, John Lintner made two important observations concerning dividend policy. First, real-world companies typically set long-term target ratios of dividends to earnings. A firm is likely to set a low target ratio if it has many positive NPV projects relative to available cash flow and a high ratio if it has few positive NPV projects. Second, managers know that only part of any change in earnings is likely to be permanent. Because managers need time to assess the permanence of any earnings rise, dividend changes appear to lag earnings changes by a number of periods.

Taken together, Lintner's observations suggest that two parameters describe dividend policy: the target payout ratio (t) and the speed of adjustment of current dividends to the target (s). Dividend changes will tend to conform to the following model:

$$\text{Dividend change} \equiv Div_1 - Div_0 = s \times (tEPS_1 - Div_0) \tag{18.6}$$

where Div_1 and Div_0 are dividends in the next year and dividends in the current year, respectively; s is the speed of adjustment coefficient; and EPS_1 is earnings per share in the next year.

Example 18.2

Dividend Smoothing

Calculator Graphics International (CGI) has a target payout ratio of 0.30. Last year's earnings per share were £10, and in accordance with the target, CGI paid cash dividends of £3 per share last year. However, earnings have jumped to £20 this year. Because the managers do not believe that this increase is permanent, they do *not* plan to raise dividends all the way to £6 (= 0.30 × £20). Rather, their speed of adjustment coefficient, s, is 0.5, implying that the *increase* in dividends from last year to this year will be

$$0.5 \times (\text{£}6 - \text{£}3) = \text{£}1.50$$

That is, the increase in dividends is the product of the speed of adjustment coefficient, 0.50, times the difference between what dividends would be with full adjustment [£6 (= 0.30 × £20)] and last year's dividends. Dividends will increase by £1.50, so dividends this year will be £4.50 (= £3 + £1.50).

Now, suppose that earnings stay at £20 next year. The increase in dividends next year will be

$$0.5 \times (\text{£}6 - \text{£}4.50) = \text{£}0.75$$

In words, the increase in dividends from this year to next year will be the speed of adjustment coefficient (0.50) times the difference between what dividends would have been next year with full adjustment (£6) and this year's dividends (£4.50). Because dividends will increase by £0.75, dividends next year will be £5.25 (= £4.50 + £0.75). In this way, dividends will slowly rise every year if earnings in all future years remain at £20. However, dividends will reach £6 only at infinity.

The limiting cases in Equation 18.6 occur when $s = 1$ and $s = 0$. If $s = 1$, the actual change in dividends will be equal to the target change in dividends. Here, full adjustment occurs immediately. If $s = 0$, $Div_1 = Div_0$. In other words, there is no change in dividends at all. Real-world companies can be expected to set s between 0 and 1.

An implication of Lintner's model is that the dividends-to-earnings ratio rises when a company begins a period of bad times, and the ratio falls when a company starts a period of good times. Thus, dividends display less variability than do earnings. In other words, firms *smooth* dividends.

Payouts Provide Information to the Market

We previously observed that the price of a firm's shares frequently rises when either its current dividend is increased or a share repurchase is announced. Conversely, the price of a firm's shares can fall significantly when its dividend is cut. This is a very strong signal that companies have less cash to pay out to shareholders and the accompanying price falls may suggest that investors are looking at current dividends for clues concerning the level of future earnings and dividends.

A Sensible Payout Policy

The knowledge of the finance profession varies across topic areas. For example, capital budgeting techniques are both powerful and precise. A single net present value equation can accurately determine whether a multimillion-pound or euro project should be accepted or rejected. The capital asset pricing model and the arbitrage pricing model provide empirically validated relationships between expected return and risk.

However, the profession has less knowledge of capital structure policy. Though a number of elegant theories relate firm value to the level of debt, no formula can be used to calculate the firm's optimal debt–equity ratio. Academics and practitioners are forced too frequently to employ rules of thumb, such as treating the industry's average ratio as the optimal one for the firm. The field's knowledge of dividend policy is, perhaps, similar to its knowledge of capital structure policy.

We do know the following:

1   The intrinsic value of a firm is reduced when positive NPV projects are rejected to pay a dividend.

2   Firms should avoid issuing shares to pay a dividend in a world with personal taxes.

3   Share repurchases represent a sensible alternative to dividends.

However, there is no formula for calculating the optimal dividend-to-earnings ratio. In addition, there is no formula for determining the optimal mix between share repurchases and dividends. It can be argued that for tax reasons, firms should always substitute share repurchases for dividends. But while the volume of repurchases has greatly increased over time, Figure 18.7 does not suggest that dividends are on the way out.

The Pros and Cons of Paying Dividends

Pros	Cons
1 Dividends may appeal to investors who desire stable cash flow but do not want to incur the transaction costs from periodically selling shares of equity.	1 Dividends are taxed as ordinary income.
2 Behavioural finance argues that investors with limited self-control can meet current consumption needs with high-dividend shares while adhering to the policy of never dipping into principal.	2 Dividends can reduce internal sources of financing. Dividends may force the firm to forgo positive NPV projects or to rely on costly external equity financing.
3 Managers, acting on behalf of shareholders, can pay dividends in order to keep cash from bondholders.	3 Once established, dividend cuts are hard to make without adversely affecting a firm's share price.
4 The board of directors, acting on behalf of shareholders, can use dividends to reduce the cash available to spendthrift managers.	
5 Managers may increase dividends to signal their optimism concerning future cash flow.	

Some Survey Evidence about Dividends

In a study surveying a large number of financial executives regarding dividend policy, one of the questions asked was this: 'Do these statements describe factors that affect your company's dividend decisions?' Table 18.3 shows some of the results.

As shown in Table 18.3, financial managers are very disinclined to cut dividends. Moreover, they are very conscious of their previous dividends and desire to maintain a relatively steady dividend. In contrast, the cost of external capital and the desire to attract 'prudent man' investors (those with fiduciary duties) are less important.

Table 18.3 Survey Responses on Dividend Decisions

Policy Statements	Percentage Who Agree or Strongly Agree
1 We try to avoid reducing dividends per share.	93.8
2 We try to maintain a smooth dividend from year to year.	89.6
3 We consider the level of dividends per share that we have paid in recent quarters.	88.2
4 We are reluctant to make dividend changes that might have to be reversed in the future.	77.9
5 We consider the change or growth in dividends per share.	66.7
6 We consider the cost of raising external capital to be smaller than the cost of cutting dividends.	42.8
7 We pay dividends to attract investors subject to 'prudent man' investment restrictions.	41.7

Survey respondents were asked the question, 'Do these statements describe factors that affect your company's dividend decisions?'

Source: Adapted from Table 4 of Brav et al. (2005).

Table 18.4 is drawn from the same survey, but here the responses are to the question, 'How important are the following factors to your company's dividend decisions?' Not surprisingly given the responses in Table 18.3 and our earlier discussion, the highest priority is maintaining a consistent dividend policy. The next several items are also consistent with our previous analysis. Financial managers are very concerned about earnings stability and future earnings levels in making dividend decisions, and they consider the availability of good investment opportunities. Survey respondents also believed that attracting both institutional and individual (retail) investors was relatively important.

Table 18.4 Survey Responses on Dividend Decisions

Policy Statements	Percentage Who Think This is Important or Very Important
1 Maintaining consistency with our historic dividend policy.	84.1
2 Stability of future earnings.	71.9
3 A sustainable change in earnings.	67.1
4 Attracting institutional investors to purchase our stock.	52.5
5 The availability of good investment opportunities for our firm to pursue.	47.6
6 Attracting retail investors to purchase our stock.	44.5
7 Personal taxes our stockholders pay when receiving dividends.	21.1
8 Flotation costs to issuing new equity.	9.3

Survey respondents were asked the question, 'How important are the following factors to your company's dividend decisions?'

Source: Adapted from Table 5 of Brav et al. (2005).

In contrast to our discussion in the earlier part of this chapter of taxes and flotation costs, the financial managers in this survey did not think that personal taxes paid on dividends by shareholders are very important. And even fewer think that equity flotation costs are relevant.

Real World Insight 18.1

Eni Dividends in the World of Collapsing Oil Prices

Eni, the Italian oil major, was one of many companies that were impacted by the 50 per cent drop in oil prices in 2015. Given that oil is both a key cost and revenue for the company, any change in the oil price can have a significant impact on the firm's operations. In March 2015, the CEO of Eni gave a press conference to present the company's 4-year strategic plan and his presentation gave great insights into the way executives think about dividends. During the press conference the CEO predicted that the Brent oil price would average out at $55 per barrel in 2015. Consequently, ENI would put significant focus into reducing capital expenditure and reducing costs in all their operations throughout the world. In terms of dividend policies, they decided to reset and lower their dividend to €0.8/share with a commitment to increase future years' dividend in line with earnings growth.

18.10   Stock Dividends and Stock Splits

Another type of dividend is paid out in shares of equity. This type of dividend is called a stock or share dividend. A stock dividend is not a true dividend because it is not paid in cash. The effect of a stock dividend is to increase the number of shares that each owner holds. Because there are more shares outstanding, each is worth less.

A stock dividend is commonly expressed as a percentage; for example, a 20 per cent stock dividend means that a shareholder receives one new share for every five currently owned (a 20 per cent increase). Because every shareholder receives 20 per cent more shares, the total number of shares outstanding rises by 20 per cent. As we will see in a moment, the result is that each share of equity is worth about 20 per cent less.

A stock split is essentially the same thing as a stock dividend, except that a split is expressed as a ratio instead of a percentage. When a split is declared, each share is split up to create additional shares. For example, in a three-for-one stock split, each old share is split into three new shares.

Some Details about Stock Splits and Stock Dividends

Stock splits and stock dividends have essentially the same impact on the corporation and the shareholder: they increase the number of shares outstanding and reduce the value per share. Unlike US accounting standards, IFRS makes no distinction between a cash dividend and a stock dividend. IFRS considers a stock dividend as being a cash dividend to shareholders with a simultaneous purchase of shares by the same shareholders.

Value of Stock Splits and Stock Dividends

The laws of logic tell us that stock splits and stock dividends can (1) leave the value of the firm unaffected, (2) increase its value, or (3) decrease its value. Unfortunately, the issues are complex enough that we cannot easily determine which of the three relationships holds.

The Benchmark Case

A strong case can be made that stock dividends and splits do not change either the wealth of any shareholder or the wealth of the firm as a whole. Consider an all-equity firm with a total market value of €660,000 and 10,000 shares. With the 10 per cent stock dividend, the number of shares increases to 11,000, so it seems that each would be worth €660,000/11,000 = €60.

For example, a shareholder who had 100 shares worth €66 each before the dividend would have 110 shares worth €60 each afterward. The total value of the equity is €6,600 either way; so the stock dividend does not really have any economic effect.

Now consider a two for one stock split. After the stock split, there are 20,000 shares outstanding, so each should be worth €660,000/20,000 = €33. In other words, the number of shares doubles and the price halves. From these calculations, it appears that stock dividends and splits are just paper transactions. This is the view taken by the International Accounting Standards Board in their International Financial Reporting Standards (IFRS).

Although these results are relatively obvious, there are reasons that are often given to suggest that there may be some benefits to these actions. The typical financial manager is aware of many real-world complexities, and for that reason the stock split or stock dividend decision is not treated lightly in practice.

Popular Trading Range

Proponents of stock dividends and stock splits frequently argue that a security has a proper trading range. When the security is priced above this level, many investors do not have the funds to buy the common trading unit of 100 shares, called a *round lot*. Although securities can be purchased in *odd-lot* form (fewer than 100 shares), the commissions are greater. Thus, firms will split the shares to keep the price in this trading range.

For example, in June 2014, Apple announced a seven-for-one stock split. This was the fourth split for Apple since the company went public in 1980. The stock had split two-for-two on each of the three previous occasions (in 2005, 2000, and 1987). So for every share of Apple you owned in 1980 when the company first went public, you would own 56 shares as of the most recent stock split in 2014.

Although this argument of a trading range is a popular one, its validity is questionable for a number of reasons. Mutual funds, pension funds and other institutions have steadily increased their trading activity since World War II and now handle a sizeable percentage of total trading volume. Because these institutions buy and sell in huge amounts, the individual share price is of little concern.

Furthermore, we sometimes observe share prices that are quite large that do not appear to cause problems. To take an extreme case, consider the Swiss chocolatier Lindt. In March 2015, Lindt shares were selling for around 56,625 Swiss francs each, or about £38,424 (€52,982). This is fairly expensive, but also consider Berkshire-Hathaway, the company run by legendary investor Warren Buffet. In April 2012, each share in the company sold for about $216,595!

Finally, there is evidence that stock splits may actually decrease the liquidity of the company's shares. Following a two-for-one split, the number of shares traded should more than double if liquidity is increased by the split. This does not appear to happen, and the reverse is sometimes observed.

Reverse Splits

A less frequently encountered financial manoeuvre is the reverse split. For example, in 2015, Ahold, the multinational retail group based in the Netherlands, underwent a twelve-for-thirteen reverse stock split. In a twelve-for-thirteen reverse split, each investor exchanges thirteen old shares for twelve new shares. As with stock splits and stock dividends, a case can be made that a reverse split has no real effect.

Given real-world imperfections, three related reasons are cited for reverse splits. First, transaction costs to shareholders may be less after the reverse split. Second, the liquidity and marketability of a company's equity might be improved when its price is raised to the popular trading range. Third, shares selling at prices below a certain level are not considered respectable, meaning that investors underestimate these firms' earnings, cash flow, growth and stability. Some financial analysts argue that a reverse split can achieve instant respectability. As was the case with stock splits, none of these reasons is particularly compelling, especially not the third one.

There are two other reasons for reverse splits. First, stock exchanges have minimum price per share requirements. A reverse split may bring the share price up to such a minimum. In 2001–2002, in the wake of a bear market, this motive became an increasingly important one in the US. In 2001, 106 companies asked their shareholders to approve reverse splits. There were 111 reverse splits in 2002 and 75 in 2003, but only 14 by mid-year 2004. The most common reason for these reverse splits is that some exchanges can delist companies whose share price drops below an acceptable value per share. In 2002 and 2003, many US companies, particularly Internet-related technology companies, found themselves in danger of being delisted and used reverse splits to boost their share prices. Second, companies sometimes perform reverse splits and, at the same time, buy out any shareholders who end up with less than a certain number of shares.

In October 2005, Sagient Research Systems, a publisher of independent financial research, announced a 1-for-101 reverse stock split. At the same time, the company would repurchase all shares held by shareholders with fewer than 100 shares. The purpose of the reverse split was to allow the company to go dark. The reverse split and share repurchase meant the company would have fewer than 300 shareholders, so it would no longer be required to file periodic reports with the SEC. What made the proposal especially imaginative was that immediately after the reverse stock split, the company underwent a 101-for-1 split to restore the equity to its original cost!

Summary and Conclusions

1 The dividend policy of a firm is irrelevant in a perfect capital market because the shareholder can effectively undo the firm's dividend strategy. If a shareholder receives a greater dividend than desired, he or she can reinvest the excess. Conversely, if the shareholder receives a smaller dividend than desired, he or she can sell off extra shares of equity. This argument is due to MM and is similar to their homemade leverage concept, discussed in a previous chapter.

2 Shareholders will be indifferent between dividends and share repurchases in a perfect capital market.

3 Because dividends are taxed, companies should not issue equity to pay out a dividend.

4 Also because of taxes, firms have an incentive to reduce dividends. For example, they might consider increasing capital expenditures, acquiring other companies, or purchasing financial assets. However, due to financial considerations and legal constraints, rational firms with large cash flows will likely exhaust these activities with plenty of cash left over for dividends.

5 In a world with personal taxes, a strong case can be made for repurchasing shares instead of paying dividends.

6 Nevertheless, there are a number of justifications for dividends even in a world with personal taxes:

   (a) Investors in no-dividend equities incur transaction costs when selling off shares for current consumption.

   (b) Behavioural finance argues that investors with limited self-control can meet current consumption needs via high-dividend equities while adhering to a policy of 'never dipping into principal'.

   (c) Managers, acting on behalf of shareholders, can pay dividends to keep cash from bondholders. The board of directors, also acting on behalf of shareholders, can use dividends to reduce the cash available to spendthrift managers.

7 The stock market reacts positively to increases in dividends (or an initial payment) and negatively to decreases in dividends. This suggests that there is information content in dividend payments.

◁

8   High (low) dividend firms should arise to meet the demands of dividend-preferring (capital gains-preferring) investors. Because of these clienteles, it is not clear that a firm can create value by changing its dividend policy.

9   Time-varying demand for dividends means that in some periods companies that pay dividends are traded at a premium and in other cases they are not. Managers will time their dividend policies to take advantage of this premium.

Questions and Problems

CONCEPT

1   **Different Types of Dividends**   Explain the difference between a cash dividend, a stock dividend, a special dividend, and a stock buyback.

2   **The Dividend Payment Process**   How is it possible that dividends are so important, but at the same time dividend policy is irrelevant? When a dividend is paid, give some reasons why the share price decline may not be the same as the actual dividend payment.

3   **Disappearing Dividends**   Explain what is meant by the disappearing dividend phenomenon. What are the competing explanations for the phenomenon?

4   **Share Repurchases**   Stock buybacks are happening in rapid succession among companies all over the world. Is this good or bad news for shareholders? Explain.

5   **Dividends, Taxes, and other Real World Factors**   Explain the importance of taxes in dividend policy. What are the real world factors that would encourage firms to follow a high dividend policy?

6   **Agency Theory and Payout Policy**   Explain the role of agency conflicts between managers, shareholders, and bondholders in corporate payout policy.

7   **Clienteles**   What is meant by dividend clienteles? If dividend clienteles exist, what does that imply for firms that adopt a new dividend policy in order to increase firm value?

8   **Catering Theory**   What is the catering theory of dividends and how would it influence a manager looking to improve the value of her firm through dividend policy? What does the empirical evidence say about the catering theory?

9   **Dividend Policy in Practice**   Under the assumptions set out by Modigliani and Miller, is a firm with a low payout dividend stream that uses retentions to finance investment more or less viable than a high payout firm that issues new issues to finance investment? Do you think dividend policy is important in practice? Justify your answer using information you have read in this chapter.

10 **Stock Dividends and Stock Splits**   Why would firms have a reverse split? Should a reverse split have any impact on the value of the firm?

REGULAR

11 **Dividend Policy**   It is sometimes suggested that firms should follow a 'residual' dividend policy. With such a policy, the main idea is that a firm should focus on meeting its investment needs and maintaining its desired debt–equity ratio. Having done so, a firm pays out any leftover, or residual, income as dividends. What do you think would be the chief drawback to a residual dividend policy?

12 **Dividends and Clientele**   Bodyswerve plc has experienced significant performance gains over previous years and there is no reason to expect any different in the future. The firm has engaged with a potential investor to purchase its shares in the open market. However, the investor has argued that a Bodyswerve investment is not good value for money because the firm has never paid a dividend and their preference is to choose equities that only pay dividends.

(a)   Does the investor's argument make sense? Explain.

(b)   What argument should be used to convince the investor that Bodyswerve equity is the investment for her?

(c)   What counter-arguments could be made?

13 Dividends and Taxes You are approaching retirement and are considering ways to minimize the tax bill from your investment portfolio. Assuming that you are only investing in equities within your own country, what is the best way to maximize your after-tax investment return? Explain.

14 Dividends versus Capital Gains It is clear in many countries that investors prefer dividend-paying stocks to those that pay no dividends. How do you explain this if dividend policy is irrelevant? Explain.

15 Dividend Irrelevancy 'We must ensure that dividends do not fall from one year to the next, even if our company makes a loss. However, if we make a profit then we should increase the dividend.' Does this statement make sense? Explain.

16 Share Repurchases MUG Company has a market capitalization of £1 billion and 20 million shares outstanding. Its Board has decided to distribute £100 million to shareholders through a repurchase programme. How many shares will be repurchased?

17 Dividends and Taxes Thesepe plc has declared a £2 per-share dividend and sells for £8.40 per share. Assuming that the tax rate on capital gains and dividends is zero, what do you think the ex-dividend price will be? Explain.

18 Stock Dividends The shareholder equity accounts for Hexagon International are shown here:

	£
Ordinary shares (£1 par value)	10,000
Capital surplus	180,000
Retained earnings	586,500
Total owners' equity	776,500

(a) If Hexagon shares currently sell for £25 per share and a 10 per cent stock dividend is declared, how many new shares will be distributed? Show how the equity accounts would change.

(b) If Hexagon declared a 25 per cent stock dividend, how would the accounts change?

19 Stock Splits For the company in Problem 18, show how the equity accounts will change if:

(a) Hexagon declares a four-for-one stock split. How many shares are outstanding now? What is the new par value per share?

(b) Hexagon declares a one-for-five reverse stock split. How many shares are outstanding now? What is the new par value per share?

20 Stock Splits and Stock Dividends Eurasion Natural Resources Corporation currently has 2.4 million shares outstanding that sell for £5.16 per share. Assuming no market imperfections or tax effects exist, what will the share price be after:

(a) A three-for-two stock split?

(b) An 8 per cent stock dividend?

(c) A 20 per cent stock dividend?

(d) A two-for-three reverse stock split?

Determine the new number of shares outstanding in parts (a) through (d).

21 Regular Dividends The balance sheet for Severn Trent plc is shown here in market value terms. There are 2.4 billion shares outstanding.

Market Value Balance Sheet (£m)			
Cash	5,045	Equity	4,022
Non-current assets	5,526	Liabilities	6,549
Total	10,571	Total	10,571

The company has declared a dividend of £0.40 per share. The equity goes ex dividend tomorrow. Ignoring any tax effects, what are the shares selling for today? What will they sell for tomorrow? What will the market value balance sheet look like after the dividends are paid?

22 Share Repurchase In the previous problem, suppose Severn Trent plc has announced it is going to repurchase £1 billion worth of equity. What effect will this transaction have on the equity of the firm?

How many shares will be outstanding? What will the price per share be after the repurchase? Ignoring tax effects, show how the share repurchase is effectively the same as a cash dividend.

23 **Stock Dividends**   The market value balance sheet for KL Air is shown here. KL Air has declared a 20 per cent stock dividend. The equity goes ex dividend tomorrow (the chronology for a stock dividend is similar to that for a cash dividend). There are 15,000 shares of equity outstanding. What will the ex-dividend price be?

Market Value Balance Sheet			
	(R)		(R)
Cash	1,290,000	Debt	1,682,500
Non-current assets	5,440,000	Equity	5,047,500
Total	6,730,000	Total	6,730,000

24 **Stock Dividends**   The company with the equity accounts shown here has declared a 12 per cent stock dividend when the market value of its equity is €20 per share. What effects on the equity accounts will the distribution of the stock dividend have?

	(€)
Ordinary shares (€1 par value)	350,000
Capital surplus	1,650,000
Retained earnings	3,000,000
Total owners' equity	5,000,000

25 **Stock Splits**   In the previous problem, suppose the company instead decides on a five-for-one stock split. The firm's 70 cents per share cash dividend on the new (post-split) shares represents an increase of 10 per cent over last year's dividend on the pre-split equity. What effect does this have on the equity accounts? What was last year's dividend per share?

26 **Residual Dividend Policy**   Hillshire plc uses a residual dividend policy. (see Question 11.) A debt–equity ratio of 0.60 is considered optimal. Earnings for the period just ended were £524,292 and a dividend of £50,000 was declared. How much in new debt was borrowed? What were total capital outlays?

27 **Residual Dividend Policy**   Worthington AG has declared an annual dividend of 1.50 Swiss Francs (SFr) per share. For the year just ended, earnings were SFr14 per share.

(a)   What is Worthington's payout ratio?

(b)   Suppose Worthington has 12 million shares outstanding. Borrowing for the coming year is planned at SFr25 million. What are planned investment outlays assuming a residual dividend policy? (See Question 11.) What target capital structure is implicit in these calculations?

28 **Residual Dividend Policy**   Red Zeppelin plc follows a strict residual dividend policy (see Question 11). Its debt–equity ratio is 3.

(a)   If earnings for the year are £180,000, what is the maximum amount of capital spending possible with no new equity?

(b)   If planned investment outlays for the coming year are £760,000, will Red Zeppelin pay a dividend? If so, how much?

(c)   Does Red Zeppelin maintain a constant dividend payout? Why or why not?

29 **Residual Dividend Policy**   Preti Rock SA predicts that earnings in the coming year will be €56 million. There are 12 million shares, and PR maintains a debt–equity ratio of 2.

(a)   Calculate the maximum investment funds available without issuing new equity and the increase in borrowing that goes along with it.

(b)   Suppose the firm uses a residual dividend policy. (See Question 11.) Planned capital expenditures total €72 million. Based on this information, what will the dividend per share be?

(c)   In part (b), how much borrowing will take place? What is the addition to retained earnings?

(d)   Suppose PR plans no capital outlays for the coming year. What will the dividend be under a residual policy? What will new borrowing be?

30 Dividends and Share Price Mann Company belongs to a risk class for which the appropriate discount rate is 10 per cent. Mann currently has 100,000 outstanding shares selling at £100 each. The firm is contemplating the declaration of a £5 dividend at the end of the fiscal year just begun. Assume there are no taxes on dividends. Answer the following questions based on the Miller and Modigliani model, which is discussed in the text.

(a) What will be the price of the shares on the ex-dividend date if the dividend is declared?

(b) What will be the price of the shares at the end of the year if the dividend is not declared?

(c) If Mann makes £2 million of new investments at the beginning of the period, earns net income of £1 million, and pays the dividend at the end of the year, how many shares of new equity must the firm issue to meet its funding needs?

(d) Is it realistic to use the MM model in the real world to value equity? Why or why not?

31 Homemade Dividends You own 2,000 shares of equity in Avondale Property plc. You will receive a £0.25 per share dividend in one year. In 2 years, Avondale will pay a liquidating dividend of £0.75 per share. The required return on Avondale shares is 18 per cent. What is the current share price of your equity (ignoring taxes)? If you would rather have equal dividends in each of the next 2 years, show how you can accomplish this by creating homemade dividends. (*Hint:* Dividends will be in the form of an annuity.)

32 Homemade Dividends In the previous problem, suppose you want only £400 total in dividends the first year. What will your homemade dividend be in 2 years?

33 Share Repurchase Flychucker SA is evaluating an extra dividend versus a share repurchase. In either case €5,000 would be spent. Current earnings are €0.95 per share, and the equity currently sells for €40 per share. There are 200 shares outstanding. Ignore taxes and other imperfections in answering parts (a) and (b).

(a) Evaluate the two alternatives in terms of the effect on the price per share of the equity and shareholder wealth.

(b) What will be the effect on Flychucker's EPS and PE ratio under the two different scenarios?

(c) In the real world, which of these actions would you recommend? Why?

34 Dividends and Firm Value The net income of Novis AS is 32,000 kroner (DKr). The company has 10,000 outstanding shares and a 100 per cent payout policy. The expected value of the firm one year from now is DKr1,545,600. The appropriate discount rate for Novis is 12 per cent, and the dividend tax rate is zero.

(a) What is the current value of firm assuming the current dividend has not yet been paid?

(b) What is the ex-dividend price of Novis's equity if the board follows its current policy?

(c) At the dividend declaration meeting, several board members claimed that the dividend is too meagre and is probably depressing Novis's price. They proposed that Novis sell enough new shares to finance a DKr4.25 dividend.

(i) Comment on the claim that the low dividend is depressing the share price. Support your argument with calculations.

(ii) If the proposal is adopted, at what price will the new shares sell? How many will be sold?

35 Dividend Policy Newcastle Autos plc has a current period cash flow of £4.2 million and pays no dividends. The present value of the company's future cash flows is £72 million. The company is entirely financed with equity and has 1 million shares outstanding. Assume the dividend tax rate is zero.

(a) What is the share price of Newcastle Autos' equity?

(b) Suppose the board of directors of Newcastle Autos announces its plan to pay out 40 per cent of its current cash flow as cash dividends to its shareholders. How could you achieve a zero payout policy on your own, if you own 1,000 shares of Newcastle Autos equity?

36 Dividend Smoothing Sharpe SA has just paid a dividend of €1.25 per share of equity. Its target payout ratio is 40 per cent. The company expects to have an earnings per share of €4.50 one year from now.

(a) If the adjustment rate is 0.3 as defined in the Lintner model, what is the dividend one year from now?

(b) If the adjustment rate is 0.6 instead, what is the dividend one year from now?

(c) Which adjustment rate is more conservative? Why?

CHALLENGE

37 **Expected Return, Dividends and Taxes** Gecko Company and Gordon Company are two firms whose business risk is the same but that have different dividend policies. Gecko pays no dividend, whereas Gordon has an expected dividend yield of 6 per cent. Suppose the capital gains tax rate is zero, whereas the dividend tax rate is 12.5 per cent. Gecko has an expected earnings growth rate of 15 per cent annually, and its share price is expected to grow at this same rate. If the after-tax expected returns on the two equities are equal (because they are in the same risk class), what is the pre-tax required return on Gordon's shares?

38 **Dividends and Taxes** As discussed in the text, in the absence of market imperfections and tax effects, we would expect the share price to decline by the amount of the dividend payment when the equity goes ex dividend. Once we consider the role of taxes, however, this is not necessarily true. One model has been proposed that incorporates tax effects into determining the ex-dividend price (Elton and Gruber, 1970):

$$(P_0 - P_X)/D = (1 - t_P)/(1 - t_G)$$

Here P_0 is the price just before the share goes ex, P_X is the ex-dividend share price, D is the amount of the dividend per share, t_P is the relevant marginal personal tax rate on dividends, and t_G is the effective marginal tax rate on capital gains.

(a) If $t_P = t_G = 0$, how much will the share price fall when the equity goes ex?

(b) If $t_P = 36.1$ per cent and $t_G = 0$ per cent, how much will the share price fall?

(c) If $t_P = 36.1$ per cent and $t_G = 28$ per cent, how much will the share price fall?

(d) What does this problem tell you about real-world tax considerations and the dividend policy of the firm?

39 **Signalling through Corporate Payout Policy** Miller and Rock (1985) put forward a signalling model of corporate payout policy. Critically evaluate this model, with specific reference to the theoretical and empirical literature that supports or contradicts the model.

40 **Dividends versus Reinvestment** After completing its capital spending for the year, Carlson Manufacturing has £1,000 extra cash. Carlson's managers must choose between investing the cash in Treasury bonds that yield 8 per cent or paying the cash out to investors who would invest in the bonds themselves.

(a) If the corporate tax rate is 23 per cent, what personal tax rate would make the investors equally willing to receive the dividend or to let Carlson invest the money?

(b) Is the answer to (a) reasonable? Why or why not?

Exam Question (45 minutes)

1 You have been asked by a client to forecast the dividend per share of Clouds plc over the next 3 years. From initial investigation, you find out that the company paid a dividend of £1.00 per share last year. An examination of analysts' earnings forecasts points to an expected earnings per share of £3 next year which is an increase from the current earnings per share of £2.75. The earnings per share 2 years from now are expected to be £3.50. Using Lintner's model, you estimate that the company has a long-term payout rate of 60 per cent and an adjustment factor of 50 per cent. (40 marks)

2 Review the reasons why corporations issue dividends when it appears from a tax perspective sub-optimal to do so. (30 marks)

3 In recent years, share repurchases have become more common than cash dividends. Explain why you think this is so, using research you have read to support your answer. (30 marks)

Mini Case

Electronic Calendrier SA

Electronic Calendrier (EC) is a small company founded 15 years ago by electronics engineers Georges Thiébald and Louis-Lucien Klotz. EC manufactures integrated circuits to capitalize on the complex mixed-signal design technology and has recently entered the market for frequency timing generators, or silicon timing devices, which provide the timing signals or 'clocks' necessary to synchronize electronic systems. Its clock products originally were used in PC video graphics applications, but the market subsequently expanded to include motherboards, PC peripheral devices, and other digital consumer electronics, such as digital television boxes and game consoles. EC also designs and markets custom application-specific integrated circuits (ASICs) for industrial customers. The ASIC's design combines analogue and digital, or mixed-signal, technology. In addition to Georges and Louis-Lucien, Katherine Pancol, who provided capital for the company, is the third primary owner. Each owns 25 per cent of the 1 million shares outstanding. Several other individuals, including current employees, own the remaining company shares.

Recently, the company designed a new computer motherboard. The company's design is both more efficient and less expensive to manufacture, and the EC design is expected to become standard in many personal computers. After investigating the possibility of manufacturing the new motherboard, EC determined that the costs involved in building a new plant would be prohibitive. The owners also decided that they were unwilling to bring in another large outside owner. Instead, EC sold the design to an outside firm. The sale of the motherboard design was completed for an after-tax payment of €30 million.

1 Georges believes the company should use the extra cash to pay a special one-time dividend. How will this proposal affect the share price? How will it affect the value of the company?

2 Louis-Lucien believes that the company should use the extra cash to pay off debt and upgrade and expand its existing manufacturing capability. How would Louis-Lucien's proposals affect the company?

3 Katherine is in favour of a share repurchase. She argues that a repurchase will increase the company's P/E ratio, return on assets and return on equity. Are her arguments correct? How will a share repurchase affect the value of the company?

4 Another option discussed by Georges, Louis-Lucien and Katherine would be to begin a regular dividend payment to shareholders. How would you evaluate this proposal?

5 One way to value a share of equity is the dividend growth, or growing perpetuity, model. Consider the following: The dividend payout ratio is 1 minus b, where b is the 'retention' or 'ploughback' ratio. So, the dividend next year will be the earnings next year, E_1, times 1 minus the retention ratio. The most commonly used equation to calculate the sustainable growth rate is the return on equity times the retention ratio. Substituting these relationships into the dividend growth model, we get the following equation to calculate the price of a share of equity today:

$$P_o = \frac{E_1(1-b)}{R_S - ROE \times b}$$

What are the implications of this result in terms of whether the company should pay a dividend or upgrade and expand its manufacturing capability? Explain.

6 Does the question of whether the company should pay a dividend depend on whether the company is organized as a corporation or partnership?

Practical Case Study

Use the annual financial statements for Man Group plc, Cairn Energy plc and TUI Group to find the dividend payout ratio for each company for the last 3 years. Why would these companies pay out a different percentage of income as dividends?

Relevant Accounting Standards

Dividend policy in itself is not affected by accounting standards. However, the presentation of dividends is affected by IAS 1 *Presentation of Financial Statements*, IAS 27 *Consolidated and Separate Financial Statements*, and IAS 33 *Earnings per Share*. Visit the IASPlus website (www.iasplus.com) for more information.

References

Allen, F., A. Bernardo and I. Welch (2002) 'A Theory of Dividends Based on Tax Clienteles', *The Journal of Finance*, Vol. 55, No. 6, 2499–2536.

Asquith, P. and D. Mullins, Jr (1983) 'The Impact of Initiating Dividend Payments on Shareholder Wealth', *Journal of Business*, Vol. 56, 77–96.

Baker, M. and J. Wurgler (2004) 'A Catering Theory of Dividends', *The Journal of Finance*, Vol. 59, No. 3, 1125–1165.

Bhattacharya, S. (1979) 'Imperfect Information, Dividend Policy, and "the Bird in the Hand" Fallacy', *Bell Journal of Economics*, Vol. 10, No. 1, 259–270.

Bhattacharya, S. (1980) 'Non-dissipative Signaling Structure and Dividend Policy', *Quarterly Journal of Economics*, Vol. 95, No. 1, 1–24.

Brav, A., J.R. Graham, C.R. Harvey and R. Michaely (2005) 'Payout Policy in the 21st Century', *Journal of Financial Economics*, Vol. 77, No. 3, 487–527.

DeAngelo, H. and L. DeAngelo (1990) 'Dividend Policy and Financial Distress: An Empirical Investigation of Troubled NYSE Firms', *The Journal of Finance*, Vol. 45, No. 5, 1415–1431.

DeAngelo, H., L. DeAngelo and D. Skinner (2004) 'Are Dividends Disappearing? Dividend Concentration and the Consolidation of Earnings', *Journal of Financial Economics*, Vol. 72, No. 3, 425–456.

Elton, N. and M. Gruber (1970) 'Marginal Stockholder Tax Rates and the Clientele Effect', *Review of Economics and Statistics*, Vol. 52, No. 1, 68–74.

Fama, E.F. and K.R. French (2001) 'Disappearing Dividends: Changing Firm Characteristics or Lower Propensity to Pay?' *The Journal of Financial Economics*, Vol. 60, 3–43.

Graham, J.R. and A. Kumar (2006) 'Do Dividend Clienteles Exist? Evidence on Dividend Preferences of Retail Investors', *The Journal of Finance*, Vol. 61, No. 3, 1305–1336.

Hansen, R.S., R. Kumar and D.K. Shome (1994) 'Dividend Policy and Corporate Monitoring: Evidence from the Regulated Electric Utility Industry', *Financial Management*, Vol. 23, No. 1, 16–22.

Jensen, M.C. (1986) 'Agency Costs of Free Cash Flows, Corporate Finance, and Takeovers', *American Economic Review*, Vol. 76, No. 2, 323–329.

Julio, B. and D. Ikenberry (2004) 'Reappearing Dividends', *Journal of Applied Corporate Finance*, Vol. 16, 89–100.

Kose, J. and J. Williams (1985) 'Dividends, Dilution and Taxes: A Signaling Equilibrium', *The Journal of Finance*, Vol. 40, No. 4, 1053–1070.

Lintner, J. (1956) 'Distribution and Incomes of Corporations among Dividends, Retained Earnings, and Taxes', *American Economic Review*, Vol. 46, No. 2, 97–113.

Michaely, R., R.H. Thaler and K. Womack (1995) 'Price Reactions to Dividend Initiations and Omissions: Overreactions to Drift', *The Journal of Finance*, Vol. 50, No. 2, 573–608.

Miller, M. and K. Rock (1985) 'Dividend Policy under Asymmetric Information', *The Journal of Finance*, Vol. 40, No. 4, 1031–1051.

Peterson, P., D. Peterson and J. Ang (1985) 'Direct Evidence on the Marginal Rate of Taxation on Dividend Income', *Journal of Financial Economics*, Vol. 14, 267–282.

Rangvid, J., M. Schmeling and A. Schrimpf (2014) 'Dividend Predictability around the World', *Journal of Financial and Quantitative Analysis*, Vol. 49, 1–46.

Ross, S. (1977) 'The Determination of Financial Structure: The Incentive Signaling Approach', *Bell Journal of Economics*, Vol. 8, No. 1, 23–40.

Rozeff, M. (1986) 'How Companies Set their Dividend Payout Ratios', in J.M. Stern and D.H. Chew (eds), *The Revolution in Corporate Finance* (New York: Basil Blackwell).

von Eije, H. and W. Megginson (2008) 'Dividends and Share Repurchases in the European Union', *Journal of Financial Economics*, Vol. 89, 347–374.

Additional Reading

Dividend policy, the reasons why firms issue dividends, the factors affecting dividend policy, and their importance to investors are issues that have been bothering academics since Modigliani and Miller published their original dividend irrelevance theorem. The papers that are referenced below consider dividends in detail.

Theoretical Developments

1   Allen, F., A.E. Bernardo and I. Welch (2000) 'A Theory of Dividends Based on Tax Clienteles', *The Journal of Finance*, Vol. 55, No. 6, 2499–2536.

2   DeAngelo, H. and L. DeAngelo (2006) 'The Irrelevance of the MM Dividend Irrelevance Theorem', *Journal of Financial Economics*, Vol. 80, No. 2, 299–315.

3   Lambrecht, B.M. and S.C. Myers (2012) 'A Lintner Model of Payout and Managerial Rents', *The Journal of Finance*, Vol. 67, No. 5, 1761–1810.

4   Ohlson, J.A., A.J. Ostaszewski and Z. Gao (2011) 'Dividend Policy Irrelevancy and the Construct of Earnings', Working Paper.

Dividend Policy, Share Repurchases and Stock Splits

5   Andres, C., A. Betzer, M. Goergen and L. Renneboog (2009) 'Dividend Policy of German Firms: A Panel Data Analysis of Partial Adjustment Models', *Journal of Empirical Finance*, Vol. 16, No. 2, 175–187. **Germany.**

6 Bargeron, L., M. Kulchania and S. Thomas (2011) 'Accelerated Share Repurchases', *Journal of Financial Economics*, Vol. 101, No. 1, 69–89.

7 Bell, L. and T. Jenkinson (2002) 'New Evidence of the Impact of Dividend Taxation and on the Identity of the Marginal Investor', *The Journal of Finance*, Vol. 57, No. 3, 1321–1346. **UK.**

8 Brav, A., J.R. Graham, C.R. Harvey and R. Michaely (2005) 'Payout Policy in the 21st Century', *Journal of Financial Economics*, Vol. 77, No. 3, 483–527. **US.**

9 Brockman, P. and E. Unlu (2009) 'Dividend Policy, Creditor Rights, and the Agency Costs of Debt', *Journal of Financial Economics*, Vol. 92, No. 2, 276–299. **International.**

10 De Cesari, A., S. Espenlaub, A. Khurshed and M. Simkovi (2012) 'The Effects of Ownership and Stock Liquidity on the Timing of Repurchase Transactions', *Journal of Corporate Finance*, Vol. 18, No. 5, 1023–1050.

11 Chan, K., D.L. Ikenberry, I. Lee and Y. Wang (2010) 'Share Repurchases as a Potential Tool to Mislead Investors', *Journal of Corporate Finance*, Vol. 16, No. 2, 137–158. **US.**

12 DeAngelo, H., L. DeAngelo and R.M. Stulz (2006) 'Dividend Policy and the Earned/Contributed Capital Mix: A Test of the Life-Cycle Theory', *Journal of Financial Economics*, Vol. 81, No. 1, 227–254. **US.**

13 Ferris, S.P., N. Jayaraman and S. Sabherwal (2009) 'Catering Effects in Corporate Dividend Policy: The International Evidence', *Journal of Banking and Finance*, Vol. 33, No. 9, 1730–1738.

14 Graham, J.R. and A. Kumar (2006) 'Do Dividend Clienteles Exist? Evidence on Dividend Preferences of Retail Investors', *The Journal of Finance*, Vol. 61, No. 3, 1305–1336. **US.**

15 Grinstein, Y. and R. Michaely (2005) 'Institutional Holdings and Payout Policy', *The Journal of Finance*, Vol. 60, No. 3, 1389–1426. **US.**

16 Henock, L. and H. White (2007) 'Do Managers Intentionally Use Repurchase Tender Offers to Signal Private Information? Evidence from Firm Financial Reporting Behavior', *Journal of Financial Economics*, Vol. 85, No. 1, 205–233. **US.**

17 Hoberg, G. and N. Prabhala (2009) 'Disappearing Dividends, Catering, and Risk', *Review of Financial Studies*, Vol. 22, No. 1, 79–116. **US.**

18 Holmen, M., J.D. Knopf and S. Peterson (2008) 'Inside Shareholders' Effective Tax Rates and Dividends', *Journal of Banking and Finance*, Vol. 32, No. 9, 1860–1869. **Sweden.**

19 Jiang, Z., K.A. Kim, E. Lie and S. Yang (2013) 'Share Repurchases, Catering, and Dividend Substitution', *Journal of Corporate Finance*, Vol. 21, 36–50.

20 Kinkki, S. (2008) 'Minority Protection and Dividend Policy in Finland', *European Financial Management*, Vol. 14, No. 3, 470–502. **Finland.**

21 Kunz, R.M. and S. Rosa-Majhensek (2008) 'Stock Splits in Switzerland: To Signal or Not to Signal', *Financial Management*, Vol. 37, No. 2, 193–226. **Switzerland.**

22 La Porta, L., F. Lopez-de-Silanes, A. Shliefer and R. Vishney (2000) 'Agency Problems and Dividend Policy around the World', *The Journal of Finance*, Vol. 55, No. 1, 1–33. **International.**

23 Li, W. and E. Lie (2006) 'Dividend Changes and Catering Incentives', *Journal of Financial Economics*, Vol. 80, No. 2, 293–308. **US.**

24 Lin, J-C., A.K. Singh and W. Yu (2009) 'Stock Splits, Trading Continuity, and the Cost of Equity Capital', *Journal of Financial Economics*, Vol. 93, No. 3, 474–489.

25 Massa, M., Z. Rehman and T. Vermaelen (2007) 'Mimicking Repurchases', *Journal of Financial Economics*, Vol. 84, No. 3, 624–666. **US.**

26 Moder, W.J. (2007) 'The Effect of Shareholder Taxes on Corporate Payout Choice', *Journal of Financial and Quantitative Analysis*, Vol. 42, No. 4, 991–1019. **US.**

27 Oswald, D. and S. Young (2008) 'Share Reacquisitions, Surplus Cash, and Agency Problems', *Journal of Banking and Finance*, Vol. 32, No. 5, 795–806. **UK.**

28 Renneboog, L. and G. Trojanowski (2011) 'Patterns in Payout Policy and Payout Channel Choice', *Journal of Banking and Finance*, Vol. 35, No. 6, 1477–1490. **UK.**

29 Rommens, A., L. Cuyvers and M. Deloof (2012) 'Dividend Policies of Privately Held Companies: Stand-Alone and Group Companies in Belgium', *European Financial Management*, Vol. 18, No. 5, 816–835.

30 Schultz, P. (2000) 'Stock Splits, Tick Size, and Sponsorship', *The Journal of Finance*, Vol. 55, No. 1, 429–450. **US.**

Other Relevant Research

31 Alzahrani, M. and M. Lasfer (2012) 'Investor Protection, Taxation, and Dividends', *Journal of Corporate Finance*, Vol. 18, No. 4, 745–762.

32 Bonaimé, A.A., K.W. Hankins and J. Harford (2014) 'Financial Flexibility, Risk Management, and Payout Choice', *Review of Financial Studies*, Vol. 27, No. 4, 1074–1101.

33 Del Brio, E.B. and A. De Miguel (2010) 'Dividends and Market Signalling: An Analysis of Corporate Insider Trading', *European Financial Management*, Vol. 16, No. 3, 480–497. **Spain.**

34 Dong, M., C. Robinson and C. Veld (2005) 'Why Individual Investors Want Dividends', *Journal of Corporate Finance*, Vol. 12, No. 1, 121–158. **The Netherlands.**

35 Liu, Y., S.H. Szewczyck and Z. Zantout (2008) 'Underreaction to Dividend Reductions and Omissions?', *The Journal of Finance*, Vol. 62, No. 2, 987–1020. **US.**

36 Pinkowitz, L., R. Stulz and R. Williamson (2006) 'Does the Contribution of Corporate Cash Holdings and Dividends to Firm Value Depend on Governance? A Cross-Country Analysis', *The Journal of Finance*, Vol. 61, No. 6, 2725–2751. **International.**

Endnotes

1   von Eije and Megginson (2008).

2   See n. 15 in Chapter 15.

3   See, for example, Jensen (1986).

4   See also Brav et al. (2005).

5   Rozeff (1986). See also Hansen et al. (1994).

6   The correct representation of Equation 18.5 involves cash flow, not earnings. However, with little loss of understanding, we could discuss dividend signalling in terms of earnings, not cash flow.

7   Papers examining fully developed models of signalling include Bhattacharya (1979); Bhattacharya (1980); Ross (1977); Miller and Rock (1985).

8   Signalling models where dividends and repurchases are not perfect substitutes are contained in Allen et al. (2002), Kose and Williams (1985) and Rangvid et al. (2014).

PART 5

Long-term Financing

Most of the material covered in the book so far has focused on applying theory to practice. Each chapter has had a theoretical foundation that is developed before practical examples and research findings are presented. The approach works well when we are talking about different aspects of valuation and firm strategy. However, it is less appropriate when we consider the behaviours and processes followed throughout the world by companies in trying to raise money for their operations. There are so many ways companies can raise money, either privately or through public routes. Moreover, practices differ across countries and geographical regions to reflect varying degrees of economic development and cultural norms. Finally, the participants in each market and country are different, ranging from very large banks to families who fund companies through informal means.

This is the setting for Part 5 of the textbook, *Corporate Finance*. Even though there is a lack of consistency and structure in the process of raising new financing, there are some commonalities in practice. In the next three chapters on long-term financing, we will draw out the areas that one is normally concerned with and the reader will be presented with an overview of what happens when companies go to the markets to raise capital for their investment decisions.

Since there are two major funding types for companies (equity and debt), we devote one chapter each to the challenges and distinctive characteristics of these securities. Chapter 19 focuses on equity financing. Companies can issue equity publicly through underwriters to be traded on stock exchanges or privately via venture capital and private equity. In Chapter 19 we discuss both types of equity financing. Chapter 20 does the same for debt financing and considers public debt issues (public listed bonds) and private debt (bank loans). Finally, in Chapter 20, we discuss an alternative financing vehicle, leasing, and show how this can substitute for debt in a company's capital structure.

Equity Financing

Chapter 5
Page 125

When a firm wishes to raise capital for new investment, it has two real choices. One option is to issue new equity (equity valuation is discussed in **Chapter 5**, Sections 5.4–5.8). Another option is to borrow funds from financial institutions or through the public issue of debt. Every day in the financial press, you will read about companies that have gone to the markets to raise new equity.

Take the Chinese online business to business auction company, Alibaba, as an example. After substantial revenue growth, the company decided to list its shares on the Hong Kong Stock Exchange. However, regulatory concerns made a Chinese listing unattractive and, as a result, the company listed on the NASDAQ stock exchange in the US. The initial public offering raised $24 billion and was the world's largest ever share issue for a new company. During the issue, investors submitted bids that vastly exceeded the number of shares on offer. The issue price of $68 per share grew by 50 per cent to $92.70 by the close of trading on the same day, and by the end of 2014 the shares were trading at $103.94.

In this chapter, we examine the process by which companies such as Alibaba sell equity to the public, the costs of doing so, and the role of intermediaries in the process. We pay particular attention to what is probably the most important stage in a company's financial life cycle – the initial public offering. Such offerings are the process by which companies convert from being privately owned to being publicly owned. For many people, starting a company, growing it and taking it public are the ultimate entrepreneurial dream.

19.1 The Public Issue

When considering the steps involved in a public issue of equity, it is important to remember that each country has its own specific regulations and traditions, although the European Union has a comprehensive directive that covers all member countries. Table 19.1 illustrates the process for the UK, which is very similar to most other European countries.

Table 19.1 The Process of Raising Capital

Steps in Public Offering	Time	Activities
1 Pathfinder prospectus	Several months before issue	An initial indicative prospectus is released that presents the proposed offering.
2 Pre-underwriting conferences	About 4 weeks before the full prospectus is issued	The amount of money to be raised and the type of security to be issued are discussed. Initial expressions of interest are collected and an issue price is set. An underwriter and approved adviser will be appointed.
3 Full prospectus	Several weeks before the offering takes place	The prospectus contains all relevant financial and business information.
4 Public offering and sale	Shortly after the last day of the registration period	In a typical firm commitment contract, the underwriter buys a stipulated amount of equity from the firm and sells it at a higher price. The selling group assists in the sale.
5 Market stabilization	Usually within 30 days of the offering	The underwriter stands ready to place orders to buy at a specified price on the market.

19.2 Alternative Issue Methods

When a company decides to issue a new security, it can sell it as a public issue or a private issue. In a public issue, the shares will be traded on a stock exchange and the firm is required to register the issue with the stock exchange on which it is listed. If the issue is sold to only a few institutions, it is called a *private placement* or *placing* and can be treated as a private issue. A registration statement is normally not required in this case.[1]

There are two kinds of public issue: the *general cash offer* and the *rights issue*. Cash offers are sold to all interested investors, and rights offers are sold to existing shareholders. Equity is sold by both the cash offer and the rights offer, though almost all debt is sold by cash offer.

The first public equity issue that is made by a company is referred to as an initial public offering (IPO) or an unseasoned new issue. All initial public offerings are cash offers because, if the firm's existing shareholders wanted to buy the shares, the firm would not need to sell them publicly. IPO activity is positively related to the performance of stock markets and this has been reflected in the slew of new issues in Europe and the US over the last few years. A seasoned issue refers to a new issue of shares for a company that is already listed on a stock exchange. A seasoned issue of ordinary shares will normally be through a rights issue.

Methods of issuing new securities are shown in Table 19.2 and discussed in the next few sections.

Table 19.2 The Methods of Issuing New Securities

Method	Type	Definition
Public		
Traditional negotiated cash offer	Firm commitment cash offer	Company negotiates an agreement with a bank to underwrite and distribute the new shares. A specified number of shares are bought by underwriters and sold at a higher price.
	Best efforts cash offer	Company has underwriters sell as many of the new shares as possible at the agreed-upon price. There is no guarantee concerning how much cash will be raised. Some best efforts offerings do not use an underwriter.
	Dutch auction cash offer	Company has underwriters auction shares to determine the highest offer price obtainable for a given number of shares to be sold.
Privileged	Pre-emptive rights issue	Company offers the new equity directly to its existing shareholders.
Subscription	Standby rights issue	Like the pre-emptive rights issue, this contains a privileged subscription arrangement with existing shareholders. The net proceeds are guaranteed by the underwriters.
Non-traditional cash offer	Shelf cash offer	Qualifying companies can authorize all the shares they expect to sell over a specified period and sell them when needed.
	Competitive firm cash offer	Company can elect to award the underwriting contract through a public auction instead of negotiation.
Private	Direct placement	Securities are sold directly to the purchaser.

19.3   The Cash Offer

As just mentioned, equity is sold to all interested investors in a **cash offer**. If the cash offer is a public one, **banks** are usually involved. Banks are financial intermediaries that perform a wide variety of services. In addition to taking deposits and making loans, they also aid in the sale of securities, facilitate mergers and other corporate reorganizations, act as brokers to both individual and institutional clients, and trade for their own accounts. Much of this activity is undertaken by the investment arm of banks.

For corporate issuers, the investment banking function includes the following:

- Formulating the method used to issue new securities.
- Pricing the new securities.
- Selling the new securities.

There are three basic methods of issuing securities for cash:

1 *Firm commitment*: Under this method, the bank (or a group of banks) buys the securities for less than the offering price and accepts the risk of not being able to sell them. Because this function involves risk, we say that the banker *underwrites* the securities in a firm commitment. In other words, when participating in a firm commitment offering, the banker acts as an *underwriter*. (Because firm commitments are so prevalent, we will use *banker* and *underwriter* interchangeably in this chapter.)

   To minimize the risks here, bankers combine to form an underwriting group (**syndicate**) to share the risk and to help sell the issue. In such a group, one or more managers arrange or co-manage the deal. The manager is designated as the lead manager or principal manager. The lead manager typically has responsibility for all aspects of the issue. The other investment bankers in the syndicate serve primarily to sell the issue to their clients.

The difference between the underwriter's buying price and the offering price is called the *spread* or *discount*. It is the basic compensation received by the underwriter. Sometimes the underwriter will get non-cash compensation in the form of warrants or equity in addition to the spread.

Firm commitment underwriting is really just a purchase–sale arrangement, and the syndicate's fee is the spread. The issuer receives the full amount of the proceeds less the spread, and all the risk is transferred to the underwriter. If the underwriter cannot sell all of the issue at the agreed-upon offering price, it may need to lower the price on the unsold shares. However, because the offering price usually is not set until the underwriters have investigated how receptive the market is to the issue, this risk is usually minimal. This is particularly true with seasoned new issues because the price of the new issue can be based on prior trades in the security.

2   *Best efforts*: The underwriter bears risk with a firm commitment because it buys the entire issue. Conversely, the syndicate avoids this risk under a best-efforts offering because it does not purchase the shares. Instead it merely acts as an agent, receiving a commission for each share sold. The syndicate is legally bound to use its best efforts to sell the securities at the agreed-upon offering price. If the issue cannot be sold at the offering price, it is usually withdrawn. This form of underwriting has become relatively rare.

3   *Dutch auction underwriting*: With Dutch auction underwriting the underwriter does not set a fixed price for the shares to be sold. Instead the underwriter conducts an auction in which investors bid for shares. The offer price is determined based on the submitted bids. A Dutch auction is also known by the more descriptive name *uniform price auction*. This approach to selling securities to the public is relatively rare in the IPO market and has not been widely used there, but it is very common in the bond markets. For example, it is the sole procedure used by the governments to sell enormous quantities of notes, bonds and bills to the public.

Dutch auction underwriting was much in the news in 2004 because Google elected to use this approach in issuing its own equity. The best way to understand a Dutch or uniform price auction is to consider a simple example. Suppose the Rial Company wants to sell 400 shares to the public. The company receives five bids as follows:

Bidder	Quantity	Price (£)
A	100 shares	16
B	100 shares	14
C	100 shares	12
D	200 shares	12
E	200 shares	10

Thus, bidder A is willing to buy 100 shares at £16 each, bidder B is willing to buy 100 shares at £14, and so on. The Rial Company examines the bids to determine the highest price that will result in all 400 shares being sold. For example, at £14, A and B would buy only 200 shares, so that price is too high. Working our way down, all 400 shares will not be sold until we hit a price of £12, so £12 will be the offer price in the IPO. Bidders A through D will receive shares; bidder E will not.

There are two additional important points to observe in our example. First, all the winning bidders will pay £12 – even bidders A and B, who actually bid a higher price. The fact that all successful bidders pay the same price is the reason for the name 'uniform price auction'. The idea in such an auction is to encourage bidders to bid aggressively by providing some protection against bidding a price that is too high.

Second, notice that at the £12 offer price, there are actually bids for 500 shares, which exceeds the 400 shares Rial wants to sell. Thus, there has to be some sort of allocation. How this is done varies a bit; but in the IPO market the approach has been to simply compute the ratio of shares offered to shares bid at the offer price or better, which, in our example, is 400/500 = 0.8, and allocate bidders that percentage of their bids. In other words, bidders A through D would each receive 80 per cent of the shares they bid at a price of £12 per share.

In most offerings, the principal underwriter is permitted to buy shares if the market price falls below the offering price. The purpose is to *support* the market and *stabilize* the price from temporary downward pressure. If the issue remains unsold after a time (for example, 30 days), members may leave the group and sell their shares at whatever price the market will allow.

Many underwriting contracts contain a Green Shoe provision, which gives the members of the underwriting group the option to purchase additional shares at the offering price.[2] The stated reason for the Green Shoe option is to cover excess demand and oversubscription. Green Shoe options usually last for about 30 days and involve no more than a percentage (usually less than 15 per cent) of the newly issued shares. The Green Shoe option is a benefit to the underwriting syndicate and a cost to the issuer. If the market price of the new issue goes above the offering price within 30 days, the underwriters can buy shares from the issuer and immediately resell the shares to the public.

The period after a new issue is initially sold to the public is called the *aftermarket*. During this period, the members of the underwriting syndicate generally do not sell shares of the new issue for less than the offer price.

Almost all underwriting agreements contain *lock-ups*. Such arrangements specify how long insiders must wait after an IPO before they can sell some of their shares. Typically, lock-up periods are set at 180 days, but can last for several years. Lock-ups are important because it is not unusual for the number of locked-up insider shares to be larger than the number of shares held by the public. Thus, there is the possibility that, when the lock-up period ends, a large number of shares will be sold by insiders, thereby depressing share prices.

Beginning well before an offering and extending for a period following an IPO, many countries require that a firm and its managing underwriters observe a 'quiet period'. This means that all communications with the public must be limited to ordinary announcements and other purely factual matters. The logic is that all relevant information should be contained in the prospectus. An important result of this requirement is that the underwriter's analysts are prohibited from making recommendations to investors. As soon as the quiet period ends, however, the managing underwriters typically publish research reports, usually accompanied by a favourable 'buy' recommendation.

Firms that do not stay quiet can have their IPOs delayed. For example, just before Google's IPO, an interview with cofounders Sergy Brin and Larry Page appeared in *Playboy*. The interview almost caused a postponement of the IPO, but Google was able to amend its prospectus in time (by including the article!).

Investment Banking

Investment banking is at the heart of new security issues. The investment banking arms of big banks provide advice, market the securities (after investigating the market's receptiveness to the issue), and underwrite the proceeds. They accept the risk that the market price may fall between the date the offering price is set and the time the issue is sold.

In addition, banks have the responsibility of pricing fairly. When a firm goes public, particularly for the first time, the buyers know relatively little about the firm's operations. After all, it is not rational for a buyer of, say, only 1,000 shares of equity to study the company at length. Instead, the buyer must rely on the judgement of the bank, which has presumably examined the firm in detail. Given this asymmetry of information, what prevents the banker from pricing the issued securities too high? Although the underwriter has a short-term incentive to price high, it has a long-term incentive to make sure its customers do not pay too much; they might desert the underwriter in future deals if they lose money on this one. Thus, as long as banks plan to stay in business over time, it is in their self-interest to price fairly.

In other words, financial economists argue that each bank has a reservoir of 'reputation capital'.[3] Mispricing of new issues or unethical dealings are likely to reduce this reputation capital.

Banks put great importance on their relative rankings and view downward movement in their placement with much distaste. While this jockeying for position may seem as unimportant as the currying of royal favour in the court of Louis XVI, it is explained by the preceding discussion. In any industry where reputation is so important, the firms in the industry must guard theirs with great vigilance.

There are two basic methods for selecting the syndicate. In a competitive offer the issuing firm can offer its securities to the underwriter bidding highest. In a negotiated offer the issuing firm works with one underwriter. Because the firm generally does not negotiate with many underwriters concurrently, negotiated deals may suffer from lack of competition.

In Their Own Words

Robert S. Hansen on the Economic Rationale for the Firm Commitment Offer

Underwriters provide four main functions: certification, monitoring, marketing and risk bearing.

Certification assures investors that the offer price is fair. Investors have concerns about whether the offer price is unfairly above the equity's intrinsic value. Certification increases issuer value by reducing investor doubt about fairness, making a better offer price possible.

Monitoring of issuing firm management and performance builds value because it adds to shareholders' ordinary monitoring. Underwriters provide collective monitoring on behalf of both capital suppliers and current shareholders. Individual shareholder monitoring is limited because the shareholder bears the entire cost, whereas all owners collectively share the benefit, pro rata. By contrast, in underwriter monitoring all shareholders share both the costs and benefits, pro rata.

Due diligence and legal liability for the proceeds give investors assurance. However, what makes certification and monitoring credible is lead bank reputation in competitive capital markets, where they are disciplined over time. Evidence that irreputable behaviour is damaging to a bank's future abounds. Capital market participants punish poorly performing banks by refusing to hire them. The participants pay banks for certification and meaningful monitoring in 'quasi-rents' in the spread, which represent the fair cost of 'renting' the reputations.

Marketing is finding long-term investors who can be persuaded to buy the securities at the offer price. This would not be needed if demand for new shares were 'horizontal'. There is much evidence that issuers and syndicates repeatedly invest in costly marketing practices, such as expensive road shows to identify and expand investor interest. Another is organizing members to avoid redundant pursuit of the same customers. Lead banks provide trading support in the issuer's equity for several weeks after the offer.

Underwriting risk is like the risk of selling a put option. The syndicate agrees to buy all new shares at the offer price and resell them at that price or at the market price, whichever is lower. Thus, once the offer begins, the syndicate is exposed to potential losses on unsold inventory should the market price fall below the offer price. The risk is likely to be small, because offerings are typically well prepared for quick sale.

Robert S. Hansen is the Freeman Senior Research Professor of Finance at Tulane University.

Whereas competitive bidding occurs frequently in other areas of commerce, it may surprise you that negotiated deals in banking occur with all but the largest issuing firms. Investment bankers argue that they must expend much time and effort learning about the issuer before setting an issue price and a fee schedule. Except in the case of large issues, these underwriters could not expend the time and effort without the near certainty of receiving the contract.

Studies generally show that issuing costs are higher in negotiated deals than in competitive ones. However, many financial economists argue that issuing firms are not necessarily hurt by negotiated deals. They point out that the underwriter gains much information about the issuing firm through negotiation – information likely to increase the probability of a successful offering.[4]

Reputation is exceptionally important in underwriting and investment banks compete with each other to get the very best quality new issues. Similarly, the number of IPOs that an investment bank is able to undertake is a good proxy for underwriter quality. The better banks get more IPO business and, by implication, are better at generating new financing. Table 19.3 presents the top ten underwriters in six major European markets for raising new financing. As can be seen, big players are active in more than one market, but there are also country-specific specialists.

The Offering Price

Determining the correct offering price is the most difficult thing the lead underwriter must do for an initial public offering. The issuing firm faces a potential cost if the offering price is set too high or too low. If the issue is priced too high, it may be unsuccessful and be withdrawn. If the issue is priced below the true market price, the issuer's existing shareholders will experience an opportunity loss.

Ljunqvist (2006) has found that unseasoned new equity issues are generally offered below their true market price in the vast majority of countries. Underpricing helps new shareholders earn a higher return on the shares they buy. However, the existing shareholders of the issuing firm are not necessarily helped by underpricing. To them it is an indirect cost of issuing new securities. Figure 19.1 shows the issue date average return on new IPOs for a variety of European countries and Table 19.4 updates and extends Ljunqvist's analysis to many other countries.

Table 19.3 Ranking Underwriters of European IPOs

Panel A: Equally weighted

	Paris Euronext (no Marché Libre)		Frankfurt		London Official List		AIM	
	Name	No. IPOs	Name	No. IPOs	Name	No. IPOs	Name	No. IPOs
1	BNP Paribas	40	Landesbanken	75	UBS	38	Evolution Sec	123
2	Crédit Mutuel	39	Commerzbank	74	JPMorgan Chase	37	Dowgate CS	98
3	Crédit Agricole	37	DZ Bank	54	Evolution Sec	25	Collins Stewart	90
4	Oddo & Cie	37	Deutsche Bank	47	Investec	23	Peel Hunt	83
5	Société Générale	35	Unicredit	37	Crédit Suisse	23	Ambrian Capital	64
6	BFBP	33	Sal. Oppenheim	36	BoA Merrill Lynch	22	WH Ireland	62
7	Crédit du Nord	28	Gontard & Metallbank	23	Commerzbank	19	Landsbanki Sec	62
8	Crédit Lyonnaise	27	VEM Aktienbank	23	Morgan Stanley	19	Grant Thornton	55
9	KBC	22	Concord Effekten	19	Goldman Sachs	19	Brewin Dolphin	53
10	Natixis	19	HSBC	16	Citigroup	15	Numis Sec	48

Panel B: Proceeds-weighted

	Paris Euronext (no Marché Libre)		Frankfurt		London Official List		AIM	
	Name	€b	Name	€b	Name	€b	Name	€b
1	Crédit Agricole	11.05	Deutsche Bank	12.84	UBS	19.87	Collins Stewart	3.94
2	Société Générale	10.39	Commerzbank	11.32	Morgan Stanley	15.59	Evolution Sec	1.83
3	BNP Paribas	7.66	UBS	6.56	Goldman Sachs	12.18	Numis Sec	1.59
4	Lazard	7.05	Goldman Sachs	6.52	BoA Merrill Lynch	11.31	Peel Hunt	1.42
5	Goldman Sachs	6.49	Morgan Stanley	4.85	Citigroup	10.07	Deutsche Bank	1.14
6	Morgan Stanley	6.35	Landesbanken	3.92	JPMorgan Chase	9.05	JPMorgan Chase	1.06
7	Abn Amro	4.42	Unicredit	2.86	Crédit Suisse	8.89	Smith & Williamson	0.86
8	Crédit Suisse	3.88	DZ Bank	2.32	Commerzbank	6.28	Cenkos Sec	0.86
9	HSBC	3.20	Sal. Oppenheim	2.22	AIB CMs	2.78	Grant Thornton	0.82
10	Commerzbank	3.04	JPMorgan Chase	2.17	Deutsche Bank	1.94	BoA Merrill Lynch	0.76

Source: Adapted from Migliorati and Vismara (2014, Table 4).

Figure 19.1 Equal Weighted Average Initial IPO Returns in per cent for 19 European Countries between 1990 and 2003

Source: Ljunqvist (2006).

Table 19.4 IPO Underpricing Around the World

Country	Sample Size	Time Period	Average First-Day Return (%)	Country	Sample Size	Time Period	Average First-Day Return (%)
Australia	1,562	1976–2011	21.8	Netherlands	181	1982–2006	10.2
Austria	103	1971–2013	6.4	New Zealand	242	1979–2013	18.6
Belgium	114	1984–2006	13.5	Nigeria	122	1989–2013	13.1
Bulgaria	9	2004–2011	36.5	Norway	209	1984–2013	8.1
Canada	720	1971–2013	7.4	Pakistan	80	2000–2013	22.1
China	2,512	1990–2012	118.4	Philippines	155	1987–2013	18.1
Cyprus	73	1999–2012	20.3	Poland	309	1991–2014	12.7
Denmark	164	1984–2011	7.4	Portugal	32	1992–2013	11.9
Egypt	62	1990–2010	10.4	Russia	64	1999–2013	3.3
Finland	168	1971–2013	16.9	Saudi Arabia	80	2003–2011	239.8
France	697	1983–2010	10.5	Singapore	609	1973–2013	25.8
Germany	736	1978–2011	24.2	South Africa	316	1980–2013	17.4
Greece	373	1976–2013	50.8	Spain	143	1986–2013	10.3
Hong Kong	1,486	1980–2013	15.8	Sri Lanka	105	1987–2008	33.5
India	2,964	1990–2011	88.5	Sweden	374	1980–2011	27.2
Indonesia	464	1990–2014	24.9	Switzerland	164	1983–2013	27.3
Iran	279	1991–2004	22.4	Taiwan	1,620	1980–2013	38.1
Ireland	38	1999–2013	21.6	Thailand	500	1987–2012	35.1
Israel	348	1990–2006	13.8	Turkey	399	1990–2013	9.7
Italy	312	1985–2013	15.2	United Kingdom	4,932	1959–2012	16.0
Korea	1,720	1980–2013	59.3	United States	12,702	1960–2014	16.9
Malaysia	474	1980–2013	56.2				

Source: Adapted from Loughran et al. (1994), updated 16 February 2015.

Underpricing: A Possible Explanation

There are several possible explanations for underpricing. But so far there is no agreement among scholars as to which explanation is correct. In our opinion, there are two important facts associated with the underpricing puzzle that are key elements to a unifying theory. First, much of the apparent underpricing is concentrated in smaller issues. This point is documented in Table 19.5, which shows that underpricing tends to be attributable to firms with few or no sales in the prior year. These firms tend to be young firms with uncertain future prospects. The increased uncertainty in some way probably attracts risk-averse investors only if underpricing exists. Second, when the price of a new issue is too low, the issue is often *oversubscribed*. This means investors will not be able to buy all of the shares they want, and the underwriters will allocate the shares among investors. The average investor will find it difficult to get shares in an oversubscribed offering because there will not be enough shares to go around. Although initial public offerings have positive initial returns on average, a significant fraction of them have price drops. An investor submitting an order for all new issues may find that he or she will be allocated more shares in issues that go down in price.

Table 19.5 Average First-Day Returns, Categorized by Sales, for IPOs: 1980–2013

	1980–1989		1990–1998		1999–2000		2001–2013	
	Return (%)	N	Return (%)	N	Return (%)	N	Return (%)	N
0 ≤ sales < $10m	10.3	422	17.2	741	68.9	333	5.9	198
$10m ≤ sales < $20m	8.7	243	18.6	395	81.7	137	12.1	55
$20m ≤ sales < $50m	7.8	500	18.8	790	74.9	154	14.4	177
$50m ≤ sales < $100m	6.4	355	12.9	588	61.2	87	19.5	217
$100m ≤ sales < $200m	5.1	234	11.8	454	35.8	56	16.3	196
$200m ≤ sales	3.4	290	8.7	645	25.2	90	12.0	500
All	7.2	2,044	14.8	3,613	64.5	857	13.3	1,343

Sales, measured in millions, are for the last 12 months prior to going public. All sales have been converted into dollars of 2003 purchasing power, using the Consumers Price Index. There are 7,857 IPOs, after excluding IPOs with an offer price of less than $5.00 per share, units, REITs, ADRs, closed-end funds, banks and S&Ls, firms not listed on CRSP within 6 months of the offering, and natural resource-related limited partnerships. Sales are from Thomson Financial's SDC, Dealogic, EDGAR, and the Graeme Howard-Todd Huxster collection of pre-EDGAR prospectuses. The average first-day return is 17.9 per cent.

Source: Professor Jay R. Ritter, University of Florida.

Consider this tale of two investors. Ms Smarts knows precisely what companies are worth when their shares are offered. Mr Average knows only that prices usually rise one month after the IPO. Armed with this information, Mr Average decides to buy 1,000 shares of every IPO. Does Mr Average actually earn an abnormally high average return across all initial offerings?

The answer is no, and at least one reason is Ms Smarts. For example, because Ms Smarts knows that company XYZ is underpriced, she invests all her money in its IPO. When the issue is oversubscribed, the underwriters must allocate the shares between Ms Smarts and Mr Average. If they do this on a pro rata basis and if Ms Smarts has bid for twice as many shares as Mr Average, she will get two shares for each one Mr Average receives. The net result is that when an issue is underpriced, Mr Average cannot buy as much of it as he wants.

Ms Smarts also knows that company ABC is overpriced. In this case, she avoids its IPO altogether, and Mr Average ends up with a full 1,000 shares. To summarize, Mr Average receives fewer shares when more knowledgeable investors swarm to buy an underpriced issue, but he gets all he wants when the smart money avoids the issue.

This is called the *winner's curse*, and it explains much of the reason why IPOs have such a large average return. When the average investor wins and gets his allocation, it is because those who knew better avoided the issue. To counteract the winner's curse and attract the average investor, underwriters underprice issues.[5]

19.4 The Announcement of New Equity and the Value of the Firm

It seems reasonable to believe that new long-term financing is arranged by firms after positive net present value projects are put together. As a consequence, when the announcement of external financing is made, the firm's market value should go up. As we mentioned in an earlier chapter, this is precisely the opposite of what actually happens in the case of new equity financing. Asquith and Mullins, Masulis and Korwar, and Mikkelson and Partch for the US, Gajewski and Ginglinger for France, Martin-Ugedo for Spain, and Barnes and Walker for the UK, have all found that the market value of existing equity drops on the announcement of a new public issue of equity.[6] Plausible reasons for this strange result include the following:

1 *Managerial information*: If managers have superior information about the market value of the firm, they may know when the firm is overvalued. If they do, they might attempt to issue new shares when the market value exceeds the correct value. This will benefit existing shareholders. However, the potential new shareholders are not stupid. They will infer overvaluation from the new issue, thereby bidding down the share price on the announcement date of the issue.

2 *Debt capacity*: The stereotypical firm chooses a debt–equity ratio that balances the tax shield from the debt with the cost of financial distress. When the managers of a firm have special information that the probability of financial distress has risen, the firm is more likely to raise capital through equity than through debt. If the market infers this chain of events, the share price should fall on the announcement date of an equity issue.

3 *Falling earnings*:[7] When managers raise capital in amounts that are unexpectedly large (as most unanticipated financings will be) and if investors have a reasonable fix on the firm's upcoming investments and dividend payouts (as they do because capital expenditure announcements are often well known, as are future dividends), the unanticipated financings are roughly equal to unanticipated shortfalls in earnings (this follows directly from the firm's sources and uses of funds identity). Therefore, an announcement of a new equity issue will also reveal a future earnings shortfall.

19.5 The Cost of New Issues

Issuing securities to the public is not free, and the costs of different issuing methods are important determinants of which will be used. The costs fall into six categories:

1 *Spread or underwriting discount*: The spread is the difference between the price the issuer receives and the price offered to the public.

2 *Other direct expenses*: These are costs incurred by the issuer that are not part of the compensation to underwriters. They include filing fees, legal fees and taxes – all reported in the prospectus.

3 *Indirect expenses*: These costs are not reported in the prospectus and include management time spent on the new issue.

4 *Abnormal returns*: In a seasoned issue of equity, the price drops upon the announcement of the issue. The drop protects new shareholders against the firm's selling overpriced equity to new shareholders.

5 *Underpricing*: For initial public offerings, the equity typically rises substantially after the issue date. This is a cost to the firm because the shares are sold for less than their efficient price in the aftermarket.[8]

6 *Green Shoe option*: The Green Shoe option gives the underwriters the right to buy additional shares at the offer price to cover over-allotments. This is a cost to the firm because the underwriter will buy additional shares only when the offer price is below the price in the aftermarket.

An interesting study by Seth Armitage (2000) reports two of these six costs – underwriting discount and other non-underwriting direct expenses. Table 19.6, which is reproduced from Table 1 of the paper, provides three main insights:

1 The total issue costs decline as the gross proceeds of the offering increase for both US and UK companies. Thus, it appears that issuance costs are subject to substantial economies of scale.[9]

2 Issue costs in the US are higher than in the UK for most levels of gross proceeds.

3   Last, and perhaps most important, the costs of issuing securities to the public are quite large. For example, total direct expenses are approximately 6 per cent in the UK and this rises to nearly 15 per cent for small issues. This implies that issuing equity is a weighty decision, especially for smaller companies. Although there are many benefits, such as raising needed capital and spreading ownership, the costs cannot be ignored.

Table 19.6 Cost of Issue by Issue Size

| UK Rights Issues and Open Offers, Purged Sample | | US SEOs | |
Gross Proceeds (£m)	Total Costs (%)	Gross Proceeds ($ m)	Total Costs (%)
312.5+	2.17	500+	3.15
125.0−312.4	2.65	200−499.9	3.47
62.5−124.9	2.79	100−199.9	4.22
50.0−62.4	3.54	80−99.9	4.73
37.5−49.9	3.07	60−79.9	5.18
25.0−37.4	3.70	40−59.9	5.87
12.5−24.9	3.68	20−39.9	6.93
6.25−12.4	5.16	10−19.9	8.72
1.25−6.24	8.27	2−9.9	13.28
0.1−1.24	14.36		
Total	5.78		7.11
Median	4.28		

Source: Adapted from Table 1 from Armitage (2000).

19.6   Rights

When new shares of equity are offered to the general public, the proportionate ownership of existing shareholders is likely to be reduced. However, if a pre-emptive right is contained in the firm's articles of incorporation, the firm must first offer any new issue of equity to existing shareholders. This assures each owner his or her proportionate owner's share.

An issue of equity to existing shareholders is called a *rights issue* or *rights offering*. Here each shareholder is issued an *option* to buy a specified number of new shares from the firm at a specified price within a specified time, after which the rights expire. For example, consider the £1.1 billion rights issue undertaken by Babcock International in April 2014 to partly fund a £1.6 billion acquisition of the helicopter firm, Avincis. The firm's equity was selling at £13.66 on the announcement date and current shareholders were able to buy a fixed number of shares at £7.90 per share within one month. The terms of the option are evidenced by certificates known as *share warrants* or *rights*. Such rights are often traded on securities exchanges or over the counter.

The Mechanics of a Rights Issue

The various considerations confronting a financial manager in a rights offering are illustrated by Babcock International. At the time, Babcock's equity was worth nearly £5 billion and had 362 million shares outstanding.

The process of issuing rights differs from the process of issuing shares of equity for cash. Existing shareholders are notified that they have been given a specific number of rights for each share of equity they own. Exercise occurs when a shareholder sends payment to the firm's subscription agent (usually a bank) and turns in the required number of rights. Shareholders of Babcock were given four choices:

1   Exercise some or all of your rights at £7.90 per right.
2   Sell all your rights.

3   Sell a proportion of your rights to generate sufficient funds to exercise the rest of your rights.

4   Do nothing and let the rights expire (this was the default option).

Babcock management had to answer the following questions:

1   What price should the existing shareholders be allowed to pay for a share of new equity?

2   How many rights will be required to purchase one share of equity?

3   What effect will the rights offering have on the existing share price of the company?

Subscription Price

In a rights issue the subscription price is the price that existing shareholders are allowed to pay for a share of equity. A rational shareholder will subscribe to the rights offering only if the subscription price is below the market price of the equity on the offer's expiration date. For example, if the share price at expiration is £5 and the subscription price is £7.90, no rational shareholder will subscribe. Why pay £7.90 for something worth only £5? Babcock International chose a price of £7.90, which was well below the existing market price of £13.66. As long as the market price did not fall below the subscription price of £7.90 before expiration, the rights offering would succeed.

Number of Rights Needed to Purchase a Share

Babcock International wanted to raise just over £1.1 billion in new equity. With a subscription price of £7.90, it needed to issue 139,259,204 new shares. This can be determined by dividing the total amount to be raised by the subscription price:

$$\text{Number of new shares} = \frac{\text{Funds to be raised}}{\text{Subscription price}} = \frac{£1,100,147,712}{£7.90} = 139,259,204 \text{ shares}$$

To determine how many rights must be exercised to get one share of equity, we can divide the number of existing outstanding shares of equity by the number of new shares:

$$\frac{\text{Number of rights needed}}{\text{to buy a share of equity}} = \frac{\text{'Old' shares}}{\text{'New' shares}} = \frac{362,073,930}{139,259,204} = 2.6 \text{ rights}$$

Clearly, it is impossible to own exactly 2.6 shares and so in a rights issue, one must construct terms so that the number of rights and shares are integers. In Babcock's case, the correct terms were 13 'old' shares for 5 'new' shares (13/5 = 2.6). In markets parlance, this would be called a '5 for 13 rights issue of 139,259,204 shares at £7.90 per share'. Thus each shareholder had to give up 13 rights plus £7.90 to receive 5 shares of new equity. If all the shareholders do this, Babcock will raise the required £1.1 billion.

   It should be clear that the subscription price, the number of new shares and the number of rights needed to buy a new share of equity are interrelated. If Babcock International lowered the subscription price, it would have had to issue more new shares to raise £1.1 billion in new equity. Several alternatives appear here:

Subscription Price (£)	Number of New Shares	Number of Rights Needed to Buy a Share of Equity
9.00	122,238,635	2.962
7.90	139,259,204	2.600
5.00	220,029,542	1.646

Effect of Rights Offering on the Share Price

Rights clearly have value. In the case of Babcock International, the right to be able to buy a share of equity worth £13.66 for £7.90 was valuable.

   Suppose a Babcock shareholder owns 13 shares of equity just before the rights offering. This situation is depicted in Table 19.7. Initially the Babcock share price was £13.66, so the shareholder's total holding is worth 13 × £13.66 = £177.58. The shareholder who has 13 shares will receive 13 rights. The Babcock rights issue gave shareholders with 13 rights the opportunity to purchase 5 additional shares for £7.90. The holding of the shareholder who exercises these rights and buys the new shares would increase to 18 shares. The value of the new holding would be £177.58 + £39.50 = £217.08 (the £177.58 initial value plus the £39.50 paid to the company). Because the shareholder now holds 18 shares, the price per share would drop to £217.08/18 = £12.06 (rounded to two decimal places).

Table 19.7 The Value to the Individual Shareholder of Babcock International's Rights

	The Shareholder
Initial position	
Number of shares	13
Share price	£13.66
Value of holding	£177.58
Terms of offer	
Subscription price	£7.90
Number of old shares for new shares	13 for 5
After offer	
Number of shares	18
Value of holding	£217.08
Share price	£12.06
Value of a right	
Old price − New price	£13.66 − £12.06 = £1.60
New price − Subscription price	(£12.06 − £7.90)/2.6 = £1.60
Number of rights for a share	

The difference between the old share price of £13.66 and the new share price of £12.06 reflects the fact that the old shares carried rights to subscribe to the new issue. The difference must be equal to the value of one right – that is, £13.66 − £12.06 = £1.60.

Just as we learned of an ex-dividend date in the previous chapter, there is an **ex-rights date** here. An individual buying the equity prior to the ex-rights date will receive the rights when they are distributed. An individual buying the equity on or after the ex-rights date will not receive the rights. In our example the price of the equity prior to the ex-rights date was £13.66. An individual buying on or after the ex-rights date is not entitled to the rights. The price on or after the ex-rights date will be £12.06.

Table 19.8 shows what happens to Babcock International. If all shareholders exercise their rights, the number of shares will increase to 501,333,134 and the value of the firm will increase to £6,046,077,601. After the rights offering the value of each share will drop to £12.06 (=£6,046,077,601/501,333,134).

Table 19.8 The Babcock International Rights Offering

Initial position	
Number of 'old' shares	362,073,930
Share price	£13.66
Value of firm	£4,945,929,889
Terms of offer	
Subscription price	£7.90
Number of 'new' shares	139,259,204
After offer	
Number of shares	501,333,134
Share price	£12.06
Value of firm	£6,046,077,601
Value of one right	£13.66 − £12.06 = £1.60 or (£12.06 − £7.90)/2.6 = £1.60

An investor holding no shares of Babcock International equity who wants to subscribe to the new issue can do so by buying rights. An outside investor buying 13 rights will pay £1.60 × 13 = £20.80 (to account for previous rounding). If the investor exercises the rights at a subscription cost of £7.90 to purchase 5 new shares, the total cost would be £20.80 + £39.50 = £60.30. In return for this expenditure, the investor will receive 5 shares of the new equity (worth £12.06 per share), totalling £60.30.

Of course, outside investors can also buy the Babcock International shares directly at £12.06 per share. In an efficient stock market it will make no difference whether new equity is obtained via rights or via direct purchase.

Effects on Shareholders

Shareholders can exercise their rights or sell them. In either case, the shareholder will neither win nor lose by the rights offering. The hypothetical holder of 13 Babcock International shares has a portfolio worth £177.58. On the one hand, if the shareholder exercises the rights, he or she ends up with 5 shares worth a total of £60.30. In other words, by spending £60.30, the investor increases the value of the holding by £60.30, which means that he or she is neither better nor worse off.

On the other hand, a shareholder who sells the 13 rights for £1.60 each obtains £1.60 × 13 = £20.80 in cash. Because the 13 shares are each worth £12.06, the holdings are valued at

$$
\begin{aligned}
\text{Shares} &= 13 \times £12.06 = £156.78 \\
\text{Sold rights} &= 13 \times £\ 1.60 = £\ \ 20.80 \\
\text{Total} &\qquad\qquad\ = £177.58
\end{aligned}
$$

The new £156.78 market value plus £20.80 in cash is exactly the same as the original holding of £177.58. Thus, shareholders can neither lose nor gain from exercising or selling rights.

It is obvious that the new market price of the firm's equity will be lower after the rights offering than it was before the rights issue. The lower the subscription price, the greater the price decline of a rights issue. However, our analysis shows that the shareholders have suffered no loss because of the rights issue.

The Underwriting Arrangements

Undersubscription can occur if investors throw away rights or if bad news causes the market price of the equity to fall below the subscription price. To ensure against these possibilities, rights offerings are typically arranged by **standby underwriting**. Here the underwriter makes a firm commitment to purchase the unsubscribed portion of the issue at the subscription price less a take-up fee. The underwriter usually receives a **standby fee** as compensation for this riskbearing function.

In practice the subscription price is usually set well below the current market price, making the probability of a rights failure quite small. Though a small percentage (less than 10 per cent) of shareholders fail to exercise valuable rights, shareholders are usually allowed to purchase unsubscribed shares at the subscription price. This **oversubscription privilege** makes it unlikely that the corporate issuer would need to turn to its underwriter for help.

Although the Babcock International rights issue was priced substantially lower than the market price, the issue was 96.62 per cent subscribed. This meant that the underwriter (also known as the bookrunner) had to purchase the 3.38 per cent unsubscribed portion of the issue. As the Babcock press release of 7 May 2014, stated:

> *In accordance with their obligations as Joint Bookrunners in respect of the Rights Issue pursuant to the Underwriting Agreement, J.P. Morgan Securities plc, Jefferies International Limited, Barclays Bank PLC and HSBC Bank plc will endeavour to procure subscribers for the remaining 4,701,180 New Ordinary Shares not validly taken up in the Rights Issue and the 5,915 New Ordinary Shares representing fractional entitlements in respect of the Rights Issue, failing which J.P. Morgan Securities plc, Jefferies International Limited, Barclays Bank PLC and HSBC Bank plc have agreed to acquire, on a several basis, any remaining New Ordinary Shares.*

19.7 Shelf Registration

To simplify the procedures for issuing securities, many stock exchanges allow **shelf registration**. Shelf registration permits a corporation to register an offering that it reasonably expects to sell within a specified number of years. A master registration statement is filed at the time of registration. The company is permitted to sell the issue whenever it wants over the shelf registration period as long as it distributes a short-form statement.

Hershman (1983) reports on the use of the *dribble* method of new equity issuance. With dribbling, a company registers the issue and hires an underwriter to be its selling agent. The company sells shares in small amounts from time to time via a stock exchange. For example, in March 2015, Mesa Laboratories filed a $130 million shelf registration to sell equity and in 2011, the Greek government filed a shelf registration for bonds.

The rule has been very controversial. Several arguments have been made against shelf registration:

1. The timeliness of disclosure is reduced with shelf registration because the master registration statement may have been prepared up to 2 years before the actual issue occurs.

2. Some bankers have argued that shelf registration will cause a market overhang because registration informs the market of future issues. It has been suggested that this overhang will depress market prices. However, an empirical analysis by Bhagat et al. (1985) found that shelf registration is less costly than conventional underwriting and found no evidence to suggest a market overhang effect.

19.8   The Private Equity Market

The previous sections of this chapter assumed that a company is big enough, successful enough and old enough to raise capital in the public equity market. Of course many firms have not reached this stage and cannot use the public equity market. For start-up firms or firms in financial trouble, the public equity market is often not available. For these companies, the private equity market, may be the best option.

Private Placement

Private placements avoid the costly procedures associated with the registration requirements that are part of public issues. Stock exchanges tend to restrict private placement issues to no more than a couple of dozen knowledgeable investors, including institutions such as insurance companies and pension funds. The biggest drawback of privately placed securities is that the securities cannot be easily resold. Most private placements involve debt securities, but equity securities can also be privately placed.

The Private Equity Firm

A large amount of private equity investment is undertaken by professional private equity managers representing large institutional investors such as mutual funds and pension funds. The limited partnership is the dominant form of intermediation in this market. Typically, the institutional investors act as the limited partners, and the professional managers act as general partners. The general partners are firms that specialize in funding and managing equity investments in closely held private firms. The private equity market has been important for both traditional start-up companies and established public firms. Thus, the private equity market can be divided into venture equity and non-venture equity markets. A large part of the non-venture market is made up of firms in financial distress. Firms in financial distress are not likely to be able to issue public equity and typically cannot use traditional forms of debt such as bank loans or public debt. For these firms, the best alternative is to find a private equity market firm. Outside of the United States, the UK is the leading centre for private equity and most private equity firms are based there. Table 19.9 lists the main European private equity firms and the value of their assets under management as at beginning of 2015.

Suppliers of Venture Capital

As we have pointed out, venture capital is an important part of the private equity market. There are at least four types of suppliers of venture capital. First, a few old-line, wealthy families have traditionally provided start-up capital to promising businesses. These families have been involved in venture capital for at least a century. For example, over the years, the Rockefeller family has made the initial capital contribution to a number of successful businesses.

Second, a number of private partnerships and corporations have been formed to provide investment funds. The organizer behind the partnership might raise capital from institutional investors, such as insurance companies and pension funds. Alternatively, a group of individuals might provide the funds to be ultimately invested with budding entrepreneurs.

Venture capital is a sub-activity of all private equity financing. The most common form of private equity financing in recent years is through buy-outs. Examples of private equity buyout activity include EMI, Boots and Chrysler. Figure 19.2 provides a breakdown of European private equity funding in 2013.[10] The majority of venture capital funds are in life sciences. Because of the global financial crisis in 2008, buy-out and venture capital activity dropped significantly on 2007 and 2006 levels, but it is now recovering slowly.

Table 19.9 Major European Private Equity Fundraisers

Fund Name	Assets under Management as at Beginning of 2015
Allianz	€7 billion
Skandia Life Insurance Company	€3.6 billion
SL Capital	€8.2 billion
Ardian	€29.1 billion
Shell Asset Management	€4.5 billion
European Investment Fund	€7.9 billion
Universities Superannuation Scheme	€5 billion
Adveq	€5 billion
Ilmarinen Mutual Pension Insurance	€1.65 billion
Danske Private Equity	€3 billion
Access Capital Partners	€5.4 billion
Swiss National Accident Insurance Institution (SUVA)	€2.3 billion
Pensionskassernes Administration	€2.5 billion
Pantheon	€29 billion
LGT Capital Partners	€14.9 billion
PGGM	€9 billion
Partners Group	€24 billion
AlpInvest	€37.7 billion
APG	€16.5 billion

Stories used to abound about how easily an individual could obtain venture capital. Though that may have been the case in an earlier era, it is certainly not the case today. Venture capital firms employ various screening procedures to prevent inappropriate funding. For example, because of the large demand for funds, many venture capitalists have at least one employee whose full-time job consists of reading business plans. Only the very best plans can expect to attract funds. Maier and Walker (1987) indicate that only about 2 per cent of requests actually receive financing.

Third, large industrial or financial corporations have established venture capital subsidiaries. Manufacturers Hanover Venture Capital Corp., Citicorp Venture Capital and Chemical Venture Capital Corporation of Chemical Bank are examples of this type. However, subsidiaries of this type appear to make up only a small portion of the venture capital market.

Fourth, there are also participants in an informal venture capital market.[11] Rather than belonging to any venture capital firm, these investors (often referred to as *angels*) act as individuals when providing financing. However, they should not, by any means, be viewed as isolated. Wetzel and others indicate that there is a rich network of angels, continually relying on each other for advice. A number of researchers have stressed that in any informal network there is likely one knowledgeable and trustworthy individual who, when backing a venture, brings a few less experienced investors in with him.

The venture capital community has unfortunately chosen to refer to these individuals as 'dumb dentists'. Although a number indeed may be dentists, their intelligence should not be called into question. Wetzel asserts that the prototypical angel has income over $100,000, net worth over $1,000,000, and substantial business experience and knowledge. As we might expect, the informal venture capitalist is able to tolerate high risks.

Though this informal market may seem small and unimportant, it is perhaps the largest of all sources of venture capital. Wetzel says that aggregate investments from this source in the US total around $50 billion, about twice the amount invested by more professional venture capitalists. The size of each contribution is smaller here. Perhaps, on average, only $250,000 per venture is raised when the informal market is tapped.

Stages of Financing

Bruno and Tyebjee (1985) identify six stages in venture capital financing:

1 *Seed money stage*: A small amount of financing needed to prove a concept or develop a product. Marketing is not included in this stage.

2 *Start-up*: Financing for firms that started within the past year. Funds are likely to pay for marketing and product development expenditures.

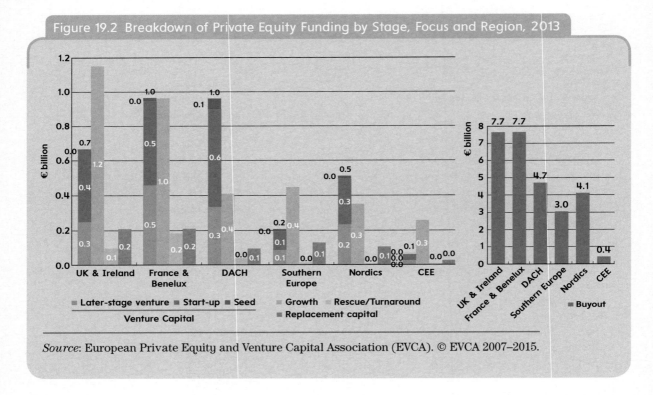

Figure 19.2 Breakdown of Private Equity Funding by Stage, Focus and Region, 2013

Source: European Private Equity and Venture Capital Association (EVCA). © EVCA 2007–2015.

3   *First-round financing*: Additional money to begin sales and manufacturing after a firm has spent its start-up funds.

4   *Second-round financing*: Funds earmarked for working capital for a firm that is currently selling its product but still losing money.

5   *Third-round financing*: Financing for a company that is at least breaking even and is contemplating an expansion. This is also known as *mezzanine financing*.

6   *Fourth-round financing*: Money provided for firms that are likely to go public within half a year. This round is also known as *bridge financing*.

Although these categories may seem vague to the reader, we have found that the terms are well-accepted within the industry. For example, the venture capital firms listed in Pratt's *Guide to Venture Capital* indicate which of these stages they are interested in financing. Figure 19.2 also presents a breakdown of where private equity funding was made in Europe in 2013. The use of venture capital varied considerably across countries and whereas in the UK and Ireland it was used to fund new growth, in continental Europe it was more associated with start-up funding.

The penultimate stage in venture capital finance is the initial public offering.[12] Venture capitalists are very important participants in initial public offerings. Venture capitalists rarely sell all of the shares they own at the time of the initial public offering. Instead they usually sell out in subsequent public offerings.

Real World Insight 19.1

Cyber Security Start-Ups

(*Excerpts taken from 'The private equity deals that fail to justify "fast buck" strategies', by Marc Goergen, Geoffrey Wood and Noel O'Sullivan*)

There is an ongoing and very heated debate between the unconditional supporters of private equity and their opponents. It's not hard to see why. On the surface, these investors can often buy fragile companies, load on debt to fund strategic change and sack workers in a bid for efficiency. It can look ruthless, but the industry claims it simply works.

The British Private Equity & Venture Capital Association (BVCA) preaches what it deems to be the undeniable benefits of private equity. For example, the trade lobby group wrote in 2010 that:

*Private equity investment has been demonstrated to contribute significantly to companies' growth.
Private equity backed companies outperform leading UK businesses.*

In contrast, Ed Miliband in his speech at the 2011 annual Labour Party conference accused private equity houses of 'stripping assets for a quick buck and … [failing to represent] the values of British business'.

To date, studies of private equity acquisitions of firms listed on the stock exchange disagree as to the effects on employment. A major issue is that the studies typically conflate very different forms of private equity acquisitions which are likely to vary significantly in terms of their impact.

It is important to realise that there are three main forms of private equity acquisitions which involve very different stakeholders and which are therefore likely to have very different effects on employment.

The most frequent form of private equity acquisition is a management buy-out or MBO. These involve management of a company taking the firm private, with the help of private equity houses which provide the cash. However, given that the existing management stays in place and carries on running the firm, the employment effects of MBOs are typically very positive or neutral at worst.

However, the other two main forms of private equity acquisitions – management buy-ins (MBIs) and institutional buy-outs (IBOs) – result in a change in the management. In the case of less-frequent MBIs, a new management team buys out the existing shareholders and takes the firm private and the input of private equity houses is typically limited to the financing. In the case of IBOs, the private equity house not only provides the financing, but also the management team. You can happily make the case for the positive employment effects of MBOs. The evidence on MBIs and IBOs, however, is much more mixed.

A new study (Goergen, M., & Wood, G., 2014, The employment consequences of private equity acquisitions: The case of institutional buy outs. *European Economic Review*, 71, 67-79) sheds new light on the employment effects of UK IBOs. The study is based on 106 IBO acquisitions of UK listed firms between 1997 and 2006 (during the same period there were 139 MBOs and six MBIs). The sample included well-known companies such as Churchill China (check the bottom of your restaurant crockery), Fox's biscuits, Goodfella's Pizza maker Northern Foods and the high street department store Debenhams.

The findings are stark reading. The most important thing is that there is a significant decrease in employment in the year following the acquisition in the target firms of IBOs, and this drop in employment is combined with a drop in wages below the market rates for the target firms.

The IBO companies' median employment growth was 11 per cent five years before acquisition, falling down to –4.80 per cent the year after the deal. Figures on salary suggest a similar trend with IBO companies seeing a salary reduction from a mean of £29,460 before the IBO to £28,520 following it.

Those cynical about the industry might not be surprised by the above, but there is more. Importantly, despite what could be perceived as a much needed cull of the work force, the target firms do not experience an improvement in their profitability and productivity following the acquisition. The suggestion is clear: the increased insecurity inherent in the shedding of jobs and the downward pressure on wages outweighs any of the potential benefits from a change in management brought about by an institutional buy-out.

While this new study uncovers negative effects on employment of a particular type of private equity acquisition – so called institutional buy-outs (IBOs) – it does not imply that all private equity acquisitions are bad for employment. What the results do suggest is that the debate on the effects of private equity acquisitions needs to be much more nuanced.

Importantly, it needs to distinguish between those types of private equity acquisitions that have undeniable positive benefits for employment – as well as the survival and competitiveness of UK businesses – and those that are likely to be mostly detrimental.

Summary and Conclusions

This chapter looked closely at how equity is issued. The main points follow:

1 Large issues have proportionately much lower costs of issuing equity than small ones.

2 Firm commitment underwriting is far more prevalent for large issues than is best-efforts underwriting. Smaller issues probably primarily use best efforts because of the greater uncertainty of these issues.

For an offering of a given size, the direct expenses of best-efforts underwriting and firm commitment underwriting are of the same magnitude.

3   Rights issues are cheaper than general cash offers and eliminate the problem of underpricing. Yet most new equity issues are underwritten general cash offers.

4   Shelf registration is a new method of issuing new debt and equity. The direct costs of shelf issues seem to be substantially lower than those of traditional issues.

5   Private equity is an increasingly important influence in start-up firms and subsequent financing.

Questions and Problems

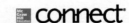

CONCEPT

1   **The Public Issue**   Review the steps involved in the public issue of equity. Do a search on Google for a public equity issue in your country, download all relevant news stories and track the issue process for the company. Is it similar to the one presented in this chapter? For IPOs, what do you think the main factors are that determine the stock exchange the company should list on?

2   **Alternative Issue Methods**   What is the difference between a public offering and a private placement? What might explain a company's decision to favour one over the other? Your discussion should make reference to the advantages and disadvantages of each.

3   **Announcement Effects**   Why do you think the share price tends to go down when an equity issue is announced?

4   **Shelf Registration**   Why would shareholders not be keen on shelf registration? What steps could they take to avoid shelf registration?

REGULAR

5   **The Private Equity Market**   Provide an overview of the private equity market. Why would firms wish to go private once they have listed on a stock exchange? In April 2015, Rangers International Football Club plc delisted from the AIM market on the London Stock Exchange. Why do you think this was? Do you think this will be beneficial to the club?

6   **IPO Underpricing**   What is meant by underpricing? Why are most IPOs underpriced? Drawing on the academic evidence, explain the main theories behind this phenomenon. Is this is a sign of market inefficiency? Explain.

7   **IPO Pricing**   Unicredit, a multinational bank, had a rights issue in January 2012. Assisted by a consortium of banks including BofA Merrill Lynch and Mediobanca, Unicredit sold 3.86 billion shares at €1.943 each, thereby raising a total of €7.5 billion. At the end of the first day of trading, the shares sold for €2.29 per share. Based on the end-of-day numbers, Unicredit shares were apparently underpriced by about 15 per cent each, meaning that the company missed out on an additional €1.34 billion. Should Unicredit be upset at BofA Merrill Lynch over the underpricing?

8   **Costs and Benefits of IPOs**   Outline the advantages and disadvantages for a company undertaking an IPO.

9   **IPO Underpricing around the World**   IPO underpricing is a worldwide phenomenon. In the United States, IPOs are on average underpriced by around 17 per cent, and in the United Kingdom they are underpriced by around 16 per cent. Most other advanced economies experience IPO underpricing of around 20 per cent. In China, IPOs are underpriced by around 137 per cent, while for emerging markets it is around 60 per cent. What do you think explains these vast differences?

10   **Cash Offer versus Rights Offer**   ThyssenKrup AG is an industrial component manufacturer based in Germany. Assume that it is considering opening a new plant in Poland. It has two choices to fund the investment: issue equity via a rights issue to its existing shareholders, or have a full public underwritten cash offer. Give advice to the management of ThyssenKrup on the best issue method. What is your recommendation and why?

11   **IPO Underpricing**   Consider the following experiment: you submit a purchase order for every firm commitment initial public offering of oil and gas exploration companies. There are 22 of these offerings,

and you submit a purchase order for approximately €1,000 in equity for each of the companies. However, for ten issues you are allocated no shares and for five issues you receive fewer than the requested number of shares. In only seven issues do you receive the number of shares you requested.

Assume that this was a very good year for oil and gas exploration company owners: on average, for the 22 companies that went public, the shares were selling for 80 per cent above the offering price a month after the initial offering date. However, you have looked at your own performance record and found that the €8,400 invested in the 12 companies had grown to €10,000, representing a return of only about 20 per cent (commissions were negligible). Did you have bad luck, or should you have expected to do worse than the average initial public offering investor? Explain.

12 **IPO Pricing** The following material represents the cover page and summary of the prospectus for the initial public offering of the Pest Investigation Control Corporation SA (PICC), which is going public tomorrow with a firm commitment initial public offering managed by the investment banking firm of Bigelli and Pindado.

(a) Assume that you know nothing about PICC other than the information contained in the prospectus. Based on your knowledge of finance, what is your prediction for the price of PICC tomorrow? Provide a short explanation of why you think this will occur.

(b) Assume that you have several thousand euros to invest. When you get home from class tonight, you find that your stockbroker, whom you have not talked to for weeks, has called. She has left a message that PICC is going public tomorrow and that she can get you several hundred shares at the offering price if you call her back first thing in the morning. Discuss the merits of this opportunity.

PROSPECTUS   PICC

200,000 shares
PEST INVESTIGATION CONTROL CORPORATION

Of the shares being offered hereby, all 200,000 are being sold by the Pest Investigation Control Corporation SA ('the Company'). Before the offering there has been no public market for the shares of PICC, and no guarantee can be given that any such market will develop.

These securities have not been approved or disapproved by the Autorité des Marchés Financiers, nor has the Authority passed judgment upon the accuracy or adequacy of this prospectus. Any representation to the contrary is a criminal offence.

	Price to Public (€)	Underwriting Discount (€)	Proceeds to Company* (€)
Per share	11.00	1.10	9.90
Total	2,200,000	220,000	1,980,000

*Before deducting expenses estimated at €27,000 and payable by the company.

This is an initial public offering. The ordinary shares are being offered, subject to prior sale, when, as, and if delivered to and accepted by the Underwriters and subject to approval of certain legal matters by their Counsel and by Counsel for the Company. The Underwriters reserve the right to withdraw, cancel, or modify such offer and to reject offers in whole or in part.

Bigelli and Pindado, Bankers
12 July 2015
Prospectus Summary

The Company	The Pest Investigation Control Corporation (PICC) breeds and markets toads and tree frogs as ecologically safe insect-control mechanisms.
The Offering	200,000 ordinary shares of equity, no par value.
Listing	The Company will seek listing on Euronext.
Shares Outstanding	As of 30 June 2015, 400,000 ordinary shares of equity were outstanding. After the offering, 600,000 ordinary shares of equity will be outstanding.
Use of Proceeds	To finance expansion of inventory and receivables and general working capital, and to pay for country club memberships for certain finance professors.

▶

Selected Financial Information (amounts in thousands except per-share data)					
	Fiscal Year Ended 30 June				As of 30 June 2015
	2013 (€)	2014 (€)	2015 (€)		Actual (€)	As Adjusted for this Offering (€)
Revenues	60.00	120.00	240.00	Working capital	0.8	1,961
Net earnings	3.80	15.90	36.10	Total assets	511	2,464
Earnings per share	0.01	0.04	0.09	Shareholders' equity	423	2,376

13 **Competitive and Negotiated Offers** Assume you have been hired by the Spanish food exporter, Distribuidora Internacional de Alimentacion SA to help progress a seasoned equity offering it plans to undertake in the autumn. You have been specifically asked to recommend either a competitive offer or a negotiated offer for the firm to undertake. What is your recommendation and why?

14 **Seasoned Equity Offers** For the same firm in Question 14, you have been asked by a reporter why you are having a seasoned equity offering when typically share prices drop when they are announced. How would you explain the price drop?

15 **Raising Capital** For the same firm in Question 14, you have been approached by a major shareholder who has asked you to consider either an underwritten cash offer or a rights issue (not underwritten) to current shareholders. The shareholder has insisted you maximize shareholder wealth. What is your decision? Explain.

16 **Shelf Registration** Explain why shelf registration has been used by many firms instead of syndication. Why is it controversial?

17 **IPOs** Every IPO is unique, but what are the basic empirical regularities in IPOs?

18 **Rights Offerings** Balmorals plc is a well-established company that has run into difficulty in recent years. Its management has recently undertaken a review of its activities and has decided to proceed with a radical restructuring of the business. To restore the company's financial stability, it has been decided it will be necessary to raise £160 million through a rights issue. After consulting its investment bankers the company is planning to make the rights issue at a discount of 20 per cent to the current market price of £5. The company has 100 million shares outstanding.

(a) What is the value of a right?

(b) What are the current terms of the rights issue?

(c) How would an investor with 10,000 shares be affected if they:
   (i) Exercised their rights?
   (ii) Sold their rights?
   (iii) Tail-swallowed their rights?

19 **Rights Offering** Faff plc has announced a rights issue to raise £50 million for a new journal, the *Journal of Financial Excess*. This journal will review potential articles after the author pays a non-refundable reviewing fee of £5,000 per page. The equity currently sells for £40 per share, and there are 5.2 million shares outstanding.

(a) What is the maximum possible subscription price? What is the minimum?

(b) If the subscription price is set at £35 per share, how many shares must be sold? How many rights will it take to buy one share?

(c) What is the ex-rights price? What is the value of a right?

(d) Show how a shareholder with 1,000 shares before the offering and no desire (or money) to buy additional shares is not harmed by the rights offer.

20 **Rights** Glasauge AB concluded that additional equity financing will be needed to expand operations and that the needed funds will be best obtained through a rights issue. It has correctly determined that as a result of the rights issue, the share price will fall from €3.38 to €3.00 (€3.38 is the 'rights-on' price; €3.00 is the ex-rights price, also known as the *when-issued* price). The company is seeking €2 million in additional funds with a per-share subscription price equal to €2. How many shares are there currently, before the offering? (Assume that the increment to the market value of the equity equals the gross proceeds from the offering.)

21 **IPO Underpricing** Carlyle plc and Mullan plc have both announced IPOs at £40 per share. One of these is undervalued by £11, and the other is overvalued by £6, but you have no way of knowing which is which. You plan on buying 1,000 shares of each issue. If an issue is underpriced, it will be rationed, and only half your order will be filled. If you *could* get 1,000 shares in Carlyle and 1,000 shares in Mullan, what would your profit be? What profit do you actually expect? What principle have you illustrated?

22 **Calculating Flotation Costs** Groene Heuvels NV has just gone public. Under a firm commitment agreement, Groene Heuvels received €19.75 for each of the 5 million shares sold. The initial offering price was €21 per share, and the equity rose to €26 per share in the first few minutes of trading. Groene Heuvels paid €800,000 in direct legal and other costs and €250,000 in indirect costs. What was the flotation cost as a percentage of funds raised?

23 **Price Dilution** Raggio SpA has 100,000 shares of equity outstanding. Each share is worth €90, so the company's market value of equity is €9,000,000. Suppose the firm issues 20,000 new shares at the following prices: €90, €85 and €70. What will the effect be of each of these alternative offering prices on the existing price per share?

24 **Stock Offerings** The Newton Company has 10,000 shares of equity that each sell for £40. Suppose the company issues 5,000 shares of the new equity at the following prices: £40, £20 and £10. What is the effect of each of the alternative offering prices on the existing price per share?

CHALLENGE

25 **Seasoned Equity Issues** What are the five methods through which a company can raise seasoned equity? What might explain a company's decision to favour one over the other? Your discussion should define each and make reference to the advantages and disadvantages of each.

26 **Dilution** Larme SA wishes to expand its facilities. The company currently has 10 million shares outstanding and no debt. The equity sells for €50 per share, but the book value per share is €40. Net income for Larme is currently €15 million. The new facility will cost €35 million, and it will increase net income by €500,000.

  (a) Assuming a constant price–earnings ratio, what will the effect be of issuing new equity to finance the investment? To answer, calculate the new book value per share, the new total earnings, the new EPS, the new share price, and the new market-to-book ratio. What is going on here?

  (b) What would the new net income for Larme have to be for the share price to remain unchanged?

27 **Dilution** Elvis Heavy Metal Mining (EHMM) plc wants to diversify its operations. Some recent financial information for the company is shown here:

Share price (£)	98
Number of shares	14,000
Total assets (£)	6,000,000
Total liabilities (£)	2,400,000
Net income (£)	630,000

EHMM is considering an investment that has the same PE ratio as the firm. The cost of the investment is £1,100,000, and it will be financed with a new equity issue. The return on the investment will equal EHMM's current ROE. What will happen to the book value per share, the market value per share, and the EPS? What is the NPV of this investment? Does dilution take place?

28 **Dilution** In the previous problem, what would the ROE on the investment have to be if we wanted the price after the offering to be £98 per share? (Assume the PE ratio remains constant.) What is the NPV of this investment? Does any dilution take place?

29 **Rights** A company's equity currently sells for £45 per share. Last week the firm issued rights to raise new equity. To purchase a new share, a shareholder must remit £10 and three rights.

  (a) What is the ex-rights share price?

  (b) What is the price of one right?

  (c) When will the price drop occur? Why will it occur then?

30 **Rights** Gipfel equity is currently selling at €13 per share. There are 1 million shares outstanding. The firm is planning to raise €2 million to finance a new project. What are the ex-rights share price, the value of a right and the appropriate subscription prices under the following scenarios?

(a) Two shares of outstanding equity are entitled to purchase one additional share of the new issue.

(b) Four shares of outstanding equity are entitled to purchase one additional share of the new issue.

(c) How does the shareholders' wealth change from part (a) to part (b)?

31 **Rights** Hoobastink Mfg. is considering a rights offer. The company has determined that the ex-rights price would be €52. The current price is €55 per share, and there are 5 million shares outstanding. The rights issue would raise a total of €60 million. What is the subscription price?

32 **Value of Right** Show that the value of a right can be written as

$$\text{Value of a right} = P_{RO} - P_X = (P_{RO} - P_S)/(N + 1)$$

where P_{RO}, P_S, and P_X stand for the 'rights-on' price, the subscription price and the ex-rights price, respectively, and N is the number of rights needed to buy one new share at the subscription price.

33 **Selling Rights** Wuttke plc wants to raise £3.65 million via a rights issue. The company currently has 490,000 ordinary shares outstanding that sell for £30 per share. Its underwriter has set a subscription price of £22 per share and will charge Wuttke a 6 per cent spread. If you currently own 6,000 shares of equity in the company and decide not to participate in the rights issue, how much money can you get by selling your rights?

34 **Valuing a Right** Mitsi Inventory Systems has announced a rights offer. The company has announced that it will take four rights to buy a new share in the offering at a subscription price of €40. At the close of business the day before the ex-rights day, the company's shares sell for €80 per share. The next morning you notice that the equity sells for €72 per share and the rights sell for €6 each. Are the equity and/or the rights correctly priced on the ex-rights day? Describe a transaction in which you could use these prices to create an immediate profit.

Exam Question (45 minutes)

1 *'In a public share issue, the probability of receiving an allocation of an underpriced security is less than or equal to the probability of receiving an allocation of an overpriced issue.'* Discuss this statement in the context of initial public offerings. (25 marks)

Ai Due Fanali SA has decided to undertake a rights issue that will raise €288 million. The current share price is €4.50 and there are 160 million shares in circulation. They have to make a decision on whether to underwrite the rights issue. The underwriting fee will be 2 per cent of proceeds if the shares are offered at a 20 per cent discount. Ai Due Fanali's finance director believes that a discount of 40 per cent will avoid the need for underwriting altogether.

2 Set out the terms of the issue under each of the two alternatives referred to above. Calculate the theoretical ex-rights price and the value of a right. (25 marks)

3 Demonstrate that in principle, a wealth maximizing shareholder owning six shares will be indifferent between the two alternative methods of raising the funds. (25 marks)

4 Discuss the benefits of using an underwriter in a rights issue. Review the factors which determine an underwriter's fee. (25 marks)

Mini Case

West Coast Yachts Goes Public

Larissa Warren and Dan Ervin have been discussing the future of West Coast Yachts. The company has been experiencing fast growth, and the future looks like clear sailing. However, the fast growth means that the company's growth can no longer be funded by internal sources, so Larissa and Dan have decided the time is right to take the company public. To this end, they have entered into discussions with the bank of Crowe & Mallard. The company has a working relationship with Robin Perry, the underwriter who assisted with the company's previous bond offering. Crowe & Mallard have helped numerous small companies in the IPO process, so Larissa and Dan feel confident with this choice.

Robin begins by telling Larissa and Dan about the process. Although Crowe & Mallard charged an underwriter fee of 4 per cent on the bond offering, the underwriter fee is 7 per cent on all initial equity offerings of the size of West Coast Yachts' initial offering. Robin tells Larissa and Dan that the company can expect to pay about £1,200,000 in legal fees and expenses, £12,000 in registration fees, and £15,000 in other filing fees. Additionally, to be listed on the London Stock Exchange, the company must pay £100,000. There are also transfer agent fees of £6,500 and engraving expenses of £450,000. The company should also expect to pay £75,000 for other expenses associated with the IPO.

Finally, Robin tells Larissa and Dan that to file with the London Stock Exchange, the company must provide 3 years' worth of audited financial statements. She is unsure of the costs of the audit. Dan tells Robin that the company provides audited financial statements as part of its bond indenture, and the company pays £300,000 per year for the outside auditor.

1   At the end of the discussion Dan asks Robin about the Dutch auction IPO process. What are the differences in the expenses to West Coast Yachts if it uses a Dutch auction IPO versus a traditional IPO? Should the company go public with a Dutch auction or use a traditional underwritten offering?

2   During the discussion of the potential IPO and West Coast Yachts' future, Dan states that he feels the company should raise £50 million. However, Larissa points out that if the company needs more cash soon, a secondary offering close to the IPO would be potentially problematic. Instead she suggests that the company should raise £80 million in the IPO. How can we calculate the optimal size of the IPO? What are the advantages and disadvantage of increasing the size of the IPO to £80 million?

3   After deliberation, Larissa and Dan have decided that the company should use a firm commitment offering with Crowe & Mallard as the lead underwriter. The IPO will be for £60 million. Ignoring underpricing, how much will the IPO cost the company as a percentage of the funds received?

4   Many of the employees of West Coast Yachts have shares of equity in the company because of an existing employee stock purchase plan. To sell the equity, the employees can tender their shares to be sold in the IPO at the offering price, or the employees can retain their equity and sell it in the secondary market after West Coast Yachts goes public (once the 180-day lockup expires). Larissa asks you to advise the employees about which option is best. What would you suggest to the employees?

Practical Case Study

Do a search on Google news for ten announcements of new funding for companies in the last year. Look at the share price between the announcement date and 5 days later. Can you see any pattern between share price reaction and funding type? In what ways could you improve this very simplistic analysis?

Relevant Accounting Standard

The most important accounting standard for equities is IAS 39 *Financial Instruments: Recognition and Measurement*. Visit the IASPlus website (www.iasplus.com) for more information.

References

Altinkilic, O. and R.S. Hansen (2000) 'Are There Scale Economies in Underwriting Spreads? Evidence of Rising External Financing Costs', *Review of Financial Studies*, Vol. 13, 191–218.

Armitage, S. (2000) 'The Direct Costs of UK Rights Issues and Open Offers', *European Financial Management*, Vol. 6, No. 1, 57–68.

Asquith, P. and D. Mullins (1986) 'Equity Issues and Offering Dilution', *Journal of Financial Economics*, Vol. 15, Nos. 1–2, 61–89.

Barnes, E. and M. Walker (2006) 'The Seasoned-Equity Issues of UK Firms: Market Reaction and Issuance Method',

Journal of Business Finance and Accounting, Vol. 33, No. 1–2, 45–78.

Barry, C., C.J. Muscarella, J.W. Peavey III and M.R. Vetsuypens (1990) 'The Role of Venture Capital in the Creation of Public Companies: Evidence from the Going Public Process', *Journal of Financial Economics*, Vol. 27, No. 2, 447–471.

Beatty, R. and J. Ritter (1986) 'Investment Banking, Reputation, and the Underpricing of Initial Public Offerings', *Journal of Financial Economics*, Vol. 15, Nos. 1–2, 213–232.

Bhagat, S. (1986) 'The Effect of Management's Choice between Negotiated and Competitive Equity Offerings on Shareholder Wealth', *Journal of Financial and Quantitative Analysis*, Vol. 21, 181–196.

Bhagat, S., M.W. Marr and G.R. Thompson (1985) 'The Rule 415 Experiment: Equity Markets', *The Journal of Finance*, Vol. 40, No. 5, 1385–1401.

Bruno, A.V. and T.T. Tyebjee (1985) 'The Entrepreneur's Search for Capital', *Journal of Business Venturing*, Vol. 1, 61–74.

Carter, R. and S. Manaster (1990) 'Initial Public Offerings and Underwriter Reputation', *The Journal of Finance*, Vol. 45, 1045–1067.

Carter, R.B., F.H. Dark and T.A. Sapp (2011) 'Underwriter Reputation and IPO Issuer Alignment 1981–2005', *The Quarterly Review of Economics and Finance*, Vol. 5, 443–455.

Gajewski, J-F. and E. Ginglinger (2002) 'Seasoned Equity Issues in a Closely Held Market: Evidence from France', *European Finance Review*, Vol. 6, No. 3, 291–319.

Hansen, R.S. and C. Crutchley (1990) 'Corporate Earnings and Financings: An Empirical Analysis', *Journal of Business*, Vol. 63, 347–372.

Hansen, R.S. and N. Khanna (1994) 'Why Negotiation with a Single Syndicate May Be Preferred to Making Syndicates Compete: The Problem of Trapped Bidders', *Journal of Business*, Vol. 67, No. 3, 423–457.

Hershman, A. (1983) 'New Strategies in Equity Financing', *Dunn's Business Monthly*, June.

Ibbotson, R. (1975) 'Price Performance of Common Stock New Issues', *Journal of Financial Economics*, Vol. 2, 235–272.

Krigman, L., W. Shaw and K. Womack (2001) 'Why Do Firms Switch Underwriters?', *Journal of Financial Economics*, Vol. 60, Nos. 2–3, 245–284.

Ljunqvist, A. (2006) 'IPO Underpricing', in B. Espen Eckbo (ed.), *Handbook of Corporate Finance: Empirical Corporate Finance*, Volume A, Chapter 7 (Amsterdam: Elsevier/North Holland).

Logue, D. and R. Jarrow (1978) 'Negotiation vs. Competitive Bidding in the Sales of Securities by Public Utilities', *Financial Management*, Vol. 7, 31–39.

Logue, D. and S. Tiniç (1999) 'Optimal Choice of Contracting Methods: Negotiated versus Competitive Underwritings Revisited', *Journal of Financial Economics*, Vol. 51, No. 3, 451–471.

Loughran, T., J. Ritter and K. Rydqvist (1994) 'Initial Public Offerings: International Insights', *Pacific-Basin Finance Journal*, Vol. 2, 165–169.

Maier, J. B. and D. Walker (1987) 'The Role of Venture Capital in Financing Small Business', *Journal of Business Venturing*, Vol. 2, No. 3, 207–214.

Martin-Ugedo, J. (2003) 'Equity Rights Issues in Spain: Flotation Costs and Wealth Effects', *Journal of Business Finance and Accounting*, Vol. 30, 1277–1304.

Masulis, R. and A.N. Korwar (1986) 'Seasoned Equity Offerings: An Empirical Investigation', *Journal of Financial Economics*, Vol. 15, Nos. 1–2, 91–118.

Migliorati, K. and S. Vismara (2014) 'Ranking Underwriters of European IPOs', *European Financial Management*, Vol. 20, 891–925.

Mikkelson, W.H. and M.M. Partch (1986) 'The Valuation Effects of Security Offerings and the Issuance Process', *Journal of Financial Economics*, Vol. 15, Nos. 1–2, 31–60.

Rock, K. (1986) 'Why New Issues Are Underpriced', *Journal of Financial Economics*, Vol. 15, Nos. 1–2, 187–212.

Wetzel, W.E. (1987) 'The Informal Venture Capital Market: Aspects of Scale and Market Efficiency', *Journal of Business Venturing*, Vol. 2, No. 4, 299–313.

Additional Reading

Research in equity financing covers many areas and this is reflected in the number of recent papers published in the area. To aid understanding and targeted reading, the reference list below is categorized into separate but overlapping topics. As with every good academic paper, its implications can span several different areas. Equity financing research is no different in this regard.

Initial Public Offerings

1   Bancel, F. and U.R. Mittoo (2009) 'Why Do European Firms Go Public?', *European Financial Management*, Vol. 15, No. 4, 844–884. **Europe**.

2   Binay, M.M., V.A. Gatchev and C.A. Pirinsky (2007) 'The Role of Underwriter–Investor Relationships in the IPO Process', *Journal of Financial and Quantitative Analysis*, Vol. 42, No. 3, 785–809. **US**.

3   Bodnaruk, A., E. Kandel and M. Massa (2008) 'Shareholder Diversification and the Decision to Go Public', *Review of Financial Studies*, Vol. 21, No. 6, 2779–2824. **Sweden**.

4   Brau, J.C. and S.E. Fawcett (2006) 'Initial Public Offerings: An Analysis of Theory and Practice', *The Journal of Finance*, Vol. 61, No. 1, 399–436. **US**.

5   Celikyurt, U., M. Sevilir and A. Shivdasani (2010) 'Going Public to Acquire? The Acquisition Motive in IPOs', *Journal of Financial Economics*, Vol. 96, No. 3, 345–363.

6   Chemmanur, T.J., S. He and D.K. Nandy (2010) 'The Going-Public Decision and the Product Market', *Review of Financial Studies*, Vol. 23, No. 5, 1855–1908.

7   Chemmanur, T.J., G. Hu and J. Huang (2010) 'The Role of Institutional Investors in Initial Public Offerings', *Review of Financial Studies*, Vol. 23, No. 12, 4496–4540. **US**.

8   Chemmanur, T.J. and I. Paeglis (2005) 'Management Quality, Certification, and Initial Public Offerings', *Journal of Financial Economics*, Vol. 76, No. 2, 331–368. **US**.

9   Cook, D.O., R. Kieschnick, and R.A. Van Ness (2006) 'On the Marketing of IPOs', *Journal of Financial Economics*, Vol. 82, No. 1, 35–61. **US**.

10 Corwin, S.A. and P. Schultz (2005) 'The Role of IPO Underpricing Syndicates: Pricing, Information Production, and Underwriter Competition', *The Journal of Finance*, Vol. 60, No. 1, 443–486. **US**.

11 Deloof, M., W. De Maeseneire and K. Inghelbrecht (2009) 'How Do Investment Banks Value Initial Public Offerings (IPOs)?', *Journal of Business Finance and Accounting*, Vol. 36, Nos. 1 and 2, 130–160. **Belgium**.

12 Derrien, F. and A. Kecskes (2007) 'The Initial Public Offering of Listed Firms', *The Journal of Finance*, Vol. 62, No. 1, 447–479. **UK**.

13 Edwards, A.K. and K. Weiss Hanley (2010) 'Short Selling in Initial Public Offerings', *Journal of Financial Economics*, Vol. 98, No. 1, 21–39. **US**.

14 Ellul, A. and M. Pagano (2006) 'IPO Underpricing and After-Market Liquidity', *Review of Financial Studies*, Vol. 19, No. 2, 381–421. **UK**.

15 Holmen, M. and P. Hogfeldt (2004) 'A Law and Finance Analysis of Initial Public Offerings', *Journal of Financial Intermediation*, Vol. 13, No. 3, 324–358. **Sweden**.

16 Jenkinson, T. and H. Jones (2009) 'IPO Pricing and Allocation: A Survey of the Views of Institutional Investors', *Review of Financial Studies*, Vol. 22, No. 4, 1477–1504. **International**.

17 Kaustia, M. and S. Knupfer (2008) 'Do Investors Overweight Personal Experience? Evidence from IPO Subscriptions', *The Journal of Finance*, Vol. 63, No. 6, 2679–2702. **Finland**.

18 Kerins, F., K. Kutsuna and R. Smith (2007) 'Why Are IPOs Underpriced? Evidence from Japan's Hybrid Auction-Method Offerings', *Journal of Financial Economics*, Vol. 85, No. 3, 637–666. **Japan**.

19 Kutsuna, K., J. Kiholm Smith and R. Smith (2009) 'Public Information, IPO Price Formation, and Long-Run Returns: Japanese Evidence', *The Journal of Finance*, Vol. 64, No. 1, 505–546. **Japan**.

20 Ljungqvist, A. and W.J. Wilhelm (2005) 'Does Prospect Theory Explain IPO Market Behavior?', *The Journal of Finance*, Vol. 60, No. 4, 1759–1790. **US**.

21 Loughran, T. and B. McDonald (2013) 'IPO First-day Returns, Offer Price Revisions, Volatility, and Form S-1 Language', *Journal of Financial Economics*, Vol. 109, No. 2, 307–326.

22 Lowry, M., M.S. Officer and G.W. Schwert (2010) 'The Variability of IPO Initial Returns', *The Journal of Finance*, Vol. 65, No. 2, 425–465.

23 Pastor, L. and P. Veronesi (2005) 'Rational IPO Waves', *The Journal of Finance*, Vol. 60, No. 4, 1713–1757. **US**.

24 Roosenboom, P. and W. Schramade (2006) 'The Price of Power: Valuing the Controlling Position of Owner-Managers in French IPO Firms', *Journal of Corporate Finance*, Vol. 12, No. 2, 270–295. **France**.

Private Equity and Venture Capital

25 Acharya, V.V., O.F. Gottschalg, M. Hahn and C. Kehoe (2013) 'Corporate Governance and Value Creation: Evidence from Private Equity', *Review of Financial Studies*, Vol. 26, No. 2, 368–402.

26 Bharath, S.T. and A.K. Dittmar (2010) 'Why Do Firms Use Private Equity to Opt Out of Public Markets?', *Review of Financial Studies*, Vol. 23, No. 5, 1771–1818.

27 Botazzi, L., M. Da Rin and T. Hellmann (2008) 'Who Are the Active Investors? Evidence from Venture Capital', *Journal of Financial Economics*, Vol. 89, No. 3, 488–512, **Europe**.

28 Cochrane, J.H. (2005) 'The Risk and Return of Venture Capital', *Journal of Financial Economics*, Vol. 75, No. 1, 3–52. **US**.

29 Cronqvist, H. and M. Nilsson (2005) 'The Choice between Rights Offerings and Private Equity Placements', *Journal of Financial Economics*, Vol. 78, No. 2, 375–407. **Sweden**.

30 Cumming, D. (2008) 'Contracts and Exits in Venture Capital Finance', *Review of Financial Studies*, Vol. 21, No. 5, 1947–1982. **Europe**.

31 Cumming, D. and U. Walz (2010) 'Private Equity Returns and Disclosure around the World', *Journal of International Business Studies*, Vol. 41, 727–754. **International**.

32 Cumming, D., D. Schmidt and U. Walz (2010) 'Legality and Venture Capital Governance around the World', *Journal of Business Venturing*, Vol. 25, No. 1, 54–72.

33 Diller, C. and C. Kaserer (2009) 'What Drives Private Equity Returns? Fund Inflows, Skilled GPs and/or Risk?', *European Financial Management*, Vol. 15, No. 3, 643–675.

34 Hochberg, Y.V., A. Ljungqvist and Y. Lu (2007) 'Whom You Know Matters: Venture Capital Networks and Investment Performance', *The Journal of Finance*, Vol. 62, No. 1, 251–301. **US**.

35 Ivashina, V. and A. Kovner (2011) 'The Private Equity Advantage: Leveraged Buyout Firms and Relationship Banking', *Review of Financial Studies*, Vol. 24, No. 7, 2462–2498.

36 Kaplan, S. and A. Schoar (2005) 'Private Equity Performance: Returns, Persistence, and Capital Flows', *The Journal of Finance*, Vol. 60, No. 4, 1791–1823. **US**.

37 Kaplan, S., S. Berk and P. Stromberg (2009) 'Should Investors Bet on the Jockey or the Horse? Evidence from the Evolution of Firms from Early Business Plans to Public Companies', *The Journal of Finance*, Vol. 64, No. 1, 75–115. **US**.

38 Kräussl, R. and S. Krause (2012) 'Has Europe Been Catching Up? An Industry Level Analysis of Venture Capital Success over 1985–2009', *European Financial Management*, Vol. 20, No. 1, 179–205. **Europe**.

39 Mettrick, A. and A. Yasuda (2010) 'The Economics of Private Equity Funds', *Review of Financial Studies*, Vol. 23, No. 6, 2303–2341. **International**.

40 Nahata, R. (2008) 'Venture Capital Reputation and Investment Performance', *Journal of Financial Economics*, Vol. 90, No. 2, 127–151. **US**.

41 Phalippou, L. and O. Gottschalg (2009) 'The Performance of Private Equity Funds', *Review of Financial Studies*, Vol. 90, No. 4, 1747–1776. **US**.

42 Renneboog, L., T. Simons and M. Wright (2007) 'Why Do Public Firms Go Private in the UK? The Impact of Private Equity Investors, Incentive Realignment and Undervaluation', *Journal of Corporate Finance*, Vol. 13, No. 4, 591–628. **UK**.

Seasoned Equity Offerings, Rights Issues and Reverse LBOs

43 Armitage, S. (2010) 'Block Buying and Choice of Issue Method in UK Seasoned Equity Offers', *Journal of Business Finance and Accounting*, Vol. 37, Nos. 3 and 4 (April/May), 422–448. **UK**.

44 Cao, J. and J. Lerner (2009) 'The Performance of Reverse Leveraged Buyouts', *Journal of Financial Economics*, Vol. 91, No. 2, 139–157. **US**.

45 Cohen, D.A. and P. Zarowin (2010) 'Accrual-Based and Real Earnings Management Activities around Seasoned Equity Offerings', *Journal of Accounting and Economics*, Vol. 50, No. 1, 2–19.

46 DeAngelo, H., L. DeAngelo and R.M. Stulz (2010) 'Seasoned Equity Offerings, Market Timing, and the Corporate Lifecycle', *Journal of Financial Economics*, Vol. 95, No. 3, 275–295. **US**.

47 Gao, X. and J.R. Ritter (2010) 'The Marketing of Seasoned Equity Offerings', *Journal of Financial Economics*, Vol. 97, No. 1, 33–52.

48 Hillier, D. (2010) 'Discussion of Block Buying and Choice of Issue Method in UK Seasoned Equity Offers', *Journal of Business Finance and Accounting*, Vol. 37, Nos. 3–4, 449–455.

49 Iqbal, A. (2008) 'The Importance of the Sequence in UK Rights Issues', *Journal of Business Finance and Accounting*, Vol. 35, Nos. 1–2, 150–176. **UK**.

50 Lee, G. and R.W. Masulis (2009) 'Seasoned Equity Offerings: Quality of Accounting Information and Expected Flotation Costs', *Journal of Financial Economics*, Vol. 92, No. 3, 443–469. **US**.

Other Relevant Research

51 Boubakri, N., J-C. Cosset and O. Guedhami (2005) 'Postprivatization Corporate Governance: The Role of Ownership Structure and Investor Protection', *Journal of Financial Economics*, Vol. 76, No. 2, 369–399. **International**.

52 Hoberg, G. (2007) 'The Underwriter Persistence Phenomenon', *The Journal of Finance*, Vol. 62, No. 3, 1169–1206. **US**.

53 Sarkissian, S. and M. Schill (2009) 'Are there Permanent Valuation Gains to Overseas Listing?', *Review of Financial Studies*, Vol. 22, No. 1, 371–412. **International**.

Endnotes

1 As with the majority of the material covered in this chapter, the specific approach to placings is different in each country. Information on country regulations can usually be found in the listing rules of each stock exchange. These are normally downloadable from the exchange's website.

2 The Green Shoe Corp. in the US was the first firm to allow this provision.

3 For example, see Carter et al. (2011); Krigman et al. (2001); Carter and Manaster (1990); and Beatty and Ritter (1986).

4 This choice has been studied by Logue and Tiniç (1999); Hansen and Khanna (1994); Bhagat (1986); and Logue and Jarrow (1978).

5 This explanation was first suggested in Rock (1986).

6 Asquith and Mullins (1986); Masulis and Korwar (1986); Mikkelson and Partch (1986); Gajewski and Ginglinger (2002); Martin-Ugedo (2003). Barnes and Walker (2006) actually find that private placings elicit a positive response in contrast to a public listing, which is associated with significant negative returns.

7 Hansen and Crutchley (1990).

8 Some people have argued that the price in the aftermarket is not efficient after all. However, Ibbotson (1975) shows that, on average, new issues exhibit no abnormal price performance over the first 5 years following issuance. This result is generally viewed as being consistent with market efficiency. That is, the equity obtains an efficient price immediately following issuance and remains at an efficient price.

9 The notion of economies of scale has been contested by Altinkilic and Hansen (2000). They provide data and analysis showing that underwriter cost will be U-shaped.

10 The majority of information in this section comes from the European Private Equity and Venture Capital Association, a non-profit trade association of around 1,300 private equity firms (www.evca.eu).

11 See Wetzel (1987).

12 A very influential paper by Barry et al. (1990) shows that venture capitalists do not usually sell shares at the time of the initial public offering, but they usually have board seats and act as advisers to managers.

CHAPTER
20

Debt Financing

In its basic form, a bond is a simple financial instrument. You lend a company some amount, say £10,000. The company pays you interest on a regular basis, and it repays the original loan amount of £10,000 at some point in the future. Bank loans can be more customized to the borrower and the terms and conditions on loans vary with the loan itself. Many bonds originating in the Middle East are Shariah compliant and do not pay interest. In Europe, government bond issues have attracted intense scrutiny by analysts looking for hints on the future direction of the Eurozone.

An example of a bond is one issued by Malaysia in March 2015. The sovereign bond (all state and government bonds are called sovereign bonds) was worth $2 billion and had a maturity of more than 5 years. An interesting feature of the bond was that it did not pay interest. Instead, they were Islamic bonds, known as *sukuk*. In this chapter, we will discuss the various characteristics of debt financing and review the different possible debt instruments corporations can use to finance their operations (you may at this point want to reread Sections 5.1 to 5.3 in **Chapter 5** to reacquaint yourself with bond valuation).

Chapter 5
Page 120

KEY NOTATIONS

r	Yield to maturity; cost of debt
C	Coupon

20.1   Bank Loans

Bank loans form a major part of debt financing across the world. Although the amount of credit available from banks has declined somewhat from pre-financial crisis levels, it still dominates other forms of financing in many countries. Figure 20.1 presents bank loans as a proportion of external financing in a number of selected countries. As can be seen, bank loans vary in popularity, with Italian firms the most favourable towards this type of debt.

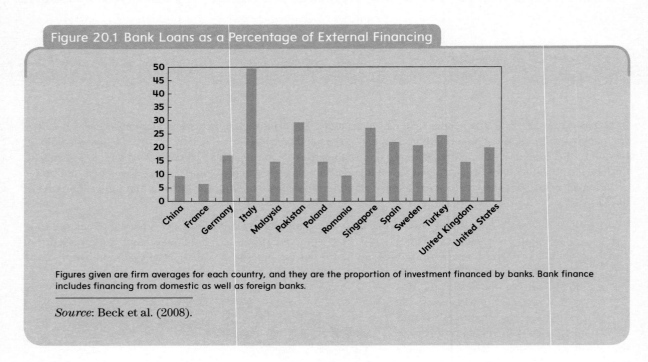

Figure 20.1 Bank Loans as a Percentage of External Financing

Figures given are firm averages for each country, and they are the proportion of investment financed by banks. Bank finance includes financing from domestic as well as foreign banks.

Source: Beck et al. (2008).

Types of Bank Loan

Bank loans come in two types: lines of credit and loan commitments. A line of credit is an arrangement between a bank and a firm, typically for a short-term loan, whereby the bank authorizes the maximum loan amount, but not the interest rate, when setting up the line of credit. Lines of credit do not in a practical sense commit the bank to lend money because the bank is free to quote any interest rate it wishes at the time the borrowing firm requests funds. If the interest rate is too high, the firm will decline the available line of credit.

A loan commitment, on the other hand, is an arrangement that requires a bank to lend up to a maximum pre-specified loan amount at a pre-specified interest rate. The commitment is in place and available at the firm's request as long as the firm meets the requirements established when the commitment was drawn up. There are two types of loan commitment. A revolver is a loan commitment in which funds flow back and forth between the bank and the firm without any predetermined schedule. Funds are drawn from the revolver whenever the company needs them, up to the maximum amount specified. Revolvers may also be subject to an annual clean-up in which the firm must retire all borrowings. A non-revolving loan commitment is one in which the firm cannot pay down the loan and then subsequently increase the amount of borrowing. Research has shown that firms with high levels of cash flow are able to obtain lines of credit but less liquid firms tend to rely on cash for their short-term capital requirements.[1]

20.2   Debt Financing

Long-term debt securities are promises by the issuing firm to pay interest and principal on the unpaid balance. The *maturity* of a long-term debt instrument refers to the length of time the debt remains outstanding with some unpaid balance. Debt securities can be *short term* (maturities of one year or less) or *long term* (maturities of more than one year). Short-term debt is sometimes referred to as *unfunded debt* and long-term debt as *funded debt*.

The two major forms of long-term debt are publicly issued and privately placed debt. We discuss public-issue bonds first, and most of what we say about them holds true for privately placed long-term debt as well. The main difference between publicly issued and privately placed debt is that private debt is directly placed with a lending institution.

There are many other attributes to long-term debt, including security, call features, sinking funds, ratings and protective covenants. The following table illustrates the features for a fixed rate bond recently issued by Vilmorin & Cie, the global agricultural firm.

	Term	Explanation
Amount of issue	€150 million	The company issued €150 million worth of bonds.
Date of issue	11 March 2015	The bonds were sold on 11 March 2015.
Maturity	26 May 2021	The bonds mature on 26 May 2021.
Face value	€100,000	The denomination of the bonds is €100,000.
Annual coupon	2.375%	Each bondholder will receive 2.375 per cent per annum
Offer price	104.802	The offer price was 104.802 per cent of the face value of the bond. This is €104,802.
Coupon payment dates	26 May	Coupons of €2,375 will be paid on this date each year until maturity.
Security	Pari Passu	Equal rank to other creditors.
Sinking fund	No	The bonds have no sinking fund.
Call provision	Yes	The bonds can only be redeemed in full.
Rating	Unrated	The bond has no credit rating.

20.3 The Public Issue of Bonds

The general procedures followed for a public issue of bonds are the same as those for equities, as described in the previous chapter. First, the offering must be approved by the board of directors. Sometimes a vote of shareholders (or supervisory board if the company operates in a country with a two-tier board system) is also required. Second, a registration statement is prepared for review by the relevant regulatory authority. Third, if accepted, the registration statement becomes *effective* at some point in the near future, and the securities are sold.

However, the registration statement for a public issue of bonds must include an indenture, a document not relevant for the issue of equities. An indenture is a written agreement between the corporation (the borrower) and a trust company. It is sometimes referred to as the *deed of trust*.[2] The trust company is appointed by the corporation to represent the bondholders. The trust company must (1) make sure the terms of the indenture are obeyed, (2) manage the sinking fund (if appropriate), and (3) represent bondholders if the company defaults on its payments.

The typical bond indenture can be a document of several hundred pages, and it generally includes the following provisions:

1 The basic terms of the bonds
2 A description of property used as security
3 Details of the protective covenants
4 The sinking fund arrangements
5 The call provision.

Each of these is discussed next.

The Basic Terms

Bonds usually have a denomination (also known as *face value* or *principal value*) denominated in multiples of 100. For example, in the UK, government bonds have a face value of £100 and corporate bonds tend to have a face value of £100,000. In Europe, the denomination is often €1,000, €10,000 or €100,000. In the US, the denomination is normally $1,000. The denomination of the bond is always stated on the bond certificate. In addition, the *par value* (i.e., initial accounting value) of a bond is almost always the same as the face value.

Transactions between bond buyers and bond sellers determine the market value of the bond. Actual bond market values depend on the general level of interest rates, among other factors, and need not equal the face value. Bond prices are quoted as a percentage of the denomination. This is illustrated in the following example.

Example 20.1

Bond Prices

Suppose Nero SpA has issued 100 bonds. The amount stated on each bond certificate is €1,000. The total denomination, face value or principal value of the bonds is €100,000. Further suppose the bonds are currently *priced* at 100, which means 100 per cent of €1,000. This means that buyers and sellers are holding bonds at a price per bond of €1,000. If interest rates rise, the price of the bond might fall to, say, 97, which means 97 per cent of €1,000, or €970.

Suppose the bonds have a stated interest rate of 12 per cent due on 1 January 2050. The bond indenture might read as follows:

> The bond will mature on 1 January 2050, and will be limited in aggregate denomination to €100,000. Each bond will bear interest at the rate of 12.0 per cent per annum from 1 January 2013, or from the most recent Interest Payment Date to which interest has been paid or provided for. Interest is payable semi-annually on 1 July and 1 January of each year.

As is typical of industrial bonds, the Nero bonds are registered. The indenture might read as follows:

> Interest is payable semi-annually on 1 July and 1 January of each year to the person in whose name the bond is registered at the close of business on 15 June or 15 December respectively.

This means that the company has a registrar who will record the ownership of each bond. The company will pay the interest and principal by cheque mailed directly to the address of the owner of record.

When a bond is registered with attached coupons, the bondholder must separate a coupon from the bond certificate and send it to the company registrar (paying agent). Some bonds are in bearer form. This means that ownership is not recorded in the company books. As with a registered bond with attached coupons, the holder of the bond certificate separates the coupons and sends them to the company to receive payment.

There are two drawbacks to bearer bonds. First, they can be easily lost or stolen. Second, because the company does not know who owns its bonds, it cannot notify bondholders of important events. Consider, for example, Mr and Mrs De Loof, who go to their safe deposit box and clip the coupon on their 12 per cent, €1,000 bond issued by Nero SpA. They send the coupon to the paying agent and feel richer. A few days later a notice comes from the paying agent that the bond was retired and its principal paid off one year earlier. In other words, the bond no longer exists. Mr and Mrs De Loof must forfeit one year of interest. (Of course, they can turn their bond in for €1,000.)

However, bearer bonds have the advantage of secrecy because even the issuing company does not know who the bond's owners are. This secrecy is particularly vexing to tax authorities because tax collection on interest is difficult if the holder is unknown.

A Note on Bond Price Quotes

If you buy a bond between coupon payment dates, the price you pay is usually more than the price you are quoted. The reason is that standard convention in the bond market is to quote prices net of 'accrued interest', meaning that accrued interest is deducted to arrive at the quoted price. This quoted price is called the clean price. The price you actually pay, however, includes the accrued interest. This price is the dirty price, also known as the 'full' or 'invoice' price.

An example is the easiest way to understand these issues. Suppose you buy a UK government bond with a 12 per cent annual coupon, payable semi-annually. You actually pay £108 for this bond, so £108 is the dirty, or invoice, price. Further, on the day you buy it, the next coupon is due in 4 months, so you are between coupon dates. Notice that the next coupon will be £6.

The accrued interest on a bond is calculated by taking the fraction of the coupon period that has passed, in this case 2 months out of 6, and multiplying this fraction by the next coupon, £6. So, the accrued interest in this example is 2/6 × £6 = £2. The bond's quoted price (i.e., its clean price) would be £108 − £2 = £106.

Security

Debt securities are also classified according to the *collateral* protecting the bondholder. Collateral is a general term for the assets that are pledged as security for payment of debt. For example, *collateral trust bonds* involve a pledge of equity held by the corporation.

Example 20.2

Collateral Trust Bonds

Suppose Railroad Holdings plc owns all of the ordinary shares of Track plc; that is, Track plc is a wholly owned subsidiary of Railroad Holdings plc. Railroad issues debt securities that pledge the equity of Track plc as collateral. The debts are collateral trust bonds; UK Sur Bank will hold them. If Railroad Holdings plc defaults on the debt, UK Sur Bank will be able to sell the equity of Track plc to satisfy Railroad's obligation.

Mortgage securities are secured by a mortgage on real estate or other long-term assets of the borrower. The legal document that describes the mortgage is called a *mortgage trust indenture* or *trust deed*. The mortgage can be *closed-end*, so that there is a limit on the amount of bonds that can be issued. More frequently it is *open-end*, without limit to the amount of bonds that may be issued.

Example 20.3

Mortgage Securities

Suppose Cuscin Bond Company has buildings and land worth £10 million and a £4 million mortgage on these properties. If the mortgage is closed-end, Cuscin Bond Company cannot issue more bonds on this property.

If the bond indenture contains no clause limiting the amount of additional bonds that can be issued, it is an open-end mortgage. In this case, Cuscin Bond Company can issue additional bonds on its property, making the existing bonds riskier. For example, if additional mortgage bonds of £2 million are issued, the property has been pledged for a total of £6 million of bonds. If Cuscin Bond Company must liquidate its property for £4 million, the original bondholders will receive 4/6, or 67 per cent, of their investment. If the mortgage had been closed-end, they would have received 100 per cent of the stated value.

The value of a mortgage depends on the market value of the underlying property. Because of this, mortgage bonds sometimes require that the property be properly maintained and insured. Of course, a building and equipment bought in 1914 for manufacturing slide rules might not have much value no matter how well the company maintains it. The value of any property ultimately depends on its next best economic use. Bond indentures cannot easily insure against losses in economic value.

Sometimes mortgages are on specific property – for example, a single building. More often, blanket mortgages are used. A blanket mortgage pledges many assets owned by the company.

Some bonds represent unsecured obligations of the company. A debenture is an unsecured bond, where no specific pledge of property is made. Debenture holders have a claim on property not otherwise pledged: the property that remains after mortgages and collateral trusts are taken into account.

Protective Covenants

A protective covenant is that part of the indenture or loan agreement that limits certain actions of the borrowing company. Protective covenants can be classified into two types: negative covenants and positive covenants. A negative covenant limits or prohibits actions that the company may take. Here are some typical examples:

1 Limitations are placed on the amount of dividends a company may pay.
2 The firm cannot pledge any of its assets to other lenders.

3　The firm cannot merge with another firm.

4　The firm may not sell or lease its major assets without approval by the lender.

5　The firm cannot issue additional long-term debt.

A **positive covenant** specifies an action that the company agrees to take or a condition the company must abide by. Here are some examples:

1　The company agrees to maintain its working capital at a minimum level.

2　The company must furnish periodic financial statements to the lender.

The financial implications of protective covenants were treated in detail in the chapters about capital structure. In that discussion, we argued that protective covenants can benefit shareholders because if bondholders are assured that they will be protected in times of financial stress, they will accept a lower interest rate.

The Sinking Fund

Bonds can be entirely repaid at maturity, at which time the bondholder will receive the stated value of the bond; or they can be repaid before maturity. Early repayment is more typical.

In a direct placement of debt, the repayment schedule is specified in the loan contract. For public issues, the repayment takes place through the use of a sinking fund and a call provision.

A *sinking fund* is an account managed by the bond trustee for the purpose of repaying the bonds. Typically, the company makes yearly payments to the trustee. The trustee can purchase bonds in the market or can select bonds randomly using a lottery and purchase them, generally at face value. There are many different kinds of sinking fund arrangements:

- Most sinking funds start between 5 and 10 years after the initial issuance.
- Some sinking funds establish equal payments over the life of the bond.
- Most high-quality bond issues establish payments to the sinking fund that are not sufficient to redeem the entire issue. As a consequence, there is the possibility of a large *balloon* payment at maturity.

Sinking funds have two opposing effects on bondholders:

1　*Sinking funds provide extra protection to bondholders.* A firm experiencing financial difficulties would have trouble making sinking fund payments. Thus, sinking fund payments provide an early warning system to bondholders.

2　*Sinking funds give the firm an attractive option.* If bond prices fall below the face value, the firm will satisfy the sinking fund by buying bonds at the lower market prices. If bond prices rise above the face value, the firm will buy the bonds back at the lower face value (or other fixed price, depending on the specific terms).

The Call Provision

A *call provision* lets the company repurchase or *call* the entire bond issue at a predetermined price over a specified period.

Generally the call price is above the bond's face value. The difference between the call price and the face value is the **call premium**. For example, if the call price is 105 – that is, 105 per cent of, say, €1,000 – the call premium is €50. The amount of the call premium usually becomes smaller over time. One typical arrangement is to set the call premium initially equal to the annual coupon payment and then make it decline to zero over the life of the bond.

Call provisions are not usually operative during the first few years of a bond's life. For example, a company may be prohibited from calling its bonds for the first 10 years. This is referred to as a **deferred call**. During this period the bond is said to be **call-protected**.

In just the last few years, a new type of call provision, a 'make-whole' call, has become widespread in the corporate bond market. With such a feature, bondholders receive approximately what the bonds are worth if they are called. Because bondholders do not suffer a loss in the event of a call, they are 'made whole'.

To determine the make-whole call price, we calculate the present value of the remaining interest and principal payments at a rate specified in the indenture. For example, assume that the Vilmorin & Cie issue was callable and that the discount rate is 'Treasury rate plus 0.20 per cent'. What this means is that we determine the discount rate by first finding a French Treasury issue with the same maturity. We calculate the yield to maturity on the Treasury issue and then add on an additional 0.20 per cent to get the discount rate we use.

20.4 Bond Refunding

Replacing all or part of an issue of outstanding bonds is called bond **refunding**. Usually, the first step in a typical bond refunding is to call the entire issue of bonds at the call price. Bond refunding raises two questions:

1 Should firms issue callable bonds?

2 Given that callable bonds have been issued, when should the bonds be called?

We attempt to answer these questions in this section, focusing on traditional fixed-price call features.

Should Firms Issue Callable Bonds?

Common sense tells us that call provisions have value. First, many publicly issued bonds have call provisions. Second, it is obvious that a call works to the advantage of the issuer. If interest rates fall and bond prices go up, the option to buy back the bonds at the call price is valuable. In bond refunding, firms will typically replace the called bonds with a new bond issue. The new bonds will have a lower coupon rate than the called bonds.

However, bondholders will take the call provision into account when they buy the bond. For this reason we can expect that bondholders will demand higher interest rates on callable bonds than on non-callable bonds. In fact, financial economists view call provisions as being zero-sum in efficient capital markets.[3] Any expected gains to the issuer from being allowed to refund the bond at lower rates will be offset by higher initial interest rates. We illustrate the zero-sum aspect to callable bonds in the following example.

Example 20.4

Suppose Scandinavian Intercable ASA intends to issue perpetual bonds of 1,000 Norwegian kroner (NKr) face value at a 10 per cent interest rate. Annual coupons have been set at NKr100. There is an equal chance that by the end of the year interest rates will do one of the following:

1 Fall to $6\frac{2}{3}$ per cent. If so, the bond price will increase to NKr1,500.

2 Increase to 20 per cent. If so, the bond price will fall to NKr500.

Non-callable Bond Suppose the market price of the non-callable bond is the expected price it will have next year plus the coupon, all discounted at the current 10 per cent interest rate.[4] The value of the non-callable bond is this:

Value of non-callable bond

$$\frac{\text{First-year coupon} + \text{Expected price at end of year}}{1 + r}$$

$$= \frac{\text{NKr}100 + (0.5 \times \text{NKr}1,500) + (0.5 \times \text{NKr}500)}{1.10}$$

$$= \text{NKr}1,000$$

Callable Bond Now suppose Scandinavian Intercable ASA decides to issue callable bonds. The call premium is set at NKr100 over par value, and the bonds can be called *only* at the end of the first year.[5] In this case, the call provision will allow the company to buy back its bonds at NKr1,100 (NKr1,000 par value plus the NKr100 call premium). Should interest rates fall, the company will buy a bond for NKr1,100 that would be worth NKr1,500 in the absence of a call provision. Of course, if interest rates rise, Scandinavian Intercable would not want to call the bonds for NKr1,100 because they are worth only NKr500 on the market.

Suppose rates fall and Scandinavian Intercable calls the bonds by paying NKr1,100. If the firm simultaneously issues new bonds with a coupon of NKr100, it will bring in NKr1,500 (NKr100/0.0667) at the $6\frac{2}{3}$ per cent interest rate. This will allow Scandinavian Intercable to pay an extra dividend to shareholders of NKr400 (NKr1,500 − NKr1,100). In other words, if rates fall from 10 per cent to $6\frac{2}{3}$ per cent, exercise of the call will transfer NKr400 of potential bondholder gains to the shareholders.

When investors purchase callable bonds, they realize that they will forfeit their anticipated gains to shareholders if the bonds are called. As a consequence, they will not pay NKr1,000 for a callable bond with a coupon of NKr100.

How high must the coupon on the callable bond be so that it can be issued at the par value of NKr1,000? We can answer this in three steps.

Step 1: Determining End-of-year Value if Interest Rates Drop   If the interest rate drops to $6\frac{2}{3}$ per cent by the end of the year, the bond will be called for NKr1,100. The bondholder will receive both this and the annual coupon payment. If we let C represent the coupon on the callable bond, the bondholder gets the following at the end of the year:

$$\text{NKr}1,100 + C$$

Step 2: Determining End-of-year Value if Interest Rates Rise   If interest rates rise to 20 per cent, the value of the bondholder's position at the end of the year is:

$$\frac{C}{0.20} + C$$

That is, the perpetuity formula tells us that the bond will sell at $C/0.20$. In addition, the bondholder receives the coupon payment at the end of the year.

Step 3: Solving for C   Because interest rates are equally likely to rise or to fall, the expected value of the bondholder's end-of-year position is:

$$(\text{NKr}1,100 + C) \times 0.5 + \left(\frac{C}{0.20} + C\right) \times 0.5$$

Using the current interest rate of 10 per cent, we set the present value of these payments equal to par:

$$\text{NKr}1,000 = \frac{(\text{NKr}1,100 + C) \times 0.5 + (C/0.20 + C) \times 0.5}{1.10}$$

C is the unknown in the equation. The equation holds if $C = \text{NKr}157.14$. In other words, callable bonds can sell at par only if their coupon rate is 15.714 per cent.

The Paradox Restated   If Scandinavian Intercable issues a non-callable bond, it will only need to pay a 10 per cent interest rate. By contrast, Scandinavian Intercable must pay an interest rate of 15.7 per cent on a callable bond. The interest rate differential makes an investor indifferent to either bond in our example. Because the return to the investor is the same with either bond, the cost of debt capital is the same to Scandinavian Intercable with either bond. Thus, our example suggests that there is neither an advantage nor a disadvantage to issuing callable bonds.

Why, therefore, are callable bonds issued in the real world? This question has vexed financial economists for a long time. We now consider four specific reasons why a company might use a call provision:

1   Superior interest rate predictions.

2   Taxes.

3   Financial flexibility for future investment opportunities.

4   Less interest rate risk.

Superior Interest Rate Forecasting

Company insiders may know more about interest rate changes on the company's bonds than does the investing public. For example, managers may be better informed about potential changes in the firm's credit rating. Thus, a company may prefer the call provision at a particular time because it believes that the expected fall in interest rates (the probability of a fall multiplied by the amount of the fall) is greater than the bondholders believe.

Although this is possible, there is reason to doubt that inside information is the rationale for call provisions. Suppose firms really had superior ability to predict changes that would affect them. Bondholders would infer that a company expected an improvement in its credit rating whenever it issued callable bonds. Bondholders would require an increase in the coupon rate to protect them against a call if this occurred. As a result, we would expect that there would be no financial advantage to the firm from callable bonds over non-callable bonds.

Of course, there are many non-company-specific reasons why interest rates can fall. For example, the interest rate level is connected to the anticipated inflation rate. But it is difficult to see how companies could have more information about the general level of interest rates than other participants in the bond markets.

Taxes

Call provisions may have tax advantages if the bondholder is taxed at a lower rate than the company. We have seen that callable bonds have higher coupon rates than non-callable bonds. Because the coupons provide a deductible interest expense to the corporation and are taxable income to the bondholder, the corporation will gain more than a bondholder in a low tax bracket will lose. Presumably, some of the tax savings can be passed on to the bondholders in the form of a high coupon.

Future Investment Opportunities

As we have explained, bond indentures contain protective covenants that restrict a company's investment opportunities. For example, protective covenants may limit the company's ability to acquire another firm or to sell certain assets (for example, a division of the company). If the covenants are sufficiently restrictive, the cost to the shareholders in lost net present value can be large. However, if bonds are callable, the company can buy back the bonds at the call price and take advantage of a superior investment opportunity.

Less Interest Rate Risk

The call provision will reduce the sensitivity of a bond's value to changes in the level of interest rates. As interest rates increase, the value of a non-callable bond will fall. Because the callable bond has a higher coupon rate, the value of a callable bond will fall less than the value of a non-callable bond. Kraus (1983) has argued that by reducing the sensitivity of a bond's value to changes in interest rates, the call provision may reduce the risk of shareholders as well as bondholders.[6] He argues that because the bond is a liability of the corporation, the shareholders bear risk as the bond changes value over time. Thus, it can be shown that, under certain conditions, reducing the risk of bonds through a call provision will also reduce the risk of equity.

Calling Bonds: When Does it Make Sense?

The value of the company is the value of the equity plus the value of the bonds. From the Modigliani–Miller theory and the pie model in earlier chapters, we know that firm value is unchanged by how it is divided between these two instruments. Therefore, maximizing shareholder wealth means minimizing the value of the callable bond. In a world with no transaction costs, it can be shown that the company should call its bonds whenever the callable bond value exceeds the call price. This policy minimizes the value of the callable bonds.

The preceding analysis is modified slightly by including the costs from issuing new bonds. These extra costs change the refunding rule to allow bonds to trade at prices above the call price. The objective of the company is to minimize the sum of the value of the callable bonds plus new issue costs. It has been observed that many real-world firms do not call their bonds when the market value of the bonds reaches the call price. Instead, they wait until the market value of the bonds exceeds the call price. Perhaps these issue costs are an explanation. Also, when a bond is called, the holder has about 30 days to surrender the bond and receive the call price in cash. In 30 days the market value of the bonds could fall below the call price. If so, the firm is giving away money. To forestall this possibility, it can be argued that firms should wait until the market value of the bond exceeds the call price before calling bonds.

20.5 Bond Ratings

Firms frequently pay to have their debt rated. The two leading bond-rating firms are Moody's Investors Service and Standard & Poor's. The debt ratings depend on (1) the likelihood that the firm will default, and (2) the protection afforded by the loan contract in the event of default. The ratings are constructed from information supplied by the corporation, primarily the financial statements of the firm. The rating classes are shown in the accompanying box.

The highest rating debt can have is AAA or Aaa. Debt rated AAA or Aaa is judged to be the best quality and to have the lowest degree of risk. The lowest rating is D, which indicates that the firm is in default. In recent years, a growing part of corporate borrowing has taken the form of *low-grade bonds*. These bonds are also known as either *high-yield bonds* or *junk bonds*. Low-grade bonds are corporate bonds that are rated below *investment grade* by the major rating agencies (that is, below BBB for Standard & Poor's or Baa for Moody's).

Bond ratings are important because bonds with lower ratings tend to have higher interest costs. However, the most recent evidence is that bond ratings merely reflect bond risk. There is no conclusive evidence that bond ratings affect risk.[7] It is not surprising that the share prices and bond prices of firms do not show any unusual behaviour on the days around a rating change. Because the ratings are based on publicly available information, they probably do not, in themselves, supply new information to the market.[8]

Example 20.5

Bond Ratings

	Very High Quality	High Quality	Speculative	Very Poor
Standard & Poor's	AAA AA	A BBB	BB B	CCC CC C D
Moody's	Aaa Aa	A Baa	Ba B	Caa Ca C D

At times both Moody's and Standard & Poor's adjust these ratings. S&P uses plus and minus signs: A+ is the strongest A rating and A− the weakest. Moody's uses a 1, 2, or 3 designation, with 1 indicating the strongest. These increments are called notches.

Moody's	S&P	
Aaa	AAA	Debt rated Aaa and AAA has the highest rating. Capacity to pay interest and principal is extremely strong.
Aa	AA	Debt rated Aa and AA has a very strong capacity to pay interest and repay principal. Together with the highest rating, this group comprises the high-grade bond class.
A	A	Debt rated A has a strong capacity to pay interest and repay principal. How ever, it is somewhat more susceptible to adverse changes in circumstances and economic conditions.
Baa	BBB	Debt rated Baa and BBB is regarded as having an adequate capacity to pay interest and repay principal. Whereas it normally exhibits adequate protection parameters, adverse economic conditions or changing circumstances are more likely to lead to a weakened capacity to pay interest and repay principal for debt in this category than in higher-rated categories. These bonds are medium-grade obligations.
Ba B	BB B	Debt rated in these categories is regarded, on balance, as predominantly speculative. Ba and BB indicate the lowest degree of speculation, and Ca and CC the highest.
Caa Ca	CCC CC	Although such debt is likely to have some quality and protective characteristics, these are outweighed by large uncertainties or major risk exposure to adverse conditions.
C	C	This rating is reserved for income bonds on which no interest is being paid.
D	D	Debt rated D is in default, and payment of interest and/or repayment of principal is in arrears.

Source: Data from various editions of *Standard & Poor's Bond Guide* and *Moody's Bond Guide.*

Rating agencies do not always agree. For example, some bonds are known as 'crossover' or '5B' bonds. The reason is that they are rated triple-B (or Baa) by one rating agency and double-B (or Ba) by another: a 'split rating'.

Junk Bonds

The investment community has labelled bonds with a Standard & Poor's rating of BB and below or a Moody's rating of Ba and below as **junk bonds**. These bonds are also called *high-yield, speculative* or *low-grade;* we shall use all three terms interchangeably. Issuance of junk bonds has grown greatly in recent years, leading to increased public interest in this form of financing.

During economic downturns, junk bonds are most likely to default because of their speculative nature. Table 20.1 presents data by Standard & Poor's on European junk bond defaults in the recent past. As can be seen,

Table 20.1 Historical Default Rates – European Junk Bonds: 2010–2014

Default rate on bonds outstanding, issued since 2009	2010	2011	2012	2013	2014
Bonds outstanding (beginning of the year)	58	158	279	441	659
Number of defaults	0	3	2	13	10
Default rate on bonds outstanding	**0.00%**	**1.90%**	**0.72%**	**2.95%**	**1.52%**
Bond called or matured	1	4	14	29	123
Bonds issued	101	128	178	260	236

Sources: Table 6 of Newsletter (16 January 2015) from Scoperatings.com, AFME, Bloomberg, Scope Ratings.

Scope's definition of European high-yield issuers follows that of Dealogic. It includes 1,042 high-yield bonds issued within Europe between 2009 and 2014. The definition excludes sovereign, sub-sovereign and supranational parent issuers, as well as ABS/MBS issuers, but also banks, funds, finance companies and insurers. Historical data is reported in euro using the exchange rate at the time of issuance. Ratings are the lowest for each bond at issuance as reported by the AFME European High-Yield bond report.

the default rate on European junk bonds in 2010 and 2011 was negligible and increased to 3.63 per cent in 2013. This fell again in 2014 but with the fall in the oil price in 2015 and concerns about the Russian economy, the expectation is that default rates will grow over 2015–2017.

Looking forward, Figure 20.2 shows that a large number of European high yield bonds are due to expire in 2018, 2019 and 2020. This suggests that there may be a spike in defaults if economic conditions in Europe are poor and lower grade borrowers struggle to refinance their debt.

Figure 20.2 European High Yield Bond Maturity Schedule for Issues since 2009 (€ bn)

Sources: Figure 8 of Newsletter (16 January 2015) from Scoperatings.com, AFME, Bloomberg, Scope Ratings.

The junk bond market took on increased importance when these instruments were used to finance mergers and other corporate restructurings. Whereas a firm can issue only a small amount of high-grade debt, the same firm can issue much more debt if low-grade financing is allowed as well. Therefore, the use of junk bonds lets acquirers effect takeovers that they could not do with only traditional bond financing techniques. Junk bonds can also be used to restructure a firm's debt or for working capital and Figure 20.3 shows the different uses for which these bonds can be used. Although mergers and restructurings are common reasons for junk bond issuance, the biggest use of junk bonds between 2010 and 2014 was to refinance existing debt. This was primarily because global interest rates were so low during this period, making junk bond coupons low for issuing companies but large enough to be attractive to lenders.

Figure 20.3 Use of European High Yield Bond Proceeds

- Repayments and Refinancing
- General Corporate Purpose
- Other
- M&A and LBO
- Dividends and Buybacks

Sources: Figure 3 of Newsletter (16 January 2015) from Scoperatings.com. AFME, Bloomberg, Scope Ratings.

At this time, it is not clear how the great growth in junk bond financing between 2010 and 2014 altered the returns on these instruments. Financial theory indicates that the expected returns on an asset should be negatively related to its marketability.[9] Because trading volume in junk bonds has greatly increased in recent years, the marketability has risen as well. This should lower the expected return on junk bonds, thereby benefiting corporate issuers.

We discussed the costs of issuing securities in a previous chapter and established that the costs of issuing debt are substantially less than the costs of issuing equity. Table 20.2 clarifies several questions regarding the costs of issuing debt securities. It contains a breakdown of direct costs for bond issues after the investment and non-investment grades have been separated.

Table 20.2 Average Gross Spreads and Total Direct Costs for Domestic Debt Issues: 1990–2003

| | Convertible Bonds | | | | Straight Bonds | | | |
| | Investment Grade | | Non-investment Grade | | Investment Grade | | Non-investment Grade | |
Proceeds ($ in millions)	Gross Spread (%)	Total Direct Cost (%)	Gross Spread (%)	Total Direct Cost (%)	Gross Spread (%)	Total Direct Cost (%)	Gross Spread (%)	Total Direct Cost (%)
2–9.99	—	—	—	—	0.62	1.90	—	—
10–19.99	—	—	4.00	5.67	0.50	1.35	2.74	4.80
20–39.99	—	—	3.47	5.02	0.58	1.21	3.06	4.36
40–59.99	1.92	2.43	3.33	4.48	0.39	0.86	3.01	3.93
60–79.99	1.65	2.09	2.78	3.40	0.57	0.97	2.99	4.07
80–99.99	0.89	1.16	2.54	3.19	0.66	0.94	2.74	3.66
100–199.99	2.22	2.55	2.57	3.00	0.55	0.80	2.71	3.39
200–499.99	1.99	2.18	2.62	2.85	0.50	0.81	2.49	2.90
500 and up	1.96	2.09	2.50	2.57	0.28	0.38	2.45	2.71
	1.99	2.26	2.81	3.47	0.51	0.85	2.68	3.35

Source: Adapted from Lee et al. (1996); updated by the authors.

First, there are substantial economies of scale here as well. Second, investment-grade issues have much lower direct costs, particularly for straight bonds. Finally, there are relatively few non-investment-grade issues in the smaller size categories, reflecting the fact that such issues are more commonly handled as private placements, which we discuss in a later section.

Bond Investors Speak

(Excerpts taken from 'Top Bond Fund Manager: How I Am Playing the "Expensive" Bond Market', The Telegraph, 21 April 2015)

Jenna Barnard and John Pattullo, who oversee a number of funds for the £1.4 billion Henderson Strategic Bond Fund, are among an elite group of highly regarded bond portfolio managers. Ms Barnard explains here how the bond fund is navigating the 'expensive' market – while delivering, at 5 per cent, one of the highest yields.

How is the fund positioned at the moment?

Given that we can invest in any type of bond we hold a mix of assets, but predominately favour high yield and riskier bonds. For the fund to yield 5 per cent we have to buy bonds with poorer credit ratings. Government bonds, which carry the highest ratings, are extremely expensive.

What changes have you been making to the portfolio recently?

We have been switching into long-dated bonds, typically with a 30-year life. As the bond market has become so expensive there is little scope for capital appreciation; the only way to make returns is through income. We favour bank and insurance debt, and both are yielding in excess of 5 per cent. These are large established businesses, so we are not worried about default risk.

What areas of the bond market are you avoiding?

We have been selling smaller-sized bonds as they are becoming more difficult to sell as yields continue to be driven lower. I would sooner own the large, high-yield bonds issued by businesses in industries such as mobile phones, packaging and health care.

How the fund is positioned

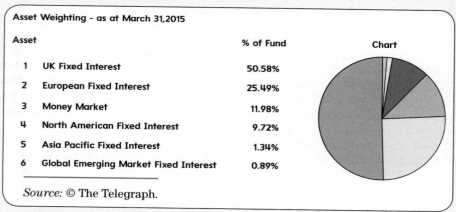

Asset Weighting - as at March 31,2015

Asset		% of Fund	Chart
1	UK Fixed Interest	50.58%	
2	European Fixed Interest	25.49%	
3	Money Market	11.98%	
4	North American Fixed Interest	9.72%	
5	Asia Pacific Fixed Interest	1.34%	
6	Global Emerging Market Fixed Interest	0.89%	

Source: © The Telegraph.

Top ten holdings

Top ten holdings	% of Fund
1 TREASURY 1.75% GILT 22/07/19 GBP0.01	2.90%
2 LLOYDS BANKING GROUP 7.881% 2049	1.80%
3 DAILY MAIL & GENERAL TRUST 5.75% BDS 7/12/18 GBP(VAR)	1.70%
4 LEGAL & GENERAL GROUP 5.50% 2064	1.70%
5 BUPA FINANCE 6.125% 2049	1.70%
6 PRUDENTIAL PLC 5.7% DATED TIER 2 NTS 19/12/63 GBP 100000	1.70%
7 BBVA INTERNATIONAL PREFERRED SAU 5.919% 2049	1.60%
8 BNP PARIBAS 7.195% 2049	1.50%
9 BARCLAYS BANK 6.278% 2049	1.50%
10 HSBC 5.844% 2049	1.30%

Source: © The Telegraph.

20.6 Some Different Types of Bonds

Until now we have considered 'plain vanilla' bonds in our discussions. In this section we look at some more unusual types: floating-rate bonds, deep-discount bonds and income bonds.

Floating-rate Bonds

The conventional bonds we have discussed in this chapter have *fixed monetary obligations*. That is, the coupon rate is set as a fixed percentage of the par value. With floating-rate bonds, the coupon payments are adjustable. The adjustments are tied to an *interest rate index* such as the Treasury bill interest rate, the London Interbank Offered Rate (LIBOR) or the European Interbank Offered Rate (EURIBOR).

In most cases the coupon adjusts with a lag to some base rate. For example, suppose a coupon rate adjustment is made on 1 June. The adjustment may be from a simple average of yields on 6-month Treasury bills issued during March, April and May. In addition, the majority of these *floaters* have put provisions and floor and ceiling provisions:

1   With a *put provision* the holder has the right to redeem his or her note at par on the coupon payment date. Frequently, the investor is prohibited from redeeming at par during the first few years of the bond's life.

2   With floor and ceiling provisions the coupon rate is subject to a minimum and maximum. For example, the minimum coupon rate might be 8 per cent and the maximum rate might be 14 per cent.

The popularity of floating-rate bonds is connected to *inflation risk*. When inflation is higher than expected, issuers of fixed-rate bonds tend to make gains at the expense of lenders; and when inflation is less than expected, lenders make gains at the expense of borrowers. Because the inflation risk of long-term bonds is borne by both issuers and bondholders, it is in their interests to devise loan agreements that minimize inflation risk.[10]

Floaters reduce inflation risk because the coupon rate is tied to the current interest rate, which, in turn, is influenced by the rate of inflation. We can see this most clearly by considering the formula for the present value of a bond. As inflation increases the interest rate (the denominator of the formula), inflation increases a floater's coupon rate (the numerator of the formula). Hence, bond value is hardly affected by inflation. Conversely, the coupon rate of fixed-rate bonds cannot change, implying that the prices of these bonds are at the mercy of inflation.

As an alternative, an individual who is concerned with inflation risk can invest in short-term notes, such as Treasury bills, and *roll them over*. The investor can accomplish essentially the same objective by buying a floater that is adjusted to the Treasury bill rate. However, the purchaser of a floater can reduce transaction costs relative to rolling over short-term Treasury bills because floaters are long-term bonds. The same type of reduction in transaction costs makes floaters attractive to some corporations.[11] They benefit from issuing a floater instead of issuing a series of short-term notes.

In an earlier section, we discussed callable bonds. Because the coupon on floaters varies with marketwide interest rates, floaters always sell at or near par. Therefore, it is not surprising that floaters do not generally have call features.

Deep-Discount Bonds

A bond that pays no coupon must be offered at a price that is much lower than its face value. Such bonds are known as original-issue discount bonds, deep-discount bonds, pure discount bonds, or zero coupon bonds. They are frequently called *zeros* for short.

Suppose DDB AG issues 1,000 Swiss francs (SFr) of 5-year deep-discount bonds when the marketwide interest rate is 10 per cent. These bonds do not pay any coupons. The initial price is set at SFr621 because SFr621 = SFr1,000/(1.10)^5.

Because these bonds have no intermediate coupon payments, they are attractive to certain investors and unattractive to others. For example, consider an insurance company forecasting death benefit payments of SFr1,000,000 five years from today. The company would like to be sure that it will have the funds to pay off the liability in 5 years' time. The company could buy 5-year zero coupon bonds with a face value of SFr1,000,000. The company is matching assets with liabilities here, a procedure that eliminates interest rate risk. That is, regardless of the movement of interest rates, the firm's set of zeros will always be able to pay off the SFr1,000,000 liability.

Conversely, the firm would be at risk if it bought coupon bonds instead. For example, if it bought 5-year coupon bonds, it would need to reinvest the coupon payments through to the fifth year. Because interest rates in the future are not known with certainty today, we cannot be sure if these bonds will be worth more or less than SFr1,000,000 by the fifth year.

Now, consider a couple saving for their child's university education in 15 years. They *expect* that, with inflation, 4 years of university should cost SFr150,000 in 15 years. Thus they buy 15-year zero coupon bonds with a face value of SFr150,000.[12] If they have forecast inflation perfectly (and if university costs keep pace with inflation), their child's tuition will be fully funded. However, if inflation rises more than expected, the tuition will be more than SFr150,000. Because the zero coupon bonds produce a shortfall, the child might end up working his way through school. As an alternative, the parents might have considered rolling over Treasury bills. Because the yields on Treasury bills rise and fall with the inflation rate, this simple strategy is likely to cause less risk than the strategy with zeros.

The key to these examples concerns the distinction between nominal and real quantities. The insurance company's liability is SFr1,000,000 in *nominal* Swiss francs. Because the face value of a zero coupon bond is a nominal quantity, the purchase of zeros eliminates risk. However, it is easier to forecast university costs in real terms than in nominal terms. Thus, a zero coupon bond is a poor choice to reduce the financial risk of a child's university education.

Income Bonds

Income bonds are similar to conventional bonds, except that coupon payments depend on company income. Specifically, coupons are paid to bondholders only if the firm's income is sufficient.

Income bonds are a financial puzzle because, from the firm's standpoint, they appear to be a cheaper form of debt than conventional bonds. Income bonds provide the same tax advantage to corporations from interest deductions that conventional bonds do. However, a company that issues income bonds is less likely to experience financial distress. When a coupon payment is omitted because of insufficient corporate income, an income bond is not in default.

Why don't firms issue more income bonds? Two explanations have been offered:

1   *The 'smell of death' explanation*: Firms that issue income bonds signal the capital markets of their increased prospect of financial distress.

2   *The 'deadweight costs' explanation*: The calculation of corporate income is crucial to determining the status of bondholders' income, and shareholders and bondholders will not necessarily agree on how to calculate the income. This creates agency costs associated with the firm's accounting methods.

Although these are possibilities, the work of McConnell and Schlarbaum (1986) suggests that no truly satisfactory reason exists for the lack of more investor interest in income bonds.

Other Types of Bonds

Many bonds have unusual or exotic features and are really limited only by the imaginations of the parties involved. Unfortunately, there are far too many variations for us to cover in detail here. We therefore mention only a few of the more common types.

A *convertible bond* can be swapped for a fixed number of shares of equity any time before maturity at the holder's option. Convertibles are relatively common, but the number has been decreasing in recent years.

A *put bond* allows the *holder* to force the issuer to buy the bond back at a stated price. For example, Skyepharma plc, a UK speciality drug company, has bonds outstanding that allow the holder to force Skyepharma to buy the bonds back at 100 per cent of face value. The put feature is therefore just the reverse of the call provision.

A given bond may have many unusual features. Two of the most recent exotic bonds are CoCo bonds, which have a coupon payment, and NoNo bonds, which are zero coupon bonds. CoCo and NoNo bonds are contingent convertible, putable, callable, subordinated bonds. The contingent convertible clause is similar to the normal conversion feature, except the contingent feature must be met. For example, a contingent feature may require that the company equity trade at 110 per cent of the conversion price for 20 out of the most recent 30 days. Valuing a bond of this sort can be quite complex, and the yield to maturity calculation is often meaningless. For example, in 2006, a NoNo issued by Merrill Lynch was selling at a price of $939.99, with a yield to maturity of negative 1.63 per cent. At the same time, a NoNo issued by Countrywide Financial was selling for $1,640, which implied a yield to maturity of negative 59 per cent!

Islamic Bonds

Having read Section 14.6 on Islamic financing, you may think it would be impossible for any type of bond to be acceptable to Islamic law. This is because any interest payment or attempt to make money from money is forbidden. With the massive increase in the price of oil over the last few years, many Islamic investment funds and banks have been seeking ways to diversify their investment portfolios in ways that are consistent with their religious beliefs. One such instrument is a *sukuk*, otherwise known as an Islamic bond.

A *sukuk* is not a simple certificate like a bond that promises set periodic payments over the period of the bond. It is more akin to a financing company that is involved in profit sharing (*musharakah*), stated cost plus profit (*murabahah*) or sale and leasebacks (*ijarah*). Taking an *ijarah sukuk* as an example, a company wishes to raise funds just now in return for a set periodic payment in the future. To be compliant with Islamic law, the financing instrument cannot have any interest, or make money from money. An *ijarah sukuk* is structured as follows:

1   The company that wishes to raise funds creates a subsidiary specifically for the *ijarah sukuk*. This is generally known as a special purpose vehicle (SPV) or special investment vehicle (SIV).

2   The company sells its own assets (for example, a manufacturing plant, technical machinery, or property) to the SPV with a value equal to the amount of financing required.

3   The SPV issues securities or *sukuk* to the market. The *sukuk* pays periodic payments (fixed or floating depending on the underlying asset) from the cash flows generated by the assets. The money raised by the *sukuk* issue is used to pay for the assets in step 2.

4   The company immediately leases the assets back from the SPV making periodic payments (fixed or floating depending on the asset) to the SPV. The payments are passed on to the *sukuk* holders.

5   At the end of the financing period, the company buys the assets back from the SPV and the SPV passes these on to the holders of the *sukuk*.

The cash flows from the *sukuk* to different parties are presented in Table 20.3. Notice how the cash flows from the *sukuk* are exactly the same as that of a bond, except that money is being generated from the underlying asset and not money in itself.

Table 20.3 Cash Flows from a *Sukuk* or Islamic Bond

Step	Company	SPV	Sukuk Holders
1. Create SPV			
2. Company sells assets	+ Asset value	− Asset value	
3. SPV issues securities to market		+ Asset value	− Asset value
4. Company leases asset from SPV	− Periodic payment	+ Periodic payment − Periodic payment	+ Periodic payment
5. Company buys assets back from SPV. SPV pays back *sukuk* holders	− Asset value	+ Asset value − Asset value	+ Asset value

20.7   Private Placement Compared to Public Issues

Earlier in this chapter we described the mechanics of issuing debt to the public. However, more than 50 per cent of all debt is privately placed. There are two basic forms of direct private long-term financing: term loans and private placement.

Term loans are direct business loans with maturities of 1–15 years. The typical term loan is amortized over the life of the loan. That is, the loan is repaid by equal annual payments of interest and principal. The lenders are banks and insurance companies. A private placement, which also involves the sale of a bond or loan directly to a limited number of investors, is similar to a term loan except that the maturity is longer.

Here are some important differences between direct long-term financing and public issues:

1   A direct long-term loan avoids the cost of registration with stock exchange authorities.

2   Direct placement is likely to have more restrictive covenants.

3   It is easier to renegotiate a term loan and a private placement in the event of a default. It is harder to renegotiate a public issue because hundreds of holders are usually involved.

4   Life insurance companies and pension funds dominate the private placement segment of the bond market. Banks are significant participants in the term loan market.

5   The costs of distributing bonds are lower in the private market.

The interest rates on term loans and private placements are usually higher than those on an equivalent public issue. Hayes et al. (1979) found that the yield to maturity on private placements was 0.46 per cent higher than on similar public issues. This finding reflects the trade-off between a higher interest rate and more flexible arrangements in the event of financial distress, as well as the lower transaction costs associated with private placements.

20.8 Long-term Syndicated Bank Loans

Most bank loans are for less than a year. They serve as a short-term 'bridge' for the acquisition of inventory and are typically self-liquidating – that is, when the firm sells the inventory, the cash is used to repay the bank loan. We talk about the need for short-term bank loans in the next section of the text. Now we focus on long-term bank loans.

First, we introduce the concept of commitment. Most bank loans are made with a commitment to a firm. That commitment establishes a line of credit and allows the firm to borrow up to a predetermined limit. Most commitments are in the form of a revolving credit commitment (i.e., a revolver) with a fixed term of up to 3 years or more. Revolving credit commitments are drawn or undrawn depending on whether the firm has a current need for the funds.

Now we turn to the concept of syndication. Very large banks such as Citigroup typically have a larger demand for loans than they can supply, and small regional banks frequently have more funds on hand than they can profitably lend to existing customers. Basically, they cannot generate enough good loans with the funds they have available. As a result, a very large bank may arrange a loan with a firm or country and then sell portions of it to a syndicate of other banks. With a syndicated loan, each bank has a separate loan agreement with the borrowers.

A syndicated loan is a corporate loan made by a group (or syndicate) of banks and other institutional investors. A syndicated loan may be publicly traded. It may be a line of credit and be 'undrawn', or it may be drawn and be used by a firm. Syndicated loans are always rated investment grade. However, a *leveraged* syndicated loan is rated speculative grade (i.e., it is 'junk'). In addition, syndicated loan prices are reported for a group of publicly traded loans. Altman and Suggitt (2000) report slightly higher default rates for syndicated loans than for comparable corporate bonds.

Summary and Conclusions

This chapter described some important aspects of long-term debt financing:

1   The written agreement describing the details of the long-term debt contract is called an *indenture*. Some of the main provisions are security, repayment, protective covenants and call provisions.

2   There are many ways that shareholders can take advantage of bondholders. Protective covenants are designed to protect bondholders from management decisions that favour equityholders at bondholders' expense.

3   Unsecured bonds are called *debentures* or *notes*. They are general claims on the company's value. Most public industrial bonds are unsecured. In contrast, utility bonds are usually secured. Mortgage bonds are secured by tangible property, and collateral trust bonds are secured by financial securities such as equities and bonds. If the company defaults on secured bonds, the trustee can repossess the assets. This makes secured bonds more valuable.

4   Long-term bonds usually provide for repayment of principal before maturity. This is accomplished by a sinking fund. With a sinking fund, the company retires a certain number of bonds each year. A sinking fund protects bondholders because it reduces the average maturity of the bond, and its payment signals the financial condition of the company.

5   Most publicly issued bonds are callable. A callable bond is less attractive to bondholders than a non-callable bond. A callable bond can be bought back by the company at a call price that is less than

the true value of the bond. As a consequence, callable bonds are priced to obtain higher stated interest rates for bondholders than non-callable bonds.

Generally, companies should exercise the call provision whenever the bond's value is greater than the call price.

There is no single reason for call provisions. Some sensible reasons include taxes, greater flexibility, management's ability to predict interest rates, and the fact that callable bonds are less sensitive to interest rate changes.

6   There are many different types of bonds, including floating-rate bonds, deep-discount bonds and income bonds. This chapter also compared private placement with public issuance.

7   Islamic businesses can invest in special types of bonds, known as *sukuk*, that are designed to be consistent with Shariah law.

Questions and Problems

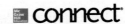

CONCEPT

1   **Debt Financing**   Review the characteristics of a bond. Why do you think short-term debt is known as unfunded debt and long-term debt as funded debt?

2   **The Public Issue of Bonds**   Explain what is meant by a bond covenant and provide examples of the different forms of covenant you may see in a bond indenture. What are the costs and benefits of bond covenants to the shareholders of the issuing firm?

3   **Bond Refunding**   Why would a firm choose to issue callable bonds? Are there any disadvantages to issuing callable bonds? Explain.

4   **Different Types of Bonds**   Explain what is meant by a *sukuk*. Why do you think it is called a bond? Global *sukuk* issuance has rapidly expanded over the last number of years. Why do you think this is? What is the unique nature of *sukuks* that make them a suitable form of finance for infrastructure projects? Explain.

5   **Private Placement versus Public Issue**   What are the benefits of a private placement over a public issue of bonds?

6   **Long-term Syndicated Bank Loans**   What are the main agency issues involved in a syndicated loan? Do you think syndicated loans should be priced differently from public debt issues? Explain.

REGULAR

7   **Credit Rating Agencies**   Since 2007 credit rating agencies have come under a lot of criticism for their role in the subprime mortgage crisis. To what extent do you think credit rating agencies were responsible for the following financial crisis? Do credit rating agencies still have an important role to play in financial markets? Explain.

8   **Call Provisions**   Assume you work for Sacyr Vallehermoso SA, a Spanish company that offers construction services. The management has decided to have a long-term bond issue to fund investment in China. It is debating whether to include a call provision. What are the benefits to Sacyr Vallehermoso from including a call provision? What are the costs? How do these answers change for a put provision? What are the other types of options that can be embedded into bond contracts?

9   **Coupon Rate**   How would Sacyr Vallehermoso decide on an appropriate coupon rate to set on its bonds given that the investment is in China? Is the coupon rate the same as the required rate of return on the bond? Explain.

10   **Credit Ratings and Financial Markets**   Empirically, share prices and bond prices have been shown to react only to a small degree to credit rating changes, if at all. Why do you think this is?

11   **Bond Ratings**   As the Eurozone crisis deepened, most of the countries in the area had their credit ratings downgraded. What impact do you think a government's credit rating has on a company that operates in that country?

12 Crossover Bonds Assume that Sacyr Vallehermoso had a bond issue and a credit rating from Moody's and S&P. However, Moody's have given a rating of Aaa and S&P have given a rating of BBB. What does this mean and why do you think it has happened? Explain.

13 Borrowing Choices Why might we expect firms with credit ratings in the middle of the spectrum to issue debt privately rather than publicly?

14 Bond Indentures Why do bonds have indentures? What, in your opinion, is the most important indenture for a bond? Are indentures more or less important for junk bond issues? Explain.

15 Rating Agencies A controversy erupted regarding bond rating agencies when some agencies began to provide unsolicited bond ratings. Why do you think this is controversial?

16 Bonds as Equity Recently several companies have issued bonds with 100-year maturities. Critics charge that the issuers are really selling equity in disguise. What are the issues here? Why would a company want to sell 'equity in disguise'?

17 Callable Bonds Do you agree or disagree with the following statement? 'In an efficient market callable and non-callable bonds will be priced in such a way that there will be no advantage or disadvantage to the call provision.' Why?

18 Bond Prices If interest rates fall, will the price of non-callable bonds move up higher than that of callable bonds? Why or why not?

19 Junk Bonds What is a 'junk bond'? What are some of the controversies created by junk bond financing?

20 Sinking Funds What is a sinking fund covenant? Sinking funds have both positive and negative characteristics for bondholders. Why?

21 Mortgage Bonds Which is riskier to a prospective creditor – an open-end mortgage or closed-end mortgage? Why?

22 Public Issues versus Direct Financing Which of the following are characteristics of public issues, and which are characteristics of direct financing?

(a) Stock exchange registration required.

(b) Higher interest cost.

(c) Higher fixed cost.

(d) Quicker access to funds.

(e) Active secondary market.

(f) Easily renegotiated.

(g) Lower flotation costs.

(h) Regular amortization required.

(i) Ease of repurchase at favourable prices.

(j) High total cost to small borrowers.

(k) Flexible terms.

(l) Less intensive investigation required.

23 Bond Ratings In general, why don't bond prices change when bond ratings change?

24 Accrued Interest You purchase an Asian Paints Ltd bond on the Bombay Stock Exchange with an invoice price of R9,342. The bond has a coupon rate of 6.45 per cent, and there are 5 months to the next semi-annual coupon date. What is the clean price of the bond?

25 Accrued Interest You purchase a bond with a coupon rate of 5.2 per cent and a clean price of £865. If the next semi-annual coupon payment is due in 2 months, what is the invoice price?

26 Bond Refunding Infineon AG plans to issue €500 million of bonds with a face value of €100,000, coupon rate of 3.5 per cent and 10 years to maturity. The current market interest rate on these bonds is 6 per cent. In one year, the interest rate on the bonds will be either 8 per cent or 5 per cent with equal probability. Assume investors are risk-neutral.

(a) If the bonds are non-callable, what is the price of the bonds today?

(b) If the bonds are callable one year from today at €120,000, will their price be greater than or less than the price you computed in (a)? Why?

27 Bond Refunding Parto SpA has an outstanding perpetual bond with a 4 per cent coupon rate that can be called in one year. The bonds make annual coupon payments. The call premium is set at 120 per cent of par value. There is a 40 per cent chance that the interest rate in one year will be 8 per cent, and a 60 per cent chance that the interest rate will be 6 per cent. If the current interest rate is 7 per cent, what is the current market price of the bond?

28 Bond Refunding Mobistar intends to issue callable, perpetual bonds with annual coupon payments. The bonds are callable at €12,500. One-year interest rates are 6 per cent. There is a 60 per cent probability that long-term interest rates one year from today will be 9 per cent, and a 40 per cent probability that long-term interest rates will be 4 per cent. Assume that if interest rates fall the bonds will be called. What coupon rate should the bonds have in order to sell at par value?

29 Bond Refunding Heineken NV has decided to borrow money by issuing perpetual bonds with a coupon rate of 6 per cent, payable annually. The one-year interest rate is 6 per cent. Next year, there is a 35 per cent probability that interest rates will increase to 7 per cent, and there is a 65 per cent probability that they will fall to 5 per cent.

(a) What will the market value of these bonds be if they are non-callable?

(b) If the company instead decides to make the bonds callable in one year, what coupon will be demanded by the bondholders for the bonds to sell at par? Assume that the bonds will be called if interest rates fall and that the call premium is equal to the annual coupon.

(c) What will be the value of the call provision to the company?

30 Bond Refunding An outstanding issue of Jeronimo Martins bonds has a call provision attached. The total principal value of the bonds is €120 million, and the bonds have an annual coupon rate of 6.6 per cent. The total cost of refunding would be 12 per cent of the principal amount raised. The appropriate tax rate for the company is 12.5 per cent. How low does the borrowing cost need to drop to justify refunding with a new bond issue?

31 Bond Refunding Charles River Associates is considering whether to refinance either of the two perpetual bond issues the company currently has outstanding. Here is information about the two bond issues:

	Bond A	Bond B
Coupon rate	8%	9%
Value outstanding	€75,000,000	€87,500,000
Call premium	8.5%	9.5%
Transaction cost of refunding	€10,000,000	€12,000,000
Current interest rate	7%	7.25%

The corporate tax rate is 12.5 per cent. What is the NPV of the refunding for each bond? Which bond should the company refinance?

CHALLENGE

32 CoCo Bonds Following the banking crisis European regulators have been encouraging banks to issue CoCo bonds, which have a bail-in structure should it get into financial difficulty. For instance, if the bank's capital goes below a pre-specified level – say, 5 per cent – then the debt converts into equity. Regulators hope this will help banks in stressed conditions, and contribute to financial stability. Do you think there are any disadvantages to CoCo bonds?

33 Valuing the Call Feature Consider the prices in the following three Treasury issues as of 24 February 2013:

6.500	16 May	106:10	106:12	−13	5.28
8.250	16 May	103:14	103:16	−3	5.24
12.000	16 May	134:25	134:31	−15	5.32

The bond in the middle is callable in February 2014. What is the implied value of the call feature? (*Hint:* Is there a way to combine the two non-callable issues to create an issue that has the same coupon as the callable bond?)

34 **Negative Yields** As of February 2015, the total stock of government bonds trading at a negative yield was $3.6 trillion. Why do you think investors are willing to buy bonds with a negative yield?

35 *Sukuk* Medhat International is a manufacturing firm operated along Islamic principles. They wish to raise 20 billion Bahrain dinars and pay this back in equal instalments over 6 years. Comparable Western bonds have 8 per cent coupons. Construct a *sukuk* that is competitive with Western bonds.

Exam Question (45 minutes)

Stature Technologies plans to issue £100 million of bonds with a face value of £100,000, coupon rate of 4.125 per cent and 10 years to maturity. The current yield to maturity of these bonds is 4 per cent. In one year, the yield to maturity on the bonds will be either 6 per cent or 3.75 per cent with equal probability. Assume investors are risk-neutral.

1 If the bonds are non-callable, what is the price of the bonds today? (30 marks)

2 If the bonds are callable one year from today at 115 per cent of face value, will their price be greater than or less than the price you computed in (1)? Why? (30 marks)

3 If Stature Technologies wished to issue the bond (without call option) in Abu Dhabi as a *sukuk*, explain, using a diagram, how you would construct the Islamic bond. (40 marks)

Mini Case

Financing West Coast Yachts' Expansion Plans with a Bond Issue

Larissa Warren, the owner of West Coast Yachts, has decided to expand her operations. She asked her newly hired financial analyst, Dan Ervin, to enlist an underwriter to help sell £30 million in new 20-year bonds to finance new construction. Dan has entered into discussions with Robin Perry, an underwriter from the firm of Crowe & Mallard, about which bond features West Coast Yachts should consider and also what coupon rate the issue will likely have. Although Dan is aware of bond features, he is uncertain of the costs and benefits of some features, so he is not sure how each feature would affect the coupon rate of the bond issue.

1 You are Robin's assistant, and she has asked you to prepare a memo to Dan describing the effect of each of the following bond features on the coupon rate of the bond. She would also like you to list any advantages or disadvantages of each feature.

(a) The security of the bond – that is, whether the bond has collateral.

(b) The seniority of the bond.

(c) The presence of a sinking fund.

(d) A call provision with specified call dates and call prices.

(e) A deferred call accompanying the call provision in (d).

(f) A make-whole call provision.

(g) Any positive covenants. Also, discuss several possible positive covenants West Coast Yachts might consider.

(h) Any negative covenants. Also, discuss several possible negative covenants West Coast Yachts might consider.

(i) A conversion feature (note that West Coast Yachts is not a publicly traded company).

(j) A floating-rate coupon.

Dan is also considering whether to issue coupon bearing bonds or zero coupon bonds. The YTM on either bond issue will be 8 per cent. The coupon bond would have an 8 per cent coupon rate. The company's tax rate is 28 per cent.

2 How many of the coupon bonds must West Coast Yachts issue to raise the £30 million? How many of the zeros must it issue?

3   In 20 years, what will be the principal repayment due if West Coast Yachts issues the coupon bonds? What if it issues the zeros?

4   What are the company's considerations in issuing a coupon bond compared to a zero coupon bond?

5   Suppose West Coast Yachts issues the coupon bonds with a make-whole call provision. The make-whole call rate is the Treasury rate plus 0.40 per cent. If West Coast calls the bonds in 7 years when the Treasury rate is 5.6 per cent, what is the call price of the bond? What if it is 9.1 per cent?

6   Are investors really made whole with a make-whole call provision?

7   After considering all the relevant factors, would you recommend a zero coupon issue or a regular coupon issue? Why? Would you recommend an ordinary call feature or a make-whole call feature? Why?

Practical Case Study

Look up the websites and financial reports for Société Générale, Crédit Agricole, Enel SpA and ING Groep and find the credit rating for each firm. For some of these companies, you will need to search closely for the information. While it may seem a bit of a bore to do this, searching for data and reading through corporate financial websites gives fantastic experience in understanding corporate finance. Which companies (if any) have an investment-grade rating? Which companies are rated below investment grade? Are any unrated? Compare the change in share price over the last year and the rating for each company. Is there a relationship? What do credit ratings say about a firm's share price performance?

Relevant Accounting Standards

The most important accounting standard for bonds is IAS 39 *Financial Instruments: Recognition and Measurement*. However, you should also know IAS 23 *Borrowing Costs*, which deals with the way interest payments and other charges are presented in the financial accounts. Visit the IASPlus website (www.iasplus.com) for more information.

References

Altman, E.I. and H.J. Suggitt (2000) 'Default Rates in the Syndicated Bank Loan Market: A Mortality Analysis', *Journal of Banking and Finance*, Vol. 24, Nos. 1–2, 229–253.

Amihud, Y. and H. Mendelson (1986) 'Asset Pricing and the Bid–Ask Spread', *Journal of Financial Economics*, Vol. 17, 223–249.

Beck, T., A. Demirgüç-Kunt and V. Maksimovic (2008) 'Financing Patterns around the World: The Role of Institutions', *Journal of Financial Economics*, Vol. 89, 467–487.

Brooks, R., R. Faff, D. Hillier and J. Hillier (2004) 'The National Market Impact of Sovereign Rating Changes', *Journal of Banking and Finance*, Vol. 28, No. 1, 233–250.

Cornell, B. (1986) 'The Future of Floating-Rate Bonds', in J.M. Stern and D.H. Chew, Jr (eds), *The Revolution in Corporate Finance* (New York: Basil Blackwell).

Cox, J., J. Ingersoll and S.A. Ross (1980) 'An Analysis of Variable Rate Loan Contracts', *The Journal of Finance*, Vol. 35, 389–403.

Hayes, P.A., M.D. Joehnk and R.W. Melicher (1979) 'Determinants of Risk Premiums in the Public and Private Bond Market', *Journal of Financial Research*, Vol. 2, 143–152.

Holthausen, R.W. and R.W. Leftwich (1986) 'The Effect of Bond Rating Changes on Common Stock Prices', *Journal of Financial Economics*, Vol. 17, No. 1, 57–89.

Kraus, A. (1983) 'An Analysis of Call Provisions and the Corporate Refunding Decision', *Midland Corporate Finance Journal*, Vol. 1, 46–60.

Lee, I., S. Lockhead, J. Ritter and Q. Zhao (1996) 'The Costs of Raising Capital', *Journal of Financial Research*, Vol. 19, No. 1, 59–74.

McConnell, J. and G. Schlarbaum (1986) 'The Income Bond Puzzle', in J.M. Stern and D.H. Chew, Jr (eds), *The Revolution in Corporate Finance* (New York: Basil Blackwell).

Ogden, J.P. (1987) 'Determinants of Relative Interest Rate Sensitivity of Corporate Bonds', *Financial Management*, Vol. 16, No. 1, 22–30.

Reilly, F. and M. Joehnk (1976) 'The Association between Market-Based Risk Measures for Bonds and Bond Ratings', *The Journal of Finance*, Vol. 31, No. 5, 1387–1403.

Sufi, A. (2009) 'Bank Lines of Credit in Corporate Finance: An Empirical Analysis', *Review of Financial Studies*, Vol. 22, 1057–1088.

Weinstein, M. (1977) 'The Effect of a Ratings Change Announcement on Bond Price', *Journal of Financial Economics*, Vol. 5, 29–44.

Weinstein, M. (1981) 'The Systematic Risk of Corporate Bonds', *Journal of Financial and Quantitative Analysis*, Vol. 16, No. 3, 257–78.

Additional Reading

The literature on debt financing can be conveniently separated into three areas: pricing, risk and structure. This is the approach we take in listing the relevant papers in the area.

Bond and Bank Loan Pricing

1 Cai, N., J. Helwege and A. Warga (2007) 'Underpricing in the Corporate Bond Market', *Review of Financial Studies*, Vol. 20, No. 6, 2021–2046. **US**.

2 Carey, M. and G. Nini (2007) 'Is the Corporate Loan Market Globally Integrated? A Pricing Puzzle', *The Journal of Finance*, Vol. 62, 2969–3007. **International**.

3 Chava, S., D. Livden and A. Purnanandam (2009) 'Do Shareholder Rights Affect the Cost of Bank Loans?', *Review of Financial Studies*, Vol. 22, 2973–3004.

4 Cremers, K.J.M., V.B. Nair and C. Wei (2007) 'Governance Mechanisms and Bond Prices', *Review of Financial Studies*, Vol. 20, No. 5, 1359–1388. **US**.

5 Ross, D.G. (2010) 'The "Dominant Bank Effect": How High Lender Reputation Affects the Information Content and Terms of Bank Loans', *Review of Financial Studies*, Vol. 23, 2730–2756.

Bond Risk and Credit Ratings

6 Avramov, D., T. Chordia, G. Jostova and A. Philipov (2009) 'Dispersion in Analysts' Earnings Forecasts and Credit Rating', *Journal of Financial Economics*, Vol. 91, No. 1, 83–101. **US**.

7 Behr, P. and A. Guttler (2008) 'The Informational Content of Unsolicited Ratings', *Journal of Banking and Finance*, Vol. 32, No. 5, 587–599. **US**.

8 Berger, A.N., M.A. Espinosa-Vega, W. Scott Frame and N.H. Miller (2005) 'Debt Maturity, Risk, and Asymmetric Information', *The Journal of Finance*, Vol. 60, No. 6, 2895–2923. **US**.

9 Brooks, R., R. Faff, D. Hillier and J. Hillier (2004) 'The National Market Impact of Sovereign Rating Changes', *Journal of Banking and Finance*, Vol. 28, No. 1, 233–250. **International**.

10 Butler, A. (2008) 'Distance Still Matters: Evidence from Municipal Bond Underwriting', *Review of Financial Studies*, Vol. 21, 763–784.

Bond Covenants and Structures

11 Billett, M.T., T. Dolly King and D.C. Mauer (2007) 'Growth Opportunities and the Choice of Leverage, Debt Maturity, and Covenants', *The Journal of Finance*, Vol. 62, No. 2, 697–730. **US**.

12 Chava, S. and M.R. Roberts (2008) 'How Does Financing Impact Investment? The Role of Debt Covenants', *The Journal of Finance*, Vol. 63, No. 5, 2085–2121. **US**.

13 Chen, Z., C.X. Mao and Y. Wang (2010) 'Why Firms Issue Callable Bonds: Hedging Investment Uncertainty', *Journal of Corporate Finance*, Vol. 16, 588–607.

14 Datta, S., M. Iskandar-Datta and K. Raman (2005) 'Managerial Stock Ownership and the Maturity Structure of Corporate Debt', *The Journal of Finance*, Vol. 60, No. 5, 2333–2350. **US**.

15 Jimenez, G., V. Salas and J. Saurina (2006) 'Determinants of Collateral', *Journal of Financial Economics*, Vol. 81, No. 1, 255–281. **Spain**.

16 Qian, J. and P.E. Strahan (2007) 'How Laws and Institutions Shape Financial Contracts: The Case of Bank Loans', *The Journal of Finance*, Vol. 62, No. 6, 2803–2834. **International**.

17 Sufi, A. (2007) 'Information Asymmetry and Financing Arrangements: Evidence from Syndicated Loans', *The Journal of Finance*, Vol. 62, No. 2, 629–668. **US**.

Other Relevant Research

18 Agarwal, S. and R. Hauswald (2010) 'Distance and Private Information in Lending', *Review of Financial Studies*, Vol. 23, 2757–2788.

19 Bonaccorsi Di Patti, E. and G. Gobbi (2007) 'Winners or Losers? The Effects of Banking Consolidation on Corporate Borrowers', *The Journal of Finance*, Vol. 62, 669–695.

20 Cho, S.S., S. El Ghoul, O. Guedhami and J. Suh (2014) 'Creditor Rights and Capital Structure: Evidence from International Data', *Journal of Corporate Finance*, Vol. 25, 40–60.

21 Colla, P., F. Ippolito and K. Li (2013) 'Debt Specialization', *The Journal of Finance*, Vol. 68, No. 5, 2117–2141.

22 Carey, M. and G. Nini (2007) 'Is the Corporate Loan Market Globally Integrated? A Pricing Puzzle', *The Journal of Finance*, Vol. 62, No. 6, 2969–3007. **International**.

23 Danielova, A., N. Smart, B. Scott and J. Boquist (2010) 'What Motivates Exchangeable Debt Offerings?', *Journal of Corporate Finance*, Vol. 16, 159–169.

24 Gillet, R. and H. de la Bruslerie (2010) 'The Consequences of Issuing Convertible Bonds: Dilution and/or Financial Restructuring?', *European Financial Management*, Vol. 16, 552–584.

25 Jang, W., L. Kai and P. Shao (2010) 'When Shareholders Are Creditors: Effects of the Simultaneous Holding of Equity and Debt by Non-commercial Banking Institutions', *Review of Financial Studies*, Vol. 23, 3595–3637.

26 Lin, C., Y. Ma, P. Malatesta and Y. Xuan (2013) 'Corporate Ownership Structure and the Choice between Bank Debt and Public Debt', *Journal of Financial Economics*, Vol. 109, No. 2, 517–534.

27 McCahery, J. and A. Schweinbacher (2010) 'Bank Reputation in the Private Debt Market', *Journal of Corporate Finance*, Vol. 16, 498–515.

28 Roberts, M.R. and A. Sufi (2009) 'Control Rights and Capital Structure: An Empirical Investigation', *The Journal of Finance*, Vol. 64, No. 4, 1657–1695. **US**.

Endnotes

1 Sufi (2009).

2 The term *loan agreement* or *loan contract* is usually used for privately placed debt and term loans.

3 See Kraus (1983), p. 1.

4 We are assuming that the current price of the non-callable bonds is the expected value discounted at the risk-free rate of 10 per cent. This is equivalent to assuming that the risk is unsystematic and carries no risk premium.

5 Normally, bonds can be called over a period of many years. Our assumption that the bond can be called only at the end of the first year was introduced for simplicity.

6 Kraus points out that the call provision will not always reduce the equity's interest rate risk. If the firm as a whole bears interest rate risk, more of this risk may be shifted from shareholders to bondholders with non-callable debt. In this case, shareholders may actually bear more risk with callable debt.

7 Weinstein (1981); Ogden (1987); and Reilly and Joehnk (1976).

8 Weinstein (1977). However, Holthausen and Leftwich (1986) find that bond rating downgrades are associated with abnormal negative returns on the equity of the issuing firm. In addition, Brooks et al. (2004) show that stock market indices react negatively to downgrades of government credit rating.

9 For example, see Amihud and Mendelson (1986).

10 See Cornell (1986).

11 Cox et al. (1980) developed a framework for pricing floating-rate notes.

12 A more precise strategy would be to buy zeros maturing in years 15, 16, 17 and 18, respectively. In this way the bonds might mature just in time to meet tuition payments.

Instead of incurring major capital expenditure through purchasing fixed assets, leasing allows a company to dispense with the need to raise capital for investment. For example, many airlines lease planes instead of owning them. The International Lease Finance Corporation (ILFC), which is the world's largest airplane leasing company by fleet value with annual revenues in excess of €4 billion, leases airplanes to airlines such as Air France-KLM, British Midland, Emirates, International Airlines Group, Lufthansa and Aer Lingus. The company currently owns around 1,000 jets. So why is ILFC in the business of buying airplanes, only to lease them out? And why don't companies that lease from ILFC simply purchase the airplanes themselves? This chapter provides answers to these and other questions associated with leasing.

Chapter 7
Page 177

In this chapter, we discuss the different types of leases that companies can use. We then illustrate how you can assess the value of a lease in the same way as a standard capital budgeting problem (see **Chapter 7**). Unlike a standard NPV analysis, the identification of the appropriate discount rate is tricky and we show that the after-tax risk-free rate is the appropriate rate to use for lease decisions. The chapter closes by presenting reasons (good and bad) for why firms lease, followed by a general review of some areas that are still being investigated by researchers. This chapter provides answers to these and other questions associated with leasing.

KEY NOTATIONS

NPV	Net present value
L	Lease payment

21.1 Types of Lease Financing

A *lease* is a contractual agreement between a lessee and lessor. The agreement establishes that the lessee has the right to use an asset and in return must make periodic payments to the lessor, the owner of the asset. The lessor is either the asset's manufacturer or an independent leasing company. If the lessor is an independent leasing company, it must buy the asset from a manufacturer. Then the lessor delivers the asset to the lessee, and the lease goes into effect.

As far as the lessee is concerned, it is the use of the asset that is most important, not who owns the asset. The use of an asset can be obtained by a lease contract. Because the user can also buy the asset, leasing and buying involve alternative financing arrangements for the use of an asset. This is illustrated in Figure 21.1.

The specific example in Figure 21.1 happens often in the computer industry. Firm U, the lessee, might be a hospital, a law firm, or any other firm that uses computers. The lessor is an independent leasing company that purchased the equipment from a manufacturer such as Dell, Sony, HP or Apple. Leases of this type are called direct leases. In the figure, the lessor issued both debt and equity to finance the purchase.

Of course, a manufacturer like Apple could lease its *own* computers, though we do not show this situation in the example. Leases of this type are called sales-type leasing. In this case, Apple would compete with the independent computer leasing company.

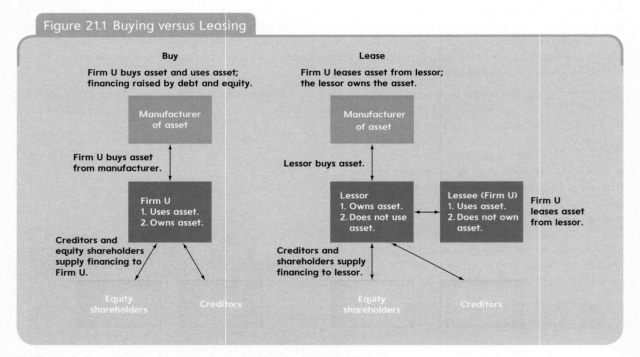

Figure 21.1 Buying versus Leasing

Operating Leases

Years ago, a lease where the lessee received an operator along with the equipment was called an operating lease. Though the operating lease defies an exact definition today, this form of leasing has several important characteristics:

1. Operating leases are usually not fully amortized. This means that the payments required under the terms of the lease are not enough to recover the full cost of the asset for the lessor. This occurs because the term or life of the operating lease is usually less than the economic life of the asset. Thus, the lessor must expect to recover the costs of the asset by renewing the lease or by selling the asset for its residual value.

2. Operating leases usually require the lessor to maintain and insure the leased assets.

3. Perhaps the most interesting feature of an operating lease is the cancellation option. This option gives the lessee the right to cancel the lease contract before the expiration date. If the option to cancel is exercised, the lessee must return the equipment to the lessor. The value of a cancellation clause depends on whether future

technological or economic conditions are likely to make the value of the asset to the lessee less than the value of the future lease payments under the lease.

To leasing practitioners, the preceding characteristics constitute an operating lease. However, accountants use the term in a slightly different way, as we will see shortly.

Financial Leases

Financial leases are the exact opposite of operating leases, as seen from their important characteristics:

1   Financial leases do not provide for maintenance or service by the lessor.
2   Financial leases are fully amortized.
3   The lessee usually has a right to renew the lease on expiration.
4   Generally, financial leases cannot be cancelled. In other words, the lessee must make all payments or face the risk of bankruptcy.

Because of these characteristics, particularly (2), this lease provides an alternative method of financing to purchase. Hence, its name is a sensible one. Two special types of financial leases are the sale and lease-back arrangement and the leveraged lease.

Sale and Leaseback

A **sale and leaseback** occurs when a company sells an asset it owns to another firm and immediately leases it back. In a sale and leaseback two things happen:

1   The lessee receives cash from the sale of the asset.
2   The lessee makes periodic lease payments, thereby retaining use of the asset.

For example, in 2015, the British retailer, Morrisons, was involved in a £500 million sale and leaseback initiative so as to raise enough capital to manage increasing competition from low cost European retailers such as Aldi and Lidl. This was only part of an increasing market for sale and leasebacks in Europe, which saw deals amounting to €3.8 billion in 2014.

Leveraged Leases

A **leveraged lease** is a three-sided arrangement among the lessee, the lessor and the lenders:

1   The lessee uses the assets and makes periodic lease payments.
2   The lessor purchases the assets, delivers them to the lessee, and collects the lease payments. However, the lessor puts up no more than 40 to 50 per cent of the purchase price.
3   The lenders supply the remaining financing and receive interest payments from the lessor. Thus, the arrangement on the right side of Figure 21.1 would be a leveraged lease if the bulk of the financing was supplied by creditors.

The lenders in a leveraged lease typically use a non-recourse loan. This means that the lessor is not obligated to the lender in case of a default. However, the lender is protected in two ways:

1   The lender has a first lien on the asset.
2   In the event of loan default, the lease payments are made directly to the lender.

The lessor puts up only part of the funds but gets the lease payments and all the tax benefits of ownership. These lease payments are used to pay the debt service of the non-recourse loan. The lessee benefits because, in a competitive market, the lease payment is lowered when the lessor saves taxes.

Real World Insight 21.1

American Airlines

(*Excerpts taken from American Airlines press release*)

AMR Corporation, the parent company of American Airlines, announced landmark agreements with Airbus and Boeing that will allow it to replace and transform American's narrowbody fleet over 5 years and solidify its fleet plan into the next decade. These new aircraft will allow American to reduce its operating and fuel costs and deliver state-of-the-art amenities to customers, while maximizing financial flexibility for the Company.

Fleet Replacement Summary:

- Under the new agreements, American plans to acquire 460 narrowbody, single-aisle aircraft from the Boeing 737 and Airbus A320 families beginning in 2013 through 2022 – the largest aircraft order in aviation history. As part of these agreements, starting in 2017 American will become the first network US airline to begin taking delivery of 'next generation' narrowbody aircraft that will further accelerate fuel-efficiency gains.

- American also will benefit from approximately $13 billion of committed financing from the manufacturers through lease transactions that will help maximize balance sheet flexibility and reduce risk. The financing fully covers the first 230 deliveries. Under the agreement with Boeing, American plans to acquire a total of 200 additional aircraft from the 737 family, with options for another 100 aircraft. American has the flexibility to convert the new deliveries into variants within the 737 family, including the 737-700, 737-800 and 737-900ER.

The agreements with Boeing and Airbus will continue American's fleet simplification efforts, allowing American to transition from four fleet types (MD-80, 737-800, 757 and 767-200) to two (the 737 and the A320 families, which offer significant commonality benefits within each family).

21.2   Accounting and Leasing

Twenty years ago, a firm could arrange to use an asset through a lease and not disclose the asset or the lease contract on the balance sheet. Lessees needed to report information on leasing activity only in the footnotes of their financial statements. Thus leasing led to off-balance-sheet financing. Things have changed significantly in recent years and leasing now has an accounting standard all to itself: IAS 17 *Leases*.

The International Accounting Standards Board (IASB) recognizes that leases have different characteristics and this affects how they should be recorded in the financial statements of a firm. The major issue relates to the effective ownership of an asset, the risks and rewards of ownership, and to whom this should be attributed. Specifically, a lease is considered a finance lease if the lessee bears the majority of risks and reward of the asset whereas it is viewed as an operating lease if the lessor bears the risk.

The accounting treatment of operating and finance leases are very different. In an operating lease, lease payments are treated as expenses and appear in a firm's income statement. In contrast, with a finance lease, the leased asset appears on the balance sheet and is depreciated in the same way as other assets. The value to be recorded in the balance sheet must be the fair or realizable value of the asset or, if lower, the present value of the lease payments. This means that, for all intents and purposes, assets that are funded by a finance lease are regarded in the exact same way as normal assets in a company without the need to undertake a substantial capital expenditure to purchase the asset.

Under IAS 17, lessors follow the opposite rule to lessees. This means that if a firm leases out an asset as an operating lease, the lessor has effective ownership of the asset and it must be recorded in the balance sheet and depreciated accordingly. Similarly, a lessor treats the income from a finance lease as revenue and it appears in the firm's income statement.

21.3   The Cash Flows of Leasing

In this section we identify the basic cash flows used in evaluating a lease. Consider the decision confronting Xomox Ltd, which manufactures long-distance gas pipes. Business has been expanding, and Xomox currently has a 5-year backlog of gas pipe orders for a trans-Scandinavian pipeline.

Global Boring Machines (GBM) makes a pipe-boring machine that can be purchased for €10,000. Xomox has determined that it needs a new machine, and the GBM model will save Xomox €6,000 per year in reduced electricity bills for the next 5 years. These savings are known with certainty because Xomox has a long-term electricity purchase agreement with French Electric Utilities SA.

Xomox has an effective corporate tax rate of 28 per cent. We assume that 20 per cent reducing balance method depreciation is used for the pipe-boring machine, and the machine has no value after 5 years.[1]

However, Friendly Leasing Ltd has offered to lease the same pipe-boring machine to Xomox for €2,500 per year for 5 years. With the lease, Xomox would remain responsible for maintenance, insurance and operating expenses.

To assess the value of the lease opportunity, one must calculate the incremental cash flows from leasing the GBM machine in lieu of buying it. Table 21.1 shows the direct cash flow consequences of buying the pipe-boring machine and also signing the lease agreement with Friendly Leasing Ltd.

Table 21.1 Cash Flows to Xomox from Using the GBM Pipe-Boring Machine: Buy versus Lease

	Year 0 (€)	Year 1 (€)	Year 2 (€)	Year 3 (€)	Year 4 (€)	Year 5 (€)
Buy						
Cost of machine	−10,000					
After-tax operating savings [€4,320 = €6,000 × (1 − 0.28)]		4,320	4,320	4,320	4,320	4,320
Depreciation tax benefit		560	448	358	287	1,147
	−10,000	4,880	4,768	4,678	4,607	5,467
Lease						
Lease payments		−2,500	−2,500	−2,500	−2,500	−2,500
Tax benefits of lease payments (€700 = €2,500 × 0.28)		700	700	700	700	700
After-tax operating savings		4,320	4,320	4,320	4,320	4,320
Total		2,520	2,520	2,520	2,520	2,520

Depreciation is 20 per cent reducing balance. Because the depreciable base is €10,000, depreciation expense and tax benefit (tax rate = 28 per cent) from depreciation per year is calculated as given in Table 21.2. Because the asset has no value at the end of 5 years, the tax benefit from depreciation is 28 per cent of €4,096 = €1,147.

Table 21.2 Depreciation Schedule for Asset

Initial Cost (€)	Depreciation (€)	Balance (€)	Tax benefit (€)
10,000	2,000	8,000	560
	1,600	6,400	448
	1,280	5,120	358
	1,024	4,096	287
			1,147

To simplify matters, Table 21.3 subtracts the direct cash flows of buying the pipe-boring machine from those of leasing it. Noting that only the net advantage of leasing is relevant to Xomox, one can conclude:

1   Operating costs are not directly affected by leasing. Xomox will save €4,320 (after taxes) from use of the GBM boring machine regardless of whether the machine is owned or leased. Thus, this cash flow stream does not appear in Table 21.3.

2   If the machine is leased, Xomox will save the €10,000 it would have used to purchase the machine. This saving shows up as an initial cash *inflow* of €10,000 in year 0.

3   If Xomox leases the pipe-boring machine, it will no longer own this machine and must give up the depreciation tax benefits. These lost tax benefits show up as an *outflow*.

4   If Xomox chooses to lease the machine, it must pay €2,500 per year for 5 years. The first payment is due at the end of the first year. (This is a break: sometimes the first payment is due immediately.) The lease payments are tax deductible and, as a consequence, generate tax benefits of €700 (= 0.28 × €2,500).

The net cash flows have been placed in the bottom line of Table 21.3. These numbers represent the cash flows from *leasing* relative to the cash flows from the purchase. It is arbitrary that we express the flows in this way. We could have expressed the cash flows from the *purchase* relative to the cash flows from leasing. These cash flows would look like this:

	Year 0 (€)	Year 1 (€)	Year 2 (€)	Year 3 (€)	Year 4 (€)	Year 5 (€)
Net cash flows from purchase alternative relative to lease alternative	−10,000	2,360	2,248	2,158	2,087	2,947

Of course, the cash flows here are the opposite of those in the bottom line of Table 21.3. Depending on our purpose, we may look at either the purchase relative to the lease or vice versa. Thus, the student should become comfortable with either viewpoint.

Table 21.3 Incremental Cash Flow Consequences for Xomox from Leasing Instead of Purchasing

Lease Minus Buy	Year 0 (€)	Year 1 (€)	Year 2 (€)	Year 3 (€)	Year 4 (€)	Year 5 (€)
Lease						
Lease payment		−2,500	−2,500	−2,500	−2,500	−2,500
Tax benefit of lease payment		700	700	700	700	700
Buy (minus)						
Cost of machine	−(−10,000)					
Lost depreciation tax benefit		−560	−448	−358	−287	−1,147
Total	10,000	−2,360	−2,248	−2,158	−2,087	−2,947

The bottom line presents the cash flows from leasing relative to the cash flows from purchase. The cash flows would be exactly the *opposite* if we considered the purchase relative to the lease.

Now that we have the cash flows, we can make our decision by discounting the flows properly. However, because the discount rate is tricky, we take a detour in the next section before moving back to the Xomox case. In this next section, we show that cash flows in the lease-versus-buy decision should be discounted at the *after-tax* interest rate (i.e., the after-tax cost of debt capital).

21.4 A Detour for Discounting and Debt Capacity with Corporate Taxes

The analysis of leases is difficult, and both financial practitioners and academics have made conceptual errors. These errors revolve around taxes. We hope to avoid their mistakes by beginning with the simplest type of example: a loan for one year. Though this example is unrelated to our lease-versus-buy situation, principles developed here will apply directly to lease–buy analysis.

Present Value of Riskless Cash Flows

Consider a corporation that lends €100 for a year. If the interest rate is 10 per cent, the firm will receive €110 at the end of the year. Of this amount, €10 is interest and the remaining €100 is the original principal. A corporate tax rate of 34 per cent implies taxes on the interest of €3.40 (0.34 × €10). Thus, the firm ends up with €106.60 (= €110 − €3.40) after taxes on a €100 investment.

Now, consider a company that borrows €100 for a year. With a 10 per cent interest rate, the firm must pay €110 to the bank at the end of the year. However, the borrowing firm can take the €10 of interest as a tax deduction. The corporation pays €3.40 (= 0.34 × €10) less in taxes than it would have paid had it not borrowed the money at all. Thus, considering this reduction in taxes, the firm must pay €106.60 (= €110 − €3.40) on a €100 loan. The cash flows from both lending and borrowing are displayed in Table 21.4.

Table 21.4 Lending and Borrowing in a World with Corporate Taxes (Interest Rate is 10 per cent and Corporate Tax Rate is 34 per cent)

Date 0		Date 1
Lending example		
Lend − €100		Receive + €100.00 of principal
		Receive + € 10.00 of interest
	6.6% lending rate	Pay −€3.40 (= −0.34 × 10) in taxes
		+€106.60
After-tax lending rate is 6.6%.		
Borrowing example		
Borrow + €100		Pay − €100.00 of principal
		Pay −€ 10.00 of interest
	6.6% borrowing rate	Receive +€3.40 (= −0.34 × 10) as a tax rebate
		−€106.60
After-tax borrowing rate is 6.6%.		

General principle: In a world with corporate taxes, riskless cash flows should be discounted at the after-tax interest rate.

The previous two paragraphs show a very important result: the firm could not care less whether it received €100 today or €106.60 next year.[2] If it received €100 today, it could lend it out, thereby receiving €106.60 after corporate taxes at the end of the year. Conversely, if it knows today that it will receive €106.60 at the end of the year, it could borrow €100 today. The after-tax interest and principal payments on the loan would be paid with the €106.60 that the firm will receive at the end of the year. Because of this interchangeability, we say that a payment of €106.60 next year has a present value of €100. Because €100 = €106.60/1.066, a riskless cash flow should be discounted at the after-tax interest rate of 0.066 [= 0.10 × (1 − 0.34)].

Of course, the preceding discussion considered a specific example. The general principle is this:

> **In a world with corporate taxes, the firm should discount riskless cash flows at the after-tax riskless rate of interest.**

Optimal Debt Level and Riskless Cash Flows

In addition, our simple example can illustrate a related point concerning optimal debt level. Consider a firm that has just determined that the current level of debt in its capital structure is optimal. Immediately following that determination, it is surprised to learn that it will receive a guaranteed payment of €106.60 in one year from, say, a tax-exempt government lottery. This future windfall is an asset that, like any asset, should raise the firm's optimal debt level. How much does this payment raise the firm's optimal level?

Our analysis implies that the firm's optimal debt level must be €100 more than it previously was. That is, the firm could borrow €100 today, perhaps paying the entire amount out as a dividend. It would owe the bank €110 at the end of the year. However, because it receives a tax rebate of €3.40 (= 0.34 × €10), its net repayment will be €106.60. Thus, its borrowing of €100 today is fully offset by next year's government lottery proceeds of €106.60. In other words, the lottery proceeds act as an irrevocable trust that can service the increased debt. Note that we need not know the optimal debt level before the lottery was announced. We are merely saying that whatever this pre-lottery optimal level was, the optimal debt level is €100 more after the lottery announcement.

Of course, this is just one example. The general principle is this:[3]

> **In a world with corporate taxes, we determine the increase in the firm's optimal debt level by discounting a future guaranteed after-tax inflow at the after-tax riskless interest rate.**

Conversely, suppose that a second, unrelated firm is surprised to learn that it must pay €106.60 next year to the government for back taxes. Clearly, this additional liability impinges on the second firm's debt capacity. By the previous reasoning, it follows that the second firm's optimal debt level must be lowered by exactly €100.

21.5   NPV Analysis of the Lease versus Buy Decision

Chapter 6
Page 151

Our detour leads to a simple method for evaluating leases: discount all cash flows at the after-tax interest rate (this section draws on the NPV discussion in **Chapter 6**, Section 6.1). From the bottom line of Table 21.3, Xomox's incremental cash flows from leasing versus purchasing are these:

	Year 0	Year 1	Year 2	Year 3	Year 4	Year 5
Net cash flows from lease alternative relative to purchase alternative	€10,000	−€2,360	−€2,248	−€2,158	−€2,087	−€2,947

Let us assume that Xomox can either borrow or lend at the interest rate of 7.8472 per cent. If the corporate tax rate is 28 per cent, the correct discount rate is the after-tax rate of 5.65 per cent [= 7.8472% × (1 − 0.28)]. When 5.65 per cent is used to compute the NPV of the lease, we have:

	Year 0	Year 1	Year 2	Year 3	Year 4	Year 5
Present value of net cash flows from lease alternative relative to purchase alternative	€10,000	−€2,233.79	−€2,013.99	−€1,830.30	−€1,674.89	−€2,238.80

$$NPV = €10,000 − €2,233.79 − €2,013.99 − €1,830.30 − €1,674.89 − €2,238.80$$
$$= €8.23 \tag{21.1}$$

Because the net present value of the incremental cash flows from leasing relative to purchasing is positive, Xomox prefers to lease the assets.

Equation 21.1 is the correct approach to lease versus buy analysis. However, students are often bothered by two things. First, they question whether the cash flows in Table 21.3 are truly riskless. We examine this issue next. Second, they feel that this approach lacks intuition. We address this concern a little later.

The Discount Rate

Because we discounted at the after-tax riskless rate of interest, we have implicitly assumed that the cash flows in the Xomox example are riskless. Is this appropriate?

A lease payment is like the debt service on a secured bond issued by the lessee, and the discount rate should be approximately the same as the interest rate on such debt. In general, this rate will be slightly higher than the riskless rate considered in the previous section. The various tax shields could be somewhat riskier than the lease payments for two reasons. First, the value of the depreciation tax benefits depends on the ability of Xomox to generate enough taxable income to use them. Second, the corporate tax rate may change in the future. For these two reasons, a firm might be justified in discounting the depreciation tax benefits at a rate higher than that used for the lease payments. However, our experience is that real-world companies discount both the depreciation shield and lease payments at the same rate. This implies that financial practitioners view these two risks as minor. We adopt the real-world convention of discounting the two flows at the same rate. This rate is the after-tax interest rate on secured debt issued by the lessee.

At this point some students still ask, 'Why not use R_{WACC} as the discount rate in lease versus buy analysis?' Of course, R_{WACC} should not be used for lease analysis because the cash flows are more like debt service cash flows than operating cash flows and, as such, the risk is much less. The discount rate should reflect the risk of the incremental cash flows.

21.6   Does Leasing Ever Pay? The Base Case

We previously looked at the lease–buy decision from the point of view of the potential lessee, Xomox. Let us now look at the decision from the point of view of the lessor, Friendly Leasing Limited. This firm faces three cash flows, all of which are displayed in Table 21.5. First, Friendly purchases the machine for €10,000 at year 0. Second, because the asset is depreciated by reducing balance over 5 years, the depreciation expense and depreciation tax shield at the end of each of the 5 years is as follows:

Initial cost (€)	Depreciation (€)	Balance (€)	Tax benefit (€)
10,000	2,000	8,000	560
	1,600	6,400	448
	1,280	5,120	358
	1,024	4,096	287
			1,147

Third, because the yearly lease payment is €2,500, the after-tax lease payments are as follows: €1,800 [= €2,500 × (1 − 0.28)].

Table 21.5 Cash Flows to Friendly Leasing Limited as Lessor of GBM Pipe-Boring Machine

	Year 0 (€)	Year 1 (€)	Year 2 (€)	Year 3 (€)	Year 4 (€)	Year 5 (€)
Cash for machine	−10,000					
Depreciation tax benefit		560	448	358	287	1,147
After-tax lease payment [€1,800 = €2,500 × (1 − 0.28)]		1,800	1,800	1,800	1,800	1,800
Total	−10,000	2,360	2,248	2,158	2,087	2,947

Now examine the total cash flows to Friendly Leasing Limited, displayed in the bottom line of Table 21.5. These cash flows are exactly the *opposite* of those of Xomox, displayed in the bottom line of Table 21.3. Those of you with a healthy sense of scepticism may be thinking something interesting: 'If the cash flows of the lessor are exactly the opposite of those of the lessee, the combined cash flow of the two parties must be zero each year. Thus, there does not seem to be any joint benefit to this lease. Because the net present value to the lessee was €8.23, the NPV to the lessor must be −€8.23. The joint NPV is £0 (= €8.23 − €8.23). There does not appear to be any way for the NPV of both the lessor and the lessee to be positive at the same time. Because one party would inevitably lose money, the leasing deal could never fly.'

This is one of the most important results of leasing. Though Table 21.5 concerns one particular leasing deal, the principle can be generalized. As long as (1) both parties are subject to the same interest and tax rates, and (2) transaction costs are ignored, there can be no leasing deal that benefits both parties. However, there is a lease payment for which both parties would calculate an NPV of zero. Given that fee, Xomox would be indifferent to whether it leased or bought, and Friendly Leasing would be indifferent to whether it leased or not.[4]

A student with an even healthier sense of scepticism might be thinking, 'This textbook appears to be arguing that leasing is not beneficial. Yet we know that leasing occurs frequently in the real world. Maybe, just maybe, the textbook is wrong.' Although we will not admit to being wrong (what authors would?!), we freely admit that our explanation is incomplete at this point. The next section considers factors that give benefits to leasing.

21.7 Reasons for Leasing

Proponents of leasing make many claims about why firms should lease assets rather than buy them. Some of the reasons given to support leasing are good, and some are not. We discuss here the reasons for leasing that we think are good and some of the ones we think are not.

Good Reasons for Leasing

Leasing is a good choice if at least one of the following is true:

1   Taxes may be reduced by leasing.

2   The lease contract may reduce certain types of uncertainty.

3   Transaction costs can be higher for buying an asset and financing it with debt or equity than for leasing the asset.

Tax Advantages

The most important reason for long-term leasing is tax reduction. If the corporate income tax were repealed, long-term leasing would probably disappear. The tax advantages of leasing exist because firms are in different tax brackets.

Should a user be in a low tax bracket purchase, he will receive little tax benefit from depreciation and interest deductions. Should the user lease, the lessor will receive the depreciation shield and the interest deductions. In a competitive market, the lessor must charge a low lease payment to reflect these tax shields. Thus, the user is likely to lease rather than purchase.

In our example with Xomox and Friendly Leasing Limited, the value of the lease to Xomox was €8.23. However, the value of the lease to Friendly was exactly the opposite (−€8.23). Because the lessee's gains came at the expense of the lessor, no deal could be arranged.

However, if Friendly Leasing Limited pays no taxes, both Friendly and Xomox will find positive NPV in leasing. The value of the lease to Xomox is still €8.23.

Given a lease payment of €2,500, the cash flows to Friendly Leasing Limited look like this:

	Year 0 (€)	Year 1 (€)	Year 2 (€)	Year 3 (€)	Year 4 (€)	Year 5 (€)
Cost of machine	−10,000					
Lease payment		2,500	2,500	2,500	2,500	2,500
Total	−10,000	2,500	2,500	2,500	2,500	2,500

The value of the lease to Friendly is:

$$\text{Value of lease} = -€10,000 - €2,500 \times A^5_{0.0784722}$$

$$= -€10,000 + €10,022.10$$

$$= €22.10$$

Notice that the discount rate is the interest rate of 7.84722 per cent because tax rates are zero. In addition, the full lease payment of €2,500 – and not some lower after-tax number – is used because there are no taxes. Finally, note that depreciation is ignored, also because no taxes apply.

As a consequence of different tax rates, the lessee (Xomox) gains €8.23 and the lessor (Friendly) gains €22.10. Both the lessor and the lessee can gain if their tax rates are different because the lessee uses the depreciation and interest tax shields that cannot be used by the lessor. The government loses tax revenue, and some of the tax gains to the lessee may be (if so desired) passed on to the lessor in the form of lower lease payments.

Because both parties can gain when tax rates differ, the lease payment is agreed upon through negotiation. Before negotiation begins, each party needs to know the *reservation* payment of both parties. This is the payment that will make one party indifferent to whether it enters the lease deal. In other words, this is the payment that makes the value of the lease zero. These payments are calculated next.

Reservation Payment of Lessee

We now solve for L_{MAX}, the payment that makes the value of the lease to the lessee zero. When the lessee is in the 28 per cent bracket, his cash flows, in terms of L_{MAX}, are as follows:

Lease Minus Buy	Year 0 (€)	Year 1 (€)	Year 2 (€)	Year 3 (€)	Year 4 (€)	Year 5 (€)
Lease						
Lease payment		$-L_{MAX}$	$-L_{MAX}$	$-L_{MAX}$	$-L_{MAX}$	$-L_{MAX}$
Tax benefit of lease payment		$L_{MAX} \times 0.28$	$L_{MAX} \times 0.28$	$L_{MAX} \times 0.28$	$L_{MAX} \times 0.28$	$L_{MAX} \times 0.28$

Lease Minus Buy	Year 0 (€)	Year 1 (€)	Year 2 (€)	Year 3 (€)	Year 4 (€)	Year 5 (€)
Buy (minus)						
Cost of machine	−(−10,000)					
Lost depreciation tax benefit		−560	−448	−358	−287	−1,147
Total	10,000	$-L_{MAX}(1-$ $0.28) - 560$	$-L_{MAX}(1-$ $0.28) - 448$	$-L_{MAX}(1-$ $0.28) - 358$	$-L_{MAX}(1-$ $0.28) - 287$	$-L_{MAX}(1-$ $0.28) - 1,147$

The only way to solve for L_{MAX} is through trial and error in a spreadsheet. A solution is presented below:

Lease Minus Buy	Year 0 (€)	Year 1 (€)	Year 2 (€)	Year 3 (€)	Year 4 (€)	Year 5 (€)
Lease						
Lease payment		−2,503	−2,503	−2,503	−2,503	−2,503
Tax benefit of lease payment		700.84	700.84	700.84	700.84	700.84
Buy (minus)						
Cost of machine	10,000					
Lost depreciation tax benefit		−560	−448	−358.40	−286.72	−1,146.88
Total	10,000	−2,362.16	−2,250.16	−2,160.56	−2,088.88	−2,949.04
PV(CF)	10,000	−2,235.84	−2,015.93	−1,832.14	−1,676.62	−2,240.44
NPV(CF)	−0.96					

The value of the lease approximately equals zero when L_{MAX} is €2,503.

After performing this calculation, the lessor knows that he will never be able to charge a payment above €2,503.

Reservation Payment of Lessor

We now solve for L_{MIN}, the payment that makes the value of the lease to the lessor zero. The cash flows to the lessor, in terms of L_{MIN}, are these:

	Year 0	Year 1	Year 2	Year 3	Year 4	Year 5
Cost of machine	−€10,000					
Lease payment		L_{MIN}	L_{MIN}	L_{MIN}	L_{MIN}	L_{MIN}

This chart implies that:

$$\text{Value of lease} = -€10,000 + L_{MIN} \times A^5_{0.0784722}$$

The value of the lease equals zero when:

$$L_{MIN} = \frac{€10,000}{A^5_{0.0784722}}$$

$$= €2,494.49$$

After performing this calculation, the lessee knows that the lessor will never agree to a lease payment below €2,494.49.

A Reduction of Uncertainty

We have noted that the lessee does not own the property when an operating lease expires. The value of the property at this time is called the *residual value,* and the lessor has a firm claim to it. When the lease contract is signed, there may be substantial uncertainty about what the residual value of the asset will be. Thus, under a lease contract, this residual risk is borne by the lessor. Conversely, the user bears this risk when purchasing.

It is common sense that the party best able to bear a particular risk should do so. If the user has little risk aversion, she will not suffer by purchasing. However, if the user is highly averse to risk, she should find a third-party lessor more capable of assuming this burden.

This latter situation frequently arises when the user is a small or newly formed firm. Because the risk of the entire firm is likely to be quite high and because the principal shareholders are likely to be undiversified, the firm desires to minimize risk wherever possible. A potential lessor, such as a large, publicly held financial institution, is far more capable of bearing the risk. Conversely, this situation is not expected to happen when the user is a blue chip corporation. That potential lessee is more able to bear risk.

Transaction Costs

The costs of changing an asset's ownership are generally greater than the costs of writing a lease agreement. Consider the choice that confronts a person who lives in Oslo but must do business in London for 2 days. It will clearly be cheaper to rent a hotel room for 2 nights than it would be to buy an apartment for 2 days and then to sell it.

Unfortunately, leases generate agency costs as well. For example, the lessee might misuse or overuse the asset because she has no interest in the asset's residual value. This cost will be implicitly paid by the lessee through a high lease payment. Although the lessor can reduce these agency costs through monitoring, monitoring itself is costly.

Thus, leasing is most beneficial when the transaction costs of purchase and resale outweigh the agency and monitoring costs of a lease. Flath (1980) argues that this occurs in short-term leases but not in long-term leases.

Bad Reasons for Leasing

Leasing and Accounting Income

In our discussion of accounting and leasing we pointed out that a firm's statement of financial position shows fewer liabilities with an operating lease than with either a finance lease or a purchase financed with debt. We indicated that a firm desiring to project a strong balance sheet might select an operating lease. In addition, the firm's return on assets (ROA) is generally higher with an operating lease than with either a finance lease or a purchase. To see this, we look at the numerator and denominator of the ROA formula in turn.

With an operating lease, lease payments are treated as an expense. If the asset is purchased, both depreciation and interest charges are expenses. At least in the early part of the asset's life, the yearly lease payment is generally less than the sum of yearly depreciation and yearly interest. Thus, accounting income, the numerator of the ROA formula, is higher with an operating lease than with a purchase. Because accounting expenses with a finance lease are analogous to depreciation and interest with a purchase, the increase in accounting income does not occur with a finance lease.

In addition, leased assets do not appear on the statement of financial position with an operating lease. Thus, the total asset value of a firm, the denominator of the ROA formula, is less with an operating lease than it is with either a purchase or a capitalized lease. The two preceding effects imply that the firm's ROA should be higher with an operating lease than with either a purchase or a finance lease.

Of course, in an efficient capital market, accounting information cannot be used to fool investors. It is unlikely, then, that leasing's impact on accounting numbers should create value for the firm. Savvy investors should be able to see through attempts by management to improve the firm's financial statements.

One Hundred Per Cent Financing

It is often claimed that leasing provides 100 per cent financing, whereas secured equipment loans require an initial down payment. However, if a firm has a target debt–equity ratio and follows International Accounting Standards, financial leases will displace debt elsewhere in the firm.

For example, a firm that purchases equipment will generally issue debt to finance the purchase. The debt becomes a liability of the firm. A lessee incurs a liability equal to the present value of all future lease payments. Because of this, there is a strong argument that leases displace debt. The statements of financial position in Table 21.6 illustrate how leasing might affect debt.

Table 21.6 Debt Displacement Elsewhere in the Firm When a Lease Is Instituted

Assets	(€)	Liabilities	(€)
Initial situation			
Current	50,000	Debt	60,000
Non-current	50,000	Equity	40,000
Total	100,000	Total	100,000
Buy with secured loan			
Current	50,000	Debt	66,000

Assets	(€)	Liabilities	(€)
Non-current	50,000	Equity	44,000
Machine	10,000	Total	110,000
Total	110,000		
Lease			
Current	50,000	Lease	10,000
Non-current	50,000	Debt	56,000
Machine	10,000	Equity	44,000
Total	110,000	Total	110,000

This example shows that leases reduce the level of debt elsewhere in the firm. Though the example illustrates a point, it is not meant to show a precise method for calculating debt displacement.

Suppose a firm initially has €100,000 of assets and a 150 per cent target debt–equity ratio. The firm's debt is €60,000, and its equity is €40,000. As in the Xomox case, suppose the firm must use a new €10,000 machine. The firm has two alternatives:

1 *The firm can purchase the machine.* If it does, it will finance the purchase with a secured loan and with equity. The debt capacity of the machine is assumed to be the same as for the firm as a whole.

2 *The firm can lease the asset and get 100 per cent financing.* That is, the present value of the future lease payments will be €10,000.

If the firm finances the machine with both secured debt and new equity, its debt will increase by €6,000 and its equity by €4,000. Its target debt–equity ratio of 150 per cent will be maintained.

Conversely, consider the lease alternative. Under International Accounting Standards, a finance lease must appear in the statement of financial position. As just mentioned, the present value of the lease liability is €10,000. If the leasing firm is to maintain a debt–equity ratio of 150 per cent, debt elsewhere in the firm must fall by €4,000 when the lease is instituted. Because debt must be repurchased, net liabilities rise by only €6,000 (= €10,000 − €4,000) when €10,000 of assets are placed under lease.

Recent research by Eisfeldt and Rampini (2009) argues that the '100 per cent financing' argument is actually an important and good reason for leasing. They show that leasing makes repossession in the case of a default of an asset easier than borrowing and that this increases the capacity of a firm to take on more debt via leases. They then provide evidence that small financially constrained firms use leases more than unconstrained firms.

Debt displacement is a hidden cost of leasing. If a firm leases, it will not use as much regular debt as it would otherwise. The benefits of debt capacity will be lost – particularly the lower taxes associated with interest expense.

Other Reasons

There are, of course, many special reasons that some companies find advantages in leasing. In one celebrated case, the US Navy leased a fleet of tankers instead of asking Congress for appropriations. Thus, leasing may be used to circumvent capital expenditure control systems set up by bureaucratic firms.

Real World Insight 21.2

Leasing Land in Emerging Markets

(*Excerpts taken from 'South Africa's land ownership proposals "are fair"', 16 February 2015, SouthAfrica. info*)

Buying land can be incredibly difficult in many parts of the world, especially in the emerging markets where land ownership rights are not well defined. In addition, political sentiment is strongly against foreign ownership of land as there is a fear that the government is selling its prime asset. As a result, leasing becomes a natural substitute to buying. In 2015, South Africa introduced new land reforms to put a stop to any purchasing of land by foreign nationals.

President Jacob Zuma was asked if the decision to disallow land ownership by foreigners would harm the country's ability to attract foreign direct investment or foreigners doing business in South Africa. He responded that many countries were very careful when it came to land ownership as it was a critical issue for any nation, and that South Africa was not an exception.

> I think we are taking a very fair decision to say if you are coming for business and you need land, we lease it [to you]… I think that is fair.

> To buy it and make it your property when a good percentage of South African cities have no land is very difficult to justify when people don't own land and part of our country is being owned by people out there.

In his Sona, Zuma announced that a proposed law, the Regulation of Land Holdings Bill, would be submitted to parliament this year. In terms of the proposal, foreign nationals and juristic persons would not be allowed to own land in South Africa, but would be eligible for a long-term lease with a minimum of 30 years.

> We now know that people come and buy the best part of the land, so local people are not going to have an opportunity to do business in their own country because it has been bought. You might end up with three quarters of the land in South Africa being owned by people out there and we end up paying rent to them.

21.8 Some Unanswered Questions about Leasing

Our analysis suggests that the primary advantage of long-term leasing results from the differential tax rates of the lessor and the lessee. Other valid reasons for leasing are lower contracting costs and risk reduction. There are several questions our analysis has not specifically answered.

Are the Uses of Leases and Debt Complementary?

Ang and Peterson (1984) find that firms with high debt tend to lease frequently as well. This result should not be puzzling. The corporate attributes that provide high debt capacity may also make leasing advantageous. Thus, even though leasing displaces debt (that is, leasing and borrowing are substitutes) for an individual firm, high debt and high leasing can be positively associated when we look at a number of firms.

Why Are Leases Offered by Both Manufacturers and Third-party Lessors?

The offsetting effects of taxes can explain why both manufacturers (for example, computer firms) and third-party lessors offer leases.

1 For manufacturer lessors, the basis for determining depreciation is the manufacturer's cost. For third-party lessors, the basis is the sales price that the lessor paid to the manufacturer. Because the sales price is generally greater than the manufacturer's cost, this is an advantage to third-party lessors.

2 However, the manufacturer must recognize a profit for tax purposes when selling the asset to the third-party lessor. The manufacturer's profit for some equipment can be deferred if the manufacturer becomes the lessor. This provides an incentive for manufacturers to lease.

Why Are Some Assets Leased More than Others?

Certain assets appear to be leased more frequently than others. Smith and Wakeman (1985) have looked at non-tax incentives that affect leasing. Their analysis suggests many asset and firm characteristics that are important in the lease-or-buy decision. The following are among the things they mention:

1 The more sensitive the value of an asset is to usage and maintenance decisions, the more likely it is that the asset will be purchased instead of leased. They argue that ownership provides a better incentive to minimize maintenance costs than does leasing.

2   Price discrimination opportunities may be important. Leasing may be a way of circumventing laws against charging too *low* a price.

Are the Reasons for Leasing Different across Firms?

At different stages in a company's life cycle, there are changing pressures and opportunities facing management. For example, small firms that are growing quickly find it difficult to regularly source new debt financing. In contrast, large established firms find it significantly easier to go to the debt markets or banks to arrange debt. Lasfer and Levis (1998) and Cosci et al. (2015) for Italian firms, show that smaller firms use leases because they are unable to get other forms of debt whereas larger firms use debt and leasing interchangeably. They also find that large lessee firms are significantly more profitable than small lessee firms, suggesting that leases are used as a complement to debt in large firms whereas they are a substitute for debt in small firms.

Lasfer and Levis's findings are supported by the recent work of Eisfeldt and Rampini (2009) who argue that leasing enhances debt capacity more than secured lending or debt. Because smaller firms are financially constrained, they value the debt capacity provided by leases and hence lease more than larger firms.

Summary and Conclusions

Off-balance-sheet financing has become a major issue for most of the world's corporations. While many may see off-balance-sheet financing as a bad thing, it has many positive characteristics. In particular, leasing can help firms increase debt capacity when they would otherwise be financially constrained. A large fraction of the corporate world's equipment is leased rather than purchased. This chapter both described the institutional arrangements surrounding leases and showed how to evaluate leases financially.

1   Leases can be separated into two polar types. Though operating leases allow the lessee to use the equipment, ownership remains with the lessor. Although the lessor in a financial lease legally owns the equipment, the lessee maintains effective ownership because financial leases are fully amortized.

2   When a firm purchases an asset with debt, both the asset and the liability appear on the firm's balance sheet. If a lease meets at least one of a number of criteria, it must be capitalized. This means that the present value of the lease appears as both an asset and a liability. A lease escapes capitalization if it does not meet any of these criteria. Leases not meeting the criteria are called *operating leases,* though the accountant's definition differs somewhat from the practitioner's definition. Operating leases do not appear on the statement of financial position (balance sheet). For cosmetic reasons, many firms prefer that a lease be called *operating.*

3   Firms generally lease for tax purposes. To protect their interests, tax authorities allow financial arrangements to be classified as leases only if a number of criteria are met.

4   We showed that risk-free cash flows should be discounted at the after-tax risk-free rate. Because both lease payments and depreciation tax shields are nearly riskless, all relevant cash flows in the lease–buy decision should be discounted at a rate near this after-tax rate. We use the real-world convention of discounting at the after-tax interest rate on the lessee's secured debt.

5   If the lessor is in the same tax bracket as the lessee, the cash flows to the lessor are exactly the opposite of the cash flows to the lessee. Thus, the sum of the value of the lease to the lessee plus the value of the lease to the lessor must be zero. Although this suggests that leases can never fly, there are actually at least three good reasons for leasing:

  (a) Differences in tax brackets between lessor and lessee.

  (b) Shift of risk bearing to the lessor.

  (c) Minimization of transaction costs.

We also documented a number of bad reasons for leasing.

Questions and Problems

CONCEPT

1 **Types of Lease Financing**   What is a lease, and what are the different types of lease financing that are available to firms?

2 **Accounting and Leasing**   What is meant by 'off-balance-sheet financing'? Why has leasing been viewed as off-balance-sheet funding when it appears in the financial statements? Is this term now a misnomer? Explain.

3 **The Cash Flows of Leasing**   If you did not have the financing to purchase an asset, would you compare it to the buy decision in your leasing analysis? Explain.

4 **Discounting and Taxes**   In a world with taxes, why is WACC not appropriate for discounting cash flows in a lease versus buy decision? What is the appropriate discount rate when evaluating a lease? Explain.

5 **Leasing**   You have recently joined the finance department of a large retail company, and your manager tells you that the company's policy is to lease its assets, instead of buying them outright. He explains that because leasing reduces risk it will reduce the firm's cost of capital. Do you agree with him? Explain.

6 **Does Leasing ever Pay?**   If the cash flows to the lessee are exactly the opposite of the cash flows to the lessor, why does leasing exist in practice? Explain, using an example.

7 **Reasons for Leasing**   Review the reasons why firms undertake leasing. Explain why some of these reasons are not beneficial for shareholders.

8 **Unanswered Questions**   Why do some firms lease and others do not? What are some of the reasons why firms may or may not lease?

REGULAR

9 **Accounting for Leases**   Discuss the accounting criteria for determining whether a lease must be reported in the statement of financial position. In each case, give a rationale for the criterion.

10 **Accounting for Leases**   The International Accounting Standards Board (IASB) and the US Financial Accounting Standards Board (FASB) have been working toward a new standard for lease accounting. Consult the websites of both these organizations and discuss what progress has been made. What impact will the agreed changes have on the lessee?

11 **Sale and Leaseback**   Why might a firm choose to engage in a sale and leaseback transaction? Give two reasons. Is a sale and leaseback good for firms in financial distress? What does the empirical evidence say? Explain.

12 **Lease or Buy**   A company could purchase a machine for £100,000. The machine has annual maintenance costs of £10,000 and an anticipated useful life of 5 years, after which it will have zero salvage value. Tax depreciation can be claimed on a 25 per cent reducing balance basis. Assume all cash flows occur at the end of the financial year. The company pays a corporation tax rate of 30 per cent, and taxes are paid one year in arrears. The opportunity cost of capital for the machine is 10 per cent, based on the company's borrowing rate for the project. The asset would be purchased today at 1 January 2015. The company's financial year end is 31 December. However, the company could alternatively lease the asset for 5 years. As this is an operating lease, maintenance costs will be borne by the lessor, and lease payments are due at the beginning of the year. Payments by the lessee are tax deductible in the company's income statement. The lease payments are £40,000 per annum. Should the company buy or lease the machine?

13 **Leasing Cash Flows**   You work for an airline that is contemplating leasing a new design plane geo-navigational system. The system costs £22 million and it will be depreciated using 20 per cent reducing balance. At the end of 4 years, the geo-navigational system will have zero value. You can lease it for £6 million per year for 4 years. What are the cash flows from the lease from the lessor's viewpoint? Assume a 23 per cent tax bracket.

14 Finding the Break-even Payment   Using the information from question 13, what would the lease payment have to be for both lessor and lessee to be indifferent about the lease? Assume that the tax rate is 23 per cent. You can borrow at 8 per cent before taxes.

15 Taxes and Leasing Cash Flows   Using the information in question 13, assume that your company does not contemplate paying taxes for the next several years. What are the cash flows from leasing in this case?

16 Setting the Lease Payment   In the previous question, over what range of lease payments will the lease be profitable for both parties? What are the minimums and maximum amounts?

17 Lease or Buy   Super Sonics Entertainment is considering buying a machine that costs NKr3,500,000. The machine will be depreciated using the 20 per cent reducing balance method. At the end of 5 years it will be sold at its accounting residual value. The company can lease the machine with year-end payments of NKr942,000. The company can issue bonds at a 9 per cent interest rate. If the corporate tax rate is 28 per cent, should the company buy or lease?

Use the following information to solve Problems 18–20. The Wildcat Oil Company is trying to decide whether to lease or buy a new computer-assisted drilling system for its oil exploration business. Management has decided that it must use the system to stay competitive; it will provide £700,000 in annual pre-tax cost savings. The system costs £6 million and will be depreciated at 20 per cent reducing balance method. At the end of 5 years, it will have no value. Wildcat's tax rate is 28 per cent, and the firm can borrow at 9 per cent. Lambert Leasing Company has offered to lease the drilling equipment to Wildcat for payments of £1,400,000 per year. Lambert's policy is to require its lessees to make payments at the start of the year.

18 Lease or Buy   What is the net advantage to leasing (NAL) for Wildcat? What is the maximum lease payment that would be acceptable to the company?

19 Leasing and Salvage Value   Suppose it is estimated that the equipment will have an after-tax residual value of £500,000 at the end of the lease. What is the maximum lease payment acceptable to Wildcat now?

20 Deposits in Leasing   Many lessors require a security deposit in the form of a cash payment or other pledged collateral. Suppose Lambert requires Wildcat to pay a £200,000 security deposit at the inception of the lease. If the lease payment is still £1,400,000, is it advantageous for Wildcat to lease the equipment now?

21 Setting the Lease Price   Raymond Rayon Corporation wants to expand its manufacturing facilities. Liberty Leasing Corporation has offered Raymond Rayon the opportunity to lease a machine for €1,500,000 for 6 years. The machine will be fully depreciated by the straight-line method. The corporate tax rate for Raymond Rayon is 25 per cent, whereas Liberty Leasing has a corporate tax rate of 40 per cent. Both companies can borrow at 8 per cent. Assume lease payments occur at year-end. What is Raymond's reservation price? What is Liberty's reservation price?

22 Setting the Lease Price   An asset costs £360,000 and will be depreciated using the 20 per cent reducing balance method. At the end of its 3-year life it will be sold for its accounting residual value. The corporate tax rate is 28 per cent, and the appropriate interest rate is 10 per cent.

(a) What set of lease payments will make the lessee and the lessor equally well off?

(b) Show the general condition that will make the value of a lease to the lessor the negative of value to the lessee.

(c) Assume that the lessee pays no taxes and the lessor is in the 28 per cent tax bracket. For what range of lease payments does the lease have a positive NPV for both parties?

23 Lease or Buy   Wolfson plc has decided to purchase a new machine that costs £4.2 million. The machine will be depreciated on a 20 per cent reducing balance basis and will be worth nothing at the end of 4 years. The corporate tax rate is 28 per cent. The Sur Bank has offered Wolfson a 4-year loan for £4.2 million. The repayment schedule is 4-yearly principal repayments of £1.05 million and an interest charge of 9 per cent on the outstanding balance of the loan at the beginning of each year. Both principal repayments and interest are due at the end of each year. Cal Leasing Corporation offers to lease the same machine to Wolfson. Lease payments of £1.2 million per year are due at the beginning of each of the 4 years of the lease.

(a) Should Wolfson lease the machine or buy it with bank financing?

(b) What is the annual lease payment that will make Wolfson indifferent to whether it leases the machine or purchases it?

CHALLENGE

24 **Lease versus Borrow** Return to the case of the geo-navigational system discussed in Problems 13 through 16. Suppose the entire £22 million purchase price of the geo-navigational system is borrowed. The rate on the loan is 8 per cent, and the loan will be repaid in equal instalments. Create a lease versus buy analysis that explicitly incorporates the loan payments. Assume that the tax rate is 23 per cent. Show that the NPV of leasing instead of buying is not changed from what it was in Problem 12. Why is this so?

25 **Lease or Buy** High electricity costs have made Farmer Corporation's chicken-plucking machine economically worthless. Only two machines are available to replace it. The International Plucking Machine (IPM) model is available only on a lease basis. The lease payments will be £2,100 for 5 years, due at the beginning of the year. This machine will save Farmer £6,000 per year through reductions in electricity costs in every year. As an alternative, Farmer can purchase a more energy-efficient machine from Basic Machine Corporation (BMC) for £15,000. This machine will save £9,000 per year in electricity costs. A local bank has offered to finance the machine with a £15,000 loan. The interest rate on the loan will be 10 per cent on the remaining balance and five annual principal payments of £3,000. Farmer has a target debt-to-asset ratio of 67 per cent. Farmer has a corporation tax rate of 28 per cent. After 5 years, both machines will be worth nothing. The depreciation method is 20 per cent reducing balance method.

(a) Should Farmer lease the IPM machine or purchase the more efficient BMC machine?

(b) Does your answer depend on the form of financing for direct purchase?

(c) How much debt is displaced by this lease?

26 **Debt Capacity** Many researchers are now coming to the conclusion that leasing has benefits from increasing the debt capacity of financially constrained firms. Explain why this is so and provide a review of the literature that proposes this idea. Present your own views on the purpose of leasing and provide a counter-argument or confirmatory evidence on your position.

27 **Moral Hazard** Schneider (2010) argues that moral hazard in leasing is a major contributor to the level of accidents that New York taxi drivers experience. Explain what is meant by moral hazard and present a case for or against the findings of Schneider (2010).

28 **Asset Liquidity** Gavazza (2010) finds that *'more-liquid assets (1) make leasing, operating leasing in particular, more likely; (2) have shorter operating leases; (3) have longer capital leases; and (4) command lower markups of operating lease rates'*. Explain the findings of Gavazza (2010) in the context of the material covered in this chapter.

29 **Leasing and Accounting Quality** Beatty et al. (2010) argue that low accounting quality firms increase the likelihood that a firm will lease assets instead of buying them. Provide a critique of this view and explain why accounting quality would have an impact on the lease versus buy decision.

Exam Question (45 minutes)

1 Andrew and Gilstad (2005) write that *'business schools typically teach that leasing is a zerosum game. However, the economic assumptions that lead to this belief often are not true. These incorrect assumptions have caused serious confusion and bias in lease evaluation for more than a generation.'* Explain this statement. Do you believe the authors are correct? Provide examples to illustrate your answer. (40 marks)

2 Parklead Leasing are a successful leasing company, specializing in the highest quality excavation equipment. They have a fleet of 300 vehicles and a repair and maintenance section. They purchase a new machine for £80,000 that they plan to lease for 6 years. They forecast that maintenance, insurance and administrative costs of the lease will be constant at £10,000 per year. Parklead Leasing pays corporation tax of 23 per cent one year in arrears and the borrowing rate is 10 per cent on assets of this type. Depreciation is charged on machinery at 25 per cent reducing balance. What should be the minimum lease payment? (30 marks)

3 Ibro Tinmines plc requires the use of excavation machinery and estimates that it would cost them £100,000 to purchase the equipment. Alternatively, they could lease the equipment for 6 years from Parklead Leasing for £25,000 per year. If Parklead Leasing can buy the equipment for a discounted price of £80,000 evaluate

the lease from the perspective of the lessee and the lessor. Ibro Tinmines will be expected to meet all repair and maintenance costs, the tax rate is 23 per cent paid one year in arrears, and the discount rate for projects of this type is 10 per cent. Depreciation is charged at 25 per cent reducing balance. It is expected that the equipment will be scrapped after 6 years. (30 marks)

Mini Case

The Decision to Lease or Buy at Warf Computers

Warf Computers has decided to proceed with the manufacture and distribution of the virtual keyboard (VK) the company has developed. To undertake this venture, the company needs to obtain equipment for the production of the microphone for the keyboard. Because of the required sensitivity of the microphone and its small size, the company needs specialized equipment for production.

Nick Warf, the company president, has found a vendor for the equipment. Clapton Acoustical Equipment has offered to sell Warf Computers the necessary equipment at a price of £5 million. The equipment will be depreciated using the 20 per cent reducing balance method. At the end of 4 years, the market value of the equipment is expected to be £600,000.

Alternatively, the company can lease the equipment from Hendrix Leasing. The lease contract calls for four annual payments of £1.3 million due at the beginning of the year. Additionally, Warf Computers must make a security deposit of £300,000 that will be returned when the lease expires. Warf Computers can issue bonds with a yield of 11 per cent, and the company has a marginal tax rate of 28 per cent.

1 Should Warf buy or lease the equipment?

2 Nick mentions to James Hendrix, the president of Hendrix Leasing, that although the company will need the equipment for 4 years, he would like a lease contract for 2 years instead. At the end of the 2 years, the lease could be renewed. Nick would also like to eliminate the security deposit, but he would be willing to increase the lease payments to £2.3 million for each of the 2 years. When the lease is renewed in 2 years, Hendrix would consider the increased lease payments in the first 2 years when calculating the terms of the renewal. The equipment is expected to have a market value of £2 million in 2 years. What is the NAL of the lease contract under these terms? Why might Nick prefer this lease? What are the potential ethical issues concerning the new lease terms?

3 In the leasing discussion, James informs Nick that the contract could include a purchase option for the equipment at the end of the lease. Hendrix Leasing offers three purchase options:

   (a) An option to purchase the equipment at the fair market value.

   (b) An option to purchase the equipment at a fixed price. The price will be negotiated before the lease is signed.

   (c) An option to purchase the equipment at a price of £250,000.

   How would the inclusion of a purchase option affect the value of the lease?

4 James also informs Nick that the lease contract can include a cancellation option. The cancellation option would allow Warf Computers to cancel the lease on any anniversary date of the contract. In order to cancel the lease, Warf Computers would be required to give 30 days' notice prior to the anniversary date. How would the inclusion of a cancellation option affect the value of the lease?

Practical Case Study

Download the financial accounts of five companies in your country. Look for information on operating leases, financial leases, and sale and leasebacks. In each case, decide whether the financing is long term or short term and how it affects the debt to equity ratio of each firm. Do you see evidence that leasing is used as a substitute for debt? Alternatively, is it used as a complement to debt? A reading of Yan (2006) may help for this case study. Write a brief report on your findings.

Relevant Accounting Standards

Because of its importance, leasing has an accounting standard all to itself, titled IAS 17 *Leasing*. Off-balance-sheet financing has received a lot of attention because of the role of special purpose vehicles in the global banking crisis in 2008 and accounting standards pertaining to off-balance-sheet financing are being actively considered by the International Accounting Standards Board. The relevant standard is IAS 27 *Consolidated and Separate Financial Statements*. However, expect to see major changes in this standard or even a complete replacement in the next few years. IAS 23 *Borrowing Costs* is of interest because it deals with financial leases.

References

Andrew, G.M. and D.J. Gilstad (2005) 'A Generation of Bias against Leasing', *Journal of Equipment Lease Financing*, Vol. 23, No. 2, 1–14.

Ang, J. and P.P. Peterson (1984) 'The Leasing Puzzle', *The Journal of Finance*, Vol. 39, 1055–1065.

Beatty, A., S. Liao and J. Weber (2010) 'Financial Reporting Quality, Private Information, Monitoring and the Lease-versus-Buy Decision', *The Accounting Review*, Vol. 85, 1215–1238.

Cosci, S., R. Guida and V. Meliciani (2015) 'Leasing Decisions and Credit Constraints: Empirical Analysis on a Sample of Italian Firms', *European Financial Management*, Vol. 21, No. 2, 377–398.

Eisfeldt, A.L. and A.A. Rampini (2009) 'Leasing, Ability to Repossess, and Debt Capacity', *Review of Financial Studies*, Vol. 22, No. 4, 1621–1657.

Flath, D. (1980) 'The Economics of Short-Term Leasing', *Economic Inquiry*, Vol. 18, 247–259.

Gavazza, A. (2010) 'Asset Liquidity and Financial Contracts: Evidence from Aircraft Leases', *Journal of Financial Economics*, Vol. 95, No. 1, 62–84.

Lasfer, M. and M. Levis (1998) 'The Determinants of the Leasing Decision of Small and Large Companies', *European Financial Management*, Vol. 4, No. 2, 159–184.

Schneider, H. (2010) 'Moral Hazard in Leasing Contracts: Evidence from the New York City Taxi Industry', *Journal of Law and Economics*, Vol. 53, No. 4, 783–805.

Smith, C.W. Jr, and L.M. Wakeman (1985) 'Determinants of Corporate Leasing Policy', *The Journal of Finance*, Vol. 40, 895–908.

Yan, A. (2006) 'Leasing and Debt Financing: Substitutes or Complements?', *Journal of Financial and Quantitative Analysis*, Vol. 41, No. 3, 709–731.

Additional Reading

The following papers are of interest:

1 Beatty, A., S. Liao and J. Weber (2010) 'Financial Reporting Quality, Private Information, Monitoring and the Lease-versus-buy Decision', *The Accounting Review*, Vol. 85, 1215–1238.

2 Eisfeldt, A.L. and A.A. Rampini (2009) 'Leasing, Ability to Repossess, and Debt Capacity', *Review of Financial Studies*, Vol. 22, No. 4, 1621–1657.

3 Gavazza, A. (2010) 'Asset Liquidity and Financial Contracts: Evidence from Aircraft Leases', *Journal of Financial Economics*, Vol. 95, No. 1, 62–84.

4 Gronlund, T., A. Louko and M. Vaihekoski (2008) 'Corporate Real Estate Sale and Leaseback Effect: Empirical Evidence from Europe', *European Financial Management*, Vol. 14, No. 4, 820–843. **Europe**.

5 Schneider, H. (2010) 'Moral Hazard in Leasing Contracts: Evidence from the New York City Taxi Industry', *Journal of Law and Economics*, Vol. 53, No. 4, 783–805.

6 Yan, A. (2006) 'Leasing and Debt Financing: Substitutes or Complements?', *Journal of Financial and Quantitative Analysis*, Vol. 41, No. 3, 709–731. **US**.

Endnotes

1 For simplicity, we have assumed that lease payments are made at the end of each year. Actually, most leases require lease payments to be made at the beginning of the year.

2 For simplicity, assume that the firm received €100 or €106.60 *after* corporate taxes. Because 0.66 = 1 − 0.34, the pre-tax inflows would be €151.52 (€100/0.66) and €161.52 (€106.60/0.66), respectively.

3 This principle holds for riskless or guaranteed cash flows only. Unfortunately, there is no easy formula for determining the increase in optimal debt level from a *risky* cash flow.

4 Both the lessor and lessee could solve for the break-even lease payment if they wish.

PART 6

Options, Futures and Corporate Finance

Derivative securities have become ubiquitous in business and now every firm with any scale will have considered using some type of derivative contract in managing its risk. Derivatives allow a company and investor to control the level of risk they are willing to bear. As such, derivatives are the standard risk management tool used by modern corporations.

There are many types of derivatives. Forward contracts, futures, options and warrants can be combined in a limitless number of innovative ways to create completely new securities to reflect the needs and desires of investors and companies. In Part 6, we will discuss derivatives in great detail. We will explore their characteristics, how a company can use them to optimize its risk profile and how these instruments can be valued. We will then look at hybrid securities, which have derivative characteristics. Finally we will consider risk management, one of the most important new areas in finance.

Specifically, Part 6 begins in Chapter 22 with a study of options and their use in corporate finance. We then extend the conceptual material in Chapter 23 to look at real world applications of options and how they can be used to make better financial decisions. Warrants and convertible bonds are investigated in Chapter 24, and Chapter 25 ends Part 6 with a very detailed look at financial risk management.

Options and Corporate Finance

On 6 February 2015 the closing share prices for the British companies Prudential plc and SSE plc were £16.16 and £16.39, respectively. Each company had a call option trading on ICE (Intercontinental Exchange owned by NYSE) with a £16.00 strike price and an expiration date of 31 March 2015. The Prudential options sold for £0.5574 and SSE options traded at £0.5900. You might expect that the prices on these call options would be much lower given that the strike price is only £0.16 and £0.39 away from the underlying share prices, respectively, but they weren't. Why did these options have a much higher value than the payoff that would have accrued if the holder decided to exercise that day? A big reason (but not the only one) is that the volatility of the underlying shares is an important determinant of an option's underlying value. In this chapter, we explore this issue – and many others – in much greater depth using the Noble Prize-winning Black–Scholes option pricing model.

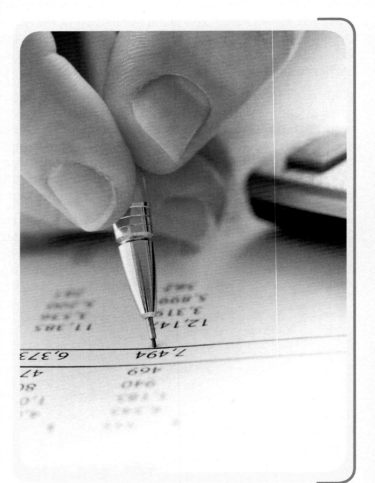

KEY NOTATIONS

C	Value of a call option
P	Value of a put option
S	Current share price
E	Exercise price of option
R	Annual risk-free rate of return, continuously compounded
σ^2	Variance (per year) of the continuous share price return
t	Time (in years) to expiration date
$N(d)$	Probability that a standardized, normally distributed, random variable will be less than or equal to d

$$d_1 = [\ln(S/E) + (R + \sigma^2/2)t]/\sqrt{\sigma^2 t}$$

$$d_2 = d_1 - \sqrt{\sigma^{2t}}$$

22.1 Options

An **option** is a contract giving its owner the right to buy or sell an asset at a fixed price on or before a given date. For example, an option on a building might give the buyer the right to buy the building for €1 million on or any time before the Saturday prior to the third Wednesday in January 2020. Options are a unique type of financial contract because they give the buyer the right, but not the *obligation,* to do something. The buyer uses the option only if it is advantageous to do so; otherwise the option can be thrown away.

There is a special vocabulary associated with options. Here are some important definitions:

1 *Exercising the option*: The act of buying or selling the underlying asset via the option contract.

2 *Strike or exercise price*: The fixed price in the option contract at which the holder can buy or sell the underlying asset.

3 *Expiration date*: The maturity date of the option; after this date, the option is dead.

4 *American and European options*: An American option may be exercised any time up to the expiration date. A European option differs from an American option in that it can be exercised only on the expiration date.

22.2 Call Options

The most common type of option is a **call option**. A call option gives the owner the right to buy an asset at a fixed price during a particular period. There is no restriction on the kind of asset, but the most common ones traded on exchanges are options on shares and bonds.

For example, call options on Associated British Foods plc shares can be purchased on ICE. Associated British Foods does not issue (that is, sell) call options on its equity. Instead, individual investors are the original buyers and sellers of call options on Associated British Foods equity. A representative call option on Associated British Foods equity enables an investor to buy 100 shares of Associated British Foods on or before 15 July at an exercise price of £7.00. This is a valuable option if there is some probability that the price of Associated British Foods equity will exceed £7.00 on or before 15 July.

The Value of a Call Option at Expiration

What is the value of a call option contract on equity at expiration? The answer depends on the value of the underlying shares at expiration.

Let us continue with the Associated British Foods example. Suppose the share price is £8.00 at expiration. The buyer[1] of the call option has the right to buy the underlying shares at the exercise price of £7.00. In other words, he has the right to exercise the call. Having the right to buy something for £7.00 when it is worth £8.00 is obviously a good thing. The value of this right is £1.00 (= £8.00 − £7.00) on the expiration day.[2]

The call would be worth even more if the share price were higher on expiration day. For example, if Associated British Foods were selling for £8.50 on the date of expiration, the call would be worth £1.50 (= £8.50 − £7.00) at that time. In fact, the call's value increases £1 for every £1 rise in the share price.

If the share price is greater than the exercise price, we say that the call is *in the money*. Of course, it is also possible that the value of the equity will turn out to be less than the exercise price, in which case we say that the call is *out of the money*. The holder will not exercise in this case. For example, if the share price at the expiration date is £6.00, no rational investor would exercise. Why pay £7.00 for shares worth only £6.00? Because the option holder has no obligation to exercise the call, she can *walk away* from the option. As a consequence, if Associated British Food's share price is less than £7.00 on the expiration date, the value of the call option will be £0. In this case, the value of the call option is not the difference between Associated British Food's share price and £7.00, as it would be if the holder of the call option had the *obligation* to exercise the call.

Here is the pay-off of this call option at expiration:

	Pay-off on the Expiration Date	
	If Share Price Is Less Than £7.00	**If Share Price Is Greater Than £7.00**
Call option value	£0	Share price − £7.00

Example 22.1

Call Option Pay-offs

Suppose Mr Optimist holds a one-year call option on equity of the Belgian imaging and IT company, Agfa Gevaert. It is a European call option and can be exercised at €1.80. Assume that the expiration date has arrived. What is the value of the Agfa Gevaert call option on the expiration date? If Agfa Gevaert is selling for €2.00 per share, Mr Optimist can exercise the option – purchase Agfa Gevaert at £1.80 – and then immediately sell the share at €2.00. Mr Optimist will have made €0.20 (= €2.00 − €1.80). Thus, the price of this call option must be €0.20 at expiration.

Instead, assume that Agfa Gevaert is selling for €1.00 per share on the expiration date. If Mr Optimist still holds the call option, he will throw it out. The value of the Agfa Gevaert call on the expiration date will be zero in this case.

Figure 22.1 plots the value of the call at expiration against the value of Associated British Foods' equity. This is referred to as the *hockey stick diagram* of call option values. If the share price is less than £7.00, the call is out of the money and worthless. If the share price is greater than £7.00, the call is in the money and its value rises one-for-one with increases in the share price. Notice that the call can never have a negative value. It is a *limited liability instrument*, which means that all the holder can lose is the initial amount she paid for it.

Figure 22.1 The Value of a Call Option on the Expiration Date

Value of call at expiration (£)

0

£7

Value of equity at expiration (£)

A call option gives the owner the right to buy an asset at a fixed price during a particular time period. If, at the expiration date, Associated British Food's share price is greater than the exercise price of £100, the call's value is

Share price – £7

If Associated British Food's share price is less than £7 at this time, the value of the call is zero.

22.3   Put Options

A **put option** can be viewed as the opposite of a call option. Just as a call gives the holder the right to buy the share at a fixed price, a put gives the holder the right to *sell* the share for a fixed exercise price.

The Value of a Put Option at Expiration

The circumstances that determine the value of the put are the opposite of those for a call option because a put option gives the holder the right to sell shares. Let us assume that the exercise price of the put is £50 and the share price at expiration is £40. The owner of this put option has the right to sell the share for *more* than it is worth, something that is clearly profitable. That is, he can buy the share at the market price of £40 and immediately sell it at the exercise price of £50, generating a profit of £10 (= £50 − £40). Thus, the value of the option at expiration must be £10.

The profit would be greater still if the share price were lower. For example, if the share price were only £30, the value of the option would be £20 (= £50 − £30). In fact, for every £1 that the share price declines at expiration, the value of the put rises by £1.

However, suppose that the equity at expiration is trading at £60 – or any price above the exercise price of £50. The owner of the put would not want to exercise here. It is a losing proposition to sell shares for £50 when they trade in the open market at £60. Instead, the owner of the put will walk away from the option. That is, he will let the put option expire.

Here is the pay-off of this put option:

	Pay-off on the Expiration Date	
	If Share Price Is Less Than £50	**If Share Price Is Greater Than £50**
Put option value	£50 − Share price	£0

Figure 22.2 plots the values of a put option for all possible values of the underlying share. It is instructive to compare Figure 22.2 with Figure 22.1 for the call option. The call option is valuable when the share price is above the exercise price, and the put is valuable when the share price is below the exercise price.

Figure 22.2 The Value of a Put Option on the Expiration Date

A put option gives the owner the right to sell an asset at a fixed price during a particular period. If the share price is greater than the exercise price of £50, the put value is zero. If the share price is less than £50, the put value is:

£50 – Share price

Example 22.2

Put Option Pay-offs

Ms Pessimist believes that the German healthcare firm, Bayer AG, will fall from its current €42.00 share price. She buys a put. Her put option contract gives her the right to sell a share of Bayer equity at €42.00 one year from now. If the price of Bayer is €44.00 on the expiration date, she will tear up the put option contract because it is worthless. That is, she will not want to sell shares worth €44.00 for the exercise price of €42.00.

On the other hand, if Bayer is selling for €40.00 on the expiration date, she will exercise the option. In this case she can buy a share of Bayer in the market for €40.00 and turn around and sell the share at the exercise price of €42.00. Her profit will be €2.00 (= €42.00 − €40.00). The value of the put option on the expiration date therefore will be €2.00.

22.4 Writing Options

An investor who sells (or *writes*) a call on equity must deliver shares of the equity if required to do so by the call option holder. Notice that the seller is *obligated* to do so.

If, at expiration date, the price of the equity is greater than the exercise price, the holder will exercise the call and the seller must give the holder shares of equity in exchange for the exercise price. The seller loses the difference between the share price and the exercise price. For example, assume that the share price is £60 and the exercise price is £50. Knowing that exercise is imminent, the option seller buys equity in the open market at £60. Because she is obligated to sell at £50, she loses £10 (= £50 − £60). Conversely, if at the expiration date the price of the equity is below the exercise price, the call option will not be exercised and the seller's liability is zero.

Why would the seller of a call place herself in such a precarious position? After all, the seller loses money if the share price ends up above the exercise price, and she merely avoids losing money if the share price ends up below the exercise price. The answer is that the seller is paid to take this risk. On the day that the option transaction takes place, the seller receives the price that the buyer pays.

Now let us look at the seller of puts. An investor who sells a put on equity agrees to purchase shares of equity if the put holder should so request. The seller loses on this deal if the share price falls below the exercise price. For example, assume that the share price is £40 and the exercise price is £50. The holder of the put will exercise in this case. In other words, she will sell the underlying share at the exercise price of £50. This means that the seller of the put must buy the underlying equity at the exercise price of £50. Because each share is worth only £40, the loss here is £10 (= £40 − £50).

The values of the 'sell-a-call' and 'sell-a-put' positions are depicted in Figure 22.3. The graph on the left side of the figure shows that the seller of a call loses nothing when the share price at expiration date is below £50. However, the seller loses a pound for every pound that the share price rises above £50. The graph in the centre of the figure shows that the seller of a put loses nothing when the share price at expiration date is above £50. However, the seller loses a pound for every pound that the share price falls below £50.

Figure 22.3 The Pay-offs to Sellers of Calls and Puts and to Buyers of Equity

It is worthwhile to spend a few minutes comparing the graphs in Figure 22.3 to those in Figures 22.1 and 22.2. The graph of selling a call (the graph in the left side of Figure 22.3) is the mirror image of the graph of buying a call (Figure 22.1).[3] This occurs because options are a zero sum game. The seller of a call loses what the buyer makes. Similarly, the graph of selling a put (the middle graph in Figure 22.3) is the mirror image of the graph of buying a put (Figure 22.2). Again, the seller of a put loses what the buyer makes.

Figure 22.3 also shows the value at expiration of simply buying equity. Notice that buying the share is the same as buying a call option on the share with an exercise price of zero. This is not surprising. If the exercise price is zero, the call holder can buy the share for nothing, which is really the same as owning it.

22.5 Option Quotes

Now that we understand the definitions for calls and puts, let us see how these options are quoted. Table 22.1 presents information, obtained from the NYSE Euronext website (www.euronext.com), about Air France-KLM options expiring in March 2015. At the time of these quotes, Air France-KLM was selling for €7.55.

Table 22.1 Information about the Options of Air France-KLM Corporation

Codes and Classification							
Code	AF1	**Market**	Euronext Paris	**Vol.**		6,600	20 Mar 2015
Exercise Type	American	**Currency**	€	**O.I.**		209,925	19 Mar 2015

Codes and Classification							
Name	AIR FRANCE-KLM	**ISIN**	FR0000031122			**Market**	Euronext Paris
Currency	€	**Best Bid**	7.547 (20 Mar 2015 12:18)			**Best Ask**	7.55 (20 Mar 2015 12:18)
Time	CET	**Last**	7.55 (20 Mar 2015 12:17)			**Last Change %**	0.16
Volume	981,099	**High**	7.63			**Low**	7.50

March 2015 Prices – 20/03/15													EXTENDED VIEW	
Calls											Puts			
SettI.	O.I.	Day Vol	Last	Bid	Ask		Strike		Bid	Ask	Last	Day Vol	O.I.	Settl.
0.35	1,724	–	–	0.32	0.38	C	7.20	P	–	0.10	–	–	5,275	0.02
0.15	1,000	–	–	0.11	0.19	C	7.40	P	–	0.05	–	–	183	0.03
0.05	1,060	–	–	0.01	0.06	C	7.60	P	0.05	0.11	–	–	1,110	0.13
0.01	–	–	–	–	0.10	C	7.80	P	0.21	0.30	–	–	545	0.29
0.01	2,192	–	–	–	0.10	C	8.00	P	0.42	0.50	–	–	1,682	0.48

There are three boxes in Table 22.1. The first relates to the option contract and it can be seen that Air France-KLM's option ticker is AF1, is denominated in euros, and is of American type (that is, it can be exercised before the expiration date). Each option contract relates to purchasing 100 shares. On 20 March 2015, the last transaction involved 6,600 contracts and the total number of contracts outstanding on 19 March 2015 was 209,925.

The second box relates to the underlying asset, which is Air France-KLM equity. This is traded on Euronext Amsterdam and is denominated in euros. There were 981,099 shares traded in the equity and the last transaction price was €7.55 on 20 March 2015 as at 12:18, which was the time the information was recorded. Other price information, such as high and low price is also presented.

The final box provides information on individual call and put contracts. 'Settl.' is the previous day's settlement price.

22.6 Option Combinations

Puts and calls can serve as building blocks for more complex option contracts. For example, Figure 22.4 illustrates the pay-off from buying a put option on a share and simultaneously buying the share.

Figure 22.4 Pay-off to the Combination of Buying a Put and Buying the Underlying Equity

If the share price is greater than the exercise price, the put option is worthless, and the value of the combined position is equal to the value of the equity. If instead the exercise price is greater than the share price, the decline in the value of the shares will be exactly offset by the rise in the value of the put.

The strategy of buying a put and buying the underlying share is called a *protective* put. It is as if we are buying insurance for the share. The share can always be sold at the exercise price, regardless of how far the market price of the share falls.

Note that the combination of buying a put and buying the underlying share has the same *shape* in Figure 22.4 as the call purchase in Figure 22.1. To pursue this point, let us consider the graph for buying a call, which is shown at the far left of Figure 22.5. This graph is the same as Figure 22.1, except that the exercise price is £50 here. Now, let us try the strategy of:

- (Leg A) Buying a call.
- (Leg B) Buying a risk-free, zero coupon bond (i.e., a T-bill) with a face value of £50 that matures on the same day that the option expires.

Figure 22.5 Pay-off to the Combination of Buying a Call and Buying a Zero Coupon Bond

The graph of buying a call and buying a zero coupon bond is the same as the graph of buying a put and buying the share in Figure 22.4

We have drawn the graph of leg A of this strategy at the far left of Figure 22.5, but what does the graph of leg B look like? It looks like the middle graph of the figure. That is, anyone buying this zero coupon bond will be guaranteed to receive £50, regardless of the price of the share at expiration.

What does the graph of *simultaneously* buying both leg A and leg B of this strategy look like? It looks like the far right graph of Figure 22.5. That is, the investor receives a guaranteed £50 from the bond, regardless of what happens to the share price. In addition, the investor receives a pay-off from the call of £1 for every £1 that the share price rises above the exercise price of £50.

The far right graph of Figure 22.5 looks *exactly* like the far right graph of Figure 22.4. Thus, an investor gets the same pay-off from the strategy of Figure 22.4 and the strategy of Figure 22.5, regardless of what happens to the price of the underlying equity. In other words, the investor gets the same pay-off from:

1 Buying a put and buying the underlying share.
2 Buying a call and buying a risk-free, zero coupon bond.

If investors have the same pay-offs from the two strategies, the two strategies must have the same cost. Otherwise, all investors will choose the strategy with the lower cost and avoid the strategy with the higher cost. This leads to the following interesting result:

$$\text{Price of underlying equity} + \text{Price of put} = \text{Price of call} + \text{Present value of exercise price} \qquad (22.1)$$

Cost of first strategy = Cost of second strategy

This relationship is known as put–call parity and is one of the most fundamental relationships concerning options. It says that there are two ways of buying a protective put. You can buy a put and buy the underlying equity simultaneously. Here, your total cost is the share price of the underlying equity plus the price of the put. Or you can buy the call and buy a zero coupon bond. Here, your total cost is the price of the call plus the price of the zero coupon bond. The price of the zero coupon bond is equal to the present value of the exercise price – that is, the present value of £50 in our example.

Equation 22.1 is a very precise relationship. It holds only if the put and the call have both the same exercise price and the same expiration date. In addition, the maturity date of the zero coupon bond must be the same as the expiration date of the options.

To see how fundamental put–call parity is, let us rearrange the formula, yielding:

$$\text{Price of underlying equity} = \text{Price of call} - \text{Price of put} + \text{Present value of exercise price}$$

This relationship now states that you can replicate the purchase of a share of equity by buying a call, selling a put, and buying a zero coupon bond. (Note that because a minus sign comes before 'Price of put', the put is sold, not bought.) Investors in this three-legged strategy are said to have purchased a *synthetic* share.

Let us do one more transformation:

Covered call strategy

$$\text{Price of underlying equity} - \text{Price of call} = - \text{Price of put} + \text{Present value of exercise price}$$

Many investors like to buy a share and write the call on the share simultaneously. This is a conservative strategy known as *selling a covered call*. The preceding put–call parity relationship tells us that this strategy is equivalent to selling a put and buying a zero coupon bond. Figure 22.6 develops the graph for the covered call. You can verify that the covered call can be replicated by selling a put and simultaneously buying a zero coupon bond.

Figure 22.6 Pay-off to the Combination of Buying a Share and Selling a Call

Of course, there are other ways of rearranging the basic put–call relationship. For each rearrangement, the strategy on the left side is equivalent to the strategy on the right side. The beauty of put–call parity is that it shows how any strategy in options can be achieved in two different ways.

To test your understanding of put–call parity, suppose Nokia shares are selling for €10.95. A three-month call option with an €10.95 strike price goes for €0.35. The risk-free rate is 0.5 per cent per month. What is the value of a 3-month put option with a €10.95 strike price?

We can rearrange the put–call parity relationship to solve for the price of the put as follows:

$$\text{Price of put} = - \text{Price of underlying equity} + \text{Price of call} + \text{Present value of strike price}$$

$$= - €10.95 + €0.35 + €10.95/1.005^3$$
$$= €0.1873$$

As shown, the value of the put is €0.1873.

A Synthetic T-Bill

Suppose shares of Kassam plc are selling for £110. A call option on Kassam with one year to maturity and a £110 strike price sells for £15. A put with the same terms sells for £5. What is the risk-free rate?

To answer, we need to use put–call parity to determine the price of a risk-free, zero coupon bond:

Price of underlying share + Price of put − Price of call = Present value of exercise price

Plugging in the numbers, we get:

$$£110 + £5 − £15 = £100$$

Because the present value of the £110 strike price is £100, the implied risk-free rate is 10 per cent.

22.7   Valuing Options

In the last section we determined what options are worth on the expiration date. Now we wish to determine the value of options when you buy them well before expiration.[4] We begin by considering the lower and upper bounds on the value of a call.

Bounding the Value of a Call

Lower Bound

Consider an American call that is in the money prior to expiration. For example, assume that the share price is £60 and the exercise price is £50. In this case, the option cannot sell below £10. To see this, note the following simple strategy if the option sells at, say, £9:

Date	Transaction	£
Today	(1) Buy call.	−9
Today	(2) Exercise call – that is, buy underlying share at exercise price.	−50
Today	(3) Sell share at current market price.	+60
Arbitrage profit		+1

The type of profit that is described in this transaction is an *arbitrage* profit. Arbitrage profits come from transactions that have no risk or cost and cannot occur regularly in normal, well-functioning financial markets. The excess demand for these options would quickly force the option price up to at least £10 (= £60 – £50).

Of course, the price of the option is likely to be above £10. Investors will rationally pay more than £10 because of the possibility that the share will rise above £60 before expiration. For example, suppose the call actually sells for £12. In this case, we say that the *intrinsic value* of the option is £10, meaning it must always be worth at least this much. The remaining £12 − £10 = £2 is sometimes called the *time premium*, and it represents the extra amount that investors are willing to pay because of the possibility that the share price will rise before the option expires.

Upper Bound

Is there an upper boundary for the option price as well? It turns out that the upper boundary is the price of the underlying share. That is, an option to buy equity cannot have a greater value than the equity itself. A call option can be used to buy equity with a payment of the exercise price. It would be foolish to buy equity this way if the shares could be purchased directly at a lower price. The upper and lower bounds are represented in Figure 22.7.

The Factors Determining Call Option Values

The previous discussion indicated that the price of a call option must fall somewhere in the shaded region of Figure 22.7. We will now determine more precisely where in the shaded region it should be. The factors that determine a call's value can be broken into two sets. The first set contains the features of the option contract. The two basic contractual features are the exercise price and the expiration date. The second set of factors affecting the call price concerns characteristics of the equity and the market.

Figure 22.7 The Upper and Lower Boundaries of Call Option Values

Value of the call must lie in the shaded region

Exercise Price

An increase in the exercise price reduces the value of the call. For example, imagine that there are two calls on a share selling at £60. The first call has an exercise price of £50 and the second one has an exercise price of £40. Which call would you rather have? Clearly, you would rather have the call with an exercise price of £40 because that one is £20 (= £60 − £40) in the money. In other words, the call with an exercise price of £40 should sell for more than an otherwise identical call with an exercise price of £50.

Expiration Date

The value of an American call option must be at least as great as the value of an otherwise identical option with a shorter term to expiration. Consider two American calls: one has a maturity of 9 months and the other expires in 6 months. Obviously, the 9-month call has the same rights as the 6-month call, and it also has an additional 3 months within which these rights can be exercised. It cannot be worth less and will generally be more valuable.[5]

Share Price

Other things being equal, the higher the share price, the more valuable the call option will be. For example, if a share is worth £80, a call with an exercise price of £100 is not worth very much. If the share soars to £120, the call becomes much more valuable.

Now consider Figure 22.8, which shows the relationship between the call price and the share price prior to expiration. The curve indicates that the call price increases as the share price increases. Furthermore, it can be shown that the relationship is represented not by a straight line, but by a *convex* curve. That is, the increase in the call price for a given change in the share price is greater when the share price is high than when the share price is low.

Figure 22.8 Value of an American Call as a Function of Share Price

The call price is positively related to the share price. In addition, the change in the call price for a given change in the share price is greater when the share price is high than when it is low.

There are two special points on the curve in Figure 22.8:

1 *The equity is worthless.* The call must be worthless if the underlying equity is worthless. That is, if the equity has no chance of attaining any value, it is not worthwhile to pay the exercise price to obtain the share.

2 *The share price is very high relative to the exercise price.* In this situation, the owner of the call knows that she will end up exercising the call. She can view herself as the owner of the share now, with one difference: she must pay the exercise price at expiration.

Thus, the value of her position – that is, the value of the call – is:

$$\text{Share price} - \text{Present value of exercise price}$$

These two points on the curve are summarized in the bottom half of Table 22.2.

Table 22.2 Factors Affecting American Option Values

Increase in	Call Option*	Put Option*
Value of underlying asset (share price)	+	−
Exercise price	−	+
Share price volatility	+	+
Interest rate	+	−
Time to expiration	+	+

In addition to the preceding, we have presented the following four relationships for American calls:
1 The call price can never be greater than the share price (*upper bound*).
2 The call price can never be less than either zero or the difference between the share price and the exercise price (*lower bound*).
3 The call is worth zero if the underlying equity is worth zero.
4 When the share price is much greater than the exercise price, the call price tends toward the difference between the share price and the present value of the exercise price.

* The signs (+, −) indicate the effect of the variables on the value of the option. For example, the two +s for share volatility indicate that an increase in volatility will increase both the value of a call and the value of a put.

The Key Factor: The Variability of the Underlying Asset

The greater the variability of the underlying asset, the more valuable the call option will be. Consider the following example. Suppose that just before the call expires, the share price will be either £100 with probability 0.5, or £80 with probability 0.5. What will be the value of a call with an exercise price of £110? Clearly, it will be worthless because no matter what happens to the equity, the share price will always be below the exercise price.

What happens if the share price is more variable? Suppose we add £20 to the best case and take £20 away from the worst case. Now the equity has a one-half chance of being worth £60 and a one-half chance of being worth £120. We have spread the share returns, but of course the expected value of the share has stayed the same:

$$(1/2 \times £80) + (1/2 \times £100) = £90 = (1/2 \times £60) + (1/2 \times £120)$$

Notice that the call option has value now because there is a one-half chance that the share price will be £120, or £10 above the exercise price of £110. This illustrates an important point. There is a fundamental distinction between holding an option on an underlying asset and holding the underlying asset. If investors in the marketplace are risk-averse, a rise in the variability of the equity will decrease its market value. However, the holder of a call receives pay-offs from the positive tail of the probability distribution. As a consequence, a rise in the variability in the underlying equity increases the market value of the call.

This result can also be seen from Figure 22.9. Consider two shares, A and B, each of which is normally distributed. For each security, the figure illustrates the probability of different share prices on the expiration date. As can be seen from the figures, share B has more volatility than does share A. This means that share B has a higher probability of both abnormally high returns and abnormally low returns. Let us assume that options on each of the two securities have the same exercise price. To option holders, a return much below average on share B is no worse than a return only moderately below average on share A. In either situation, the option expires out of the money. However, to option holders, a return much above average on share B is better than a return only moderately above average on share A. Because a call's price at the expiration date is the difference between the share price and the exercise price, the value of the call on B at expiration will be higher in this case.

Figure 22.9 Distribution of Equity Price at Expiration for Both Security *A* and Security *B*. Options on the Two Securities Have the Same Exercise Price

The call on share B is worth more than the call on share A because share B is more volatile. At expiration, a call that is deep in the money is more valuable than a call that is only slightly in the money. However, at expiration, a call way out of the money is worth zero, just as is a call only slightly out of the money.

The Interest Rate

Call prices are also a function of the level of interest rates. Buyers of calls do not pay the exercise price until they exercise the option, if they do so at all. The ability to delay payment is more valuable when interest rates are high and less valuable when interest rates are low. Thus, the value of a call is positively related to interest rates.

A Quick Discussion of Factors Determining Put Option Values

Given our extended discussion of the factors influencing a call's value, we can examine the effect of these factors on puts very easily. Table 22.2 summarized the five factors influencing the prices of both American calls and American puts. The effect of three factors on puts are the opposite of the effect of these three factors on calls:

1   The put's market value *decreases* as the share price increases because puts are in the money when the equity sells below the exercise price.

2   The value of a put with a high exercise price is *greater* than the value of an otherwise identical put with a low exercise price for the reason given in (1).

3   A high interest rate *adversely* affects the value of a put. The ability to sell a share at a fixed exercise price sometime in the future is worth less if the present value of the exercise price is reduced by a high interest rate.

The effect of the other two factors on puts is the same as the effect of these factors on calls:

4   The value of an American put with a distant expiration date is greater than an otherwise identical put with an earlier expiration.[6] The longer time to maturity gives the put holder more flexibility, just as it did in the case of a call.

5   Volatility of the underlying share price increases the value of the put. The reasoning is analogous to that for a call. At expiration, a put that is way in the money is more valuable than a put only slightly in the money. However, at expiration, a put way out of the money is worth zero, just as is a put only slightly out of the money.

22.8   An Option Pricing Formula

We have explained *qualitatively* that the value of a call option is a function of five variables:

1   The current price of the underlying asset, which for equity options is the share price.

2   The exercise price.

3   The time to expiration date.

4   The variance of the underlying asset.

5   The risk-free interest rate.

It is time to replace the qualitative model with a precise option valuation model. The model we choose is the famous Black–Scholes option pricing model. You can put numbers into the Black–Scholes model and get values back.

The Black–Scholes model is represented by a rather imposing formula. A derivation of the formula is simply not possible in this textbook, as many students will be happy to learn. However, some appreciation for the achievement as well as some intuitive understanding is in order.

Chapter 6
Page 151

In the early chapters of this book, we showed how to discount capital budgeting projects using the net present value formula (see **Chapter 6**, section 6.1). We also used this approach to value shares and bonds. Why, students sometimes ask, can't the same NPV formula be used to value puts and calls? This is a good question: the earliest attempts at valuing options used NPV. Unfortunately the attempts were not successful because no one could determine the appropriate discount rate. An option is generally riskier than the underlying share, but no one knew exactly how much riskier.

Black and Scholes attacked the problem by pointing out that a strategy of borrowing to finance an equity purchase duplicates the risk of a call. Then, knowing the price of an equity already, we can determine the price of a call such that its return is identical to that of the share-with-borrowing alternative.

We illustrate the intuition behind the Black–Scholes approach by considering a simple example where a combination of a call and an equity eliminates all risk. This example works because we let the future share price be one of only *two* values. Hence, the example is called a *two-state* or *binomial option pricing model*. By eliminating the possibility that the share price can take on other values, we are able to duplicate the call exactly.

A Two-state Option Model

Consider the following example. Suppose the current market price of a share is £50 and the share price will be either £60 or £40 at the end of the year. Further, imagine a call option on this share with a one-year expiration date and a £50 exercise price. Investors can borrow at 10 per cent. Our goal is to determine the value of the call.

To value the call correctly, we need to examine two strategies. The first is to simply buy the call. The second is to:

1   Buy one-half of a share of equity.
2   Borrow £18.18, implying a payment of principal and interest at the end of the year of £20 (= £18.18 × 1.10).

As you will see shortly, the cash flows from the second strategy match the cash flows from buying a call. (A little later, we will show how we came up with the exact fraction of a share of equity to buy and the exact borrowing amount.) Because the cash flows match, we say that we are *duplicating* the call with the second strategy.

At the end of the year, the future pay-offs are set out as follows:

	Future Pay-offs	
Initial Transactions	**If Share Price Is £60**	**If Share Price Is £40**
1. Buy a call	£60 − £50 = £ 10	£ 0
2. Buy 1/2 share of equity	1/2 × £60 = £30	1/2 × £40 = £20
Borrow £18.18 at 10%	− (£18.18 × 1.10) = −£20	− £20
Total from equity and borrowing strategy	£ 10	£ 0

Note that the future pay-off structure of the 'buy-a-call' strategy is duplicated by the strategy of 'buy share and borrow'. That is, under either strategy an investor would end up with £10 if the share price rose and £0 if the share price fell. Thus these two strategies are equivalent as far as traders are concerned.

If two strategies always have the same cash flows at the end of the year, how must their initial costs be related? The two strategies must have the *same* initial cost. Otherwise, there will be an arbitrage possibility. We can easily calculate this cost for our strategy of buying share and borrowing:

Buy 1/2 share of equity	1/2 × £50 = £25.00
Borrow £18.18	− 18.18
	£ 6.82

Because the call option provides the same pay-offs at expiration as does the strategy of buying equity and borrowing, the call must be priced at £6.82. This is the value of the call option in a market without arbitrage profits.

We left two issues unexplained in the preceding example.

Determining the Delta

How did we know to buy one-half share of equity in the duplicating strategy? Actually, the answer is easier than it might at first appear. The call price at the end of the year will be either £10 or £0, whereas the share price will be either £60 or £40. Thus, the call price has a potential swing of £10 (= £10 − £0) next period, whereas the share price has a potential swing of £20 (= £60 − £40). We can write this in terms of the following ratio:

$$\text{Delta} = \frac{\text{Swing of call}}{\text{Swing of equity}} = \frac{£10 - £0}{£60 - £40} = \frac{1}{2}$$

As indicated, this ratio is called the *delta* of the call. In words, a £1 swing in the share price gives rise to a £1/2 swing in the price of the call. Because we are trying to duplicate the call with the equity, it seems sensible to buy one-half share of equity instead of buying one call. In other words, the risk of buying one-half share of equity should be the same as the risk of buying one call.

Determining the Amount of Borrowing

How did we know how much to borrow? Buying one-half share of equity brings us either £30 or £20 at expiration, which is exactly £20 more than the pay-offs of £10 and £0, respectively, from the call. To duplicate the call through a purchase of equity, we should also borrow enough money so that we have to pay back exactly £20 of interest and principal. This amount of borrowing is merely the present value of £20, which is £18.18 (= £20/1.10).

Now that we know how to determine both the delta and the borrowing, we can write the value of the call as follows:

$$\text{Value of call} = \text{Share price} \times \text{Delta} - \text{Amount borrowed}$$
$$£6.82 = £10 \times 1/2 - £18.18 \tag{22.2}$$

We will find this intuition useful in explaining the Black–Scholes model.

Risk-neutral Valuation

Before leaving this simple example, we should comment on a remarkable feature. We found the exact value of the option without even knowing the probability that the equity would go up or down! If an optimist thought the probability of an up move was high and a pessimist thought it was low, they would still agree on the option value. How can that be? The answer is that the current £50 share price already balances the views of the optimists and the pessimists. The option reflects that balance because its value depends on the share price.

This insight provides us with another approach to valuing the call. If we do not need the probabilities of the two states to value the call, perhaps we can select *any* probabilities we want and still come up with the right answer. Suppose we selected probabilities such that the return on the equity is equal to the risk-free rate of 10 per cent. We know that the equity return given a rise is 20 per cent (= £60/£50 − 1) and the equity return given a fall is − 20 per cent (= £40/£50 − 1). Thus, we can solve for the probability of a rise necessary to achieve an expected return of 10 per cent as follows:

$$10\% = \text{Probability of a rise} \times 20\% + (1 - \text{Probability of rise}) \times -20\%$$

Solving this formula, we find that the probability of a rise is 3/4 and the probability of a fall is 1/4. If we apply these probabilities to the call, we can value it as:

$$\text{Value of call} = \frac{\frac{3}{4} \times £10 + \frac{1}{4} \times £0}{1.10} = £6.82$$

which is the same value we got from the duplicating approach.

Why did we select probabilities such that the expected return on the equity is 10 per cent? We wanted to work with the special case where investors are *risk-neutral*. This case occurs when the expected return on *any* asset (including both the share and the call) is equal to the risk-free rate. In other words, this case occurs when investors demand no additional compensation beyond the risk-free rate, regardless of the risk of the asset in question.

What would have happened if we had assumed that the expected return on a share of equity was greater than the risk-free rate? The value of the call would still be £6.82. However, the calculations would be difficult. For example, if we assumed that the expected return on the equity was, say 11 per cent, we would have had to derive the expected return on the call. Although the expected return on the call would be higher than 11 per cent, it would take a lot of work to determine the expected return precisely. Why do any more work than you have to? Because we cannot think of any good reason, we (and most other financial economists) choose to assume risk neutrality.

Thus, the preceding material allows us to value a call in the following two ways:

1 Determine the cost of a strategy duplicating the call. This strategy involves an investment in a fractional share of equity financed by partial borrowing.

2 Calculate the probabilities of a rise and a fall under the assumption of risk neutrality. Use these probabilities, in conjunction with the risk-free rate, to discount the pay-offs of the call at expiration.

The Black–Scholes Model

The preceding example illustrates the duplicating strategy. Unfortunately, a strategy such as this will not work in the real world over, say, a one-year time frame because there are many more than two possibilities for next year's share price. However, the number of possibilities is reduced as the period is shortened. Is there a time period over which the share price can only have two outcomes? Academics argue that the assumption that there are only two possibilities for the share price over the next infinitesimal instant is quite plausible.[7]

In our opinion, the fundamental insight of Black and Scholes is to shorten the time period. They show that a specific combination of equity and borrowing can indeed duplicate a call over an infinitesimal time horizon. Because the share price will change over the first instant, another combination of equity and borrowing is needed to duplicate the call over the second instant and so on. By adjusting the combination from moment to moment, they can continually duplicate the call. It may boggle the mind that a formula can (1) determine the duplicating combination at any moment, and (2) value the option based on this duplicating strategy. Suffice it to say that their dynamic strategy allows them to value a call in the real world, just as we showed how to value the call in the two-state model.

This is the basic intuition behind the Black–Scholes (BS) model. Because the actual derivation of their formula is, alas, far beyond the scope of this text, we simply present the formula itself:

Black–Scholes model

$$C = SN(d_1) - Ee^{-Rt} N(d_2)$$

where

$$d_1 = [\ln(S/E) + (R + \sigma^2/2)t]/\sqrt{\sigma^2 t}$$
$$d_2 = d_1 - \sqrt{\sigma^2 t}$$

This formula for the value of a call, C, is one of the most complex in finance. However, it involves only five parameters:

1 S = Current share price
2 E = Exercise price of call
3 R = Annual risk-free rate of return, continuously compounded
4 σ^2 = Variance (per year) of the continuous share price return
5 t = Time (in years) to expiration date.

In addition, there is this statistical concept:

$$N(d) = \text{Probability that a standardized, normally distributed,}$$
$$\text{random variable will be less than or equal to } d.$$

Rather than discuss the formula in its algebraic state, we illustrate the formula with an example.

Example 22.4

Black–Scholes

Consider Private Equipment Company (PEC). On 4 October of year 0, the PEC 21 April call option (exercise price = £49) had a closing value of £4. The equity itself was selling at £50. On 4 October, the option had 199 days to expiration (maturity date = 21 April, year 1). The annual risk-free interest rate, continuously compounded, was 7 per cent.

This information determines three variables directly:

1 The share price, S, is £50
2 The exercise price, E, is £49
3 The risk-free rate, R, is 0.07.

In addition, the time to maturity, t, can be calculated quickly: the formula calls for t to be expressed in *years*.

4 We express the 199-day interval in years as $t = 199/365$.

In the real world, an option trader would know S and E exactly. Traders generally view government Treasury bills as riskless, so a current quote from newspapers, such as the *Financial Times* or a similar source, would be obtained for the interest rate. The trader would also know (or could count) the number of days to expiration exactly. Thus, the fraction of a year to expiration, t, could be calculated quickly.

The problem comes in determining the variance of the underlying equity's return. The formula calls for the variance between the purchase date of 4 October and the expiration date. Unfortunately, this represents the future, so the correct value for variance is not available. Instead, traders frequently estimate variance from past data, just as we calculated variance in an earlier chapter. In addition, some traders may use intuition to adjust their estimate. For example, if anticipation of an upcoming event is likely to increase the volatility of the share price, the trader might adjust her estimate of variance upward to reflect this.

The preceding discussion was intended merely to mention the difficulties in variance estimation, not to present a solution. For our purposes, we assume that a trader has come up with an estimate of variance:

5 The variance of Private Equipment Corporation has been estimated to be 0.09 per year.

Using these five parameters, we calculate the Black–Scholes value of the PEC option in three steps:

Step 1: Calculate d_1 and d_2

These values can be determined by a straightforward, albeit tedious, insertion of our parameters into the basic formula. We have

$$d_1 = \left[\ln\left(\frac{S}{E}\right) + (R + \sigma^2/2)t\right]\Big/\sqrt{\sigma^2 t}$$
$$= \left[\ln\left(\frac{50}{49}\right) + (0.07 + 0.09/2) \times \frac{199}{365}\right]\Big/\sqrt{0.09 \times \frac{199}{365}}$$
$$= [0.0202 + 0.0627]/0.2215 = 0.3742$$
$$d_2 = d_1 - \sqrt{\sigma^2 t}$$
$$= 0.1527$$

Step 2: Calculate $N(d_1)$ and $N(d_2)$

We can best understand the values $N(d_1)$ and $N(d_2)$ by examining Figure 22.10. The figure shows the normal distribution with an expected value of 0 and a standard deviation of 1. This is frequently called the standardized normal distribution. We mentioned in an earlier chapter that the probability that a drawing from this distribution will be between −1 and +1 (within one standard deviation of its mean, in other words) is 68.26 per cent.

Shaded area represents cumulative probability. Because the probability is 0.6459 that a drawing from the standard normal distribution will be below 0.3742, we say that N(0.3742) = 0.6459. That is, the cumulative probability of 0.3742 is 0.6459.

Figure 22.10 Graph of Cumulative Probability

Now let us ask a different question: What is the probability that a drawing from the standardized normal distribution will be *below* a particular value? For example, the probability that a drawing will be below 0 is clearly 50 per cent because the normal distribution is symmetric. Using statistical terminology, we say that the cumulative probability of 0 is 50 per cent. Statisticians also say that N(0) = 50 per cent. It turns out that:

$$N(d_1) = N(0.3742) = 0.6459$$
$$N(d_2) = N(0.1527) = 0.5607$$

The first value means that there is a 64.59 per cent probability that a drawing from the standardized normal distribution will be below 0.3742. The second value means that there is a 56.07 per cent probability that a drawing from the standardized normal distribution will be below 0.1527. More generally, N(d) is the probability that a drawing from the standardized normal distribution will be below d. In other words, N(d) is the cumulative probability of d. Note that d_1 and d_2 in our example are slightly above zero, so N(d_1) and N(d_2) are slightly greater than 0.50.

Perhaps the easiest way to determine N(d_1) and N(d_2) is from the EXCEL function NORMSDIST. In our example, NORMSDIST(0.3742) and NORMSDIST(0.1527) are 0.6459 and 0.5607, respectively.

We can also determine the cumulative probability from Table 22.3. For example, consider $d = 0.37$. This can be found in the table as 0.3 on the vertical and 0.07 on the horizontal. The value in the table for $d = 0.37$ is 0.1443. This value is *not* the cumulative probability of 0.37. We must first make an adjustment to determine cumulative probability. That is:

$$N(0.37) = 0.50 + 0.1443 = 0.6443$$
$$N(-0.37) = 0.50 - 0.1443 = 0.3557$$

d	0.00	0.01	0.02	0.03	0.04	0.05	0.06	0.07	0.08	0.09
0.0	0.0000	0.0040	0.0080	0.0120	0.0160	0.0199	0.0239	0.0279	0.0319	0.0359
0.1	0.0398	0.0438	0.0478	0.0517	0.0557	0.0596	0.0636	0.0675	0.0714	0.0753
0.2	0.0793	0.0832	0.0871	0.0910	0.0948	0.0987	0.1026	0.1064	0.1103	0.1141
0.3	0.1179	0.1217	0.1255	0.1293	0.1331	0.1368	0.1406	0.1443	0.1480	0.1517
0.4	0.1554	0.1591	0.1628	0.1664	0.1700	0.1736	0.1772	0.1808	0.1844	0.1879
0.5	0.1915	0.1950	0.1985	0.2019	0.2054	0.2088	0.2123	0.2157	0.2190	0.2224

N(d) represents areas under the standard normal distribution function. Suppose that $d_1 = 0.24$. The table implies a cumulative probability of 0.5000 + 0.0948 = 0.5948. If d_1 is equal to 0.2452, we must estimate the probability by interpolating between N(0.25) and N(0.24).

Table 22.3 Cumulative Probabilities of the Standard Normal Distribution Function

Unfortunately, our table handles only two significant digits, whereas our value of 0.3742 has four significant digits. Hence we must interpolate to find N(0.3742). Because N(0.37) = 0.6443 and N(0.38) = 0.6480, the difference between the two values is 0.0037 (= 0.6480 − 0.6443). Since 0.3742 is 42 per cent of the way between 0.37 and 0.38, we interpolate as:[8]

$$N(0.3742) = 0.6443 + 0.42 \times 0.0037 = 0.6459$$

Step 3: Calculate C

We have:

$$C = S \times [N(d_1)] - E_e^{-Rt} \times [N(d_2)]$$
$$= \pounds50 \times [N(d_1)] - \pounds49 \times e^{-0.07 \times (199/365)}] \times N(d_2)$$
$$= (\pounds50 \times 0.6459) - (\pounds49 \times 0.9626 \times 0.5607)$$
$$= \pounds32.295 - \pounds26.447$$
$$= \pounds5.85$$

The estimated price of £5.85 is greater than the £4 actual price, implying that the call option is underpriced. A trader believing in the Black–Scholes model would buy a call. Of course the Black–Scholes model is fallible. Perhaps the disparity between the model's estimate and the market price reflects error in the trader's estimate of variance.

The previous example stressed the calculations involved in using the Black–Scholes formula. Is there any intuition behind the formula? Yes, and that intuition follows from the share purchase and borrowing strategy in our binomial example. The first line of the Black–Scholes equation is:

$$C = S \times N(d_1) - Ee^{-Rt} N(d_2)$$

which is exactly analogous to Equation 22.2:

$$\text{Value of call} = \text{Share price} \times \text{Delta} - \text{Amount borrowed} \tag{22.2}$$

We presented this equation in the binomial example. It turns out that $N(d_1)$ is the delta in the Black–Scholes model. $N(d_1)$ is 0.6459 in the previous example. In addition, $Ee^{-Rt} N(d_2)$ is the amount that an investor must borrow to duplicate a call. In the previous example, this value is £26.45 (= £49 × 0.9626 × 0.5607). Thus, the model tells us that we can duplicate the call of the preceding example by both:

1   Buying 0.6459 share of equity.

2   Borrowing £26.45.

It is no exaggeration to say that the Black–Scholes formula is among the most important contributions in finance. It allows anyone to calculate the value of an option given a few parameters. The attraction of the formula is that four of the parameters are observable: the current share price, S; the exercise price, E; the interest rate, R; and the time to expiration date, t. Only one of the parameters must be estimated: the variance of return, σ^2.

To see how truly attractive this formula is, note what parameters are not needed. First, the investor's risk aversion does not affect value. The formula can be used by anyone, regardless of willingness to bear risk. Second, it does not depend on the expected return on the equity! Investors with different assessments of the equity's expected return will nevertheless agree on the call price. As in the two-state example, this is because the call depends on the share price, and that price already balances investors' divergent views.

Black–Scholes with Dividends

Chapter 18
Page 480

The Black–Scholes model assumes that a company does not pay dividends. What happens when dividends are paid? Assume that a firm pays a regular dividend with a constant continuous dividend yield, q. From **Chapter 18**, we showed that dividends cause share prices to fall by the same amount as the dividend to reflect cash leaving the company. So if a share price grows from S to S_t when paying dividends, it will have to grow to $S_t e^{qt}$ if it does not pay any dividends. This is because the equity will have a higher growth rate because it isn't paying out any cash to shareholders.

An alternative way to express this argument is that we can say that the share price will grow from S to S_t when dividends are paid and Se^{-qt} to S_t if no dividends are paid. In the second formulation, we are anchoring time at t, the exercise date.

All this complexity simply means that we substitute S for Se^{-qt} in the standard Black–Scholes formula. The revised formula is:

$$C = Se^{-qt} N(d_1) - Ee^{-Rt} N(d_2)$$

$$d_1 = \left[\ln\left(\frac{Se^{-qt}}{E} \right) + \left(R + \frac{\sigma^2}{2} \right)t \right] \Big/ \sqrt{\sigma^2 t} = \left[\ln\left(\frac{S}{E} \right) + \left(R - q + \frac{\sigma^2}{2} \right)t \right] \Big/ \sqrt{\sigma^2 t}$$

$$d_2 = d_1 - \sqrt{\sigma^2 t}$$

Real World Insight 22.1

Energy Options

When energy companies plan new large-scale investments, they need to forecast energy prices for at least 5 years. However, volatility in oil and gas prices can have a massive impact on the risk of these investments. One way to reduce investment risk is to anchor future prices so that risk is associated with the general investment without being exacerbated by temporary fluctuations in energy prices. This is what many oil companies have done in response to the massive drop in energy prices in 2015. The question that is being asked is whether we will see a return to $100 a barrel over the next few years. Oil call options give companies that need oil the right to buy it at a set price by a certain date and oil put options give companies that sell oil the right to sell it at a set price by a certain date.

An assessment of the market in May 2015 for Brent crude oil options with expiry dates of December 2018, showed that call option open interest was 1.98 times that of put option open interest, suggesting that almost twice as many investors were betting that the Brent crude oil price would be above $100. The positive sentiment in the markets is the exact opposite of that in the financial media, where news is replete with companies scaling back investments and mothballing oil drilling sites. Only time will tell if investors in 2015 were too optimistic.

22.9   The 'Greeks'

In the previous section, you were introduced to the ratio, delta, which is the change in the option price with respect to a change in the value of the underlying asset. This measure of risk is one of four measures in option pricing that are important to corporate finance practitioners.

Table 22.2 presented the main factors that influence the price of an option. These are the value of the underlying asset (the share price), the exercise price, volatility in the value of the underlying asset, the interest rate and time to expiry. While we know that the exercise price will not change during the lifetime of the option, it is certain that the other factors will vary to some extent during this period.

The 'Greeks' measure the rate of change in the value of a call or put with respect to these major factors. Fortunately for you, their derivation and calculation (with the exception of delta) are beyond the scope of this book. However, it is important that the reader is aware of the 'Greeks' and what they represent.

Delta measures the rate of change in the value of an option with respect to a change in the underlying equity's share price. The delta for call options will always be between 0 and 1 and for put options it will always be between 0 and −1. Thus, if a delta is 0.8, this means that the call will increase in value by €0.80 for every €1.00 increase in the underlying equity's share price. Clearly, since put option values fall when the value of the underlying equity goes up, the delta of put options will be negative.

Gamma measures the rate of change in delta with respect to a change in the value of the underlying share price. Since delta is central to the valuation of options, it is also important to understand how delta behaves during the lifetime of an option. Consider a call option that has a gamma of 0.05 and a delta of 0.8. If the underlying share price increases in value by €1.00, the delta of the option will grow by 0.05 to 0.85. Similarly, if the underlying share price falls by €1.00, the delta of the option will fall by 0.05 to 0.75.

Gamma has several important characteristics:

1   Gamma is very small when options are deep out of the money (that is, when the share price is low relative to the exercise price for call options or when the share price is high relative to the exercise price for put options).

2   Gamma is very small when options are deep in the money (that is, when the share price is high relative to the exercise price for call options or when the share price is low relative to the exercise price for put options).

3   Gamma is at its highest when options are at the money (that is, when the share price is equal to the exercise price of the option).

4   Gamma is positive when you hold the option (that is, you are long in the option) and negative when you have written the option (that is, you are short in the option).

Theta measures the rate of change in the value of an option with respect to the change in time to maturity of the option. An option will necessarily lose value as the exercise date gets closer and, as a result, theta is always negative. Options lose value faster the closer they are to expiry.

Finally, **vega** measures the rate of change in an option's value with respect to changes in its implied volatility. Implied volatility can be calculated using the Black–Scholes option-pricing model when both the underlying share price and option value are available. It is useful as a measure of expected volatility during the remaining life of an option. Many traders take the market's estimate of an option value to be the correct estimate and use this to calculate the volatility of the asset. Call and put options increase in value when volatility increases and, as a result, vega will always be positive.

22.10   Shares and Bonds as Options

The previous material in this chapter described, explained and valued publicly traded options. This is important material to any finance student because much trading occurs in these listed options. However, the study of options has another purpose for the student of corporate finance.

   You may have heard the one-liner about the elderly gentleman who was surprised to learn that he had been speaking prose all of his life. The same can be said about the corporate finance student and options. Although options were formally defined for the first time in this chapter, many corporate policies discussed earlier in the text were actually options in disguise. Though it is beyond the scope of this chapter to recast all of corporate finance in terms of options, the rest of the chapter considers three examples of implicit options:

1   Shares and bonds as options
2   Capital structure decisions as options
3   Capital budgeting decisions as options.

We begin by illustrating the implicit options in shares and bonds.

Example 22.5

Shares and Bonds as Options

A British firm, Jenkins Brothers Ice Creams, has been awarded the contract for football-related ice cream packaging at the 2018 World Cup in Russia. Because it is unlikely that there will be much need for football-related ice cream after the World Cup, their enterprise will disband afterwards. The firm has issued debt to help finance this venture. Interest and principal due on the debt next year will be £800, at which time the debt will be paid off in full. The firm's cash flows next year are forecast as follows:

	Jenkins Brothers Cash Flow Schedule			
	Very Successful World Cup (£)	Moderately Successful World Cup (£)	Moderately Unsuccessful World Cup (£)	Outright Failure (£)
Cash flow before interest and principal	1,000	850	700	550
Interest and principal	−800	−800	−700	−550
Cash flow to shareholders	200	50	0	0

As can be seen, there are four equally likely scenarios. If either of the first two scenarios occurs, the bondholders will be paid in full. The extra cash flow goes to the shareholders. However, if either of the last two scenarios occurs, the bondholders will not be paid in full. Instead they will receive the firm's entire cash flow, leaving the shareholders with nothing.

This example is similar to the bankruptcy examples presented in our chapters about capital structure. Our new insight is that the relationship between the equity and the firm can be expressed in terms of options. We consider call options first because the intuition is easier. The put option scenario is treated next.

The Firm Expressed in Terms of Call Options

The Shareholders

We now show that equity can be viewed as a call option on the firm. To illustrate this, Figure 22.11 graphs the cash flow to the shareholders as a function of the cash flow to the firm. The shareholders receive nothing if the firm's cash flows are less than £800; here all of the cash flows go to the bondholders. However, the shareholders earn a pound for every pound that the firm receives above £800. The graph looks exactly like the call option graphs that we considered earlier in this chapter.

Figure 22.11 Cash Flow to Shareholders of Jenkins Brothers Ice Creams as a Function of Cash Flow of Firm

The shareholders can be viewed as having a call option on the firm. If the cash flows of the firm exceed £800, the shareholders pay £800 in order to receive the firm's cash flows. If the cash flows of the firm are less than £800, the shareholders do not exercise their option. They walk away from the firm, receiving nothing.

But what is the underlying asset upon which the equity is a call option? The underlying asset is the firm itself. That is, we can view the *bondholders* as owning the firm. However, the shareholders have a call option on the firm with an exercise price of £800.

If the firm's cash flow is above £800, the shareholders would choose to exercise this option. In other words, they would buy the firm from the bondholders for £800. Their net cash flow is the difference between the firm's cash flow and their £800 payment. This would be £200 (= £1,000 − £800) if the World Cup is very successful and £50 (= £850 − £800) if the World Cup is moderately successful.

Should the value of the firm's cash flows be less than £800, the shareholders would not choose to exercise their option. Instead, they would walk away from the firm, as any call option holder would do. The bondholders would then receive the firm's entire cash flow.

This view of the firm is a novel one, and students are frequently bothered by it on first exposure. However, we encourage students to keep looking at the firm in this way until the view becomes second nature to them.

The Bondholders

What about the bondholders? Our earlier cash flow schedule showed that they would get the entire cash flow of the firm if the firm generates less cash than £800. Should the firm earn more than £800, the bondholders would receive only £800. That is, they are entitled only to interest and principal. This schedule is graphed in Figure 22.12.

Figure 22.12 Cash Flow to Bondholders of Jenkins Brothers Ice Creams as a Function of Cash Flow of Firm

The bondholders can be viewed as owning the firm but writing a call option on the firm to the shareholders as well. If the cash flows of the firm exceed £800, the call is exercised against the bondholders. The bondholders give up the firm and receive £800. If the cash flows are less than £800, the call expires. The bondholders receive the cash flows of the firm in this case.

In keeping with our view that the shareholders have a call option on the firm, what does the bondholders' position consist of? The bondholders' position can be described by two claims:

1   They own the firm.
2   They have written a call on the firm with an exercise price of £800.

As we mentioned before, the shareholders walk away from the firm if cash flows are less than £800. Thus, the bondholders retain ownership in this case. However, if the cash flows are greater than £800, the shareholders exercise their option. They call the equity away from the bondholders for £800.

The Firm Expressed in Terms of Put Options

The preceding analysis expresses the positions of the shareholders and the bondholders in terms of call options. We can now express the situation in terms of put options.

The Shareholders

The shareholders' position can be expressed by three claims:

1   They own the firm.

2   They owe £800 in interest and principal to the bondholders.

If the debt were risk-free, these two claims would fully describe the shareholders' situation. However, because of the possibility of default, we have a third claim as well:

3   The shareholders own a put option on the firm with an exercise price of £800. The group of bondholders is the seller of the put.

Now consider two possibilities.

Cash Flow Is Less than £800

Because the put has an exercise price of £800, the put is in the money. The shareholders 'put' – that is, sell – the firm to the bondholders. Normally, the holder of a put receives the exercise price when the asset is sold. However, the shareholders already owe £800 to the bondholders. Thus, the debt of £800 is simply cancelled – and no money changes hands – when the equity is delivered to the bondholders. Because the shareholders give up the equity in exchange for extinguishing the debt, the shareholders end up with nothing if the cash flow is below £800.

Cash Flow Is Greater than £800

Because the put is out of the money here, the shareholders do not exercise. Thus, the shareholders retain ownership of the firm but pay £800 to the bondholders as interest and principal.

The Bondholders

The bondholders' position can be described by two claims:

1   The bondholders are owed £800.

2   They have sold a put option on the firm to the shareholders with an exercise price of £800.

Cash Flow Is Less than £800

As mentioned before, the shareholders will exercise the put in this case. This means that the bondholders are obligated to pay £800 for the firm. Because they are owed £800, the two obligations offset each other. Thus, the bondholders simply end up with the firm in this case.

Cash Flow Is Greater than £800

Here, the shareholders do not exercise the put. Thus, the bondholders merely receive the £800 that is due them.

Expressing the bondholders' position in this way is illuminating. With a riskless default-free bond, the bondholders are owed £800. Thus, we can express the risky bond in terms of a riskless bond and a put:

$$\text{Value of risky bond} = \text{Value of default-free bond} - \text{Value of put option}$$

That is, the value of the risky bond is the value of the default-free bond less the value of the shareholders' option to sell the company for £800.

A Resolution of the Two Views

We have argued that the positions of the shareholders and the bondholders can be viewed either in terms of calls or in terms of puts. These two viewpoints are summarized in Table 22.4.

Table 22.4 Positions of Shareholders and Bondholders in Jenkins Brothers Ice Creams in Terms of Calls and Puts

Shareholders	Bondholders
Positions viewed in terms of call options	
1 Shareholders own a call on the firm with an exercise price of £800.	1 Bondholders own the firm.
	2 Bondholders have sold a call on the firm to the shareholders.
Positions viewed in terms of put options	
1 Shareholders own the firm.	1 Bondholders are owed £800 in interest and principal.
2 Shareholders owe £800 in interest and principal to bondholders.	2 Bondholders have sold a put on the firm to the shareholders.
3 Shareholders own a put option on the firm with an exercise price of £800.	

We have found from experience that it is generally harder for students to think of the firm in terms of puts than in terms of calls. Thus, it would be helpful if there were a way to show that the two viewpoints are equivalent. Fortunately there is *put–call parity*. In an earlier section, we presented the put–call parity relationship as Equation 22.1, which we now repeat:

$$\begin{matrix} \text{Price of underlying} \\ \text{equity} \end{matrix} + \begin{matrix} \text{Price} \\ \text{of put} \end{matrix} = \begin{matrix} \text{Price of} \\ \text{call} \end{matrix} + \begin{matrix} \text{Present value} \\ \text{of exercise price} \end{matrix} \qquad (22.1)$$

Using the results of this section, Equation 22.1 can be rewritten like this:

$$\begin{matrix} \text{Value of call} \\ \text{on firm} \end{matrix} = \begin{matrix} \text{Value of} \\ \text{firm} \end{matrix} = \begin{matrix} \text{Value of put} \\ \text{on firm} \end{matrix} = \begin{matrix} \text{Value of} \\ \text{default-free bond} \end{matrix} \qquad (22.2)$$

$$\begin{matrix} \text{Shareholders' position} \\ \text{in terms of call options} \end{matrix} = \begin{matrix} \text{Shareholders' position} \\ \text{in terms of put options} \end{matrix}$$

Going from Equation 22.1 to Equation 22.2 involves a few steps. First, we treat the firm, not the equity, as the underlying asset in this section. (In keeping with common convention, we refer to the *value* of the firm and the *price* of the equity.) Second, the exercise price is now £800, the principal and interest on the firm's debt. Taking the present value of this amount at the riskless rate yields the value of a default-free bond. Third, the order of the terms in Equation 22.1 is rearranged in Equation 22.2.

Note that the left side of Equation 22.2 is the shareholders' position in terms of call options, as shown in Table 22.3. The right side of Equation 22.2 is the shareholders' position in terms of put options, as shown in the same table. Thus, put–call parity shows that viewing the shareholders' position in terms of call options is equivalent to viewing the shareholders' position in terms of put options.

Now let us rearrange the terms in Equation 22.2 to yield the following:

$$\begin{matrix} \text{Value of} \\ \text{firm} \end{matrix} - \begin{matrix} \text{Value of call} \\ \text{on firm} \end{matrix} = \begin{matrix} \text{Value of} \\ \text{default-free bond} \end{matrix} - \begin{matrix} \text{Value of put} \\ \text{on firm} \end{matrix} \qquad (22.3)$$

$$\begin{matrix} \text{Bondholders' position in} \\ \text{terms of call options} \end{matrix} = \begin{matrix} \text{Boldholders' position in} \\ \text{terms of put options} \end{matrix}$$

The left side of Equation 22.3 is the bondholders' position in terms of call options, as shown in Table 22.4. (The minus sign on this side of the equation indicates that the bondholders are *writing* a call.) The right side of the equation is the bondholders' position in terms of put options, as shown in Table 22.4. Thus, put–call parity shows that viewing the bondholders' position in terms of call options is equivalent to viewing the bondholders' position in terms of put options.

A Note about Loan Guarantees

In the Jenkins Brothers example given earlier, the bondholders bore the risk of default. Of course, bondholders generally ask for an interest rate that is high enough to compensate them for bearing risk. When firms experience financial distress, they can no longer attract new debt at moderate interest rates. Thus, firms experiencing distress have frequently sought loan guarantees from the government. Our framework can be used to understand these guarantees.

If the firm defaults on a guaranteed loan, the government must make up the difference. In other words, a government guarantee converts a risky bond into a riskless bond. What is the value of this guarantee?

Recall that with option pricing:

$$\text{Value of default-free bond} = \text{Value of risky bond} + \text{Value of put firm}$$

This equation shows that the government is assuming an obligation that has a cost equal to the value of a put option.

This analysis differs from that of either politicians or company spokespeople. They generally say that the guarantee will cost the taxpayers nothing because the guarantee enables the firm to attract debt, thereby staying solvent. However, it should be pointed out that although solvency may be a strong possibility, it is never a certainty. Thus, when the guarantee is made, the government's obligation has a cost in terms of present value. To say that a government guarantee costs the government nothing is like saying a put on the equity of Apple plc has no value because the equity is *likely* to rise in price.

Several governments (such as Britain, France, Germany and the US) used loan guarantees to help firms get through the major recession that began in 2008. Under the guarantees, if a company defaulted on new loans, the lenders could obtain the full value of their claims from the company's government. From the lender's point of view, the loans became as risk-free as Treasury bonds. Loan guarantees enable firms to borrow cash to get through a difficult time.

Who benefits from a typical loan guarantee?

1   If existing risky bonds are guaranteed, all gains accrue to the existing bondholders. The shareholders gain nothing because the limited liability of corporations absolves the shareholders of any obligation in bankruptcy.

2   If new debt is issued and guaranteed, the new debtholders do not gain. Rather, in a competitive market, they must accept a low interest rate because of the debt's low risk. The shareholders gain here because they are able to issue debt at a low interest rate. In addition, some of the gains accrue to the old bondholders because the firm's value is greater than would otherwise be true. Therefore, if shareholders want all the gains from loan guarantees, they should renegotiate or retire existing bonds before the guarantee is in place.

3   Obviously, employees of distressed firms benefit because otherwise the firm may go into bankruptcy if new funding is not provided from lenders. In addition, employees of firms that are suppliers and customers of distressed firms would also benefit. This was the main rationale underlying the government rescue packages of 2008 and 2009.

Summary and Conclusions

This chapter serves as an introduction to options.

1   The most familiar options are puts and calls. These options give the holder the right to sell or buy shares of equity at a given exercise price. American options can be exercised any time up to and including the expiration date. European options can be exercised only on the expiration date.

2   We showed that a strategy of buying a share and buying a put is equivalent to a strategy of buying a call and buying a zero coupon bond. From this, the put–call parity relationship was established:

$$\text{Value of stock} + \text{Value of put} - \text{Value of call} = \text{Present value of exercise price}$$

3   The value of an option depends on five factors:
   (a)   The price of the underlying asset
   (b)   The exercise price
   (c)   The expiration date
   (d)   The variability of the underlying asset
   (e)   The interest rate on risk-free bonds.

The Black–Scholes model can determine the intrinsic price of an option from these five factors.

4   The 'Greeks' (delta, gamma, theta and vega) measure different aspects of the risk of options.

5   Much of corporate financial theory can be presented in terms of options. In this chapter, we pointed out that:

   (a) Equity can be represented as a call option on the firm.

   (b) Shareholders enhance the value of their call by increasing the risk of their firm.

Questions and Problems

CONCEPT

1   **Options**   Many laypeople find the whole concept of options difficult to understand. Use a non-financial example to explain how options work and why they are so important for flexible decision-making. What are the types of option contracts corporations can buy? Why would a corporation buy these options? Explain.

2   **American versus European Options**   What is the difference between an American and European option? Is an American call option on a dividend-paying stock always worth at least as much as its intrinsic value? How about for a European call option? Explain.

3   **American Versus European Options**   Why is it that an American option is always worth the same as a European option? If it were not, what strategy could an arbitrageur use to profit?

4   **Options and Asset Values**   Suppose that UK government bond yields unexpectedly rise. Ceteris paribus, what would happen to the value of call options and put options?

5   **Option Quotes**   Look at Table 22.1. Normally the settlement price falls as the strike price increases for call options. Conversely, the settlement price generally increases as the strike price gets higher for put options. Why do you think this is not the case with Air France-KLM? Explain.

6   **Option Combinations**   Why would a corporation wish to combine put and call options on a commodity? Provide an example of a case where this might happen.

7   **Valuing Options**   Review the factors that affect the value of call and put options.

8   **Option Pricing**   Why can't you just value an option using discounted cash flows, as in net present value?

9   **The Greeks**   What are the Greeks? Why are they important to a corporation?

10   **Shares and Bonds as Options**   Show how a share of equity can be viewed as an option. Why is this perspective helpful?

11   **Options and Corporate Decisions**   In many countries, governments have encouraged bank mergers to reduce their risk. Use option analysis to show why this may be bad news for the bank's shareholders. Does this mean that you should not buy the shares of a newly merged bank? Explain.

REGULAR

12   **Option Pricing**   The Pirelli & C. SpA share price is €8.895. A call option with an exercise price of €9 sells for €0.35 and a put option with the same exercise price sells for €0.65. Does this make sense? Explain.

13   **Two-state Option Pricing Model**   T-bills currently yield 2.1 per cent and the Man Group plc share price is £0.97. There is no possibility that the equity will be worth less than £0.50 per share in one year.

   (a)   What is the value of a call option with a £0.97 exercise price? What is the intrinsic value?

   (b)   What is the value of a call option with a £0.70 exercise price? What is the intrinsic value?

   (c)   What is the value of a put option with a £1.10 exercise price? What is the intrinsic value?

14   **Understanding Option Quotes**   Use the option quote information from Euronext Liffe shown here for Xstrata plc to answer the questions that follow. The equity is currently selling for £11.025.

	Calls								Puts					
Settl.	O.I.	Day Vol	Last	Bid	Ask		Strike		Bid	Ask	Last	Day Vol	O.I.	Settl.
463.00	–	–	–	431.50	490.00	C	6.40	P	–	5.50	–	–	62	0.50
423.00	558	–	–	391.50	450.00	C	6.80	P	–	6.00	–	–	781	0.50
383.00	35	–	–	352.50	410.00	C	7.20	P	–	6.50	–	–	1,276	1.00
343.00	27	–	–	312.50	370.00	C	7.60	P	–	5.50	–	–	47	2.50
303.00	419	–	–	272.00	330.50	C	8.00	P	0.50	7.00	–	–	641	3.50
263.50	88	–	–	233.50	291.50	C	8.40	P	2.50	8.50	–	–	135	5.50
225.50	583	–	–	208.00	238.00	C	8.80	P	7.00	12.50	–	–	944	9.50
188.50	16	–	–	171.00	201.00	C	9.20	P	12.50	17.50	–	–	1,339	14.50
153.50	149	–	–	144.00	159.00	C	9.60	P	20.00	22.50	–	–	1,017	21.00
122.00	2,620	–	–	112.00	127.00	C	10.00	P	30.00	33.50	–	–	1,830	31.00
80.50	154	–	–	76.00	82.00	C	10.60	P	50.50	55.00	49.00	15	1,095	51.00
58.50	699	–	–	55.00	60.00	C	11.00	P	69.00	74.50	66.00	15	4,477	69.50
38.00	4,742	20	43.50	34.50	39.00	C	11.50	P	97.50	104.00	–	–	1,729	99.00
22.50	3,537	47	21.00	20.00	23.50	C	12.00	P	130.00	142.50	127.00	3	3,038	134.00
8.00	2,456	–	–	5.50	9.50	C	13.00	P	205.00	235.00	205.00	5	973	219.00
1.50	1,679	–	–	–	5.00	C	14.00	P	285.50	345.00	–	–	454	313.00
0.00	140	–	–	–	3.50	C	15.00	P	384.00	443.00	–	–	8	412.00
0.00	116	–	–	–	5.00	C	16.00	P	484.00	543.50	–	–	22	512.00

(a) Are the call options in the money? What is the intrinsic value of an Xstrata plc call option?

(b) Are the put options in the money? What is the intrinsic value of an Xstrata plc put option?

(c) Looking at the quotes on their own, do you think that the market expects the price of Xstrata to increase or decrease during the period of the option? What range of prices are anticipated? Look at the share price history for Xstrata on Yahoo! Finance and find out what actually happened. Who made a profit from their trading – the call or put holders?

15 **Calculating Pay-offs** Use the option quote information on Ageas from Euronext Liffe shown here to answer the questions that follow.

Codes and Classification						
Code	**FOR**	Market	**NYSE Liffe Amsterdam**	Vol.	**125**	13/04/12
Exercise Type	**American**	Currency	€	O.I	**507,670**	12/04/12

Underlying						
Name	**FORTIS**	ISIN	**BE0003801181**	Market	**Euronext Amsterdam**	
Currency	€	Best Bid	–	Best Ask	–	
Time	CET	Last	**1.493**	Last Change %	**14.93**	
Volume	**70,649,448**	High	**1.68**	Low	**1.332**	

June 2012 Prices - 13/04/12												EXTENDED VIEW		
	Calls											Puts		
Settl.	O.I.	Day Vol	Last	Bid	Ask		Strike		Bid	Ask	Last	Day Vol	O.I.	Settl.
0.28	1,191	–	–	0.25	0.29	C	1.20	P	0.03	0.05	–	–	1,453	0.04
0.11	759	–	–	0.10	0.12	C	1.40	P	0.09	0.12	–	–	662	0.11
0.06	20	–	–	0.05	0.08	C	1.50	P	0.15	0.18	–	–	–	0.17
0.03	1,300	–	–	0.02	0.05	C	1.60	P	0.21	0.26	–	–	1,777	0.24
0.02	110	–	–	–	0.04	C	1.70	P	0.29	0.35	–	–	80	0.33

(a) Suppose you buy 20 contracts of the June €1.50 call option. How much will you pay, ignoring commissions?

(b) In part (a), suppose that Ageas equity is selling for €1.70 per share on the expiration date. How much is your options investment worth? What if the terminal share price is €1.35? Explain.

(c) Suppose you buy 10 contracts of the June €1.20 put option. What is your maximum gain? On the expiration date, Ageas is selling for €1.14 per share. How much is your options investment worth? What is your net gain?

(d) In part (c), suppose you *sell* 10 of the June €1.20 put contracts. What is your net gain or loss if Ageas is selling for €1.14 at expiration? For €1.32? What is the break-even price – that is, the terminal share price that results in a zero profit?

16 **Two-state Option Pricing Model**   The share price of ABC plc will be either £2 or £1.5 at the end of the year. Call options are available with one year to expiration. UK government bond yields are currently at 3 per cent.

(a) Suppose the current share price of ABC plc is £1.74. What is the value of the call option if the exercise price is £1.75 per share?

(b) Suppose the exercise price is £1.9 in part (a). What is the value of the call option now?

17 **Two-state Option Pricing Model**   The price of National Bank of Greece shares will be either €1.74 or €1.43 at the end of the year. Call options are available with one year to expiration. T-bills currently yield 7 per cent.

(a) Suppose the current price of National Bank of Greece shares is €1.68. What is the value of the call option if the exercise price is €1.50 per share?

(b) Suppose the exercise price is €1.68 in part (a). What is the value of the call option now?

18 **Put–Call Parity**   BP plc shares are currently selling for £4.29 per share. A put option with an exercise price of £4.40 sells for £0.25 and expires in 3 months. If the risk-free rate of interest is 2.6 per cent per year, compounded continuously, what is the price of a call option with the same exercise price?

19 **Put–Call Parity**   Alcatel-Lucent put option and a call option with an exercise price of €1 and 3 months to expiration sell for €0.28 and €0.11, respectively. If the risk-free rate is 2.5 per cent per year, compounded continuously, what is the current share price?

20 **Put–Call Parity**   Arcellormittal call and put options with an exercise price of €17 expire in 4 months and sell for €2.07 and €2.03, respectively. If the equity is currently priced at €17.03, what is the annual continuously compounded rate of interest?

21 **Black–Scholes and Asset Value**   Coal mining is becoming more popular because of the demand for energy in Asia. Assume that you have the rights to a coal mine and the most recent valuation of the mine was £6.7 million. Because of increasing demand from Asia, the price of similar mines has grown by 15 per cent per annum, with an annual standard deviation of 20 per cent. A buyer has recently approached you and wants an option to buy the mine in the next 12 months for £7 million. The risk-free rate of interest is 3 per cent per year, compounded continuously. How much should you charge for the option?

22 **Black–Scholes and Asset Value**   In the previous problem, suppose you wanted the option to sell the mine to the buyer in one year. Assuming all the facts are the same, describe the transaction that would occur today. What is the price of the transaction today?

23 **Black–Scholes**   The spot price of XYZ plc is 394.5p, with a standard deviation of 20 per cent. A call option on the stock expires in 219 days, and it has a strike price of 400p, with a quoted price of 18p. The risk-free rate is 1 per cent.

(a) Find the Black–Scholes value of the call.

(b) Why does the Black–Scholes value not match the quoted price of the call?

24 **Black–Scholes**   Xstrata plc is currently priced at £10.52. A call option with an expiration of 6 months has an exercise price of £9.00. The risk-free rate is 3 per cent per year, compounded continuously, and the standard deviation of the equity's return is infinitely large. What is the price of the call option?

25 **Equity as an Option**   Shire plc has a zero coupon bond issue outstanding with £12 billion face value that matures in 5 years. The current market value of the firm's assets is £20 billion. The standard deviation of the return on the firm's assets is 23 per cent per year, and the annual risk-free rate is 3 per cent per year, compounded continuously. Based on the Black–Scholes model, what is the market value of the firm's equity and debt?

26 Equity as an Option and NPV Suppose Shire plc (see Question 25) is considering two mutually exclusive investments. Project A has an NPV of £700 million, and project B has an NPV of £1.2 billion. As the result of taking project A, the standard deviation of the return on the firm's assets will increase to 55 per cent per year. If project B is taken, the standard deviation will fall to 19 per cent per year.

(a) What is the value of the firm's equity and debt if project A is undertaken? If project B is undertaken?

(b) Which project would the shareholders prefer? Can you reconcile your answer with the NPV rule?

(c) Suppose the shareholders and bondholders are in fact the same group of investors. Would this affect your answer to (b)?

(d) What does this problem suggest to you about shareholder incentives?

27 Mergers and Equity as an Option Suppose Shire plc (Question 25) decides to reorient its operations and, as a result, the return on assets now has a standard deviation of 30 per cent per year.

(a) What is the value of Shire plc equity now? The value of debt?

(b) What was the gain or loss for shareholders? For bondholders?

(c) What happened to shareholder value here?

28 Equity as an Option and NPV A company has a single zero coupon bond outstanding that matures in 10 years with a face value of £30 million. The current value of the company's assets is £22 million, and the standard deviation of the return on the firm's assets is 39 per cent per year. The risk-free rate is 6 per cent per year, compounded continuously.

(a) What is the current market value of the company's equity?

(b) What is the current market value of the company's debt?

(c) What is the company's continuously compounded cost of debt?

(d) The company has a new project available. The project has an NPV of £750,000. If the company undertakes the project, what will be the new market value of equity? Assume volatility is unchanged.

(e) Assuming the company undertakes the new project and does not borrow any additional funds, what is the new continuously compounded cost of debt? What is happening here?

29 Two-state Option Pricing Model Ken is interested in buying a European call option written on Southeastern Airlines plc, a non-dividend-paying equity, with a strike price of £110 and one year until expiration. Currently, Southeastern's equity sells for £100 per share. In one year Ken knows that Southeastern's shares will be trading at either £125 per share or £80 per share. Ken is able to borrow and lend at the risk-free EAR of 2.5 per cent.

(a) What should the call option sell for today?

(b) If no options currently trade on the equity, is there a way to create a synthetic call option with identical pay-offs to the call option just described? If there is, how would you do it?

(c) How much does the synthetic call option cost? Is this greater than, less than, or equal to what the actual call option costs? Does this make sense?

30 Two-state Option Pricing Model Maverick Manufacturing plc must purchase gold in 3 months for use in its operations. Maverick's management has estimated that if the price of gold were to rise above $875 per ounce, the firm would go bankrupt. The current price of gold is $850 per ounce. The firm's chief financial officer believes that the price of gold will either rise to $900 per ounce or fall to $825 per ounce over the next 3 months. Management wishes to eliminate any risk of the firm going bankrupt. Maverick can borrow and lend at the risk-free APR of 16.99 per cent.

(a) Should the company buy a call option or a put option on gold? To avoid bankruptcy, what strike price and time to expiration would the company like this option to have?

(b) How much should such an option sell for in the open market?

(c) If no options currently trade on gold, is there a way for the company to create a synthetic option with identical pay-offs to the option just described? If there is, how would the firm do it?

(d) How much does the synthetic option cost? Is this greater than, less than, or equal to what the actual option costs? Does this make sense?

31 Black–Scholes and Collar Cost An investor is said to take a position in a 'collar' if she buys the asset, buys an out-of-the-money put option on the asset, and sells an out-of-the-money call option on the asset. The two options should have the same time to expiration. Suppose Marie wishes to purchase a collar on Zurich Re, a non-dividend-paying equity, with 6 months until expiration. She would like the put to have a strike price of 50 Swiss francs (SFr) and the call to have a strike price of SFr120. The current price of Zurich Re's equity is SFr80 per share. Marie can borrow and lend at the continuously compounded risk-free rate of 10 per cent per annum, and the annual standard deviation of the equity's return is 50 per cent. Use the Black–Scholes model to calculate the total cost of the collar that Marie is interested in buying. What is the effect of the collar?

CHALLENGE

32 **Debt Valuation and Time to Maturity** McLemore Industries has a zero coupon bond issue that matures in 2 years with a face value of £30,000. The current value of the company's assets is £13,000, and the standard deviation of the return on assets is 60 per cent per year.

  (a) Assume the risk-free rate is 5 per cent per year, compounded continuously. What is the value of a risk-free bond with the same face value and maturity as the company's bond?

  (b) What price would the bondholders have to pay for a put option on the firm's assets with a strike price equal to the face value of the debt?

  (c) Using the answers from (a) and (b), what is the value of the firm's debt? What is the continuously compounded yield on the company's debt?

  (d) From an examination of the value of the assets of McLemore Industries, and the fact that the debt must be repaid in 2 years, it seems likely that the company will default on its debt. Management has approached bondholders and proposed a plan whereby the company would repay the same face value of debt, but the repayment would not occur for 5 years. What is the value of the debt under the proposed plan? What is the new continuously compounded yield on the debt? Explain why this occurs.

33 **Debt Valuation and Asset Variance** Brozik plc has a zero coupon bond that matures in 5 years with a face value of £60,000. The current value of the company's assets is £57,000, and the standard deviation of its return on assets is 50 per cent per year. The risk-free rate is 6 per cent per year, compounded continuously.

  (a) What is the value of a risk-free bond with the same face value and maturity as the current bond?

  (b) What is the value of a put option on the firm's assets with a strike price equal to the face value of the debt?

  (c) Using the answers from (a) and (b), what is the value of the firm's debt? What is the continuously compounded yield on the company's debt?

  (d) Assume the company can restructure its assets so that the standard deviation of its return on assets increases to 60 per cent per year. What happens to the value of the debt? What is the new continuously compounded yield on the debt? Reconcile your answers in (c) and (d).

  (e) What happens to bondholders if the company restructures its assets? What happens to shareholders? How does this create an agency problem?

34 **Two-state Option Pricing and Corporate Valuation** Strudler Property plc, a construction firm financed by both debt and equity, is undertaking a new project. If the project is successful, the value of the firm in one year will be £500 million but if the project is a failure, the firm will be worth only £320 million. The current value of Strudler is £400 million, a figure that includes the prospects for the new project. Strudler has outstanding zero coupon bonds due in one year with a face value of £380 million. Treasury bills that mature in one year yield 7 per cent EAR. Strudler pays no dividends.

  (a) Use the two-state option pricing model to find the current value of Strudler's debt and equity.

  (b) Suppose Strudler has 500,000 shares of equity outstanding. What is the price per share of the firm's equity?

  (c) Compare the market value of Strudler's debt to the present value of an equal amount of debt that is riskless with one year until maturity. Is the firm's debt worth more than, less than, or the same as the riskless debt? Does this make sense? What factors might cause these two values to be different?

  (d) Suppose that in place of the preceding project, Strudler's management decides to undertake a project that is even more risky. The value of the firm will either increase to £800 million or decrease to £200 million by the end of the year. Surprisingly, management concludes that the value of the firm today will remain at exactly £400 million if this risky project is substituted for the less risky one. Use the two-state option pricing model to determine the value of the firm's debt and equity if the firm plans on undertaking this new project. Which project do bondholders prefer?

35 **Black–Scholes and Dividends** In addition to the five factors discussed in the chapter, dividends also affect the price of an option. The Black–Scholes option pricing model with dividends is:

$$C = S \times e^{-dt} \times N(d_1) - E \times e^{-Rt} \times N(d_2)$$

$$d_1 = [\ln(S/E) + (R - d + \sigma^2/2) \times t]/(\sigma \times \sqrt{t}).$$

$$d_2 = d_1 - \sigma \times \sqrt{t}$$

All of the variables are the same as the Black–Scholes model without dividends except for the variable d, which is the continuously compounded dividend yield on the share.

(a) What effect do you think the dividend yield will have on the price of a call option? Explain.

(b) Genmab A/S is currently priced at 2.26 Danish Kroner (DKr) per share, the standard deviation of its return is 50 per cent per year, and the risk-free rate is 5 per cent per year compounded continuously. What is the price of a call option with a strike price of DKr2.00 and a maturity of 6 months if the share has a dividend yield of 2 per cent per year?

36 **Put–Call Parity and Dividends** The put–call parity condition is altered when dividends are paid. The dividend adjusted put–call parity formula is:

$$S \times e^{-dt} + P = E \times e^{-Rt} + C$$

where d is again the continuously compounded dividend yield.

(a) What effect do you think the dividend yield will have on the price of a put option? Explain.

(b) From the previous question, what is the price of a call option with a strike price of DKr2.00 and a maturity of 6 months if the share has a dividend yield of 2 per cent per year? What is the price of a put option with the same strike price and time to expiration as the call option?

37 **Put Delta** In the chapter, we noted that the delta for a put option is $N(d_1) - 1$. Is this the same thing as $-N(-d_1)$? (*Hint:* Yes, but why?)

38 **Black–Scholes Put Pricing Model** Use the Black–Scholes model for pricing a call, put–call parity, and the previous question to show that the Black–Scholes model for directly pricing a put can be written as follows:

$$P = E \times e^{-Rt} \times N(-d_2) - S \times N(-d_1)$$

39 **Black–Scholes** An equity is currently priced at £50. The share will never pay a dividend. The risk-free rate is 12 per cent per year, compounded continuously, and the standard deviation of the share's return is 60 per cent. A European call option on the share has a strike price of £100 and no expiration date, meaning that it has an infinite life. Based on Black–Scholes, what is the value of the call option? Do you see a paradox here? Do you see a way out of the paradox?

40 **Delta** You purchase one call and sell one put with the same strike price and expiration date. What is the delta of your portfolio? Why?

Exam Question (45 minutes)

A developer has just acquired 60 acres of property in Ngorongoro to develop a safari wildlife centre. The safari centre will also include a hotel development. In order to generate operating capital, the developer is selling rights. The rights give the holder of the contract the right to purchase a lodge in the hotel development for a fixed price. Each lodge is half an acre. The agreements expire 6 months after they are signed.

The developer is offering the following inducement. A potential lodge owner can purchase the lodge for TSh25million at the end of 6 months if the lodge owner enters into the contract this week. The purchase price for a lodge increases to TSh40million on all contracts signed after this week.

1 Describe and explain the type of option being sold by the developer. (15 marks)

2 Describe and explain the position held by the potential lodge owner as an option. (15 marks)

3 Discuss the risks associated with this transaction to both the developer and the lodge owner. (15 marks)

4   Suppose we purchased a right on one of the lodges during the inducement period, and it has just been discovered that a very rare type of lion has been discovered close to the lodge. Explain what you think will happen to the value of the right that you own. Is this contract in the money? Explain. (15 marks)

5   Suppose that the developer was selling two contracts. One contract permits you to purchase a lodge any time during the 6-month period, and the other allows you to purchase the lodge only at the end of 6 months. Which of the two contracts is worth more? Explain. (15 marks)

6   To reduce your cash outflows shortly before it became public knowledge that the rare lions live near the lodge, you sign a contract with a colleague. This contract gives you the right to sell the lodge at any time in the next 6 months to your friend for TSh35million. Describe your position and that of your friend. (15 marks)

7   Describe the potential obligations associated with the options involving the developer and the two friends. Use diagrams to illustrate your answer. (10 marks)

Mini Case

Clissold Industries Options

You are currently working for Clissold Industries. The company, which went public 5 years ago, engages in the design, production and distribution of lighting equipment and speciality products worldwide. Because of recent events, Mal Clissold, the company president, is concerned about the company's risk, so he asks for your input.

In your discussion with Mal, you explain that the CAPM proposes that the market risk of the company's equity is the determinant of its expected return. Even though Mal agrees with this, he argues that his portfolio consists entirely of Clissold Industry shares and options, so he is concerned with the total risk, or standard deviation, of the company's equity. Furthermore, even though he has calculated the standard deviation of the company's equity for the past 5 years, he would like an estimate of the share's volatility moving forward.

Mal states that you can find the estimated volatility of the share for future periods by calculating the implied standard deviation of option contracts on the company equity. When you examine the factors that affect the price of an option, all of the factors except the standard deviation of the shares are directly observable in the market. You can also observe the option price as well. Mal states that because you can observe all of the option factors except the standard deviation, you can simply solve the Black–Scholes model and find the implied standard deviation.

To help you find the implied standard deviation of the company's equity, Mal has provided you with the following option prices on four call options that expire in 6 months. The risk-free rate is 6 per cent, and the current share price is £50.

Strike Price (£)	Option Price (£)
30	23.00
40	16.05
50	9.75
55	7.95

1   How many different volatilities would you expect to see for the equity?

2   Unfortunately, solving for the implied standard deviation is not as easy as Mal suggests. In fact, there is no direct solution for the standard deviation of the equity even if we have all other variables for the Black–Scholes model. Mal would still like you to estimate the implied standard deviation of the share. To do this, set up a spreadsheet using the Solver function in Excel to calculate the implied volatilities for each of the options.

3   Are all of the implied volatilities for the options the same? (*Hint:* No.) What are the possible reasons that can cause different volatilities for these options?

4   After you discuss the importance of volatility on option prices, your boss mentions that he has heard of the FTSE 100 Volatility Index (VFTSE) on Euronext. What is the VFTSE and what does it represent?

FTSE100 VOLAT.INDX			
NYSE EURONEXT			[Realtime data]
Last −0.82% **20.55** € 13/04/12 18:05:01 CEST	**Open** 20.72	**High** 21.56	**Low** 19.71

Codes and classification			
ISIN **Euronext code**	QS0011052162 QS0011052162	**Market** **Mnemo**	Amsterdam Local - VFTSE
Market type	Indice	**Calculation mode**	-

Market data DLY	13/04/12 18:05 CEST	
Last (€)		**20.55**
Change D/D-1 (%)		−0.82%
Day		
First (€)	09:00	20.72
High (€)	09:43	21.56
Low (€)	09:43	19.71
/31-12		
High	12/04/12	24.24
Low	14/03/12	10.20

FTSE100 VOLAT.INDX - Intraday 13/04/2012 17:32 (CEST)

Source: Data from Euronext

5   Look for current option quotes for the FTSE 100 Volatility Index on Euronext. To find these, search on the Euronext website for the ISIN: QS0011052162. What does the implied volatility of a VFTSE option represent?

Relevant Accounting Standards

IAS 39 *Financial Instruments: Recognition and Measurement* and IFRS 7 *Financial Instruments: Disclosure* are exceptionally important for options. Since the potential exposure to losses from options can be significant, it is important their impact is reflected in a firm's accounting statements. Visit the IASPlus website (www.iasplus.com) for more information.

Reference

Hull, J.C. (2012) *Options, Futures and Other Derivatives*, 8th edn (Upper Saddle River, NJ: Prentice Hall).

Additional Reading

A very rich empirical and theoretical research field considers option pricing dynamics. The reference list below focuses on options as they relate to corporate finance.

1   Amram, M., F. Li and C.A. Perkins (2006) 'How Kimberly-Clark Uses Real Options', *Journal of Applied Corporate Finance*, Vol. 18, No. 2, 40–47.

2   Giaccotto, C., G.M. Goldberg and S.P. Hegde (2007) 'The Value of Embedded Real Options: Evidence from Consumer Automobile Lease Contracts', *The Journal of Finance*, Vol. 62, No. 1, 411–445.

3   Granadier, S.R. and A. Malenko (2011) 'Real Options Signaling Games with Applications to Corporate Finance', *Review of Financial Studies*, Vol. 24, No. 2, 3993–4036.

4   Lambrecht, B.M. and G. Pawlina (2010) 'Corporate Finance and the (In)efficient Exercise of Real Options', *Multinational Finance Journal*, Vol. 14, No. 1/2, 129–156.

5   McDonald, R.L. (2006) 'The Role of Real Options in Capital Budgeting: Theory and Practice', *Journal of Applied Corporate Finance*, Vol. 18, No. 2, 28–39.

Endnotes

1   We use *buyer, owner* and *holder* interchangeably.

2   This example assumes that the call lets the holder purchase one share at £7.00. In reality, one call option contract would let the holder purchase 100 shares. The profit would then equal £100 [= (£8.00 − £7.00) × 100].

3   Actually, because of differing exercise prices, the two graphs are not quite mirror images of each other.

4   Our discussion in this section is of American options because they are more commonly traded in the real world. As necessary, we will indicate differences for European options. American options are differentiated from European options through their ability to be exercised at any time before the expiration date. The terminology has nothing to do with where the options are traded.

5   This relationship need not hold for a European call option. Consider a firm with two otherwise identical European call options, one expiring at the end of May and the other expiring a few months later. Further assume that a *huge* dividend is paid in early June. If the first call is exercised at the end of May, its holder will receive the underlying share. If he does not sell the share, he will receive the large dividend shortly thereafter. However, the holder of the second call will receive the share through exercise after the dividend is paid. Because the market knows that the holder of this option will miss the dividend, the value of the second call option could be less than the value of the first.

6   Though this result must hold in the case of an American put, it need not hold for a European put.

7   A full treatment of this assumption can be found in Hull (2012).

8   This method is called *linear interpolation*. It is only one of a number of possible methods of interpolation.

Options and Corporate Finance: Extensions and Applications

In recent years, many companies have exchanged their employee share options for restricted stock units (RSUs). An RSU is a share of equity that cannot be sold or exchanged until it is vested. The vesting period can vary, but is usually between 3 and 5 years. When an RSU vests, the employee receives a full share of equity. The biggest advantage of RSUs for employees is that they receive the equity no matter what the share price. In comparison, with employee share options the employee may receive nothing.

The reason for this change in policy was that most executive share options were worthless as a result of the major market falls in the immediate aftermath of the global financial crisis. The main purpose for executive share options is that they reward employees for good performance and loyalty to their company. If the options are worth nothing, there is no financial reason why the best executives should stay in a company if their services are demanded elsewhere. Restricted stock units are therefore better in a down market because executives always receive something for their efforts.

KEY NOTATIONS

C	Value of a call option
P	Value of a put option
S	Current share price
E	Exercise price of option
R	Annual risk-free rate of return, continuously compounded
σ^2	Variance (per year) of the continuous share price return
t	Time (in years) to expiration date
$N(d)$	Probability that a standardized, normally distributed, random variable will be less than or equal to d

$$d_1 = [\ln(S/E) + (R + \sigma^2/2)t]/\sqrt{\sigma^2 t}$$

$$d_2 = d_1 - \sqrt{\sigma^2 t}$$

23.1 Executive Share Options

Why Options?

Chapter 2
Page 32

Executive compensation (see **Chapter 2**, section 2.2 for more on executive compensation) is usually made up of base salary plus some or all of the following elements:

1 Base salary.

2 Annual bonuses.

3 Long-term incentives, such as retirement contributions, options and restricted stock units.

When stock markets are on an upward trajectory, the final component of compensation, options, is by far the biggest part of total compensation for many top executives. In many parts of Europe, full disclosure of executive pay is not yet normal practice. However, this has not stopped politicians and the media from decrying the total pay of executives, whose share options are a major component of their total remuneration. Figure 23.1 presents a breakdown of chief executive pay in Europe in 2010. Bonuses represent any payments paid for performance during the year and LTI is long-term incentives, which include executive share options.

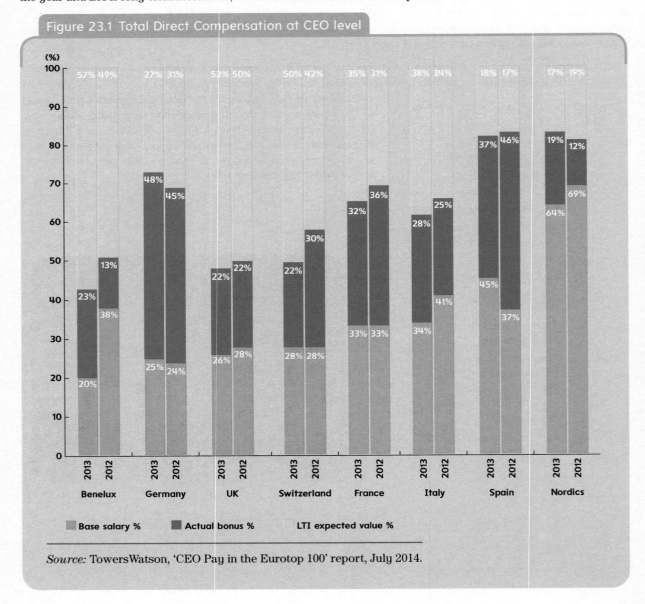

Figure 23.1 Total Direct Compensation at CEO level

Source: TowersWatson, 'CEO Pay in the Eurotop 100' report, July 2014.

As can be seen, long-term incentives, such as executive share options, have been extremely popular in European countries, particularly in Benelux, France, UK and Switzerland. Some of the reasons given for using executive share options were these:

1   Options align executives' interests to that of the shareholders. By aligning interests, executives are more likely to make decisions for the benefit of the shareholders.

2   Options allow the company to lower the executives' base pay. This removes pressures on morale caused by disparities between the salaries of executives and those of other employees.

3   Options put an executive's pay at risk, rather than guaranteeing it regardless of the performance of the firm.

At the same time, there are a number of significant criticisms of executive share options. The most notable criticism is that share options encourage managers to take on more risky projects so as to increase the size of their personal remuneration. Given the role of executive compensation in the banking sector and the perverse incentives to maximize bank share price at the expense of bank risk, regulators across the world have moved to limit top executive pay. However, as it stands, regulators have only been successful in constraining executive pay and not reducing it.

Valuing Executive Compensation

In this section, we value executive share options. Not surprisingly, the complexity of the total compensation package often makes valuation a difficult task. The economic value of the options depends on factors such as the volatility of the underlying equity and the exact terms of the option grant.

Only a few countries fully disclose the details of executive pay and in Example 23.1, we will estimate the economic value of the options held by the chief executive of a hypothetical company. Example 23.1 is necessarily simplistic but it serves to illustrate the way we can value executive share options. Simple matters such as requiring the executive to hold the option for a fixed period, the freeze-out period, before exercising, can significantly diminish the value of a standard option.

Example 23.1

Executive Options

Consider Ray Davies, the chief executive officer (CEO) of KinKins, who has been granted 2 million executive share options. The average share price at the time of the options grant was €39.71. We will assume that his options are at the money. The risk-free rate is 5 per cent and the options expire in 5 years. The preceding information implies that:

1   The share price (S) of €39.71 equals the exercise price (E).

2   The risk-free rate $R = 0.05$.

3   The time interval $t = 5$.

In addition, the variance of KinKins is estimated to be $(0.2168)^2 = 0.0470$.

This information allows us to value Ray Davies's options using the Black–Scholes model:

$$C = SN(d_1) - Ee^{-Rt}N(d_2)$$

$$d_1 = [(R + 1/2\sigma^2)t]/\sqrt{\sigma^2 t} = 0.758$$

$$d_2 = d_1 - \sqrt{\sigma^2 t} = 0.273$$

$$N(d_1) = 0.776$$

$$N(d_2) = 0.608$$

$$e^{-0.05 \times 5} = 0.7788$$

$$C = €39.71 \times 0.776 - €39.71 \times (0.778 \times 0.608) = €12.03$$

Thus the value of a call option on one share of KinKins equity is €12.03. Because Mr Davies was granted options on 2 million shares, the market value of his options, as estimated by the Black–Scholes formula, is about €24 million (= 2 million × €12.03).

Equally important, the Black–Scholes formula has to be modified if the equity pays dividends and is no longer applicable if the volatility of the equity is changing randomly over time. Intuitively, a call option on a dividend-paying equity is worth less than a call on an equity that pays no dividends: all other things being equal, the dividends will lower the share price. Nevertheless, let us see what we can do.

The value of the options we computed in Example 23.1 is the economic value of the options if they were to trade in the market. The real question is this: whose value are we talking about? Are these the costs of the options to the company? Are they the values of the options to the executives?

The total value of €24 million for Ray Davies's options in Example 23.1 is the amount that the options would trade at in the financial markets and that traders and investors would be willing to pay for them.[1] If KinKins was very large, it would not be unreasonable to view this as the cost of granting the options to the CEO, Ray Davies. Of course, in return, the company would expect Mr Davies to improve the value of the company to its shareholders by more than this amount. As we have seen, perhaps the main purpose of options is to align the interests of management with those of the shareholders of the firm. Under no circumstances, though, is the €24 million necessarily a fair measure of what the options are worth to Mr Davies.

As an illustration, suppose that the CEO of London Conversation plc has options on 1 million shares with an exercise price of €30 per share, and the current share price of London Conversation is €50. If the options were exercised today, they would be worth €20 million (an underestimation of their market value). Suppose, in addition, that the CEO owns €5 million in company equity and has €5 million in other assets. The CEO clearly has a very undiversified personal portfolio. By the standards of modern portfolio theory, having 25/30 or about 83 per cent of your personal wealth in one equity and its options is unnecessarily risky.

Although the CEO is wealthy by most standards, shifts in share price impact the CEO's economic well-being. If the price drops from €50 per share to €30 per share, the current exercise value of the options on 1 million shares drops from €20 million down to zero. Ignoring the fact that if the options had more time to mature they might not lose all of this value, we nevertheless have a rather startling decline in the CEO's net worth from about €30 million to €8 million (€5 million in other assets plus equity that is now worth €3 million). But that is the purpose of giving the options and the equity holdings to the CEO – namely, to make the CEO's fortunes rise and fall with those of the company. It is why the company requires the executive to hold the options for at least a freeze-out period rather than letting the executive sell them to realize their value.

The implication is that when options are a large portion of an executive's net worth, the total value of the position to the executive is less than market value. As a purely financial matter, an executive might be happier with €5 million in cash rather than €20 million in options. At least the executive could then diversify his personal portfolio. The recent shift from executive share options to restricted stock units suggests that in practice, the effective minimum value of executive share options is not zero. If companies systematically respond to deep out-of-the-money options by converting them to RSUs, the firms are exercising another option: to exchange the share option for an RSU. As with any option, this has value to the holder, in this case the senior executive.

23.2   Investment in Real Projects and Options

Chapter 8
Page 204

In **Chapter 8**, we considered projects where forecasts for future cash flows were made at date 0. The expected cash flow in each future period was discounted at an appropriate risky rate, yielding an NPV calculation. For independent projects, a positive NPV meant acceptance and a negative NPV meant rejection. This approach treated risk through the discount rate.

We later considered decision tree analysis, an approach that handles risk in a more sophisticated way. We pointed out that the firm will make investment and operating decisions on a project over its entire life. We value a project today, assuming that future decisions will be optimal. However, we do not yet know what these decisions will be because much information remains to be discovered. The firm's ability to delay its investment and operating decisions until the release of information is an option. We now illustrate this option through an example.

This example presents an approach that is similar to our decision tree analysis in a previous chapter. Our purpose in this section is to discuss this type of decision in an option framework. When BP purchases the land, it is actually purchasing a call option. That is, once the land has been purchased, the firm has an option to buy an active oil field at an exercise price of £500,000. As it turns out, one should generally not exercise a call option immediately. In this case, the firm should delay exercise until relevant information concerning future oil prices is released.

Example 23.2

Options and Capital Budgeting

Consider a hypothetical issue that could face BP plc, the British energy company. BP is considering the purchase of an oil field in the Hammerfest-Varanger Basin, to the north of Norway. The seller has listed the property for £10,000 (Norwegian Kroner equivalent) and is eager to sell immediately. Initial drilling costs are £500,000. BP anticipates that 10,000 barrels of oil can be extracted each year for many decades. Because the termination date is so far in the future and so hard to estimate, the firm views the cash flow stream from the oil as a perpetuity. With oil prices at £50 per barrel and extraction costs at £46 a barrel, the firm anticipates a net margin of £4 per barrel. Because oil prices are expected to rise at the inflation rate, the firm assumes that its cash flow per barrel will always be £4 in real terms. The appropriate real discount rate is 10 per cent. Assume that BP has enough tax credits from bad years in the past that it will not need to pay taxes on any profits from the oil field. Should BP buy the property?

The NPV of the oil field to BP is:

$$-£110,000 = -£10,000 - £500,000 + \frac{£4 \times 10,000}{0.10}$$

According to this analysis, BP should not purchase the land.

Though this approach uses the standard capital budgeting techniques of this and other textbooks, it is actually inappropriate for this situation. To see this, consider the analysis of Professor I.M. Jolly, a consultant to BP. He agrees that the price of oil is *expected* to rise at the rate of inflation. However, he points out that the next year is quite perilous for oil prices. On the one hand, OPEC is considering a long-term agreement that would raise oil prices to £65 per barrel in real terms for many years in the future. On the other hand, the economic recession may last a lot longer than analysts and politicians predict. Professor Jolly argues that oil will be priced at £35 in real terms for many years should this scenario play out. Full information about both these developments will be known in exactly one year.

Should oil prices rise to £65 a barrel, the NPV of the project would be:

$$£1,390,000 = -£10,000 - £500,000 + \frac{(£45 - £46) \times 10,000}{0.10}$$

However, should oil prices fall to £35 a barrel, the NPV of the oil field will be even more negative than it is today.

Professor Jolly makes two recommendations to BP's board. He argues that:

1   The land should be purchased.

2   The drilling decision should be delayed until information about both OPEC's new agreement and the extent of the global recession is known.

Professor Jolly explains his recommendations to the board by first assuming that the land has already been purchased. He argues that under this assumption, the drilling decision should be delayed. Second, he investigates his assumption that the land should have been purchased in the first place. This approach of examining the second decision (whether to drill) after assuming that the first decision (to buy the land) has been made was also used in our earlier presentation on decision trees. Let us now work through Professor Jolly's analysis.

Assume the land has already been purchased. If the land has already been purchased, should drilling begin immediately? If drilling begins immediately, the NPV is −£110,000. If the drilling decision is delayed until new information is released in a year, the optimal choice can be made at that time. If oil prices drop to £35 a barrel, BP should not drill. Instead the firm should walk away from the project, losing nothing beyond its £10,000 purchase price for the land. If oil prices rise to £65, drilling should begin.

Professor Jolly points out that by delaying, the firm will invest the £500,000 of drilling costs only if oil prices rise. Thus, by delaying, the firm saves £500,000 in the case where oil prices drop. Jolly concludes that once the land is purchased, the drilling decision should be delayed.

Should the land have been purchased in the first place? We now know that if the land has been purchased, it is optimal to defer the drilling decision until the release of information. Given that we know this optimal decision concerning drilling, should the land be purchased in the first place? Without knowing the exact probability that oil prices will rise, Professor Jolly is nevertheless confident that the land should be purchased. The NPV of the project at £65 oil prices is £1,390,000, whereas the cost of the land is only £10,000. Professor Jolly believes that an oil price rise is possible, though by no means probable. Even so, he argues that the high potential return is clearly worth the risk.

This section points out a serious deficiency in classical capital budgeting: net present value calculations typically ignore the flexibility that real-world firms have. In our example, the standard techniques generated a negative NPV for the land purchase. Yet, by allowing the firm the option to change its investment policy according to new information, the land purchase can easily be justified.

We encourage the reader to look for hidden options in projects. Because options are beneficial, managers are short-changing their firm's projects if capital budgeting calculations ignore flexibility.

23.3 Valuing a Start-up

Ralph Simmons was not your typical Master's student. Since childhood he had one ambition: to open a restaurant that sold wild boar meat. He went to business school because he realized that although he knew 101 ways to cook wild boars, he did not have the business skills necessary to run a restaurant. He was extremely focused, with each course at graduate school being important to him only to the extent that it could further his dream.

While taking his school's course in entrepreneurship, he began to develop a business plan for his restaurant, which he now called Wild Boar for Everyone. He thought about marketing; he thought about raising capital; he thought about dealing with future employees. He even devoted a great deal of time to designing the physical layout of the restaurant. Against the professor's advice in his entrepreneurship class, he designed the restaurant in the shape of a wild boar, where the front door went through the animal's mouth. Of course his business plan would not be complete without financial projections. After much thought, he came up with the projections shown in Table 23.1.

Table 23.1 Financial Projections for Wild Boar for Everyone

	Year 1 (£)	Year 2 (£)	Year 3 (£)	Year 4 (£)	All Future Years (£)
(1) Sales	300,000	600,000	900,000	1,000,000	1,000,000
(2) Cash flows from operations	−100,000	−50,000	+75,000	+250,000	+250,000
(3) Increase in working capital	50,000	20,000	10,000	10,000	0
(4) Net cash flows [(2) − (3)]	−150,000	−70,000	65,000	240,000	250,000

Present value of net cash flows in years 1–4 (discounted at 20%)	−20,255
Present value of terminal value	$\dfrac{£250,000}{0.20} \times \dfrac{1}{(1.20)^4} = £602,816$
Present value of restaurant	£602,816 − £20,255 = £582,561
−Cost of building	−£700,000
Net present value of restaurant	−£117,439

The table starts with sales projections, which rise from £300,000 in the first year to a steady state of £1 million a year. Cash flows from operations are shown in the next line, although we leave out the intermediate calculations needed to move from line (1) to line (2). After subtracting working capital, the table shows net cash flows in line (4). Net cash flows are negative initially, which is quite common in start-ups, but they become positive by year 3. However, the rest of the table presents the unfortunate truth. The cash flows from the restaurant yield a present value of £582,561, assuming a discount rate of 20 per cent. Unfortunately, the cost of the building is greater, at £700,000, implying a negative net present value of −£117,439.

The projections indicate that Ralph's lifelong dream may not come to pass. He cannot expect to raise the capital needed to open his restaurant; and if he did obtain the funding, the restaurant would likely go under anyway. Ralph checked and rechecked the numbers, hoping vainly to discover either a numerical error or a cost-saving omission that would move his venture from the red to the black. In fact, Ralph saw that, if anything, his forecasts are generous: a 20 per cent discount rate and an infinitely lived building are on the optimistic side.

It was not until Ralph took a course in corporate strategy that he saw the hidden value in his venture. In that course, his instructor repeatedly stated the importance of positioning a firm to take advantage of new opportunities. Although Ralph did not see the connection at first, he finally realized the implications for Wild Boar for Everyone. His financial projections were based on expectations. There was a 50 per cent probability that wild boar meat would be more popular than he thought, in which case actual cash flows would exceed projections. And there was a 50 per cent probability that the meat would be less popular, in which case the actual flows would fall short of projections.

If the restaurant did poorly, it would probably fold in a few years because he would not want to keep losing money forever. However, if the restaurant did well, he would be in a position to expand. With wild boar meat being popular in one locale, it would likely prove popular in other locales as well. Thus, he recognized two options: the option to abandon under bad conditions and the option to expand under good conditions. Although both options can be valued according to the principles of the previous chapter, we focus on the option to expand because it is probably much more valuable.

Ralph reasoned that as much as he personally liked wild boar meat, consumer resistance in some regions of the United Kingdom would doom Wild Boar for Everyone. So he developed a strategy of catering only to those regions where wild boar meat is somewhat popular already. He forecast that although he could expand quickly if the first restaurant proved successful, the market would limit him to 30 additional restaurants.

Ralph believes that this expansion will occur about 4 years from now. He believes that he will need 3 years of operating the first restaurant to (1) get the initial restaurant running smoothly, and (2) have enough information to place an accurate value on the restaurant. If the first restaurant is successful enough, he will need another year to obtain outside capital. Thus, he will be ready to build the 30 additional units around the fourth year.

Ralph will value his enterprise, including the option to expand, according to the Black–Scholes model. From Table 23.1 we see that each unit costs £700,000, implying a total cost over the 30 additional units of £21,000,000 (= 30 × £700,000). The present value of the cash inflows from these 30 units is £17,476,830 (=30 × £582,561), according to the table. However, because the expansion will occur around the fourth year, this present value calculation is provided from the point of view of 4 years in the future. The present value as of today is £8,428,255 [= £17,476,830/(1.20)^4], assuming a discount rate of 20 per cent per year. Thus, Ralph views his potential restaurant business as an option, where the exercise price is £21,000,000 and the value of the underlying asset is £8,428,255. The option is currently out of the money, a result that follows from the negative value of a typical restaurant, as calculated in Table 23.1. Of course, Ralph is hoping that the option will move into the money within 4 years.

Ralph needs three additional parameters to use the Black–Scholes model: R, the continuously compounded interest rate; t, the time to maturity; and σ, the standard deviation of the underlying asset. Ralph uses the yield on a 4-year zero coupon bond, which is 3.5 per cent, as the estimate of the interest rate. The time to maturity is 4 years. The estimate of standard deviation is a little trickier because there is no historical data on wild boar restaurants. Ralph finds that the average annual standard deviation of the returns on publicly traded restaurants is 0.35. Because Wild Boar for Everyone is a new venture, he reasons that the risk here would be somewhat greater. He finds that the average annual standard deviation for restaurants that have gone public in the last few years is 0.45. Ralph's restaurant is newer still, so he uses a standard deviation of 0.50.

There is now enough data to value Ralph's venture. The value according to the Black–Scholes model is £1,455,196. The actual calculations are shown in Example 23.3. Of course Ralph must start his pilot restaurant before he can take advantage of this option. Thus, the net value of the call option plus the negative present value of the pilot restaurant is £1,337,757 (= £1,455,196 − £117,439). Because this value is large and positive, Ralph decides to stay with his dream of Wild Boar for Everyone. He knows that the probability that the restaurant will fail is greater than 50 per cent. Nevertheless, the option to expand is important enough that his restaurant business has value. And if he needs outside capital, he probably can attract the necessary investors.

This finding leads to the appearance of a paradox. If Ralph approaches investors to invest in a single restaurant with no possibility of expansion, he will probably not be able to attract capital. After all, Table 23.1 shows a net present value of −£117,439. However, if Ralph thinks bigger, he will likely be able to attract all the capital he needs. But this is really not a paradox at all. By thinking bigger, Ralph is offering investors the option – not the obligation – to expand.

The example we have chosen may seem frivolous, and certainly we added offbeat characteristics for interest. However, if you think that business situations involving options are unusual or unimportant, let us state emphatically that nothing is further from the truth. The notion of embedded options is at the heart of business. There are two possible outcomes for virtually every business idea. On the one hand, the business may fail, in which case the managers will probably try to shut it down in the most cost-efficient way. On the other hand, the business may prosper, in which case the managers will try to expand. Thus, virtually every business has both the option to abandon and the option to expand. You may have read pundits claiming that the net present value approach to capital budgeting is wrong or incomplete. Although criticism of this type frequently irritates the finance establishment, the pundits definitely have a point. If virtually all projects have embedded options, only an approach such as the one we have outlined can be appropriate. Ignoring the options is likely to lead to serious undervaluation.

Example 23.3

Valuing a Start-up Firm (Wild Boar for Everyone) as an Option

1   The value of a single restaurant is negative, as indicated by the net present value calculation in Table 23.1 of −£117,439. Thus, the restaurant would not be funded if there was no possibility of expansion.

2   If the pilot restaurant is successful, Ralph Simmons plans to create 30 additional restaurants around year 4. This leads to the following observations:

   (a) The total cost of 30 units is £21,000,000 (= 30 × £700,000).

   (b) The present value of future cash flows as of year 4 is £17,476,830 (= 30 × £582,561).

   (c) The present value of these cash flows today is £8,428,255 [= £17,476,830/(1.20)⁴].

Here we assume that cash flows from the project are discounted at 20 per cent per annum.

   Thus, the business is essentially a call option, where the exercise price is £21,000,000 and the underlying asset is worth £8,428,255.

3   Ralph Simmons estimates the standard deviation of the annual return on Wild Boar for Everyone's equity to be 0.50.
   Parameters of the Black–Scholes model:

$$S \text{ (share price)} = £8,428,255$$

$$E \text{ (exercise price)} = £21,000,000$$

$$t \text{ (time to maturity)} = 4 \text{ years}$$

$$\sigma \text{ (standard deviation)} = 0.50$$

$$R \text{ (continuously compounded interest rate)} = 3.5\%$$

Calculation from the Black–Scholes model:

$$C = SN(d_1) - Ee^{-Rt}N(d_2)$$

$$d_1 = [\ln(S/E) + (R + 1/2\sigma^2)t]/\sqrt{\sigma^2 t}$$

$$d_2 = d_1 - \sqrt{\sigma^2 t}$$

$$d_1 = \left[\ln \frac{8,428,255}{21,000,000} + \left(0.035 + \frac{1}{2}(0.50)^2\right)4\right]/\sqrt{(0.50)^2\, 4} = -0.27293$$

$$d_2 = -0.27293 - \sqrt{(0.50)^2\, 4} = -1.27293$$

$$N(d_1) = N(-0.27293) = 0.3936$$

$$N(d_2) = N(-1.27293) = 0.1020$$

$$C = £8,428,555 \times 0.3936 - £21,000,000 \times e^{-0.035 \times 4} \times 0.1020$$

$$= £1,455,196$$

Value of the business including the cost of the pilot restaurant is £1,337,757 (= £1,455,196 − £117,439).

23.4 More about the Binomial Model

Chapter 22
Page 586

Earlier in this chapter, we examined three applications of options: executive compensation, options to abandon or expand, and the start-up decision. In two cases we valued the option using the Black–Scholes model. Although this model is justifiably well known, it is not the only approach to option valuation. As mentioned in the previous chapter (see **Chapter 22**, Section 22.8), the two-state or binomial model is an alternative and – in some situations – a superior approach to valuation. The rest of this chapter examines two applications of the binomial model.

Heating Oil

Two-date Example

Consider Anthony Meyer, a typical heating oil distributor, whose business consists of buying heating oil at the wholesale level and reselling the oil to homeowners at a somewhat higher price. Most of his revenue comes from sales during the winter. Today, 1 September, heating oil sells for €2.00 per litre. Of course this price is not fixed. Rather, oil prices will vary from 1 September until 1 December, the time when his customers will probably make their big winter purchases of heating oil. Let us simplify the situation by assuming that Mr Meyer believes that oil prices will be at either €2.74 or €1.46 on 1 December. Figure 23.2 portrays this possible price movement. This potential price range represents a great deal of uncertainty because Mr Meyer has no idea which of the two possible prices will actually occur. However, this price variability does not translate into that much risk because he can pass price changes on to his customers. That is, he will charge his customers more if he ends up paying €2.74 per litre than if he ends up paying €1.46 per litre.

Figure 23.2 Movement of Heating Oil Prices from 1 September to 1 December in a Two-Date Example

€2.74
(€0.64 = €2.74 − 2.10)

€2.00

The price of heating oil on 1 December will be either €2.74 or €1.46. Because the price on 1 September is €2.00, we say that $u = 1.37$ (= €2.74/€2.00) and $d = 0.73$ (= €1.46/€2.00). The loss per litre to Mr Meyer (or, equivalently, the gain per litre to CECO) of €0.64 in the up state or €0 in the down state is shown in parentheses.

€1.46
(€0)

1 September   1 December

Of course, Mr Meyer is avoiding risk by passing on that risk to his customers. His customers accept the risk, perhaps because they are each too small to negotiate a better deal. This is not the case with CECO, a large electric utility in his area. CECO approaches Mr Meyer with the following proposition. The utility would like to be able to buy *up to* 6 million litres of oil from him at €2.10 per litre on 1 December.

Although this arrangement represents a lot of oil, both Mr Meyer and CECO know that Mr Meyer can expect to lose money on it. If prices rise to €2.74 per litre, the utility will happily buy all 6 million litres at only €2.10 per litre, clearly creating a loss for the distributor. However, if oil prices decline to €1.46 per litre, the utility will not buy any oil. After all, why should CECO pay €2.10 per litre to Mr Meyer when the utility can buy all the oil it wants at €1.46 per litre in the open market? In other words, CECO is asking for a *call option* on heating oil. To compensate Mr Meyer for the risk of loss, the two parties agree that CECO will pay him €1,000,000 up front for the right to buy up to 6 million litres of oil at €2.10 per litre.

Is this a fair deal? Although small distributors may evaluate a deal like this by gut feel, we can evaluate it more quantitatively by using the binomial model described in the previous chapter. In that chapter, we pointed out that option problems can be handled most easily by assuming *risk-neutral pricing*. In this approach, we first note that oil will either rise 37 per cent (= €2.74/€2.00 − 1) or fall −27 per cent (= €1.46/€2.00 − 1) from 1 September to

1 December. We can think of these two numbers as the possible returns on heating oil. In addition, we introduce two new terms, u and d. We define u as $1 + 0.37 = 1.37$ and d as $1 - 0.27 = 0.73$.[2] Using the methodology of the previous chapter, we value the contract in the following two steps.

Step 1: Determining the Risk-Neutral Probabilities

We determine the probability of a price rise such that the expected return on oil exactly equals the risk-free rate. Assuming an 8 per cent annual interest rate, which implies a 2 per cent rate over the next 3 months, we can solve for the probability of a rise as follows:[3]

$$2\% = \text{Probability of rise} \times 0.37 + (1 - \text{Probability of rise}) \times (-0.27)$$

Solving this equation, we find that the probability of a rise is approximately 45 per cent, implying that the probability of a fall is 55 per cent. In other words, if the probability of a price rise is 45 per cent, the expected return on heating oil is 2 per cent. In accordance with what we said in the previous chapter, these are the probabilities that are consistent with a world of risk neutrality. That is, under risk neutrality, the expected return on any asset would equal the riskless rate of interest. No one would demand an expected return above this riskless rate, because risk-neutral individuals do not need to be compensated for bearing risk.

Step 2: Valuing the Contract

If the price of oil rises to €2.74 on 1 December, CECO will want to buy oil from Mr Meyer at €2.10 per litre. Mr Meyer will lose €0.64 per litre because he buys oil in the open market at €2.74 per litre, only to resell it to CECO at €2.10 per litre. This loss of €0.64 is shown in parentheses in Figure 23.2. Conversely, if the market price of heating oil falls to €1.46 per litre, CECO will not buy any oil from Mr Meyer. That is, CECO would not want to pay €2.10 per litre to him when the utility could buy heating oil in the open market at €1.46 per litre. Thus, we can say that Mr Meyer neither gains nor loses if the price drops to €1.46. The gain or loss of zero is placed in parentheses under the price of €1.46 in Figure 23.2. In addition, as mentioned earlier, Mr Meyer receives €1,000,000 up front.

Given these numbers, the value of the contract to Mr Meyer can be calculated as:

$$\underbrace{[0.45 \times (\text{€}2.10 - \text{€}2.74) \times 6 \text{ million} + 0.55 \times 0]/1.02}_{\text{Value of the call option}} + \text{€}1,000,000,000 = -\text{€}694,118$$

$$(23.1)$$

As in the previous chapter, we are valuing an option using risk-neutral pricing. The cash flows of −€0.64 (= €2.10 − €2.74) and €0 per litre are multiplied by their risk-neutral probabilities. The entire first term in Equation 23.1 is then discounted at €1.02 because the cash flows in that term occur on 1 December. The €1,000,000 is not discounted because Mr Meyer receives it today, 1 September. Because the present value of the contract is negative, Mr Meyer would be wise to reject the contract.

As stated before, the distributor has sold a call option to CECO. The first term in the preceding equation, which equals −€1,694,118, can be viewed as the value of this call option. It is a negative number because the equation looks at the option from Mr Meyer's point of view. Therefore, the value of the call option would be +€1,694,118 to CECO. On a per-litre basis, the value of the option to CECO is:

$$[0.45(\text{€}2.74 - \text{€}2.10) + 0.55 \times 0]/1.02 = \text{€}0.282$$

$$(23.2)$$

Equation 23.2 shows that CECO will gain €0.64 (= €2.74 − €2.10) per litre in the up state because CECO can buy heating oil worth €2.74 for only €2.10 under the contract. By contrast, the contract is worth nothing to CECO in the down state because the utility will not pay €2.10 for oil selling for only €1.46 in the open market. Using risk-neutral pricing, the formula tells us that the value of the call option on one litre of heating oil is €0.282.

Three-date Example

Although the preceding example captures a number of aspects of the real world, it has one deficiency. It assumes that the price of heating oil can take on only two values on 1 December. This is clearly not plausible: oil can take on essentially any value in reality. Although this deficiency seems glaring at first glance, it is easily correctable. All we have to do is to introduce more intervals over the 3-month period of our example.

For example, consider Figure 23.3, which shows the price movement of heating oil over two intervals of 1½ months each.[4] As shown in the figure, the price will be either €2.50 or €1.60 on 15 October. We refer to €2.50 as the price in the *up state* and €1.60 as the price in the *down state*. Thus, heating oil has returns of 25 per cent (= €2.50/€2.00) and −20 per cent (= €1.60/€2) in the two states.

Figure 23.3   Movement of Heating Oil Prices in a Three-Date Model

€3.12
(€1.02 = €3.12 − €2.10)

€2.50
(€0.474)

€2.00
(€0.220)

€2.00
(€0)

€1.60
(€0)

€1.28
(€0)

1 September   15 October   1 December

The figure shows the prices of a litre of heating oil on three dates, given $u = 1.25$ and $d = 0.80$. There are three possible prices for heating oil on 1 December. For each one of these three prices, we calculate the price on 1 December of a call option on a litre of heating oil with an exercise price of €2.10. These numbers are in parentheses. Call prices at earlier dates are determined by the binomial model and are also shown in parentheses.

We assume the same variability as we move forward from 15 October to 1 December. That is, given a price of €2.50 on 15 October, the price on 1 December will be either €3.12 (= €2.50 × 1.25) or €2 (= €2.50 × 0.80). Similarly, given a price of €1.60 on 15 October, the price on 1 December will be either €2 (= €1.60 × 1.25) or €1.28 (= €1.60 × 0.80). This assumption of constant variability is quite plausible because the rate of new information impacting heating oil (or most commodities or assets) is likely to be similar from month to month.

Note that there are three possible prices on 1 December, but there are two possible prices on 15 October. Also note that there are two paths to a price of €2 on 1 December. The price could rise to €2.50 on 15 October before falling back down to €2 on 1 December. Alternatively, the price could fall to €1.60 on 15 October before going back up to €2 on 1 December. In other words the model has symmetry, where an up movement followed by a down movement yields the same price on 1 December as a down movement followed by an up movement.

How do we value CECO's option in this three-date example? We employ the same procedure that we used in the two-date example, although we now need an extra step because of the extra date.

Step 1: Determining the Risk-Neutral Probabilities

As we did in the two-date example, we determine what the probability of a price rise would be such that the expected return on heating oil exactly equals the riskless rate. However, in this case, we work with an interval of 1½ months. Assuming an 8 per cent annual rate of interest, which implies a 1 per cent rate over a 1½ month interval,[5] we can solve for the probability of a rise like this:

$$1\% = \text{Probability of rise} \times 0.25 + (1 - \text{Probability of rise}) \times (-0.20)$$

Solving the equation, we find that the probability of a rise here is 47 per cent, implying that the probability of a fall is 53 per cent. In other words, if the probability of a rise is 47 per cent, the expected return on heating oil is 1 per cent per each 1½-month interval. Again these probabilities are determined under the assumption of risk-neutral pricing.

Note that the probabilities of 47 per cent and 53 per cent hold for both the interval from 1 September to 15 October and the interval from 15 October to 1 December. This is the case because the return in the up state is 25 per cent and the return in the down state is −20 per cent for each of the two intervals. Thus, the preceding equation must apply to each of the intervals separately.

Step 2: Valuing the Option as of 15 October

As indicated in Figure 23.3, the option to CECO will be worth €1.02 per litre on 1 December if the price of heating oil has risen to €3.12 on that date. That is, CECO can buy oil from Mr Meyer at €2.10 when it would otherwise have to pay €3.12 in the open market. However, the option will be worthless on 1 December if the price of a litre of heating oil is either €2 or €1.28 on that date. Here the option is out of the money because the exercise price of €2.10 is above either €2 or €1.28.

Using these option prices on 1 December, we can calculate the value of the call option on 15 October. If the price of a litre of heating oil is €2.50 on 15 October, Figure 23.3 shows us that the call option will be worth either €1.02 or €0 on 1 December. Thus if the price of heating oil is €2.50 on 15 October, the value of the option on one litre of heating oil at that time is:

$$[0.47 \times €1.02 + 0.53 \times €0]/1.01 = €0.474$$

Here we are valuing an option using the same risk-neutral pricing approach that we used in the earlier two-date example. This value of €0.474 is shown in parentheses in Figure 23.3.

We also want to value the option on 15 October if the price at that time is €1.60. However, the value here is clearly zero, as indicated by this calculation:

$$[0.47 \times €0 + 0.53 \times €0]/1.01 = 0$$

This is obvious once we look at Figure 23.3. We see from the figure that the call must end up out of the money on 1 December if the price of heating oil is €1.60 on 15 October. Thus, the call must have zero value on 15 October if the price of heating oil is €1.60 on that date.

Step 3: Valuing the Option on 1 September

In the previous step, we saw that the price of the call on 15 October would be €0.474 if the price of a litre of heating oil were €2.50 on that date. Similarly, the price of the option on 15 October would be €0 if oil were selling at €1.60 on that date. From these values, we can calculate the call option value on 1 September:

$$[0.47 \times €0.474 + 0.53 \times €0]/1.01 = €0.220$$

Notice that this calculation is completely analogous to the calculation of the option value in the previous step, as well as the calculation of the option value in the two-date example that we presented earlier. In other words, the same approach applies regardless of the number of intervals used. As we will see later, we can move to many intervals, which produces greater realism, yet still maintains the same basic methodology.

The previous calculation has given us the value to CECO of its option on one litre of heating oil. Now we are ready to calculate the value of the contract to Mr Meyer. Given the calculations from the previous equation, the contract's value can be written as:

$$-€0.220 \times 6,000,000 + €1,000,000 = -€320,000$$

That is, Mr Meyer is giving away an option worth €0.220 for each of the 6 million litres of heating oil. In return, he is receiving only €1,000,000 up front. On balance, he is losing €320,000. Of course, the value of the contract to CECO is the opposite, so the value to this utility is €320,000.

Extension to Many Dates

We have looked at the contract between CECO and Mr Meyer using both a two-date example and a three-date example. The three-date case is more realistic because more possibilities for price movements are allowed here. However, why stop at just three dates? Moving to 4 dates, 5 dates, 50 dates, 500 dates, and so on should give us ever more realism. Note that as we move to more dates, we are merely shortening the interval between dates without increasing the overall time period of 3 months (1 September to 1 December).

For example, imagine a model with 90 dates over the 3 months. Here each interval is approximately one day long because there are about 90 days in a 3-month period. The assumption of two possible outcomes in the binomial model is more plausible over a one-day interval than it is over a 1½-month interval, let alone a 3-month interval. Of course, we could probably achieve greater realism still by going to an interval of, say, one hour or one minute.

How do we adjust the binomial model to accommodate increases in the number of intervals? It turns out that two simple formulas relate u and d to the standard deviation of the return of the underlying asset:[6]

$$u = e^{\sigma/\sqrt{n}} \quad \text{and} \quad d = 1/u$$

where σ is the standard deviation of the annualized return on the underlying asset (heating oil, in this case) and n is the number of intervals over a year.

When we created the heating oil example, we assumed that the annualized standard deviation of the return on heating oil was 0.63 (or, equivalently, 63 per cent). Because there are four quarters in a year, $u = e^{0.63/\sqrt{4}} = 1.37$ and $d = 1/1.37 = 0.73$, as shown in the two-date example of Figure 23.2. In the three-date example of Figure 23.3, where each interval is 1½ months long, $u = e^{0.63/\sqrt{8}} = 1.25$ and $d = 1/1.25 = 0.80$. Thus the binomial model can be applied in practice if the standard deviation of the return of the underlying asset can be estimated.

We stated earlier that the value of the call option on a litre of heating oil was estimated to be €0.282 in the two-date model and €0.220 in the three-date model. How does the value of the option change as we increase the number of intervals while keeping the time period constant at 3 months (from 1 September to 1 December)? We have calculated the value of the call for various time intervals in Table 23.2.[7] The realism increases with the number of intervals because the restriction of only two possible outcomes is more plausible over a short interval than over a long one. Thus, the value of the call when the number of intervals is 99 or infinity is likely more realistic than this value when the number of intervals is, say, 1 or 2.

Table 23.2 Value of a Call on One Litre of Heating Oil

Number of Intervals*	Call Value (€)
1	0.282
2	0.220
3	0.244
4	0.232
6	0.228
10	0.228
20	0.228
30	0.228
40	0.228
50	0.226
99	0.226
Black–Scholes infinity	0.226

In this example, the value of the call according to the binomial model varies as the number of intervals increases. However, the value of the call converges rapidly to the Black–Scholes value. Thus the binomial model, even with only a few intervals, appears to be a good approximation to Black–Scholes.
*The number of intervals is always one less than the number of dates.

However, a very interesting phenomenon can be observed from the table. Although the value of the call changes as the number of intervals increases, convergence occurs quite rapidly. The call's value with 6 intervals is almost identical to the value with 99 intervals. Thus, a small number of intervals appears serviceable for the binomial model. Six intervals in a 3-month period implies that each interval is 2 weeks long. Of course the assumption that heating oil can take on only one of two prices in 2 weeks is simply not realistic. The paradox is that this unrealistic assumption still produces a realistic call price.

What happens when the number of intervals goes to infinity, implying that the length of the interval goes to zero? It can be proved mathematically that we end up with the value of the Black–Scholes model. This value is also presented in Table 23.2. Thus, we can argue that the Black–Scholes model is the best approach to value the heating oil option. It is also quite easy to apply. We can use a calculator to value options with

Black–Scholes, whereas we must generally use a computer program for the binomial model. However, as shown in Table 23.2, the values from the binomial model, even with relatively few intervals, are quite close to the Black–Scholes value. Thus, although Black–Scholes may save us time, it does not materially affect our estimate of value.

At this point it seems as if the Black–Scholes model is preferable to the binomial model. Who would not want to save time and still get a slightly more accurate value? However, such is not always the case. There are plenty of situations where the binomial model is preferred to the Black–Scholes model. One such situation is presented in the next section.

23.5   Shutdown and Reopening Decisions

Some of the earliest and most important examples of special options have occurred in the natural resources and mining industries.

Valuing a Palladium Mine

The Woborov palladium mine was founded in 1878 on one of the richest veins of palladium in Russia. Palladium is a platinum-like metal that is used for industrial purposes across the world. Thirty years later, by 1908, the mine had been played out; but occasionally, depending on the price of palladium, it is reopened. Currently, palladium is not actively mined at Woborov, but its equity is still traded on the Russian Stock Exchange and Euronext under the ticker symbol WOB. WOB has no debt and, with about 20 million outstanding shares, its market value (share price times number of shares outstanding) exceeds €1 billion. WOB owns about 160 acres of land surrounding the mine and has a 100-year government lease to mine palladium there. However, land in the Russian tundra has a market value of only a few thousand euros (rouble equivalent). WOB holds cash securities, and other assets worth about €30 million. What could possibly explain why a company with €30 million in assets and a closed palladium mine with no cash flow has the market value that WOB has?

The answer lies in the options that WOB implicitly owns in the form of a palladium mine. Assume that the current price of palladium is about €320 per ounce, and the cost of extraction and processing at the mine is about €350 per ounce. It is no wonder that the mine is closed. Every ounce of palladium extracted costs €350 and can be sold for only €320, for a loss of €30 per ounce. Presumably, if the price of palladium were to rise, the mine could be opened. It costs €2 million to open the mine; when it is opened, production is 50,000 ounces per year. Geologists believe that the amount of palladium in the mine is essentially unlimited, and WOB has the right to mine it for the next 100 years. Under the terms of its lease, WOB cannot stockpile palladium and must sell each year all the palladium it mines that year. Closing the mine, which costs €1 million, requires equipment to be mothballed and some environmental precautions to be put in place. We will refer to the €2 million required to open the mine as the entry fee or investment and the €1 million to close it as the closing or abandonment cost. (We cannot avoid the abandonment cost by simply keeping the mine open and not operating.)

From a financial perspective, WOB is really just a package of options on the price of palladium disguised as a company and a mine. The basic option is a call on the price of palladium where the exercise price is the €350 extraction cost. The option is complicated by having an exercise fee of €2 million – the opening cost – whenever it is exercised and a closing fee of €1 million when it is abandoned. It is also complicated by the fact that it is a perpetual option with no final maturity.

The Abandonment and Opening Decisions

Before valuing the option implicit in WOB, it is useful to see what we can say by just applying common sense. To begin with, the mine should be opened only when the price of palladium is sufficiently above the extraction cost of €350 per ounce. Because it costs €2 million to open the mine, the mine should not be opened whenever the price of palladium is only slightly above €350. At a palladium price of, say, €350.10, the mine would not be opened because the ten-cent profit per ounce translates into €5,000 per year (= 50,000 ounces × €0.10/ounce). This would not begin to cover the €2 million opening costs. More significantly, though, the mine probably would not be opened if the price rose to €360 per ounce, even though a €10 profit per ounce – €500,000 per year – would pay the €2 million opening costs at any reasonable discount rate. The reason is that here, as in all option problems, volatility (in this case the volatility of palladium) plays a significant role. Because the palladium price is volatile, the price has to rise sufficiently above €350 per ounce to make it worth opening the mine. If the price at which the mine is opened is too close to the extraction price of €350 per ounce, say at €360 per ounce, we would open the mine every time the price jogged above €360. Unfortunately, we would then find ourselves operating at a loss or facing a closing decision whenever palladium jogged back down €10 per ounce (or only 3 per cent) to €350.

The estimated volatility of the return on palladium is about 15 per cent per year. This means that a single annual standard deviation movement in the palladium price is 15 per cent of €320 or €48 per year. Surely with this amount of random movement in the palladium price, a threshold of, for example, €352 is much too low at which to open the mine. A similar logic applies to the closing decision. If the mine is open, we will clearly keep it open as long as the palladium price is above the extraction cost of €350 per ounce because we are profiting on every ounce of palladium mined. But we also will not close the mine down simply because the palladium price drops below €350 per ounce. We will tolerate a running loss because palladium may later rise back above €350. If, alternatively, we closed the mine, we would pay the €1 million abandonment cost, only to pay another €2 million to reopen the mine if the price rose again.

To summarize, if the mine is currently closed, then it will be opened – at a cost of €2 million – whenever the price of palladium rises *sufficiently* above the extraction cost of €350 per ounce. If the mine is currently operating, then it will be closed down – at a cost of €1 million – whenever the price of palladium falls *sufficiently* below the extraction cost of €350 per ounce. WOB's problem is to find these two threshold prices at which it opens a closed mine and closes an open mine. We call these prices p_{open} and p_{close}, respectively, where:

$$p_{open} > €350/\text{ounce} > p_{close}$$

In other words, WOB will open the mine if the palladium price option is sufficiently in the money and will close it when the option is sufficiently out of the money.

We know that the more volatile the palladium price, the further away p_{open} and p_{close} will be from €350 per ounce. We also know that the greater the cost of opening the mine, the higher p_{open} will be; and the greater the cost of abandoning the mine, the lower will be p_{close}. Interestingly, we should also expect that p_{open} will be higher if the abandonment cost is increased. After all, if it costs more to abandon the mine, WOB will need to be more assured that the price will stay above the extraction cost when it decides to open the mine. Otherwise WOB will face the costly choice between abandonment and operating at a loss if the price falls below €350 per ounce. Similarly, raising the cost of opening the mine will make WOB more reluctant to close an open mine. As a result, p_{close} will be lower.

The preceding arguments have enabled us to reduce the problem of valuing WOB to two stages. First, we have to determine the threshold prices, p_{open} and p_{close}. Second, given the best choices for these thresholds, we must determine the value of a palladium option that is exercised for a cost of €2 million when the palladium price rises above p_{open} and is shut down for a cost of €1 million whenever the palladium price is below p_{close}.

When the mine is open – that is, when the option is exercised – the annual cash flow is equal to the difference between the palladium price and the extraction cost of €350 per ounce times 50,000 ounces. When the mine is shut down, it generates no cash flow.

The following diagram describes the decisions available at each point in time:

How do we determine the critical values for p_{open} and p_{close} and then the value of the mine? It is possible to get a good approximation by using the tools we have currently developed.

Valuing the Simple Palladium Mine

Here is what has to be done both to determine p_{open} and p_{close} and to value the mine.

Step 1

Find the risk-free interest rate and the volatility. We assume a semi-annual interest rate of 3.4 per cent and a volatility of 15 per cent per year for palladium.

Step 2

Construct a binomial tree and fill it in with palladium prices. Suppose, for example, that we set the steps of the tree 6 months apart. If the annual volatility is 15 per cent, u is equal to $e^{0.15/\sqrt{2}}$, which is approximately equal to 1.11. The other parameter, d, is 0.90 (= 1/1.11). Figure 23.4 illustrates the tree. Starting at the current price of €320, the first 11 per cent increase takes the price to €355 in 6 months. The first 10 per cent decrease takes the price to €288. Subsequent steps are up 11 per cent or down 10 per cent from the previous price. The tree extends for the 100-year life of the lease or 200 six-month steps.

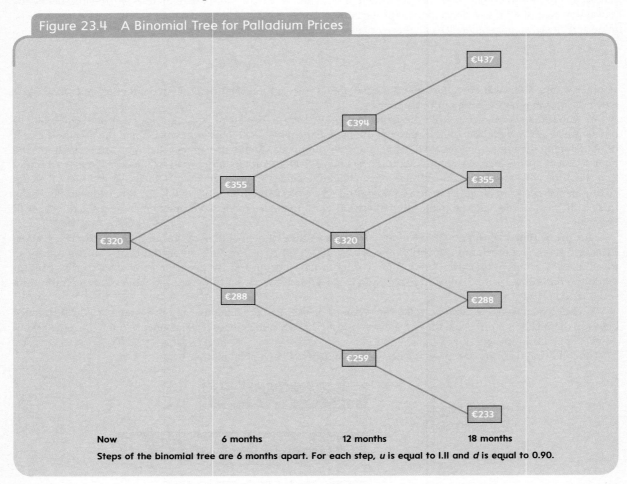

Figure 23.4   A Binomial Tree for Palladium Prices

| €437 |
| €394 |
| €355 |
| €320 |
| €288 |
| €259 |
| €233 |

Now   6 months   12 months   18 months

Steps of the binomial tree are 6 months apart. For each step, *u* is equal to 1.11 and *d* is equal to 0.90.

Using our analysis from the previous section, we now compute the risk-adjusted probabilities for each step. Given a semi-annual interest rate of 3.4 per cent, we have:

$$3.4\% = \text{Probability of a rise} \times 0.11 + (1 - \text{Probability of a rise}) \times -0.10$$

Solving this equation gives us 0.64 for the probability of a rise, implying that the probability of a fall is 0.36. These probabilities are the same for each 6-month interval. In other words, if the probability of a rise is 0.64, the expected return on palladium is 3.4 per cent per each 6-month interval. These probabilities are determined under the assumption of risk-neutral pricing. In other words, if investors are risk-neutral, they will be satisfied with an expected return equal to the risk-free rate because the extra risk of palladium will not concern them.

Step 3

Now we turn the computer on and let it simulate, say, 5,000 possible paths through the tree. At each node, the computer has a 0.64 probability of picking an 'up' movement in the price and a corresponding 0.36 probability of picking a 'down' movement in the price. A typical path might be represented by whether the price rose or fell each 6-month period over the next 100 years; it would be a list like:

$$\text{up, up, down, up, down, down,} \ldots \text{, down}$$

where the first 'up' means the price rose from €320 to €355 in the first 6 months, the next 'up' means it again went up in the second half of the year from €355 to €394, and so on, ending with a down move in the last half of year 100.

With 5,000 such paths we will have a good sample of all the future possibilities for movement in the palladium price.

Step 4

Next we consider possible choices for the threshold prices, p_{open} and p_{close}. For p_{open}, we let the possibilities be:

$$p_{open} = €360 \text{ or } €370 \text{ or } \ldots \text{ or } €500$$

a total of 15 values. For p_{close} we let the possibilities be:

$$p_{close} = €340 \text{ or } €330 \text{ or } \ldots \text{ or } €100$$

a total of 25 values.

We picked these choices because they seemed reasonable and because increments of €10 for each seemed sensible. To be precise, though, we should let the threshold prices change as we move through the tree and get closer to the end of 100 years. Presumably, for example, if we decided to open the mine with one year left on the lease, the price of palladium should be at least high enough to cover the €2 million opening costs in the coming year. Because we mine 50,000 ounces per year, we will open the mine in year 99 only if the palladium price is at least €40 above the extraction cost, or €390.

Although this will become important at the end of the lease, using a constant threshold should not have too big an impact on the value with 100 years to go. Therefore, we will stick with our approximation of constant threshold prices.

Step 5

We calculate the value of the mine for each pair of choices of p_{open} and p_{close}. For example, if $p_{open} = €410$ and $p_{close} = €290$, we use the computer to keep track of the cash flows if we opened the mine whenever it was previously closed and the palladium price rose to €410, and closed the mine whenever it was previously open and the palladium price fell to €290. We do this for each of the 5,000 paths we simulated in Step 4.

For example, consider the path illustrated in Figure 23.5:

$$\text{up, up, down, up, up, down, down, down, down}$$

As can be seen from the figure, the price reaches a peak of €437 in 2½ years, only to fall to €288 over the following four 6-month intervals. If $p_{open} = €410$ and $p_{close} = €290$, the mine will be opened when the price reaches €437, necessitating a cost of €2 million. However, the firm can sell 25,000 ounces of palladium at €437 at that time, producing a cash flow of €2.175 million [= 25,000 × (€437 − €350)]. When the price falls to €394 six months later, the firm sells another 25,000 ounces, yielding a cash flow of €1.1 million [= 25,000 × (€394 − €350)]. The price continues to fall, reaching €320 a year later. Here, the firm experiences a cash outflow because production costs are €350 per ounce. Next, the price falls to €288. Because this price is below p_{close} of €290, the mine is closed at a cost of €1 million. Of course, the price of palladium will fluctuate in further years, leading to the possibility of future mine openings and closings.

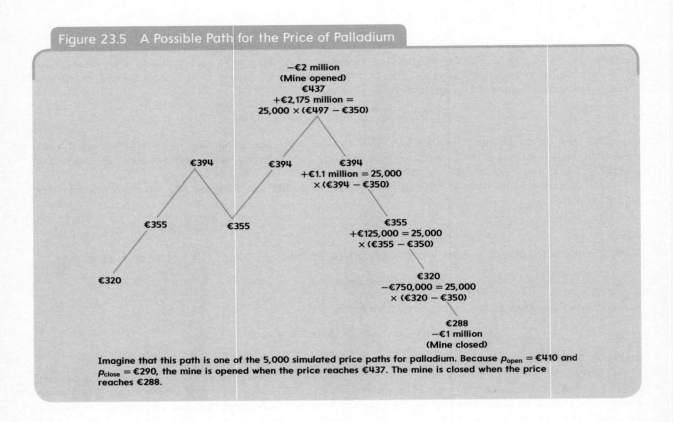

Figure 23.5 A Possible Path for the Price of Palladium

Imagine that this path is one of the 5,000 simulated price paths for palladium. Because p_{open} = €410 and p_{close} = €290, the mine is opened when the price reaches €437. The mine is closed when the price reaches €288.

This path is just a possibility. It may or may not occur in any simulation of 5,000 paths. For each of the 5,000 paths that the computer simulated, we have a sequence of semi-annual cash flows using a p_{open} of €410 and a p_{close} of €290. We calculate the present value of each of these cash flows, discounting at the interest rate of 3.4 per cent. Summing across all the cash flows, we have the present value of the palladium mine for one path.

We then take the average present value of the palladium mine across all the 5,000 simulated paths. This number is the expected value of the mine from following a policy of opening the mine whenever the palladium price hits €410 and closing it at a price of €290.

Step 6

The final step is to compare the different expected discounted cash flows from Step 5 for the range of possible choices for p_{open} and p_{close} and to pick the highest one. This is the best estimate of the expected value of the mine. The values for p_{close} and p_{open} corresponding to this estimate are the points at which to open a closed mine and to shut an open one.

As mentioned in Step 3, there are 15 different values for p_{open} and 25 different values for p_{close}, implying 375 (= 15 × 25) different pairs. Consider Table 23.3, which shows the present values associated with the 20 best pairs. The table indicates that the best pair is p_{open} = €400 and p_{close} = €140, with a present value of €1.467 billion. This number represents the average present value across 5,000 simulations, all assuming the preceding values of p_{open} and p_{close}. The next best pair is p_{open} = €460 and p_{close} = €300, with a present value of €1.459 billion. The third best pair has a somewhat lower present value, and so on.

Table 23.3 Valuation of Woborov (WOB) Palladium Mine for the 20 Best Choices of p_{open} and p_{close}

p_{open} (€)	p_{close} (€)	Estimated value of palladium mine (€)
400	140	1,466,720,900
460	300	1,459,406,200
380	290	1,457,838,700
370	100	1,455,131,900
360	190	1,449,708,200
420	150	1,448,711,400
430	340	1,448,450,200
430	110	1,445,396,500
470	200	1,435,687,400
500	320	1,427,512,000
410	290	1,426,483,500
420	290	1,423,865,300
400	160	1,423,061,900
360	320	1,420,748,700
360	180	1,419,112,000
380	280	1,417,405,400
450	310	1,416,238,000
450	280	1,409,709,800
440	220	1,408,269,100
440	240	1,403,398,100

For our simulation, WOB opens the mine whenever the palladium price rises above p_{open} and closes the mine whenever the palladium price falls below p_{close}.

Of course, our estimate of the value of the mine is €1.467 billion, the present value of the best pair of choices. The market capitalization (price × number of shares outstanding) of WOB should reach this value if the market makes the same assumptions that we did. Note that the value of the firm is quite high using an option framework. However, as stated earlier, WOB would appear worthless if a regular discounted cash flow approach were used. This occurs because the initial palladium price of €320 is below the extraction cost of €350.

This example is not easy, either in concepts or in implementation. However, the extra work involved in mastering this example is worth it because the example illustrates the type of modelling that actually occurs in corporate finance departments in the real world.

Furthermore, the example illustrates the benefits of the binomial approach. We merely calculate the cash flows associated with each of a number of simulations, discount the cash flows from each simulation, and average present values across the simulations. Because the Black–Scholes model is not amenable to simulations, it cannot be used for this type of problem. In addition, there are a number of other situations where the binomial model is more appropriate than the Black–Scholes model. For example, it is well known that the Black–Scholes model cannot properly handle options with dividend payments prior to the expiration date. This model also does not adequately handle the valuation of an American put. By contrast, the binomial model can easily handle both of these situations.

Thus, any student of corporate finance should be well versed in both models. The Black–Scholes model should be used whenever appropriate because it is simpler to use than is the binomial model. However, for the more complex situations where the Black–Scholes model breaks down, the binomial model becomes a necessary tool.

23.6   Mergers and Diversification

Chapter 28
Page 755

In **Chapter 28**, we discuss mergers and acquisitions. There we mention that diversification is frequently cited as a reason for two firms to merge. Is diversification a good reason to merge? It might seem so. After all, in an earlier chapter, we spent a lot of time explaining why diversification is valuable for investors in their own portfolios because of the elimination of unsystematic risk.

To investigate this issue, let us consider two companies, Sunshine Swimwear (SS) and Polar Winterwear (PW). For obvious reasons, both companies have highly seasonal cash flows; and, in their respective off-seasons, both companies worry about cash flow. If the two companies were to merge, the combined company would have a much more stable cash flow. In other words, a merger would diversify away some of the seasonal variation and, in fact, would make bankruptcy much less likely.

Notice that the operations of the two firms are very different, so the proposed merger is a purely 'financial' merger. This means that there are no 'synergies' or other value-creating possibilities except, possibly, gains from risk reduction. Here is some pre-merger information:

	Sunshine Swimwear	Polar Winterwear
Market value of assets	€30 million	€10 million
Face value of pure discount debt	€12 million	€4 million
Debt maturity	3 years	3 years
Asset return standard deviation	50%	60%

The risk-free rate, continuously compounded, is 5 per cent. Given this, we can view the equity in each firm as a call option and calculate the following using Black–Scholes to determine equity values (check these for practice):

	Sunshine Swimwear (€)	Polar Winterwear (€)
Market value of equity	20.394 million	6.992 million
Market value of debt	9.606 million	3.008 million

If you check these, you may get slightly different answers if you use Table 22.3 (we used a spreadsheet). Notice that we calculated the market value of debt using the market value balance sheet identity.

After the merger, the combined firm's assets will simply be the sum of the pre-merger values, €30 + €10 = €40, because no value was created or destroyed. Similarly, the total face value of the debt is now €16 million. However, we will assume that the combined firm's asset return standard deviation is 40 per cent. This is lower than for either of the two individual firms because of the diversification effect.

So, what is the impact of this merger? To find out, we compute the post-merger value of the equity. Based on our discussion, here is the relevant information:

Combined Firm	
Market value of assets	€40 million
Face value of pure discount debt	€16 million
Debt maturity	3 years
Asset return standard deviation	40%

Once again, we can calculate equity and debt values:

Combined Firm (€)	
Market value of equity	26.602 million
Market value of debt	13.398 million

What we notice is that this merger is a terrible idea, at least for the shareholders! Before the merger, the equity in the two separate firms was worth a total of €20.394 + €6.992 = €27.386 million compared to only €26.602 million post-merger; so the merger vaporized €27.386 − €26.602 = €0.784 million.

Where did €0.784 million in equity go? It went to the bondholders. Their bonds were worth €9.606 + €3.008 = €12.614 million before the merger and €13.398 million after, a gain of exactly €0.784 million. Thus this merger neither created nor destroyed value, but it shifted it from the shareholders to the bondholders.

Our example shows that pure financial mergers are a bad idea, and it also shows why. The diversification works in the sense that it reduces the volatility of the firm's return on assets. This risk reduction benefits the bondholders by making default less likely. This is sometimes called the 'coinsurance' effect. Essentially, by merging, the firms insure each other's bonds. The bonds are thus less risky, and they rise in value. If the bonds increase in value, and there is no net increase in asset values, then the equity must decrease in value. Thus, pure financial mergers are good for creditors but not for shareholders.

Another way to see this is that because the equity is a call option, a reduction in return variance on the underlying asset has to reduce its value. The reduction in value in the case of a purely financial merger has an interesting interpretation. The merger makes default (and thus bankruptcy) *less* likely to happen. That is obviously a good thing from a bondholder's perspective, but why is it a bad thing from a shareholder's perspective? The answer is simple: the right to go bankrupt is a valuable shareholder option. A purely financial merger reduces the value of that option.

Real World Insight 23.1

Valuing Internet Firms

(*Excerpts taken from 'Twitter's IPO and the dark side of valuing companies', The Conversation, 11 November 2013*)

Social media darling Twitter ended last week with US$2.3 billion wiped off its market valuation, following a 7.24 per cent fall in its share price on the second day it traded. Despite the slip, the share price ended at US$41.64, significantly higher than the issue price of US$26.

The problems of valuing companies like Twitter are not new. Twitter is the latest example of a difficult to value business, but the same can be said of many listed companies including Google, Facebook and LinkedIn.

As indicated by Mary Jo White, Chair of the US Securities Exchange Commission, the metrics used in selling recent IPOs like Google and Twitter to the public are not closely related to profits or even to sales of product. She identifies some of the recent measures that companies have touted as proof of their value.

> ... the number of users of the service, the number of players of an online game, or the number of people who quote 'liked' the company or something the company does.

To get a better sense of the problems faced in valuing these firms it is worth revisiting the internet crisis of 2000. During this period it was often argued there was a pricing bubble in the internet industry with market prices arguably no longer reflecting value. Yet, when the crunch came it was not the result of new disclosures about the various measures of internet activity but earnings reports issued in 2000 for the 1999 year. These showed that predicted profits had not eventuated.

The real issue in valuing internet companies is in achieving some sensible understanding of the cash flows that the business is capable of achieving. Reliance on simple counts makes little sense even when touted by the spruikers of these new companies as the only available information on which to base valuations. Valuation requires the identification of expected cash flows that the company can reasonably be expected to generate, and while this may be related in some sense to website visits, it must ultimately be linked to expected profits and cash distributed to shareholders, either as dividends or capital gains.

Most internet companies rely on advertising revenues to drive their profits and so it is critical for analysts to estimate future advertising demand in the industry and identify the share that the internet company will be able to capture. Advertisers are usually careful with their advertising spending and tend to follow up on expenditures to see whether sales of product or service are actually affected by the advertising.

If the internet company has not fully developed its product or if there are issues with competition in the future then the valuation task becomes more complex as there are different scenarios that could occur. Valuation of these more complex businesses involves an attempt to capture the complexity of the business. This is a challenging task and might be solved using complex mathematical tools or careful thought and research into the key value drivers. The valuation of these companies is unlikely to be driven by "the number of people who 'liked' the company", for example.

Scenario analysis is one approach to dealing with the uncertainty of the valuation of these companies. With this approach the firm is valued under a number of situations and the analyst attempts to identify those elements of the company's business that most affect its value. For example, the development of an internet

▷

business might be particularly sensitive to government interference in terms of restricting access to citizens or from government oversight of how the system is used by citizens. Entry of competitors could also be a problem.

So the company might be valued on the basis of free entry to all countries as well as access restrictions in some key countries. 'Real option valuation' is also used and this involves identifying the key options that the business faces and then valuing these options. This can be complex as options become more valuable as uncertainty increases.

Real options are often called managerial options as the value of the option rests on the ability of management to exercise them at the best time for the firm. It is generally best for the firm if management do nothing in periods of extreme uncertainty and indeed the value of real options is greatest during periods of great uncertainty. In effect the market rewards management for doing nothing during these periods. As uncertainty reduces managers are able to make more informed decisions and so certain real options might then be exercised. Classic examples of real options include the option to grow the business, the option to reduce the business and the option to abandon the business altogether.

23.7   Options and Capital Budgeting

We now consider two issues regarding capital budgeting. What we will show is that, for a leveraged firm, the shareholders might prefer a lower NPV project to a higher one. We then show that they might even prefer a *negative* NPV project to a positive NPV project.

As usual, we will illustrate these points first with an example. Here is the basic background information for the firm:

Market value of assets	£20 million
Face value of pure discount debt	£40 million
Debt maturity	5 years
Asset return standard deviation	50%

The risk-free rate is 4 per cent. As we have now done several times, we can calculate equity and debt values:

	£
Market value of equity	5.724 million
Market value of debt	14.276 million

This firm has a fairly high degree of leverage: the debt–equity ratio based on market values is £14.276/£5.724 = 2.5, or 250 per cent. This is high, but not unheard of. Notice also that the option here is out of the money; as a result, the delta is 0.546.

The firm has two mutually exclusive investments under consideration. The projects affect both the market value of the firm's assets and the firm's asset return standard deviation as follows:

	Project A	Project B
NPV	£4	£2
Market value of firm's assets (£20 + NPV)	£24	£22
Firm's asset return standard deviation	40%	60%

Which project is better? It is obvious that project A has the higher NPV, but by now you are wary of the change in the firm's asset return standard deviation. One project reduces it; the other increases it. To see which project the shareholders like better, we have to go through our by now familiar calculations:

	Project A (£)	Project B (£)
Market value of equity	5.938	8.730
Market value of debt	18.062	13.270

There is a dramatic difference between the two projects. Project A benefits both the shareholders and the bondholders, but most of the gain goes to the bondholders. Project B has a huge impact on the value of the equity, plus it reduces the value of the debt. Clearly the shareholders prefer B.

What are the implications of our analysis? Basically, we have discovered two things. First, when the equity has a delta significantly smaller than 1.0, any value created will go partially to bondholders. Second, shareholders have a strong incentive to increase the variance of the return on the firm's assets. More specifically, shareholders will have a strong preference for variance-increasing projects as opposed to variance-decreasing ones, even if that means a lower NPV.

Let us do one final example. Here is a different set of numbers:

Market value of assets	£20 million
Face value of pure discount debt	£100 million
Debt maturity	5 years
Asset return standard deviation	50%

The risk-free rate is 4 per cent, so the equity and debt values are these:

	£
Market value of equity	2 million
Market value of debt	18 million

Notice that the change from our previous example is that the face value of the debt is now £100 million, so the option is far out of the money. The delta is only 0.24, so most of any value created will go to the bondholders.

The firm has an investment under consideration that must be taken now or never. The project affects both the market value of the firm's assets and the firm's asset return standard deviation as follows:

Project NPV	−£1 million
Market value of firm's assets (£20 million + NPV)	£19 million
Firm's asset return standard deviation	70%

Thus, the project has a negative NPV, but it increases the standard deviation of the firm's return on assets. If the firm takes the project, here is the result:

	£
Market value of equity	4.821 million
Market value of debt	14.179 million

This project more than doubles the value of the equity! Once again, what we are seeing is that shareholders have a strong incentive to increase volatility, particularly when the option is far out of the money. What is happening is that the shareholders have relatively little to lose because bankruptcy is the likely outcome. As a result, there is a strong incentive to go for a long shot, even if that long shot has a negative NPV. It is a bit like using your very last euro on a lottery ticket. It is a bad investment, but there are not a lot of other options!

Summary and Conclusions

Real options, which are pervasive in business, are not captured by net present value analysis. **Chapter 8** valued real options via decision trees. Given the work on options in the previous chapter, we are now able to value real options according to the Black–Scholes model and the binomial model.

In this chapter, we described seven different types of options:

1 Executive share options, which are technically not real options.
2 The option to expand and abandon operations.
3 The embedded option in a start-up company.
4 The option in simple business contracts.
5 The option to shut down and reopen a project.
6 Mergers and diversification.
7 Options and capital budgeting.

We tried to keep the presentation simple and straightforward from a mathematical point of view. The binomial approach to option pricing in Chapter 22 was extended to many periods. This adjustment brings us closer to the real world because the assumption of only two prices at the end of an interval is more plausible when the interval is short.

Questions and Problems

CONCEPT

1 **Executive Share Options**   Why do companies issue options to executives if they cost the company more than they are worth to the executive? Why not just give cash and split the difference? Wouldn't that make both the company and the executive better off?

2 **Real Options**   What are the two options that many businesses have? Why does a traditional NPV analysis tend to underestimate the value of an investment opportunity? Explain.

3 **Valuing a Start-up**   Given that anything is possible in the future, why can't an entrepreneur who is seeking funding choose assumptions that make a start-up look good when it isn't? Is this more a danger with real option analysis than with normal capital budgeting analysis?

4 **The Binomial Model**   Why is the binomial model more appropriate for real option analysis than Black–Scholes?

5 **Executive Stock Options**   Do you think that executive stock options motivate executives to act in the best interests of the company? Explain.

REGULAR

6 **Stock Option Exercises and Share Prices**   The stock price of ABC plc is currently at £30, and the company has 2 million shares outstanding. The company's CEO exercises 200,000 stock options with a strike price of £20. What will happen to the share price of ABC plc?

7 **Real Options**   Utility companies often face a decision to build new plants that burn coal, oil, or both. If the prices of both coal and gas are highly volatile, how valuable is the decision to build a plant that can burn either coal or oil? What happens to the value of this option as the correlation between coal and oil prices increases?

8 **Real Options**   Your company owns a vacant plot in a suburban area. What is the advantage of waiting to develop the plot?

9 **Real Options**   Ventiora SpA has a disused warehouse it is holding till land prices increase before selling to potential buyers. In option terminology, what type of option(s) does the company have on the warehouse?

10 **Real Options and Capital Budgeting**   Most companies use traditional capital budgeting techniques, such as payback period and net present value. Why do you think this is the case? How would you justify the use of real option methodology to a reluctant chief executive?

11 **Insurance as an Option**   Insurance, whether purchased by a corporation or an individual, is in essence an option. What type of option is an insurance policy?

12 **Real Options**   How would the analysis of real options change if a company has competitors?

13 **Employee Share Options**   Kevin Swinson is the finance director of Mountainbrook Trading plc. The board of directors has just granted Mr Swinson 30,000 at-the-money European call options on the company's equity, which is currently trading at £30 per share. The equity pays no dividends. The options will expire in 4 years, and the standard deviation of the returns on the shares is 55 per cent. Treasury bills that mature in 4 years currently yield a continuously compounded interest rate of 3 per cent.

   (a)   Use the Black–Scholes model to calculate the value of the share options.

   (b)   You are Mr Swinson's financial adviser. He must choose between the previously mentioned share option package and an immediate £500,000 bonus. If he is risk-neutral, which would you recommend?

   (c)   How would your answer to (b) change if Mr Swinson were risk-loving and he could not sell the options prior to expiration?

14 **Employee Share Options**   Joseph-Benoit Suvee has just been named the new chief executive officer of BluBell Fitness NV. In addition to an annual salary of €400,000, his 3-year contract states that his compensation will include 10,000 at-the-money European call options on the company's shares that expire in 3 years. The current share price is €40 per share, and the standard deviation of the returns on the firm's equity is 68 per cent. The company does not pay a dividend. Treasury bills that mature in 3 years yield a continuously compounded interest rate of 5 per cent. Assume that Mr Suvee's annual salary payments occur

at the end of the year and that these cash flows should be discounted at a rate of 9 per cent. Using the Black–Scholes model to calculate the value of the share options, determine the total value of the compensation package on the date the contract is signed.

15 Binomial Model   Gasworks AG has been approached to sell up to 5 million litres of gasoline in 3 months at a price of €1.85 per litre. Gasoline is currently selling on the wholesale market at €1.65 per litre and has a standard deviation of 46 per cent. If the risk-free rate is 6 per cent per year, what is the value of this option?

16 Real Options   Webber plc is an international conglomerate with a real estate division that owns the right to erect an office building on a parcel of land in the outskirts of Leeds over the next year. This building would cost £10.5 million to construct. Due to low demand for office space in the area, such a building is worth approximately £10 million today. If demand increases, the building would be worth £12.5 million a year from today. If demand decreases, the same office building would be worth only £8 million in a year. The company can borrow and lend at the risk-free rate of 2.5 per cent effective annual rate. A local competitor in the real estate business has recently offered £750,000 for the right to build an office building on the land. Should the company accept this offer? Use a two-state model to value the real option.

17 Real Options   Eurocargoair is a British private air courier firm that has been given the option to purchase three new small jets at the price of £3 million per plane. The purchase agreement is only valid for the next 3 months before the offer is removed from the table. The company is also in negotiation with another firm for three similar jets but the purchase price has not yet been agreed. The firm's financial managers believe that there is an 80 per cent chance that they can purchase the planes elsewhere for £2.7 million each. If they are unsuccessful in negotiations, they will only be able to arrange a deal of £3.6 million per plane elsewhere. Negotiations will conclude in 3 months and the outcome will be unknown until then. Eurocargoair can borrow or lend at 3.5 per cent per annum. What is the value of the option to buy the jets at £3 million per plane?

18 Real Options   Jet Black is an international conglomerate with a petroleum division and is currently competing in an auction to win the right to drill for crude oil on a large piece of land in one year. The current market price of crude oil is $55 per barrel, and the land is believed to contain 125,000 barrels of oil. If found, the oil would cost $10 million to extract. Treasury bills that mature in one year yield a continuously compounded interest rate of 6.5 per cent, and the standard deviation of the returns on the price of crude oil is 50 per cent. Use the Black–Scholes model to calculate the maximum bid that the company should be willing to make at the auction.

19 Real Options   Sardano and Sons is a large, publicly held company that is considering leasing a warehouse. One of the company's divisions specializes in manufacturing steel and this particular warehouse is the only facility in the area that suits the firm's operations. The current price of steel is £3,600 per ton. If the price of steel falls over the next 6 months, the company will purchase 400 tons of steel and produce 4,800 steel rods. Each steel rod will cost £120 to manufacture, and the company plans to sell the rods for £360 each. It will take only a matter of days to produce and sell the steel rods. If the price of steel rises or remains the same, it will not be profitable to undertake the project, and the company will allow the lease to expire without producing any steel rods. Treasury bills that mature in 6 months yield a continuously compounded interest rate of 4.5 per cent, and the standard deviation of the returns on steel is 45 per cent. Use the Black–Scholes model to determine the maximum amount that the company should be willing to pay for the lease.

20 Real Options   Mouillez Pour L'été SA (MPLE) manufactures filters for swimming pools. The company is deciding whether to implement a new technology in its pool filters. One year from now the company will know whether the new technology is accepted in the market. If the demand for the new filters is high, the present value of the cash flows in one year will be €10 million. Conversely, if the demand is low, the value of the cash flows in one year will be €6 million. The value of the project today under these assumptions is €9.1 million, and the risk-free rate is 6 per cent. Suppose that in one year, if the demand for the new technology is low, the company can sell the technology for €7 million. What is the value of the option to abandon?

CHALLENGE

21 Binomial Model   There is an American put option on an equity that expires in 2 months. The share price is €13.20, and the standard deviation of the share price returns is 35 per cent. The option has a strike price of €14.00, and the risk-free interest rate is a 3.5 per cent annual percentage rate. What is the price of the put option today using one-month steps? (*Hint:* How will you find the value of the option if it can be exercised early? When would you exercise the option early?)

22 **Real Options** You are in discussions to purchase an option on an office building with a strike price of £47 million. The building is currently valued at £45 million. The option will allow you to purchase the building either 6 months from today or 1 year from today. Six months from today, accrued rent payments from the building in the amount of £500,000 will be made to the owners. If you exercise the option in 6 months, you will receive the accrued rent payments; otherwise the payment will be made to the current owners. A second accrued rent payment of £500,000 will be paid 1 year from today with the same payment terms. The standard deviation of the value of the building is 25 per cent, and the risk-free rate is an 8 per cent annual percentage rate. What is the price of the option today using 6-month steps? (*Hint:* The value of the building in 6 months will be reduced by the accrued rent payment if you do not exercise the option at that time.)

23 **Overseas Oil Exploration** Fan and Zhu (2010) propose a real options framework to value oil exploration projects in the presence of three sources of uncertainty: the overseas investment environment, the exchange rate and the oil price. Explain how the real options methodology can aid in investment evaluation for these types of projects.

24 **Downsizing and Shared Services** In today's global economic environment, many firms have chosen to downsize operations and share services or facilities with another firm. An example is the joint venture by Fiat and Chrysler to share their manufacturing facilities in Europe and North America. Explain how the real options approach can be used to assess the value of this type of investment decision.

25 **Electrical Interconnectors** In the electricity industry, interconnectors give the owner the option to transmit electricity to one of two locations. Show, using your own example, how real option analysis can be used to value an electrical interconnector.

26 **Research and Development** You have recently been employed as a finance consultant to a growing company, R&D Industries, which consistently develops successful products. After a meeting with the company's management, you estimate that the company produces, on average, two new product proposals every three years. The company's management informs you that the investment opportunities the company produces typically have an initial investment requirement of £10 million, and return annual cash flows of £1 million in perpetuity. After conducting a scenario analysis, you estimate that these cash flows could grow at one of three possible rates, which have an equal probability of occurring: −3%, 0%, and 3%. The company's management tell you that the projects are 'take it or leave it' opportunities. In other words, the company does not have the option to wait to invest under more favourable circumstances.

(a) If the company's cost of capital is 12 per cent, what is the present value of the company's future growth opportunities under each scenario?

(b) Which projects would be accepted or rejected?

Exam Question (45 minutes)

1 Your firm is considering a bid for a financially distressed football firm that is in administration. The administrators have said you must pay an exclusivity fee of £500,000 to develop the bid further, show the seriousness of your bid and present your commitment to resolving the issue. There are three potential bidders and the exclusivity fee will guarantee you a period of 1 month in which you will be sole bidder. Since the firm is in administration, your investment will be used to pay off all the outstanding creditors of the firm, who are owed a total of £134 million. Your plan is to enter into a company voluntary agreement (CVA) with the creditors where they will receive £0.06 for every £1 of debt and you have estimated that there is a 50 per cent probability that they will accept. If this were to happen, you estimate the NPV of the bid is £3 million. However, if they do not accept the CVA, the bid will not go ahead and your exclusivity fee will be lost. Your company can borrow and lend at the risk-free rate of 6 per cent per annum. Is it worthwhile for you to pay the exclusivity fee? Explain. (40 marks)

2 What are the benefits of real option methodology over traditional methods? Why, in your opinion, do many firms not use real options to value investments? Explain. (30 marks)

3 In real options analysis, why is the binomial model preferred to Black-Scholes? Explain your answer, using a quantitative example. (30 marks)

Mini Case

Exotic Cuisines Employee Share Options

As a new university graduate, you have taken a management position with Exotic Cuisines plc, a restaurant chain that just went public last year. The company's restaurants specialize in exotic main dishes, using ingredients such as wild boar, crocodile and pheasant. A concern you had going in was that the restaurant business is very risky. However, after some due diligence, you discovered a common misperception about the restaurant industry. It is widely thought that 90 per cent of new restaurants close within 3 years; however, recent evidence suggests the failure rate is closer to 60 per cent over 3 years. So it is a risky business, although not as risky as you originally thought.

During your interview process, one of the benefits mentioned was employee share options. Upon signing your employment contract, you received options with a strike price of £50 for 10,000 shares of company equity. As is fairly common, your share options have a 3-year vesting period and a 10-year expiration, meaning that you cannot exercise the options for 3 years, and you lose them if you leave before they vest. After the 3-year vesting period, you can exercise the options at any time. Thus, the employee share options are European (and subject to forfeit) for the first 3 years and American afterward. Of course, you cannot sell the options, nor can you enter into any sort of hedging agreement. If you leave the company after the options vest, you must exercise within 90 days or forfeit.

Exotic Cuisines equity is currently trading at £24.38 per share, a slight increase from the initial offering price last year. There are no market-traded options on the company's equity. Because the company has been traded for only about a year, you are reluctant to use the historical returns to estimate the standard deviation of the equity's return. However, you have estimated that the average annual standard deviation for restaurant company shares is about 55 per cent. Because Exotic Cuisines is a newer restaurant chain, you decide to use a 60 per cent standard deviation in your calculations. The company is relatively young, and you expect that all earnings will be reinvested back into the company for the near future. Therefore, you expect no dividends will be paid for at least the next 10 years. A 3-year Treasury note currently has a yield of 3.8 per cent, and a 10-year Treasury note has a yield of 4.4 per cent.

1   You are trying to value your options. What minimum value would you assign? What is the maximum value you would assign?

2   Suppose that in 3 years the company's equity is trading at £60. At that time should you keep the options or exercise them immediately? What are some of the important determinants in making such a decision?

3   Your options, like most employee share options, are not transferable or tradable. Does this have a significant effect on the value of the options? Why?

4   Why do you suppose employee share options usually have a vesting provision? Why must they be exercised shortly after you depart the company even after they vest?

5   As we have seen, much of the volatility in a company's share price is due to systematic or marketwide risks. Such risks are beyond the control of a company and its employees. What are the implications for employee share options? In light of your answer, can you recommend an improvement over traditional employee share options?

Practical Case Study

Consider the Cement example from Chapter 7. What are the real options that exist for the project? How would you incorporate these into your consultancy work? What would be the process you would follow to arrive at future decisions and what would be the main inputs into your analysis?

Relevant Accounting Standards

The important standard for executive share options is IFRS 2 *Share-based Payment*. Although not directly linked to real option analysis, there is an accounting standard for exploration and mining activities. This is IFRS 6 *Exploration for and Evaluation of Mineral Resources*. Visit the IASPlus website (www.iasplus.com) for more information.

References

Fan, Y. and L. Zhu (2010) 'A Real Options Based Study on Overseas Oil Investment and its Application in China's Overseas Oil Investment', *Energy Economics*, Vol. 32, 627–637.

Hull, J. C. (2012) *Options, Futures, and Other Derivatives*, 8th edn (Upper Saddle River, NJ: Prentice Hall).

Additional Reading

This chapter focuses on practical applications of real option analysis and, consequently, the reading list reflects this. The references are categorized into executive compensation research (which should also be read in conjunction with material in Chapter 2) and other research related to the application of real option analysis.

Executive Compensation

1 Babenko, L. (2009) 'Share Repurchases and Pay-Performance Sensitivity of Employee Compensation Contracts', *The Journal of Finance*, Vol. 64, No. 1, 117–150. **US**.

2 Brockman, P., X. Martin and E. Unlu (2010) 'Executive Compensation and the Maturity Structure of Corporate Debt', *The Journal of Finance*, Vol. 65, No. 3, 1123–1161.

3 Burns, N. and S. Kedia (2006) 'The Impact of Performance-Based Compensation on Misreporting', *Journal of Financial Economics*, Vol. 79, No. 1, 35–57. **US**.

4 Chhaochharia, V. and Y. Grinstein (2009) 'CEO Compensation and Board Structure', *The Journal of Finance*, Vol. 64, No. 1, 231–261. **US**.

5 Coles, J.L., N.D. Daniel and L. Naveen (2006) 'Managerial Incentives and Risk Taking', *Journal of Financial Economics*, Vol. 80, No. 2, 431–468. **US**.

6 Cvitanic, J., Z. Wiener and F. Zapatero (2008) 'Analytic Pricing of Employee Stock Options', *Review of Financial Studies*, Vol. 21, No. 2, 683–724. **US**.

7 Efendi, J., A. Srivastava and E.P. Swanson (2007) 'Why Do Corporate Managers Misstate Financial Statements? The Role of Option Compensation and Other Factors', *Journal of Financial Economics*, Vol. 85, No. 3, 667–708. **US**.

8 Frydman, C. and R.E. Saks (2010) 'Executive Compensation: A New View from a Long-Term Perspective, 1930–2005', *Review of Financial Studies*, Vol. 23, No. 5, 2099–2138.

9 Graham, J.R., S. Li and J. Qiu (2012) 'Managerial Attributes and Executive Compensation', *Review of Financial Studies*, Vol. 25, No. 1, 144–186.

10 Gregoric, A., S. Polanec and S. Slapnicar (2010) 'Pay Me Right: Reference Values and Executive Compensation', *European Financial Management*, Vol. 16, No. 5, 778–804. **Europe**.

11 Kato, H.K., M. Lemmon, M. Luo and J. Schalheim (2005) 'An Empirical Examination of the Costs and Benefits of Executive Stock Options: Evidence from Japan', *Journal of Financial Economics*, Vol. 78, No. 2, 435–461. **Japan**.

12 Narayanan, M.P. and H.N. Seyhun (2008) 'The Dating Game: Do Managers Designate Option Grant Dates to Increase the Compensation?', *Review of Financial Studies*, Vol. 21, No. 5, 1907–1945. **US**.

Other Relevant Research

13 Ang, A. and N.P.B. Bollen (2010) 'Locked Up by a Lockup: Valuing Liquidity as a Real Option', *Financial Management*, Vol. 39, No. 3, 1069–1096.

14 Fan, Y. and L. Zhu (2010) 'A Real Options Based Model and its Application to China's Overseas Oil Investment Decisions', *Energy Economics*, Vol. 32, No. 3, 627–637. **China**.

15 Hackbarth, D. and E. Morellec (2008) 'Stock Returns in Mergers and Acquisitions', *The Journal of Finance*, Vol. 63, No. 3, 1213–1252. **US**.

16 Hillier, D. and A. Marshall (1998) 'A Model of Complex Equity Funding for Contingent Acquisitions – A Case Study of Non-Interest Bearing Convertible Unsecured Loan Stock', *Journal of Corporate Finance*, Vol. 4, No. 2, 133–152. **UK**.

17 Su, N., R. Akkiraju, N. Nayak and R. Goodwin (2009) 'Shared Services Transformation: Conceptualization and Valuation from the Perspective of Real Options', *Decision Sciences*, Vol. 40, No. 3, 381–402.

Endnotes

1 We ignore warrant dilution in this example. See **Chapter 24** for a discussion of warrant dilution.

2 As we will see later, here u and d are consistent with a standard deviation of the annual return on heating oil of 0.63.

3 For simplicity, we ignore both storage costs and a convenience yield.

4 Though it is not apparent at first glance, we will see later that the price movement in Figure 23.3 is consistent with the price movement in Figure 23.2.

5 For simplicity, we ignore interest compounding.

6 See Hull (2012) for a derivation of these formulas.

7 In this discussion we have used both *intervals* and *dates*. To keep the terminology straight, remember that the number of intervals is always one less than the number of dates. For example, if a model has two dates, it has only one interval.

CHAPTER 24

Warrants and Convertibles

In the last few years, there has been a major paradigm shift in the way in which corporate finance is practised. We have come through a sustained period of deregulation and globalization in the world's markets. Financial innovation and the introduction of new securities has been commonplace as a result of the free markets that have spread throughout the world. However, things are very much different going into the second decade of the twenty-first century.

The financial world has seen a glut of corporate insolvencies. Governments of the major developed economies have all reduced interest rates to near zero and pumped cash into their ailing firms. Whole industries have effectively been nationalized and purchased by governments. Corporate strategies that were successful because of the availability of cheap debt are no longer possible. Finally, financial instruments that may have been viable and popular in a vibrant economy have become obsolete.

Convertible bonds are part of many companies' capital structure. They allow bondholders to convert the debt instruments into equity during a specified window in the future. The conversion feature is an embedded option that holders will exercise if the convertible is in the money. At the turn of the century, these became exceptionally popular investment targets of hedge funds that looked for a quick return from conversion and although we have seen much market volatility in recent times, convertible bonds are more popular than ever.

KEY NOTATIONS

#	Number of shares outstanding
$\#_w$	Number of warrants
c_w	Value of a call option written on the equity of a firm *without* warrants
S	Current share price
E	Exercise price of option
R	Annual risk-free rate of return, continuously compounded.
σ^2	Variance (per year) of the continuous share price return
t	Time (in years) to expiration date.
$N(d)$	Probability that a standardized, normally distributed, random variable will be less than or equal to d

$$d_1 = [\ln(S/E) + (R + \sigma^2/2)t]/\sqrt{\sigma^2 t}$$
$$d_2 = d_1 - \sqrt{\sigma^2 t}$$

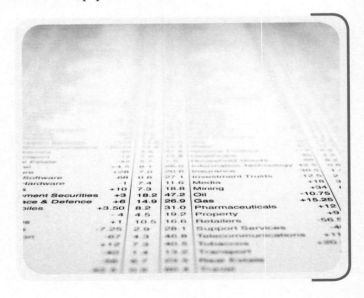

Warrants are similar to standard call options, except that the company must issue new shares if the holder chooses to exercise them. Because of changes in the global financial environment they have become less popular. However, they are present in the financial structure of many companies and tend to be issued in conjunction with standard bond issues.

This chapter is concerned with valuing the option embedded in these financial instruments.

24.1 Warrants

Warrants are securities that give holders the right, but not the obligation, to buy shares of equity directly from a company at a fixed price for a given period. Each warrant specifies the number of shares of equity that the holder can buy, the exercise price and the expiration date.

From the preceding description of warrants, it is clear that they are similar to call options. The differences in contractual features between warrants and the call options that trade on Euronext Liffe are small. For example, warrants have longer maturity periods. Some warrants are actually perpetual, meaning that they never expire.

Warrants are referred to as *equity kickers* because they are usually issued in combination with privately placed bonds.[1] In most cases, warrants are attached to the bonds when issued. The loan agreement will state whether the warrants are detachable from the bond – that is, whether they can be sold separately. Usually, the warrant can be detached immediately.

In the last few years, only a very few corporations have issued warrants and these have largely been in the United States. In recent times, governments purchased warrants from banks that needed financial assistance, and in the 2012 Greek sovereign debt bailout, bondholders received GDP-linked warrants which pay off if the Greek economy beats growth expectations.[2]

To illustrate warrants, we will focus on a hypothetical example of a firm, Hellas Shipping, which has issued warrants. Each warrant gives the holder the right to purchase one share of equity at an exercise price of €19.32 and the warrants expire in 4 years. The share price of Hellas Shipping is €17.57, and the price of a warrant is €4.05.

The relationship between the value of Hellas Shipping's warrants and its share price can be viewed as similar to the relationship between a call option and the share price, described in a previous chapter. Figure 24.1 depicts this relationship. The lower limit on the value of the warrants is zero if Hellas Shipping's share price is below €19.32 per share. If the price of Hellas Shipping's equity rises above €19.32 per share, the lower limit is the share price minus €19.32. The upper limit is the share price of Hellas Shipping. A warrant to buy one share of equity cannot sell at a price above the price of the underlying shares.

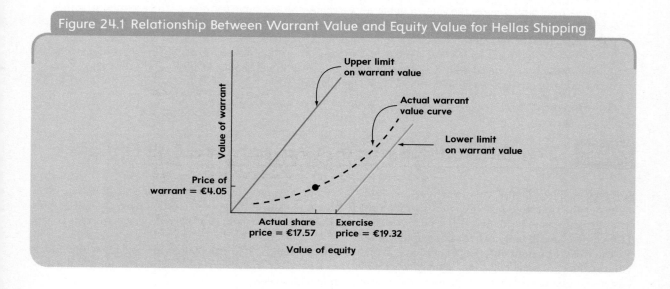

Figure 24.1 Relationship Between Warrant Value and Equity Value for Hellas Shipping

The price of Hellas Shipping's warrants was higher than the lower limit. The height of the warrant price above the lower limit will depend on the following:

1 The variance of Hellas Shipping's share price returns.
2 The time to expiration date.
3 The risk-free rate of interest.
4 The share price of Hellas Shipping.
5 The exercise price.
6 Cash dividends.

With the exception of cash dividends, these are the same factors that determine the value of a call option.[3]

Warrants can also have unusual features. For example, when the French specialist metals group Carbone Lorraine was unable to raise financing for solar power acquisitions, it entered into a financing deal with Société Générale. Under the deal, Carbone Lorraine issued convertible warrants to SocGen that allowed the French bank to buy up to 17.5 per cent of Carbone Lorraine's equity at a 10 per cent discount whenever the metals company needed funds. This innovative financing deal was a warrant, where the decision to exercise was with the issuer, not the holder. In effect, it mimicked an equity-linked credit line that bypassed the credit squeeze in the markets at the time.

Real World Insight 24.1

The Bonduelle Group

(Excerpts from a Bonduelle Press Release 27 March 2015)

On 27 March 2015, Bonduelle SCA made a block purchase of redeemable equity warrants from its main shareholder, Pierre et Benoit Bonduelle SAS and initiated a buyout offer to the other warrant holders. The objective of this transaction, made possible by the vast improvement of the Group's financial profile and justified by the increase in its stock price, was to limit the creation of equity and the dilution that could be caused if the redeemable equity warrants issued in 2009 were exercised.

Reasons for the transaction

In July 2007, Bonduelle issued 150,000 bonds with redeemable warrants for an amount of €150 million, with five warrants attached to each bond, i.e. a total of 750,000 redeemable equity warrants. This issue allowed Bonduelle to improve its financial structure by optimizing the cost of its debt, with the option to increase its equity if new shares are issued when the bonds are exercised.

In April 2009, Bonduelle issued 233,333 additional bonds with redeemable warrants for an amount of €140 million, with three warrants attached to each bond, i.e. a total of 699,999 redeemable equity warrants issued. The financial benefits of the transaction were the same for Bonduelle as those during the 2007 issue, i.e. the cost of debt was optimized with the option to increase its equity.

At the time of this new issue, Bonduelle had also offered to exchange the 750,000 redeemable equity warrants from 2007 against the same number of warrants with the same features as the warrants attached to the 2009 OBSAARs, i.e. maturing on 8 April 2016 and with a strike price of €80. Following this operation, there was a total of 1,449,999 redeemable equity warrants in circulation.

In view of the continued improvement in its financial profile, making a capital increase irrelevant, the Bonduelle Group decided to limit the dilution which would be brought about by the exercising of the redeemable equity warrants and the associated equity creation.

Reproduced with permission of Groupe Bonduelle

24.2 The Difference between Warrants and Call Options

From the holder's point of view, warrants are similar to call options on equity. A warrant, like a call option, gives its holder the right to buy shares at a specified price. Warrants usually have an expiration date, though in most cases they are issued with longer lives than call options. From the firm's point of view, however, a warrant is very different from a call option on the company's equity.

The most important difference between call options and warrants is that call options are issued by individuals and warrants are issued by firms. When a warrant is exercised, a firm must issue new shares of equity. Each time a warrant is exercised, then the number of shares outstanding increases.

To illustrate, suppose Endrun Ltd issues a warrant giving holders the right to buy one share of equity at €25. Further, suppose the warrant is exercised. Endrun must print one new share certificate. In exchange for the share certificate, it receives €25 from the holder.

In contrast, when a call option is exercised, there is no change in the number of shares outstanding. Suppose Ms Eager holds a call option on the equity of Endrun. The call option gives Ms Eager the right to buy one share of the equity of Endrun for €25. If Ms Eager chooses to exercise the call option, a seller, say Mr Swift, is obligated to give her one share of Endrun's equity in exchange for €25. If Mr Swift does not already own a share, he must enter the stock market and buy one. The call option is a side bet between buyers and sellers on the value of Endrun shares. When a call option is exercised, one investor gains and the other loses. The total number of shares outstanding of the Endrun Company remains constant, and no new funds are made available to the company.

Warrants also affect accounting numbers. Warrants and (as we shall see) convertible bonds cause the number of shares to increase. This causes the firm's net income to be spread over more shares, thereby decreasing earnings per share. Firms with significant amounts of warrants and convertible issues must report earnings on a primary basis and a fully diluted basis.

24.3 Warrant Pricing and the Black–Scholes Model

Chapter 22
Page 597

We now wish to express the gains from exercising a call and a warrant in more general terms (reread **Chapter 22**, Section 22.8 for the Black–Scholes model). The gain on a call can be written like this:

Gain from exercising a single call

$$\underbrace{\frac{\text{Firm's value net of debt}}{\#}}_{\text{(Value of a share of equity)}} - \text{Exercise price} \tag{24.1}$$

We define the *firm's value net of debt* to be the total firm value less the value of the debt. The # stands for the number of shares outstanding. The ratio on the left is the value of a share of equity. The gain on a warrant can be written as follows:

Gain from exercising a single warrant

$$\underbrace{\frac{\text{Firm's value net of debt} + \text{Exercise price} \times \#_w}{\# + \#_w}}_{\text{(Value of a share of equity after warrant is exercised)}} - \text{Exercise price} \tag{24.2}$$

The numerator of the left term is the firm's value net of debt *after* the warrant is exercised. It is the sum of the firm's value net of debt *prior* to the warrant's exercise plus the proceeds the firm receives from the exercise. The proceeds equal the product of the exercise price multiplied by the number of warrants. The number of warrants appears as $\#_w$. (Our analysis uses the plausible assumption that all warrants in the money will be exercised.) The denominator, $\# + \#_w$, is the number of shares outstanding *after* the exercise of the warrants. The ratio on the left is the value of a share of equity after exercise. By rearranging terms, we can rewrite Equation 24.2 as [4]

Gain from exercising a single warrant

$$\frac{\#_w}{\# + \#_w} \times \underbrace{\left(\frac{\text{Firm's value net of debt}}{\#} - \text{Exercise price} \right)}_{\text{(Gain from a call on a firm with no warrants)}} \tag{24.3}$$

Formula 24.3 relates the gain on a warrant to the gain on a call. Note that the term within parentheses is Equation 24.1. Thus, the gain from exercising a warrant is a proportion of the gain from exercising a call in a firm without warrants. The proportion $\#/(\# + \#_w)$ is the ratio of the number of shares in the firm without warrants to the number of shares after all the warrants have been exercised. This ratio must always be less than 1. Thus, the gain on a warrant must be less than the gain on an identical call in a firm without warrants.

The preceding implies that we can value a warrant using the Black–Scholes model, adjusted for the dilution effect:

$$w = \frac{1}{\left(1 + \frac{\#_w}{\#} \right)} c_w \tag{24.4}$$

where c_w is the value of a call option written on the equity of a firm *without* warrants.[5]

Warrant Valuation

Veld NV is planning to issue 10,000 warrants that, when exercised, can be converted on a one-for-one basis. The proceeds of the warrant issuance will be distributed to the existing shareholders. Besides this dividend, the company is not planning to pay out any other cash dividend during the lifetime of the warrants. The company currently has 50,000 shares outstanding. If the share price of Veld NV is €2.50 and the exercise price of the warrants is €2.30, what is the value of the warrant today? The continuously compounded annual risk free rate of interest is 7 per cent, the variance of returns of Veld NV is 0.09 and the time to expiry is 1 year.

Step 1. First we need to calculate the value of a comparable call option on the firm's equity. This is done by simply plugging the relevant values into the Black–Scholes Option Pricing Formula (see Chapter 22).

Step 1a. Calculate d_1 and d_2.

$$d_1 = \left[1n\left(\frac{S}{E}\right) + (R + \sigma^2/2)t \right] / \sqrt{\sigma^2 t}$$

$$= \left[1n\left(\frac{€2.30}{€2.30}\right) + (0.07 + 0.09/2)1 \right] / \sqrt{0.09}$$

$$= [0.0834 + 0.115]/0.3 = 0.6613$$

$$d_2 = d_1 - \sqrt{\sigma^2 t}$$

$$= 0.3613$$

Step 1b. Calculate $N(d_1)$ and $N(d_2)$ using a spreadsheet or tables.

$$N(d_1) = N(0.6613) = 0.7458$$

$$N(d_2) = N(0.3613) = 0.6411$$

Step 1c. Calculate c_w.

$$c_w = S \times [N(d_1)] - E_e^{-Rt} \times [N(d_2)]$$

$$= €2.50 \times [N(d_1)] - €2.30 \times e^{-0.07} \times N(d_2)$$

$$= (€2.50 \times 0.7458) - (€2.30 \times 0.9324 \times 0.6411)$$

$$= €1.8645 - €1.3749$$

$$= €0.49$$

Step 2. The value of the Veld NV warrant is thus:

$$W = \frac{1}{\left(1 + \frac{\#_w}{\#}\right)} c_w = \frac{1}{\left(1 + \frac{10,000}{50,000}\right)} €0.49$$

$$= 0.8333(€0.49)$$

$$= €0.4083$$

24.4   Convertible Bonds

A convertible bond is similar to a bond with warrants. The most important difference is that a bond with warrants can be separated into distinct securities and a convertible bond cannot. A convertible bond gives the holder the right to exchange it for a given number of shares any time up to and including the maturity date of the bond.

Preference shares can frequently be converted into equity. A convertible preference share is the same as a convertible bond except that it has an infinite maturity date.

Convertibles

In November 2013, Swiss Life AG launched a zero coupon convertible bond to raise 500 million Swiss francs. The face value of each bond was 5,000 Swiss francs, which means that 100,000 convertible bonds were issued by the firm. If redeemed by the bondholder, each bond would be converted into ordinary shares of Swiss Life.

Bond traders speak of the *conversion price* of the bond, which is equal to the share price at which the bond can be converted into equity. The conversion price of the Swiss Life bond was 243.97 Swiss francs, which represented a *conversion premium* of 31 per cent over the price (186.24 Swiss francs) that was recorded on the date of issue. The premium reflects the fact that the conversion option in Swiss Life convertible bonds was *out of the money*. This conversion premium is typical.

The number of shares received for each bond is called the *conversion ratio*. Since the face value of each Swiss Life bond was 5,000 Swiss francs and the conversion price was 243.97 Swiss francs, 20.49 shares (= 5,000/243.97) would be received for each bond.

Convertibles are almost always protected against stock splits and share dividends. If Swiss Life's equity had been split two for one, the conversion ratio would have been increased from 20.49 to 40.98.

Conversion ratio, conversion price and conversion premium are well-known terms in the real world. For that reason alone, the student should master the concepts. However, conversion price and conversion premium implicitly assume that the bond is selling at par. If the bond is selling at another price, the terms have little meaning. By contrast, conversion ratio can have a meaningful interpretation regardless of the price of the bond.

24.5 The Value of Convertible Bonds

Chapter 5
Page 120

The value of a convertible bond can be described in terms of three components: straight bond value (see **Chapter 5**, Sections 5.1–5.3), conversion value and option value. We examine these three components next.

Straight Bond Value

The straight bond value is what the convertible bonds would sell for if they could not be converted into equity. It will depend on the general level of interest rates and on the default risk. Consider a convertible bond issued by a hypothetical firm, Cold Dawn plc. On 1 November 2015, Cold Dawn plc raised £300 million by issuing 6.75 per cent convertible subordinated debentures due in 2031. It planned to use the proceeds to invest in new plant and equipment. Like typical debentures, they had a sinking fund and were callable. Cold Dawn's bonds differed from other debentures in their convertible feature: each bond was convertible into 2,353 shares of Cold Dawn equity any time before maturity. When Cold Dawn issued its convertible bonds, its share price was £22.625. The conversion price of £42.50 (=£100,000/2,353) was 88 per cent higher than the actual equity price. Suppose that straight debentures issued by Cold Dawn plc had been rated A, and A-rated bonds were priced to yield 4 per cent per 6 months on 1 November 2015. The straight bond value of Cold Dawn convertible bonds can be determined by discounting the £3,375 semi-annual coupon payment and principal amount at 4 per cent:

$$\text{Straight bond} = \sum_{t=1}^{32} \frac{£3,375}{1.04^t} + \frac{£100,000}{(1.04)^{32}}$$

$$= £3,375 \times A_{0.04}^{32} + \frac{£100,000}{(1.04)^{32}}$$

$$= £60,323 + £28,506$$

$$= £88,829$$

The straight bond value of a convertible bond is a minimum value. The price of Cold Dawn's convertible could not have gone lower than the straight bond value.

Figure 24.2 illustrates the relationship between straight bond value and share price. In Figure 24.2 we have been somewhat dramatic and implicitly assumed that the convertible bond is default free. In this case, the straight bond value does not depend on the share price, so it is graphed as a straight line.

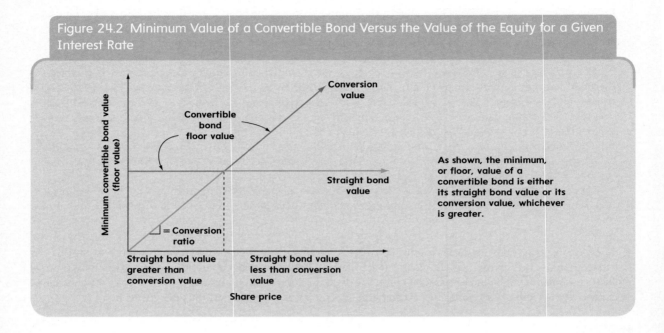

Figure 24.2 Minimum Value of a Convertible Bond Versus the Value of the Equity for a Given Interest Rate

As shown, the minimum, or floor, value of a convertible bond is either its straight bond value or its conversion value, whichever is greater.

Conversion Value

The value of convertible bonds depends on conversion value. Conversion value is what the bonds would be worth if they were immediately converted into equity at current prices. Typically, we compute conversion value by multiplying the number of shares of equity that will be received when the bond is converted by the current price of the equity.

On 1 November 2015, each Cold Dawn convertible bond could have been converted into 2,353 shares of Cold Dawn equity. Cold Dawn shares were selling for £22.625. Thus, the conversion value was $2,353 \times £22.625 = £53,237$. A convertible cannot sell for less than its conversion value. Arbitrage prevents this from happening. If Cold Dawn's convertible sold for less than £53,237, investors would have bought the bonds and converted them into equity and sold the shares. The profit would have been the difference between the value of the shares sold and the bond's conversion value.

Thus, convertible bonds have two minimum values: the straight bond value and the conversion value. The conversion value is determined by the value of the firm's underlying equity. This is illustrated in Figure 24.2. As the value of equity rises and falls, the conversion price rises and falls with it. When the value of Cold Dawn's equity increased by £1, the conversion value of its convertible bonds increased by £2,353.

Option Value

The value of a convertible bond will generally exceed both the straight bond value and the conversion value.[6] This occurs because holders of convertibles need not convert immediately. Instead, by waiting they can take advantage of whichever is greater in the future: the straight bond value or the conversion value. This option to wait has value, and it raises the value over both the straight bond value and the conversion value.

When the value of the firm is low, the value of convertible bonds is most significantly influenced by their underlying value as straight debt. However, when the value of the firm is very high, the value of convertible bonds is mostly determined by their underlying conversion value. This is illustrated in Figure 24.3

The bottom portion of the figure implies that the value of a convertible bond is the maximum of its straight bond value and its conversion value, plus its option value:

$$\text{Value of convertible bond} = \text{The greater of (Straight bond value, Conversion value)} + \text{Option value}$$

Figure 24.3 Value of a Convertible Bond Versus the Value of the Equity for a Given Interest Rate

As shown, the value of a convertible bond is the sum of its floor value and its option value.

Example 24.2

Conversion

Suppose Avaya plc has outstanding 1,000 shares of equity and 100 bonds. Each bond has a face value of £100,000 at maturity. They are discount bonds and pay no coupons. At maturity each bond can be converted into 10 shares of newly issued equity.

What circumstances will make it advantageous for the holders of Avaya convertible bonds to convert to equity at maturity?

If the holders of the convertible bonds convert, they will receive $100 \times 10 = 1,000$ shares of equity. Because there were already 1,000 shares, the total number of shares outstanding becomes 2,000 upon conversion. Thus, converting bondholders own 50 per cent of the value of the firm, V. If they do not convert, they will receive £10,000,000 or V, whichever is less. The choice for the holders of the Avaya bonds is obvious. They should convert if 50 per cent of V is greater than £10,000,000. This will be true whenever V is greater than £20,000,000. This is illustrated as follows:

Pay-off to Convertible Bondholders and Shareholders of Avaya plc			
	(1) $V \leq £10,000,000$	(2) $£10,000,000 < V \leq £20,000,000$	(3) $V > £20,000,000$
Decision:	Bondholders will not convert	Bondholders will not convert	Bondholders will convert
Convertible bondholders	V	£10,000,000	$0.5V$
Shareholders	0	$V - £10,000,000$	$0.5V$

HSBC CoCos

In April 2015, the multinational bank, HSBC, issued US$2.25 billion of bonds that convert into shares if the bank's risk rises above a certain level. The contingent convertible bonds, or 'CoCos', have an annual coupon of 6.375 per cent, which will be converted into equity if the bank's regulatory capital falls below a specified benchmark. CoCos are becoming more popular because of regulatory requirements that banks keep below a certain level of risk. If a bank becomes financially risky, CoCos convert into equity and their financial leverage risk is subsequently lowered.

24.6　Reasons for Issuing Warrants and Convertibles

Probably there is no other area of corporate finance where real-world practitioners disagree as they do on the reasons for issuing convertible debt. To separate fact from fantasy, we present a rather structured argument. We first compare convertible debt with straight debt. Then we compare convertible debt with equity. For each comparison, we ask in what situations is the firm better off with convertible debt and in what situations is it worse off.

Convertible Debt versus Straight Debt

Convertible debt pays a lower interest rate than does otherwise identical straight debt. For example, if the interest rate is 10 per cent on straight debt, the interest rate on convertible debt might be 9 per cent. Investors will accept a lower interest rate on a convertible because of the potential gain from conversion.

Imagine a firm that seriously considers both convertible debt and straight debt, finally deciding to issue convertibles. When would this decision have benefited the firm and when would it have hurt the firm? We consider two situations.

The Share Price Later Rises so that Conversion Is Indicated

The firm clearly likes to see the share price rise. However, it would have benefited even more had it previously issued straight debt instead of a convertible. Although the firm paid out a lower interest rate than it would have with straight debt, it was obligated to sell the convertible holders a chunk of the equity at a below-market price.

The Share Price Later Falls or Does Not Rise Enough to Justify Conversion

The firm hates to see the share price fall. However, as long as the share price does fall, the firm is glad that it had previously issued convertible debt instead of straight debt. This is because the interest rate on convertible debt is lower. Because conversion does not take place, our comparison of interest rates is all that is needed.

Summary

Compared to straight debt, the firm is worse off having issued convertible debt if the underlying equity subsequently does well. The firm is better off having issued convertible debt if the underlying equity subsequently does poorly. In an efficient market, we cannot predict future share prices. Thus, we cannot argue that convertibles either dominate or are dominated by straight debt.

Convertible Debt versus Equity

Next, imagine a firm that seriously considers both convertible debt and equity but finally decides to issue convertibles. When would this decision benefit the firm and when would it hurt the firm? We consider our two situations.

The Share Price Later Rises so that Conversion Is Indicated

The firm is better off having previously issued a convertible instead of equity. To see this, consider the Cold Dawn case. The firm could have issued equity for £22. Instead, by issuing a convertible, the firm effectively received £42.50 for a share upon conversion.

The Share Price Later Falls or Does Not Rise Enough to Justify Conversion

No firm wants to see its share price fall. However, given that the price did fall, the firm would have been better off if it had previously issued equity instead of a convertible. The firm would have benefited by issuing equity above its later market price. That is, the firm would have received more than the subsequent worth of the equity. However, the drop in share price did not affect the value of the convertible much because the straight bond value serves as a floor.

Summary

Compared with equity, the firm is better off having issued convertible debt if the underlying equity subsequently does well. The firm is worse off having issued convertible debt if the underlying equity subsequently does poorly. We cannot predict future share prices in an efficient market. Thus, we cannot argue that issuing convertibles is better or worse than issuing equity. The preceding analysis is summarized in Table 24.1.

Table 24.1 The Case For and Against Convertible Bonds (CBs)

	If Firm Subsequently Does Poorly	If Firm Subsequently Prospers
Convertible bonds (CBs)	No conversion because of low share price.	Conversion because of high share price.
Compared to:		
Straight bonds	CBs provide cheap financing because coupon rate is lower.	CBs provide expensive financing because bonds are converted, which dilutes existing equity.
Equity	CBs provide expensive financing because firm could have issued equity at high prices.	CBs provide cheap financing because firm issues equity at high prices when bonds are converted.

Modigliani–Miller (MM) pointed out that, abstracting from taxes and bankruptcy costs, the firm is indifferent to whether it issues equity or issues debt. The MM relationship is a quite general one. Their pedagogy could be adjusted to show that the firm is indifferent to whether it issues convertibles or issues other instruments. To save space (and the patience of students) we have omitted a full-blown proof of MM in a world with convertibles. However, our results are perfectly consistent with MM. Now we turn to the real-world view of convertibles.

The 'Free Lunch' Story

The preceding discussion suggests that issuing a convertible bond is no better and no worse than issuing other instruments. Unfortunately, many corporate executives fall into the trap of arguing that issuing convertible debt is actually better than issuing alternative instruments. This is a free lunch type of explanation, of which we are quite critical.

Example 24.3

Are Convertibles Always Better?

The share price of RW SE is €20. Suppose this company can issue subordinated debentures at 10 per cent. It can also issue convertible bonds at 6 per cent with a conversion value of €800. The conversion value means that the holders can convert a convertible bond into 40 (= €800/€20) shares of equity.

A company treasurer who believes in free lunches might argue that convertible bonds should be issued because they represent a cheaper source of financing than either subordinated bonds or equity. The treasurer will point out that if the company does poorly and the price does not rise above €20, the convertible bondholders will not convert the bonds into equity. In this case the company will have obtained debt financing at below-market rates by attaching worthless equity kickers. On the other hand, if the firm does well and the price of its equity rises to €25 or above, convertible holders will convert. The company will issue 40 shares. The company will receive a bond with face value of €1,000 in exchange for issuing 40 shares of equity, implying a conversion price of €25. The company will have issued equity at €25 per share, or 20 per cent above the €20 equity price prevailing when the convertible bonds were issued. This enables it to lower its cost of equity capital. Thus, the treasurer happily points out, regardless of whether the company does well or poorly, convertible bonds are the cheapest form of financing.

Although this argument may sound quite plausible at first, there is a flaw. The treasurer is comparing convertible financing *with straight debt* when the share price subsequently falls. However, the treasurer compares convertible financing *with equity* when the share price subsequently rises. This is an unfair mixing of comparisons. By contrast, our analysis of Table 24.1 was fair because we examined both share price increases and decreases when comparing a convertible with each alternative instrument. We found that no single alternative dominated convertible bonds in *both* up and down markets.

The 'Expensive Lunch' Story

Suppose we stand the treasurer's argument on its head by comparing (1) convertible financing with straight debt when share prices rise, and (2) convertible financing with equity when share prices fall.

From Table 24.1, we see that convertible debt is more expensive than straight debt when share prices subsequently rise. The firm's obligation to sell convertible holders a chunk of equity at a below-market price more than offsets the lower interest rate on a convertible.

Also from Table 24.1, we see that convertible debt is more expensive than equity when share prices subsequently fall. Had the firm issued equity, it would have received a price higher than its subsequent worth. Therefore, the expensive lunch story implies that convertible debt is an inferior form of financing. Of course, we dismiss both the free lunch and the expensive lunch arguments.

A Reconciliation

In an efficient financial market there is neither a free lunch nor an expensive lunch. Convertible bonds can be neither cheaper nor more expensive than other instruments. A convertible bond is a package of straight debt and an option to buy equity. The difference between the market value of a convertible bond and the value of a straight bond is the price investors pay for the call option feature. In an efficient market, this is a fair price.

In general, if a company prospers, issuing convertible bonds will turn out to be worse than issuing straight bonds and better than issuing equity. In contrast, if a company does poorly, convertible bonds will turn out to be better than issuing straight bonds and worse than issuing equity.

24.7   Why Are Warrants and Convertibles Issued?

From studies it is known that firms that issue convertible bonds are different from other firms. Here are some of the differences:

1   The bond ratings of firms using convertibles are lower than those of other firms.[7]
2   Convertibles tend to be used by smaller firms with high growth rates and more financial leverage.[8]
3   Convertibles are usually subordinated and unsecured.

The kind of company that uses convertibles provides clues to why they are issued. Here are some explanations that make sense.

Matching Cash Flows

If financing is costly, it makes sense to issue securities whose cash flows match those of the firm. A young, risky and (it hopes) growing firm might prefer to issue convertibles or bonds with warrants because these will have lower initial interest costs. When the firm is successful, the convertibles (or warrants) will be converted. This causes expensive dilution, but it occurs when the firm can most afford it.

Risk Synergy

Another argument for convertible bonds and bonds with warrants is that they are useful when it is very costly to assess the risk of the issuing company. Suppose you are evaluating a new product by a start-up company. The new product is a genetically engineered virus that may increase the yields of corn crops in northern climates. It may also cause cancer. This type of product is difficult to value properly. Thus, the risk of the company is very hard to determine: it may be high, or it may be low. If you could be sure the risk of the company was high, you would price the bonds for a high yield, say 15 per cent. If it was low, you would price them at a lower yield, say 10 per cent.

Convertible bonds and bonds with warrants can protect somewhat against mistakes of risk evaluation. Convertible bonds and bonds with warrants have two components: straight bonds and call options on the company's underlying equity. If the company turns out to be a low-risk company, the straight bond component will have high value and the call option will have low value. However, if the company turns out to be a high-risk company, the straight bond component will have low value and the call option will have high value. This is illustrated in Table 24.2.

Table 24.2 A Hypothetical Case of the Yields on Convertible Bonds*

	Firm risk	
	Low (%)	High (%)
Straight bond yield	10	15
Convertible bond yield	6	7

*The yields on straight bonds reflect the risk of default. The yields on convertibles are not sensitive to default risk.

However, although risk has effects on value that cancel each other out in convertibles and bonds with warrants, the market and the buyer nevertheless must make an assessment of the firm's potential to value securities, and it is not clear that the effort involved is that much less than is required for a straight bond.

Agency Costs

Convertible bonds can resolve agency problems associated with raising money. In a previous chapter, we showed that straight bonds are like risk-free bonds minus a put option on the assets of the firm. This creates an incentive for creditors to force the firm into low-risk activities. In contrast, holders of equity have incentives to adopt high-risk projects. High-risk projects with negative NPV transfer wealth from bondholders to shareholders. If these conflicts cannot be resolved, the firm may be forced to pass up profitable investment opportunities. However, because convertible bonds have an equity component, less expropriation of wealth can occur when convertible debt is issued instead of straight debt.[9] In other words, convertible bonds mitigate agency costs. One implication is that convertible bonds have less restrictive debt covenants than do straight bonds in the real world. Casual empirical evidence seems to bear this out.

Backdoor Equity

A popular theory of convertibles views them as backdoor equity.[10] The basic story is that young, small, high-growth firms cannot usually issue debt on reasonable terms due to high financial distress costs. However, the owners may be unwilling to issue equity if current share prices are too low.

Lewis et al. (1998) examine the risk shifting and backdoor equity theories of convertible bond debt. They find evidence for both theories.

The European Puzzle

Until very recently, there has been no research on convertible bond issuance in Europe. However, two recent papers that have explored this issue provide additional insights into why European managers issue convertibles. Bancel and Mittoo (2004) and Dutordoir and Van de Gucht (2009) both ask the question 'Why do European firms issue convertible debt instead of straight debt or equity?' Surprisingly, their findings differ somewhat from the established view of convertible issuance that has been propagated by US researchers.

Bancel and Mittoo (2004) surveyed 229 firms in 16 European countries that issued convertible bonds. This sample represented 295 convertible bond issues amounting to a total of €97,933 million. Only 29 firms responded to the sample and most of these were French. Normally, such a small sample would be problematic but given that this was the first study of its type, we can be forgiving. They found that there was no one reason why firms opt for convertibles over other forms of financing. French respondents argued that the liquidity of the convertibles market was a strong motivator for issuing convertibles. Clearly, this appears to be consistent with the situation in financial markets as we move into the second decade of the twenty-first century. In addition, firms whose equity appears to be overvalued opt for convertibles to avoid the share price falling because of equity dilution.

Dutordoir and Van de Gucht (2009) act as an interesting counterpoint to the work of Bancel and Mittoo and earlier US research. Using a much larger sample of security issues, they find that European issuers of convertible bonds are actually large companies with low financing costs. This is the opposite to US convertible issuers who tend to be small and highly levered. Again, unlike the US, convertible bonds in Europe are rarely callable and only 27 per cent have been converted into equity. In Europe, it appears that convertible bonds are not used as backdoor equity but instead as 'sweetened debt', to reduce financing costs of raising debt.

The findings of Dutordoir and Van de Gucht (2009) raise important questions about the motivation for European firms that issue convertible bonds. Given that issuers tend to be large, financially healthy and mature, the explanations relating to financing costs that have been proposed do not appear to explain the reality in Europe. A possible reason may simply be due to market timing, as argued by Baker and Wurgler (2002) and discussed in an earlier chapter. The contrast in findings between the US and Europe highlight the need to recognize differences in environment, culture and motivations of corporate managers in these two very heterogeneous regions.

Finally, Dong et al. (2012) asked top executives from Australia, Canada, UK and US why their firms issued convertible bonds. Although the findings were not conclusive, most support was given to the 'risk synergy' rationale. The executives also stated that they issued convertible bonds because debt was too costly or covenant-heavy and their share price was too low.

Who Buys Convertible Bonds?

Because of their hybrid debt and equity characteristics, convertible bonds attract two main types of investors. Originally, financial institutions bought convertibles because they provided exposure to upside share price growth and limited downside credit risk. However, a new type of investor, hedge funds, now comprise a major part of the convertible market. Hedge funds buy the convertible bond and short the equity of the issue to take advantage of any undervaluation in the convertible bond price. Unfortunately, this can lead to falls in the share price of the convertible issuing firm because of the short-selling activity.[11]

24.8 Conversion Policy

There is one aspect of convertible bonds that we have omitted so far. Firms are sometimes granted a call option on the bond. It should be noted that in the US, call features are significantly more common than in Europe. The typical arrangements for calling a convertible bond are simple. When the bond is called, the holder has about 30 days to choose between the following:

1 Converting the bond to equity at the conversion ratio
2 Surrendering the bond and receiving the call price in cash.

What should bondholders do? It should be obvious that if the conversion value of the bond is greater than the call price, conversion is better than surrender; and if the conversion value is less than the call price, surrender is better than conversion. If the conversion value is greater than the call price, the call is said to force conversion.

What should financial managers do? Calling the bonds does not change the value of the firm as a whole. However, an optimal call policy can benefit the shareholders at the expense of the bondholders. Because we are speaking about dividing a pie of fixed size, the optimal call policy is simple: do whatever the bondholders do not want you to do.

Bondholders would love the shareholders to call the bonds when the bonds' market value is below the call price. Shareholders would be giving bondholders extra value. Alternatively, should the value of the bonds rise above the call price, the bondholders would love the shareholders not to call the bonds because bondholders would be allowed to hold onto a valuable asset.

There is only one policy left. This is the policy that maximizes shareholder value and minimizes bondholder value:

Call the bond when its value is equal to the call price.

It is a puzzle that firms do not always call convertible bonds when the conversion value reaches the call price. Ingersoll (1977) examined the call policies of 124 firms between 1968 and 1975.[12] In most cases he found that the company waited to call the bonds until the conversion value was much higher than the call price. The median company waited until the conversion value of its bonds was 44 per cent higher than the call price. This is not even close to our optimal strategy. Why?

One reason is that if firms attempt to implement the optimal strategy, it may not be truly optimal. Recall that bondholders have 30 days to decide whether to convert bonds to equity or to surrender bonds for the call price in cash. In 30 days the share price could drop, forcing the conversion value below the call price. If so, the convertible is 'out of the money' and the firm is giving away money. The firm would be giving up cash for equity worth much less. Because of this possibility, firms in the real world usually wait until the conversion value is substantially above the call price before they trigger the call.[13] This is sensible.

Summary and Conclusions

1   A warrant gives the holder the right to buy shares of equity at an exercise price for a given period. Typically, warrants are issued in a package with privately placed bonds. Afterwards they may become detached and trade separately.

2   A convertible bond is a combination of a straight bond and a call option. The holder can give up the bond in exchange for shares.

3   Convertible bonds and warrants are like call options. However, there are some important differences:

   (a)   Warrants and convertible securities are issued by corporations. Call options are traded between individual investors.

      (i)   Warrants are usually issued privately and are combined with a bond. In most cases the warrants can be detached immediately after the issue. In some cases, warrants are issued with preference shares, with equity, or in executive compensation programmes.

      (ii) Convertibles are usually bonds that can be converted into equity.

      (iii) Call options are sold separately by individual investors (called *writers* of call options).

   (b)   Warrants and call options are exercised for cash. The holder of a warrant gives the company cash and receives new shares of the company's equity. The holder of a call option gives another individual cash in exchange for shares. When someone converts a bond, it is exchanged for equity. As a consequence, bonds with warrants and convertible bonds have different effects on corporate cash flow and capital structure.

   (c)   Warrants and convertibles cause dilution to the existing shareholders. When warrants are exercised and convertible bonds converted, the company must issue new shares of equity. The percentage ownership of the existing shareholders will decline. New shares are not issued when call options are exercised.

4   Many arguments, both plausible and implausible, are given for issuing convertible bonds and bonds with warrants. One plausible rationale for such bonds has to do with risk. Convertibles and bonds with warrants are associated with risky companies. Lenders can do several things to protect themselves from high-risk companies:

   (a)   They can require high yields.

   (b)   They can lend less or not at all to firms whose risk is difficult to assess.

   (c)   They can impose severe restrictions on such debt.

   Another useful way to protect against risk is to issue bonds with equity kickers. This gives the lenders the chance to benefit from risks and reduces the conflicts between bondholders and shareholders concerning risk.

5   A puzzle particularly vexes financial researchers: convertible bonds may have call provisions. Companies appear to delay calling convertibles until the conversion value greatly exceeds the call price. From the shareholders' standpoint, the optimal call policy would be to call the convertibles when the conversion value equals the call price.

Questions and Problems

CONCEPT

1. **Warrants**   What are warrants? Why are warrants sometime referred to as equity kickers? What does this mean?

2. **Warrants and Options**   What is the primary difference between a warrant and a traded call option? Why is the dilution factor important in warrant pricing?

3. **Warrants**   What are the advantages and disadvantages of issuing warrants?

4. **Convertible Bonds**   What is a convertible bond? What are the key features of such a security?

5. **Reasons for Issuing Warrants and Convertibles**   Why do firms issue convertibles? What impact do convertibles have on firms with target debt to equity ratios? Discuss convertible bonds in the context of the trade-off, pecking order and market timing theories of capital structure.

6. **Reasons for Buying Convertible Bonds**   Why might an investor buy a convertible security?

7. **Conversion Policy**   Why will convertible bonds not be voluntarily converted to equity before expiration? When and why should a firm force conversion of convertibles?

REGULAR

8. **Warrants**   Explain the following limits on the prices of warrants:

   (a) If the share price is below the exercise price of the warrant, the lower bound on the price of a warrant is zero.

   (b) If the share price is above the exercise price of the warrant, the lower bound on the price of a warrant is the difference between the share price and the exercise price.

   (c) An upper bound on the price of any warrant is the current value of the firm's equity.

9. **Convertible Bonds and Equity Volatility**   Assume that Barclays plc has just issued a callable convertible bond. You are concerned that the share price of Barclays is going to become more volatile over the next year. Should you buy the bond? Explain.

10. **Convertible Bond Value**   Using the same bond as in Question 9, assume that you believe interest rates are going to increase. What do you think will happen to the value of the bond? What if the bond was a putable convertible bond? Explain.

11. **Dilution**   What is dilution, and why does it occur when warrants are exercised?

12. **Warrants and Convertibles**   What is wrong with the simple view that it is cheaper to issue a bond with a warrant or a convertible feature because the required coupon is lower?

13. **Warrants and Convertibles**   You are employed as a finance consultant to a company which has undergone severe financial distress over the last number of years. Lacking in internal financing resources, the company tells you that it must go to the market to obtain funds, and has suggested issuing a convertible bond with a warrant attached to it. What are your thoughts on this?

14. **Convertible Bonds and Financial Distress**   Read the paper 'The Role of Convertible Bonds in Alleviating Contracting Costs' in the *Quarterly Review of Economics and Finance* by Krishnaswami and Yaman (2008). What are the authors' main findings? Does this surprise you? Explain.

15. **Warrant Valuation**   A warrant with 5 months until expiration entitles its owner to buy 100 shares of the issuing firm's equity for an exercise price of €23 per share. If the current market price of the equity is €10 per share, will the warrant be worthless?

16. **Convertible Bonds**   Why do you think executives believe the risk synergy rationale for issuing convertibles and not the other explanations? Explain.

17. **Conversion Price**   A convertible bond with a face value of €1,000 has a conversion ratio of 16.4. What is the conversion price?

18. **Conversion Ratio**   A convertible bond with a face value of SKr10,000 has a conversion price of SKr356. What is the conversion ratio of the bond?

19 Conversion Value A convertible bond has a conversion ratio of 100. If the shares are currently priced at £9.20, what is the conversion value of the bond?

20 Conversion Premium Citic Securities recently issued bonds with a face value of 100,000 renminbi and conversion ratio of 420. If the share price at the bond issue was 124 renminbi, what was the conversion premium?

21 Convertible Bonds Hannon Home Products recently issued £43,000,000 worth of 8 per cent convertible debentures. Each convertible bond has a face value of £100,000. Each convertible bond can be converted into 2,425 shares of equity any time before maturity. The share price is £31.25, and the market value of each bond is £118,000.

(a) What is the conversion ratio?

(b) What is the conversion price?

(c) What is the conversion premium?

(d) What is the conversion value?

(e) If the stock price increases by £2, what is the new conversion value?

22 Warrant Value A warrant gives its owner the right to purchase three shares of equity at an exercise price of 32 Swedish krona per share. The current market price of the equity is 39 Swedish krona. What is the minimum value of the warrant?

23 Convertible Bond Value An analyst has recently informed you that at the issuance of a company's convertible bonds, one of the two following sets of relationships existed:

	Scenario A (€)	Scenario B (€)
Face value of bond	1,000	1,000
Straight value of convertible bond	900	950
Market value of convertible bond	1,000	900

Assume the bonds are available for immediate conversion. Which of the two scenarios do you believe is more likely? Why?

24 Convertible Bond Value Tvep plc issued convertible bonds with a conversion price of £20. The bonds are available for immediate conversion. The current price of the company's equity is £18 per share. The current market price of the convertible bonds is £990. The convertible bonds' straight value is not known.

(a) What is the minimum price for the convertible bonds?

(b) Explain the difference between the current market price of each convertible bond and the value of the equity into which it can be immediately converted.

25 Convertible Bonds You own a callable, convertible bond with a conversion ratio of 500. The equity is currently selling for £22 per share. The issuer of the bond has announced a call at a call price of 105 on a face value of £100. What are your options here? What should you do?

26 Warrant Value General Modems has 5-year warrants that currently trade in the open market. Each warrant gives its owner the right to purchase one share of equity for an exercise price of £35.

(a) Suppose the equity is currently trading for £33 per share. What is the lower limit on the price of the warrant? What is the upper limit?

(b) Suppose the equity is currently trading for £39 per share. What is the lower limit on the price of the warrant? What is the upper limit?

27 Convertible Bonds Trichet SA has just issued a 30-year callable, convertible bond with a coupon rate of 7 per cent annual coupon payments. The bond has a conversion price of €125. The company's equity is selling for €32 per share. The owner of the bond will be forced to convert if the bond's conversion value is ever greater than or equal to €1,100. The required return on an otherwise identical non-convertible bond is 12 per cent.

(a) What is the minimum value of the bond?

(b) If the share price were to grow by 15 per cent per year forever, how long would it take for the bond's conversion value to exceed €1,100?

28 Convertible Bonds Rob Stevens is the chief executive officer of Isner Construction plc and owns 500,000 shares. The company currently has 4 million shares and convertible bonds with a face value of £20 million outstanding. The convertible bonds have a conversion price of £20, and the equity is currently selling for £25.

(a) What percentage of the firm's equity does Mr Stevens own?

(b) If the company decides to call the convertible bonds and force conversion, what percentage of the firm's equity will Mr Stevens own? He does not own any convertible bonds.

29 **Warrants**   Survivor NV, an all-equity firm, has three shares outstanding. Yesterday, the firm's assets consisted of 5 ounces of platinum, currently worth €1,000 per ounce. Today, the company issued Ms Wu a warrant for its fair value of €1,000. The warrant gives Ms Wu the right to buy a single share of the firm's equity for €2,100 and can be exercised only on its expiration date one year from today. The firm used the proceeds from the issuance to immediately purchase an additional ounce of platinum.

(a) What was the price of a single share of equity *before* the warrant was issued?

(b) What was the price of a single share of equity immediately *after* the warrant was issued?

(c) Suppose platinum is selling for €1,100 per ounce on the warrant's expiration date in one year. What will be the value of a single share of equity on the warrant's expiration date?

30 **Warrants**   The capital structure of Ricketti Enterprises plc consists of 10 million shares of equity and 1 million warrants. Each warrant gives its owner the right to purchase one share of equity for an exercise price of £15. The current share price is £17, and each warrant is worth £3. What is the new share price if all warrant holders decide to exercise today?

CHALLENGE

31 **Convertible Calculations**   You have been hired to value a new 25-year callable, convertible bond. The bond has a 6.80 per cent coupon rate, payable annually. The conversion price is £150, and the equity currently sells for £44.75. The stock price is expected to grow at 12 per cent per year. The bond is callable at £1,200 but based on prior experience it will not be called unless the conversion value is £1,300. The required return on this bond is 10 per cent. What value would you assign to this bond?

32 **Warrant Value**   Superior Clamps AB has a capital structure consisting of 4 million shares of equity and 500,000 warrants. Each warrant gives its owner the right to purchase one share of newly issued equity for an exercise price of €20. The warrants are European and will expire one year from today. The market value of the company's assets is €88 million, and the annual variance of the returns on the firm's assets is 0.04. Treasury bills that mature in one year yield a continuously compounded interest rate of 7 per cent. The company does not pay a dividend. Use the Black–Scholes model to determine the value of a single warrant.

33 **Warrant Value**   Omega Airline's capital structure consists of 1.5 million shares of equity and zero coupon bonds with a face value of $10 million that mature in 6 months. The firm just announced that it will issue warrants with an exercise price of $95 and 6 months until expiration to raise the funds to pay off its maturing debt. Each warrant can be exercised only at expiration and gives its owner the right to buy a single newly issued share of equity. The firm will place the proceeds from the warrant issue immediately into Treasury bills.

The market value balance sheet shows that the firm will have assets worth $160 million after the announcement. The company does not pay dividends. The standard deviation of the returns on the firm's assets is 65 per cent, and Treasury bills with a 6-month maturity yield 6 per cent. How many warrants must the company issue today to be able to use the proceeds from the sale to pay off the firm's debt obligation in 6 months?

Exam Question (45 minutes)

1 You have been hired to value a new 10-year callable, convertible bond. The bond has a 5.6 per cent coupon rate, payable annually. The conversion price is £150, and the equity currently sells for £44.75. The share price is expected to grow at 8 per cent per year. The bond is callable at £1,100 but based on prior experience it will not be called unless the conversion value is £1,200. The required return on this bond is 6 per cent. What value would you assign to this bond? (30 marks)

2   Your firm has 3 million shares of equity and 100,000 warrants. Each warrant gives its owner the right to purchase one share of newly issued equity for an exercise price of €15. The warrants are European and will expire one year from today. The market value of the company's assets is €60 million, and the annual standard deviation of the returns on the firm's assets is 24 per cent. Treasury bills that mature in one year yield a continuously compounded interest rate of 2 per cent. The company does not pay a dividend. Use the Black–Scholes model to determine the value of a single warrant. (30 marks)

3   Review the reasons given for why firms issue convertible bonds. Which one do you think is the most valid? Explain. (40 marks)

Mini Case

S&S Air's Convertible Bond

Kartner Meister was recently hired by S&S Air AB to assist the company with its short-term financial planning and to evaluate the company's performance. Kartner graduated from university 5 years ago with a finance degree. He has been employed in the finance department of a major German company since then.

S&S Air was founded 10 years ago by two friends, Stephan Lochner and Hans Multscher. The company has manufactured and sold light airplanes over this period, and the company's products have received high reviews for safety and reliability. The company has a niche market in that it sells primarily to individuals who own and fly their own airplanes. The company has two models: the Birdie, which sells for €53,000, and the Eagle, which sells for €78,000.

S&S Air is not publicly traded, but the company needs new funds for investment opportunities. In consultation with Conrad Witz of underwriter Koerbecke and Pleydenwurff, Kartner decided that a convertible bond issue with a 20-year maturity is the way to go. He met with the owners, Stephan and Hans, and presented his analysis of the convertible bond issue. Because the company is not publicly traded, Kartner looked at comparable publicly traded companies and determined that the average PE ratio for the industry is 12.5. Earnings per share for the company are €1.60. With this in mind, Kartner concluded that the conversion price should be €25 per share.

Several days later Stephan, Hans and Kartner met again to discuss the potential bond issue. Both Hans and Stephan have researched convertible bonds and have questions for Kartner. Hans begins by asking Kartner if the convertible bond issue will have a lower coupon rate than a comparable bond without a conversion feature. Kartner replies that to sell the bond at par value, the convertible bond issue would require a 6 per cent coupon rate with a conversion value of €800, while a plain vanilla bond would have a 7 per cent coupon rate. Hans nods in agreement, and he explains that the convertible bonds are a win–win form of financing. He states that if the value of the company equity does not rise above the conversion price, the company has issued debt at a cost below the market rate (6 per cent instead of 7 per cent). If the company's equity does rise to the conversion value, the company has effectively issued shares at above the current value.

Stephan immediately disagrees, arguing that convertible bonds are a no-win form of financing. He argues that if the value of the company equity rises to €25, the company is forced to sell shares at the conversion price. This means the new shareholders (those who bought the convertible bonds) benefit from a bargain price. Put another way, if the company prospers, it would have been better to have issued straight debt so that the gains would not be shared.

Kartner has gone back to Conrad for help. As Conrad's assistant, you have been asked to prepare another memo answering the following questions:

1   Why do you think Kartner is suggesting a conversion price of €25? Given that the company is not publicly traded, does it even make sense to talk about a conversion price?

2   What is the floor value of the S&S Air convertible bond?

3   What is the conversion ratio of the bond?

4   What is the conversion premium of the bond?

5   What is the value of the option?

6   Is there anything wrong with Hans' argument that it is cheaper to issue a bond with a convertible feature because the required coupon is lower?

7 Is there anything wrong with Stephan's argument that a convertible bond is a bad idea because it allows new shareholders to participate in gains made by the company?

8 How can you reconcile the arguments made by Hans and Stephan?

9 During the debate, a question comes up concerning whether the bonds should have an ordinary (not make-whole) call feature. Kartner confuses everybody by stating, 'The call feature lets S&S Air force conversion, thereby minimizing the problem Stephan has identified.' What is he talking about? Is he making sense?

Practical Case Study

Download the financial accounts of ten companies and look for any issues of warrants or convertibles. You may find examples of bonds that have conversion options or warrant-like properties. Are convertibles an important part of your firms' capital structures? Write a brief report on the use of convertibles and warrants for your sample of firms.

Relevant Accounting Standard

The most important accounting standard for warrants and convertibles is IAS 39 *Financial Instruments: Recognition and Measurement*. IAS 39 provides definitions for different types of financial securities and states how the different components of a security should be valued and presented in a firm's financial accounts. Visit the IASPlus website (www.iasplus.com) for more information.

References

Altintig, Z.A. and A.W. Butler (2005) 'Are They Still Called Late? The Effect of Notice Period on Calls of Convertible Bonds', *Journal of Corporate Finance*, Vol. 11, 337–350.

Asquith, P. (1995) 'Convertible Bonds Are Not Called Late', *The Journal of Finance*, Vol. 50, 1275–1289.

Baker, M. and J. Wurgler (2002) 'Market Timing and Capital Structure', *The Journal of Finance*, Vol. 57, No. 1, 1–32.

Bancel, F. and Mittoo, U.R. (2004) 'Why Do European Firms Issue Corporate Debt?', *European Financial Management*, Vol. 10, 339–373.

Barnea, A., R.A. Haugen and L. Senbet (1985) *Agency Problems and Financial Contracting*, Prentice Hall Foundations of Science Series (New York: Prentice Hall).

Brigham, E.F. (1966) 'An Analysis of Convertible Debentures', *The Journal of Finance*, Vol. 21, 35–54.

Choi, D., M. Getmansky, B. Henderson and H. Tookes (2010) 'Convertible Bond Arbitrageurs as Suppliers of Capital', *Review of Financial Studies*, Vol. 23, 2492–2522.

Dong, M., M. Dutordoir and C. Veld (2012) 'Why Do Firms Issue Convertible Bonds? Evidence from the Field', Working Paper.

Duca, E., M. Dutordoir, C. Veld and P. Verwijmeren (2012) 'Why Are Convertible Bond Announcements Associated with Increasingly Negative Issuer Stock Returns? An Arbitrage-based Explanation', *Journal of Banking and Finance*, Vol. 36, No. 11, 2884–2899.

Dutordoir, M. and L. Van de Gucht (2009) 'Why Do Western European Firms Issue Convertibles Instead of Straight Debt or Equity?', *European Financial Management*, Vol. 15, No. 3, 563–583.

Ederington, L.H., G.L. Caton and C.J. Campbell (1997) 'To Call or Not to Call Convertible Debt', *Financial Management*, Vol. 26, No. 1, 26–31.

Harris, M. and A. Raviv (1985) 'A Sequential Signalling Model of Convertible Debt Policy', *The Journal of Finance*, Vol. 40, 1263–1281.

Ingersoll, J. (1977) 'An Examination of Corporate Call Policies on Convertible Bonds', *The Journal of Finance*, Vol. 32, 463–478.

Krishnaswami, S. and D. Yaman (2008) 'The Role of Convertible Bonds in Alleviating Contracting Costs', *Quarterly Review of Economics and Finance*, Vol. 48, No. 4, 792–816.

Lewis, C.M., R.J. Rogalski and J.K. Seward (1998) 'Understanding the Design of Convertible Debt', *Journal of Applied Corporate Finance*, Vol. 11, No. 1, 45–53.

Lewis, C.M. and P. Verwijmeren (2011) 'Convertible Security Design and Contract Innovation', *Journal of Corporate Finance*, Vol. 17, 809–831.

Mazzeo, M.A. and W.T. Moore (1992) 'Liquidity Costs and Stock Price Response to Convertible Security Calls', *Journal of Business*, Vol. 65, 353–369.

Mikkelson, W.H. (1981) 'Convertible Calls and Security Returns', *Journal of Financial Economics*, Vol. 9, 237–264.

Schulz, G.U. and S. Trautmann (1994) 'Robustness of Option-like Warrant Valuation', *Journal of Banking and Finance*, Vol. 18, No. 5, 841–859.

Singh, A.K., A.R. Cowan and N. Nayar (1991) 'Underwritten Calls of Convertible Bonds', *Journal of Financial Economics*, Vol. 29, 173–196.

Stein, J. (1992) 'Convertible Bonds as Backdoor Equity Financing', *Journal of Financial Economics*, Vol. 32, 3–21.

Ter Horst, J. and C. Veld (2008) 'An Empirical Analysis of the Pricing of Bank Issued Options Versus Options Exchange Options', *European Financial Management*, Vol. 14, No. 2, 288–314.

Additional Reading

Much of the recent research in this area has already been discussed in the main text. The following papers will add to your understanding. In 2014, the *Journal of Corporate Finance* issued a full special issue on convertible bonds, edited by Craig Lewis and Chris Veld. The issue (Volume 24) contained a number of papers on the area and should be read first if you are wanting to get an up-to-date insight into convertible bond financing. In particular, the following paper gives a review of research in this area to date:

Dutordoir, M., C. Lewis, J. Seward and C. Veld (2014) 'What We Do and Do Not Know about Convertible Bond Financing', *Journal of Corporate Finance*, Vol. 24, 3–20. Other interest papers include:

1 Agarwal, V., W.H. Fung, Y.C. Loon and N.Y. Naik (2011) 'Risk and Return in Convertible Arbitrage: Evidence from the Convertible Bond Market', *Journal of Empirical Finance*, Vol. 18, No. 2, 175–194.

2 Choi, D., M. Getmansky and H. Tookes (2009) 'Convertible Bond Arbitrage, Liquidity Externalities, and Stock Prices', *Journal of Financial Economics*, Vol. 91, No. 2, 227–251. **US**.

3 Choi, D., M. Getmansky, B. Henderson and H. Tookes (2010) 'Convertible Bond Arbitrageurs as Suppliers of Capital', *Review of Financial Studies*, Vol. 23, No. 6, 2492–2522.

4 Gajewski, J-F., E. Ginglinger and M. Lasfer (2007) 'Why Do Companies Include Warrants in Seasoned Equity Offerings?', *Journal of Corporate Finance*, Vol. 13, No. 1, 25–42. **France**.

5 Gillet, R. and H. De La Bruslerie (2010) 'The Consequences of Issuing Convertible Bonds: Dilution and/or Financial Restructuring', *European Financial Management*, Vol. 16, No. 4, 552–584. **France**.

6 Jarrow, R.A. and S. Trautmann (2011) 'A Reduced-Form Model for Warrant Valuation', *Financial Review*, Vol. 46, No. 3, 413–425.

7 Loncarski, I., J. ter Horst and C. Veld (2009) 'The Rise and Demise of the Convertible Arbitrage Strategy', *Financial Analysts Journal*, Vol. 65, 35–50.

8 Zabolotnyuk, Y., R. Jones and C. Veld (2010) 'An Empirical Comparison of Convertible Bond Valuation Models', *Financial Management*, Vol. 39, No. 2, 675–706.

9 Zeidler, F., M. Mietzner and D. Schiereck (2012) 'Risk Dynamics Surrounding the Issuance of Convertible Bonds', *Journal of Corporate Finance*, Vol. 18, No. 2, 273–290.

Endnotes

1 Warrants are also issued with publicly distributed bonds and new issues of equity.

2 At the turn of the twenty-first century many banks began issuing options on other companies under the name 'call warrants'. These are not warrants in the real sense because the companies on which the call warrants are written do not issue new equity in response to an exercise of the call warrants. In this chapter, we will not consider the valuation of these call warrants. See Ter Horst and Veld (2008) for more information on call warrants.

3 Just like call options, warrants are protected against stock splits and stock dividends, but not against cash dividends. The latter generally does not cause a problem for the valuation of call options, since these only have short maturities and therefore a relatively small amount of dividends are paid during their lifetime. Given that warrants generally have maturities of several years, the effect of cash dividends can be significant.

4 To derive Formula 24.3, we separate 'Exercise price' in Equation 24.2. This yields

$$\frac{\text{Firm's value net of debt}}{\# + \#_w} - \frac{\#}{\# + \#_w} \times \text{Exercise price}$$

By rearranging terms, we can obtain Formula 24.3.

5 Equation 24.4 is not exactly correct. After a warrant is issued, the share price and volatility of returns will change to reflect the warrant's existence. However, Schulz and Trautmann (1994) report that Equation 24.4 performs just as well as more complex valuation models, except when the warrant is deep out of the money.

6 The most plausible exception is when conversion would provide the investor with a dividend much greater than the interest available prior to conversion. The optimal strategy here could very well be to convert immediately, implying that the market value of the bond would exactly equal the conversion value. Other exceptions occur when the firm is in default or the bondholders are forced to convert.

7 Brigham (1966).

8 Mikkelson (1981).

9 Barnea et al. (1985), Chapter VI.

10 Stein (1992). See also Lewis et al. (1998); Lewis and Verwijmeren (2011).

11 See Duca et al. (2012); Choi et al. (2010).

12 See also Harris and Raviv (1985). Harris and Raviv describe a signal equilibrium that is consistent with Ingersoll's result. They show that managers with favourable information will delay calls to avoid depressing stock prices.

13 See Altintig and Butler (2005); Asquith (1995). On the other hand, the stock market usually reacts negatively to the announcement of a call. For example, see Singh et al. (1991); Mazzeo and Moore (1992). Ederington et al. (1997) tested various theories about when it is optimal to call convertibles. They found evidence consistent for the preceding 30-day 'safety margin' theory. They also found that calls of in-the-money convertibles are highly unlikely if dividends to be received (after conversion) exceed the company's interest payment.

Financial Risk Management with Derivatives

Anyone studying corporate finance must be familiar with the principles of financial risk management. Many students think that only financial institutions use derivatives such as futures and swaps. However, every company that does business overseas, sources raw materials from other countries, borrows or lends money, or buys commodities today for delivery in the future will use risk management techniques to manage risk and optimize their business.

For example, automobile exporters, such as BMW and Fiat, are regularly faced with uncertainty regarding the value of currencies. Since automobiles are manufactured in one country and exported to the rest of the world, currency depreciation or appreciation can be a major issue. The same concerns are had by firms in many industries. This chapter will review some of the methods open to exporters and importers to manage their financial risk.

KEY NOTATIONS

P	Price
R	Discount rate; yield to maturity

25.1 Derivatives, Hedging and Risk

Chapter 22
Page 586

The name *derivatives* is self-explanatory. A derivative is a financial instrument whose pay-offs and values are derived from, or depend on, something else. Often, we speak of the thing that the derivative depends on as the *primitive* or the *underlying*. For example, in **Chapter 22** we studied how options work. An option is a derivative. The value of a call option depends on the value of the underlying equity on which it is written. Actually, call options are quite complicated examples of derivatives. The vast majority of derivatives are simpler than call options. Most derivatives are forward or futures agreements or what are called *swaps*, and we will study each of these in some detail.

Why do firms use derivatives? The answer is that derivatives are tools for changing the firm's risk exposure. Someone once said that derivatives are to finance what scalpels are to surgery. By using derivatives, the firm can cut away unwanted portions of risk exposure and even transform the exposures into quite different forms. However, scalpels can also be exceptionally dangerous in the hands of the unskilled or unethical!

A central point in finance is that risk is undesirable. In our chapters about risk and return, we pointed out that individuals would choose risky securities only if the expected return compensated for the risk. Similarly, a firm will accept a project with high risk only if the return on the project compensates for this risk. Not surprisingly, then, firms are usually looking for ways to reduce their risk. When the firm reduces its risk exposure with the use of derivatives, it is said to be hedging. Hedging offsets the firm's risk, such as the risk in a project, by one or more transactions in the financial markets.

Derivatives can also be used to merely change or even increase the firm's risk exposure. When this occurs, the firm is speculating on the movement of some economic variables – those that underlie the derivative. For example, if a derivative is purchased that will rise in value if interest rates rise, and if the firm has no offsetting exposure to interest rate changes, then the firm is speculating that interest rates will rise and give it a profit on its derivatives position. Using derivatives to translate an opinion about whether interest rates or some other economic variable will rise or fall is the opposite of hedging – it is risk enhancing. Speculating on your views on the economy and using derivatives to profit if that view turns out to be correct is not necessarily wrong, but the speculator should always remember that sharp tools cut deep: if the opinions on which the derivatives position is based turn out to be incorrect, then the consequences can prove costly. Efficient market theory teaches how difficult it is to predict what markets will do. Most of the disastrous experiences with derivatives have occurred not from their use as instruments for hedging and offsetting risk, but rather from speculation.

25.2 Forward Contracts

We can begin our discussion of hedging by considering forward contracts. You have probably been dealing in forward contracts your whole life without knowing it. Suppose you walk into a bookstore on, say, 1 February to buy the best-seller, *Learn to Play Silky Football: The Bobo Philosophy*. The cashier tells you that the book is currently sold out, but he takes your phone number, saying that he will reorder it for you. He says the book will cost £10.00. If you agree on 1 February to pick up and pay £10.00 for the book when called, you and the cashier have engaged in a forward contract. That is, you have agreed both to pay for the book and to pick it up when the bookstore notifies you. Because you are agreeing to buy the book at a later date, you are *buying* a forward contract on 1 February. In commodity parlance, you will be taking delivery when you pick up the book. The book is called the deliverable instrument.

The cashier, acting on behalf of the bookstore, is selling a forward contract. (Alternatively, we say that he is writing a forward contract.) The bookstore has agreed to turn the book over to you at the predetermined price of £10.00 as soon as the book arrives. The act of turning the book over to you is called making delivery. Table 25.1 illustrates the book purchase. Note that the agreement takes place on 1 February. The price is set and the conditions for sale are set at that time. In this case, the sale will occur when the book arrives. In other cases, an exact date of sale would be given. However, *no* cash changes hands on 1 February; cash changes hands only when the book arrives.

Table 25.1 Illustration of Book Purchase as a Forward Contract

1 February	Date When Book Arrives
Buyer	
Buyer agrees to	**Buyer**
1 Pay the purchase price of £10.00.	1 Pays purchase price of £10.00.
2 Receive book when book arrives.	2 Receives book.
Seller	
Seller agrees to	**Seller**
1 Give up book when book arrives.	1 Gives up book.
2 Accept payment of £10.00 when book arrives.	2 Accepts payment of £10.00.

Note that cash does not change hands on 1 February. Cash changes hands when the book arrives.

Though forward contracts may have seemed exotic to you before you began this chapter, you can see that they are quite commonplace. Dealings in your personal life probably have involved forward contracts. Similarly, forward contracts occur all the time in business. Every time a firm orders an item that cannot be delivered immediately, a forward contract takes place. Sometimes, particularly when the order is small, an oral agreement will suffice. Other times, particularly when the order is larger, a written agreement is necessary.

Note that a forward contract is not an option. Both the buyer and the seller are obligated to perform under the terms of the contract. Conversely, the buyer of an option *chooses* whether to exercise the option.

A forward contract should be contrasted with a cash transaction – that is, a transaction where exchange is immediate. Had the book been on the bookstore's shelf, your purchase of it would constitute a cash transaction.

In Islamic financing, the equivalent hedge transaction is called a *bai salam*. The difference between a *bai salam* and a forward contract is that money is transferred today in a *bai salam*, but is transferred at a future date with a forward. See **Chapter 14** for more information on the *bai salam*.

Chapter 14
Page 376

25.3 Futures Contracts

A variant of the forward contract takes place on financial exchanges. Contracts on exchanges are usually called futures contracts. There are a number of futures exchanges around the world, and more are being established. The big three futures exchanges are the Chicago Mercantile Exchange, the Intercontinental Exchange, and Eurex. While trading on these exchanges spans whole geographic regions, there are many smaller exchanges, such as Nasdaq OMX (Nordic and Baltic markets), National Stock Exchange of India, BM&FBovespa (Brazil), the Moscow Exchange (Russia), and the Dalian Commodity Exchange (China).

Table 25.2 gives the specification for cocoa futures contracts from ICE, the Intercontinental Exchange. Note that the contracts are for delivery of 10 tonnes of cocoa and are quoted in dollars per tonne. The contracts are traded in New York, London and Singapore. If the futures contract is held till expiry, the cocoa will actually be delivered to a warehouse in the US. Almost always, however, the futures trader will take an opposite position on the futures to cancel it out. For example, a trader who is long in the futures and will buy the cocoa could take an opposite position to sell the cocoa, thereby closing out the contract.

Table 25.2 Cocoa futures contract specification

Description	The Cocoa contract is the world benchmark for the global cocoa market. The contract prices the physical delivery of exchange-grade product from a variety of African, Asian and Central and South American origins to any of five US delivery ports.
Symbol	CC

Contract Size	10 metric tons
Price Quotation	$/metric ton
Contract Listing	March, May, July, September, December
Minimum Price Movement	$1.00/metric ton, equivalent to $10.00 per contract
Settlement	Physical delivery
Daily Price Limit	None
Deliverable Growths	The growth of any country or clime, including new or yet unknown growths. Growths are divided into three classifications. Group A-Deliverable at a premium of $160/ton (including main crops of Ghana, Lomé, Nigeria, Côte d'Ivoire and Sierra Leone). Group B-Deliverable at a premium of $80/ton (includes Bahia, Arriba, Venezuela, Sanchez, among others). Group C-Deliverable at par (includes Haiti, Malaysia and all others). Commencing with the July 2015 expiry, the growths of Peru and Colombia will be included in Group B.
Delivery Points	At licensed warehouses in the Port of New York District, Delaware River Port District, Port of Hampton Roads, Port of Albany or Port of Baltimore.

In Table 25.3, the price and volumes of cocoa futures contracts are provided. The price of cocoa for delivery in the future is expected to steadily fall over the next year. For example, the price of a May 2015 cocoa futures contract is $2,766, falling to $2,719 for a July 2016 contract.

Table 25.3 Cocoa Futures Price and Volume Data

Month	May 2015	July 2015	September 2015	December 2015	March 2016	May 2016	July 2016
Price	2,766	2,763	2,757	2,750	2,741	2,733	2,719
Volume	5,126	1,931	246	196	47	15	9

Source: ICE, April 2015.

For the cocoa contract with a May 2015 maturity, the first number in the row is the *last price* ($2,766), and it is essentially the most recent transaction price in the cocoa contract. The final price of the day is known as the *settlement price* and for the purposes of marking to market, this is the figure used. The volume of 5,126 contracts represents the number of cocoa contracts traded that day. Notice that the futures volume falls as the length of the contract grows. This is because most of the hedging requirements are for the next few months after the quote (April, 2015).

Though we are discussing a futures contract, let us work with a forward contract first. Suppose you wrote a *forward* contract for September cocoa at $2,757. From our discussion of forward contracts, this would mean that you would agree to turn over 10 tonnes of cocoa beans for $2,757 per tonne on some specified date in the month of September.

A futures contract differs somewhat from a forward contract. First, the seller can choose to deliver the cocoa on any day during the delivery month – that is, the month of September. This gives the seller leeway that he would not have with a forward contract. When the seller decides to deliver, he notifies the exchange clearinghouse that he wants to do so. The clearinghouse then notifies an individual who bought a September cocoa contract that she must stand ready to accept delivery within the next few days. Though each exchange selects the buyer in a different way, the buyer is generally chosen in a random fashion. Because there are so many buyers at any one time, the buyer selected by the clearinghouse to take delivery almost certainly did not originally buy the contract from the seller now making delivery.

Second, futures contracts are traded on an exchange, whereas forward contracts are generally traded off an exchange. Because of this, there is generally a liquid market in futures contracts. A buyer can net out her futures position with a sale. A seller can net out his futures position with a purchase. If a buyer of a futures contract does not subsequently sell her contract, she must take delivery.

Third, and most important, the prices of futures contracts are marked to the market daily. That is, suppose the price falls to $2,754 on Monday's close. Because all buyers lost $30 per contract on that day, they each must turn over the $30 per contract to their brokers within 24 hours, who subsequently remit the proceeds to the clearinghouse. All sellers gained $30 per contract on that day, so they each receive $30 per contract from their brokers. Their brokers are subsequently compensated by the clearinghouse. Because there is a buyer for every seller, the clearinghouse must break even every day.

Now suppose that the price rises to $2,760 on the close of the following Tuesday. Each buyer receives $60 ($27,600 − $27,540) per contract, and each seller must pay $60 per contract. Finally, suppose that on Tuesday a seller notifies his broker of his intention to deliver.[1] The delivery price will be $2,760, which is Tuesday's close.

There are clearly many cash flows in futures contracts. However, after all the dust settles, the *net price* to the buyer must be the price at which she bought originally. That is, an individual buying at Friday's closing price of $2,757 and being called to take delivery on Tuesday pays $30 per contract on Monday, receives $60 per contract on Tuesday, and takes delivery at $2,760. Her net outflow per 10 tonnes is −$27,570 (= −$30 + $60 − $27,600) or $2,757 per tonne, which is the price at which she contracted on Friday. (Our analysis ignores the time value of money.) Conversely, an individual selling at Friday's closing price of $2,757 and notifying his broker concerning delivery the following Tuesday receives $30 per contract on Monday, pays $60 per contract on Tuesday, and makes delivery at $2,760. His net inflow per contract is $27,570 (= $30 − $60 + $27,600) or $2,757 per tonne, which is the price at which he contracted on Friday. These details are presented in the box below.

Illustration of Example Involving Marking to Market in Futures Contracts

Both buyer and seller originally transact at Friday's closing price. Delivery takes place at Tuesday's closing price.*

	Friday, 13 April	Monday, 16 April	Tuesday, 17 April	Delivery (Notification Given by Seller on Tuesday)
Closing price	$2,757	$2,754	$2,760	
Buyer	Buyer purchases futures contract for 10 tonnes at closing price of $2,757/tonne.	Buyer must pay $30 per contract to clearinghouse within one business day.	Buyer receives $60 per contract from clearinghouse within one business day.	Buyer pays $27,600 per contract and receives cocoa within one business day.

Buyer's net payment of −$27,570 (= −$30 + $60 − $27,600) is the same as if buyer purchased a forward contract for $2,757 per tonne.

Seller	Seller sells futures contract for 10 tonnes at closing price of $2,757/tonne.	Seller receives $30 per contract from clearing-house within one business day.	Seller pays $60 per contract to clearinghouse within one business day.	Seller receives $27,600 per contract and delivers cocoa within one business day.

Seller's net receipts of $27,570 (= $30 − $60 + $27,600) are the same as if seller sold a forward contract for $2,757 per tonne.

*For simplicity, we assume that buyer and seller both (1) initially transact at the same time, and (2) meet in the delivery process. This is actually very unlikely to occur in the real world because the clearinghouse assigns the buyer to take delivery in a random manner.

For simplicity, we assumed that the buyer and seller who initially transact on Friday's close meet in the delivery process. The point in the example is that the buyer's net payment of $27,570 per contract is the same as if she purchased a forward contract for $27,570. Similarly, the seller's net receipt of $27,570 per contract is the same as if he sold a forward contract for $27,570. The only difference is the timing of the cash flows. The buyer of a forward contract knows that he will make a single payment of $27,570 on the expiration date. He will not need to worry about any other cash flows in the interim. Conversely, though the cash flows to the buyer of a futures contract will net to exactly $27,570 as well, the pattern of cash flows is not known ahead of time.

The mark-to-the-market provision on futures contracts has two related effects. The first concerns differences in net present value. For example, a large price drop immediately following purchase means an immediate payout for the buyer of a futures contract. Though the net outflow of $27,570 is still the same as under a forward contract, the present value of the cash outflows is greater to the buyer of a futures contract. Of course, the present value of the cash outflows is less to the buyer of a futures contract if a price rise follows purchase.[2] Though this effect could be substantial in certain theoretical circumstances, it appears to be of quite limited importance in the real world.[3]

Second, the firm must have extra liquidity to handle a sudden outflow prior to expiration. This added risk may make the futures contract less attractive.

Students frequently ask, 'Why in the world would managers of the commodity exchanges ruin perfectly good contracts with these bizarre mark-to-the-market provisions?' Actually, the reason is a very good one. Consider the forward contract of Table 25.1 concerning the bookstore. Suppose the public quickly loses interest in *Learn to Play Silky Football: The Bobo Philosophy*. By the time the bookstore calls the buyer, other stores may have dropped the price of the book to £6.00. Because the forward contract was for £10.00, the buyer has an incentive not to take delivery on the forward contract. Conversely, should the book become a hot item selling at £15.00, the bookstore may simply not call the buyer.

Mark-to-the-market provisions minimize the chance of default on a futures contract. If the price rises, the seller has an incentive to default on a forward contract. However, after paying the clearinghouse, the seller of a futures contract has little reason to default. If the price falls, the same argument can be made for the buyer. Because changes in the value of the underlying asset are recognized daily, there is no accumulation of loss, and the incentive to default is reduced.

Because of this default issue, forward contracts generally involve individuals and institutions who know and can trust each other. However, lawyers earn a handsome living writing supposedly airtight forward contracts, even among friends. The genius of the mark-to-the-market system is that it can prevent default where it is most likely to occur – among investors who do not know each other.

25.4   Hedging

Now that we have determined how futures contracts work, let us talk about hedging. There are two types of hedges, long and short. We discuss the short hedge first.

Example 25.1

Futures Hedging

In March, Simon Agyei-Ampomah, a Ghanaian farmer, anticipates a harvest of 5,000 tonnes of cocoa at the end of September. He has two alternatives.

1 *Write futures contracts against his anticipated harvest.* The September cocoa contract on ICE is trading at $27,570/per contract (10 tonnes) on 13 April. He executes the following transaction:

Date of Transaction	Transaction	Price per 10 tonnes
13 April	Write 500 September futures contracts	$27,570

He notes that transportation costs to the designated delivery point in London are $100 per 10 tonnes. Thus, his net price per contract is $27,470 = $27,570 − $100.

2 *Harvest the cocoa without writing a futures contract.* Alternatively, Mr Agyei-Ampomah could harvest the cocoa without benefit of a futures contract. The risk would be quite great here because no one knows what the cash price in September will be. If prices rise, he will profit. Conversely, he will lose if prices fall.

We say that strategy 2 is an unhedged position because there is no attempt to use the futures markets to reduce risk. Conversely, strategy 1 involves a hedge. That is, a position in the futures market offsets the risk of a position in the physical – that is, in the actual – commodity.

Though hedging may seem quite sensible to you, it should be mentioned that not everyone hedges. Mr Agyei-Ampomah might reject hedging for at least two reasons.

First, he may simply be uninformed about hedging. We have found that not everyone in business understands the hedging concept. Many executives have told us that they do not want to use futures markets for hedging their inventories because the risks are too great. However, we disagree. While there are large price fluctuations in these markets, hedging actually reduces the risk that an individual holding inventories bears.

Second, Mr Agyei-Ampomah may have a special insight or some special information that commodity prices will rise. He would not be wise to lock in a price of $2,757 if he expects the cash price in September to be well above this price.

The hedge of strategy 1 is called a short hedge because Mr Agyei-Ampomah reduces his risk by *selling* a futures contract. The short hedge is very common in business. It occurs whenever someone either anticipates receiving inventory or is holding inventory. Mr Agyei-Ampomah is anticipating the harvest of cocoa. A manufacturer of soybean meal and oil may hold large quantities of raw soybeans that are already paid for. However, the prices to be received for meal and oil are not known because no one knows what the market prices will be when the meal and oil are produced. The manufacturer may write futures contracts in meal and oil to lock in sales prices. An oil company may hold large inventories of petroleum to be processed into heating oil. The firm could sell futures contracts in heating oil to lock in the sales price. A mortgage banker may assemble mortgages slowly before selling them in bulk to a financial institution. Movements of interest rates affect the value of the mortgages while they are in inventory. The mortgage banker could sell Treasury bond futures contracts to offset this interest rate risk. (This last example is treated later in this chapter.)

Example 25.2

More Hedging

On 1 April, Maan Chemical agreed to sell petrochemicals (in US dollars) to the Dutch government in the future. The delivery dates and prices have been determined. Because oil is a basic ingredient of the production process, Maan Chemical will need to have large quantities of oil on hand. The firm can get the oil in one of two ways:

1 *Buy the oil as the firm needs it.* This is an unhedged position because, as of 1 April, the firm does not know the prices it will later have to pay for the oil. Oil is quite a volatile commodity, so Maan Chemical is bearing a good bit of risk. The key to this risk bearing is that the sales price to the Dutch government has already been fixed. Thus, Maan Chemical cannot pass on increased costs to the consumer.

2 *Buy futures contracts.*[4] The firm can buy futures contracts with expiration months corresponding to the dates the firm needs inventory. The futures contracts lock in the purchase price to Maan Chemical. Because there is a crude oil futures contract for every month, selecting the correct futures contract is not difficult. Many other commodities have only five contracts per year, frequently necessitating buying contracts one month away from the month of production.

As mentioned earlier, Maan Chemical is interested in hedging the risk of fluctuating oil prices because it cannot pass any cost increases on to the consumer. Suppose, alternatively, that Maan Chemical was not selling petrochemicals on fixed contract to the Dutch government. Instead, imagine that the petrochemicals were to be sold to private industry at currently prevailing prices. The price of petrochemicals should move directly with oil prices because oil is a major component of petrochemicals. Because cost increases are likely to be passed on to the consumer, Maan Chemical would probably not want to hedge in this case. Instead, the firm is likely to choose strategy 1, buying the oil as it is needed. If oil prices increase between 1 April and 1 September, Maan Chemical will, of course, find that its inputs have become quite costly. However, in a competitive market, its revenues are likely to rise as well.

Strategy 2 is called a long hedge because one *purchases* a futures contract to reduce risk. In other words, one takes a long position in the futures market. In general, a firm institutes a long hedge when it is committed to a fixed sales price. One class of situations involves actual written contracts with customers, such as Maan Chemical had with the Dutch government. Alternatively, a firm may find that it cannot easily pass on costs to consumers or does not want to pass on these costs.

25.5 Interest Rate Futures Contracts

In this section we consider interest rate futures contracts. Our examples deal with futures contracts on Treasury bonds because of their high popularity. We first price Treasury bonds and Treasury bond forward contracts. Differences between futures and forward contracts are explored. Hedging examples are provided next.

Pricing of Treasury Bonds

As mentioned earlier in the text, a Treasury bond pays semi-annual interest over its life. In addition, the face value of the bond is paid at maturity. Consider a 20-year, 8 per cent coupon bond that was issued on 1 March. The first payment is to occur in 6 months – that is, on 1 September. The value of the bond can be determined as follows:

Pricing of Treasury bond

$$P_{TB} = \frac{€40}{1 + R_1} + \frac{€40}{(1 + R_2)^2} + \frac{€40}{(1 + R_3)^3} + \cdots + \frac{€40}{(1 + R_{39})^{39}} + \frac{€1,040}{(1 + R_{40})^{40}} \qquad (25.1)$$

Because an 8 per cent coupon bond pays interest of €80 a year, the semi-annual coupon is €40. The principal and semi-annual coupons are both paid at maturity. As we mentioned in a previous chapter, the price of the Treasury bond, P_{TB}, is determined by discounting each payment on a bond at the appropriate spot rate. Because the payments are semi-annual, each spot rate is expressed in semi-annual terms. That is, imagine a horizontal term structure where the effective annual yield is 12 per cent for all maturities. Because each spot rate, R, is expressed in semi-annual terms, each spot rate is $\sqrt{1.12} - 1 = 5.83$ per cent. Coupon payments occur every 6 months, so there are 40 spot rates over the 20-year period.

Pricing of Forward Contracts

Now imagine a *forward* contract where, on 1 March, you agree to buy a new 20-year, 8 per cent coupon Treasury bond in 6 months (on 1 September). As with typical forward contracts, you will pay for the bond on 1 September, not 1 March. The cash flows from both the Treasury bond issued on 1 March and the forward contract that you purchase on 1 March are presented in Figure 25.1. The cash flows on the Treasury bond begin exactly 6 months earlier than do the cash flows on the forward contract. The Treasury bond is purchased with cash on 1 March (date 0). The first coupon payment occurs on 1 September (date 1). The last coupon payment occurs at date 40, along with the face value of €1,000. The forward contract compels you to pay $P_{FORW.\ CONT.}$, the price of the forward contract, on 1 September (date 1). You receive a new Treasury bond at that time. The first coupon payment you receive from the bond occurs on 1 March of the following year (date 2). The last coupon payment occurs at date 41, along with the face value of €1,000.

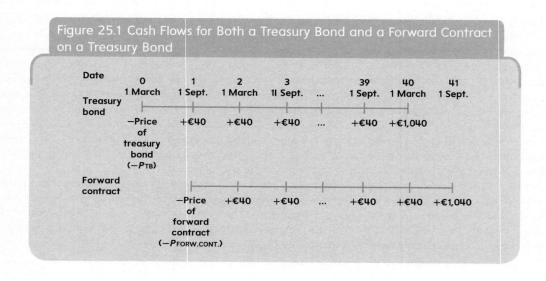

Figure 25.1 Cash Flows for Both a Treasury Bond and a Forward Contract on a Treasury Bond

Given the 40 spot rates, Equation 25.1 showed how to price a Treasury bond. How do we price the forward contract on a Treasury bond? Just as we saw earlier in the text that net present value analysis can be used to price bonds, we will now show that net present value analysis can be used to price forward contracts. Given the cash flows for the forward contract in Figure 25.1, the price of the forward contract must satisfy the following equation:

$$\frac{P_{\text{FORW.CONT}}}{1 + R_1} = \frac{€40}{(1 + R_2)^2} + \frac{€40}{(1 + R_3)^3} + \frac{€40}{(1 + R_4)^4} + \cdots + \frac{€40}{(1 + R_{40})^{40}} + \frac{€1,040}{(1 + R_{41})^{41}} \quad (25.2)$$

The right side of Equation 25.2 discounts all the cash flows from the delivery instrument (the Treasury bond issued on 1 September) back to date 0 (1 March). Because the first cash flow occurs at date 2 (March 1 of the subsequent year), it is discounted by $1/(1 + R_2)^2$. The last cash flow of €1,040 occurs at date 41, so it is discounted by $1/(1 + R_{41})^{41}$. The left side represents the cost of the forward contract as of date 0. Because the actual out-payment occurs at date 1, it is discounted by $1/(1 + R_1)$.

Students often ask, 'Why are we discounting everything back to date 0, when we are actually paying for the forward contract on 1 September?' The answer is simply that we apply the same techniques to Equation 25.2 that we apply to all capital budgeting problems: we want to put everything in today's (date 0's) euros. Given that the spot rates are known in the marketplace, traders should have no more trouble pricing a forward contract by Equation 25.2 than they would have pricing a Treasury bond by Equation 25.1.

Forward contracts are similar to the underlying bonds themselves. If the entire term structure of interest rates unexpectedly shifts upward on 2 March, the Treasury bond issued the previous day should fall in value. This can be seen from Equation 25.1. A rise in each of the spot rates lowers the present value of each of the coupon payments. Hence, the value of the bond must fall. Conversely, a fall in the term structure of interest rates increases the value of the bond.

The same relationship holds with forward contracts, as we can see by rewriting Equation 25.2 like this:

$$P_{\text{FORW.CONT}} = \frac{€40 \times (1 + R_1)}{(1 + R_2)^2} + \frac{€40 \times (1 + R_1)}{(1 + R_3)^3} + \frac{€40 \times (1 + R_1)}{(1 + R_4)^4}$$
$$+ \cdots + \frac{€40 \times (1 + R_1)}{(1 + R_{40})^{40}} + \frac{€1,040 \times (1 + R_1)}{(1 + R_{41})^{41}} \quad (25.3)$$

We went from Equation 25.2 to 25.3 by multiplying both the left and the right sides by $(1 + R_1)$. If the entire term structure of interest rates unexpectedly shifts upward on 2 March, the *first* term on the right side of Equation 25.3 should fall in value.[5] That is, both R_1 and R_2 will rise an equal amount. However, R_2 enters as a *squared* term, $1/(1 + R_2)^2$, so an increase in R_2 more than offsets the increase in R_1. As we move further to the right, an increase in any spot rate, R_i, more than offsets an increase in R_1. Here R_i enters as the *i*th power, $1/(1 + R_i)^i$. Thus, as long as the entire term structure shifts upward an equal amount on 2 March, the value of a forward contract must fall on that date. Conversely, as long as the entire term structure shifts downward an equal amount on 2 March, the value of a forward contract must rise.

Futures Contracts

The previous discussion concerned a forward contract in Treasury bonds – that is, a forward contract where the deliverable instrument is a Treasury bond. What about a futures contract on a Treasury bond?[6] We mentioned earlier that futures contracts and forward contracts are quite similar, though there are a few differences between the two. First, futures contracts are generally traded on exchanges, whereas forward contracts are not traded on an exchange. Second, futures contracts generally allow the seller a period of time in which to deliver, whereas forward contracts generally call for delivery on a particular day. The seller of a Treasury bond futures contract can choose to deliver on any business day during the delivery month.[7] Third, futures contracts are subject to the mark-to-the-market convention, whereas forward contracts are not. Traders in Treasury bill futures contracts must adhere to this convention. Fourth, there is generally a liquid market for futures contracts allowing contracts to be quickly netted out. That is, a buyer can sell his futures contract at any time, and a seller can buy back her futures contract at any time. Conversely, because forward markets are generally quite illiquid, traders cannot easily net out their positions. The popularity of the Treasury bond futures contract has produced liquidity even higher than that on other futures contracts. Positions in that contract can be netted out quite easily.

This discussion is not intended to be an exhaustive list of differences between a forward contract and a futures contract on Treasury bonds. Rather, it is intended to show that both contracts share fundamental characteristics. Though there are differences, the two instruments should be viewed as variations of the same species, not different species. Thus, the pricing equation 25.3, which is exact for the forward contract, should be a decent approximation for the futures contract.

Hedging in Interest Rate Futures

Now that we have the basic institutional details under our belts, we are ready for examples of hedging using either futures contracts or forward contracts on Treasury bonds. Because the T-bond futures contract is extremely popular whereas the forward contract is traded sporadically, our examples use the futures contract.

Example 25.3

Interest Rate Hedging

Erik Werenskiold owns a mortgage banking company. On 1 March he made a commitment to lend a total of €1 million to various homeowners on 1 May. The loans are 20-year mortgages carrying a 12 per cent coupon, the going interest rate on mortgages at the time. Thus, the mortgages are made at par. Though homeowners would not use the term, we could say that he is buying a *forward contract* on a mortgage. That is, he agrees on 1 March to give €1 million to his borrowers on 1 May in exchange for principal and interest from them every month for the next 20 years.

Like many mortgage bankers, he has no intention of paying the €1 million out of his own pocket. Rather, he intends to sell the mortgages to an insurance company. Thus, the insurance company will actually lend the funds and will receive principal and interest over the next 20 years. Mr Werenskiold does not currently have an insurance company in mind. He plans to visit the mortgage departments of insurance companies over the next 60 days to sell the mortgages to one or many of them. He sets 30 April as a deadline for making the sale because the borrowers expect the funds on the following day.

Suppose Mr Werenskiold sells the mortgages to Superbe Insurance on 15 April. What price will Superbe pay for the bonds?

You may think the insurance company will obviously pay €1 million for the loans. However, suppose interest rates have risen above 12 per cent by 15 April. The insurance company will buy the mortgage at a discount. For example, suppose the insurance company agrees to pay only €940,000 for the mortgages. Because the mortgage banker agreed to lend a full €1 million to the borrowers, the mortgage banker must come up with the additional €60,000 (= €1 million − €940,000) out of his own pocket.

Alternatively, suppose interest rates fall below 12 per cent by 15 April. The mortgages can be sold at a premium under this scenario. If the insurance company buys the mortgages at €1.05 million, the mortgage banker will have made an unexpected profit of €50,000 (= €1.05 million − €1 million).

Because Erik Werenskiold is unable to forecast interest rates, this risk is something that he would like to avoid. The risk is summarized in Table 25.4.

	Mortgage Interest Rate on 15 April	
	Above 12%	Below 12%
Sale Price to Superbe Insurance	Below €1 million (we assume €940,000).	Above €1 million (we assume €1.05 million).
Effect on Mortgage Banker	He loses because he must lend the full €1 million to borrowers.	He gains because he lends only €1 million to borrowers.
Euro Gain or Loss	Loss of €60,000 (= €1 million − 940,000).	Gain of €50,000 (= €1.05 million − €1 million).

The interest rate on 1 March, the date when the loan agreement was made with the borrowers, was 12 per cent. The mortgages were sold to Superbe Insurance on 15 April.

Table 25.4 Effects of Changing Interest Rates on Erik Werenskiold, Mortgage Banker

Seeing the interest rate risk, students at this point may ask, 'What does the mortgage banker get out of this loan to offset his risk bearing?' Mr Werenskiold wants to sell the mortgages to the insurance company so that he can get two fees. The first is an *origination fee*, which is paid to the mortgage banker by the insurance company on 15 April – that is, on the date the loan is sold. An industry standard in certain locales is 1 per cent of the value of the loan, which is €10,000 (= 1% × €1 million). In addition, Mr Werenskiold will act as a collection agent for the insurance company. For this service he will receive a small portion of the outstanding balance of the loan each month. For example, if he is paid 0.03 per cent of the loan each month, he will receive €300 (= 0.03% × €1 million) in the first month. As the outstanding balance of the loan declines, he will receive less.

Though Mr Werenskiold will earn profitable fees on the loan, he bears interest rate risk. He loses money if interest rates rise after 1 March, and he profits if interest rates fall after 1 March. To hedge this risk, he writes June Treasury bond futures contracts on 1 March. As with mortgages, Treasury bond futures contracts fall in value if interest rates rise. Because he *writes* the contract, he makes money on these contracts if they fall in value. Therefore, with an interest rate rise, the loss he endures in the mortgages is offset by the gain he earns in the futures market. Conversely, Treasury bond futures contracts rise in value if interest rates fall. Because he writes the contracts, he suffers losses on them when rates fall. With an interest rate fall, the profit he makes on the mortgages is offset by the loss he suffers in the futures markets.

The details of this hedging transaction are presented in Table 25.5. The column on the left is labelled 'cash markets' because the deal in the mortgage market is transacted off an exchange. The column on the right shows the offsetting transactions in the futures market. Consider the first row. The mortgage banker enters into a forward contract on 1 March. He simultaneously writes Treasury bond futures contracts. Ten contracts are written because the deliverable instrument on each contract is €100,000 of Treasury bonds. The total is €1 million (= 10 × €100,000), which is equal to the value of the mortgages. Mr Werenskiold would prefer to write May Treasury bond futures contracts. Here, Treasury bonds would be delivered on the futures contract during the same month that the loan is funded. Because there is no May T-bond futures contract, Mr Werenskiold achieves the closest match through a June contract.

	Cash Markets	Futures Markets
1 March	Mortgage banker makes forward contracts to lend €1 million at 12 per cent for 20 years. The loans are to be funded on 1 May. No cash changes hands on 1 March.	Mortgage banker writes 10 June Treasury bond futures contracts.
15 April	Loans are sold to Superbe Insurance. Mortgage banker will receive sale price from Superbe on the 1 May funding date.	Mortgage banker buys back all the futures contracts.
If interest rates rise:	Loans are sold at a price below €1 million. Mortgage banker loses because he receives less than the €1 million he must give to borrowers.	Each futures contract is bought back at a price below the sales price, resulting in *profit*. Mortgage banker's profit in futures market offsets loss in cash market.
If interest rates fall:	Loans are sold at a price above €1 million. Mortgage banker *gains* because he receives more than the €1 million he must give to borrowers.	Each futures contract is bought back at a price above the sales price, resulting in *loss*. Mortgage banker's loss in futures market offsets gain in cash market.

Table 25.5 Illustration of Hedging Strategy for Erik Werenskiold, Mortgage Banker

If held to maturity, the June contract would obligate the mortgage banker to deliver Treasury bonds in June. Interest rate risk ends in the cash market when the loans are sold. Interest rate risk must be terminated in the futures market at that time. Thus, Mr Werenskiold nets out his position in the futures contract as soon as the loan is sold to Superbe Insurance.

As our example shows, risk is clearly reduced via an offsetting transaction in the futures market. However, is risk totally eliminated? Risk would be totally eliminated if losses in the cash markets were *exactly* offset by gains in the futures markets and vice versa. This is unlikely to happen because mortgages and Treasury bonds are not identical instruments. First, mortgages may have different maturities from Treasury bonds. Second, Treasury bonds have a different payment stream from mortgages. Principal is paid only at maturity on T-bonds, whereas principal is paid every month on mortgages. Because mortgages pay principal continuously, these instruments have a shorter *effective* time to maturity than do Treasury bonds of equal maturity.[8] Third, mortgages have default risk whereas Treasury bonds do not. The term structure applicable to instruments with default risk may change even when the term structure for risk-free assets remains constant. Fourth, mortgages may be paid off early and hence have a shorter *expected maturity* than Treasury bonds of equal maturity.

Because mortgages and Treasury bonds are not identical instruments, they are not identically affected by interest rates. If Treasury bonds are less volatile than mortgages, financial consultants may advise Mr Werenskiold to write more than 10 T-bond futures contracts. Conversely, if these bonds are more volatile, the consultant may state that fewer than 10 futures contracts are indicated. An optimal ratio of futures to mortgages will reduce risk as much as possible. However, because the price movements of mortgages and Treasury bonds are not *perfectly correlated*, Mr Werenskiold's hedging strategy cannot eliminate all risk.

The preceding strategy is called a *short hedge* because Mr Werenskiold sells futures contracts to reduce risk. Though it involves an interest rate futures contract, this short hedge is analogous to short hedges in agricultural and metallurgical futures contracts. We argued at the beginning of this chapter that individuals and firms institute short hedges to offset inventory price fluctuation. Once Mr Werenskiold makes a contract to lend money to borrowers, the mortgages effectively become his inventory. He writes a futures contract to offset the price fluctuation of his inventory.

We now consider an example where a mortgage banker institutes a long hedge.

Example 25.4

Short versus Long Hedging

Margaret Boswell is another mortgage banker. Her firm faces problems similar to those facing Mr Werenskiold's firm. However, she tackles the problems through the use of advance commitments, a strategy the opposite of Mr Werenskiold's. That is, she promises to deliver loans to a financial institution *before* she lines up borrowers. On 1 March her firm agreed to sell mortgages to No-State Insurance. The agreement specifies that she must turn over 12 per cent coupon mortgages with a face value of €1 million to No-State by 1 May. No-State is buying the mortgages at par, implying that they will pay Ms Boswell €1 million on 1 May. As of 1 March, Ms Boswell had not signed up any borrowers. Over the next 2 months, she will seek out individuals who want mortgages beginning 1 May.

As with Mr Werenskiold, changing interest rates will affect Ms Boswell. If interest rates fall before she signs up a borrower, the borrower will demand a premium on a 12 per cent coupon loan. That is, the borrower will receive more than par on 1 May.[9] Because Ms Boswell receives par from the insurance company, she must make up the difference.

Conversely, if interest rates rise, a 12 per cent coupon loan will be made at a discount. That is, the borrower will receive less than par on 1 May. Because Ms Boswell receives par from the insurance company, the difference is pure profit to her.

The details are provided in Table 25.6. As did Mr Werenskiold, Ms Boswell finds the risk burdensome. Therefore, she offsets her advance commitment with a transaction in the futures markets. Because she *loses* in the cash market when interest rates fall, she *buys* futures contracts to reduce the risk. When interest rates fall, the value of her futures contracts increases. The gain in the futures market offsets the loss in the cash market. Conversely, she gains in the cash markets when interest rates rise. The value of her futures contracts decreases when interest rates rise, offsetting her gain.

	Cash Markets	Futures Markets
1 March	Mortgage banker makes a forward contract (advance commitment) to deliver €1 million of mortgages to No-State Insurance. The insurance company will pay par to Ms Boswell for the loans on 1 May. The borrowers are to receive their funding from the mortgage banker on 1 May. The mortgages are to be 12 per cent coupon loans for 20 years.	Mortgage banker buys 10 June Treasury bond futures contracts.
15 April	Mortgage banker signs up borrowers to 12 per cent coupon, 20-year mortgages. She promises that the borrowers will receive funds on 1 May.	Mortgage banker sells all futures contracts.
If interest rates rise:	Mortgage banker issues mortgages to borrowers at a discount. Mortgage banker gains because she receives par from the insurance company.	Futures contracts are sold at a price below purchase price, resulting in loss. Mortgage banker's loss in futures market offsets gain in cash market.
If interest rates fall:	Loans to borrowers are issued at a premium. Mortgage banker loses because she receives only par from insurance company.	Futures contracts are sold at a price above purchase price, resulting in gain. Mortgage banker's gain in futures market offsets loss in cash market.

Table 25.6 Illustration of Advance Commitment for Margaret Boswell, Mortgage Banker

We call this a *long hedge* because Ms Boswell offsets risk in the cash markets by buying a futures contract. Though it involves an interest rate futures contract, this long hedge is analogous to long hedges in agricultural and metallurgical futures contracts. We argued at the beginning of this chapter that individuals and firms institute long hedges when their finished goods are to be sold at a fixed price. Once Ms Boswell makes the advance commitment with No-State Insurance, she has fixed her sales price. She buys a futures contract to offset the price fluctuation of her raw materials – that is, her mortgages.

25.6   Duration Hedging

The last section concerned the risk of interest rate changes. We now want to explore this risk in a more precise manner. In particular, we want to show that the concept of duration is a prime determinant of interest rate risk. We begin by considering the effect of interest rate movements on bond prices.

The Case of Zero Coupon Bonds

Imagine a world where the interest rate is 10 per cent across all maturities. A 1-year pure discount bond pays €110 at maturity. A 5-year pure discount bond pays €161.05 at maturity. Both of these bonds are worth €100, as given by the following:

Value of 1-year pure discount bond

$$€100 = \frac{€110}{1.10}$$

Value of 5-year pure discount bond

$$€100 = \frac{€161.05}{(1.10)^5}$$

Which bond will change more when interest rates move? To find out, we calculate the value of these bonds when interest rates are either 8 or 12 per cent. The results are presented in Table 25.7. As can be seen, the 5-year bond has greater price swings than does the 1-year bond. That is, both bonds are worth €100 when interest rates are 10 per cent. The 5-year bond is worth more than the 1-year bond when interest rates are 8 per cent and worth less than the 1-year bond when interest rates are 12 per cent. We state that the 5-year bond is subject to more price volatility. This point, which was mentioned in passing in an earlier section of the chapter, is not difficult to understand. The interest rate term in the denominator, $1 + R$, is taken to the fifth power for a 5-year bond and only to the first power for the 1-year bond. Thus, the effect of a changing interest rate is magnified for the 5-year bond. The general rule is this:

The percentage price changes in long-term pure discount bonds are greater than the percentage price changes in short-term pure discount bonds.

Table 25.7 Value of a Pure Discount Bond as a Function of Interest Rate

Interest Rate (%)	One-Year Pure Discount Bond	Five-Year Pure Discount Bond
8	$€101.85 = \frac{€110}{1.08}$	$€109.61 = \frac{€161.05}{(1.08)^5}$
10	$€100.00 = \frac{€110}{1.10}$	$€100.00 = \frac{€161.05}{(1.10)^5}$
12	$€98.21 = \frac{€110}{1.12}$	$€91.38 = \frac{€161.05}{(1.12)^5}$

For a given interest rate change, a 5-year pure discount bond fluctuates more in price than does a 1-year pure discount bond.

The Case of Two Bonds with the Same Maturity but with Different Coupons

The previous example concerned pure discount bonds of different maturities. We now want to see the effect of different coupons on price volatility. To abstract from the effect of differing maturities, we consider two bonds with the same maturity but with different coupons.

Consider a 5-year, 10 per cent coupon bond and a 5-year, 1 per cent coupon bond. When interest rates are 10 per cent, the bonds are priced like this:

Value of 5-year, 10 per cent coupon bond

$$€100 = \frac{€10}{1.10} + \frac{€10}{(1.10)^2} + \frac{€10}{(1.10)^3} + \frac{€10}{(1.10)^4} + \frac{€110}{(1.10)^5}$$

Value of 5-year, 1 per cent coupon bond

$$€65.88 = \frac{€1}{1.10} + \frac{€1}{(1.10)^2} + \frac{€1}{(1.10)^3} + \frac{€1}{(1.10)^4} + \frac{€101}{(1.10)^5}$$

Which bond will change more in *percentage terms* if interest rates change?[10] To find out, we first calculate the value of these bonds when interest rates are either 8 or 12 per cent. The results are presented in Table 25.8. As we would expect, the 10 per cent coupon bond always sells for more than the 1 per cent coupon bond. Also as we would expect, each bond is worth more when the interest rate is 8 per cent than when the interest rate is 12 per cent.

Table 25.8 Value of Coupon Bonds at Different Interest Rates

Interest Rate (%)	Value
5-Year, 10% Coupon Bond	
8	$€107.99 = \frac{€10}{1.08} + \frac{€10}{(1.08)^2} + \frac{€10}{(1.08)^3} + \frac{€10}{(1.08)^4} + \frac{€110}{(1.08)^5}$
10	$€100.00 = \frac{€10}{1.10} + \frac{€10}{(1.10)^2} + \frac{€10}{(1.10)^3} + \frac{€10}{(1.10)^4} + \frac{€110}{(1.10)^5}$
12	$€92.79 = \frac{€10}{1.12} + \frac{€10}{(1.12)^2} + \frac{€10}{(1.12)^3} + \frac{€10}{(1.12)^4} + \frac{€110}{(1.12)^5}$
5-Year, 1% Coupon Bond	
8	$€72.05 = \frac{€1}{1.08} + \frac{€1}{(1.08)^2} + \frac{€1}{(1.08)^3} + \frac{€1}{(1.08)^4} + \frac{€101}{(1.08)^5}$
10	$€65.88 = \frac{€1}{1.10} + \frac{€1}{(1.10)^2} + \frac{€1}{(1.10)^3} + \frac{€1}{(1.10)^4} + \frac{€101}{(1.10)^5}$
12	$€60.35 = \frac{€1}{1.12} + \frac{€1}{(1.12)^2} + \frac{€1}{(1.12)^3} + \frac{€1}{(1.12)^4} + \frac{€101}{(1.12)^5}$

We calculate percentage price changes for both bonds as the interest rate changes from 10 to 8 per cent and from 10 to 12 per cent:

	10% Coupon Bond	1% Coupon Bond
Interest rate changes from 10% to 8%:	$7.99\% = \frac{€107.99}{€100} - 1$	$9.37\% = \frac{€72.05}{€65.88} - 1$
Interest rate changes from 10% to 12%:	$-7.21\% = \frac{€92.79}{€100} - 1$	$-8.39\% = \frac{€60.35}{€65.88} - 1$

As we can see, the 1 per cent coupon bond has a greater percentage price increase than does the 10 per cent coupon bond when the interest rate falls. Similarly, the 1 per cent coupon bond has a greater percentage price decrease than does the 10 per cent coupon bond when the interest rate rises. Thus, we say that the percentage price changes on the 1 per cent coupon bond are greater than are the percentage price changes on the 10 per cent coupon bond.

Duration

The question, of course, is 'Why?' We can answer this question only after we have explored a concept called *duration*. We begin by noticing that any coupon bond is actually a combination of pure discount bonds. For example, the 5-year, 10 per cent coupon bond is made up of five pure discount bonds:

1 A pure discount bond paying €10 at the end of year 1.
2 A pure discount bond paying €10 at the end of year 2.
3 A pure discount bond paying €10 at the end of year 3.
4 A pure discount bond paying €10 at the end of year 4.
5 A pure discount bond paying €110 at the end of year 5.

Similarly, the 5-year, 1 per cent coupon bond is made up of five pure discount bonds. Because the price volatility of a pure discount bond is determined by its maturity, we would like to determine the average maturity of the five pure discount bonds that make up a 5-year coupon bond. This leads us to the concept of duration.

We calculate average maturity in three steps. For the 10 per cent coupon bond, we have these:

1 *Calculate present value of each payment.* We do this as follows:

Year	Payment (€)	Present Value of Payment by Discounting at 10% (€)
1	10	9.091
2	10	8.264
3	10	7.513
4	10	6.830
5	110	68.302
		100.00

2 *Express the present value of each payment in relative terms.* We calculate the relative value of a single payment as the ratio of the present value of the payment to the value of the bond. The value of the bond is €100. We obtain these values:

Year	Payment (€)	Present Value of Payment (€)	Relative Value = $\dfrac{\text{Present Value of Payment}}{\text{Value of Bond}}$
1	10	9.091	9.091/100 = 0.09091
2	10	8.264	0.08264
3	10	7.513	0.07513
4	10	6.830	0.06830
5	110	68.302	0.68302
		100.00	1.0

The bulk of the relative value, 68.302 per cent, occurs at year 5 because the principal is paid back at that time.

3 *Weight the maturity of each payment by its relative value:*

$$4.1699 \text{ year} = 1 \text{ year} \times 0.09091 + 2 \text{ year} \times 0.08264 + 3 \text{ year} \times 0.07513$$
$$+ 4 \text{ year} \times 0.6830 + 5 \text{ year} \times 0.68302$$

There are many ways to calculate the average maturity of a bond. We have calculated it by weighting the maturity of each payment by the payment's present value. We find that the *effective* maturity of the bond is 4.1699 years. *Duration* is a commonly used word for effective maturity. Thus, the bond's duration is 4.1699 years. Note that duration is expressed in units of time.[11]

Because the 5-year, 10 per cent coupon bond has a duration of 4.1699 years, its percentage price fluctuations should be the same as those of a zero coupon bond with a duration of 4.1699 years.[12] It turns out that the 5-year,

1 per cent coupon bond has a duration of 4.8742 years. Because the 1 per cent coupon bond has a higher duration than the 10 per cent bond, the 1 per cent coupon bond should be subject to greater price fluctuations. This is exactly what we found earlier. In general we say the following:

The percentage price changes of a bond with high duration are greater than the percentage price changes of a bond with low duration.

A final question: why *does* the 1 per cent bond have a greater duration than the 10 per cent bond, even though they both have the same 5-year maturity? As mentioned earlier, duration is an average of the maturity of the bond's cash flows, weighted by the present value of each cash flow. The 1 per cent coupon bond receives only €1 in each of the first 4 years. Thus the weights applied to years 1 through 4 in the duration formula will be low. Conversely, the 10 per cent coupon bond receives €10 in each of the first 4 years. The weights applied to years 1 through 4 in the duration formula will be higher.

Matching Liabilities with Assets

Earlier in this chapter, we argued that firms can hedge risk by trading in futures. Because some firms are subject to interest rate risk, we showed how they can hedge with interest rate futures contracts. Firms may also hedge interest rate risk by matching liabilities with assets. This ability to hedge follows from our discussion of duration.

Example 25.5

Using Duration
The Bank of Amsterdam has the following market value balance sheet:

BANK OF AMSTERDAM Market Value Balance Sheet		
	Market Value (€)	Duration
Assets		
Overnight money	35 million	0
Accounts receivable–backed loans	500 million	3 months
Inventory loans	275 million	6 months
Industrial loans	40 million	2 years
Mortgages	150 million	14.8 years
	1,000 million	
Liabilities and Owners' Equity		
Chequing and savings accounts	400 million	0
Certificates of deposit	300 million	1 year
Long-term financing	200 million	10 years
Equity	100 million	
	1,000 million	

The bank has €1,000 million of assets and €900 million of liabilities. Its equity is the difference between the two: €100 million (= €1,000 million − €900 million). Both the market value and the duration of each individual item are provided in the balance sheet. Both overnight money and chequing and savings accounts have a duration of zero. This is because the interest paid on these instruments adjusts immediately to changing interest rates in the economy.

The bank's managers think that interest rates are likely to move quickly in the coming months. Because they do not know the direction of the movement, they are worried that their bank is vulnerable to changing rates. They call in a consultant, Jan Mandyn, to determine a hedging strategy.

Mr Mandyn first calculates the duration of the assets and the duration of the liabilities:[13]

Duration of assets

$$2.56 \text{ years} = 0 \text{ year} \times \frac{€35 \text{ million}}{€1,000 \text{ million}} + \frac{1}{4} \text{ year} \times \frac{€35 \text{ million}}{€1,000 \text{ million}}$$

$$+ \frac{1}{2} \text{ year} \times \frac{€275 \text{ million}}{€1,000 \text{ million}} + 2 \text{ year} \times \frac{€40 \text{ million}}{€1,000 \text{ million}} \qquad (25.4)$$

$$+ 14.8 \text{ years} (25.4) + \frac{€150 \text{ million}}{€1,000 \text{ million}}$$

Duration of liabilities

$$2.56 \text{ years} = 0 \text{ year} \times \frac{€400 \text{ million}}{€900 \text{ million}} + 1 \text{ year} \times \frac{€300 \text{ million}}{€900 \text{ million}} + 10 \text{ years} \times \frac{€200 \text{ million}}{€900 \text{ million}} \qquad (25.5)$$

The duration of the assets, 2.56 years, equals the duration of the liabilities. Because of this, Mr Mandyn argues that the firm is immune to interest rate risk.

Just to be on the safe side, the bank calls in a second consultant, Gabrielle Aertsen. Ms Aertsen argues that it is incorrect to simply match durations because assets total €1,000 million and liabilities total only €900 million. If both assets and liabilities have the same duration, the price change on a *euro* of assets should be equal to the price change on a euro of liabilities. However, the *total* price change will be greater for assets than for liabilities because there are more assets than liabilities in this bank. The firm will be immune from interest rate risk only when the duration of the liabilities is greater than the duration of the assets. Ms Aertsen states that the following relationship must hold if the bank is to be immunized – that is, immune to interest rate risk:

$$\begin{array}{c}\text{Duration of} \\ \text{assets}\end{array} \times \begin{array}{c}\text{Market value of} \\ \text{assets}\end{array} = \begin{array}{c}\text{Duration of} \\ \text{liabilities}\end{array} \times \begin{array}{c}\text{Market value of} \\ \text{liabilities}\end{array} \qquad (25.6)$$

She says that the bank should not *equate* the duration of the liabilities with the duration of the assets. Rather, using Equation 25.6, the bank should match the duration of the liabilities to the duration of the assets. She suggests two ways to achieve this match.

1 *Increase the duration of the liabilities without changing the duration of the assets.* Ms Aertsen argues that the duration of the liabilities could be increased to:

$$\text{Duration of assets} \times \frac{\text{Market value of assets}}{\text{Market value of liabilities}} = 2.56 \text{ years} \times \frac{€1,000 \text{ million}}{€900 \text{ million}}$$

$$= 2.84 \text{ years}$$

Equation 25.5 then becomes:

$$2.56 \times €1 \text{ billion} = 2.84 \times €900 \text{ million}$$

2 *Decrease the duration of the assets without changing the duration of the liabilities.* Alternatively, Ms Aertsen points out that the duration of the assets could be decreased to:

$$\text{Duration of liabilities} \times \frac{\text{Market value of liabilities}}{\text{Market value of assets}} = 2.56 \text{ years} \times \frac{€900 \text{ million}}{€1,000 \text{ million}}$$

$$= 2.30 \text{ years}$$

Equation 25.6 then becomes:

$$2.30 \times €1 \text{ billion} = 2.56 \times €900 \text{ million}$$

Duration and the accompanying immunization strategies are useful in other areas of finance. For example, many firms establish pension funds to meet obligations to retirees. If the assets of a pension fund are invested in bonds and other fixed-income securities, the duration of the assets can be computed. Similarly, the firm views the obligations to retirees as analogous to interest payments on debt. The duration of these liabilities can be calculated as well. The manager of a pension fund would commonly choose pension assets so that the duration of the assets is matched with the duration of the liabilities. In this way, changing interest rates would not affect the net worth of the pension fund.

Life insurance companies receiving premiums today are legally obligated to provide death benefits in the future. Actuaries view these future benefits as analogous to interest and principal payments of fixed-income securities. The duration of these expected benefits can be calculated. Insurance firms frequently invest in bonds where the duration of the bonds is matched to the duration of the future death benefits.

The business of a leasing company is quite simple. The firm issues debt to purchase assets, which are then leased. The lease payments have a duration, as does the debt. Leasing companies frequently structure debt financing so that the duration of the debt matches the duration of the lease. If a firm did not do this, the market value of its equity could be eliminated by a quick change in interest rates.

25.7   Swaps Contracts

Swaps are close cousins to forwards and futures contracts. Swaps are arrangements between two counterparts to exchange cash flows over time. There is enormous flexibility in the forms that swaps can take, but the two basic types are interest rate swaps and currency swaps. Often these are combined when interest received in one currency is swapped for interest in another currency.

Interest Rate Swaps

Like other derivatives, swaps are tools that firms can use to easily change their risk exposures and their balance sheets. Consider a firm that has borrowed and carried on its books an obligation to repay a 10-year loan for €100 million of principal with a 9 per cent coupon rate paid annually. Ignoring the possibility of calling the loan, the firm expects to have to pay coupons of €9 million every year for 10 years and a balloon payment of €100 million at the end of the 10 years. Suppose, though, that the firm is uncomfortable with having this large fixed obligation on its books. Perhaps the firm is in a cyclical business where its revenues vary and could conceivably fall to a point where it would be difficult to make the debt payment.

Suppose, too, that the firm earns a lot of its revenue from financing the purchase of its products. Typically, for example, a manufacturer might help its customers finance their purchase of its products through a leasing or credit subsidiary. Usually these loans are for relatively short periods and are financed at some premium over the prevailing short-term rate of interest. This puts the firm in the position of having revenues that move up and down with interest rates while its costs are relatively fixed.

What the firm would really prefer is to have a floating-rate loan rather than a fixed-rate loan. That way, when interest rates rise, the firm would have to pay more on the loan, but it would be making more on its product financing. An interest rate swap is ideal in this situation.

Of course, the firm could also just go into the capital markets and borrow €100 million at a variable interest rate and then use the proceeds to retire its outstanding fixed-rate loan. Although this is possible, it is generally quite expensive, requiring underwriting a new loan and the repurchase of the existing loan. The ease of entering a swap is its inherent advantage.

The particular swap would be one that exchanged its fixed obligation for an agreement to pay a floating rate. Every year it would agree to pay a coupon based on whatever the prevailing interest rate was at the time in exchange for an agreement from a counterparty to pay the firm's fixed coupon.

A common reference point for floating-rate commitments is called LIBOR. LIBOR stands for the London Interbank Offered Rate, and it is the rate that most international banks charge one another for sterling and US dollar loans in the London market. LIBOR is commonly used as the reference rate for a floating-rate commitment, and, depending on the creditworthiness of the borrower, the rate can vary from LIBOR to LIBOR plus one point or more over LIBOR. For euro-denominated loans, the applicable rate is EURIBOR.

If we assume that our firm has a credit rating that requires it to pay EURIBOR plus 50 basis points, then in a swap it would be exchanging its fixed 9 per cent obligation for the obligation to pay whatever the prevailing EURIBOR rate is plus 50 basis points. Table 25.9 displays how the cash flows on this swap would work. In the table, we have assumed that EURIBOR starts at 8 per cent and rises for 3 years to 11 per cent and then drops to 7 per cent. As the table illustrates, the firm would owe a coupon of 8.5% × €100 million = €8.5 million in year 1, €9.5 million in year 2, €10.5 million in year 3, and €11.5 million in year 4. The precipitous drop to 7 per cent lowers the annual payments to €7.5 million thereafter. In return, the firm receives the fixed payment of €9 million each year. Actually, rather than swapping the full payments, the cash flows would be netted. Because the firm is paying variable and receiving fixed – which it uses to pay its lender – in the first year, for example, the firm owes €8.5 million and is owed by its counterparty, who is paying fixed, €9 million. Hence, net, the firm would receive a payment of €0.5 million. Because the firm has to pay its lender €9 million but gets a net payment from the swap of €0.5 million, it really pays out only the difference, or €8.5 million. In each year, then, the firm would effectively pay only EURIBOR plus 50 basis points.

Table 25.9 Fixed for Floating Swap: Cash Flows (€ million)

Year	Coupons									
	1	2	3	4	5	6	7	8	9	10
Swap										
Fixed obligation	9	9	9	9	9	9	9	9	9	9
EURIBOR floating	−8.5	−9.5	−10.5	−11.5	−7.5	−7.5	−7.5	−7.5	−7.5	−7.5
Original loan										
Fixed obligation	−9	−9	−9	−9	−9	−9	−9	−9	−9	109
Net effect	−8.5	−9.5	10.5	11.5	7.5	7.5	7.5	7.5	7.5	−107.5

Notice, too, that the entire transaction can be carried out without any need to change the terms of the original loan. In effect, by swapping, the firm has found a counterparty that is willing to pay its fixed obligation in return for the firm paying a floating obligation.

Currency Swaps

FX stands for foreign exchange, and currency swaps are sometimes called FX swaps. Currency swaps are swaps of obligations to pay cash flows in one currency for obligations to pay in another currency.

Currency swaps arise as a natural vehicle for hedging the risk in international trade. For example, consider the problem of BMW, that sells a broad range of its product line in the United States market. Every year the firm can count on receiving revenue from the United States in dollars. We will study international finance later in this book, but for now we can just observe that because exchange rates fluctuate, this subjects the firm to considerable risk.

If BMW produces its products in Germany and exports them to the US, then the firm has to pay its workers and its suppliers in euros. But it is receiving some of its revenues in dollars. The €/$ exchange rate changes over time. As the dollar rises in value, the US revenues are worth more euros, but as it falls they decline. Suppose the firm can count on selling $100 million of automobiles each year in the United States. If the exchange rate is $2 for each €, then the firm will receive €50 million. But if the exchange rate were to rise to $3 for each €, the firm would receive only €33.333 million for its $100 million. Naturally the firm would like to protect itself against these currency swings.

To do so BMW can enter a currency swap. We will learn more about exactly what the terms of such a swap might be, but for now we can assume that the swap is for 5 years at a fixed term of $100 million for €50 million each year. Now, no matter what happens to the exchange rate between the dollar and the euro over the next 5 years, as long as BMW makes $100 million each year from the sale of its automobiles, it will swap this for €50 million each year.

We have not addressed the question of how the market sets prices for swaps – either interest rate swaps or currency swaps. In the fixed for floating example and in the currency swap, we just quoted some terms. We will not go into great detail on exactly how it is done, but we can stress the most important points.

Swaps, like forwards and futures, are essentially zero-sum transactions, which is to say that in both cases the market sets prices at a fair level, and neither party has any substantial bargain or loss at the moment the deal is struck. For example, in the currency swap, the swap rate is some average of the market expectation of what the exchange rate will be over the life of the swap. In the interest rate swap, the rates are set as the fair floating and fixed rates for the creditor, taking into account the creditworthiness of the counterparties. We can actually price swaps fairly once we know how to price forward contracts. In our interest rate swap example, the firm swapped EURIBOR plus 50 basis points for a 9 per cent fixed rate, all on a principal amount of €100 million. This is equivalent to a series of forward contracts extending over the life of the swap. In year 1, for example, having made the swap, the firm is in the same position that it would be if it had sold a forward contract entitling the buyer to receive EURIBOR plus 50 basis points on €100 million in return for a fixed payment of €9 million (9 per cent of €100 million). Similarly, the currency swap can also be viewed as a series of forward contracts.

Exotics

Up to now we have dealt with the meat and potatoes of the derivatives markets, swaps, options, forwards and futures. Exotics are the complicated blends of these that often produce surprising results for buyers.

One of the more interesting types of exotics is called an *inverse floater*. In our fixed for floating swap, the floating payments fluctuated with EURIBOR. An inverse floater is one that fluctuates inversely with some rate such as EURIBOR or LIBOR. For example, the floater might pay an interest rate of 20 per cent minus EURIBOR. If EURIBOR is 9 per cent, then the inverse pays 11 per cent, and if EURIBOR rises to 12 per cent, the payments on the inverse would fall to 8 per cent. Clearly the purchaser of an inverse profits from the inverse if interest rates fall.

Both floaters and inverse floaters have a supercharged version called *superfloaters* and *superinverses* that fluctuate more than one for one with movements in interest rates. As an example of a superinverse floater, consider a floater that pays an interest rate of 30 per cent minus *twice* LIBOR. When LIBOR is 10 per cent, the inverse pays

$$30\% - 2 \times 10\% = 30\% - 20\% = 10\%$$

And if LIBOR falls by 3 per cent to 7 per cent, then the return on the inverse rises by 6 per cent from 10 per cent to 16 per cent:

$$30\% - 2 \times 7\% = 30\% - 14\% = 16\%$$

Sometimes derivatives are combined with options to bound the impact of interest rates. The most important of these instruments are called *caps* and *floors*. A cap is so named because it puts an upper limit or a cap on the impact of a rise in interest rates. A floor, conversely, provides a floor below which the interest rate impact is insulated.

To illustrate the impact of these, consider a firm that is borrowing short term and is concerned that interest rates might rise. For example, using LIBOR as the reference interest rate, the firm might purchase a 7 per cent cap. The cap pays the firm the difference between LIBOR and 7 per cent on some principal amount, provided that LIBOR is greater than 7 per cent. As long as LIBOR is below 7 per cent, the holder of the cap receives no payments.

By purchasing the cap the firm has assured itself that even if interest rates rise above 7 per cent, it will not have to pay more than a 7 per cent rate. Suppose that interest rates rise to 9 per cent. While the firm is borrowing short term and paying 9 per cent rates, this is offset by the cap, which is paying the firm the difference between 9 per cent and the 7 per cent limit. For any LIBOR rate above 7 per cent, the firm receives the difference between LIBOR and 7 per cent, and, as a consequence, it has capped its cost of borrowing at 7 per cent.

On the other side, consider a financial firm that is in the business of lending short term and is concerned that interest rates – and consequently its revenues – might fall. The firm could purchase a floor to protect itself from such declines. If the limit on the floor is 7 per cent, then the floor pays the difference between 7 per cent and LIBOR whenever LIBOR is below 7 per cent, and nothing if LIBOR is above 7 per cent. Thus, if interest rates were to fall to, say, 5 per cent while the firm is receiving only 5 per cent from its lending activities, the floor is paying it the difference between 7 per cent and 5 per cent, or an additional 2 per cent. By purchasing the floor, the firm has assured itself of receiving no less than 7 per cent from the combination of the floor and its lending activities.

We have only scratched the surface of what is available in the world of derivatives. Derivatives are designed to meet marketplace needs, and the only binding limitation is the human imagination. Nowhere should the buyer's warning *caveat emptor* be taken more seriously than in the derivatives markets, and this is especially true for the exotics. If swaps are the meat and potatoes of the derivatives markets, then caps and floors are the meat and potatoes of the exotics. As we have seen, they have obvious value as hedging instruments. But much attention has been focused on truly exotic derivatives, some of which appear to have arisen more as the residuals that were left over from more straightforward deals. We will not examine these in any detail, but suffice it to say that some of these are so volatile and unpredictable that market participants have dubbed them 'toxic waste'.

Real World Insight 25.1

Hedging Oil

(Excerpts from 'Drillers' $26 billion oil-hedge gain spreads price-drop pain', Bloomberg, 9 April 2015)

For US shale drillers, the crash in oil prices came with a $26 billion safety net. That's how much they stand to get paid on insurance they bought to protect themselves against a bear market – as long as prices stay low.

The flip side is that those who sold the price hedges now have to make good. At the top of the list are the same Wall Street banks that financed the biggest energy boom in history, including JPMorgan Chase & Co., Bank of America Corp., Citigroup Inc. and Wells Fargo & Co.

While it is standard practice for them to sell some of that risk to third parties, it is nearly impossible to identify who exactly is on the hook because there are no rules requiring disclosure of all transactions. The buyers come from groups like hedge funds, airlines, refiners and utilities.

The swift decline in US oil prices – $107.26 on 20 June, $46.39 seven months later – caught market participants by surprise. Harold Hamm, the billionaire founder of Continental Resources Inc., cashed out his company's protection in October, betting on a rebound. Instead, crude kept falling.

The fair value of hedges held by 57 US companies in the Bloomberg Intelligence North America Independent Explorers and Producers index rose to $26 billion as of 31 December, a fivefold increase from the end of September, according to data compiled by Bloomberg.

Though it is difficult to determine who will ultimately lose money on the trades and how much, a handful of drillers do reveal the names of their counterparties, offering a glimpse of how the risk of falling oil prices moved through the financial system. More than a dozen energy companies say they buy hedges from their lenders, including JPMorgan, Wells Fargo, Citigroup and Bank of America.

Danielle Romero-Apsilos, a Citigroup spokeswoman, said the bank actively hedges and manages its risk. Representatives of JPMorgan, Wells Fargo and Bank of America declined to comment.

US oil companies already netted at least $2.4 billion in the fourth quarter of 2014 on their hedges, according to data compiled on 57 US companies in the Bloomberg Intelligence index. Oil companies would rather be losing money on the trades and making money selling crude at higher prices, Kilduff said. 'It's like homeowners' insurance,' he said. 'You don't buy it hoping the house burns down.'

The $26 billion of protection won't last forever. Most hedging contracts expire this year, according to company reports. Buying new insurance today means locking in prices below $60 a barrel. The alternative is following Hamm's example and having no cushion if crude keeps falling.

Financial institutions act as a go-between, selling oil derivatives to one company and buying from another while pocketing fees and profiting on the spread, said Charles Peabody, an analyst at Portales Partners LLC in New York. The question is whether the banks were able to adequately offset their risk when the market took a nosedive, he said.

'The banks always tell us that they try to lay off the risk,' Peabody said. 'I know from history and practice that it's great in concept, but it's hard to do in reality.'

25.8 Financial Risk Management in Practice

Because the true extent of derivatives does not usually appear in financial statements, it is much more difficult to observe the use of derivatives by firms compared to, say, bank debt. Much of our knowledge of corporate derivative use comes from academic surveys. Most surveys report that the use of derivatives appears to vary widely among large publicly traded firms. Large firms are far more likely to use derivatives than are small firms. Table 25.10 shows the percentage of firms across the world that use derivatives, where it can be seen that foreign currency and interest rate derivatives are most popular.

Table 25.10 Derivative Usage Around the World

	Number of Firms	All Types of Derivatives	Foreign Exchange Derivatives	Interest Rate Derivatives	Commodity Price Derivatives
Australia	305	66.6	51.5	42.3	14.1
Germany	413	47.0	39.2	24.2	4.6
United Kingdom	886	64.2	54.5	36.6	3.8
United States	2,231	64.9	37.7	40.4	16.3
United States and Canada	2,830	63.8	39.3	37.6	16.8
Europe	2,530	61.4	50.9	32.4	5.0
Asia & Pacific	1,743	51.2	44.1	27.3	6.0
Africa/Middle East	127	78.0	74.8	22.0	7.9
OECD	6,133	64.3	47.3	37.4	11.4
Non-OECD	1,186	39.6	34.6	10.8	3.0
Non-US	5,088	58.3	48.5	29.9	7.3

Source: Adapted from Table 2, Bartram et al. (2009).

The prevailing view is that derivatives can be very helpful in reducing the variability of firm cash flows, which, in turn, reduces the various costs associated with financial distress. Therefore, it is somewhat puzzling that large firms use derivatives more often than small firms – because large firms tend to have less cash flow variability than small firms. Also some surveys report that firms occasionally use derivatives when they want to speculate about future prices and not just to hedge risks. However, most of the evidence is consistent with the theory that derivatives are most frequently used by firms where financial distress costs are high and access to the capital markets is constrained. Finally, because derivatives hedge distress risk, firms who hedge have lower costs of equity and higher values.[14]

Summary and Conclusions

1   Firms hedge to reduce risk. This chapter showed a number of hedging strategies.

2   A forward contract is an agreement by two parties to sell an item for cash at a later date. The price is set at the time the agreement is signed. However, cash changes hands on the date of delivery. Forward contracts are generally not traded on organized exchanges.

3   Futures contracts are also agreements for future delivery. They have certain advantages, such as liquidity, that forward contracts do not. An unusual feature of futures contracts is the mark-to-the-market convention. If the price of a futures contract falls on a particular day, every buyer of the contract must pay money to the clearinghouse. Every seller of the contract receives money from the clearinghouse. Everything is reversed if the price rises. The mark-to-the-market convention prevents defaults on futures contracts.

4   We divided hedges into two types: short hedges and long hedges. An individual or firm that sells a futures contract to reduce risk is instituting a short hedge. Short hedges are generally appropriate for holders of inventory. An individual or firm that buys a futures contract to reduce risk is instituting a long hedge. Long hedges are typically used by firms with contracts to sell finished goods at a fixed price.

5   An interest rate futures contract employs a bond as the deliverable instrument. Because of their popularity, we worked with Treasury bond futures contracts. We showed that Treasury bond futures contracts can be priced using the same type of net present value analysis that is used to price Treasury bonds themselves.

6   Many firms face interest rate risk. They can reduce this risk by hedging with interest rate futures contracts. As with other commodities, a short hedge involves the sale of a futures contract. Firms that are committed to buying mortgages or other bonds are likely to institute short hedges. A long hedge involves the purchase of a futures contract. Firms that have agreed to sell mortgages or other bonds at a fixed price are likely to institute long hedges.

7   Duration measures the average maturity of all the cash flows in a bond. Bonds with high duration have high price variability. Firms frequently try to match the duration of their assets with the duration of their liabilities.

8   Swaps are agreements to exchange cash flows over time. The first major type is an interest rate swap in which one pattern of coupon payments, say, fixed payments, is exchanged for another, say, coupons that float with LIBOR. The second major type is a currency swap, in which an agreement is struck to swap payments denominated in one currency for payments in another currency over time.

Questions and Problems

■■ connect

CONCEPT

1   **Derivatives: Hedging and Risk**   Discuss the differences between hedging and speculation with derivatives. Many corporations' risk management divisions earn significant profits each year. What does this say about derivative use in large corporations?

2   **Forward Contracts**   Explain what is meant by a forward contract. Use a non-financial example to illustrate how a forward contract works. What are the advantages and disadvantages of forward contracts?

3 **Futures Contracts**   What is a futures contract? What are the advantages and disadvantages of futures contracts?

4 **Interest Rate Futures Contracts**   Explain how interest rates can be hedged by futures contracts. Provide an example of how you could use one to hedge against an increase in interest rates.

5 **Duration Hedging**   What is duration and how can it be used to hedge against interest rate changes? Use an example to illustrate your answer.

6 **Swaps**   Explain why a swap is effectively a series of forward contracts. Suppose a firm enters a swap agreement with a swap dealer. Describe the nature of the default risk faced by both parties.

7 **Financial Risk Management**   Using Table 25.10, discuss the main concerns of corporations when using derivatives to manage risk.

REGULAR

8 **Hedging**   Provide an overview of the empirical determinants of hedging. If you were the corporate treasurer for a company, would you recommend hedging as a risk management strategy? Explain.

9 **Hedging Strategies**   If a firm is buying futures contracts on lumber as a hedging strategy, what must be true about the firm's exposure to lumber prices? What if a firm is writing call options on cocoa futures as a hedging strategy, what must be true about the firm's exposure to cocoa prices?

10 **Hedging Strategies**   What are the three strategies a firm has at its disposal to deal with currency risk? What are the advantages and disadvantages of each? Explain.

11 **Hedging Risks**   Vestas Wind Systems A/S, the Danish wind energy company, would like to consider hedging the risk of its operations. What are the main risks the company faces and how would it hedge these risks? Provide at least two reasons why it probably will not be possible to achieve a completely flat risk profile with respect to their identified risks.

12 **Sources of Risk**   A company produces an energy-intensive product and uses natural gas as the energy source. The competition primarily uses oil. Explain why this company is exposed to fluctuations in both oil and natural gas prices.

13 **Hedging Commodities**   If a textile manufacturer wanted to hedge against adverse movements in cotton prices, it could buy cotton futures contracts or buy call options on cotton futures contracts. What would be the pros and cons of the two approaches?

14 **Option**   Explain why a put option on a bond is conceptually the same as a call option on interest rates.

15 **Hedging Interest Rates**   A company has a large bond issue maturing in one year. When it matures, the company will float a new issue. Current interest rates are attractive, and the company is concerned that rates next year will be higher. What are some hedging strategies that the company might use in this case?

16 **Swaps**   Suppose a firm enters a fixed for floating interest rate swap with a swap dealer. Using an example and a diagram, illustrate the cash flows that will occur as a result of the swap. Why would a swap be preferable to other derivative transactions?

17 **Transaction versus Economic Exposure**   What is the difference between transactions and economic exposure? Which can be hedged more easily? Why?

18 **Hedging Exchange Rate Risk**   If a Dutch company exports its goods to the UK, how would it use a futures contract on sterling to hedge its exchange rate risk? Would it buy or sell sterling futures? Does the way the exchange rate is quoted in the futures contract matter?

19 **Hedging Strategies**   You are the finance director of a British company which is expecting a payment in euros of €200 million at the end of September and wish to hedge against currency risk. However, the nearest maturity date for a euro futures contract is on 13 December and it is now 29 January. The face value of one euro futures contract is €100,000. The spot rate today is £0.9/€ and the futures rate is £0.85/€.

(a) Estimate the number of futures contracts required.

(b) Assume that at the end of September, the spot rate turns out to be £0.95/€ and a futures contract taken out at the end of September to expire on 13 December is quoted at £0.92/€. Estimate the total gain or loss earned by your company.

(c) Estimate the effective exchange rate received by your company.

20 **Swaps** Syco SA, a distributor of food and food-related products, has announced it has signed an interest rate swap. The interest rate swap effectively converts the company's €100 million, 4.6 per cent interest rate bonds for a variable rate payment, which is the 6-month EURIBOR minus 0.52 per cent. Why would Syco use a swap agreement? In other words, why didn't Syco just go ahead and issue floating-rate bonds because the net effect of issuing fixed-rate bonds and then doing a swap is to create a variable rate bond?

21 **Currency Swaps** Consider two firms, Larss plc and Sousa plc. Larss plc has a better credit rating and can borrow cheaper than Sousa plc in both fixed and floating rate markets. Specifically, Larss pays 6.35 per cent fixed and LIBOR plus 0.5 per cent floating. Sousa plc pays 9.85 per cent fixed and LIBOR plus 1.5 per cent floating.

(a) If Larss plc prefers to borrow floating and Sousa plc prefers to borrow fixed, determine the spread differential that they will split if they do a swap with each other.

(b) Construct a swap in which both Larss plc and Sousa plc can exploit Sousa plc's comparative advantage. Your answer should include a swap diagram and a description of the cash flows transferred as a result of the swap.

(c) Describe what is meant by a currency swap and the conditions under which a company may wish to undertake this type of transaction.

22 **Hedging Strategies** Suntharee Lhaopadchan is a Thai student who is planning a one-year stay in the United Kingdom. She expects to arrive in the United Kingdom in 8 months. She is worried about depreciation in the Thai baht relative to the British pound over the next 8 months and wishes to take a position in foreign exchange futures to hedge this risk. What should Miss Lhaopadchan's hedging position be? Assume the exchange rate between the baht and sterling is quoted as baht/pound.

23 **Future Quotes** Suppose you purchase a May 2015 cocoa futures contract on 16 April 2015, at the last price of the day. What will your profit or loss be if the cocoa prices turn out to be $3,000 per metric ton at expiration? (Refer to Table 25.2 to help answer this question.)

24 **Futures Quotes** Suppose you sell five May 2015 gold futures contracts on 16 April 2015, at the last price of the day at $1,648.6 per ounce. What will your profit or loss be if gold prices turn out to be $1,500 per ounce at expiration and $1,300 per ounce at expiration? Assume each contract is for 100 ounces.

25 **Put and Call Pay-offs** Suppose a financial manager buys call options on 35,000 barrels of oil with the same exercise price of £120 per barrel. She simultaneously sells a put option on 35,000 barrels of oil with the same exercise price of £120 per barrel. Consider her gains and losses if oil prices are £115, £120, £125, £130 and £135. What do you notice about the payoff profile?

26 **Marking to Market** You are long 10 gold futures contracts, established at an initial settle price of €1,000 per ounce, where each contract represents 100 ounces. Over the subsequent four trading days, gold settles at €1,003, €1,009, €1,012 and €1,004, respectively. Compute the cash flows at the end of each trading day, and compute your total profit or loss at the end of the trading period.

27 **FRA Quotes** Rock Spring plc decides it wants to borrow capital for a 6-month period in two 3-month instalments. The company can borrow at LIBOR + 2 per cent. LIBOR rates today are 4 per cent. However, because the firm must agree the contract in advance and pay later, it will be exposed to the risk of interest rates over the next 3 months, since the level of its second interest payment will not be established until the end of the first period. In order to manage this risk, the firm decides to acquire FRA from an investment bank. The company receives the following FRA quotes:

Period	Dealer 1	Dealer 2
3 v 6	1.8% – 1.85%	1.9% – 1.95%
3 v 6	1.7% – 1.86%	1% – 1.82%
6 v 9	2% – 2.3%	2.1% – 2.5%
6 v 9	3% – 3.5%	2.9% – 3.3%
9 v 12	3.2% – 3.9%	3% – 3.7%
9 v 12	3.7% – 4%	3.8% – 4.2%

Which quote should the firm use to hedge its exposure and at what interest rate?

28 **Duration** What is the duration of a bond with 4 years to maturity and a coupon of 9 per cent paid annually if the bond sells at par?

29 Duration   Pillow Private Bank has the following market value balance sheet:

Asset or Liability	Market Value (in £ billions)	Duration (in years)
Government deposits	28	0
Trade receivables	580	1.20
Short-term loans	390	2.65
Long-term loans	84	7.25
Mortgages	315	16.25
Liabilities		
Chequing and savings deposits	520	0
Certificates of deposit	340	2.60
Long-term financing	260	17.80
Equity	277	N/A

(a) What is the duration of the assets?

(b) What is the duration of the liabilities?

(c) Is the bank immune from interest rate risk?

30 Hedging with Futures   Suppose today is 16 April 2015, and your firm produces chocolate and needs 75,000 tonnes of cocoa in July 2015 for an upcoming promotion. You would like to lock in your costs today because you are concerned that cocoa prices might go up between now and June. The closing price for July 2015 futures is £1,468 per ton of cocoa.

(a) How could you use cocoa futures contracts to hedge your risk exposure?

(b) Suppose cocoa prices are £1,500 per contract in July. What is the profit or loss on your futures position? Explain how your futures position has eliminated your exposure to price risk in the cocoa market.

31 Interest Rate Swaps   ABC Company and XYZ Company need to raise funds to pay for capital improvements at their manufacturing plants. ABC Company is a well-established firm with an excellent credit rating in the debt market; it can borrow funds either at 11 per cent fixed rate or at EURIBOR + 1 per cent floating rate. XYZ Company is a fledgling start-up firm without a strong credit history. It can borrow funds either at 10 per cent fixed rate or at EURIBOR + 3 per cent floating rate.

(a) Is there an opportunity here for ABC and XYZ to benefit by means of an interest rate swap?

(b) Suppose you have just been hired at a bank that acts as a dealer in the swaps market, and your boss has shown you the borrowing rate information for your clients ABC and XYZ. Describe how you could bring these two companies together in an interest rate swap that would make both firms better off while netting your bank a 2.0 per cent profit.

32 Duration   Per and Birthe Clausen have a son who will begin university 3 years from today. Expenses of €30,000 will need to be paid at the beginning of each of the 4 years that their son plans to attend university. What is the duration of this liability to the couple if they can borrow and lend at the market interest rate of 10 per cent?

33 Duration   What is the duration of a bond with 2 years to maturity if the bond has a coupon rate of 8 per cent paid semi-annually, and the market interest rate is 7 per cent?

CHALLENGE

34 Forward Pricing   The forward price (F) of a contract on an asset with neither carrying costs nor convenience yield is the current spot price of the asset (S_0) multiplied by 1 plus the appropriate interest rate between the initiation of the contract and the delivery date of the asset. Derive this relationship by comparing the cash flows that result from the following two strategies:

Strategy 1:   Buy silver on the spot market today and hold it for one year. (*Hint:* Do not use any of your own money to purchase the silver.)

Strategy 2:   Take on a long position in a silver forward contract for delivery in one year. Assume that silver is an asset with neither carrying costs nor convenience yield.

35 Forward Pricing   You enter into a forward contract to buy a 10-year, zero coupon bond that will be issued in one year. The face value of the bond is £100,000, and the 1-year and 11-year spot interest rates are 5 per cent and 9 per cent, respectively.

(a) What is the forward price of your contract?

(b) Suppose both the 1-year and 11-year spot rates unexpectedly shift downward by 2 per cent. What is the new price of the forward contract?

36 **Forward Pricing** This morning you agreed to buy a 1-year Treasury bond in 6 months. The bond has a face value of £100,000. Use the spot interest rates listed here to answer the following questions:

Time (Months)	EAR (%)
6	7.42
12	8.02
18	8.79
24	9.43

(a) What is the forward price of this contract?

(b) Suppose shortly after you purchased the forward contract, all rates increased by 30 basis points. For example, the 6-month rate increased from 7.42 per cent to 7.72 per cent. What is the price of a forward contract otherwise identical to yours given these changes?

37 **Financial Engineering** Suppose there were call options and forward contracts available on coal, but no put options. Show how a financial engineer could synthesize a put option using the available contracts. What does your answer tell you about the general relationship between puts, calls and forwards?

Exam Question (45 minutes)

Malaika plc, a British company, is planning to make a payment in euros of €150 million at the end of September. However, the nearest maturity date for a euro futures contract is at 13 December and it is now 29 January. The face value of one euro futures contract is €250,000. The spot rate today is €1.49/£ and the futures rate is €1.45/£.

1 Estimate the number of futures contracts required. (25 marks)

2 Assume that at the end of September, the spot rate turns out to be €1.55/£ and a futures contract taken out at the end of September to expire on 13 December is quoted at €1.50/£. Estimate the total gain or loss earned by Malaika plc. (25 marks)

3 Review the primary differences between hedging with futures and hedging with forwards. (25 marks)

4 Explain what is meant by a currency option. Provide a worked example of a currency option strategy and the reasons for its use. Explain why currency put options are not necessarily a bearish investment. (25 marks)

Mini Case

McAfee Mortgages Ltd

Jennifer McAfee recently received her university Master's degree and has decided to enter the mortgage brokerage business. Rather than work for someone else, she has decided to open her own shop. Her cousin Finn has approached her about a mortgage for a house he is building. The house will be completed in 3 months, and he will need the mortgage at that time. Finn wants a 25-year, fixed-rate mortgage for the amount of £500,000 with monthly payments.

Jennifer has agreed to lend Finn the money in 3 months at the current market rate of 8 per cent. Because Jennifer is just starting out, she does not have £500,000 available for the loan, so she approaches Ian MacDuff, the president of IM Insurance, about purchasing the mortgage from her in 3 months. Ian has agreed to purchase the mortgage in 3 months, but he is unwilling to set a price on the mortgage. Instead, he has agreed in writing to purchase the mortgage at the market rate in 3 months. There are Treasury bond futures contracts available for delivery in 3 months. A Treasury bond contract is for £100,000 in face value of Treasury bonds.

1 What is the monthly mortgage payment on Finn's mortgage?
2 What is the most significant risk Jennifer faces in this deal?
3 How can Jennifer hedge this risk?
4 Suppose that in the next 3 months the market rate of interest rises to 9 per cent.
   (a) How much will Ian be willing to pay for the mortgage?
   (b) What will happen to the value of Treasury bond futures contracts? Will the long or short position increase in value?
5 Suppose that in the next 3 months the market rate of interest falls to 7 per cent.
   (a) How much will Ian be willing to pay for the mortgage?
   (b) What will happen to the value of T-bond futures contracts? Will the long or short position increase in value?
6 Are there any possible risks Jennifer faces in using Treasury bond futures contracts to hedge her interest rate risk?

Practical Case Study

Every company that uses international accounting standards must have a statement on their hedging activity. Download the financial accounts of a company from your country. Read through the risk section and write a report on their hedging activity, if any.

Relevant Accounting Standards

The derivative positions held by all companies that follow IFRS must be reported at fair value. Guidance is contained in IAS 39 *Financial Instruments: Recognition and Measurement*. You should also be familiar with IFRS 7 *Financial Instruments: Disclosures*. Visit the IASPlus website for more information (www.iasplus.com).

References

Aretz, K. and S.M. Bartram (2010) 'Corporate Hedging and Shareholder Value', *Journal of Financial Research*, Vol. 33, No. 4, 317–371.

Bartram, S.M., G.W. Brown and F.R. Rehle (2009) 'International Evidence on Financial Derivatives Usage', *Financial Management*, Vol. 38, No. 1, 185–206.

Cox, J.C., J.E. Ingersoll and S.A. Ross (1981) 'The Relationship between Forward and Future Prices', *Journal of Financial Economics*, Vol. 9, 321–346.

Gay, G.D., C-M. Lin and S.D. Smith (2011) 'Corporate Derivatives Use and the Cost of Equity', *Journal of Banking and Finance*, Vol. 35, No. 6, 1491–1506.

Additional Reading

With the exception of Nocco and Stulz (2006) and Gates and Nantes (2006), the papers listed below relate to corporate hedging activity. Nocco and Stulz (2006) and Gates and Nantes (2006) provide interesting reviews of enterprise risk management, which integrates all the disparate risks a company faces into one cohesive policy.

Corporate Hedging

1 Aretz, K., and S.M. Bartram (2010) 'Corporate Hedging and Shareholder Value', *Journal of Financial Research*, Vol. 33, No. 4, 317–371.

2 Bartram, S.M., G.W. Brown and F.R. Fehle (2009) 'International Evidence on Financial Derivatives Usage', *Financial Management*, Vol. 38, No. 1, 185–206.

3 Campello, M., C. Lin, Y. Ma and H. Zou (2011) 'The Real and Financial Implications of Corporate Hedging', *The Journal of Finance*, Vol. 66, No. 5, 1615–1647.

4 Clark, E. and A. Judge (2009) 'Foreign Currency Derivatives versus Foreign Currency Debt and the Hedging Premium', *European Financial Management*, Vol. 15, No. 3, 606–642. **UK.**

5   Faulkender, M. (2005) 'Hedging or Market Timing? Selecting the Interest Rate Exposure of Corporate Debt', *The Journal of Finance*, Vol. 60, No. 2, 931–962. **US.**

6   Graham, J.R. and D.A. Rogers (2002) 'Do Firms Hedge in Response to Tax Incentives?', *The Journal of Finance*, Vol. 57, No. 2, 815–839. **US.**

7   Guay, W. and S.P. Kothari (2003) 'How Much Do Firms Hedge with Derivatives?', *Journal of Financial Economics*, Vol. 70, No. 3, 423–461. **US.**

8   Haushalter, G.D. (2000) 'Financing Policy, Basis Risk, and Corporate Hedging: Evidence from Oil and Gas Producers', *The Journal of Finance*, Vol. 55, No. 1, 107–152. **US.**

9   Jin, Y. and P. Jorion (2006) 'Firm Value and Hedging: Evidence from U.S. Oil and Gas Producers', *The Journal of Finance*, Vol. 61, No. 2, 893–929. **US.**

10 Lel, U. (2012) 'Currency Hedging and Corporate Governance: A Cross-Country Analysis', *Journal of Corporate Finance*, Vol. 18, No. 2, 221–237. **International**.

11 Marshall, A. (2000) 'Foreign Exchange Risk Management in UK, USA, and Asia Pacific Multinational Companies', *Journal of Multinational Financial Management*, Vol. 10, No. 2, 185–211. **International.**

Enterprise Risk Management

12 Gates, S. and A. Nantes (2006), 'Incorporating Strategic Risk into Enterprise Risk Management: A Survey of Current Corporate Practice', *Journal of Applied Corporate Finance*, Vol. 18, No. 4, 81–90. **US.**

13 Nocco, B.W. and R.M. Stulz (2006) 'Enterprise Risk Management: Theory and Practice', *Journal of Applied Corporate Finance*, Vol. 18, No. 4, 8–20.

Endnotes

1   He will deliver on Thursday, 2 days later.

2   The direction is reversed for the seller of a futures contract. However, the general point that the net present value of cash flows may differ between forward and futures contracts holds for sellers as well.

3   See Cox et al. (1981).

4   Alternatively, the firm could buy the oil on 1 April and store it. This would eliminate the risk of price movements because the firm's oil costs would be fixed upon the immediate purchase. However, this strategy would be inferior to strategy 2 in the common case where the difference between the futures contract quoted on 1 April and the 1 April cash price is less than the storage costs.

5   We are assuming that each spot rate shifts by the same amount. For example, suppose that on 1 March $R_1 = 5\%$, $R_2 = 5.4\%$, and $R_3 = 5.8\%$. Assuming that all rates increase by 1/2 per cent on 2 March, R_1 becomes 5.5 per cent (0.5% + 1/2%), R_2 becomes 5.9 per cent, and R_3 becomes 6.3 per cent.

6   Futures contracts on bonds are also called *interest rate futures contracts*.

7   Delivery occurs 2 days after the seller notifies the clearinghouse of her intention to deliver.

8   Alternatively, we can say that mortgages have shorter duration than do Treasury bonds of equal maturity. A precise definition of duration is provided later in this chapter.

9   Alternatively, the mortgage would still be at par if a coupon rate below 12 per cent were used. However, this is not done because the insurance company wants to buy only 12 per cent mortgages.

10 The bonds are at different prices initially. Thus, we are concerned with percentage price changes, not absolute price changes.

11 The mathematical formula for duration is:

$$\text{Duration} = \frac{PV(C_1)1 + PV(C_2)2 + \cdots + PV(C_T)T}{PV}$$

and

$$PV = PV(C_1) + PV(C_2) + \cdots + PV(C_T)$$
$$PV(C_T) = \frac{C_T}{(1 + R)^T}$$

where C_T is the cash to be received in time T and R is the current discount rate.

Also note that in our numerical example, we discounted each payment by the interest rate of 10 per cent. This was done because we wanted to calculate the duration of the bond before a change in the interest rate occurred. After a change in the rate to, say, 8 or 12 per cent, all three of our steps would need to reflect the new interest rate. In other words, the duration of a bond is a function of the current interest rate.

12 Actually, this relationship exactly holds only in the case of a one-time shift in a flat yield curve, where the change in the spot rate is identical for all maturities.

13 Note that the duration of a group of items is an average of the duration of the individual items, weighted by the market value of each item. This is a simplifying step that greatly increases duration's practicality.

14 See Aretz and Bartram (2010); Gay et al. (2011).

PART 7

Financial Planning and Short-term Finance

More and more companies are coming to view short-term financial planning to be just as important to firm welfare as long-term investment appraisal. In past years, the most efficient ways to raise capital for strategic investments was to use retained earnings from previous years or to get new financing via bond or equity issues. However, with many firms now at debt capacity and unwilling to give up an ownership stake, short-term financial planning has become much more significant.

Focusing on short-term finance, improving cash management, proactively implementing appropriate inventory control and strategically following an optimal trade credit policy can have a substantial impact on cash generation.

Part 7 consists of two chapters. In Chapter 26, we look at short-term financial planning and inventory control. Cash management and trade credit are covered in the following chapter. By the end of Part 7, you will have a much better understanding of the issues involved in controlling short-term capital and releasing cash from a firm's operations via cash, working capital, and trade credit management.

Short-term Finance and Planning

Technological and digital advances in recent years have led to a revolution in corporate operational reach. With smartphones, executives in the field can make complex decisions using phone applications as if they were sitting in front of their computer in the office. Digital technologies have also transformed manufacturing by allowing the development of fully automated factories that are more efficient, have better quality control and are more environmentally sustainable than similar operations with armies of manual workers.

To fully exploit the improvement in digital technologies, many companies have adapted their business models to realize the benefits such advances provide. Examples include the development of mobile and embedded devices to improve production efficiency, such as radio-frequency identification (RFID) tags. RFID tags are essentially high-tech replacements for bar codes. The advantage is that they can be read from a distance, so an entire warehouse can be scanned in seconds.

RFID tag sales now exceed $9 billion and have been used in a wide variety of areas to improve operational efficiency, including mobile phone payment systems, asset and inventory management, product tracking, logistics and passports. In particular, using digital technologies allows for a more efficient management of short-term assets such as inventory, and this can have a significant impact on the profitability of a company and the value investors place on it.

Short-term financial planning is one activity that concerns everyone in business. As this chapter illustrates, such planning demands, among other things, sales projections from marketing, cost numbers from accounting, and inventory requirements from operations.

26.1 Tracing Cash and Net Working Capital

In this section we trace the components of cash and net working capital as they change from one year to the next. Our goal is to describe the short-term operating activities of the firm and their impact on cash and working capital.

Current assets are cash and other assets that are expected to be converted to cash within the year. Current assets are presented in the balance sheet in order of their accounting liquidity – the ease with which they can be converted to cash at a fair price and the time it takes to do so. Table 26.1 gives the current assets and current liabilities of the global mining firm, Antofagasta plc, for 2014. The items found in the current assets section of the Antofagasta balance sheet include inventories, trade debtors, bank and other deposits, and short-term investments for sale within one year.

Table 26.1 Current Assets and Liabilities of Antofagasta plc for Year Ending 2014

Current Assets	$millions	Current Liabilities	$millions
		Trade creditors	793.8
Inventories	369.3	Short-term loans and overdrafts	284.5
Trade debtors	810.3	Corporation tax	77.6
Bank and deposits	845.4	Derivatives	7.5
Derivatives	0.2	**Current liabilities**	1,163.4
Deferred taxation	106.9		
Investments	1,529.1		
Current assets	3,661.2		

Analogous to their investment in current assets, firms use several kinds of short-term debt, called current liabilities. Current liabilities are obligations that are expected to require cash payment within one year or within the operating cycle, whichever is shorter.[1] The items found as *current liabilities* are trade creditors, short-term loans or overdrafts, and accrued expenses to be paid off within one year.

26.2 Defining Cash in Terms of Other Elements

Now we will define cash in terms of the other elements of the *statement of financial position* or *balance sheet*. The balance sheet equation is:

$$\text{Net working capital} + \text{Non-current assets} = \text{Non-current liabilities} + \text{Equity} \qquad (26.1)$$

Net working capital is cash plus the other elements of net working capital:

$$\text{Net working capital} = \text{Cash} + \text{Other current assets} - \text{Current liabilities} \qquad (26.2)$$

Substituting Equation 26.2 into 26.1 yields:

$$\text{Cash} + \text{Other current assets} - \text{Current liabilities} = \text{Non-current liabilities} + \text{Equity} - \text{Non-current assets} \qquad (26.3)$$

and rearranging, we find that:

$$\text{Cash} = \text{Non-current liabilities} + \text{Equity} - \text{Net working capital (excluding cash)} - \text{Non-current assets} \qquad (26.4)$$

The natural interpretation of Equation 26.4 is that increasing non-current liabilities and equity and decreasing non-current assets and net working capital (excluding cash) will increase cash to the firm.

The Sources and Uses of Cash

We first introduced the statement of cash flows in Chapter 3. This is the accounting statement that describes the sources and uses of cash. In this section we look at where cash comes from and how it is used. From the right side of Equation 26.4 we can see that an increase in non-current liabilities or equity leads to an increase in cash. Moreover, a decrease in net working capital or non-current assets leads to an increase in cash. In addition, the sum of net income and depreciation increases cash, whereas dividend payments decrease cash. This reasoning allows an accountant to create a statement of cash flows, which shows all the transactions that affect a firm's cash position.

Let us trace the changes in cash for Antofagasta during 2014. From the firm's statement of cash flows (Table 26.2), we find that Antofagasta generated cash as follows:

1 Generated cash flow of $1.820.9 billion from operations.
2 Raised new financing of $1.583.4 billion.

Antofagasta plc used cash for the following reasons:

1 Paid off existing borrowings of $583.1 million.
2 Invested $1.235.4 billion in non-current assets such as land and machinery.
3 Paid dividends of $1,376.6 billion.

This example illustrates the difference between a firm's cash position on the balance sheet and its cash flows from operations.

Table 26.2 Sources and Uses of Cash in Antofagasta plc

	$millions
Net cash inflow from operating activities	1,820.9
Net cash flow from investing activities	−1,235.4
Equity dividends paid	−1,376.6
Proceeds from new borrowings	1,583.4
Repayments of borrowings and other obligations	−583.1
Net cash flow from other financing activities	50.0
Net cash flow	81,114

26.3 The Operating Cycle and the Cash Cycle

Short-term finance is concerned with the firm's short-term operating activities. A typical manufacturing firm's short-term operating activities consist of a sequence of events and decisions:

Events	Decisions
1 Buying raw materials.	1 How much inventory to order?
2 Paying cash for purchases.	2 To borrow or draw down cash balance?
3 Manufacturing the product.	3 What choice of production technology?
4 Selling the product.	4 To offer cash terms or credit terms to customers?
5 Collecting cash.	5 How to collect cash?

These activities create patterns of cash inflows and cash outflows that are both unsynchronized and uncertain. They are unsynchronized because the payment of cash for raw materials does not happen at the same time as the receipt of cash from selling the product. They are uncertain because future sales and costs are not known with certainty.

Figure 26.1 depicts the short-term operating activities and cash flows for a typical manufacturing firm along the cash flow time line. The operating cycle is the interval between the arrival of inventory stock and the date when cash is collected from receivables.

Figure 26.1 Cash Flow Time Line and the Short-term Operating Activities of a Typical Manufacturing Firm

The *operating cycle* is the period from the arrival of stock until the receipt of cash. (Sometimes the operating cycle is defined to include the time from placement of the order until arrival of the stock.) The *cash cycle* begins when cash is paid for materials, and ends when cash is collected from receivables.

The cash cycle begins when cash is paid for materials and ends when cash is collected from receivables. The cash flow time line consists of an operating cycle and a cash cycle. The need for short-term financial decision-making is suggested by the gap between the cash inflows and cash outflows. This is related to the lengths of the operating cycle and the accounts or trades payable period. This gap can be filled either by borrowing or by holding a liquidity reserve for marketable securities. The gap can be shortened by changing the inventory, receivable and payable periods. Now we take a closer look at the operating cycle.

The length of the operating cycle is equal to the sum of the lengths of the inventory and accounts receivable periods. The inventory period is the length of time required to order raw materials, produce and sell a product. The accounts receivable period is the length of time required to collect cash receipts.

The cash cycle is the time between cash disbursement and cash collection. It can be thought of as the operating cycle less the accounts payable period:

$$\text{Cash cycle} = \text{Operating cycle} - \text{Accounts payable period}$$

The accounts payable period is the length of time the firm is able to delay payment on the purchase of various resources, such as labour and raw materials.

In practice, the inventory period, the accounts receivable period and the accounts payable period are measured by days in inventory, days in receivables and days in payables, respectively. We illustrate how the operating cycle and the cash cycle can be measured in the following example.

Example 26.1

Cash Cycle

We will return to Antofagasta plc, a firm we considered earlier in this chapter. We can determine the operating cycle and the cash cycle for Antofagasta after calculating the appropriate ratios for inventory, receivables and payables. Consider inventory first. The inventory levels for the firm in 2014 and 2013 were $369,300,000 and $402,100,000, respectively. The average inventory is

$$\text{Average inventory} = \frac{\$369,300,000 + \$402,100,000}{2} = \$385,700,000$$

We next calculate the inventory turnover ratio. The cost of goods sold for Antofagasta in 2014 was $3,650,700,000.

$$\text{Inventory turnover ratio} = \frac{\text{Cost of goods sold}}{\text{Average inventory}} = \frac{\$3,650,700,000}{\$385,700,000} = 9.47$$

This implies that the inventory cycle occurs 9.47 times a year. Finally, we calculate days in inventory:

$$\text{Days in inventory} = \frac{365 \text{ days}}{9.47} = 38.54 \text{ days}$$

Our calculation implies that the inventory cycle is slightly more than 38 days. We perform analogous calculations for receivables and payables:[2]

$$\frac{\text{Average}}{\text{trade receivables}} = \frac{\$810,300,000 + \$904,600,000}{2} = \$857,450,000$$

$$\frac{\text{Average}}{\text{receivables turnover}} = \frac{\text{Credit sales}}{\text{Average trade receivables}} = \frac{\$5,290,400,000}{\$857,450,000} = 6.17$$

$$\frac{\text{Days in}}{\text{receivables}} = \frac{365}{6.17} = 59.16 \text{ days}$$

$$\frac{\text{Average}}{\text{trade payables}} = \frac{\$793,800,000 + \$776,600,000}{2} = \$785,200,000$$

$$\frac{\text{Trade payables}}{\text{deferral period}} = \frac{\text{Cost of goods sold}}{\text{Average trade payables}} = \frac{\$3,650,700,000}{\$785,200,000} = 4.65$$

$$\frac{\text{Days in}}{\text{payables}} = \frac{365}{4.65} = 78.49 \text{ days}$$

The preceding calculations allow us to determine both the operating cycle and the cash cycle:

$$\frac{\text{Operating}}{\text{cycle}} = \frac{\text{Days in}}{\text{inventory}} + \frac{\text{Days in}}{\text{receivables}}$$

$$= 38.54 \text{ days} + 59.16 \text{ days} = 97.70 \text{ days}$$

$$\text{Cash cycle} = \text{Operating cycle} - \text{Days in payables}$$

$$= 97.70 \text{ days} - 78.49 \text{ days} = 19.21 \text{ days}$$

The cash cycle is longer in some industries than in others because of different products and industry practices. Table 26.3 illustrates this point by comparing the current assets and current liabilities for four different companies. Of the four, Wal-Mart has the highest level of inventories. Does this mean Wal-Mart is less efficient? Probably not; instead, it is likely that the relatively high inventory levels are consistent with the industry. Wal-Mart needs a higher level of inventory to satisfy customers who walk into its stores. In contrast, Dell makes products to order, so its inventory levels are lower. What might seem surprising is Boeing's relatively low level of inventory, especially given that much of its inventory consists of aircraft under construction. However, notice that the current assets for Boeing are only 37 per cent of total assets, implying that fixed assets are large, as you would expect from such a capital-intensive company – plus Boeing has been aggressive in recent years in reducing its inventory. In contrast, Amazon's fixed assets are small relative to its current assets, which again is what we would expect given the nature of its business.

Table 26.3 Current Assets and Current Liabilities as a Percentage of Total Assets for Selected Companies

	Amazon.com (%)	Boeing (%)	Dell (%)	Wal-Mart (%)
Cash and near cash	27.41	11.04	30.47	4.56
Marketable securities	26.70	0.94	8.72	0.00
Accounts receivable	9.82	8.17	17.69	1.43

	Amazon.com (%)	Boeing (%)	Dell (%)	Wal-Mart (%)
Inventories	15.31	12.42	2.49	24.49
Other current assets	0.00	4.49	17.24	1.53
Total current assets	<u>79.25</u>	<u>37.07</u>	<u>76.62</u>	<u>32.02</u>
Accounts payable	52.19	27.23	42.58	29.20
Short-term borrowings	0.00	3.20	26.34	6.47
Other short-term liabilities	0.00	4.32	0.00	0.00
Current liabilities	<u>52.19</u>	<u>34.75</u>	<u>68.92</u>	<u>35.67</u>

26.4 Some Aspects of Short-term Financial Policy

The policy that a firm adopts for short-term finance will be composed of at least two elements:

1 *The size of the firm's investment in current assets*: This is usually measured relative to the firm's level of total operating revenues. A flexible or accommodative short-term financial policy would maintain a high ratio of current assets to sales. A restrictive short-term financial policy would entail a low ratio of current assets to sales.

2 *The financing of current assets*: This is measured as the proportion of short-term debt to long-term debt. A restrictive short-term financial policy means a high proportion of short-term debt relative to long-term financing, and a flexible policy means less short-term debt and more long-term debt.

The Size of the Firm's Investment in Current Assets

Flexible short-term financial policies include:

1 Keeping large balances of cash and marketable securities.
2 Making large investments in inventory.
3 Granting liberal credit terms, which results in a high level of accounts receivable.

Restrictive short-term financial policies are:

1 Keeping low cash balances and no investment in marketable securities.
2 Making small investments in inventory.
3 Allowing no credit sales and no accounts receivable.

Determining the optimal investment level in short-term assets requires an identification of the different costs of alternative short-term financing policies. The objective is to trade off the cost of restrictive policies against those of the flexible ones to arrive at the best compromise.

Current asset holdings are highest with a flexible short-term financial policy and lowest with a restrictive policy. Thus, flexible short-term financial policies are costly in that they require higher cash outflows to finance cash and marketable securities, inventory and accounts receivable. However, future cash inflows are highest with a flexible policy. Sales are stimulated by the use of a credit policy that provides liberal financing to customers. A large amount of inventory on hand ('on the shelf') provides a quick delivery service to customers and increases in sales.[3] In addition, the firm can probably charge higher prices for the quick delivery service and the liberal credit terms of flexible policies. A flexible policy also may result in fewer production stoppages because of inventory shortages.[4]

Managing current assets can be thought of as involving a trade-off between costs that rise with the level of investment and costs that fall with the level of investment. Costs that rise with the level of investment in current assets are called carrying costs. Costs that fall with increases in the level of investment in current assets are called shortage costs.

Carrying costs are generally of two types. First, because the rate of return on current assets is low compared with that of other assets, there is an opportunity cost. Second, there is the cost of maintaining the economic value of the item. For example, the cost of warehousing inventory belongs here.

Determinants of Corporate Liquid Asset Holdings

Firms with High Holdings of Liquid Assets Will Have	Firms with Low Holdings of Liquid Assets Will Have
High-growth opportunities	Low-growth opportunities
High-risk investments	Low-risk investments
Small firms	Large firms
Low-credit firms	High-credit firms

Firms will hold more liquid assets (i.e., cash and marketable securities) to ensure that they can continue investing when cash flow is low relative to positive NPV investment opportunities. Firms that have good access to capital markets will hold less liquid assets.

Source: Opler et al. (1999).

Shortage costs are incurred when the investment in current assets is low. If a firm runs out of cash, it will be forced to sell marketable securities. If a firm runs out of cash and cannot readily sell marketable securities, it may need to borrow or default on an obligation. (This general situation is called *cash-out*.) If a firm has no inventory (a *stockout*) or if it cannot extend credit to its customers, it will lose customers.

There are two kinds of shortage costs:

1   *Trading or order costs*: Order costs are the costs of placing an order for more cash (*brokerage costs*) or more inventory (*production set-up costs*).

2   *Costs related to safety reserves*: These are costs of lost sales, lost customer goodwill and disruption of production schedules.

Figure 26.2 illustrates the basic nature of carrying costs. The total costs of investing in current assets are determined by adding the carrying costs and the shortage costs. The minimum point on the total cost curve (CA*) reflects the optimal balance of current assets. The curve is generally quite flat at the optimum, and it is difficult, if not impossible, to find the precise optimal balance of shortage and carrying costs. Usually, we are content with a choice near the optimum.

If carrying costs are low or shortage costs are high, the optimal policy calls for substantial current assets. In other words, the optimal policy is a flexible one. This is illustrated in the second graph of Figure 26.2.

If carrying costs are high or shortage costs are low, the optimal policy is a restrictive one. That is, the optimal policy calls for modest current assets. This is illustrated in the third graph of the figure.

Opler et al. (1999) examine the determinants of holdings of cash and marketable securities by publicly traded firms. They find evidence that firms behave according to the static tradeoff model described earlier. Their study focuses only on liquid assets (i.e., cash and market securities), so that carrying costs are the opportunity costs of

Figure 26.2 Carrying Costs and Shortage Costs

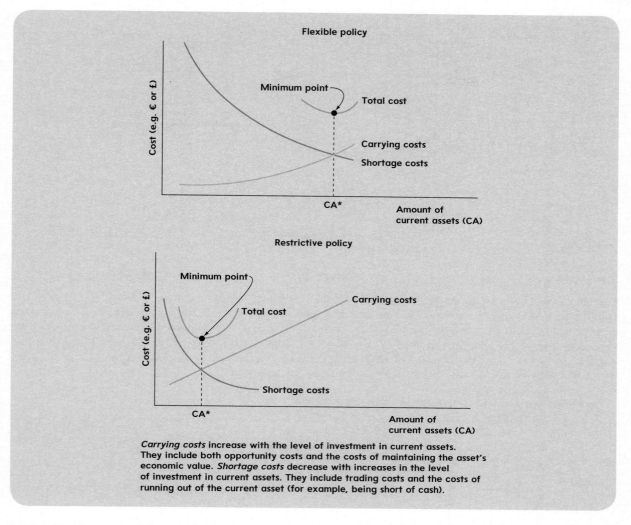

Carrying costs increase with the level of investment in current assets. They include both opportunity costs and the costs of maintaining the asset's economic value. Shortage costs decrease with increases in the level of investment in current assets. They include trading costs and the costs of running out of the current asset (for example, being short of cash).

holding liquid assets and shortage costs are the risks of not having cash when investment opportunities are good. In a study of UK firms, Gogineni et al. (2012) find similar results and report private firms have lower cash holdings when firms are large, there is high net working capital and leverage. Cash is higher when dividends are large, capital expenditure is high and cash flow is more volatile.

Alternative Financing Policies for Current Assets

In the previous section, we examined the level of investment in current assets. Now we turn to the level of current liabilities, assuming the investment in current assets is optimal.

An Ideal Model

In an ideal economy, short-term assets can always be financed with short-term debt, and long-term assets can be financed with long-term debt and equity. In this utopian economy, net working capital is always zero.

Imagine the simple case of a grain elevator operator. Grain elevator operators buy crops after harvest, store them and sell them during the year. They have high inventories of grain after the harvest and end with low inventories just before the next harvest.

Bank loans with maturities of less than one year are used to finance the purchase of grain. These loans are paid with the proceeds from the sale of grain.

The situation is shown in Figure 26.3. Long-term assets are assumed to grow over time, whereas current assets increase at the end of the harvest and then decline during the year. Short-term assets end at zero just before the next harvest. These assets are financed by short-term debt, and long-term assets are financed with long-term debt and equity. Net working capital – current assets minus current liabilities – is always zero.

Figure 26.3 Financing Policy for an Idealized Economy

Different Strategies in Financing Current Assets

Current assets cannot be expected to drop to zero in the real world because a long-term rising level of sales will result in some permanent investment in current assets. A growing firm can be thought of as having a permanent requirement for both current assets and long-term assets. This total asset requirement will exhibit balances over time reflecting (1) a secular growth trend, (2) a seasonal variation around the trend, and (3) unpredictable day-to-day and month-to-month fluctuations. This is depicted in Figure 26.4. (We have not tried to show the unpredictable day-to-day and month-to-month variations in the total asset requirement.)

Figure 26.4 The Total Asset Requirement over Time

Now let us look at how this asset requirement is financed. First, consider the strategy (strategy F in Figure 26.5) where long-term financing covers more than the total asset requirement, even at seasonal peaks. The firm will have excess cash available for investment in marketable securities when the total asset requirement falls from peaks. Because this approach implies chronic short-term cash surpluses and a large investment in net working capital, it is considered a flexible strategy.

When long-term financing does not cover the total asset requirement, the firm must borrow short term to make up the deficit. This restrictive strategy is labelled strategy R in Figure 26.5.

Which Is Best?

What is the most appropriate amount of short-term borrowing? There is no definitive answer. Several considerations must be included in a proper analysis:

1   *Cash reserves*: The flexible financing strategy implies surplus cash and little short-term borrowing. This strategy reduces the probability that a firm will experience financial distress. Firms may not need to worry as

Figure 26.5 Alternative Asset Financing Policies

Strategy F always implies a short-term cash surplus and a large investment in cash and marketable securities. Strategy R uses long-term financing for secular asset requirements only, and short-term borrowing for seasonal variations.

much about meeting recurring short-term obligations. However, investments in cash and marketable securities are zero net present value investments at best.

2   *Maturity hedging*: Most firms finance inventories with short-term bank loans and fixed assets with long-term financing. Firms tend to avoid financing long-lived assets with short-term borrowing. This type of maturity mismatching would necessitate frequent financing and is inherently risky because short-term interest rates are more volatile than longer rates. This type of activity was precisely the reason why many banks found themselves in difficulty during the global credit crunch of 2007 and 2008. Banks financed long-term assets (loans and mortgages granted to borrowers) by short-term borrowing. In some cases, this borrowing had just a 30-day maturity. For example, Northern Rock plc, the British bank that requested emergency central bank funding in September 2007, funded its loans and mortgages by 61 per cent short-term borrowing and 39 per cent deposits just before it made the request to the Bank of England. Because of the collapse in credit, the funding base of Northern Rock collapsed.

3   *Term structure*: Short-term interest rates are normally lower than long-term interest rates. This implies that, on average, it is more costly to rely on long-term borrowing than on short-term borrowing.

Managing Cash Flow

(Excerpts taken from 'Top 10 cashflow tips for SMEs', The Telegraph, 2 June 2014)

Imagine the worst

Managing cashflow means having enough money coming in to cover what you have to pay out. But getting the balance right can be tricky, because suppliers and customers have different priorities. Work out what a late or non-payment would mean for your business, and have a backup plan in place.

Make a plan

'It's amazing how few businesses bother to create profit and cashflow forecasts, and they get themselves into trouble because they don't have an organised approach,' says chartered accountant and business coach Michael Ogilvie. 'Planning gives you the opportunity to ask the right questions of your business to avoid unnecessary costs, and to charge the right price,' he adds.

Be brutally honest

After you've made forecasts you might have to accept that cashflow problems aren't always the fault of late paying customers. 'Sometimes poor cashflow can mask something more fundamentally wrong – an unpopular product, flabby costs or under-performing sales team,' says Stephen Bence, chairman of Beauhurst, a company which tracks the performance of growing businesses: 'If you see a problem, do something about it before it's too late.'

Protect yourself against bad debt

At the very least, learn as much as you can about potential customers – are they creditworthy? – and work out whether you have the cash reserves, overdraft or credit facilities to cover a bad debt. Credit insurance can provide peace of mind.

Do your bit

Most customers will be happy to pay for good products or services. 'Don't give the customer any excuse not to pay,' says Harrop. Make sure orders are on time and complete.

Get paid promptly

Don't let the glow of a significant sale or a lucrative new contract blind you from the need to ensure prompt payment. When you're well established you also have some sway with suppliers. 'Speak to suppliers and renegotiate terms. Pay less and pay slower,' says Ogilvie.

Incentivise early payment

'Try offering customers a small (one to two per cent) discount or free delivery, for early payment,' says Bence. 'Such inducements build loyalty and they can give a real boost to cashflow in times of need.' At the same time, charge interest on late payments.

Choose your preferred method of payment carefully

Credit card payments can be quite time consuming and expensive for small businesses, says Stuart Hibbert, CEO of icomplete.com, an SME that provides CRM, e-marketing and telephony web-based services to other SMEs. 'Encourage faster payments – so the money is in your account within a few hours.'

Practise what you preach

You expect to be paid in a timely manner, so make sure your suppliers receive timely payment from you, within the terms of your contract. It is the right thing to do, but it also makes sound business sense.

Think differently

If cash is tight, why not lease assets rather than buy outright? Or consider alternative methods of finance. 'Traditional finance tools are often difficult to arrange, costly to administer and, importantly, usually tie up or require pledges of company assets,' says Toby Lanyon, chief operating officer of TradeRiver Finance. Alternative finance can be used to finance trade with multiple suppliers without security from either party.

Source: © The Telegraph.

26.5 | Cash Budgeting

The cash budget is a primary tool of short-term financial planning. It allows the financial manager to identify short-term financial needs (and opportunities). It will tell the manager the required borrowing for the short term. It is the way of identifying the cash flow gap on the cash flow time line. The idea of the cash budget is simple: it records estimates of cash receipts and disbursements. We illustrate cash budgeting with the following example of Fun Toys.

Example 26.2

Cash Collections

All of Fun Toys' cash inflows come from the sale of toys. Cash budgeting for Fun Toys starts with a sales forecast for the next year, by quarter:

	First Quarter	Second Quarter	Third Quarter	Fourth Quarter
Sales (€ millions)	100	200	150	100

Fun Toys' fiscal year starts on 1 July. Fun Toys' sales are seasonal and are usually very high in the second quarter due to holiday sales. But Fun Toys sells to department stores on credit, and sales do not generate cash immediately. Instead, cash comes later from collections on accounts receivable. Fun Toys has a 90-day collection period, and 100 per cent of sales are collected in the following quarter. In other words:

$$\text{Collections} = \text{Last quarter's sales}$$

This relationship implies that:

$$\text{Accounts receivable at end of last quarter} = \text{Last quarter's sales} \qquad (26.5)$$

We assume that sales in the fourth quarter of the previous fiscal year were €100 million. From Equation 26.5 we know that accounts receivable at the end of the fourth quarter of the previous fiscal year were €100 million, and collections in the first quarter of the current fiscal year are €100 million.

The first quarter sales of the current fiscal year of €100 million are added to the accounts receivable, but €100 million of collections are subtracted. Therefore, Fun Toys ended the first quarter with accounts receivable of €100 million. The basic relation is:

$$\text{Ending accounts receivable} = \text{Starting accounts receivable} + \text{Sales} - \text{Collections}$$

Table 26.4 shows cash collections for Fun Toys for the next four quarters. Though collections are the only source of cash here, this need not always be the case. Other sources of cash could include sales of assets, investment income and long-term financing.

	First Quarter	Second Quarter	Third Quarter	Fourth Quarter
Sales	100	200	150	100
Cash collections	100	100	200	150
Starting receivables	100	100	200	150
Ending receivables	100	200	150	100

Table 26.4 Sources of Cash (in € millions)

Cash Outflow

Next, we consider cash disbursements. They can be put into four basic categories, as shown in Table 26.5.

1 *Payments of accounts payable*: These are payments for goods or services, such as raw materials. These payments will generally be made after purchases. Purchases will depend on the sales forecast. In the case of Fun Toys, assume that:

$$\text{Payments} = \text{Last quarter's purchases}$$

$$\text{Purchases} = 1/2 \text{ next quarter's sales forecast}$$

2 *Wages, taxes and other expenses*: This category includes all other normal costs of doing business that require actual expenditures. Depreciation, for example, is often thought of as a normal cost of business, but it requires no cash outflow.

3 *Capital expenditures*: These are payments of cash for long-lived assets. Fun Toys plans a major capital expenditure in the fourth quarter.

4 *Long-term financing*: This category includes interest and principal payments on long-term outstanding debt and dividend payments to shareholders.

The total forecast outflow appears in the last line of Table 26.5.

Table 26.5 Disbursement of Cash (in € millions)

	First Quarter	Second Quarter	Third Quarter	Fourth Quarter
Sales	100	200	150	100
Purchases	100	75	50	50
Uses of cash				
Payments of accounts payable	50	100	75	50
Wages, taxes and other expenses	20	40	30	20
Capital expenditures	0	0	0	100
Long-term financing expenses: interest and dividends	10	10	10	10
Total uses of cash	80	150	115	180

The Cash Balance

The net cash balance appears in Table 26.6, and a large net cash outflow is forecast in the second quarter. This large outflow is not caused by an inability to earn a profit. Rather, it results from delayed collections on sales. This results in a cumulative cash shortfall of €30 million in the second quarter.

Table 26.6 The Cash Balance (in € millions)

	First Quarter	Second Quarter	Third Quarter	Fourth Quarter
Total cash receipts	100	100	200	150
Total cash disbursements	80	150	115	180
Net cash flow	20	(50)	85	(30)
Cumulative excess cash balance	20	(30)	55	25
Minimum cash balance	5	5	5	5
Cumulative finance surplus (deficit)				
Requirement	15	(35)	50	20

Fun Toys had established a minimum operating cash balance equal to €5 million to facilitate transactions, protect against unexpected contingencies, and maintain compensating balances at its banks. This means that it has a cash shortfall in the second quarter equal to €35 million.

26.6 The Short-term Financial Plan

Fun Toys has a short-term financing problem. It cannot meet the forecast cash outflows in the second quarter from internal sources. Its financing options include (1) unsecured bank borrowing, (2) secured borrowing, and (3) other sources.

Unsecured Loans

The most common way to finance a temporary cash deficit is to arrange a short-term unsecured bank loan. Firms that use short-term bank loans usually ask their bank for either a non-committed or a committed *line of credit*. A *non-committed* line is an informal arrangement that allows firms to borrow up to a previously specified limit without going through the normal paperwork. The interest rate on the line of credit is usually set equal to the bank's prime lending rate plus an additional percentage.

Committed lines of credit are formal legal arrangements and usually involve a commitment fee paid by the firm to the bank (usually the fee is approximately 0.25 per cent of the total committed funds per year). For larger firms, the interest rate is often tied to the Interbank Offered Rate (LIBOR or EURIBOR) or to the bank's cost of funds, rather than the benchmark rate. Mid-sized and smaller firms often are required to keep compensating balances in the bank.

Compensating balances are deposits the firm keeps with the bank in low-interest or non-interest-bearing accounts. Compensating balances are commonly in the order of 2 to 5 per cent of the amount used. By leaving these funds with the bank without receiving interest, the firm increases the effective interest earned by the bank on the line of credit. For example, if a firm borrowing £100,000 must keep £5,000 as a compensating balance, the firm effectively receives only £95,000. A stated interest rate of 10 per cent implies yearly interest payments of £10,000 (=£100,000 × 0.10). The effective interest rate is 10.53 per cent (=£10,000/£95,000).

Secured Loans

Banks and other finance companies often require *security* for a loan. Security for short-term loans usually consists of accounts receivable or inventories.

Under accounts receivable financing, receivables are either *assigned* or *factored*. Under assignment, the lender not only has a lien on the receivables but also has recourse to the borrower. Factoring involves the sale of accounts receivable. The purchaser, who is called a *factor*, must then collect on the receivables. The factor assumes the full risk of default on bad accounts.

As the name implies, an inventory loan uses inventory as collateral. Some common types of inventory loans are:

1 *Blanket inventory lien*: The blanket inventory lien gives the lender a lien against all the borrower's inventories.

2 *Trust receipt*: Under this arrangement the borrower holds the inventory in trust for the lender. The document acknowledging the loan is called the trust receipt. Proceeds from the sale of inventory are remitted immediately to the lender.

3 *Field warehouse financing*: In field warehouse financing, a public warehouse company supervises the inventory for the lender.

Other Sources

A variety of other sources of short-term funds are employed by corporations. The most important of these are the issuance of commercial paper and financing through banker's acceptances. Commercial paper consists of short-term notes issued by large, highly rated firms. Typically these notes are of short maturity, ranging up to 270 days (beyond that limit the firm will normally be required to file a registration statement with the appropriate stock exchange). Because the firm issues these directly and because it usually backs the issue with a special bank line of credit, the rate the firm obtains is often significantly below the rate the bank would charge it for a direct loan.

A banker's acceptance is an agreement by a bank to pay a sum of money. These agreements typically arise when a seller sends a bill or draft to a customer. The customer's bank *accepts* this bill and notes the acceptance on it, which makes it an obligation of the bank. In this way a firm that is buying something from a supplier can effectively arrange for the bank to pay the outstanding bill. Of course, the bank charges the customer a fee for this service.

Summary and Conclusions

1 This chapter introduced the management of short-term finance. Short-term finance involves short-lived assets and liabilities. We traced and examined the short-term sources and uses of cash as they appear on the firm's financial statements. We saw how current assets and current liabilities arise in the short-term operating activities and the cash cycle of the firm. From an accounting perspective, short-term finance involves net working capital.

2 Managing short-term cash flows involves the minimization of costs. The two major costs are carrying costs (the interest and related costs incurred by over-investing in short-term assets such as cash) and shortage costs (the cost of running out of short-term assets). The objective of managing short-term finance and short-term financial planning is to find the optimal trade-off between these costs.

3 In an ideal economy, a firm could perfectly predict its short-term uses and sources of cash, and net working capital could be kept at zero. In the real world, net working capital provides a buffer that lets the firm meet its ongoing obligations. The financial manager seeks the optimal level of each of the current assets.

4 The financial manager can use the cash budget to identify short-term financial needs. The cash budget tells the manager what borrowing is required or what lending will be possible in the short term. The firm has a number of possible ways of acquiring funds to meet short-term shortfalls, including unsecured and secured loans.

Questions and Problems

CONCEPT

1 **Net Working Capital**   What is short-term financial planning? Why is short-term financial planning crucial to a company? Provide an example of a company that has either undergone an insolvency event or is in financial distress due to poor short-term financial planning.

2 **Cash**   Review the different ways in which cash can increase or decrease in a firm. Use the accounting equation to support your answer. What are some of the characteristics of a firm with a long operating cycle? Similarly, what are some of the characteristics of a firm with a long cash cycle?

3 **Short-term Financing Needs**   Which of the following companies are likely to have high short-term financing needs? Why?

   (a)   The Hilton.

   (b)   British Gas.

   (c)   Manchester United.

   (d)   Thomas Cook.

   (e)   Private Infrastructure Development Group.

4 **Short-term Financial Policy**   Your friend has recently started up a new ice-cream shop business, but he is worried about the seasonality of cash flows his business will face, because the demand for ice cream will most likely be higher in summer than in other seasons, particularly winter. Aware you are studying for a finance degree, he asks you for help on how he should manage this risk. What would your advice to him be?

5 **Financing Strategies**   Give an overview of different working capital financing strategies. What are the advantages and disadvantages of each?

6 **The Short-term Financial Plan**   Explain what is meant by cash budgeting. Review the various ways a firm can finance a short-term cash deficit and the various financing policies to manage current assets.

REGULAR

7 **Sources and Uses**   For the year ending 2015, you have gathered the following information about Rock Spring plc:

   (a)   The company undertook a £200 million share buyback programme.

   (b)   £300 million was invested in property, plant and equipment.

   (c)   Deferred revenue increased by £400 million.

   (d)   Corporation tax payments were £500 million.

   (e)   Staff redundancy payments of £50 million were made.

Label each as a source or use of cash and describe its effect on the firm's cash balance.

8 **Short-term Financial Management** A bank has recently installed a new embedded mobile phone payment system for rural communities. Describe the effect this is likely to have on the company's short-term financial management.

9 **Operating and Cash Cycles** You have just been appointed as financial manager of a food processing and manufacturing firm. The production engineer has said that the cash cycle of your firm should always be longer than its operating cycle. Do you agree with this? Explain why or why not.

10 **Shortage Costs** Assume you work for Evraz plc, the coal and iron ore miner. What would be the costs of shortages in such a firm? Explain using examples.

11 **Reasons for Net Working Capital** Why is net working capital always zero in an ideal economy, but positive in the real economy? Does this introduce any risks to a company?

Use the following information to answer Questions 12–15: In the last year, Power Assets Holdings Limited reduced its bill payments to 60 days from 82 days. The reason given was that the company wanted to 'control costs and optimize cash flow'. The reduced payable period will be in effect for all of the company's 4,000 suppliers.

12 **Operating and Cash Cycles** What impact did this change in payables policy have on Power Assets' operating cycle? Its cash cycle?

13 **Operating and Cash Cycles** What impact do you think the policy change had on Power Assets' suppliers?

14 **Corporate Ethics** Is it ethical for large firms to unilaterally lengthen their payable periods, particularly when dealing with smaller suppliers? Is an 82-day payables period necessarily bad? Explain.

15 **Payables Period** Why do you think Power Assets really reduced their payables period? Is their explanation that it would 'control costs and optimize cash flow' sensible? Will there be any direct or indirect cash benefits to Power Assets from the change in payables period? Explain.

16 **Accounts Receivable** In April 2014, and with just £3.5 million in the bank and a monthly cost base of around £1 million, the Board of Directors of Rangers FC asked supporters to pay for the 2014/15 season tickets up front and in full by May 2014. This was despite the fact that the football season does not start until August. Do you think this was a wise strategy? Explain.

17 **Changes in the Cash Account** Indicate the impact of the following corporate actions on cash, using the letter *I* for an increase, *D* for a decrease, or *N* when no change occurs.

(a) A dividend is paid with funds received from a sale of debt.

(b) Property is purchased and paid for with short-term debt.

(c) Inventory is bought on credit.

(d) A short-term bank loan is repaid.

(e) Next year's taxes are prepaid.

(f) Preference shares are redeemed.

(g) Sales are made on credit.

(h) Interest on long-term debt is paid.

(i) Payments for previous sales are collected.

(j) The trade payables balance is reduced.

(k) A dividend is paid.

(l) Production supplies are purchased and paid with a short-term note.

(m) Utility bills are paid.

(n) Cash is paid for raw materials purchased for inventory.

(o) Marketable securities are sold.

18 **Cash Equation** Eurasian Natural Resources plc, a Kazakhstani firm listed on the London Stock Exchange, has total non-current assets of $4,938 million. Non-current liabilities are $1,038 million. Current assets, other than cash, are $2,098 million. Current liabilities are $1,161 million. Total equity is worth $7,176 million. How much cash does the company have?

19 **Changes in the Operating Cycle** Indicate the effect that the following will have on the operating cycle. Use the letter *I* to indicate an increase, the letter *D* for a decrease, and the letter *N* for no change.

(a) Receivables average goes up.

(b) Credit repayment times for customers are increased.

(c) Inventory turnover goes from 3 times to 6 times.

(d) Payables turnover goes from 6 times to 11 times.

(e) Receivables turnover goes from 7 times to 9 times.

(f) Payments to suppliers are accelerated.

20 **Changes in Cycles**   Indicate the impact of the following on the cash and operating cycles, respectively. Use the letter I to indicate an increase, the letter D for a decrease, and the letter N for no change.

(a) The terms of cash discounts offered to customers are made less favourable.

(b) The cash discounts offered by suppliers are increased; thus, payments are made earlier.

(c) An increased number of customers begin to pay in cash instead of with credit.

(d) Fewer raw materials than usual are purchased.

(e) A greater percentage of raw material purchases are purchased on credit.

(f) More finished goods are produced for inventory instead of for order.

21 **Calculating Cash Collections**   Assume that Next plc has projected the following quarterly sales amounts for the coming year:

	Q1	Q2	Q3	Q4
Sales	£824m	£920m	£620m	£1,600m

(a) Trade receivables at the beginning of the year are £145 million. Next plc has a 10-day collection period. Calculate cash collections in each of the four quarters by completing the following:

	Q1	Q2	Q3	Q4
Beginning receivables				
Sales				
Cash collections				
Ending receivables				

(b) Rework (a) assuming a collection period of 20 days.

(c) Rework (a) assuming a collection period of 30 days.

22 **Calculating Cycles**   Consider the following financial statement information for Bulldog Ice plc. Calculate the operating and cash cycles. How do you interpret your answer?

Item	Beginning (£)		Ending (£)
Inventory	8,413		10,158
Accounts receivable	5,108		5,439
Accounts payable	6,927		7,625
Net sales		67,312	
Cost of goods sold		52,827	

23 **Calculating Payments**   Lewellen Products has projected the following sales for the coming year:

	Q1	Q2	Q3	Q4
Sales (£)	540	630	710	785

Sales in the year following this one are projected to be 15 per cent greater in each quarter.

(a) Calculate payments to suppliers assuming that Lewellen places orders during each quarter equal to 30 per cent of projected sales for the next quarter. Assume that the company pays immediately. What is the payables period in this case?

	Q1	Q2	Q3	Q4
Payment of accounts (£)				

(b) Rework (a) assuming a 90-day payables period.

	Q1	Q2	Q3	Q4
Payment of accounts (£)				

(c) Rework (a) assuming a 60-day payables period.

	Q1	Q2	Q3	Q4
Payment of accounts (£)				

24 Calculating Payments Marshall plc's purchases from suppliers in a quarter are equal to 75 per cent of the next quarter's forecast sales. The payables period is 60 days. Wages, taxes and other expenses are 20 per cent of sales, and interest and dividends are £60 per quarter. No capital expenditures are planned.

Here are the projected quarterly sales:

	Q1	Q2	Q3	Q4
Sales (£)	750	920	890	790

Sales for the first quarter of the following year are projected at £970. Calculate the company's cash outlays by completing the following:

	Q1	Q2	Q3	Q4
Payment of accounts				
Wages, taxes, other expenses				
Long-term financing expenses (interest and dividends)				
Total				

25 Calculating Cash Collections The following is the sales budget for Freezing Snow plc for the first quarter of 2015:

	January	February	March
Sales budget (£)	150,000	173,000	194,000

Credit sales are collected as follows:

65 per cent in the month of the sale.

20 per cent in the month after the sale.

15 per cent in the second month after the sale.

The accounts receivable balance at the end of the previous quarter was £57,000 (£41,000 of which was uncollected December sales).

(a) Compute the sales for November.

(b) Compute the sales for December.

(c) Compute the cash collections from sales for each month from January through March.

CHALLENGE

26 Calculating the Cash Budget Here are some important figures from the budget of Sagmo AB for the first quarter of 2015:

	January (NKr)	February (NKr)	March (NKr)
Credit sales	380,000	396,000	438,000
Credit purchases	147,000	175,500	200,500
Cash disbursements			
Wages, taxes and expenses	39,750	48,210	50,300
Interest	11,400	11,400	11,400
Equipment purchases	83,000	91,000	0

The company predicts that 5 per cent of its credit sales will never be collected, 35 per cent of its sales will be collected in the month of the sale, and the remaining 60 per cent will be collected in the following month. Credit purchases will be paid in the month following the purchase.

In December 2014, credit sales were NKr210,000, and credit purchases were NKr156,000. Using this information, complete the following cash budget:

	January 2015 (NKr)	February	March
Beginning cash balance	280,000		
Cash receipts			
Cash collections from credit sales			
Total cash available			
Cash disbursements			
Purchases			
Wages, taxes and expenses			
Interest			
Equipment purchases			
Total cash disbursements			
Ending cash balance			

27 **Sources and Uses** Here are the most recent balance sheets for the multinational mining firm, Anglo American plc. Excluding accumulated depreciation, determine whether each item is a source or a use of cash, and the amount:

CONSOLIDATED BALANCE SHEET as at 31 December 2015		
US$ million	2015	2014
Intangible assets	2,322	2,316
Property, plant and equipment	40,549	39,810
Environmental rehabilitation trusts	360	379
Investments in associates	5,240	4,900
Financial asset investments	2,896	3,220
Trade and other receivables	437	321
Deferred tax assets	530	389
Other financial assets (derivatives)	668	465
Other non-current assets	138	178
Total non-current assets	**53,140**	**51,978**
Inventories	3,517	3,604
Trade and other receivables	3,674	3,731
Current tax assets	207	235
Other financial assets (derivatives)	172	377
Cash and cash equivalents	11,732	6,401
Total current assets	**19,302**	**14,348**
Assets classified as held for sale	–	330
Total assets	**72,442**	**66,656**
Trade and other payables	(5,098)	(4,950)
Short term borrowings	(1,018)	(1,535)
Provisions for liabilities and charges	(372)	(446)
Current tax liabilities	(1,528)	(871)
Other financial liabilities (derivatives)	(162)	(80)
Total current liabilities	**(8,178)**	**(7,882)**

CONSOLIDATED BALANCE SHEET as at 31 December 2015		
US$ million	2015	2014
Medium and long term borrowings	(11,855)	(11,904)
Retirement benefit obligations	(639)	(591)
Deferred tax liabilities	(5,730)	(5,641)
Other financial liabilities (derivatives)	(950)	(755)
Provisions for liabilities and charges	(1,830)	(1,666)
Other non-current liabilities	(71)	(104)
Total non-current liabilities	**(21,075)**	**(20,661)**
Liabilities directly associated with assets classified as held for sale	–	(142)
Total liabilities	**(29,253)**	**(28,685)**
Net assets	**43,189**	**37,971**
Equity		
Called-up share capital	738	738
Share premium account	2,714	2,713
Other reserves	283	3,642
Retained earnings	35,357	27,146
Equity attributable to equity shareholders of the Company	**39,092**	**34,239**
Non-controlling interests	4,097	3,732
Total equity	**43,189**	**37,971**

28 Cash Budgeting The sales budget for your company in the coming year is based on a 20 per cent quarterly growth rate with the first-quarter sales projection at £100 million. In addition to this basic trend, the seasonal adjustments for the four quarters are 0, −£10, −£5 and £15 million, respectively. Generally, 50 per cent of the sales can be collected within the quarter and 45 per cent in the following quarter; the rest of sales are bad debt. The bad debts are written off in the second quarter after the sales are made. The beginning accounts payable balance is £81 million. Assuming all sales are on credit, compute the cash collections from sales for each quarter.

29 Calculating the Cash Budget Wildcat SA has estimated sales (in millions) for the next four quarters as follows:

	Q1	Q2	Q3	Q4
Sales (€m)	230	195	270	290

Sales for the first quarter of the year after this one are projected at €250 million. Accounts receivable at the beginning of the year were €79 million. Wildcat has a 45-day collection period.

Wildcat's purchases from suppliers in a quarter are equal to 45 per cent of the next quarter's forecast sales, and suppliers are normally paid in 36 days. Wages, taxes and other expenses run at about 30 per cent of sales. Interest and dividends are €15 million per quarter.

Wildcat plans a major capital outlay in the second quarter of €90 million. Finally, the company started the year with a €73 million cash balance and wishes to maintain a €30 million minimum balance.

(a) Complete a cash budget for Wildcat by filling in the following:

WILDCAT SA Cash Budget (in € millions)				
	Q1	Q2	Q3	Q4
Beginning cash balance	73			
Net cash inflow				
Ending cash balance				
Minimum cash balance	30			
Cumulative surplus (deficit)				

(b) Assume that Wildcat can borrow any needed funds on a short-term basis at a rate of 3 per cent per quarter, and can invest any excess funds in short-term marketable securities at a rate of 2 per cent per quarter. Prepare a short-term financial plan by filling in the following schedule. What is the net cash cost (total interest paid minus total investment income earned) for the year?

WILDCAT SA Short-Term Financial Plan (in € millions)				
	Q1	Q2	Q3	Q4
Beginning cash balance	73			
Net cash inflow				
New short-term investments				
Income from short-term investments				
Short-term investments sold				
New short-term borrowing				
Interest on short-term borrowing				
Short-term borrowing repaid				
Ending cash balance				
Minimum cash balance	30			
Cumulative surplus (deficit)				
Beginning short-term investments				
Ending short-term investments				
Beginning short-term debt				
Ending short-term debt				

30 **Cash Management Policy**   Rework Problem 29 assuming the following:

(a) Wildcat maintains a minimum cash balance of €45 million.

(b) Wildcat maintains a minimum cash balance of €15 million.

Based on your answers in (a) and (b), do you think the firm can boost its profit by changing its cash management policy? Should other factors be considered as well? Explain.

31 **Short-term Finance Policy**   Renault SA and Peugeot SA are competing automobile manufacturing firms. Download their annual financial accounts for the most recent period from each company's website.

(a) How are the current assets of each firm financed?

(b) Which firm has the larger investment in current assets? Why?

(c) Which firm is more likely to incur carrying costs, and which is more likely to incur shortage costs? Why?

Exam Question (45 minutes)

1   Consider the following financial statement information for Orologio SpA: Calculate the operating and cash cycles. How do you interpret your answer? (40 marks)

Item	Beginning (€)		Ending (€)
Inventory	44,234		34,048
Accounts receivable	43,211		35,532
Accounts payable	35,603		53,503
Net sales		360,302	
Cost of goods sold		120,400	

2   You have been hired by a manufacturing firm that is currently experiencing significant levels of financial distress. The managers have asked you to find ways in which the company can increase its cash levels so as to improve liquidity. Write a report to the managers, using figures to illustrate your answer, on how they can achieve this most efficiently. (60 marks)

Mini Case

Wolgemut Manufacturing Working Capital Management

You have recently been hired by Wolgemut Manufacturing to work in its established treasury department. Wolgemut Manufacturing is a small company that produces highly customized cardboard boxes in a variety of sizes for different purchasers. Adam Wolgemut, the owner of the company, works primarily in the sales and production areas of the company. Currently, the company basically puts all receivables in one pile and all payables in another, and a part-time accountant periodically comes in and attacks the piles. Because of this disorganized system, the finance area needs work, and that is what you have been brought in to do.

The company currently has a cash balance of €115,000, and it plans to purchase new machinery in the third quarter at a cost of €200,000. The purchase of the machinery will be made with cash because of the discount offered for a cash purchase. Adam wants to maintain a minimum cash balance of €90,000 to guard against unforeseen contingencies. All of Wolgemut's sales to customers and purchases from suppliers are made with credit, and no discounts are offered or taken.

The company had the following sales each quarter of the year just ended:

	Q1	Q2	Q3	Q4
Gross sales (€)	565,000	585,000	628,000	545,000

After some research and discussions with customers, you are projecting that sales will be 8 per cent higher in each quarter next year. Sales for the first quarter of the following year are also expected to grow at 8 per cent. You calculate that Wolgemut currently has an accounts receivable period of 57 days and an accounts receivable balance of €426,000. However, 10 per cent of the accounts receivable balance is from a company that has just entered bankruptcy, and it is likely that this portion will never be collected.

You have also calculated that Wolgemut typically orders supplies each quarter to the amount of 50 per cent of the next quarter's projected gross sales, and suppliers are paid in 53 days on average. Wages, taxes and other costs run at about 25 per cent of gross sales. The company has a quarterly interest payment of €120,000 on its long-term debt. Finally, the company uses a local bank for its short-term financial needs. It currently pays 1.2 per cent per quarter on all short-term borrowing and maintains a money market account that pays 0.5 per cent per quarter on all short-term deposits.

Adam has asked you to prepare a cash budget and short-term financial plan for the company under the current policies. He has also asked you to prepare additional plans based on changes in several inputs.

1   Use the numbers given to complete the cash budget and short-term financial plan.

2   Rework the cash budget and short-term financial plan assuming Wolgemut changes to a minimum cash balance of €70,000.

3   Rework the sales budget assuming an 11 per cent growth rate in sales and a 5 per cent growth rate in sales. Assume a €90,000 target cash balance.

4   Assuming the company maintains its target cash balance at €90,000, what sales growth rate would result in a zero need for short-term financing? To answer this question, you may need to set up a spreadsheet and use the 'Solver' function.

Practical Case Study

1   **Cash and Operating Cycles** Find the most recent financial statements for ArcelorMittal and Nokia. Calculate the cash and operating cycle for each company for the most recent year. Are the numbers similar for these companies? Why or why not?

2   **Cash and Operating Cycles** Download the most recent quarterly financial statements for Rio Tinto plc. Calculate the operating and cash cycle for Rio Tinto over each of the last four quarters. Comment on any changes in the operating or cash cycle over this period.

Relevant Accounting Standards

The relevant accounting standards are those that apply to the presentation of financial statements and cash flow. These are IAS 1 *Presentation of Financial Statements* and IAS 7 *Statement of Cash Flows*.

References

Gogineni, S., S. Linn and P. Yadav (2012) 'Evidence on the Determinants of Cash Holdings By Private and Public Companies', Working Paper.

Opler, T., L. Pinkowitz, R. Stulz and R. Williamson (1999) 'The Determinants and Implication of Corporate Cash Holdings', *Journal of Financial Economics*, Vol. 52, No. 1, 3–46.

Additional Reading

The literature on cash holdings has exploded in recent years and the papers below give a flavour of the work in this area.

1 Bigelli, M. and J. Sánchez-Vidal (2012) 'Cash Holdings in Private Firms', *Journal of Banking and Finance*, Vol. 36, No. 1, 26–35.

2 Brown, J.R. and B.C. Petersen (2011) 'Cash Holdings and R&D Smoothing', *Journal of Corporate Finance*, Vol. 17, No. 3, 694–709.

3 Denis, D.J. and V. Sinilkov (2010) 'Financial Constraints, Investment, and the Value of Cash Holdings', *Review of Financial Studies*, Vol. 23, No. 1, 247–269.

4 Duchin, R. (2010) 'Cash Holdings and Corporate Diversification', *The Journal of Finance*, Vol. 65, No. 3, 955–992.

5 Fresard, L. (2010) 'Financial Strength and Product Market Behavior: The Real Effects of Corporate Cash Holdings', *The Journal of Finance*, Vol. 65, No. 3, 1097–1122.

6 Klasa, S., W.F. Maxwell and H. Ortiz-Molina (2009) 'The Strategic Use of Corporate Cash Holdings in Collective Bargaining with Labor Unions', *Journal of Financial Economics*, Vol. 92, No. 3, 421–442.

7 Lins, K.V., H. Servaes and P. Tufano (2010) 'What Drives Corporate Liquidity? An International Survey of Cash Holdings and Lines of Credit', *Journal of Financial Economics*, Vol. 98, No. 1, 160–176.

8 Palazzo, B. (2012) 'Cash Holdings, Risk and Expected Returns', *Journal of Financial Economics*, Vol. 104, No. 1, 162–185.

9 Paul, S. and C. Guermat (2010) 'Trade Credit as Short-Term Finance, in the UK' *Accounting and Finance*, Working Paper.

10 Schauten, M.B.J., D. van Dijk and P. van der Waal (2013) 'Corporate Governance and the Value of Excess Cash Holdings of Large European Firms', *European Financial Management*, Vol. 19, No. 5, 991–1016.

11 Yun, H. (2009) 'The Choice of Corporate Liquidity and Corporate Governance', *Review of Financial Studies*, Vol. 22, No. 4, 1447–1475.

Endnotes

1 As we will learn in this chapter, the operating cycle begins when inventory is received and ends when cash is collected from the sale of inventory.

2 We assume that Antofagasta makes no cash sales.

3 This is true of some types of finished goods.

4 This is true of inventory of raw material but not of finished goods.

CHAPTER 27

Short-term Capital Management

Even if a firm is growing and has excellent performance, if it runs out of cash or does not manage its short-term capital properly it cannot survive. In any sale, one of the most important decisions made by the seller is whether to grant credit and, if credit is granted, the terms of the credit sale. As with many other decisions, there is variation from company to company, but credit policies tend to be similar within industries.

One way to examine a company's credit policy is to look at the days' sales in receivables, or the length of time from the sale until the company is paid. In 2015, the receivables period for a typical firm in Europe was about 35 days, or a little over a month. For some firms, the period is much shorter. For example, British retailer Sainsbury's was about 5 days and Tesco's was about 9 days. Although both firms have operations in several industries, neither routinely grants credit to its customers and so these numbers come as no surprise. In contrast, in the mining sector, credit periods are longer. Antofagasta, for example, had a credit period of about 59 days in 2014 (see **Chapter 26**).

Chapter 26
Page 698

In this chapter, we examine cash management and the various issues a firm must consider. We also examine how a firm sets its credit policy, including when to grant credit and for how long. Taken together, cash and credit policy represent the firm's short-term capital management.

KEY NOTATIONS

C	Cash balance
C^*	Optimal cash balance
R	Opportunity cost of holding cash
F	Fixed cost of selling securities to replenish cash
T	Total amount of new cash needed for transaction purposes over the relevant planning period
TC	Total cost of cash-balance policy
$U; L$	upper (U) and lower (L) control limits
Z	Target cash balance
Z^*	Optimal target cash balance
P_0	Price per unit received at time 0
C_0	Cost per unit paid at time 0
Q_0	Quantity sold at time 0
NCF	Net cash flow
h	Probability that customers will pay outstanding credit

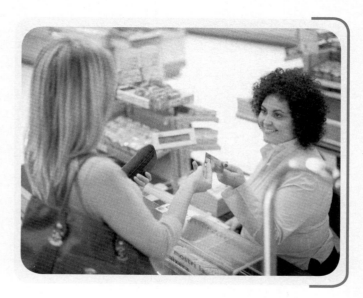

27.1   Reasons for Holding Cash

The term *cash* is a surprisingly imprecise concept. The economic definition of cash includes currency, savings account deposits at banks and undeposited cheques. However, financial managers often use the term *cash* to include short-term marketable securities. Short-term marketable securities are frequently referred to as *cash equivalents* and include Treasury bills, certificates of deposit and repurchase agreements. (Several different types of short-term marketable securities are described at the end of this chapter.) The balance sheet item 'cash' usually includes cash equivalents.

The previous chapter discussed the management of net working capital. Net working capital includes both cash and cash equivalents. This chapter is concerned with cash, not net working capital, and it focuses on the narrow economic definition of cash.

The basic elements of net working capital management such as carrying costs, shortage costs and opportunity costs are relevant for cash management. However, cash management is more concerned with how to minimize cash balances by collecting and disbursing cash effectively.

There are two primary reasons for holding cash. First, cash is needed to satisfy the transactions motive. Transaction-related needs come from normal disbursement and collection activities of the firm. The disbursement of cash includes the payment of wages and salaries, trade debts, taxes and dividends. Cash is collected from sales from operations, sales of assets and new financing. The cash inflows (*collections*) and outflows (*disbursements*) are not perfectly synchronized, and some level of cash holdings is necessary as a buffer. If the firm maintains too small a cash balance, it may run out of cash. If so, it must sell marketable securities or borrow. Selling marketable securities and borrowing involve *trading costs*.

Another reason to hold cash is for compensating balances. Cash balances are kept at banks to compensate for banking services rendered to the firm. The cash balance for most firms can be thought of as consisting of transaction balances and compensating balances. However, it would not be correct for a firm to add the amount of cash required to satisfy its transaction needs to the amount of cash needed to satisfy its compensatory balances to produce a target cash balance. The same cash can be used to satisfy both requirements.

The cost of holding cash is, of course, the opportunity cost of lost interest. To determine the target cash balance, the firm must weigh the benefits of holding cash against the costs. It is generally a good idea for firms to figure out first how much cash to hold to satisfy transaction needs. Next, the firm must consider compensating balance requirements, which will impose a lower limit on the level of the firm's cash holdings. Because compensating balances merely provide a lower limit, we ignore compensating balances for the following discussion of the target cash balance.

In general, firms have been holding more cash in recent years. Table 27.1 presents average statistics on general cash holdings of firms across the world. There is clearly significant variation across countries, with firms in some countries having very low average cash balances and others holding cash in excess of 10 per cent of its total assets.

Table 27.1 Average Corporate Cash Holdings by Country

Country	Number of firms	Market-to-book ratio		Cash holdings	
		Mean	Median	Mean	Median
Austria	96	0.855	0.761	0.105	0.074
Belgium	126	0.938	0.779	0.115	0.074
Canada	821	1.150	0.946	0.092	0.039
China	639	1.218	1.040	0.177	0.149
Czech Rep.	16	0.570	0.481	0.072	0.047
Denmark	130	1.035	0.839	0.119	0.081
Egypt	29	1.355	1.146	0.130	0.112
Finland	155	0.989	0.839	0.102	0.067
France	832	0.951	0.759	0.119	0.088
Germany	708	0.948	0.777	0.104	0.061
Greece	235	0.971	0.837	0.072	0.042
Hong Kong	690	0.897	0.682	0.178	0.148
Hungary	25	0.850	0.738	0.097	0.055

Country	Number of firms	Market-to-book ratio		Cash holdings	
		Mean	Median	Mean	Median
India	635	1.245	0.856	0.066	0.031
Indonesia	239	0.924	0.755	0.116	0.083
Ireland	61	1.207	0.993	0.145	0.096
Israel	126	1.044	0.885	0.171	0.135
Italy	275	0.880	0.713	0.117	0.083
Jordan	17	1.438	1.173	0.126	0.091
South Korea	922	0.766	0.635	0.125	0.088
Malaysia	807	0.912	0.739	0.107	0.072
Netherlands	215	1.060	0.868	0.092	0.051
New Zealand	100	1.176	0.979	0.050	0.020
Norway	182	1.047	0.875	0.131	0.102
Pakistan	96	0.899	0.758	0.108	0.061
Philippines	105	0.821	0.679	0.094	0.059
Poland	152	1.161	0.905	0.091	0.062
Portugal	73	0.791	0.714	0.055	0.033
Russia	61	1.206	0.996	0.076	0.062
Singapore	525	0.930	0.773	0.155	0.121
South Africa	297	1.048	0.899	0.115	0.090
Spain	149	0.987	0.837	0.078	0.048
Sri Lanka	21	0.728	0.648	0.105	0.068
Sweden	323	1.131	0.897	0.116	0.081
Switzerland	217	1.087	0.869	0.135	0.107
Thailand	403	0.907	0.780	0.082	0.047
Turkey	161	1.021	0.836	0.093	0.060
U.K.	1727	1.154	0.942	0.109	0.073
U.S.A.	3372	1.416	1.132	0.121	0.063
Venezuela	12	0.537	0.489	0.063	0.056

The table shows the number of firms per country, the mean and median market-to-book ratio (V_0, the sum of the year end market capitalization and the book value of debt, divided by total assets) and the mean and median cash holdings (L_0, cash and short-term investments divided by total assets).

Source: Adapted from Table 1, Panel B of Kyröläinen et al. (2013).

27.2   Determining the Target Cash Balance

The target cash balance involves a trade-off between the opportunity costs of holding too much cash and the trading costs of holding too little. Figure 27.1 presents the problem graphically. If a firm tries to keep its cash holdings too low, it will find itself selling marketable securities (and perhaps later buying marketable securities to replace those sold) more frequently than if the cash balance was higher. Thus, trading costs will tend to fall as the cash balance becomes larger. In contrast, the opportunity costs of holding cash rise as the cash holdings rise. At point C^* in Figure 27.1, the sum of both costs, depicted as the total cost curve, is at a minimum. This is the target or optimal cash balance.

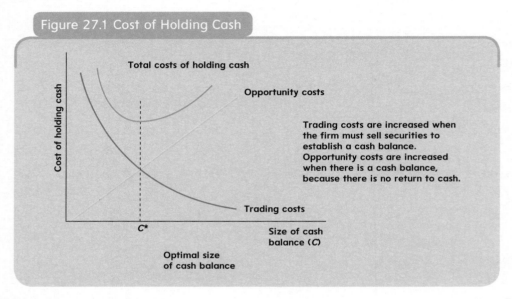

Figure 27.1 Cost of Holding Cash

The Baumol Model

William Baumol (1952) was the first to provide a formal model of cash management incorporating opportunity costs and trading costs. His model can be used to establish the target cash balance.

Suppose Golden Socks plc began week 0 with a cash balance of $C = £1.2$ million, and outflows exceed inflows by £600,000 per week. Its cash balance will drop to zero at the end of week 2, and its average cash balance will be $C/2 = £1.2$ million$/2 = £600,000$ over the two-week period. At the end of week 2, Golden Socks must replace its cash either by selling marketable securities or by borrowing. Figure 27.2 shows this situation.

Figure 27.2 Cash Balances for Golden Socks Plc

If C were set higher, say at £2.4 million, cash would last 4 weeks before the firm would need to sell marketable securities, but the firm's average cash balance would increase to £1.2 million (from £600,000). If C were set at £600,000, cash would run out in one week and the firm would need to replenish cash more frequently, but its average cash balance would fall from £600,000 to £300,000.

Because transaction costs must be incurred whenever cash is replenished (for example, the brokerage costs of selling marketable securities), establishing large initial cash balances will lower the trading costs connected with cash management. However, the larger the average cash balance, the greater the opportunity cost (the return that could have been earned on marketable securities).

To solve this problem, Golden Socks needs to know the following three things:

1 The fixed cost of selling securities to replenish cash (F).

2 The total amount of new cash needed for transaction purposes over the relevant planning period – say, one year (T).

3 The opportunity cost of holding cash; this is the interest rate on marketable securities (R).

With this information, Golden Socks can determine the total costs of any particular cash-balance policy. It can then determine the optimal cash-balance policy.

The Opportunity Costs

The total opportunity costs of cash balances, in monetary terms, must be equal to the average cash balance multiplied by the interest rate:

$$\text{Opportunity costs (£)} = (C/2) \times R$$

The opportunity costs of various alternatives are given here:

Initial Cash Balance C(£)	Average Cash Balance C/2(£)	Opportunity Costs (R = 0.10) (C/2) × R(£)
4,800,000	2,400,000	240,000
2,400,000	1,200,000	120,000
1,200,000	600,000	60,000
600,000	300,000	30,000
300,000	150,000	15,000

The Trading Costs

We can determine total trading costs by calculating the number of times that Golden Socks must sell marketable securities during the year. The total amount of cash disbursement during the year is £600,000 × 52 weeks = £31.2 million. If the initial cash balance is set at £1.2 million, Golden Socks will sell £1.2 million of marketable securities every 2 weeks. Thus, trading costs are given by:

$$\frac{£31.2 \text{ million}}{£1.2 \text{ million}} \times F = 26F$$

The general formula is:

$$\text{Trading costs (£)} = (T/C) \times F$$

A schedule of alternative trading costs follows:

Total Disbursements during Relevant Period T(£)	Initial Cash Balance C(£)	Trading Costs (F = £1,000) (T/C) × F(£)
31,200,000	4,800,000	6,500
31,200,000	2,400,000	13,000
31,200,000	1,200,000	26,000
31,200,000	600,000	52,000
31,200,000	300,000	104,000

The Total Cost

The total cost of cash balances consists of the opportunity costs plus the trading costs:

$$\text{Total cost} = \text{Opportunity costs} + \text{Trading costs}$$

$$= (C/2) \times R + (T/C) \times F$$

Cash balance (£)	Total cost (£)	=	Opportunity costs (£)	+	Trading costs (£)
4,800,000	246,500		240,000		6,500
2,400,000	133,000		120,000		13,000
1,200,000	86,000		60,000		26,000
600,000	82,000		30,000		52,000
300,000	119,000		15,000		104,000

The Solution

We can see from the preceding schedule that a £600,000 cash balance results in the lowest total cost of the possibilities presented: £82,000. But what about £700,000 or £500,000 or other possibilities? To determine minimum total costs precisely, Golden Socks must equate the marginal reduction in trading costs as balances rise with the marginal increase in opportunity costs associated with cash balance increases. The target cash balance should be the point where the two offset each other. This can be calculated with either numerical iteration or calculus. We will use calculus; but if you are unfamiliar with such an analysis, you can skip to the solution.

Recall that the total cost equation is:

$$\text{Total cost } (TC) = (C/2) \times R + (T/C) \times F$$

If we differentiate the TC equation with respect to the cash balance and set the derivative equal to zero, we will find:

$$\frac{\mathrm{d}TC}{\mathrm{d}C} = \frac{R}{2} - \frac{TF}{C^2} = 0$$

We obtain the solution for the general cash balance, C^*, by solving this equation for C:

$$\frac{R}{2} = \frac{TF}{C^2}$$

$$C^* = \sqrt{2TF/R}$$

If $F = £1,000$, $T = £31,200,000$, and $R = 0.10$, then $C^* = £789,936.71$. Given the value of C^*, opportunity costs are:

$$(C^*/2) \times R = \frac{£789,936.71}{2} \times 0.10 = £39,496.84$$

Trading costs are:

$$(TC^*) \times F = \frac{£31,200,000}{£789,936.71} \times 1,000 = £39,496.84$$

Hence, total costs are:

$$£39,496.84 + £39,496.84 = £78,993.68$$

Limitations

The Baumol model represents an important contribution to cash management. The limitations of the model include the following:

1 *The model assumes the firm has a constant disbursement rate.* In practice, disbursements can be only partially managed because due dates differ and costs cannot be predicted with certainty.

2 *The model assumes there are no cash receipts during the projected period.* In fact, most firms experience both cash inflows and outflows daily.

3 *No safety stock is allowed.* Firms will probably want to hold a safety stock of cash designed to reduce the possibility of a cash shortage or *cash-out*. However, to the extent that firms can sell marketable securities or borrow in a few hours, the need for a safety stock is minimal.

The Baumol model is possibly the simplest and most stripped-down sensible model for determining the optimal cash position. Its chief weakness is that it assumes discrete, certain cash flows. We next discuss a model designed to deal with uncertainty.

The Miller–Orr Model

Merton Miller and Daniel Orr (1966) developed a cash balance model to deal with cash inflows and outflows that fluctuate randomly from day to day. In the Miller–Orr model, both cash inflows and cash outflows are included. The model assumes that the distribution of daily net cash flows (cash inflow minus cash outflow) is normally distributed. On each day the net cash flow could be the expected value or some higher or lower value. We will assume that the expected net cash flow is zero.

Figure 27.3 shows how the Miller–Orr model works. The model operates in terms of upper (U) and lower (L) control limits and a target cash balance (Z). The firm allows its cash balance to wander randomly within the lower and upper limits. As long as the cash balance is between U and L, the firm makes no transaction. When the cash balance reaches U, such as at point X, the firm buys $U - Z$ units (e.g. euros or pounds) of marketable securities.

Figure 27.3 The Miller–Orr Model

U is the upper control limit.
L is the lower control limit.
The target cash balance is Z.
As long as cash is between L and U, no transaction is made.

This action will decrease the cash balance to Z. In the same way, when cash balances fall to L, such as at point Y (the lower limit), the firm should sell $Z - L$ securities and increase the cash balance to Z. In both situations, cash balances return to Z. Management sets the lower limit, L, depending on how much risk of a cash shortfall the firm is willing to tolerate.

Like the Baumol model, the Miller–Orr model depends on trading costs and opportunity costs. The cost per transaction of buying and selling marketable securities, F, is assumed to be fixed. The percentage opportunity cost per period of holding cash, R, is the daily interest rate on marketable securities. Unlike in the Baumol model, the number of transactions per period is a random variable that varies from period to period, depending on the pattern of cash inflows and outflows.

As a consequence, trading costs per period depend on the expected number of transactions in marketable securities during the period. Similarly, the opportunity costs of holding cash are a function of the expected cash balance per period.

Given L, which is set by the firm, the Miller–Orr model solves for the target cash balance, Z, and the upper limit, U. Expected total costs of the cash balance return policy (Z, U) are equal to the sum of expected transaction costs and expected opportunity costs. The values of Z (the return cash point) and U (the upper limit) that minimize the expected total cost have been determined by Miller and Orr:

$$Z^* = \sqrt[3]{3F\sigma^2/(4R)} + L$$

$$U^* = 3Z^* - 2L$$

Here * denotes optimal values, and σ^2 is the variance of net daily cash flows.

The average cash balance in the Miller–Orr model is:

$$\text{Average cash balance} = \frac{4Z - L}{3}$$

Example 27.1

Miller–Orr

To clarify the Miller–Orr model, suppose $F = £1{,}000$, the interest rate is 10 per cent annually, and the standard deviation of daily net cash flows is £2,000. The daily opportunity cost, R, is:

$$(1 + R)^{365} - 1 = 0.10$$

$$1 + R = \sqrt[365]{1.10} = 1.000261$$

$$R = 0.000261$$

The variance of daily net cash flows is:

$$\sigma^2 = (2,000)^2 = 4,000,000$$

Let us assume that $L = 0$:

$$Z^* = \sqrt[3]{(3 \times £1,000 \times 4,000,000)/(4 \times 0.000261) + 0}$$

$$= \sqrt[3]{(£11,493,900,000,000)} = £22,568$$

$$U^* = 3 \times £22,568 = £67,704$$

$$\text{Average cash balance} = \frac{4 \times £22,568}{3} = £30,091$$

Implications of the Miller–Orr Model

To use the Miller–Orr model, the manager must do four things:

1   Set the lower control limit for the cash balance. This lower limit can be related to a minimum safety margin decided on by management.
2   Estimate the standard deviation of daily cash flows.
3   Determine the interest rate.
4   Estimate the trading costs of buying and selling marketable securities.

These four steps allow the upper limit and return point to be computed. Miller and Orr tested their model using 9 months of data for cash balances for a large industrial firm. The model was able to produce average daily cash balances much lower than the averages actually obtained by the firm.

The Miller–Orr model clarifies the issues of cash management. First, the model shows that the best return point, Z^*, is positively related to trading costs, F, and negatively related to R. This finding is consistent with and analogous to the Baumol model. Second, the Miller–Orr model shows that the best return point and the average cash balance are positively related to the variability of cash flows. That is, firms whose cash flows are subject to greater uncertainty should maintain a larger average cash balance.

Other Factors Influencing the Target Cash Balance

Borrowing

In our previous examples, the firm obtained cash by selling marketable securities. Another alternative is to borrow cash. Borrowing introduces additional considerations to cash management:

1   Borrowing is likely to be more expensive than selling marketable securities because the interest rate is likely to be higher.
2   The need to borrow will depend on management's desire to hold low cash balances. A firm is more likely to need to borrow to cover an unexpected cash outflow with greater cash flow variability and lower investment in marketable securities.

Compensating Balance

The costs of trading securities are well below the lost income from holding cash for large firms. Consider a firm faced with either selling £2 million of Treasury bills to replenish cash or leaving the money idle overnight. The daily opportunity cost of £2 million at a 10 per cent annual interest rate is $0.10/365 = 0.027$ per cent per day. The daily return earned on £2 million is $0.00027 \times £2$ million $= £540$. The cost of selling £2 million of Treasury bills is much less than £540. As a consequence, a large firm will buy and sell securities many times a day before it will leave substantial amounts idle overnight.

However, most large firms hold more cash than cash balance models imply, suggesting that managers disagree with this logic. Here are some possible reasons:

1   Firms have cash in the bank as a compensating balance in payment for banking services.
2   Large corporations have thousands of accounts with several dozen banks. Sometimes it makes more sense to leave cash alone than to manage each account daily.

27.3   Managing the Collection and Disbursement of Cash

A firm's cash balance as reported in its financial statements (*book cash* or *ledger cash*) is not the same thing as the balance shown in its bank account (*bank cash* or *collected bank cash*). The difference between bank cash and book cash is called float and represents the net effect of cheques in the process of collection.

Example 27.2

Float

Imagine that Great Mechanics International plc (GMI) currently has £100,000 on deposit with its bank. It purchases some raw materials, paying its vendors with a cheque written on 8 July for £100,000. The company's books (that is, ledger balances) are changed to show the £100,000 reduction in the cash balance. But the firm's bank will not find out about this cheque until it has been deposited at the vendor's bank and has been presented to the firm's bank for payment on, say, 15 July. Until the cheque's presentation, the firm's bank cash is greater than its book cash, and it has *positive float*.

Position prior to 8 July

$$\text{Float} = \text{Firm's bank cash} - \text{Firm's book cash}$$
$$= £100,000 - £100,000$$
$$= 0$$

Position from 8 July through 14 July

$$\text{Disbursement float} = \text{Firm's bank cash} - \text{Firm's book cash}$$
$$= £100,000 - 0$$
$$= £100,000$$

While the cheque is *clearing*, GMI has a balance with the bank of £100,000 and can obtain the benefit of this cash. For example, the bank cash could be invested in marketable securities. Cheques written by the firm generate *disbursement float*, causing an immediate decrease in book cash but no immediate change in bank cash.

Cheques received by the firm represent *collection float*, which increases book cash immediately but does not immediately change bank cash. The firm is helped by disbursement float and is hurt by collection float. The sum of disbursement float and collection float is *net float*.

Example 27.3

More Float

Imagine that GMI receives a cheque from a customer for £100,000. Assume, as before, that the company has £100,000 deposited at its bank and has a *neutral float position*. It deposits the cheque and increases its book cash by £100,000 on 8 November. However, the cash is not available to GMI until its bank has presented the cheque to the customer's bank and received £100,000 on, say, 15 November. In the meantime, the cash position at GMI will reflect a collection float of £100,000.

Position prior to 8 November

$$\text{Float} = \text{Firm's bank cash} - \text{Firm's book cash}$$
$$= £100,000 - £100,000$$
$$= 0$$

Position from 8 November through 14 November

$$\text{Collection float} = \text{Firm's bank cash} - \text{Firm's book cash}$$
$$= £100,000 - £200,000$$
$$= -£100,000$$

A firm should be more concerned with net float and bank cash than with book cash. If a financial manager knows that a cheque will not clear for several days, he or she will be able to keep a lower cash balance at the bank than might be true otherwise. Good float management can generate a great deal of money. For example, suppose the average daily sales of the power distribution firm, Schneider Electric SA, are about €400 million. If Schneider Electric speeds up the collection process or slows down the disbursement process by one day, it frees up €400 million, which can be invested in marketable securities. With an interest rate of 4 per cent, this represents overnight interest of approximately €44,000 [= (€400 million/365) × 0.04].

Float management involves controlling the collection and disbursement of cash. The objective in cash collection is to reduce the lag between the time customers pay their bills and the time the cheques are collected. The objective in cash disbursement is to slow down payments, thereby increasing the time between when cheques are written and when cheques are presented. In other words, collect early and pay late. Of course, to the extent that the firm succeeds in doing this, the customers and suppliers lose money, and the trade-off is the effect on the firm's relationship with them.

Collection float can be broken down into three parts: mail float, in-house processing float, and availability float:

1   *Mail float* is the part of the collection and disbursement process where cheques are trapped in the postal system.

2   *In-house processing float* is the time it takes the receiver of a cheque to process the payment and deposit it in a bank for collection.

3   *Availability float* refers to the time required to clear a cheque through the banking system. The clearing process takes place using the central clearing system of the country in which the bank operates (e.g. the Central Exchange in the UK), clearing banks, or local clearinghouses.

Example 27.4

Float

A cheque for £1,000 is mailed from a customer on Monday, 1 September. Because of mail, processing and clearing delays, it is not credited as available cash in the firm's bank until the following Monday, 7 days later. The float for this cheque is:

$$\text{Float} = £1,000 \times 7 \text{ days} = £7,000$$

Another cheque for £7,000 is mailed on 1 September. It is available on the next day. The float for this cheque is:

$$\text{Float} = £7,000 \times 1 \text{ day} = £7,000$$

The measurement of float depends on the time lag and the amount of money involved. The cost of float is an opportunity cost: the cash is unavailable for use while cheques are tied up in the collection process. The cost of float can be determined by (1) estimating the average daily receipts, (2) calculating the average delay in obtaining the receipts, and (3) discounting the average daily receipts by the *delay-adjusted cost of capital*.

Example 27.5

Average Float

Suppose that Fundamentals Ltd has two receipts each month:

	Amount (£)	Number of Days' Delay	Float (£)
Item 1	5,000,000	× 3 =	15,000,000
Item 2	3,000,000	× 5 =	15,000,000
Total	8,000,000		30,000,000

Here is the average daily float over the month:

Average daily float

$$\frac{\text{Total float}}{\text{Total days}} = \frac{£30,000,000}{30} = £1,000,000$$

Another procedure we can use to calculate average daily float is to determine average daily receipts and multiply by the average daily delay:

Average daily receipts

$$\frac{\text{Total receipts}}{\text{Total days}} = \frac{£8,000,000}{30} = £266,666.67$$

$$\text{Weighted average delay} = (5/8) \times 3 + (3/8) \times 5$$

$$= 1.875 + 1.875 = 3.75 \text{ days}$$

$$\text{Average daily float} = \text{Average daily receipts} \times \text{Weighted average delay}$$

$$= £266,666.67 \times 3.75 = £1,000,000$$

Example 27.6

Cost of Float

Suppose Fundamentals Ltd has average daily receipts of £266,667. The float results in this amount being delayed 3.75 days. The present value of the delayed cash flow is:

$$V = \frac{£266,667}{1 + R_B}$$

where R_B is the cost of debt capital for Fundamentals, adjusted to the relevant time frame. Suppose the annual cost of debt capital is 10 per cent. Then:

$$R_B = 0.1 \times (3.75/365) = 0.00103$$

and

$$V = \frac{£266,667}{1 + 0.00103} = £266,392.62$$

Thus, the net present value of the delay float is £266,392.62 − £266,667 = −£274.38 per day. For a year, this is −£274.38 × 365 = −£100,148.70.

Accelerating Collections

The following is a depiction of the basic parts of the cash collection process:

The total time in this process is made up of mailing time, cheque processing time and cheque clearing time. The amount of time cash spends in each part of the cash collection process depends on where the firm's customers and banks are located and how efficient the firm is at collecting cash. Some of the techniques used to accelerate collections and reduce collection time are lockboxes, concentration banking and wire transfers.

Lockboxes

The lockbox is the most widely used device in the US to speed up collections of cash. It is a special post office box set up to intercept trade receivables payments. In Europe, it is generally not used and other methods are substantially more commonplace.

The collection process is started by customers mailing their cheques to a post office box instead of sending them to the firm. The lockbox is maintained by a local bank and is typically located no more than several hundred miles away. In the typical lockbox system, the local bank collects the lockbox cheques from the post office several times a day. The bank deposits the cheques directly to the firm's account. Details of the operation are recorded (in some computer-usable form) and sent to the firm.

A lockbox system reduces mailing time because cheques are received at a nearby post office instead of at corporate headquarters. Lockboxes also reduce the firm's processing time because they reduce the time required for a corporation to physically handle receivables and to deposit cheques for collection. A bank lockbox should enable a firm to get its receipts processed, deposited and cleared faster than if it were to receive cheques at its headquarters and deliver them itself to the bank for deposit and clearing.

Concentration Banking

Another way to speed up collection is to get the cash from the bank branches to the firm's main bank more quickly. This is done by a method called concentration banking.

With a concentration banking system, the firm's sales offices are usually responsible for collecting and processing customer cheques. The sales office deposits the cheques into a local deposit bank account. Surplus funds are transferred from the deposit bank to the concentration bank. The purpose of concentration banking is to obtain customer cheques from nearby receiving locations. Concentration banking reduces mailing time because the firm's sales office is usually nearer than corporate headquarters to the customer. Furthermore, bank clearing time will be reduced because the customer's cheque is usually drawn on a local bank. Figure 27.4 illustrates this process, where concentration banks are combined with lockboxes in a total cash management system.

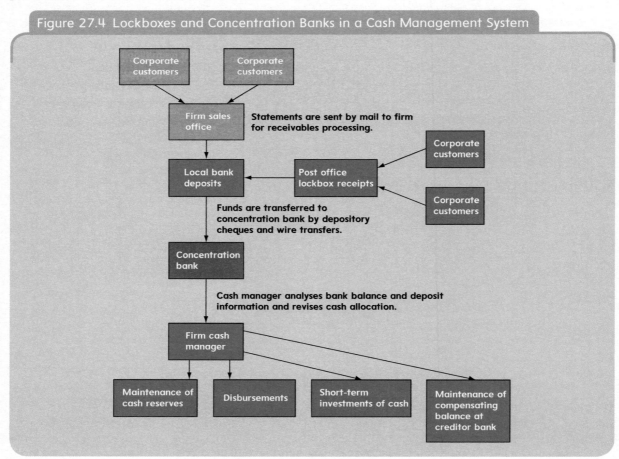

Figure 27.4 Lockboxes and Concentration Banks in a Cash Management System

The corporate cash manager uses the pools of cash at the concentration bank for short-term investing or for some other purpose. The concentration banks usually serve as the source of short-term investments. They also serve as the focal point for transferring funds to disbursement banks.

Wire Transfers

Wire transfers are the most common method of transferring cash in Europe. After the customers' cheques get into the local banking network, the objective is to transfer the surplus funds (funds in excess of required compensating balances) from the local branch to the concentration bank. The fastest and most expensive way is by wire transfer. Wire transfers take only a few minutes, and the cash becomes available to the firm upon receipt of a wire notice at the concentration bank. Wire transfers take place electronically, from one computer to another, and eliminate the mailing and cheque clearing times associated with other cash transfer methods.

The main wire service is SWIFT (operated by the Society for Worldwide Interbank Financial Telecommunication).

Delaying Disbursements

Accelerating collections is one method of cash management; paying more slowly is another. The cash disbursement process is illustrated in Figure 27.5. Techniques to slow down disbursement will attempt to increase mail time and cheque clearing time.

Figure 27.5 Cash Disbursement

Disbursement process

Firm prepares cheque to supplier.

↓

Delivery of cheque to supplier.

↓

Deposit goes to supplier's bank.

↓

Bank collects funds.

Devices to delay cheque clearing

1. Write cheque on distant bank.
2. Hold payment for several days after postmarked in office.
3. Call supplier firm to verify statement accuracy for large amounts.

Disbursement Float ('Playing the Float Game')

Even though the cash balance at the bank may be €1 million, a firm's books may show only €500,000 because it has written €500,000 in payment cheques. The disbursement float of €500,000 is available for the corporation to use until the cheques are presented for payment. Float in terms of slowing down payment cheques comes from mail delivery, cheque processing time, and collection of funds. This is illustrated in Figure 27.5. Disbursement float can be increased by writing a cheque on a geographically distant bank. For example, a British supplier might be paid with cheques drawn on an Italian bank. This will increase the time required for the cheques to clear through the banking system.

Zero Balance Accounts

Some firms set up a zero balance account (ZBA) to handle disbursement activity. The account has a zero balance as cheques are written. As cheques are presented to the zero balance account for payment (causing a negative balance), funds are automatically transferred in from a central control account. The master account and the ZBA are located in the same bank. Thus, the transfer is automatic and involves only an accounting entry in the bank.

Drafts

Firms sometimes use drafts instead of cheques. Drafts differ from cheques because they are drawn not on a bank but on the issuer (the firm) and are payable by the issuer. The bank acts only as an agent, presenting the draft to the issuer for payment. When a draft is transmitted to a firm's bank for collection, the bank must present the draft to the issuing firm for acceptance before making payment. After the draft has been accepted, the firm must deposit the necessary cash to cover the payment. The use of drafts rather than cheques allows a firm to keep lower cash balances in its disbursement accounts because cash does not need to be deposited until the drafts are presented for payment.

Ethical and Legal Questions

The cash manager must work with cash balances collected by the bank and not the firm's book balance, which reflects cheques that have been deposited but not collected. If not, a cash manager could be drawing on uncollected cash as a source for making short-term investments. Most banks charge a penalty for use of uncollected funds. However, banks may not have good enough accounting and control procedures to be fully aware of the use of uncollected funds. This raises some ethical and legal questions for the firm.

Electronic Data Interchange and the Single Euro Payments Area: The End of Float?

Electronic data interchange (EDI) is a general term that refers to the growing practice of direct electronic information exchange between all types of businesses. One important use of EDI, often called financial EDI, or FEDI, is to electronically transfer financial information and funds between parties, thereby eliminating paper invoices, paper cheques, mailing and handling. For example, it is possible to arrange to have your cheque account directly debited each month to pay many types of bills, and corporations now routinely directly deposit pay cheques into employee accounts. More generally, EDI allows a seller to send a bill electronically to a buyer, thereby avoiding the mail. The buyer can then authorize payment, which also occurs electronically. Its bank then transfers the funds to the seller's account at a different bank. The net effect is that the length of time required to initiate and complete a business transaction is shortened considerably, and much of what we normally think of as float is sharply reduced or eliminated. As the use of FEDI increases (which it will), float management will evolve to focus much more on issues surrounding computerized information exchange and fund transfers.

The Single Euro Payments Area (SEPA) is a European initiative to reduce payment times across most countries in Europe. SEPA aims to harmonize payments across Europe by treating the different countries within the region as a single area. This has already resulted in significant reductions in business transaction times.

27.4   Investing Idle Cash

If a firm has a temporary cash surplus, it can invest in short-term marketable securities. The market for short-term financial assets is called the *money market*. The maturity of short-term financial assets that trade in the money market is one year or less.

Most large firms manage their own short-term financial assets, transacting through banks and dealers. Some large firms and many small firms use money market funds. These are funds that invest in short-term financial assets for a management fee. The management fee is compensation for the professional expertise and diversification provided by the fund manager. Among the many money market mutual funds, some specialize in corporate customers. Banks also offer *sweep accounts*, where the bank takes all excess available funds at the close of each business day and invests them for the firm.

Firms have temporary cash surpluses for these reasons: to help finance seasonal or cyclical activities of the firm, to help finance planned expenditures of the firm, and to provide for unanticipated contingencies.

Seasonal or Cyclical Activities

Some firms have a predictable cash flow pattern. They have surplus cash flows during part of the year and deficit cash flows the rest of the year. For example, Toys 'R' Us, a retail toy firm, has a seasonal cash flow pattern influenced by holiday sales. Such a firm may buy marketable securities when surplus cash flows occur and sell marketable securities when deficits occur. Of course bank loans are another short-term financing device. Figure 27.6 illustrates the use of bank loans and marketable securities to meet temporary financing needs.

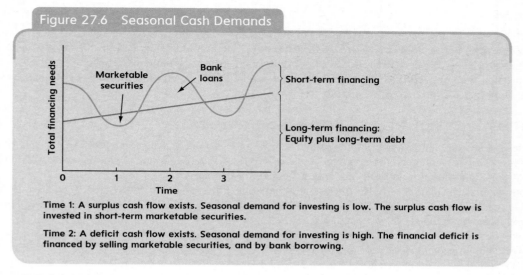

Figure 27.6   Seasonal Cash Demands

Time 1: A surplus cash flow exists. Seasonal demand for investing is low. The surplus cash flow is invested in short-term marketable securities.

Time 2: A deficit cash flow exists. Seasonal demand for investing is high. The financial deficit is financed by selling marketable securities, and by bank borrowing.

Planned Expenditures

Firms frequently accumulate temporary investments in marketable securities to provide the cash for a plant construction programme, dividend payment and other large expenditures. Thus, firms may issue bonds and shares before the cash is needed, investing the proceeds in short-term marketable securities and then selling the securities to finance the expenditures.

The important characteristics of short-term marketable securities are their maturity, default risk, marketability and taxability.

Maturity

Maturity refers to the time period over which interest and principal payments are made. For a given change in the level of interest rates, the prices of longer-maturity securities will change more than those for shorter-maturity securities. As a consequence, firms that invest in long-maturity securities are accepting greater risk than firms that invest in securities with short-term maturities. This type of risk is usually called *interest rate risk*. Most firms limit their investments in marketable securities to those maturing in less than 90 days. Of course, the expected return on securities with short-term maturities is usually less than the expected return on securities with longer maturities.

Default Risk

Chapter 20
Page 549

Default risk refers to the probability that interest or principal will not be paid on the due date and in the promised amount. In **Chapter 20**, Section 20.5, we observed that various financial reporting agencies, such as Moody's and Standard & Poor's, compile and publish ratings of various corporate and public securities. These ratings are connected to default risk. Of course, some securities have negligible default risk, such as Treasury bills. Given the purposes of investing idle corporate cash, firms typically avoid investing in marketable securities with significant default risk.

Marketability

Marketability refers to how easy it is to convert an asset to cash. Sometimes marketability is referred to as *liquidity*. It has two characteristics:

1   *No price pressure effect*: If an asset can be sold in large amounts without changing the market price, it is marketable. Price pressure effects are those that come about when the price of an asset must be lowered to facilitate the sale.

2   *Time*: If an asset can be sold quickly at the existing market price, it is marketable. In contrast, a Renoir painting or antique desk appraised at €1 million will likely sell for much less if the owner must sell on short notice.

In general, marketability is the ability to sell an asset for its face market value quickly and in large amounts. The most marketable of all securities are Treasury bills of developed countries.

Taxability

Several kinds of securities have varying degrees of tax exemption. The interest on the bonds of governments tends to be exempt from taxes. Pre-tax expected returns on government bonds must be lower than on similar taxable investments and therefore are more attractive to corporations in high marginal tax brackets.

The market price of securities will reflect the total demand and supply of tax influences. The position of the firm may be different from that of the market.

Different Types of Money Market Securities

Money market securities are generally highly marketable and short term. They usually have low risk of default. They are issued by governments (for example, Treasury bills), domestic and foreign banks (for example, certificates of deposit), and business corporations (commercial paper, for example).

Treasury bills are obligations of the government that mature in 90, 180, 270 or 360 days. They are pure discount securities. The 90-day and 180-day bills will be sold by auction every week, and 270-day and 360-day bills will be sold at a longer interval, such as every month.

Treasury notes and bonds have original maturities of more than one year. They are interest-bearing securities. The interest may be exempt from state and local taxes.

Commercial paper refers to short-term securities issued by finance companies, banks and corporations. Commercial paper typically is unsecured. Maturities range from a few weeks to 270 days. There is no active secondary market in commercial paper. As a consequence, their marketability is low. (However, firms that issue commercial paper will directly repurchase before maturity.) The default risk of commercial paper depends on the financial strength of the issuer. Moody's and Standard & Poor's publish quality ratings for commercial paper.

Certificates of deposit (CDs) are short-term loans to commercial banks. There are active markets in CDs of 3-month, 6-month, 9-month and 12-month maturities.

Repurchase agreements are sales of government securities (for example, Treasury bills) by a bank or securities dealer with an agreement to repurchase. An investor typically buys some Treasury securities from a bond dealer and simultaneously agrees to sell them back at a later date at a specified higher price. Repurchase agreements are usually very short term – overnight to a few days.

Eurodollar CDs are deposits of cash with foreign banks.

Banker's acceptances are time drafts (orders to pay) issued by a business firm (usually an importer) that have been accepted by a bank that guarantees payment.

Real World Insight 27.1

Vivendi

In 2015, Vivendi had a major disagreement with one of its shareholders, P. Schoenfeld Asset Management (PSAM), a US hedge fund, over the amount of cash it was holding. PSAM believed that the cash should have been paid out to investors in the form of a special dividend.

'PSAM believes that Vivendi is significantly undervalued due to its excessive cash holdings, inadequate capital return policy and the uncertainty over Vivendi's future use of its capital,' it said.

27.5 Terms of Sale

The *terms of sale* refer to the period for which credit is granted, the cash discount and the type of credit instrument. For example, suppose a customer is granted credit with terms of 2/10, net 30. This means that the customer has 30 days from the invoice date within which to pay. In addition, a cash discount of 2 per cent from the stated sales price is to be given if payment is made in 10 days. If the stated terms are net 60, the customer has 60 days from the invoice date to pay and no discount is offered for early payment.

When sales are seasonal, a firm might use seasonal dating. O.M. Scott and Sons is a manufacturer of lawn and garden products with a seasonal dating policy that is tied to the growing season. Payments for winter shipments of fertilizer might be due in the spring or summer. A firm offering 3/10, net 60, 1 May dating, is making the effective invoice date 1 May. The stated amount must be paid on 30 June, regardless of when the sale is made. The cash discount of 3 per cent can be taken until 10 May.

A trade or account receivable is created when credit is granted; a trade or account payable is created when a firm receives credit. These accounts are illustrated in Figure 27.7. The term 'trade credit' refers to credit granted to other firms.

Figure 27.7 Trade Credit

Trade credit extended to a customer by a firm appears as a trade receivable.
Trade credit extended by the firm's supplier to the firm appears as a trade payable.

Credit Period

Credit periods vary among different industries. For example, a jewellery store may sell diamond engagement rings for 5/30, net 4 months. A food wholesaler, selling fresh fruit and produce, might use net 7. Generally, a firm must consider three factors in setting a credit period:

1   *The probability that the customer will not pay*: A firm whose customers are in high-risk businesses may find itself offering restrictive credit terms.

2   *The size of the account*: If the account is small, the credit period will be shorter. Small accounts are more costly to manage, and small customers are less important.

3   *The extent to which the goods are perishable*: If the collateral values of the goods are low and cannot be sustained for long periods, less credit will be granted.

Lengthening the credit period effectively reduces the price paid by the customer. Generally, this increases sales. Figure 27.8 illustrates the cash flows from granting credit.

Figure 27.8 The Cash Flows of Granting Credit

Cash Discounts

Cash discounts are often part of the terms of sale. One reason they are offered is to speed up the collection of receivables. The firm must trade this off against the cost of the discount.

Example 27.7

Credit Policy

Edward Manalt, the chief financial officer of Ruptbank, is considering the request of the company's largest customer, who wants to take a 3 per cent discount for payment within 20 days on a £10,000 purchase. In other words, he intends to pay £9,700 [= £10,000 × (1 − 0.03)]. Normally, this customer pays in 30 days with no discount. The cost of debt capital for Ruptbank is 10 per cent. Edward has worked out the cash flow implications illustrated in Figure 27.9. He assumes that the time required to cash the cheque when the customer receives it is the same under both credit arrangements. He has calculated the present value of the two proposals:

Figure 27.9 Cash Flows for Different Credit

Current policy

$$PV = \frac{£10,000}{1 + (0.1 \times 30/365)} = £9,918.48$$

Proposed policy

$$PV = \frac{£9,700}{1 + (0.1 \times 20/365)} = £9,647.14$$

His calculation shows that granting the discount would cost Ruptbank £271.34 (= £9,918.48 − £9,647.14) in present value. Consequently, Ruptbank is better off with the current credit arrangement.

In the previous example, we implicitly assumed that granting credit had no side effects. However, the decision to grant credit may generate higher sales and involve a different cost structure. The next example illustrates the impact of changes in the level of sales and costs in the credit decision.

Example 27.8

More Credit Policy

Suppose that Ruptbank has variable costs of £0.50 per £1 of sales. If offered a discount of 3 per cent, customers will increase their order size by 10 per cent. This new information is shown in Figure 27.10.

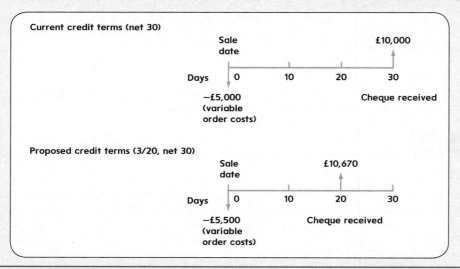

Figure 27.10 Cash Flows for Different Credit Terms: The Impact of New Sales and Costs

That is, the customer will increase the order size to £11,000 and, with the 3 per cent discount, will remit £10,670 [= £11,000 × (1 − 0.03)] to Ruptbank in 20 days. It will cost more to fill the larger order because variable costs are £5,500. The net present values are worked out here:

Current policy

$$NPV = -£5,000 + \frac{£10,000}{1 + (0.1 \times 30/365)} = £4,918.48$$

Proposed policy

$$NPV = -£5,500 + \frac{£10,670}{1 + (0.1 \times 20/365)} = £5,111.85$$

Now it is clear that the firm is better off with the proposed credit policy. This increase is the net effect of several different factors including the larger initial costs, the earlier receipt of the cash inflows, the increased sales level and the discount.

Credit Instruments

Most credit is offered on *open account*. This means that the only formal credit instrument is the invoice, which is sent with the shipment of goods, and which the customer signs as evidence that the goods have been received. Afterwards, the firm and its customers record the exchange on their accounting books.

At times, the firm may require that the customer sign a *promissory note* or IOU. This is used when the order is large and when the firm anticipates a problem in collections. Promissory notes can eliminate controversies later about the existence of a credit agreement.

One problem with promissory notes is that they are signed after delivery of the goods. One way to obtain a credit commitment from a customer before the goods are delivered is through the use of a *commercial draft*. The selling firm typically writes a commercial draft calling for the customer to pay a specific amount by a specified date. The draft is then sent to the customer's bank with the shipping invoices. The bank has the buyer sign the draft before turning over the invoices. The goods can then be shipped to the buyer. If immediate payment is required, it is called a *sight draft*. Here, funds must be turned over to the bank before the goods are shipped.

Frequently, even a signed draft is not enough for the seller. In this case she might demand that the banker pay for the goods and collect the money from the customer. When the banker agrees to do so in writing, the document is called a *banker's acceptance*. That is, the banker *accepts* responsibility for payment. Because banks generally are well-known and well-respected institutions, the banker's acceptance becomes a liquid instrument. In other words, the seller can then sell (*discount*) the banker's acceptance in the secondary market.

A firm can also use a *conditional sales contract* as a credit instrument. This is an arrangement where the firm retains legal ownership of the goods until the customer has completed payment. Conditional sales contracts usually are paid off in instalments and have interest costs built into them.

27.6   The Decision to Grant Credit: Risk and Information

Locust Industries has been in existence for 2 years. It is one of several successful firms that develop computer programs. The present financial managers have set out two alternative credit strategies: the firm can offer credit, or the firm can refuse credit.

Suppose Locust has determined that if it offers no credit to its customers, it can sell its existing computer software for €50 per program. It estimates that the costs to produce a typical computer program are €20 per program.

The alternative is to offer credit. In this case, customers of Locust will pay one period later. With some probability, Locust has determined that if it offers credit, it can charge higher prices and expect higher sales.

Strategy 1: Refuse Credit

If Locust refuses to grant credit, cash flows will not be delayed, and period 0 net cash flows, *NCF,* will be:

$$P_0Q_0 - C_0Q_0 = NCF$$

The subscripts denote the time when the cash flows are incurred, where P_0 is the price per unit received at time 0; C_0 is the cost per unit paid at time 0; and Q_0 is the quantity sold at time 0.

The net cash flows at period 1 are zero, and the net present value to Locust of refusing credit will simply be the period 0 net cash flow:

$$NPV = NCF$$

For example, if credit is not granted and $Q_0 = 100$, the NPV can be calculated as:

$$(\text{€}50 \times 100) - (\text{€}20 \times 100) = \text{€}3,000$$

Strategy 2: Offer Credit

Alternatively, let us assume that Locust grants credit to all customers for one period. The factors that influence the decision are listed here:

	Strategy 1 Refuse Credit	Strategy 2 Offer Credit
Price per unit	$P_0 = \text{€}50$	$P_0' = \text{€}50$
Quantity sold	$Q_0 = 100$	$Q_0' = 200$
Cost per unit	$C_0 = \text{€}20$	$C_0' = \text{€}25$
Probability of payment	$h = 1$	$h = 0.90$
Credit period	0	1 period
Discount rate	0	$R_B = 0.01$

The prime (') denotes the variables under the second strategy. If the firm offers credit and the new customers pay, the firm will receive revenues of $P_0'Q_0'$ one period hence, but its costs, $C_0'Q_0'$ are incurred in period 0. If new customers do not pay, the firm incurs costs, $C_0'Q_0'$ and receives no revenues. The probability that customers will pay, h, is 0.90 in the example. Quantity sold is higher with credit because new customers are attracted. The cost per unit is also higher with credit because of the costs of operating a credit policy.

The expected cash flows for each policy are set out as follows:

	Expected Cash Flows	
	Time 0	Time 1
Refuse credit	$P_0Q_0 - C_0Q_0$	0
Offer credit	$-C_0'Q_0'$	$h \times P_0'Q_0'$

Note that granting credit produces delayed expected cash inflows equal to $h \times P_0'Q_0'$. The costs are incurred immediately and require no discounting. The net present value if credit is offered is:

$$NPV(\text{offer}) = \frac{h \times P_0'Q_0'}{1 + R_B} - C_0'Q_0'$$

$$= \frac{0.9 \times \text{€}50 \times 200}{1.01} - \text{€}5,000 = \text{€}3,910.89$$

Locust's decision should be to adopt the proposed credit policy. The NPV of granting credit is higher than that of refusing credit. This decision is very sensitive to the probability of payment. If it turns out that the probability of payment is 81 per cent, Locust Software is indifferent to whether it grants credit or not. In this case, the NPV of granting credit is €3,000, which we previously found to be the NPV of not granting credit:

$$\text{€}3,000 = h \times \frac{\text{€}50 \times 200}{1.01} - \text{€}5,000$$

$$\text{€}8,000 = h \times \frac{\text{€}50 \times 200}{1.01}$$

$$h = 80.8\%$$

The decision to grant credit depends on four factors:

1   The delayed revenues from granting credit, $P_0'Q_0'$.
2   The immediate costs of granting credit, $C_0'Q_0'$.
3   The probability of payment, h.
4   The appropriate required rate of return for delayed cash flows, R_B.

The Value of New Information about Credit Risk

Obtaining a better estimate of the probability that a customer will default can lead to a better decision. How can a firm determine when to acquire new information about the creditworthiness of its customers?

It may be sensible for Locust to determine which of its customers are most likely not to pay. The overall probability of non-payment is 10 per cent. But credit checks by an independent firm show that 90 per cent of Locust's customers (computer stores) have been profitable over the last 5 years and that these customers have never defaulted on payments. The less profitable customers are much more likely to default. In fact, 100 per cent of the less profitable customers have defaulted on previous obligations.

Locust would like to avoid offering credit to the deadbeats. Consider its projected number of customers per year of $Q_0' = 200$ if credit is granted. Of these customers, 180 have been profitable over the last 5 years and have never defaulted on past obligations. The remaining 20 have not been profitable. Locust Software expects that all of these less profitable customers will default. This information is set out here:

Type of Customer	Number	Probability of Non-Payment (%)	Expected Number of Defaults
Profitable	180	0	0
Less profitable	20	100	20
Total customers	200	10	20

The NPV of granting credit to the customers who default is:

$$\frac{hP_0'Q_0'}{1+R_B} - C_0'Q_0' = \frac{0 \times €50 \times 20}{1.01} - €25 \times 20 = -€500$$

This is the cost of providing them with the software. If Locust can identify these customers without cost, it would certainly deny them credit.

In fact, it actually costs Locust €3 per customer to figure out whether a customer has been profitable over the last 5 years. The expected pay-off of the credit check on its 200 customers is then:

$$\underset{€500}{\underset{\text{extending credit}}{\text{Gain from not}}} - \underset{€3 \times 200}{\underset{\text{credit checks}}{\text{Cost of}}} = -€100$$

For Locust, credit is not worth checking. It would need to pay €600 to avoid a €500 loss.

Future Sales

Up to this point, Locust has not considered the possibility that offering credit will permanently increase the level of sales in future periods (beyond next month). In addition, payment and non-payment patterns in the current period will provide credit information that is useful for the next period. These two factors should be analysed.

In the case of Locust, there is a 90 per cent probability that the customer will pay in period 1. But, if payment is made, there will be another sale in period 2. The probability that the customer will pay in period 2, if the customer has paid in period 1, is 100 per cent. Locust can refuse to offer credit in period 2 to customers who have refused to pay in period 1. This is diagrammed in Figure 27.11.

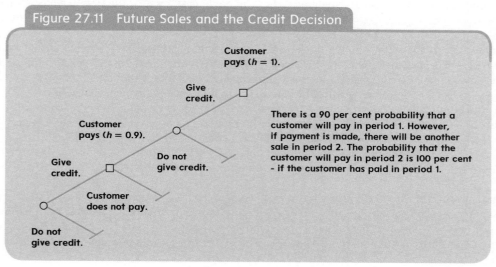

Figure 27.11 Future Sales and the Credit Decision

27.7   Optimal Credit Policy

So far, we have discussed how to compute net present value for two alternative credit policies. However, we have not discussed the optimal amount of credit. At the optimal amount of credit, the incremental cash flows from increased sales are exactly equal to the carrying costs from the increase in accounts receivable.

Consider a firm that does not currently grant credit. This firm has no bad debts, no credit department and relatively few customers. Now consider another firm that grants credit. This firm has lots of customers, a credit department and a bad debt expense account.

It is useful to think of the decision to grant credit in terms of carrying costs and opportunity costs:

1   *Carrying costs* are the costs associated with granting credit and making an investment in receivables. Carrying costs include the delay in receiving cash, the losses from bad debts and the costs of managing credit.

2   *Opportunity costs* are the lost sales from refusing to offer credit. These costs drop as credit is granted.

We represent these costs in Figure 27.12.

Figure 27.12   The Costs of Granting Credit

The sum of the carrying costs and the opportunity costs of a particular credit policy is called the *total credit cost curve*. A point is identified as the minimum of the total credit cost curve. If the firm extends more credit than the minimum, the additional net cash flow from new customers will not cover the carrying costs of this investment in receivables.

The concept of optimal credit policy in the context of modern principles of finance should be somewhat analogous to the concept of the optimal capital structure discussed earlier in the text. In perfect financial markets, there should be no optimal credit policy. Alternative amounts of credit for a firm should not affect the value of the firm. Thus, the decision to grant credit would be a matter of indifference to financial managers.

Just as with optimal capital structure, we could expect taxes, monopoly power, bankruptcy costs and agency costs to be important in determining an optimal credit policy in a world of imperfect financial markets. For example, customers in high tax brackets would be better off borrowing and taking advantage of cash discounts offered by firms than would customers in low tax brackets. Corporations in low tax brackets would be less able to offer credit because borrowing would be relatively more expensive than for firms in high tax brackets.

In general, a firm will extend trade credit if it has a comparative advantage in doing so. Trade credit is likely to be advantageous if the selling firm has a cost advantage over other potential lenders, if the selling firm has monopoly power it can exploit, if the selling firm can reduce taxes by extending credit, and if the product quality of the selling firm is difficult to determine. Firm size may be important if there are size economies in managing credit.

The Decision to Grant Credit

Trade credit is more likely to be granted by the selling firm if

1 The selling firm has a cost advantage over other lenders.

Example: York Manufacturing Ltd produces widgets. In a default, it is easier for York Manufacturing Ltd to repossess widgets and resell them than for a finance company to arrange for it with no experience in selling widgets.

2 The selling firm can engage in price discrimination.

Example: National Motors can offer below-market interest rates to lower-income customers who must finance a large portion of the purchase price of cars. Higher-income customers pay the list price and do not generally finance a large part of the purchase.

3 The selling firm can obtain favourable tax treatment.

Example: A.B. Production offers long-term credit to its best customers. This form of financing may qualify as an instalment plan and allow A.B. Production to book profits of the sale over the life of the loan. This may save taxes because the present value of the tax payments will be lower if spread over time.

4 The selling firm has no established reputation for quality products or services.

Example: Advanced Micro Instruments (AMI) manufactures sophisticated measurement instruments for controlling electrical systems on commercial airplanes. The firm was founded by two engineering graduates from the University of Amsterdam in 2005. It became a public firm in 2013. To hedge their bets, aircraft manufacturers will ask for credit from AMI. It is very difficult for customers of AMI to assess the quality of its instruments until the instruments have been in place for some time.

5 The selling firm perceives a long-term strategic relationship.

Example: Food.com is a fast-growing, cash-constrained Internet food distributor. It is currently not profitable. Fantastic Food will grant Food.com credit for food purchased because Food.com will generate profits in the future.

6 The selling firm has more differentiated products.

Example: TUI Travel, the holiday firm, has gradually concentrated more and more on differentiated and unusual holiday destinations and themes. Because of their distinctiveness, demand directly related to the holiday characteristics is high and customers can only deal with TUI for specific holidays. This makes it easier to provide credit to customers.

Source: Mian and Smith (1994); Deloof and Jegers (1996); Long et al. (1993); Petersen and Rajan (1997); Giannetti et al. (2011).

The optimal credit policy depends on characteristics of particular firms. Assuming that the firm has more flexibility in its credit policy than in the prices it charges, firms with excess capacity, low variable operating costs, high tax brackets and repeat customers should extend credit more liberally than others.

27.8 Credit Analysis

When granting *credit*, a firm tries to distinguish between *customers* who will pay and customers who will not pay. There are a number of sources of information for determining creditworthiness.

Credit Information

Information commonly used to assess creditworthiness includes the following:

1 *Financial statements*: A firm can ask a customer to supply financial statements. Rules of thumb based on calculated financial ratios can be used.

2 *Credit reports on customer's payment history with other firms*: Many organizations sell information on the credit strength of business firms. Firms such as Experian, Equifax and Dun & Bradstreet provide subscribers with credit reports on individual firms.

3 *Banks*: Banks will generally provide some assistance to their business customers in acquiring information on the creditworthiness of other firms.

4 *The customer's payment history with the firm*: The most obvious way to obtain an estimate of a customer's probability of non-payment is whether he or she has paid previous bills.

Credit Scoring

Once information has been gathered, the firm faces the hard choice of either granting or refusing credit. Many firms use the traditional and subjective guidelines referred to as the 'five Cs of credit':

1 *Character*: The customer's willingness to meet credit obligations.

2 *Capacity*: The customer's ability to meet credit obligations out of operating cash flows.

3 *Capital*: The customer's financial reserves.

4 *Collateral*: A pledged asset in the case of default.

5 *Conditions*: General economic conditions.

Conversely, firms such as credit card issuers have developed elaborate statistical models (called credit scoring models) for determining the probability of default. Usually, all the relevant and observable characteristics of a large pool of customers are studied to find their historic relation to default. Because these models determine who is and who is not creditworthy, not surprisingly they have been the subject of government regulation. For example, if a statistical model were to find that women default more than men, it might be used to deny women credit. Regulation removes such models from the domain of the statistician and makes them the subject of politicians.

27.9 Collection Policy

Collection refers to obtaining payment of past-due accounts. The credit manager keeps a record of payment experiences with each customer.

Average Collection Period

Paragon Blu-Ray Disc Players sells 100,000 Blu-Ray disc players a year at €300 each. All sales are for credit with terms of 2/20, net 60.

Suppose that 80 per cent of Paragon's customers take the discounts and pay on day 20; the rest pay on day 60. The average collection period (ACP) measures the average amount of time required to collect a trade or account receivable. The ACP for Paragon is 28 days:

$$0.8 \times 20 \text{ days} + 0.2 + 60 \text{ days} = 28 \text{ days}$$

(The average collection period is frequently referred to as *days' sales outstanding* or *days in receivables*.)

Of course, this is an idealized example where customers pay on either one of two dates. In reality, payments arrive in a random fashion, so the average collection period must be calculated differently.

To determine the ACP in the real world, firms first calculate average daily sales. The average daily sales (ADS) equal annual sales divided by 365. The ADS of Paragon are:

$$\text{Average daily sales} = \frac{€300 \times 100,000}{365 \text{ days}} = €82,192$$

If receivables today are €2,301,376, the average collection period is:

$$\text{Average collection period} = \frac{\text{Accounts receivable}}{\text{Average daily sales}}$$
$$= \frac{€2,301,376}{€82,192}$$
$$= 28 \text{ days}$$

In practice, firms observe sales and receivables daily. Consequently, an average collection period can be computed and compared to the stated credit terms. For example, suppose Paragon had computed its ACP at 40 days for several weeks, versus its credit terms of 2/20, net 60. With a 40-day ACP, some customers are paying later than usual. Some accounts may be overdue.

However, firms with seasonal sales will often find the *calculated* ACP changing during the year, making the ACP a somewhat flawed tool. This occurs because receivables are low before the selling season and high after the season. Thus, firms may keep track of seasonal movement in the ACP over past years. In this way, they can compare the ACP for today's date with the average ACP for that date in previous years. To supplement the information in the ACP, the credit manager may make up an accounts receivable ageing schedule.

Ageing Schedule

The ageing schedule tabulates receivables by age of account. In the following schedule, 75 per cent of the accounts are on time, but a significant number are more than 60 days past due. This signifies that some customers are in arrears.

Age of Account	Percentage of Total Value of Accounts Receivable
0–20 days	50
21–60 days	25
61–80 days	20
Over 80 days	5
	100

The ageing schedule changes during the year. Comparatively, the ACP is a somewhat flawed tool because it gives only the yearly average. Some firms have refined it so that they can examine how it changes with peaks and valleys in their sales. Similarly, the ageing schedule is often augmented by the payments pattern. The *payments pattern* describes the lagged collection pattern of receivables. Like a mortality table that describes the probability that a 23-year-old will live to be 24, the payments pattern describes the probability that a 67-day-old account will still be unpaid when it is 68 days old.

Collection Effort

The firm usually employs the following procedures for customers that are overdue:

1   Send a delinquency letter informing the customer of the past-due status of the account.
2   Make a telephone call to the customer.
3   Employ a collection agency.
4   Take legal action against the customer.

At times, a firm may refuse to grant additional credit to customers until arrears are paid. This may antagonize a normally good customer and points to a potential conflict of interest between the collections department and the sales department.

Factoring

Factoring refers to the sale of a firm's trade receivables to a financial institution known as a *factor*. The firm and the factor agree on the basic credit terms for each customer. The customer sends payment directly to the factor, and the factor bears the risk of non-paying customers. The factor buys the receivables at a discount, which usually ranges from 0.35 to 4 per cent of the value of the invoice amount. The average discount throughout the economy is probably about 1 per cent.

One point should be stressed. We have presented the elements of credit policy as though they were somewhat independent of each other. In fact, they are closely interrelated. For example, the optimal credit policy is not independent of collection and monitoring policies. A tighter collection policy can reduce the probability of default, and this in turn can raise the NPV of a more liberal credit policy.

27.10   How to Finance Trade Credit

In addition to the unsecured debt instruments described earlier in this chapter, there are three general ways of financing accounting receivables: secured debt, a captive finance company and securitization.

Use of secured debt is usually referred to as asset-based receivables financing. This is the predominant form of receivables financing. Many lenders will not lend without security to firms with substantive uncertainty or little equity. With secured debt, if the borrower gets into financial difficulty, the lender can repossess the asset and sell it for its fair market value.

Many large firms with good credit ratings use captive finance companies. The captive finance companies are subsidiaries of the parent firm. This is similar to the use of secured debt because the creditors of the captive finance company have a claim on its assets and, as a consequence, the accounts receivable of the parent firm. A captive finance company is attractive if economies of scale are important and if an independent subsidiary with limited liability is warranted.

Securitization occurs when the selling firm sells its accounts receivable to a financial institution. The financial institution pools the receivables with other receivables and issues securities to finance items.

Summary and Conclusions

The chapter discussed how firms manage cash.

1 A firm holds cash to conduct transactions and to compensate banks for the various services they render.

2 The optimal amount of cash for a firm to hold depends on the opportunity cost of holding cash and the uncertainty of future cash inflows and outflows. The Baumol model and the Miller–Orr model are two transaction models that provide rough guidelines for determining the optimal cash position.

3 The firm can use a variety of procedures to manage the collection and disbursement of cash to speed up the collection of cash and slow down payments. Some methods to speed collection are lockboxes, concentration banking and wire transfers. The financial manager must always work with collected company cash balances and not with the company's book balance. To do otherwise is to use the bank's cash without the bank knowing it, raising ethical and legal questions.

4 Because of seasonal and cyclical activities, to help finance planned expenditures, or as a reserve for unanticipated needs, firms temporarily find themselves with cash surpluses. The money market offers a variety of possible vehicles for parking this idle cash.

5 The components of a firm's credit policy are the terms of sale, the credit analysis and the collection policy.

6 The terms of sale describe the amount and period of time for which credit is granted and the type of credit instrument.

7 The decision to grant credit is a straightforward NPV decision that can be improved by additional information about customer payment characteristics. Additional information about the customers' probability of defaulting is valuable, but this value must be traded off against the expense of acquiring the information.

8 The optimal amount of credit the firm offers is a function of the competitive conditions in which it finds itself. These conditions will determine the carrying costs associated with granting credit and the opportunity costs of the lost sales from refusing to offer credit. The optimal credit policy minimizes the sum of these two costs.

9 We have seen that knowledge of the probability that customers will default is valuable. To enhance its ability to assess customers' default probability, a firm can score credit. This relates the default probability to observable characteristics of customers.

10 The collection policy is the method of dealing with past-due accounts. The first step is to analyse the average collection period and to prepare an ageing schedule that relates the age of accounts to the proportion of the accounts receivable they represent. The next step is to decide on the collection method and to evaluate the possibility of factoring – that is, selling the overdue accounts.

Questions and Problems

CONCEPT

1 **Reasons for Holding Cash**   Why do firms hold cash? What are the consequences of holding too little cash? Is it possible for a firm to have too much cash? Why would shareholders care if a firm accumulates large amounts of cash? Explain

2 **Determining the Target Cash Balance**   Show, using both the Baumol Model and the Miller–Orr Model, how a firm can determine its optimal cash balance. What are the advantages and disadvantages of each?

3 **Collection and Disbursement of Cash**   Which would a firm prefer: a net collection float or a net disbursement float? Why?

4 **Investing Idle Cash**   What options are available to a firm if it believes it has too much cash? How about too little?

5 **Terms of the Sale**   Explain what is meant by the credit terms of a sale. Provide an example of a typical trade credit agreement.

6 **Establishing a Credit Policy**   What steps are involved in establishing a credit policy?

7 **Optimal Credit Policy**   Is it possible to have an optimal credit policy? In this context, discuss the total credit curve and its impact on a firm's approach to trade credit.

8 **Credit Analysis**   What are the five 'C's of credit? Give an example of what happens when one of the 5Cs is not met. Are there any other factors a firm should consider?

9 **Collection Policy**   How can a firm use an ageing schedule of payments to maximize its total collection of outstanding debtors?

REGULAR

10 **Opportunity versus Trading Costs**   Konyagi plc has an average daily cash balance of £10,500. Total cash needed for the year is £65,000. The interest rate is 3 per cent, and replenishing the cash costs €17 each time. What are the opportunity cost of holding cash, the trading cost, and the total cost? What do you think of Konyagi's strategy?

11 **Costs and the Baumol Model**   Saint-Michel SA needs a total of €54,000 in cash during the year for transactions and other purposes. Whenever cash runs low, it sells off €20,000 in securities and transfers the cash in. The interest rate is 3 per cent per year, and selling off securities costs €100 per sale.

(a) What is the opportunity cost under the current policy? The trading cost? With no additional calculations, would you say that Saint-Michel keeps too much or too little cash? Explain.

(b) What is the target cash balance derived using the Baumol model?

12 **Calculating Net Float**   Each business day, on average, a company writes cheques totalling €125,000 to pay its suppliers. The usual clearing time for the cheques is 3 days. Meanwhile, the company is receiving payments from its customers each day, in the form of cheques, totalling €140,000. The cash from the payments is available to the firm after 4 days.

(a) Calculate the company's disbursement float, collection float and net float.

(b) What would be company's net float if the collected funds were available in 2 days instead of 4?

13 **Float and Weighted Average Delay**   Every month, your neighbour receives three cheques, one for £12,000, one for £7,000 and one for £3,000. The largest cheque takes 4 days to clear after it is deposited; the smallest one takes 5 days; and the £7,000 cheque takes 6 days because it is sent from overseas. Assume 30 days in a month, on an average.

(a) What is the total float for the month?

(b) What is the average daily float?

(c) What are the average daily receipts and weighted average delay?

14 **Using Weighted Average Delay** A mail-order firm processes 50,000 cheques per month. Of these, 34 per cent are for €20 and 66 per cent are for €30. The €20 cheques are delayed 2 days on average; the €30 cheques are delayed 3 days on average. Assume 30 days in a month, on an average.

   (a) What is the average daily collection float? How do you interpret your answer?

   (b) What is the weighted average delay? Use the result to calculate the average daily float.

   (c) How much should the firm be willing to pay to eliminate the float?

   (d) If the interest rate is 3 per cent per year, calculate the daily cost of the float.

   (e) How much should the firm be willing to pay to reduce the weighted average float by 1.5 days?

15 **Collections** It takes Transocean about 8 days to receive and deposit cheques from customers. Transocean's management is considering a new system to reduce the firm's collection times. It is expected that the new system will reduce receipt and deposit times to 4 days total. Average daily collections are SFr640,000, and the required rate of return is 12 per cent per year.

   (a) What is the reduction in outstanding cash balances as a result of implementing the new system?

   (b) What monetary return could be earned on these savings?

   (c) What is the maximum monthly charge Transocean should pay for this new system?

16 **Value of Delay** Vedant plc disburses cheques every 2 weeks that average £370,000 and take 7 days to clear. How much interest can the company earn annually if it delays transfer of funds from an interest-bearing account that pays 0.03 per cent per day for these 7 days? Ignore the effects of compounding interest.

17 **NPV and Reducing Float** Starthub Ltd has an agreement with its bank whereby the bank handles Rm500 million in collections a day and requires a Rm40,000,000 compensating balance. Starthub is contemplating cancelling the agreement and dividing its Malaysian activities so that two other banks will handle its business. Banks A and B will each handle Rm200 million of collections a day, and each requires a compensating balance of Rm12 million. Starthub's financial manager expects that collections will be accelerated by one day if the Malaysian activities are divided between two banks. Should the company proceed with the new system? What will be the annual net savings? Assume that the T-bill rate is 2 per cent annually.

18 **Determining Optimal Cash Balances** TByrne Ltd is currently holding €700,000 in cash. It projects that over the next year its cash outflows will exceed cash inflows by €360,000 per month. How much of the current cash holding should be retained, and how much should be used to increase the company's holdings of marketable securities? Each time these securities are bought or sold through a broker, the company pays a fee of €500. The annual interest rate on money market securities is 6.5 per cent. After the initial investment of excess cash, how many times during the next 12 months will securities be sold? Use the Baumol model.

19 **Using Miller–Orr** SlapShot plc has a fixed cost associated with buying and selling marketable securities of £100. The interest rate is currently 0.021 per cent per day, and the firm has estimated that the standard deviation of its daily net cash flows is £75. Management has set a lower limit of £1,100 on cash holdings. Calculate the target cash balance and upper limit using the Miller–Orr model, and describe how the system will work.

20 **Using Baumol** Grampian plc has a weekly cash requirement of £60,000. The cost of selling marketable securities to raise cash is £50. The interest rate is 7 per cent per annum. Determine the optimal order quantity and the optimal order period.

21 **Cash Discounts** You place an order for 200 units of inventory at a unit price of £95. The supplier offers terms of 2/10, net 30.

   (a) How long do you have to pay before the account is overdue? If you take the full period, how much should you remit?

   (b) What is the discount being offered? How quickly must you pay to get the discount? If you take the discount, how much should you remit?

   (c) If you do not take the discount, how much interest are you paying implicitly? How many days' credit are you receiving?

22 **ACP and Accounts Receivable** Dalglish plc sells earnings forecasts for British securities. Its credit terms are 2/10, net 30. Based on experience, 65 per cent of all customers will take the discount.

   (a) What is the average collection period for Dalglish?

   (b) If Dalglish sells 1,200 forecasts every month at a price of £2,200 each, what is its average balance sheet amount in accounts receivable?

23 Terms of Sale A firm offers terms of 2/9, net 40. What effective annual interest rate does the firm earn when a customer does not take the discount? Without doing any calculations, explain what will happen to this effective rate if:

(a) The discount is changed to 3 per cent.

(b) The credit period is increased to 60 days.

(c) The discount period is increased to 15 days.

24 ACP and Receivables Turnover Muziek Stad NV has an average collection period of 52 days. Its average daily investment in receivables is €46,000. What are its annual credit sales? What is the receivables turnover?

25 Early Payment Discount XYZ plc has recently won a very large order to supply a retail chain, called TT Ltd, with items over the next two years. The size of any order may vary considerably and XYZ are obliged to deliver within two days of an order being placed. This will mean that XYZ has to invest heavily in stocks. TT Ltd also usually requires 90 days' credit from any of its suppliers. XYZ are considering either debt factoring, loan financing, or offering TT Ltd a 3 per cent discount to settle within 10 days in order to meet its operational requirements. Calculate whether it is better for XYZ to offer the discount to get payment within 10 days or to finance its operational requirements via a loan. XYZ's bank charges 12 per cent per annum for a loan.

26 Size of Accounts Receivable Baker Ginger Ltd sells on credit terms of net 25. Its accounts are, on average, 9 days past due. If annual credit sales are £8 million, what is the company's balance sheet amount in accounts receivable?

27 Evaluating Credit Policy Air Spares is a wholesaler that stocks engine components and test equipment for the commercial aircraft industry. A new customer has placed an order for eight high-bypass turbine engines, which increase fuel economy. The variable cost is €1.5 million per unit, and the credit price is €1.8 million each. Credit is extended for one period, and based on historical experience, payment for about 1 out of every 200 such orders is never collected. The required return is 2.5 per cent per period.

(a) Assuming that this is a one-time order, should it be filled? The customer will not buy if credit is not extended.

(b) What is the break-even probability of default in part (a)?

(c) Suppose that customers who do not default become repeat customers and place the same order every period forever. Further assume that repeat customers never default. Should the order be filled? What is the break-even probability of default?

(d) Describe in general terms why credit terms will be more liberal when repeat orders are a possibility.

28 Credit Policy Evaluation Champions SA is considering a change in its cash-only sales policy. The new terms of sale would be net one month. Based on the following information, determine if Champions should proceed. Describe the build-up of receivables in this case. The required return is 1.5 per cent per month.

	Current Policy	New Policy
Price per unit	€800	€800
Cost per unit	€475	€475
Unit sales per month	1,130	1,195

29 Evaluating Credit Policy Bruce Jacks plc is in the process of considering a change in its terms of sale. The current policy is cash only; the new policy will involve one period's credit. Sales are 70,000 units per period at a price of £530 per unit. If credit is offered, the new price will be £552. Unit sales are not expected to change, and all customers are expected to take the credit. Bruce Jacks estimates that 2 per cent of credit sales will be uncollectible. If the required return is 2 per cent per period, is the change a good idea?

30 Credit Policy Evaluation Clapton Erich GmbH sells 3,000 pairs of running shoes per month at a cash price of €90 per pair. The firm is considering a new policy that involves 30 days' credit and an increase in price to €91.84 per pair on credit sales. The cash price will remain at €90, and the new policy is not expected to affect the quantity sold. The discount period will be 10 days. The required return is 1 per cent per month.

(a) How would the new credit terms be quoted?

(b) What is the investment in receivables required under the new policy?

(c) Explain why the variable cost of manufacturing the shoes is not relevant here.

(d) If the default rate is anticipated to be 10 per cent, should the switch be made? What is the break-even credit price? The break-even cash discount?

31 Factoring The factoring department of Inter Scandinavian Bank (ISB) is processing 100,000 invoices per year with an average invoice value of €1,500. ISB buys the accounts receivable at 3.5 per cent off the invoice value. Currently 2.5 per cent of the accounts receivable turns out to be bad debt. The annual operating expense of this department is €400,000. What are the EBIT for the factoring department of ISB?

32 Factoring Receivables Your firm has an average collection period of 34 days. Current practice is to factor all receivables immediately at a 2 per cent discount. What is the effective cost of borrowing in this case? Assume that default is extremely unlikely.

33 Credit Analysis Silicon Wafers plc (SW), is debating whether to extend credit to a particular customer. SW's products, primarily used in the manufacture of semiconductors, currently sell for £1,850 per unit. The variable cost is £1,200 per unit. The order under consideration is for 12 units today; payment is promised in 30 days.

    (a) If there is a 20 per cent chance of default, should SW fill the order? The required return is 2 per cent per month. This is a one-time sale, and the customer will not buy if credit is not extended.

    (b) What is the break-even probability in part (a)?

    (c) This part is a little harder. In general terms, how do you think your answer to part (a) will be affected if the customer will purchase the merchandise for cash if the credit is refused? The cash price is £1,700 per unit.

34 Credit Analysis Consider the following information about two alternative credit strategies:

	Refuse Credit	Grant Credit
Price per unit	£51	£55
Cost per unit	£29	£31
Quantity sold per quarter	3,300	3,500
Probability of payment	1.0	0.90

The higher cost per unit reflects the expense associated with credit orders, and the higher price per unit reflects the existence of a cash discount. The credit period will be 90 days, and the cost of debt is 0.75 per cent per month.

    (a) Based on this information, should credit be granted?

    (b) In part (a), what does the credit price per unit have to be to break even?

    (c) In part (a), suppose we can obtain a credit report for £2 per customer. Assuming that each customer buys one unit and that the credit report correctly identifies all customers who will not pay, should credit be extended?

35 NPV of Credit Policy Switch Suppose a corporation currently sells Q units per month for a cash-only price of P. Under a new credit policy that allows one month's credit, the quantity sold will be Q' and the price per unit will be P'. Defaults will be π per cent of credit sales. The variable cost is ν per unit and is not expected to change. The percentage of customers who will take the credit is α, and the required return is R per month. What is the NPV of the decision to switch? Interpret the various parts of your answer.

36 Credit Policy The Wiggins Bicycle Shop has decided to offer credit to its customers during the spring selling season. Sales are expected to be 400 bicycles. The average cost to the shop of a bicycle is £280. The owner knows that only 97 per cent of the customers will be able to make their payments. To identify the remaining 3 per cent, she is considering subscribing to a credit agency. The initial charge for this service is £500, with an additional charge of £4 per individual report. Should she subscribe to the agency?

37 Credit Policy Evaluation Dschungel AG is considering a change in its cash-only policy. The new terms would be net one period. Based on the following information, determine if Dschungel should proceed. The required return is 3 per cent per period.

	Current Policy	New Policy
Price per unit	€75	€80
Cost per unit	€43	€43
Unit sales per month	3,200	3,500

CHALLENGE

38 Baumol Model Lisa Tylor, CFO of Purple Rain Co., concluded from the Baumol model that the optimal cash balance for the firm is $10 million. The annual interest rate on marketable securities is 5.8 per cent. The fixed cost of selling securities to replenish cash is $5,000. Purple Rain's cash flow pattern is well approximated by the Baumol model. What can you infer about Purple Rain's average weekly cash disbursement?

39 Miller–Orr Model Gold Star Ltd and Silver Star Ltd both manage their cash flows according to the Miller–Orr model. Gold Star's daily cash flow is controlled between £95,000 and £205,000, whereas Silver Star's daily cash flow is controlled between £120,000 and £230,000. The annual interest rates Gold Star and Silver Star can get are 5.8 per cent and 6.1 per cent, respectively, and the costs per transaction of trading securities are £2,800 and £2,500, respectively.

(a) What are their respective target cash balances?

(b) Which firm's daily cash flow is more volatile?

40 Credit Policy Netal Ltd has annual sales of 50 million rand, all of which are on credit. The current collection period is 45 days, and the credit terms are net 30. The company is considering offering terms of 2/10, net 30. It anticipates that 70 per cent of its customers will take advantage of the discount. The new policy will reduce the collection period to 28 days. The appropriate interest rate is 6 per cent. Should the new credit policy be adopted? How does the level of credit sales affect this decision?

Exam Question (45 minutes)

1 Leon Dung SA, a large fertilizer distributor based in the north of Spain, is planning to use a lockbox system to speed up collections from its customers located in the Castille y Leon region. A Vallidolid-area bank will provide this service for an annual fee of €25,000 plus 10 cents per transaction. The estimated reduction in collection and processing time is one day. If the average customer payment in this region is €5,500, how many customers each day, on average, are needed to make the system profitable for Leon Dung? Treasury bills are currently yielding 5 per cent per year. (40 marks)

2 Based on the Miller–Orr model, describe what will happen to the lower limit, the upper limit, and the spread (the distance between the two) if the variation in net cash flow grows. Give an intuitive explanation for why this happens. What happens if the variance drops to zero? (30 marks)

3 Given an annual interest rate of 4 per cent, a fixed order cost of €10, and total cash needed of €5,000, calculate the target cash balance using the Baumol model. How do you interpret your answer? (30 marks)

Mini Case

Cash Management at Seglem Ltd

Seglem Ltd was founded 20 years ago by its president, Trygve Seglem. The company originally began as a mail-order company but has grown rapidly in recent years, in large part due to its website. Because of the wide geographical dispersion of the company's customers, it currently employs a lockbox system with collection centres in Trondheim, Stavanger, Hammerfest, Molde and Tromsø.

Arne Austreid, the company's treasurer, has been examining the current cash collection policies. On average, each lockbox centre handles NKr130,000 in payments each day. The company's current policy is to invest these payments in short-term marketable securities daily at the collection centre banks. Every 2 weeks the investment accounts are swept, and the proceeds are wire-transferred to Seglem's headquarters in Oslo to meet the company's payroll. The investment accounts each pay 0.015 per cent per day, and the wire transfers cost 0.15 per cent of the amount transferred.

Arne has been approached by Third National Bank, located just outside Oslo, about the possibility of setting up a concentration banking system for Seglem Ltd. Third National will accept the lockbox centres' daily payments via automated clearinghouse (ACH) transfers in lieu of wire transfers. The ACH-transferred funds will not be available for use for one day. Once cleared, the funds will be deposited in a short-term account, which will also yield 0.015 per cent per day. Each ACH transfer will cost NKr700. Trygve has asked Arne to determine which cash management system will be the best for the company. Arne has asked you, his assistant, to answer the following questions:

1   What is Seglem's total net cash flow from the current lockbox system available to meet payroll?

2   Under the terms outlined by Third National Bank, should the company proceed with the concentration banking system?

3   What cost of ACH transfers would make the company indifferent between the two systems?

Credit Policy at Schwarzwald AG

Dagmar Bamberger, the president of Schwarzwald AG, has been exploring ways of improving the company's financial performance. Schwarzwald manufactures and sells office equipment to retailers. The company's growth has been relatively slow in recent years, but with an expansion in the economy, it appears that sales may increase more quickly in the future. Dagmar has asked Johann Rüstow, the company's treasurer, to examine Schwarzwald's credit policy to see if a different credit policy can help increase profitability.

The company currently has a policy of net 30. As with any credit sales, default rates are always of concern. Because of Schwarzwald's screening and collection process, the default rate on credit is currently only 1.5 per cent. Johann has examined the company's credit policy in relation to other vendors, and he has determined that three options are available.

The first option is to relax the company's decision on when to grant credit. The second option is to increase the credit period to net 45, and the third option is a combination of the relaxed credit policy and the extension of the credit period to net 45. On the positive side, each of the three policies under consideration would increase sales. The three policies have the drawbacks that default rates would increase, the administrative costs of managing the firm's receivables would increase, and the receivables period would increase. The credit policy change would impact all four of these variables in different degrees. Johann has prepared the following table outlining the effect on each of these variables:

	Annual Sales (€millions)	Default Rate (% of Sales)	Administrative Costs (% of Sales)	Receivables Period (Days)
Current policy	120	1.5	2.1	38
Option 1	140	2.4	3.1	41
Option 2	137	1.7	2.3	51
Option 3	150	2.1	2.9	49

Schwarwald's variable costs of production are 45 per cent of sales, and the relevant interest rate is a 6 per cent effective annual rate. Which credit policy should the company use? Also, notice that in option 3 the default rate and administrative costs are below those in option 2. Is this plausible? Why or why not?

References

Baumol, W.S. (1952) 'The Transactions Demand for Cash: An Inventory Theoretic Approach', *Quarterly Journal of Economics*, Vol. 66, No. 4, 545–556.

Deloof, M. and M. Jegers (1996) 'Trade Credit, Product Quality, and Intragroup Trade: Some European Evidence', *Financial Management*, Vol. 25, No. 3, 33–43.

Giannetti, M., M. Burkart and T. Ellingsen (2011) 'What You Sell Is What You Lend? Explaining Trade Credit

Contracts', *The Review of Financial Studies*, Vol. 24, No. 4, 1261–1298.

Kyröläinen, P., I. Tan and P. Karjalainen (2013) 'How Creditor Rights Affect the Value of Cash: A Cross-Country Study', *Journal of Corporate Finance*, Vol. 22, 278–298.

Long, M., I.B. Malitz and S.A. Ravid (1993) 'Trade Credit, Quality Guarantees, and Product Marketability', *Financial Management*, Vol. 22, No. 4, 117–127.

Mian, S.I. and C.W. Smith (1994) 'Extending Trade Credit and Financing Receivables', *Journal of Applied Corporate Finance*, Vol. 7, No. 1, 75–84.

Miller, M.H. and Orr, D. (1966) 'A Model of the Demand for Money by Firms', *Quarterly Journal of Economics*, Vol. 80, 413–435.

Petersen, M.A. and R.G. Rajan (1997) 'Trade Credit: Theories and Evidence', *Review of Financial Studies*, Vol. 10, No. 3, 661–691.

Additional Reading

Many papers on cash holdings are presented in Chapter 26. The following papers also consider the cash management function in firms. In addition, recent important papers on trade credit are presented.

1 Aktas, N., E. Croci and D. Petmezas (2015) 'Is Working Capital Management Value-enhancing? Evidence from Firm Performance and Investments', *Journal of Corporate Finance*, Vol. 30, 98–113.

2 Almeida, H., M. Campello and M.S. Weisbach (2004) 'The Cash Flow Sensitivity of Cash', *The Journal of Finance*, Vol. 59, No. 4, 1777–1804. **US**.

3 Atanasova, C. (2007) 'Access to Institutional Finance and the Use of Trade Credit', *Financial Management*, Vol. 36, No. 1, 49–67. **UK**.

4 Bates, T.W., K.M. Kahle and R.M. Stulz (2009) 'Why Do U.S. Firms Hold so Much More Cash than They Used To?', *The Journal of Finance*, Vol. 64, No. 5, 1985–2021. **US**.

5 Bougheas, S., S. Mateut and P. Mizen (2009) 'Corporate Trade Credit and Inventories: New Evidence of a Trade-Off from Accounts Payable and Receivable', *Journal of Banking and Finance*, Vol. 33, No. 2, 300–307.

6 Cunat, V. (2007) 'Trade Credit: Suppliers as Debt Collectors and Insurance Providers', *Review of Financial Studies*, Vol. 20, No. 2, 491–527. **UK**.

7 Dittmar, A. and J. Mahrt-Smith (2007) 'Corporate Governance and the Value of Cash Holdings', *Journal of Financial Economics*, Vol. 83, No. 3, 599–634. **US**.

8 Fabbri, D. and A.M.C. Menichini (2010) 'Trade Credit, Collateral Liquidation, and Borrowing Constraints', *Journal of Financial Economics*, Vol. 96, No. 3, 413–432.

9 Foley, C.F., J.C. Hartzell, S. Titman and G. Twite (2007) 'Why Do Firms Hold so Much Cash? A Tax Based Explanation', *Journal of Financial Economics*, Vol. 86, No. 4, 579–607. **US**.

10 Gao, H., J. Harford and K. Li (2013) 'Determinants of Corporate Cash Policy: Insights from Private Firms', *Journal of Financial Economics*, Vol. 109, No. 3, 623–639.

11 Garcia-Teruel, P.J. and P. Martinez-Solano (2009) 'A Dynamic Approach to Accounts Receivable: A Study of Spanish SMEs', *European Financial Management*, Vol. 16, No. 3, 400–421. **Spain**.

12 Giannetti, M., M. Burkart and T. Ellingsen (2011) 'What You Sell Is What You Lend? Explaining Trade Credit Contracts', *Review of Financial Studies*, Vol. 24, No. 4, 1261–1298.

13 Harford, J., S. Klasa and W.F. Maxwell (2014) 'Refinancing Risk and Cash Holdings', *The Journal of Finance*, Vol. 69, No. 3, 975–1012.

14 Howorth, C. and B. Reber (2003) 'Habitual Late Payment of Trade Credit: An Empirical Examination of UK Small Firms', *Managerial and Decision Economics*, Vol. 24, Nos. 6 and 7, 471–482. **UK**.

15 Kalcheva, I. and K.V. Lins (2007) 'International Evidence on Cash Holdings and Expected Managerial Agency Problems', *Review of Financial Studies*, Vol. 20, No. 4, 1087–1112. **International**.

16 Klapper, L.F., L. Laeven and R. Rajan (2012) 'Trade Credit Contracts', *Review of Financial Studies*, Vol. 25, No. 3, 838–886.

17 Klasa, S., W.F. Maxwell and H. Ortiz-Molina (2009) 'The Strategic Use of Corporate Cash Holdings in Collective Bargaining with Labor Unions', *Journal of Financial Economics*, Vol. 92, 421–442. **US**.

18 Love, I., L.A. Preve and V. Sarria-Allende (2007) 'Trade Credit and Bank Credit: Evidence from Recent Financial Crises', *Journal of Financial Economics*, Vol. 83, No. 2, 453–469. **International**.

19 Pinkowitz, L., R. Stulz and R. Williamson (2007) 'Cash Holdings, Dividend Policy, and Corporate Governance: A Cross-Country Analysis', *Journal of Applied Corporate Finance*, Vol. 19, No. 1, 81–87. **International**.

20 Qiu, J. and C. Wan (2015) 'Technology Spillovers and Corporate Cash Holdings', *Journal of Financial Economics*, Vol. 115, No. 3, 558–573.

21 Sufi, A. (2009) 'Bank Lines of Credit in Corporate Finance: An Empirical Analysis', *Review of Financial Studies*, Vol. 22, No. 3, 1057–1088. **UK**.

22 Wilner, B.S. (2000) 'The Exploitation of Relationships in Financial Distress: The Case of Trade Credit', *The Journal of Finance*, Vol. 55, No. 1, 153–178. **US**.

PART 8

Special Topics

Part 8 finishes our comprehensive tour of Corporate Finance by considering three very important topics in finance. In Chapter 28, mergers and acquisitions are discussed in depth. As firms respond to the rapidly changing corporate environment, many managers have opted to restructure their operations through buying or merging with another firm. There are many good reasons for restructuring through combining with another firm, but there are also a number of not-so-good reasons. This chapter discusses these and considers the value implications of merger activity.

Merger and acquisitions have been used as one strategy for a firm to emerge from financial distress. Bigger is safer and acquiring a new company can provide some risk mitigation. However, mergers and acquisitions are not the only tactic a firm can follow if it is in financial distress. Chapter 29 covers all the different ways a firm can respond to being in financial difficulty. We also look at methods to identify if a firm is at risk of financial distress.

The final chapter of Part 8 as well as the book is concerned with international corporate finance and the challenges and opportunities involved in doing business within an international context. Chapter 30 shows how to adapt capital budgeting methods to assessing international projects. It also considers the different issues one must be aware of when working in countries of different cultures.

Mergers and Acquisitions

The $19.4 billion acquisition of WhatsApp by Facebook in 2014 was just one of many corporate restructurings, mergers, and acquisitions that have taken place over the last few years. Facebook had just gone through its own $16 billion initial public offering and WhatsApp was the first major investment since the company became public. Analysts were perplexed as to why Facebook had paid so much money to a firm that had only made $300 million in revenues, virtually no profit, and employed 55 people. It should also be noted that $19.4 billion was more than twice the gross revenues Facebook earned that year and larger than the annual GDP of Honduras, Iceland and Nepal. Without doubt, the purchase price was eye-watering and the valuation multiple was enormous. Whereas very successful technology companies like Google and Apple are priced at 33 and 13 times earnings, respectively, Facebook priced WhatsApp at 66 times gross revenues and an almost infinite valuation multiple against net income.

A number of reasons have been put forward for the acquisition. First, Facebook wished to create a social media conglomerate that spans all areas of the Internet world. A second is that Facebook wishes to dominate mobile Internet and WhatsApp is one of the most successful companies on that medium. An interesting perspective is that WhatsApp provides Facebook with a very strong presence in the developing world, where Facebook has not had as much success as it has in Europe and the US. Finally, WhatsApp provides Facebook with an immensely huge database of conversations that will allow it to exploit future 'big data' opportunities that present themselves to the combined firm.

How do companies like Facebook determine whether an acquisition or merger is a good idea? This chapter explores the reasons why corporate restructurings, such as acquisitions, should take place. Just as important, it also presents reasons why they should not.

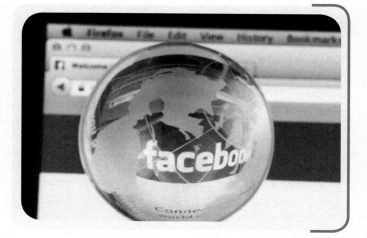

KEY NOTATION

V	Value of firm

28.1 The Basic Forms of Acquisition

Acquisitions follow one of three basic forms: (1) merger or consolidation; (2) acquisition of shares; and (3) acquisition of assets.

Merger or Consolidation

A *merger* refers to the absorption of one firm by another. The acquiring firm retains its name and identity, and it acquires all of the assets and liabilities of the acquired firm. After a merger, the acquired firm ceases to exist as a separate business entity.

A *consolidation* is the same as a merger except that an entirely new firm is created. In a consolidation both the acquiring firm and the acquired firm terminate their previous legal existence and become part of the new firm.

Example 28.1

Merger Basics

Suppose firm A acquires firm B in a merger. Further, suppose firm B's shareholders are given one share of firm A's equity in exchange for two shares of firm B's equity. From a legal standpoint, firm A's shareholders are not directly affected by the merger. However, firm B's shares cease to exist. In a consolidation, the shareholders of firm A and firm B exchange their shares for shares of a new firm (e.g., firm C).

Because of the similarities between mergers and consolidations, we shall refer to both types of reorganization as mergers. Here are two important points about mergers and consolidations:

1 A merger is legally straightforward and does not cost as much as other forms of acquisition. It avoids the necessity of transferring title of each individual asset of the acquired firm to the acquiring firm.

2 The shareholders of each firm must approve a merger.[1] Typically, votes of the owners of two-thirds of the shares are required for approval. In addition, shareholders of the acquired firm have *appraisal rights*. This means that they can demand that the acquiring firm purchase their shares at a fair value. Often the acquiring firm and the dissenting shareholders of the acquired firm cannot agree on a fair value, which results in expensive legal proceedings.

Acquisition of Shares

A second way to acquire another firm is to purchase the firm's voting shares in exchange for cash, or shares of equity and other securities. This process may start as a private offer from the management of one firm to another. At some point the offer is taken directly to the selling firm's shareholders, often by a tender offer. A *tender offer* is a public offer to buy shares of a target firm. It is made by one firm directly to the shareholders of another firm. The offer is communicated to the target firm's shareholders by public announcements such as newspaper advertisements. Sometimes a general mailing is used in a tender offer. However, a general mailing is difficult because the names and addresses of the shareholders of record are not usually available.

The following factors are involved in choosing between an acquisition of shares and a merger:

1 In an acquisition of shares, shareholder meetings need not be held and a vote is not required. If the shareholders of the target firm do not like the offer, they are not required to accept it and need not tender their shares.

2 In an acquisition of shares, the bidding firm can deal directly with the shareholders of a target firm via a tender offer. The target firm's management and board of directors are bypassed.

3 Target managers often resist acquisition. In such cases, acquisition of shares circumvents the target firm's management. Resistance by the target firm's management often makes the cost of acquisition by shares higher than the cost by merger.

4 Frequently a minority of shareholders will hold out in a tender offer, and thus the target firm cannot be completely absorbed.

5 Complete absorption of one firm by another requires a merger. Many acquisitions of shares end with a formal merger.

Acquisition of Assets

One firm can acquire another by buying all of its assets. The selling firm does not necessarily vanish because its 'shell' can be retained. A formal vote of the target shareholders is required in an acquisition of assets. An advantage here is that although the acquirer is often left with minority shareholders in an acquisition of shares, this does not happen in an acquisition of assets. Minority shareholders often present problems, such as holdouts. However, asset acquisition involves transferring title to individual assets, which can be costly.

A Classification Scheme

Financial analysts have typically classified acquisitions into three types:

1   *Horizontal acquisition*: Here, both the acquirer and acquired are in the same industry. Lloyds TSB's merger with HBOS in 2009 is an example of a horizontal merger in the banking industry.

2   *Vertical acquisition*: A vertical acquisition involves firms at different steps of the production process. The acquisition by an airline company of a travel agency would be a vertical acquisition.

3   *Conglomerate acquisition*: The acquiring firm and the acquired firm are not related to each other. The acquisition of WhatsApp by Facebook would be considered a conglomerate acquisition.

A Note about Takeovers

Takeover is a general and imprecise term referring to the transfer of control of a firm from one group of shareholders to another.[2] A firm that has decided to take over another firm is usually referred to as the bidder. The bidder offers to pay cash or securities to obtain the equity or assets of another company. If the offer is accepted, the target firm will give up control over its equity or assets to the bidder in exchange for *consideration* (i.e., its equity, its debt or cash).

Takeovers can occur by acquisition, proxy contests and going-private transactions. Thus, takeovers encompass a broader set of activities than acquisitions, as depicted in Figure 28.1.

Figure 28.1 Varieties of Takeovers

If a takeover is achieved by acquisition, it will be by merger, tender offer for shares of equity, or purchase of assets. In mergers and tender offers, the acquiring firm buys the voting ordinary shares of the acquired firm.

Proxy contests can result in takeovers as well. Proxy contests occur when a group of shareholders attempts to gain seats on the board of directors. A *proxy* is written authorization for one shareholder to vote for another shareholder. In a proxy contest, an insurgent group of shareholders solicits proxies from other shareholders.

In *going-private transactions*, a small group of investors purchases all the equity shares of a public firm. The group usually includes members of incumbent management and some outside investors. The shares of the firm are delisted from the stock exchange and can no longer be purchased in the open market.

28.2   Synergy

The previous section discussed the basic forms of acquisition. We now examine why firms are acquired. (Although the previous section pointed out that acquisitions and mergers have different definitions, these differences will be unimportant in this, and many of the following, sections. Thus, unless otherwise stated, we will refer to acquisitions and mergers synonymously.)

Much of our thinking here can be organized around the following four questions:

1   Is there a rational reason for mergers? Yes – in a word, *synergy*.

Suppose firm A is contemplating acquiring firm B. The value of firm A is V_A and the value of firm B is V_B. (It is reasonable to assume that for public companies, V_A and V_B can be determined by observing the market prices of the outstanding securities.) The difference between the value of the combined firm (V_{AB}) and the sum of the values of the firms as separate entities is the synergy from the acquisition:

$$\text{Synergy} = V_{AB} - (V_A + V_B)$$

In words, synergy occurs if the value of the combined firm after the merger is greater than the sum of the value of the acquiring firm and the value of the acquired firm before the merger.

2   Where does this magic force, synergy, come from?

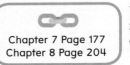

Chapter 7 Page 177
Chapter 8 Page 204

Increases in cash flow create value (see **Chapters 7 and 8** for more information). We define ΔCF_t as the difference between the cash flows at date t of the combined firm and the sum of the cash flows of the two separate firms. From the chapters about capital budgeting, we know that the cash flow in any period t can be written as:

$$\Delta CF_t = \Delta Rev_t - \Delta Costs_t - \Delta Taxes_t - \Delta Capital\ Requirements_t$$

where ΔRev_t is the incremental revenue of the acquisition, $\Delta Costs_t$ is the incremental costs of the acquisition, $\Delta Taxes_t$ is the incremental acquisition taxes, and $\Delta Capital\ Requirements_t$ is the incremental new investment required in working capital and fixed assets.

It follows from our classification of incremental cash flows that the possible sources of synergy fall into four basic categories: revenue enhancement, cost reduction, lower taxes and lower capital requirements. Improvements in at least one of these four categories create synergy. Each of these categories will be discussed in detail in the next section.

In addition, reasons are often provided for mergers where improvements are not expected in any of these four categories. These 'bad' reasons for mergers will be discussed in Section 28.4.

3   How are these synergistic gains shared?

In general, the acquiring firm pays a premium for the acquired, or target, firm. For example, if the equity of the target is selling for €50, the acquirer might need to pay €60 a share, implying a premium of €10 or 20 per cent. The gain to the target in this example is €10. Suppose that the synergy from the merger is €30. The gain to the acquiring firm, or bidder, would be €20 (=€30 − €10). The bidder would actually lose if the synergy were less than the premium of €10. A more detailed treatment of these gains or losses will be provided in Section 28.6.

4   Are there other motives for a merger besides synergy? Yes.

As we have said, synergy is a source of benefit to shareholders. However, the *managers* are likely to view a potential merger differently. Even if the synergy from the merger is less than the premium paid to the target, the managers of the acquiring firm may still benefit. For example, the revenues of the combined firm after the merger will almost certainly be greater than the revenues of the bidder before the merger. The managers may receive higher compensation once they are managing a larger firm. Even beyond the increase in compensation, managers generally experience greater prestige and power when managing a larger firm. Conversely, the managers of the target could lose their jobs after the acquisition and they might very well oppose the takeover even if their shareholders would benefit from the premium. These issues will be discussed in more detail in Section 28.9.

28.3   Sources of Synergy

In this section, we discuss sources of synergy.

Revenue Enhancement

A combined firm may generate greater revenues than two separate firms. Increased revenues can come from marketing gains, strategic benefits and market power.

Marketing Gains

It is frequently claimed that, due to improved marketing, mergers and acquisitions can increase operating revenues. Improvements can be made in the following areas:

1 Previously ineffective media programming and advertising efforts.
2 A weak existing distribution network.
3 An unbalanced product mix.

Strategic Benefits

Some acquisitions promise a *strategic* benefit, which is more like an option than a standard investment opportunity. For example, imagine that a sewing machine company acquires a computer company. The firm will be well positioned if technological advances allow computer-driven sewing machines in the future.

Michael Porter (1998) has used the word *beachhead* to denote the strategic benefits from entering a new industry. He uses the example of Procter & Gamble's acquisition of the Charmin Paper Company as a beachhead that allowed Procter & Gamble to develop a highly interrelated cluster of paper products – disposable nappies, paper towels, feminine hygiene products and bathroom tissue.

Market or Monopoly Power

One firm may acquire another to reduce competition. If so, prices can be increased, generating monopoly profits. However, mergers that reduce competition do not benefit society, and the government regulators may challenge them.

Cost Reduction

A combined firm may operate more efficiently than two separate firms. This was the primary reason for many mergers and acquisitions. A merger can increase operating efficiency in the following ways.

Economies of Scale

An economy of scale means that the average cost of production falls as the level of production increases. Figure 28.2 illustrates the relation between cost per unit and size for a typical firm. As can be seen, average cost first falls and then rises. In other words, the firm experiences economies of scale until optimal firm size is reached. Diseconomies of scale arise after that.

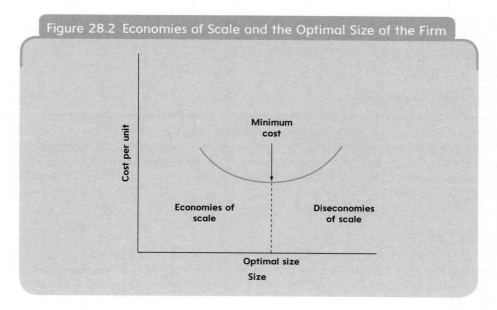

Figure 28.2 Economies of Scale and the Optimal Size of the Firm

Though the precise nature of economies of scale is not known, it is one obvious benefit of horizontal mergers. The phrase *spreading overhead* is frequently used in connection with economies of scale. This refers to sharing central facilities such as corporate headquarters, top management, and computer systems.

Economies of Vertical Integration

Operating economies can be gained from vertical combinations as well as from horizontal combinations. The main purpose of vertical acquisitions is to make coordination of closely related operating activities easier. This is probably why most forest product firms that cut timber also own sawmills and hauling equipment. The Glencore International–Xstrata merger attempt in 2012 was motivated by vertical integration because Glencore sold many of Xstrata's mining products. Similarly, Starbucks purchased Chinese farms so that it could produce its own coffee beans rather than buying them in the market. Economies from vertical integration probably also explain why most airline companies own airplanes. They also may explain why some airline companies have purchased hotels and car rental companies.

Technology Transfer

Technology transfer is another reason for merger. An automobile manufacturer might well acquire an aircraft company if aerospace technology can improve automotive quality. This technology transfer was the motivation behind the acquisition of Nokia devices and services by Microsoft in 2014.

Complementary Resources

Some firms acquire others to improve usage of existing resources. A ski equipment store merging with a tennis equipment store will smooth sales over both the winter and summer seasons, thereby making better use of store capacity.

Elimination of Inefficient Management

A change in management can often increase firm value. Some managers overspend on perquisites and pet projects, making them ripe for takeover. Alternatively, incumbent managers may not understand changing market conditions or new technology, making it difficult for them to abandon old strategies. Although the board of directors should replace these managers, the board is often unable to act independently. Thus, a merger may be needed to make the necessary replacements.

Mergers and acquisitions can be viewed as part of the labour market for top management. Michael Jensen and Richard Ruback (1983) have used the phrase 'market for corporate control', in which alternative management teams compete for the rights to manage corporate activities.

Tax Gains

Tax reduction may be a powerful incentive for some acquisitions. This reduction can come from:

1 The use of tax losses.
2 The use of unused debt capacity.
3 The use of surplus funds.
4 Tax differentials across countries.

One of the biggest reasons for cross-border mergers in recent years has been an activity called tax inversion. This happens when the country in which a firm is domiciled has a very high corporate tax rate. In a tax inversion, a firm will merge with or acquire a competitor in a low tax regime and transfer its headquarters to the low tax country to minimize tax payments. Tax inversion is suspected to be the main motivation for a number of US cross border mergers and acquisitions, such as Medtronic (US) and Covidien (Ireland); AbbVie (US) and Shire (Ireland); and Burger King (US) and Tim Hortons (Canada). As you would expect, the US government has actively tried to disincentivize this type of tax arbitrage via a number of new tax code changes and regulations.

Net Operating Losses

A firm with a profitable division and an unprofitable one will have a low tax bill because the loss in one division offsets the income in the other. However, if the two divisions are actually separate companies, the profitable firm will not be able to use the losses of the unprofitable one to offset its income. Thus, in the right circumstances, a merger can lower taxes.

Consider Table 28.1, which shows pre-tax income, taxes and after-tax income for firms A and B. Firm A earns €200 in state 1 but loses money in state 2. The firm pays taxes in state 1 but is not entitled to a tax rebate in state 2. Conversely, firm B turns a profit in state 2 but not in state 1. This firm pays taxes only in state 2. The table shows that the combined tax bill of the two separate firms is always €68, regardless of which state occurs.

Table 28.1 Tax Effect of Merger of Firms A and B

| | Before Merger | | | | After Merger | |
| | Firm A | | Firm B | | Firm AB | |
	If State 1	If State 2	If State 1	If State 2	If State 1	If State 2
Taxable income (€)	200	−100	−100	200	100	100
Taxes (€)	68	0	0	68	34	34
Net income (€)	132	−100	−100	132	66	66

Neither firm will be able to deduct its losses prior to the merger. The merger allows the losses from A to offset the taxable profits from B – and vice versa.

However, the last two columns of the table show that after a merger, the combined firm will pay taxes of only €34. Taxes drop after the merger, because a loss in one division offsets the gain in the other.

The message of this example is that firms need taxable profits to take advantage of potential losses. These losses are often referred to as *net operating losses* or NOL for short. Mergers can sometimes bring losses and profits together. However, there are two qualifications to the previous example:

1   Many country tax laws permit firms that experience alternating periods of profits and losses to equalize their taxes by carry-back and carry-forward provisions. For example, a firm that has been profitable but has a loss in the current year may be able to get refunds of income taxes paid in *three previous years* and can carry the loss *forward for 15 years*. Thus, a merger to exploit unused tax shields must offer tax savings over and above what can be accomplished by firms via carryovers.[3]

2   Tax authorities in many countries are likely to disallow an acquisition if its principal purpose is to avoid the payment of taxes.

Debt Capacity

There are at least two cases where mergers allow for increased debt and a larger tax shield. In the first case, the target has too little debt, and the acquirer can infuse the target with the missing debt. In the second case, both target and acquirer have optimal debt levels. A merger leads to risk reduction, generating greater debt capacity and a larger tax shield. We treat each case in turn.

Case 1: Unused Debt Capacity

Chapter 16
Page 428

In **Chapter 16**, we pointed out that every firm has a certain amount of debt capacity. This debt capacity is beneficial because greater debt leads to a greater tax shield. More formally, every firm can borrow a certain amount before the marginal costs of financial distress equal the marginal tax shield. This debt capacity is a function of many factors, perhaps the most important being the risk of the firm. Firms with high risk generally cannot borrow as much as firms with low risk. For example, a utility or a supermarket, both firms with low risk, can have a higher debt-to-value ratio than can a technology firm.

Some firms, for whatever reason, have less debt than is optimal. Perhaps the managers are risk-averse, or perhaps the managers simply do not know how to assess debt capacity properly. Is it bad for a firm to have too little debt? The answer is yes. As we have said, the optimal level of debt occurs when the marginal cost of financial distress equals the marginal tax shield. Too little debt reduces firm value.

This is where mergers come in. A firm with little or no debt is an inviting target. An acquirer could raise the target's debt level after the merger to create a bigger tax shield.

Case 2: Increased Debt Capacity

Chapter 10
Page 253

Let us move back to the principles of modern portfolio theory, as presented in **Chapter 10**. Consider two equities in different industries, where both equities have the same risk or standard deviation. A portfolio of these two equities has lower risk than that of either equity separately. In other words, the two-equity portfolio is somewhat diversified, whereas each equity by itself is completely undiversified.[4]

Now, rather than considering an individual buying both equities, consider a merger between the two underlying firms. Because the risk of the combined firm is less than that of either one separately, banks should be willing to lend more money to the combined firm than the total of what they would lend to the two firms separately. In other words, the risk reduction that the merger generates leads to greater debt capacity.

For example, imagine that each firm can borrow £100 on its own before the merger. Perhaps the combined firm after the merger will be able to borrow £250. Debt capacity has increased by £50 (= £250 − £200).

Remember that debt generates a tax shield. If debt rises after the merger, taxes will fall. That is, simply because of the greater interest payments after the merger, the tax bill of the combined firm should be less than the sum of the tax bills of the two separate firms before the merger. In other words, the increased debt capacity from a merger can reduce taxes.

To summarize, we first considered the case where the target had too little leverage. The acquirer could infuse the target with more debt, generating a greater tax shield. Next, we considered the case where both target and acquirer began with optimal debt levels. A merger leads to more debt even here. That is, the risk reduction from the merger creates greater debt capacity and thus a greater tax shield.

Surplus Funds

Another quirk in the tax laws involves surplus funds. Consider a firm that has *free cash flow*. That is, it has cash flow available after payment of all taxes and after all positive net present value projects have been funded. In this situation, aside from purchasing securities, the firm can either pay dividends or buy back shares.

We have already seen in our previous discussion of dividend policy that an extra dividend will increase the income tax paid by some investors. Investors pay lower taxes in a share repurchase.[5] However, a share repurchase is not normally a legal option if the sole purpose is to avoid taxes on dividends.

Instead, the firm might make acquisitions with its excess funds. Here, the shareholders of the acquiring firm avoid the taxes they would have paid on a dividend.[6]

Reduced Capital Requirements

Earlier in this chapter, we stated that due to economies of scale, mergers can reduce operating costs. It follows that mergers can reduce capital requirements as well. Accountants typically divide capital into two components: fixed capital and working capital.

When two firms merge, the managers will likely find duplicate facilities. For example, if both firms had their own headquarters, all executives in the merged firm could be moved to one headquarters building, allowing the other headquarters to be sold. Some plants might be redundant as well. Or two merging firms in the same industry might consolidate their research and development, permitting some R&D facilities to be sold.

The same goes for working capital. The inventory-to-sale ratio and the cash-to-sales ratio often decrease as firm size increases. A merger permits these economies of scale to be realized, allowing a reduction in working capital.

28.4   Two 'Bad' Reasons for Mergers

Earnings Growth

An acquisition can create the appearance of earnings growth, perhaps fooling investors into thinking that the firm is worth more than it really is. Let us consider two companies, Global Resources and Regional Enterprises, as depicted in the first two columns of Table 28.2. As can be seen, earnings per share are €1 for both companies. However, Global sells for €25 per share, implying a price–earnings (PE) ratio of 25 (= 25/1). By contrast, Regional sells for €10, implying a PE ratio of 10. This means that an investor in Global pays €25 to get €1 in earnings, whereas an investor in Regional receives the same €1 in earnings on only a €10 investment. Are investors getting a

Chapter 5
Page 120

better deal with Regional? Not necessarily. Perhaps Global's earnings are expected to grow faster than are Regional's earnings. If this is the case, an investor in Global will expect to receive high earnings in later years, making up for low earnings in the short term. In fact, **Chapter 5** argues that the primary determinant of a firm's PE ratio is the market's expectation of the firm's growth rate in earnings.

Table 28.2 Financial Positions of Global Resources Ltd and Regional Enterprises

	Global Resources Before Merger	Regional Enterprises Before Merger	Global Resources After Merger	
			The Market is 'Smart'	The Market is 'Fooled'
Earnings per share (€)	1.00	1.00	1.43	1.43
Price per share (€)	25.00	10.00	25.00	35.71
Price–earnings ratio	25	10	17.5	25
Number of shares	100	100	140	140
Total earnings (€)	100	100	200	200
Total value (€)	2,500	1,000	3,500	5,000

Exchange ratio: 1 share in Global for 2.5 shares in Regional.

Now let us imagine that Global acquires Regional, with the merger creating no value. If the market is smart, it will realize that the combined firm is worth the sum of the values of the separate firms. In this case, the market value of the combined firm will be €3,500, which is equal to the sum of the values of the separate firms before the merger.

At these values, Global will acquire Regional by exchanging 40 of its shares for 100 shares of Regional, so that Global will have 140 shares outstanding after the merger.[7] Global's share price remains at €25 (= €3,500/140). With 140 shares outstanding and €200 of earnings after the merger, Global earns €1.43 (= €200/140) per share after the merger. Its PE ratio becomes 17.5 (= 25/1.43), a drop from 25 before the merger. This scenario is represented by the third column of Table 28.2. Why has the PE dropped? The combined firm's PE will be an average of Global's high PE and Regional's low PE before the merger. This is common sense once you think about it. Global's PE should drop when it takes on a new division with low growth.

Let us now consider the possibility that the market is fooled. As we just said, the acquisition enables Global to increase its earnings per share from €1 to €1.43. If the market is fooled, it might mistake the 43 per cent increase in earnings per share for true growth. In this case, the price–earnings ratio of Global may not fall after the merger. Suppose the price–earnings ratio of Global remains at 25. The total value of the combined firm will increase to €5,000 (= 25 × €200), and the share price of Global will increase to €35.71 (= €5,000/140). This is reflected in the last column of the table.

This is earnings growth magic. Can we expect this magic to work in the real world? Managers of a previous generation certainly thought so, with firms such as LTV Industries, ITT and Litton Industries all trying to play the PE-multiple game in the 1960s. However, in hindsight it looks as if they played the game without much success. These operators have all dropped out with few, if any, replacements. It appears that the market is too smart to be fooled this easily.

Diversification

Diversification is often mentioned as a benefit of one firm acquiring another. However, we argue that diversification, by itself, cannot produce increases in value. To see this, recall that a business's variability of return can be separated into two parts: (1) what is specific to the business and called *unsystematic*, and (2) what is *systematic* because it is common to all businesses.

Systematic variability cannot be eliminated by diversification, so mergers will not eliminate this risk at all. By contrast, unsystematic risk can be diversified away through mergers. However, the investor does not need widely diversified companies such as Unilever to eliminate unsystematic risk. Shareholders can diversify more easily than corporations by simply purchasing equity in different corporations. For example, instead of Air France and KLM merging to form Air France-KLM, the shareholders of Air France could have purchased shares in KLM if they believed there would be diversification gains in doing so. Thus, diversification through merger may not benefit shareholders.[8]

Diversification can produce gains to the acquiring firm only if one of two things is true:

1 Diversification decreases the unsystematic variability at a lower cost than by investors' adjustments to personal portfolios. This seems very unlikely.

2 Diversification reduces risk and thereby increases debt capacity. This possibility was mentioned earlier in the chapter.

28.5 A Cost to Shareholders from Reduction in Risk

In **Chapter 23** we used option pricing theory to show that pure financial mergers are bad for shareholders. In this section, we will revisit this idea from an alternative perspective and show that the diversification effects of mergers can benefit bondholders at the expense of shareholders.

The Base Case

Consider an example where firm A acquires firm B. Panel I of Table 28.3 shows the net present values of firm A and firm B prior to the merger in the two possible states of the economy. Because the probability of each state is 0.50, the market value of each firm is the average of its values in the two states. For example, the market value of firm A is:

$$0.5 \times £80 + 0.5 \times £20 = £50$$

Now imagine that the merger of the two firms generates no synergy. The combined firm AB will have a market value of £75 (= £50 + £25), the sum of the values of firm A and firm B. Further imagine that the shareholders of firm B receive equity in AB equal to firm B's standalone market value of £25. In other words, firm B receives no premium. Because the value of AB is £75, the shareholders of firm A have a value of £50 (= £75 − £25) after the merger – just what they had before the merger. Thus, the shareholders of both firms A and B are indifferent to the merger.

Table 28.3 Equity-Swap Mergers

	NPV		Market Value
	State 1	State 2	
Probability	0.5	0.5	
I. Base case (no debt in either firm's capital structure)			
Values before merger:			
Firm A	£80	£20	£50
Firm B	10	40	25
Values after merger:*			
Firm AB	£90	£60	£75
II. Debt with face value of £30 in firm A's capital structure **Debt with face value of £15 in firm B's capital structure**			
Values before merger:			
Firm A	£80	£20	£50
Debt	30	20	25
Equity	50	0	25
Firm B	£10	£40	£25
Debt	10	15	12.50
Equity	0	25	12.50
Values after merger:†			
Firm AB	£90	£60	£75
Debt	45	45	45
Equity	45	15	30

Values of both firm A's debt and firm B's debt rise after merger. Values of both firm A's equity and firm B's equity fall after merger.
*Shareholders in firm A receive £50 of equity in firm AB. Shareholders in firm B receive £25 of equity in firm AB. Thus shareholders in both firms are indifferent to the merger.
†Shareholders in firm A receive equity in firm AB worth £20. Shareholders in firm B receive equity in firm AB worth £10. Gains and losses from merger are:

Loss to equityholders in firm A: £20 − £25 = −£5
Loss to equityholders in firm B: £10 − £12.50 = −£2.50
Combined gain to bondholders in both firms: £45.00 − £37.50 = £7.50

Both Firms Have Debt

Alternatively, imagine that firm A has debt with a face value of £30 in its capital structure, as shown in Panel II of Table 28.3. Without a merger, firm A will default on its debt in state 2 because the value of firm A in this state is £20, less than the face value of the debt of £30. As a consequence, firm A cannot pay the full value of the debt claim; the bondholders receive only £20 in this state. The creditors take the possibility of default into account, valuing the debt at £25 (= 0.5 × £30 + 0.5 × £20).

Firm B's debt has a face value of £15. Firm B will default in state 1 because the value of the firm in this state is £10, less than the face value of the debt of £15. The value of firm B's debt is £12.50 (= 0.5 × £10 + 0.5 × £15). It follows that the sum of the value of firm A's debt and the value of firm B's debt is £37.50 (= £25 + £12.50).

Now let us see what happens after the merger. Firm AB is worth £90 in state 1 and £60 in state 2, implying a market value of £75 (= 0.5 × £90 + 0.5 × £60). The face value of the debt in the combined firm is £45 (= £30 + £15). Because the value of the firm is greater than £45 in either state, the bondholders always get paid in full. Thus, the value of the debt is its face value of £45. This value is £7.50 greater than the sum of the values of the two debts before the merger, which we just found to be £37.50. Therefore, the merger benefits the bondholders.

What about the shareholders? Because the equity of firm A was worth £25 and the equity of firm B was worth £12.50 before the merger, let us assume that firm AB issues two shares to firm A's shareholders for every share issued to firm B's shareholders. Firm AB's equity is £30, so firm A's shareholders get shares worth £20 and firm B's shareholders get shares worth £10. Firm A's shareholders lose £5 (= £20 − £25) from the merger. Similarly, firm B's shareholders lose £2.50 (= £10 − £12.50). The total loss to the shareholders of both firms is £7.50, exactly the gain to the bondholders from the merger.

There are a lot of numbers in this example. The point is that the bondholders gain £7.50 and the shareholders lose £7.50 from the merger. Why does this transfer of value occur? To see what is going on, notice that when the two firms are separate, firm B does not guarantee firm A's debt. That is, if firm A defaults on its debt, firm B does not help the bondholders of firm A. However, after the merger the bondholders can draw on the cash flows from both A and B. When one of the divisions of the combined firm fails, creditors can be paid from the profits of the other division. This mutual guarantee, which is called the *coinsurance effect*, makes the debt less risky and more valuable than before.

There is no net benefit to the firm as a whole. The bondholders gain the coinsurance effect, and the shareholders lose the coinsurance effect. Some general conclusions emerge from the preceding analysis:

1 Mergers usually help bondholders. The size of the gain to bondholders depends on the reduction in the probability of bankruptcy after the combination. That is, the less risky the combined firm is, the greater are the gains to bondholders.

2 Shareholders of the acquiring firm are hurt by the amount that bondholders gain.

3 Conclusion 2 applies to mergers without synergy. In practice, much depends on the size of the synergy.

How Can Shareholders Reduce their Losses from the Coinsurance Effect?

The coinsurance effect raises bondholder values and lowers shareholder values. However, there are at least two ways in which shareholders can reduce or eliminate the coinsurance effect. First, the shareholders in firm A could retire its debt *before* the merger announcement date and reissue an equal amount of debt after the merger. Because debt is retired at the low premerger price, this type of refinancing transaction can neutralize the coinsurance effect to the bondholders.

Also, note that the debt capacity of the combined firm is likely to increase because the acquisition reduces the probability of financial distress. Thus, the shareholders' second alternative is simply to issue more debt after the merger. An increase in debt following the merger will have two effects, even without the prior action of debt retirement. The interest tax shield from new corporate debt raises firm value, as discussed in an earlier section of this chapter. In addition, an increase in debt after the merger raises the probability of financial distress, thereby reducing or eliminating the bondholders' gain from the coinsurance effect.

Some Final Thoughts on the Coinsurance Effect

The coinsurance effect only arises if organizational restructuring has no impact on the systematic risk of a company. Diversification reduces unsystematic risk but since systematic risk is the only important risk to investors, there is no overall value impact to the firm. However, Hann et al. (2013) argue that corporate diversification may allow a firm to (a) avoid financial distress costs; (b) reduce the cost of raising external finance; or (c) retain important stakeholders such as suppliers, customers, or employees. If this is the case, the coinsurance effect will reduce a firm's systematic risk and therefore lower its cost of capital. Hann et al. (2013) test this hypothesis and find it to be true. Specifically, diversified firms have a significantly lower cost of capital than comparable portfolios of stand-alone firms and this will have clear value implications for the diversified firm.

So, is the coinsurance effect a real issue or do other factors drive mergers and acquisitions from a diversification motive as Hann et al. (2013) suggest? Time will tell. Certainly, many believe that the coinsurance effect means diversification motives for mergers and acquisitions are bad. However, if there are strategic justifications to diversify, then coinsurance will actually enhance firm value.

28.6 The NPV of a Merger

Firms typically use NPV analysis when making acquisitions. The analysis is relatively straightforward when the consideration is cash. The analysis becomes more complex when the consideration is equity.

Cash

Suppose firm A and firm B have values as separate entities of £500 and £100, respectively. They are both all-equity firms. If firm A acquires firm B, the merged firm AB will have a combined value of £700 due to synergies of £100. The board of firm B has indicated that it will sell firm B if it is offered £150 in cash.

Should firm A acquire firm B? Assuming that firm A finances the acquisition out of its own retained earnings, its value after the acquisition is:[9]

$$\text{Value of firm A after the acquisition} = \text{Value of combined firm} - \text{Cash paid}$$
$$= £700 - £150$$
$$= £550$$

Because firm A was worth £500 prior to the acquisition, the NPV to firm A's equityholders is:

$$£50 = £550 - £500 \tag{28.1}$$

Assuming that there are 25 shares in firm A, each share of the firm is worth £20 (= £500/25) prior to the merger and £22 (= £550/25) after the merger. These calculations are displayed in the first and third columns of Table 28.4. Looking at the rise in equity price, we conclude that firm A should make the acquisition.

Table 28.4 Cost of Acquisition: Cash versus Equity

| | Before Acquisition | | | After Acquisition: Firm A | |
| | (1) | (2) | (3) | (4) Equity[†] Exchange Ratio (0.75:1) | (5) Equity[†] Exchange Ratio (0.6819:1) |
	Firm A	Firm B	Cash*		
Market value (V_A, V_B) (£)	500	100	550	700	700
Number of shares	25	10	25	32.5	31.819
Price per share (£)	20	10	22	21.54	22

*Value of firm A after acquisition: cash
$$V_A = V_{AB} - \text{cash}$$
$$£550 = £700 - £150$$

[†]Value of firm A after acquisition: equity
$$V_A = V_{AB}$$
$$£700 = £700$$

We spoke earlier of both the synergy and the premium of a merger. We can also value the NPV of a merger to the acquirer:

$$\text{NPV of a merger to acquirer} = \text{Synergy} - \text{Premium}$$

Because the value of the combined firm is £700 and the pre-merger values of A and B were £500 and £100, respectively, the synergy is £100 [= £700 − (£500 + £100)]. The premium is £50 (= £150 − £100). Thus, the NPV of the merger to the acquirer is:

$$\text{NPV of merger to firm A} = £100 − £50 = £50$$

One caveat is in order. This textbook has consistently argued that the market value of a firm is the best estimate of its true value. However, we must adjust our analysis when discussing mergers. If the true price of firm A *without the merger* is £500, the market value of firm A may actually be above £500 when merger negotiations take place. This happens because the market price reflects the possibility that the merger will occur. For example, if the probability is 60 per cent that the merger will take place, the market price of firm A will be:

		Market value of firm A with merger	×	Probability of merger	+	Market value of firm A without merger	×	Probability of no merger
£530	=	£550	×	0.60	+	£500	×	0.40

The managers would underestimate the NPV from the merger in Equation 28.1 if the market price of firm A is used. Thus, managers face the difficult task of valuing their own firm without the acquisition.

Equity

Of course, firm A could purchase firm B with equity instead of cash. Unfortunately, the analysis is not as straightforward here. To handle this scenario, we need to know how many shares are outstanding in firm B. We assume that there are 10 shares outstanding, as indicated in column 2 of Table 28.4.

Suppose firm A exchanges 7.5 of its shares for the entire 10 shares of firm B. We call this an exchange ratio of 0.75:1. The value of each share of firm A's equity before the acquisition is £20. Because 7.5 × £20 = £150, this exchange *appears* to be the equivalent of purchasing firm B in cash for £150.

This is incorrect: the true cost to firm A is greater than £150. To see this, note that firm A has 32.5 (= 25 + 7.5) shares outstanding after the merger. Firm B shareholders own 23 per cent (= 7.5/32.5) of the combined firm. Their holdings are valued at £161 (= 23 per cent × £700). Because these shareholders receive equity in firm A worth £161, the cost of the merger to firm A's shareholders must be £161, not £150.

This result is shown in column 4 of Table 28.4. The value of each share of firm A's equity after an equity-for-equity transaction is only £21.54 (= £700/32.5). We found out earlier that the value of each share is £22 after a cash-for-equity transaction. The difference is that the cost of the equity-for-equity transaction to firm A is higher.

This non-intuitive result occurs because the exchange ratio of 7.5 shares of firm A for 10 shares of firm B was based on the *premerger* prices of the two firms. However, because the equity of firm A rises after the merger, firm B equityholders receive more than £150 in firm A equity.

What should the exchange ratio be so that firm B equityholders receive only £150 of firm A's equity? We begin by defining α, the proportion of the shares in the combined firm that firm B's shareholders own. Because the combined firm's value is £700, the value of firm B shareholders after the merger is:

Value of firm B shareholders after merger

$$\alpha \times £700$$

Setting $\alpha \times £700 = £150$, we find that $\alpha = 21.43$ per cent. In other words, firm B's shareholders will receive equity worth £150 if they receive 21.43 per cent of the firm after merger.

Now we determine the number of shares issued to firm B's shareholders. The proportion, α, that firm B's shareholders have in the combined firm can be expressed as follows:

$$\alpha = \frac{\text{New shares issued}}{\text{Old shares} + \text{New shares issued}} = \frac{\text{New shares issued}}{25 + \text{New shares issued}}$$

Plugging our value of α into the equation yields:

$$0.2143 = \frac{\text{New shares issued}}{25 + \text{New shares issued}}$$

Solving for the unknown, we have:

$$\text{New shares} = 6.819 \text{ shares}$$

Total shares outstanding after the merger are 31.819 (= 25 + 6.819). Because 6.819 shares of firm A are exchanged for 10 shares of firm B, the exchange ratio is 0.6819:1.

Results at the exchange ratio of 0.6819:1 are displayed in column 5 of Table 28.4. Because there are now 31.819 shares, each share of equity is worth £22 (= £700/31.819), exactly what it is worth in the equity-for-cash transaction. Thus, given that the board of firm B will sell its firm for £150, this is the fair exchange ratio, not the ratio of 0.75:1 mentioned earlier.

Cash versus Equity

In this section, we have examined both cash deals and equity-for-equity deals. Our analysis leads to the following question: when do bidders want to pay with cash and when do they want to pay with equity? There is no easy formula: the decision hinges on a few variables, with perhaps the most important being the price of the bidder's equity.

In the example of Table 28.4, firm A's market price per share prior to the merger was £20. Let us now assume that at the time firm A's managers believed the 'true' price was £15. In other words, the managers believed that their equity was overvalued. Is it likely for managers to have a different view from that of the market? Yes – managers often have more information than does the market. After all, managers deal with customers, suppliers and employees daily and are likely to obtain private information.

Now imagine that firm A's managers are considering acquiring firm B with either cash or equity. The overvaluation would have no impact on the merger terms in a cash deal; firm B would still receive £150 in cash. However, the overvaluation would have a big impact on a share-for-share deal. Although firm B receives £150 worth of A's equity as calculated at market prices, firm A's managers know that the true value of the equity is less than £150.

How should firm A pay for the acquisition? Clearly, firm A has an incentive to pay with equity because it would end up giving away less than £150 of value. This conclusion might seem rather cynical because firm A is, in some sense, trying to cheat firm B's shareholders. However, both theory and empirical evidence suggest that firms are more likely to acquire with equity when their own equities are overvalued.[10]

The story is not quite this simple. Just as the managers of firm A think strategically, firm B's managers will likely think this way as well. Suppose that in the merger negotiations, firm A's managers push for a share-for-share deal. This might tip off firm B's managers that firm A is overpriced. Perhaps firm B's managers will ask for better terms than firm A is currently offering. Alternatively, firm B may resolve to accept cash or not to sell at all. And just as firm B learns from the negotiations, the market learns also. Empirical evidence shows that the acquirer's equity price generally falls upon the announcement of an equity-for-equity deal.[11]

28.7 Valuation of Mergers in Practice

The previous section provided the tools of merger valuation. However, in practice, the approach to valuation is significantly more complex and subjective. Mergers and acquisitions have two distinct differences from the typical investment project that a firm will undertake. First, the size of a merger will be significantly larger, which means that the risks of mis-evaluation are substantially higher. If an acquiring firm arrives at the wrong value of a target, it may destroy both companies. A good example of this is the Royal Bank of Scotland acquisition of the Dutch bank, ABN AMRO in 2007, when the Royal Bank of Scotland (with Fortis Bank and Banco Santander) bought ABN AMRO for £49 billion. The acquisition took place just before the collapse in bank valuations because of the global credit crunch. Two years later, in 2009, the Royal Bank of Scotland revalued the acquisition and reported a resultant £28 billion loss. The bank was subsequently bailed out by the British government and most of the directors lost their jobs.

The second difference is that if the target company is listed on a stock exchange, the share price can be used as an indicator of the value of the target's equity. While this makes things intuitively easier, because of the run-up in target valuations when takeover bids are rumoured, share price valuations may be too high if the current share price is used. As the previous section shows, this may lead to the wrong bid price being tabled.

Chapter 8
Page 204

When considering a potential target for acquisition or merger, both firms should evaluate a variety of scenarios and consider the various embedded options that exist in most firms (see **Chapter 8**). We suggest that acquiring firms take the following steps to evaluate prospective targets.

Stage 1: Value the Target as a Stand-alone Firm

The first stage in the valuation process is to consider the target as a stand-alone entity. This is the base case valuation upon which the merger can be assessed. To value a company requires estimates of future cash flows and the appropriate rates for discounting the cash flows. The initial valuation should then be compared to the current share price of the target to form an initial opinion of the merger.

Stage 2: Calibrate the Valuation

It is very unlikely that your initial valuation of the target firm will be equal to its share price and any differential in valuations needs to be explained. As mentioned in the previous section, share prices may also reflect takeover probabilities and potential takeover premiums. In addition, the share price may not incorporate private information that has been gained as a result of your in-depth analysis. For example, private information could be provided by the management of the target firm if the merger is friendly and fully supported by the target's board. Alternatively, new information may have been discovered in the course of your investigations. Because the effort in this phase is so great and the analysis so extensive, it is possible that your valuation may be better than the share price of the market. This is especially true if the target firm is listed on a small exchange or emerging market where valuations may not be so accurate.

If you do not have more information than the market and there is still a difference between your valuation and the share price, it is highly probable that your valuation is incorrect. In other words, your estimates of future cash flows and discount rates will be different from that of the market. At this point, it is strongly recommended that you revisit your assumptions to see if anything can be improved. It is imperative that you get your assumptions right because they are the building blocks for the rest of your analysis.

Stage 3: Value the Synergies

Whereas stages 1 and 2 focus on your initial valuation of the target, stage 3 concerns your assessment of the benefits of a possible merger or acquisition. To do this, you must value the synergies associated with combining the target and the acquirer. In the same way as you initially valued the target firm, you value synergies by estimating the cash flows generated by the synergies along with the appropriate discount rates. Some synergies are easier to predict while others are considerably more difficult. For example, synergies that come from tax savings or reductions in fixed costs are easier to predict than increased sales or reductions in variable costs.

The future cash flows and the discount rates used in the base case valuation are likely to be used in valuing risky synergies. For example, you may believe that the proposed merger will lead to a 10 per cent increase in the target's cash flows in the 5 years after the merger. Valuing this synergy will require both the pre-acquisition discount rate and the cash flows of the target. In addition, valuing synergies may also require an estimate of the acquiring firm's cost of capital and expected cash flows. Hence, the acquiring firm will want to use the procedures outlined in steps 1 and 2 to value its own equity and calibrate its cost of capital and cash flows.

When synergies are valued, it is important to discount cash flows arising from the synergy using the weighted average of both firms' cost of capital. For example, as a result of declining population in Japan and an increasingly competitive global whisky industry, Suntory (the Japanese alcoholic spirits firm) acquired the US whisky firm, Beam Inc. in 2014. Assume that, as a result of the acquisition, both companies would increase their pre-tax profits by 10 per cent per year. Given that the gain in each year is proportional to the pre-acquisition cash flows of both firms, the appropriate discount rate would be an equally weighted average of the two firm's costs of capital.

The Suntory-Beam example illustrates a case where synergies affect both parties to the merger equally. However, this will not always be the case. If the acquisition was expected to result in a proportional increase in Suntory's profits, but not Beam's, then you would use Suntory's cost of capital to value the synergy.

If the major gain from the acquisition is Suntory's penetration of the Americas, there will be many strategic options open to the company once it starts operations. Consequently, it might be better to consider valuing the synergy as a strategic option, using the real options methodology in **Chapters 8 and 22**, instead of the risk-adjusted discount rate method. When a firm expands into a new market, it has the option to expand further if prospects turn out to be more favourable than originally anticipated, and to exit if the situation turns out to be unfavourable. In these situations, an investment may be substantially undervalued when such options are ignored.

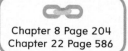

Chapter 8 Page 204
Chapter 22 Page 586

Stage 4: Value the Merger

The final part of the analysis is to add the base case valuation of the target to the value of the synergies from the merger or acquisition. The rule of thumb is that the merger or acquisition should go ahead if the costs of the merger, which includes the bid premium as well as all transaction costs, are lower than the combined value of the merger.

28.8 Friendly versus Hostile Takeovers

Mergers are generally initiated by the acquiring, not the acquired, firm. Thus, the acquirer must decide to purchase another firm, select the tactics to effectuate the merger, determine the highest price it is willing to pay, set an initial bid price, and make contact with the target firm. Often the CEO of the acquiring firm simply calls on the CEO of the target and proposes a merger. Should the target be receptive, a merger eventually occurs. Of course there may be many meetings, with negotiations over price, terms of payment and other parameters. The target's board of directors generally has to approve the acquisition. Sometimes the bidder's board must also give its approval. Finally, an affirmative vote by the shareholders is needed. But when all is said and done, an acquisition that proceeds in this way is viewed as *friendly*.

Of course, not all acquisitions are friendly. The target's management may resist the merger, in which case the acquirer must decide whether to pursue the merger and, if so, what tactics to use. Facing resistance, the acquirer may begin by purchasing some of the target's equity in secret. This position is often called a *toehold*. Regulation in almost every country requires that an institution or individual disclose their holding in a company once a specific percentage ownership threshold is passed. For example, in the UK, an acquiring company must disclose any holdings above 3 per cent and provide detailed information, including its intentions and its position in the target. Secrecy ends at this point because the acquirer must state that it plans to acquire the target. The price of the target's shares will probably rise after the disclosure, with the new equity price reflecting the possibility that the target will be bought out at a premium.

Although the acquirer may continue to purchase shares in the open market, an acquisition is unlikely to be effectuated in this manner. Rather, the acquirer is more likely at some point to make a *tender offer* (an offer made directly to the shareholders to buy shares at a premium above the current market price). The tender offer may specify that the acquirer will purchase all shares that are tendered – that is, turned in to the acquirer. Alternatively, the offer may state that the acquirer will purchase all shares up to, say, 50 per cent of the number of shares outstanding. If more shares are tendered, prorating will occur. For example, if, in the extreme case, all of the shares are tendered, each shareholder will be allowed to sell one share for every two shares tendered. The acquirer may also say that it will accept the tendered shares only if a minimum number of shares have been tendered.

National regulators normally require that tender offers be held open for a minimum period. This delay gives the target time to respond. For example, the target may want to notify its shareholders not to tender their shares. It may release statements to the press criticizing the offer. The target may also encourage other firms to enter the bidding process.

At some point, the tender offer ends, at which time the acquirer finds out how many shares have been tendered. The acquirer does not necessarily need 100 per cent of the shares to obtain control of the target. In some companies, a holding of 20 per cent or so may be enough for control. In others the percentage needed for control is much higher. *Control* is a vague term, but you might think of it operationally as control over the board of directors. Shareholders elect members of the board, who, in turn, appoint managers. If the acquirer receives enough equity to elect a majority of the board members, these members can appoint the managers whom the acquirer wants. And effective control can often be achieved with less than a majority. As long as some of the original board members vote with the acquirer, a few new board members can gain the acquirer a working majority.

Sometimes, once the acquirer gets working control, it proposes a merger to obtain the few remaining shares that it does not already own. The transaction is now friendly because the board of directors will approve it. Mergers of this type are often called *clean-up* mergers.

A tender offer is not the only way to gain control of a *hostile* target. Alternatively, the acquirer may continue to buy more shares in the open market until control is achieved. This strategy, often called a *street sweep*, is infrequently used, perhaps because of the difficulty of buying enough shares to obtain control. Also, as mentioned, tender offers often allow the acquirer to return the tendered shares if fewer shares than the desired number are tendered. By contrast, shares purchased in the open market cannot be returned.

Another means to obtain control is a *proxy fight* – a procedure involving corporate voting. Elections for seats on the board of directors are generally held at the annual shareholders' meeting, perhaps 4–5 months after the end of the firm's fiscal year. After purchasing shares in the target company, the acquirer nominates a slate of candidates to run against the current directors. The acquirer generally hires a proxy solicitor, who contacts shareholders prior to the shareholders' meeting, making a pitch for the insurgent slate. Should the acquirer's candidates win a majority of seats on the board, the acquirer will control the firm. And as with tender offers, effective control can often be achieved with less than a majority. The acquirer may just want to change a few specific policies of the firm, such as the firm's capital budgeting programme or its diversification plan. Or it may simply want to replace management.

If some of the original board members are sympathetic to the acquirer's plans, a few new board members can give the acquirer a working majority.

Whereas mergers end up with the acquirer owning all of the target's equity, the victor in a proxy fight does not gain additional shares. The reward to the proxy victor is simply share price appreciation if the victor's policies prove effective. In fact, just the threat of a proxy fight may raise the share price because management may improve operations to head off the fight.

28.9 Defensive Tactics

Target firm managers frequently resist takeover attempts. Actions to defeat a takeover may benefit the target shareholders if the bidding firm raises its offer price or another firm makes a bid. Alternatively, resistance may simply reflect self-interest at the shareholders' expense. That is, the target managers might fight a takeover to preserve their jobs. Sometimes management resists while simultaneously improving corporate policies. Shareholders can benefit in this case, even if the takeover fails.

In this section, we describe various ways in which target managers resist takeovers. A company is said to be 'in play' if one or more suitors are currently interested in acquiring it. It is useful to separate defensive tactics before a company is in play from tactics after the company is in play.

Deterring Takeovers before Being in Play

Corporate Charters

The corporate charter refers to the articles of incorporation and corporate bylaws governing a firm. Among other provisions, the charter establishes conditions allowing a takeover. Firms frequently amend charters to make acquisitions more difficult. As examples, consider the following two amendments:

1 *Classified or staggered board*: In an unclassified board of directors, shareholders elect all of the directors each year. In a staggered board, only a fraction of the board is elected each year, with terms running for multiple years. For example, one-third of the board might stand for election each year, with terms running for 3 years. Staggered boards increase the time an acquirer needs to obtain a majority of seats on the board. In the previous example, the acquirer can gain control of only one-third of the seats in the first year after acquisition. Another year must pass before the acquirer is able to control two-thirds of the seats. Therefore, the acquirer may not be able to change management as quickly as it would like. However, some argue that staggered boards are not necessarily effective because the old directors often choose to vote with the acquirer.

2 *Supermajority provisions*: Corporate charters determine the percentage of voting shares needed to approve important transactions such as mergers. A supermajority provision in the charter means that this percentage is above 50 per cent. Two-thirds majorities are common, though the number can be much higher. A supermajority provision clearly increases the difficulty of acquisition in the face of hostile management. Many charters with supermajority provisions have what is known as a *board out* clause as well. Here supermajority does not apply if the board of directors approves the merger. This clause makes sure that the provision hinders only hostile takeovers.

Golden Parachutes

This colourful term refers to generous severance packages provided to management in the event of a takeover. The argument is that golden parachutes will deter takeovers by raising the cost of acquisition. However, some authorities point out that the deterrence effect is likely to be unimportant because a severance package, even a generous one, is probably a small part of the cost of acquiring a firm. In addition, some argue that golden parachutes actually *increase* the probability of a takeover. The reasoning here is that management has a natural tendency to resist any takeover because of the possibility of job loss. A large severance package softens the blow of takeover, reducing management's inclination to resist.

Golden parachutes are very controversial in economic downturns as there is nothing the media likes more than to splash an incredibly generous severance package all over the front pages when the company is in financial distress. This has been the case in recent years when many outgoing executives bowed to public pressure and rescinded their golden parachutes. A good example concerns the chief executives of the Royal Bank of Scotland and HBOS, the big British banks that succumbed to the credit crisis in 2009. Fred Goodwin (RBS) and Andy Hornby (HBOS) gave up their golden parachutes of £1.2 million and £1 million respectively when they left their banks after intense political and public criticism.

Mylan's Golden Parachute

In April 2015, the global pharmaceuticals firm, Mylan, was the target of a hostile takeover by Teva Pharmaceutical Industries Ltd. A major cost of the bid being successful was the presence of golden parachutes for Mylan's executive board. In the event of a change in ownership, the chairman of Mylan was due $72.1 million in the form of benefits, compensation and option exercises. The CEO of Mylan was also due $45.9 million in a similar package.

Shareholder Rights Plans

A shareholder rights plan (or poison pill) is a sophisticated defensive tactic that is common in the US but illegal in Europe without shareholder approval. In the event of a hostile bid, a poison pill allows the target firm to issue new shares to every shareholder *except the bidder* at a deep discount.

Perhaps the example of PeopleSoft (PS) will illustrate the general idea. At one point in 2005, PS's poison pill provision stated that once a bidder acquired 20 per cent or more of PeopleSoft's shares, all shareholders except the acquirer could buy new shares from the corporation at half price. At the time, PS had about 400 million shares outstanding. Should some bidder acquire 20 per cent of the company (80 million shares), every shareholder *except the bidder* would be able to buy 16 new shares for every one previously held. If all shareholders exercised this option, PeopleSoft would have to issue 5.12 billion (= 0.8×400 million $\times 16$) new shares, bringing its total to 5.52 billion. The share price would drop because the company would be selling shares at half price. The bidder's percentage of the firm would drop from 20 per cent to 1.45 per cent (= 80 million/5.52 billion). Dilution of this magnitude causes some critics to argue that poison pills are insurmountable.

Since poison pills are illegal or actively discouraged in many countries, this has led to greater frequency of hostile takeovers, especially by hedge funds looking to quickly take over a company and sell it on at a profit. Outlawing poison pills has also led to some criticism because acquiring firms can quickly take control of a target firm before other, possibly better, bids are being prepared by other firms.

Deterring a Takeover after the Company Is in Play

Greenmail and Standstill Agreements

Managers may arrange a *targeted repurchase* to forestall a takeover attempt. In a targeted repurchase, a firm buys back its own equity from a potential bidder, usually at a substantial premium, with the proviso that the seller promises not to acquire the company for a specified period. Critics of such payments label them *greenmail*.

A *standstill agreement* occurs when the acquirer, for a fee, agrees to limit its holdings in the target. As part of the agreement, the acquirer often promises to offer the target a right of first refusal in the event that the acquirer sells its shares. This promise prevents the block of shares from falling into the hands of another would-be acquirer.

Greenmail has been a colourful part of the financial lexicon since its first application in the late 1970s. Since then, pundits have commented numerous times on either its ethical or unethical nature. Greenmail is predominantly a strategy undertaken by US firms and is not common in the rest of the world.

White Knight and White Squire

A firm facing an unfriendly merger offer might arrange to be acquired by a friendly suitor, commonly referred to as a *white knight*. The white knight might be favoured simply because it is willing to pay a higher purchase price. Alternatively, it might promise not to lay off employees, fire managers or sell off divisions.

Management instead may wish to avoid any acquisition at all. A third party, termed a *white squire*, might be invited to make a significant investment in the firm, under the condition that it vote with management and not purchase additional shares. White squires are generally offered shares at favourable prices. Billionaire investor Warren Buffett has acted as a white squire to many firms, including Champion International and Gillette.

Recapitalizations and Repurchases

Target management will often issue debt to pay out a dividend – a transaction called a *leveraged recapitalization*. A *share repurchase*, where debt is issued to buy back shares, is a similar transaction. The two transactions fend off takeovers in a number of ways. First, the equity price may rise, perhaps because of the increased tax shield from greater debt. A rise in share price makes the acquisition less attractive to the bidder. However, the price will rise only if the firm's debt level before the recapitalization was below the optimum, so a levered recapitalization is not recommended for every target. Consultants point out that firms with low debt but with stable cash flows are ideal candidates for 'recaps'. Second, as part of the recapitalization, management may issue new securities that give management greater voting control than it had before the recap. The increase in control makes a hostile takeover more difficult. Third, firms with a lot of cash are often seen as attractive targets. As part of the recap, the target may use this cash to pay a dividend or buy back equity, reducing the firm's appeal as a takeover candidate.

Exclusionary Self-Tenders

An *exclusionary self-tender* is the opposite of a targeted repurchase. Here, the firm makes a tender offer for a given amount of its own equity while excluding targeted shareholders.

In a particularly celebrated case, Unocal, a large integrated oil firm, made a tender offer for 29 per cent of its shares while excluding its largest shareholder, Mesa Partners II (led by T. Boone Pickens). Unocal's self-tender was for $72 per share, which was $16 over the prevailing market price. It was designed to defeat Mesa's attempted takeover of Unocal by transferring wealth, in effect, from Mesa to Unocal's other equityholders. This type of activity is almost non-existent in most countries outside of the United States because of the existence of pre-emptive rights. A notable example is Barclays Bank plc and Unicredit Bank who attempted in 2008 to bypass the pre-emptive rights of existing shareholders in order to raise cash quickly. Not surprisingly, the management of both companies came under intense pressure from institutional shareholders to change their decisions.

Asset Restructurings

In addition to altering capital structure, firms may sell off existing assets or buy new ones to avoid takeover. Targets generally sell, or divest, assets for two reasons. First, a target firm may have assembled a hodgepodge of assets in different lines of business, with the various segments fitting together poorly. Value might be increased by placing these divisions into separate firms. Academics often emphasize the concept of *corporate focus*. The idea here is that firms function best by focusing on those few businesses that they really know. A rise in equity price following a divestiture will reduce the target's appeal to a bidder.

The second reason is that a bidder might be interested in a specific division of the target. The target can reduce the bidder's interest by selling off this division. Although the strategy may fend off a merger, it can hurt the target's shareholders if the division is worth more to the target than to the division's buyer. Authorities frequently talk of selling off the *crown jewels* or pursuing a *scorched earth policy*.

While some targets divest existing assets, others buy new ones. Two reasons are generally given here. First, the bidder may like the target as is. The addition of an unrelated business makes the target less appealing to the acquirer. However, a bidder can always sell off the new business, so the purchase is likely not a strong defence. Second, antitrust legislation is designed to prohibit mergers that reduce competition. Antitrust law is enforced at both country level and regional level. For example, in the UK, mergers are governed by the Takeover Panel (UK regulator) and the European Commission (Europe). A target may purchase a company, knowing that this new division will pose antitrust problems for the bidder. However, this strategy might not be effective because, in its filings with the respective regulatory authorities, the bidder can state its intention to sell off the unrelated business.

28.10 The Diary of a Takeover: AbbVie Inc. and Shire plc

In May 2014, the global pharmaceuticals firm, AbbVie Inc., made a number of private approaches to London Stock Exchange-listed Irish pharmaceutical firm, Shire plc with a view to acquire the company. Over the next few months an enthralling saga of bid and counterbid, interspersed with regulatory interference, took place.

May 2014: Rumours of a Bid for Shire Filter through the Market

During the month of May, numerous rumours built up around the company, especially after Citigroup and Deutsche Bank both announced 'Buy' recommendations for Shire. Although these were ostensibly because of a new dry-eye treatment that Shire had submitted for approval to regulators, commentators felt that potential buyers were considering a bid. In particular, Ireland's very low corporate tax rate suggested that it would be a target for a large US firm hoping to undertake a tax inversion. In the latter half of May 2014, the Shire plc price rose from £32.80 to £34.14 without any specific news being released by the company, valuing the company at around £20 billion.

First Half of June 2014: Rumours Continue to Grow of a Bid

At the beginning of the month, the first company to be linked with Shire was Allergan, which makes botox. Allergan were thought to be keen on a Shire bid to avoid being taken over themselves by the Canadian pharma firm, Valeant, who had made a bid for them in May. As the bid rumours heated up, Shire hired Citi to help draw up a defence strategy to protect the firm against any takeover bid. By 19 June and with no specific news relating to Shire, the company's share price had risen further to £37.38.

20 June 2014: Shire Announces that it Has Rejected Three Unsolicited Takeover Bids

On 20 June, Shire announced that it had spurned three unsolicited bids from AbbVie. Although there was no mention of tax inversion (acquiring an overseas firm to take advantage of a lower corporate tax rate), this was the reason that was put forward for the bid by the financial media. Shire's share price closed the day at £43.71.

21/22 June 2014: Shire Sets Out its Defensive Stall

Between 20 and 21 June, more information came out regarding the AbbVie bid. The details consisted of a £46.11 per share combined cash and equity offer equivalent to £27 billion. AbbVie justified the approach on the basis that it wished to reduce its reliance from its revenues from the rheumatoid arthritis drug, Humira, and Shire would provide the necessary diversified product base. However, it was clear that the company could take advantage of the big difference in tax rates between Ireland and US by shifting its headquarters to Dublin if the bid was successful.

On 22 June, Shire's Danish chief executive, Flemming Ornskov, set out a very optimistic 10-year growth plan and argued that the company was expecting significant growth in revenues from its ADHD drug, Vyanse, as well as drugs for other rare diseases. Any bid for Shire would have to take these future growth opportunities into account and a much higher price was expected if the management was to even consider recommending acceptance of an offer to the company's shareholders.

25 June 2014: AbbVie Puts Forward its Case

Over the next three days, Shire's share price continued to grow and was now sitting at £45.17, very close to AbbVie's original offer price of £46.11. According to the *Financial Times*, Richard Gonzalez, AbbVie's chief executive, admitted that the company would take advantage of Ireland's low corporate tax rate and shift its headquarters from the US. However, he argued that there was a clear strategic rationale for acquiring Shire because it allowed AbbVie to '…widen the reach of Shire's products and accelerate drug development'.

Mr Gonzalez said AbbVie was 'willing to move quickly and co-operatively to engage … with a view to achieving a transaction for the benefit of all shareholders', but did not rule out a hostile bid if Shire continued to resist, and said AbbVie planned talks with the UK company's shareholders to seek their backing for a deal.[12]

8–14 July 2014: AbbVie Raises its Offer

After two weeks of negotiation, AbbVie raised its offer from £46.11 per share to £51.15 per share. The make-up of the bid was similar to the earlier bid with it combining £22.44 in cash with 0.8568 AbbVie Shares to make a total offer of £51.15 per share. At the time, both boards were in friendly negotiations, but AbbVie made it clear that should discussions break down, they would consider going direct to the shareholders of Shire with the bid.

Talks between the two boards intensified over the next few days and by 13 July, Shire had pushed AbbVie to increase their bid a second time to £53.20 per share (consisting of 46 per cent cash and 54 per cent AbbVie shares). At this point, the Shire plc board recommended to shareholders that they accept AbbVie's bid.

The AbbVie–Shire takeover bid provides many insights into the process of a takeover. First, the bidder will justify why it feels the offer is a sensible one. It may argue on the basis of performance improvements or criticize the target in terms of its performance, value, or management. Second, the target firm's management, if it does not wish to be taken over, will respond in a negative manner and defend their business model and performance. Third, the market will have its own view on the viability and likelihood of a merger. Finally, it is clear that much effort on the part of both management teams was expended over the period. This time could have been spent elsewhere improving the value of each firm's business operations.

In the end and after all the discussions between the two companies, AbbVie pulled out of the takeover. The reasons were nothing to do with Shire and everything to do with US regulatory changes. Because many American firms were using tax inversion to reduce their tax payments, the US government amended its regulation to reduce

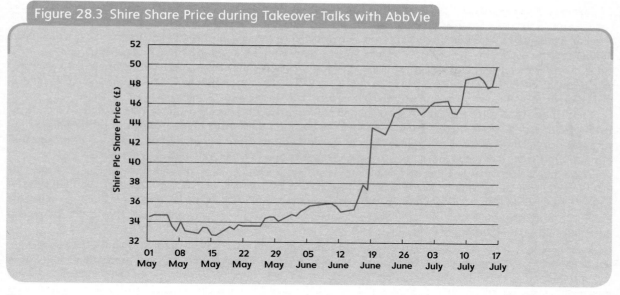

Figure 28.3 Shire Share Price during Takeover Talks with AbbVie

the attractiveness of this activity. This caused AbbVie to reassess the value benefit from tax inversion and the purchase price of £53.20 was consequently no longer attractive to AbbVie's shareholders.

28.11   Do Mergers Add Value?

In Section 28.2, we stated that synergy occurs if the value of the combined firm after the merger is greater than the sum of the value of the acquiring firm and the value of the acquired firm before the merger. Section 28.3 provided a number of sources of synergy in mergers, implying that mergers *can* create value. We now want to know whether mergers actually create value in practice. This is an empirical question and must be answered by empirical evidence.

There are a number of ways to measure value creation, but many academics favour *event studies*. These studies estimate abnormal equity returns on, and around, the merger announcement date. An *abnormal return* is usually defined as the difference between an actual equity return and the return on a market index or control group of equities. This control group is used to net out the effect of marketwide or industrywide influences.

Consider Table 28.5, where returns around the announcement days of mergers in the US are reported. The average abnormal percentage return across all mergers from 1980 to 2001 is 0.0135. This number combines the returns on both the acquiring company and the acquired company. Because 0.0135 is positive, the market believes that mergers on average create value. The other three returns in the first column are positive as well, implying value creation in the different subperiods. Many other academic studies have provided similar results. Thus, it appears from this column that the synergies we mentioned in Section 28.3 show up in the real world.

Table 28.5 Percentage and Dollar Returns for Mergers

Time Period	Gain or Loss to Merger (Both Acquired and Acquiring Firms)		Gain or Loss to Acquiring Firms	
	Abnormal Percentage Return	Aggregate Dollar Gain or Loss	Abnormal Percentage Return	Aggregate Dollar Gain or Loss
1980–2001	0.0135	−79 billion	0.0110	−220 billion
1980–1990	0.0241	12 billion	0.0064	−4 billion
1991–2001	0.0104	−90 billion	0.0120	−216 billion
1998–2001	0.0029	−134 billion	0.0069	−240 billion

Source: Modified from Moeller et al. (2005), Table 1.

However, the next column tells us something different. Across all mergers from 1980 to 2001, the aggregate dollar change around the day of merger announcement is −$79 billion. This means that the market is, on average, *reducing* the combined equity value of the acquiring and acquired companies around the merger announcement date. Though the difference between the two columns may seem confusing, there is an explanation. Although most mergers have created value, mergers involving the very largest firms have lost value. The abnormal percentage return is an unweighted average in which the returns on all mergers are treated equally. A positive return here reflects all those small mergers that created value. However, losses in a few large mergers cause the aggregate dollar change to be negative.

But there is more. The rest of the second column indicates that the aggregate dollar losses occurred only in the 1998 to 2001 period. While there were losses of −$134 billion in this period, there were gains of $12 billion from 1980 to 1990. And interpolation of the table indicates that there were gains of $44 billion (= $134 − $90) from 1991 through 1997. Thus, it appears that some large mergers lost a great deal of value from 1998 to 2001.

The analysis presented in Table 28.5 considers the effect of mergers on shareholders. It does not consider the effect of mergers on the whole firm, that is equity and debt. Recall from Section 28.5 that mergers may transfer value from equityholders to debtholders because of the reduction in risk of the combined company. Doukas and Kan (2006) show this to be the case for cross-border mergers involving US firms and find that overall firm value is not reduced from this activity.

Most research on mergers and acquisitions has focused on US firms. This is largely because the activity has not been particularly common elsewhere. For example, in Europe, merger activity only grew significantly after the introduction of the euro. The exception to this is the UK, where mergers have been commonplace and come in waves in a similar way to the US. Figure 28.4 presents the total volume and number of European mergers over time. There was a massive spike in the late twentieth century as the high-tech boom took hold, which then fell after the bubble burst. In recent years, the value of mergers across the world has dropped drastically with the disappearance of credit in the financial markets. Admittedly, there has been a consolidation of companies that were forced to merge as a result of financial distress or economic necessity (for example, HBOS with Lloyds TSB, and Merrill Lynch with Bank of America) but, on the whole, there has been little interest in large acquisitions.

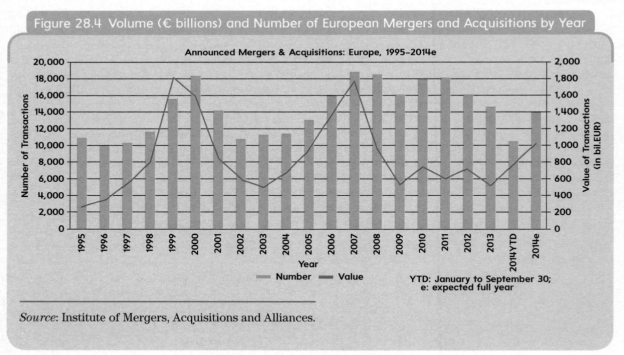

Figure 28.4 Volume (€ billions) and Number of European Mergers and Acquisitions by Year

Source: Institute of Mergers, Acquisitions and Alliances.

When one considers the value benefits of mergers and acquisitions, it is important to remember that every country has a different regulatory and legal framework for dealing with acquisitions. In some places, foreign ownership is only allowed up to a certain pre-specified percentage of shares. This can significantly affect the success of merger bids. Europe is particularly interesting because although it operates under a cohesive regulation system, corporate cultures are very different across the area. Campa and Hernando (2004) show that differences in the institutional environment can affect the benefits of mergers and acquisitions. They found that European mergers in regulated industries or those that were under government control were significantly less successful than in unregulated industries.

The results in a table such as Table 28.5 should have important implications for public policy because regulators are always wondering whether mergers are to be encouraged or discouraged. However, the results in that table are, unfortunately, ambiguous. On the one hand, you could focus on the first column, saying that mergers create value on average. Proponents of this view might argue that the great losses in the few large mergers were flukes, not likely to occur again. On the other hand, we cannot easily ignore the fact that over the entire period, mergers destroyed more value than they created.

Jarrad Harford, Mark Humphery-Jenner and Ronan Powell (2012) investigated how entrenched managers destroy value from their acquisition decisions. They found that poor managers avoided private targets, overpaid for firms, and chose companies with poor synergy opportunities.

It is important to remember that mergers and acquisitions are often driven by different agenda. For example, the mergers and acquisitions of recent times have been in response to the economic woes facing world economies. Economies of scale and risk reduction are the main factors underlying these mergers. If you go several years back in time, the mergers and acquisitions were largely a result of growth into new markets and exploitation of different synergies. Naturally, the performance of mergers in recent times will be very different from earlier periods because of the different objectives of the activity.

Before we move on, some final thoughts are in order. Readers may be bothered that abnormal returns are taken only around the time of the acquisition, well before all of the acquisition's impact is revealed. Academics look at long-term returns but they have a special fondness for short-term returns. If markets are efficient, the short-term return provides an unbiased estimate of the total effect of the merger. Long-term returns, while capturing more information about a merger, also reflect the impact of many unrelated events.

Returns to Bidders

The preceding results combined returns on both bidders and targets. Investors want to separate the bidders from the targets. Columns 4 and 5 of Table 28.5 provide returns for acquiring companies alone. The third column shows that abnormal percentage returns for bidders have been positive for the entire sample period and for each of the individual subperiods – a result similar to that for bidders and targets combined. The fourth column indicates aggregate losses, suggesting that large mergers did worse than small ones. The time pattern for these aggregate losses to bidders is presented in Figure 28.5. Again, the large losses occurred from 1998 to 2001, with the greatest loss in 2000.

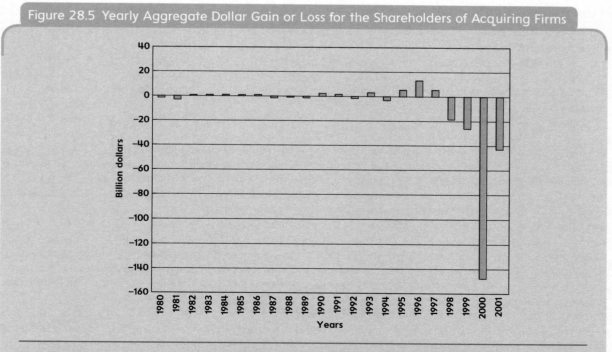

Figure 28.5 Yearly Aggregate Dollar Gain or Loss for the Shareholders of Acquiring Firms

Note: The graph shows the aggregate dollar gain or loss across all acquiring firms each year from 1980 to 2001.

Source: Taken from Fig. 1, Moeller et al. (2005).

Let us fast-forward a few decades and imagine that you are the CEO of a company. In that position you will certainly be faced with potential acquisitions. Does the evidence in Table 28.5 and Figure 28.5 encourage you to make acquisitions or not? Again, the evidence is ambiguous. On the one hand, you could focus on the averages in Column 4 of the table, likely increasing your appetite for acquisitions. On the other hand, Column 5 of the table, as well as the figure, might give you pause.

Target Companies

Although the evidence just presented for both the combined entity and the bidder alone is ambiguous, the evidence for targets is crystal-clear. Acquisitions benefit the target's equityholders. Consider the following chart, which shows the median merger *premium* over different periods in the United States:[13]

Time Period	1973–1998	1973–1979	1980–1989	1990–1998
Premium	42.1%	47.2%	37.7%	34.5%

The premium is the difference between the acquisition price per share and the target's pre-acquisition share price, divided by the target's pre-acquisition share price. The average premium is quite high for the entire sample period and for the various subsamples. For example, a target company selling at $100 per share before the acquisition that is later acquired for $142.1 per share generates a premium of 42.1 per cent. The results are similar in other countries. For example, in the UK, the average premium is 45 per cent.[14]

Though other studies may provide different estimates of the average premium, all studies show positive premiums. Thus, we can conclude that mergers benefit the target shareholders. This conclusion leads to at least two implications. First, we should be somewhat sceptical of target managers who resist takeovers. These managers may claim that the target's share price does not reflect the true value of the company. Or they may say that resistance will induce the bidder to raise its offer. These arguments could be true in certain situations, but they may also provide cover for managers who are simply scared of losing their jobs after acquisition. Second, the premium creates a hurdle for the acquiring company. Even in a merger with true synergies, the acquiring shareholders will lose if the premium exceeds the value of these synergies.

The Managers versus the Shareholders

Managers of Bidding Firms

The preceding discussion was presented from the shareholders' point of view. Because, in theory, shareholders pay the salaries of managers, we might think that managers would look at things from the shareholders' point of view. However, it is important to realize that individual shareholders have little clout with managers. For example, the typical shareholder is simply not in a position to pick up the phone and give the managers a piece of her mind. It is true that the shareholders elect the board of directors, which monitors the managers. However, an elected director has little contact with individual shareholders.

Thus, it is fair to ask whether managers are held fully accountable for their actions. This question is at the heart of what economists call *agency theory*. Researchers in this area often argue that managers work less hard, get paid more, and make worse business decisions than they would if shareholders had more control over them. And there is a special place in agency theory for mergers. Managers frequently receive bonuses for acquiring other companies. In addition, their pay is often positively related to the size of their firm. Finally, managers' prestige is also tied to firm size. Because firm size increases with acquisitions, managers are disposed to look favourably on acquisitions, perhaps even ones with negative NPV.

A fascinating study[15] compared companies where managers received a lot of options on their own company's equity as part of their compensation package with companies where the managers did not. Because option values rise and fall in tandem with the firm's equity price, managers receiving options have an incentive to forgo mergers with negative NPVs. The paper reported that the acquisitions by firms where managers receive lots of options (termed *equity-based compensation* in the paper) create more value than the acquisitions by firms where managers receive few or no options.

Agency theory may also explain why the biggest merger failures have involved large firms. Managers owning a small fraction of their firm's equity have less incentive to behave responsibly because the great majority of any losses are borne by other shareholders. Managers of large firms likely have a smaller percentage interest in their firm's equity than do managers of small firms (a large percentage of a large firm is too costly to acquire). Thus, the merger failures of large acquirers may be due to the small percentage ownership of the managers.

An earlier chapter of this text discussed the free cash flow hypothesis. The idea here is that managers can spend only what they have. Managers of firms with low cash flow are likely to run out of cash before they run out of good (positive NPV) investments. Conversely, managers of firms with high cash flow are likely to have cash on hand even after all the good investments are taken. Managers are rewarded for growth, so managers with cash flow above that needed for good projects have an incentive to spend the remainder on bad (negative NPV) projects. A paper tested this conjecture, finding that 'cash-rich firms are more likely than other firms to attempt acquisitions. . . . cash-rich bidders destroy seven cents in value for every dollar of cash reserves held. . . . consistent with the equity return evidence, mergers in which the bidder is cash-rich are followed by abnormal declines in operating performance.'[16]

The previous discussion has considered the possibility that some managers were knaves – more interested in their own welfare than in the welfare of their shareholders. However, a recent paper entertained the idea that other managers were more fools than knaves. Malmendier and Tate (2008) classified certain CEOs as overconfident, either because they refused to exercise equity options on their own company's equity when it was rational to do so or because the press portrayed them as confident or optimistic. The authors find that these overconfident managers are more likely to make acquisitions than are other managers. In addition, the equity market reacts more negatively to announcements of acquisitions when the acquiring CEO is overconfident.

Managers of Target Firms

Our discussion has just focused on the managers of acquiring firms, finding that these managers sometimes make more acquisitions than they should. However, that is only half of the story. Shareholders of target firms may have just as hard a time controlling their managers. While there are many ways that managers of target firms can put themselves ahead of their shareholders, two seem to stand out. First, we said earlier that because premiums are positive, takeovers are beneficial to the target's shareholders. However, if managers may be fired after their firms are acquired, they may resist these takeovers.[17] Tactics employed to resist takeover, generally called defensive tactics, were discussed in an earlier section of this chapter. Second, managers who cannot avoid takeover may bargain with the bidder, getting a good deal for themselves at the expense of their shareholders.

Consider Wulf's (2004) fascinating work on *mergers of equals* (MOEs). Some deals are announced as MOEs, primarily because both firms have equal ownership in and equal representation on the board of directors of the merged entity. AOL and Time Warner, Daimler-Benz and Chrysler, Morgan Stanley and Dean Witter, and Fleet Financial Group and BankBoston are generally held out as examples of MOEs. Nevertheless, authorities point out that in any deal one firm is typically 'more equal' than the other. That is, the target and the bidder can usually be distinguished in practice. For example, Daimler-Benz is commonly classified as the bidder and Chrysler as the target in their merger.

Wulf finds that targets get a lower percentage of the merger gains, as measured by abnormal returns around the announcement date, in MOEs than in other mergers. And the percentage of the gains going to the target is negatively related to the representation of the target's officers and directors on the postmerger board. These and other findings lead Wulf to conclude, 'they [the findings of the paper] suggest that CEOs trade power for premium in MOE transactions'.

28.12 Accounting and Tax Considerations

Many mergers involve companies in two different countries, which presents difficulties in assessing the value of acquisitions. This is because accounting and tax rules can be very different across countries. In recent years, there has been a concerted effort by accounting standard setters and regulatory authorities to streamline the administrative and bureaucratic challenges that face merging firms. In the subsequent discussion, we will try to be as generic as possible about the accounting and tax considerations without losing the necessary important detail. However, given the heterogeneity of regulations across countries, it is impossible to be specific about every regulation in place regarding mergers.

In Europe and many other countries (but not the US), International Financial Reporting Standards govern the way that companies account for transactions. To improve the efficiency of the accounting treatment of cross-border mergers, the International Accounting Standards Board (IASB) and the US Financial Accounting Standards Board (FASB) have been working together to converge the standards of both systems. This is an ongoing project and developments will continue in the future.

In a similar way that the accounting treatment of mergers and acquisitions is converging to one basic standard across the world, governments have also attempted to integrate country-level tax laws. The taxation of mergers and acquisitions across national borders can be extremely complex and prohibitive in cost and this deters many corporations from pursuing cross-border mergers. Each national tax system is different but in recent years there have been a number of treaties that smooth out these differences.

Chapter 2
Page 25

In Europe, the main treaty is the Cross-Border Merger Directive that was fully implemented at the end of 2007. As **Chapter 2** attests, the governance systems across Europe are quite varied and employee participation is stronger in some countries (e.g. Germany, France and Belgium) than in others (e.g. the United Kingdom). Combining the operations of corporations that are based in countries with different governance cultures and taxation systems presents some difficulty. The EU Merger Directive presents a cohesive framework that allows European national taxation systems to fully operate within a broader international context.

28.13   Going Private and Leveraged Buyouts

Going-private transactions and leveraged buyouts have much in common with mergers, and it is worthwhile to discuss them in this chapter. A publicly traded firm *goes private* when a private group, usually composed of existing management, purchases its equity. As a consequence, the firm's equity is taken off the market (if it is an exchange-traded equity, it is delisted) and is no longer traded. Thus, in going-private transactions, shareholders of publicly held firms are forced to accept cash for their shares.

Going-private transactions are frequently *leveraged buyouts* (LBOs). In a leveraged buyout the cash offer price is financed with large amounts of debt. Part of the appeal of LBOs is that the arrangement calls for little equity capital. This equity capital is generally supplied by a small group of investors, some of whom are likely to be managers of the firm being purchased.

The selling shareholders are invariably paid a premium above market price in an LBO, just as in a merger. As with a merger, the acquirer profits only if the synergy created is greater than the premium. Synergy is quite plausible in a merger of *two* firms, and we delineated a number of types of synergy earlier in the chapter. However, it is more difficult to explain synergy in an LBO because only *one* firm is involved.

Two reasons are generally given for value creation in an LBO. First, the extra debt provides a tax deduction, which, as earlier chapters suggested, leads to an increase in firm value. Most LBOs are of firms with stable earnings and with low to moderate debt. The LBO may simply increase the firm's debt to its optimum level.

The second source of value comes from increased efficiency and is often explained in terms of 'the carrot and the stick'. Managers become owners under an LBO, giving them an incentive to work hard. This incentive is commonly referred to as the carrot. Interest payments from the high level of debt constitute the stick. Large interest payments can easily turn a profitable firm before an LBO into an unprofitable one after the LBO. Management must make changes, either through revenue increases or cost reductions, to keep the firm in the black. Agency theory, a topic mentioned earlier in this chapter, suggests that managers can be wasteful with a large free cash flow. Interest payments reduce this cash flow, forcing managers to curb the waste.

Though it is easy to measure the additional tax shields from an LBO, it is difficult to measure the gains from increased efficiency. Nevertheless, this increased efficiency is considered at least as important as the tax shield in explaining the LBO phenomenon.

Academic research suggests that LBOs have, on average, created value. First, premiums are positive, as they are with mergers, implying that selling shareholders benefit. Second, studies indicate that LBOs that eventually go public generate high returns for the management group. Finally, other studies show that operating performance increases after the LBO. However, we cannot be completely confident of value creation because researchers have difficulty obtaining data about LBOs that do not go public. If these LBOs generally destroy value, the sample of firms going public would be a biased one.

Regardless of the average performance of firms undertaking an LBO, we can be sure of one thing: because of the great leverage involved, the risk is huge. On the one hand, LBOs have created many large fortunes. On the other hand, a number of bankruptcies and near-bankruptcies have occurred as well.

28.14   Divestitures

This chapter has primarily been concerned with acquisitions but it is also worthwhile to consider their opposite – divestitures. Divestitures come in a number of different varieties, the most important of which we discuss next.

Sale

The most basic type of divestiture is the *sale* of a division, business unit, segment, or set of assets to another company. The buyer generally, but not always, pays in cash. A number of reasons are provided for sales. First, in an earlier section of this chapter we considered asset sales as a defence against hostile takeovers. It was pointed out in that section that sales often improve corporate focus, leading to greater overall value for the seller. This same rationale applies when the selling company is not in play. Second, asset sales provide needed cash to liquidity-poor firms. Third, it is often argued that the paucity of data about individual business segments makes large, diversified firms hard to value. Investors may discount the firm's overall value because of this lack of transparency. Sell-offs streamline a firm, making it easier to value. However, this argument is inconsistent with market efficiency because it implies that large, diversified firms sell below their true value. Fourth, firms may simply want to sell unprofitable divisions. However, unprofitable divisions are likely to have low values to everyone. A division should be sold only if its value is greater to the buyer than to the seller.

There has been a fair amount of research on sell-offs, with academics reaching two conclusions. First, event studies show that returns on the seller's equity are positive around the time of the announcement of sale, suggesting that sell-offs create value to the seller. Second, acquisitions are often sold off down the road. For example, Kaplan and Weisbach (1992) found that over 40 per cent of acquisitions were later divested, a result that does not reflect well on mergers. The average time between acquisition and divestiture was about 7 years.

Spin-off

In a spin-off a parent firm turns a division into a separate entity and distributes shares in this entity to the parent's shareholders. Spin-offs differ from sales in at least two ways. First, the parent firm receives no cash from a spin-off: shares are sent for free to the shareholders. Second, the initial shareholders of the spun-off division are the same as the parent's shareholders. By contrast, the buyer in a sell-off is most likely another firm. However, because the shares of the division are publicly traded after the spin-off, the identities of the shareholders will change over time.

At least four reasons are generally given for a spin-off. First, as with a sell-off, the spin-off may increase corporate focus. Second, because the spun-off division is now publicly traded, stock exchange regulators require additional information to be disseminated – so investors may find it easier to value the parent and subsidiary after the spin-off. Third, corporations often compensate executives with shares of equity in addition to cash. The equity acts as an incentive: good performance from managers leads to share price increases. However, prior to the spin-off, executives can receive equity only in the parent company. If the division is small relative to the entire firm, price movement in the parent's equity will be less related to the performance of the manager's division than to the performance of the rest of the firm. Thus, divisional managers may see little relation between their effort and equity appreciation. However, after the spin-off, the manager can be given equity in the subsidiary. The manager's effort should directly impact price movement in the subsidiary's equity. Fourth, the tax consequences from a spin-off are generally better than from a sale because the parent receives no cash from a spin-off.

Carve-out

In a carve-out, the firm turns a division into a separate entity and then sells shares in the division to the public. Generally the parent retains a large interest in the division. This transaction is similar to a spin-off, and the first three benefits listed for a spin-off apply to a carve-out as well. However, the big difference is that the firm receives cash from a carve-out, but not from a spinoff. The receipt of cash can be both good and bad. On the one hand, many firms need cash. Michaely and Shaw (1995) find that large, profitable firms are more likely to use carve-outs, whereas small, unprofitable firms are more likely to use spin-offs. One interpretation is that firms generally prefer the cash that comes with a carve-out. However, small and unprofitable firms have trouble issuing equity. They must resort to a spin-off, where equity in the subsidiary is merely given to their own equityholders.

Unfortunately, there is also a dark side to cash, as developed in the free cash flow hypothesis. That is, firms with cash exceeding that needed for profitable capital budgeting projects may spend it on unprofitable ones. Allen and McConnell (1998) find that the equity market reacts positively to announcements of carve-outs if the cash is used to reduce debt. The market reacts neutrally if the cash is used for investment projects.

Summary and Conclusions

1   One firm can acquire another in several different ways. The three legal forms of acquisition are merger and consolidation, acquisition of equity and acquisition of assets. Mergers and consolidations are the least costly from a legal standpoint, but they require a vote of approval by the shareholders. Acquisition by equity does not require a shareholder vote and is usually done via a tender offer. However, it is difficult to obtain 100 per cent control with a tender offer. Acquisition of assets is comparatively costly because it requires more difficult transfer of asset ownership.

2   The synergy from an acquisition is defined as the value of the combined firm (V_{AB}) less the value of the two firms as separate entities (V_A and V_B):

$$\text{Synergy} = V_{AB} - (V_A + V_B)$$

The shareholders of the acquiring firm will gain if the synergy from the merger is greater than the premium.

3   The possible benefits of an acquisition come from the following:

   (a)   Revenue enhancement.

   (b)   Cost reduction.

   (c)   Lower taxes.

   (d)   Reduced capital requirements.

4   Shareholders may not benefit from a merger that is done only to achieve diversification or earnings growth. And the reduction in risk from a merger may actually help bondholders and hurt shareholders.

5   A merger is said to be friendly when the managers of the target support it. A merger is said to be hostile when the target managers do not support it. Some of the most colourful language of finance stems from defensive tactics in hostile takeover battles. *Poison pills*, *golden parachutes*, *crown jewels* and *greenmail* are terms that describe various anti-takeover tactics.

6   The empirical research on mergers and acquisitions is extensive. On average, the shareholders of acquired firms fare very well. The effect of mergers on acquiring shareholders is less clear.

7   In a *going-private* transaction, a buyout group, usually including the firm's management, buys all the shares of the other equityholders. The equity is no longer publicly traded. A *leveraged buyout* is a going-private transaction financed by extensive leverage.

Questions and Problems

CONCEPT

1   **The Basic Forms of Acquisitions**   Describe the three main types of acquisitions and provide a real life example of each type. Which type of merger do you think creates more value for shareholders? Explain.

2   **Synergy**   Explain the concept of synergy and provide examples of sources of synergy. Where does synergy come from? Is it possible that a merged company will not benefit from synergies? Discuss.

3   **M&A Waves**   Why do you think that M&A activity often clusters in time, causing M&A waves? What M&A waves can you identify from history? Are there any factors which you think are uniquely favourable to M&A activity today? Explain.

4   **Bad Reasons for Mergers**

   (a)   Many explanations and justifications are made by acquiring (and sometimes target) managers for a merger. Review these justifications and discuss whether they are good or bad for shareholders.

   (b)   An argument has been made that financial mergers are bad for shareholders because bondholders benefit from the reduction in risk. However, are there situations where a financial merger can be good for shareholders?

5 **Method of Payment in M&As**   Outline the two broad methods of payment in M&A transactions. What might determine the method of payment, and what impact does this have on both the acquiring and the target firm?

6 **NPV of a Merger**   Describe the main uncertainties that are involved in a merger analysis. Are mergers an ideal activity in which to use real option valuation? Discuss some of the ways in which a real option analysis could be used to value a merger.

7 **Merger Valuation in Practice**   Discuss the main steps that are involved in a merger analysis.

8 **Friendly versus Hostile Takeovers**   What types of actions might the management of a firm take to fight a hostile acquisition bid from an unwanted suitor? How do the target firm shareholders benefit from the defensive tactics of their management team? How are the target firm shareholders harmed by such actions? Explain.

9 **Defensive Tactics**   Review the various tactics that a target firm's management may use when trying to deter a hostile takeover attempt. For each tactic, provide a balanced discussion of whether they are good or bad for the target's shareholders.

10 **The Diary of a Takeover**   Compare and contrast a successful merger or acquisition with a failed one. What were the factors that contributed to the success and failure of the deal?

11 **Managerial Motives for Takeovers**   Outline the managerial motives for takeovers.

12 **Accounting for Mergers and Takeovers**   Explain the acquisition method of accounting for mergers and acquisitions. What effect does expensing merger costs have on the viability of a potential merger or acquisition?

13 **Divestitures**   Why would a firm wish to sell off its assets? If the sold divisions are so bad, why are buyers found for them?

REGULAR

14 **Mergers**   Indicate whether you think the following claims regarding takeovers are true or false. In each case, provide a brief explanation for your answer.

  (a) By merging competitors, takeovers have created monopolies that will raise product prices, reduce production and harm consumers.

  (b) Managers act in their own interests at times and in reality may not be answerable to shareholders. Takeovers may reflect runaway management.

  (c) In an efficient market, takeovers would not occur because market prices would reflect the true value of corporations. Thus, bidding firms would not be justified in paying premiums above market prices for target firms.

  (d) Traders and institutional investors, having extremely short time horizons, are influenced by their perceptions of what other market traders will be thinking of equity prospects and do not value takeovers based on fundamental factors. Thus, they will sell shares in target firms despite the true value of the firms.

  (e) Mergers are a way of avoiding taxes because they allow the acquiring firm to write up the value of the assets of the acquired firm.

  (f) Acquisitions analysis frequently focuses on the total value of the firms involved. An acquisition, however, will usually affect relative values of equities and bonds, as well as their total value.

15 **Merger Rationale**   During the financial crisis that engulfed most of Europe, two large banks, Lloyds TSB Group and HBOS, merged with each other to diversify risk. Is this a good or bad idea? Explain.

16 **Corporate Split**   In 2012 News Corp was rumoured to be considering selling off its newspaper line. What is the benefit of a spin-off of this type? Why would another company buy the assets?

17 **Shareholder Rights Plans**   Are shareholder rights plans good or bad for equity-holders? How do you think acquiring firms are able to get around them? What effect do you think the legal dubiety of shareholder rights plans in Europe has had on hostile takeovers?

18 **Merger and Taxes**   Many commentators have argued that differences in tax regulations, especially regarding mergers and acquisitions, have reduced the viability of this corporate activity. Do you agree with this? Explain.

19 **Economies of Scale**   Iberdrola, the Spanish electricity giant, has in recent years pursued an aggressive acquisition strategy throughout the world. Companies that have been acquired by the firm include Scottish Power (UK, 2006), Energy East (US, 2008), and Elektro (Brazil, 2011). During peak times each firm operates

at 100 per cent capacity and during off-peak times, the average usage of electricity amounts to about 60 per cent of total capacity per firm. The peak periods begin at 9:00 a.m. and 5:00 p.m. local time and last about 45 minutes. Explain why Iberdrola's acquisition strategy may make sense.

20 **Bid Offers** In 2012, a consortium of investors put forward a bid for Rangers Football Club plc. The bid details were as follows: £5,000,000 in cash; cancellation of an existing Rangers debt worth £8,000,000; an additional sum of £500,000 payable for the shares of the major owner; the assumption of the football debts (up to a maximum of aggregate amount of £1,000,000) owed by the company to Scottish football clubs; on Rangers Football Club successfully qualifying for the group stages of the UEFA Champions League competition to be held in seasons 2012/13 and/or 2013/14, an additional £500,000; and on Rangers Football Club successfully qualifying for the quarter final stages of either of the UEFA Champions League competition to be held in seasons 2012/13 or 2013/14, an additional £1,000,000. How much cash was actually offered? Why do you think the bid was structured in this way? What are the benefits to the bidders? What are the benefits to the sellers?

21 **Bid Offers**   Falcon plc and Thor plc have entered into a stock swap merger agreement whereby Falcon will pay a 30 per cent premium over Thor's pre-merger price of £30. If Falcon's pre-merger price was £40, what exchange ratio will Falcon need to offer?

22 **Calculating Synergy**   Assume that ABC plc is planning to offer £30 billion cash for all of the equity in XYZ plc. Based on recent market information, XYZ is worth £20 billion as an independent operation. If the merger makes economic sense for ABC, what is the minimum estimated value of the synergistic benefits from the merger?

23 **Balance Sheets for Mergers**   Consider the following pre-merger information about firm X and firm Y:

	Firm X	Firm Y
Total earnings (£)	74,000	35,000
Shares outstanding	21,000	10,000
Per share values:		
Market (£)	25	28
Book (£)	20	7

Assume that firm X acquires firm Y by paying cash for all the shares outstanding at a merger premium of £5 per share. Assuming that neither firm has any debt before or after the merger, calculate the total assets of the combined firm.

24 **Balance Sheets for Mergers**   Assume that the following balance sheets are stated at book value. Construct a post-merger balance sheet assuming that Reflection plc purchases Lhanger plc, and both sets of accounts are presented according to International Financial Reporting Standards.

REFLECTION plc			
	(£)		(£)
Current assets	12,000	Current liabilities	2,100
Non-current assets	17,000	Non-current liabilities	5,900
		Equity	21,000
Total	29,000	Total	29,000

LHANGER plc			
	(£)		(£)
Current assets	6,400	Current liabilities	1,600
Non-current assets	2,600	Non-current liabilities	2,900
		Equity	4,500
Total	9,000	Total	9,000

The fair market value of Lhangers's non-current assets is £10,000 versus the £2,600 book value shown. Reflection pays £18,000 for Lhanger and raises the needed funds through an issue of long-term debt. Construct the post-merger balance sheet.

25 Balance Sheets for Mergers Silver Enterprises has acquired All Gold Mining in a merger transaction. Construct the balance sheet for the new corporation. The following balance sheets represent the pre-merger book values for both firms:

SILVER ENTERPRISES			
	(£)		(£)
Current assets	6,600	Current liabilities	4,800
Goodwill	800	Non-current liabilities	5,900
Net non-current assets	7,900	Equity	4,600
Total	15,300	Total	15,300

ALL GOLD MINING			
	(£)		(£)
Current assets	1,100	Current liabilities	900
Goodwill	350	Non-current liabilities	0
Non-current assets	2,800	Equity	3,350
Total	4,250	Total	4,250

The market value of All Gold Mining's non-current assets (excluding goodwill) is £5,800; the market values for current assets and goodwill are the same as the book values. Assume that Silver Enterprises issued £8,400 in new long-term debt to finance the acquisition.

26 Cash versus Equity Payment Fresnillo plc, the silver and gold mining firm, is analysing the possible acquisition of Weir Group plc, the Scottish-based engineering firm. Assume both firms have no debt. Fresnillo believes the acquisition will increase its total after-tax annual cash flows by £183 million indefinitely. The current market value of Weir Group is £1.3 billion and that of Fresnillo is £2.9 billion. The appropriate discount rate for the incremental cash flows is 12 per cent. Fresnillo is trying to decide whether it should offer 50 per cent of its equity or £1.6 billion in cash to Weir Group's shareholders.

(a) What is the cost of each alternative?

(b) What is the NPV of each alternative?

(c) Which alternative should Fresnillo choose?

27 EPS, PE and Mergers The shareholders of Flannery SA have voted in favour of a buyout offer from Stultz Corporation. Information about each firm is given here:

	Flannery	Stultz
Price–earnings ratio	5.25	21
Shares outstanding	60,000	180,000
Earnings	£300,000	£675,000

Flannery's shareholders will receive one share of Stultz equity for every three shares they hold in Flannery.

(a) What will the EPS of Stultz be after the merger? What will the PE ratio be if the NPV of the acquisition is zero?

(b) What must Stultz feel is the value of the synergy between these two firms? Explain how your answer can be reconciled with the decision to go ahead with the takeover.

28 Merger Rationale Ziff Electrics (ZE) is a public utility that provides electricity to the whole Yorkshire region. Recent events at its Mile-High Nuclear Station have been discouraging. Several shareholders have expressed concern over last year's financial statements.

Income Statement Last Year (in £ millions)		Balance Sheet End of Year (in £ millions)	
Revenue	110	Assets	400
Fuel	50	Debt	300
Other expenses	30	Equity	100
Interest	30		
Net income	0		

Recently, a wealthy group of individuals has offered to purchase half of ZE's assets at fair market price. Management recommends that this offer be accepted because 'We believe our expertise in the energy industry can be better exploited by ZE if we sell our electricity generating and transmission assets and enter the telecommunication business. Although telecommunications is a riskier business than providing electricity as a public utility, it is also potentially very profitable.'

Should the management approve this transaction? Why or why not?

29 **Cash versus Equity as Payment** Consider the following pre-merger information about a bidding firm (firm B) and a target firm (firm T). Assume that both firms have no debt outstanding.

	Firm B	Firm T
Shares outstanding	1,500	900
Price per share	£34	£24

Firm B has estimated that the value of the synergistic benefits from acquiring firm T is £3,000.

(a) If firm T is willing to be acquired for £27 per share in cash, what is the NPV of the merger?

(b) What will the price per share of the merged firm be assuming the conditions in (a)?

(c) In part (a), what is the merger premium?

(d) Suppose firm T is agreeable to a merger by an exchange of equity. If B offers three of its shares for every one of T's shares, what will the price per share of the merged firm be?

(e) What is the NPV of the merger assuming the conditions in (d)?

30 **Cash versus Equity as Payment** In Problem 29, are the shareholders of firm T better off with the cash offer or the equity offer? At what exchange ratio of B shares to T shares would the shareholders in T be indifferent between the two offers?

31 **Effects of an Equity Exchange** Consider the following pre-merger information about firm A and firm B:

	Firm A	Firm B
Total earnings (DKr)	900	600
Shares outstanding	550	220
Price per share (DKr)	40	15

Assume that firm A acquires firm B via an exchange of equity at a price of DKr20 for each share of B's equity. Both A and B have no debt outstanding.

(a) What will the earnings per share, EPS, of firm A be after the merger?

(b) What will firm A's price per share be after the merger if the market incorrectly analyses this reported earnings growth (that is, the price–earnings ratio does not change)?

(c) What will the price–earnings ratio of the post-merger firm be if the market correctly analyses the transaction?

(d) If there are no synergy gains, what will the share price of A be after the merger? What will the price–earnings ratio be? What does your answer for the share price tell you about the amount A bid for B? Was it too high? Too low? Explain.

32 **Merger NPV** Show that the NPV of a merger can be expressed as the value of the synergistic benefits, ΔV, less the merger premium.

33 **Merger NPV** Tazza is analysing the possible acquisition of Bichiery. Neither firm has debt. The forecasts of Tazza show that the purchases would increase its annual after-tax cash flow by £1.3 million indefinitely. The current market value of Bichiery is £500 million. The current market value of Tazza is £1.5 billion. The appropriate discount rate for the incremental cash flows is 8 per cent. Tazza is trying to decide whether it would offer 40 per cent of its equity or £600 million in cash to Bichiery.

(a) What is the synergy from the merger?

(b) What is the value of Bichiery to Tazza?

(c) What is the cost to Tazza of the share offer?

(d) What is the NPV to Tazza of each alternative?

(e) What alternative should Tazza use?

34 Merger NPV Farrods PLC has a market value of £800 million and 35 million shares outstanding. Redridge department store has a market value of £300 million and 25 million shares outstanding. Farrods is contemplating acquiring Redridge. Farrods' CFO concludes that the combined firm with synergy will be worth £1.5 billion, and Redridge can be acquired at a premium of £200 million.

(a) If Farrods offers 20 million shares of its equity in exchange for the 25 million shares of Redridge, what will the equity price of Farrods be after the acquisition?

(b) What exchange ratio between the two equities would make the value of an equity offer equivalent to a cash offer of £350 million?

35 Mergers and Shareholder Value Gentley plc and Rolls Manufacturing are considering a merger. The possible states of the economy and each company's value in that state are shown here:

State	Probability	Gentley	Rolls
Boom	0.45	£300,000	£260,000
Recession	0.55	£110,000	£ 80,000

Gentley currently has a bond issue outstanding with a face value of £140,000. Rolls is an all equity company.

(a) What is the value of each company before the merger?

(b) What are the values of each company's debt and equity before the merger?

(c) If the companies continue to operate separately, what are the total value of the companies, the total value of the equity, and the total value of the debt?

(d) What would be the value of the merged company? What would be the value of the merged company's debt and equity?

(e) Is there a transfer of wealth in this case? Why?

(f) Suppose that the face value of Gentley's debt was £100,000. Would this affect the transfer of wealth?

CHALLENGE

36 Calculating NPV Plant AG is considering making an offer to purchase Palmer AG. Plant's vice president of finance has collected the following information:

	Plant	Palmer
Price–earnings ratio	12.5	9
Shares outstanding	1,000,000	550,000
Earnings	€2,000,000	€580,000
Dividends	€600,000	€290,000

Plant also knows that securities analysts expect the earnings and dividends of Palmer to grow at a constant rate of 5 per cent each year. Plant management believes that the acquisition of Palmer will provide the firm with some economies of scale that will increase this growth rate to 7 per cent per year.

(a) What is the value of Palmer to Plant?

(b) What would Plant's gain be from this acquisition?

(c) If Plant were to offer €18 in cash for each share of Palmer, what would the NPV of the acquisition be?

(d) What is the most Plant should be willing to pay in cash per share for the equity of Palmer?

(e) If Plant were to offer 100,000 of its shares in exchange for the outstanding equity of Palmer, what would the NPV be?

(f) Should the acquisition be attempted? If so, should it be as in (c) or as in (e)?

(g) Plant's outside financial consultants think that the 7 per cent growth rate is too optimistic and a 6 per cent rate is more realistic. How does this change your previous answers?

37 Mergers and Shareholder Value The Chocolate Ice Cream Company and the Vanilla Ice Cream Company have agreed to merge and form Fudge Swirl Consolidated. Both companies are exactly alike except that they are located in different towns. The end-of-period value of each firm is determined by the weather, as shown below. There will be no synergy to the merger.

State	Probability	Value (£)
Rainy	0.1	100,000
Warm	0.4	200,000
Hot	0.5	400,000

The weather conditions in each town are independent of those in the other. Furthermore, each company has an outstanding debt claim of £200,000. Assume that no premiums are paid in the merger.

(a) What are the possible values of the combined company?

(b) What are the possible values of end-of-period debt values and equity values after the merger?

(c) Show that the bondholders are better off and the equityholders are worse off in the combined firm than they would have been if the firms had remained separate.

Exam Question (45 minutes)

1   Linfrae plc is a computer software development firm and is considering a hostile takeover of Jaffikake plc, a software distribution firm. Linfrae has been advised by its investment bankers that a combined development and distribution firm would lead to annual cost savings of £7 million for the foreseeable future (in perpetuity). Both firms are financed entirely by equity. Linfrae has 29 million shares outstanding at a price of £4.70 each whereas Jaffikake has 10 million shares outstanding at a price of £10.07 each. The investment bank that is advising Linfrae suggests that an initial bid with a premium of 33 per cent would be sufficiently high as to persuade Jaffikake's shareholders to sell their holdings to Linfrae. Linfrae has enough cash reserves to fund the takeover bid. If the cost of capital of the combined firm is 20 per cent, evaluate the proposed takeover from the perspective of Linfrae's shareholders. (30 marks)

2   It has been proposed that Linfrae plc should bid for Jaffikake using equity instead of cash. Linfrae's investment bankers advise Linfrae to offer three shares of Linfrae for every one share of Jaffikake. What is the percentage premium offered to Jaffikake's shareholders? Evaluate the takeover from the perspective of Linfrae's shareholders. (30 marks)

3   Explain what is meant by vertical, horizontal and conglomerate mergers. Review the motives for undertaking each type of merger and provide real examples of each case. (40 marks)

Mini Case

The Birdie Golf–Hybrid Golf Merger

Birdie Golf has been in merger talks with Hybrid Golf Company for the past 6 months. After several rounds of negotiations, the offer under discussion is a cash offer of €550 million for Hybrid Golf. Both companies have niche markets in the golf club industry, and the companies believe a merger will result in significant synergies due to economies of scale in manufacturing and marketing, as well as significant savings in general and administrative expenses.

Bryce Bichon, the financial officer for Birdie, has been instrumental in the merger negotiations. Bryce has prepared the following pro forma financial statements for Hybrid Golf assuming the merger takes place. The financial statements include all synergistic benefits from the merger:

	2010 (€)	2011 (€)	2012 (€)	2013 (€)	2014 (€)
Sales	800,000,000	900,000,000	1,000,000,000	1,125,000,000	1,250,000,000
Productions costs	562,000,000	630,000,000	700,000,000	790,000,000	875,000,000
Depreciation	75,000,000	80,000,000	82,000,000	83,000,000	83,000,000
Other expenses	80,000,000	90,000,000	100,000,000	113,000,000	125,000,000
EBIT	83,000,000	100,000,000	118,000,000	139,000,000	167,000,000
Interest	19,000,000	22,000,000	24,000,000	25,000,000	27,000,000

	2010 (€)	2011 (€)	2012 (€)	2013 (€)	2014 (€)
Taxable income	64,000,000	78,000,000	94,000,000	114,000,000	140,000,000
Taxes (40%)	25,600,000	31,200,000	37,600,000	45,600,000	56,000,000
Net income	38,400,000	46,800,000	56,400,000	68,400,000	84,000,000

Bryce is also aware that the Hybrid Golf division will require investments each year for continuing operations, along with sources of financing. The following table outlines the required investments and sources of financing:

	2010 (€)	2011 (€)	2012 (€)	2013 (€)	2014 (€)
Investments:					
Net working capital	20,000,000	25,000,000	25,000,000	30,000,000	30,000,000
Non-current assets	15,000,000	25,000,000	18,000,000	12,000,000	7,000,000
Total	35,000,000	50,000,000	43,000,000	42,000,000	37,000,000
Sources of financing:					
New debt	35,000,000	16,000,000	16,000,000	15,000,000	12,000,000
Profit retention	0	34,000,000	27,000,000	27,000,000	25,000,000
Total	35,000,000	50,000,000	43,000,000	42,000,000	37,000,000

The management of Birdie Golf feels that the capital structure at Hybrid Golf is not optimal. If the merger takes place, Hybrid Golf will immediately increase its leverage with a €110 million debt issue, which would be followed by a €150 million dividend payment to Birdie Golf. This will increase Hybrid's debt-to-equity ratio from 0.50 to 1.00. Birdie Golf will also be able to use a €25 million tax loss carry-forward in 2011 and 2012 from Hybrid Golf's previous operations. The total value of Hybrid Golf is expected to be €900 million in 5 years, and the company will have €300 million in debt at that time.

Equity in Birdie Golf currently sells for €94 per share, and the company has 18 million shares of equity outstanding. Hybrid Golf has 8 million shares of equity outstanding. Both companies can borrow at an 8 per cent interest rate. The risk-free rate is 6 per cent, and the expected return on the market is 13 per cent. Bryce believes the current cost of capital for Birdie Golf is 11 per cent. The beta for Hybrid Golf equity at its current capital structure is 1.30.

Bryce has asked you to analyse the financial aspects of the potential merger. Specifically, he has asked you to answer the following questions:

1 Suppose Hybrid shareholders will agree to a merger price of €68.75 per share. Should Birdie proceed with the merger?

2 What is the highest price per share that Birdie should be willing to pay for Hybrid?

3 Suppose Birdie is unwilling to pay cash for the merger but will consider an equity exchange. What exchange ratio would make the merger terms equivalent to the original merger price of €68.75 per share?

4 What is the highest exchange ratio Birdie would be willing to pay and still undertake the merger?

Practical Case Study

The HBOS–Lloyds TSB merger was one of the biggest in European banking history. Both banks had been hit hard by the global banking crisis in 2008 and the British government strongly encouraged them to merge in order to be safe enough to ride out the forthcoming recession. Both companies argued that there would be cost savings and the merger would be good for both sets of shareholders. However, within months of the merger, the British government had to bail out the new Lloyds Banking Group and effectively nationalize it.

Carry out your own research into the merger and use the merger techniques in this chapter to ascertain, from an *ex ante* perspective, whether the merger was good for either set of shareholders. Write a brief report on your analysis.

Relevant Accounting Standards

The main accounting standard for mergers and acquisitions is IFRS 3 *Business Combinations*. For restructuring activities, the relevant standard is IAS 37 *Provisions, Contingent Liabilities, and Contingent Assets*.

References

Allen, J. and J. McConnell (1998) 'Equity Carve-outs and Managerial Discretion', *The Journal of Finance*, Vol. 53, 163–186.

Andrade, G., M. Mitchell and E. Stafford (2001) 'New Evidence and Perspectives on Mergers', *Journal of Economic Perspectives*, Vol. 15, No. 2, 103–120.

Antoniou, A., P. Arbour and H. Zhang (2008) 'How Much Is too Much? Are Merger Premiums too High?', *European Financial Management*, Vol. 14, No. 2, 268–287.

Campa, J.M. and I. Hernando (2004) 'Shareholder Value Creation in European M&As', *European Financial Management*, Vol. 10, 47–81.

Datta, S., M. Iskandar-Datta and K. Raman (2001) 'Executive Compensation and Corporate Acquisition Decisions', *The Journal of Finance*, Vol. 56, 2299–2336.

Doukas, J. and O.B. Kan (2006) 'Does Global Diversification Destroy Firm Value?', *Journal of International Business Studies*, Vol. 37, 352–371.

Hann, R.N., M. Ogneva and O. Ozbas (2013) 'Corporate Diversification and the Cost of Capital', *The Journal of Finance*, Vol. 68, No. 5, 1961–1999.

Harford, J. (1999) 'Corporate Cash Reserves and Acquisitions', *The Journal of Finance*, Vol. 54, 1969–1997.

Harford, J., M. Humphery-Jenner and R. Powell (2012) 'The Sources of Value Destruction in Acquisitions by Entrenched Managers', *Journal of Financial Economics*, Vol. 106, No. 2, 247–261.

Heron, R. and E. Lie (2002) 'Operating Performance and the Method of Payment in Takeovers', *Journal of Financial and Quantitative Analysis*, Vol. 37, 137–155.

Jensen, M.C. and R.S. Ruback (1983) 'The Market for Corporate Control: The Scientific Evidence', *Journal of Financial Economics*, Vol. 11, 5–50.

Kaplan, S. and M. Weisbach (1992) 'The Success of Acquisitions: Evidence from Divestitures', *The Journal of Finance*, Vol. 47, 107–138.

Malmendier, U. and G. Tate (2008) 'Who Makes Acquisitions? CEO Overconfidence and the Market's Reaction', *Journal of Financial Economics*, Vol. 89, 20–43.

Michaely, R. and W. Shaw (1995) 'The Choice of Going Public: Spinoffs vs. Carveouts', *Financial Management*, Vol. 24, No. 3, 5–21.

Moeller, S., F. Schlingemann and R. Stulz (2005) 'Wealth Destruction on a Massive Scale? A Study of Acquiring-Firm Returns in the Recent Merger Wave', *The Journal of Finance*, Vol. 60, 757–780.

Myers, S. and N. Majluf (1984) 'Corporate Financing and Investment Decisions When Firms Have Information that Investors Do Not Have', *Journal of Financial Economics*, Vol. 13, No. 2, 187–221.

Porter, M. (1998) *Competitive Advantage* (New York: Free Press).

Wulf, J. (2004) 'Do CEOs in Mergers Trade Power for Premium? Evidence from "Mergers of Equals"', *Journal of Law, Economics, and Organization*, Vol. 20, 60–101.

Additional Reading

As the size of this chapter attests, the study of mergers, acquisitions and corporate restructuring is huge. Below is a list of recent papers in the area. Naturally, the categorization of papers is not mutually exclusive and papers do overlap categories. However, hopefully the groupings will aid the reading effort.

The Merger, Acquisition and Corporate Restructuring Process

1   Aktas, N., E. De Bodt and R. Roll (2013) 'MicroHoo: Deal Failure, Industry Rivalry, and Sources of Overbidding', *Journal of Corporate Finance*, Vol. 19, 20–35.

2   Aktas, N., E. De Bodt and R. Roll (2013) 'Learning from Repetitive Acquisitions: Evidence from the Time between Deals', *Journal of Financial Economics*, Vol. 108, No. 1, 99–117.

3   Alexandridis, G., D. Petmezas and N.G. Travlos (2010) 'Gains from Mergers and Acquisitions Around the World: New Evidence', *Financial Management*, Vol. 39, No. 4, 1671–1695.

4   Antoniou, A., P. Arbour and H. Zhao (2008) 'How Much Is too Much: Are Merger Premiums too High?', *European Financial Management*, Vol. 14, No. 2, 268–287. **UK.**

5 Baker, M., X. Pan and J. Wurgler (2012) 'The Effect of Reference Point Prices on Mergers and Acquisitions', *Journal of Financial Economics*, Vol. 106, No. 1, 49–71.

6 Betton, S., B.E. Eckbo and K.S. Thorburn (2009) 'Merger Negotiations and the Toehold Puzzle', *Journal of Financial Economics*, Vol. 91, No. 2, 158–178. **US**.

7 Boone, A.L. and J.H. Mulherin (2007) 'How Are Firms Sold?', *The Journal of Finance*, Vol. 62, No. 2, 847–875. **US**.

8 Bouwman, C., K. Fuller and A. Nain (2009) 'Market Valuation and Acquisition Quality: Empirical Evidence', *Review of Financial Studies*, Vol. 22, No. 2, 633–679. **US.**

9 Deng, X., J.K. Kang and B.S. Low (2013) 'Corporate Social Responsibility and Stakeholder Value Maximization: Evidence from Mergers', *Journal of Financial Economics*, Vol. 110, No. 1, 87–109.

10 Dittmann, I., E. Maug and C. Schneider (2008) 'How Preussag Became TUI: A Clinical Study of Institutional Blockholders and Restructuring in Europe', *Financial Management*, Vol. 37, No. 3, 571–598. **Germany**.

11 Duchin, R. and B. Schmidt (2013) 'Riding the Merger Wave: Uncertainty, Reduced Monitoring, and Bad Acquisitions', *Journal of Financial Economics*, Vol. 107, No. 1, 69–88.

12 Eckbo, B.E. (2009) 'Bidding Strategies and Takeover Premiums: A Review', *Journal of Corporate Finance*, Vol. 15, No. 1, 10–29. **International.**

13 Edmans, A., I. Goldstein and W. Jiang (2012) 'The Real Effects of Financial Markets: The Impact of Prices on Takeovers', *The Journal of Finance*, Vol. 67, No. 3, 933–971.

14 Ekkayokkaya, M., P. Holmes and K. Paudyal (2009) 'The Euro and the Changing Face of European Banking: Evidence from Mergers and Acquisitions', *European Financial Management*, Vol. 15, No. 2, 451–476. **Europe**.

15 Erel, I., R.C. Liao and M.S. Weisbach (2012) 'Determinants of Cross-Border Mergers and Acquisitions', *The Journal of Finance*, Vol. 67, No. 3, 1045–1082.

16 Erel, I., Y. Jang and M.S. Weisbach (2015) 'Do Acquisitions Relieve Target Firms' Financial Constraints?', *The Journal of Finance*, Vol. 70, No. 1, 289–328.

17 Fu, F., L. Lin and M.S. Officer (2013) 'Acquisitions Driven by Stock Overvaluation: Are They Good Deals?', *Journal of Financial Economics*, Vol. 109, No. 1, 24–39.

18 Faccio, M. and R. Masulis (2005) 'The Choice of Payment Method in European Mergers and Acquisitions', *The Journal of Finance*, Vol. 60, No. 3, 1345–1388. **Europe.**

19 Ferreira, M.A., M. Massa and P. Matos (2010) 'Shareholders at the Gate? Institutional Investors and Cross-Border Mergers and Acquisitions', *Review of Financial Studies*, Vol. 23, No. 2, 601–644.

20 Di Giuli, A. (2013) 'The Effect of Stock Misvaluation and Investment Opportunities on the Method of Payment in Mergers', *Journal of Corporate Finance*, Vol. 21, 196–215.

21 Hann, R.N., M. Ogneva and O. Ozbas (2013) 'Corporate Diversification and the Cost of Capital', *The Journal of Finance*, Vol. 68, No. 5, 1961–1999.

22 Harford, J. (2005) 'What Drives Merger Waves?', *Journal of Financial Economics*, Vol. 77, No. 3, 529–560. **US**.

23 Hoberg, G. and G. Phillips (2010) 'Product Market Synergies and Competition in Mergers and Acquisitions: A Text-Based Analysis', *Review of Financial Studies*, Vol. 23, No. 10, 3773–3811.

24 Hodgkinson, L. and G.H. Partington (2008) 'The Motivation for Takeovers in the UK', *Journal of Business Finance and Accounting*, Vol. 35, Nos. 1 and 2, 102–126. **UK.**

25 Holmen, M. and J. Knopf (2004) 'Minority Shareholder Protection and Private Benefits of Control for Swedish Mergers', *Journal of Financial and Quantitative Analysis*, Vol. 39, 167–191.

26 Kisgen, D.J., J. Qian and W. Song (2009) 'Are Fairness Opinions Fair? The Case of Mergers and Acquisitions', *Journal of Financial Economics*, Vol. 91, No. 2, 179–207.

27 Laeven, L. and R. Levine (2007) 'Is There a Diversification Discount in Financial Conglomerates?', *Journal of Financial Economics*, Vol. 85, No. 2, 331–367. **US**.

28 Lambrecht, B.M. and S.C. Myers (2007) 'A Theory of Takeovers and Disinvestment', *The Journal of Finance*, Vol. 62, No. 2, 809–845. **Theoretical Paper.**

29 Luo, Y. (2005) 'Do Insiders Learn from Outsiders? Evidence from Mergers and Acquisitions', *The Journal of Finance*, Vol. 60, No. 3, 1951–1982. **US**.

30 Maksimovic, V. and G. Phillips (2008) 'The Industry Life Cycle, Acquisitions and Investment: Does Firm Organisation Matter?', *The Journal of Finance*, Vol. 62, No. 2, 673–708. **US**.

31 Martynova, M. and L. Renneboog (2008) 'A Century of Corporate Takeovers: What Have We Learned and Where Do We Stand?', *Journal of Banking and Finance*, Vol. 32, No. 10, 2148–2177.

32 Martynova, M. and L. Renneboog (2009) 'What Determines the Financing Decision in Corporate Takeovers: Cost of Capital, Agency Problems, or the Means of Payment?', *Journal of Corporate Finance*, Vol. 15, No. 3, 290–315. **Europe.**

33 Rhodes-Kropf, M., D.T. Robinson and S. Viswanathan (2005) 'Valuation Waves and Merger Activity: The Empirical Evidence', *Journal of Financial Economics*, Vol. 77, No. 3, 561–603. **US**.

34 Rossi, S., and P.F. Volpin (2005) 'Cross-Country Determinants of Mergers and Acquisitions', *Journal of Financial Economics*, Vol. 74, No. 2, 277–304. **International.**

35 Serdar Dinc, I. and I. Erel (2013) 'Economic Nationalism in Mergers and Acquisitions', *The Journal of Finance*, Vol. 68, No. 6, 2471–2514.

36 Veld, C. and Y.V. Veld-Merkoulova (2004) 'Do Spin-offs Really Create Value? The European Case', *Journal of Banking and Finance*, Vol. 28, No. 5, 1111–1135. **Europe.**

37 Wright, M., L. Renneboog, T. Simons and L. Scholes (2006) 'Leveraged Buyouts in the UK and Continental Europe: Retrospect and Prospect', *Journal of Applied Corporate Finance*, Vol. 18, No. 3, 38–55. **Europe.**

Pre-restructuring

38 Atanassov, J. and E.H. Kim (2009) 'Labor and Corporate Governance: International Evidence from Restructuring Decisions', *The Journal of Finance*, Vol. 64, No. 1, 341–374.

39 Botsari, A. and G. Meeks (2008) 'Do Acquirers Manage Earnings Prior to a Share for Share Bid?', *Journal of Business Finance and Accounting*, Vol. 35, Nos. 5 and 6, 633–670. **UK.**

40 Dong, M., D. Hirshleifer, S. Richardson and S.H. Teoh (2006) 'Does Investor Mis-valuation Drive the Takeover Market?', *The Journal of Finance*, Vol. 61, No. 2, 725–762. **US.**

41 Field, L.C. and J.M. Karpoff (2002) 'Takeover Defenses of IPO Firms', *The Journal of Finance*, Vol. 57, No. 5, 1857–1889. **US.**

42 Huang, Q., F. Jiang, E. Lie and Ke Yang (2014) 'The Role of Investment Banker Directors in M&A', *Journal of Financial Economics*, Vol. 112, No. 2, 269–286.

43 Jenkinson, T. and H. Jones (2004) 'Bids and Allocations in European IPO Bookbuilding', *The Journal of Finance*, Vol. 59, No. 5, 2309–2338. **Europe.**

44 Kisgen, D.J., J. Qian and W. Song (2009) 'Are Fairness Opinions Fair? The Case of Mergers and Acquisitions', *Journal of Financial Economics*, Vol. 91, No. 2, 179–207. **US.**

45 Liu, B. and J.J. McConnell (2013) 'The Role of the Media in Corporate Governance: Do the Media Influence Managers' Capital Allocation Decisions?' *Journal of Financial Economics*, Vol. 110, No. 1, 1–17.

46 Veld, C. and Y.V. Veld-Merkoulova (2008) 'An Empirical Analysis of the Stockholder-Bondholder Conflict in Corporate Spin-Offs', *Financial Management*, Vol. 37, No. 1, 103–124. **US.**

Post-restructuring

47 Alexandridis, G., K.P. Fuller, L. Terhaar and N.G. Travlos (2013) 'Deal Size, Acquisition Premia and Shareholder Gains', *Journal of Corporate Finance*, Vol. 20, 1–13.

48 Custódio, C. and D. Metzger (2013) 'How Do CEOs Matter? The Effect of Industry Expertise on Acquisition Returns', *Review of Financial Studies*, Vol. 26, No. 8, 2008–2047.

49 Devos, E., P. Kadapakkam and S. Krishnamurthy (2009) 'How do Mergers Create Value? A Comparison of Taxes, Market Power, and Efficiency Improvements as Explanations for Synergies', *Review of Financial Studies*, Vol. 22, No. 3, 1179–1211. **US.**

50 Draper, P. and K. Paudyal (2008) 'Information Asymmetry and Bidders' Gains', *Journal of Business Finance and Accounting*, Vol. 35, Nos. 3 and 4, 376–405. **UK.**

51 Hagendorff, J., M. Collins and K. Keasey (2008) 'Investor Protection and the Value Effects of Bank Merger Announcements in Europe and the US', *Journal of Banking and Finance*, Vol. 32, No. 7, 1333–1348. **Europe.**

52 Harford, J., M. Humphery-Jenner and R. Powell (2012) 'The Sources of Value Destruction in Acquisitions by Entrenched Managers', *Journal of Financial Economics*, Vol. 106, No. 2, 247–261.

53 Harford, J. and R.J. Schonlau (2013) 'Does the Director Labor Market Offer Ex Post Settling-up for CEOs? The Case of Acquisitions', *Journal of Financial Economics*, Vol. 110, No. 1, 18–36.

54 Li, X. (2013) 'Productivity, Restructuring, and the Gains from Takeovers', *Journal of Financial Economics*, Vol. 109, No. 1, 250–271.

55 Masulis, R.W., C. Wang and F. Xie (2007) 'Corporate Governance and Acquirer Returns', *The Journal of Finance*, Vol. 62, No. 4, 1851–1889. **US.**

56 Moeller, S.B., F.P. Schlingemann and R.M. Stulz (2005) 'Wealth Destruction on a Massive Scale? A Study of Acquiring-Firm Returns in the Recent Merger Wave', *The Journal of Finance*, Vol. 60, No. 2, 757–782. **US.**

57 Paul, D.L. (2007) 'Board Composition and Corrective Action: Evidence from Corporate Responses to Bad Acquisition Bids', *Journal of Financial and Quantitative Analysis*, Vol. 42, No. 3, 759–78. **US.**

58 Rajan, R., H. Servaes and L. Zingales (2000) 'The Cost of Diversity: The Diversification Discount and Inefficient Investment', *The Journal of Finance*, Vol. 55, No. 1, 35–80. **US.**

59 Renneboog, L. and P.G. Szilagyi (2008) 'Corporate Structuring and Bondholder Wealth', *European Financial Management*, Vol. 14, No. 4, 792–819.

60 Santalo, J. and M. Becerra (2008) 'Competition from Specialized Firms and the Diversification–Performance Linkage', *The Journal of Finance*, Vol. 62, No. 2, 851–883. **US.**

61 Sheen, A. (2014) 'The Real Product Market Impact of Mergers', *The Journal of Finance*, Vol. 69, 2651–2688.

62 Wang, C. and F. Xie (2009) 'Corporate Governance Transfer and Synergistic Gains from Mergers and Acquisitions', *Review of Financial Studies*, Vol. 22, No. 2, 829–858. **US.**

Endnotes

1 Mergers between corporations require compliance with government laws. In virtually all countries, the shareholders of each corporation must give their assent.

2 *Control* can usually be defined as having a majority vote on the board of directors.

3 Every country's tax system is different and almost always complex. The best place to find up-to-date information is by visiting the website of the country's tax authority. A good site with summary information on many countries' tax system is www.worldwide-tax.com.

4 Although diversification is most easily explained by considering equities in different industries, the key is really that the returns on the two equities are less than perfectly correlated – a relationship that should occur even for equities in the same industry.

5 A dividend is taxable to all tax-paying recipients. A repurchase creates a tax liability only for those who choose to sell (and do so at a profit).

6 The situation is actually a little more complex: the target's shareholders must pay taxes on their capital gains. These shareholders will likely demand a premium from the acquirer to offset this tax.

7 This ratio implies a fair exchange because a share of Regional is selling for 40 per cent (= €10/€25) of the price of a share of Global.

8 In fact, a number of scholars have argued that diversification can *reduce* firm value by weakening corporate focus, a point to be developed in a later section of this chapter.

9 The analysis will be essentially the same if new equity is issued. However, the analysis will differ if new debt is issued to fund the acquisition because of the tax shield to debt. An adjusted present value (APV) approach would be necessary here.

10 The basic theoretical ideas are presented in Myers and Majluf (1984).

11 For example, see Andrade et al. (2001); and Heron and Lie (2002).

12 FT.com, 'AbbVie lays out case for Shire takeover', 25 June 2015.

13 Taken from Andrade et al. (2001), Table 1.

14 Antoniou et al. (2008).

15 Datta et al. (2001).

16 From Harford (1999), p. 1969.

17 However, as stated earlier, managers may resist takeovers to raise the offer price, not to prevent the merger.

CHAPTER 29

Financial Distress

The global economy is continually changing and what seems certain today can quickly become a major risk factor tomorrow. Oil is a very good example that has caused many firms to become financially distressed. For many years, economies and companies lived with an oil price of at least $100 per barrel. This allowed financial managers to factor costs and revenues on the basis of this value. However, in 2015, the oil price collapsed to $50 a barrel resulting in significant financial difficulties for companies that generate revenues from the commodity. This led to cancellations of major strategic investments, redundancies, dividend cancellations and a wave of mergers and acquisitions across the oil-related industries.

A firm that does not generate enough cash flow to make a contractually required payment, such as an interest payment, will experience financial distress. A firm that defaults on a required payment may be forced to liquidate its assets. More often, a defaulting firm will reorganize its financial structure. Financial restructuring involves replacing old financial claims with new ones and takes place with private workouts or legal bankruptcy. Private workouts are voluntary arrangements to restructure a company's debt, such as postponing a payment or reducing the size of the payment. If a private workout is not possible, formal bankruptcy is usually required.

KEY NOTATION

Z	Altman's Z-Score

29.1   What Is Financial Distress?

Financial distress is surprisingly hard to define precisely. This is true partly because of the variety of events befalling firms under financial distress. The list of events is almost endless, but here are some examples:

- Dividend reductions
- Plant closings
- Losses
- Layoffs
- CEO resignation
- Plummeting share prices.

Financial distress is a situation where a firm's operating cash flows are not sufficient to satisfy current obligations (such as trade credits or interest expenses) and the firm is forced to take corrective action (**Chapter 16** discusses the costs of financial distress from taking on too much debt).[1] Financial distress may lead a firm to default on a contract, and it may involve financial restructuring between the firm, its creditors and its equity investors. Usually the firm is forced to take actions that it would not have taken if it had sufficient cash flow.

Chapter 16
Page 428

Our definition of financial distress can be expanded somewhat by linking it to insolvency. Insolvency is defined in *Black's Law Dictionary* as:[2]

> Inability to pay one's debts; lack of means of paying one's debts. Such a condition of a woman's (or man's) assets and liability that the former made immediately available would be insufficient to discharge the latter.

This definition has two general themes: value and flows.[3] These two ways of thinking about insolvency are depicted in Figure 29.1. Value-based insolvency occurs when a firm has negative net worth, so the value of assets is less

Figure 29.1   Insolvency

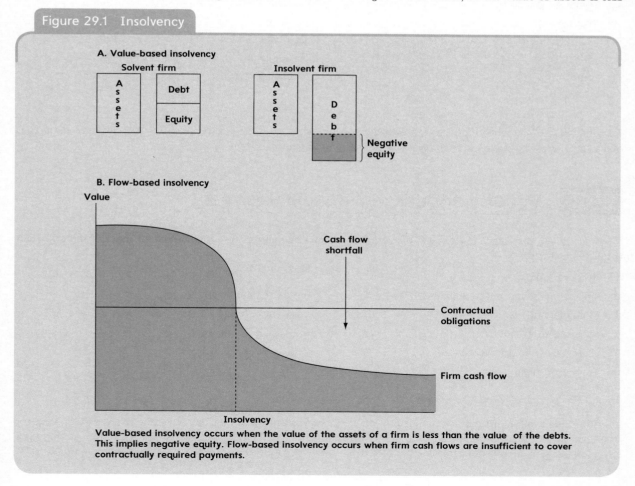

Value-based insolvency occurs when the value of the assets of a firm is less than the value of the debts. This implies negative equity. Flow-based insolvency occurs when firm cash flows are insufficient to cover contractually required payments.

Table 29.1 Large Corporate Bankruptcies Since 2001

Company	Country	Year
Energy Future Holdings	United States	2014
Cengage Learning	United States	2013
AMR (American Airlines)	United States	2011
MF Global	United States	2011
Chrysler	United States	2009
SsangYong Motor Company	South Korea	2009
Nortel Networks	United States	2009
General Motors	United States	2009
CIT Group	United States	2009
Washington Mutual	United States	2008
Sterling Airlines	Denmark	2008
Sanlu Group	China	2008
Lehman Brothers Holdings Inc.	United States	2008
Kaupthing Bank	Iceland	2008
Hypo Real Estate	Germany	2008
Yukos	Russia	2006
MG Rover	United Kingdom	2005
Delta Air Lines, Inc.	United States	2005
Parmalat	Italy	2004
Worldcom Inc.	United States	2002
Sabena	Belgium	2001
Enron Corp.	United States	2001

than the value of its debts. Flow-based insolvency occurs when operating cash flow is insufficient to meet current obligations. Flow-based insolvency refers to the inability to pay one's debts.

29.2 What Happens in Financial Distress?

There are many responses to financial distress that a firm can make. These include one or more of the following turnaround strategies:

1 Asset expansion policies
2 Operational contraction policies
3 Financial policies
4 External control activity
5 Changes in managerial control
6 Wind up company.

Asset Expansion Policies

If a firm finds itself in difficulty, it may try to reduce the risk of its operations by increasing the size of its business or assets. Asset expansion policies include the full acquisition of another firm, a partial acquisition, setting up a new joint venture, increasing capital expenditure, higher levels of production or expansion of existing facilities.

With the collapse in oil price in 2015, many oil producing and exploration firms sought potential targets to merge with so as to reduce their financial distress risk. This led to a wave of merger and acquisition deals in the sector in Europe and across the world. The largest such merger attempt was between Royal Dutch Shell and BG Group to create one of the largest oil firms in the world.

Operational Contraction Policies

Chapter 28
Page 755

The opposite of expansion is contraction and many firms choose to focus on their most profitable businesses during a downturn. Operational contraction policies include asset sales, spin-offs and divestitures (see **Chapter 28**). Plants may also be closed, production can be cut, and employees made redundant. Redundancies are politically very sensitive and many countries have very strong trade unions that can dramatically constrain the flexibility of firms when dealing with their own workforce.

Staying with the energy theme, because of sustained low oil and gas prices in 2015, the oil industry underwent a significant contraction of operations, including the cancellation of strategic investments and large scale redundancy programmes of specialized staff.

Financial Policies

Financially distressed firms will definitely face some type of cash liquidity problem. Several remedies are available. One, the company can reduce its annual dividend. Another option is to restructure its existing debt facilities so that less interest is paid. The equity and debt markets may also be tapped to raise further funding.

During the global credit crunch, many banks had to be bailed out by their governments with loan guarantees and equity share issues. In addition, almost every bank slashed its dividend to zero.

External Control Activity

External control activity means that the firm has been taken over or an outside investor takes a significant stake in the firm. A change in external control means that one or more major shareholders sell their shares to another investor with a larger capital base and greater access to capital. The European football industry has seen many deals of this type.

Changes in Managerial Control

The ultimate penalty for poor performance is losing your job and many firms opt to remove their chairman, chief executive or other directors when they are in financial distress. This will normally go hand in hand with other forms of restructuring. Examples include Fred Goodwin, the former chief executive of Royal Bank of Scotland, who had to step down after the bank found itself in serious financial difficulty as a result of the acquisition of Dutch bank, ABN AMRO, in 2007.

Wind Up Company

The final and least desirable strategy a financially distressed firm will follow is to wind up its operations and go into some form of bankruptcy. Bankruptcy laws differ on a country-by-country basis and even within the United Kingdom, bankruptcy law is different in Scotland from the rest of the country. Growth in corporate bankruptcies has rocketed as a result of the harsh economic conditions facing businesses in Europe. However, bankruptcy may not always end in the disappearance of a company, and firms may be split up, sold on to a new buyer, or restructured during the process.

Figure 29.2 shows how large public firms will normally move through financial distress. Approximately half of financial restructurings are done via private workouts. Most large public firms (approximately 70 per cent) that file for bankruptcy are able to reorganize and continue to do business.[4]

Firms in Europe follow a very similar process when they are financially distressed. For example, Table 29.2 presents the turnaround strategies of British firms that faced financial distress. The majority of firms reduced their scope of operations and underwent some form of financial restructuring.

Financial distress can serve as a firm's 'early warning' system for trouble. Firms with more debt will experience financial distress earlier than firms with less debt. However, firms that experience financial distress earlier will have more time for private workouts and reorganization. Firms with low leverage will experience financial distress later and, in many instances, be forced to liquidate.

The supermarket price war is being blamed for doubling the number of food and drink manufacturing companies in 'significant' financial distress, raising fears for farmers in the supply chain.

Figure 29.2   What Happens in Financial Distress

Source: Wruck (1990), Figure 2. See also Gilson et al. (1990); and Weiss (1990).

Table 29.2 Turnaround Strategies of Financially Distressed UK Firms 1992–1998

Reported Action	Percentage of Firms
Asset expansion policies	
Full acquisition	32.46
Partial acquisition	4.55
Joint venture	8.44
Increase investment expenditures	0.65
Increase output / expand production facilities	2.60
Total	40.26
Asset contraction policies	
Asset sale / spin-off / divestiture	29.87
Plant closure	1.30
Withdrawal from line of business	7.14
Unspecified cost-cutting programme	16.23
Cut in employment	13.64
Total	65.58
Financial policies	
Cut dividend	45.45

Reported Action	Percentage of Firms
Debt restructuring / renegotiation	1.95
Issue debt	4.55
Rights issue	3.90
Placing	6.49
Total	54.55
External control activity	
Non-financial block purchase	0.65
Negotiations	4.55
Unsuccessful offer	0
Total	4.55
Change in managerial control	
CEO turnover	20.78
Forced CEO turnover	8.44
Total	20.78

Source: Hillier and McColgan (2007).

Real World Insight 29.1

Financial Distress in the Food and Drink Industry

(Excerpts from 'Supermarkets blamed as food companies in financial distress doubles', Farmers Weekly, 20 April 2015)

A study by business recovery specialists Begbies Traynor has revealed that food and drinks manufacturers saw a 92 per cent increase in the number of companies facing significant financial distress in the fourth quarter of 2014 – up to 1,410 businesses compared to 733 in Q4 of 2013.

Julie Palmer, partner at Begbies and Traynor, warned:

A perfect storm is brewing for SME food suppliers at the bottom of the food supply chain, with many suffering a double hit from larger suppliers demanding 'loyalty' payments as well as vanishing margins as a result of the inevitable aggressive supermarket price war.

The food and drink manufacturing industry was the worst performing of all in the study, which covered a large range of sectors including construction, telecoms, financial services and general retailing.

Since the beginning of 2014 the big four retailers have cut millions of pounds off shelf prices in an effort to keep up with the rapid rise of the discounters and have promised more still. The knock-on effect, say consultants, has seen enormous pressure piled on suppliers including farmers and growers as retailers have used different methods to reduce their costs.

29.3 Bankruptcy, Liquidation and Reorganization

Firms that cannot or choose not to make contractually required payments to creditors have two basic options: liquidation or reorganization.

Liquidation means termination of the firm as a going concern; it involves selling the assets of the firm for salvage value. The proceeds, net of transactions costs, are distributed to creditors in order of established priority.

Reorganization is the option of keeping the firm as a going concern; it sometimes involves issuing new securities to replace old securities.

Liquidation and formal reorganization may be done by bankruptcy. *Bankruptcy* is a legal proceeding and can be done voluntarily with the corporation filing the petition or involuntarily with the creditors filing the petition.

Bankruptcy Law

Bankruptcy law across the world is converging to a similar process. However, there are important country level differences. The European Union introduced its bankruptcy regulation in 2002, 'Regulation on Insolvency Proceedings', which is followed by all EU countries, with the exception of Denmark. This was updated in 2014 to accommodate new thinking on financial distress and recovery. Since European bankruptcy law is very similar, the regulations facing British bankruptcy will be discussed in detail, followed by an overview of the salient differences in other countries.

Financially distressed firms in the UK can be voluntarily or compulsorily dissolved or liquidated. Liquidation means that the firm's assets are sold to allow payment of the outstanding liabilities of the firm. However, this is the very last and least desirable option and it will only be considered when all other strategies have been exhausted. An alternative is to appoint an administrator, who will attempt to restructure the firm's outstanding claims, introduce a viable business model or look for a potential buyer. It is important to note that when a firm is in administration, it will continue business until a solution (which may be liquidation) is found.

Liquidation

For a firm to be liquidated or made insolvent, a creditor, the directors or the shareholders must petition a court for a winding-up order. If a judge decides that there is a case for liquidation, an official receiver will be appointed who liquidates the assets of the firm and distributes the proceeds to all creditors. Normally, creditors will not be paid all that they are due because of direct bankruptcy costs from legal and administration fees.

Priority of Claims

Once a corporation is determined to be bankrupt, liquidation takes place. The distribution of the proceeds of the liquidation occurs according to the following general priority:

1   Administration expenses associated with liquidating the bankrupt's assets.
2   Unsecured claims arising after the filing of an involuntary bankruptcy petition.
3   Wages, salaries and commissions.
4   Contributions to employee benefit plans arising within a set period before the filing date.
5   Consumer claims.
6   Tax claims.
7   Secured and unsecured creditors' claims.
8   Preference shareholder claims.
9   Ordinary shareholder claims.

The priority rule in liquidation is known as the absolute priority rule (APR).

One qualification to this list concerns secured creditors. Liens on property are outside APR ordering. However, if the secured property is liquidated and provides cash insufficient to cover the amount owed them, the secured creditors join with unsecured creditors in dividing the remaining liquidating value. In contrast, if the secured property is liquidated for proceeds greater than the secured claim, the net proceeds are used to pay unsecured creditors and others.

Example 29.1

APR

The B.O. Deodorant Company is to be liquidated. Its liquidating value is £2.7 million. Bonds worth £1.5 million are secured by a mortgage on the B.O. Deodorant Company corporate headquarters building, which is sold for £1 million; £200,000 is used to cover administrative costs and other claims (including unpaid wages, pension benefits, consumer claims and taxes). After paying £200,000 to the administrative priority claims, the amount available to pay secured and unsecured creditors is £2.5 million. This is less than the amount of unpaid debt of £4 million.

Under APR, all creditors must be paid before shareholders, and the mortgage bondholders have first claim on the £1 million obtained from the sale of the headquarters building.

The trustee has proposed the following distribution:

Type of Claim	Prior Claim (£)	Cash Received Under Liquidation (£)
Bonds (secured by mortgage)	1,500,000	1,500,000
Subordinated debentures	2,500,000	1,000,000
Ordinary shareholders	10,000,000	0
Total	14,000,000	2,500,000
Calculation of the Distribution		
Cash received from sale of assets available for distribution		2,500,000
Cash paid to secured bondholders on sale of mortgaged property		1,000,000
Available to bond and debenture holders		1,500,000
Total claims remaining (£4,000,000 less payment of £1,000,000 on secured bonds)		3,000,000
Distribution of remaining £1,500,000 to cover total remaining claims of £3,000,000		

	Claim on Liquidation	
Type of Claim Remaining	Proceeds (£)	Cash Received (£)
Bonds	500,000	500,000
Debentures	2,500,000	1,000,000
Total	3,000,000	1,500,000

Administration

When a company enters administration, the administrator will attempt to restructure the company's liabilities, look for a buyer or break up the company into viable parts. Possible strategies also include exchanging debt for equity, which allows the financially distressed firm to dispense with paying interest on debt and at the same time gives the creditor a stake in the company should it recover.

The legal agreement which details how the firm's liabilities are to be restructured is known as a Company Voluntary Agreement (CVA). If creditors reject the CVA or the company does not submit a CVA to the court, the judge can give the corporation an extension during which it must come up with an acceptable plan or ask the creditors to come up with their own reorganization plan. In most cases, at least one extension is granted. Under UK bankruptcy law, a CVA will be accepted if at least 75 per cent of the company's claimholders, including shareholders, vote in favour of it. Once accepted, the agreement is legally binding.

In Scotland, bankruptcy law is slightly more complex. In addition to administration and insolvency procedures, firms may also go into receivership. This is also a characteristic of bankruptcy law in England and Wales for firms that have outstanding securities issued before 2003. The differences between administration and receivership are important. When in administration, the financially distressed firm is legally protected from its creditors while a CVA is prepared. An insolvency practitioner, such as an accounting firm, is normally appointed to run the business while the agreement is being drawn up. A firm will go into receivership if its creditors do not believe that the company can recover and repay its liabilities. A receiver, again normally an accounting firm, will thus be appointed to sell the assets of the firm so that the creditors can be paid.

Example 29.2

Suppose B.O. Deodorant Co. decides to go into administration and reorganize. Generally, senior claims are honoured in full before various other claims receive anything. Assume that the 'going concern' value of B.O. Deodorant Co. is £3 million and that its statement of financial position is as shown:

	£
Assets	3,000,000
Liabilities	
Mortgage bonds	1,500,000
Subordinated debentures	2,500,000
Shareholders' equity	−1,000,000

The firm has proposed the following reorganization plan:

Old Security	Old Claim (£)	New Claim with Reorganization Plan (£)
Mortgage bonds	1,500,000	1,500,000
Subordinated debentures	2,500,000	1,500,000

and a distribution of new securities under a new claim with this reorganization plan:

Old Security	Received under Proposed Reorganization Plan
Mortgage bonds	£1,000,000 in 9% senior debentures
	£500,000 in 11% subordinated debentures
Debentures	£1,000,000 in 8% preference shares
	£500,000 in ordinary shares

However, it will be difficult for the firm to convince secured creditors (mortgage bonds) to accept unsecured debentures of equal face value. In addition, the corporation may wish to allow the old shareholders to retain some participation in the firm. Needless to say, this would be a violation of the absolute priority rule, and the holders of the debentures would not be happy.

Bankruptcy in Other Countries

Bankruptcy procedures in most countries follow the same model as that in the United Kingdom. In the United States, financially distressed firms may file for Chapter 11 bankruptcy (equivalent to administration) or for Chapter 7 bankruptcy (equivalent to liquidation). All other aspects of the system are practically the same.

Countries in the European Union follow the 2002 'Regulation on Insolvency Proceedings', which was updated in 2014 by the European Commission's recommendation on 'A New Approach to Business Failure and Insolvency'.

Some country-level differences do exist, however. France has a three-stage process. The first stage involves pre-insolvency hearings, which can occur if the firm's auditor is concerned about the financial health of the firm. If the hearings cannot resolve the auditor's concerns, a petition will be made to a commercial court. The firm may at this point request a 3-month window to draw up a CVA that will be acceptable to all parties. If this is unsuccessful, the firm will be wound up. Finally, although South Africa follows a similar system to other countries, there is no administration process. Thus, creditors, shareholders or the company itself will go directly to the South African High Court to request that the firm be placed in liquidation. The process is then worked through the system and restructuring or winding-up may be an outcome of this process.

In Their Own Words

Edward I. Altman* on Corporate Financial Distress and Bankruptcy

As we entered the new millennium, corporate distress and bankruptcy were no longer a niche area of corporate evolution. The average company is far riskier today than it was just two decades ago, and the roles of the bankruptcy courts and restructuring specialists have never been more important. Financial distress of private and public entities throughout the world is a frequent occurrence with important implications to their many stakeholders. While the role of corporate bankruptcy laws is clear – either to provide a legal procedure that permits firms, which have temporary liquidity problems, to restructure and successfully emerge as continuing entities or to provide an orderly process to liquidate assets for the benefit of creditors before asset values are dissipated – bankruptcy laws differ markedly from country to country.

It is generally agreed that the US Chapter 11 provisions under the Bankruptcy Reform Act of 1978 provide the most protection for bankrupt firms' assets and result in a greater likelihood of successful reorganization than is found in other countries where liquidation and sale of the assets for the benefit of creditors is more likely the result. But the US code's process is usually lengthy (averaging close to 2 years, except where a sufficient number of creditors agree in advance via a prepackaged Chapter 11) and expensive, and the reorganized entity is not always successful in avoiding subsequent distress. If the reorganization is not successful, then liquidation under Chapter 7 will usually ensue.

Bankruptcy processes in the industrialized world outside the United States strongly favour senior creditors who obtain control of the firm and seek to enforce greater adherence to debt contracts. The UK process, for example, is speedy and less costly, but the reduced costs can result in undesirable liquidations, unemployment and underinvestment. The new bankruptcy code in Germany attempts to reduce the considerable power of secured creditors but it is still closer to the UK system.

Regardless of the location, one of the objectives of bankruptcy and other distressed workout arrangements is that creditors and other suppliers of capital clearly know their rights and expected recoveries in the event of a distressed situation. When these are not transparent and/or are based on outdated processes with arbitrary and possibly corrupt outcomes, then the entire economic system suffers and growth is inhibited. Such is the case in several emerging market countries. Revision of these outdated systems should be a priority.

Edward I. Altman is Max L. Heine Professor of Finance, NYU Stern School of Business. He is widely recognized as one of the world's experts on bankruptcy and credit analysis as well as the distressed debt and high-yield bond markets.

29.4 Private Workout or Bankruptcy: Which Is Best?

A firm that defaults on its debt payments will need to restructure its financial claims. The firm will have two choices: formal bankruptcy or private workout. The previous section described two types of formal bankruptcies: bankruptcy liquidation and bankruptcy reorganization. This section compares private workouts with bankruptcy reorganizations. Both types of financial restructuring involve exchanging new financial claims for old financial claims. Usually senior debt is replaced with junior debt and debt is replaced with equity. Much recent academic research has described what happens in private workouts and formal bankruptcies.[5]

- Historically, half of financial restructurings have been private, but recently formal bankruptcy has dominated.

- Firms that emerge from private workouts experience share price increases that are much greater than those for firms emerging from formal bankruptcies.

- The direct costs of private workouts are much less than the costs of formal bankruptcies.

- Top management usually loses pay and sometimes jobs in both private workouts and formal bankruptcies.

These facts, when taken together, seem to suggest that a private workout is much better than a formal bankruptcy. We then ask: why do firms ever use formal bankruptcies to restructure?

The Marginal Firm

For the average firm, a formal bankruptcy is more costly than a private workout, but for some firms formal bankruptcy is better. Formal bankruptcy allows firms to issue debt that is senior to all previously incurred debt. This new debt is 'debtor in possession' (DIP) debt. For firms that need a temporary injection of cash, DIP debt makes bankruptcy reorganization an attractive alternative to a private workout. There are some tax advantages to bankruptcy. Firms do not lose tax carry-forwards in bankruptcy, and the tax treatment of the cancellation of indebtedness is better in bankruptcy. Also, interest on pre-bankruptcy unsecured debt stops accruing in formal bankruptcy.

Holdouts

Bankruptcy is usually better for the equity investors than it is for the creditors. Using DIP debt and stopping pre-bankruptcy interest on unsecured debt helps the shareholders and hurts the creditors. As a consequence, equity investors can usually hold out for a better deal in bankruptcy. The absolute priority rule, which favours creditors over equity investors, is usually violated in formal bankruptcies. One recent study found that in 81 per cent of recent bankruptcies the equity investor obtained some compensation.[6] When a firm is in administration, the creditors are often forced to give up some of their seniority rights to get management and the equity investors to agree to a deal.

Complexity

A firm with a complicated capital structure will have more trouble putting together a private workout. Firms with secured creditors and trade creditors will usually use formal bankruptcy because it is too hard to reach an agreement with many different types of creditors.

Lack of Information

There is an inherent conflict of interest between equity investors and creditors, and the conflict is accentuated when both have incomplete information about the circumstances of financial distress. When a firm initially experiences a cash flow shortfall, it may not know whether the shortfall is permanent or temporary. If the shortfall is permanent, creditors will push for a formal reorganization or liquidation. However, if the cash flow shortfall is temporary, formal reorganization or liquidation may not be necessary. Equity investors will push for this viewpoint. This conflict of interest cannot easily be resolved.

These last two points are especially important. They suggest that financial distress will be more expensive (cheaper) if complexity is high (low) and information is incomplete (complete). Complexity and lack of information make cheap workouts less likely.

Institutional Factors

Most research on corporate bankruptcies has looked at single countries, such as the United States and United Kingdom. However, an examination of only one country can mask the effect of important institutional factors that relate to the legal and corporate system. Davydenko and Franks (2008) look at the French, German and British systems of bankruptcy and investigate whether their country-specific regulations impact upon the likelihood of firms going into and surviving formal administration.

The legal bankruptcy systems in France, Germany and UK fall under the umbrella of EU regulation. However, France and the UK represent two extremes in their approaches to resolving bankruptcy. Whereas France's approach focuses on the debtor or borrowing firm, the UK is very much creditor or lender friendly. In France, lenders have no input, beyond an advisory role, into the reorganization plan. This contrasts with the situation in the UK, where creditors can veto any reorganization plan that is put forward by the company. Germany is somewhere in between these two extremes.

Davydenko and Franks found that banks required higher levels of collateral when lending to French companies to offset the lower likelihood of receiving outstanding debts in the event of a default. Moreover, recovery rates (i.e. the percentage of outstanding debts that are received by creditors) are significantly higher in the United Kingdom (92 per cent) than in Germany (67 per cent) or France (56 per cent). Interestingly, British firms are more likely to survive administration because their creditors, normally banks, are more likely to work with the financially distressed company to see them through the administration period.

29.5 Predicting Financial Distress: The *Z*-score Model

Many potential lenders use credit scoring models to assess the creditworthiness of prospective borrowers. The general idea is to find statistical factors that enable the lenders to discriminate between good and bad credit risks. To put it more precisely, lenders want to identify attributes of the borrower that can be used to predict default or bankruptcy.

Edward Altman (1993) has developed a model using financial statement ratios and multiple discriminant analyses to predict bankruptcy for publicly traded manufacturing firms. The resultant model for US companies is of the form:

$$Z = 3.3 \frac{\text{EBIT}}{\text{Total assets}} + 1.2 \frac{\text{Net working capital}}{\text{Total assets}}$$

$$+ 1.0 \frac{\text{Sales}}{\text{Total assets}} + 0.6 \frac{\text{Market value of equity}}{\text{Book value of debt}}$$

$$+ 1.4 \frac{\text{Accumulated retained earnings}}{\text{Total assets}}$$

where *Z* is an index of bankruptcy.

A score of *Z* less than 2.675 indicates that a firm has a 95 per cent chance of becoming bankrupt within one year. However, Altman's results show that in practice scores between 1.81 and 2.99 should be thought of as a grey area. In actual use, bankruptcy would be predicted if $Z \leq 1.81$ and non-bankruptcy if $Z \geq 2.99$. Altman shows that bankrupt firms and non-bankrupt firms have very different financial profiles one year before bankruptcy. These different financial profits are the key intuition behind the *Z*-score model and are depicted in Table 29.3.

Table 29.3 Financial Statement Ratios One Year Before Bankruptcy: Manufacturing Firms

	Bankrupt Firms (%)	Non-Bankrupt Firms (%)
Networking capital / Total assets	−6.1	41.4
Accumulated retained earnings / Total assets	−62.6	35.5
EBIT / Total assets	−31.8	15.4
Market value of equity / Total liabilities	40.1	247.7
Sales / Assets	150	190

Source: Altman (1993), Table 3.1, p. 109.

Altman's original *Z*-score model requires a firm to have publicly traded equity and be a manufacturer. He uses a revised model to make it applicable for private firms and non-manufacturers. The resulting model for non-manufacturing and emerging market firms is this:

$$Z = 6.56 \frac{\text{Net working capital}}{\text{Total assets}} + 3.26 \frac{\text{Accumulated retained earnings}}{\text{Total assets}}$$

$$+ 6.72 \frac{\text{EBIT}}{\text{Total assets}} + 1.05 \frac{\text{Book value of equity}}{\text{Total liabilities}}$$

where $Z < 1.1$ indicates a bankruptcy prediction, $1.1 \geq Z \leq 2.60$ indicates a grey area, and $Z > 2.60$ indicates no bankruptcy.

The resulting model for private firms is given below:

$$Z = 0.717 \frac{\text{Net working capital}}{\text{Total assets}} + 0.847 \frac{\text{Accumulated retained earnings}}{\text{Total assets}}$$

$$+ 3.10 \frac{\text{EBIT}}{\text{Total assets}} + 0.420 \frac{\text{Book value of equity}}{\text{Total liabilities}} + 0.998 \frac{\text{Sales}}{\text{Total Assets}}$$

where $Z < 1.23$ indicates a bankruptcy prediction, $1.23 \geq Z \leq 2.90$ indicates a grey area, and $Z > 2.90$ indicates no bankruptcy.

Real World Insight 29.2

In 2012, European football was rocked when Rangers Football Club entered administration. Although the club had the 14th largest match-day revenues in Europe, a lack of commercial and television opportunities led to its demise. What about other Scottish football clubs? Were they living beyond their means as well? In the table below, we present the Z-scores for each club using the most recent set of accounts. Almost all Scottish clubs are private firms and so the modified Z-score model will be used.

Team	T1	T2	T3	T4	T5	Z-score
Aberdeen	−0.442	−0.608	−0.063	0.037	0.337	−0.675
Celtic	−0.110	−0.269	0.010	0.917	0.628	0.736
Dundee Utd	−1.191	−0.949	−0.041	−0.350	0.773	−1.161
Dunfermline	−0.410	−7.819	−0.173	−0.796	1.093	−6.697
Hearts	0.955	−2.381	0.085	−0.551	0.405	−0.896
Hibernian	−0.121	0.195	0.009	1.204	0.257	0.868
Inverness CT	−0.218	−3.337	−0.188	−0.153	3.523	−0.115
Kilmarnock	−0.233	−0.527	0.021	0.220	0.450	−0.008
Motherwell	0.003	0.322	0.169	0.866	1.776	2.938
Rangers	−0.158	−0.996	0.041	1.080	0.413	0.036
St Johnstone	0.545	0.688	0.000	3.606	0.000	2.488
St Mirren	−0.030	0.827	−0.030	13.846	0.275	6.676

Where the following variables are used:

Liquidity	T1 = (Current assets − current liabilities)/Total assets
LT profitability	T2 = Retained earnings/Total assets
Operating efficiency	T3 = EBIT/Total assets
Shareholder value	T4 = Book value of equity/Total liabilities
Asset turnover	T5 = Sales/Total assets

Most clubs in Scotland appear to be in some form of financial distress or operating close to their financial limits. What is causing this? The main reason is that clubs have racked up losses over many years and this is reflected in the negative long-term profitability ratios. In addition, many clubs have negative working capital which means that they are also exceptionally illiquid.

An alert reader will wonder why US Z-score coefficients can be used for a firm that is based in Europe. This would be a very good observation. In practice, banks use a variety of propriety prediction models when assessing the creditworthiness of potential borrowers, and Altman's Z-score model is just one of these. Another approach is to use neural networks to predict failure in borrowers. Irrespective of the model used, good quality data on credit defaults is required in order to calibrate the coefficients. The coefficients in any model will clearly be a function of the borrower and lender demographics, institutional factors and the quality of data that the analyst has in her possession. In practice, each country will have its own set of important variables and coefficients. All Altman's model does is provide a prediction of failure, which is not a perfect prediction of the future. As a general indicator, the US coefficients can be used to provide some insight on the bankruptcy risk of corporations in other countries. Only, do not take the outcome as particularly precise.

Summary and Conclusions

This chapter examined what happens when firms experience financial distress.

1   Financial distress is a situation where a firm's operating cash flow is not sufficient to cover contractual obligations. Financially distressed firms are often forced to take corrective action and undergo financial restructuring. Financial restructuring involves exchanging new financial claims for old ones.

2   Financial restructuring can be accomplished with a private workout or formal bankruptcy. Financial restructuring can involve liquidation or reorganization. However, liquidation is not common.

3   Corporate bankruptcy involves liquidation or reorganization. An essential feature of bankruptcy codes is the absolute priority rule. The absolute priority rule states that senior creditors are paid in full before junior creditors receive anything. However, in practice the absolute priority rule is often violated.

Questions and Problems

CONCEPT

1   **Financial Distress**   Define *financial distress* using the value-based and flow-based approaches. Do you think these are appropriate definitions for financial distress? Explain.

2   **What Happens in Financial Distress**   Review the turnaround strategies that firms can follow when in financial distress. Which do you think are most effective? Why?

3   **Bankruptcy Liquidation and Administration**   What is the difference between administration and reorganization? What are some benefits of financial distress?

4   **Private Workouts and Bankruptcy**   Do you think country-level institutional factors affect the turnaround strategies that financially distressed firms may adopt? What is the trade-off for policymakers between debtor-friendly and creditor-friendly bankruptcy law? Explain.

5   **Predicting Financial Distress**   Review the variables and decision rule in Altman's Z -score model. Why do you think these variables are important in predicting financial distress? Is Altman's Z-score successful in correctly categorizing distressed and non-distressed firms?

REGULAR

6   **Financial Distress**   What do you think are the main causes of financial distress? Explain your answer using a case study firm of your choice.

7   **APR and DIP Loans**   What is the absolute priority rule? What are DIP loans? Where do DIP loans fall in the APR?

8   **Costs of Bankruptcy**   What are the costs to a company of financial distress? Discuss your answer using a case study company of your choice.

9   **Bankruptcy Ethics**   Firms that are in financial distress can use 'prepack' arrangements, where the financially distressed firm sells its assets and then immediately declares that it wishes to stop trading. This action transfers the assets to a completely new firm but without the debts of the old firm. Is this an ethical tactic?

10   **Bankruptcy Ethics**   Several firms have entered bankruptcy, or threatened to enter bankruptcy, at least in part, as a means of reducing labour costs. Whether this move is ethical, or proper, is hotly debated. Is this an ethical use of bankruptcy?

11   **Bankruptcy versus Private Workouts**   Empirical evidence has shown that private workouts are faster and more cost-effective than a Chapter 11 bankruptcy procedure. Yet, according to Wruck (1990), over half of financial restructurings in the United States occur in Chapter 11 rather than through a private workout. Why do you think this is?

12   **Administration**   When Beacon Computers entered insolvency, it had the following balance sheet information:

Liquidating Value (£)		Claims (£)	
		Trade credit	3,000
		Secured mortgage notes	6,000
		Senior debentures	5,000
		Junior debentures	9,000
Total assets	15,500	Book equity	−7,500

Assuming there are no legal fees associated with the bankruptcy, as trustee, what distribution of liquidating value do you propose?

13 **Administration** When Masters Printing filed for bankruptcy, it entered administration. Key information is shown below. As trustee, what reorganization plan would you accept?

Assets (£)		Claims (£)	
		Mortgage bonds	10,000
		Senior debentures	6,000
		Junior debentures	4,000
Going concern value	15,000	Book equity	−5,000

Refer to Real World Insight 29.2 for questions 14 to 17.

14 **Insolvency** Look at the club Z-scores. If you were the financial manager of a Scottish football club, what would you view as being the most important issue for the future viability of the industry? Develop a turnaround plan for one of the clubs and justify your proposals. Refer to Real World Insight 29.2.

15 **Z-score Models** Many analysts argue that football clubs are special cases and you cannot blindly apply standard Z-score models to the industry. Critically assess this argument and discuss why you think it may or may not be valid. Which variables do you perceive to be most important for football clubs? Which ones do you think are less relevant? Explain your answer. Refer to Real World Insight 29.2.

16 **Negative Equity** Four of the 12 Scottish clubs have a negative value for T4. Does this mean they are insolvent? Explain. Refer to Real World Insight 29.2.

17 **Net Working Capital** Nine of the 12 Scottish clubs have a negative value for net working capital. Does this mean that these clubs are in danger of insolvency? Can you explain why in football, negative net working capital for most clubs can be explained as normal? Refer to Real World Insight 29.2.

18 **Turnaround Strategies** Firms that are in financial distress sometimes increase the size of their assets. Explain why firms would pursue such a strategy instead of a more standard cost-cutting approach.

19 **Financially Distressed Firms** In 2012, Rangers Football Club went into administration with over £100 million in debt. The owner of the firm, Craig Whyte, held 85.3 per cent of the club's shares and was also its only secured creditor, holding an £18 million floating charge over the assets of Rangers. Why do you think Mr Whyte chose to be the secured creditor and owner of the firm? Does this make sense? Provide a rationale for Mr Whyte holding such a position in Rangers.

20 **Private Equity** Many publicly traded financially distressed firms are purchased by private equity funds and delisted from the stock exchange. Several years later they are brought back to the exchange for a new share listing. Why do you think private equity firms delist financially distressed firms? Why do they bring them back to market?

Exam Question (45 minutes)

In 2012, the Game Group filed for insolvency. Using Altman's Z-score analysis, would you have been able to predict its financial distress? What is your interpretation of the results? Are there any figures that would have given you cause for concern? Explain. (100 marks)

	2011 £000	2010 £000	2009 £000	2008 £000	2007 £000
Fixed assets	322,644	344,870	350,614	303,533	203,628
Current assets	349,696	310,489	377,044	336,785	161,131
Current liabilities	320,069	289,848	397,075	370,244	175,526
Long-term liabilities	25,277	33,956	40,175	66,152	31,897
Book value of equity	326,994	331,555	290,408	203,922	157,336
Market value of equity	26,059	243,222	368,308	441,275	868,652
Retained earnings	156,714	164,426	130,472	61,276	23,852
Sales	1,625,034	1,772,358	1,971,905	1,491,914	801,306
EBIT	28,850	89,128	128,345	76,703	33,212

Mini Case

In March 2012, the spread betting firm, Worldspreads Ltd, applied to go into administration. The decision was made when the company realized its cash balance of £16.6 million could not meet its liabilities of £29.7 million. The firm's key statistics, income statement and balance sheet for a number of years are given below.

Key statistics:

	31/03/2011 £000	31/03/2010 £000	31/03/2009 £000	31/03/2008 £000	31/03/2007 £000
	12 months Uncons. Unqualified IFRS	12 months Uncons. Unqualified IFRS	12 months Uncons. Unqualified	12 months Uncons. Unqualified	12 months Uncons. Unqualified
Turnover	13,665	11,420	5,809	4,187	1,914
Profit (loss) before taxation	−520	2,396	421	887	−476
Net tangible assets (liab.)	8,114	8,454	2,208	3,824	1,317
Shareholders' funds	8,450	6,866	2,440	2,186	1,626
Profit margin	−3.81	20.98	7.25	21.18	−24.89
Return on shareholders' funds	−6.15	34.90	17.25	40.58	−29.29
Return on capital employed	−6.13	27.65	17.25	21.85	−29.29
Liquidity ratio (x)	1.20	1.26	1.06	1.15	1.06
Gearing (%)	82.97	140.64	363.40	210.75	77.85
Number of employees	44	26	18	15	14

Income statement:

	31/3/2011	31/3/2010	31/3/2009	31/3/2008
Turnover	13,665	11,420	5,809	4,187
Cost of sales	−3,997	−3,279	−2,443	−736
Gross profit	9,668	8,141	3,366	3,451
Administration expenses	−10,553	−5,770	−2,990	−2,632
Other operating income pre OP	382	54		
Operating profit	−504	2,425	376	820
Total other income and interest received	33	29	110	113
Profit (loss) before interest paid	−471	2,454	486	933
Interest received	33	29		
Interest paid	−49	−58	−65	−46
Net interest	−16	−29	−65	−46
Profit (loss) before tax	−520	2,396	421	887
Taxation	104	−670	−153	−337
Profit (loss) for period	−416	1,726	268	550

Balance sheet:

Fixed assets	2011	2010	2009	2008
Tangible assets	1,270	734	254	189
Intangible assets	372	212	232	236
Investments		27	364	489
Fixed assets	3,653	2,956	2,495	2,433

Current assets				
Trade debtors	2,318	4,139	2,389	2,254
Bank and deposits	27,371	23,260	16,567	16,572
Other debtors	8,944	0	0	365
Prepayments	1,589	1,289		
Deferred taxation	133			
Investments		7,238	3,953	5,176
Current assets	40,356	36,816	26,674	24,367
Current liabilities				
Trade creditors	−20,588	−14,207	−12,802	−12,067
Short-term loans and overdrafts	−6,974	−7,856	−8,867	−2,733
Corporation tax	0	−333	−28	−29
Accruals and Def. Inc. (sh. t.)	−869	−569	−336	−245
Other current liabilities	−5,079	−6,157	−3,051	−6,147
Current liabilities	−33,511	−29,123	−25,083	−21,221
Total assets	41,997	37,789	27,523	25,281
Long-term liabilities				
Long-term debt		−1,800		−1,700
Provisions for other liabilities	−37			−174
Long-term liabilities	−37	−1,800		−1,874
Shareholders' funds				
Issued capital	8,012	6,012	3,312	3,312
Profit (loss) account	319	735	−991	−1,258
Other reserves	118	118	118	132
Shareholders' funds	8,450	6,866	2,440	2,186

1   Assume that you had taken over the financial manager's role in 2010. Would you have predicted that Worldspreads Limited would be in financial distress within a year? Explain.

2   Assume now that you are in 2011 and the company has experienced a torrid year. What is the Z-score for the firm? Does this give you any insight into the risk or insolvency status of the firm?

3   Now that you know Worldspreads is in financial distress, what are the different types of strategies you would follow? What do you think is most appropriate in this particular case? Explain.

Practical Case Study

It is not difficult to find firms that are in financial distress. Download the financial accounts for five firms in your country that have performed poorly over the last year. Carry out a Z-score analysis for these companies. Now download the financial accounts for five firms that performed strongly in the past year and carry out a similar analysis. Are the Z-scores for the poor performance sample different from the good performance sample? Write a report on your analysis.

Relevant Accounting Standards

Many financially distressed firms choose to restructure their assets and sell off poorly performing divisions. An important standard in this regard is IAS 37 *Provisions, Contingent Liabilities and Contingent Assets*. If firms wish to sell off divisions or non-current assets, they should also be familiar with IFRS 5 *Non-Current Assets Held for Sale and Discontinued Operations*.

References

Altman, E. (1993) *Corporate Financial Distress: A Complete Guide to Predicting, Avoiding, and Dealing with Bankruptcy*, 2nd edn (New York: John Wiley & Sons).

Beranek, W., R. Boehmer and B. Smith (1996) 'Much Ado about Nothing: Absolute Priority Deviations in Chapter 11', *Financial Management*, Vol. 25, No. 3, 102–109.

Davydenko, S.A. and J. Franks (2008) 'Do Bankruptcy Codes Matter? A Study of Defaults in France, Germany and the UK', *The Journal of Finance*, Vol. 63, 565–609.

Gilson, S. (1991) 'Managing Default: Some Evidence on How Firms Choose between Workouts and Bankruptcy', *Journal of Applied Corporate Finance*, Vol. 4, No. 2, 62–70.

Gilson, S.C., J. Kose and L.N.P. Lang (1990) 'Troubled Debt Restructuring: An Empirical Study of Private Reorganization of Firms in Defaults', *Journal of Financial Economics*, Vol. 27, 315–353.

Hillier, D. and P. McColgan (2007) 'Managerial Discipline and Firm Responses to a Decline in Operating Performance', Working Paper.

Weiss, L.A. (1990) 'Bankruptcy Resolution: Direct Costs and Violation of Priority and Claims', *Journal of Financial Economics*, Vol. 27, 285–314.

Wruck, K. (1990) 'Financial Distress: Reorganization and Organization Efficiency', *Journal of Financial Economics*, Vol. 27, No. 2, 419–444.

Additional Reading

Financial distress is another topic that has taken on a new lease of life in recent years because of the unprecedented events in the world economy. The literature can be separated into factors that influence financial distress and turnaround strategies once a company is in trouble.

Predictors of Distress

1   Acharya, V.V., S.T. Bharath and A. Srinivasan (2007) 'Does Industry-wide Distress Affect Defaulted Firms? Evidence from Credit Recoveries', *Journal of Financial Economics*, Vol. 85, No. 3, 787–821. **US**.

2   Agarwal, V. and R. Taffler (2008) 'Comparing the Performance of Market-Based and Accounting-based Bankruptcy Prediction Models', *Journal of Banking and Finance*, Vol. 32, No. 8, 1541–1551. **UK**.

3   Braun, M. and B. Larrain (2005) 'Finance and the Business Cycle: International, Inter-Industry Evidence', *The Journal of Finance*, Vol. 60, No. 3, 1097–1127. **International**.

4   Campbell, J.Y., J. Hilscher and J. Szilagyi (2008) 'In Search of Distress Risk', *The Journal of Finance*, Vol. 63, No. 6, 2899–2939. **US**.

5   Garlappi, L. and H. Yan (2011) 'Financial Distress and the Cross-Section of Equity Returns', *The Journal of Finance*, Vol. 66, No. 3, 789–822.

6   Yang, L. (2008) 'The Real Determinants of Asset Sales', *The Journal of Finance*, Vol. 63, No. 5, 2231–2262. **US**.

Turnaround Strategies and the Bankruptcy Process

7   Ang, J., A. De Jong and M. Van der Poel (2014) 'Does Familiarity with Business Segments Affect CEOs' Divestment Decisions?', *Journal of Corporate Finance*, Vol. 29, 58–74.

8   Bates, T.W. (2005) 'Asset Sales, Investment Opportunities, and the Use of Proceeds', *The Journal of Finance*, Vol. 60, No. 1, 105–135. **US**.

9   Bris, A., I. Welch and N. Zhu (2006) 'The Costs of Bankruptcy: Chapter 7 Liquidation versus Chapter 11 Reorganization', *The Journal of Finance*, Vol. 61, No. 3, 1253–1303. **US**.

10   Brown, D.T., B.A. Ciochetti and T.J. Riddiough (2006) 'Theory and Evidence on the Resolution of Financial Distress', *Review of Financial Studies*, Vol. 19, No. 4, 1357–1397. **US**.

11 Davydenko, S.A. and J.R. Franks (2008) 'Do Bankruptcy Codes Matter? A Study of Defaults in France, Germany and the UK', *The Journal of Finance*, Vol. 62, No. 2, 565–608. **Europe**.

12 Eckbo, B.E. and K. Thorburn (2009) 'Creditor Financing and Overbidding in Bankruptcy Auctions: Theory and Tests', *Journal of Corporate Finance*, Vol. 15, No. 1, 10–29. **Sweden**.

13 Eisdorfer, A. (2008) 'Empirical Evidence of Risk Shifting in Financially Distressed Firms', *The Journal of Finance*, Vol. 62, No. 2, 609–637. **US**.

14 Faccio, M., R.W. Masulis and J.J. McConnell (2006) 'Political Connections and Corporate Bailouts', *The Journal of Finance*, Vol. 16, No. 6, 2597–2635. **International**.

15 Hillier, D., A. Marshall, P. McColgan and S. Werema (2007) 'Employee Layoffs, Shareholder Wealth and Firm Performance: Evidence from the UK', *Journal of Business Finance and Accounting*, Vol. 34, Nos. 3 and 4, 467–494. **UK**.

16 Jostarndt, P. and Z. Sautner (2008) 'Financial Distress, Corporate Control, and Management Turnover', *Journal of Banking and Finance*, Vol. 32, No. 10, 2188–2204. **Germany**.

17 Lee, E. and S. Lin (2008) 'Corporate Sell-offs in the UK: Use of Proceeds, Financial Distress and the Long-Run Impact on Shareholder Wealth', *European Financial Management*, Vol. 14, No. 2, 222–242. **UK**.

18 Molina, C.A. and L. A. Preve (2009) 'Trade Receivables Policy of Distressed Firms and its Effect on the Costs of Financial Distress', *Financial Management*, Vol. 38, No. 2, 663–686.

Other Relevant Research

19 Davydenko, S.A., I.A. Strebulaev and X. Zhao (2012) 'A Market-based Study of the Cost of Default', *Review of Financial Studies*, Vol. 25, No. 10, 2959–2999.

20 Gennaioli, N. and S. Rossi (2013) 'Contractual Resolutions of Financial Distress', *Review of Financial Studies*, Vol. 26, No. 3, 602–634.

21 Ongena, S., D.C. Smith and D. Michalsen (2003) 'Firms and their Distressed Banks: Lessons from the Norwegian Banking Crisis', *Journal of Financial Research*, Vol. 67, No. 1, 81–112. **Norway**.

Endnotes

1 This definition is close to the one used by Wruck (1990), p. 425.

2 *Black's Law Dictionary*, 5th ed. (St Paul, MN: West Publishing Company), p. 716.

3 Edward Altman (1993) was one of the first to distinguish between stock-based insolvency and flow-based insolvency.

4 However, only less than 20 per cent of all firms (public or private) going through a bankruptcy are successfully reorganized.

5 For example, see Gilson (1991); and Gilson et al. (1990).

6 Weiss (1990). However, Beranek et al. (1996), find that 33.8 per cent of bankruptcy reorganizations leave shareholders with nothing.

International Corporate Finance

Relatively few large companies operate in a single country. As a financial manager in a corporation, even if your sales are not overseas, it is very likely that your competitors or suppliers are from overseas. In most industries, raw materials and components are sourced and imported from overseas, and many services and products are sold to different countries.

For example, an analysis of import and export revenue for the United Kingdom shows that most of Britain's export revenue comes from Germany (11.3 per cent), US (10.5 per cent), the Netherlands (8.8 per cent), France (7.4 per cent), Ireland (6.2 per cent) and Belgium (5.1 per cent). Similarly, the United Kingdom's main import partners are Germany (12.6 per cent), China (8 per cent), the Netherlands (7.5 per cent), US (6.7 per cent), France (5.4 per cent), Belgium (4.4 per cent), and Norway (4 per cent). Table 30.1 presents the main import and export partners for other selected countries.

KEY NOTATIONS

P	Price
S_0	Spot exchange rate
$E(S_t)$	Expected exchange rate in t periods
h_{HC}	Inflation rate in the home currency
h_{FC}	Foreign country inflation rate
F_t	Forward exchange rate for settlement at time t
R_{HC}	Home currency nominal risk-free interest rate
R_{FC}	Foreign country nominal risk-free interest rate

Table 30.1 Main Import and Export Partners of Selected Countries

	Top three export partners	Top three import partners
Australia	China, Japan, South Korea	China, US, Japan
Austria	Germany, Italy, Switzerland	Germany, Italy, Switzerland
Bahrain	Saudi Arabia, India, UAE	Saudi Arabia, US, China

	Top three export partners	Top three import partners
Belgium	Germany, France, Netherlands	Netherlands, Germany, France
China	Hong Kong, US, Japan	South Korea, Japan, Taiwan
Denmark	Germany, Sweden, UK	Germany, Sweden, Netherlands
Finland	Sweden, Russia, Germany	Russia, Sweden, Germany
France	Germany, Belgium, Italy	German, Belgium, Italy
Germany	France, US, UK	Netherlands, France, China
Greece	Turkey, Italy, Germany	Russia, Germany, Italy
Hong Kong	China, US, Japan	China, Japan, Taiwan
India	UAE, US, China	China, UAE, Saudi Arabia
Ireland	US, UK, Belgium	UK, US, Germany
Italy	Germany, France, US	Germany, France, China
Japan	China, US, South Korea	China, US, Australia
Malaysia	Singapore, China, Japan	China, Singapore, Japan
Netherlands	Germany, Belgium, France	Germany, China, Belgium
Norway	UK, Germany, Netherlands	Sweden, Germany, China
Oman	China, Japan, UAE	UAE, Japan, India
Poland	Germany, UK, Czech Republic	Germany, Russia, Netherlands
Portugal	Spain, Germany, France	Spain, Germany, France
Russia	Netherlands, China, Germany	China, Germany, Ukraine
Singapore	Malaysia, Hong Kong, China	Malaysia, China, US
Slovenia	Germany, Italy, Austria	Italy, Germany, Austria
South Africa	China, US, Japan	China, Germany, Saudi Arabia
Spain	France, Germany, Italy	Germany, France, Italy
Sweden	Norway, Germany, UK	Germany, Denmark, Norway
Switzerland	Germany, US, Italy	Germany, Italy, France
Tanzania	India, China, Japan	China, India, South Africa
Thailand	China, Japan, US	Japan, China, UAE
Turkey	Germany, Iraq, Iran	Russia, Germany, China
United Arab Emirates	Japan, India, Iran	India, China, US
United Kingdom	Germany, US, Netherlands	Germany, China, Netherlands
United States	Canada, Mexico, China	China, Canada, Mexico

Source: CIA World Factbook, 2015.

Currency fluctuations will clearly have an impact on firms. For example, if the euro strengthens against the British pound, British exports become more competitive in Europe. Similarly, raw materials sourced from Europe will become more expensive and British corporations will look elsewhere for cheaper inputs. One of the reasons why European Monetary Union was introduced was precisely because many countries in the Eurozone traded heavily with each other. With a single currency, the risk of fluctuations is eradicated. In this chapter, we explore the roles played by currencies and exchange rates, along with a number of other key topics in international corporate finance.

Corporations with significant foreign operations are often called *international corporations* or *multinationals*. Such corporations must consider many financial factors that do not directly affect purely domestic firms. These include foreign exchange rates, differing interest rates from country to country, different and possibly more complex accounting methods for foreign operations, foreign tax rates and foreign government intervention.

The basic principles of corporate finance still apply to international corporations; like domestic companies, these firms seek to invest in projects that create more value for the shareholders than they cost and to arrange financing that raises cash at the lowest possible cost. In other words, the net present value principle holds for both foreign and domestic operations, although it is usually more complicated to apply the NPV rule to foreign investments.

One of the most significant complications of international finance is foreign exchange. The foreign exchange markets provide important information and opportunities for an international corporation when it undertakes capital budgeting and financing decisions. As we will discuss, international exchange rates, interest rates and inflation rates are closely related. We will spend much of this chapter exploring the connection between these financial variables.

We will not have much to say here about the role of cultural and social differences in international business. Neither will we be discussing the implications of differing political and economic systems. These factors are of great importance to international businesses, but it would take another book to do them justice. Consequently we will focus only on some purely financial considerations in international finance and some key aspects of foreign exchange markets.

30.1 Terminology

A common buzzword for the student of business finance is *globalization*. The first step in learning about the globalization of financial markets is to conquer the new vocabulary. As with any specialized field, international finance is rich in jargon. Accordingly, we get started on the subject with a highly eclectic vocabulary exercise.

The terms that follow are presented alphabetically, and they are not all of equal importance. We choose these particular ones because they appear frequently in the financial press or because they illustrate the colourful nature of the language of international finance.

1   An American depositary receipt (ADR) is a security issued in the United States that represents shares of a foreign equity, allowing that equity to be traded in the United States. Foreign companies use ADRs, which are issued in US dollars, to expand the pool of potential US investors. ADRs are available in two forms for a large and growing number of foreign companies: company sponsored, which are listed on an exchange, and unsponsored, which usually are held by the investment bank that makes a market in the ADR. Both forms are available to individual investors, but only company-sponsored issues are quoted daily in newspapers. A global depositary receipt (GDR) is an equivalent security denominated in sterling or euros, and issued and traded in financial centres such as London or Frankfurt.

2   The cross-rate is the implicit exchange rate between two currencies (usually an emerging or transitional economy) when both are quoted in some third currency, usually the US dollar, euro or British pound.

3   A Eurobond is a bond issued in multiple countries but denominated in a single currency, usually the issuer's home currency. Such bonds have become an important way to raise capital for many international companies and governments. Eurobonds are issued outside the restrictions that apply to domestic offerings and are syndicated and traded mostly from London. Trading can and does take place anywhere there are buyers and sellers.

4   Eurocurrency is money deposited in a financial centre outside of the country whose currency is involved. For instance, Eurodollars – the most widely used Eurocurrency – are US dollars deposited in banks outside the US banking system. Eurosterling and euroyen are British and Japanese equivalents.

5   Foreign bonds, unlike Eurobonds, are issued in a single country and are usually denominated in that country's currency. Often, the country in which these bonds are issued will draw distinctions between them and bonds issued by domestic issuers – including different tax laws, restrictions on the amount issued, and tougher disclosure rules.

Foreign bonds often are nicknamed for the country where they are issued: Yankee bonds (United States), Samurai bonds (Japan), Rembrandt bonds (the Netherlands), and Bulldog bonds (Britain). Partly because of tougher regulations and disclosure requirements, the foreign bond market hasn't grown in past years with the vigour of the Eurobond market.

30.2   Foreign Exchange Markets and Exchange Rates

The foreign exchange market is undoubtedly the world's largest financial market. It is the market where one country's currency is traded for another's. Most of the trading takes place in a few currencies: the US dollar ($), the British pound sterling (£), the Japanese yen (¥), and the euro (€). Table 30.2 lists some of the more common currencies and their symbols.

Table 30.2 International Currency Symbols

Country	Currency	Symbol
Australia	Australian dollar	A$
Canada	Canadian dollar	C$
Denmark	Danish krone	DKr
Eurozone	Euro	€
Hungary	Forint	F$_t$
India	Indian rupee	₹
Iran	Rial	IR
Japan	Yen	¥
Kuwait	Kuwaiti dinar	KD
Norway	Norwegian krone	NKr
Saudi Arabia	Saudi riyal	SR
South Africa	Rand	R
Sweden	Swedish krona	SKr
Switzerland	Swiss franc	SFr
Tanzania	Tanzanian shilling	TSh
United Kingdom	Pound sterling	£
United States	Dollar	$

The foreign exchange market is an over-the-counter market, so there is no single location where traders get together. Instead, market participants are located in the major commercial and investment banks around the world. They communicate using computers, telephones and other telecommunications devices. For example, one communications network for foreign transactions is maintained by the Society for Worldwide Interbank Financial Telecommunications (SWIFT), a Belgian not-for-profit cooperative. Using data transmission lines, a bank in Berlin can send messages to a bank in London via SWIFT regional processing centres.

The many different types of participants in the foreign exchange market include the following:

1 Importers who pay for goods using foreign currencies.
2 Exporters who receive foreign currency and may want to convert to the domestic currency.
3 Portfolio managers who buy or sell foreign equities and bonds.
4 Foreign exchange brokers who match buy and sell orders.
5 Traders who 'make a market' in foreign currencies.
6 Speculators who try to profit from changes in exchange rates.

Exchange Rates

An exchange rate is simply the price of one country's currency expressed in terms of another country's currency. In practice, almost all trading of currencies takes place in terms of the US dollar, yen or euro.

Exchange Rate Quotations

Figure 30.1 reproduces an excerpt of exchange rate quotations as they appeared in the *Financial Times* on 7 April 2015. The four main columns give the number of units of foreign currency it takes to buy one pound, dollar, euro and yen (× 100), respectively. Because this is the price in foreign currency with respect to pounds, dollars, euros

Figure 30.1 Exchange Rate Quotations

Apr 7	Currency	POUND		DOLLAR		EURO		YEN (x100)	
		Closing Mid	Day's Change	Closing Mid	Day's Change	Closing Mid	Day's Change	Closing Mid	Day's Change
Pakistan	(Pak Rupee)	151.6042	−1.0744	101.9250	−0.0200	110.6954	−1.7857	84.7151	−0.9673
Panama	(Balboa)	1.4874	−0.0102	1.0000	−	1.0860	−0.0173	0.8312	−0.0093
Papua New Guinea	(Kina)	3.9840	−0.0274	2.6785	−	2.9089	−0.0463	2.2262	−0.0250
Paraguay	(Guarani)	7189.5636	−58.6778	4833.6150	−6.1050	5249.5367	−90.3754	4017.4667	−50.2086
Peru	(New Sol)	4.6072	−0.0190	3.0975	0.0085	3.3640	−0.0442	2.5745	−0.0217
Philippines	(Peso)	66.1600	−0.3210	44.4800	0.0900	48.3074	−0.6704	36.9696	−0.3392
Pitcairn Is	(Sterling £)	1.0000	−	0.6723	0.0046	0.7302	−0.0066	0.5588	−0.0024
Poland	(Zloty)	5.5387	0.0144	3.7237	0.0351	4.0441	−0.0257	3.0950	−0.0052
Portugal	(Euro)	1.3696	0.0122	0.9208	0.0144	1.0000	−	0.7653	0.0035
Puerto Rico	(US $)	1.4874	−0.0102	1.0000	−	1.0860	−0.0173	0.8312	−0.0093
Qatar	(Riyal)	5.4150	−0.0372	3.6406	0.0001	3.9538	−0.0629	3.0258	−0.0339
Reunion Is de la	(Euro)	11.3696	0.0122	0.9208	0.0144	1.0000	−	0.7653	0.0035
Romania	(New Leu)	6.0487	0.0522	4.0666	0.0627	4.4165	−0.0012	3.3800	0.0148
Russia	(Rouble)	81.7406	−1.3569	54.9550	−0.5300	59.6837	−1.5357	45.6759	−0.9580
Rwanda	(Fr)	1028.5434	−3.3417	691.5000	2.5000	751.0019	−9.2069	574.7413	−4.3476
St Christopher	(E Carib $)	4.0160	−0.0277	2.7000	−	2.9323	−0.0467	2.2441	−0.0252
St Helena	(£)	1.0000	−	0.6723	0.0046	0.7302	−0.0066	0.5588	−0.0024
St Lucia	(E Carib $)	4.0160	−0.0277	2.7000	−	2.9323	−0.0467	2.2441	−0.0252
St Pierre & Miquelon	(Euro)	1.3696	0.0122	0.9208	0.0144	1.0000	−	0.7653	0.0035
St Vincent	(E Carib $)	4.0160	−0.0277	2.7000	−	2.9323	−0.0467	2.2441	−0.0252
San Marino	(Euro)	1.3696	0.0122	0.9208	0.0144	1.0000	−	0.7653	0.0035
Sao Tome	(Dobra)	32529.6366	−156.7092	21870.0000	45.0000	23751.8599	−328.7730	18177.2846	−166.1344
Saudi Arabia	(Riyal)	5.5796	−0.0384	3.7513	−	4.0740	−0.0649	3.1179	−0.0350
Senegal	(CFA Fr)	898.3716	7.9940	603.9842	9.4702	655.9556	−0.0020	502.0024	2.3268
Serbia	(Dinar)	164.2843	1.3094	110.4500	1.6300	119.9540	−0.1127	91.8007	0.3399
Seychelles	(Rupee)	19.9313	−0.0774	13.4000	0.0400	14.5530	−0.1877	11.1374	−0.0913
Sierra Leone	(Leone)	6477.6699	−29.6499	4355.0000	10.0000	4729.7380	−64.3235	3619.6651	−32.2092
Singapore	($)	2.0212	−0.0007	1.3589	0.0088	1.4758	−0.0138	1.1295	−0.0053
Slovakia	(Euro)	1.3696	0.0122	0.9208	0.0144	1.0000	−	0.7653	0.0035
Slovenia	(Euro)	1.3696	0.0122	0.9208	0.0144	1.0000	−	0.7653	0.0035
Solomon Is	($)	11.5842	−0.0526	7.7882	0.0182	8.4583	−0.1147	6.4731	−0.0574
Somali Rep	(Shilling)	11.8993	−1006.5069	8.0000	−672.0000	8.6884	−741.5902	6.6492	−564.8754
South Africa	(Rand)	17.5886	0.0630	11.8250	0.1230	12.8425	−0.0689	9.8284	−0.0069
Spain	(Euro)	1.3696	0.0122	0.9208	0.0144	1.0000	−	0.7653	0.0035
Spanish Ports N Af	(Euro)	1.3696	0.0122	0.9208	0.0144	1.0000	−	0.7653	0.0035
Sri Lanka	(Rupee)	197.8998	−1.5131	133.0500	−0.1000	144.4986	−2.4125	110.5847	−1.3248
Sudan Rep	(£)	8.8159	0.0667	5.9270	0.0851	6.4370	−0.0087	4.9262	0.0163
Surinam	(Dollar)	4.9084	−0.0338	3.3000	−	3.5840	−0.571	2.7428	−0.0308
Swaziland	(Lilangeni)	17.5886	0.0630	11.8250	0.1230	12.8425	−0.0689	9.8284	−0.0069
Sweden	(Krona)	12.8381	0.1344	8.6312	0.1488	9.3739	0.0148	7.1738	0.0446
Switzerland	(Fr)	1.4312	0.0077	0.9622	0.0117	10450	−0.0037	0.7997	0.0009
Taiwan	($)	46.1536	−0.6130	31.0295	−0.1970	33.6995	−0.7543	25.7902	−0.4549
Tanzania	(Shilling)	2759.1444	−19.0085	1855.0000	−	2014.6185	−32.0974	1541.7861	−17.2994
Thailand	(Baht)	48.4449	−0.2139	32.5700	0.0800	35.3726	−0.4753	27.0706	−0.2365
Togo Rep	(CFA Fr)	898.3716	7.9940	603.9842	9.4702	655.9556	−0.0020	502.0024	2.3268
Tonga Is	(Pa'anga)	2.9492	−0.0203	1.9828	−	2.1534	−0.0343	1.6480	−0.0185
Trinidad & Tobago	($)	9.4763	−0.0653	6.3710	−	6.91192	−0.1102	5.2953	−0.0594
Tunisia	(Dinar)	2.8993	0.0126	1.9492	0.0217	2.1169	−0.0097	1.6201	0.0001
Turkey	(New Lira)	3.8522	0.0118	2.5899	0.0256	2.8128	−0.0166	2.1526	−0.0026
Turkmenistan	(New Manat)	4.9828	−0.0343	3.3500	−	3.6383	−0.0580	2.7844	−0.0312
Turks & Caicos	(US $)	1.4874	−0.0102	1.0000	−	1.0860	−0.0173	0.8312	−0.0093
Tuvalu	(Australian $)	1.9437	−0.0105	1.3068	0.0020	1.4192	−0.0204	1.0861	−0.0105
Uganda	(New Shilling)	4447.3540	−45.6165	2990.0000	−10.0000	3247.2825	−62.7712	2485.1432	−36.2890
Ukraine	(Hryvnia)	34.9913	−0.1287	23.5250	0.0750	25.5493	−0.3243	19.5528	−0.1564
UAE	(Dirham)	5.4633	−0.0376	3.6731	−	3.9891	−0.0636	3.0529	−0.0343
United Kingdom	(£)	1.0000	−	0.6723	0.0046	0.7302	−0.0066	0.5588	−0.0024
United States	($)	1.4874	−0.0102	1.0000	−	1.0860	−0.0173	0.8312	−0.0093
Uruguay	(Peso Uruguay)	38.0851	−0.4121	25.6050	−0.1000	27.8082	−0.5534	21.2816	−0.3228
Uzbekistan	(Sum)	3712.8111	−25.5793	2496.1600	−	2710.9491	−43.1913	2074.6873	−23.2788

or yen, it is called an *indirect* quote. For example, the Thai baht (Bt) is quoted at 48.4449 against the pound, which means that you can buy one British pound with 48.4449 Thai baht.

If you were a Thai person and the quote was Bt48.4449/£, the quote would be a *direct* quote because it is in the home currency (baht) with respect to the foreign currency (£).

Example 30.1

Rand for Euros

Suppose you have £1,000. Based on the rates in Figure 30.1, how many South African rand can you get? Alternatively, if a Porsche costs €100,000, how many pounds will you need to buy it?

The exchange rate in terms of rand per pound is 17.5886. Your £1,000 will thus get you

$$£1,000 \times 17.5886 \text{ rand per } £1 = 17,5886 \text{ rand}$$

Because the exchange rate in terms of pound per euro is 0.7302, you will need

$$€100,000 \times £0.7302 \text{ per } € = £73,020$$

Cross-Rates and Triangle Arbitrage

The *Financial Times* quotes exchange rates in terms of the British pound, US dollar, euro and Japanese yen. Using any of these currencies as the common denominator in quoting exchange rates greatly reduces the number of possible cross-currency quotes. For example, with five major currencies, there would potentially be 10 exchange rates instead of just 4.[1] Also, the fact that the one currency (pound, dollar, euro or yen) is used throughout cuts down on inconsistencies in the exchange rate quotations.

Earlier, we defined the cross-rate as the exchange rate for a foreign currency expressed in terms of another foreign currency. For example, suppose we observe the following for the Russian rouble and the Bahraini dinar:

$$\text{Russian rouble per } €1 = 45.8022$$
$$\text{Bahraini dinar per } €1 = 0.4831$$

Suppose the cross-rate is quoted as:

$$\text{Dinar per rouble} = 0.01$$

What do you think?

The cross-rate here is inconsistent with the exchange rates. To see this, suppose you have €100. If you convert this to Russian roubles, you will receive:

$$€100 \times 45.8022 \text{ roubles per } €1 = 4,580.22 \text{ roubles}$$

If you convert this to dinar at the cross-rate, you will have:

$$4,580.22 \text{ roubles} \times 0.01 \text{ per rouble} = 45.8022 \text{ dinar}$$

However, if you just convert your euros to dinar without going through Russian roubles, you will have:

$$€100 \times 0.4831 \text{ dinar per } €1 \doteq 48.31 \text{ dinar}$$

What we see is that the dinar has two prices, 0.4831 dinar per €1 and 0.4580 dinar per €1, with the price we pay depending on how we get the dinar.

To make money, we want to buy low and sell high. The important thing to note is that dinar are cheaper if you buy them with euros because you get 0.4831 dinar instead of just 0.4580 dinar. You should proceed as follows:

1   Buy 48.31 dinar for €100.

2   Use the 48.31 dinar to buy Russian roubles at the cross-rate. Because it takes 0.01 dinar to buy a Russian rouble, you will receive 48.31 dinar/0.01 roubles = 4,831 roubles.

3   Use the 4,831 roubles to buy euros. Because the exchange rate is 45.8022 roubles per euro, you receive 4,831 roubles/45.8022 = €105.48, for a round-trip profit of €5.48.

4   Repeat steps 1 through 3.

This particular activity is called *triangle arbitrage* because the arbitrage involves moving through three different exchange rates:

To prevent such opportunities, it is not difficult to see that because a euro will buy you either 45.8022 Russian roubles or 0.4831 Bahraini dinar, the cross-rate must be:

$$(\text{€}1/0.4831 \text{ dinar})/(45.8922 \text{ rouble/€}1) = 0.010527 \text{ dinar/rouble}$$

That is, the cross-rate must be 0.010527 Bahraini dinar per 1 Russian rouble. If it were anything else, there would be a triangle arbitrage opportunity.

Example 30.2

Shedding Some Pounds

According to Figure 30.1, the exchange rates for the British pound against the euro and dollar are:

$$\text{€/£} = 1.3696$$
$$\text{\$/£} = 1.4874$$

The cross-rate is \$1.0860/€. Show that the exchange rates are consistent.

Types of Transactions

There are two basic types of trades in the foreign exchange market: spot trades and forward trades. A spot trade is an agreement to exchange currency 'on the spot', which actually means that the transaction will be completed or settled within two business days. The exchange rate on a spot trade is called the spot exchange rate. Implicitly, all of the exchange rates and transactions we have discussed so far have referred to the spot market.

A forward trade is an agreement to exchange currency at some time in the future. The exchange rate that will be used is agreed upon today and is called the forward exchange rate. A forward trade will normally be settled sometime in the next 12 months.

If you look back at Figure 30.1, you will see forward exchange rates quoted for the dollar, euro and pound. For example, the spot €/£ exchange rate is €1.3696/£. Assume that the 1-year forward exchange rate is €1.3121/£. This means that you can buy a pound today for €1.3696, or you can agree to take delivery of a pound in one year and pay €1.3121 at that time.

Notice that the British pound is cheaper in the forward market (€1.3121 versus €1.3696). Because the British pound is less expensive in the future than it is today, it is said to be selling at a *discount* relative to the euro. For the same reason, the euro is said to be selling at a *premium* relative to the British pound.

Why does the forward market exist? One answer is that it allows businesses and individuals to lock in a future exchange rate today, thereby eliminating any risk from unfavourable shifts in the exchange rate.

Example 30.3

Looking Forward

Suppose you are a British business and expecting to receive €1 million in 3 months, and you agree to a forward trade to exchange your euros for pounds. Based on Figure 30.1 and assuming that the 3-month forward rate is €1.35/£, how many pounds will you get in 3 months? Is the euro selling at a discount or a premium relative to the pound?

In Figure 30.1, the spot exchange rate in terms of pound per euro is £0.7302 = €1. If the 3-month forward rate is €1.35/£, this means that you can get £0.7407 (= 1/1.35) for every euro. If you expect €1 million in 3 months, then you will get €1 million × 0.7407 per pound = £740,700. Because it is cheaper to buy a pound in the forward market than in the spot market (£0.7407 versus £0.7302), the euro is said to be selling at a premium relative to the pound.

As we mentioned earlier, it is standard practice around the world (with a few exceptions) to quote exchange rates in terms of the pound, dollar, euro and yen. This means that rates are quoted as the amount of currency per pound, dollar, euro or yen. For the remainder of this chapter, we will stick with this form. Things can get extremely confusing if you forget this. Thus, when we say things like 'the exchange rate is expected to rise', it is important to remember that we are talking about the exchange rate quoted as units of foreign currency per dollar, euro or pound.

30.3   Purchasing Power Parity

Now that we have discussed what exchange rate quotations mean, we can address an obvious question: what determines the level of the spot exchange rate? In addition, because we know that exchange rates change through time, we can ask the related question, what determines the rate of change in exchange rates? At least part of the answer in both cases goes by the name of purchasing power parity (PPP), the idea that the exchange rate adjusts to keep purchasing power constant among currencies. As we discuss next, there are two forms of PPP, *absolute* and *relative*.

Absolute Purchasing Power Parity

The basic idea behind *absolute purchasing power parity* is that a commodity costs the same regardless of what currency is used to purchase it or where it is selling. This is a very straightforward concept. If a beer costs NKr 50 in Oslo, and the exchange rate is NKr10 per pound, then a beer costs NKr50/10 = £5 in London. In other words, absolute PPP says that £1 or €1 will buy you the same number of, say, cheeseburgers anywhere in the world.

More formally, let S_0 be the spot exchange rate between the euro and the dollar today (time 0), and we are quoting exchange rates as the amount of foreign currency per euro. Let P_{US} and P_{Euro} be the current US and euro prices, respectively, on a particular commodity, say, apples. Absolute PPP simply says that:

$$P_{US} = S_0 \times P_{Euro}$$

This tells us that the US price for something is equal to the euro price for that same something multiplied by the exchange rate.

The rationale behind PPP is similar to that behind triangle arbitrage. If PPP did not hold, arbitrage would be possible (in principle) if apples were moved from one country to another. For example, suppose apples are selling in Milan for €2 per bushel, whereas in New York the price is $3 per bushel. Absolute PPP implies that:

$$P_{US} = S_0 \times P_{Euro}$$
$$\$3 = S_0 \times \text{€}2$$
$$S_0 = \$3/\text{€}2 = \$1.50/\text{€}$$

That is, the implied spot exchange rate is $1.50 per euro. Equivalently, a dollar is worth €1/$1.5 = €0.667/$.

Suppose instead that the actual exchange rate is $1.2815/€. Starting with €2, a trader could buy a bushel of apples in Madrid, ship it to New York, and sell it there for $3. Our trader could then convert the $3 into euros at the prevailing exchange rate, $S_0 = \$1.2815/\text{€}$, yielding a total of $3/€1.2815 = €2.34. The round-trip gain would be 34 cents.

Because of this profit potential, forces are set in motion to change the exchange rate and/or the price of apples. In our example, apples would begin moving from Madrid to New York. The reduced supply of apples in Madrid would raise the price of apples there, and the increased supply in the US would lower the price of apples in New York.

In addition to moving apples around, apple traders would be busily converting dollars back into euros to buy more apples. This activity would increase the supply of dollars and simultaneously increase the demand for euros. We would expect the value of a dollar to fall. This means that the euro would be getting more valuable, so it would take more dollars to buy one euro. Because the exchange rate is quoted as dollars per euro, we would expect the exchange rate to rise from $1.2815/£.

For absolute PPP to hold absolutely, several things must be true:

1   The transaction costs of trading apples – shipping, insurance, spoilage, and so on – must be zero.

2   There must be no barriers to trading apples – no tariffs, taxes or other political barriers.

3   Finally, an apple in New York must be identical to an apple in Madrid. It will not do for you to send red apples to Madrid if the Spanish eat only green apples.

Given the fact that the transaction costs are not zero and that the other conditions are rarely met exactly, it is not surprising that absolute PPP is really applicable only to traded goods, and then only to very uniform ones.

For this reason, absolute PPP does not imply that a Mercedes costs the same as a Ford or that a nuclear power plant in France costs the same as one in New York. In the case of the cars, they are not identical. In the case of the power plants, even if they were identical, they are expensive and would be very difficult to ship. On the other hand, we would be very surprised to see a significant violation of absolute PPP for gold.

Violations of PPP are actually sought out by corporations. For example, in the middle of 2004, Alcoa announced that it would build a $1 billion aluminium smelter plant on the Caribbean island of Trinidad. At the same time, the company was breaking ground on another $1 billion plant in Iceland and looking into other locations including China, Brunei, Bahrain, Brazil and Canada. In all cases, low energy costs were the attraction (aluminium smelting is very energy-intensive). Meanwhile, the company had several plants in the Pacific Northwest that were closed because higher electricity prices in this region made the plants unprofitable.

One of the more famous violations of absolute PPP is the Big Mac Index constructed by *The Economist*. To construct the index, prices for a Big Mac in different countries are gathered from McDonald's. Below you will find the January 2015 Big Mac index from www.economist.com. (We will leave it to you to find the most recent index.)

As you can see from the index, absolute PPP does not seem to hold, at least for the Big Mac. In fact, in very few currencies surveyed by *The Economist* is the exchange rate within 20 per cent of that predicted by absolute PPP. The largest disparity is in Switzerland, where the currency is apparently overvalued by about 57 per cent. And many currencies are 'incorrectly' priced by more than 35 per cent. Why?

There are several reasons. First, a Big Mac is not really transportable. Yes, you can load a ship with Big Macs and send it to Norway where the currency is supposedly overvalued by more than 30 per cent. But do you really think people would buy your Big Macs? Probably not. Even though it is relatively easy to transport a Big Mac, it would be relatively expensive, and the hamburger would suffer in quality along the way.

2015 Big Mac Index

Country	Big Mac Prices in Local Currency	Big Mac Prices in Dollars	Implied PPP of the Dollar	Actual Dollar Exchange Rate January 2015	Under (−)/over (+) Valuation Against the Dollar (%)
Australia	5.3	4.32	1.11	1.23	−9.84
Britain	2.89	4.37	0.60	0.66	−8.81
China	17.2	2.77	3.59	6.21	−42.19
Denmark	34.5	5.38	7.20	6.42	12.23
Euro area	3.68	4.26	0.77	0.86	−10.98
Hong Kong	18.8	2.43	3.92	7.75	−49.37
India	116.25	1.89	24.27	61.62	−60.61
Japan	370	3.14	77.24	117.77	−34.41
Malaysia	7.63	2.11	1.59	3.62	−55.94
New Zealand	5.9	4.49	1.23	1.31	−6.21
Norway	48	6.30	10.02	7.62	31.46
Poland	9.2	2.48	1.92	3.71	−48.18
Russia	89	1.36	18.58	65.23	−71.51
Saudi Arabia	11	2.93	2.30	3.76	−38.87
Singapore	4.7	3.53	0.98	1.33	−26.40
South Africa	25.5	2.22	5.32	11.48	−53.62
Sweden	40.7	4.97	8.50	8.19	3.73
Switzerland	6.5	7.54	1.36	0.86	57.49

Country	Big Mac Prices in Local Currency	Big Mac Prices in Dollars*	Implied PPP of the Dollar	Actual Dollar Exchange Rate January 2015	Under (−)/over (+) Valuation Against the Dollar (%)
Thailand	99	3.04	20.67	32.61	−36.61
Turkey	9.25	3.96	1.93	2.33	−17.24
UAE	13	3.54	2.71	3.67	−26.11
United States	4.79	4.79	1.00	1.00	0.00
Austria	3.39	3.93	0.71	0.86	−18.00
Belgium	3.7	4.29	0.77	0.86	−10.50
Finland	4.1	4.75	0.86	0.86	−0.83
France	3.9	4.52	0.81	0.86	−5.66
Germany	3.67	4.25	0.77	0.86	−11.23
Greece	3.05	3.53	0.64	0.86	−26.22
Ireland	3.49	4.04	0.73	0.86	−15.58
Italy	3.85	4.46	0.80	0.86	−6.87
Netherlands	3.45	4.00	0.72	0.86	−16.55
Portugal	3	3.48	0.63	0.86	−27.43
Spain	3.65	4.23	0.76	0.86	−11.71

Also, if you look, the price of the Big Mac is the average price from each of the countries in the Eurozone. The reason is that Big Macs do not sell for the same price in Europe, where presumably they are all purchased with the euro. The cost of living and competition are only a few of the factors that affect the price of a Big Mac in Europe. If Big Macs are not priced the same in the same currency, would we expect absolute PPP to hold across currencies?

Finally, differing tastes can account for the apparent discrepancy. In the United States, hamburgers and fast food have become a staple of the American diet. In other countries, hamburgers have not become as entrenched. We would expect the price of the Big Mac to be lower in the United States because there is much more competition.

Having examined the Big Mac, we can say that absolute PPP should hold more closely for more easily transportable items. For instance, there are many companies with equity listed on exchanges in more than one country. If you examine the share prices on the two exchanges you will find that the price of the shares is almost exactly what absolute PPP would predict. The reason is that a share of equity in a particular company is (usually) the same wherever you buy it and whatever currency you use.

Relative Purchasing Power Parity

As a practical matter, a relative version of purchasing power parity has evolved. *Relative purchasing power parity* does not tell us what determines the absolute level of the exchange rate. Instead, it tells us what determines the *change* in the exchange rate over time.

The Basic Idea

Suppose the British pound–US dollar exchange rate is currently $S_0 = \$1.30$. Further suppose that the inflation rate in the US is predicted to be 10 per cent over the coming year, and (for the moment) the inflation rate in the United Kingdom is predicted to be zero. What do you think the exchange rate will be in a year?

If you think about it, you see that a pound currently costs $1.30 in the US. With 10 per cent inflation, we expect prices in the US to generally rise by 10 per cent. So we expect that the price of a pound will go up by 10 per cent, and the exchange rate should rise to $1.30 × 1.1 = $1.43.

If the inflation rate in the United Kingdom is not zero, then we need to worry about the *relative* inflation rates in the two countries. For example, suppose the UK inflation rate is predicted to be 4 per cent. Relative to prices in the

United Kingdom, prices in the US are rising at a rate of 10 per cent − 4 per cent = 6 per cent per year. So we expect the price of the pound to rise by 6 per cent, and the predicted exchange rate is $1.30 × 1.06 = $1.378.

The Result

In general, relative PPP says that the change in the exchange rate is determined by the difference in the inflation rates of the two countries. To be more specific, we will use the following notation:

- S_0 = Current (time 0) spot exchange rate (foreign currency per home currency).
- $E(S_t)$ = Expected exchange rate in t periods.
- h_{HC} = Inflation rate in the home currency.
- h_{FC} = Foreign country inflation rate.

Based on our discussion just preceding, relative PPP says that the expected percentage change in the exchange rate over the next year, $[E(S_1) − S_0]/S_0$, is:

$$[E(S_1) − S_0]/S_0 = h_{FC} − h_{HC} \qquad (30.1)$$

In words, relative PPP simply says that the expected percentage change in the exchange rate is equal to the difference in inflation rates. If we rearrange this slightly, we get:

$$E(S_1) = S_0 × [1 + (h_{FC} − h_{HC})] \qquad (30.2)$$

This result makes a certain amount of sense, but care must be used in quoting the exchange rate.

In our example involving United States and Britain, relative PPP tells us that the exchange rate will rise by $h_{FC} − h_{HC}$ = 10 per cent − 4 per cent = 6 per cent per year. Assuming the difference in inflation rates does not change, the expected exchange rate in 2 years, $E(S_2)$, will therefore be:

$$\begin{aligned} E(S_2) &= E(S_1) × (1 + 0.06) \\ &= 1.378 × 1.06 \\ &= 1.461 \end{aligned}$$

Notice that we could have written this as:

$$\begin{aligned} E(S_2) &= 1.378 × 1.06 \\ &= 1.30 × (1.06 × 1.06) \\ &= 1.30 × 1.06^2 \end{aligned}$$

In general, relative PPP says that the expected exchange rate at some time in the future, $E(S_t)$, is:

$$E(S_t) = S_0 × [1 + (h_{FC} − h_{HC})]^t \qquad (30.3)$$

As we will see, this is a very useful relationship.

Because we do not really expect absolute PPP to hold for most goods, we will focus on relative PPP in our following discussion. Henceforth, when we refer to PPP without further qualification, we mean relative PPP.

Example 30.4

It Is All Relative

From Figure 30.1, the Turkish lira–euro exchange rate is 2.8128 lira per euro. The inflation rate in Turkey over the next 3 years will run at, say, 10 per cent per year, whereas the Eurozone inflation rate will be 2 per cent. Based on relative PPP, what will the exchange rate be in 3 years?

Because the Eurozone inflation rate is lower, we expect that a euro will become more valuable. The exchange rate change will be 10 per cent −2 per cent = 8 per cent per year. Over 3 years the exchange rate will rise to:

$$\begin{aligned} E(S_3) &= S_0 × [1 + (h_{FC} − h_{HC})]^3 \\ &= 2.8128 × [1 + (0.08)]^3 \\ &= 3.5433 \end{aligned}$$

Currency Appreciation and Depreciation

We frequently hear things like 'the euro strengthened (or weakened) in financial markets today' or 'the euro is expected to appreciate (or depreciate) relative to the pound'. When we say that the euro strengthens or appreciates, we mean that the value of a euro rises, so it takes more foreign currency to buy a euro.

What happens to the exchange rates as currencies fluctuate in value depends on how exchange rates are quoted. Because we are quoting them as units of foreign currency per home currency, the exchange rate moves in the same direction as the value of the home currency: it rises as the home currency strengthens, and it falls as the home currency weakens.

Relative PPP tells us that the exchange rate will rise if the home currency inflation rate is lower than the foreign country's inflation rate. This happens because the foreign currency depreciates in value and therefore weakens relative to the home currency.

30.4 Interest Rate Parity, Unbiased Forward Rates and the International Fisher Effect

The next issue we need to address is the relationship between spot exchange rates, forward exchange rates and interest rates. To get started, we need some additional notation:

- F_t = Forward exchange rate for settlement at time t.
- R_{HC} = Home currency nominal risk-free interest rate.
- R_{FC} = Foreign country nominal risk-free interest rate.

As before, we will use S_0 to stand for the spot exchange rate. You can take the home currency nominal risk-free rate, R_{HC}, to be the home country T-bill rate.

Covered Interest Arbitrage

Assume we observe the following information about the British pound and the US dollar in the market:

- $S_0 = \$1.6117$
- $F_1 = \$1.6064$
- $R_{HC} = 2.13\%$
- $R_{FC} = 0.27\%$

where R_{FC} is the nominal risk-free rate in the United States. The period is one year, so F_1 is the 360-day forward rate.

Do you see an arbitrage opportunity here? Suppose you have £10,000 to invest, and you want a riskless investment. One option you have is to invest the £10,000 in a riskless UK investment such as a 360-day T-bill. If you do this, then in one period your £1 will be worth:

$$\text{£ value in 1 period} = \text{£1} \times (1 + R_{HC})$$
$$= \text{£10,213}$$

Alternatively, you can invest in the US risk-free investment. To do this, you need to convert your £10,000 to US dollars and simultaneously execute a forward trade to convert dollars back to pounds in one year. The necessary steps would be as follows:

1 Convert your £10,000 to £10,000 × S_0 = $16,117.

2 At the same time, enter into a forward agreement to convert US dollars back to pounds in one year. Because the forward rate is $1.6064, you will get £1 for every $1.6064 that you have in one year.

3 Invest your $16,117 in the United States at R_{FC}. In one year, you will have:

$$\text{\$ value in 1 year} = \$16,117 \times (1 + R_{FC})$$
$$= \$16,117 \times 1.0027$$
$$= \$16,161$$

4   Convert your \$16,161 back to pounds at the agreed-upon rate of \$1.6064 = £1. You end up with:

$$\text{£ value in 1 year} = \$16,161/1.6064$$
$$= £10,060$$

Notice that the value in one year resulting from this strategy can be written as:

$$\text{£ value in 1 year} = £10,000 \times S_0 \times (1 + R_{FC})/F_1$$
$$= £10,000 \times 1.6117 \times 1.0027/1.6064$$
$$= £10,060$$

The return on this investment is apparently 0.60 per cent. This is lower than the 2.13 per cent we get from investing in the United Kingdom. Because both investments are risk-free, there is an arbitrage opportunity.

To exploit the difference in interest rates, you need to borrow, say, \$10 million at the lower US rate and invest it at the higher British rate. What is the round-trip profit from doing this? To find out, we can work through the steps outlined previously:

1   Convert the \$10 million at \$1.6064/£ to get £6,225,100.
2   Agree to exchange dollars for pounds in one year at \$1.6161 to the pound.
3   Invest the £6,225,100 for one year at $R_{UK} = 2.13$ per cent. You end up with £6,357,694.
4   Convert the £6,357,694 back to dollars to fulfil the forward contract. You receive £6,357,694 × \$1.6161/£ = \$10,274,670.
5   Repay the loan with interest. You owe \$10 million plus 0.27 per cent interest, for a total of \$10,027,000. You have \$10,274,670, so your round-trip profit is a risk-free \$247,670.

The activity that we have illustrated here goes by the name of *covered interest arbitrage*. The term *covered* refers to the fact that we are covered in the event of a change in the exchange rate because we lock in the forward exchange rate today.

Interest Rate Parity

If we assume that significant covered interest arbitrage opportunities do not exist, then there must be some relationship between spot exchange rates, forward exchange rates and relative interest rates. To see what this relationship is, note that in general strategy 1 from the preceding discussion, investing in a riskless home currency investment, gives us $1 + R_{HC}$ for every unit of home currency we invest. Strategy 2, investing in a foreign risk-free investment, gives us $S_0 \times (1 + R_{FC})/ F_1$ for every unit of home currency we invest. Because these have to be equal to prevent arbitrage, it must be the case that:

$$1 + R_{HC} = S_0 \times (1 + R_{FC})/F_1$$

Rearranging this a bit gets us the famous interest rate parity (IRP) condition:

$$F_1/S_0 = (1 + R_{FC})/(1 + R_{HC}) \tag{30.4}$$

There is a very useful approximation for IRP that illustrates clearly what is going on and is not difficult to remember. If we define the percentage forward premium or discount as $(F_1 - S_0) / S_0$, then IRP says that this percentage premium or discount is *approximately* equal to the difference in interest rates:

$$(F_1 - S_0)/S_0 \times R_{FC} - R_{HC} \tag{30.5}$$

Loosely, what IRP says is that any difference in interest rates between two countries for some period is just offset by the change in the relative value of the currencies, thereby eliminating any arbitrage possibilities. Notice that we could also write:

$$F_1 = S_0 \times [1 + (R_{FC} - R_{HC})] \tag{30.6}$$

In general, if we have t periods instead of just one, the IRP approximation is written like this:

$$F_t = S_0 \times [1 + (R_{FC} - R_{HC})]^t \tag{30.7}$$

Example 30.5

Parity Check

Suppose the exchange rate for the South African rand, S_0, is currently R10.2992 = €1. If the interest rate in the Eurozone is $R_{Euro} = 2.12$ per cent and the interest rate in South Africa is $R_{SA} = 10.95$ per cent, then what must the forward rate be to prevent covered interest arbitrage?

From IRP, we have

$$
\begin{aligned}
F_1 &= S_0 \times [1 + (R_{SA} - R_{Euro})] \\
&= \text{R}10.2992 \times [1 + (0.1095 - 0.0212)] \\
&= \text{R}10.2992 \times 1.0883 \\
&= \text{R}11.2086
\end{aligned}
$$

Notice that the rand will sell at a discount relative to the euro. (Why?)

Forward Rates and Future Spot Rates

In addition to PPP and IRP, there is one more basic relationship we need to discuss. What is the connection between the forward rate and the expected future spot rate? The **unbiased forward rates (UFR)** condition says that the forward rate, F_1, is equal to the *expected* future spot rate, $E(S_1)$:

$$F_1 = E(S_1)$$

With t periods, UFR would be written as:

$$F_t = E(S_t)$$

Loosely, the UFR condition says that, on average, the forward exchange rate is equal to the future spot exchange rate.

If we ignore risk, then the UFR condition should hold. Suppose the forward rate for the South African rand is consistently lower than the future spot rate by, say, 10 rand. This means that anyone who wanted to convert euros to rand in the future would consistently get more rand by not agreeing to a forward exchange. The forward rate would have to rise to get anyone interested in a forward exchange.

Similarly, if the forward rate were consistently higher than the future spot rate, then anyone who wanted to convert rand to euros would get more euros per rand by not agreeing to a forward trade. The forward exchange rate would have to fall to attract such traders.

For these reasons, the forward and actual future spot rates should be equal to each other on average. What the future spot rate will actually be is uncertain, of course. The UFR condition may not hold if traders are willing to pay a premium to avoid this uncertainty. If the condition does hold, then the one year forward rate that we see today should be an unbiased predictor of what the exchange rate will actually be in one year.

Putting it All Together

We have developed three relationships – PPP, IRP and UFR – that describe the interactions between key financial variables such as interest rates, exchange rates and inflation rates. We now explore the implications of these relationships as a group.

Uncovered Interest Parity

To start, it is useful to collect our international financial market relationships in one place:

$$\text{PPP:} \quad E(S_1) = S_0 \times [1 + (h_{FC} - h_{HC})]$$
$$\text{IRP:} \quad F_1 = S_0 \times [1 + (R_{FC} - R_{HC})]$$
$$\text{UFR:} \quad F_1 = E(S_1)$$

We begin by combining UFR and IRP. Because we know that $F_1 = E(S_1)$ from the UFR condition, we can substitute $E(S_1)$ for F_1 in IRP. The result is:

$$\text{UIP:} \quad E(S_1) = S_0 \times [1 + (R_{FC} - R_{HC})] \tag{30.8}$$

This important relationship is called uncovered interest parity (UIP), and it will play a key role in our international capital budgeting discussion that follows. With t periods, UIP becomes:

$$E(S_t) = S_0 \times [1 + (R_{FC} - R_{HC})]^t \qquad (30.9)$$

The International Fisher Effect

Next we compare PPP and UIP. Both of them have $E(S_1)$ on the left side, so their right sides must be equal. We thus have:

$$S_0 \times [1 + (h_{FC} - h_{HC})] = S_0 \times [1 + (R_{FC} - R_{HC})]$$
$$h_{FC} - h_{HC} = R_{FC} - R_{HC}$$

This tells us that the difference in returns between the home country and a foreign country is just equal to the difference in inflation rates. Rearranging this slightly gives us the international Fisher effect (IFE):

$$\text{IFE: } R_{HC} - h_{HC} = R_{FC} - h_{FC} \qquad (30.10)$$

The IFE says that *real* rates are equal across countries. The conclusion that real returns are equal across countries is really basic economics. If real returns were higher in, say, Britain than in the Eurozone, money would flow out of Eurozone financial markets and into British markets. Asset prices in Britain would rise and their returns would fall. At the same time, asset prices in Europe would fall and their returns would rise. This process acts to equalize real returns.

Having said all this, we need to note a couple of things. First, we have not explicitly dealt with risk in our discussion. We might reach a different conclusion about real returns once we do, particularly if people in different countries have different tastes and attitudes toward risk. Second, there are many barriers to the movement of money and capital around the world. Real returns might be different in two different countries for long periods if money cannot move freely between them.

Despite these problems, we expect that capital markets will become increasingly internationalized. As this occurs, any differences in real rates will probably diminish. The laws of economics have little respect for national boundaries.

30.5 International Capital Budgeting

Chapter 7
Page 177

For any foreign investment, one must consider the impact of changing exchange rates on the home currency net present value (see **Chapter 7** for general capital budgeting). Take, for example, Kihlstrom Equipment, a US-based international company that is evaluating an overseas investment. Kihlstrom's exports of drill bits have increased to such a degree that it is considering building a distribution centre in France. The project will cost €2 million to launch. The cash flows are expected to be €0.9 million a year for the next 3 years.

The current spot exchange rate for euros is €0.5/$. Recall that this is euros per dollar, so a euro is worth $1/0.5 = $2. The risk-free rate in the United States is 5 per cent, and the risk-free rate in France is 7 per cent. Note that the exchange rate and the two interest rates are observed in financial markets, not estimated. Kihlstrom's required return on dollar investments of this sort is 10 per cent.

Should Kihlstrom take this investment? As always, the answer depends on the NPV; but how do we calculate the net present value of this project in US dollars? There are two basic methods:

1 *The home currency approach*: Convert all the euro cash flows into dollars, and then discount at 10 per cent to find the NPV in dollars. Notice that for this approach we have to come up with the future exchange rates to convert the future projected euro cash flows into dollars.

2 *The foreign currency approach*: Determine the required return on euro investments, and then discount the euro cash flows to find the NPV in euros. Then convert this euro NPV to a dollar NPV. This approach requires us to somehow convert the 10 per cent dollar required return to the equivalent euro required return.

Chapter 6
Page 150

The difference between these two approaches is primarily a matter of when we convert from euros to dollars. In the first case, we convert before estimating the NPV. In the second case, we convert after estimating NPV (NPV is discussed in detail in **Chapter 6**).

It might appear that the second approach is superior because for it we have to come up with only one number, the euro discount rate. Furthermore, because the first approach requires us to forecast future exchange rates, it probably seems that there is greater room for error with this approach. As we illustrate next, however, based on our previous results, the two approaches are really the same.

Method 1: The Home Currency Approach

To convert the project future cash flows into dollars, we will invoke the uncovered interest parity, or UIP, relation to come up with the projected exchange rates. Remember that the euro is the foreign currency in this example. Based on our earlier discussion, the expected exchange rate at time t, $E(S_t)$, is:

$$E(S_t) = S_0 \times [1 + (R_\epsilon - R_{US})]^t$$

where R_ϵ stands for the nominal risk-free rate in France. Because R_ϵ is 7 per cent, R_{US} is 5 per cent, and the current exchange rate (S_0) is €0.5:

$$E(S_t) = 0.5 \times [1 + (0.07 - 0.05)]^t$$
$$= 0.5 \times 1.02^t$$

The projected exchange rates for the drill bit project are thus as shown here:

Year	Expected Exchange Rate
1	€0.5 × 1.02^1 = €0.5100
2	€0.5 × 1.02^2 = €0.5202
3	€0.5 × 1.02^3 = €0.5306

Using these exchange rates, along with the current exchange rate, we can convert all of the euro cash flows to dollars (note that all of the cash flows in this example are in millions):

Year	(1) Cash Flow in €m	(2) Expected Exchange Rate	(3) Cash Flow in $m (1)/(2)
0	−2.0	0.5000	−4.00
1	0.9	0.5100	1.76
2	0.9	0.5202	1.73
3	0.9	0.5306	1.70

To finish off, we calculate the NPV in the ordinary way:

$$NPV_\$ = -\$4 + \$1.76 / 1.10 + \$1.73 / 1.10^2 + \$1.70 / 1.10^3$$
$$= \$0.3 \text{ million}$$

So, the project appears to be profitable.

Method 2: The Foreign Currency Approach

Kihlstrom requires a nominal return of 10 per cent on the dollar-denominated cash flows. We need to convert this to a rate suitable for euro-denominated cash flows. Based on the international Fisher effect, we know that the difference in the nominal rates is:

$$R_\epsilon - R_{US} = h_\epsilon - h_{US}$$
$$= 7\% - 5\% = 2\%$$

The appropriate discount rate for estimating the euro cash flows from the drill bit project is approximately equal to 10 per cent plus an extra 2 per cent to compensate for the greater euro inflation rate.

If we calculate the NPV of the euro cash flows at this rate, we get:

$$NPV_\epsilon = -€2 + €0.9/1.12 + €0.9/1.12^2 + €0.9/1.12^3$$
$$= €0.16 \text{ million}$$

The NPV of this project is €0.16 million. Taking this project makes us €0.16 million richer today. What is this in dollars? Because the exchange rate today is €0.5, the dollar NPV of the project is

$$NPV\$ = NPV_\epsilon/S_0 = €0.16/0.5 = \$0.3 \text{ million}$$

This is the same dollar NPV that we previously calculated.

The important thing to recognize from our example is that the two capital budgeting procedures are actually the same and will always give the same answer. In this second approach, the fact that we are implicitly forecasting exchange rates is simply hidden. Even so, the foreign currency approach is computationally a little easier.

Unremitted Cash Flows

The previous example assumed that all after-tax cash flows from the foreign investment could be remitted to (paid out to) the parent firm. Actually, substantial differences can exist between the cash flows generated by a foreign project and the amount that can be remitted, or 'repatriated', to the parent firm.

A foreign subsidiary can remit funds to a parent in many forms, including the following:

1 Dividends.

2 Management fees for central services.

3 Royalties on the use of trade names and patents.

However cash flows are repatriated, international firms must pay special attention to remittances because there may be current and future controls on remittances. Many governments are sensitive to the charge of being exploited by foreign national firms. In such cases, governments are tempted to limit the ability of international firms to remit cash flows. Funds that cannot currently be remitted are sometimes said to be *blocked*.

30.6　Exchange Rate Risk

Exchange rate risk is the natural consequence of international operations in a world where relative currency values move up and down. Managing exchange rate risk is an important part of international finance. As we discuss next, there are three different types of exchange rate risk or exposure: short-term exposure, long-term exposure and translation exposure.

Short-Term Exposure

The day-to-day fluctuations in exchange rates create short-term risks for international firms. Most such firms have contractual agreements to buy and sell goods in the near future at set prices. When different currencies are involved, such transactions have an extra element of risk.

For example, imagine that you are importing imitation pasta from Italy and reselling it in the United Kingdom under the Impasta brand name. Your largest customer has ordered 10,000 cases of Impasta. You place the order with your supplier today, but you will not pay until the goods arrive in 60 days. Your selling price is £6 per case. Your cost is €8.40 per case, and the exchange rate is currently €1.50, so it takes 1.50 euros to buy £1.

At the current exchange rate, your cost in pounds of filling the order is €8.40/1.5 = £5.60 per case, so your pre-tax profit on the order is $10,000 \times (£6 - 5.60) = £4,000$. However, the exchange rate in 60 days will probably be different, so your profit will depend on what the future exchange rate turns out to be.

For example, if the rate goes to €1.60, your cost is €8.40/1.60 = £5.25 per case. Your profit goes to £7,500. If the exchange rate goes to, say, €1.40, then your cost is €8.40/1.40 = £6, and your profit is zero.

The short-term exposure in our example can be reduced or eliminated in several ways. The most obvious way is by entering into a forward exchange agreement to lock in an exchange rate. For example, suppose the 60-day forward rate is €1.58. What will be your profit if you hedge? What profit should you expect if you do not hedge?

If you hedge, you lock in an exchange rate of €1.58. Your cost in pounds will thus be €8.40/1.58 = £5.32 per case, so your profit will be $10,000 \times (£6 - 5.32) = £6,800$. If you do not hedge, then, assuming that the forward rate is an unbiased predictor (in other words, assuming the UFR condition holds), you should expect that the exchange rate will actually be €1.58 in 60 days. You should expect to make £6,800.

Alternatively, if this strategy is not feasible, you could simply borrow the pounds today, convert them into euros, and invest the euros for 60 days to earn some interest. Based on IRP, this amounts to entering into a forward contract.

Long-term Exposure

In the long term, the value of a foreign operation can fluctuate because of unanticipated changes in relative economic conditions. For example, imagine that we own a labour-intensive assembly operation located in another country to take advantage of lower wages. Through time, unexpected changes in economic conditions can raise the foreign wage levels to the point where the cost advantage is eliminated or even becomes negative.

Hedging long-term exposure is more difficult than hedging short-term risks. For one thing, organized forward markets do not exist for such long-term needs. Instead, the primary option that firms have is to try to match up foreign currency inflows and outflows. The same thing goes for matching foreign currency-denominated assets and liabilities. For example, a firm that sells in a foreign country might try to concentrate its raw material purchases and labour expense in that country. That way, the home currency values of its revenues and costs will move up and down together. Probably the best examples of this type of hedging are the so-called transplant auto manufacturers such as BMW, Honda, Mercedes and Toyota, which now build a substantial portion of the cars they sell in the United States at plants located in the United States, thereby obtaining some degree of immunization against exchange rate movements.

For example, the German firm, BMW, produces 160,000 cars in South Carolina, US, and exports about 100,000 of them. The costs of manufacturing the cars are paid mostly in dollars, and when BMW exports the cars to Europe it receives euros. When the dollar weakens, these vehicles become more profitable for BMW. At the same time, BMW exports about 217,000 cars to the United States each year. The costs of manufacturing these imported cars are mostly in euros, so they become less profitable when the dollar weakens. Taken together, these gains and losses tend to offset each other and give BMW a natural hedge.

Similarly, a firm can reduce its long-term exchange rate risk by borrowing in the foreign country. Fluctuations in the value of the foreign subsidiary's assets will then be at least partially offset by changes in the value of the liabilities.

Translation Exposure

When a British company calculates its accounting net income and EPS for some period, it must translate everything into pounds. Similarly, a Eurozone firm must translate all overseas income into euros. This can create some problems for the accountants when there are significant foreign operations. In particular, two issues arise:

1   What is the appropriate exchange rate to use for translating each account in the statement of financial position?

2   How should accounting gains and losses from foreign currency translation be handled?

To illustrate the accounting problem, suppose we started a small foreign subsidiary in Lilliputia a year ago. The local currency is the gulliver, abbreviated GL. At the beginning of the year, the exchange rate was GL2 = €1, and the statement of financial position for gulliver looked like this:

	GL		GL
Assets	1,000	Liabilities	500
		Equity	500

At 2 gullivers to the euro, the beginning statement of financial position in euros was as follows:

	€		€
Assets	500	Liabilities	250
		Equity	250

Lilliputia is a quiet place, and nothing at all actually happened during the year. As a result, net income was zero (before consideration of exchange rate changes). However, the exchange rate did change to 4 gullivers = €1 purely because the Lilliputian inflation rate is much higher than the Eurozone inflation rate.

Because nothing happened, the ending statement in financial position in gullivers is the same as the beginning one. However, if we convert it to euros at the new exchange rate, we get these figures:

	€		€
Assets	250	Liabilities	125
		Equity	125

Notice that the value of the equity has gone down by €125, even though net income was exactly zero. Despite the fact that absolutely nothing happened, there is a €125 accounting loss. How to handle this €125 loss has been a controversial accounting question.

The current approach to handling translation gains and losses is based on rules set out in the International Accounting Standards Board (IASB) *International Accounting Standard 21* (IAS 21). For the most part, IAS 21 requires that all assets and liabilities be translated from the subsidiary's currency into the parent's currency using the exchange rate that currently prevails. Income and expenses are treated differently and these are translated at the exchange rate that prevails at the time of the transaction or at the average rate for the period when this is a reasonable approximation.

Managing Exchange Rate Risk

For a large multinational firm, the management of exchange rate risk is complicated by the fact that there can be many different currencies involved in many different subsidiaries. It is likely that a change in some exchange rate will benefit some subsidiaries and hurt others. The net effect on the overall firm depends on its net exposure.

For example, suppose a firm has two divisions. Division A buys goods in Italy for euros and sells them in Britain for pounds. Division B buys goods in Britain for pounds and sells them in Italy for euros. If these two divisions are of roughly equal size in terms of their inflows and outflows, then the overall firm obviously has little exchange rate risk.

In our example, the firm's net position in pounds (the amount coming in less the amount going out) is small, so the exchange rate risk is small. However, if one division, acting on its own, were to start hedging its exchange rate risk, then the overall firm's exchange rate risk would go up. The moral of the story is that multinational firms have to be conscious of the overall position that the firm has in a foreign currency. For this reason, management of exchange rate risk is probably best handled on a centralized basis.

30.7   Political Risk

One final element of risk in international investing is *political risk.* That is, changes in value that arise as a consequence of political actions. This is not a problem faced exclusively by international firms. For example, changes in British tax laws and regulations may benefit some British firms and hurt others, so political risk exists nationally as well as internationally.

Some countries have more political risk than others, however. When firms have operations in these riskier countries, the extra political risk may lead the firms to require higher returns on overseas investments to compensate for the possibility that funds may be blocked, critical operations interrupted, and contracts abrogated. In the most extreme case, the possibility of outright confiscation may be a concern in countries with relatively unstable political environments.

Political risk also depends on the nature of the business: some businesses are less likely to be confiscated because they are not particularly valuable in the hands of a different owner. An assembly operation supplying subcomponents that only the parent company uses would not be an attractive takeover target, for example. Similarly, a manufacturing operation that requires the use of specialized components from the parent is of little value without the parent company's cooperation.

Natural resource developments, such as copper mining or oil drilling, are just the opposite. Once the operation is in place, much of the value is in the commodity. The political risk for such investments is much higher for this reason. Also, the issue of exploitation is more pronounced with such investments, again increasing the political risk.

Corruption is a very big issue in many countries and the payment of kickbacks or 'business facilitation fees' is the norm in many areas. Government officials, petty bureaucrats and cumbersome administrative regulations can significantly restrict the efficiency of international operations.

Chapter 2
Page 46

Many organizations present rankings of political risk in countries and it is paramount that these are considered before any foreign direct investment takes place. *Transparency International*'s 'perceptions of corruption' ranking is an example of such an assessment and is presented in Figure 2.4 of **Chapter 2**.

Political risk can be hedged in several ways, particularly when confiscation or nationalization is a concern. The use of local financing, perhaps from the government of the foreign country in question, reduces the possible loss because the company can refuse to pay the debt in the event of unfavourable political activities. Based on our discussion in this section, structuring the operation in such a way that it requires significant parent company involvement to function is another way to reduce political risk.

Real World Insight 30.1

Doing Business in Emerging Markets

(*Excerpts from 'Shell wins £1.9bn India tax case', The Guardian with AFP, 19 November 2014*)

There are many challenges when running a business in emerging markets. Many parts of the supply chain are inefficient and unreliable, there is corruption between companies and with government employees, and regulations can be cumbersome.

In recent years, India has worked hard to shed its image as a difficult place for foreign firms to operate. Unfortunately, there are still massive difficulties in terms of cultural differences and the regulatory red tape that seems ever present. However, this may be changing. In 2014, the Anglo-Dutch oil firm Shell won a multimillion-dollar court battle against the Indian authorities, marking a significant victory for multinationals involved in tax wrangles in the country.

The high court in Mumbai ruled in favour of Shell, whose Indian unit had been accused of underpricing shares issued to its parent firm by about 180bn rupees (£1.9 billion). The company had challenged a demand by Indian authorities for tax on the interest that would have been earned. The judges quashed the income tax department order. 'This is a positive outcome which should provide a further boost to the government initiatives to improve the investment climate,' Shell said in a statement.

The high tax claim was one in a series ordered by Indian authorities on foreign firms including HSBC, IBM and Nokia. A court ruled in October in favour of the British mobile phone company Vodafone, which had been engaged in a £317 million tax battle with Indian authorities after they accused it of also underpricing its shares.

Foreign companies claim India's tax laws are sometimes applied in an uneven and capricious manner, making it difficult to do business in the country. Vikram Dhawan, director of equities at Equentis Capital, described the ruling in the Shell case as 'a very positive development', which showed India 'is walking the talk of being friendly and fair to businesses'.

Source: The Guardian with AFP.

Summary and Conclusions

The international firm has a more complicated life than the purely domestic firm. Management must understand the connection between interest rates, foreign currency exchange rates and inflation, and it must become aware of many different financial market regulations and tax systems. This chapter is intended to be a concise introduction to some of the financial issues that come up in international investing.

Our coverage has been necessarily brief. The main topics we discussed are the following:

1 *Some basic vocabulary*: We briefly defined some exotic terms in international finance.

2 *The basic mechanics of exchange rate quotations*: We discussed the spot and forward markets and how exchange rates are interpreted.

3 *The fundamental relationships between international financial variables*:

   (a) Absolute and relative purchasing power parity, PPP.

   (b) Interest rate parity, IRP.

   (c) Unbiased forward rates, UFR.

   Absolute purchasing power parity states that a currency, such as the euro, should have the same purchasing power in each country. This means that an orange costs the same whether you buy it in Brussels or in Oslo.

   Relative purchasing power parity means that the expected percentage change in exchange rates between the currencies of two countries is equal to the difference in their inflation rates.

   Interest rate parity implies that the percentage difference between the forward exchange rate and the spot exchange rate is equal to the interest rate differential. We showed how covered interest arbitrage forces this relationship to hold.

   The unbiased forward rates condition indicates that the current forward rate is a good predictor of the future spot exchange rate.

4 *International capital budgeting*: We showed that the basic foreign exchange relationships imply two other conditions:

   (a) Uncovered interest parity.

   (b) The international Fisher effect.

   By invoking these two conditions, we learned how to estimate NPVs in foreign currencies and how to convert foreign currencies into the home currency to estimate NPV in the usual way.

5 *Exchange rate and political risk*: We described the various types of exchange rate risk and discussed some common approaches to managing the effect of fluctuating exchange rates on the cash flows and value of the international firm. We also discussed political risk and some ways of managing exposure to it.

Questions and Problems

1 **Terminology** Explain the difference between a domestic bond, a foreign bond and a Eurobond, and give an example of each.

2 **Foreign Exchange Markets and Exchange Rates** What is meant by triangular arbitrage? Is this likely to occur in real life? Explain.

3 **Purchasing Power Parity** Do you think purchasing power parity exists in the world economies? As country barriers fall, is purchasing power parity likely to become more prevalent? Does the empirical evidence support the PPP theory? Discuss.

4 **Interest Rate Parity, Unbiased Forward Rates and the International Fisher Effect** Review the international parity conditions. Which ones do you think are likely to exist and which are less likely to be valid? During a global recession, do you think they are less or more likely to be valid? Explain.

5 **International Capital Budgeting** Should international capital budgeting projects be assessed from the perspective of a multinational's subsidiary, or from the parent company? Are there any circumstances under which this would change? Explain.

6 **Exchange Rate Risk** In 2008/09 the British pound depreciated by approximately 25 per cent on a trade-weight basis after the Bank of England reduced interest rates to a historically low level. In your opinion, did the depreciation in sterling damage the UK economy? Are exchange rate movements necessarily good or bad for a country? Explain.

7 **Political Risk** Why is country risk analysis important? Can multinationals reduce their exposure to country risk? Before the 2014 Scottish independence referendum, the Royal Bank of Scotland announced contingency plans to move their headquarters to elsewhere in the United Kingdom, should there have been a 'yes' vote to leave. Why did you think they did this? Explain.

8 **Spot and Forward Rates** Suppose the exchange rate for the Australian dollar is quoted as \$AUS3/£ in the spot market and \$AUS4/£ in the 90-day forward market.

(a) Is the British pound selling at a premium or a discount relative to the Australian dollar?

(b) Does the financial market expect the Australian dollar to weaken relative to the pound? Explain.

(c) What do you suspect is true about relative economic conditions in the United Kingdom and Australia?

9 **Purchasing Power Parity** Suppose the rate of inflation in the Eurozone will run about 3 per cent higher than the UK inflation rate over the next several years. All other things being the same, what will happen to the euro versus pound exchange rate? What relationship are you relying on in answering?

10 **Exchange Rates** The exchange rate for the Australian dollar is currently A\$0.9641/US\$. This exchange rate is expected to rise by 10 per cent over the next year.

(a) Is the Australian dollar expected to get stronger or weaker?

(b) What do you think about the relative inflation rates in the US and Australia?

(c) What do you think about the relative nominal interest rates in the US and Australia? Relative real rates?

11 **Bulldog Bonds** Which of the following most accurately describes a Bulldog bond?

(a) A bond issued by Vodafone in Frankfurt with the interest payable in British pounds.

(b) A bond issued by Vodafone in Frankfurt with the interest payable in euros.

(c) A bond issued by BMW in Germany with the interest payable in British pounds.

(d) A bond issued by BMW in London with the interest payable in British pounds.

(e) A bond issued by BMW worldwide with the interest payable in British pounds.

12 **International Risks** At one point, Duracell International confirmed that it was planning to open battery manufacturing plants in China and India. Manufacturing in these countries allows Duracell to avoid import duties of between 30 and 35 per cent that have made alkaline batteries prohibitively expensive for some consumers. What additional advantages might Duracell see in this proposal? What are some of the risks to Duracell?

13 **Multinational Corporations** Given that many multinationals based in many countries have much greater sales outside their domestic markets than within them, what is the particular relevance of their domestic currency?

14 **Exchange Rate Movements** Are the following statements true or false? Explain why.

(a) If the central bank decreases interest rates in the United Kingdom, but holds them constant in the United States, then we would expect the pound to depreciate relative to the dollar.

(b) Suppose you are a German machine tool exporter, and you invoice all of your sales in foreign currency. Further suppose that there are higher inflation rates in Germany relative to those in other countries, then you should use the forward markets to protect yourself against future losses resulting from the deterioration in the value of the euro.

(c) The 2015 UK general election was widely anticipated to produce a hung parliament. Instead, a Conservative majority government was elected. Against this backdrop, we should expect the pound to appreciate relative to the euro.

15 **Exchange Rate Movements** Some countries encourage movements in their exchange rate relative to those of some other country as a short-term means of addressing foreign trade imbalances. For each of the following scenarios, evaluate the impact the announcement would have on a Danish importer and a Danish exporter doing business with the foreign country:

(a) Officials in the Danish government announce that they are comfortable with a rising krone relative to the euro.

(b) The Bank of England announce that they feel the krone has been driven too low by currency speculators relative to the British pound.

(c) The European Central Bank announces that it will print billions of new euros and inject them into the economy in an effort to reduce the country's unemployment rate.

16 **International Capital Market Relationships** We discussed five international capital market relationships: relative PPP, IRP, UFR, UIP and the international Fisher effect. Which of these would you expect to hold most closely? Which do you think would be most likely to be violated?

17 **Exchange Rate Risk** If you are an exporter who must make payments in foreign currency 3 months after receiving each shipment and you predict that the domestic currency will appreciate in value over this period, is there any value in hedging your currency exposure?

18 **International Capital Budgeting** Suppose it is your task to evaluate two different investments in new subsidiaries for your company, one in your own country and the other in a foreign country. You calculate the cash flows of both projects to be identical after exchange rate differences. Under what circumstances might you choose to invest in the foreign subsidiary? Give an example of a country where certain factors might influence you to alter this decision and invest at home.

19 **FX Risk** What are the types of foreign exchange risk a multinational faces? How do these risks arise? Explain.

20 **International Borrowing** If a South African firm raises funds for a foreign subsidiary, what are the disadvantages to borrowing in South Africa? How would you overcome them?

21 **International Investment** If financial markets are perfectly competitive and the Eurodollar rate is above that offered in the US loan market, you would immediately want to borrow money in the United States and invest it in Eurodollars. True or false? Explain.

22 **Eurobonds** Explain motives companies might have for raising money on the international bond markets.

23 **Using Exchange Rates** Take a look back at Figure 30.1 to answer the following questions:

(a) If you have €100, how many British pounds can you get?

(b) How much is one pound worth against the euro?

(c) If you have £5 million, how many euros do you have?

(d) Which is worth more, a Trinidad and Tobago dollar or a Singapore dollar?

(e) Which is worth more, a Pakistani rupee or a Sri Lankan rupee?

(f) How many Swiss francs can you get for a Swedish krona? What do you call this rate?

(g) Per unit, what is the most valuable currency of those listed? The least valuable?

24 **Using the Cross-Rate**   Use the information in Figure 30.1 to answer the following questions:

(a) Which would you rather have, €100 or £100? Why?

(b) Which would you rather have, 100 Swiss francs (SFr) or 100 Swedish krona (SKr)? Why?

(c) What is the cross-rate for Swiss francs in terms of Swedish krona? For Swedish krona in terms of Swiss francs?

25 **Forward Exchange Rates**   Use the information in Figure 30.1 to answer the following questions:

(a) If the 3-month forward rate for the US dollar per euro F90 = $1.3215 (per €), is the dollar selling at a premium or a discount? Explain.

(b) If the 3-month forward rate for British pounds in euros per pound is F90 = €1.2198, is the euro selling at a premium or a discount? Explain.

26 **Using Spot and Forward Exchange Rates**   Suppose the spot exchange rate for the South African rand is R15/£ and the 6-month forward rate is R16/£.

(a) Which is worth more, the British pound or South African rand?

(b) Assuming absolute PPP holds, what is the cost in the United Kingdom of a Castle beer if the price in South Africa is R20? Why might the beer actually sell at a different price in the United Kingdom?

(c) Is the British pound selling at a premium or a discount relative to the South African rand?

(d) Which currency is expected to appreciate in value?

(e) Which country do you think has higher interest rates – the United Kingdom or South Africa? Explain.

27 **Cross-Rates and Arbitrage**   Use Figure 30.1 to answer the following questions:

(a) What is the cross-rate in terms of Rwandan franc per Thai baht?

(b) Suppose the cross-rate is 12 Rwandan franc = 1 Thai baht. Is there an arbitrage opportunity here? If there is, explain how to take advantage of the mispricing.

28 **Interest Rate Parity**   Use Figure 30.1 to answer the following question. Suppose interest rate parity holds, and the current annual risk-free rate in the Eurozone is 3.8 per cent. Assume the UK one year forward rate is £0.8251. What must the annual risk-free rate be in Great Britain?

29 **Interest Rates and Arbitrage**   The treasurer of a major British firm has £30 million to invest for 3 months. The annual interest rate in the United Kingdom is 0.45 per cent per month. The interest rate in the Eurozone is 0.6 per cent per month. The spot exchange rate is €1.12/£, and the 3-month forward rate is €1.15/£. Ignoring transaction costs, in which country would the treasurer want to invest the company's funds? Why?

30 **Inflation and Exchange Rates**   Suppose the current exchange rate for the Polish zloty is Z5.1134/£. The expected exchange rate in 3 years is Z5.2/£. What is the difference in the annual inflation rates for the United Kingdom and Poland over this period? Assume that the anticipated rate is constant for both countries. What relationship are you relying on in answering?

31 **Exchange Rate Risk**   Suppose your company, which is based in Nantes, imports computer motherboards from Singapore. The exchange rate is given in Figure 30.1. You have just placed an order for 30,000 motherboards at a cost to you of 158.5 Singapore dollars each. You will pay for the shipment when it arrives in 90 days. You can sell the motherboards for €100 each. Calculate your profit if the exchange rate goes up or down by 10 per cent over the next 90 days. What is the breakeven exchange rate? What percentage rise or fall does this represent in terms of the Singapore dollar versus the euro?

32 **Exchange Rates and Arbitrage**   Suppose the spot and 6-month forward rates on the Swedish krona are SKr10.7917/£ and SKr12.00/£, respectively. The annual risk-free rate in the United Kingdom is 2.5 per cent, and the annual risk-free rate in Sweden is 1.13 per cent.

(a) Is there an arbitrage opportunity here? If so, how would you exploit it?

(b) What must the 6-month forward rate be to prevent arbitrage?

33 **The International Fisher Effect**   You observe that the inflation rate in the United Kingdom is 3.5 per cent per year and that T-bills currently yield 3.9 per cent annually. What do you estimate the inflation rate to be in

(a) Australia if short-term Australian government securities yield 5 per cent per year?

(b) Canada if short-term Canadian government securities yield 7 per cent per year?

(c) Taiwan if short-term Taiwanese government securities yield 10 per cent per year?

34 **Spot versus Forward Rates** Suppose the spot and 3-month forward rates for the Indian rupee are R68.81/€ and R61.8/€, respectively.

(a) Is the rupee expected to get stronger or weaker?

(b) What would you estimate is the difference between the inflation rates of the Eurozone and India?

35 **Expected Spot Rates** Suppose the spot exchange rate for the Tanzanian shilling is TSh2500/£. The inflation rate in the United Kingdom is 3.5 per cent and it is 8.6 per cent in Tanzania. What do you predict the exchange rate will be in 1 year? In 2 years? In 5 years? What relationship are you using?

36 **Forward Rates** The spot rate of foreign exchange between the United States and the United Kingdom is $1.6117/£. If the interest rate in the United States is 13 per cent and it is 8 per cent in the United Kingdom, what would you expect the one-year forward rate to be if no immediate arbitrage opportunities existed?

37 **Capital Budgeting** The Dutch firm, ABS Equipment, has an investment opportunity in the United Kingdom. The project costs £12 million and is expected to produce cash flows of £2.7 million in year 1, £3.5 million in year 2, and £3.3 million in year 3. The current spot exchange rate is €1.12/£ and the current risk-free rate in the Eurozone is 2.12 per cent, compared to that in the United Kingdom of 2.13 per cent. The appropriate discount rate for the project is estimated to be 13 per cent, the Eurozone cost of capital for the company. In addition, the subsidiary can be sold at the end of 3 years for an estimated £7.4 million. What is the NPV of the project?

38 **Capital Budgeting** As a German company, you are evaluating a proposed expansion of an existing subsidiary located in Switzerland. The cost of the expansion would be SFr 27.0 million. The cash flows from the project would be SFr 7.5 million per year for the next 5 years. The euro required return is 13 per cent per year, and the current exchange rate is SFr 1.48/€. The going rate on EURIBOR is 8 per cent per year. It is 7 per cent per year on Swiss francs.

(a) What do you project will happen to exchange rates over the next 4 years?

(b) Based on your answer in (a), convert the projected franc flows into euro cash flows and calculate the NPV.

(c) What is the required return on franc cash flows? Based on your answer, calculate the NPV in francs and then convert to euros.

CHALLENGE

39 **Using the Exact International Fisher Effect** From our discussion of the Fisher effect in this chapter, we know that the actual relationship between a nominal rate, R, a real rate, r, and an inflation rate, h, can be written as follows:

$$1 + r = (1 + R)/(1 + h)$$

This is the *domestic* Fisher effect.

(a) What is the non-approximate form of the international Fisher effect?

(b) Based on your answer in (a), what is the exact form for UIP? (*Hint*: Recall the exact form of IRP and use UFR.)

(c) What is the exact form for relative PPP? (*Hint*: Combine your previous two answers.)

(d) Recalculate the NPV for the Kihlstrom drill bit project (discussed in Section 30.5) using the exact forms for the UIP and the international Fisher effect. Verify that you get precisely the same answer either way.

Exam Question (45 minutes)

On 29 March 2004, the €/$ exchange rate was €0.82/$ compared to €0.94/$ exactly one year before. On the same day, the £/$ exchange rate was £0.56/$ compared with £0.62/$ one year earlier.

1 Calculate the percentage appreciation of the euro against the dollar over the previous year. Calculate the percentage appreciation of sterling against the dollar over the previous year. (20 marks)

2   Calculate the percentage appreciation or depreciation of sterling against the euro over the previous year. Calculate the percentage appreciation or depreciation of the euro against sterling over the previous year. (20 marks)

3   Does the percentage appreciation or depreciation of sterling in (1) equal the euro depreciation or appreciation in (2) multiplied by negative one? Explain your answer. (20 marks)

4   Review the international parity conditions. Do you believe they work? Explain. (40 marks)

Mini Case

West Coast Yachts Goes International

Larissa Warren, the owner of West Coast Yachts, has been in discussions with a yacht dealer in Monaco about selling the company's yachts in Europe. Jarek Jachowicz, the dealer, wants to add West Coast Yachts to his current retail line. Jarek has told Larissa that he feels the retail sales will be approximately €5 million per month. All sales will be made in euros, and Jarek will retain 5 per cent of the retail sales as commission, which will be paid in euros. Because the yachts will be customized to order, the first sales will take place in one month. Jarek will pay West Coast Yachts for the order 90 days after it is filled. This payment schedule will continue for the length of the contract between the two companies.

Larissa is confident the company can handle the extra volume with its existing facilities, but she is unsure about any potential financial risks of selling yachts in Europe. In her discussion with Jarek she found that the current exchange rate is €1.12/£. At this exchange rate the company would spend 70 per cent of the sales income on production costs. This number does not reflect the sales commission to be paid to Jarek.

Larissa has decided to ask Dan Ervin, the company's financial analyst, to prepare an analysis of the proposed international sales. Specifically she asks Dan to answer the following questions:

1   What are the pros and cons of the international sales plan? What additional risks will the company face?

2   What will happen to the company's profits if the British pound strengthens? What if the British pound weakens?

3   Ignoring taxes, what are West Coast Yachts' projected gains or losses from this proposed arrangement at the current exchange rate of €1.12/£? What will happen to profits if the exchange rate changes to €1.20/£? At what exchange rate will the company break even?

4   How can the company hedge its exchange rate risk? What are the implications for this approach?

5   Taking all factors into account, should the company pursue international sales further? Why or why not?

Practical Case Study

Search on Google for the price of a specific model of car (your choice) that is sold in the United Kingdom, Ireland, France, Italy, Spain and Germany. Does absolute purchasing power parity hold?

Relevant Accounting Standards

When investing or doing business overseas, companies need to be sure of the accounting standards to which the target country adheres. Although over 100 countries follow international accounting standards, many countries do not follow these standards, including the US. Foreign currency earnings need to be translated according to IAS 21 *The Effects of Changes in Foreign Exchange Rates*. Further, if a company is carrying out business in countries with a hyperinflationary environment (examples are Zimbabwe, Angola and Myanmar) they may have to adhere to IAS 29 *Financial Reporting in Hyperinflationary Economies*. Sometimes, overseas investments are in the form of joint ventures. If this is the case, IAS 31 *Interests in Joint Ventures* is also important.

Additional Reading

1. Bekaert, G., C.R. Harvey, C.T. Lundblad and S. Siegel (2013) 'The European Union, the Euro, and Equity Market Iintegration', *Journal of Financial Economics*, Vol. 109, No. 3, 583–603.

2. Bekaert, G., C.R. Harvey, C.T. Lundblad and S. Siegel (2014) 'Political Risk Spreads', *Journal of International Business Studies*, Vol. 45, No. 4, 471–493.

3. Brennan, M.J. and Y. Xia (2006) 'International Capital Markets and Foreign Exchange Risk', *Review of Financial Studies*, Vol. 19, No. 3, 753–795. **International**.

4. Xu, J. (2012) 'Profitability and Capital Structure: Evidence from Import Penetration', *Journal of Financial Economics*, Vol. 106, No. 2, 427–446.

Very few papers exist that examine international capital budgeting in any detail. However, there are a few:

5   Greene, W.H., A.S. Hornstein and L.J. White (2009) 'Multinationals Do it Better: Evidence on the Efficiency of Corporations' Capital Budgeting', *Journal of Empirical Finance*, Vol. 16, No. 5, 703–720.

6   Holmén, M. and B. Pramborg (2009) 'Capital Budgeting and Political Risk: Empirical Evidence', *Journal of International Financial Management and Accounting*, Vol. 20, No. 2, 105–134.

Endnote

1   There are four exchange rates instead of five because one exchange rate would involve the exchange of a currency for itself. More generally, it might seem that there should be 25 exchange rates with five currencies. There are 25 different combinations, but, of these, 5 involve the exchange of a currency for itself. Of the remaining 20, half are redundant because they are just the reciprocals of another exchange rate. Of the remaining 10, 6 can be eliminated by using a common denominator.

Index